T0140063

Lecture Notes in Computer Science 11692

More information about this series at http://www.springer.com/series/7410

Alexandra Boldyreva · Daniele Micciancio (Eds.)

Advances in Cryptology – CRYPTO 2019

39th Annual International Cryptology Conference
Santa Barbara, CA, USA, August 18–22, 2019
Proceedings, Part I

 Springer

Editors
Alexandra Boldyreva
Georgia Institute of Technology
Atlanta, GA, USA

Daniele Micciancio
University of California at San Diego
La Jolla, CA, USA

ISSN 0302-9743   ISSN 1611-3349 (electronic)
Lecture Notes in Computer Science
ISBN 978-3-030-26947-0   ISBN 978-3-030-26948-7 (eBook)
https://doi.org/10.1007/978-3-030-26948-7

LNCS Sublibrary: SL4 – Security and Cryptology

This Springer imprint is published by the registered company Springer Nature Switzerland AG
The registered company address is: Gewerbestrasse 11, 6330 Cham, Switzerland

Preface

The 39th International Cryptology Conference (Crypto 2019) was held at the University of California, Santa Barbara, California, USA, during August 18–22, 2019. It was sponsored by the International Association for Cryptologic Research (IACR). As in the previous year, a number of workshops took place on the days (August 17 and August 18, 2019) immediately before the conference. This year, the list of affiliated events included a Workshop on Attacks in Cryptography organized by Juraj Somorovsky (Ruhr University Bochum); a Blockchain Workshop organized by Rafael Pass (Cornell Tech) and Elaine Shi (Cornell); a Workshop on Advanced Cryptography Standardization organized by Daniel Benarroch (QEDIT) and Tancrède Lepoint (Google); a workshop on New Roads to Cryptopia organized by Amit Sahai (UCLA); a Privacy Preserving Machine Learning Workshop organized by Gilad Asharov (JP Morgan AI Research), Rafail Ostrovsky (UCLA) and Antigoni Polychroniadou (JP Morgan AI Research); and the Mathcrypt Workshop organized by Kristin Lauter (Microsoft Research), Yongsoo Song (Microsoft Research) and Jung Hee Cheon (Seoul National University).

Crypto continues to grow, year after year, and Crypto 2019 was no exception. The conference set new records for both submissions and publications, with a whopping 378 papers submitted for consideration. It took a Program Committee (PC) of 51 cryptography experts working with 333 external reviewers for over two months to select the 81 papers which were accepted for the conference.

As usual, papers were reviewed in the double-blind fashion, with each paper assigned to three PC members. Initially, papers received independent reviews, without any communication between PC members. After the initial review stage, authors were given the opportunity to comment on all available preliminary reviews. Finally, the PC discussed each submission, taking all reviews and author comments into account, and selecting the list of papers to be included in the conference program. PC members were limited to two submissions, and their submissions were held to higher standards. The two Program Chairs were not allowed to submit papers.

The PC recognized three papers and their authors for standing out amongst the rest. "Cryptanalysis of OCB2: Attacks on Authenticity and Confidentiality", by Akiko Inoue, Tetsu Iwata, Kazuhiko Minematsu and Bertram Poettering was voted Best Paper of the conference. Additionally, the papers "Quantum cryptanalysis in the RAM model: Claw-finding attacks on SIKE" by Samuel Jaques and John M. Schanck, and "Fully Secure Attribute-Based Encryption for t-CNF from LWE" by Rotem Tsabary, were voted Best Papers Authored Exclusively By Young Researchers.

Beside the technical presentations, Crypto 2019 featured a Rump session, and two invited talks by Jonathan Katz from University of Maryland, and Helen Nissenbaum from Cornell Tech.

We would like to express our sincere gratitude to all the reviewers for volunteering their time and knowledge in order to select a great program for 2019. Additionally, we are very appreciative of the following individuals and organizations for helping make Crypto 2019 a success:

- Muthu Venkitasubramaniam (University of Rochester) Crypto 2019 General Chair
- Carmit Hazay (Bar-Ilan University) - Workshop Chair
- Jonathan Katz (University of Maryland) - Invited Speaker
- Helen Nissenbaum (Cornell Tech) - Invited Speaker
- Shai Halevi - Author of the IACR Web Submission and Review System
- Anna Kramer and her colleagues at Springer
- Whitney Morris and UCSB Conference Services

We would also like to say thank you to our numerous sponsors, the workshop organizers, everyone who submitted papers, the session chairs, and the presenters. Lastly, a big thanks to everyone who attended the conference at UCSB.

August 2019

Alexandra Boldyreva
Daniele Micciancio

CRYPTO 2019

The 39th International Cryptology Conference

University of California, Santa Barbara, CA, USA
August 18–22, 2019

Sponsored by the *International Association for Cryptologic Research*

General Chair

Muthu Venkitasubramaniam University of Rochester, USA

Program Chairs

Alexandra Boldyreva   Georgia Institute of Technology, USA
Daniele Micciancio   University of California at San Diego, USA

Program Committee

Manuel Barbosa   INESC TEC, University of Porto, Portugal
Zvika Brakerski   Weizmann Institute of Science, Israel
Mark Bun   Simons Institute, Boston University, USA
Ran Canetti   Tel Aviv University, Israel, and Boston University,
                           USA
Dario Catalano   University of Catania, Italy
Alessandro Chiesa   UC Berkeley, USA
Sherman S. M. Chow   Chinese University of Hong Kong, SAR China
Kai-Min Chung   Academia Sinica, Taiwan
Jean-Sebastien Coron   Luxembourg University, Luxembourg
Jean Paul Degabriele   TU Darmstadt, Germany
Nico Döttling   Cispa Helmholtz Center (i.G.), Germany
Orr Dunkelman   University of Haifa, Israel
Rosario Gennaro   City College, CUNY, USA
Tim Güneysu   Ruhr University Bochum, DFKI, Germany
Felix Günther   UC San Diego, USA
Siyao Guo   NYU Shanghai, China
Sean Hallgren   Pennsylvania State University, USA
Carmit Hazay   Bar-Ilan University, Israel
Susan Hohenberger   Johns Hopkins University, USA
Sorina Ionica   Université de Picardie, France
Bhavana Kanukurthi   Indian Institute of Science, India
Vladimir Kolesnikov   Georgia Institute of Technology, USA

Additional Reviewers

Cecilia Boschini
Katharina Boudgoust
Florian Bourse
Elette Boyle
Jacqueline Brendel
Anne Broadbent
Wouter Castryck
Andrea Cerulli
Yilei Chen
Nai-Hui Chia
Ilaria Chillotti
Arka Rai Choudhuri
Michele Ciampi
Benoit Cogliati
Ran Cohen
Sandro Coretti
Craig Costello
Geoffroy Couteau
Jan Czajkowski
Dana Dachaman-Soled
Wei Dai
Anders Dalskov
Hannah Davis
Akshay Degwekar
Ioannis Demertzis
Patrick Derbez
David Derler
Itai Dinur
Mario Di Raimondo
Benjamin Dowling
Minxin Du
Léo Ducas
Yfke Dulek
Francois Dupressoir
Frédéric Dupuis
Stefan Dziembowski
Gautier Eberhart
Christoph Egger
Maria Eichlseder
Daniel Escudero
Antonio Faonio
Franz Aguirre Farro
Pooya Farshim
Omar Fawzi
Katharina Fech
Ben Fisch

Marc Fischlin
Emmanuel Fouotsa
Danilo Francati
Daniele Friolo
Ariel Gabizon
Tommaso Gagliardoni
Steven Galbraith
Chaya Ganesh
Lydia Garms
Romain Gay
Ran Gelles
Adela Georgescu
David Gerault
Essam Ghadafi
Satrajit Ghosh
Federico Giacon
Aarushi Goel
Junqing Gong
Alonso Gonzalez
Rishab Goyal
Vipul Goyal
Nicola Greco
Daniel Grosse
Zichen Gui
Tim Güneysu
Chethan Kamath Hosdurg
Mohammad Hajiabadi
Lucjan Hanzlik
Patrick Harasser
Carmit Hazay
Julia Hesse
Minki Hhan
Kuan-Yi Ho
Justin Holmgren
Akinori Hosoyamada
Patrick Hough
James Howe
Pavel Hubácek
Shih-Han Hung
Kathrin Hövelmanns
Takanori Isobe
Mitsugu Iwamoto
Malika Izabachène
Joseph Jaeger
Christian Janson
Dirmanto Jap

Stas Jarecki
Zhengzhong Jin
Charanjit Jutla
Guillaume Kaim
Mustafa Kairallah
Yael Kalai
Chethan Kamath
Marc Kaplan
Shuichi Katsumata
Shinagawa Kazumasa
Mojtaba Khalili
Dmitry Khovratovich
Ryo Kikuchi
Sam Kim
Elena Kirshanova
Fuyuki Kitagawa
Susumu Kiyoshima
Karen Klein
Michael Klooss
Kamil Kluczniak
Markulf Kohlweiss
Ilan Komargodski
Venkata Koppula
Evgenios Kornaropoulos
Takeshi Koshiba
Luke Kowalczyk
Stephan Krenn
Mukul Kulkarni
Ranjit Kumaresan
Gijs Van Laer
Russell W. F. Lai
Thalia Laing
Changmin Lee
Eysa Lee
Moon Sung Lee
Tancrède Lepoint
Jyun-Jie Liao
Han-Hsuan Lin
Huijia (Rachel) Lin
Helger Lipmaa
Qipeng Liu
Tianren Liu
Alex Lombardi
Patrick Longa
Julian Loss
Atul Luykx

Julio López
Fermi Ma
Jack P. K. Ma
Bernardo Magri
Mohammad Mahmoody
Christian Majenz
Hemanta Maji
Giulio Malavolta
Mary Maller
Nathan Manohar
Peter Manohar
Daniel Masny
Takahiro Matsuda
Alexander May
Sogol Mazaheri
Jeremias Mechler
Simon-Philipp Merz
Peihan Miao
Romy Minko
Takaaki Mizuki
Amir Moradi
Kirill Morozov
Travis Morrison
Nicky Mouha
Tamer Mour
Pratyay Mukherjee
Jörn Müller-Quade
Kartik Nayak
Gregory Neven
Ka-Lok Ng
Ruth Ng
Ngoc Khanh Nguyen
Ventzislav Nikov
Ariel Nof
Sai Lakshmi Bhavana
    Obbattu
Maciej Obremski
Tobias Oder
Sabine Oechsner
Wakaha Ogata
Miyako Ohkubo
Cristina Onete
Claudio Orlandi
Emmanuela Orsini
Carles Padro
Jiaxin Pan

Lorenz Panny
Dimitris Papadopoulos
Anat Paskin-Cherniavsky
Christopher Patton
Alice Pellet-Mary
Zack Pepin
Jeroen Pijnenburg
Oxana Poburinnaya
Antigoni Polychroniadou
Bart Preneel
Ben Pring
Emmanuel Prouff
Chen Qian
Luowen Qian
Willy Quach
Srinivasan Raghuraman
Adrián Ranea
Divya Ravi
Vincent Rijmen
Peter Rindal
Felix Rohrbach
Razvan Rosie
Dragos Rotaru
Ron Rothblum
Arnab Roy
Paul Rösler
Luisa Siniscalchi
Mohamed Sabt
Rajeev Anand Sahu
Cyprien de Saint Guilhem
Kazuo Sakiyama
Pratik Sarkar
Pascal Sasdrich
Alessandra Scafuro
Falk Schellenberg
Thomas Schneider
Tobias Schneider
Jacob Schuldt
Gregor Seiler
Sruthi Sekar
Karn Seth
Yannick Seurin
Aria Shahverdi
Abhishek Shetty
Sina Shiehian
Javier Silva

Siang Meng Sim
Mark Simkin
Luisa Siniscalchi
Fang Song
Pratik Soni
Katerina Sotiraki
Nicholas Spooner
Caleb Springer
Akshayaram Srinivasan
François-Xavier Standaert
Douglas Stebila
Damien Stehlé
Ron Steinfeld
Noah
    Stephens-Davidowitz
Christoph Striecks
Patrick Struck
Banik Subhadeep
Gelo Noel Tabia
Stefano Tessaro
Sri Aravinda Krishnan
    Thyagarajan
Mehdi Tibouchi
Elmar W. Tischhauser
Yosuke Todo
Junichi Tomida
Patrick Towa
Monika Trimoska
Itay Tsabary
Rotem Tsabary
Sulamithe Tsakou
Ida Tucker
Dominique Unruh
Bogdan Ursu
Vinod Vaikuntanathan
Kerem Varici
Prashant Vasudevan
Muthu
    Venkitasubramaniam
Fernando Virdia
Madars Virza
Ivan Visconti
Satyanarayana Vusirikala
Riad Wahby
Adrian Waller
Alexandre Wallet

Michael Walter
Haoyang Wang
Jiafan Wang
Meiqin Wang
Xiuhua Wang
Yuyu Wang
Gaven Watson
Hoeteck Wee
Weiqiang Wen

Harry W. H. Wong
Tim Wood
Joanne Woodage
Huangting Wu
Keita Xagawa
Shota Yamada
Takashi Yamakawa
Avishay Yanai
Kenji Yasunaga

Kevin Yeo
Eylon Yogev
Yu Yu
Mark Zhandry
Jiapeng Zhang
Yupeng Zhang
Yongjun Zhao
Yu Zheng

Sponsors

Contents – Part I

Mathematical Cryptanalysis

Proofs of Storage

Non-Malleable Codes

SNARKs and Blockchains

Homomorphic Cryptography

Leakage Models and Key Reuse

Contents – Part II

Leakage Resilience

Memory Hard Functions and Privacy Amplification

Attribute Based Encryption

Foundations

Contents – Part III

Watermarking

Secure Computation

Various Topics

Award Papers

Cryptanalysis of OCB2: Attacks on Authenticity and Confidentiality

Akiko Inoue[1]($\boxtimes$), Tetsu Iwata[2]📵, Kazuhiko Minematsu[1]($\boxtimes$)📵, and Bertram Poettering[3,4]📵

[1] NEC Corporation, Kawasaki, Japan
a-inoue@cj.jp.nec.com, k-minematsu@ah.jp.nec.com
[2] Nagoya University, Nagoya, Japan
tetsu.iwata@nagoya-u.jp
[3] Royal Holloway, University of London, London, UK
[4] IBM Research Zurich, Zurich, Switzerland
poe@zurich.ibm.com

Abstract. We present practical attacks on OCB2. This mode of operation of a blockcipher was designed with the aim to provide particularly efficient and provably-secure authenticated encryption services, and since its proposal about 15 years ago it belongs to the top performers in this realm. OCB2 was included in an ISO standard in 2009.

An internal building block of OCB2 is the tweakable blockcipher obtained by operating a regular blockcipher in XEX* mode. The latter provides security only when evaluated in accordance with certain technical restrictions that, as we note, are not always respected by OCB2. This leads to devastating attacks against OCB2's security promises: We develop a range of very practical attacks that, amongst others, demonstrate universal forgeries and full plaintext recovery. We complete our report with proposals for (provably) repairing OCB2. To our understanding, as a direct consequence of our findings, OCB2 is currently in a process of removal from ISO standards. Our attacks do not apply to OCB1 and OCB3, and our privacy attacks on OCB2 require an active adversary.

Keywords: OCB2 · Authenticated encryption · Cryptanalysis · Forgery · Plaintext recovery · XEX

1 Introduction

Authenticated encryption (AE) is a form of symmetric-key encryption that simultaneously protects the confidentiality and authenticity of messages. The primitive is widely accepted as a fundamental tool in practical cryptography, finding application in many settings, including in SSH and TLS.

© International Association for Cryptologic Research 2019
A. Boldyreva and D. Micciancio (Eds.): CRYPTO 2019, LNCS 11692, pp. 3–31, 2019.
https://doi.org/10.1007/978-3-030-26948-7_1

Constructions of the AE primitive include the OCB family of blockcipher modes of operation. Its three members (OCB1, OCB2, OCB3) are celebrated for their beautiful and innovative architecture, and their almost unrivaled efficiency. In fact, the modes are fully parallelizable and thus effectively as efficient as the fastest known confidentiality-only modes. The first version (OCB1) was proposed at ACM CCS 2001 by Rogaway et al. [34], the second version (OCB2) at ASIACRYPT 2004 by Rogaway [30] (hereafter Rog04), and the third version (OCB3) at FSE 2011 by Krovetz and Rogaway [20]. While all three designs share roughly the same construction principles, differences to note include both the external interface (while OCB1 is a pure AE mode, its successors OCB2 and OCB3 are AEAD modes where encryption and decryption is performed with respect to an auxiliary associated data input), and a core internal building block (while OCB1 and OCB3 are driven by look-up tables, OCB2 relies on the so-called powering-up construction).

Each version of OCB has received significant attention from researchers, standardization bodies, and the industry. In particular, OCB1 is listed in the IEEE 802.11 standard as an option for the protection of wireless networks, OCB2 was included in the ISO/IEC 19772:2009 [15] standard, and OCB3 is specified as document RFC 7253 [21] as an IETF Internet standard. Moreover, OCB3 is included in the final portfolio of the CAESAR competition[1]. Various versions of OCB have been implemented in popular cryptographic libraries, including in Botan, BouncyCastle, LibTomCrypt, OpenSSL, and SJCL.

The security of (all versions of) OCB has been extensively studied. For each version, the designer(s) provided security reductions to the security of the underlying blockcipher, with additive birthday-bound tightness of roughly the form $O(\sigma^2/2^n)$, where σ indicates the number of processed blocks (message and associated data) and n is the block size of the cipher. Note that this bound formally becomes pointless if $\sigma = 2^{n/2}$ blocks are involved, and indeed Ferguson [10] and Sun et al. [36] showed collision attacks that get along with this many processed blocks, implying that the bound is tight. (The attacks do not seem to be practical, though, as they require processing 300 EB (exabytes) of data with a single key, assuming $n = 128$.) As discussed below, all further known attacks against the members of the OCB family are in relaxed security settings (e.g. involving nonce misuse), with the conclusion being that their security is widely believed to hold (up to the birthday bound, in classic security models).

In this article we invalidate this belief by presenting a series of attacks against OCB2. The most basic attack requires one encryption and one decryption (of short messages and ciphertexts, respectively) to create an existential forgery with success probability one. No heavy computation or large amount of memory is needed for this; rather performing a couple of XOR computations is sufficient to craft the forgery. The attack is independent of the blockcipher E over which OCB2 is defined, including of its key and block length. Further, the message to which the forged ciphertext decrypts is strongly dependent on the message involved in the first encryption query, so that most parts of it can be assumed

---

[1] https://competitions.cr.yp.to/caesar.html.

to be known to, or influenced by, the adversary. Extended versions of our attack achieve forgeries for arbitrary messages (including full control over nonces and associated data), and full plaintext recovery, at the expense of a slight increase in the number of required encryption and decryption queries. Long story short: Our attacks on OCB2 are as critical as attacks on AE schemes could ever be.

We turn to technical details of our attacks. All members of the OCB family can be seen as modes of operation of a tweakable blockcipher (TBC, [22]): For encrypting a message consisting of one or multiple blocks, each message block is enciphered independently of the others using a tweak that reflects the position of the block in the message. Special tweaking rules are deployed for the last (possibly padded) message block and the checksum used for tag generation. In OCB2, the tweakable blockcipher itself is derived from an underlying regular blockcipher (e.g. AES) using the XEX^* transform. The latter is a hybrid of XE ("XOR-encipher", $C = E_K(\Delta \oplus M)$) and XEX ("XOR-encipher-XOR", $C = \Delta \oplus E_K(\Delta \oplus M)$) where it can be decided on a per-evaluation basis which of the two is used. We emphasize that the flaw of OCB2 that we identify and exploit is located neither in the general method the AEAD scheme is constructed from a tweakable blockcipher nor in the security of the XEX^* primitive. The problem is rather hidden in the interplay between the former and a technical peculiarity of the latter: If XEX^* is ever evaluated twice on the same input but in different modes (XE vs. XEX), it gives up on all security promises. While the corresponding access rule was already identified as necessary by Rog04, it was overlooked that OCB2 actually does not always satisfy it. Indeed, as we expose in this paper, an attacker can arrange that an XEX evaluation occurring when encrypting a regular message block and an XE evaluation occurring when decrypting a (padded) last block of an *unauthentic* ciphertext are on the same inputs. This issue, that was overlooked by the cryptographic community for the past 15 years, not only devalidates the formal security argument for OCB2 but ultimately leads to attacks that completely break the security of this primitive. As it turns out, OCB2 can be provably fixed by replacing certain XE invocations by XEX invocations. While the price to pay for this is minor (one additional XOR operation per encryption/decryption operation), unfortunately the fixed version loses backward compatibility with (unmodified) OCB2 implementations.

Our attacks are technical and fairly complex, so we confirmed their effectivity by implementing them: For our most relevant attacks we have C code that breaks the OCB2 reference implementation[2] with the reported high efficiency and success rate. We finally note that OCB1 and OCB3 do not combine the XE and XEX modes in the way OCB2 does, and we did not find them affected by our attacks.

1.1   Impact

OCB2 has been standardized in ISO/IEC 19772:2009 for about a decade [15]. As the scheme offers exceptional performance that was and still is challenging

---

[2] By Krovetz, http://web.cs.ucdavis.edu/~rogaway/ocb/code-2.0.htm.

to rival for AES-based constructions, it has to be assumed that industry has widely picked up on it, ultimately incorporating the scheme into products. The consequences of this might be severe. We have thus been in contact with members of ISO/IEC SC 27 Working Group 2, which is responsible for the standard, to advise on the right interpretation of our findings. The working group has issued a document [10] that acknowledges our findings and makes it clear that OCB2 should no longer be used. Moves are nearing completion to remove the scheme from the international standard.

OCB2 was and possibly still is covered by Intellectual Property claims. While such claims don't necessarily manifest a noticeable obstacle for deployment in industry, for open source software development efforts they routinely are. As a consequence, a number of relevant open source crypto libraries do not have an implementation of OCB2 and are thus not affected by our findings (an exception to this is Stanford's SJCL library[3]). The lack of open implementations suggests that most affected parties have industrial background. By the very nature of (IND$ secure) encryption, spotting products that rely on OCB2 for security and now became vulnerable remains a challenge.

1.2   Further Related Work

Besides the already mentioned attacks by Ferguson and Sun et al. (that show tightness of the birthday bound claimed for OCB), the following analyses in less classic attack settings have been conducted: Attacks in scenarios where the AE scheme is deployed in a somewhat sloppy way, e.g. where nonces are repeated (nonce-misuse setting) or where message fragments emerging from partially decrypted (possibly invalid) ciphertexts are leaked (release of unverified plaintext setting) are proposed by Andreeva et al. [1] and Ashur et al. [3]. In the same vein, but also considering attacks against the birthday bound of security claims, Vaudenay and Vizár [37] studied all third-round CAESAR candidates, including OCB3.

Not with the aim of breaking a particular version of OCB, but with the goal of better understanding the security of the schemes by refining the set of necessary security requirements on the underlying blockcipher, Aoki and Yasuda [2] show that relaxed assumptions are sufficient to establish the security of OCB. (Note that our attacks are in conflict with their claims on OCB2, indicating that their security arguments have to be reconsidered; the authors of [2] confirmed this view to us.)

Attacks in the *reforgeability setting* [6,11] deliver a series of existential forgeries with the specific property that creating the first forgery is the hardest part. While in most cases hardness is measured in terms of computation time, also our attacks can be seen in the reforgeability setting, but with a different complexity measure: While crafting the first OCB2 forgery requires two queries (one encryption, one decryption) and the forgery is only existential, all further forgeries can be universal (on arbitrary messages and associated data), and only require one further query (encryption). In fact, one can create hundreds of universal forgeries from the second encryption query.

---

[3] http://bitwiseshiftleft.github.io/sjcl/.

1.3   Organization and Contributions

We recall notions of tweakable blockciphers and authenticated encryption in Sect. 2. After specifying the OCB2 algorithms in Sect. 3 we present simple authenticity and confidentiality attacks against them in Sect. 4. While the latter achieve overwhelming advantages with respect to formal notions of unforgeability and indistinguishability and thus make evident that OCB2 is *academically* broken, certain restrictions on the format of forged or distinguished messages remain. We hence develop, in Sect. 5, a set of advanced attacks (including universal forgery and arbitrary decryption) that break the scheme also in most *real-world* settings. In Sect. 6 we explore which technical component of OCB2 is responsible for its insecurity; as many other schemes in symmetric cryptography use structures similar to those of OCB2, these reflections might also guide future cryptanalysis attempts of such schemes. In Sect. 7 we survey the applicability of our attack strategies to related encryption modes, including to OCB1 and OCB3; however we do not identify any further weak candidate. Finally, in Sect. 8 we consider a couple of ways to repair OCB2.

2   Preliminaries

2.1   Notations

If A is a set we write $a \xleftarrow{\$} A$ for the operation of picking an element of A uniformly at random and assigning it to the variable a. If B, B' are sets we write $B \xleftarrow{\cup} B'$ as shorthand for $B \leftarrow B \cup B'$.

STRINGS AND PADDING. Let $\{0,1\}^*$ be the set of all binary strings, including the empty string ε. The bit length of $X \in \{0,1\}^*$ is denoted by $|X|$, and in particular we have $|\varepsilon| = 0$. The sequence of c zeros is denoted with 0^c, with the convention that $0^0 = \varepsilon$. The concatenation of two bit strings X and Y is written $X \parallel Y$, or XY when no confusion is possible. The XOR combination of two same-length bit strings X, Y is denoted $X \oplus Y$. We denote with $\mathrm{msb}_c(X)$ and $\mathrm{lsb}_c(X)$ the first and last $c \leq |X|$ bits of X, respectively.

For X, n with $|X| \leq n$ we define the zero padding, $X \parallel 0^*$, and the one-zero padding, $X \parallel 10^*$. Both are X when $|X| = n$. They are $X \parallel 0^* = X \parallel 0^{n-|X|}$ and $X \parallel 10^* = X \parallel 10^{n-|X|-1}$, respectively, when $0 \leq |X| < n$.

For $X \in \{0,1\}^*$, we also define the parsing of a string into n-bit blocks denoted by

$$(X[1], X[2], \ldots, X[m]) \xleftarrow{n} X,$$

where $m = |X|_n \stackrel{\text{def}}{=} \lceil |X|/n \rceil$, $X[1] \parallel X[2] \parallel \ldots \parallel X[m] = X$, $|X[i]| = n$ for $1 \leq i < m$ and $0 < |X[m]| \leq n$ when $|X| > 0$. When $|X| = 0$, we let $X[1] \xleftarrow{n} X$ with $X[1] = \varepsilon$.

2.2 (Tweakable) Blockciphers

A tweakable blockcipher (TBC) [22] is a keyed function $\widetilde{E}\colon \mathcal{K}\times\mathcal{T}\times\mathcal{M} \to \mathcal{M}$ such that for each $(K,T) \in \mathcal{K} \times \mathcal{T}$, the partial function $\widetilde{E}(K,T,\cdot)$ is a permutation of $\mathcal{M}$. Here, K is the key and T is a public value called tweak, and typically we have $\mathcal{M} = \{0,1\}^n$ where n is called the block length. (It is safe to assume $n = 128$ from here on.) A conventional blockcipher is a TBC with $\mathcal{T}$ being a singleton, and specifically written as $E\colon \mathcal{K} \times \mathcal{M} \to \mathcal{M}$. The enciphering of $X \in \mathcal{M}$ under key $K \in \mathcal{K}$ and tweak $T \in \mathcal{T}$ is denoted, equivalently, $\widetilde{E}(K,T,X)$ or $\widetilde{E}_K(T,X)$ or $\widetilde{E}_K^T(X)$. For blockciphers we correspondingly write $E(K,X)$ or $E_K(X)$. The deciphering is written as $\widetilde{E}_K^{-1,T}(Y)$ for TBCs and $E_K^{-1}(Y)$ for blockciphers. For any $T \in \mathcal{T}$ and $K \in \mathcal{K}$, when $Y = \widetilde{E}_K^T(X)$ we have $\widetilde{E}_K^{-1,T}(Y) = X$.

When the key K used with a blockcipher or TBC invocation is obvious from the context, we may omit writing it. Moreover, for a mode of operation that depends on a keyed blockcipher instance E_K, we may treat E_K as the key and write Mode_E (and correspondingly for a TBC $\widetilde{E}$).

SECURITY OF (TWEAKABLE) BLOCKCIPHERS. Consider a TBC of the form $\widetilde{E}\colon \mathcal{K}\times\mathcal{T}\times\mathcal{M} \to \mathcal{M}$. A tweakable uniform random permutation (TURP) for sets $\mathcal{T}, \mathcal{M}$ is an information-theoretic TBC that behaves like uniformly distributed over all $\mathcal{T}$-tweaked permutations over $\mathcal{M}$ (i.e., like a uniformly picked function $f\colon \mathcal{T} \times \mathcal{M} \to \mathcal{M}$ such that $f(T,*)$ is a permutation over $\mathcal{M}$ for all $T \in \mathcal{T}$.) We denote TURP instances for $\widetilde{E}$ with $\widetilde{\mathsf{P}}$.

We define the Tweakable Pseudorandom Permutation (TPRP) advantage and the Tweakable Strong PRP (TSPRP) advantage of an adversary $\mathcal{A}$ as follows:

$$\mathbf{Adv}_{\widetilde{E}}^{\mathsf{tprp}}(\mathcal{A}) \overset{\text{def}}{=} \Pr\left[K \xleftarrow{\$} \mathcal{K} : \mathcal{A}^{\widetilde{E}_K} \Rightarrow 1\right] - \Pr\left[\mathcal{A}^{\widetilde{\mathsf{P}}} \Rightarrow 1\right]$$

$$\mathbf{Adv}_{\widetilde{E}}^{\mathsf{tsprp}}(\mathcal{A}) \overset{\text{def}}{=} \Pr\left[K \xleftarrow{\$} \mathcal{K} : \mathcal{A}^{\widetilde{E}_K, \widetilde{E}_K^{-1}} \Rightarrow 1\right] - \Pr\left[\mathcal{A}^{\widetilde{\mathsf{P}}, \widetilde{\mathsf{P}}^{-1}} \Rightarrow 1\right]$$

Here, the adversaries perform chosen-plaintext attacks and chosen-ciphertext attacks, respectively, and in both cases with chosen tweak. (That is, they can query any (T, X) in the enciphering direction and any (T, Y) in the deciphering direction (if applicable), with freely chosen T.)

For blockciphers $E\colon \mathcal{K} \times \mathcal{M} \to \mathcal{M}$ we analogously define the PRP advantage $\mathbf{Adv}_E^{\mathsf{prp}}(\mathcal{A})$ and SPRP advantage $\mathbf{Adv}_E^{\mathsf{sprp}}(\mathcal{A})$, using a URP P as information-theoretic reference point. (A URP uniformly distributes over all permutations over $\mathcal{M}$.)

GALOIS FIELDS. Following [18,30], bit strings $a \in \{0,1\}^n$ can be considered elements of $\mathrm{GF}(2^n)$, assuming a representation of the latter with a polynomial basis and seeing the bits of a as polynomial coefficients. The strings $0^{n-2}10$ and $0^{n-2}11$ correspond with the polynomials 'x' and 'x+1', and we denote these field elements with '2' and '3', respectively. It is common to refer to the multiplication of a field element with 2 (read: x) as *doubling*. For instance, $2^i a$ denotes i-times doubling a. Standard calculation rules (for fields) apply; in particular we have $3a = 2a \oplus a$ and $2^i 3a = 3(2^i a) = 2^{i+1}a \oplus 2^i a$ for all i.

In the spirit of the above, OCB2 considers the domain $\mathcal{M} = \{0,1\}^n$ of the blockcipher it is based on a Galois field. More precisely, the fixed block length $n = 128$ is assumed (which matches AES), and as the (irreducible) reduction polynomial of the $\mathrm{GF}(2^n)$ representation the lexicographically-first *primitive* polynomial is used, which is $\mathbf{x}^{128} + \mathbf{x}^7 + \mathbf{x}^2 + \mathbf{x} + 1$. This choice implies that all non-zero elements of $\mathrm{GF}(2^n)$ are (cyclically) obtained by continuously doubling the element 2, and further that the doubling mapping $a \mapsto 2a$ can be efficiently implemented as $\mathtt{lsb}_n(a \ll 1)$ if $\mathtt{msb}_1(a) = 0$ and $\mathtt{lsb}_n(a \ll 1) \oplus (0^{120}10000111)$ if $\mathtt{msb}_1(a) = 1$, where $(a \ll 1)$ denotes the left-shift of a by one bit. For more details on this representation, see [30].

2.3 AE and AEAD

For simplicity we refer with the term AE to both: schemes implementing (pure) Authenticated Encryption and schemes implementing Authenticated Encryption with Associated Data (AEAD) [29]. An AE scheme $\Pi = (\Pi.\mathcal{E}, \Pi.\mathcal{D})$ is defined over a key space $\mathcal{K}$, a nonce space $\mathcal{N}$, an associated data (AD) space $\mathcal{A}$, a message space $\mathcal{M}$, and a tag space $\mathcal{T} = \{0,1\}^\tau$ for some fixed tag length τ. The understanding of AD is that it is an input to the encryption and decryption algorithms that is not to be kept confidential; rather it reflects the context in which the encryption happens and is authenticated along with the encrypted message.[4] Formally, the AEAD encryption algorithm is a function $\Pi.\mathcal{E} \colon \mathcal{K} \times \mathcal{N} \times \mathcal{A} \times \mathcal{M} \to \mathcal{M} \times \mathcal{T}$, and the decryption (incl. verification) algorithm is a function $\Pi.\mathcal{D} \colon \mathcal{K} \times \mathcal{N} \times \mathcal{A} \times \mathcal{M} \times \mathcal{T} \to \mathcal{M} \cup \{\bot\}$, where symbol $\bot$ is used to report verification failures.

To encrypt plaintext M with nonce N, associated data A, and key K, compute $(C, T) \leftarrow \Pi.\mathcal{E}_K(N, A, M)$ to produce ciphertext C and tag T. The tuple (N, A, C, T) is communicated to the receiver[5] and the original message M recovered by computing $\Pi.\mathcal{D}_K(N, A, C, T)$.

SECURITY NOTIONS. The security of AE is typically captured with two notions: privacy and authenticity. Following the definitions of [5,32], authenticity requires that ciphertexts (including nonce, associated data, and tag) cannot be forged, and privacy requires their indistinguishability (including the tag). More precisely, while [32, Sec. 3] defines privacy as the inability of a passive adversary to distinguish ciphertext-tag pairs from random strings, [32, Sec. 6] gives a second definition that formalizes privacy against active adversaries (that can pose decryption queries). As noted in [32, Sec. 6], if authenticity is provided by a scheme, the two privacy notions turn out to be equivalent. Since the current article considers an AE scheme that does *not* provide authenticity, we emphasize that for this scheme the equivalence of the two notions cannot be assumed (and in fact they differ!). We correspondingly reproduce the two definitions separately.

---

[4] For example, if network payloads are to be encrypted, it is useful to include network header information in the AD.

[5] In many practical cases, receivers can reproduce N and/or A by themselves so that these values do not need to be transmitted.

We formalize privacy against passive attacks with a pair of games where a nonce-respecting adversary interacts with an oracle that is called on inputs (N, A, M) and either implements a keyed AEAD instance that returns the ciphertext $(C, T) = \mathcal{E}_K(N, A, M)$, or implements a random-bits oracle that returns a uniformly picked string of length $|M| + \tau$. The privacy advantage of an adversary $\mathcal{A}$ is defined as

$$\mathbf{Adv}_{\Pi}^{\mathrm{priv}}(\mathcal{A}) \stackrel{\mathrm{def}}{=} \Pr\left[K \stackrel{\$}{\leftarrow} \mathcal{K} : \mathcal{A}^{\Pi.\mathcal{E}_K(\cdot,\cdot,\cdot)} \Rightarrow 1\right] - \Pr\left[\mathcal{A}^{\$(\cdot,\cdot,\cdot)} \Rightarrow 1\right].$$

Privacy against active adversaries is defined similarly, but with an added decryption oracle that the adversary may query on arbitrary tuples (N, A, C, T) except those where (C, T) was returned by a $\mathcal{E}_K(N, A, \cdot)$ or $\$(N, A, \cdot)$ query before. The corresponding advantage definition is

$$\mathbf{Adv}_{\Pi}^{\mathrm{priv\text{-}cca}}(\mathcal{A}) \stackrel{\mathrm{def}}{=} \Pr_{K}\left[\mathcal{A}^{\Pi.\mathcal{E}_K(\cdot,\cdot,\cdot),\Pi.\mathcal{D}_K(\cdot,\cdot,\cdot,\cdot)} \Rightarrow 1\right] - \Pr_{K}\left[\mathcal{A}^{\$(\cdot,\cdot,\cdot),\Pi.\mathcal{D}_K(\cdot,\cdot,\cdot,\cdot)} \Rightarrow 1\right].$$

where the probabilities are over the random choice $K \stackrel{\$}{\leftarrow} \mathcal{K}$.

With respect to the authenticity notion, we deem adversaries $\mathcal{A}$ with access to $\mathcal{E}_K$ and $\mathcal{D}_K$ oracles successful if they are effective with creating forgeries. Formally, the authenticity advantage is defined as

$$\mathbf{Adv}_{\Pi}^{\mathrm{auth}}(\mathcal{A}) \stackrel{\mathrm{def}}{=} \Pr\left[K \stackrel{\$}{\leftarrow} \mathcal{K} : \mathcal{A}^{\Pi.\mathcal{E}_K(\cdot,\cdot,\cdot),\Pi.\mathcal{D}_K(\cdot,\cdot,\cdot,\cdot)} \text{ forges }\right], \tag{1}$$

where $\mathcal{A}$ forges if it receives a value $M' \neq \perp$ from the $\Pi.\mathcal{D}_K$ oracle, conditioned on it being nonce respecting and not querying tuples (N, A, C, T) to the $\Pi.\mathcal{D}_K$ oracle if it made a query (N, A, M) to $\Pi.\mathcal{E}_K$ with result (C, T) before.

3   The OCB2 Mode of Operation

The OCB2 authenticated encryption scheme was initially, in [30], described as a pure (nonce-based) AE mode without support for AD processing.[6] Like its predecessor OCB1 it is fully parallelizable and rate-1 (requiring one blockcipher invocation per message block), but it replaced the table-driven design of OCB1 with the 'powering-up' construction to compute a sequence of tweaks by continuously doubling them. Further, in [30, Sec. 11] it was suggested that the OCB2 AE mode can be generalized into an AEAD mode (dubbed AEM) by XOR-ing, in all cases where the AD is non-empty, a MAC of the AD into the authentication tag of OCB2. The OCB2-related PMAC construction was identified as a particularly interesting option as it would allow sharing its blockcipher instance with that of the OCB2 encryption core.[7]

---

[6] In that paper the mode was actually referred to as OCB1; what we call OCB1 was referred to as OCB in [30].

[7] The PMAC version from [31] is slightly different from the initial version [7] in that it uses doublings for mask generation and was further adapted to be computationally independent from the encryption part when combined with OCB2.

Algorithm OCB2.$\mathcal{E}_E(N, A, M)$	Algorithm OCB2.$\mathcal{D}_E(N, A, C, T)$
1. $L \leftarrow E(N)$	1. $L \leftarrow E(N)$
2. $(M[1], \ldots, M[m]) \xleftarrow{n} M$	2. $(C[1], \ldots, C[m]) \xleftarrow{n} C$
3. **for** $i \leftarrow 1$ **to** $m-1$	3. **for** $i \leftarrow 1$ **to** $m-1$
4. $\quad C[i] \leftarrow 2^i L \oplus E(2^i L \oplus M[i])$	4. $\quad M[i] \leftarrow 2^i L \oplus E^{-1}(2^i L \oplus C[i])$
5. Pad $\leftarrow E(2^m L \oplus \text{len}(M[m]))$	5. Pad $\leftarrow E(2^m L \oplus \text{len}(C[m]))$
6. $C[m] \leftarrow M[m] \oplus \text{msb}_{|M[m]|}(\text{Pad})$	6. $M[m] \leftarrow C[m] \oplus \text{msb}_{|C[m]|}(\text{Pad})$
7. $\Sigma \leftarrow C[m] \,\|\, 0^* \oplus \text{Pad}$	7. $\Sigma \leftarrow C[m] \,\|\, 0^* \oplus \text{Pad}$
8. $\Sigma \leftarrow M[1] \oplus \cdots \oplus M[m-1] \oplus \Sigma$	8. $\Sigma \leftarrow M[1] \oplus \cdots \oplus M[m-1] \oplus \Sigma$
9. $T \leftarrow E(2^m 3L \oplus \Sigma)$	9. $T^* \leftarrow E(2^m 3L \oplus \Sigma)$
10. **if** $A \neq \varepsilon$ **then** $T \leftarrow T \oplus \text{PMAC}_E(A)$	10. **if** $A \neq \varepsilon$ **then** $T^* \leftarrow T^* \oplus \text{PMAC}_E(A)$
11. $T \leftarrow \text{msb}_\tau(T)$	11. $T^* \leftarrow \text{msb}_\tau(T^*)$
12. **return** (C, T)	12. **if** $T = T^*$ **return** M
	13. **else return** $\perp$

Fig. 1. Algorithms of OCB2. See Appendix B for the specifications of len and PMAC_E. Blockcipher E is implicitly parameterized with the AEAD key.

Our specification of OCB2 is taken from [31, Fig. 3] and supports associated data. The key space $\mathcal{K}$ is that of the underlying blockcipher E, the latter is required to have block length $n = 128$ (in particular, AES is suitable), the nonce space is $\mathcal{N} = \{0,1\}^n$, the message space $\mathcal{M}$ and the AD space $\mathcal{A}$ are the sets of strings of arbitrary length, and the tag space is $\mathcal{C} = \{0,1\}^\tau$ for any fixed parameter $\tau \leq n$.

The OCB2 algorithms $\mathcal{E}_E$ and $\mathcal{D}_E$ are detailed in Fig. 1 (and algorithm $\mathcal{E}_E$ is further illustrated in Fig. 2). In the code, for $X \in \{0,1\}^{\leq n}$, expression $\text{len}(X)$ denotes an n-bit encoding of $|X|$, $\text{PMAC}_E(A)$ denotes the PMAC of A computed with the (keyed) blockcipher instance E, and the field operations are with respect to the $\text{GF}(2^n)$ setup described in Sect. 2.2. The details of functions len and PMAC are ultimately not relevant for our attacks, so we omit their description here. (For completeness we reproduce them in Appendix B.)

4 Basic Attacks

We prove by example that, in the formal sense, OCB2 provides neither authenticity nor confidentiality. We start with specifying a minimal attack on unforgeability that gets along with a single encryption query to produce an existential forgery with probability 1. This attack, while formally valid, is rather limited with respect to the choice of involved parameters like message length and tag length. We thus proceed with giving a more general version that extends the basic attack in terms of these parameters.

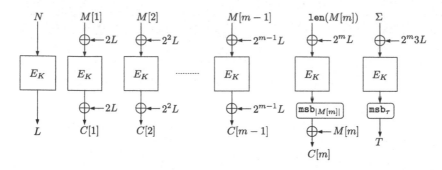

Fig. 2. OCB2 encryption for the case of empty AD.

We then focus on the confidentiality of OCB2 and observe that our attacks against authenticity effectively also break the privacy of OCB2 (requiring one encryption and one decryption query).

The attacks considered here neither craft universal forgeries nor decrypt arbitrary ciphertexts. These more powerful attacks are described in Sect. 5.

4.1 Minimal Forgery

We give the minimal example of our forgery attacks against OCB2. For simplicity, assume $\tau = n$, i.e., that tags have maximum length. Note that the attack is independent of both the AD processing function (PMAC) and the details of the length encoding function len.

The following steps of our attack are also illustrated in Fig. 3 and specified in pseudocode in Fig. 4.

1. Encrypt (N, A, M) where N is any nonce, $A = \varepsilon$ is empty, and M is the $2n$-bit message $M = M[1] \, \| \, M[2]$ where

$$M[1] = \text{len}(0^n)$$

   and $M[2]$ is any n-bit block. The encryption oracle returns the pair (C, T) consisting of a $2n$-bit ciphertext $C = C[1] \, \| \, C[2]$ and a tag T.
2. Decrypt (N', A', C', T') with $|C'| = n$ such that

$$\begin{aligned}
N' &= N, \\
A' &= \varepsilon, \\
C' &= C[1] \oplus \text{len}(0^n) \\
T' &= M[2] \oplus C[2]
\end{aligned}$$

(2)

Note that $C' \neq C$ (they have different lengths), so we have a successful forgery if (N', A', C', T') is accepted by the decryption algorithm. To see that this is the case, observe first that by the encryption algorithm we have

$$C[1] = 2L \oplus E(2L \oplus \mathtt{len}(0^n))$$
$$C[2] = M[2] \oplus \mathrm{Pad}, \qquad (3)$$

where $L = E(N)$ and $\mathrm{Pad} = E(2^2 L \oplus \mathtt{len}(0^n))$. Let Pad' and Σ' be the intermediate values computed during decryption. Then C' is decrypted to

$$
\begin{aligned}
M' &= C' \oplus \mathrm{Pad}' \\
&= C' \oplus E(2L \oplus \mathtt{len}(0^n)) \\
&= C[1] \oplus \mathtt{len}(0^n) \oplus E(2L \oplus \mathtt{len}(0^n)) \\
&= 2L \oplus E(2L \oplus \mathtt{len}(0^n)) \oplus \mathtt{len}(0^n) \oplus E(2L \oplus \mathtt{len}(0^n)) \\
&= 2L \oplus \mathtt{len}(0^n),
\end{aligned}
$$

and the tag is recovered as

$$
\begin{aligned}
T^* &= E(2 \cdot 3L \oplus \Sigma') \\
&= E(2 \cdot 3L \oplus C' \oplus \mathrm{Pad}') \\
&= E(2 \cdot 3L \oplus M') \\
&= E(2 \cdot 3L \oplus 2L \oplus \mathtt{len}(0^n)) \\
&= E(2^2 L \oplus \mathtt{len}(0^n)) \qquad (4) \\
&= \mathrm{Pad} \\
&= T', \qquad (5)
\end{aligned}
$$

where (4) follows from the identity $2 \cdot 3L = 2^2 L \oplus 2L$ and (5) follows from (2) and (3). The conclusion is: We have $T^* = T'$ and thus tuple (N', A', C', T') is falsely accepted as an authentic ciphertext.

4.2   Forgery of Longer Messages

We next show that the attack of Sect. 4.1 can be generalized, without increasing the number of encryption or decryption queries, to allow forging ciphertexts for arbitrarily long messages. The generalized attack further drops the requirement for $A = \varepsilon$ for the encryption query, and relaxes the $\tau = n$ requirement for the tag length.

1. Encrypt (N, A, M) where N and A are arbitrary, $M = M[1] \| \cdots \| M[m-1] \| M[m]$ is an m-block message satisfying

$$M[m-1] = \mathtt{len}(0^n),$$

and $M[m]$ is any s-bit string such that $\tau \leq s \leq n$. The encryption oracle returns a pair (C, T) where $C = C[1] \| \cdots \| C[m-1] \| C[m]$.

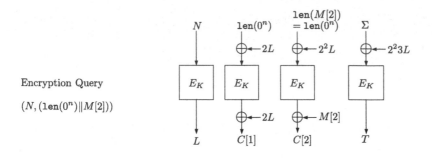

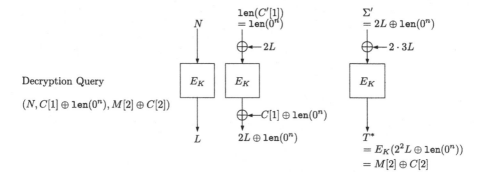

Fig. 3. Minimal forgery attack (see Sect. 4.1).

2. Decrypt (N', A', C', T') where $N' = N$, $A' = \varepsilon$, and $C' = C'[1] \| \cdots \| C'[m-2] \| C'[m-1]$ has $m-1$ blocks such that

$$C'[i] = C[i] \text{ for } 1 \leq i \leq m-2$$

$$C'[m-1] = \sum_{i=1}^{m-2} M[i] \oplus C[m-1] \oplus \text{len}(M[m])$$

$$T' = \text{msb}_\tau(M[m] \oplus C[m]).$$

To see that this tuple is accepted as authentic (and thus manifests a forgery), let $\overline{T}'$ be the reconstructed (untruncated) tag in the decryption query. We have

$$\overline{T}' = E(\Sigma' \oplus 3 \cdot 2^{m-1} L)$$

$$= E\left(\sum_{i=1}^{m-2} M'[i] \oplus C'[m-1] \oplus \text{Pad}' \oplus 3 \cdot 2^{m-1} L \right)$$

$$= E\left(\sum_{i=1}^{m-2} M[i] \oplus C'[m-1] \oplus C[m-1] \oplus 2^{m-1} L \oplus 3 \cdot 2^{m-1} L \right), \quad (6)$$

where $M'[i] = M[i]$ is the i-th decrypted plaintext block, and $\text{Pad}' = C[m-1] \oplus 2^{m-1}L$. Since $2^{m-1}L \oplus 3 \cdot 2^{m-1}L = 2^m L$, the last term of (6) is further expanded as

$$E \left(\sum_{i=1}^{m-2} M[i] \oplus C'[m-1] \oplus C[m-1] \oplus 2^m L \right)$$

$$= E \left(\sum_{i=1}^{m-2} M[i] \oplus \left(\sum_{i=1}^{m-2} M[i] \oplus C[m-1] \oplus \texttt{len}(M[m]) \right) \oplus C[m-1] \oplus 2^m L \right)$$

$$= E \left(\texttt{len}(M[m]) \oplus 2^m L \right)$$

$$= \text{Pad} .$$

Finally, we have

$$\begin{aligned}
T^* &= \texttt{msb}_\tau(\overline{T}') \\
&= \texttt{msb}_\tau(\text{Pad}) \\
&= \texttt{msb}_\tau(M[m] \oplus C[m]) \quad (\because \tau \leq |M[m]| \leq n) \\
&= T' .
\end{aligned}$$

4.3   Confidentiality Attack

In Sect. 4.1 we have seen a basic attack that breaks the authenticity of OCB2. Perhaps surprisingly at first, the very same attack (formally) also breaks the privacy of the scheme. More precisely, we describe a two-query adversary against the PRIV-CCA notion that achieves a distinguishing advantage of almost 1.

The intuition behind our adversary is quite simple: It poses the same encryption and decryption queries as adversary $\mathcal{A}$ in Sect. 4.1, but then considers whether the value M' returned by the decryption oracle indicates that the ciphertext was valid or not: $\mathcal{A}$ outputs $b = 1$ if $M' \in \mathcal{M}$; otherwise, if $M' = \bot$, it outputs $b = 0$. Note that if $\mathcal{A}$ interacts with legit $\mathcal{E}$ and $\mathcal{D}$ oracles then the forgery will be successful (by what we proved) and we have the $b = 1$ case. On the other hand, if $\mathcal{A}$ interacts with \$ and $\mathcal{D}$, the probability that $M' \neq \bot$ and thus $\mathcal{A}$ outputs $b = 1$, is only $2^{-\tau}$.

ATTACKING THE PRIV-CV NOTION. In Sect. 2.3 we formalized the privacy notions PRIV and PRIV-CCA, where the former did not have a decryption oracle and targeted fully passive adversaries. We note that a version that is like the plain PRIV notion but adds a *ciphertext verification oracle* would interpolate between the two; we call this notion PRIV-CV (for ciphertext verification). The new oracle tries to decrypt any provided ciphertext and returns a bit (encoded as ⊤/⊥) indicating whether the ciphertext was valid. It is not hard to see that our attack against PRIV-CCA is actually an attack against PRIV-CV. (Note that this increases its applicability and thus makes it more powerful.) We give the full details of the attack in Fig. 4, where we denote the verification oracle with $\mathcal{V}$.

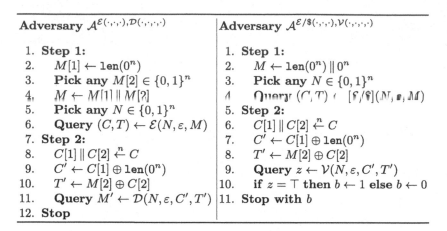

Fig. 4. Left: Minimal attack on authenticity. **Right:** Minimal attack on privacy (version with ciphertext verification oracle).

ATTACKING THE IND-CCA NOTION. A different formalization of confidentiality is given by the IND-CCA notion [32] which does not require that ciphertexts look like random strings but focuses on the bare semantic security aspect of encryption. It is easy to modify our above attack to be successful in the IND-CCA sense: In the classic left-or-right setting, the left message would be chosen according to our authenticity attack, while the right message would be chosen to be the all-zero message (of the same length). As above, the adversary would output $b = 1$ iff its forgery attempt is deemed valid.

4.4 Observations

The attacks of Sects. 4.1 and 4.2 can be extended to several directions.

TRUNCATED TAG. Since the tag T returned by the first encryption query is not needed by our attacks, they also work if AD is chosen non-empty (for the encryption query). However, the decryption query needs the empty AD. For the same reason, our attacks also work when $\tau < n$; we just set $T' = \mathrm{msb}_\tau(M[2] \oplus C[2])$ and the forgery will be accepted with probability one.

ALMOST-ARBITRARY MESSAGE. Most of the blocks of the message involved in the first encryption query can be freely chosen by the attacker. Only the last but one block requires a special format: $\mathrm{len}(0^n) = 0^{120}10^7$ (see Appendix B). This format is not too special and could even occur naturally, e.g. if plaintexts receive a certain padding before being encrypted.

THE CONDITION ON $M[m-1]$. Our attacks also work for some values $M[m-1]$ that differ from $\mathrm{len}(0^n)$. When $M[m-1] = \mathrm{len}(0^{n-s})$ for some $0 < s < n$, by making $(n-s)$-bit $C'[m-1] = \mathrm{msb}_{n-s}(C[m-1]) \oplus \mathrm{msb}_{n-s}(\mathrm{len}(0^n))$ the forgery is still successful if s is small. In more detail, the success probability is

$1/2^s$ which is the probability that $\mathtt{lsb}_s(\mathrm{Pad})$ equals to $\mathtt{lsb}_s(2L \oplus \mathtt{len}(0^n))$. If we create 2^s forgeries for 2^s encryption queries, there will be at least one successful forgery with a high probability.

When $\mathtt{len}(M[m]) < \tau$, the adversary can forge T^* with probability $1/2^{\tau - \mathtt{len}(M[m])}$, since the adversary only knows $\mathtt{msb}_{\mathtt{len}(M[m])}(\mathrm{Pad})$ and has to guess the remaining $(\tau - \mathtt{len}(M[m]))$ bits.

5 Advanced Attacks

In this section we target some of the most powerful goals of encryption scheme cryptanalysis: We contribute a universal forgery attack and a full plaintext recovery attack for arbitrary ciphertexts.

5.1 Universal Forgeries

In a universal forgery attack the adversary freely chooses any $M^\$ \in \{0,1\}^*$, any $A^\$ \in \{0,1\}^*$, and any $N^\$ \in \{0,1\}^n$, and creates a forgery $(C^\$, T^\$)$ such that $\mathrm{OCB2}.\mathcal{D}_E(N^\$, A^\$, C^\$, T^\$)$ returns $M^\$$. We present a universal forgery attack for OCB2 that is based on two sub-routines that we describe first.

EXTRACTING RANDOM BLOCKCIPHER MAPPINGS. Given a fixed blockcipher instance $E = E_K$, we refer to any pair $(X, Y) \in (\{0,1\}^n)^2$ satisfying $E(X) = Y$ as an *input-output pair* or *mapping* of the blockcipher. Note that the regular deployment of OCB2 does not expose such pairs. (This is not a coincidence as the XEX* construction becomes insecure when such pairs become public.) However, as we observe and explore in the following, if forged OCB2 ciphertexts surface and are decrypted then the resulting messages *do* leak one or more input-output pairs. We develop pseudocode for a procedure that, on input an integer m, performs a specific OCB2 forgery and extracts roughly m-many input-output pairs from the result. As our procedure does not control the positions X, Y for which it finds the pairs we refer to the process as 'random mapping extraction'.

Recall that in our authenticity attack from Sect. 4.1 the adversary learns value $M' = 2L \oplus \mathtt{len}(0^n)$ and thus $E(N) = L = (M' \oplus \mathtt{len}(0^n))/2$ from the forgery. Note that (N, L) is the first example of an extracted input-output pair. In fact, inspection of the OCB2 algorithms in Fig. 1 shows that also $(2L \oplus \mathtt{len}(0^n), 2L \oplus C[1])$ and $(2^2 L \oplus \mathtt{len}(0^n), C[2] \oplus M[2])$ are input-output pairs of E. (In addition, but only if $\tau = n$, we can obtain one more such pair from Σ and T; however, for generality we ignore this observation in the following.)

Similar observations hold for our long-message forgery attack of Sect. 4.2, and the number of extractable input-output pairs is even higher (linear in the length of the message). Our SamplePairs procedure, specified in Fig. 5 (left), mechanizes the input-output pair gathering by crafting, in the spirit of Sect. 4.2, a forgery for a long all-zero message. More precisely, the procedure takes on input a value $m \geq 2$ and extracts $m+1$ input-output pairs[8], assuming it is provided with access

---

[8] The number of pairs can be fewer than $m + 1$ when collisions occur, however this event has a negligible probability.

to $\mathcal{E}$ and $\mathcal{D}$ oracles. (Again we ignore the extra pair obtainable when $\tau = n$.) The resulting pairs (X, Y) are collected in a global set $\mathbb{E}$. While the latter is shared with other algorithms that we describe below, the set can be characterized by the implication $(X, Y) \in \mathbb{E} \Rightarrow E(X) = Y$ (for one fixed blockcipher key K).

EXTRACTING SPECIFIC BLOCKCIPHER MAPPINGS. Once a non-empty set $\mathbb{E}$ is obtained with the SamplePairs procedure, we can implement a second procedure that takes an arbitrary vector $(X_1, X_2, \ldots)$ of blockcipher inputs and returns the vector $(Y_1, Y_2, \ldots)$ such that $E(X_i) = Y_i$ for all i. The underlying idea is to pick from $\mathbb{E}$ a random input-output pair (N, L), to use N as a (hopefully fresh) nonce in an encryption query of a message M, and to exploit the a priori knowledge of value L (that would normally remain hidden) to carefully prepare message M such that the blockcipher invocations induced by the encryption process coincide exactly with the points X_i. The corresponding values Y_i can then be extracted from the ciphertext.

The specification of the corresponding Encipher procedure is in Fig. 5 (right). The nonce generation in line 2 assumes that set $\mathbb{E}$ was populated before by at least one invocation of procedure SamplePairs. The likely most interesting detail of the procedure is that while the first $m - 1$ values X_i are embedded directly into (the first $m - 1$ blocks of) the message M, the one remaining value X_m is only implicitly embedded: We carefully choose the last message block $M[m]$ such that the sum $\Sigma = M[1] \oplus \ldots \oplus M[m]$ used to derive the authentication tag is such that the tag is computed as $T = E(X_m)$. Observe that the full T, and thus Y_m, is visible to the adversary only if $\tau = n$, i.e., if the tag is not truncated. Correspondingly, our procedure translates X_m to Y_m only in this case. Otherwise, if $\tau < n$, only for $X_1, \ldots, X_{m-1}$ the corresponding value Y_i is identified and returned. Note that we feed back all extracted pairs (X_i, Y_i) into the set $\mathbb{E}$, giving more choice to pick a fresh nonce in line 2 of a later invocation of Encipher.

UNIVERSAL FORGERY ATTACK. Note that with the development of the Encipher algorithm it became trivial to compute forgeries on any combination of nonce N, message M, and AD A: It simply suffices to execute OCB2's encryption algorithm $\mathcal{E}$ from Fig. 1 on input N, A, M, emulating all blockcipher evaluations with invocations of Encipher. The resulting forgeries are perfect. Note further that OCB2 is parallelizable, i.e., most of the blockcipher evaluations of an encryption operation happen concurrently of each other. This property makes forging very efficient (in terms of the number of required encryption queries), as all concurrent enciphering operations can be batch-processed with a single Encipher call.

When closely looking at the details it however becomes apparent that universally forging cannot be performed with a single Encipher invocation. As a matter of fact, not all enciphering operations related to an encryption are concurrent: In OCB2's $\mathcal{E}$ algorithm, tag T is computed by enciphering a value dependent on Pad which is a blockcipher output by itself. These computations cannot be parallelized, and it becomes clear that universal forging requires at least two succeeding Encipher invocations. A similar observation can be made for the PMAC algorithm (see Fig. 9 in Appendix) where the finalization step requires enciphering an intermediate sum

Procedure SamplePairs$^{\mathcal{E}(),\mathcal{D}()}(m)$	**Procedure** Encipher$^{\mathcal{E}()}(X_1,\ldots,X_{m-1},X_m)$
1. **Global variable:** $\mathbb{E}$	
2. $M[1,\ldots,m-2,m] \leftarrow 0^n$	1. **Global variable:** $\mathbb{E}$
3. $M[m-1] \leftarrow \mathtt{len}(0^n)$	2. $(N,L) \xleftarrow{\$} \mathbb{E}$
4. $M \leftarrow M[1] \| \ldots \| M[m]$	3. **for** $i \leftarrow 1$ **to** $m-1$:
5. $N \xleftarrow{\$} \{0,1\}^n$	4. $\quad M[i] \leftarrow 2^i L \oplus X_i$
6. $(C,T) \leftarrow \mathcal{E}(N,\varepsilon,M)$	5. $\Sigma \leftarrow 2^m 3L \oplus X_m$
7. $C[1] \| \ldots \| C[m] \xleftarrow{n} C$	6. $M[m] \leftarrow M[1] \oplus \ldots \oplus M[m-1] \oplus \Sigma$
8. $C[m-1] \leftarrow C[m-1] \oplus \mathtt{len}(0^n)$	7. $M \leftarrow M[1] \| \ldots \| M[m]$
9. $C' \leftarrow C[1] \| \ldots \| C[m-1]$	8. $(C,T) \leftarrow \mathcal{E}(N,\varepsilon,M)$
10. $T' \leftarrow \mathtt{msb}_\tau(C[m])$	9. $C[1] \| \ldots \| C[m] \xleftarrow{n} C$
11. $M' \leftarrow \mathcal{D}(N,\varepsilon,C',T')$	10. **for** $i \leftarrow 1$ **to** $m-1$:
12. $M'[1] \| \ldots \| M'[m-1] \xleftarrow{n} M'$	11. $\quad Y_i \leftarrow 2^i L \oplus C[i]$
13. $L \leftarrow 2^{-(m-1)}(M'[m-1] \oplus \mathtt{len}(0^n))$	12. $X' \leftarrow 2^m L \oplus \mathtt{len}(0^n)$
14. **for** $i \leftarrow 1$ **to** $m-1$:	13. $Y' \leftarrow M[m] \oplus C[m]$
15. $\quad (X_i,Y_i) \leftarrow (2^i L \oplus M[i], 2^i L \oplus C[i])$	14. $\mathbb{E} \xleftarrow{\cup} \{(X_1,Y_1),\ldots,(X_{m-1},Y_{m-1})\}$
16. $X_m \leftarrow 2^m L \oplus \mathtt{len}(0^n)$	15. $\mathbb{E} \xleftarrow{\cup} \{(X',Y')\}$
17. $Y_m \leftarrow C[m]$	16. **if** $\tau = n$ **then**
18. $\mathbb{E} \xleftarrow{\cup} \{(N,L)\}$	17. $\quad Y_m \leftarrow T$
19. $\mathbb{E} \xleftarrow{\cup} \{(X_1,Y_1),\ldots,(X_m,Y_m)\}$	18. $\quad \mathbb{E} \xleftarrow{\cup} \{(X_m,Y_m)\}$
20. **if** $\tau = n$ **then**	19. **return** $(Y_1,\ldots,Y_{m-1},Y_m)$
21. $\quad X_T \leftarrow \mathtt{len}(0^n) \oplus 2^m 3L$	
22. $\quad Y_T \leftarrow T$	
23. $\quad \mathbb{E} \xleftarrow{\cup} \{(X_T,Y_T)\}$	
24. **return**	

Fig. 5. Left: Procedure that generates a random collection of $m+1$ pairs (X_i,Y_i) such that $E(X_i) = Y_i$ for all i. If $\tau = n$ (gray part) then this is improved to $m+2$ pairs. **Right:** Procedure that given $X_1,\ldots,X_{m-1}$ finds $Y_1,\ldots,Y_{m-1}$ such that $E(X_i) = Y_i$ for all i. If $\tau = n$ (gray part) then one more mapping $X_m \to Y_m$ can be processed. (If $\tau < n$ use any value for X_m in line 5, e.g., $X_m = 0$.) **Both:** The procedures share a common set variable $\mathbb{E}$ that is assumed to initially be empty. Procedure Encipher may only be invoked after SamplePairs has been (this is to ensure well-defined behavior in line 2 of the former).

that is computed by adding up outputs of other enciphering operations. The latter, by themselves depend on the value $E(0^n)$, so the minimal number of Encipher invocations increases to three. (Of course $E(0^n)$ could be cached from a prior forgery but a worst-case analysis cannot assume that.)

We complete this discussion by showing that three Encipher invocations are sufficient in all cases. We do this by describing the full set of instructions to compute a forgery $(C^\$,T^\$)$ for input data $N^\$, M^\$, A^\$$.

The attack successively calls SamplePairs and Encipher. The first call is to obtain $E(N^\$)$ and $E(0^n)$, the second is to obtain those needed for encryption of

$M^\$$ and PMAC of $A^\$$ *except the tag and the last AD block*, and the third is for the tag and the last AD block. Specifically, the steps for the universal forgery are as follows:

1. The adversary performs SamplePairs(2). With overwhelming probability, we assume nonce sampled in SamplePairs(2), N', is different from $N^\$$. Then she obtains a set of distinct pairs written as $\mathbb{E} = \{(N', L'), (X', Y'), (X'', Y'')\}$.
2. If $(N^\$, E_K(N^\$)), (0^n, E_K(0^n)) \in \mathbb{E}$, she goes to the next step. Otherwise, she performs Encipher($N^\$, 0^n, 0^n$) and obtains $L := E_K(N^\$)$ and $V := 3^2 E_K(0^n)$.
3. Let

$$X_i := M^\$[i] \oplus 2^i L \text{ for } 1 \le i \le m - 1,$$

$$X_m := \texttt{len}(M^\$[m]) \oplus 2^m L,$$

$$X_i^A := A^\$[i] \oplus 2^i V, \text{ for } 1 \le i \le a - 1,$$

where $M^\$[1], \ldots, M^\$[m] \xleftarrow{n} M^\$$ and $A^\$[1], \ldots, A^\$[a] \xleftarrow{n} A^\$$. She obtains $Y_i = E_K(X_i)$ $(1 \le i \le m)$ and $Y_i^A = E_K(X_i^A)$ $(1 \le i \le a - 1)$ by performing Encipher($X_1, \cdots, X_m, X_1^A, \cdots, X_{a-1}^A, 0^n$).
4. Let $X_{m+1} := \Sigma^\$ \oplus 2^m \cdot 3L$, where

$$\Sigma^\$ = \bigoplus_{i=1}^{m-1} M^\$[i] \oplus (M^\$[m] \parallel \texttt{lsb}_{n-|M^\$[m]|}(Y_m)).$$

If $|A^\$[a]| = n$, let $X_a^A := \Sigma_{i=1}^{a-1} Y_i^A \oplus A^\$[a] \oplus 2^a \cdot 3V$ and else, $X_a^A := \Sigma_{i=1}^{a-1} Y_i^A \oplus$ ozp($A^\$[a]$) $\oplus 2^a \cdot 3^2 V$. She obtains $Y_{m+1} = E_K(X_{m+1})$ and $Y_a^A = E_K(X_a^A)$ by calling Encipher($X_{m+1}, X_a^A, 0^n$).
5. She creates $(N^\$, A^\$, C^\$, T^\$)$, where

$$C^\$ = (Y_1 \oplus 2L) \parallel \cdots \parallel (Y_{m-1} \oplus 2^{m-1}L) \parallel (\texttt{msb}_{|M^\$[m]|}(Y_m) \oplus M^\$[m]),$$

$$T^\$ = \texttt{msb}_\tau(Y_{m+1} \oplus Y_a^A).$$

This tuple $(N^\$, A^\$, C^\$, T^\$)$ will be accepted as valid by $\mathcal{D}$, with return value $M^\$$.

5.2 Plaintext Recovery

SECURITY MODEL OF PLAINTEXT RECOVERY ATTACK. We consider an attack model that closely follows [25]. A challenger has a secret key K. Let (C^*, T^*) be the encryption of (N^*, A^*, M^*), where a nonce N^*, associated data A^*, and a plaintext M^* are arbitrarily chosen by the challenger.

Then (N^*, A^*, C^*, T^*) is given to the adversary as a challenge. She has access to the encryption and decryption oracles, and the goal is to recover M^*. She cannot use N^* as a nonce in encryption queries (as N^* was already used in encryption to generate the challenge). Also, the adversary is nonce-respecting and hence cannot repeat the same nonce in encryption queries. To avoid a trivial win, she cannot use the challenge (N^*, A^*, C^*, T^*) in decryption queries.

PLAINTEXT RECOVERY ATTACK. (C^*, T^*) is the encryption of (N^*, A^*, M^*), and (N^*, A^*, C^*, T^*) is given to the adversary as a challenge. We first make an assumption that M^* is long and C^* has many blocks (for instance 3 or more blocks), and the goal is to recover M^* (We will later show how to recover short plaintexts).

We first recover $L^* := E_K(N^*)$. This can be done by using SamplePairs and Encipher as follows: The adversary first calls SamplePairs(2), and with overwhelming probability, we assume nonce N' sampled in SamplePairs(2) is different from N^*. Then she obtains a set of distinct pairs $\mathbb{E} = \{(N', L'), (X', Y'), (X'', Y'')\}$. If $(N^*, E_K(N^*)) \in \mathbb{E}$, then we have L^*. Otherwise, she performs Encipher($N^*, 0^n$) and obtains L^* from the first block of the output of Encipher($N^*, 0^n$).

With the knowledge of L^*, we modify C^* to make a decryption query. Specifically, let $C^* = (C^*[1], \ldots, C^*[m^*])$ be the challenge ciphertext broken into blocks, and we first fix two distinct indices $j, k \in \{1, \ldots, m^*-1\}$. Note that we are assuming that M^* is long and $m^* \geq 3$. We then define $C^\$ = (C^\$[1], \ldots, C^\$[m^*])$ as follows:

- $C^\$[i] := C^*[i]$ for $i \in \{1, \ldots, m^*\} \setminus \{j, k\}$
- $C^\$[j] := C^*[k] \oplus 2^k L^* \oplus 2^j L^*$
- $C^\$[k] := C^*[j] \oplus 2^k L^* \oplus 2^j L^*$

Next, the adversary makes a decryption query $(N^*, A^*, C^\$, T^*)$, i.e, this is almost the same as the challenge, but the j-th and k-th blocks of C^* are modified. This step can fail only with a negligible probability (e.g., if $C^*[j] = C^*[k]$ and $L^* = 0^n$). We see that the query will be accepted since the checksum remains the same, and the adversary obtains $M^\$$. The goal of the attack, M^*, is obtained by swapping the j-th and k-th blocks of $M^\$$ and making necessary modifications. More precisely, from $M^\$ = (M^\$[1], \ldots, M^\$[m^*])$, we obtain $M^* = (M^*[1], \ldots, M^*[m^*])$ as follows:

- $M^*[i] := M^\$[i]$ for $i \in \{1, \ldots, m^*\} \setminus \{j, k\}$
- $M^*[j] := M^\$[k] \oplus 2^k L^* \oplus 2^j L^*$
- $M^*[k] := M^\$[j] \oplus 2^k L^* \oplus 2^j L^*$

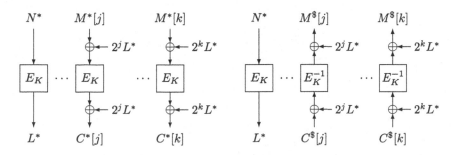

Fig. 6. Left: The encryption process of (N^*, A^*, M^*). **Right:** The decryption process of $(N^*, A^*, C^\$, T^*)$. In the right figure, we have $C^\$[j] = C^*[k] \oplus 2^k L^* \oplus 2^j L^*$ and $C^\$[k] = C^*[j] \oplus 2^k L^* \oplus 2^j L^*$, and it follows that $M^*[j] = M^\$[k] \oplus 2^k L^* \oplus 2^j L^*$ and $M^*[k] = M^\$[j] \oplus 2^k L^* \oplus 2^j L^*$. We see that the checksum remains the same.

See Fig. 6 for the encryption process of (N^*, A^*, M^*) and the decryption process of $(N^*, A^*, C^\$, T^*)$.

EMULATING BLOCKCIPHER DECRYPTION. We show that, for any Y^*, the adversary can compute $X^* = E_K^{-1}(Y^*)$. This complements the extraction of a specific blockcipher mapping in Sect. 5.1, and this will be useful in the plaintext recovery for plaintexts of two blocks.

The adversary first calls SamplePairs(2), and let N be the nonce sampled in the call. Then she obtains $\mathbb{E} = \{(N, L), (X[1], Y[1]), (X[2], Y[2])\}$.

Let $(N', L') = (X[1], Y[1])$, where we assume that $N' \neq N$, and define

$$M^* = (X^* \oplus 2L', X^* \oplus 2^2 L', 0^n) \in \{0, 1\}^{3n}.$$

The approach we take is to compute C^* and T^* under the nonce N' and empty A^*, and make a decryption query (N', A^*, C^*, T^*). The adversary obtains M^*, and X^* can be obtained in an obvious way.

The observation here is that the checksum of M^* is $\Sigma^* := 2L' \oplus 2^2 L'$, which is independent of X^*, and we know all the blockcipher input values to compute C^* and T^*. See Fig. 7 for the encryption process of (N', A^*, M^*). We need to derive the values of $C^*[3]$ and T^* in Fig. 7. This can be done by calling Encipher$(X[1], X[2], 0^n)$, where $X[1] = \text{len}(0^n) \oplus 2^3 L'$ and $X[2] = 2L' \oplus 2^2 L' \oplus 2^3 3L'$. From the output $(Y[1], Y[2], Y[3])$ of Encipher$(X[1], X[2], 0^n)$, $C^*[3]$ is $Y[1]$ and T^* is $\text{msb}_\tau(Y[2])$.

The final step is to make a decryption query (N', A^*, C^*, T^*), where A^* is empty, $C^* = (Y^* \oplus 2L', Y^* \oplus 2^2 L', C^*[3])$, and $C^*[3]$ and T^* are obtained as above. The query will be accepted, and the oracle returns $M^* = (X^* \oplus 2L', X^* \oplus 2^2 L', 0^n)$. The adversary can compute X^* from the knowledge of L', and we see that the entire process succeeds with an overwhelming probability.

PLAINTEXT RECOVERY ATTACK (SHORT PLAINTEXT). Here, we show that the plaintext recovery is possible even for short plaintexts. We first consider the case where $M^* = (M^*[1], M^*[2])$ is the target plaintext of two blocks. Let (N^*, A^*, C^*, T^*) be a challenge, where $C^* = (C^*[1], C^*[2])$ has two blocks.

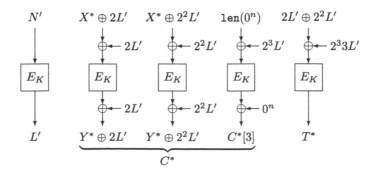

Fig. 7. The encryption process of (N', A^*, M^*). $C^*[3]$ and T^* are unknown.

$L^* := E_K(N^*)$ can be recovered as in case for the plaintext recovery for long plaintexts. We can then compute $\text{Pad}^* := E_K(\text{len}(C^*[2]) \oplus 2^2 L^*)$ by calling $\text{Encipher}(\text{len}(C^*[2]) \oplus 2^2 L^*, 0^n)$, and $M^*[2]$ can be obtained as $\text{msb}_{|C^*[2]|}(\text{Pad}^*) \oplus C^*[2]$. To recover $M^*[1]$, we need to compute $E_K^{-1}(C^*[1] \oplus 2L^*) \oplus 2L^*$, which can be done with the emulation of the blockcipher decryption we have just described.

When the target plaintext $M^* = M^*[1]$ has one block, we first recover $L^* := E_K(N^*)$, and then compute $\text{Pad}^* := E_K(\text{len}(C^*[1]) \oplus 2L^*)$ by calling $\text{Encipher}(\text{len}(C^*[1]) \oplus 2L^*, 0^n)$. This gives $M^*[1] = \text{msb}_{|C^*[1]|}(\text{Pad}^*) \oplus C^*[1]$.

Therefore, it is possible to mount a plaintext recovery attack against any challenge (N^*, A^*, C^*, T^*).

6   Design Flaw of OCB2

The root of the flaw in OCB2 is in the instantiation of AE using XEX*. For blockcipher E_K, let

$$\text{XEX}_E^{N,i,j}(X) \stackrel{\text{def}}{=} E(2^i L \oplus X) \oplus 2^i L,$$
$$\text{XE}_E^{N,i,j}(X) \stackrel{\text{def}}{=} E(2^i 3^j L \oplus X),$$

where $L = E(N)$ for nonce N, for $i = 1, 2, \ldots$ and $j = 0, 1, \ldots$. Here, j is always set to 0 for XEX. XEX* unifies them by introducing one bit b to the tweak. That is,

$$\text{XEX}_E^{*,b,N,i,j}(X) = \begin{cases} \text{XEX}_E^{N,i,j}(X) & \text{if } b = 1; \\ \text{XE}_E^{N,i,j}(X) & \text{if } b = 0. \end{cases}$$

Decryption is trivially defined, and is never invoked when $b = 0$. Rog04 refers b to *tag*; not to be confused with the tag in the global interface of AE.

Suppose an encryption query (N, A, M), where $A = \varepsilon$ and M is parsed as $(M[1], \ldots, M[m])$, is given to OCB2. It encrypts M by using $\text{XEX}_E^{*,1,N,i,0}$ for $M[i]$ with $i = 1, \ldots, m-1$, and $\text{XEX}_E^{*,0,N,m,0}$ for $M[m]$. The checksum, Σ, is encrypted by $\text{XEX}_E^{*,0,N,m,1}$ to create the (untrancated) tag.

In the proof of OCB2, we first apply the standard conversion from computational to information theoretic security [4] and focus on the security of OCB2 instantiated by an n-bit uniform random permutation (URP), P, denoted by OCB2$_\text{P}$. Then, the proof of OCB2$_\text{P}$ has two main steps: the indistinguishability of XEX$^*_\text{P}$, and the privacy and authenticity of AE[9] which replaces XEX$^*_\text{P}$ in OCB2$_\text{P}$ with an ideal primitive, a tweakable random permutation $\widetilde{\text{P}}$. The latter step is not relevant to our attacks.

For the first step, Rog04 proved that XEX$^*_\text{P}$ is indistinguishable from $\widetilde{\text{P}}$ for any adversary who queries to both encryption and decryption of XEX$^*_\text{P}$ and respects the semantics of tag b. More precisely, the conditions for the adversary are as follows.

---
[9] An equivalent mode for OCB3 is called ΘCB3 [20].

Definition 1. *We say an adversary querying* XEX^* *is tag-respecting when*

1. $\mathrm{XEX}^{*,0,N,i,j}$ *is only queried in encryption queries for any* (N,i,j);
2. *Once* $\mathrm{XEX}^{*,b,N,i,j}$ *is queried in either encryption or decryption, then it is not allowed to query* $\mathrm{XEX}^{*,1-b,N,i,j}$, *for any* (N,i,j).

Let $\Theta\mathrm{CB2}_{\widetilde{E}}$ be the mode of operations of TBC $\widetilde{E}_K$ which has the same interface as XEX^*_E. The pseudocode is shown in Fig. 8. Then, $\Theta\mathrm{CB2}_{\mathrm{XEX}^*_E}$ is equivalent to $\mathrm{OCB2}_E$.

Let $\widetilde{\mathsf{P}}$ be TURP which has the same interface as XEX^*. Rog04 showed that, for any privacy-adversary $\mathcal{A}$ and authenticity-adversary $\mathcal{A}_\pm$,

$$\mathbf{Adv}^{\mathrm{priv}}_{\mathrm{OCB2}_{\mathsf{P}}}(\mathcal{A}) = \mathbf{Adv}^{\mathrm{priv}}_{\Theta\mathrm{CB2}_{\mathrm{XEX}^*_{\widetilde{\mathsf{P}}}}}(\mathcal{A}) \leq \mathbf{Adv}^{\mathrm{tprp}}_{\mathrm{XEX}^*_{\widetilde{\mathsf{P}}}}(\mathcal{B}) + \mathbf{Adv}^{\mathrm{priv}}_{\Theta\mathrm{CB2}_{\widetilde{\mathsf{P}}}}(\mathcal{A}), \qquad (7)$$

$$\mathbf{Adv}^{\mathrm{auth}}_{\mathrm{OCB2}_{\mathsf{P}}}(\mathcal{A}_\pm) = \mathbf{Adv}^{\mathrm{auth}}_{\Theta\mathrm{CB2}_{\mathrm{XEX}^*_{\widetilde{\mathsf{P}}}}}(\mathcal{A}_\pm) \leq \mathbf{Adv}^{\mathrm{tsprp}}_{\mathrm{XEX}^*_{\widetilde{\mathsf{P}}}}(\mathcal{B}_\pm) + \mathbf{Adv}^{\mathrm{auth}}_{\Theta\mathrm{CB2}_{\widetilde{\mathsf{P}}}}(\mathcal{A}_\pm) \qquad (8)$$

hold for some CPA-adversary $\mathcal{B}$ and CCA-adversary $\mathcal{B}_\pm$, which are tag-respecting and can simulate the privacy and the authenticity games involving $\Theta\mathrm{CB2}_{\mathrm{XEX}^*_{\widetilde{\mathsf{P}}}}$ and $\mathcal{A}$ and $\mathcal{A}_\pm$, respectively. From Rog04, we have

$$\mathbf{Adv}^{\mathrm{tprp}}_{\mathrm{XEX}^*_{\widetilde{\mathsf{P}}}}(\mathcal{B}) \leq \frac{4.5q^2}{2^n}, \text{ and } \mathbf{Adv}^{\mathrm{tsprp}}_{\mathrm{XEX}^*_{\widetilde{\mathsf{P}}}}(\mathcal{B}_\pm) \leq \frac{9.5q^2}{2^n} \qquad (9)$$

for any $\mathcal{B}$ and $\mathcal{B}_\pm$ that are tag-respecting and use at most q queries. The last terms of (7) and (8) are proved to be almost ideally small: zero for privacy and $2^{n-\tau}/(2^n-1)$ for authenticity with single decryption query.

The privacy bound is obtained from (9) and (7). However, to derive the authenticity bound, we need to identify $\mathcal{B}_\pm$ that can simulate $\mathcal{A}_\pm$, where $\mathcal{A}_\pm$ must compute the decryption of $\Theta\mathrm{CB2}$, even with single decryption query[10]. Depending on $\mathcal{A}_\pm$, there are cases that no tag-respecting $\mathcal{B}_\pm$ can simulate $\mathcal{A}_\pm$. For example, let us assume that $\mathcal{A}_\pm$ first queries (N, A, M) of $|M| = 2n$ to the encryption oracle and then queries (N', A', C', T') to the decryption oracle, where $N' = N$, $A' = \varepsilon$ and $|C'| = n$, as well as the attack of Sect. 4.1. Then, $\mathcal{B}_\pm$ who simulates $\mathcal{A}_\pm$ first queries to $\mathrm{XEX}^{*,1,N,1,0}$ and $\mathrm{XEX}^{*,0,N,2,0}$ and $\mathrm{XEX}^{*,0,N,2,1}$. For the second query, it queries to $\mathrm{XEX}^{*,0,N,1,0}$ and $\mathrm{XEX}^{*,0,N,1,1}$. Thus both $\mathrm{XEX}^{*,1,N,1,0}$ and $\mathrm{XEX}^{*,0,N,1,0}$ are queried, which implies a violation of the second condition of Definition 1. Consequently, the authenticity proof of Rog04 does not work, hence our attacks. At the same time, this also implies that the privacy (confidentiality) attack *under CPA*, i.e. distinguishing the ciphertext from random using only encryption queries, is not possible. This shows a sharp difference between CPA and CCA queries, where the latter easily breaks confidentiality (Sect. 4.3).

---

[10] Rog04 defines the authenticity notion in the game that the adversary queries to the encryption oracle then outputs a query to the decryption oracle, but the response is not returned. The decryption oracle is not involved in the game and the success or failure of the forgery is determined outside the game. This definition itself is essentially the same as Eq. (1), and has no problem. However, because the adversary's final output does not tell whether the adversary wins or loses, we do not know how to apply a hybrid argument of (8) using this definition.

Algorithm $\Theta\text{CB2}.\mathcal{E}_{\widetilde{E}}(N, A, M)$	**Algorithm** $\Theta\text{CB2}.\mathcal{D}_{\widetilde{E}}(N, A, C, T)$
1. $(M[1], \ldots, M[m]) \xleftarrow{n} M$	1. $(C[1], \ldots, C[m]) \xleftarrow{n} C$
2. **for** $i = 1$ **to** $m - 1$	2. **for** $i = 1$ **to** $m - 1$
3. $C[i] \leftarrow \widetilde{E}^{*,1,N,i,0}(M[i])$	3. $M[i] \leftarrow (\widetilde{E}^{*,1,N,i,0})^{-1}(C[i])$
4. $\text{Pad} \leftarrow \widetilde{E}^{*,0,N,m,0}(\text{len}(M[m]))$	4. $\text{Pad} \leftarrow \widetilde{E}^{*,0,N,m,0}(\text{len}(C[m]))$
5. $C[m] \leftarrow M[m] \oplus \text{msb}_{|M[m]|}(\text{Pad})$	5. $M[m] \leftarrow C[m] \oplus \text{msb}_{|C[m]|}(\text{Pad})$
6. $\Sigma \leftarrow C[m] \parallel 0^* \oplus \text{Pad}$	6. $\Sigma \leftarrow C[m] \parallel 0^* \oplus \text{Pad}$
7. $\Sigma \leftarrow M[1] \oplus \cdots \oplus M[m-1] \oplus \Sigma$	7. $\Sigma \leftarrow M[1] \oplus \cdots \oplus M[m-1] \oplus \Sigma$
8. $T \leftarrow \widetilde{E}^{*,0,N,m,1}(\Sigma)$	8. $T^* \leftarrow \widetilde{E}^{*,0,N,m,1}(\Sigma)$
9. **return** (C, T)	9. **if** $T = T^*$ **return** M
	10. **else return** $\perp$

Fig. 8. Algorithms of ΘCB2. For simplicity, $\tau = n$ and $A = \varepsilon$.

7 Applicability to Related Schemes

OTHER OCB VERSIONS. Our attacks are only applicable to OCB2. For OCB1, the last block is encrypted by XE with a clearly separated mask. For OCB3, the last block is encrypted by XEX when it is n bits and otherwise by XE with a mask separated from those used by XEX.

OTHER DESIGNS BASED ON OCB. We have not found other AE algorithms based on OCB that could be affected by our attacks. OTR [24] is an inverse-free (for the absence of the blockcipher decryption in the scheme) parallelizable AE having a similar structure as OCB. As it only uses XE for the whole process, it is safe from our attacks. OPP [12] is a permutation-based AE based on OCB. It always uses XEX, or more precisely, a variant of XPX [23], because otherwise an offline permutation inverse query easily breaks the scheme. It is safe because of this consistent use of XPX.

Aoki and Yasuda [2] presented security bounds of OCB when the block cipher has indistinguishability against encryption queries, however only unpredictability for decryption queries (thus is weaker than normal SPRPs). The presented bounds were claimed to cover all versions of OCB including OCB2. Therefore, our attacks invalidated them regarding OCB2.

8 Fixing OCB2

We discuss several ways to prevent our attacks in practice. In principle each of our suggestions would require its own formal security analysis, but we provide one only for the "XEX for the last plaintext block" fix presented in Sect. 8.1. While also our other proposals intuitively lead to a secure scheme, without conducting further research we cannot fully vouch for their security.

ALWAYS USING AD. Our forgery attacks from Sect. 4 have the property that the AD of the forgeries have to be the empty string. This was unavoidable as for $A \neq \varepsilon$ we would have had to predict PMAC(A) but we are not aware of a way to do so. (Of course, if we could use the Encipher algorithm of Sect. 5.1 then computing PMAC values is not a challenge; however, Encipher can only be invoked after SamplePairs, and the latter implicitly conducts a forgery with $A = \varepsilon$.) Overall we note that a forgery with $A = \varepsilon$ is a key component of *all* our attacks on OCB2. This observation immediately suggests a fix: If the involved users agree that all encryption/decryption operations are with respect to a non-empty AD, then it seems (to us) that all problems go away. An easy way to implement this strategy generically is to prepend a fixed string (e.g. the single letter "A" or the all-zero block 0^n) to every occurring AD (including the empty AD).

ALWAYS USING PMAC. Recall from Line 10 of $\mathcal{E}$ in Fig. 1 that PMAC(A) is XOR-ed into the tag only if $A \neq \varepsilon$. We discuss the case that this condition is removed, and PMAC(A) is *always* XOR-ed into the tag, also when $A = \varepsilon$. An initial analysis of the PMAC algorithm (see Fig. 9 in Appendix) shows that the value PMAC(ϵ) is unpredictable, and also cannot be replayed from other ciphertexts, so that also this modification of OCB2 promises to be a secure candidate.

COUNTER-CRYPTANALYSIS. The two countermeasures just discussed require that the code of both the sender and the receiver would have to be adapted. It might be impossible to do so for instance if OCB2 is included in already shipped products that cannot be updated remotely. In such settings the following two options might be interesting: The sender is modified to never encrypt a message where the second-last block is $\texttt{len}(0^n)$ while the receiver remains unchanged, or the sender remains unchanged and the receiver is modified to never decrypt to a message where the last block would be of the form $2^m L \oplus \texttt{len}(0^n)$.[11] While such changes would (marginally) influence the correctness of the encryption scheme, they seem to make our attacks impossible. To patch a live system this might be a viable option.

USE XEX$^+$. Minematsu and Matsushima [26] proposed an extension of XEX* called XEX$^+$. The latter allows to use plain blockcipher calls in combination with XEX and XE. The authors in particular suggest how to use XEX$^+$ to instantiate a variant of OCB, where the last message block is encrypted by an unmasked blockcipher. This variant of OCB is not affected by our attacks and provably secure.

---

[11] We caution that this change might not be sufficient. Our results from Sect. 4.4 indicate that more plaintexts and ciphertexts have to be rejected: on the encryptor's side all messages with $M[m-1] = \texttt{len}(0^{n-s})$ for some $s = 1, \ldots, n$, and on the decryptor's side all ciphertexts that would result in $M^*[m-1] = \texttt{len}(0^{n-s})$ for some $s = 1, \ldots, n$. We are still investigating which conditions would be necessary/sufficient for security.

8.1   XEX for the Last Message Block

Recall that the vulnerabilities of OCB2 stem from a bad interaction of the XE and XEX components in XEX* and the fact that XE is used for the last block of encryption. A simple way to fix OCB2 is to use XEX also for the last block. We call the resulting scheme OCB2f. Its pseudocode is obtained by changing line 5 of OCB2.$\mathcal{E}_E$ and OCB2.$\mathcal{D}_E$ in Fig. 1 to

$$\text{Pad} \leftarrow 2^m L \oplus E(2^m L \oplus \texttt{len}(M[m]))$$

and

$$\text{Pad} \leftarrow 2^m L \oplus E(2^m L \oplus \texttt{len}(C[m])),$$

respectively. As well as OCB2, OCB2f is a mode of XEX*, since the tweak spaces of XE and XEX in OCB2f are distinct. Specifically, we define $\Theta\text{CB2f}_{\widetilde{E}}$ as a mode obtained by changing $\widetilde{E}^{*,0,N,m,0}$ to $\widetilde{E}^{*,1,N,m,0}$ in line 4 of $\Theta\text{CB2}.\mathcal{E}_{\widetilde{E}}$ and $\Theta\text{CB2}.\mathcal{D}_{\widetilde{E}}$ in Fig. 8. Then $\Theta\text{CB2f}_{\widetilde{E}}$ is equivalent to OCB2f$_E$ if $\widetilde{E}_K$ is XEX$_E^*$. To handle a non-empty AD, we also define $\mathbb{PMAC}_{\widetilde{E}}$ as a mode of TBC $\widetilde{E}_K$ defined in the same way as ΘCB2 so that $\mathbb{PMAC}_{\text{XEX}_E^*}$ is equivalent to PMAC$_E$ (see Fig. 9 in Appendix). We finally add the following line after line 8 (for $\Theta\text{CB2}.\mathcal{E}_{\widetilde{E}}$ and $\Theta\text{CB2}.\mathcal{D}_{\widetilde{E}}$) in Fig. 8

$$\text{if } A \neq \varepsilon \text{ then } T \leftarrow \texttt{msb}_\tau(T \oplus \mathbb{PMAC}_{\widetilde{E}}(A))$$

to make it AEAD. We prove the security of OCB2f using a hybrid argument involving ΘCB2f. To simplify the argument, we also define $\Theta\text{CB2f}'$ by converting $\mathbb{PMAC}_{\widetilde{E}}$ in ΘCB2f to a URF (uniform random function) R : $\{0,1\}^* \rightarrow \{0,1\}^n$.

The security bounds of OCB2f are the same as those claimed for OCB2:

Theorem 1. *Let $\mathcal{A}$ and $\mathcal{A}_\pm$ denote the adversary against AEAD in the privacy and authenticity games. We assume $\mathcal{A}_\pm$ uses q_v decryption queries. We have*

$$\mathbf{Adv}^{\text{priv}}_{\text{OCB2f}_{\text{P}}}(\mathcal{A}) = \mathbf{Adv}^{\text{priv}}_{\Theta\text{CB2f}_{\text{XEX}_{\text{P}}^*}}(\mathcal{A}) \leq \frac{5\sigma^2_{\text{priv}}}{2^n},$$

$$\mathbf{Adv}^{\text{auth}}_{\text{OCB2f}_{\text{P}}}(\mathcal{A}_\pm) = \mathbf{Adv}^{\text{auth}}_{\Theta\text{CB2f}_{\text{XEX}_{\text{P}}^*}}(\mathcal{A}_\pm) \leq \frac{5\sigma^2_{\text{auth}}}{2^n} + \frac{4q_v}{2^\tau},$$

where σ_{priv} and σ_{auth} are the number of queried blocks (the number of invocations of XEX) in the privacy game and the authenticity game, respectively.*

Intuitively, the security of OCB2f holds because (1) OCB2f is ΘCB2f using $\widetilde{E}$ instantiated by XEX*, and (2) ΘCB2f and $\Theta\text{CB2f}'$ are indistinguishable (up to collision), and (3) $\Theta\text{CB2f}'$ in the privacy and authenticity games do not force the adversary to violate the access rules (Definition 1). Combining the known bounds of XEX* and $\mathbb{PMAC}_{\widetilde{E}}$ and the proofs of $\Theta\text{CB2}_{\widetilde{\text{P}}}$ with minor changes gives the desired results. A full proof is given in the full version of this article [13].

9   Conclusions

We have presented practical forgery and decryption attacks against OCB2, a high-profile ISO-standard authenticated encryption scheme. This was possible due to the discrepancy between the proof of OCB2 and the actual construction, in particular the interpretation of OCB2 as a mode of a TBC which combines XEX and XE. While the latest OCB3 has a superior software performance than the previous ones, and is clearly recommended by the designers, we think OCB2 is still quite influential for its simple description and the sophisticated modular design based on a TBC. Our attacks show that, while the approach introduced by Rog04 is invaluable, we could not directly derive a secure AE from it without applying a fix.

We comment that, due to errors in proofs, 'provably-secure schemes' sometimes still can be broken, or schemes remain secure but the proofs need to be fixed. Even if we limit our focus to AE, we have many examples, such as NSA's Dual CTR [9,33], EAX-prime [25], GCM [19], and some of the CAESAR submissions [8,27,35] and more. We believe our work emphasizes the need for quality of security proofs, and their active verification.

Acknowledgements. The authors would like to thank Phil Rogaway for his response to our findings, and officials of ISO SC 27 for feedback and suggestions. We also would like to thank the reviewers of CRYPTO 2019 for useful comments.

A   Brief History of This Paper

A frequent question we have received is how we came to find the flaws, and how they lead to the devastating attacks. The current article is based on three prior ones [14,17,28] that appeared in late 2018 on the IACR ePrint archive. That OCB2 might be flawed was first identified by the authors of [14] when they re-examined the proofs of OCB2 for educational purposes and searched for potential improvements. Instead they came to find a seemingly tiny crack in the proof that they first tried to fix as they strongly believed OCB2 was a secure design, but after several tries they ended up with existential and (near-)universal forgeries. Only two weeks after these findings became public (in [14]), the author of the second ePrint article [28] announced an IND-CCA vulnerability and first steps towards plaintext recovery, and again three days later, the author of the third ePrint article [17] announced full plaintext recovery. This series of happenings is a good example of "attacks only get better" and how seemingly minor error conditions can rapidly grow to nullify the security of a renowned scheme.

Algorithm $\text{PMAC}_E(A)$	**Algorithm** $\mathbb{PMAC}_{\widetilde{E}}(A)$
1. $S \leftarrow 0^n$	1. $S \leftarrow 0^n$
2. $V \leftarrow 3^2 E(0^n)$	2. $(A[1], \dots, A[a]) \xleftarrow{n} A$
3. $(A[1], \dots, A[a]) \xleftarrow{n} A$	3. **for** $i \leftarrow 1$ **to** $a - 1$
4. **for** $i \leftarrow 1$ **to** $a - 1$	4. $S \leftarrow S \oplus \widetilde{E}^{*,0,0^n,i,2}(A[i])$
5. $S \leftarrow S \oplus E(2^i V \oplus A[i])$	5. $S \leftarrow S \oplus A[a] \,\|\, 10^*$
6. $S \leftarrow S \oplus A[a] \,\|\, 10^*$	6. **if** $|A[a]| = n$
7. **if** $|A[a]| = n$	7. $Q \leftarrow \widetilde{E}^{*,0,0^n,a,3}(S)$
8. $Q \leftarrow E(2^a 3 V \oplus S)$	8. **else** $Q \leftarrow \widetilde{E}^{*,0,0^n,a,4}(S)$
9. **else** $Q \leftarrow E(2^a 3^2 V \oplus S)$	9. **return** Q
10. **return** Q	

Fig. 9. Left: The algorithm PMAC_E for the use in OCB2. **Right:** A TBC-based PMAC, $\mathbb{PMAC}_{\widetilde{E}}$.

B   Left-out Details of OCB2

We complete our OCB2 description from Sect. 3 by specifying the details of the PMAC and len functions. For the former see Fig. 9. The latter takes a string $X \in \{0,1\}^{\leq n}$ and encodes its lengths $|X|$ as per $\text{len}(X) = 0^{n-8}\|\ell_X$, where ℓ_X denotes the standard binary encoding of $|X|$. For example, $\text{len}(0^n)$ for $n = 128$ is $0^{120}10^7$.

References

1. Andreeva, E., Bogdanov, A., Luykx, A., Mennink, B., Mouha, N., Yasuda, K.: How to securely release unverified plaintext in authenticated encryption. In: Sarkar, P., Iwata, T. (eds.) ASIACRYPT 2014, Part I. LNCS, vol. 8873, pp. 105–125. Springer, Heidelberg (2014). https://doi.org/10.1007/978-3-662-45611-8_6

2. Aoki, K., Yasuda, K.: The security of the OCB mode of operation without the SPRP assumption. In: Susilo, W., Reyhanitabar, R. (eds.) ProvSec 2013. LNCS, vol. 8209, pp. 202–220. Springer, Heidelberg (2013). https://doi.org/10.1007/978-3-642-41227-1_12

3. Ashur, T., Dunkelman, O., Luykx, A.: Boosting authenticated encryption robustness with minimal modifications. In: Katz, J., Shacham, H. (eds.) CRYPTO 2017, Part III. LNCS, vol. 10403, pp. 3–33. Springer, Cham (2017). https://doi.org/10.1007/978-3-319-63697-9_1

4. Bellare, M., Desai, A., Jokipii, E., Rogaway, P.: A concrete security treatment of symmetric encryption. In: 38th FOCS, pp. 394–403. IEEE Computer Society Press, Miami Beach, 19–22 October 1997. https://doi.org/10.1109/SFCS.1997.646128

5. Bellare, M., Rogaway, P., Wagner, D.: The EAX mode of operation. In: Roy, B., Meier, W. (eds.) FSE 2004. LNCS, vol. 3017, pp. 389–407. Springer, Heidelberg (2004). https://doi.org/10.1007/978-3-540-25937-4_25

6. Black, J., Cochran, M.: MAC reforgeability. In: Dunkelman, O. (ed.) FSE 2009. LNCS, vol. 5665, pp. 345–362. Springer, Heidelberg (2009). https://doi.org/10.1007/978-3-642-03317-9_21

7. Black, J., Rogaway, P.: A block-cipher mode of operation for parallelizable message authentication. In: Knudsen, L.R. (ed.) EUROCRYPT 2002. LNCS, vol. 2332, pp. 384–397. Springer, Heidelberg (2002). https://doi.org/10.1007/3-540-46035-7_25
8. Bost, R., Sanders, O.: Trick or tweak: on the (In)security of OTR's tweaks. In: Cheon, J.H., Takagi, T. (eds.) ASIACRYPT 2016, Part I. LNCS, vol. 10031, pp. 333–353. Springer, Heidelberg (2016). https://doi.org/10.1007/978-3-662-53887-6_12
9. Donescu, P., Gligor, V.D., Wagner, D.: A Note on NSA's Dual Counter Mode of Encryption (2001). http://www.cs.berkeley.edu/~daw/papers/dcm-prelim.ps/
10. Ferguson, N.: Collision attacks on OCB. Comments to NIST (2002). https://csrc.nist.gov/CSRC/media/Projects/Block-Cipher-Techniques/documents/BCM/Comments/general-comments/papers/Ferguson.pdf/
11. Forler, C., List, E., Lucks, S., Wenzel, J.: Reforgeability of authenticated encryption schemes. In: Pieprzyk, J., Suriadi, S. (eds.) ACISP 2017, Part II. LNCS, vol. 10343, pp. 19–37. Springer, Cham (2017). https://doi.org/10.1007/978-3-319-59870-3_2
12. Granger, R., Jovanovic, P., Mennink, B., Neves, S.: Improved masking for tweakable blockciphers with applications to authenticated encryption. In: Fischlin, M., Coron, J.-S. (eds.) EUROCRYPT 2016, Part I. LNCS, vol. 9665, pp. 263–293. Springer, Heidelberg (2016). https://doi.org/10.1007/978-3-662-49890-3_11
13. Inoue, A., Iwata, T., Minematsu, K., Poettering, B.: Cryptanalysis of OCB2: Attacks on authenticity and confidentiality. IACR Cryptology ePrint Archive 2019, 311 (2019). https://eprint.iacr.org/2019/311
14. Inoue, A., Minematsu, K.: Cryptanalysis of OCB2. IACR Cryptology ePrint Archive 2018, 1040 (2018). https://eprint.iacr.org/2018/1040
15. ISO: Information Technology - Security techniques - Authenticated encryption, ISO/IEC 19772:2009. International Standard ISO/IEC 19772 (2009)
16. ISO/IEC JTC 1/SC 27: STATEMENT ON OCB2.0 - Major weakness found in a standardised cipher scheme 09 January 2019, press release. https://www.din.de/blob/321470/da3d9bce7116deb510f6aded2ed0b4df/20190107-press-release-19772-2009-1st-ed-ocb2-0-data.pdf
17. Iwata, T.: Plaintext Recovery Attack of OCB2. IACR Cryptology ePrint Archive 2018, 1090 (2018). https://eprint.iacr.org/2018/1090
18. Iwata, T., Kurosawa, K.: OMAC: one-key CBC MAC. In: Johansson, T. (ed.) FSE 2003. LNCS, vol. 2887, pp. 129–153. Springer, Heidelberg (2003). https://doi.org/10.1007/978-3-540-39887-5_11
19. Iwata, T., Ohashi, K., Minematsu, K.: Breaking and repairing GCM security proofs. In: Safavi-Naini, R., Canetti, R. (eds.) CRYPTO 2012. LNCS, vol. 7417, pp. 31–49. Springer, Heidelberg (2012). https://doi.org/10.1007/978-3-642-32009-5_3
20. Krovetz, T., Rogaway, P.: The software performance of authenticated-encryption modes. In: Joux, A. (ed.) FSE 2011. LNCS, vol. 6733, pp. 306–327. Springer, Heidelberg (2011). https://doi.org/10.1007/978-3-642-21702-9_18
21. Krovetz, T., Rogaway, P.: The OCB Authenticated-Encryption Algorithm. IRTF RFC 7253 (2014)
22. Liskov, M., Rivest, R.L., Wagner, D.: Tweakable block ciphers. In: Yung, M. (ed.) CRYPTO 2002. LNCS, vol. 2442, pp. 31–46. Springer, Heidelberg (2002). https://doi.org/10.1007/3-540-45708-9_3
23. Mennink, B.: XPX: generalized tweakable Even-Mansour with improved security guarantees. In: Robshaw, M., Katz, J. (eds.) CRYPTO 2016, Part I. LNCS, vol. 9814, pp. 64–94. Springer, Heidelberg (2016). https://doi.org/10.1007/978-3-662-53018-4_3

24. Minematsu, K.: Parallelizable rate-1 authenticated encryption from pseudorandom functions. In: Nguyen, P.Q., Oswald, E. (eds.) EUROCRYPT 2014. LNCS, vol. 8441, pp. 275–292. Springer, Heidelberg (2014). https://doi.org/10.1007/978-3-642-55220-5_16
25. Minematsu, K., Lucks, S., Morita, H., Iwata, T.: Attacks and security proofs of EAX-prime. In: Moriai, S. (ed.) FSE 2013. LNCS, vol. 8424, pp. 327–347. Springer, Heidelberg (2014). https://doi.org/10.1007/978-3-662-43933-3_17
26. Minematsu, K., Matsushima, T.: Generalization and Extension of XEX* Mode. IEICE Trans. **92–A**(2), 517–524 (2009)
27. Nandi, M.: Forging attacks on two authenticated encryption schemes COBRA and POET. In: Sarkar, P., Iwata, T. (eds.) ASIACRYPT 2014, Part I. LNCS, vol. 8873, pp. 126–140. Springer, Heidelberg (2014). https://doi.org/10.1007/978-3-662-45611-8_7
28. Poettering, B.: Breaking the confidentiality of OCB2. IACR Cryptology ePrint Archive 2018, 1087 (2018). https://eprint.iacr.org/2018/1087
29. Rogaway, P.: Authenticated-encryption with associated-data. In: Atluri, V. (ed.) ACM CCS 2002, pp. 98–107. ACM Press, Washington, DC, 18–22 November 2002. https://doi.org/10.1145/586110.586125
30. Rogaway, P.: Efficient instantiations of tweakable blockciphers and refinements to modes OCB and PMAC. In: Lee, P.J. (ed.) ASIACRYPT 2004. LNCS, vol. 3329, pp. 16–31. Springer, Heidelberg (2004). https://doi.org/10.1007/978-3-540-30539-2_2
31. Rogaway, P.: Efficient Instantiations of Tweakable Blockciphers and Refinements to Modes OCB and PMAC. Full version of [30] (2004). http://www.cs.ucdavis.edu/~rogaway/papers/
32. Rogaway, P.: Nonce-based symmetric encryption. In: Roy, B., Meier, W. (eds.) FSE 2004. LNCS, vol. 3017, pp. 348–358. Springer, Heidelberg (2004). https://doi.org/10.1007/978-3-540-25937-4_22
33. Rogaway, P.: On the role definitions in and beyond cryptography. In: Maher, M.J. (ed.) ASIAN 2004. LNCS, vol. 3321, pp. 13–32. Springer, Heidelberg (2004). https://doi.org/10.1007/978-3-540-30502-6_2
34. Rogaway, P., Bellare, M., Black, J., Krovetz, T.: OCB: a block-cipher mode of operation for efficient authenticated encryption. In: Reiter, M.K., Samarati, P. (eds.) ACM CCS 2001, pp. 196–205. ACM Press, Philadelphia, 5–8 November 2001. https://doi.org/10.1145/501983.502011
35. Schroé, W., Mennink, B., Andreeva, E., Preneel, B.: Forgery and Subkey recovery on CAESAR candidate iFeed. In: Dunkelman, O., Keliher, L. (eds.) SAC 2015. LNCS, vol. 9566, pp. 197–204. Springer, Cham (2016). https://doi.org/10.1007/978-3-319-31301-6_11
36. Sun, Z., Wang, P., Zhang, L.: Collision attacks on variant of OCB mode and its series. In: Kutyłowski, M., Yung, M. (eds.) Inscrypt 2012. LNCS, vol. 7763, pp. 216–224. Springer, Heidelberg (2013). https://doi.org/10.1007/978-3-642-38519-3_14
37. Vaudenay, S., Vizár, D.: Can caesar beat galois? In: Preneel, B., Vercauteren, F. (eds.) ACNS 2018. LNCS, vol. 10892, pp. 476–494. Springer, Cham (2018). https://doi.org/10.1007/978-3-319-93387-0_25

Quantum Cryptanalysis in the RAM Model: Claw-Finding Attacks on SIKE

Samuel Jaques[✉] and John M. Schanck[✉]

Institute for Quantum Computing, Department of Combinatorics and Optimization,
University of Waterloo, Waterloo, ON N2L 3G1, Canada
sam.e.jaques@gmail.com, jschanck@uwaterloo.ca

Abstract. We introduce models of computation that enable direct comparisons between classical and quantum algorithms. Incorporating previous work on quantum computation and error correction, we justify the use of the gate-count and depth-times-width cost metrics for quantum circuits. We demonstrate the relevance of these models to cryptanalysis by revisiting, and increasing, the security estimates for the Supersingular Isogeny Diffie–Hellman (SIDH) and Supersingular Isogeny Key Encapsulation (SIKE) schemes. Our models, analyses, and physical justifications have applications to a number of memory intensive quantum algorithms.

1 Introduction

The US National Institute of Standards and Technology (NIST) is currently standardising post-quantum cryptosystems. As part of this process, NIST has asked cryptographers to compare the security of such cryptosystems to the security of standard block ciphers and hash functions. Complicating this analysis is the diversity of schemes under consideration, the corresponding diversity of attacks, and stark differences in attacks on post-quantum schemes versus attacks on block ciphers and hash functions. Chief among the difficulties is a need to compare classical and quantum resources.

NIST has suggested that one quantum gate can be assigned a cost equivalent to $\Theta(1)$ classical gates [34, Section 4.A.5]. However, apart from the notational similarity between boolean circuits and quantum circuits, there seems to be little justification for this equivalence.

Even if an adequate cost function were defined, many submissions rely on proxies for quantum gate counts. These will need to be re-analyzed before comparisons can be made. Some submissions use query complexity as a lower bound on gate count. Other submissions use a non-standard circuit model that includes a unit-cost random access gate. The use of these proxies may lead to conservative security estimates. However,

1. they may produce severe security underestimates—and correspondingly large key size estimates—especially when they are used to analyze memory intensive algorithms; and

A. Boldyreva and D. Micciancio (Eds.): CRYPTO 2019, LNCS 11692, pp. 32–61, 2019.
https://doi.org/10.1007/978-3-030-26948-7_2

2. they lead to a proliferation of incomparable units.

We aim to provide cryptographers with tools for making justified comparisons between classical and quantum computations.

1.1 Contributions

In Sect. 2 we review the quantum circuit model and discuss the role that classical computers play in performing quantum gates and preserving quantum memories. We then introduce a model of computation in which a classical random access machine (RAM) acts as a controller for a *memory peripheral* such as an array of bits or an array of qubits. This model allows us to clearly distinguish between costly memory operations, which require the intervention of the controller, and free operations, which do not.

We then describe how to convert a quantum circuit into a parallel RAM (PRAM) program that could be executed by a collection of memory peripheral controllers. The complexity of the resulting program depends on the physical assumptions in the definition of the memory peripheral. We give two sets of assumptions that lead to two distinct cost metrics for quantum circuits. Briefly, we say that G quantum gates arranged in a circuit of depth D and width (number of qubits) W has a cost of

- $\Theta(G)$ RAM operations under the *G-cost metric*, which assumes that quantum memory is *passively corrected*; and
- $\Theta(DW)$ RAM operations under the *DW-cost metric*, which assumes that quantum memory is *actively corrected* by the memory peripheral controller.

These metrics allow us to make direct comparisons between quantum circuits and classical PRAM programs.

In the remainder of the paper we apply our cost metrics to algorithms of cryptographic significance. In Sect. 6 we review the known classical and quantum *claw-finding* attacks on the Supersingular Isogeny Key Encapsulation scheme (SIKE). Our analysis reveals an attack landscape that is shaped by numerous trade-offs between time, memory, and RAM operations. We find that attackers with limited memory will prefer the known quantum attacks, whereas attackers with limited time will prefer the known classical attacks. In terms of the SIKE public parameter p, there are low-memory quantum attacks that use $p^{1/4+o(1)}$ RAM operations, and there are low-depth classical attacks that use $p^{1/4+o(1)}$ RAM operations. Simultaneous time and memory constraints push the cost of all known claw-finding attacks higher. We are not aware of any attack that can be parameterized to use fewer than $p^{1/4+o(1)}$ RAM operations, although some algebraic attacks may also achieve this complexity.

We build toward our analysis of SIKE by considering the cost of prerequisite quantum data structures and algorithms. In Sect. 4 we introduce a new dynamic set data structure, which we call a Johnson vertex. In Sect. 5 we analyze the cost of quantum algorithms based on random walks on Johnson graphs. We find that data structure operations limit the range of time-memory trade-offs that are available in these algorithms. Previous analyses of SIKE [20, 21] ignore data structure operations and assume that time-memory trade-offs enable an attack of cost $p^{1/6+o(1)}$. After accounting for data structure operations, we find that the claimed $p^{1/6+o(1)}$ attack has cost $p^{1/3+o(1)}$.

In Sect. 6.3, we give non-asymptotic cost estimates for claw-finding attacks on SIKE-n (SIKE with an n-bit public parameter p). This analysis lends further support to the parameter recommendations of Adj et al. [1], who suggest that a 434-bit p provides 128-bit security and that a 610-bit p provides 192-bit security. Adj et al. base their recommendation on the cost of memory-constrained classical attacks. We complement this analysis by considering depth-constrained quantum attacks (with depth $< 2^{96}$). Under mild assumptions on the cost of some subroutines, we find that the best known depth-limited quantum claw-finding attack on SIKE-434 uses at least 2^{143} RAM operations. Likewise, we find that the best known depth-limited quantum claw-finding attack on SIKE-610 uses at least 2^{232} RAM operations.

Our methods have immediate applications to the analysis of other quantum algorithms that use large quantum memories and/or classical co-processors. We list some directions for future work in Sect. 7.

2   Machine Models

We begin with some quantum computing background in Sect. 2.1, including the physical assumptions behind Deutsch's circuit model. We elaborate on the circuit model to construct *memory peripheral models* in Sect. 2.2. We specify classical control costs, with units of RAM operations, for memory peripheral models in Sect. 2.3. On a first read, the examples of memory peripherals given in Sect. 2.4 may be more informative than the general description of memory peripheral models in Sect. 2.2. Section 2.4 justifies the cost functions that are used in the rest of the paper.

2.1   Preliminaries on Quantum Computing

Quantum states and time-evolution. Let Γ be a set of observable configurations of a computer memory, e.g. binary strings. A quantum state for that memory is a unit vector $|\psi\rangle$ in a complex euclidean space $\mathcal{H} \cong \mathbb{C}^\Gamma$. Often Γ will have a natural cartesian product structure reflecting subsystems of the memory, e.g. an ideal n-bit memory has $\Gamma = \{0,1\}^n$. In such a case, $\mathcal{H}$ has a corresponding tensor product structure, e.g. $\mathcal{H} \cong (\mathbb{C}^2)^{\otimes n}$. The scalar product on $\mathcal{H}$ is denoted $\langle \cdot | \cdot \rangle$ and is Hermitian symmetric, $\langle \phi | \psi \rangle = \overline{\langle \psi | \phi \rangle}$. The notation $|\psi\rangle$ for unit vectors is meant to look like the right "half" of the scalar product. Dual vectors are denoted $\langle \psi |$. The set $\{|x\rangle \mid x \in \Gamma\}$ is the *computational basis* of $\mathcal{H}$. The *Hermitian adjoint* of a linear operator A is denoted $A^\dagger$. A linear operator is *self-adjoint* if $A = A^\dagger$ and *unitary* if $AA^\dagger = A^\dagger A = 1$.

One of the postulates of quantum mechanics is that the observable properties of a state correspond to self-adjoint operators. A self-adjoint operator can be written as $A = \sum_i \lambda_i P_i$ where $\lambda_i \in \mathbb{R}$ and P_i is a projector onto an eigenspace with eigenvalue λ_i. Measurement of a quantum state $|\psi\rangle$ with respect to A yields outcome λ_i with probability $\langle\psi|\,P_i\,|\psi\rangle$. The post-measurement state is an eigenvector of P_i.

Quantum computing is typically concerned with only two observables: the configurations of the memory, and the total energy of the system. The operator associated to the memory configuration has the computational basis vectors as eigenvectors; it can be written as $\sum_{x \in \Gamma} \lambda_x |x\rangle\langle x|$. If the state of the memory is given by $|\psi\rangle = \sum_{x \in \Gamma} \psi_x |x\rangle$, then measuring the memory configuration of $|\psi\rangle$ will leave the memory in configuration x with probability $|\langle x|\,\psi\rangle|^2 = |\psi_x|^2$. The total energy operator is called the *Hamiltonian* of the system and is denoted H. Quantum states evolve in time according to the Schrödinger equation[1]

$$\frac{\mathrm{d}}{\mathrm{d}t} |\psi(t)\rangle = -iH \, |\psi(t)\rangle .\tag{1}$$

Time-evolution for a duration δ yields $|\psi(t_0 + \delta)\rangle = U_\delta |\psi(t_0)\rangle$ where $U_\delta = \exp(-iH\delta)$. Note that since H is self-adjoint we have $U_\delta^\dagger = \exp(iH\delta)$ so U_δ is unitary. In general, the Hamiltonian of a system may vary in time, and one may write $H(t)$ in Eq. 1. The resulting time-evolution operator is also unitary. The Schrödinger equation applies only to closed systems. A time-dependent Hamiltonian is a convenient fiction that allows one to model an interaction with an external system without modeling the interaction itself.

Quantum circuits. Deutsch introduced the quantum circuit model in [15]. A quantum circuit is a collection of *gates* connected by *unit-wires*. Each wire represents the motion of a *carrier* (a physical system that encodes information). A carrier has both physical and logical (i.e. computational) degrees of freedom. External inputs to a circuit are provided by *sources*, and outputs are made available at *sinks*. The computation proceeds in time with the carriers moving from the sources to the sinks. A gate with k inputs represents a unitary transformation of the logical state space of k carriers. For example, if the carriers encode qubits, then a gate with k inputs is a unitary transformation of $(\mathbb{C}^2)^{\otimes k}$. Each gate takes some non-zero amount of time. Gates that act on disjoint sets of wires may be applied in parallel. The inputs to any particular gate must arrive simultaneously; wires may be used to delay inputs until they are needed.

Carriers feature prominently in Deutsch's description of quantum circuits [15, p. 79], as does time evolution according to an explicitly time-dependent Hamiltonian [15, p. 88]. However, while Deutsch used physical reasoning to justify his model, in particular his choice of gates, this reasoning was not encoded into the circuit diagrams themselves. The gates that appear in Deutsch's diagrams are defined entirely by the logical transformation that they perform. Gates, including the unit-wire, are deemed *computationally equivalent* if they enact the same logical transformation. Two gates can be equivalent even if they act on different carriers, take different amounts of time, etc. Computationally equivalent gates

---

[1] Here we are taking Planck's constant equal to 2π, i.e. $\hbar = 1$.

are given the same representation in a circuit diagram. Today it is common to think of quantum circuits as describing transformations of logical states alone.

2.2 Memory Peripheral Models

The *memory peripheral models* that we introduce in this section generalize the circuit model by making carriers explicit. We depart from the circuit model as follows:

1. We associate a carrier to each unit-wire and to each input and output wire of each gate. Wires can only be connected if they act on the same carrier.
2. We assume that the logical state of a computation emerges entirely from the physical state of its carriers.
3. Our unit-wire acts on its associated carrier by time evolution according to a given time-independent Hamiltonian for a given duration.
4. We interpret our diagrams as programs for classical controllers. Every gate (excluding the unit-wire) represents an intervention from the controller.

In sum, these changes allow us to give some physical justification for how a circuit is executed, and they allow us to assign different costs depending on the justification provided. In particular, they allow us to separate free operations—those that are due to natural time-independent evolution—from costly operations—those that are due to interventions from the classical controller.

Our model has some potentially surprising features. A unit-wire that acts on a carrier with a non-trivial Hamiltonian does not necessarily enact the logical identity transformation. Consequently, wires of different lengths may not be computationally equivalent in Deutsch's sense. In fact, since arbitrary computations can be performed *ballistically*, i.e. by time-independent Hamiltonians [16,24,28], the unit-wire can enact any transformation of the computational state. We do not take advantage of this in our applications; the unit-wires that we consider in Sect. 2.4 enact the logical identity transformation (potentially with some associated cost).

A carrier, in our model, is represented by a physical state space $\mathcal{H}$ and a Hamiltonian $H : \mathcal{H} \to \mathcal{H}$. To avoid confusion with Deutsch's carriers, we refer to $(\mathcal{H}, H)$ as a memory peripheral.

Definition 2.1. *A memory peripheral is a tuple* $\mathsf{A} = (\mathcal{H}, H)$ *where* $\mathcal{H}$ *is a finite dimensional state space and* H *is a Hermitian operator on* $\mathcal{H}$. *The operator* H *is referred to as the Hamiltonian of* A.

The reader may like to keep in mind the example of an ideal qubit memory $\mathsf{Q} = (\mathbb{C}^2, 0)$.

Parallel wires carry the parallel composition of their associated memory peripherals. The memory peripheral that results from parallel composition of A and B is denoted $\mathsf{A} \otimes \mathsf{B}$. The state space associated with $\mathsf{A} \otimes \mathsf{B}$ is $\mathcal{H}^{\mathsf{A}} \otimes \mathcal{H}^{\mathsf{B}}$, and the Hamiltonian is $H^{\mathsf{A}} \otimes I^{\mathsf{B}} + I^{\mathsf{A}} \otimes H^{\mathsf{B}}$. We say that A and B are *subperipherals* of $\mathsf{A} \otimes \mathsf{B}$. We say that a memory peripheral is *irreducible* if it has no sub-peripherals. The *width* of a memory peripheral is the number of irreducible sub-peripherals it contains.

A quantum circuit on n qubits may be thought of as a program for the memory peripheral $\mathsf{Q}^{\otimes n}$. Programs for other memory peripherals may involve more general memory operations.

Definition 2.2. *A* memory operation *is a morphism of memory peripherals* $f :$ $\mathsf{A} \to \mathsf{B}$ *that acts as a quantum channel between* $\mathcal{H}^{\mathsf{A}}$ *and* $\mathcal{H}^{\mathsf{B}}$*, i.e. it takes quantum states on* $\mathcal{H}^{\mathsf{A}}$ *to quantum states on* $\mathcal{H}^{\mathsf{B}}$*.*

The *arity* of a memory operation is the number of irreducible sub-peripherals on which it acts. If there is no potential for ambiguity, we will refer to memory operations as gates. Examples of memory operations include: unitary transformations of a single state space, isometries between state spaces, state preparation, measurement, and changes to the Hamiltonian of a carrier.

In order to define state preparation and measurement it is convenient to introduce a void peripheral 1. State preparation is a memory operation of the form $1 \to \mathsf{A}$, and measurement is a memory operation of the form $\mathsf{A} \to 1$. The reader may assume that $1 = (\mathbb{C}, 0)$ in all of our examples.

Networks of memory operations can be represented by diagrams that are almost identical to quantum circuits. Memory peripherals must be clearly labelled, and times must be given for gates, but no other diagrammatic changes are necessary. An example is given in Fig. 1.

Just as it is useful to specify a gate set for quantum circuits, it is useful to define collections of memory peripherals that are closed under parallel composition and under sequential composition of memory operations. The notion of a symmetric monoidal category captures the relevant algebraic structure. The following definition is borrowed from [13, Definition 2.1] and, in the language of that paper, makes a memory peripheral model into a type of *resource theory*. The language of resource theories is not strictly necessary for our purposes, but we think this description may have future applications.

Definition 2.3. *A* memory peripheral model *is a symmetric monoidal category* $(\mathbf{C}, \circ, \otimes, 1)$ *where*

- *the objects of* $\mathbf{C}$ *are memory peripherals,*
- *the morphisms between objects of* $\mathbf{C}$ *are memory operations,*
- *the binary operation* $\circ$ *denotes sequential composition of memory operations,*
- *the binary operation* $\otimes$ *denotes parallel composition of memory peripherals and of memory operations, and*
- *the void peripheral* 1 *satisfies* $\mathsf{A} \otimes 1 = 1 \otimes \mathsf{A} = \mathsf{A}$ *for all* $\mathsf{A} \in \mathbf{C}$*.*

2.3 Parallel RAM Controllers for Memory Peripheral Models

A memory peripheral diagram can be viewed as a program that tells a classical computer where, when, and how to interact with its memory. We will now specify a computer that executes these programs.

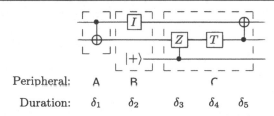

Peripheral: A   B   C

Duration: δ_1 δ_2 δ_3 δ_4 δ_5

(a) A memory peripheral diagram with $A = A_1 \otimes A_2$, $B = A_1 \otimes A_2 \otimes B_3$, and $C = C_1 \otimes A_2 \otimes B_3$ (numbered top to bottom). The memory peripheral changes from A to B in the second time step because of the new qubit. The change from B to C in the third time step is marked by a carrier change that enacts the logical identity gate. Note that truly instantaneous changes are not possible, but the δ_i could be very small.

Controller one	Controller two	Controller three
1. APPLY "CNOT" (1,2)	1. no op.	1. APPLY "INIT" (0,3)
2. no op.	2. STEP	2. no op.
3. APPLY "A_1 to C_1" (0,1)	3. no op.	3. no op.
4. no op.	4. no op.	4. STEP
5. no op.	5. APPLY "CZ" (3,2)	5. no op.
6. no op.	6. APPLY "T" (0,2)	6. no op.
7. APPLY "CNOT" (2,1)	7. no op.	7. no op.
8. no op.	8. no op.	8. STEP

(b) A PRAM program for the memory peripheral diagram of Fig. 1a using the notation of Section 2.3.

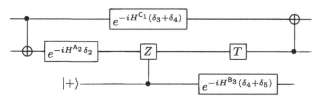

(c) A quantum circuit for the memory peripheral diagram of Fig. 1a. Note that the I gate is absent, and explicit time-evolution with respect to the wire Hamiltonians has been added.

Fig. 1. Three representations of a quantum algorithm.

Following Deutsch, we have assumed that all gates take a finite amount of time, that each gate acts on a bounded number of subsystems, and that gates that act on disjoint subsystems can be applied in parallel. Circuits can be of arbitrary width, so a control program may need to execute an unbounded number of operations in a finite amount of time. Hence, we must either assume that the classical control computer can operate arbitrarily quickly or in parallel.

We opt to treat controllers as parallel random access machines (PRAMs). Several variants of the PRAM exist [26]. The exact details of the instruction set and concurrency model are largely irrelevant here. For our purposes, a PRAM is a collection of RAMs that execute instructions in synchrony. Each RAM executes (at most) one instruction per time step. At time step i each RAM can assume that the other RAMs have completed their step $i - 1$ instructions. We assume that synchronization between RAMs and memory peripherals is free.

We assign a unique positive integer to each wire in a diagram, so that an ordered collection of k memory peripherals can be identified by a k-tuple of integers. We use a k-tuple to specify an input to a k-ary gate. The memory operations that are available to a controller are also assigned unique positive integers.

We add two new instructions to the RAM instruction set: APPLY and STEP. These instructions enable parallel and sequential composition of memory operations, respectively. APPLY takes three arguments: a k-tuple of addresses, a memory operation, and an (optional) k-tuple of RAM addresses in which to store measurement results. STEP takes no arguments; it is only used to impose a logical sequence on steps of the computation.

When a processor calls APPLY the designated memory operation is scheduled to be performed during the next STEP call. In one layer of circuit depth, each RAM processor schedules some number of memory operations to be applied in parallel and then one processor calls STEP. If memory operations with overlapping addresses are scheduled for the same step, the behaviour of the memory peripheral is undefined and the controller halts. This ensures that only one operation is applied per subsystem per call to STEP.

A quantum circuit of width W can be converted into $O(W)$ RAM programs by assigning gates to processors according to a block partition of $\{1, \ldots, W\}$. The blocks should be of size $O(1)$, otherwise a single processor could need to execute an unreasonable number of operations in a fixed amount of time. If a gate involves multiple qubits that are assigned to different processors, the gate is executed by the processor that is responsible for the qubit of lowest address. We have provided an example in Fig. 1b.

To apply a multi-qubit gate, a RAM processor must be able to address arbitrary memory peripherals. This is a strong capability. However, each peripheral is involved in at most one gate per step, so this type of random access is analogous to the exclusive-read/exclusive-write random access that is typical of PRAMs.

The cost of a PRAM computation. Every RAM instruction has unit cost, except for the placeholder "no operation" instruction, no op, which is free. The cost of a PRAM computation is the total number of RAM operations executed.

2.4 Examples of Memory Peripheral Models

Here we give three examples of memory peripheral models. Example 2.4.1 is classical and primarily an illustration of the model. It shows that our framework can accommodate classical memory without changing the PRAM costs. Example 2.4.2 is a theoretical self-corrected quantum memory that justifies the G-cost. Example 2.4.3 is a more realistic actively-corrected quantum memory that justifies the DW-cost.

2.4.1 Non-volatile Classical Memories

A non-volatile bit-memory can store a bit indefinitely without periodic error correction or read/write cycles. As a memory peripheral, this can simulate other classical computation models and gives the expected costs.

Technologies. The historically earliest example of a non-volatile bit memory is the "core memory" of Wang and Woo [41]. A modern example is Ferroelectric RAM (FeRAM). The DRAM found in common consumer electronics requires a periodic read/write cycle, which should be included in a cost analysis. While there may be technological and economic barriers to using non-volatile memory at all stages of the computing process, there are no physical barriers.

Hamiltonian of a memory cell. A logical bit can be encoded in the net magnetization of a ferromagnet. A ferromagnet can be modelled as a collection of *spins*. Each spin is oriented up or down, and has state $|\uparrow\rangle$ or $|\downarrow\rangle$. The self-adjoint operator associated to the orientation of a spin is $\sigma_z = |\uparrow\rangle\langle\uparrow| - |\downarrow\rangle\langle\downarrow|$; measuring $|\uparrow\rangle$ with respect to σ_z yields outcome $+1$ with probability 1, and measuring $|\downarrow\rangle$ yields outcome -1 with probability 1.

In the d-dimensional Ising model of ferromagnetism, L^d spins are arranged in a regular square lattice of diameter L in d-dimensional space. The Ising Hamiltonian imposes an energy penalty on adjacent spins that have opposite orientations:

$$H_{Ising} = -\sum_{(i,j)} \sigma_z^{(i)} \otimes \sigma_z^{(j)}.$$

In 1936 [35] Peierls showed that the Ising model is *thermally stable* in dimensions $d \geq 2$. The two ground states, all spins pointing down and all spins pointing up, are energetically separated. The energy required to map the logical zero (all down) to logical one (all up) grows with L, and the probability of this happening (under a reasonable model of thermal noise) decreases with L. The phenomenon of thermal stability in dimensions 2 and 3 provides an intuitive explanation for why we are able to build classical non-volatile memories like core-memory (see also [14, Section X.A]).

Memory peripheral model. A single non-volatile bit, encoded in the net magnetization of an $L \times L$ grid of spins, can be represented by a memory peripheral $\mathsf{B}_L = ((\mathbb{C}^2)^{\otimes L^2}, H_{Ising})$. From a single bit we can construct w-bit word peripherals $\mathsf{W}_{L,w} = \mathsf{B}_L^{\otimes w}$.

Turing machines, boolean circuits, PRAMs, and various other classical models can be simulated by controllers for word memory peripheral models. The only strictly necessary memory operations are those for reading and writing individual words.

2.4.2   Self-correcting Quantum Memories

A self-correcting quantum memory is the quantum analogue of a non-volatile bit memory. The Hamiltonian of the carrier creates a large energy barrier between logical states. At a sufficiently low temperature the system does not have enough energy for errors to occur.

The thermal stability of the Ising model in $d \geq 2$ spatial dimensions seems to have inspired Kitaev's search for geometrically local quantum stabilizer codes [27]. The two-dimensional toric code that Kitaev defined in [27] is not thermally stable [2]. However, a four-dimensional variant is thermally stable [3,14]. The question of whether there exists a self-correcting quantum memory with a Hamiltonian that is geometrically local in <4 spatial dimensions remains open.

In two spatial dimensions, various "no-go theorems" suggest that self-correcting quantum memories may not exist. For example, a stabilizer code defined on a two-dimensional lattice of qubits cannot self-correct [11]. Brown et al. [12] summarize generalizations of this no-go result and survey the remaining avenues toward self-correcting memory in low dimensions.

At present, a model of quantum computation that assumes non-volatile memory, i.e. a free identity gate, and <4 spatial dimensions is making a physical assumption about the existence of two- or three-dimensional self-correcting memories. Here we will simply ignore geometric locality and write down a memory peripheral for the four-dimensional toric code. Because real devices are limited to three spatial dimensions, this is purely a theoretical example.

Memory peripheral model. The Hamiltonian for the four-dimensional toric code can be found in [14, Section X.B]. We will denote it H_{toric}. Like the four-dimensional Ising Hamiltonian it is defined on L^4 spins arranged in a square lattice. The memory peripheral $Q_{toric} = (\mathbb{C}^{L^4}, H_{toric})$ can serve as a drop-in replacement for the ideal qubit memory peripheral Q for the purpose of describing the unit-wire.

To execute arbitrary quantum computations on a collection of logical qubits encoded in Q_{toric} peripherals, we need memory operations for a universal gate set, initialization, and measurement. Initialization and Clifford+T gates are described for the two-dimensional toric code in [14, Section IX] and the four-dimensional versions are similar. A measurement procedure for the four-dimensional toric code is in [14, Section X.B]. Treating any of these procedures as a single memory operation will mask some classical control cost that is polynomial in L. Treating the T gate as a single memory operation masks the use of an additional memory peripheral to hold a resource state.

Cost function. A quantum circuit on n qubits can be converted into a memory peripheral diagram for $Q_{toric}^{\otimes n}$ and then interpreted as a PRAM program. In this way we can assign a cost, in units of RAM operations, to the quantum circuit itself. Each wire in the quantum circuit is assigned a length in the memory peripheral diagram. The quantum circuit and memory peripheral diagram are otherwise identical. Each gate in the diagram (including state-preparation and measurement gadgets, but not unit-wires) is expanded into at least one APPLY instruction. The wires themselves incur no RAM cost, but one STEP instruction is needed per layer of circuit depth for synchronization. The number of STEP instructions is no more than the number of APPLY instructions. The following cost function, the G-cost, is justified by assuming that each gate expands to $O(1)$ RAM operations.

Definition 2.4 (G-cost). *A logical Clifford+T quantum circuit that uses G gates (in any arrangement) has a G-cost of $\Theta(G)$ RAM operations.*

Remark 2.1. The depth and width of a circuit do not directly affect its G-cost, but these quantities are often relevant in practice. A PRAM controller for a circuit that uses G gates in an arrangement that is D gates deep and W qubits wide uses $O(W)$ RAM processors for $\Omega(D)$ time. Various G-cost-preserving trade-offs between time and number of processors may be possible. For example, a circuit can be re-written so that no two gates are applied at the same time. In this way, a single RAM processor can execute any G gate circuit in $\Theta(G)$ time. This trade-off is only possible because self-correcting memory allows us to assign an arbitrary duration to a unit-wire.

2.4.3   Actively Corrected Quantum Memories

It should be possible to build quantum computers even if it is not possible to build self-correcting quantum memories. Active error correction strategies are nearing technological realizability; several large companies and governments are currently pursuing technologies based on the surface code.

Memory peripheral model. When using an active error correction scheme, a logical Clifford+T circuit has to be compiled to a physical circuit that includes active error correction. We may assume that the wires carry the ideal qubit memory peripheral Q. A more detailed analysis might start from the Hamiltonians used in circuit QED [9].

Memory operations. The compiled physical circuit will not necessarily use the Clifford+T gate set. The available memory operations will depend on the physical architecture, e.g. in superconducting nano-electronic architectures one typically has arbitrary single qubit rotations and one two-qubit gate [42].

Cost function. We can assume that every physical gate takes $\Theta(1)$ RAM operations to apply. This may mask a large constant; a proposal for a hardware implementation of classical control circuitry can be found in [32]. A review of active quantum error correction for the purpose of constructing memories can be found in [39].

An active error correction routine is applied, repeatedly, to all physical qubits regardless of the logical workload. If we assume that logical qubits can be encoded in a constant number of physical qubits, and that logical Clifford+T gates can be implemented with a constant number of physical gates, then the above considerations justify the DW-cost for quantum circuits.

Definition 2.5 (DW-cost). *A logical Clifford+T quantum circuit that is D gates deep, W qubits wide, and uses any number of gates within that arrangement has a DW-cost of $\Theta(DW)$ RAM operations.*

Remark 2.2. In contrast with the G-cost, there are no DW-cost preserving trade-offs between time and number of processors when constructing a PRAM program from a quantum circuit. A circuit of depth D and width W uses $\Theta(W)$ processors for time $\Theta(D)$.

Technologies. Fowler et al. provide a comprehensive overview of the surface code [17]. Importantly, to protect a circuit of depth D and width W, the surface code requires $\Theta(\log^2(DW))$ physical qubits per logical qubit. The active error correction is applied in a regular cycle (once every 200 ns in [17]). In each cycle a constant fraction of the physical qubits are measured and re-initialized. The measurement results are processed with a non-trivial classical computation [18]. The overall cost of surface code computation is $\Omega(\log^2(DW))$ RAM operations per logical qubit per layer of logical circuit depth. Nevertheless, future active error correction techniques may bring this more in line with the DW-cost.

3   Cost Analysis: Quantum Random Access

Our memory peripheral models provide classical controllers with random access to individual qubits. A controller can apply a memory operation—e.g. a Clifford+T gate or a measurement—to any peripheral in any time step. However, a controller does not have quantum random access to individual qubits. A controller cannot call APPLY with a superposition of addresses. Quantum random access must be built from memory operations.

In [4], Ambainis considers a data structure that makes use of a "random access gate." This gate takes an index i, an input b, and an R element array $A = (a_1, a_2, \ldots, a_R)$. It computes the XOR of a_i and b:

$$|i\rangle |b\rangle |A\rangle \mapsto |i\rangle |b \oplus a_i\rangle |A\rangle. \tag{2}$$

Assuming that each $|a_j\rangle$ is encoded in $O(1)$ irreducible memory peripherals, a random access gate has arity that grows linearly with R. If the underlying memory peripheral model only includes gates of bounded arity, then an implementation of a random access gate clearly uses $\Omega(R)$ operations. Beals et al. have noted that a circuit for random access to an R-element array of m-bit strings must have width $\Omega(Rm)$ and depth $\Omega(\log R)$ [5, Theorem 4]. Here we give a Clifford+T construction that is essentially optimal[2].

Rather than providing a full circuit, we will describe how the circuit acts on $|i\rangle\,|0\rangle\,|A\rangle$. The address is $\log R$ bits and each register of A is m bits. We use two ancillary arrays $|A'\rangle$ and $|A''\rangle$, both initialized to 0. The array A' holds R address-sized registers and $O(R)$ additional qubits for intermediary results, a total of $O(R \log R)$ qubits. The array A'' is $O(Rm)$ qubits.

We use a standard construction of R-qubit fan-out and R-qubit parity due to Moore [33]. The fan-out is a tree of $O(R)$ CNOT gates arranged in depth $O(\log R)$. Parity is fan-out conjugated by Hadamard gates. We also use a $\log R$-bit comparison circuit due to Thapliyal, Ranganathan, and Ferreir [40]. This circuit uses $O(\log R)$ gates in depth $O(\log \log R)$.

Our random access circuit acts as follows:

1. *Fan-out address:* Fan-out circuits copy the address i to each register of A'. This needs a total of $\log R$ fan-outs, one for each bit of address. These can all be done in parallel.
2. *Controlled copy:* For each $1 \le j \le R$, the boolean value $A'[j] = j$ is stored in the scratch space associated to A'. The controller knows the address of each register, so it can apply a dedicated circuit for each comparison. Controlled-CNOTs are used to copy $A[j]$ to $A''[j]$ when $A'[j] = j$. Since $A'[j] = j$ if and only if $j = i$, this copies $A[i]$ to $A''[i]$ but leaves $A''[j] = 0$ for $j \ne i$.
3. *Parity:* Since $A''[j]$ is 0 for $j \ne i$, the parity of the low-order bit of all the A'' registers is equal to the low-order bit of just $A''[i]$. Likewise for the other $m-1$ bits. So parallel R-qubit parity circuits can be used to copy $A''[i]$ to an m-qubit output register.
4. *Uncompute:* The controlled copy and fan-out steps are applied in reverse, returning A'', A', and the scratch space to zero.

The entire circuit can be implemented in width $O(Rm + R \log R)$. Step 1 dominates the depth and Step 2 dominates the gate cost. The comparison circuits use $O(R \log R)$ gates with depth $O(\log \log R)$. To implement the controlled-CNOTs used to copy $A[i]$ to $A''[i]$ in constant depth, instead of $O(m)$ depth, each of the R comparison results can be fanned out to $(m-1)$ qubits in the scratch space of A''. This fan-out has depth $O(\log m)$.

The total cost of random access is given in Cost 1. Observe that there is more than a constant factor gap between the G- and DW-cost.

Cost 1. Random access to R registers of m bits each.

   Gates: $O(Rm + R \log R)$
   Depth: $O(\log m + \log R)$
   Width: $O(Rm + R \log R)$

---

[2] Actually, here and elsewhere, we use a gate set that includes Toffoli gates and controlled-swap gates. These can be built from $O(1)$ Clifford+T gates.

4 Cost Analysis: The Johnson Vertex Data Structure

We expect to find significant gaps between the G- and DW-costs of algorithms that use a large amount of memory. Candidates include quantum algorithms for element distinctness [4], subset-sum [7], claw-finding [38], triangle-finding [30], and information set decoding [25]. All of these algorithms are based on quantum random walks on Johnson graphs—graphs in which each vertex corresponds to a subset of a finite set.

In this section we describe a quantum data structure for representing a vertex of a Johnson graph. Essentially, we need a dynamic set that supports membership testing, uniform sampling from the encoded set, insertion, and deletion. These operations can be fine-tuned for quantum walk applications. In particular, insertion and deletion only need to be defined on inputs that would change the size of the encoded set. To avoid ambiguity, we will refer to these special cases as *guaranteed insertion* and *guaranteed deletion*.

4.1 History-Independence

Fix a finite set $\mathcal{X}$. A quantum data structure for subsets of $\mathcal{X}$ consists of two parts: a presentation of subsets as quantum states, and unitary transformations representing set operations. The presentation must assign a *unique* quantum state $|\mathcal{A}\rangle$ to each $\mathcal{A} \subset \mathcal{X}$. Uniqueness is a strong condition, but it is necessary for quantum interference. Different sequences of insertions and deletions that produce the same set will only interfere if each sequence presents the output in exactly the same way. The set $\{0, 1\}$ cannot be stored as $|0\rangle |1\rangle$ or $|1\rangle |0\rangle$ depending on the order in which the elements were inserted. Some valid alternatives are to fix an order (e.g. always store $|0\rangle |1\rangle$) or to coherently randomize the order (e.g. always store $\frac{1}{\sqrt{2}}(|0\rangle |1\rangle + |1\rangle |0\rangle)$). Data structures that allow for interference between computational paths are called *history-independent*.

Ambainis describes a history-independent data structure for sets in [4]. His construction is based on a combined hash table and skip list. Bernstein, Jeffery, Lange, and Meurer [7], and Jeffery [22], provide a simpler solution based on radix trees. Both of these data structures use random access gates extensively. Our Johnson vertices largely avoid random access gates, and in Sect. 4.4 we show that our data structure is more efficient as a result.

4.2 Johnson Vertices

The Johnson graph $J(X, R)$ is a graph whose vertices are R-element subsets of $\{1, \ldots, X\}$. Subsets $\mathcal{U}$ and $\mathcal{V}$ are adjacent in $J(X, R)$ if and only if $|\mathcal{U} \cap \mathcal{V}| = R-1$. In algorithms it is often useful to fix a different base set, so we will define our data structure with this in mind: A *Johnson vertex* of capacity R, for a set of m-bit strings, is a data structure that represents an R-element subset of some set $\mathcal{X} \subseteq \{1, \ldots, 2^m - 1\}$. This implies $\log_2 R \leq m$.

In our implementation below, a subset is presented in lexicographic order in an array of length R. This ensures that every R element subset has a unique presentation.

We describe circuits parameterized by m and R for membership testing, uniform sampling, guaranteed insertion, and guaranteed deletion. Since R is a circuit parameter, our circuits cannot be used in situations where R varies between computational paths[3]. This is fine for quantum walks on Johnson graphs, but it prevents our data structure from being used as a generic dynamic set.

Memory allocation. The set is stored in a length R array of m-bit registers that we call A. Every register is initialized to the m-bit zero string, $\perp$. The guaranteed insertion/deletion and membership testing operations require auxiliary arrays A' and A''. Both contain $O(Rm)$ bits and are initialized to zero. It is helpful to think of these as length R arrays of m-bit registers that each have some scratch space. We will not worry about the exact layout of the scratch space.

Guaranteed insertion/deletion. Let $\mathcal{U}$ be a set of m-bit strings with $|\mathcal{U}| = R-1$, and suppose x is an m-bit string not in $\mathcal{U}$. The capacity $R-1$ guaranteed insertion operation performs

$$|\mathcal{U}\rangle\,|\perp\rangle\,|x\rangle \mapsto |\mathcal{U} \cup \{x\}\rangle\,|x\rangle.$$

Capacity R guaranteed deletion is the inverse operation.

Figure 2 depicts the following implementation of capacity $R-1$ guaranteed insertion. For concreteness, we assume that the correct position of x is at index k with $1 \le k \le R$. At the start of the routine, the first $R-1$ entries of A represent a sorted list. Entry R is initialized to $|\perp\rangle = |0\rangle^{\otimes m}$.

(a). *Fan-out:* Fan-out the input x to the R registers of A' and also to $A[R]$, the blank cell at the end of A. The fan-out can be implemented with $O(Rm)$ gates in depth $O(\log R)$ and width $O(Rm)$.

(b). *Compare:* For i in 1 to R, flip all m bits of $A''[i]$ if and only if $A'[i] \le A[i]$. The comparisons are computed using the scratch space in A''. Each comparison costs $O(m)$ gates, and has depth $O(\log m)$ and width $O(m)$ [40]. The single bit result of each comparison is fanned out to all m bits of $A''[i]$ using $O(m)$ gates in depth $O(\log m)$. The total cost is $O(Rm)$ gates, $O(\log m)$ depth.

(c). *First conditional swap:* For i in 1 to $R-1$, if $A''[i]$ is $11\ldots1$ swap $A'[i+1]$ and $A[i]$. After this step, cells k through R of A hold copies of x. The values originally in $A[k],\ldots,A[R-1]$ are in $A'[k+1],\ldots,A'[R]$. Each register swap uses m controlled-swap gates. All of the swaps can be performed in parallel. The cost is $O(Rm)$ gates in $O(1)$ depth.

(d). *Second conditional swap:* For i in 1 to $R-1$, if $A''[i]$ is $11\ldots1$ then swap $A'[i+1]$ and $A[i+1]$. After this step, the values originally in $A'[k+1],\ldots,A'[R]$ are in $A[k+1],\ldots,A[R]$. The cost is again $O(Rm)$ gates in $O(1)$ depth.

---

[3] One can handle a range of capacities using controlled operations, but the size of the resulting circuit grows linearly with the number of capacities it must handle.

(e). *Clear comparisons:* Repeat the comparison step to reset A''.
(f). *Clear fan-out:* Fan-out the input x to the array A'. This will restore A' back to the all 0 state. Note that the fan-out does not include $A[R]$ this time.

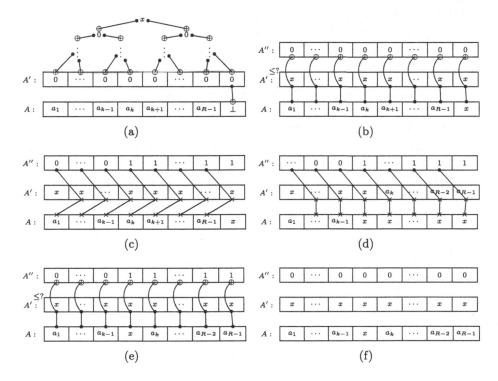

Fig. 2. Insertion into a Johnson vertex. See text for full description.

Cost 2. Guaranteed insertion/deletion for a Johnson vertex of capacity R with m-bit elements.

 Gates: $O(Rm)$
 Depth: $O(\log m + \log R)$
 Width: $O(Rm)$

Membership testing and relation counting. The capacity R membership testing operation performs

$$|\mathcal{U}\rangle\,|x\rangle\,|b\rangle \;\mapsto\; \begin{cases} |\mathcal{U}\rangle\,|x\rangle\,|b \oplus 1\rangle & \text{if } x \in \mathcal{U} \\ |\mathcal{U}\rangle\,|x\rangle\,|b\rangle & \text{otherwise.} \end{cases}$$

As in guaranteed insertion/deletion, the routine starts with a fan-out followed by a comparison. In the comparison step we flip the leading bit of $A''[i]$ if and only if $A'[i] = A[i]$. This will put at most one 1 bit into the A'' array. Computing the parity of the A'' array will extract the result. The comparisons use $O(Rm)$ gates in depth $O(\log m)$ [40], as does the parity check [33]. Thus the cost of membership testing matches that of guaranteed insertion: $O(Rm)$ gates in depth $O(\log m + \log R)$.

The above procedure is easily modified to test other relations and return the total number of matches. In place of the parity circuit, we would use a binary tree of $O(\log R)$-bit addition circuits. With the adders of [37], the cost of the addition tree is $O(R \log R)$ gates in depth $O(\log^2 R)$. The ancilla bits for the addition tree do not increase the overall width beyond $O(Rm)$. As such, the gate cost of the addition tree is no more than a constant factor more than the cost of a guaranteed insertion. The full cost of relation counting will also depend on the cost of evaluating the relation.

Cost 3. Membership testing and relation counting for a Johnson vertex of capacity R with m-bit elements. The terms T_G, T_D, and T_W denote the gates, depth, and width of evaluating a relation.

	Membership testing	Relation counting
Gates:	$O(Rm)$	$O(Rm + R\mathsf{T}_G)$
Depth:	$O(\log m + \log R)$	$O(\log^2 R + \mathsf{T}_D)$
Width:	$O(Rm)$	$O(Rm + R\mathsf{T}_W)$

Uniform sampling. The capacity R uniform sampling operation performs $|\mathcal{A}\rangle |0\rangle = |\mathcal{A}\rangle \left(\frac{1}{\sqrt{R}} \sum_{x \in \mathcal{A}} |x\rangle \right)$. We use a random access to the array A with a uniform superposition of addresses. By Cost 1, this uses $O(Rm)$ gates in depth $O(\log m + \log R)$.

4.3   Random Replacement

A quantum walk on a Johnson graph needs a subroutine to replace $\mathcal{U}$ with a neighbouring vertex in order to take a step. Intuitively, this procedure just needs to delete $u \in \mathcal{U}$, sample $x \in \mathcal{X} \backslash \mathcal{U}$, then insert x. The difficulty lies in sampling x in such a way that it can be uncomputed even after subsequent insertion/deletion operations. The naive rejection sampling approach will entangle x with $\mathcal{U}$.

The applications that we consider below can tolerate a replacement procedure that leaves $\mathcal{U}$ unchanged with probability R/X. We first sample x uniformly from $\mathcal{X}$ and perform a membership test. This yields $\sqrt{1/X} \sum_{x \in \mathcal{X}} |\mathcal{U}\rangle |x\rangle |x \in \mathcal{U}\rangle$. Conditioned on non-membership, we uniformly sample some $u \in \mathcal{U}$, delete u, and insert x. Conditioned on membership, we copy x into the register that would otherwise hold u. The membership bit can be uncomputed using the "u" register. This yields $\sqrt{1/X} \sum_{x \in \mathcal{U}} |\mathcal{U}\rangle |x\rangle |x\rangle + \sqrt{1/RX} \sum_{v \sim \mathcal{U}} |\mathcal{V}\rangle |x\rangle |u\rangle$. The cost of random replacement is $O(1)$ times the cost of guaranteed insertion plus the cost of uniform sampling in $\mathcal{X}$.

4.4 Comparison with Quantum Radix Trees

In [7] a quantum radix tree is constructed as a uniform superposition over all possible memory layouts of a classical radix tree. This solves the problem of history-dependence, but relies heavily on random access gates. The internal nodes of a radix tree store the memory locations of its two children. In the worst case, membership testing, insertion, and deletion follow paths of $\Theta(m)$ memory locations. Because a quantum radix tree is stored in all possible memory layouts, these are genuine random accesses to an R register array. Note that a radix tree of m-bit strings cannot have more than 2^m leaves. As such, $\log R = O(m)$ and Cost 1 matches the lower bound for random access gates given by Beals et al. [5]. Cost 4 is obtained by using Cost 1 for each of the $O(\log R)$ random accesses. The lower bound in Cost 4 exceeds the upper bound in Cost 2.

Cost 4. Membership testing, insertion, and deletion for quantum radix trees.

Gates: $\Omega(Rm^2)$
Depth: $\Omega(m \log m + m \log R)$
Width: $\Omega(Rm)$

---

5   Cost Analysis: Claw-Finding by Quantum Walk

5.1 Quantum Walk Based Search Algorithms

Let $\mathcal{S}$ be a finite set with a subset $\mathcal{M}$ of "marked" elements. We focus on a generic search problem: to find some $x \in \mathcal{M}$. A simple approach is to repeatedly guess elements of $\mathcal{S}$. This can be viewed as a random walk. At each step, one transitions from the current guess to another with uniform probability. The random walk starts with a *setup* routine that produces an initial element $\mathcal{S}$. It then repeats a loop of (1) *checking* if the current element is marked, and (2) *walking* to another element. Of course, one need not use the uniform distribution. In a Markov chain, the transition probabilities can be arbitrary, so long as they only depend on the current guess. The probability of transitioning from a guess of u to a guess of v can be viewed as a weighted edge in a graph with vertex set $\mathcal{S}$. The weighted adjacency matrix of this graph is called the *transition matrix* of the Markov chain.

Quantum random walks perform analogous operations. The elements of $\mathcal{S}$ are encoded into pairwise orthogonal quantum states. A setup circuit produces an initial superposition of these states. A check circuit applies a phase to marked elements. An additional *diffusion* circuit amplifies the probability of success. It uses a walk circuit, which samples a new element of $\mathcal{S}$.

Grover's algorithm is a quantum walk with uniform transition probabilities. It finds a marked element after $\Theta(\sqrt{|\mathcal{S}| / |\mathcal{M}|})$ check steps. Szegedy's algorithm can decide whether or not $\mathcal{M}$ is empty for a larger class of Markov chains [36]. Magniez, Nayak, Roland, and Santha (MNRS) generalize Szegedy's algorithm to admit even more general Markov chains [31]. They also describe a routine that can find a marked element [31, "Tolerant RAA" algorithm]. We will not describe these algorithms in detail; we will only describe the subroutines that applications of quantum walks must implement. We do not present these in full generality.

Quantum walk subroutines. Szegedy- and MNRS-style quantum walks use circuits for the following transformations. The values u and v are elements of $\mathcal{S}$, and $\mathcal{M}$ is the subset of marked elements. The values p_{vu} are matrix entries of the transition matrix of a Markov chain P. We assume $p_{vu} = p_{uv}$, and that the corresponding graph is connected.

$$\textbf{Set-up:} |0\cdots 0\rangle \mapsto \frac{1}{\sqrt{|\mathcal{S}|}}\sum_{u\in\mathcal{S}}|u\rangle|0\rangle. \tag{3}$$

$$\textbf{Check:} |u\rangle|v\rangle \mapsto \begin{cases} -|u\rangle|v\rangle & \text{if } u\in\mathcal{M}, \\ |u\rangle|v\rangle & \text{otherwise.} \end{cases} \tag{4}$$

$$\textbf{Update:} |u\rangle|0\rangle \mapsto \sum_{u\in\mathcal{S}}\sqrt{p_{vu}}|u\rangle|v\rangle \tag{5}$$

$$\textbf{Reflect:} |u\rangle|v\rangle \mapsto \begin{cases} |u\rangle|v\rangle & \text{if } v=0, \\ -|u\rangle|v\rangle & \text{otherwise.} \end{cases} \tag{6}$$

The walk step applies $(\text{Update})^{-1}(\text{Reflect})(\text{Update})$. After this, it swaps $|u\rangle$ and $|v\rangle$, repeats $(\text{Update})^{-1}(\text{Reflect})(\text{Update})$, then swaps the vertices back.

Following MNRS, we write S for the cost of the Set-up circuit, U for the cost of the Update and C for the cost of the check. The reflection cost is insignificant in our applications. The cost of a quantum walk also depends on the fraction of marked elements, $\epsilon = |\mathcal{M}|/|\mathcal{S}|$, and the spectral gap of P. With our assumptions, the spectral gap is $\delta(P) = 1 - |\lambda_2(P)|$ where $\lambda_2(P)$ is the second largest eigenvalue of P, in absolute value.

Szegedy's algorithm repeats the check and walk steps for $O(1/\sqrt{\epsilon\delta})$ iterations. MNRS uses $O(1/\sqrt{\epsilon\delta})$ iterations of the walk step, but then only $O(1/\sqrt{\epsilon})$ iterations of the check step. MNRS also uses $O(\log(1/\epsilon\delta))$ ancilla qubits. Cost 5 shows the costs of both algorithms.

Cost 5. Quantum Random Walks. The tuples S, C, and U are the costs of random walk subroutines, ϵ is the fraction of marked vertices, and δ is the spectral gap of the underlying transition matrix.

	Szegedy	MNRS
Gates:	$O\left(\mathsf{S}_G + \frac{1}{\sqrt{\epsilon\delta}}(\mathsf{U}_G + \mathsf{C}_G)\right)$	$O\left(\mathsf{S}_G + \frac{1}{\sqrt{\epsilon}}\left(\frac{1}{\sqrt{\delta}}\mathsf{U}_G + \mathsf{C}_G\right)\right)$
Depth:	$O\left(\mathsf{S}_D + \frac{1}{\sqrt{\epsilon\delta}}(\mathsf{U}_D + \mathsf{C}_D)\right)$	$O\left(\mathsf{S}_D + \frac{1}{\sqrt{\epsilon}}\left(\frac{1}{\sqrt{\delta}}\mathsf{U}_D + \mathsf{C}_D\right)\right)$
Width:	$O(\max\{\mathsf{S}_W, \mathsf{U}_W, \mathsf{C}_W\})$	$O\left(\max\{\mathsf{S}_W, \mathsf{U}_W + \log\left(\frac{1}{\epsilon\delta}\right), \mathsf{C}_W + \log\left(\frac{1}{\epsilon\delta}\right)\}\right)$

5.2   The Claw-Finding Problem

We will now consider a quantum walk algorithm with significant cryptanalytic applications. The claw-finding problem is defined as follows.

Problem 5.1 (Claw Finding). *Given finite sets $\mathcal{X}$, $\mathcal{Y}$, and $\mathcal{Z}$ and functions $f : \mathcal{X} \to \mathcal{Z}$ and $g : \mathcal{Y} \to \mathcal{Z}$ find $x \in \mathcal{X}$ and $y \in \mathcal{Y}$ such that $f(x) = g(y)$.*

In a so-called *golden* claw-finding problem the pair (x, y) is unique.

Tani applied Szegedy's algorithm to solve the decisional version of the claw-finding problem (detecting the presence of a claw) [38]. He then applied a binary search strategy to solve the search problem. As noted in [38], the MNRS algorithm can solve the claw-finding problem directly. The core idea is the same in either case. Parallel walks are taken on Johnson graphs $J(X, R_f)$ and $J(Y, R_g)$, and the checking step looks for claws.

There are a few details to address. First, since the claw property is defined in terms of the set $\mathcal{Z}$, we will need to augment the base sets with additional data. Second, we need to formalize the notion of parallel walks. Fortunately, this does not require any new machinery. Tani's algorithm perfoms a walk on the graph product $J(X, R_f) \times J(Y, R_g)$. A graph product $G_1 \times G_2$ is a graph with vertex set $V(G_1) \times V(G_2)$ which includes an edge between (v_1, v_2) and (u_1, u_2) if and only if v_1 is adjacent to u_1 in G_1 and v_2 is adjacent to u_2 in G_2. Our random replacement routine adds self-loops to both Johnson graphs.

5.3   Tracking Claws Between a Pair of Johnson Vertices

In order to track claws we will store Johnson vertices over the base sets $\mathcal{X}_f = \{(x, f(x)) : x \in \mathcal{X}\}$ and $\mathcal{Y}_g = \{(y, g(y)) : y \in \mathcal{Y}\}$. Alongside each pair of Johnson vertices for $\mathcal{U} \subset \mathcal{X}_f$ and $\mathcal{V} \subset \mathcal{Y}_g$, we will store a counter for the total number of claws between $\mathcal{U}$ and $\mathcal{V}$.

This counter can be maintained using the relationship counting routine of Sect. 4. Before a guaranteed insertion of $(x, f(x))$ into $\mathcal{U}$ we count the number of $(y, g(y))$ in $\mathcal{V}$ with $f(x) = g(y)$. Evaluating the relation costs no more than equality testing and so the full relation counting procedure uses $O(R_g m)$ gates in depth $O(\log m + \log^2 R_g)$. Assuming that $R_f \approx R_g$, counting claws before insertion into $\mathcal{U}$ is the dominant cost. We maintain the claw counter when deleting from $\mathcal{U}$, inserting into $\mathcal{V}$, and deleting from $\mathcal{V}$.

5.4   Analysis of Tani's Claw-Finding Algorithm

We will make a few assumptions in the interest of brevity. We assume that elements of $\mathcal{X}_f$ and $\mathcal{Y}_g$ have the same bit-length m. We write $X = |\mathcal{X}|$, $Y = |\mathcal{Y}|$, and $R = \max\{R_f, R_g\}$. We also assume that the circuits for f and g are identical; we write E_G, E_D, and E_W for the gates, depth, and width of either.

In Tani's algorithm a single graph vertex is represented by two Johnson vertex data structures. Szegedy's algorithm and MNRS store a pair of adjacent graph vertices, so here we are working with two pairs of adjacent Johnson vertices $\mathcal{U}_\mathcal{X} \sim \mathcal{V}_\mathcal{X}$ and $\mathcal{U}_\mathcal{Y} \sim \mathcal{V}_\mathcal{Y}$. The main subroutines are as follows.

Set-up. The Johnson vertices $\mathcal{U}_\mathcal{X}$ and $\mathcal{U}_\mathcal{Y}$ are populated by sampling R elements of $\mathcal{X}$ and inserting these while maintaining the claw counter. We defer the full cost as it is essentially $O(R)$ times the update cost.

Update. The update step applies the random replacement of Sect. 4.3 to each of the Johnson vertices. The insertions and deletions within the replacement routine must maintain the claw counter, so relation counting is the dominant cost of either. Replacement has a cost of $O(1)$ guaranteed insertion/deletions (from the larger of the two sets) and $O(1)$ function evaluations. Based on Cost 3 and the cost of evaluating f, the entire procedure uses $O(Rm + \mathsf{E}_G)$ gates in a circuit of depth $O(\log m + \log^2 R + \mathsf{E}_D)$ and width $O(Rm + \mathsf{E}_W)$.

Check. A phase is applied if the claw-counter is non-zero, with negligible cost.

Walk parameters. Let P be the transition matrix for a random walk on $J(X, R_f)$, formed by normalizing the adjacency matrix. The second largest eigenvalue of P is $\lambda_2 = O(1 - \frac{1}{R_f})$, and is positive. Our update step introduces self-loops with probability R/X into the random walk. The transition matrix with self-loops is $P' = \frac{R}{X}I + (1 - \frac{R}{X})P$. The second-largest eigenvalue of P' is $\lambda_2' = \frac{R}{X} + (1 - \frac{R}{X})\lambda_2$. Since λ_2 is positive, the spectral gap of the walk with self-loops is $\delta_f' = 1 - |\lambda_2'| = \Omega\left(\frac{1}{R_f} - \frac{1}{X}\right)$. In general, the spectral gap of a random walk on $G_1 \times G_2$ is the minimum of the spectral gap of a walk on G_1 or G_2. Thus the spectral gap of our random walk on $J(X, R_f) \times J(Y, R_g)$ is

$$\delta = \Omega\left(\frac{1}{R} - \frac{1}{X}\right).$$

The marked elements are vertices $(\mathcal{U}_\mathcal{X}, \mathcal{U}_\mathcal{Y})$ that contain a claw. In the worst case there is one claw between the functions and

$$\epsilon = \frac{R_f R_g}{XY}.$$

The walk step will then be applied $1/\sqrt{\epsilon\delta} \geq \sqrt{XY/R}$ times.

In Cost 6 we assume $R \leq (XY)^{1/3}$. This is because the query-optimal parameterization of Tani's algorithm uses $R \approx (XY)^{1/3}$ [38], and the set-up routine dominates the cost of the algorithm when $R > (XY)^{1/3}$. The optimal values of R for the G- and DW-cost will typically be much smaller than $(XY)^{1/3}$. The G-cost is minimized when $R = \mathsf{E}_G/m$, and the DW-cost is minimized when $R = \mathsf{E}_W/m$.

Cost 6. Claw-finding using Tani's algorithm with $|\mathcal{X}_f| = X$; $|\mathcal{Y}_g| = Y$; $R = \max\{R_f, R_g\} \leq (XY)^{1/3}$; m large enough to encode an element of $\mathcal{X}_f$ or $\mathcal{Y}_g$; and E_G, E_D, and E_W the gates, depth, and width of a circuit to evaluate f or g.

Gates: $O\left(m\sqrt{XYR} + \mathsf{E}_G\sqrt{\frac{XY}{R}}\right)$

Depth: $O\left(\log m\sqrt{\frac{XY}{R}} + \log^2 R\sqrt{\frac{XY}{R}} + \mathsf{E}_D\sqrt{\frac{XY}{R}}\right)$

Width: $O\left(Rm + \mathsf{E}_W\right)$

5.5 Comparison with Grover's Algorithm

Cost 7 gives the costs of Grover's algorithm applied to claw-finding. It requires $O(\sqrt{XY})$ Grover iterations. Each iteration evaluates f and g, and we assume this is the dominant cost of each iteration. Note that the cost is essentially that of Tani's algorithm with $R = 1$.

Grover's and Tani's algorithms have the same square root relationship to XY. Tani's algorithm can achieve a slightly lower cost when the functions f and g are expensive.

Cost 7. Claw-finding using Grover's algorithm with the notation of Cost 6.

Gates: $O\left(\mathsf{E}_G\sqrt{XY}\right)$

Depth: $O\left(\mathsf{E}_D\sqrt{XY}\right)$

Width: $O\left(\mathsf{E}_W\right)$

5.6 Effect of Parallelism

The naive method to parallelise either algorithm over P processors is to divide the search space into P subsets, one for each processor. For both algorithms, parallelising will reduce the depth and gate cost for *each* processor by $1/\sqrt{P}$. Accounting for costs across all P processors shows that parallelism increases the total cost of either algorithm by a factor of $\sqrt{P}$. This is true in both the G- and the DW-cost metric. This is optimal for Grover's algorithm [43], but may not be optimal for Tani's algorithm. The parallelisation strategy of Jeffery et al. [23] is better, but uses substantial communication between processors in the check step. A detailed cost analysis would need to account for the physical geometry of the processors, which we leave for future work.

6 Application: Cryptanalysis of SIKE

The Supersingular Isogeny Key Encapsulation (SIKE) scheme [20] is based on Jao and de Feo's Supersingular Isogeny Diffie–Helman (SIDH) protocol [21]. In this section we describe the G- and DW-costs of an attack on SIKE. Our analysis can be applied to SIDH as well.

SIKE has public parameters p and E where p is a prime of the form $2^{e_A} 3^{e_B} - 1$ and E is a supersingular elliptic curve defined over $\mathbb{F}_{p^2}$. Typically e_A and e_B are chosen so that $2^{e_A} \approx 3^{e_B}$; we will assume this is the case. For each prime $\ell \neq p$, one can associate a graph, *the ℓ-isogeny graph*, to the set of supersingular elliptic curves defined over $\mathbb{F}_{p^2}$. This graph has approximately $p/12$ vertices. Each vertex represents an equivalence class of elliptic curves with the same *j-invariant*. Edges between vertices represent *degree-ℓ isogenies* between the corresponding curves[4]. A SIKE public key is a curve E_A, and a private key is a path of length e_A that connects E and E_A in the 2-isogeny graph; only one path of this length is expected to exist.

The ℓ-isogeny graph is $(\ell + 1)$-regular. So the set of paths of length c that start at some fixed vertex in the 2-isogeny graph is of size $3 \cdot 2^{c-1}$. This suggests the following golden claw-finding problem. Let $\mathcal{X}$ be the set of paths of length $\lfloor e_A/2 \rfloor$ that start at E, and let $\mathcal{Y}$ be the set of paths of length $\lceil e_A/2 \rceil$ that start at E_A. Let $f : \mathcal{X} \to \mathbb{F}_{p^2}$ and $g : \mathcal{Y} \to \mathbb{F}_{p^2}$ be functions that compute the j-invariant corresponding to the curve reached by a path. Recovering the private key corresponding to E_A is no more difficult than finding a claw between f and g. With the typical parameterisation of $2^{e_A} \approx 3^{e_B}$, both $\mathcal{X}$ and $\mathcal{Y}$ are of size approximately $p^{1/4}$.

We will fix these definitions of $\mathcal{X}$, $\mathcal{Y}$, f, and g for the remainder. We will also assume that E_G, E_D, and E_W—the gates, depth, and width of a circuit for evaluating f or g—are all $p^{o(1)}$.

6.1   Quantum Claw-Finding Attacks

Let us first consider a parallel Grover search with P quantum processors using the parallelisation strategy of Sect. 5.6. Processor i performs a Grover search on $\mathcal{X}_i \times \mathcal{Y}_i$ where $\mathcal{X}_i$ is a subset of $\mathcal{X}$ of size $p^{1/4}/\sqrt{P}$, and $\mathcal{Y}_i$ is a subset of $\mathcal{Y}$ of size $p^{1/4}/\sqrt{P}$. Based on Cost 7 the circuit for all P processors uses $p^{1/4+o(1)}\sqrt{P}$ gates, has depth $p^{1/4+o(1)}/\sqrt{P}$, and has width $p^{o(1)}P$. The only benefit to using more than 1 processor is a reduction in depth. The G- and the DW-cost both increase with P.

Tani's algorithm admits time vs. memory trade-offs using both the Johnson graph parameter R and the number of parallel instances P. With any number of instances, both the G- and the DW-cost are minimized when $R = p^{o(1)}$. Based on Cost 6 the circuit for P processors uses $p^{1/4+o(1)}\sqrt{P}$ gates, has depth $p^{1/4+o(1)}/\sqrt{P}$, and has width $p^{o(1)}P$. This is identical to Grover search up to the $p^{o(1)}$ factors. However, there may be a benefit to using $R > 1$ if function evaluations are sufficiently expensive.

6.2   Classical Claw-Finding Attacks

In a recent analysis of SIKE, Adj et al. [1] conclude that the best known classical claw-finding attack on the scheme is based on the van Oorschot–Wiener (VW)

---

[4] We are being slightly imprecise, as the ℓ-isogeny graph is actually directed. However, if there is an edge from u to v corresponding to an isogeny ϕ, then there is an edge from v to u corresponding to the dual isogeny $\hat{\phi}$.

parallel collision search algorithm. We defer to [1] for a full description of the attack. The VW method uses a PRAM with P processors and M registers. Each register must be large enough to store an element of $\mathcal{X}$ or $\mathcal{Y}$ and a small amount of additional information.

From [1], a claw-finding attack on SIKE using VW on a PRAM with 1 processor and M registers of memory performs

$$\max\left\{\frac{p^{3/8+o(1)}}{M^{1/2}},\ p^{1/4+o(1)}\right\} \tag{7}$$

RAM operations. The $o(1)$ term hides the cost of evaluating f, g, and a hash function. The algorithm parallelizes perfectly so long as $P < M \le p^{1/4}$. This restriction is to avoid a backlog of operations on the shared memory. The algorithm performs $p^{1/4+o(1)}$ shared memory operations in total, and $M^{1/2}P/p^{1/8+o(1)}$ shared memory operations simultaneously. Using memory $M > p^{1/4+o(1)}$ does not reduce the total number of shared memory operations, hence the second term in Eq. 7.

It is natural to treat the P processors in this attack as a memory peripheral controller for M registers of non-volatile memory. Each processor needs an additional $p^{o(1)}$ bits of memory for its internal state, and each of the M registers are of size $p^{o(1)}$. Unlike the quantum claw-finding attacks that we have considered, the RAM operation cost of the VW method decreases as the amount of available hardware increases.

The query-optimal parameterisation of Tani's algorithm has $p^{1/6+o(1)}$ qubits of memory. In our models this implies $p^{1/6+o(1)}$ classical processors for control with a combined $p^{1/6+o(1)}$ bits of classical memory. A RAM operation for these processors is equivalent to a quantum gate in cost and time. Repurposed to run VW, these processors would solve the claw-finding problem in time $p^{1/8+o(1)}$ with $p^{7/24+o(1)}$ RAM operations. Our conclusion is that an adversary with enough quantum memory to run Tani's algorithm with the query-optimal parameters could break SIKE faster by using the classical control hardware to run van Oorschot–Wiener.

6.3   Non-asymptotic Cost Estimates

The claw-finding attacks that we have described above can all break SIKE in $p^{1/4+o(1)}$ RAM operations. However, they achieve this complexity using different amounts of time and memory. Both quantum attacks achieve their minimal cost in time $p^{1/4+o(1)}$ on a machine with $p^{o(1)}$ qubits. The van Oorschot–Wiener method achieves its minimal cost in time $p^{o(1)}$ on a machine with $p^{1/4+o(1)}$ memory and processors. A more thorough accounting of the low order terms could identify the attack (and parameterization) of least cost, but real attackers have resource constraints that might make this irrelevant.

We use SIKE-n to denote a parameterisation of SIKE using an n-bit prime. We focus on SIKE-434 and SIKE-610, parameters introduced as alternatives to the original submission to NIST [1]. Figure 3 depicts the attack landscape for

SIKE-434. Figure 4 gives the cost of breaking SIKE-434 and SIKE-610 under various constraints. These cost estimates are based on assumptions that we describe below.

Cost of function evaluations. The functions f and g involve computing isogenies of (2-smooth) degree approximately $p^{1/4}$. We assume that the cost of evaluating f is equal to the cost of evaluating g, and we let E_G, E_D, and E_W denote the gate-count, depth, and width of a circuit for either. We assume that the classical and quantum gate counts are equal, which may lead us to underestimate the quantum cost.

The SIKE specification describes a method for computing a degree-2^e isogeny that uses approximately $e \log e$ curve operations [20]. Each operation is either a point doubling or a degree-2 isogeny evaluation. We assume that it costs the attacker at least $4 \log p \log \log p$ gates to compute either curve operation. This is a very conservative estimate given that both operations involve multiplication in $\mathbb{F}_{p^2}$, and a single multiplication in $\mathbb{F}_{p^2}$ involves 3 multiplications in $\mathbb{F}_p$. Based on this, we assume that computing an isogeny of degree $\approx p^{1/4}$ costs the attacker at least $(\log p)^2 \left((\log \log p)^2 - 2 \log \log p \right)$ gates. We assume that the attacker's circuit has width $2 \log p$, which is just enough space to represent its output. We assume that the gates parallelize perfectly so that $\mathsf{E}_D = \mathsf{E}_G / \mathsf{E}_W$.

For an attack on SIKE-434 our assumptions give $\mathsf{E}_G = 2^{23.4}$, $\mathsf{E}_D = 2^{13.7}$, and $\mathsf{E}_W = 2^{9.8}$. For an attack on SIKE-610, they give $\mathsf{E}_G = 2^{24.6}$, $\mathsf{E}_D = 2^{14.3}$, and $\mathsf{E}_W = 2^{10.3}$. We assume that elements of $\mathcal{X}_f$ and $\mathcal{Y}_g$ can be represented in $m = (\log p)/2$ bits.

Grover. Each Grover iteration computes two function evaluations. However, to avoid the issue of whether these evaluations are done in parallel or in series, we only cost a single evaluation. We ignore the cost of the diffusion operator. We partition the search space into P parts and distribute the subproblems to P processors. Each processor performs approximately $p^{1/4}/\sqrt{P}$ Grover iterations. This gives a total gate count of at least $p^{1/4}\sqrt{P}\mathsf{E}_G$, depth of at least $p^{1/4}\mathsf{E}_D/\sqrt{P}$, and width of at least $P\mathsf{E}_W$.

For depth-constrained computations we use the smallest P that is compatible with the constraint. For memory-constrained computations we take P large enough to use all of the available memory.

Tani. A single instance of Tani's algorithm stores two lists of size R and needs scratch space for computing two function evaluations. We only cost a single function evaluation. We assume that only $2Rm + \mathsf{E}_W$ qubits are needed.

We parallelise the gate-optimal parameterisation, i.e. we take $R = \mathsf{E}_G/m$. We partition the search space into P parts and distribute subproblems to P processors. Each processor performs roughly $p^{1/4}/\sqrt{RP}$ walk iterations. Each walk iteration performs at least one guaranteed insertion with claw-tracking and at least one function evaluation. Each insertion costs at least Rm gates. Each function evaluation has depth E_D and width E_W. The total gate cost across all P processors is at least $p^{1/4}\sqrt{P/R}(Rm + \mathsf{E}_G) = p^{1/4}\sqrt{2m\mathsf{E}_G P}$ gates in depth at least $p^{1/4}\mathsf{E}_D/\sqrt{RP} = p^{1/4}\mathsf{E}_D\sqrt{m/P\mathsf{E}_G}$ and uses width at least $P(2Rm + \mathsf{E}_W) = P(2\mathsf{E}_G + \mathsf{E}_W)$.

For depth-constrained computations we use the smallest P that is compatible with the constraint. For memory-constrained computations we take P large enough to use all of the available memory. If the parallelisation is such that $R = \mathsf{E}_G/m \geq (p^{1/2}/P)^{1/3}$, which would cause the setup cost to exceed the cost of the walk iteration, we decrease R.

van Oorschot–Wiener. Each processor iterates a cycle of computing a function evaluation and storing the result. We only cost a single function evaluation per iteration. Our quantum machine models assume a number of RAM controllers that is proportional to memory. We make the same assumption here. When the attacker has M bits of memory we assume they also have $P = M/(\mathsf{E}_W + m)$ processors. Intuitively, each processor needs space to evaluate a function and is responsible for one unit of shared memory. This gives a total gate count of at least $(p^{3/8}/M^{1/2})\mathsf{E}_G$, a depth of at least $(p^{3/8}/M^{3/2})(\mathsf{E}_W + m)\mathsf{E}_D$, and a width of M.

For depth constrained-computations we use the smallest amount of memory that satisfies the constraint. Unlike the quantum attacks, the gate cost of VW decreases with memory use, so Fig. 4a and b do not show the best gate count that VW can achieve with a depth constraint. For memory-constrained computations we use the maximum amount of memory allowed.

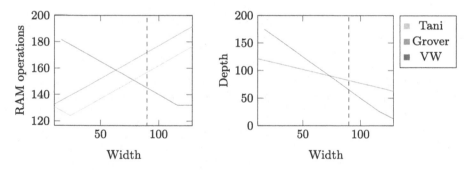

Fig. 3. G-cost and depth of claw-finding attacks on SIKE-434, with the isogeny costs of Sect. 6.3. The dashed lines are at the width of the query-optimal parameterisation including storage, $(p^{1/6}\log p)/2$. Axes are in base-2 logarithms.

7 Conclusions and Future Work

7.1 Impact of Our Work on the NIST Security Level of SIKE

The SIKE submission recommends SIKE-503, SIKE-751, and SIKE-964 for security matching AES-128, AES-192, and AES-256, respectively. NIST suggests that an attack on AES-128 costs 2^{143} classical gates (in a non-local boolean circuit model). NIST also suggests that attacks on AES-192 and AES-256 cost 2^{207} and

Attack	SIKE-434			SIKE-610		
	G	D	W	G	D	W
Grover	190	64	127	280	64	216
Tani	175	63	126	264	64	216
VW	145	64	91	189	63	136

(a) MAXDEPTH $= 2^{64}$

Attack	SIKE-434			SIKE-610		
	G	D	W	G	D	W
Grover	158	96	63	248	96	152
Tani	143	95	62	232	96	152
VW	155	95	70	200	95	115

(b) MAXDEPTH $= 2^{96}$

Attack	SIKE-434			SIKE-610		
	G	D	W	G	D	W
Grover	159	95	64	204	140	64
Tani	144	94	64	188	140	64
VW	158	104	64	225	172	64

(c) MAXMEMORY $= 2^{64}$

Attack	SIKE-434			SIKE-610		
	G	D	W	G	D	W
Grover	175	79	96	220	124	96
Tani	160	78	96	204	124	96
VW	142	56	96	209	124	96

(d) MAXMEMORY $= 2^{96}$

Attack	SIKE-434			SIKE-610		
	G	D	W	G	D	W
Grover	132	122	10	177	167	10
Tani	124	114	25	169	159	25
VW	132	14	128	177	14	173

(e) G-cost optimal

Attack	SIKE-434			SIKE-610		
	G	D	W	G	D	W
Grover	132	122	10	177	167	10
Tani	131	122	10	177	166	10
VW	132	14	128	177	14	173

(f) DW-cost optimal

Fig. 4. Cost estimates for claw finding attacks on SIKE. All numbers are expressed as base-2 logarithms.

2^{272} classical gates, respectively. We have used "RAM operations" throughout to refer to non-local bit/qubit operations; our G-cost is directly comparable with these estimates.

Adj et al. [1] recommend slightly smaller primes: SIKE-434 for security matching AES-128 and SIKE-610 for security matching AES-192. Their analysis is based on the cost of van Oorschot–Wiener with less than 2^{80} registers of memory. NIST's recommended machine model does not impose a limit on classical memory, but it does impose a limit on the depth of quantum circuits. Our cost estimates (Fig. 4) suggests that known quantum attacks do not break SIKE-434 using less than 2^{143} classical gates, or SIKE-610 using less than 2^{207} classical gates, when depth is limited to 2^{96}. We agree with the conclusions of Adj et al., and believe that NIST's machine model should include a width constraint.

We caution that claw-finding attacks may not be optimal. Biasse, Jao, and Sankar [8] present a quantum attack that exploits the algebraic structure of supersingular curves defined over $\mathbb{F}_p$. This attack uses $p^{1/4+o(1)}$ quantum gates and $2^{O(\sqrt{\log p})}$ qubits of memory. Given our analysis of Tani's algorithm, this attack may be competitive with other quantum attacks.

7.2 Further Applications of Our Memory Peripherals

Our analysis should be immediately applicable to other cryptanalytic algorithms that use quantum walks on Johnson graphs. These include algorithms for subset sum [7], information set decoding [25], and quantum Merkle puzzles [10].

The G- and DW-cost metrics have applications to classical algorithms that use quantum subroutines, such as the quantum number field sieve [6], and to quantum algorithms that use classical subroutines, such as Shor's algorithm.

Our analysis of quantum random access might affect memory-intensive algorithms like quantum lattice sieving [29]. However, we only looked at quantum access to quantum memory. There may be physically realistic memory peripherals that enable inexpensive quantum access to classical memory (e.g. [19]).

7.3 Geometrically Local Memory Peripherals

Neither of our memory peripheral models account for communication costs. We allow non-local quantum communication in the form of long-range CNOT gates. We allow non-local classical communication in the controllers. The distributed computing model of Beals et al. [5] might serve as a useful guide for eliminating non-local quantum communication. Note that the resulting circuits are, at present, only compatible with the DW-cost metric. The known self-correcting qubit memories are built out of physical qubit interactions that cannot be implemented locally in 3 dimensional space.

Acknowledgements. We thank Alfred Menezes for helpful comments on this paper. Samuel Jaques acknowledges the support of the Natural Sciences and Engineering Research Council of Canada (NSERC). This work was supported by Canada's NSERC CREATE program. IQC is supported in part by the Government of Canada and the Province of Ontario.

References

1. Adj, G., Cervantes-Vázquez, D., Chi-Domínguez, J.-J., Menezes, A., Rodríguez-Henríquez, F.: On the cost of computing isogenies between supersingular elliptic curves. In: Cid, C., Jacobson Jr., M. (eds.) SAC 2018. LNCS, vol. 11349, pp. 322–343. Springer, Cham (2018). https://doi.org/10.1007/978-3-030-10970-7_15
2. Alicki, R., Fannes, M., Horodecki, M.: On thermalization in Kitaev's 2D model. J. Phys. A **42**, 065303 (2009)
3. Alicki, R., Horodecki, M., Horodecki, P., Horodecki, R.: On thermal stability of topological qubit in Kitaev's 4d model. Open Syst. Inf. Dyn. **17**, 1–20 (2010)
4. Ambainis, A.: Quantum walk algorithm for element distinctness. SIAM J. Comput. **37**, 210–239 (2007)
5. Beals, R., et al.: Efficient distributed quantum computing. Proc. R. Soc. Lond. A: Math. Phys. Eng. Sci. **469**, 20120686 (2013)
6. Bernstein, D.J., Biasse, J.-F., Mosca, M.: A low-resource quantum factoring algorithm. In: Lange, T., Takagi, T. (eds.) PQCrypto 2017. LNCS, vol. 10346, pp. 330–346. Springer, Cham (2017). https://doi.org/10.1007/978-3-319-59879-6_19

7. Bernstein, D.J., Jeffery, S., Lange, T., Meurer, A.: Quantum algorithms for the subset-sum problem. In: Gaborit, P. (ed.) PQCrypto 2013. LNCS, vol. 7932, pp. 16–33. Springer, Heidelberg (2013). https://doi.org/10.1007/978-3-642-38616-9_2
8. Biasse, J.-F., Jao, D., Sankar, A.: A quantum algorithm for computing isogenies between supersingular elliptic curves. In: Meier, W., Mukhopadhyay, D. (eds.) INDOCRYPT 2014. LNCS, vol. 8885, pp. 428–442. Springer, Cham (2014). https://doi.org/10.1007/978-3-319-13039-2_25
9. Blais, A., Huang, R.-S., Wallraff, A., Girvin, S.M., Schoelkopf, R.J.: Cavity quantum electrodynamics for superconducting electrical circuits: an architecture for quantum computation. Phys. Rev. A **69**, 14 pages (2004)
10. Brassard, G., Høyer, P., Kalach, K., Kaplan, M., Laplante, S., Salvail, L.: Merkle puzzles in a quantum world. In: Rogaway, P. (ed.) CRYPTO 2011. LNCS, vol. 6841, pp. 391–410. Springer, Heidelberg (2011). https://doi.org/10.1007/978-3-642-22792-9_22
11. Bravyi, S., Terhal, B.: A no-go theorem for a two-dimensional self-correcting quantum memory based on stabilizer codes. New J. Phys.**11** (2009)
12. Brown, B.J., Loss, D., Pachos, J.K., Self, C.N., Wootton, J.R.: Quantum memories at finite temperature. Rev. Modern Phys. **88**, 045005 (2016)
13. Coecke, B., Fritz, T., Spekkens, R.W.: A mathematical theory of resources. Inf. Comput. **250**, 59–86 (2016)
14. Dennis, E., Kitaev, A., Landahl, A., Preskill, J.: Topological quantummemory. J. Math. Phys. **43**, 4452–4505 (2002)
15. Deutsch, D.E.: Quantum computational networks. Proc. R. Soc. Lond. A **425**, 73–90 (1989)
16. Feynman, R.P.: Quantum mechanical computers. Found. Phys. **16**, 507–531 (1986)
17. Fowler, A.G., Mariantoni, M., Martinis, J.M., Cleland, A.N.: Surfacecodes: towards practical large-scale quantum computation. Phys. Rev. A **86**, 032324 (2012)
18. Fowler, A.G., Whiteside, A.C., Hollenberg, L.C.L.: Towards practical classical processing for the surface code. Phys. Rev. Lett. **108**, 180501 (2012)
19. Giovannetti, V., Lloyd, S., Maccone, L.: Architectures for a quantum random access memory. Phys. Rev. A **78**, 052310 (2008)
20. Jao, D., et al.: Supersingular isogeny key encapsulation. Submission to NIST post-quantum project (2017). https://sike.org/#nist-submission
21. Jao, D., De Feo, L.: Towards quantum-resistant cryptosystems from supersingular elliptic curve isogenies. In: Yang, B.-Y. (ed.) PQCrypto 2011. LNCS, vol. 7071, pp. 19–34. Springer, Heidelberg (2011). https://doi.org/10.1007/978-3-642-25405-5_2
22. Jeffery, S.: Frameworks for quantum algorithms. Ph.D. thesis, University of Waterloo (2014)
23. Jeffery, S., Magniez, F., De Wolf, R.: Optimal parallel quantum query algorithms. Algorithmica **79**, 509–529 (2017)
24. Jordan, S.P.: Fast quantum computation at arbitrarily low energy. Phys. Rev. A **95**, 032305 (2017)
25. Kachigar, G., Tillich, J.-P.: Quantum information set decoding algorithms. In: Lange, T., Takagi, T. (eds.) PQCrypto 2017. LNCS, vol. 10346, pp. 69–89. Springer, Cham (2017). https://doi.org/10.1007/978-3-319-59879-6_5
26. Karp, R.M., Ramachandran, V.: A survey of parallel algorithms for shared-memory machines, Technical report UCB/CSD-88-408, EECS Department, University of California, Berkeley, March 1988
27. Kitaev, A.: Fault-tolerant quantum computation by anyons. Ann. Phys. **303**, 2–30 (2003)

28. Kitaev, A., Shen, A., Vyalyi, M.N.: Classical and Quantum Computation, no. 47. American Mathematical Society, Providence (2002)
29. Laarhoven, T., Mosca, M., van de Pol, J.: Finding shortest lattice vectors faster using quantum search. Des. Codes Crypt. **77**, 375–400 (2015)
30. Le Gall, F., Nakajima, S.: Quantum algorithm for triangle finding in sparse graphs. Algorithmica **79**, 941–959 (2017)
31. Magniez, F., Nayak, A., Roland, J., Santha, M.: Search via quantum walk. SIAM J. Comput. **40**, 142–164 (2011)
32. McDermott, R., et al.: Quantum-classical interface based onsingle flux quantum digital logic. Quantum Sci. Technol. **3**, 024004 (2018)
33. Moore, C.: Quantum circuits: Fanout, parity, and counting, arXiv preprint (1999). https://arxiv.org/abs/quant-ph/9903046
34. National Institute of Standards and Technology, Submission requirements and evaluation criteria or the post-quantum cryptography standardization process (2017). https://csrc.nist.gov/csrc/media/projects/post-quantum-cryptography/documents/call-for-proposals-final-dec-2016.pdf
35. Peierls, R.: On Ising's model of ferromagnetism. In: Mathematical Proceedings Cambridge Philosophical Society, vol. 32, pp. 477–481. Cambridge University Press, Cambridge (1936)
36. Szegedy, M.: Quantum speed-up of Markov chain based algorithms. In: 2004 IEEE Symposium on Foundations of Computer Science, pp. 32–41, October 2004
37. Takahashi, Y., Tani, S., Kunihiro, N.: Quantum addition circuits and unbounded fan-out. Quantum Inf. Comput. **10**, 872–890 (2010)
38. Tani, S.: An improved claw finding algorithm using quantum walk. In: Kučera, L., Kučera, A. (eds.) MFCS 2007. LNCS, vol. 4708, pp. 536–547. Springer, Heidelberg (2007). https://doi.org/10.1007/978-3-540-74456-6_48
39. Terhal, B.M.: Quantum error correction for quantum memories. Rev. Modern Phys. **87**, 307 (2015)
40. Thapliyal, H., Ranganathan, N., Ferreira, R.: Design of a comparator tree based on reversible logic. In: 2010 IEEE International Conference on Nanotechnology, pp. 1113–1116 (2010)
41. Wang, A., Woo, W.D.: Static magnetic storage and delay line. J. Appl. Phys. **21**, 49–54 (1950)
42. Wendin, G.: Quantum information processing with superconducting circuits: a review. Rep. Prog. Phys. **80**, 106001 (2017)
43. Zalka, C.: Grover's quantum searching algorithm is optimal. Phys. Rev. A **60**, 2746 (1999)

Fully Secure Attribute-Based Encryption for t-CNF from LWE

Rotem Tsabary[✉]

Weizmann Institute of Science, Rehovot, Israel
rotem.tsabary@weizmann.ac.il

Abstract. Attribute-based Encryption (ABE), first introduced by [SW05,GPSW06], is a public key encryption system that can support multiple users with varying decryption permissions. One of the main properties of such schemes is the supported function class of policies. While there are fully secure constructions from bilinear maps for a fairly large class of policies, the situation with lattice-based constructions is less satisfactory and many efforts were made to close this gap. Prior to this work the only known fully secure lattice construction was for the class of point functions (also known as IBE).

In this work we construct for the first time a lattice-based (ciphertext-policy) ABE scheme for the function class t-CNF, which consists of CNF formulas where each clause depends on at most t bits of the input, for any constant t. This class includes NP-verification policies, bit-fixing policies and t-threshold policies. Towards this goal we also construct a fully secure single-key constrained PRF from OWF for the same function class, which might be of independent interest.

1 Introduction

Atrribute-based Encryption (ABE), first introduced in [SW05,GPSW06], is a public key encryption system that can support multiple users with varying decryption permissions. In this work we focus on ciphertext-policy ABE schemes, where each ciphertext is associated with a public policy f and each decryption key is associated with a public attribute x, such that decryption succeeds conditioned on $f(x) = 1$. One of the main properties of an ABE scheme is the function class of policies that can be attached to ciphertexts. In fact, ABE was originally suggested as a generalization of identity-based encryption (IBE), in which each ciphertext is destined to a single attribute x (i.e. the policies are point functions).

Supported by the Israel Science Foundation (Grant No. 468/14), Binational Science Foundation (Grants No. 2016726, 2014276), and by the European Union Horizon 2020 Research and Innovation Program via ERC Project REACT (Grant 756482) and via Project PROMETHEUS (Grant 780701).

A. Boldyreva and D. Micciancio (Eds.): CRYPTO 2019, LNCS 11692, pp. 62–85, 2019.
https://doi.org/10.1007/978-3-030-26948-7_3

Bilinear Maps Constructions. It was shown in a long line of works that bilinear maps prove to be useful for the task of constructing IBE and ABE under varying group assumptions. [BF03, Coc01] constructed the first IBE schemes in the random oracle model. [CHK03, BB04a] showed constructions in the standard model, however their security was proven under a weaker notion, called *selective security*.

A few approaches were suggested to go beyond selective security. [BB04b, Wat05] introduced the first constructions with full security in the standard model, using a *partitioning* technique. Their solutions were proved to be secure via a lossy reduction, where the simulator aborts with probability that grows with the number of keys owned by the adversary. [Gen06] introduced the *tagging* technique, with which he managed to construct a fully secure IBE scheme with a tight reduction, however the hardness assumption was still related to the number of keys. Finally, [Wat09] introduced the *dual system encryption* technique and achieved the first fully secure IBE scheme with a tight reduction to a fixed assumption.

The first ABE construction was suggested by [SW05] and supported threshold policies. Later, [GPSW06] constructed a key-policy[1] ABE scheme for policies that can be expressed as a linear secret-sharing (LSSS) access structure and [OSW07] constructed a key-policy ABE scheme for all formulas. [Wat11] showed a ciphertext-policy ABE construction for LSSS access structures. All of those works were proved to be secure in the weaker *selective* mode. The works of [LOS+10, LW12, KL15, CGKW18] expand the dual system technique of [Wat09] to derive fully secure ABE for LSSS and recently [KW19] showed a construction for all monotone access structures in NC^1.

Lattice-Based Constructions. The emerging interest in hard problems over lattices, which are believed to be hard even at the presence of quantum machines, led to the development of a cryptographic toolbox [Ajt96, Ajt99, Reg05] that allows to base the security of various systems over random instances of such problems. This gave rise to a line of works about lattice-based IBE and ABE schemes. The first lattice-based IBE constructions were introduced by [GPV08, CHKP12, ABB10a] and were secure in the *selective* model. Shortly after, [ABB10b] presented a construction with full security and [BL16] constructed a fully secure scheme with a tight reduction.

The first schemes to support richer classes of polices were [AFV11, ABV+12], which constructed ABE for inner product policies and threshold policies respectively. [Boy13] showed key-policy ABE schemes for LSSS access structures. Lastly, the works of [GVW13, BGG+14] constructed key-policy ABE for all policies that can be described by a bounded-depth polynomial-size circuit.

All of the aforementioned ABE constructions were proved to be selectively secure. The works of [BV16, GKW16] showed how to boost the security of [GVW13, BGG+14] to an intermediate notion, named *semi-adaptive* security,

---

[1] In *key-policy* ABE the policies are attached to the keys and the attributes are attached to the ciphertexts.

however it is not clear how to further develop those techniques. The question of whether it is possible to construct fully-secure ABE schemes from lattices beyond point functions remained open.

Our Contribution. In this work we construct for the first time a lattice-based ciphertext-policy ABE scheme for the ensemble of function classes t-CNF, which consists of formulas in conjunctive normal form where each clause depends on at most t bits of the input, for any constant t. Our construction supports functions of unbounded size, that is, every function consisting of polynomial number of clauses. Those function classes includes NP-verification policies, bit-fixing policies and t-threshold policies. Towards this goal we also construct a fully secure single-key constrained PRF from OWF for the same function class, which might be of independent interest.

1.1 Technical Background

Let us first describe the difference between full security and selective security. The former is modeled as a game between an adversary $\mathcal{A}$ and a challenger $\mathcal{C}$ as follows. At the beginning of the game, $\mathcal{C}$ publishes the public parameters of the scheme. At any point of the game, $\mathcal{A}$ can query for multiple decryption keys to attributes x of its choice. In the challenge phase, $\mathcal{A}$ chooses a challenge policy f^* and $\mathcal{C}$ returns a ciphertext respective to f^*. The goal of $\mathcal{A}$ is to determine whether this is an encryption of 0 or 1, and the scheme is secure if it cannot do that as long as none of its queried keys x are authorized by f^*. The selective security game is identical, except that $\mathcal{A}$ has to announce the challenge policy f^* before the game begins.

In the latter game the security reduction has the opportunity to generate the public parameters according to f^*. Selective security proofs usually follow a similar structure, where f^* introduces a partitioning of the identity space. The public parameters are generated in the security reduction such that for all x for which $f^*(x) = 0$ (i.e. not authorized by f^*) it is possible to simulate a decryption key, and for all x for which $f^*(x) = 1$, a key for x would allow to break the hard problem. Since $\mathcal{A}$ can only query for keys of the first type, the reduction can still answer all of the queries appropriately.

Tagging. In [Gen06] Gentry presented an adaptively secure IBE scheme from bilinear maps, using a tagging technique as follows. In the real scheme, every ciphertext is associated with a random tag r_{ct} and every key is associated with a random tag r_{sk}. Decryption works as long as the IBE condition is satisfied *and* $r_{ct} \neq r_{sk}$. The probability that decryption fails is negligible since the tags are random. In the security proof, a random degree-Q polynomial P is embedded into the public parameters, such that it is possible to generate a challenge ciphertext respective to any x with the tag $r_{ct} = P(x)$ and similarly it is possible to generate a key respective to any x with the tag $r_{sk} = P(x)$. That is, the security reduction can answer any key query and can generate a challenge ciphertext respective to any x, however if it generates a ciphertext and a key for the same identity then the decryption fails because they both have the same tag. Recall that in the security game $\mathcal{A}$ is not allowed to query for a challenge and a key respective to the same attribute and therefore it cannot detect that case. Since P is a random polynomial, the values of P on up to Q points are distributed uniformly. For that reason security is guaranteed as long as $\mathcal{A}$ can only query for up to $Q-1$ keys. The evaluation of P has to be performed on a secret element in the exponent of a group. Since it is only possible to compute linear functions over the exponent, the reduction needs to get information that grows linearly with Q and makes the assumption stronger.

The BGG+ Lattice-Based Construction. A long sequence of works [ABB10b, MP12, GSW13, AP14, BGG+14] led to a selectively secure key-policy ABE scheme with security based on LWE, for the function class of all policies that can be described as a bounded-depth polynomial-size circuit. We now give an overview of their technique.

The public parameters consist of a matrix $\mathbf{A}$, and for each attribute x (resp. policy f) there is a related efficiently computable matrix $\mathbf{A}_x \leftarrow \mathsf{EncodeX}(\mathbf{A}, x)$ (resp. $\mathbf{A}_f \leftarrow \mathsf{EncodeF}(\mathbf{A}, f)$). Encryption for an attribute x is a Dual-Regev encryption (see [GPV08]) respective to the public matrix $\mathbf{A}_x$, while a decryption key for f is a Dual-Regev key respective to the public matrix $\mathbf{A}_f$. The matrices $\mathbf{A}_x, \mathbf{A}_f$ are cleverly defined s.t., informally, for all x, f

$$f(x) = 1 \quad \longleftrightarrow \quad \text{It is possible to convert a ciphertext respective to } \mathbf{A}_x$$
$$\text{to a ciphertext respective to } \mathbf{A}_f.$$

Let $\mathsf{Convert}$ be the "ciphertext conversion algorithm" that satisfies the above condition, then we can informally say that

$$f(x) = 1 \quad \longleftrightarrow \quad \mathsf{Convert}(\mathbf{A}_x, x, f) = \mathbf{A}_f .$$

The property that is important to us, is that $\mathsf{Convert}$ works gate-by-gate and therefore respects function composition. That is, if $f = g_2 \circ g_1$, then for all x it holds that

$$\mathsf{Convert}(\mathbf{A}_x, x, f) = \mathsf{Convert}\left(\mathsf{Convert}(\mathbf{A}_x, x, g_1), g_1(x), g_2\right) \tag{1}$$

and therefore

$$f(x) = 1 \quad \longleftrightarrow \quad \mathsf{Convert}\left(\mathsf{Convert}(\mathbf{A}_x, x, g_1), g_1(x), g_2\right) = \mathbf{A}_f .$$

The security proof follows similar lines to other selectively-secure schemes as described at the beginning of this section. That is, the challenge attribute x^* is embedded into the public parameters $\mathbf{A}$ such that it is possible to create a challenge ciphertext only respective to $\mathbf{A}_{x^*} = \mathsf{EncodeX}(\mathbf{A}, x^*)$, and it is possible to generate keys only respective to $\mathbf{A}_f = \mathsf{EncodeF}(\mathbf{A}, f)$ for which $f(x^*) = 0$.

1.2 Our Techniques

Identity-Based Encryption. We first describe how to construct a fully secure IBE scheme with our approach. The main idea is to use the tagging technique of [Gen06], but with a PRF instead of a random polynomial. The rich function class supported by [BGG+14] allows us to compute a PRF over a seed that is secretly embedded into the public parameters in the security proof. The tag of a key for an attribute x is the value of the PRF on the input x, i.e. r_x. That is, a key for x can decrypt any ciphertext respective to x unless the ciphertext tag is equivalent to r_x. In the real scheme the tags of ciphertexts are sampled uniformly, while in the security reduction they are determined by the PRF seed that is embedded into the public parameters. Details follow.

For all x we let U_x denote the circuit that on inuput σ evaluates the PRF on the point x with the seed σ. For all r we let $\bar{I}_r$ denote the circuit that on input r' returns 1 if and only if $r' \neq r$.

The public parameters of the IBE scheme are identical to [BGG+14] and the master secret key includes a PRF seed σ. To encrypt respective to x, one samples a fresh PRF seed σ' and computes the Dual-Regev encryption with the public matrix $\mathbf{A}'_x = \mathsf{Convert}(\mathbf{A}_{\sigma'}, \sigma', U_x)$ where $\mathbf{A}_{\sigma'} = \mathsf{EncodeX}(\mathbf{A}, \sigma')$. To generate a key respective to x, one first computes $r_x = U_x(\sigma)$ and then generates the Dual-Regev key respective to the matrix $\mathbf{A}_{f_x} = \mathsf{EncodeF}(\mathbf{A}, f_x)$, where $f_x = \bar{I}_{r_x} \circ U_x$. Note that $f_x(\sigma') = \bar{I}_{r_x}(U_x(\sigma'))$ where $r_x = U_x(\sigma)$. Therefore, if $\sigma = \sigma'$ then $f_x(\sigma) = 0$, but for any uniformly sampled σ', $U_x(\sigma') \neq U_x(\sigma)$ with high probability and therefore $f_x(\sigma') = 1$. That is, with high probability over a uniform σ' it holds that

$$f_x(\sigma') = 1 \quad \longleftrightarrow \quad \sigma' \neq \sigma$$

i.e.

$$\bar{I}_{r_x} \circ U_x(\sigma') = 1 \quad \longleftrightarrow \quad \sigma' \neq \sigma \ .$$

By the properties of [BGG+14] described above, it holds that

$$\bar{I}_{r_x} \circ U_x(\sigma') = 1 \quad \longleftrightarrow \quad \mathsf{Convert}\left(\mathsf{Convert}(\mathbf{A}_{\sigma'}, \sigma', U_x), U_x(\sigma'), \bar{I}_{r_x}\right) = \mathbf{A}_{f_x}$$

and therefore

$$\sigma' \neq \sigma \quad \longleftrightarrow \quad \mathsf{Convert}\left(\mathbf{A}'_x, U_x(\sigma'), \bar{I}_{r_x}\right) = \mathbf{A}_{f_x} \ .$$

That is, whenever $\sigma' \neq \sigma$ it is possible to convert a ciphertext respective to $\mathbf{A}'_x$ to a ciphertext respective to $\mathbf{A}_{f_x}$ and thus to decrypt. However, when $\sigma' = \sigma$ there is no such conversion algorithm.

In the security proof we encode σ in the public parameters, such that it is only possible to simulate Dual-Regev encryptions respective to matrices of the form $\mathbf{A}_x = \mathsf{Convert}(\mathbf{A}_\sigma, \sigma, U_x)$ (where $\mathbf{A}_\sigma = \mathsf{EncodeX}(\mathbf{A}, \sigma)$) but not respective to any other σ'. The indistinguishability relies on the pseudorandomness of the PRF and the properties of [BGG+14].

Expanding the Function Class. The main idea here is to replace the PRF with a constrained PRF. A constrained PRF, first defined in [BW13, KPTZ13, BGI14], allows the key owner to generate *constrained keys* σ_f respective to functions f, with which it is possible to compute the value of the PRF only on points x where $f(x) = 1$. More formally, there are two additional algorithms (Constrain, ConstrainEval) such that if $\sigma_f = \mathsf{Constrain}(\sigma, f)$, then for all x for which $f(x) = 1$ it holds that $\mathsf{ConstrainEval}(\sigma_f, f, x) = \mathsf{Eval}(\sigma, x)$, while for all x for which $f(x) = 0$, σ_f does not reveal information about $\mathsf{Eval}(\sigma, x)$.

Our construction uses a cPRF for policies in a function class $\mathcal{F}$ in order to construct an ABE scheme for policies in $\mathcal{F}$. The cPRF has to be single-key adaptively secure, and in addition it has to satisfy two properties as follows.

- *Gradual Evaluation* requires that for any f, x for which $f(x) = 1$, the circuit descriptions of the algorithms $\mathsf{Eval}(\cdot, x)$ and $\mathsf{ConstrainEval}(\mathsf{Constrain}(\cdot, f), f, x)$ are identical.
- *Key Simulation* requires an additional public algorithm $\mathsf{KeySim}(f) \to \sigma'_f$ that allows to simulate constrained keys. The keys should be indistinguishable from real constrained keys to a distinguisher with no access to evaluations on points x where $f(x) = 1$.

We call a cPRF that satisfies all of those properties a *conforming* cPRF. The ABE construction from a cPRF is a generalization of the IBE construction from a PRF. Details follow.

In the encryption algorithm, in order to encrypt respective to a policy f we compute a Dual-Regev encryption with the public matrix $\mathbf{A}'_f = \mathsf{Convert}(\mathbf{A}_{\sigma'}, \sigma', U_f)$, where $\mathbf{A}_{\sigma'} = \mathsf{EncodeX}(\mathbf{A}, \sigma')$ (as in the IBE construction) and U_f is the circuit description of $\mathsf{Constrain}(\cdot, f)$. The key generation algorithm remains the same as in the IBE construction. To decrypt with a key respective to x, one has to first convert the ciphertext to be respective to the matrix $\mathbf{A}'_x$. This is done by computing $\mathsf{Convert}(\mathbf{A}'_f, U_f(\sigma'), U_{f\to x})$, where $U_{f\to x}$ is the circuit description of $\mathsf{ConstrainEval}(\cdot, f, x)$. Note that

$$
\begin{aligned}
\mathsf{Convert}(\mathbf{A}'_f, U_f(\sigma'), U_{f\to x}) &= \mathsf{Convert}(\mathsf{Convert}(\mathbf{A}_{\sigma'}, \sigma', U_f), U_f(\sigma'), U_{f\to x}) \\
&= \mathsf{Convert}(\mathbf{A}_{\sigma'}, \sigma', U_x) \\
&= \mathbf{A}'_x
\end{aligned}
\tag{2}
$$

where the last equation holds by definition, and Eq. (2) holds since $U_{f\to x} \circ U_f = U_x$ by the gradual evaluation property of the cPRF, and since $\mathsf{Convert}$ respects function composition as described in Eq. (1).

The rest of the analysis is very similar to the IBE case. The key-simulation property guarantees that the adversary cannot tell whether the challenge ciphertext f^* is generated respective to σ or to a random σ', as long as it cannot query for evaluations of σ on points x where $f^*(x) = 1$ (which is indeed guaranteed by the ABE security game).

Constructing a Conforming cPRF. We construct a conforming cPRF for the function class t-CNF for any constant t. A policy f is in the class t-CNF if it can be described by a conjunctive normal form (CNF) formula, where each clause depends on t bits of the input. Our construction is inspired by the [DKNY18] construction of bit-fixing cPRF for a constant number of keys. In fact, their technique can be generalized to instantiate a family of cPRF schemes with a tradeoff between the "CNF locality" of the supported policies and the number of keys. They instantiate it with CNF locality 1 (i.e. bit-fixing) and t keys, while we instantiate it with CNF locality t and a single key. Details follow.

Let ℓ be the input length of the cPRF. We consider the set $S = \{(T, v)\}$ of all pairs (T, v) such that $T \subseteq [\ell]$, $|T| = t$, $v \in \{0, 1\}^t$. For any input $x \in \{0, 1\}^\ell$ we define the set $S_x = \{(T, x_T)\}_T$ where x_T is the substring of x on indices T. For all f we define the set $S_f \subseteq S$ of all of the pairs (T, v) that do not violate any of the clauses of f. It is easy to verify that for all x and f,

$$f(x) = 1 \quad \longleftrightarrow \quad S_x \subseteq S_f . \tag{3}$$

The master secret key is a key σ of a standard PRF. Evaluation on a point x returns the value r_x, computed as

$$r_x = \bigoplus_{(T,v) \in S_x} \mathsf{Eval}(\sigma_{(T,v)}, x) \qquad \text{where } \sigma_{(T,v)} = \mathsf{Eval}(\sigma, (T, v)) .$$

A constrained key for f consists of the values $\{\sigma_{(T,v)}\}_{(T,v) \in S_f}$. Correctness holds by Eq. (3), security and key simulation holds by the pseudorandomness of the underlying PRF and gradual evaluation holds since the circuit $\mathsf{CPRF.Eval}(\cdot, x)$ is a sub-circuit of $\mathsf{CPRF.ConstrainEval}(\mathsf{Constrain}(\cdot, f), f, x)$.

1.3 Related Work

The idea to embed a PRF seed in a [BGG+14]-like construction was previously suggested by [BV16, BL16].

Comparison with BV16. The work of [BV16] focuses on key-policy ABE with unbounded attribute length. In their scheme, the evaluation of the PRF allows to dynamically increase the width of the $\mathbf{A}$ matrix, so that $\mathbf{A}_x \leftarrow \mathsf{EncodeX}(\mathbf{A}, x)$ can be computed for x of varying length. In particular, the PRF is evaluated over values that only depend on the length of the attribute, where in our scheme the PRF is evaluated over the attribute value itself. Their ciphertexts contain two "pieces" for every bit of the attribute and they use an additional ABE scheme in a black-box manner in order to control the access that keys have to those pieces.

Their construction achieves *semi-adaptive* security, which means that the challenge attribute x^* has to be announced before the first key query, but possibly after seeing the public parameters. This property is due to the fact that in their ciphertexts the attribute value is implicitly XORed with a hidden random string Δ, that can be chosen in the security reduction at the first key generation. We note that if one desires a semi-adaptive scheme for a fixed attribute length ℓ, their technique can be instantiated with a PRG with poly(ℓ) stretch instead of a PRF. That is, the incentives for using a PRF are different in their work and ours.

Comparison with BL16. The work of [BL16] focuses on fully-secure signatures and IBE schemes with tight reductions. Their usage of a PRF in the IBE scheme has some similarities to an IBE instantiation of our approach, however the technicalities are different and the cPRF expansion is not applicable to their approach. They use a PRF with tight security that on input x outputs a single bit b_x. A ciphertext for an identity x contains two independent Dual-Regev encryptions of the message under two matrices $\mathbf{A}_{x,0}, \mathbf{A}_{x,1}$, and a key for x can only decrypt one of them $\mathbf{A}_{x,b_x}$. In the security proof the PRF seed is encoded into the public parameters such that it is possible to simulate keys for $\mathbf{A}_{x,b_x}$ without the master secret key, while it is only possible to simulate the "undecryptable" ciphertext part respective to $\mathbf{A}_{x,1-b_x}$.

1.4 Paper Organization

In Sect. 2 we go over the definitions of ABE and cPRF, and summarize lattice techniques from previous works. In Sect. 3 we define the conforming cPRF and provide a construction for policies in t-CNF. In Sect. 4 we construct a fully secure ABE scheme that can be instantiated with any conforming cPRF.

2 Preliminaries

2.1 Constrained PRF, Attribute-Based Encryption, t-CNF Policies

Definition 1 ((Standard) PRF). *A pseudo-random function family (PRF) is a pair of* PPT *algorithms* (Setup, Eval) *with the following syntax.* $\mathsf{Setup}(1^\lambda) \to \mathsf{sk}$ *takes as input a security parameter* λ *and outputs a secret key* sk. $\mathsf{Eval}_{\mathsf{sk}}(x) \to r_x$ *takes as input a secret key* sk *and a bit-string* $x \in \{0,1\}^\ell$, *and outputs a bit-sting* $r_x \in \{0,1\}^k$.

Pseudorandomness. A PRF family is secure if for any PPT *adversary* $\mathcal{A}$ *it holds that*
$$\left| Pr[\mathcal{A}^{\mathsf{Eval}_{\mathsf{sk}}(\cdot)}(1^\lambda) = 1] - Pr[\mathcal{A}^{\mathcal{O}(\cdot)}(1^\lambda) = 1] \right| = \mathrm{negl}(\lambda)$$
where $\mathsf{sk} \leftarrow \mathsf{Setup}(1^\lambda)$ *and* $\mathcal{O}$ *is a random oracle.*

Definition 2 (Constrained PRF). *Let* $\mathcal{F}$ *be a function class such that* $\mathcal{F} \subseteq \{0,1\}^\ell \to \{0,1\}$. *A constrained pseudo-random function (cPRF) for policies in* $\mathcal{F}$ *is a tuple of* PPT *algorithms with the following syntax.*

- $\mathsf{Setup}(1^\lambda) \to \mathsf{pp}, \mathsf{msk}$ *takes as input a security parameter* λ *and outputs public parameters* pp *along with a master secret key* msk.
- $\mathsf{Eval}_{\mathsf{msk}}(x) \to r_x$ *is a deterministic algorithm that takes as input a master secret key* msk *and a bit-string* $x \in \{0,1\}^\ell$, *and outputs a bit-sting* $r_x \in \{0,1\}^k$.
- $\mathsf{Constrain}_{\mathsf{msk}}(f) \to \mathsf{sk}_f$ *takes as input a master secret key* msk *and a function* $f \in \mathcal{F}$, *and outputs a constrained key* sk_f.
- $\mathsf{ConstrainEval}_{\mathsf{sk}_f}(x)$ *is a deterministic algorithm that takes as input a constrained key* sk_f *and a bit-string* $x \in \{0,1\}^\ell$, *and outputs a bit-string* $r'_x \in \{0,1\}^k$.

Correctenss. A *cPRF scheme is* correct *if for all* $x \in \{0,1\}^\ell$ *and* $f \in \mathcal{F}$ *for which* $f(x) = 1$, *it holds that* $\mathsf{Eval}_{\mathsf{msk}}(x) = \mathsf{ConstrainEval}_{\mathsf{sk}_f}(x)$ *where* $(\mathsf{pp}, \mathsf{msk}) \leftarrow \mathsf{Setup}(1^\lambda)$ *and* $\mathsf{sk}_f \leftarrow \mathsf{Constrain}_{\mathsf{msk}}(f)$.

Pseudorandomness. The adaptive security game of a cPRF scheme between an adversary $\mathcal{A}$ and a challenger $\mathcal{C}$ is as follows.

1. Initialization: $\mathcal{C}$ *generates* $(\mathsf{pp}, \mathsf{msk}) \leftarrow \mathsf{Setup}(1^\lambda)$ *and sends* pp *to* $\mathcal{A}$.
2. Queries Phase I: $\mathcal{A}$ *makes (possibly many) queries in an arbitrary order:*
   - Evaluation Queries: $\mathcal{A}$ *sends a bit-string* $x \in \{0,1\}^\ell$, $\mathcal{C}$ *returns* $r_x \leftarrow$ $\mathsf{Eval}_{\mathsf{msk}}(x)$.
   - Key Queries: $\mathcal{A}$ *sends a function* $f \in \mathcal{F}$, $\mathcal{C}$ *returns* $\mathsf{sk}_f \leftarrow \mathsf{Constrain}_{\mathsf{msk}}(f)$.
3. Challenge Phase: $\mathcal{A}$ *sends the challenge bit-string* $x^* \in \{0,1\}^\ell$. $\mathcal{C}$ *uniformly samples* $b \xleftarrow{\$} \{0,1\}$. *If* $b = 0$ *then* $\mathcal{C}$ *returns* $r^* \xleftarrow{\$} \{0,1\}^k$. *Otherwise it returns* $r^* \leftarrow \mathsf{Eval}_{\mathsf{msk}}(x^*)$.
4. Queries Phase II: *same as the first queries phase.*
5. End of Game: $\mathcal{A}$ *outputs a bit* b'.

$\mathcal{A}$ *wins the game if (1)* $b' = b$, *(2) all of the evaluation queries are not for* x^* *and (3) all of the key queries* f *are such that* $f(x^*) = 0$. The single-key *adaptive security game is as described above, except that* $\mathcal{A}$ *can only make a single key query throughout the entire game.* A cPRF scheme is secure *(resp.* single-key secure*) if for any* PPT *adversary* $\mathcal{A}$, *the probability that* $\mathcal{A}$ *wins in the adaptive (resp. single-key adaptive) security game is at most* $1/2 + \mathrm{negl}(\lambda)$.

Definition 3 (Attribute-Based Encryption). *Let* $\mathcal{F}$ *be a function class such that* $\mathcal{F} \subseteq \{0,1\}^\ell \rightarrow \{0,1\}$. *A (ciphertext-policy) attribute-based encryption (ctpABE) for policies in* $\mathcal{F}$ *is a tuple of* PPT *algorithms with the following syntax.*

- $\mathsf{Setup}(1^\lambda) \rightarrow \mathsf{pp}, \mathsf{msk}$ *takes as input a security parameter* λ *and outputs public parameters* pp *along with a master secret key* msk.
- $\mathsf{KeyGen}_{\mathsf{msk}}(x) \rightarrow \mathsf{sk}_x$ *takes as input a master secret key* msk *and a bit-string* $x \in \{0,1\}^\ell$, *and outputs a key* sk_x.
- $\mathsf{Enc}(f, \mu) \rightarrow \mathsf{ct}$ *takes as input a function* $f \in \mathcal{F}$ *and plaintext* $\mu \in \{0,1\}$, *and outputs a ciphertext* ct.
- $\mathsf{Dec}_{\mathsf{sk}_x}(\mathsf{ct}, f)$ *takes as input a key* sk_x, *a ciphertext* ct *and a function* $f \in \mathcal{F}$, *and outputs a bit* $\mu' \in \{0,1\}$.

Correctenss. A *ctpABE scheme is* correct *if for all* $x \in \{0,1\}^\ell$ *and* $f \in \mathcal{F}$ *for which* $f(x) = 1$, *and for all* $\mu \in \{0,1\}$, *it holds that*

$$Pr[\mathsf{Dec}_{\mathsf{sk}_x}(\mathsf{Enc}(f, \mu), f) \neq \mu] = \mathrm{negl}(\lambda)$$

where $(\mathsf{pp}, \mathsf{msk}) \leftarrow \mathsf{Setup}(1^\lambda)$ *and* $\mathsf{sk}_x \leftarrow \mathsf{KeyGen}_{\mathsf{msk}}(x)$.

Security. The adaptive security game of a ctpABE scheme between an adversary $\mathcal{A}$ and a challenger $\mathcal{C}$ is as follows.

1. Initialization: $\mathcal{C}$ generates $(\mathsf{pp}, \mathsf{msk}) \leftarrow \mathsf{Setup}(1^\lambda)$ and sends pp to $\mathcal{A}$.
2. Queries Phase I: $\mathcal{A}$ makes (possibly many) key queries. For each query, $\mathcal{A}$ sends a string $x \in \{0,1\}^\ell$ and $\mathcal{C}$ returns $\mathsf{sk}_x \leftarrow \mathsf{KeyGen}_{\mathsf{msk}}(x)$.
3. Challenge Phase: $\mathcal{A}$ sends the challenge function $f^* \in \mathcal{F}$. $\mathcal{C}$ uniformly samples $b \xleftarrow{\$} \{0,1\}$ and returns $\mathsf{ct}^* \leftarrow \mathsf{Enc}(f^*, b)$.
4. Queries Phase II: same as the first queries phase.
5. End of Game: $\mathcal{A}$ outputs a bit b'.

$\mathcal{A}$ wins the game if (1) $b' = b$ and (2) all of the key queries x are such that $f^*(x) = 0$. A ctpABE scheme is secure if for any PPT adversary $\mathcal{A}$, the probability that $\mathcal{A}$ wins in the adaptive security game is at most $1/2 + \mathsf{negl}(\lambda)$.

In this work we focus on the class of functions that can be described in a conjunctive normal form (CNF), where each clause is of constant locality. We give now a definition.

Definition 4 (t-CNF). A t-CNF policy $f : \{0,1\}^\ell \to \{0,1\}$ is a set of clauses $f = \{(T_i, f_i)\}_i$, where for all i, $T_i \subseteq [\ell]$, $|T_i| = t$ and $f_i : \{0,1\}^t \to \{0,1\}$. For all $x \in \{0,1\}^\ell$ the value of $f(x)$ is computed as

$$f(x) = \bigwedge_i f_i(x_{T_i})$$

where x_T is the length-t bit-string consisting of the bits of x in the indices T. A function class $\mathcal{F}$ is t-CNF if it consists only of t-CNF policies for some fixed $\ell \in \mathbb{N}$ and a constant $t \leq \ell$. If $\mathcal{F}$ is a t-CNF function class, we say that t is the CNF locality of $\mathcal{F}$.

2.2 Lattice Trapdoors, Bounded Distributions, LWE

Lattice Trapdoors. Let $n, q \in \mathbb{Z}$, $\mathbf{g} = (1, 2, 4, \ldots, 2^{\lceil \log q \rceil - 1}) \in \mathbb{Z}_q^{\lceil \log q \rceil}$ and $m = n\lceil \log q \rceil$. The *gadget matrix* $\mathbf{G}$ is defined as the diagonal concatenation of $\mathbf{g}$ n times. Formally, $\mathbf{G} = \mathbf{g} \otimes \mathbf{I}_n \in \mathbb{Z}_q^{n \times m}$. For any $t \in \mathbb{Z}$, the function $\mathbf{G}^{-1} : \mathbb{Z}_q^{n \times t} \to \{0,1\}^{m \times t}$ expands each entry $a \in \mathbb{Z}_q$ of the input matrix into a column of size $\lceil \log q \rceil$ consisting of the bits representation of a. For any matrix $\mathbf{A} \in \mathbb{Z}_q^{n \times t}$, it holds that $\mathbf{G} \cdot \mathbf{G}^{-1}(\mathbf{A}) = \mathbf{A}$.

The (centered) discrete Gaussian distribution over $\mathbb{Z}^m$ with parameter τ, denoted $D_{\mathbb{Z}^m, \tau}$, is the distribution over $\mathbb{Z}^m$ where for all $\mathbf{x}$, $\Pr[\mathbf{x}] \propto e^{-\pi \|\mathbf{x}\|^2 / \tau^2}$. Let $n, m, q \in \mathbb{N}$ and consider a matrix $\mathbf{A} \in \mathbb{Z}_q^{n \times m}$. For all $\mathbf{v} \in \mathbb{Z}_q^n$ we let $\mathbf{A}_\tau^{-1}(\mathbf{v})$ denote the random variable whose distribution is the Discrete Gaussian $D_{\mathbb{Z}^m, \tau}$ conditioned on $\mathbf{A} \cdot \mathbf{A}_\tau^{-1}(\mathbf{v}) = \mathbf{v}$.

A τ-trapdoor for $\mathbf{A}$ is a procedure that can sample from a distribution within 2^{-n} statistical distance of $\mathbf{A}_\tau^{-1}(\mathbf{v})$ in time $\mathsf{poly}(n, m, \log q)$, for any $\mathbf{v} \in \mathbb{Z}_q^n$. We slightly overload notation and denote a τ-trapdoor for $\mathbf{A}$ by $\mathbf{A}_\tau^{-1}$. The following properties had been established in a long sequence of works.

Corollary 1 (Trapdoor Generation [Ajt96, MP12]). *There exists an efficiently computable value* $m_0 = O(n \log q)$ *and an efficient procedure* TrapGen$(1^n, q, m)$ *such that for all* $m \geq m_0$ *outputs* $(\mathbf{A}, \mathbf{A}_{\tau_0}^{-1})$*, where* $\mathbf{A} \in \mathbb{Z}_q^{n \times m}$ *is* 2^{-n}*-uniform and* $\tau_0 = O(\sqrt{n \log q \log n})$.

We use the most general form of trapdoor extension as formalized in [MP12].

Theorem 1 (Trapdoor Extension [ABB10b, MP12]). *Given* $\mathbf{A} \in \mathbb{Z}_q^{n \times m}$ *with a trapdoor* $\mathbf{A}_\tau^{-1}$*, and letting* $\mathbf{B} \in \mathbb{Z}_q^{n \times m'}$ *be s.t.* $\mathbf{A} = \mathbf{B}\mathbf{S} \pmod{q}$ *where* $\mathbf{S} \in \mathbb{Z}^{m' \times m}$ *with largest singular value* $s_1(\mathbf{S})$*, then* $(\mathbf{A}_\tau^{-1}, \mathbf{S})$ *can be used to sample from* $\mathbf{B}_{\tau'}^{-1}$ *for any* $\tau' \geq \tau \cdot s_1(\mathbf{S})$.

A few additional important corollaries are derived from this theorem. We recall that $s_1(\mathbf{S}) \leq \sqrt{m'm} \, \|\mathbf{S}\|_\infty$ and that a trapdoor $\mathbf{G}_{O(1)}^{-1}$ is trivial. The first is a trapdoor extension that follows by taking $\mathbf{S} = [\mathbf{I}_{m'} \| \mathbf{0}_m]^T$.

Corollary 2. *Given* $\mathbf{A} \in \mathbb{Z}_q^{n \times m'}$*, with a trapdoor* $\mathbf{A}_\tau^{-1}$*, it is efficient to generate a trapdoor* $[\mathbf{A}\|\mathbf{B}]_{\tau'}^{-1}$ *for all* $\mathbf{B} \in \mathbb{Z}_q^{n \times m}$*, for any* $m \in \mathbb{N}$ *and any* $\tau' \geq \tau$.

Next is a trapdoor extension that had been used extensively in prior work. It follows from Theorem 1 with $\mathbf{S} = [-\mathbf{R}^T \| \mathbf{I}_m]^T$.

Corollary 3. *Given* $\mathbf{A} \in \mathbb{Z}_q^{n \times m'}$*, and* $\mathbf{R} \in \mathbb{Z}^{m' \times m}$ *with* $m = n\lceil \log q \rceil$*, it is efficient to compute* $[\mathbf{A}\|\mathbf{A}\mathbf{R} + \mathbf{G}]_\tau^{-1}$ *for* $\tau = O(\sqrt{mm'} \, \|\mathbf{R}\|_\infty)$.

Note that by taking $\mathbf{A}$ uniformly and $\mathbf{R}$ to be a high entropy small matrix, e.g. uniform in $\{-1, 0, 1\}$, and relying on the leftover hash lemma, Corollary 1 is in fact a special case of this one.

Lattice Evaluation. The following is an abstraction of the evaluation procedure in previous LWE based FHE and ABE schemes, that developed in a long sequence of works [ABB10b, MP12, GSW13, AP14, BGG+14, GVW15].

Theorem 2. *There exist efficient deterministic algorithms* EvalF *and* EvalFX *such that for all* $n, q, \ell \in \mathbb{N}$ *and* $m = n\lceil \log q \rceil$*, for any depth* d *boolean circuit* $f : \{0,1\}^\ell \to \{0,1\}^k$ *and for every* $x \in \{0,1\}^\ell$*, for any matrix* $\mathbf{A} \in \mathbb{Z}_q^{n \times m \cdot \ell}$*, the outputs* $\mathbf{H} \leftarrow$ EvalF$(f, \mathbf{A})$ *and* $\widehat{\mathbf{H}} \leftarrow$ EvalFX$(f, x, \mathbf{A})$ *are both in* $\mathbb{Z}^{m \cdot \ell \times m \cdot k}$ *and it holds that* $\|\mathbf{H}\|_\infty, \left\|\widehat{\mathbf{H}}\right\|_\infty \leq (2m)^d$ *and*

$$[\mathbf{A} - x \otimes \mathbf{G}]\widehat{\mathbf{H}} = \mathbf{A}\mathbf{H} - f(x) \otimes \mathbf{G} \pmod{q}^2 \, .$$

Moreover, for any pair of circuits $f : \{0,1\}^\ell \to \{0,1\}^k$*,* $g : \{0,1\}^k \to \{0,1\}^t$ *and for any matrix* $\mathbf{A} \in \mathbb{Z}_q^{n \times m \cdot \ell}$*, the outputs* $\mathbf{H}_f \leftarrow$ EvalF$(f, \mathbf{A})$*,* $\mathbf{H}_g \leftarrow$ EvalF$(g, \mathbf{A}\mathbf{H}_f)$ *and* $\mathbf{H}_{g \circ f} \leftarrow$ EvalF$(g \circ f, \mathbf{A})$ *satisfy* $\mathbf{H}_f \mathbf{H}_g = \mathbf{H}_{g \circ f}$.

---

[2] For all $n \in \mathbb{Z}$ and $v \in \{0,1\}^n$ the term $v \otimes \mathbf{G}$ denotes a tensor product of the binary row-vector $v = (v_1, \ldots, v_n)$ and the matrix $\mathbf{G}$. That is, $v \otimes \mathbf{G} = [v_1 \cdot \mathbf{G} \| \ldots \| v_n \cdot \mathbf{G}]$.

Bounded Distributions. The following definitions and corollaries, taken from [BV16], will allow us to properly set the parameters of our scheme.

Definition 5. *A distribution χ supported over $\mathbb{Z}$ is (B, ϵ)-bounded if $Pr_{x \xleftarrow{\$} \chi}[|x| > B] < \epsilon$.*

Definition 6. *A distribution $\tilde{\chi}$ supported over $\mathbb{Z}$ is (B, ϵ)-swallowing if for all $y \in [-B, B] \cap \mathbb{Z}$ it holds that $\tilde{\chi}$ and $y + \tilde{\chi}$ are within ϵ statistical distance.*

Corollary 4. *For every B, ϵ, δ there exists an efficiently sampleable distribution that is both (B, ϵ)-swallowing and $(B \cdot \sqrt{\log(1/\delta)}/\epsilon, O(\delta))$-bounded.*

Definition 7. *A distribution $\tilde{\chi}$ supported over $\mathbb{Z}$ is (χ, ϵ)-swallowing, for a distribution χ, if it holds that $\tilde{\chi}$ and $\chi + \tilde{\chi}$ are within ϵ statistical distance. We omit the ϵ when it indicates a negligible function in a security parameter that is clear from the context.*

Corollary 5. *Let $B(\lambda)$ be some function and let $\tilde{B}(\lambda) = B(\lambda) \cdot \lambda^{\omega(1)}$, then there exists an efficiently sampleable ensemble $\{\tilde{\chi}_\lambda\}_\lambda$ such that $\tilde{\chi}$ is χ-swallowing for any $B(\lambda)$-bounded $\{\chi_\lambda\}_\lambda$, and also $\tilde{B}(\lambda)$-bounded.*

Learning With Errors. The *Learning with Errors* (LWE) problem was introduced by Regev [Reg05]. In this work we will use its decisional version.

Definition 8 (Decisional LWE (DLWE) [Reg05] and its HNF [ACPS09]). *Let λ be the security parameter, $n = n(\lambda)$ and $q = q(\lambda)$ be integers and let $\chi = \chi(\lambda)$ be a probability distribution over $\mathbb{Z}$. The $\mathrm{DLWE}_{n,q,\chi}$ problem states that for all $m = \mathrm{poly}(n)$, letting $\mathbf{A} \leftarrow \mathbb{Z}_q^{n \times m}$, $\mathbf{s} \leftarrow \mathbb{Z}_q^n$, $\mathbf{e} \leftarrow \chi^m$, and $\mathbf{u} \leftarrow \mathbb{Z}_q^m$, it holds that $(\mathbf{A}, \mathbf{s}\mathbf{A} + \mathbf{e})$ and $(\mathbf{A}, \mathbf{u})$ are computationally indistinguishable.*

In this work we only consider the case where $q \leq 2^n$. Recall that GapSVP_γ is the (promise) problem of distinguishing, given a basis for a lattice and a parameter d, between the case where the lattice has a vector shorter than d, and the case where the lattice doesn't have any vector shorter than $\gamma \cdot d$. SIVP is the search problem of finding a set of "short" vectors. The best known algorithms for GapSVP_γ ([Sch87]) require at least $2^{\tilde{\Omega}(n/\log \gamma)}$ time. We refer the reader to [Reg05, Pei09] for more information. The following corollary allows us to appropriately choose the LWE parameters for our scheme according to known reductions from GapSVP_γ and SIVP_γ to $\mathrm{DLWE}_{n,q,\chi}$.

Corollary 6 ([Reg05, Pei09, MM11, MP12, BLP+13]). *For all $\epsilon > 0$ there exists functions $q = q(n) \leq 2^n$, $\chi = \chi(n)$ such that χ is B-bounded for some $B = B(n)$, $q/B \geq 2^{n^\epsilon}$ and such that $\mathrm{DLWE}_{n,q,\chi}$ is at least as hard as the classical hardness of GapSVP_γ and the quantum hardness of SIVP_γ for $\gamma = 2^{\Omega(n^\epsilon)}$.*

3   Conforming cPRF

Our ABE construction in the next section instantiates a constrained PRF that
has to satisfy some special properties, gathered under the following definition.

Definition 9 (Conforming cPRF). *A cPRF scheme is* conforming *if, in
addition to the correctness and single-key adaptive security properties (see Definition 2), the following holds.*

Gradual Evaluation. The algorithm Constrain *(in addition to* Eval, ConstrainEval*)
is deterministic and the following holds. For any fixing of* pp ← Setup(1^λ), $f \in \mathcal{F}$
and $x \in \{0,1\}^\ell$ *for which* $f(x) = 1$, *define the following circuits:*

- $U_{\sigma \to x} : \{0,1\}^\lambda \to \{0,1\}^k$ *takes as input* msk *and computes* Eval$_{\mathsf{msk}}(x)$.
- $U_{\sigma \to f} : \{0,1\}^\lambda \to \{0,1\}^{\ell_f}$ *takes as input* msk *and computes* Constrain$_{\mathsf{msk}}(f)$.
- $U_{f \to x}$: $\{0,1\}^{\ell_f}$ → $\{0,1\}^k$ *takes as input* sk$_f$ *and computes*
  ConstrainEval$_{\mathsf{sk}_f}(x)$.

We require that for all pp, f, x *as defined above, the circuit* $U_{\sigma \to x}$ *and the effective
sub-circuit of* $U_{f \to x} \circ U_{\sigma \to f}$ *are the same. That is, the description of* $U_{\sigma \to x}$ *as
a sequence of gates is identical to the sequence of gates that go from the input
wires to the output wires of the circuit* $U_{f \to x} \circ U_{\sigma \to f}$.

Key Simulation. We require a PPT *algorithm* KeySim$_{\mathsf{pp}}(f) \to$ sk$_f$ *such that any*
PPT *adversary* $\mathcal{A}$ *has at most* $1/2 + \mathrm{negl}(\lambda)$ *probability to win the following game
against a challenger* $\mathcal{C}$.

- Initialization: $\mathcal{C}$ *generates* (pp, msk) ← Setup(1^λ) *and sends* pp *to* $\mathcal{A}$.
- Evaluation Queries I: $\mathcal{A}$ *makes (possibly multiple) queries. In each query it
  sends a bit-string* $x \in \{0,1\}^\ell$ *and* $\mathcal{C}$ *returns* $r_x \leftarrow$ Eval$_{\mathsf{msk}}(x)$.
- Challenge Phase: $\mathcal{A}$ *sends the challenge constraint* $f^* \in \mathcal{F}$. $\mathcal{C}$ *uniformly samples* $b \xleftarrow{\$} \{0,1\}$. *If* $b = 0$ *then* $\mathcal{C}$ *returns* sk$_{f^*} \leftarrow$ Constrain$_{\mathsf{msk}}(f)$, *otherwise it
  returns* sk$_{f^*} \leftarrow$ KeySim$_{\mathsf{pp}}(f)$.
- Evaluation Queries II: *same as the first queries phase.*
- End of Game: $\mathcal{A}$ *outputs a bit* b'.

$\mathcal{A}$ *wins the game if (1)* $b' = b$ *and (2) all of the evaluation queries* x *are such
that* $f^*(x) = 0$.

Remark 1. The requirement for a deterministic Constrain algorithm is for simplicity of exposition and since in our construction this requirement holds trivially.
We note, however, that our ABE scheme can be extended to support a randomized Constrain algorithm. Alternatively, any cPRF scheme with a randomized
Constrain algorithm can be converted to one with a deterministic algorithm by
generating the randomness with an additional standard PRF.

Example. The [GGM86] PRF is a conforming cPRF for prefix policies. Gradual evaluation holds since for any $x \in \{0,1\}^\ell$ and any length-t prefix $f \in \{0,1\}^t$, it holds that $U_{\sigma \to x}(\cdot) = G_{x_\ell}(\cdots G_{x_2}(G_{x_1}(\cdot)))$ while $U_{\sigma \to f}(\cdot) = G_{f_t}(\cdots G_{f_2}(G_{f_1}(\cdot)))$ and $U_{f \to x}(\cdot) = G_{x_\ell}(\cdots G_{x_{t+2}}(G_{x_{t+1}}(\cdot)))$. Key simulation holds since a constrained key for f is indistinguishable from uniform to any adversary that cannot query for evaluations on points accepted by f.

3.1   Construction for t-CNF Policies

We now describe our single key construction for the function class $\mathcal{F}$ consisting of CNF formulas where each clause depends on t bits of the input (see Definition 4). Our construction is inspired by the [DKNY18] construction of bit-fixing cPRF for a constant number of keys. In fact, their technique can be generalized to instantiate a family of cPRF schemes with a tradeoff between the *CNF locality* of the supported policies and the number of keys. They instantiate it with CNF locality 1 (i.e. bit-fixing) and t keys, while we instantiate it with CNF locality t and a single key.

Let (P.Setup, P.Eval) be a (standard) PRF (Definition 1), let $t \leq \ell$ be a fixed constant and let S denote the set of all (T, v) pairs where $T \subseteq [\ell]$, $|T| = t$ and $v \in \{0,1\}^t$.

- Setup(1^λ): Sample and output (pp, msk) $\leftarrow$ P.Setup(1^λ).
- Eval(msk, x): Let $S_x \subseteq S$ denote the set of all $(T, v) \in S$ pairs that "agree" with x, that is, $S_x = \{(T, x_T) \in S\}$ where x_T is the length-t bit-string consisting of the bits of x in the indices T. For all $(T, v) \in S_x$ compute $\mathsf{sk}_{T,v} \leftarrow \mathsf{P.Eval}_{\mathsf{msk}}(T\|v)$. Output

$$r_x = \bigoplus_{(T,v) \in S_x} \mathsf{P.Eval}_{\mathsf{sk}_{T,v}}(x) \ . \tag{4}$$

- Constrain$_{\mathsf{msk}}(f)$: Parse f as a set of clauses $f = \{(T_i, f_i)\}$ and recall that for all i, $T_i \subseteq [\ell]$, $|T_i| = t$ and $f_i : \{0,1\}^t \to \{0,1\}$. For any clause $(T_i, f_i) \in f$ let $S_i^f \subseteq S$ be the set of all $(T, v) \in S$ pairs that "agree" with (T_i, f_i), that is,

$$S_i^f = \{(T_i, v) \in S : f_i(v) = 1\} \ .$$

Moreover, let $S_{rest}^f \subseteq S$ be the set of all $(T, v) \in S$ pairs such that f does not have a clause respective to T. That is,

$$S_{rest}^f = \{(T, v) \in S : \forall i\ T_i \neq T\} \ .$$

Finally let $S_f = S_{rest}^f \cup \bigcup_{(T_i, f_i) \in f} S_i^f$. For all $(T, v) \in S_f$ compute $\mathsf{sk}_{T,v} \leftarrow \mathsf{P.Eval}_{\mathsf{msk}}(T\|v)$. Output $\mathsf{sk}_f = \{\mathsf{sk}_{T,v}\}_{(T,v) \in S_f}$.
- Eval$_{\mathsf{sk}_f}(x)$: If $f(x) = 0$ then abort, o.w. note that $S_x \subseteq S_f$ and compute r_x as in Eq. (4).

Correctness. Fix $x \in \{0,1\}^\ell$ and $f \in \mathcal{F}$ for which $f(x) = 1$. It is enough to prove that $S_x \subseteq S_f$. Note that $S_x = \{(T, x_T) \in S\}$ and parse $f = \{(T_i, f_i)\}$. For each $(T, x_T) \in S_x$ consider two options. If f has a clause respective to T, i.e. there exists i such that $T_i = T$, then since $f(x) = \bigwedge f_i(x_{T_i})$ and $f(x) = 1$, it also holds that $f_i(x_{T_i}) = 1$, and therefore $(T, x_T) = (T_i, x_{T_i}) \in S_i^f \subseteq S_f$. Otherwise, f does not have a clause respective to T, i.e. $\forall i \; T_i \neq T$, and therefore $(T, x_T) \in S_{rest}^f \subseteq S_f$.

Single-Key Adaptive Security. We sketch here the proof, which follows similar lines to [DKNY18]. Consider the single-key adaptive security game and let x^* and f be the challenge query and (single) key query respectively. It is guaranteed by the game that $f(x^*) = 0$, therefore there exists at least one clause $(T_i, f_i) \in f$ such that $f_i(x_{T_i}^*) = 0$ and therefore $(T_i, x_{T_i}^*) \notin S_f$.

In the simulated security game, the challenger guesses the value $(T_i, x_{T_i}^*)$ at the beginning of the game by sampling a random pair $(T', v') \xleftarrow{\$} S$. When a key for f is queried, if there is no clause $(T_i, f_i) \in f$ such that $T_i = T'$ and $f_i(v') = 0$, then the challenger aborts. When a challenge for x^* is queried, if $x_{T'}^* \neq v'$ then the challenger aborts. Since there must exist an element $(T', v') \in S$ that does not cause an abort, and since (T', v') is chosen uniformly from S where $|S| = O((2\ell)^t)$, there is a significant probability $1/O((2\ell)^t)$ that the challenger does not abort when t is constant.

If the challenger does not abort, it replaces the element $\mathsf{Eval}_{\mathsf{sk}_{T',v'}}(x^*)$ in the challenge ciphertext with a uniform bit-string. This is indistinguishable by the pseudorandomness of P (respective to the key $\mathsf{sk}_{T',v'}$) and since the challenger does not have to provide $\mathsf{sk}_{T',v'}$ in the constrained key. At this point the challenge ciphertext is completely uniform, which completes the proof.

Gradual Evaluation. Fix $x \in \{0,1\}^\ell$ and $f \in \mathcal{F}$ for which $f(x) = 1$ and note that $S_x \subseteq S_f$. The circuit $U_{\sigma \to x}(\cdot)$ can be divided to two layers, where the first layer computes $\mathsf{sk}_x = \{sk_{T,x_T}\}_{(T,x_T) \in S_x}$ and the second layer computes r_x from sk_x. Moreover, letting $U_{f \to x}^* \circ U_{\sigma \to f}^*$ denote the effective sub-circuit of $U_{f \to x} \circ U_{\sigma \to f}$ (see Definition 9), it holds that $U_{\sigma \to f}^*$ (resp. $U_{f \to x}^*$) is exactly the first (resp. second) layer of $U_{\sigma \to x}(\cdot)$.

Key Simulation. The simulator $\mathsf{KeySim}(f)$ simply samples all of the components $\mathsf{sk}_f = \{\mathsf{sk}_{T,v}\}_{(T,v) \in S_f}$ uniformly. We sketch now the indistinguishability proof, which goes via a sequence of hybrids $\mathcal{H}_0, \ldots, \mathcal{H}_Q, \mathcal{H}_{Q+1}$ where Q is the number of evaluation queries made by $\mathcal{A}$. For $i = 0 \ldots Q$, in hybrid $\mathcal{H}_i$ the challenger answers the first i evaluation queries with uniformly sampled values and answers the challenge key query as in the real game. In hybrid $\mathcal{H}_{Q+1}$, the challenger answers all of the evaluation queries uniformly and answers the challenge key query with $\mathsf{KeySim}(f^*)$ regardless of the value of b. Note that hybrid $\mathcal{H}_0$ is identical to the key simulation game and that in hybrid $\mathcal{H}_{Q+1}$ the adversary wins the game with probability $1/2$. For all $i = 1 \ldots Q$, the indistinguishability of $\mathcal{H}_i$ and $\mathcal{H}_{i-1}$ follows from the single-key adaptive security of the scheme. Lastly, in hybrid $\mathcal{H}_Q$ the components of the key challenge $\mathsf{sk}_f = \{\mathsf{sk}_{T,v}\}_{(T,v) \in S_f}$ are either uniform (if $b = 1$) or from the distribution $\{\mathsf{sk}_{(T,v)} \leftarrow \mathsf{P.Eval}_{\mathsf{msk}}(T, v)\}_{(T,v) \in S_f}$ (if $b = 0$), while in $\mathcal{H}_{Q+1}$ they are always uniform. Those hybrids are indistinguishable by the pseudorandomness of P and since $|S_f| \in \mathrm{poly}(\lambda)$.

4   Fully Secure ABE from Conforming cPRF

4.1   The Construction

We now construct a ciphertext-policy ABE scheme for a function class $\mathcal{F}$ from a conforming cPRF (Definition 9) for $\mathcal{F}$. Our construction has adaptive security under the LWE assumption, and assuming that the underlying cPRF maintains single-key adaptive security.

Let $\mathsf{P} = (\mathsf{P.Setup}, \mathsf{P.Eval}, \mathsf{P.Constrain}, \mathsf{P.ConstrainEval})$ be a conforming cPRF for a class family $\mathcal{F}$ with input length ℓ and output length k. W.l.o.g. assume that the master secret key length of P is λ. For all $f \in \mathcal{F}$ let ℓ_f denote the size of a constrained key for the function f. Note that ℓ_f is constant and is efficiently computable given f and the description of P.Constrain. Let $U_{\sigma \to x}, U_{\sigma \to f}$ and $U_{f \to x}$ be the circuits as in Definition 9. Define $\mathsf{ABE} = (\mathsf{Setup}, \mathsf{Enc}, \mathsf{KeyGen}, \mathsf{Dec})$ as follows.

- $\mathsf{Setup}(1^\lambda)$: Sample $(\mathsf{P.msk}, \mathsf{P.pp}) \leftarrow \mathsf{P.Setup}(1^\lambda)$ and denote $\sigma = \mathsf{P.msk}$. Fix the parameters $n, q, m', \tau, \chi, \tilde{\chi}$ as explained below and let $m = n\lceil \log q \rceil$. Sample a matrix with its trapdoor $(\mathbf{B}, \mathbf{B}_{\tau_0}^{-1}) \leftarrow \mathsf{TrapGen}(1^n, m', q)$. Sample uniformly a matrix $\mathbf{A} \xleftarrow{\$} \mathbb{Z}_q^{n \times m \cdot \lambda}$ and a vector $\mathbf{v} \xleftarrow{\$} \mathbb{Z}_q^n$. Output $\mathsf{pp} = (\mathbf{B}, \mathbf{A}, \mathbf{v}, \mathsf{P.pp})$ and $\mathsf{msk} = (\mathbf{B}_{\tau_0}^{-1}, \sigma)$.
- $\mathsf{Enc}_{\mathsf{pp}}(f, \mu)$: Sample $\mathsf{sk}_f \leftarrow \mathsf{P.KeySim}_{\mathsf{P.pp}}(f)$ and denote $s_f = \mathsf{sk}_f$. Sample $\mathbf{s} \xleftarrow{\$} \mathbb{Z}_q^n, \mathbf{e}_0 \xleftarrow{\$} \chi^m, \mathbf{e}_1 \xleftarrow{\$} \tilde{\chi}^{m \cdot \ell_f}, e_2 \xleftarrow{\$} \chi$, and output $\mathsf{ct} = (s_f, u_0, \mathbf{u}_1, u_2)$ such that

$$u_0 = \mathbf{s}^T \mathbf{B} + \mathbf{e}_0^T, \qquad \mathbf{u}_1 = \mathbf{s}^T [\mathbf{A}_f - s_f \otimes \mathbf{G}] + \mathbf{e}_1^T, \qquad u_2 = \mathbf{s}^T \mathbf{v} + e_2 + \mu \lfloor q/2 \rceil,$$

where $\mathbf{A}_f = \mathbf{A} \mathbf{H}_{\sigma \to f}$ for $\mathbf{H}_{\sigma \to f} \leftarrow \mathsf{EvalF}(U_{\sigma \to f}, \mathbf{A})$.
- $\mathsf{KeyGen}_{\mathsf{msk}}(x)$: Compute the matrix $\mathbf{H}_{\sigma \to x} \leftarrow \mathsf{EvalF}(U_{\sigma \to x}, \mathbf{A})$ and denote $\mathbf{A}_x = \mathbf{A} \mathbf{H}_{\sigma \to x}$. Compute $r \leftarrow \mathsf{P.Eval}_\sigma(x)$ and let $I_r : \{0,1\}^k \to \{0,1\}$ be the function that on input r' returns 1 if and only if $r = r'^3$. Compute $\mathbf{H}_r \leftarrow \mathsf{EvalF}(I_r, \mathbf{A}_x)$, denote $\mathbf{A}_{x,r} = \mathbf{A}_x \mathbf{H}_r$ and use $\mathbf{B}_{\tau_0}^{-1}$ to compute $[\mathbf{B} \| \mathbf{A}_{x,r}]_\tau^{-1}$. Sample $\mathbf{k} \leftarrow [\mathbf{B} \| \mathbf{A}_{x,r}]_\tau^{-1}(\mathbf{v})$ and output $\mathsf{sk}_x = (r, \mathbf{k})$.
- $\mathsf{Dec}_{\mathsf{sk}_x}(\mathsf{ct}, f)$: Parse $\mathsf{sk}_x = (r, \mathbf{k})$ and $\mathsf{ct} = (s_f, u_0, \mathbf{u}_1, u_2)$. Compute $r' \leftarrow U_{f \to x}(s_f)$ and if $r = r'$ then abort. Otherwise, compute $\mathbf{A}_f$ and $\mathbf{A}_x$ as in $\mathsf{Enc}, \mathsf{KeyGen}$ respectively, then compute

$$\widehat{\mathbf{H}}_{s_f \to r'} \leftarrow \mathsf{EvalFX}(U_{f \to x}, s_f, \mathbf{A}_f) \qquad \text{and} \qquad \widehat{\mathbf{H}}_{r,r'} \leftarrow \mathsf{EvalFX}(I_r, r', \mathbf{A}_x).$$

Lastly, compute $u = u_2 - [u_0 \| \mathbf{u}_1 \widehat{\mathbf{H}}_{s_f \to r'} \widehat{\mathbf{H}}_{r,r'}] \mathbf{k}$ and output 1 if and only if $|u| \geq q/4$.

---

[3] Previous works used an ABE definition where the decryption succeeds conditioned on $f(x) = 0$, while we require that $f(x) = 1$. Note that in our scheme the decryption succeeds conditioned on $f(x) = 1 \wedge r \neq r'$, i.e. $f(x) = 1 \wedge I_r(r') = 0$.

Choice of Parameters. We set the parameters according to constraints that rise up in the security and correctness analysis. Choose $k = \lambda$, let $d = \text{poly}(\lambda)$ denote the depth of $U_{\sigma \to x}$ and note that since P is gradual the depths of $U_{\sigma \to f}$, $U_{f \to x}$ are bounded by d. Choose $n \geq \lambda$ such that $(2n^2)^{2d+4} \leq 2^{n^\epsilon}$, where $\epsilon \in (0, 1)$ is a security/efficiency tradeoff parameter. Note that $n \leq d^{O(1/\epsilon)}$ which is polynomial in λ for any constant ϵ. Moreover, $E' \leq 2^{n^\epsilon}$ where E' is as defined in Eq. (5). Choose q, B, χ according to Corollary 6 and note that $q/B \geq 2^{n^\epsilon}$ and that χ is B-bounded. Choose $m' = (n+1)\lceil \log q \rceil + 2\lambda$ and $\tau = \max\{\tau_0, \tau'\}$, where τ_0 is as in Corollary 1 and τ' is as in Eq. (6). Set $\tilde{\chi}$ to be a B'-swallowing distribution, where $B' = (m' + m)\lambda B(2m)^d$. By Corollary 5, $\tilde{\chi}$ can be chosen such that it is $\tilde{B}$-bounded for some $\tilde{B} \in O(B', \lambda)$.

4.2   Correctness

Lemma 1. *If* P *be a conforming cPRF for a class family* $\mathcal{F}$ *as per Definition 9, then* ABE *is a correct ciphertext policy attribute-based encryption scheme as per Definition 3 for the class family* $\mathcal{F}$.

Proof. Fix $\mu \in \{0, 1\}$, $(\text{pp}, \text{msk}) \leftarrow \text{Setup}(1^\lambda)$, $f \in \mathcal{F}$ and $x \in \{0, 1\}^\ell$ such that $f(x) = 1$. Consider $\text{ct} \leftarrow \text{Enc}(f, \mu)$ and $\text{sk}_x \leftarrow \text{KeyGen}_{\text{msk}}(x)$, and parse $\text{sk}_x = (r, \mathbf{k})$ and $\text{ct} = (s_f, \mathbf{u}_0, \mathbf{u}_1, u_2)$. Consider the execution of $\text{Dec}_{\text{sk}_x}(\text{ct}, f)$.

We first prove that with all but negligible probability $r \neq r'$ via a reduction to the pseudorandomness game of P. Recall that r' is computed as $\text{P.ConstrainEval}_{\text{sk}'_f}(x)$ where $\text{sk}'_f \leftarrow \text{P.KeySim}(f)$, while r is computed as $\text{P.Eval}_{\text{msk}}(x)$. Consider an adversary $\mathcal{A}$ in the pseudorandomness game of P as follows. Upon receiving P.pp, it computes $\text{sk}'_f \leftarrow \text{P.KeySim}(f)$ and then $r'_x \leftarrow \text{P.ConstrainEval}_{\text{sk}'_f}(x)$. It then requests for a challenge on x, and upon receiving the challenge r^*_x it outputs 1 if and only if $r^*_x = r'_x$. The advantage of $\mathcal{A}$ is at least $Pr[r = r']$ and therefore if P is pseudorandom then $Pr[r = r']$ is negligible.

We now prove that if $r \neq r'$ then the decryption succeeds with all but negligible probability. Denote $\mathbf{H}_{f \to x} = \text{EvalF}(U_{f \to x}, \mathbf{A}_f)$. Since P has gradual evaluation (see Definition 9), the effective sub-circuit of $U_{f \to x} \circ U_{\sigma \to f}$ and the circuit $U_{\sigma \to x}$ are identical. By Theorem 2 it follows that $\mathbf{H}_{\sigma \to f} \mathbf{H}_{f \to x} = \mathbf{H}_{\sigma \to x}$, and therefore $\mathbf{A}_f \mathbf{H}_{f \to x} = \mathbf{A} \mathbf{H}_{\sigma \to f} \mathbf{H}_{f \to x} = \mathbf{A} \mathbf{H}_{\sigma \to x} = \mathbf{A}_x$.

By applying Theorem 2 on $(\mathbf{H}_{f \to x}, \widehat{\mathbf{H}}_{s_f \to r'})$ and $(\mathbf{H}_r, \widehat{\mathbf{H}}_{r, r'})$, we get respectively

$$[\mathbf{A}_f - s_f \otimes \mathbf{G}] \widehat{\mathbf{H}}_{s_f \to r'} = \mathbf{A}_f \mathbf{H}_{f \to x} - U_{f \to x}(s_f) \otimes \mathbf{G} = \mathbf{A}_x - r' \otimes \mathbf{G}$$

and

$$[\mathbf{A}_x - r' \otimes \mathbf{G}] \widehat{\mathbf{H}}_{r, r'} = \mathbf{A}_x \mathbf{H}_r - I_r(r')\mathbf{G} = \mathbf{A}_{x, r}$$

where the last equation holds since $r \neq r'$ and thus $I_r(r') = 0$. Therefore,

$$
\begin{aligned}
\mathbf{u}_1 \widehat{\mathbf{H}}_{s_f \to r'} \widehat{\mathbf{H}}_{r,r'} &= \left(\mathbf{s}^T [\mathbf{A}_f - s_f \otimes \mathbf{G}] + \mathbf{e}_1^T\right) \widehat{\mathbf{H}}_{s_f \to r'} \widehat{\mathbf{H}}_{r,r'} \\
&= \mathbf{s}^T [\mathbf{A}_f - s_f \otimes \mathbf{G}] \widehat{\mathbf{H}}_{s_f \to r'} \widehat{\mathbf{H}}_{r,r'} + \mathbf{e}_1' && \text{where } \mathbf{e}_1' = \mathbf{e}_1^T \widehat{\mathbf{H}}_{s_f \to r'} \widehat{\mathbf{H}}_{r,r'} \\
&= \mathbf{s}^T [\mathbf{A}_x - r' \otimes \mathbf{G}] \widehat{\mathbf{H}}_{r,r'} + \mathbf{e}_1' \\
&= \mathbf{s}^T \mathbf{A}_{x,r} + \mathbf{e}_1' \ .
\end{aligned}
$$

Hence,

$$
\begin{aligned}
u_2 - [\mathbf{u}_0 \| \mathbf{u}_1 \widehat{\mathbf{H}}_{s_f \to r'} \widehat{\mathbf{H}}_{r,r'}] \mathbf{k} &= \mathbf{s}^T \mathbf{v} + e_2 + \mu \lfloor q/2 \rceil - \mathbf{s}^T [\mathbf{B} \| \mathbf{A}_{x,r}] \mathbf{k} - [\mathbf{e}_0^T \| \mathbf{e}_1'] \mathbf{k} \\
&= \mu \lfloor q/2 \rceil + e_2 - [\mathbf{e}_0^T \| \mathbf{e}_1'] \mathbf{k} \ .
\end{aligned}
$$

Note that

$$
\|\mathbf{e}_1'\|_\infty \leq m^2 \ell_f k \left\|\mathbf{e}_1^T\right\|_\infty \left\|\widehat{\mathbf{H}}_{s_f \to r'}\right\|_\infty \left\|\widehat{\mathbf{H}}_{r,r'}\right\|_\infty \leq m^2 \ell_f k \tilde{B} (2m)^{d_{\mathsf{ConEv}}+1}
$$

and that by the properties of discrete Gaussians, $\|\mathbf{k}\|_\infty \leq \tau \sqrt{m' + m}$ with all but $2^{-(m'+m)} = \mathsf{negl}(\lambda)$ probability.

Therefore, if $m', k, \ell_f \in O(n, \lceil \log q \rceil)$, $\tilde{B} \in O(B, n)$ and $\tau \in O\left(k, \lambda, (2m)^{d+3}\right)$, then with all but negligible probability

$$
\begin{aligned}
\left| e_2 - [\mathbf{e}_0^T \| \mathbf{e}_1'] \mathbf{k} \right| &\leq |e_2| + (m' \left\|\mathbf{e}_0^T\right\|_\infty + m \|\mathbf{e}_1'\|_\infty) \cdot \|\mathbf{k}\|_\infty \\
&\leq B + (m' B + m^3 \ell_f k \tilde{B} (2m)^{d_{\mathsf{ConEv}}+1}) \tau \sqrt{m' + m} \\
&\leq B \cdot \mathsf{poly}(n, \lceil \log q \rceil) \cdot (2m)^{d_{\mathsf{ConEv}}+d+4} \ .
\end{aligned}
$$

Denoting

$$
E = B \cdot \mathsf{poly}(n, \lceil \log q \rceil) \cdot (2m)^{d_{\mathsf{ConEv}}+d+4}
$$

and

$$
E' = 4E/B = 4 \cdot \mathsf{poly}(n, \lceil \log q \rceil) \cdot (2m)^{d_{\mathsf{ConEv}}+d+4} \ , \tag{5}
$$

by our choice of parameters E' is bounded by q/B, and therefore $E = BE'/4$ is bounded by $q/4$. Therefore, if $\mu = 0$ then $|u| \leq q/4$ and if $\mu = 1$ then $|u| > q/4$.

4.3 Security

Lemma 2. *If* P *be a conforming cPRF for a class family* $\mathcal{F}$ *as per Definition 9, then* ABE *is a secure ciphertext policy attribute-based encryption scheme as per Definition 3 for the class family* $\mathcal{F}$ *under the* $\mathrm{DLWE}_{n,q,\chi}$ *assumption.*

Proof. We prove via a sequence of hybrids.

Hybrid $\mathcal{H}_0$. This is the adaptive security game from Definition 3.

Hybrid $\mathcal{H}_1$. We change the way $\mathcal{C}$ answers the challenge query f^*. Instead of computing $s_f \leftarrow \mathsf{P.KeySim}_{\mathsf{P.pp}}(f^*)$, it computes $s_f \leftarrow \mathsf{P.Constrain}_\sigma(f^*)$. Note that now $s_f = U_{\sigma \to f}(\sigma)$.

We show computational indistinguishability via a reduction to the key simulation game of P (see Definition 9). Let $\mathcal{A}_\mathsf{P}$ be an adversary in the key simulation game. It operates as the challenger in the ABE security game as follows. For every key query x sent by $\mathcal{A}$, $\mathcal{A}_\mathsf{P}$ queries the P challenger for an evaluation over the input x and proceeds with computing the ABE key for x as in the scheme. Note that it is guaranteed by the ABE game that $f^*(x) = 0$ and therefore this query is valid in the P game. When $\mathcal{A}$ asks for the challenge ciphertext, $\mathcal{A}_\mathsf{P}$ asks for the challenge constrained key sk'_f and proceeds with the encryption algorithm as in the scheme. Any advantage of $\mathcal{A}$ at distinguishing between those hybrids translates to identical advantage of $\mathcal{A}_\mathsf{P}$ in the key simulation game.

Hybrid $\mathcal{H}_2$. We change the way $\mathcal{C}$ generates the matrix $\mathbf{A}$ as follows. It samples uniformly a matrix $\mathbf{R} \xleftarrow{\$} \{0,1\}^{m' \times m \cdot \lambda}$ and sets $\mathbf{A} = \mathbf{BR} + \sigma \otimes \mathbf{G}$. Indistinguishability follows from the extended leftover hash lemma, since $m' \geq (n+1)\lceil \log q \rceil + 2\lambda$ and $\mathbf{B}$ is statistically-close to uniform by Corollary 1.

Hybrid $\mathcal{H}_3$. We change again the way $\mathcal{C}$ answers the challenge query f^*, specifically the way it generates $\mathbf{u}_1$. Note that now

$$
\begin{aligned}
\mathbf{A}_f - s_f \otimes \mathbf{G} &= \mathbf{AH}_{\sigma \to f} - U_{\sigma \to f}(\sigma) \otimes \mathbf{G} \\
&= [\mathbf{A} - \sigma \otimes \mathbf{G}]\widehat{\mathbf{H}}_{\mathsf{msk} \to s_f} \qquad \text{where } \widehat{\mathbf{H}}_{\mathsf{msk} \to s_f} \leftarrow \mathsf{EvalFX}(U_{\sigma \to f}, \sigma, \mathbf{A}) \\
&= \mathbf{BR}\widehat{\mathbf{H}}_{\mathsf{msk} \to s_f} .
\end{aligned}
$$

The values $\mathbf{u}_0$ and u_2 will be generated as before, by sampling $\mathbf{s} \xleftarrow{\$} \mathbb{Z}_q^n$, $\mathbf{e}_0 \xleftarrow{\$} \chi^m$, $e_2 \xleftarrow{\$} \chi$ and computing $\mathbf{u}_0 = \mathbf{s}^T\mathbf{B} + \mathbf{e}_0^T$ and $u_2 = \mathbf{s}^T\mathbf{v} + e_2 + \mu\lfloor q/2 \rfloor$.

Recall that previously $\mathbf{u}_1$ was computed as $\mathbf{u}_1 = \mathbf{s}^T[\mathbf{A}_f - s_f \otimes \mathbf{G}] + \mathbf{e}_1^T$, where $\mathbf{e}_1 \xleftarrow{\$} \tilde{\chi}^{m \cdot \ell_f}$. In this hybrid, it will be computed as $\mathbf{u}_1 = \mathbf{u}_0\mathbf{R}\widehat{\mathbf{H}}_{\mathsf{msk} \to s_f} + \mathbf{e}_1^T$. Note that now

$$
\begin{aligned}
\mathbf{u}_1 &= \mathbf{u}_0\mathbf{R}\widehat{\mathbf{H}}_{\mathsf{msk} \to s_f} + \mathbf{e}_1^T \\
&= (\mathbf{s}^T\mathbf{B} + \mathbf{e}_0^T)\mathbf{R}\widehat{\mathbf{H}}_{\mathsf{msk} \to s_f} + \mathbf{e}_1^T \\
&= \mathbf{s}^T[\mathbf{A}_f - s_f \otimes \mathbf{G}] + \mathbf{e}_0^T\mathbf{R}\widehat{\mathbf{H}}_{\mathsf{msk} \to s_f} + \mathbf{e}_1^T
\end{aligned}
$$

and that $B' = \left\| \mathbf{e}_0^T\mathbf{R}\widehat{\mathbf{H}}_{\mathsf{msk} \to s_f} \right\|_\infty \leq (m' + m)\lambda \left\| \mathbf{e}_0^T \right\|_\infty \| \mathbf{R} \|_\infty \left\| \widehat{\mathbf{H}}_{\mathsf{msk} \to s_f} \right\|_\infty \leq (m' + m)\lambda B(2m)^{d_{\mathsf{Con}}}$, where d_{Con} is the depth of $U_{\sigma \to f}$. Therefore, if $\tilde{\chi}$ is B'-swallowing then this change is statistically indistinguishable.

Hybrid $\mathcal{H}_4$. We change the way $\mathcal{C}$ answers key queries. Let x be a query and fix $r \leftarrow \mathsf{P.Eval}_\sigma(x)$ and $\widehat{\mathbf{H}}_{\mathsf{msk} \to r} \leftarrow \mathsf{EvalFX}(U_{\sigma \to x}, \sigma, \mathbf{A})$. Note that

$$
\begin{aligned}
[\mathbf{A} - \sigma \otimes \mathbf{G}]\widehat{\mathbf{H}}_{\mathsf{msk} \to r} &= \mathbf{AH}_{\sigma \to x} - r \otimes \mathbf{G} \\
&= \mathbf{A}_x - r \otimes \mathbf{G} \qquad \text{where } \widehat{\mathbf{H}}_{\mathsf{msk} \to r} \leftarrow \mathsf{EvalFX}(U_{\sigma \to x}, \sigma, \mathbf{A}) ,
\end{aligned}
$$

and since $I_r(r) = 1$,

$$
[\mathbf{A}_x - r \otimes \mathbf{G}]\widehat{\mathbf{H}}_{r,r} = \mathbf{A}_x\mathbf{H}_r - I_r(r)\mathbf{G} = \mathbf{A}_{x,r} - \mathbf{G} \qquad \text{where } \widehat{\mathbf{H}}_{r,r} \leftarrow \mathsf{EvalFX}(I_r, r, \mathbf{A}_x) .
$$

Therefore, since $\mathbf{A} - \sigma \otimes \mathbf{G} = \mathbf{B}\mathbf{R}$ it holds that $\mathbf{B}\mathbf{R}\widehat{\mathbf{H}}_{\mathsf{msk}\to r}\widehat{\mathbf{H}}_{r,r} = \mathbf{A}_{x,r} - \mathbf{G}$ and hence

$$[\mathbf{B}\|\mathbf{A}_{x,r}] = [\mathbf{B}\|\mathbf{B}\mathbf{R}\widehat{\mathbf{H}}_{\mathsf{msk}\to r}\widehat{\mathbf{H}}_{r,r} + \mathbf{G}] \ .$$

Note that

$$\left\|\mathbf{R}\widehat{\mathbf{H}}_{\mathsf{msk}\to r}\widehat{\mathbf{H}}_{r,r}\right\|_\infty \le m^2 k\lambda \left\|\mathbf{R}\right\|_\infty \left\|\widehat{\mathbf{H}}_{\mathsf{msk}\to r}\right\|_\infty \left\|\widehat{\mathbf{H}}_{r,r}\right\|_\infty$$

$$\le m^2 k\lambda(2m)^{d+1} \ ,$$

and that Corollary 3, given $\mathbf{B}$ and $\mathbf{R}\widehat{\mathbf{H}}_{\mathsf{msk}\to r}\widehat{\mathbf{H}}_{r,r}$ it is efficient to compute $[\mathbf{B}\|\mathbf{A}_{x,r}]_{\tau'}^{-1}$ for some

$$\tau' = O\left(\left\|\mathbf{R}\widehat{\mathbf{H}}_{\mathsf{msk}\to r}\widehat{\mathbf{H}}_{r,r}\right\|_\infty\right) = O\left(k, \lambda, (2m)^{d+3}\right) \ . \tag{6}$$

Therefore, if $\tau \ge \tau'$ then $\mathcal{C}$ can now sample from $[\mathbf{B}\|\mathbf{A}_{x,r}]_\tau^{-1}(\mathbf{v})$ without $\mathbf{B}_{\tau_0}^{-1}$. The distribution remains identical to the previous hybrid.

Hybrid $\mathcal{H}_5$. We change the way $\mathbf{B}$ is generated. Instead of sampling it via TrapGen, sample uniformly $\mathbf{B} \xleftarrow{\$} \mathbb{Z}_q^{n\times m}$. By Corollary 1 this change is statistically indistinguishable.

Hybrid $\mathcal{H}_6$. We change again the way $\mathcal{C}$ answers the challenge query. It now samples uniformly $\mathbf{u}_0 \xleftarrow{\$} \mathbb{Z}_q^{m'}$ and $u_2 \xleftarrow{\$} \mathbb{Z}_q$. This change is computationally indistinguishable under the $\mathrm{DLWE}_{n,q,\chi}$ assumption. At this step the challenge completely hides b and so $\mathcal{A}$ has no advantage.

Acknowledgements. We thank Sina Shiehian for pointing out that the construction in Sect. 4 can be initialized with a polynomial modulus q whenever the depth of the conforming cPRF is logarithmic, which in turn implies that a low-depth PRF from LWE with a polynomial modulus suffices to derive an ABE construction for t-CNF with similar parameters.

References

[ABB10a] Agrawal, S., Boneh, D., Boyen, X.: Efficient lattice (H)IBE in the standard model. In: Gilbert, H. (ed.) EUROCRYPT 2010. LNCS, vol. 6110, pp. 553–572. Springer, Heidelberg (2010). https://doi.org/10.1007/978-3-642-13190-5_28

[ABB10b] Agrawal, S., Boneh, D., Boyen, X.: Lattice basis delegation in fixed dimension and shorter-ciphertext hierarchical IBE. In: Rabin, T. (ed.) CRYPTO 2010. LNCS, vol. 6223, pp. 98–115. Springer, Heidelberg (2010). https://doi.org/10.1007/978-3-642-14623-7_6

[ABV+12] Agrawal, S., Boyen, X., Vaikuntanathan, V., Voulgaris, P., Wee, H.: Functional encryption for threshold functions (or fuzzy IBE) from lattices. In: Fischlin, M., Buchmann, J., Manulis, M. (eds.) PKC 2012. LNCS, vol. 7293, pp. 280–297. Springer, Heidelberg (2012). https://doi.org/10.1007/978-3-642-30057-8_17

[ACPS09] Applebaum, B., Cash, D., Peikert, C., Sahai, A.: Fast cryptographic primitives and circular-secure encryption based on hard learning problems. In: Halevi, S. (ed.) CRYPTO 2009. LNCS, vol. 5677, pp. 595–618. Springer, Heidelberg (2009). https://doi.org/10.1007/978-3-642-03356-8_35

[AFV11] Agrawal, S., Freeman, D.M., Vaikuntanathan, V.: Functional encryption for inner product predicates from learning with errors. In: Lee, D.H., Wang, X. (eds.) ASIACRYPT 2011. LNCS, vol. 7073, pp. 21–40. Springer, Heidelberg (2011). https://doi.org/10.1007/978-3-642-25385-0_2

[Ajt96] Ajtai, M.: Generating hard instances of lattice problems (extended abstract). In: STOC, pp. 99–108 (1996)

[Ajt99] Ajtai, M.: Generating hard instances of the short basis problem. In: Wiedermann, J., van Emde Boas, P., Nielsen, M. (eds.) ICALP 1999. LNCS, vol. 1644, pp. 1–9. Springer, Heidelberg (1999). https://doi.org/10.1007/3-540-48523-6_1

[AP14] Alperin-Sheriff, J., Peikert, C.: Faster bootstrapping with polynomial error. In: Garay, J.A., Gennaro, R. (eds.) CRYPTO 2014. LNCS, vol. 8616, pp. 297–314. Springer, Heidelberg (2014). https://doi.org/10.1007/978-3-662-44371-2_17

[BB04a] Boneh, D., Boyen, X.: Efficient selective-ID secure identity-based encryption without random oracles. In: Cachin, C., Camenisch, J.L. (eds.) EUROCRYPT 2004. LNCS, vol. 3027, pp. 223–238. Springer, Heidelberg (2004). https://doi.org/10.1007/978-3-540-24676-3_14

[BB04b] Boneh, D., Boyen, X.: Secure identity based encryption without random oracles. In: Franklin, M. (ed.) CRYPTO 2004. LNCS, vol. 3152, pp. 443–459. Springer, Heidelberg (2004). https://doi.org/10.1007/978-3-540-28628-8_27

[BF03] Boneh, D., Franklin, M.K.: Identity-based encryption from the Weil pairing. SIAM J. Comput. **32**(3), 586–615 (2003). Preliminary version in CRYPTO '01

[BGG+14] Boneh, D., et al.: Fully key-homomorphic encryption, arithmetic circuit ABE and compact garbled circuits. In: Nguyen, P.Q., Oswald, E. (eds.) EUROCRYPT 2014. LNCS, vol. 8441, pp. 533–556. Springer, Heidelberg (2014). https://doi.org/10.1007/978-3-642-55220-5_30

[BGI14] Boyle, E., Goldwasser, S., Ivan, I.: Functional signatures and pseudorandom functions. In: Krawczyk, H. (ed.) PKC 2014. LNCS, vol. 8383, pp. 501–519. Springer, Heidelberg (2014). https://doi.org/10.1007/978-3-642-54631-0_29

[BL16] Boyen, X., Li, Q.: Towards tightly secure lattice short signature and ID-based encryption. In: Cheon, J.H., Takagi, T. (eds.) ASIACRYPT 2016. LNCS, vol. 10032, pp. 404–434. Springer, Heidelberg (2016). https://doi.org/10.1007/978-3-662-53890-6_14

[BLP+13] Brakerski, Z., Langlois, A., Peikert, C., Regev, O., Stehlé, D.: Classical hardness of learning with errors. In: Boneh, D., et al. (ed.) [BRF13], pp. 575–584

[Boy13] Boyen, X.: Attribute-based functional encryption on lattices. In: Sahai, A. (ed.) TCC 2013. LNCS, vol. 7785, pp. 122–142. Springer, Heidelberg (2013). https://doi.org/10.1007/978-3-642-36594-2_8

[BRF13] Boneh, D., Roughgarden, T., Feigenbaum, J. (eds.): Symposium on Theory of Computing Conference, STOC 2013, Palo Alto, CA, USA, 1–4 June 2013. ACM (2013)

[BV16]   Brakerski, Z., Vaikuntanathan, V.: Circuit-ABE from LWE: unbounded attributes and semi-adaptive security. In: Robshaw, M., Katz, J. (eds.) CRYPTO 2016. LNCS, vol. 9816, pp. 363–384. Springer, Heidelberg (2016). https://doi.org/10.1007/978-3-662-53015-3_13

[BW13]   Boneh, D., Waters, B.: Constrained pseudorandom functions and their applications. In: Sako, K., Sarkar, P. (eds.) ASIACRYPT 2013. LNCS, vol. 8270, pp. 280–300. Springer, Heidelberg (2013). https://doi.org/10.1007/978-3-642-42045-0_15

[CGKW18] Chen, J., Gong, J., Kowalczyk, L., Wee, H.: Unbounded ABE via bilinear entropy expansion, revisited. In: Nielsen, J.B., Rijmen, V. (eds.) EUROCRYPT 2018. LNCS, vol. 10820, pp. 503–534. Springer, Cham (2018). https://doi.org/10.1007/978-3-319-78381-9_19

[CHK03]   Canetti, R., Halevi, S., Katz, J.: A forward-secure public-key encryption scheme. In: Biham, E. (ed.) EUROCRYPT 2003. LNCS, vol. 2656, pp. 255–271. Springer, Heidelberg (2003). https://doi.org/10.1007/3-540-39200-9_16

[CHKP12] Cash, D., Hofheinz, D., Kiltz, E., Peikert, C.: Bonsai trees, or how to delegate a lattice basis. J. Cryptol. **25**(4), 601–639 (2012)

[Coc01]   Cocks, C.: An identity based encryption scheme based on quadratic residues. In: Honary, B. (ed.) Cryptography and Coding 2001. LNCS, vol. 2260, pp. 360–363. Springer, Heidelberg (2001). https://doi.org/10.1007/3-540-45325-3_32

[DKNY18] Davidson, A., Katsumata, S., Nishimaki, R., Yamada, S.: Constrained PRFs for bit-fixing from OWFs with constant collusion resistance. IACR Cryptology ePrint Archive 2018:982 (2018)

[Gen06]   Gentry, C.: Practical identity-based encryption without random oracles. In: Vaudenay, S. (ed.) EUROCRYPT 2006. LNCS, vol. 4004, pp. 445–464. Springer, Heidelberg (2006). https://doi.org/10.1007/11761679_27

[GGM86]   Goldreich, O., Goldwasser, S., Micali, S.: How to construct random functions. J. ACM **33**(4), 792–807 (1986). Extended abstract in FOCS 84

[GKW16]   Goyal, R., Koppula, V., Waters, B.: Semi-adaptive security and bundling functionalities made generic and easy. In: Hirt, M., Smith, A. (eds.) TCC 2016. LNCS, vol. 9986, pp. 361–388. Springer, Heidelberg (2016). https://doi.org/10.1007/978-3-662-53644-5_14

[GPSW06] Goyal, V., Pandey, O., Sahai, A., Waters, B.: Attribute-based encryption for fine-grained access control of encrypted data. In: Juels, A., Wright, R.N., De Capitani di Vimercati, S. (eds.) Proceedings of the 13th ACM Conference on Computer and Communications Security, CCS 2006, Alexandria, VA, USA, 30 October–3 November 2006, pp. 89–98. ACM (2006)

[GPV08]   Gentry, C., Peikert, C., Vaikuntanathan, V.: Trapdoors for hard lattices and new cryptographic constructions. In: Dwork, C. (ed.) Proceedings of the 40th Annual ACM Symposium on Theory of Computing, Victoria, British Columbia, Canada, 17–20 May 2008, pp. 197–206. ACM (2008)

[GSW13]   Gentry, C., Sahai, A., Waters, B.: Homomorphic encryption from learning with errors: conceptually-simpler, asymptotically-faster, attribute-based. In: Canetti, R., Garay, J.A. (eds.) CRYPTO 2013. LNCS, vol. 8042, pp. 75–92. Springer, Heidelberg (2013). https://doi.org/10.1007/978-3-642-40041-4_5

[GVW13]   Gorbunov, S., Vaikuntanathan, V., Wee, H.: Attribute-based encryption for circuits. In: Boneh, D., et al. (eds.) [BRF13], pp. 545–554

[GVW15] Gorbunov, S., Vaikuntanathan, V., Wichs, D.: Leveled fully homomorphic signatures from standard lattices. In: Servedio, R.A., Rubinfeld, R. (eds.) Proceedings of the Forty-Seventh Annual ACM on Symposium on Theory of Computing, STOC 2015, Portland, OR, USA, 14–17 June 2015, pp. 469–477. ACM (2015)

[KL15] Kowalczyk, L., Lewko, A.B.: Bilinear entropy expansion from the decisional linear assumption. In: Gennaro, R., Robshaw, M. (eds.) CRYPTO 2015. LNCS, vol. 9216, pp. 524–541. Springer, Heidelberg (2015). https://doi.org/10.1007/978-3-662-48000-7_26

[KPTZ13] Kiayias, A., Papadopoulos, S., Triandopoulos, N., Zacharias, T.: Delegatable pseudorandom functions and applications. In: Sadeghi, A.-R., Gligor, V.D., Yung, M., (eds.) 2013 ACM SIGSAC Conference on Computer and Communications Security, CCS 2013, Berlin, Germany, 4–8 November 2013, pp. 669–684. ACM (2013)

[KW19] Kowalczyk, L., Wee, H.: Compact adaptively secure ABE for NC1 from k-Lin. IACR Cryptology ePrint Archive 2019:224 (2019)

[LOS+10] Lewko, A., Okamoto, T., Sahai, A., Takashima, K., Waters, B.: Fully secure functional encryption: attribute-based encryption and (Hierarchical) inner product encryption. In: Gilbert, H. (ed.) EUROCRYPT 2010. LNCS, vol. 6110, pp. 62–91. Springer, Heidelberg (2010). https://doi.org/10.1007/978-3-642-13190-5_4

[LW12] Lewko, A., Waters, B.: New proof methods for attribute-based encryption: achieving full security through selective techniques. In: Safavi-Naini, R., Canetti, R. (eds.) CRYPTO 2012. LNCS, vol. 7417, pp. 180–198. Springer, Heidelberg (2012). https://doi.org/10.1007/978-3-642-32009-5_12

[MM11] Micciancio, D., Mol, P.: Pseudorandom knapsacks and the sample complexity of LWE search-to-decision reductions. In: Rogaway, P. (ed.) CRYPTO 2011. LNCS, vol. 6841, pp. 465–484. Springer, Heidelberg (2011). https://doi.org/10.1007/978-3-642-22792-9_26

[MP12] Micciancio, D., Peikert, C.: Trapdoors for lattices: simpler, tighter, faster, smaller. In: Pointcheval, D., Johansson, T. (eds.) EUROCRYPT 2012. LNCS, vol. 7237, pp. 700–718. Springer, Heidelberg (2012). https://doi.org/10.1007/978-3-642-29011-4_41

[OSW07] Ostrovsky, R., Sahai, A., Waters, B.: Attribute-based encryption with non-monotonic access structures. In: Proceedings of the 2007 ACM Conference on Computer and Communications Security, CCS 2007, Alexandria, Virginia, USA, October 28–31, pp. 195–203 (2007)

[Pei09] Peikert, C.: Public-key cryptosystems from the worst-case shortest vector problem: extended abstract. In: Proceedings of the 41st Annual ACM Symposium on Theory of Computing, STOC 2009, Bethesda, MD, USA, 31 May–2 June 2009, pp. 333–342 (2009)

[Reg05] Regev, O.: On lattices, learning with errors, random linear codes, and cryptography. In: Proceedings of the 37th Annual ACM Symposium on Theory of Computing, Baltimore, MD, USA, 22–24 May 2005, pp. 84–93 (2005)

[Sch87] Schnorr, C.-P.: A hierarchy of polynomial time lattice basis reduction algorithms. Theor. Comput. Sci. **53**, 201–224 (1987)

[SW05] Sahai, A., Waters, B.: Fuzzy identity-based encryption. In: Cramer, R. (ed.) EUROCRYPT 2005. LNCS, vol. 3494, pp. 457–473. Springer, Heidelberg (2005). https://doi.org/10.1007/11426639_27

[Wat05] Waters, B.: Efficient identity-based encryption without random oracles. In: Cramer, R. (ed.) EUROCRYPT 2005. LNCS, vol. 3494, pp. 114–127. Springer, Heidelberg (2005). https://doi.org/10.1007/11426639_7

[Wat09] Waters, B.: Dual system encryption: realizing fully secure IBE and HIBE under simple assumptions. In: Halevi, S. (ed.) CRYPTO 2009. LNCS, vol. 5677, pp. 619–636. Springer, Heidelberg (2009). https://doi.org/10.1007/978-3-642-03356-8_36

[Wat11] Waters, B.: Ciphertext-policy attribute-based encryption: an expressive, efficient, and provably secure realization. In: Catalano, D., Fazio, N., Gennaro, R., Nicolosi, A. (eds.) PKC 2011. LNCS, vol. 6571, pp. 53–70. Springer, Heidelberg (2011). https://doi.org/10.1007/978-3-642-19379-8_4

Lattice-Based ZK

Noninteractive Zero Knowledge for NP from (Plain) Learning with Errors

Chris Peikert[(✉)] and Sina Shiehian[(✉)]

Computer Science and Engineering, University of Michigan, Ann Arbor, USA
{cpeikert,shiayan}@umich.edu

Abstract. We finally close the long-standing problem of constructing a noninteractive zero-knowledge (NIZK) proof system for any NP language with security based on the *plain Learning With Errors* (LWE) problem, and thereby on worst-case lattice problems. Our proof system instantiates the framework recently developed by Canetti *et al.* [EUROCRYPT'18], Holmgren and Lombardi [FOCS'18], and Canetti *et al.* [STOC'19] for soundly applying the Fiat–Shamir transform using a hash function family that is *correlation intractable* for a suitable class of relations. Previously, such hash families were based either on "exotic" assumptions (e.g., indistinguishability obfuscation or optimal hardness of certain LWE variants) or, more recently, on the existence of circularly secure fully homomorphic encryption (FHE). However, none of these assumptions are known to be implied by plain LWE or worst-case hardness.

Our main technical contribution is a hash family that is correlation intractable for arbitrary size-S circuits, for any polynomially bounded S, based on plain LWE (with small polynomial approximation factors). The construction combines two novel ingredients: a correlation-intractable hash family for *log-depth* circuits based on LWE (or even the potentially harder Short Integer Solution problem), and a "bootstrapping" transform that uses (leveled) FHE to promote correlation intractability for the FHE decryption circuit to *arbitrary* (bounded) circuits. Our construction can be instantiated in two possible "modes," yielding a NIZK that is either *computationally* sound and *statistically* zero knowledge in the common *random* string model, or vice-versa in the common *reference* string model.

1 Introduction

A *zero-knowledge* (ZK) proof system [27] is a protocol by which a prover can convince a verifier that a particular statement is true, while revealing nothing

This material is based upon work supported by the National Science Foundation under CAREER Award CCF-1054495 and CNS-1606362. The views expressed are those of the authors and do not necessarily reflect the official policy or position of the National Science Foundation or the Sloan Foundation.

A. Boldyreva and D. Micciancio (Eds.): CRYPTO 2019, LNCS 11692, pp. 89–114, 2019.
https://doi.org/10.1007/978-3-030-26948-7_4

more than that fact. Such a system is *noninteractive* [8] (NIZK) if both parties have access to some common string (e.g., a public source of randomness), and the prover just sends a single message to the verifier. In the three decades since the introduction of NIZK, several works have constructed such protocols for *arbitrary NP languages* based on various cryptographic structures (such as quadratic residuosity, bilinear pairings, and code obfuscation) [9,20,26,29,43], and used them in a variety of important cryptographic settings, like encryption that withstands chosen-ciphertext attacks [9,36], digital signatures [6], ZAPs [19] cryptocurrencies [7], and low-interaction protocols in general.

In recent years, cryptography based on *lattices* has seen enormous growth. Among its attractions are apparent resistance to quantum attacks, advanced functionality like fully homomorphic encryption (FHE) [23], and strong theoretical guarantees like security under *worst-case* hardness assumptions, usually via the well-known Short Integer Solution (SIS) [1] and Learning With Errors (LWE) problems [42]. Yet while (non-)interactive zero-knowledge protocols for *specific* lattice problems have been known for some time [2,18,35,39], the goal of obtaining NIZK for *general NP languages* based on standard, worst-case lattice assumptions (which was explicitly posed in [39]) has frustratingly remained out of reach. The past year has seen impressive progress toward this goal [15,16,32], but the current constructions either satisfy a relaxed notion of NIZK or are based on assumptions that are not yet known to be implied by LWE or worst-case hardness.

More specifically, a fascinating recent line of research [15,16,30,31] develops a framework for instantiating the Fiat–Shamir transform [21], which removes interaction from a public-coin protocol by replacing each random verifier message with a hash of the transcript so far. In particular, these works show that if the hash function satisfies a property called *correlation intractability* [17], then the Fiat–Shamir transform can be applied soundly to many interactive protocols, including some zero-knowledge ones. Roughly speaking, a hash family H is correlation intractable for a relation R if, given a hash key k, it is hard to find an input-output pair $(x, H_k(x)) \in R$. In the context of Fiat–Shamir, this ensures that a cheating prover cannot find a message that hashes to a verifier message that admits an accepting transcript.

The works [15,16,30] construct correlation-intractable hash functions for various *sparse* relations, and use them to soundly instantiate the Fiat–Shamir transform, obtaining NIZK proofs for all of NP (among other results). Of particular interest is the beautiful work of [15], which shows that for this purpose, it suffices to have correlation intractability for arbitrary (bounded) *polynomial-time computations*, i.e., for the special class of *efficiently searchable* relations. These are relations where each input has at most a single output (witness) that is computable within some desired polynomial time bound.

The hash families constructed in [15,16] are proved to be correlation intractable under various lattice-related assumptions. However, these assumptions are somehow non-standard, involving either "optimal hardness" (e.g., of LWE with uniform error in an interval) against polynomial-time attacks [15,16], or the existence of circularly secure FHE [15]. Although the latter assumption seems tantalizingly close to plain LWE (and remains the only known way of obtaining FHE that supports *unbounded*, as opposed to just *leveled*, homomorphic computations), none of these assumptions are known to be supported by the hardness of LWE, nor the conjectured worst-case hardness of lattice problems.

1.1 Contributions

Our main result is a noninteractive zero-knowledge proof system for any NP language, based on the *plain LWE* problem with *(small) polynomial* approximation factors. This finally closes (following much recent progress) the central open problem of basing NIZK for NP on worst-case lattice assumptions. Our system instantiates the NIZK framework recently developed in [15,16], but with a new primary ingredient: a correlation-intractable hash family for arbitrary size-S circuits (i.e., relations searchable in size S), for any desired $S = \mathrm{poly}(\lambda)$, based on plain LWE with small polynomial factors.

Just like the correlation-intractable hash family constructed in [15], ours also can be instantiated in two "intractability modes," *computational* and *statistical*, by constructing the hash key in one of two computationally indistinguishable ways. In the statistical mode, input-output pairs that satisfy the relation simply *do not exist* (so obviously one cannot be found); in the computational mode, the hash key is *uniformly random* and security can be based merely on *SIS*, a potentially harder problem for which we have even stronger worst-case hardness theorems than for LWE. In either case, this is the first known construction of CI hash families for "rich" functions from plain LWE/SIS, or any worst-case lattice assumption. As shown in [15], the choice of intractability mode determines the precise properties of the NIZK system: the computational mode yields a *statistically* zero knowledge, (selectively) *computationally* sound (i.e., argument) system in the common *random* string model, while the statistical mode yields a *computationally* zero knowledge, *statistically sound* (i.e., proof) system in the common *reference* string model.

Our correlation-intractable hash family for bounded circuits is obtained by combining two new ingredients that are interesting in their own right:

1. a correlation-intractable hash family for bounded circuits based on plain SIS/LWE, where in particular for *log-depth* circuits the associated approximation factor is a (small) *polynomial*; and
2. a "bootstrapping" transform that uses (leveled) fully homomorphic encryption to promote CI for the FHE *decryption* circuit to CI for *arbitrary bounded* circuits. (This transformation is inspired by other bootstrapping techniques for code obfuscation [22], and is in some sense dual to Gentry's bootstrapping technique for FHE [23].)

In particular, a suitable FHE scheme having log-depth decryption can be instantiated based on plain LWE with small polynomial factors [3,13], which yields our ultimate LWE-based CI hash family.

1.2 Techniques

Here we summarize the main ideas and techniques underlying our constructions.

Bootstrapping Correlation Intractability. In Sect. 4 we give a generic transform that uses (leveled) fully homomorphic encryption to convert a correlation-intractable hash family for "simple" relations related to the FHE decryption function, into one for complex relations induced by circuits of any size S. For simplicity, here we focus on correlation intractability for *functions* f, i.e., for searchable relations $R_f = \{(x, f(x))\}$, but everything easily generalizes to more general relations.

Let $\mathsf{FHE} = (\mathsf{Gen}, \mathsf{Enc}, \mathsf{Dec}, \mathsf{Eval})$ denote a (symmetric-key) fully homomorphic encryption scheme.[1] Let $\mathsf{CIH} = (\mathsf{Gen}, \mathsf{Hash})$ denote a hash family that is correlation intractable for the class $\{\mathsf{Dec}_{sk}(\cdot)\}$ of FHE decryption functions, taken over all valid "hard-wired" secret keys. We define a new hash family $\mathsf{CIH}' = (\mathsf{Gen}', \mathsf{Hash}')$ for circuits of size S as follows:

- $\mathsf{Gen}'(1^\lambda)$ generates a CIH key $k \leftarrow \mathsf{CIH}.\mathsf{Gen}(1^\lambda)$, an FHE key pair $(sk, ek) \leftarrow \mathsf{FHE}.\mathsf{Gen}(1^\lambda)$, and a "dummy" ciphertext $c \leftarrow \mathsf{Enc}(sk, 0^S)$. It outputs the hash key $k' = (k, ek, c)$.
- $\mathsf{Hash}'(k' = (k, ek, c), x)$ outputs $\mathsf{Hash}(k, \mathsf{Eval}(ek, U_x, c))$, where $U_x(\cdot) = U(\cdot, x)$ is a universal circuit for size-S circuits with x "hard-coded" in.

In words, Hash' homomorphically evaluates an encrypted (dummy) circuit on the input x, then hashes the resulting ciphertext using the underlying Hash algorithm.

We now sketch why CIH' is correlation intractable for any function f having circuit size S. As a thought experiment, imagine replacing the "dummy" ciphertext with $c \leftarrow \mathsf{Enc}(sk, f)$. By the security of the FHE scheme, this does not noticeably change the probability that the adversary, given the key $k' = (k, ek, c)$, can find an input x that violates correlation intractability of $\mathsf{Hash}'(k', \cdot)$ for f, i.e.,

$$\mathsf{Hash}'(k', x) = \mathsf{Hash}(k, \underbrace{\mathsf{Eval}(ek, U_x, c)}_{c_x}) = f(x).$$

Suppose for the purpose of contradiction that the adversary is able to find such an x. Then because c_x is an FHE encryption of $f(x)$ by construction, we have $\mathsf{Hash}(k, c_x) = f(x) = \mathsf{Dec}_{sk}(c_x)$. Therefore, we have found an input c_x that violates the correlation intractability of $\mathsf{Hash}(k, \cdot)$ for the function Dec_{sk}, which is the desired contradiction.[2]

---

[1] For simplicity, here we assume that FHE supports unbounded, not just leveled, homomorphic evaluation. Adapting the construction to leveled FHE is straightforward because Eval is used only on circuits of bounded depth.

[2] The reader might notice that the specific function Dec_{sk} is not fixed in advance, but is instead chosen at random by the reduction. This is addressed in the non-uniform setting by "fixing coins" for $\mathsf{FHE}.\mathsf{Gen}$ that maximize the attacker's success probability, or in the uniform setting by adopting a security definition that lets the adversary declare a (valid) target function before receiving the hash key.

Correlation Intractability from SIS/LWE. In Sect. 3 we construct a public-coin, correlation-intractable hash family for arbitrary functions of bounded circuit size based on plain SIS, with a complementary *statistically* intractable mode based on LWE. Our construction works for arbitrary functions, and the circuit size, depth, and output length induce corresponding SIS/LWE parameters. More specifically, the dimension n grows linearly in the output length, and the approximation factor (and hence modulus q) grows exponentially with the depth and polynomially with the size. Due to our bootstrapping transformation, the main parameterization of interest is *log-depth* circuits, for which the approximation factors can be made (small) polynomials. In addition, for the NIZK application, log-depth circuits are sufficient even *without* using bootstrapping (see Remark 5).

Our construction is based upon the fully homomorphic *commitment* scheme implicit in GSW homomorphic encryption [25], which was made explicit in subsequent work on fully homomorphic signatures [28], and is inspired by the construction based on circularly secure FHE from [15]. The construction works as follows:

- A hash key is a commitment $k = \widehat{D}$ to a "dummy" circuit D of the desired output length L and size S.
- To evaluate the hash function at an input x:
  1. First, homomorphically evaluate a commitment $\widehat{D(x)}$ of $D(x)$.
  2. Then, homomorphically apply a certain special, public linear function G from $\{0,1\}^L$ to the SIS/LWE range $\mathbb{Z}_q^n$, to get an "inert commitment" $c_x = \overline{G(D(x))}$ that itself belongs to $\mathbb{Z}_q^n$.
     The name "inert," and the different notation for it, reflect that it is a *different kind of commitment* that (i) does not appear to support full homomorphism, and (ii) hides a value from the *same domain* $\mathbb{Z}_q^n$ as the commitment itself; this turns out to be central to the security argument.
  3. Finally, output $\mathrm{bin}(c_x)$, the binary representation (in $\{0,1\}^L$) of c_x.

The special linear function G just needs to satisfy $G(\mathrm{bin}(\mathbf{u})) = \mathbf{u}$ for all $\mathbf{u} \in \mathbb{Z}_q^n$. (This implies that G is surjective, so the circuit output length L must be at least $n \log q$.) For example, G can map each of n groups of $\ell = \lceil \lg q \rceil$ bits to the mod-q integers they represent in binary.[3]

Relation to [15]. We now summarize the main similarities and differences between our construction and proof, and those based on circularly secure FHE from [15]. In [15], the hash key is an FHE encryption $\widehat{D}$ of a "dummy" circuit D, along with an FHE encryption $\widehat{sk}$ of the secret decryption key sk; this is what requires the circularity assumption. Our construction elides this second component, and since it has no need for a decryption key at all, fully homomorphic commitment suffices.

---

[3] Those familiar with the literature will recognize this as the linear transform induced by the "gadget" matrix $\mathbf{G}$.

For hash evaluation, Step 1 is the same in both constructions, but then they diverge. In [15], one uses $\widehat{sk}$ to homomorphically evaluate (the complement of) the decryption circuit on $\widehat{D(x)}$, yielding the hash output $y = \overline{\mathsf{Dec}_{sk}(D(x)) \oplus 1}$. The security proof employs a clever diagonalization argument: using the FHE's security, it replaces $\widehat{D}$ in the hash key with $\widehat{f}$ for the function f of interest. This makes it so that *there does not exist* any x that hashes to $y = f(x)$. For if there were, then by applying Dec_{sk} to both sides and by the FHE's correctness, we would get $\mathsf{Dec}_{sk}(y) = \mathsf{Dec}_{sk}(f(x)) \oplus 1 = \mathsf{Dec}_{sk}(f(x))$, a contradiction.

Our construction after Step 1 proceeds quite differently: it homomorphically applies the special *public* function $G \colon \{0,1\}^L \to \mathbb{Z}_q^n$, which has a *large range* (not just a single bit, as for FHE decryption), and just as importantly, it "collapses" the result to an inert commitment $\overline{G(D(x))} \in \mathbb{Z}_q^n$ that lies in the same domain as $G(D(x)) \in \mathbb{Z}_q^n$ itself. As we will see next, in the security proof this allows us to *directly compare* the inert commitment to the value it hides, rather than only reasoning about the latter (as in [15]).

Security. Security is argued as follows, where for the moment we focus on the proof from SIS. Suppose that an adversary is able to violate correlation intractability for some function f of size S and output length L, i.e., given a hash key it finds an input x that hashes to $f(x)$. By the (statistical) security of the commitment scheme, the adversary has essentially the same probability of succeeding if the hash key is a commitment $\widehat{f}$ to f. When it does succeed we have $\mathrm{bin}(\overline{G(f(x))}) = f(x)$, and so by applying G to both sides we get

$$\overline{G(f(x))} = G(f(x)) \in \mathbb{Z}_q^n. \tag{1}$$

To see why this yields an SIS solution, we need to understand the particular form of the commitments in a little more detail. All commitments are with respect to a random SIS matrix $\mathbf{A}$ over $\mathbb{Z}_q$. The commitment scheme has the property that, given the randomness used to form the original commitment $\widehat{f}$, it is possible to efficiently compute randomness that is consistent with the homomorphically evaluated commitment $\widehat{f(x)}$, and likewise for the inert commitment $c_x = \overline{G(f(x))}$. Concretely, this derived randomness is a *short* integer vector $\mathbf{r}$ such that

$$\overline{G(f(x))} = \mathbf{A}\mathbf{r} + G(f(x)) \pmod{q}.$$

But because $\overline{G(f(x))} = G(f(x))$ by Eq. (1), it follows that $\mathbf{A}\mathbf{r} = \mathbf{0} \in \mathbb{Z}_q^n$. Therefore, the short vector $\mathbf{r}$ is a solution to the SIS problem for the random instance $\mathbf{A}$, as desired. (We also need to ensure that $\mathbf{r}$ is nonzero; this is easily done via standard techniques.)

To get *statistical* correlation intractability based on LWE, we need to slightly tweak the construction, defining the hash function to evaluate an inert commitment $c_x = \overline{G(D(x))} + \lfloor q/2 \rfloor \mathbf{u}_n$, where $\mathbf{u}_n$ is the nth standard basis vector.[4] For a particular f of interest, we again replace the commitment to D with one to f.

---

[4] With this change, the SIS-based proof still goes through, thanks to the technique for ensuring that $\mathbf{r} \neq \mathbf{0}$.

Then, to get a hash key for which an x that hashes to $f(x)$ simply *does not exist*, we switch $\mathbf{A}$ to be an LWE matrix whose bottom row $\mathbf{b}^t$ is a noisy linear combination of the others, i.e., $\mathbf{b}^t = \mathbf{s}^t\mathbf{A}' + \mathbf{e}^t$ where $\mathbf{A}'$ consists of the top $n-1$ rows of $\mathbf{A}$ and $\mathbf{e}$ is a "short" error vector; by the LWE assumption, this change is unnoticeable by the attacker.[5] Much like above, a hypothetical input x which hashes to $f(x)$ now yields $\mathbf{A}\mathbf{r} = -\lfloor q/2 \rfloor \mathbf{u}_n$, which implies that $\mathbf{A}'\mathbf{r} = \mathbf{0}$ and hence

$$-\lfloor q/2 \rfloor = \mathbf{b}^t \cdot \mathbf{r} = (\mathbf{s}^t\mathbf{A}' + \mathbf{e}^t)\mathbf{r} = \mathbf{s}^t(\mathbf{A}'\mathbf{r}) + \mathbf{e}^t \cdot \mathbf{r} = \langle \mathbf{e}, \mathbf{r} \rangle \pmod{q}.$$

But because both $\mathbf{e}$ and $\mathbf{r}$ are relatively short, by taking q to be large enough this equation simply cannot hold, hence no such x exists.

1.3   Discussion and Open Problems

We conclude this introduction with a few additional remarks about our constructions and their implications, and list some open problems for further research.

Other applications. Our NIZK implies the first entirely LWE-based, standard-model construction of an encryption scheme that is secure for key-dependent messages and under chosen-ciphertext attacks (called KDM-CCA), by applying the generic transform from [14] to the LWE-based KDM-CPA-secure construction from [4] and any of the known LWE-based IND-CCA-secure constructions of, e.g., [33,37,41]. Just as in [15], our CI hash family also suffices for proving that the parallelized quadratic residuosity protocol of [27] is *not* zero knowledge (assuming that QR is not in BPP), but now under plain SIS/LWE assumptions instead of circularly secure FHE.

Compact hashing. We emphasize that our CI hash family is *non-compact*: the size of the hash key, and hence the evaluation time as well, grow with the description size S of the circuits for which it is correlation intractable. This property is shared by all other prior constructions except those based on highly "exotic" assumptions like indistinguishability obfuscation or optimal key-dependent message security, e.g., [15,16,31]. A compact construction based on more standard assumptions would be very interesting, and presumably quite powerful.

SIS versus LWE. Our SIS-based CI hash family works for circuits of any depth, but is only supported by polynomial SIS factors for *log-depth* circuits. Dealing with deeper circuits while retaining polynomial approximation factors requires us to use our bootstrapping theorem with (leveled) FHE, which brings in the LWE assumption. (In addition, the NIZK construction also uses LWE for lossy encryption.) It is an interesting open problem to get a CI hash family for super-logarithmic depth based on just SIS with polynomial factors.

---

[5] This change also turns the fully homomorphic commitment scheme into the GSW FHE scheme [25,28], but we do not need its decryption capability.

Multi-theorem (statistical) zero knowledge. The zero-knowledge property of our NIZK constructions holds for a *single* statement and proof. We can use the generic "OR" trick from [20] to convert our single-theorem NIZK systems to multi-theorem ones. However, the resulting NIZK systems are *computational* zero knowledge, even if the original ones are statistical zero knowledge. Therefore, an interesting open problem is to construct a noninteractive, multi-theorem, statistical zero-knowledge system based on LWE. We note that such NIZK systems, having an even stricter *perfect* zero-knowledge property, can be constructed from bilinear pairings [29].

Compact proofs. A final interesting open problem is to construct a noninteractive *statistical* zero-knowledge argument system with *compact* proofs, i.e., with proof size that is both asymptotically smaller than the size of the underlying verifier circuit for the NP relation and only linear in the length of the witness. Assuming leveled or unbounded FHE, such compact proofs having *computational* zero knowledge exist [24]. In the construction based on leveled FHE (and hence based only on LWE), the proof size exceeds the witness length by $\text{poly}(\lambda, d)$, where d is the depth of verifier circuit. Unbounded FHE yields proofs that are longer than the witness by only an additive $\text{poly}(\lambda)$ term.

2   Preliminaries

We denote column vectors by lower-case bold letters, e.g., $\mathbf{a}$. We denote matrices by upper-case bold letters, e.g., $\mathbf{A}$. For integral vectors and matrices (i.e., those over $\mathbb{Z}$), we use the notation $|\mathbf{r}|, |\mathbf{R}|$ to denote the maximum absolute value over all the entries.

The Kronecker product $\mathbf{A} \otimes \mathbf{B}$ of two matrices (or vectors) $\mathbf{A}$ and $\mathbf{B}$ is obtained by replacing each entry $a_{i,j}$ of $\mathbf{A}$ with the block $a_{i,j}\mathbf{B}$. This obeys the *mixed-product* property: $(\mathbf{A} \otimes \mathbf{B})(\mathbf{C} \otimes \mathbf{D}) = (\mathbf{AC}) \otimes (\mathbf{BD})$ for any matrices $\mathbf{A}, \mathbf{B}, \mathbf{C}, \mathbf{D}$ with compatible dimensions.

2.1   Noninteractive Zero Knowledge

Definition 1. *Let R be a relation. A* noninteractive proof system *for R is a tuple of PPT algorithms* (Setup, Prove, Verify) *having the following interfaces (where $1^n, 1^\lambda$ are implicit inputs to* Prove, Verify*):*

- Setup$(1^n, 1^\lambda)$, *given a statement length n and a security parameter λ, outputs a string σ.*
- Prove(σ, x, w), *given a string σ and a statement-witness pair $(x, w) \in R$, outputs a proof π.*
- Verify(σ, x, π), *given a string σ, a statement x, and a proof π, either accepts or rejects.*

Definition 2. *Let $\Pi =$ (Setup, Prove, Verify) be a noninteractive proof system for a relation R, and let L be the language defined by R. In this work we focus on systems that satisfy some subset of the following properties:*

1. Completeness: *for every $(x, w) \in R$ and every $\lambda \in \mathbb{N}$, $\mathsf{Verify}(\sigma, x, \pi)$ accepts with probability 1, over the choice of $\sigma \leftarrow \mathsf{Setup}(1^{|x|}, 1^\lambda)$ and $\pi \leftarrow \mathsf{Prover}(\sigma, x, w)$.*

2. Common random string: *$\mathsf{Setup}(1^n, 1^\lambda)$ simply outputs a uniformly random string.*

3. Statistical soundness: *there exists a negligible function $\nu(\lambda)$ such that for any $n \in \mathbb{N}$,*

$$\Pr_{\sigma \leftarrow \mathsf{Setup}(1^n, 1^\lambda)} [\exists (x, \pi^*) \text{ s.t. } \mathsf{Verify}(\sigma, x, \pi^*) \text{ accepts} \wedge x \notin L] \leq \nu(\lambda). \quad (2)$$

4. Computational soundness: *for every non-uniform polynomial-size "cheating" prover $P^* = \{P^*_\lambda\}$ there exists a negligible function $\nu(\lambda)$ such that for any $n \in \mathbb{N}$ and any $x \notin L$,*

$$\Pr_{\substack{\sigma \leftarrow \mathsf{Setup}(1^n, 1^\lambda) \\ \pi^* = P^*_\lambda(\sigma, x)}} [\mathsf{Verify}(\sigma, x, \pi^*)] \leq \nu(\lambda). \quad (3)$$

5. Statistical zero knowledge: *there exists a PPT simulator $\mathcal{S}$ such that for every $(x, w) \in R$ the following two distribution ensembles are statistically indistinguishable:*

$$\{\mathcal{S}(1^\lambda, x)\}_\lambda \overset{s}{\approx} \{(\sigma, \mathsf{Prover}(\sigma, x, w)) : \sigma \leftarrow \mathsf{Setup}(1^{|x|}, 1^\lambda)\}_\lambda. \quad (4)$$

6. Adaptive (computational) zero knowledge: *there exists a PPT simulator $\mathcal{S} = (\mathcal{S}_1, \mathcal{S}_2)$ such that for every non-uniform polynomial-size "cheating" verifier $V^* = (V_1^*, V_2^*)$, for every $n \in \mathbb{N}$ the probabilities*

$$\Pr[V_2^*(\sigma, x, \pi, \zeta) = 1 \wedge (x \in L)]$$

in the following two experiments differ only by $\mathrm{negl}(\lambda)$:
   - *in the "real" experiment, $\sigma \leftarrow \mathsf{Setup}(1^n, 1^\lambda), (x, w, \zeta) \leftarrow V_1^*(\sigma), \pi \leftarrow \mathsf{Prove}(\sigma, x, w)$;*
   - *in the "simulation" experiment, $(\sigma, \tau) \leftarrow \mathcal{S}_1(1^\lambda), (x, w, \zeta) \leftarrow V_1^*(\sigma), \pi \leftarrow \mathcal{S}_2(\sigma, x, \tau)$.*

2.2   Correlation Intractability

As in [15] we define efficiently searchable relations and recall the definitions of correlation intractability, in their computational and statistical versions.

Definition 3. *We say that a relation $R \subseteq \mathcal{X} \times \mathcal{Y}$ is searchable in size S if there exists a function $f \colon \mathcal{X} \to \mathcal{Y}$ that is implementable as a boolean circuit of size S, such that if $(x, y) \in R$ then $y = f(x)$. (In other words, $f(x)$ is the unique witness for x, if such a witness exists.)*

Definition 4. *Let* $\mathcal{R} = \{\mathcal{R}_\lambda\}$ *be a relation class, i.e., a set of relations for each* λ. *A hash function family* (Gen, Hash) *is* correlation intractable (CI) *for* $\mathcal{R}$ *if for every non-uniform polynomial-size adversary* $\mathcal{A} = \{\mathcal{A}_\lambda\}$ *there exists a negligible function* $\nu(\lambda)$ *such that for every* $R \in \mathcal{R}_\lambda$

$$\Pr_{\substack{k \leftarrow \text{Gen}(1^\lambda) \\ x = \mathcal{A}_\lambda(k)}} [(x, \text{Hash}(k, x)) \in R] \leq \nu(\lambda). \tag{5}$$

Definition 5. *Let* $\mathcal{R} = \{\mathcal{R}_\lambda\}$ *be a relation class. A hash function family* (Gen, Hash) *with a fake-key generation algorithm* StatGen *is* somewhere statistically correlation intractable *for* $\mathcal{R}$ *if*

1. $\text{StatGen}(1^\lambda, z)$, *where* z *is an auxiliary input, outputs a key* k,
2. *there exists a negligible function* $\nu(\lambda)$ *and a class of auxiliary inputs* $\mathcal{Z} = \{\mathcal{Z}_\lambda\}$ *such that*
   - *the distribution ensembles* $\{\text{StatGen}(1^\lambda, z_\lambda)\}$ *and* $\{\text{Gen}(1^\lambda)\}$ *are computationally indistinguishable for every sequence of* $z_\lambda \in \mathcal{Z}_\lambda$, *and*
   - *for every* $R \in \mathcal{R}_\lambda$ *there exists* $z_R \in \mathcal{Z}_\lambda$ *such that*

$$\Pr_{k \leftarrow \text{StatGen}(1^\lambda, z_R)} [\exists x \ s.t. \ (x, \text{Hash}(k, x)) \in R] \leq \nu(\lambda). \tag{6}$$

We call z_R *the* intractability guarantee *for* R.

2.3   (Leveled) Fully Homomorphic Encryption

We recall the notion of leveled FHE from [23].

Definition 6. *A* leveled fully homomorphic encryption *scheme is a tuple of algorithms* (Gen, Enc, Dec, Eval) *with the following interfaces (we use only a symmetric-key version, which is sufficient for our purposes):*

- $\text{Gen}(1^\lambda, 1^d)$ *outputs a secret key* sk *and an evaluation key* ek.
- $\text{Enc}(sk, m \in \{0, 1\}^*)$, *where* m *is a message, outputs a ciphertext* c.
- $\text{Eval}(C, c)$, *where* C *is a boolean circuit of depth (at most)* d, *deterministically outputs a ciphertext* c'.
- $\text{Dec}(sk, c)$ *outputs a message (deterministically).*

It should satisfy the following properties:

1. Completeness: *For any circuit* C *of depth at most* d *and message* m, $\text{Dec}(sk, \text{Eval}(C, c)) = C(m)$ *with probability 1, over the random choice of* $sk \leftarrow \text{Gen}(1^\lambda, 1^d)$ *and* $c \leftarrow \text{Enc}(sk, m)$.
2. CPA security: *for any sequence of message pairs* $\{(m_{0,\lambda}, m_{1,\lambda})\}_\lambda$ *where* $|m_{0,\lambda}| = |m_{1,\lambda}|$, *and any sequence* $\{d_\lambda\}$, *the distribution ensembles*

$$\{\text{Enc}(sk, m_{b,\lambda}) : sk \leftarrow \text{Gen}(1^\lambda, 1^{d_\lambda})\}_\lambda \tag{7}$$

are computationally indistinguishable for $b = 0, 1$.
3. Compactness: *the complexity of* Dec *is a fixed polynomial in* λ *alone. (This implies that the output of* Eval *has a fixed polynomial size in* λ *alone, and does not depend on the evaluated circuit or* d.)

2.4   Branching Programs

A width-w boolean permutation branching program BP of length L with input space $\{0,1\}^\ell$ consists of $2L$ permutations $\{\pi_{i,b}\colon [w] \to [w]\}_{i \in [L], b \in \{0,1\}}$ along with an index-to-input map $v\colon [L] \to [\ell]$. To compute the output of BP on an input $x \in \{0,1\}^\ell$ we first initialize a state variable $st_0 = 1$. Then, for each $i \in [L]$ we set $st_i = \pi_{i,x_{v(i)}}(st_{i-1})$. Finally, if $st_L = 1$ we output 1; otherwise, we output 0. More generally, a branching program can have multi-bit output by just having a separate branching program for each output bit; its length is the maximum length of all the component programs.

Barrington's theorem [5] states that every depth-d boolean circuit can be efficiently converted into a width-5 permutation branching program of length 4^d. In particular, any NC^1 circuit can be converted into a polynomial-length, constant-width permutation branching program.

2.5   Short Integer Solution and Learning with Errors

We recall the Short Integer Solution (SIS) and Learning With Errors (LWE) problems, and their hardness based on worst-case lattice problems.

Definition 7. *The $SIS_{n,m,q,\beta}$ problem is: given a uniformly random matrix $\mathbf{A} \in \mathbb{Z}_q^{n \times m}$, find a non-zero integral vector $\mathbf{z} \in \mathbb{Z}^m$ such that $\mathbf{A} \cdot \mathbf{z} = 0 \bmod q$ and $\|\mathbf{z}\| \leq \beta$.*

We sometimes drop the subscript m when it is an unspecified polynomial in n and $\log q$. When $q \geq \beta \cdot \tilde{O}(\sqrt{n})$, solving $SIS_{n,q,\beta}$ is at least as hard as approximating certain worst-case lattice problems on n-dimensional lattices to within a $\beta \cdot \tilde{O}(\sqrt{n})$ factor [34].

For a positive integer dimension n and modulus q, and an error distribution χ over $\mathbb{Z}$, the LWE distribution and decision problem are defined as follows. For an $\mathbf{s} \in \mathbb{Z}^n$, the LWE distribution $A_{\mathbf{s},\chi}$ is sampled by choosing a uniformly random $\mathbf{a} \leftarrow \mathbb{Z}_q^n$ and an error term $e \leftarrow \chi$, and outputting $(\mathbf{a}, b = \langle \mathbf{s}, \mathbf{a} \rangle + e) \in \mathbb{Z}_q^{n+1}$. If we have m samples $(\mathbf{a}_i, b_i)$, we can gather them as a uniformly random matrix $\mathbf{A} \in \mathbb{Z}_q^{n \times m}$ and vector $\mathbf{b}^t = \mathbf{s}^t \mathbf{A} + \mathbf{e}^t \in \mathbb{Z}_q^m$.

Definition 8. *The $LWE_{n,m,q,\chi}$ problem is to distinguish, with non-negligible advantage, between m independent samples drawn from $A_{\mathbf{s},\chi}$ for a single $\mathbf{s} \leftarrow \mathbb{Z}_q^n$, and m uniformly random and independent samples over $\mathbb{Z}_q^{n+1}$.*

(As with SIS, we sometimes drop the subscript m.) A standard instantiation of LWE is to let χ be a *discrete Gaussian* distribution over $\mathbb{Z}$ with parameter $r = 2\sqrt{n}$. A sample drawn from this distribution has magnitude bounded by, say, $r\sqrt{n} = \Theta(n)$ except with probability at most 2^{-n}, and hence this tail of the distribution can be entirely removed. For this parameterization, it is known that LWE is at least as hard as *quantumly* approximating certain "short vector" problems on n-dimensional lattices, in the worst case, to within $\tilde{O}(q\sqrt{n})$ factors [38,42]. Classical reductions are also known for different parameterizations [12,37]. It is also well-known folklore that for such parameters, $LWE_{n,m,q,\chi}$ reduces to $SIS_{n,m,q,\beta}$ for every $\beta \leq q/r$.

2.6   Lattice Gadgets

Here we recall lattice "gadgets" [33] over $\mathbb{Z}_q$. For a positive integer modulus q, let $\ell = \lceil \lg q \rceil$. The "gadget" vector over $\mathbb{Z}_q$ is defined as

$$\mathbf{g}^t = (1, 2, 4, \ldots, 2^{\ell-1}) \in \mathbb{Z}_q^{\ell}. \tag{8}$$

For every $u \in \mathbb{Z}_q$, there is an efficiently computable binary vector $\mathbf{g}^{-1}[u] \in \{0, 1\}^{\ell}$ such that $\langle \mathbf{g}, \mathbf{g}^{-1}[u] \rangle = u \pmod{q}$. Specifically, $\mathbf{g}^{-1}[u]$ corresponds to the binary representation of the distinguished representative of u in $\{0, 1, \ldots, q-1\}$. We stress that $\mathbf{g}^{-1} \colon \mathbb{Z}_q \to \{0, 1\}^{\ell}$ is a *function*; its name reflects the essential property $\langle \mathbf{g}, \mathbf{g}^{-1}[u] \rangle = u$.

For a dimension n, the gadget matrix is defined as

$$\mathbf{G}_n = \mathbf{I}_n \otimes \mathbf{g}^t \in \mathbb{Z}_q^{n \times m},$$

where $m = n\ell$. We often drop the subscript n when it is clear from context. Similarly to above, we define the function $\mathbf{G}^{-1} = (\mathbf{I} \otimes \mathbf{g}^{-1}) \colon \mathbb{Z}_q^n \to \{0, 1\}^m$, which applies $\mathbf{g}^{-1}$ to each coordinate and appends the results. This has the essential property, which is also reflective of the mixed-product property, that for every $\mathbf{u} \in \mathbb{Z}_q^n$,

$$\mathbf{G} \cdot \mathbf{G}^{-1}[\mathbf{u}] = (\mathbf{I} \otimes \mathbf{g}^t) \cdot (\mathbf{I} \otimes \mathbf{g}^{-1})[\mathbf{u}] = \mathbf{u}.$$

2.7   Fully Homomorphic Commitments

Here we recall the relevant homomorphic properties of gadgets, some of which were implicit in [25], and which were developed and exploited further in [3,10,13,28]. We particularly focus on their application to fully homomorphic commitments, as laid out in [28], and refer to that work for full details.

Let $\mathbf{A} \in \mathbb{Z}_q^{n \times w}$ be an arbitrary matrix for some dimension w. Let $\mathbf{C}_i = \mathbf{A}\mathbf{R}_i + x_i\mathbf{G}$ for some integral matrix $\mathbf{R}_i \in \mathbb{Z}^{w \times m}$ and scalar $x_i \in \mathbb{Z}_q$ for $i = 1, 2$. We view $\mathbf{C}_i$ as a commitment (relative to $\mathbf{A}$) to x_i under randomness $\mathbf{R}_i$. Observe that these commitments satisfy the following homomorphic properties:

$$\mathbf{G} - \mathbf{C}_1 = \mathbf{A}(-\mathbf{R}_1) + (1 - x_1)\mathbf{G}$$

$$\mathbf{C}_+ := \mathbf{C}_1 + \mathbf{C}_2 = \mathbf{A}(\underbrace{\mathbf{R}_1 + \mathbf{R}_2}_{\mathbf{R}_+}) + (x_1 + x_2)\mathbf{G}$$

$$\mathbf{C}_\times := \mathbf{C}_1 \cdot \mathbf{G}^{-1}[\mathbf{C}_2] = \mathbf{A}(\mathbf{R}_1 \cdot \mathbf{G}^{-1}[\mathbf{C}_2]) + x_1\mathbf{G} \cdot \mathbf{G}^{-1}[\mathbf{A}\mathbf{R}_2 + x_2\mathbf{G}]$$

$$= \mathbf{A}(\underbrace{\mathbf{R}_1 \cdot \mathbf{G}^{-1}[\mathbf{C}_2] + x_1\mathbf{R}_2}_{\mathbf{R}_\times}) + x_1 x_2 \mathbf{G}.$$

In words, $\mathbf{G} - \mathbf{C}_1, \mathbf{C}_+, \mathbf{C}_\times$ are commitments to $1 - x_1, x_1 + x_2, x_1 x_2$ under randomness $-\mathbf{R}_1, \mathbf{R}_+, \mathbf{R}_\times$, respectively. Moreover, if the original committed values x_i and randomness $\mathbf{R}_i$ are "small" in norm, then so are the new values and randomness (though they are somewhat larger), because $\mathbf{G}^{-1}[\mathbf{C}_2]$ is small.

In particular, if the original committed values $x_i \in \{0, 1\}$ are restricted to *bits*, then the above homomorphic operations yield a complete set of logical gates with which we can homomorphically evaluate any boolean circuit. For example, we can implement $\text{NAND}(x, y) = 1 - xy$ using the third equation, then the first one. Of course, the size of the randomness in the final committed result depends on the depth and size of the circuit. Similarly, as shown in [3,13], the asymmetric factors applied to the commitment randomness $\mathbf{R}_1$ versus $\mathbf{R}_2$ in $\mathbf{R}_\times$ can be exploited to implement other models of computation, like branching programs, with tighter control over the magnitude of the derived randomness. In particular, the magnitude can be limited to just polynomial in the length of the branching program.

For our purposes, we need one more simple homomorphic property. Suppose we have a commitment

$$\mathbf{C} = \mathbf{A}\mathbf{R} + \mathbf{x}^t \otimes \mathbf{G} = \mathbf{A}\mathbf{R} + \mathbf{x}^t \otimes \mathbf{I}_n \otimes \mathbf{g}^t$$

to a vector $\mathbf{x} \in \mathbb{Z}_q^L$. (Observe that the ith m-column chunk of $\mathbf{C}$ is $\mathbf{C}_i = \mathbf{A}\mathbf{R}_i + x_i\mathbf{G} \in \mathbb{Z}_q^{n \times m}$, where $\mathbf{R}_i$ is the analogous chunk of $\mathbf{R}$.) Any matrix $\mathbf{M} \in \mathbb{Z}_q^{n \times L}$ can be "vectorized" as an $\mathbf{m} \in \mathbb{Z}_q^{nL}$, so that $(\mathbf{x}^t \otimes \mathbf{I}_n) \cdot \mathbf{m} = \mathbf{M}\mathbf{x}$. Then

$$\mathbf{c}_{\mathbf{M}} := \mathbf{C} \cdot \mathbf{G}_{Ln}^{-1}[\mathbf{m}] = \mathbf{A}(\underbrace{\mathbf{R} \cdot \mathbf{G}_{Ln}^{-1}[\mathbf{m}]}_{\mathbf{r}_{\mathbf{M}}}) + (\mathbf{x}^t \otimes \mathbf{I}_n \otimes \mathbf{g}^t) \cdot (\mathbf{I}_L \otimes \mathbf{I}_n \otimes \mathbf{g}^{-t})[\mathbf{m}]$$

$$= \mathbf{A}\mathbf{r}_{\mathbf{M}} + (\mathbf{x}^t \otimes \mathbf{I}_n) \cdot \mathbf{m}$$

$$= \mathbf{A}\mathbf{r}_{\mathbf{M}} + \mathbf{M}\mathbf{x} \in \mathbb{Z}_q^n .$$

We view $\mathbf{c}_{\mathbf{M}}$ as an "inert commitment" to $\mathbf{M}\mathbf{x} \in \mathbb{Z}_q^n$, under randomness $\mathbf{r}_{\mathbf{M}}$, which is small if $\mathbf{R}$ is small. (We call it an inert commitment because it does not appear to support any nonlinear homomorphic operations.)

We summarize all of the above in the following fully homomorphic commitment scheme.

Construction 1. The commitment scheme FHC is parameterized by n and q, and is defined as follows. Each input in square brackets is optional, and when provided, the algorithm also produces the additional described output. The algorithm's main output is the same whether or not the optional input is provided.

- Gen chooses a uniformly random $\mathbf{A} \leftarrow \mathbb{Z}_q^{n \times w}$, where $w = 2m = 2n\ell$.
- $\text{Com}(\mathbf{A} \in \mathbb{Z}_q^{n \times w}, \mathbf{x} \in \mathbb{Z}_q^S; \mathbf{R} \leftarrow \mathbb{Z}^{w \times Sm})$ outputs a commitment $\mathbf{C} = \mathbf{A}\mathbf{R} + \mathbf{x}^t \otimes \mathbf{G} \in \mathbb{Z}_q^{n \times Sm}$. If the randomness $\mathbf{R}$ is not provided explicitly, it is chosen uniformly from $\{0, 1\}^{w \times Sm}$ (but note that it is not required to be binary in general).
- $\text{CircuitEval}(C, \mathbf{C} \in \mathbb{Z}_q^{n \times Sm}[, \mathbf{R} \in \mathbb{Z}^{w \times Sm}])$, for a boolean circuit $C\colon \{0, 1\}^t \to \{0, 1\}^L$, deterministically outputs a commitment matrix $\mathbf{C}_C \in \mathbb{Z}^{n \times Lm}$ [and additionally an integral matrix $\mathbf{R}_C \in \mathbb{Z}^{w \times Lm}$].

- BranchEval(B, $\mathbf{C} \in \mathbb{Z}_q^{n \times Sm}[, \mathbf{R} \in \mathbb{Z}^{w \times Sm}]$), for a branching program
  $B: \{0,1\}^S \to \{0,1\}^L$, deterministically outputs a commitment matrix $\mathbf{C}_B \in \mathbb{Z}^{n \times Lm}$ [and additionally an integral matrix $\mathbf{R}_B \in \mathbb{Z}^{w \times Lm}$].
- InertEval($\mathbf{M} \in \mathbb{Z}_q^{n \times L}, \mathbf{C} \in \mathbb{Z}_q^{n \times Lm}[, \mathbf{R} \in \mathbb{Z}^{w \times Lm}]$) deterministically outputs
  an "inert commitment" vector $\mathbf{c}_{\mathbf{M}} \in \mathbb{Z}_q^n$ [and additionally an integral vector $\mathbf{r}_{\mathbf{M}} \in \mathbb{Z}^w$].

Proposition 1. *The above commitment scheme* FHC *satisfies the following properties:*

1. *By the leftover hash lemma, for any* $\mathbf{x} \in \mathbb{Z}_q^{\text{poly}(m)}$ *the distribution of* $(\mathbf{A}, \mathbf{C})$ *has* negl(m) *statistical distance from uniformly random, where* $\mathbf{A} \leftarrow$ Gen(1^n) *and* $\mathbf{C} \leftarrow$ Com($\mathbf{A}, \mathbf{x}$).
2. *For any boolean circuit* $C: \{0,1\}^S \to \{0,1\}^L$ *of depth* d, *any* $\mathbf{x} \in \{0,1\}^S$, *any* $\mathbf{A} \in \mathbb{Z}_q^{n \times w}$ *and any* $\mathbf{R} \in \mathbb{Z}^{w \times Sm}$, *for commitment* $\mathbf{C} = $ Com($\mathbf{A}, \mathbf{x}; \mathbf{R}$) *we have*

$$\text{CircuitEval}(C, \mathbf{C}) = \text{Com}(\mathbf{A}, C(x); \mathbf{R}_C), \qquad (9)$$

where $\mathbf{R}_C \in \mathbb{Z}^{w \times Lm}$ *is the additional output of* CircuitEval($C, \mathbf{C}, \mathbf{R}$), *and* $|\mathbf{R}_C| = |\mathbf{R}| \cdot m^{O(d)}$.
3. *For any branching program* $B: \{0,1\}^S \to \{0,1\}^L$ *of length* D, *any* $\mathbf{x} \in \mathcal{X}$, *any* $\mathbf{A} \in \mathbb{Z}_q^{n \times w}$ *and any* $\mathbf{R} \in \mathbb{Z}^{w \times Sm}$, *for commitment* $\mathbf{C} = $ Com($\mathbf{A}, \mathbf{x}; \mathbf{R}$) *we have*

$$\text{BranchEval}(B, \mathbf{C}) = \text{Com}(\mathbf{A}, B(x); \mathbf{R}_B), \qquad (10)$$

where $\mathbf{R}_B \in \mathbb{Z}^{w \times Lm}$ *is the additional output of* BranchEval($B, \mathbf{C}, \mathbf{R}$), *and* $|\mathbf{R}_B| = |\mathbf{R}| \cdot m^{O(1)} D$.
4. *For any matrix* $\mathbf{M} \in \mathbb{Z}_q^{n \times L}$, *any* $\mathbf{x} \in \{0,1\}^L$, *any* $\mathbf{A} \in \mathbb{Z}_q^{n \times w}$ *and any* $\mathbf{R} \in \mathbb{Z}^{w \times Lm}$, *for commitment* $\mathbf{C} = \mathbf{A}\mathbf{R} + \mathbf{x}^t \otimes \mathbf{G}$ *we have*

$$\text{InertEval}(\mathbf{M}, \mathbf{C}) = \mathbf{A}\mathbf{r}_{\mathbf{M}} + \mathbf{M}\mathbf{x}, \qquad (11)$$

where $\mathbf{r}_{\mathbf{M}} \in \mathbb{Z}^w$ *is the additional output of* InertEval($\mathbf{M}, \mathbf{C}, \mathbf{R}$), *and* $|\mathbf{r}_{\mathbf{M}}| \leq |\mathbf{R}| \cdot Lm$.

3   Correlation-Intractable Hashing from SIS/LWE

In this section we construct correlation-intractable hash families for (searchable relations defined by) arbitrary functions of bounded complexity, based on SIS. Particular cases of interest are functions computable by *log-depth* (i.e., NC^1) circuits, and polynomial-length *branching programs*, either of which are sufficient to invoke our bootstrapping transform in Sect. 4.

3.1   Construction for Circuits

Let FHC be the fully homomorphic commitment scheme from Sect. 2.7. Recall that FHC is parameterized by an SIS dimension n and a modulus q, which we instantiate below as functions of the security parameter λ based on the targeted class of functions. Our hash families work for functions of arbitrary input length, and output length *exactly* $m = n\ell = n\lceil \log q \rceil$. Correlation intractability immediately extends to functions of output length greater than m, simply by appending zeros to the length-m hash output.

We start with a construction that is correlation intractable for boolean *circuits*.

Construction 2 (CIH for circuits). The hash family $\mathsf{CIH} = (\mathsf{Gen}, \mathsf{Hash})$ with fake-key generation algorithm $\mathsf{StatGen}$ is parameterized by an arbitrary circuit size $S = S(\lambda) = \mathrm{poly}(\lambda)$ and depth $d = d(\lambda) \leq S(\lambda)$. Let $U(C, x) = C(x)$ denote a depth-universal circuit for size-S circuits.

- $\mathsf{Gen}(1^\lambda)$: generate $\mathbf{A} \leftarrow \mathsf{FHC.Gen}$ and $\mathbf{C} \leftarrow \mathsf{Com}(\mathbf{A}, 0^{S(\lambda)})$, choose a uniformly random $\mathbf{a} \leftarrow \mathbb{Z}_q^n$, and output the hash key $k = (\mathbf{a}, \mathbf{C})$.
- $\mathsf{StatGen}(1^\lambda, C)$: given a circuit C of size S, choose a uniformly random $\bar{\mathbf{A}} \leftarrow \mathbb{Z}_q^{(n-1)\times m}$ and $\bar{\mathbf{a}} \leftarrow \mathbb{Z}_q^{n-1}$. Choose $\mathbf{s} \leftarrow \mathbb{Z}_q^{n-1}$, $\mathbf{e} \leftarrow \chi^m$ and $e \leftarrow \chi$, where χ is an LWE error distribution. Let

$$\mathbf{A} := \begin{bmatrix} \bar{\mathbf{A}} \\ \mathbf{s}^t\bar{\mathbf{A}} + \mathbf{e}^t \end{bmatrix} \in \mathbb{Z}_q^{n\times m}, \quad \mathbf{a} := \begin{bmatrix} \bar{\mathbf{a}} \\ \mathbf{s}^t \cdot \bar{\mathbf{a}} + e - \lfloor q/2 \rfloor \end{bmatrix} \in \mathbb{Z}_q^n . \quad (12)$$

Compute $\mathbf{C} \leftarrow \mathsf{Com}(\mathbf{A}, C)$ and output the hash key $k = (\mathbf{a}, \mathbf{C})$.
- $\mathsf{Hash}(k = (\mathbf{a}, \mathbf{C}), x)$: let circuit $U_x(\cdot) = U(\cdot, x)$, and output

$$\mathbf{G}_n^{-1}[\mathbf{a} + \mathsf{InertEval}(\mathbf{G}_n, \mathsf{CircuitEval}(U_x, \mathbf{C}))] \in \{0, 1\}^m.$$

Remark 1. By Item 1 of Proposition 1, the hash key $k = (\mathbf{a}, \mathbf{C})$ produced by Gen is statistically close to uniformly random, so CIH is public coin.

Remark 2. In Construction 2, the circuit "size" means the length of a bit string required to describe a member of the particular circuit family $\mathcal{C} = \{\mathcal{C}_\lambda\}$ for which we seek correlation intractability. In more detail, we assume that every circuit $C \in \mathcal{C}_\lambda$ can be efficiently described by a $S(\lambda)$-bit string s_C, and that there is a (uniformly generated) depth-universal circuit family $U = \{U_\lambda\}$ for $\mathcal{C}$ for which $U_\lambda(s_C, x) = C(x)$ for every $C \in \mathcal{C}_\lambda$ and input x. For certain circuit families there may be more compact ways of specifying a member of the family than the general circuit representation; this can yield more compact hash keys.

3.2   Correlation Intractability

We now prove that Construction 2 is *computationally* correlation intractable under an appropriate SIS assumption (Theorem 1), and *statistically* correlation intractable under an appropriate LWE assumption (Theorem 2).

Theorem 1. *Assuming the hardness of $SIS_{n,m+1,q,\beta}$ for a sufficiently large $\beta = m^{O(d)}$, Construction 2 is correlation intractable for the class of functions with output length m that can be implemented by size-S, depth-d boolean circuits.*

Proof. Let $\mathcal{A} = \{\mathcal{A}_\lambda\}$ be any non-uniform polynomial-size adversary, and fix any sequence of functions $\{f_\lambda\}$, where f_λ has output length $m = m(\lambda)$ and can be implemented by a circuit of size $S = S(\lambda)$ and depth $d = d(\lambda)$. To show that Construction 2 is correlation intractable with respect to f, we first define a hybrid experiment and show that it is statistically indistinguishable from the real experiment. Then we show that in this hybrid, it is hard for an adversary to break correlation intractability against $\{f_\lambda\}$.

In the hybrid experiment we merely modify how $\mathbf{C}$ is generated, letting it be $\mathbf{C} \leftarrow \mathsf{Com}(\mathbf{A}, f)$ for $f = f_\lambda$. By Item 1 of Proposition 1, this experiment is within statistical distance $\mathrm{negl}(m) = \mathrm{negl}(\lambda)$ from the real one, so $\mathcal{A}$'s success probability can differ by at most this much between the real and hybrid experiments.

We now show that under the hardness hypothesis, $\nu(\lambda) := \Pr_k[x = \mathcal{A}_\lambda(k) : \mathsf{Hash}(k, x) = f(x)]$ is a negligible function that depends only on $\mathcal{A}$ (not $\{f_\lambda\}$). To do this we use $\mathcal{A}$ to construct a non-uniform polynomial-size attacker $\mathcal{S} = \{\mathcal{S}_\lambda\}$ against SIS that also has success probability $\nu(\lambda)$, as follows.

The attacker $\mathcal{S}_\lambda$, given an SIS instance $\mathbf{A}' = [\mathbf{a} \mid \mathbf{A}] \in \mathbb{Z}_q^{n \times (m+1)}$, generates $\mathbf{C} \leftarrow \mathsf{Com}(\mathbf{A}, f)$ and retains the commitment randomness $\mathbf{R} \in \{0,1\}^{w \times Sm}$. It defines a hash key $k = (\mathbf{a}, \mathbf{C})$ and lets $x = \mathcal{A}_\lambda(k)$. If $\mathsf{Hash}(k, x) = f(x)$, then $\mathcal{S}$ lets $(\mathbf{C}_x, \mathbf{R}_x) = \mathsf{CircuitEval}(U_x, \mathbf{C}, \mathbf{R})$ and then lets $\mathbf{r}_x$ be the additional output of $\mathsf{InertEval}(\mathbf{G}_n, \mathbf{C}_x, \mathbf{R}_x)$. It outputs $\mathbf{z}_x = (1, \mathbf{r}_x) \in \mathbb{Z}^{m+1}$ as the nonzero SIS solution.

We now analyze $\mathcal{S}$. First observe that the distribution of the hash key k it provides to $\mathcal{A}_\lambda$ is exactly as in the hybrid experiment, by the uniform distribution of the SIS instance $\mathbf{A}' = [\mathbf{a} \mid \mathbf{A}]$. We claim that $\mathbf{z}_x = (1, \mathbf{r}_x)$ is a valid SIS solution whenever $\mathsf{Hash}(k, x) = f(x)$. To see this, observe that this condition implies that

$$\begin{aligned}
\mathbf{G}_n \cdot f(x) &= \mathbf{G}_n \cdot \mathsf{Hash}(k, x) \\
&= \mathbf{a} + \mathsf{InertEval}(\mathbf{G}_n, \mathsf{CircuitEval}(U_x, \mathbf{C})) \\
&= \mathbf{a} + (\mathbf{A}\mathbf{r}_x + \mathbf{G}_n \cdot f(x)) \\
&= \mathbf{A}'\mathbf{z}_x + \mathbf{G}_n \cdot f(x)
\end{aligned}$$

and that $\|\mathbf{z}_x\| = m^{O(d)} \leq \beta$, both by Eqs. (9) and (11) of Proposition 1. Therefore, $\mathbf{A}'\mathbf{z}_x = 0$ and $\mathbf{z}_x$ satisfies the norm bound, as desired.

Theorem 2. *Assuming the hardness of $LWE_{n-1,m+1,q,\chi}$ for a $\mathrm{poly}(n)$-bounded χ and a sufficiently large $q = m^{O(d)}$, Construction 2 is somewhere statistically correlation intractable for the class of functions with output length m that can be implemented by size-S, depth-d boolean circuits; each circuit serves as the intractability guarantee for itself.*

Proof. First, it follows immediately from the LWE assumption that the outputs of $\mathsf{Gen}(1^\lambda)$ and $\mathsf{Gen}(1^\lambda, C_\lambda)$ are computationally indistinguishable for any sequence of circuits C_λ of size S.

Now fix any sequence of functions $\{f_\lambda\}$, where f_λ has output length $m = m(\lambda)$ and can be implemented by a circuit of size $S = S(\lambda)$ and depth $d = d(\lambda)$. We will show that

$$\Pr_{k \leftarrow \mathsf{StatGen}(1^\lambda, f_\lambda)} [\exists x \text{ s.t. } \mathsf{Hash}(k, x) = f(x)] = 0. \tag{13}$$

Using the notation from $\mathsf{StatGen}$, let $\mathbf{A}' = [\mathbf{a} \mid \mathbf{A}] \in \mathbb{Z}_q^{n \times (m+1)}$ and let $\bar{\mathbf{A}}' = [\bar{\mathbf{a}} \mid \bar{\mathbf{A}}] \in \mathbb{Z}_q^{(n-1) \times (m+1)}$ be its top $(n-1)$ rows. Similarly, let $\mathbf{e}' = [\mathbf{e} \mid e] \in \mathbb{Z}^{m+1}$. For any hash input x, define $\mathbf{r}_x$ and $\mathbf{z}_x = (1, \mathbf{r}_x) \in \mathbb{Z}^{m+1}$ exactly as in the proof of Theorem 1 above. Now, notice that if $\mathsf{Hash}(k, x) = f(x)$ then as above we have

$$\mathbf{G}_n \cdot f(x) = \mathbf{A}' \mathbf{z}_x + \mathbf{G}_n \cdot f(x).$$

This implies that

$$\begin{bmatrix} \bar{\mathbf{A}}' \cdot \mathbf{z}_x \\ \mathbf{s}^t \cdot \bar{\mathbf{A}}' \cdot \mathbf{z}_x + \mathbf{e}'^t \cdot \mathbf{z}_x \end{bmatrix} = \begin{bmatrix} \mathbf{0} \\ \lfloor q/2 \rfloor \end{bmatrix} \tag{14}$$

and hence $\langle \mathbf{e}', \mathbf{z}_x \rangle = \lfloor q/2 \rfloor$. But this is impossible because $|\langle \mathbf{e}', \mathbf{z}_x \rangle| \leq \|\mathbf{e}'\| \cdot \|\mathbf{z}_x\| = n^{O(1)} \cdot m^{O(d)} = m^{O(d)}$, which is smaller than $q/2$ for a sufficiently large choice of $q = m^{O(d)}$.

3.3 Construction for Branching Programs

We now describe a correlation-intractable hash family for *branching programs* of arbitrary length $D(\lambda) = \mathrm{poly}(\lambda)$. By Barrington's Theorem [5] this is sufficient for evaluating *log-depth* (i.e., NC^1) circuits, and in particular the decryption functions of known FHE schemes. (It is also possible to express the decryption functions more efficiently, directly using branching programs [3].)

The construction is almost identical to Construction 2, except that it uses a universal branching program (in place of the universal circuit U) and $\mathsf{BranchEval}$ (in place of $\mathsf{CircuitEval}$). The proof of security is also essentially identical to those above, but due to Eq. (10) of Proposition 1, the derived randomness for the ultimate inert commitment grows only polynomially, as $m^{O(1)} \cdot D$. This yields the following two security theorems.

Theorem 3. *Assuming the hardness of $SIS_{n,m+1,q,\beta}$ for a sufficiently large $\beta = m^{O(1)} \cdot D$, the above-described construction is correlation intractable for the class of functions with output length m that can be implemented by length-D branching programs.*

Theorem 4. *Assuming the hardness of $LWE_{n-1,m,q,\chi}$ for a $\mathrm{poly}(n)$-bounded χ and a sufficiently large $q = m^{O(1)} \cdot D$, the above-described construction is somewhere statistically correlation intractable for the class of functions with output length m that can be implemented by length-D branching programs; each branching program serves as the intractability guarantee of itself.*

3.4 Parameter Instantiations

Here we show how the parameters n, q (with $\ell := \lceil \log q \rceil$ and $m := n\ell$) can be chosen, with a focus on the SIS problem and the branching program instantiation; a very similar process can be followed for LWE and/or circuits. For a branching program of length $D = \lambda^d$ and desired output size of (at most) $L = \lambda^c$ for some constants $c, d > 0$, let $\beta = m^{c_1} \cdot D$ for the (small) constant $c_1 > 0$ be the norm bound given by Theorem 3. To invoke worst-case hardness theorems, we can take some $q = \beta \cdot \tilde{O}(\sqrt{n})$ and $n = \lfloor L/\ell \rfloor$, so that the true output size $m = n\ell \le L$.

With these choices, we have $q = \mathrm{poly}(\lambda)$, $n = L/\Theta(\log \lambda) = \lambda^{c-o(1)}$, and $D = n^{d/c+o(1)}$. This corresponds to a worst-case approximation factor

$$\gamma(n) = \beta \cdot \tilde{O}(\sqrt{n}) = n^{c_1+d/c+1/2+o(1)} = \mathrm{poly}(n) \tag{15}$$

for the underlying n-dimensional lattice problem.

Two noteworthy extremes are as follows. We can obtain a very short hash output length of λ^c for arbitrarily small $c > 0$, where security is supported by (large) $\mathrm{poly}(n)$-approximate lattice problems in $n = \lambda^{c-o(1)}$ dimensions, which are plausibly subexponentially hard. On the other extreme, in our NIZK application using the bootstrapping transform, the value of d is fixed by the FHE scheme and we may choose $L = \lambda^c$ freely. So, by taking a large enough constant c, security is supported by (small) $n^{c_1+1/2+\epsilon}$ approximation factors for any desired constant $\epsilon > 0$.

4 Bootstrapping Correlation Intractability

In this section we present our bootstrapping theorem for correlation-intractable hash functions.

Construction 3. Let $\mathcal{C} = \{\mathcal{C}_\lambda\}$ be a circuit class and $U_\lambda(C, x) = C(x)$ denote a universal circuit for $\mathcal{C}_\lambda$. Let $\mathsf{FHE} = (\mathsf{Gen}, \mathsf{Enc}, \mathsf{Dec}, \mathsf{Eval})$ be a (symmetric-key) encryption scheme supporting homomorphic computation of the class $\{U_x(\cdot) = U_\lambda(\cdot, x)\}_\lambda$. Let $\mathsf{CIH} = (\mathsf{Gen}, \mathsf{Hash})$ be a hash function family with fake-key generation algorithm $\mathsf{StatGen}$. Define a new hash family $\mathsf{CIH}' = (\mathsf{Gen}', \mathsf{Hash}')$ with fake-key generation algorithm $\mathsf{StatGen}'$ as follows:

- $\mathsf{Gen}'(1^\lambda)$: generate $k \leftarrow \mathsf{CIH}.\mathsf{Gen}(1^\lambda)$ and $(sk, ek) \leftarrow \mathsf{FHE}.\mathsf{Gen}(1^\lambda)$. Generate $c \leftarrow \mathsf{Enc}(pk, D)$ for some arbitrary "dummy" circuit $D \in \mathcal{C}_\lambda$, and output hash key $k' = (k, ek, c)$.
- $\mathsf{StatGen}'(1^\lambda, C \in \mathcal{C}_\lambda)$: generate $(sk, ek) \leftarrow \mathsf{FHE}.\mathsf{Gen}(1^\lambda)$ and $k \leftarrow \mathsf{StatGen}(1^\lambda, \mathsf{FHE}.\mathsf{Dec}(sk, \cdot))$. Generate $c \leftarrow \mathsf{Enc}(pk, C)$ and output hash key $k' = (k, ek, c)$.
- $\mathsf{Hash}'(k' = (k, ek, c), x)$: output $\mathsf{Hash}(k, \mathsf{Eval}(ek, U_x, c))$.

Remark 3. Observe that if the original CIH family has (pseudo)random hash keys, and FHE has jointly pseudorandom evaluation keys and ciphertexts, then CIH' has pseudorandom hash keys as well.

Let $\mathcal{R} = \{\mathcal{R}_\lambda = \{R_\lambda\}\}$ be a class of relations. For each $R_\lambda \in \mathcal{R}_\lambda$, each secret key sk that may be output by FHE.Gen(1^λ), and each circuit $C \in \mathcal{C}_\lambda$, define the associated relations

$$R_{\lambda,sk} = \{(c,y) : (\text{FHE.Dec}(sk, c), y) \in R_\lambda\}$$
$$R_{\lambda,C} = \{(x,y) : (C(x), y) \in R_\lambda\}.$$

Essentially, these relations first apply some computation (either decryption with a certain fixed secret key, or some circuit C) to the input, then check whether the provided witness is valid (under the original relation) for the result. They naturally yield the associated relation classes $\mathcal{R}^{\text{Dec}} := \{\mathcal{R}^{\text{Dec}}_\lambda = \{R_{\lambda,sk} : R_\lambda \in \mathcal{R}_\lambda\}\}$ and $\mathcal{R}^{\mathcal{C}} := \{\mathcal{R}^{\mathcal{C}}_\lambda = \{R_{\lambda,C} : R_\lambda \in \mathcal{R}_\lambda, C \in \mathcal{C}_\lambda\}\}$.

Remark 4. Similar to Remark 2, the size of the CIH$'$ hash key is affected by the choice of FHE and the description size of members of the circuit family $\{\mathcal{C}_\lambda\}$. To analyze the size of the hash key $k' = (k, ek, c)$, first notice that as shown below in Theorem 5, the underlying hash function CIH need only be CI for a circuit class whose members can be described by FHE secret keys. With a (leveled or unbounded) FHE, secret keys have a fixed poly(λ) length, regardless of the supported family $\mathcal{C}$. But depending on the FHE scheme, the size of the evaluation key ek and the ciphertext c can have various dependencies on the circuit family $\mathcal{C}$. Specifically, with an unbounded FHE, the size of ek is a fixed polynomial in λ independent of the circuit family, and the size of c is a fixed polynomial in λ and the description size of members of $\mathcal{C}$. In a leveled FHE, the sizes of ek and c may additionally depend (polynomially) on the depth of the supported circuit class.

Theorem 5. *If* FHE *is CPA-secure (for the sequence of message spaces $\{\mathcal{C}_\lambda\}$) and* CIH *is correlation intractable for the relation class* $\mathcal{R}^{\text{Dec}}$, *then* CIH$'$ *is correlation intractable for the relation class* $\mathcal{R}^{\mathcal{C}}$.

Proof. Let $\mathcal{A}' = \{\mathcal{A}'_\lambda\}$ be a non-uniform polynomial-size adversary against the correlation intractability of CIH$'$ for $\mathcal{R}^{\mathcal{C}}$, and fix any sequence of relations $\{R_{\lambda,C_\lambda}\}$ for some choice of $C_\lambda \in \mathcal{C}_\lambda$ for each λ.

We first define a hybrid experiment and show that it is computationally indistinguishable from the real experiment. In the hybrid experiment we modify only how the c component of the hash key is generated, letting $c \leftarrow \text{Enc}(pk, C_\lambda)$. By the CPA-security of FHE, the success probability of $\mathcal{A}'$ can differ by only a negligible amount between the real and the hybrid experiments. (The reduction showing this is straightforward, because sk is not used in the experiment.)

Our goal is prove that in the hybrid experiment,

$$\nu(\lambda) := \Pr_{k'}[x \leftarrow \mathcal{A}'(k') : (x, \text{Hash}'(k', x)) \in R_{\lambda,C_\lambda}]$$

is a negligible function that depends only on $\mathcal{A}'$ (and not R_{λ,C_λ}). First, observe that by construction of CIH$'$,

$$\Pr\left[\begin{array}{c} k \leftarrow \mathsf{CIH.Gen}(1^\lambda) \\ (sk, ek) \leftarrow \mathsf{FHE.Gen}(1^\lambda) \\ c \leftarrow \mathsf{Enc}(ek, C_\lambda) \\ x - \mathcal{A}'_\lambda(k' = (k, ek, c)) \\ c_x = \mathsf{Eval}(ek, U_x, c) \end{array} \middle| (C_\lambda(x), \mathsf{Hash}(k, c_x)) \in R_{\lambda,C_\lambda} \right] = \nu(\lambda). \quad (16)$$

By an averaging argument, there exists (sk_λ, ek_λ) in the support of $\mathsf{FHE.Gen}(1^\lambda)$ such that

$$\Pr\left[\begin{array}{c} k \leftarrow \mathsf{CIH.Gen}(1^\lambda) \\ c \leftarrow \mathsf{Enc}(ek_\lambda, C_\lambda) \\ x = \mathcal{A}'_\lambda(k' = (k, ek_\lambda, c)) \\ c_x = \mathsf{Eval}(ek_\lambda, U_x, c) \end{array} \middle| (C_\lambda(x), \mathsf{Hash}(k, c_x)) \in R_{\lambda,C_\lambda} \right] \geq \nu(\lambda). \quad (17)$$

We use $\mathcal{A}'$ to construct a non-uniform polynomial-size attacker $\mathcal{A} = \{\mathcal{A}_\lambda\}$ against the correlation intractability of CIH for $\mathcal{R}^{\mathsf{Dec}}$, and specifically the sequence of relations $\{R_{\lambda,sk_\lambda}\}$. Given a CIH key k, $\mathcal{A}_\lambda$ generates $c \leftarrow \mathsf{Enc}(ek_\lambda, C_\lambda)$, lets $x = \mathcal{A}'_\lambda(k' = (k, ek_\lambda, c))$, and outputs $c_x = \mathsf{Eval}(ek_\lambda, U_x, c)$.

We now prove that $\mathcal{A}_\lambda$ succeeds with probability at least $\nu(\lambda)$, hence $\nu(\lambda)$ is a negligible function (that does not depend on the choice of relations). First, notice that the distribution of k' that $\mathcal{A}_\lambda$ passes to $\mathcal{A}'_\lambda$ is exactly as in Eq. (17). Next, observe that by the correctness of FHE, we have $\mathsf{Dec}(sk_\lambda, c_x) = C_\lambda(x)$. Therefore, whenever $(C_\lambda(x), \mathsf{Hash}(k, c_x)) \in R_{\lambda,C_\lambda}$ we have $(x, \mathsf{Hash}(k, c_x)) \in R_\lambda$ and hence $(c_x, \mathsf{Hash}(k, c_x)) \in R_{\lambda,sk_\lambda}$, as needed.

Theorem 6. *If FHE is CPA-secure (for the sequence of message spaces $\{\mathcal{C}_\lambda\}$) and CIH is somewhere statistical correlation intractable for the relation class $\mathcal{R}^{\mathsf{Dec}}$, where for each $R_{\lambda,sk}$ the intractability guarantee is the description of the circuit $\mathsf{FHE.Dec}(sk, \cdot)$, then CIH$'$ is somewhere statistical correlation intractable for the relation class $\mathcal{R}^C$, and for each $R_{\lambda,C}$ the intractability guarantee is the circuit C.*

Proof. First we have to argue that the outputs of $\mathsf{Gen}'(1^\lambda)$ and $\mathsf{StatGen}'(1^\lambda, C_\lambda)$ are computationally indistinguishable for any $C_\lambda \in \mathcal{C}_\lambda$. This follows immediately from the CPA-security of FHE and the fact that CIH is somewhere statistically correlation intractable with fake-key generation StatGen.

Now fix any sequence of relations $\{R_{\lambda,C_\lambda}\}$ for some choice of $C_\lambda \in \mathcal{C}_\lambda$ for each λ. We need to show that

$$\nu(\lambda) := \Pr_{k' \leftarrow \mathsf{StatGen}'(1^\lambda, C_\lambda)}[\exists x \text{ s.t. } (x, \mathsf{Hash}'(k', x)) \in R_{\lambda,C_\lambda}]$$

is a negligible function (that does not depend on R_{λ,C_λ}). First, observe that by construction of CIH$'$,

$$\Pr\left[\begin{array}{c} (sk, ek) \leftarrow \mathsf{FHE.Gen}(1^\lambda) \\ k \leftarrow \mathsf{StatGen}(1^\lambda, \mathsf{FHE.Dec}(sk, \cdot)) \\ c \leftarrow \mathsf{Enc}(ek, C_\lambda) \end{array} \middle| \begin{array}{c} \exists x \text{ s.t.} \\ (C_\lambda(x), \mathsf{Hash}(k, c_x)) \in R_{\lambda, C_\lambda} \text{ where} \\ c_x = \mathsf{Eval}(ek, U_x, c) \end{array}\right] = \nu(\lambda). \quad (18)$$

By an averaging argument, there exists (sk_λ, ek_λ) in the support of $\mathsf{FHE.Gen}(1^\lambda)$ such that

$$\Pr\left[\begin{array}{c} k \leftarrow \mathsf{StatGen}(1^\lambda, \mathsf{FHE.Dec}(sk_\lambda, \cdot)) \\ c \leftarrow \mathsf{Enc}(ek_\lambda, C_\lambda) \end{array} \middle| \begin{array}{c} \exists x \text{ s.t.} \\ (C_\lambda(x), \mathsf{Hash}(k, c_x)) \in R_{\lambda, C_\lambda} \text{ where} \\ c_x = \mathsf{Eval}(ek_\lambda, U_x, c) \end{array}\right] \geq \nu(\lambda). \quad (19)$$

Next, observe that by the correctness of FHE, we have $\mathsf{Dec}(sk_\lambda, c_x) = C_\lambda(x)$. Therefore, whenever $(C_\lambda(x), \mathsf{Hash}(k, c_x)) \in R_{\lambda, C_\lambda}$ we have $(x, \mathsf{Hash}(k, c_x)) \in R_\lambda$ and hence $(c_x, \mathsf{Hash}(k, c_x)) \in R_{\lambda, sk_\lambda}$. So, Eq. (19) implies that

$$\Pr_{k \leftarrow \mathsf{StatGen}(1^\lambda, \mathsf{Dec}(sk_\lambda, \cdot))}[\exists c_x \text{ s.t. } (c_x, \mathsf{Hash}(k, c_x)) \in R_{\lambda, C_\lambda}] \geq \nu(\lambda). \quad (20)$$

The theorem follows by the somewhere statistical correlation intractability of CIH.

5   Putting It All Together

In this section we assemble the components from the previous sections and prior works to obtain correlation-intractable hash families for all bounded circuits, and our main result of noninteractive zero knowledge for all of NP. (Throughout this section, for simplicity we assume the standard LWE error distribution χ, i.e., a discrete Gaussian of parameter $r = 2\sqrt{n}$ for LWE dimension n.)

5.1   Correlation-Intractable Hashing for All Circuits

In this subsection let $L = L(\lambda)$, $S = S(\lambda)$, and $d = d(\lambda)$ be arbitrary $\mathrm{poly}(\lambda)$-bounded functions, and define the relation class $\mathcal{R}_{L,S,d} = \{\mathcal{R}_{\lambda,L,S,d}\}$, where $\mathcal{R}_{\lambda,L,S,d} = \{R_f = \{(x, f(x))\}\}$ is the set of all efficiently searchable relations whose search functions f can be computed by a circuit with output length $L(\lambda)$, size $S(\lambda)$, and depth $d(\lambda)$.

Let FHE be a leveled fully homomorphic encryption scheme instantiated to support circuits of depth at most $d = d(\lambda)$, with decryption circuit having size $S_{\mathsf{Dec}}(\lambda)$ and logarithmic depth $d_{\mathsf{Dec}}(\lambda) = O(\log \lambda)$. Let CIH denote Construction 2 for circuit size $S = L \cdot S_{\mathsf{Dec}}(\lambda)$ (allowing for the decryption of L ciphertexts) and depth $d = d_{\mathsf{Dec}}(\lambda)$, and with FHC parameters n, q satisfying $L \geq n\lceil \lg q \rceil$.

Theorem 7. *Assuming the hardness of $SIS_{n,q,\beta}$ for a suitable $\beta = \mathrm{poly}(S)$ (respectively $LWE_{n-1,q,\chi}$ for a $\mathrm{poly}(n)$-bounded χ and a suitable $q = \mathrm{poly}(S)$)*

and the CPA-security of FHE, *Construction 3 instantiated with* FHE *and* CIH *is correlation intractable with respect to* $\mathcal{R}_{L,S,d}$ *(respectively, somewhere statistically correlation intractable with respect to* $\mathcal{R}_{L,S,d}$, *where for each* $R_f \in \mathcal{R}_{L,S,d}$ *the intractability guarantee is* f).

Proof. Let $\mathcal{I} = \{I_\lambda = \{(x, x) : x \in \{0, 1\}^{L(\lambda)}\}\}$ be the class of equality relations. Because FHE.Dec has circuit depth $d_{\mathsf{Dec}} = O(\log \lambda)$, by Theorem 3 CIH is correlation intractable (respectively, somewhere statistically correlation intractable) for the relation class $\mathcal{I}^{\mathsf{Dec}}$ (as defined in Sect. 4). The theorem follows by noticing that $\mathcal{R}_{L,S,d} = \mathcal{I}^{\mathcal{C}}$ where $\mathcal{C}$ is the class of circuits used to define $\mathcal{R}_{L,S,d}$, and applying Theorem 5.

Using any known leveled FHE scheme based on LWE with polynomial factors that has jointly pseudorandom evaluation keys and ciphertexts (e.g., [13]), we get the following corollary.

Corollary 1. *Assuming the hardness of LWE with suitable polynomial factors, there exists a somewhere statistically correlation-intractable hash family (with pseudorandom hash keys) for* $\mathcal{R}_{L,S,d}$, *where for each* $R_f \in \mathcal{R}_{L,S,d}$ *the intractability guarantee is* f.

5.2   Noninteractive Zero Knowledge for NP

We are now ready to instantiate the noninteractive zero-knowledge protocol from [15] with our correlation-intractable hash functions. We first recall the following theorem; see Definition 2 for a reminder of the NIZK modifiers.

Theorem 8 ([15]). *Assuming the existence of*

- *a lossy public-key encryption scheme with uniformly random lossy public keys (respectively, an ordinary CPA-secure public-key encryption scheme), and*
- *a hash family with (pseudo)random keys which is CI for all circuits of output length* $L(\lambda) \geq \lambda^c$ *for some constant* $c > 0$ *and size bounded by some sufficiently large* $S(\lambda) = \mathrm{poly}(\lambda)$ *(respectively, a hash family that is somewhere statistically correlation intractable for all such circuits, where the intractability guarantee for each circuit is itself),*

there exists a computationally sound, statistically zero-knowledge noninteractive argument system with common random string for any NP language (respectively, a statistically sound, adaptively computational zero-knowledge noninteractive proof system with common reference string).

A lossy encryption scheme satisfying the requirements of Theorem 8 can be constructed based on LWE with polynomial factors (see, e.g., [40,42]). So, by Corollary 1 we get our main result:

Theorem 9. *Assuming the hardness of LWE with suitable polynomial factors, for any NP language there exists*

- a computationally sound, statistically zero-knowledge noninteractive argument system having a common random string, and
- a statistically sound, adaptively computational zero-knowledge noninteractive proof system having a common reference string.

Remark 5. We remark that intractability bootstrapping and leveled FHE are not actually necessary for the NIZK construction, because we just need a hash family that is correlation intractable for the class of "bad challenge" functions of the underlying graph-Hamiltonicity protocol of [20]. As pointed out by Alex Lombardi, a trick from [15] allows the bad-challenge functions to be implemented in NC^1 (i.e., logarithmic depth), so we can obtain the required correlation intractability merely from SIS with small polynomial factors. (However, we still use LWE for the lossy encryption ingredient.)

In short, the bad-challenge function decrypts the prover's ciphertexts to recover a graph, then checks whether the graph is a cycle. Decryption of LWE-based lossy encryption in NC^1 is standard. To implement the cycle check, we additionally require the prover to (de)commit to a permutation between its committed graph and a canonical cycle graph. The bad-challenge function (and verifier) performs the appropriate checks, which can be done in logarithmic depth by brute force. (Without the explicit permutation, the best known parallel complexity for cycle checking is NC^2, which is not good enough for the present purpose.)

Remark 6. When using a CI hash family arising from our bootstrapping transform of Construction 3, either NIZK system of Theorem 9 can have a *compact* common random/reference string, i.e., a string whose length does not depend on the size of the statement being proved. In fact, the CRS generation algorithm does not need to get the size (or any other parameter) of the statement as an input.

To see this, we first observe that for any statement length, the "bad challenge" circuits making up the family C for which Theorem 8 needs correlation intractability can be represented by strings of a *fixed* poly(λ) length. Specifically, these circuits can be fully specified by the secret key of the (lossy) public-key encryption scheme used in Theorem 8. We next observe that the universal circuit $U(\cdot, \cdot)$ for this representation (and a given statement length) is uniformly generated and has a fixed logarithmic depth in its input length. Therefore, it suffices to instantiate the FHE in Construction 3 using any leveled FHE scheme (e.g., [11,25]) for some arbitrary $\ell = \omega(\log(\lambda))$ levels. Then, by Remark 4 the hash key and hence the CRS is completely independent of the statement size.

For comparison, we also point out that there is a generic transformation from [24] which converts any NIZK to one with a compact CRS. However, this transformation does not preserve statistical zero knowledge, i.e., the resulting NIZK system is always computational zero knowledge. On the other hand, our construction has a compact CRS and is also statistical zero knowledge.

Acknowledgments. We thank Alex Lombardi and Daniel Wichs for useful comments.

References

1. Ajtai, M.: Generating hard instances of lattice problems. Quaderni di Matematica **13**, 1–32 (2004). Preliminary version in STOC 1996
2. Alamati, N., Peikert, C., Stephens-Davidowitz, N.: New (and old) proof systems for lattice problems. In: Abdalla, M., Dahab, R. (eds.) PKC 2018. LNCS, vol. 10770, pp. 619–643. Springer, Cham (2018). https://doi.org/10.1007/978-3-319-76581-5_21
3. Alperin-Sheriff, J., Peikert, C.: Faster bootstrapping with polynomial error. In: Garay, J.A., Gennaro, R. (eds.) CRYPTO 2014. LNCS, vol. 8616, pp. 297–314. Springer, Heidelberg (2014). https://doi.org/10.1007/978-3-662-44371-2_17
4. Applebaum, B., Cash, D., Peikert, C., Sahai, A.: Fast cryptographic primitives and circular-secure encryption based on hard learning problems. In: Halevi, S. (ed.) CRYPTO 2009. LNCS, vol. 5677, pp. 595–618. Springer, Heidelberg (2009). https://doi.org/10.1007/978-3-642-03356-8_35
5. Barrington, D.A.M.: Bounded-width polynomial-size branching programs recognize exactly those languages in NC^1. J. Comput. Syst. Sci. **38**(1), 150–164 (1989). Preliminary version in STOC 1986
6. Bellare, M., Goldwasser, S.: New paradigms for digital signatures and message authentication based on non-interactive zero knowledge proofs. In: Brassard, G. (ed.) CRYPTO 1989. LNCS, vol. 435, pp. 194–211. Springer, New York (1990). https://doi.org/10.1007/0-387-34805-0_19
7. Ben-Sasson, E., et al.: Zerocash: decentralized anonymous payments from Bitcoin. In: 2014 IEEE Symposium on Security and Privacy, SP 2014, Berkeley, 18–21 May 2014, pp. 459–474 (2014)
8. Blum, M., De Santis, A., Micali, S., Persiano, G.: Noninteractive zero-knowledge. SIAM J. Comput. **20**(6), 1084–1118 (1991). Preliminary version in STOC 1988
9. Blum, M., Feldman, P., Micali, S.: Non-interactive zero-knowledge and its applications (extended abstract). In: STOC, pp. 103–112 (1988)
10. Boneh, D., et al.: Fully key-homomorphic encryption, arithmetic circuit ABE and compact garbled circuits. In: Nguyen, P.Q., Oswald, E. (eds.) EUROCRYPT 2014. LNCS, vol. 8441, pp. 533–556. Springer, Heidelberg (2014). https://doi.org/10.1007/978-3-642-55220-5_30
11. Brakerski, Z., Gentry, C., Vaikuntanathan, V.: (Leveled) fully homomorphic encryption without bootstrapping. In: ITCS, pp. 309–325 (2012)
12. Brakerski, Z., Langlois, A., Peikert, C., Regev, O., Stehlé, D.: Classical hardness of learning with errors. In: STOC, pp. 575–584 (2013)
13. Brakerski, Z., Vaikuntanathan, V.: Lattice-based FHE as secure as PKE. In: ITCS, pp. 1–12 (2014)
14. Camenisch, J., Chandran, N., Shoup, V.: A public key encryption scheme secure against key dependent chosen plaintext and adaptive chosen ciphertext attacks. In: Joux, A. (ed.) EUROCRYPT 2009. LNCS, vol. 5479, pp. 351–368. Springer, Heidelberg (2009). https://doi.org/10.1007/978-3-642-01001-9_20
15. Canetti, R., et al.: Fiat-Shamir: from practice to theory. In: STOC, pp. 1082–1090 (2019)
16. Canetti, R., Chen, Y., Reyzin, L., Rothblum, R.D.: Fiat-Shamir and correlation intractability from strong KDM-secure encryption. In: Nielsen, J.B., Rijmen, V. (eds.) EUROCRYPT 2018. LNCS, vol. 10820, pp. 91–122. Springer, Cham (2018). https://doi.org/10.1007/978-3-319-78381-9_4

17. Canetti, R., Goldreich, O., Halevi, S.: The random oracle methodology, revisited. J. ACM **51**(4), 557–594 (2004). Preliminary version in STOC 1998
18. Chung, K., Dadush, D., Liu, F., Peikert, C.: On the lattice smoothing parameter problem. In: IEEE Conference on Computational Complexity, pp. 230–241 (2013)
19. Dwork, C., Naor, M.: Zaps and their applications. SIAM J. Comput. **36**(6), 1513–1543 (2007)
20. Feige, U., Lapidot, D., Shamir, A.: Multiple noninteractive zero knowledge proofs under general assumptions. SIAM J. Comput. **29**(1), 1–28 (1999). Preliminary version in FOCS 1990
21. Fiat, A., Shamir, A.: How to prove yourself: practical solutions to identification and signature problems. In: Odlyzko, A.M. (ed.) CRYPTO 1986. LNCS, vol. 263, pp. 186–194. Springer, Heidelberg (1987). https://doi.org/10.1007/3-540-47721-7_12
22. Garg, S., Gentry, C., Halevi, S., Raykova, M., Sahai, A., Waters, B.: Candidate indistinguishability obfuscation and functional encryption for all circuits. In: FOCS, pp. 40–49 (2013)
23. Gentry, C.: A fully homomorphic encryption scheme. Ph.D. thesis, Stanford University (2009). http://crypto.stanford.edu/craig
24. Gentry, C., Groth, J., Ishai, Y., Peikert, C., Sahai, A., Smith, A.D.: Using fully homomorphic hybrid encryption to minimize non-interative zero-knowledge proofs. J. Cryptol. **28**(4), 820–843 (2015)
25. Gentry, C., Sahai, A., Waters, B.: Homomorphic encryption from learning with errors: conceptually-simpler, asymptotically-faster, attribute-based. In: Canetti, R., Garay, J.A. (eds.) CRYPTO 2013. LNCS, vol. 8042, pp. 75–92. Springer, Heidelberg (2013). https://doi.org/10.1007/978-3-642-40041-4_5
26. Goldreich, O., Oren, Y.: Definitions and properties of zero-knowledge proof systems. J. Cryptol. **7**(1), 1–32 (1994)
27. Goldwasser, S., Micali, S., Rackoff, C.: The knowledge complexity of interactive proof systems. SIAM J. Comput. **18**(1), 186–208 (1989). Preliminary version in STOC 1985
28. Gorbunov, S., Vaikuntanathan, V., Wichs, D.: Leveled fully homomorphic signatures from standard lattices. In: STOC, pp. 469–477 (2015)
29. Groth, J., Ostrovsky, R., Sahai, A.: New techniques for noninteractive zero-knowledge. J. ACM **59**(3), 11:1–11:35 (2012). Preliminary version in EUROCRYPT 2006
30. Holmgren, J., Lombardi, A.: Cryptographic hashing from strong one-way functions (or: One-way product functions and their applications). In: FOCS, pp. 850–858 (2018)
31. Kalai, Y.T., Rothblum, G.N., Rothblum, R.D.: From obfuscation to the security of Fiat-Shamir for proofs. In: Katz, J., Shacham, H. (eds.) CRYPTO 2017. LNCS, vol. 10402, pp. 224–251. Springer, Cham (2017). https://doi.org/10.1007/978-3-319-63715-0_8
32. Kim, S., Wu, D.J.: Multi-theorem preprocessing NIZKs from lattices. In: Shacham, H., Boldyreva, A. (eds.) CRYPTO 2018. LNCS, vol. 10992, pp. 733–765. Springer, Cham (2018). https://doi.org/10.1007/978-3-319-96881-0_25
33. Micciancio, D., Peikert, C.: Trapdoors for lattices: simpler, tighter, faster, smaller. In: Pointcheval, D., Johansson, T. (eds.) EUROCRYPT 2012. LNCS, vol. 7237, pp. 700–718. Springer, Heidelberg (2012). https://doi.org/10.1007/978-3-642-29011-4_41
34. Micciancio, D., Regev, O.: Worst-case to average-case reductions based on Gaussian measures. SIAM J. Comput. **37**(1), 267–302 (2007). Preliminary version in FOCS 2004

35. Micciancio, D., Vadhan, S.P.: Statistical zero-knowledge proofs with efficient provers: lattice problems and more. In: Boneh, D. (ed.) CRYPTO 2003. LNCS, vol. 2729, pp. 282–298. Springer, Heidelberg (2003). https://doi.org/10.1007/978-3-540-45146-4_17

36. Naor, M., Yung, M.: Public-key cryptosystems provably secure against chosen ciphertext attacks. In: STOC, pp. 427–437 (1990)

37. Peikert, C.: Public-key cryptosystems from the worst-case shortest vector problem. In: STOC, pp. 333–342 (2009)

38. Peikert, C., Regev, O., Stephens-Davidowitz, N.: Pseudorandomness of Ring-LWE for any ring and modulus. In: STOC, pp. 461–473 (2017)

39. Peikert, C., Vaikuntanathan, V.: Noninteractive statistical zero-knowledge proofs for lattice problems. In: Wagner, D. (ed.) CRYPTO 2008. LNCS, vol. 5157, pp. 536–553. Springer, Heidelberg (2008). https://doi.org/10.1007/978-3-540-85174-5_30

40. Peikert, C., Vaikuntanathan, V., Waters, B.: A framework for efficient and composable oblivious transfer. In: Wagner, D. (ed.) CRYPTO 2008. LNCS, vol. 5157, pp. 554–571. Springer, Heidelberg (2008). https://doi.org/10.1007/978-3-540-85174-5_31

41. Peikert, C., Waters, B.: Lossy trapdoor functions and their applications. SIAM J. Comput. 40(6), 1803–1844 (2011). Preliminary version in STOC 2008

42. Regev, O.: On lattices, learning with errors, random linear codes, and cryptography. J. ACM 56(6), 1–40 (2009). Preliminary version in STOC 2005

43. Sahai, A., Waters, B.: How to use indistinguishability obfuscation: deniable encryption, and more. In: STOC, pp. 475–484 (2014)

Lattice-Based Zero-Knowledge Proofs: New Techniques for Shorter and Faster Constructions and Applications

Muhammed F. Esgin[1,2]([✉]), Ron Steinfeld[1]([✉]), Joseph K. Liu[1], and Dongxi Liu[2]

[1] Faculty of Information Technology, Monash University, Clayton, Australia
{Muhammed.Esgin,Ron.Steinfeld,Joseph.Liu}@monash.edu
[2] Data61, CSIRO, Marsfield, Australia
Dongxi.Liu@data61.csiro.au

Abstract. We devise new techniques for design and analysis of efficient lattice-based zero-knowledge proofs (ZKP). First, we introduce *one-shot* proof techniques for non-linear polynomial relations of degree $k \geq 2$, where the protocol achieves a negligible soundness error in a single execution, and thus performs significantly better in both computation and communication compared to prior protocols requiring multiple repetitions. Such proofs with degree $k \geq 2$ have been crucial ingredients for important privacy-preserving protocols in the discrete logarithm setting, such as Bulletproofs (IEEE S&P '18) and arithmetic circuit arguments (EUROCRYPT '16). In contrast, one-shot proofs in lattice-based cryptography have previously only been shown for the linear case ($k = 1$) and a very specific quadratic case ($k = 2$), which are obtained as a special case of our technique.

Moreover, we introduce two speedup techniques for lattice-based ZKPs: a CRT-packing technique supporting "inter-slot" operations, and "NTT-friendly" tools that permit the use of fully-splitting rings. The former technique comes at almost no cost to the proof length, and the latter one barely increases it, which can be compensated for by tweaking the rejection sampling parameters while still having faster computation overall.

To illustrate the utility of our techniques, we show how to use them to build efficient relaxed proofs for important relations, namely proof of commitment to bits, one-out-of-many proof, range proof and set membership proof. Despite their relaxed nature, we further show how our proof systems can be used as building blocks for advanced cryptographic tools such as ring signatures.

Our ring signature achieves a dramatic improvement in length over all the existing proposals from lattices at the same security level. The computational evaluation also shows that our construction is highly likely to outperform all the relevant works in running times. Being efficient in both aspects, our ring signature is particularly suitable for both small-scale and large-scale applications such as cryptocurrencies and e-voting systems. No trusted setup is required for any of our proposals.

ⓒ International Association for Cryptologic Research 2019
A. Boldyreva and D. Micciancio (Eds.): CRYPTO 2019, LNCS 11692, pp. 115–146, 2019.
https://doi.org/10.1007/978-3-030-26948-7_5

Keywords: Lattice-based cryptography · Zero-knowledge proof ·
CRT packing · Ring signature · One-out-of-many proof · Range proof ·
Set membership proof

1   Introduction

Zero-knowledge proofs (ZKP) are fundamental building blocks used in many
privacy-preserving applications such as anonymous cryptocurrencies and anonymous credentials [10], and the underlying advanced cryptographic primitives
such as ring signatures [26]. They enable a prover to convince a verifier that
a certain statement regarding a secret is true with minimal secret information
leakage. A core property of ZKPs is *soundness*, that is, a cheating prover should
not be able to create a convincing "proof". In the context of proofs of knowledge
(PoK), this means successful provers know a relevant secret (i.e., a *witness*),
and this is usually proven by using an *extractor* that efficiently recovers the witness given two accepting protocol transcripts with the same initial message. We
call this procedure *"basic" witness extraction* (also known as "2-special soundness", see Definition 3). A natural behaviour that is trivially observed in discrete
logarithm (DL) based ZKPs is that they achieve a convincing soundness level
(i.e., a negligible *soundness error*) in a single protocol run (i.e., they are *one-
shot*). However, this natural behaviour turns out to be unexpectedly hard to
achieve in lattice-based proofs. There are some works [3,6,22–24] that address
this problem in lattice-based cryptography and provide one-shot proofs in the
context of protocols that work with "basic" witness extraction. On the other
hand, recent research in the DL setting [7–9,16] has shown that it is possible
to construct more efficient proofs that *require* a *"complex"* witness extraction
involving more than two accepting protocol transcripts (and thus more than two
challenges) for recovering prover's secret (i.e., the protocols are *many*-special
sound). Such proofs rely on higher degree relations to obtain compact results,
unlike the 2-special sound proofs that can only check linear (first degree) relations (we refer to the aforementioned works for the motivation behind proving
high-degree relations). Again, in the DL setting, these proofs work smoothly and
are easily one-shot. However, in the lattice setting, the situation is much more
complicated, and, to the best of our knowledge, there is no one-shot witness
extraction technique for non-linear relations.

1.1   Related Work – Lattice-Based Zero-Knowledge Proofs

In being one-shot proofs, the most relevant works for our zero-knowledge proofs
are [6] and [3], where the protocols explicitly make use of lattice-based commitments. In fact, the ideas date back to the works by Lyubashevsky [22,23]
introducing the "Fiat-Shamir with Aborts" technique in lattice-based cryptography. The advantage of these works is that the (underlying) protocols achieve
a negligible soundness error in a single run, which makes them very efficient
in practice. However, all these approaches are limited to working with "basic"

witness extraction except for a specific multiplicative (second degree) relation in [6]. The multiplicative argument in [6] is to prove that the coefficient of a quadratic term is zero and no explicit witness extraction from this non-linear relation is provided (and, indeed, no witness extraction from this second degree relation is needed as witnesses are extracted from the linear relations). All these one-shot proofs introduce new complications (more precisely, *relaxations* in the relation being proved) as we discuss in detail in Sect. 3. One can get asymptotically efficient lattice-based proofs for arithmetic circuits when the circuit size is large compared to the security parameter λ using the amortization techniques from [2]. However, these techniques do not seem to be helpful in our case as the proved relations do not necessarily require a large circuit.

Another line of research makes use of *multi-shot* proofs that require multiple protocol repetitions to get a negligible soundness error. Stern-like combinatorial protocols [29] and proofs using binary challenges fall into this category, where one needs at least λ protocol repetitions for λ-bit security. Therefore, even though these approaches have a wide range of applications (e.g. logarithmic-sized group and ring signatures as in [20]), they currently seem to fall far behind practical expectations (see Table 1 for the concrete results of [20]).

In the ring $R = \mathbb{Z}[X]/(X^d + 1)$, it is possible to achieve a soundness error of $1/(2d)$ using the *monomial challenges* from [5]. Here the challenges are of the form X^i for some $0 \leq i < 2d$ (i.e., there are $2d$ possible challenges in total), and it is shown in [5] that doubled inverses of challenge differences are short (more precisely, $\|2(X^i - X^j)^{-1}\| \leq \sqrt{d}$ for $i \neq j$). Still proofs using monomial challenges require at least 10 repetitions for a typical ring dimension $d \leq 2048$. To summarize, for a soundness goal of $2^{-\lambda}$, all the above multi-shot approaches produce proofs of length $\widetilde{O}(\lambda^2)$, as a function of the security parameter λ.

1.2 Asymptotic Costs of Existing Lattice-Based ZKP Techniques

First, let us assume that one relies on computational hardness assumptions, particularly, Module-SIS (M-SIS) and Module-LWE (M-LWE) for the security of a commitment scheme and let $d_{\text{SIS}}, d_{\text{LWE}}$ be the dimension parameters required for M-SIS and M-LWE security, respectively. It is known that one needs $d_{\text{SIS}} = O(\lambda \frac{\log^2 \beta_{\text{SIS}}}{\log q})$ for λ-bit security based on M-SIS where β_{SIS} is the norm of a valid M-SIS solution (see Appendix F.4 in the full version [13] for more). Letting $\beta_{\text{SIS}} = q^\varepsilon$ for $0 < \varepsilon \leq 1$, we get $\log \beta_{\text{SIS}} = \varepsilon \log q$ and, for a balanced security,

$$d_{\text{LWE}} \approx d_{\text{SIS}} = O(\lambda \varepsilon^2 \log q). \tag{1}$$

In lattice-based cryptography, the most commonly used commitment schemes for algebraic proofs are Unbounded-Message Commitment (UMC) and Hashed-Message Commitment (HMC) (see Sect. 2.4). These commitment schemes have different tradeoffs as discussed in the full version. Let n, m, d, v be the module rank for M-SIS, the randomness vector dimension in a commitment, the polynomial ring dimension and the message vector dimension in a commitment, respectively. The commitment vector is of dimension $n + v$ for UMC and n for

HMC, which means the space costs of a commitment are $(n + v)d \log q$ and $nd \log q$ for UMC and HMC, respectively. Letting κ be the number of protocol repetitions, we get the formulae for space costs in Table 2.

The commitment matrix dimensions are $(n+v) \times m$ for UMC and $n \times (m+v)$ for HMC, and both of the commitments are computed as a matrix-vector multiplication.[1] Therefore, we also get the formulae for the time costs as given in Table 2 assuming a degree-d polynomial multiplication can be performed in time $\widetilde{O}(d)$ (more precisely, $O(d \log d)$) using, e.g., FFT-like methods.

Further, we have $d_{\text{LWE}} = (m - n - v)d$ and thus $md > d_{\text{LWE}}$ for UMC, and $d_{\text{SIS}} = nd$ for both HMC and UMC. As a result, using (1), we get

$$md = O(\lambda \varepsilon^2 \log q) \text{ for UMC, and } nd = O(\lambda \varepsilon^2 \log q) \text{ for UMC/HMC.} \quad (2)$$

Now, suppose that we want to prove a relation that involves commitment to $k = O(\log q)$ messages (for example, to prove knowledge of $m_1, \ldots m_k$ such that $\sum_{i=1}^{k} \alpha_i m_i = 0$ for public values $\alpha_1, \ldots, \alpha_k$). Clearly, if we commit to these messages independently, then the overall cost of both time and space increase by a factor of k. Alternatively, we can pack multiple messages in a commitment by setting $v = k$ and hope that this gives a better performance. If an existing multi-shot technique such as Stern-based proofs, or those using binary or monomial challenges, is used, the number of protocol repetitions κ will be $\widetilde{O}(\lambda)$, and thus we get the asymptotic costs in the "multi-shot" column of Table 2 (using (2)). On the other hand, if one can make the proof one-shot, then we get the complexities in the "one-shot" column of Table 2, where there is a clear saving of $\widetilde{O}(\lambda)$.

1.3   Our Contributions

One-shot proof techniques for non-linear polynomial relations via adjugate matrices. We introduce new techniques that provide the first solution to the problem of building efficient *one-shot* lattice-based ZKPs that require a "complex" witness extraction. In particular, we introduce witness extraction from non-linear polynomial relations of degree $k \geq 2$ (i.e., "$(k+1)$-special sound protocols", see Definition 3) while still having a one-shot proof. Our proofs reach a negligible soundness error in a single run of the protocol. In comparison to relevant multi-shot prior works such as [14, 20], we improve the asymptotic computation and communication costs by a factor of $\widetilde{O}(\lambda)$ for the security parameter λ (see Table 2), and also achieve a dramatic practical efficiency improvement in both costs (see Table 1). The previous one-shot ideas [3, 6, 22, 23] are obtained as a special case of our technique (see Sect. 3.2).

Speedup Technique 1: CRT-packing supporting inter-slot operations. Drawing inspiration from the CRT-packing techniques [15, 27] used in fully homomorphic encryption, we introduce the first CRT-packing technique in lattice-based ZKPs that supports "inter-slot" and a *complete* set of operations. That

---

[1] Here, we overlook the fact that some parts of the commitment matrix are zero or identity, but this does not change the asymptotic behaviour in Table 2.

is, our technique supports operations between messages stored in separate CRT "slots", and gives the ability to commit to/encode multiple messages at once and then "extract" all the messages in a way that permits interoperability among extracted values. In its full potential, it provides an asymptotic improvement of $O(\log q)$ in computation costs of proofs involving $O(\log q)$ messages at no additional cost to the proof length (see Table 2).

Table 1. Size comparison of ring signatures for "post-quantum" 128-bit security with N ring participants (the challenge space size is 2^{256}). Signature lengths are in KB. See Appendix A in the full version [13] for more details.

Ring Size (N) :	2	2^3	2^6	2^{12}	2^{21}	Security basis
[20]	23000	52000	94000	179000	306000	SIS
[14]	1000	1200	1600	2400	4100	M-LWE & M-SIS
[12]	236	477	839	1561	2645	LowMC (Sym-key)
[18]	?	?	~ 250	~ 456	?	LowMC (Sym-key)
This Work	**36**	**41**	**58**	**103**	**256**	M-LWE & M-SIS
[30]	> 38	> 124	> 900	61000	$> 2^{24}$	Ring-SIS
[4]	35	83	~ 600	40000	$> 2^{24}$	M-LWE & M-SIS

Speedup Technique 2: "NTT-friendly" tools for fully-splitting rings.
An important obstacle to computational efficiency of lattice-based ZKPs is that one often requires invertibility of short elements in a ring. A common solution to meeting this criterion is to choose a modulus q of a special form (such as $q \equiv 5 \bmod 8$) at the cost of disabling the ring $R_q = \mathbb{Z}_q[X]/(X^d + 1)$ to fully-split, and thus preventing the (full) use of fast computational algorithms such as Number Theoretic Transform (NTT). We introduce a new result (Lemma 7) that can be used as an alternative to enforcing invertibility, and show how it can be made used of while still supporting the use of NTT-like algorithms. The only requirement of our lemma is for the modulus q to be sufficiently large, without putting any assumptions on its "shape". One can see from, e.g., [25, Table 2] that full NTT provides a speedup of a factor between 6–8 in comparison to plain Karatsuba multiplication (with no FFT).

Design of shorter and faster lattice-based protocols. Our techniques enable the construction of communication and computation efficient lattice-based analogues of DL-based protocols for important applications, where there was previously no efficient lattice-based solutions known. To illustrate this utility of our techniques, we design an efficient range proof that uses speedup technique 1, and an efficient one-out-of-many proof that uses speedup technique 2, where our one-shot proof technique is also applied in both of the proofs.

Application to advanced cryptographic tools. Despite their relaxed nature, we show that our ZKPs are sufficient for important practical applications. Our one-out-of-many proof is used as a building block for lattice-based ring signatures, and our relaxed aggregated range proof is shown to be sufficient for an application in a form of privacy-preserving linkable anonymous credentials.

In Table 1, we compare our ring signature size results to the other potential post-quantum proposals.[2] Most of these schemes, including ours, are only analyzed in the classical random oracle model (ROM), and all the results provided in Table 1 are those in ROM. [12,18] are recent proposals from symmetric-key primitives using LowMC cipher [1] and all the rest are lattice-based proposals. As can be seen from the table, we achieve a dramatic improvement in comparison to all these post-quantum solutions. Our scheme even reaches the same performance of the linear-sized proposals (bottom two rows), which are tailored to be efficient for small ring sizes, for the smallest possible ring size $N = 2$.[3]

As detailed in the full version [13], our ring signature achieves a signature length quasi-linear in the security parameter λ, and poly-logarithmic in the ring size N. In practice, its length is proportional to $\lambda \log^2 \lambda \log^c N$ for some constant $c \approx 1.67$. This improves on the quadratic dependence on λ in [12,14,18,20].[4] In terms of the dependence on $\log N$, our scheme grows slightly faster, however, it still outperforms all these works for N as big as billions and beyond.

We further analyze the computational efficiency of our ring signature in Appendix F.5 of the full version [13]. The analysis based on reasonable assumptions shows that our construction also greatly improves practical signing/verification times over the existing ring signature proposals with concrete computational efficiency results. For $N = 1024$, we estimate the signing/verification times of our scheme to be below 30 ms whereas [18] reports 2.8 s for both of the running times. Our ring signature as well as its underlying protocols, namely binary proof and one-out-of-many proof, do not require any assumption on the "shape" of the modulus q, and thus permit the use of NTT-like algorithms.

---

[2] A concurrent work [21] has recently been put on ePrint, and it builds a linear-sized (linkable) ring signature. Even though "a less efficient version that is based on standard lattice problems" (in particular, SIS and Inhomogeneous SIS) is described, there are no concrete parameters provided for that scheme. The provided concrete instantiation, of size $1.3N$ KB for N ring members, relies on NTRU assumption and claims 103-bit security against quantum attackers. We restrict our comparison in Table 1 to those based on "standard lattice problems". Nevertheless, even the NTRU-based scheme produces longer ring signatures than ours when $N \geq 43$.

[3] Note that $N = 1$ would simply give an *ordinary* signature, and there is no reason for using a ring signature for that purpose.

[4] In [20], the soundness goal of $\lambda^{\omega(1)}$ is used and so the number of protocol repetitions for Stern's framework is taken to be $\omega(\log \lambda)$, which disappears in $\widetilde{O}(\cdot)$ notation. But, we consider a practice-oriented goal for the soundness error of $2^{-\lambda}$, and thus the number of protocol repetitions for Stern-based proofs must be $\Omega(\lambda)$. Also, it is stated in [18] that they have the same asymptotic signature growth with [20].

1.4   Our Techniques

One-shot witness extraction for non-linear polynomial relations. The main challenge in designing *efficient* lattice-based ZKPs is that the extracted witness is required to be *short* as mandated by computational lattice problems (in particular, *Short* Integer Solution – SIS problem). Traditional witness extraction techniques involve the inverse of challenge differences as a multiplicative factor in extracted witnesses, and such an approach is problematic in lattice-based protocols as these inverse terms need not be short in general. This causes one to either resort to more inefficient techniques such as aforementioned multi-shot proofs or introduce relaxations in the proofs. Our solution falls into the latter.

The target problem reduces to the question of extracting useful information from a system of equations of the form $V \cdot c = b$ where V is a matrix (a Vandermonde matrix in our case) constructed by challenges, c is a vector of commitments with unknown openings and b is a vector of commitments with known openings. Our idea is to introduce the use of *adjugate* matrices instead of inverse matrices in the "complex" witness extraction of lattice-based ZKPs. This technique, in one hand, enables us to extract *useful* information about the openings of the commitments in c without the involvement of inverse terms, and on the other hand, is the main cause of relaxations. Here, it is crucial that the relaxed proof proves a *useful* relation, is *sound*, and also *efficient*. These piece together nicely when the use of adjugate matrices is accompanied by a good choice of challenge space, and we provide an analysis of our technique with a family of commonly used challenge spaces. We emphasize that straightforward soundness proofs do not work, and one needs special tools such as those introduced in this work to overcome the complications. Our one-shot proof approach is detailed in Sect. 3 after introducing necessary preliminaries.

Table 2. The (minimal) asymptotic time and space complexities of lattice-based protocols involving commitment to $k = O(\log q)$ messages. β_{SIS}: M-SIS solution norm, q: modulus, κ: the number of protocol repetitions, n: module rank for M-SIS, v: message vector dimension in a commitment, d: polynomial ring dimension, m: randomness vector dimension in a commitment. Assume: $\log q < \log^2 \beta_{\text{SIS}}/2$ and degree-d polynomial multiplication costs $\widetilde{O}(d)$. To optimize both costs, one would set $n = v$ in all cases.

	Formula	Multi-shot [14,20] $\kappa = \widetilde{O}(\lambda), v = k$	One-shot $\kappa = 1, v = k$	One-shot + CRT $\kappa = 1, v = O(1)$
Space UMC	$\kappa(n+v)d\log q$	$\widetilde{O}(\lambda^2 \log^2 \beta_{\text{SIS}})$	$\widetilde{O}(\lambda \log^2 \beta_{\text{SIS}})$	$\widetilde{O}(\lambda \log^2 \beta_{\text{SIS}})$
Time UMC	$\kappa(n+v)md$	$\widetilde{O}(\lambda^2 \log^2 \beta_{\text{SIS}})$	$\widetilde{O}(\lambda \log^2 \beta_{\text{SIS}})$	$\widetilde{O}(\lambda \log^2 \beta_{\text{SIS}}/\log q)$
Space HMC	$\kappa nd\log q$	$\widetilde{O}(\lambda^2 \log^2 \beta_{\text{SIS}})$	$\widetilde{O}(\lambda \log^2 \beta_{\text{SIS}})$	N/A
Time HMC	$\kappa n(m+v)d$	$\widetilde{O}(\lambda^2 \log^2 \beta_{\text{SIS}})$	$\widetilde{O}(\lambda \log^2 \beta_{\text{SIS}})$	N/A

CRT-packing supporting inter-slot operations. Let $R = \mathbb{Z}[X]/(X^d + 1)$ and $R_q = \mathbb{Z}_q[X]/(X^d + 1)$ for a usual choice of power-of-two d. It is known that $X^d + 1$ factors linearly (and thus R_q fully splits) for certain choices of q (e.g., a prime $q \equiv 1 \mod 2d$) and, in that case, one can use NTT for polynomial multiplication in R_q in time $O(d \log d)$. Assume that we choose such an "NTT-friendly" q. For $1 \leq s \leq d$ where s is a power of two, let $R_q^{(0)}, \ldots, R_q^{(s-1)}$ be the polynomial rings of dimension d/s such that $R_q = R_q^{(0)} \times \cdots \times R_q^{(s-1)}$ and $R_q^{(i)} = \mathbb{Z}_q[X]/(P^{(i)}(X))$ for some polynomial $P^{(i)}(X)$ of degree d/s for all $0 \leq i < s$ (which is obtained by the Chinese Remainder Theorem – CRT). We use these CRT "slots" to store s messages in a single ring element. Thus, if we have k messages in total, we can set the message vector dimension in a commitment as $v = k/s$ (instead of $v = k$ in previous approaches).

This initial part of the CRT-packing idea seems easy, and indeed a possible application of CRT in lattice-based ZKPs is mentioned in [25] to perform parallel proofs where there is no interaction between the messages in different slots. We are, on the other hand, interested in applications such as range proofs requiring "inter-slot" operations between messages in separate CRT slots, and get a *complete* set of operations (see [15] for a discussion in the context of FHE).

First thing to note about the CRT-packing technique is that even if the messages to be stored in CRT slots are short, the resulting element in R_q representing s messages need not be so. This makes the technique inapplicable to HMC, which require short message inputs (at least in the general case). More importantly, there are two crucial hurdles we need to overcome: (1) it is not clear how to enable inter-slot operations and make the ZKP work in this setting, and (2) we need to make the proof one-shot in order not to lose the factor λ gained.

Let us write $m = \langle m_0, \ldots, m_{s-1} \rangle$ where $m \in R_q$ and $m_i \in R_q^{(i)}$ for $0 \leq i < s$ if m maps to $(m_0, \ldots, m_{s-1})$ under the CRT-mapping. In general, to prove knowledge of a message b, the prover in the protocol needs to send some "encoding" of the message as $f = \text{Enc}_x(b) = x \cdot b + \rho$ where x is a challenge and ρ is a random masking value. Clearly, we do not want to send k encodings in R_q as it does not result in any savings. Instead, our idea is to send k/s elements in R_q, each encoding s messages, *in a way* that enables the verifier to "extract" all k messages out of them. When the prover sends $f = x \cdot m + \rho$ (there may be multiple such f's), for each $0 \leq i < s$, the verifier can compute $f_i = f \mod (q, P^{(i)}(X)) = x_i \cdot m_i + \rho_i$ as the extracted encodings where $x = \langle x_0, \ldots, x_{s-1} \rangle$ and $\rho = \langle \rho_0, \ldots, \rho_{s-1} \rangle$. The main problem here is now that f_i's are encodings of m_i's, but under possibly *different* x_i's, which circumvents interoperability of distinct f_i's. For example, the sum $f_i + f_j$ for $i \neq j$ does not result in an encoding of the sum of messages under a common challenge x if $x_i \neq x_j$.

To overcome this problem, our idea is to choose the challenge $x = \langle x, \ldots, x \rangle$ for $x \in \bigcap_{i=0}^{s-1} R_q^{(i)}$ such that all extracted encodings are under the same challenge x. This means x must be of degree smaller than d/s and thus the challenge space size is possibly greatly decreased.[5] To make the proof one-shot, we choose the

---

[5] We remark that earlier works [6,28] also considered choosing a challenge of degree d/s for some $s > 1$ for the purpose of invertibility of challenges. However, our motivation here is to make sure that x has the same element in all CRT slots.

challenges to be polynomials of degree at most $d/s - 1$ with coefficients in $\mathbb{Z}_p$ such that $p^{d/s} = 2^{2\lambda}$ (i.e., there are $2^{2\lambda}$ challenges in total).[6] Therefore, we need $d/s \cdot \log p = 2\lambda$, which is satisfied by choosing $d/s = \lambda\varepsilon^2$ and $\log p = 2/\varepsilon^2$. We should also ensure $\log q > \log p = 2/\varepsilon^2 = 2\log^2 q/\log^2 \beta_{\mathrm{SIS}}$. This holds assuming $\log q < \log^2 \beta_{\mathrm{SIS}}/2$, which is easily satisfied in most of the practical applications.

To have fast computation, we also set $d = d_{\mathrm{SIS}} = O(\lambda\varepsilon^2 \log q)$, and hence get $s = O(\log q)$. Recall that we have k messages in total and s slots in a single ring element. As a result, for $k = O(\log q)$, it is enough to have $v = k/s = O(1)$. Overall, we end up with the asymptotic costs in the last column of Table 2, where our technique has a factor $\log q$ saving in asymptotic computational time in comparison to previous approaches *without* any compromise in communication.

An attractive example in practice where one would need a commitment to $k = O(\log q)$ messages is a range proof on $[0, 2^k - 1]$. Let us take a range proof on $\ell \in [0, 2^{64} - 1]$ as a running example. In this case, our proof proceeds as follows. We allow R_q to split into at least 64 factors, and thus use a *single* R_q element to commit to all the bits of ℓ (so committing to all the bits of ℓ only cost a single commitment with message vector dimension $v = 1$). In its initial move, the prover sends some commitments and gets a challenge from the verifier. Then, the prover responds with a *single* encoding in R_q (or 64 small encodings that costs as much as a single element in R_q). From here, the verifier extracts the encodings of all the bits, reconstructs the masked integer value ℓ and checks whether it matches the input commitment to ℓ. In this setting, it is clear that we require operability between different slots, and thus set the encodings of all the bits to be under the same challenge x. For a ring dimension $d = 512$, the infinity norm of a challenge can be as large as 2^{31}, which seems quite large.

Table 3. Comparison of non-interactive range proof sizes (in KB). "Ideal w/o CRT" is a hypothetical scheme optimized for proof length. FFT denotes the maximum number of FFT levels supported. Our proof sizes can be slightly reduced at the cost of reducing the FFT levels. The full parameter setting details are given in the full version [13].

range width (N)	$N = 2^{32}$				$N = 2^{64}$			
# of batched proofs (ψ)	1	5	10	(d, FFT)	1	5	10	(d, FFT)
with "norm-optimal" challenges from [25]	161	745	1484	(256, 1)	443	2131	4274	(256, 2)
Ideal w/o CRT	52	113	180	(32, 5)	86	201	302	(16, 4)
Our Work: CRT-packed	58	130	202	(512, 5)	93	216	319	(512, 6)

An alternative to this approach is to use "norm-optimal" challenges from [25] (named "optimal" in [25]) such that the infinity norm of a challenge is set to 1, and thus the overall Euclidean norm of a challenge is minimized. In this case, one needs to set the ring dimension $d \geq 256$ to get a challenge space size of at least 2^{256}. However, this results in significantly longer proofs as shown in Table 3. The reason behind this phenomenon is that one needs to encode

---

[6] In this work, we consider a challenge space size of $2^{2\lambda}$ for λ-bit post-quantum security.

64 values and with the "norm-optimal" challenges the cost of these encodings and the commitments grow too much. The use of challenges with larger (even much larger) norm does not seem to cause significant increase in the proof length, which can be explained as follows. To do a range proof on 64-bit range, the modulus q must be at least 2^{64}. Using UMC, where the message part does not affect the hardness of finding binding collisions (in particular, M-SIS hardness), such a large q already makes M-SIS very hard and M-LWE very easy. Therefore, having a challenge with a large norm only brings the hardness level of M-SIS to that of M-LWE, and results in a very compact proof.

We also add for comparison a hypothetical idealized range proof scheme optimized for proof length in Table 3, where for this scheme we only check two conditions: (1) $q \geq N$ and (2) M-SIS and M-LWE root Hermite factors are less than or equal to 1.0045. More specifically, we go over all the values of the ring dimension $d \in \{8, 16, \ldots, 1024\}$, $\log q \in \{\log N, \ldots, 100\}$ and initial noise distribution $\mathcal{U}(\{-\mathcal{B}, \ldots, \mathcal{B}\})$ for $\mathcal{B} \in \{1, 2, 3\}$, and set the remaining parameters so that the above security condition (2) is satisfied. Therefore, for the "ideal w/o CRT" scheme we do not check whether the soundness proof of the protocol works with the parameters set. Even with this advantage given, we see from Table 3 that our range proof, as expected, has approximately the same proof length as "ideal w/o CRT", and also achieves a significant speedup as the ring dimension as well as the number of FFT levels supported is higher. One can see from [25, Table 2] that going from 2 levels of FFT to 6 levels of FFT alone results in a speedup of a factor more than 3.

When we allow the ring R_q to split into more than 64 factors, then the 64 subrings in which the message bits are encoded will not be fields and the structure of R_q in these subring is lost. We are currently unable to make the soundness proof of the binary proof go through in these subrings, whose structure is unclear. On the other hand, we can make the binary proof work both in R_q using our new result (Lemma 7) and in any field. Thus, we allow R_q to split into exactly $\log N$ *fields* for a range proof of width N, which also gives the invertibility of challenges and challenge differences at no cost. The reason why the scheme with "norm-optimal" challenges cannot split into more than $2^2 = 4$ factors is because the invertibility of polynomials with coefficients as large as 2^{16} is required when one relies solely on the results of [25].

"NTT-friendly" tools for fully-splitting rings. [25] studies in detail how cyclotomic rings split and the required invertibility conditions for short ring elements. A main motivation in [25] for the invertibility of short elements can be sketched as follows. In the hope of proving knowledge of a secret s (which is usually a message-randomness pair (m, r)) that satisfies a certain relation $g(s) = t$ for public homomorphic function g and public t, one-shot proofs can only convince the verifier of knowledge of $\bar{s}$ such that $g(\bar{s}) = \bar{x}t$, where $\bar{x} = x - x'$ for some (distinct) challenges x, x'. If g is a commitment scheme and one later opens t to a valid s' such that $g(s') = t$, then one can show that $s' = \bar{s}/\bar{x}$ using the binding property of the commitment scheme provided that $\bar{x}$ is invertible. In our protocols, however, the relaxed relation proves knowledge of a secret *message* m such that

$$g'(\bar{x}m) = \bar{x}t'$$

where g' and t' are the parts dependent on the message (see Definitions 4 and 6). When one gets two relaxed openings $(\bar{x}_0, m_0)$ and $(\bar{x}_1, m_1)$, we have

$$\begin{aligned}
g'(\bar{x}_0 m_0) &= \bar{x}_0 t' \\
g'(\bar{x}_0 m_1) &= \bar{x}_1 t'
\end{aligned} \implies \begin{aligned}
g'(\bar{x}_1 \bar{x}_0 m_0) &= \bar{x}_1 \bar{x}_0 t' \\
g'(\bar{x}_0 \bar{x}_1 m_1) &= \bar{x}_0 \bar{x}_1 t'
\end{aligned} \implies \bar{x}_1 \bar{x}_0 m_0 = \bar{x}_0 \bar{x}_1 m_1, \quad (3)$$

due to the binding property of the commitment scheme. On contrary to the invertibility requirement, if the norm of each term is small relative to q, which is often the case, we use our new result Lemma 7 to show that,

$$\bar{x}_0 \bar{x}_1 (m_0 - m_1) = 0 \text{ in } \mathbb{Z}_q[X]/(X^d + 1) \implies m_0 = m_1. \quad (4)$$

That is, we can conclude the equality of two message openings even for non-invertible challenge differences. The lemma only requires q to be sufficiently large without putting any condition on its "shape", and thus enables the use of an "NTT-friendly" modulus q.

Open Problems. Our CRT technique only allows us to gain an improvement in terms of computation. A very interesting result would be to also have an asymptotic/practical advantage in communication costs, which remains as an open problem. Another interesting question is whether one can make the binary proof work while having a fully-splitting R_q. This would allow us to exploit the full potential of our CRT technique in its application to range proofs.

Roadmap. Section 3 is devoted to the introduction of the one-shot proof technique for non-linear polynomial relations. Our CRT-packing technique and other new tools that enable faster proofs are detailed in Sect. 4, followed by an application to range proofs. We apply our one-shot proof techniques to build efficient ZKPs of useful relations such as one-out-of-many proofs in Sect. 5. Further applications to advanced cryptographic tools such as ring signatures and anonymous credentials are discussed under Sect. 6. Some formal definitions, further discussions and proofs of lemmas/theorems are given in the full version [13].

2   Preliminaries

In addition to the standard notations, for a vector of polynomials $\boldsymbol{p}$, $\mathsf{HW}(\boldsymbol{p})$ denotes the Hamming weight of the coefficient vector of $\boldsymbol{p}$, and D_σ^r denotes the discrete normal distribution with center zero and standard deviation σ over $\mathbb{Z}^r$. The formal definition and the norm bounds of normal distribution, and relations between different norms are recalled in the full version. We summarize the rejection sampling [23], used to make prover's responses independent of secret information, in Algorithm 1 and its full statement is given in the full version.

2.1   Vandermonde Matrices and Some Basics of Linear Algebra

We recall some basics about Vandermonde matrices and from Linear Algebra relevant to our discussions (see e.g. [17] for more details). We denote the n-dimensional identity matrix by I_n, and assume that the matrices are defined over a ring $\mathfrak{R}$. Let A be a $n \times n$ square matrix and $\det(A)$ denote its determinant. The adjugate $\mathrm{adj}(A)$ of A, defined as the transpose of the cofactor matrix of A, satisfies the following property

$$\mathrm{adj}(A) \cdot A = A \cdot \mathrm{adj}(A) = \det(A) \cdot I_n. \tag{5}$$

Therefore, if A is non-singular, $\mathrm{adj}(A) = \det(A) \cdot A^{-1}$. A $(k+1)$-dimensional Vandermonde matrix V is defined as below for some $x_0, \ldots, x_k \in \mathfrak{R}$, with its determinant satisfying the following property

$$V = \begin{pmatrix} 1 & x_0 & x_0^2 & \cdots & x_0^k \\ 1 & x_1 & x_1^2 & \cdots & x_1^k \\ \vdots & \vdots & \vdots & \vdots & \vdots \\ 1 & x_k & x_k^2 & \cdots & x_k^k \end{pmatrix}, \quad \text{and} \quad \det(V) = \prod_{0 \le i < j \le k} (x_j - x_i). \tag{6}$$

The following is an easy consequence of (6).

Fact 1. *The Vandermonde determinant $\det(V)$ has $\binom{k+1}{2}$ multiplicands of the form $x_j - x_i$ with $j \ne i$.*

As given in [14], the Vandermonde matrix inverse V^{-1}, when it exists, has the following structure

$$\begin{pmatrix} \frac{*}{(x_0-x_1)(x_0-x_2)\cdots(x_0-x_k)} & \frac{*}{(x_0-x_1)(x_1-x_2)\cdots(x_1-x_k)} & \cdots & \frac{*}{(x_0-x_k)(x_1-x_k)\cdots(x_{k-1}-x_k)} \\ \frac{*}{(x_0-x_1)(x_0-x_2)\cdots(x_0-x_k)} & \frac{*}{(x_0-x_1)(x_1-x_2)\cdots(x_1-x_k)} & \cdots & \frac{*}{(x_0-x_k)(x_1-x_k)\cdots(x_{k-1}-x_k)} \\ \vdots & \vdots & \vdots & \vdots \\ \frac{1}{(x_0-x_1)(x_0-x_2)\cdots(x_0-x_k)} & \frac{-1}{(x_0-x_1)(x_1-x_2)\cdots(x_1-x_k)} & \cdots & \frac{(-1)^k}{(x_0-x_k)(x_1-x_k)\cdots(x_{k-1}-x_k)} \end{pmatrix}, \tag{7}$$

where $*$ denotes some element in the ring $\mathfrak{R}$, computed as a function of x_i's. It is clear from this structure that V^{-1} exists over $\mathfrak{R}$ if and only if the differences $x_i - x_j$ for $0 \le i < j \le k$ are invertible over $\mathfrak{R}$. The structure in (7) helps us to visualize the structure of $\mathrm{adj}(V)$ using the fact that $\mathrm{adj}(V) = \det(V) \cdot V^{-1}$ if V is non-singular. In particular, we have the following fact.

Fact 2. *Let $(\Gamma_0, \ldots, \Gamma_k)$ be the last row of $\mathrm{adj}(V)$. Then,*

$$\Gamma_i = (-1)^{i+k} \prod_{0 \le l < j \le k \,\wedge\, j,l \ne i} (x_j - x_l),$$

Algorithm 1. $\mathrm{Rej}(z, c, \phi, T)$

1: $\sigma = \phi T$; $\mu(\phi) = e^{12/\phi + 1/(2\phi^2)}$; $u \leftarrow [0,1)$
2: **if** $u > (\frac{1}{\mu(\phi)}) \cdot \exp\left(\frac{-2\langle z, c \rangle + \|c\|^2}{2\sigma^2}\right)$ **then return** 0 ▷ means abort in the protocols.
3: **else return** 1

---

and Γ_i has $\left[\binom{k+1}{2} - k\right] = \frac{k(k-1)}{2}$ *multiplicands for all* $0 \le i \le k$.

Fact 2 follows by observing that k multiplicands in $\det(\boldsymbol{V})$ are cancelled out by the corresponding denominator in $\boldsymbol{V}^{-1}$.

2.2   Module-SIS and Module-LWE Problems

Our schemes' security relies on the hardness of Module-SIS (M-SIS) (defined in "Hermite normal form" as in [3]) and Module-LWE (M-LWE) problems [19].

Definition 1. (M-SIS$_{n,m,q,\beta_{SIS}}$). *Given* $\boldsymbol{A} = [\,\boldsymbol{I}_n \,\|\, \boldsymbol{A}'\,]$ *with* $\boldsymbol{A}' \leftarrow \mathcal{U}(R_q^{n \times (m-n)})$, *the goal is to find* $\boldsymbol{z} \in R_q^m$ *such that* $\boldsymbol{A}\boldsymbol{z} = \boldsymbol{0} \bmod q$ *and* $0 < \|\boldsymbol{z}\| \le \beta_{SIS}$.

Definition 2. (M-LWE$_{n,m,q,\chi}$). *Let* χ *be a distribution over* R_q *and* $\boldsymbol{s} \leftarrow \chi^n$ *be a secret key. Define* $\mathrm{LWE}_{q,\boldsymbol{s}}$ *as the distribution obtained by sampling* $\boldsymbol{a} \leftarrow R_q^n$, $e \leftarrow \chi$ *and outputting* $(\boldsymbol{a}, \langle \boldsymbol{a}, \boldsymbol{s} \rangle + e)$. *The goal is to distinguish between* m *given samples from either* $\mathrm{LWE}_{q,\boldsymbol{s}}$ *or* $\mathcal{U}(R_q^n, R_q)$.

The above definition is a standard variant of decision M-LWE problem where the secret is sampled from the error distribution. More discussion about the security aspects is given in the full version [13].

2.3 Σ-protocols

Σ-protocols are a type of interactive proof systems between a prover $\mathcal{P}$ and a verifier $\mathcal{V}$. It is 3-move as in Protocol 1. A protocol transcript is *accepting* if it is accepted by the verifier. Σ-protocols are defined for a relation $\mathcal{R}$, and for a $(v, w) \in \mathcal{R}$, the quantity w is said to be a witness for v. We use the generalized definition of Σ-protocols from [14] that extends the one in [5].

Definition 3 ([14, Definition 4]). *For relations* $\mathcal{R}, \mathcal{R}'$ *with* $\mathcal{R} \subseteq \mathcal{R}'$, $(\mathcal{P}, \mathcal{V})$ *is called a Σ-protocol for* $\mathcal{R}, \mathcal{R}'$ *with completeness error* α, *a challenge space* $\mathcal{C}$, *public-private inputs* (v, w), *if the following properties are satisfied.*

- **Completeness:** *An interaction between an honest prover and an honest verifier is accepted with probability at least* $1 - \alpha$ *whenever* $(v, w) \in \mathcal{R}$.
- $(k+1)$-**special soundness:** *There exists an efficient PPT extractor* $\mathcal{E}$ *that computes w' satisfying* $(v, w') \in \mathcal{R}'$ *given* $(k+1)$ *accepting protocol transcripts* $(a, x_0, z_0), \ldots, (a, x_k, z_k)$ *with distinct x_i's for* $0 \le i \le k$. *We refer to this process as witness extraction.*
- **Special honest-verifier zero-knowledge (SHVZK):** *There exists an efficient PPT simulator $\mathcal{S}$ that outputs (a, z) given v in the language of $\mathcal{R}$ and $x \in \mathcal{C}$ such that (a, x, z) is indistinguishable from an accepting transcript produced by a real run of the protocol.*

As seen from above, the special soundness is *relaxed* in the sense the verifier is only convinced of the proof of knowledge of a witness for the relation $\mathcal{R}'$. This is usually referred to as the *soundness gap*. This relaxation is necessary for efficient algebraic proofs and such relaxed proofs are sufficient for our applications.

2.4   Commitment Schemes

We define the commitment schemes UMC (Unbounded-Message Commitment) [3,6] and HMC (Hashed-Message Commitment) (see, e.g., [3,14]). Both hiding and binding properties are computational (see the full version [13] for formal definitions of commitments, their properties and more discussion). Let $n, m, \mathcal{B}, q$ be positive integers, and assume that we commit to v-dimensional vectors over R_q for $v \geq 1$. As in [3,6], the opening algorithm Open is *relaxed* in the sense that there is an additional input $y \in R_q$, called *relaxation factor*, to Open algorithm along with a message-randomness pair $(\boldsymbol{m'}, \boldsymbol{r'})$ such that Open checks if $y \cdot C = \text{Com}_{ck}(\boldsymbol{m'}; \boldsymbol{r'})$. The instantiation of HMC with $m > n$ is as follows.

- CKeygen(1^λ): Pick $\boldsymbol{G_r'} \leftarrow R_q^{n \times (m-n)}$ and $\boldsymbol{G_m} \leftarrow R_q^{n \times v}$. Output $ck = \boldsymbol{G} = [\boldsymbol{G_r} \,\|\, \boldsymbol{G_m}] \in R_q^{n \times (m+v)}$ where $\boldsymbol{G_r} = [\boldsymbol{I_n} \,\|\, \boldsymbol{G_r'}]$. We assume that Commit and Open takes ck as an input implicitly.
- Commit($\boldsymbol{m}$): Pick $\boldsymbol{r} \leftarrow \{-\mathcal{B}, \dots, \mathcal{B}\}^{md}$. Output

$$\text{Com}_{ck}(\boldsymbol{m}; \boldsymbol{r}) = \boldsymbol{G} \cdot (\boldsymbol{r}, \boldsymbol{m}) = \boldsymbol{G_r} \cdot \boldsymbol{r} + \boldsymbol{G_m} \cdot \boldsymbol{m}.$$

- Open($C, (y, \boldsymbol{m'}, \boldsymbol{r'})$): If $\text{Com}_{ck}(\boldsymbol{m'}; \boldsymbol{r'}) = yC$ and $\|(\boldsymbol{r'}, \boldsymbol{m'})\| \leq \gamma_{\text{com}}$, return 1. Otherwise, return 0.

Lemma 1. *If M-LWE$_{m-n,n,q,\mathcal{U}(\{-\mathcal{B},\dots,\mathcal{B}\}^d)}$ problem is hard, then HMC is computationally hiding. If M-SIS$_{n,m+v,q,2\gamma_{com}}$ is hard, then HMC is computationally strong γ_{com}-binding with respect to the same relaxation factor y.*

The instantiation of UMC is also similar and defined as below for $m > n + v$.

- CKeygen(1^λ): Pick $\boldsymbol{G_1'} \leftarrow R_q^{n \times (m-n)}$ and $\boldsymbol{G_2'} \leftarrow R_q^{v \times (m-n-v)}$. Set $\boldsymbol{G_1} = [\boldsymbol{I_n} \,\|\, \boldsymbol{G_1'}]$ and $\boldsymbol{G_2} = [\boldsymbol{0}^{v \times n} \| \boldsymbol{I_v} \,\|\, \boldsymbol{G_2'}]$. Output $ck = \boldsymbol{G} = \begin{bmatrix} \boldsymbol{G_1} \\ \boldsymbol{G_2} \end{bmatrix} \in R_q^{(n+v) \times m}$. We assume that Commit and Open takes ck as an input implicitly.
- Commit($\boldsymbol{m}$): Pick $\boldsymbol{r} \leftarrow \{-\mathcal{B}, \dots, \mathcal{B}\}^{md}$. Output

$$\text{Com}_{ck}(\boldsymbol{m}; \boldsymbol{r}) = \boldsymbol{G} \cdot \boldsymbol{r} + (\boldsymbol{0}^n, \boldsymbol{m}).$$

- Open($C, (y, \boldsymbol{m'}, \boldsymbol{r'})$): If $\text{Com}_{ck}(\boldsymbol{m'}; \boldsymbol{r'}) = yC$ and $\|\boldsymbol{r'}\| \leq \gamma_{\text{com}}$, return 1. Otherwise, return 0.

Observe from the above definition that only the norm of $\boldsymbol{r'}$ is checked in the Open algorithm of UMC whereas that of $(\boldsymbol{m'}, \boldsymbol{r'})$ is checked in HMC. Also, our definition of Open for UMC is slightly different than that in [3] because we do not multiply the relaxation factor with the message as the invertibility of the relaxation factor is not guaranteed in our case.

Lemma 2. ([3]). *If M-LWE$_{m-n-v,n+v,q,\mathcal{U}(\{-\mathcal{B},\dots,\mathcal{B}\}^d)}$ problem is hard, then UMC is computationally hiding. If M-SIS$_{n,m,q,2\gamma_{com}}$ is hard, then UMC is computationally γ_{com}-binding with respect to the same relaxation factor y.*

We use the same notation for both of the commitment schemes and will clarify in the relevant sections which specific instantiation is used. We say that $(y, \boldsymbol{m}', \boldsymbol{r}')$ is a *valid* opening of C if $\mathsf{Open}(C, (y, \boldsymbol{m}', \boldsymbol{r}')) = 1$. A valid opening $(y, \boldsymbol{m}', \boldsymbol{r}')$ with $y = 1$ is called an *exact valid* opening. We call the message part $\boldsymbol{m}'$ of an opening as *message opening*, and if $(y, \boldsymbol{m}', \boldsymbol{r}')$ is a valid opening such that $yC = \mathsf{Com}_{ck}(y\boldsymbol{m}'; \boldsymbol{r}')$, then we call $\boldsymbol{m}'$ a *relaxed message opening* with relaxation factor y. It is also straightforward that both UMC and HMC satisfy the following homomorphic properties: $\mathsf{Com}_{ck}(\boldsymbol{m}_0; \boldsymbol{r}_0) + \mathsf{Com}_{ck}(\boldsymbol{m}_1; \boldsymbol{r}_1) = \mathsf{Com}_{ck}(\boldsymbol{m}_0 + \boldsymbol{m}_1; \boldsymbol{r}_0 + \boldsymbol{r}_1)$ and $c \cdot \mathsf{Com}_{ck}(\boldsymbol{m}; \boldsymbol{r}) = \mathsf{Com}_{ck}(c \cdot \boldsymbol{m}; c \cdot \boldsymbol{r})$ for $c \in R_q$.

3   One-Shot Proofs for Non-Linear Polynomial Relations

In this section, we focus on lattice-based zero-knowledge proofs in a general framework using homomorphic commitments, and introduce our techniques to get efficient proofs. Even though such a setting is also mostly shared with DL-based Σ-protocols using homomorphic commitments, the main challenges described here are not encountered in those cases. Since our main concern is about the soundness of the protocol, in this section, we omit the discussion about the zero-knowledge property, which is later obtained using a standard rejection sampling technique. We always consider homomorphic commitments when referring to "commitment" and assume that all the elements are in a ring $\mathfrak{R}$.

3.1   The Case for Linear Relations (2-Special Soundness)

If we investigate the (underlying) one-shot Σ-protocols from [3,6,22,23], we see the following. The common input of the protocol is a commitment C_1 to the prover's witness and the prover sends an initial commitment C_0.[7] Then, the verifier sends a random challenge $x \leftarrow \mathcal{C}$, which is responded by the prover as $(\boldsymbol{f}, \boldsymbol{z})$, and $(\boldsymbol{f}, \boldsymbol{z})$ is used by the verifier as a message-randomness pair for a commitment computation.[8] More precisely, the verification checks if $C_0 + xC_1 = \mathsf{Com}_{ck}(\boldsymbol{f}; \boldsymbol{z})$ holds and $\boldsymbol{f}, \boldsymbol{z}$ have small norm. This is equivalent to the structure represented in Protocol 1 for $k = 1$. From here, when the extractor gets two valid protocol transcripts $(C_0, x_0, \boldsymbol{f}_0, \boldsymbol{z}_0), (C_0, x_1, \boldsymbol{f}_1, \boldsymbol{z}_1)$ using the same initial message C_0, and different challenges x_0 and x_1, the extractor obtains

$$\begin{matrix} C_0 + x_0 C_1 = \mathsf{Com}_{ck}(\boldsymbol{f}_0; \boldsymbol{z}_0) \\ C_0 + x_1 C_1 = \mathsf{Com}_{ck}(\boldsymbol{f}_1; \boldsymbol{z}_1) \end{matrix} \implies (x_1 - x_0)C_1 = \mathsf{Com}_{ck}(\boldsymbol{f}_1 - \boldsymbol{f}_0; \boldsymbol{z}_1 - \boldsymbol{z}_0). \quad (8)$$

At this stage, it is not possible to obtain a *valid exact* opening of C_1 unless $(x_1 - x_0)^{-1}$ is guaranteed to be short due to the shortness requirements of valid

---

[7] The reason behind indexing becomes clear in what follows.

[8] In certain proofs, the use of UMC allows the prover to respond only with the randomness part $\boldsymbol{z}$. In such a case, $\boldsymbol{f}$ need not be transmitted and can be assumed to be set appropriately by the verifier.

$$\begin{array}{ll}
\mathcal{P}((ck, C_0, \ldots, C_k), (m_k, r_k)) & \mathcal{V}(ck, C_0, \ldots, C_k) \\
\hline
& \qquad\qquad x \qquad\qquad \quad x \leftarrow \mathcal{C} \\
& \xleftarrow{\hspace{4cm}} \\
f, z \leftarrow F(\cdots) & \qquad\quad f, z \\
& \xrightarrow{\hspace{4cm}} \\
& \qquad\qquad \|f\| \overset{?}{\leq} \mathcal{T}_f, \ \|z\| \overset{?}{\leq} \mathcal{T}_z \\
& \qquad\qquad C_0 + xC_1 + \cdots + x^k C_k \overset{?}{=} fz
\end{array}$$

Protocol 1. Structure of a $(k+1)$-special sound Σ-protocol. $\mathcal{T}_f, \mathcal{T}_z \in \mathbb{R}^+$ are some pre-determined values that vary among different proofs.

openings for lattice-based commitment schemes.[9] Unless ensured by design, there is no particular reason why the inverse term $(x_1 - x_0)^{-1}$ would be short. In the current state of affairs, the largest set of challenges with short challenge difference inverses is monomial challenges [5] used with ring variants of lattice assumptions. Here, only $2(x_1 - x_0)^{-1}$ is guaranteed to be short and thus the extractor can only get the openings of $2C_1$. As discussed previously, for a ring dimension of d, the cardinality of the monomial challenge space is only $2d$, which is typically smaller than 2^{12} in practice. This small challenge space problem causes major efficiency drawbacks in terms of both computation and communication as the protocol is required to be repeated many times to get a negligible soundness error (that is, the same computation and communication steps are repeated multiple times, resulting in a multi-fold increase in both computation and communication). The situation is even worse in terms of the number of repetitions when binary challenges or Stern's framework [29] is used where the protocol is required to be repeated at least λ times for λ-bit security.

The idea for a one-shot proof is to make use of (8) without any inverse computation by observing that $(f_1 - f_0, z_1 - z_0)$ is a valid opening of $(x_1 - x_0)C_1$ as long as $f_1 - f_0$ and $z_1 - z_0$ are short, which is ensured by norm checks on f, z in each verification. If one can prove that having this *relaxed* case is sufficient and also violates the binding property of the commitment (i.e., that it allows one to solve a computationally hard problem), then the soundness of the protocol is achieved (with a relaxed relation $\mathcal{R}'$ as in Definition 3) with no challenge difference inverses involved. This eliminates the need for challenge differences to have short inverses and enables one to use exponentially large challenge spaces, resulting in *one-shot* proofs. The main technical difficulty here is handling soundness gap, where the extractor only obtains an exact opening of $(x_1 - x_0)C_1$ (rather than C_1, which is the commitment to the prover's witness).

---

[9] Recall that UMC allows an unbounded *message* opening, but still the randomness is required to be short.

3.2   Generalization to Degree $k > 1$ $((k + 1)$-Special Soundness)

As can be seen from (8), the 2-special sound case is quite restrictive as it only allows witness extraction from linear (first degree) relations. On the other hand, the ability to work with non-linear relations is a must in recent efficient proofs [7–9,16], which renders the existing lattice-based one-shot techniques inapplicable. Therefore, we generalize our setting, and suppose that we have a degree-k polynomial relation $((k + 1)$-special sound Σ-protocol), $k \geq 1$, with the structure given in Protocol 1. Note that since the extractor only knows that verification steps hold, unaware of how any component is generated, other steps but those in the verification is not important. Therefore, we write all the C_i's as a common input whereas in the actual protocol a subset of them can be generated during a protocol run. The commitment to the prover's witness $(\boldsymbol{m}_k, \boldsymbol{r}_k)$ is C_k.

The witness extraction, in this case, works by the extractor obtaining $k + 1$ accepting protocol transcripts for distinct challenges $x_0, \ldots, x_k$ with the same input $(C_0, \ldots, C_k)$, and responses $(\boldsymbol{f}_0, \boldsymbol{z}_0), \ldots, (\boldsymbol{f}_k, \boldsymbol{z}_k)$, represented as below.

$$\begin{pmatrix} 1 & x_0 & x_0^2 & \cdots & x_0^k \\ 1 & x_1 & x_1^2 & \cdots & x_1^k \\ \vdots & \vdots & \vdots & \vdots & \vdots \\ 1 & x_k & x_k^2 & \cdots & x_k^k \end{pmatrix} \cdot \begin{pmatrix} C_0 \\ C_1 \\ \vdots \\ C_k \end{pmatrix} = \begin{pmatrix} \mathrm{Com}_{ck}(\boldsymbol{f}_0; \boldsymbol{z}_0) \\ \mathrm{Com}_{ck}(\boldsymbol{f}_1; \boldsymbol{z}_1) \\ \vdots \\ \mathrm{Com}_{ck}(\boldsymbol{f}_k; \boldsymbol{z}_k) \end{pmatrix}. \qquad (9)$$

We have seen that using the aforementioned *relaxed* opening approach, one can extract a witness from a linear relation (8) in *one shot*. Now a natural generalization is to ask "Can we extract a witness from a non-linear relation (9) as in Protocol 1 in *one shot*?"

Naive approach and previous *multi-shot* approach. Denoting (9) as $\boldsymbol{V} \cdot \boldsymbol{c} = \boldsymbol{b}$, the matrix $\boldsymbol{V}$ is a Vandermonde matrix. A straightforward idea to obtain the openings of C_i's is to multiply both sides of (9) by $\boldsymbol{V}^{-1}$, which gives $\boldsymbol{c} = \boldsymbol{V}^{-1} \cdot \boldsymbol{b}$. From here, using the homomorphic properties of the commitment scheme, we can get *potential* "openings" of C_i's. However, one needs to make sure that $\boldsymbol{V}^{-1}$ exists over $\mathfrak{R}$ and that it has *short* entries so that these "openings" are valid. The way [14] deals with this issue is by making use of monomial challenges from [5]. Using the structure of $\boldsymbol{V}^{-1}$ in (7), it is argued in [14] that the entries in $2^k \boldsymbol{V}^{-1}$ are short by the fact that doubled inverse of challenge differences (i.e., $2(x_j - x_i)^{-1}$) are short *when* monomial challenges are used. Thus, this approach still maintains the drawback of requiring multiple protocol repetitions to achieve a negligible soundness error, and does not address our question.

Our *one-shot* solution. Now, let us see how we develop a one-shot proof technique for non-linear relations. Using (5), we multiply both sides of (9) by $\mathrm{adj}(\boldsymbol{V})$, and obtain

$$\mathrm{adj}(\boldsymbol{V}) \cdot \boldsymbol{V} \cdot \boldsymbol{c} = \mathrm{adj}(\boldsymbol{V}) \cdot \boldsymbol{b} \quad \implies \quad \det(\boldsymbol{V}) \cdot \boldsymbol{c} = \mathrm{adj}(\boldsymbol{V}) \cdot \boldsymbol{b}. \qquad (10)$$

Note that $\det(\boldsymbol{V})$ is just some scalar in $\mathfrak{R}$, and we obtain *potential relaxed* "openings" of C_i's as a result of the commitment adj$(\boldsymbol{V}) \cdot \boldsymbol{b}$. In particular, for the commitment C_k of the *witness*, we have

$$\det(\boldsymbol{V}) \cdot C_k = \sum_{i=0}^{k} \Gamma_i \cdot \mathrm{Com}_{ck}(\boldsymbol{f}_i; \boldsymbol{z}_i) = \mathrm{Com}_{ck}(\sum_{i=0}^{k} \Gamma_i \cdot \boldsymbol{f}_i; \sum_{i=0}^{k} \Gamma_i \cdot \boldsymbol{z}_i), \quad (11)$$

where $\Gamma_i = (-1)^{i+k} \prod_{0 \le l < j \le k \wedge j, l \ne i} (x_j - x_l)$ by Fact 2. As a result, we get a *relaxed* opening of C_k, or more precisely, an *exact* opening of $\det(\boldsymbol{V}) \cdot C_k$ as $(\hat{\boldsymbol{m}}_k, \hat{\boldsymbol{r}}_k) = \left(\sum_{i=0}^{k} \Gamma_i \boldsymbol{f}_i, \sum_{i=0}^{k} \Gamma_i \boldsymbol{z}_i \right)$. Provided that the norms of $\hat{\boldsymbol{m}}_k$ and $\hat{\boldsymbol{r}}_k$ are small, this gives a *valid* opening and thus can be related to a hard lattice problem (M-SIS, in particular). It is important to observe here that $\hat{\boldsymbol{m}}_k$ and $\hat{\boldsymbol{r}}_k$ do not involve any inverse term and can be guaranteed to be short by ensuring that Γ_i's are short. The opening of other C_i's can also be recovered in a similar fashion, but the case for C_k is sufficient for our applications.

When $k = 1$, i.e., when the protocol is 2-special sound, $\det(\boldsymbol{V}) = (x_1 - x_0)$ and $(\Gamma_0, \Gamma_1) = (-1, 1)$. Therefore, we exactly obtain (8) as a special case of (11) with $k = 1$. That is, we get the results of the previous approaches from [3,6,22,23] as a special case of ours.

3.3   New Tools for Compact Proofs

Let us analyze our generalized solution and introduce our new tools to get compact proofs. The results can be easily used in other protocols that use a challenge space of the form defined in (12) as they are independent of the low-level details of a protocol. Since the most commonly used challenge spaces (e.g., in [3,4,11,24,25]) for one-shot proofs are special cases of (12), our results are widely applicable. Let $\mathfrak{R} = R = \mathbb{Z}[X]/(X^d + 1)$ and $R_q = \mathbb{Z}_q[X]/(X^d + 1)$ for $q \in \mathbb{Z}^+$. For $w \le d$ and $p \le q/2$, let $\mathcal{C}_{w,p}^d$ be the challenge space defined as

$$\mathcal{C}_{w,p}^d = \{ x \in \mathbb{Z}[X] : \deg(x) \le d - 1 \wedge \mathsf{HW}(x) = w \wedge \|x\|_\infty = p \}. \quad (12)$$

It is easy to observe that $\|x\|_1 \le pw$ for any $x \in \mathcal{C}_{w,p}^d$ and $|\mathcal{C}_{w,p}^d| = \binom{d}{w} \cdot (2p)^w$, which is, for example, larger than 2^{256} for $(d, w, p) = (256, 60, 1)$. We define $\Delta\mathcal{C}_{w,p}^d$ to be the set of challenge differences excluding zero.

Bound on the product of challenge differences.

Lemma 3. *For any $y_1, \ldots, y_n \in \Delta\mathcal{C}_{w,p}^d$, the following holds*

$$\left\| \prod_{i=1}^{n} y_i \right\|_\infty \le (2p)^n \cdot w^{n-1}, \quad \text{and} \quad \left\| \prod_{i=1}^{n} y_i \right\| \le \sqrt{d} \cdot (2p)^n \cdot w^{n-1}.$$

Bound on the relaxation factor: $\det(\boldsymbol{V})$.

Lemma 4. *Let* $\kappa = \binom{k+1}{2} = \frac{k(k+1)}{2}$. *For the* $(k+1)$-*dimensional Vandermonde matrix* $\boldsymbol{V}$ *defined in (9) using the challenge space* $\mathcal{C}^d_{w,p}$ *in (12),*

$$\|\det(\boldsymbol{V})\|_\infty \leq (2p)^\kappa \cdot w^{\kappa-1}.$$

Proof. By Fact 1, $\det(\boldsymbol{V})$ has $\kappa = \binom{k+1}{2}$ multiplicands where each multiplicand is in $\Delta\mathcal{C}^d_{w,p}$. The result follows from Lemma 3. $\qquad\square$

Bound on the extracted witness norm: $\mathrm{adj}(V) \times$ (**openings of** b).

Lemma 5. *For* $k \geq 1$ *and* $(\hat{\boldsymbol{m}}_k, \hat{\boldsymbol{r}}_k) = \left(\sum_{i=0}^k \Gamma_i \boldsymbol{f}_i, \sum_{i=0}^k \Gamma_i \boldsymbol{z}_i\right)$ *where* $\Gamma_i = \prod_{0 \leq l < j \leq k \wedge j,l \neq i}(x_j - x_l)$, *the following holds, for* $\kappa' = k(k-1)/2$,

- $\|\hat{\boldsymbol{m}}_k\| \leq (k+1) \cdot d \cdot (2p)^{\kappa'} \cdot w^{\kappa'-1} \cdot \max_i \|\boldsymbol{f}_i\|$, *and*
- $\|\hat{\boldsymbol{r}}_k\| \leq (k+1) \cdot d \cdot (2p)^{\kappa'} \cdot w^{\kappa'-1} \cdot \max_i \|\boldsymbol{z}_i\|$.

The proofs of Lemmas 3 and 5 are provided in the full version [13].

Reducing extracted witness norm in proofs with non-linear relations. In some proofs with non-linear polynomial relations such as our one-out-of-many proof, the extractor obtains an opening with a relaxation factor y of some component that is witness of a sub-protocol. Since the invertibility of y is not ensured, when this opening is used in the non-linear polynomial relation, the relaxation factor also gets exponentiated by the degree $k > 1$. In the end, instead of getting $\det(\boldsymbol{V})$ as the overall relaxation factor, we end up with relaxation factor $y^k \cdot \det(\boldsymbol{V})$. We use the lemma below to show that even though we cannot completely eliminate the extra term y^k, we can eliminate its exponent k. This results in obtaining an extracted witness with a smaller norm, and in turn, helps in getting shorter proofs. The proof of Lemma 6 is given in the full version.

Lemma 6. *Let* $f, g \in R = \mathbb{Z}[X]/(X^d + 1)$. *If* $f \cdot g^k = 0$ *in* $R_q = \mathbb{Z}_q[X]/(X^d + 1)$ *for some* $k \in \mathbb{Z}^+$, *then* $f \cdot g = 0$ *in* R_q.

4 New Techniques for Faster Lattice-Based Proofs

In this section, we go into the details of our new techniques to get computation-efficient proofs. We first show a lemma that enables one to prove that if a product of polynomials is equal to zero in R_q and the norm of each factor is sufficiently small, then there must be a factor which is exactly equal to zero. This result works for any sufficiently large q, enabling the use of a modulus suitable for fast computation such as an "NTT-friendly" modulus.

Lemma 7. *Let* $f_1, \ldots, f_n \in R$ *for some* $n \geq 1$. *If* $\prod_{i=1}^n f_i = 0$ *in* R_q *and* $q/2 > \|f_1\|_\infty \cdot \prod_{i=2}^n \|f_i\|_1$, *then there exists* $1 \leq j \leq n$ *such that* $f_j = 0$.

Proof. *(Lemma 7).* Using standard norm relations in R and the assumption on q, we have

$$\|\prod_{i=1}^{s} f_i\|_{\infty} \leq \|f_1\|_{\infty} \cdot \prod_{i=2}^{n} \|f_i\|_1 < q/2.$$

Therefore, $\prod_{i=1}^{n} f_i = 0$ holds over R. Since $X^d + 1$ is irreducible over $\mathbb{Q}$, (at least) one of the multiplicand f_i's must be zero. $\qquad\square$

Note that Lemma 7 requires all the multiplicands to have bounded norm whereas there is no such requirement in Lemma 6. Therefore, we are unable to use Lemma 7 for the purpose of the use of Lemma 6 described previously as there is no norm-bound on a multiplicand in the place Lemma 6 is used (see how these lemmas are used in the soundness proofs for more details). Lemma 7 is used in the binary proof to argue that $y_0 y_1 y_2 \hat{b}(y - \hat{b}) = 0$ in R_q for some (non-zero) challenge differences y, y_0, y_1, y_2 implies $\hat{b} = yb$ for a bit $b \in \{0, 1\}$ without requiring invertibility of any challenge difference (see Sect. 5.1).

4.1 Supporting Inter-slot Operations on CRT-packed Messages

Now, we can go into the details of our CRT packing technique. Define $f = \mathrm{Enc}_x(m) = x \cdot m + \rho \in R_q$ as an encoding of a message m under a challenge x. This encoding is widely used in proofs of knowledge as a "masked" response to a challenge x. An important advantage of this encoding over a commitment is that the storage cost of an encoding is at most $d \log q$ whereas that of a commitment is $nd \log q$ for HMC and $(n + v)d \log q$ for UMC. Therefore, for a typical module rank of, say, 4, a commitment is 4× more costly than an encoding.

There are known methods to choose a modulus q such that $X^d + 1$ splits into s factors, in which case, R_q splits into s fields and we get $R_q = R_q^{(0)} \times \cdots \times R_q^{(s-1)}$. In the case that $X^d + 1$ splits into more than s factors, but we only want to use s slots, we still have $R_q = R_q^{(0)} \times \cdots \times R_q^{(s-1)}$ where $R_q^{(i)} = \mathbb{Z}_q[X]/(P^{(i)}(X))$ for some polynomial $P^{(i)}(X)$ of degree d/s. However, $R_q^{(i)}$'s are not a field in that case as $P^{(i)}(X)$'s are not irreducible over $\mathbb{Z}_q$.

As discussed previously, when we use these s slots to pack s messages in a single ring element, we have

$$f = \mathrm{Enc}_x(m) = x \cdot m + \rho = \langle x_0 m_0 + \rho_0, \ldots, x_{s-1} m_{s-1} + \rho_{s-1} \rangle, \qquad (13)$$

where $x = \langle x_0, \ldots, x_{s-1} \rangle$, $m = \langle m_0, \ldots, m_{s-1} \rangle$ and $\rho = \langle \rho_0, \ldots, \rho_{s-1} \rangle$ in the CRT-packed representation. In this case, parallel additions are easy as

$$\mathrm{Enc}_x(\langle m_0, \ldots, m_{s-1} \rangle) + \mathrm{Enc}_x(\langle m'_0, \ldots, m'_{s-1} \rangle) = \mathrm{Enc}_x(\langle m_0 + m'_0, \ldots, m_{s-1} + m'_{s-1} \rangle).$$

Parallel multiplication is also possible as $\mathrm{Enc}_x(m) \cdot \mathrm{Enc}_x(m') = m \cdot m' \cdot x^2 + c_1 x + c_0$ for c_0, c_1 only dependent on m, m', ρ, ρ', all of which are known to the prover in advance of his first move. Therefore, the prover can prove that the coefficient of x^2 is the product of m and m', and thus proving the relation in parallel for all CRT slots.[10] Addition and multiplication alone, however, do not provide a complete set of operations (see [15] for a discussion in the context of FHE). Given an encoding of m, our main requirement is to have the ability to extract all encodings in the CRT slots of m in a way that allows further operations among extracted encodings. That is, all extracted encodings must be under the same challenge x, which translates to requiring $x = \langle x, \ldots, x \rangle$ for $x \in \bigcap_{i=0}^{s-1} R_q^{(i)}$. As a result, when we use s slots, the degree of a challenge can be at most $d/s - 1$. With this, from an encoding $f = \mathrm{Enc}_x(\langle m_0, \ldots, m_{s-1} \rangle)$, anyone can extract encodings by computing

$$f_i = \mathrm{Enc}_x(m_i) = f \bmod (q, P^{(i)}(X)) = x \cdot m_i + \rho_i = \mathrm{Enc}_x(m_i)$$

for all $0 \le i \le s - 1$. Conversely, given encoding $\mathrm{Enc}_x(m_i)$'s for all $0 \le i \le s - 1$, anyone can compute an encoding $\mathrm{Enc}_x(\langle m_0, \ldots, m_{s-1} \rangle)$.

Even more, with this choice of the challenge $x = \langle x, \ldots, x \rangle$ for $x \in \bigcap_{i=0}^{s-1} R_q^{(i)}$, we get invariance of the challenge under *any* permutation σ on CRT slots. That is, for any permutation σ, we have $\sigma(\mathrm{Enc}_x(m)) = \mathrm{Enc}_x(\sigma(m))$. From here, one can perform any inter-slot operation, and may even not require packing/unpacking of the messages in some applications. In our application to the range proof, extraction of the slots is sufficient and we refer to [15] for more on permutations. In our approach, an encoding and a commitment per message slot costs, respectively, at most $d \log q/s$ bits and $(n+v) \log q/s$ bits, which are much cheaper than a commitment to a single message.

4.2 Using CRT-packed Inter-slot Operations in Relaxed Range Proof

In this section, we introduce the first application of our ideas to Σ-protocols where the proof is *relaxed* as described in Sect. 2.3. In all of our protocols, the prover aborts if any rejection sampling step (Algorithm 1) returns 0, and our protocols are honest-verifier zero-knowledge for *non-aborting* interactions. For most of the practical applications, the protocol is made non-interactive, and thus having only non-aborting protocols with the zero-knowledge property does not cause an issue. Nevertheless, the protocols can be easily adapted to be zero-knowledge for the aborting cases using a standard technique from [5].

Our first application is a range proof that allows an efficient aggregation in the sense that the prover can prove that a set of committed values packed in a *single* commitment falls within a set of certain ranges. Let $\psi \in \mathbb{Z}^+$, $\ell^{(i)} \in [0, N_i)$ be prover's values for $1 \le i \le \psi$ and $N_i = 2^{k_i}$ with $k = k_1 + \cdots + k_\psi$, and s be the smallest power of two such that $s \ge \max\{k_1, \ldots, k_\psi\}$. For simplicity, we use base $\beta = 2$, but the result can be generalized to other base values β. Binary case gives the the most compact proofs in practice. Assume that $R_q = \mathbb{Z}_q[X]/(X^d + 1)$ splits into exactly s fields such that $R_q = R_q^{(0)} \times \cdots \times R_q^{(s-1)}$ and $R_q^{(i)} = \mathbb{Z}_q[X]/(P^{(i)}(X))$ for some *irreducible* polynomial $P^{(i)}(X)$

---

[10] We believe this is the application of CRT mentioned in [25].

of degree d/s for all $0 \leq i < s$. Write $\ell^{(i)} = (b_0^{(i)}, \ldots, b_{k_i-1}^{(i)})$ in the binary representation and define $\ell_{\mathrm{crti}}^{(i)} = \langle b_0^{(i)}, \ldots, b_{k_i-1}^{(i)} \rangle$. The exact relations proved by our "simultaneous" range proof is given in Definition 4. We show in the full version of the manuscript [13] that the relaxed range proof is sufficient for an application in anonymous credentials. Such a "simultaneous" range proof is useful when showing a credential that a set of attributes such as age, expiry date, residential postcode etc. fall into some respective ranges, and this can be achieved with a single commitment and a single proof using our techniques.

Definition 4. *The following defines the relations for Protocol 2 for* $\mathcal{T}, \hat{\mathcal{T}} \in \mathbb{R}^+$.

$$\mathcal{R}_{range}(\mathcal{T}) = \left\{ \begin{array}{c} ((ck, V), (\ell^{(1)}, \ldots, \ell^{(\psi)}, \boldsymbol{r})) : \|\boldsymbol{r}\| \leq \mathcal{T} \wedge \\ V = \mathrm{Com}_{ck}(\ell^{(1)}, \ldots, \ell^{(\psi)}; \boldsymbol{r}) \wedge \ell^{(i)} \in [0, N_i) \ \forall 1 \leq i \leq \psi \end{array} \right\},$$

$$\mathcal{R}'_{range}(\hat{\mathcal{T}}) = \left\{ \begin{array}{c} ((ck, V), (\bar{x}, \ell^{(1)}, \ldots, \ell^{(\psi)}, \hat{\boldsymbol{r}})) : \|\hat{\boldsymbol{r}}\| \leq \hat{\mathcal{T}} \wedge \bar{x} \in \Delta C_{w,p}^{d/s} \wedge \\ \bar{x}V = \mathrm{Com}_{ck}(\bar{x}\ell^{(1)}, \ldots, \bar{x}\ell^{(\psi)}; \hat{\boldsymbol{r}}) \wedge \ell^{(i)} \in [0, N_i) \ \forall 1 \leq i \leq \psi \end{array} \right\}.$$

The full description of the range proof is given in Protocol 2 where the commitment scheme is instantiated with UMC and ϕ_1, ϕ_2 are parameters determining the rejection sampling rate. The first part of the proof (Steps 4 and 5 in the verification, and its relevant components) uses the binary proof idea from [7,14] to show that $f_j^{(i)}$'s are encodings of bits, but the proof is done in parallel CRT slots. Observe in Protocol 2 that $f^{(i)} = x \cdot \langle b_0^{(i)}, \ldots, b_{k_i-1}^{(i)}, \mathbf{0}^{s-k_i} \rangle + \langle a_0^{(i)}, \ldots, a_{k_i-1}^{(i)}, \mathbf{0}^{s-k_i} \rangle = x \cdot \ell_{\mathrm{crti}}^{(i)} + a_{\mathrm{crti}}^{(i)}$ where $\mathbf{0}^{s-k_i}$ denotes a zero vector of dimension $s - k_i$. Therefore, we have, for each $1 \leq i \leq \psi$,

$$f^{(i)}(x - f^{(i)}) = x^2 \cdot \ell_{\mathrm{crti}}^{(i)}(1 - \ell_{\mathrm{crti}}^{(i)}) + x \cdot a_{\mathrm{crti}}^{(i)}(1 - 2\ell_{\mathrm{crti}}^{(i)}) - (a_{\mathrm{crti}}^{(i)})^2$$

Since there is no x^2 term (i.e., the coefficient of x^2 is zero) on the left hand side of Step 5 in the verification, we get $\ell_{\mathrm{crti}}^{(i)}(1 - \ell_{\mathrm{crti}}^{(i)}) = 0$ when Step 5 is satisfied for 3 distinct challenges x. This gives us

$$\langle b_0^{(i)}(1-b_0^{(i)}), \ldots, b_{k_i-1}^{(i)}(1-b_{k_i-1}^{(i)}), \mathbf{0}^{s-k_i} \rangle = 0 \implies b_j^{(i)}(1-b_j^{(i)}) = 0 \text{ in } R_q^{(j)} \quad (14)$$

for each $0 \leq j < s - k_i$. This fact is then used to prove that $b_j^{(i)}$'s are binary. However, since the proof is relaxed, we need to deal with more complicated issues and give the full details in the proofs of Theorem 1.

The second part of the proof is a standard argument to show that the bits $b_0^{(i)}, \ldots, b_{k_i-1}^{(i)}$ construct a value $\ell^{(i)}$ for each $1 \leq i \leq \psi$. We assumed N_i's are of the form $N_i = 2^{k_i}$ for $k_i \geq 1$. This can be extended to work for any range as described in the full version [13], where we also discuss about the practical aspects of the range proof. The following states the properties of Protocol 2.

Theorem 1. *Let* $\gamma_{range} = 4\sqrt{3}\phi_2 p w \mathcal{B} m d$. *Assume* $q > \max\{N_1, \ldots, N_\psi\}$, $d \geq 128$,[11] R_q *splits into exactly s fields and UMC is hiding and* γ_{range}-*binding.*

---

[11] The assumption $d \geq 128$ is put merely to use a constant factor of 2 when bounding the Euclidean norm of a vector following normal distribution.

$\mathcal{P}_{\text{range}}((ck, V), (\ell^{(1)}, \ldots, \ell^{(\psi)}; r))$ $\qquad\qquad\qquad$ $\mathcal{V}_{\text{range}}(ck, V)$

1: $r_b, r_c \leftarrow \{-\mathcal{B}, \ldots, \mathcal{B}\}^{md}$

2: $r_a, r_d, r_e \leftarrow D_{\phi_2 T_2}^{md}$ for $T_2 = pw\mathcal{B}\sqrt{3md}$

3: **for** $i = 1, \ldots, \psi$ **do**

4: $\quad a_0^{(i)}, \ldots, a_{k_i-1}^{(i)} \leftarrow D_{\phi_1 T_1}^{d/s}$ for $T_1 = p\sqrt{kw}$

5: $\quad a_{\text{crti}}^{(i)} = \text{CRT}^{-1}(a_0^{(i)}, \ldots, a_{k_i-1}^{(i)}, \mathbf{0}^{s-k_i})$

6: $\quad \ell_{\text{crti}}^{(i)} = \text{CRT}^{-1}(b_0^{(i)}, \ldots, b_{k_i-1}^{(i)}, \mathbf{0}^{s-k_i})$

7: $B = \text{Com}_{ck}(\ell_{\text{crti}}^{(1)}, \ldots, \ell_{\text{crti}}^{(\psi)}; r_b)$

8: $A = \text{Com}_{ck}(a_{\text{crti}}^{(1)}, \ldots, a_{\text{crti}}^{(\psi)}; r_a)$

9: $C = \text{Com}_{ck}(a_{\text{crti}}^{(1)}(1 - 2\ell_{\text{crti}}^{(1)}), \ldots, a_{\text{crti}}^{(\psi)}(1 - 2\ell_{\text{crti}}^{(\psi)}); r_c)$

10: $D = \text{Com}_{ck}(-(a_{\text{crti}}^{(1)})^2, \ldots, -(a_{\text{crti}}^{(\psi)})^2; r_d)$

11: $E = \text{Com}_{ck}(e; r_e)$ $\qquad \dfrac{A, B, C, D, E}{}\!\!\longrightarrow$

$\qquad\qquad\qquad\qquad \longleftarrow\!\!\dfrac{x}{}$ $\quad x \leftarrow \mathcal{C}_{w,p}^{d'}$ for $d' = d/s$

12: **for** $i \in [1, \psi], j \in [0, k_i)$ **do**

13: $\quad f_j^{(i)} = x \cdot b_j^{(i)} + a_j^{(i)}$

$\boldsymbol{f}_{\text{crt}} := (f_0^{(1)}, \ldots, f_{k_\psi-1}^{(\psi)}), \boldsymbol{b} := (b_0^{(1)}, \ldots, b_{k_\psi-1}^{(\psi)})$

14: $\text{Rej}(\boldsymbol{f}_{\text{crt}}, x\boldsymbol{b}, \phi_1, p\sqrt{kw})$

15: $\boldsymbol{z}_b = x \cdot \boldsymbol{r}_b + \boldsymbol{r}_a, \ \boldsymbol{z}_c = x \cdot \boldsymbol{r}_c + \boldsymbol{r}_d$

16: $\boldsymbol{z} = x \cdot \boldsymbol{r} + \boldsymbol{r}_e$

17: $\text{Rej}((\boldsymbol{z}_b, \boldsymbol{z}_c, \boldsymbol{z}), x(\boldsymbol{r}_b, \boldsymbol{r}_c, \boldsymbol{r}), \phi_2, T_2)$

If aborted, return $\perp$. $\qquad \dfrac{\boldsymbol{f}_{\text{crt}}, \boldsymbol{z}_b, \boldsymbol{z}_c, \boldsymbol{z}}{}\!\!\longrightarrow$

$\qquad\qquad\qquad$ 1: **for** $i = 1, \ldots, \psi$ **do**

$\qquad\qquad\qquad$ 2: $\quad f^{(i)} = \text{CRT}^{-1}(f_0^{(i)}, \ldots, f_{k_i-1}^{(i)}, \mathbf{0}^{s-k_i})$

$\qquad\qquad\qquad$ 3: $\|\boldsymbol{z}_b\|, \|\boldsymbol{z}_c\|, \|\boldsymbol{z}\| \overset{?}{\leq} 2\phi_2 T_2 \sqrt{md}$

$\qquad\qquad\qquad$ 4: $xB + A \overset{?}{=} \text{Com}_{ck}(f^{(0)}, \ldots, f^{(\psi)}; \boldsymbol{z}_b)$

$\qquad\qquad\qquad$ $\boldsymbol{g} := (f^{(0)}(x - f^{(0)}), \ldots, f^{(\psi)}(x - f^{(\psi)}))$

$\qquad\qquad\qquad$ 5: $xC + D \overset{?}{=} \text{Com}_{ck}(\boldsymbol{g}; \boldsymbol{z}_c)$

$\qquad\qquad\qquad$ 6: $xV + E \overset{?}{=} \text{Com}_{ck}(\boldsymbol{v}; \boldsymbol{z})$

Protocol 2. Σ-protocol for $\mathcal{R}_{\text{range}}$ and $\mathcal{R}'_{\text{range}}$. The vectors e and v are defined below.

$$e := \left(\sum_{j=0}^{k_1-1} 2^j a_j^{(1)}, \ldots, \sum_{j=0}^{k_\psi-1} 2^j a_j^{(\psi)} \right), \ v := \left(\sum_{j=0}^{k_1-1} 2^j f_j^{(1)}, \ldots, \sum_{j=0}^{k_\psi-1} 2^j f_j^{(\psi)} \right) \text{ over } R_q.$$

Then, Protocol 2 is a 3-special sound Σ-protocol (as in Definition 3) for the relations $\mathcal{R}_{range}(\mathcal{B}\sqrt{md})$ and $\mathcal{R}'_{range}(\gamma_{range})$ with a completeness error $1 - 1/(\mu(\phi_1)\mu(\phi_2))$ for $\mu(\phi_i) = e^{12/\phi_i + 1/(2\phi_i^2)}$, $i = 1, 2$.

Proof (Theorem 1). Completeness and SHVZK proofs are in the full version.

3-special soundness: Given 3 accepting protocol transcripts, we have $(A, B, C, D, E, x, \boldsymbol{f}_{crt}, \boldsymbol{z}_b, \boldsymbol{z}_c, \boldsymbol{z}), (A, B, C, D, E, x', \boldsymbol{f}'_{crt}, \boldsymbol{z}'_b, \boldsymbol{z}'_c, \boldsymbol{z}'), (A, B, C, D, E, x'', \boldsymbol{f}''_{crt}, \boldsymbol{z}''_b, \boldsymbol{z}''_c, \boldsymbol{z}'')$, with $\boldsymbol{f} = (f^{(1)}, \ldots, f^{(\psi)})$, $\boldsymbol{f}' = (f'^{(1)}, \ldots, f'^{(\psi)})$ and $\boldsymbol{f}'' = (f''^{(1)}, \ldots, f''^{(\psi)})$ computed as in the verification. We split the proof into two parts: binary proof and range proof.

Binary proof. By Step 4 in the verification, we have

$$xB + A = \text{Com}_{ck}(\boldsymbol{f}; \boldsymbol{z}_b), \tag{15}$$

$$x'B + A = \text{Com}_{ck}(\boldsymbol{f}'; \boldsymbol{z}'_b), \tag{16}$$

$$x''B + A = \text{Com}_{ck}(\boldsymbol{f}''; \boldsymbol{z}''_b). \tag{17}$$

Subtracting (16) from (15), we get $(x - x') \cdot B = \text{Com}_{ck}(\boldsymbol{f} - \boldsymbol{f}'; \boldsymbol{z}_b - \boldsymbol{z}'_b)$. Thus, for $y := x - x'$, we get exact valid openings of yB such that

$$yB = \text{Com}_{ck}(\boldsymbol{f} - \boldsymbol{f}'; \boldsymbol{z}_b - \boldsymbol{z}'_b) =: \text{Com}_{ck}(\hat{\boldsymbol{b}}; \hat{\boldsymbol{r}}_b). \tag{18}$$

Note that $\|\hat{\boldsymbol{r}}_b\| = \|\boldsymbol{z}_b - \boldsymbol{z}'_b\| \leq 4\sqrt{3}\phi_2 pw\mathcal{B}md = \gamma_{range}$, proving the claimed bound for $\mathcal{R}'_{range}$. Multiplying (15) by y and using (18) gives

$$yA = \text{Com}_{ck}(y\boldsymbol{f}; y\boldsymbol{z}_b) - xyB = \text{Com}_{ck}(y\boldsymbol{f} - x\hat{\boldsymbol{b}}; y\boldsymbol{z}_b - x\hat{\boldsymbol{r}}_b)$$
$$= \text{Com}_{ck}(x\boldsymbol{f}' - x'\boldsymbol{f}; x\boldsymbol{z}'_b - x'\boldsymbol{z}_b) =: \text{Com}_{ck}(\hat{\boldsymbol{a}}; \hat{\boldsymbol{r}}_a). \tag{19}$$

Observe that $y\boldsymbol{f} = x\hat{\boldsymbol{b}} + \hat{\boldsymbol{a}}$ by the definition of $\hat{\boldsymbol{a}}$. By the Chinese Remainder Theorem, the equality holds in each CRT slot. Using Step 5 of the verification in a similar manner, we get exact message openings $\hat{\boldsymbol{c}}$ and $\hat{\boldsymbol{d}}$ of yC and yD such that $y\boldsymbol{g} = x\hat{\boldsymbol{c}} + \hat{\boldsymbol{d}}$. Writing these equations coordinate-wise in each CRT slot, we have the following for all $1 \leq i \leq \psi$ and $0 \leq j \leq s - 1$

$$yf_j^{(i)} = x\hat{b}_j^{(i)} + \hat{a}_j^{(i)} \quad \text{in } R_q^{(j)}, \text{ and} \tag{20}$$

$$yg_j^{(i)} = yf_j^{(i)}(x - f_j^{(i)}) = x\hat{c}_j^{(i)} + \hat{d}_j^{(i)} \quad \text{in } R_q^{(j)}, \tag{21}$$

since all the challenges and their differences are the same in each CRT slot. Now, by the γ_{range}-binding property of UMC, except with negligible probability, the PPT prover cannot output a new valid exact opening of yA, yB, yC or yD in any of its rewinds. Thus, except with negligible probability, responses with respect to x' and x'' will have the same form. That is, the following holds

$$yf_j'^{(i)} = x'\hat{b}_j^{(i)} + \hat{a}_j^{(i)}, \qquad yf_j'^{(i)}(x' - f_j'^{(i)}) = x'\hat{c}_j^{(i)} + \hat{d}_j^{(i)},$$
$$\qquad\qquad\qquad\qquad\qquad\qquad\qquad\qquad\qquad\qquad\quad \text{in } R_q^{(j)}. \tag{22}$$
$$yf_j''^{(i)} = x''\hat{b}_j^{(i)} + \hat{a}_j^{(i)}, \qquad yf_j''^{(i)}(x'' - f_j''^{(i)}) = x''\hat{c}_j^{(i)} + \hat{d}_j^{(i)},$$

Now, multiplying (21) by y and using (20), we get

$$
y \cdot \left(x \cdot \hat{c}_j^{(i)} + \hat{d}_j^{(i)} \right) = y \cdot \left(y f_j^{(i)} (x - f_j^{(i)}) \right) = y f_j^{(i)} (yx - y f_j^{(i)})
$$
$$
= (x \hat{b}_j^{(i)} + \hat{a}_j^{(i)})(yx - x \hat{b}_j^{(i)} - \hat{a}_j^{(i)}) = (x \hat{b}_j^{(i)} + \hat{a}_j^{(i)})(x(y - \hat{b}_j^{(i)}) - \hat{a}_j^{(i)}) \quad (23)
$$
$$
= x^2 \left[\hat{b}_j^{(i)}(y - \hat{b}_j^{(i)}) \right] + x \left[\hat{a}_j^{(i)}(y - 2\hat{b}_j^{(i)}) \right] - (\hat{a}_j^{(i)})^2,
$$

and thus

$$
x^2 \left[\hat{b}_j^{(i)}(y - \hat{b}_j^{(i)}) \right] + x \left[\hat{a}_j^{(i)}(y - 2\hat{b}_j^{(i)}) - y \hat{c}_j^{(i)} \right] - (\hat{a}_j^{(i)})^2 - y \hat{d}_j^{(i)} = 0 \quad \text{in } R_q^{(j)}. \quad (24)
$$

Repeating the same steps of (23) with the equations in (22), we get two copies of (24) where x is replaced with x' in one and with x'' in the other. That is, we have the following system

$$
\begin{pmatrix} 1 & x & x^2 \\ 1 & x' & x'^2 \\ 1 & x'' & x''^2 \end{pmatrix} \cdot \begin{pmatrix} -(\hat{a}_j^{(i)})^2 - y \hat{d}_j^{(i)} \\ \hat{a}_j^{(i)}(y - 2\hat{b}_j^{(i)}) - y \hat{c}_j^{(i)} \\ \hat{b}_j^{(i)}(y - \hat{b}_j^{(i)}) \end{pmatrix} = \mathbf{0} \quad \text{in } R_q^{(j)}. \quad (25)
$$

Since $R_q^{(j)}$ is a field, Vandermonde matrix on the left is invertible for distinct challenges, and we get $\hat{b}_j^{(i)}(y - \hat{b}_j^{(i)}) = 0$, which implies $\hat{b}_j^{(i)} \in \{0, y\}$ in a field, i.e.

$$
\hat{b}_j^{(i)} = y b_j^{(i)} \quad \text{for } b_j^{(i)} \in \{0, 1\}. \quad (26)
$$

The range proof part is rather easier and is given in the full version [13].   □

Remark 1. The first rejection sampling at Step 14 of Protocol 2 is not necessary as UMC allows unbounded-length messages. However, when rejection sampling is done, the bitsize of $f_j^{(i)}$'s are smaller (about a factor 3) than $d \log q / s$, which is the bitsize of a random element in $R_q^{(j)}$. Further, there is no mod q reduction in the prover's response, and also no mod $P^{(j)}(X)$ at Step 13 of Protocol 2 since $b_j^{(i)}$'s are binary.

5   Efficient One-Shot Proofs for Useful Relations

5.1   Relaxed Proof of Commitment to Sequences of Bits

Using our new techniques, we extend the multi-shot proof of commitment to bits from [14] to a one-shot proof. Our protocol, called Protocol Bin, proves a weaker relation but, the relaxation is tailored in a way that the soundness proof of higher level proofs (Protocol 3) still work. It proves that a commitment B opens to sequences of binary values such that there is a single 1 in each sequence, i.e., Hamming weight of each sequence is exactly 1. The relations of Protocol Bin are defined in Definition 5 where $\boldsymbol{b} = (b_{0,0}, \dots, b_{k-1,\beta-1})$ for $k \geq 1, \beta \geq 2$.

Definition 5. *The following defines the relations for Protocol Bin* $\mathcal{T}, \hat{\mathcal{T}} \in \mathbb{R}^+$.

$$\mathcal{R}_{bin}(\mathcal{T}) = \left\{ \begin{array}{c} ((ck, B), (\boldsymbol{b}, \boldsymbol{r})) \; : \; \|\boldsymbol{r}\| \leq \mathcal{T} \; \wedge \; (b_{j,i} \in \{0, 1\} \; \forall j, i) \\ \wedge \; B = \mathrm{Com}_{ck}(\boldsymbol{b}; \boldsymbol{r}) \; \wedge \; (\sum_{i=0}^{\beta-1} b_{j,i} = 1 \; \forall j) \end{array} \right\}.$$

$$\mathcal{R}'_{bin}(\hat{\mathcal{T}}) = \left\{ \begin{array}{c} ((ck, B), (y, \boldsymbol{b}, \hat{\boldsymbol{r}})) : \|\hat{\boldsymbol{r}}\| \leq \hat{\mathcal{T}} \; \wedge \; (b_{j,i} \in \{0, 1\} \; \forall j, i) \; \wedge \\ y \in \Delta \mathcal{C}^d_{w,p} \; \wedge \; yB = \mathrm{Com}_{ck}(y\boldsymbol{b}; \hat{\boldsymbol{r}}) \; \wedge \; (\sum_{i=0}^{\beta-1} b_{j,i} = 1 \; \forall j) \end{array} \right\}.$$

The idea of the binary proof (combined with the CRT-packing technique) is already used in Protocol 2. The condition on the Hamming weight is the difference to Protocol 2 and is handled with a small modification. We defer the full description of Protocol Bin to the full version of the manuscript and show below the crucial part in making the binary proof work in a fully-splitting ring R_q.

Handling binary proof for NTT-friendly modulus q. As in (25) in the soundness proof of Theorem 1, we get the same system of equations below in the soundness proof of Protocol Bin

$$\begin{pmatrix} 1 & x & x^2 \\ 1 & x' & x'^2 \\ 1 & x'' & x''^2 \end{pmatrix} \cdot \begin{pmatrix} -(\hat{a}_{j,i})^2 - y\hat{d}_{j,i} \\ \hat{a}_{j,i}(y - 2\hat{b}_{j,i}) - y\hat{c}_{j,i} \\ \hat{b}_{j,i}(y - \hat{b}_{j,i}) \end{pmatrix} = 0 \qquad \text{in } R_q,$$

where $\hat{b}_{j,i}$ are the values we want to prove to be of the form $\hat{b}_{j,i} = yb_{j,i}$ for $b_{j,i} \in \{0, 1\}$. The difference now is that all equations now hold in R_q, and we cannot use any invertibility argument. Multiplying both sides of the above system by $\mathrm{adj}(\boldsymbol{V})$ where $\boldsymbol{V}$ is the Vandermonde matrix on the left, we get

$$\det(\boldsymbol{V})\hat{b}_{j,i}(y - \hat{b}_{j,i}) = (x'' - x')(x' - x)(x'' - x)\hat{b}_{j,i}(y - \hat{b}_{j,i}) = 0 \quad \text{in } R_q. \quad (27)$$

We show in the proof of Theorem 2 that $\|(x'' - x')(x' - x)(x'' - x)\hat{b}_{j,i}(y - \hat{b}_{j,i})\|_\infty \leq 2^7 \phi_1^2 p^5 w^3 d^2 k \beta$. Therefore assuming $q/2 > 2^7 \phi_1^2 p^5 w^3 d^2 k \beta$, one of the factors in (27) must be zero by Lemma 7. As challenge differences are non-zero, this gives either $\hat{b}_{j,i}$ or $y - \hat{b}_{j,i}$ is zero. Thus, we get $\hat{b}_{j,i} \in \{0, y\}$. That is, $\hat{b}_{j,i} = yb_{j,i}$ for $b_{j,i} \in \{0, 1\}$ as needed for $\mathcal{R}'_{\mathrm{bin}}$. We state the results in the theorem below, and defer its full proof to the full version of the manuscript [13].

Theorem 2. *Let* $\gamma_{bin} = 2p\sqrt{dw} \left(16\phi_1^4 p^4 d^3 k^3 w^2 \beta(\beta + 1) + 12\phi_2^2 p^2 w^2 \mathcal{B}^2 m^2 d^2 \right)^{1/2}$. *Assume that* $d \geq 128$, $q/2 > 2^7 \phi_1^2 p^5 w^3 d^2 k \beta$ *and HMC is hiding and* γ_{bin}-*binding. Then, Protocol Bin is a 3-special sound* Σ-*protocol (as in Definition 3) for the relations* $\mathcal{R}_{bin}(\mathcal{B}\sqrt{md})$ *and* $\mathcal{R}'_{bin}(4\sqrt{2}\phi_2 pw\mathcal{B}md)$ *with a completeness error* $1 - 1/(\mu(\phi_1)\mu(\phi_2))$ *for* $\mu(\phi_i) = e^{12/\phi_i + 1/(2\phi_i^2)}$, $i = 1, 2$.

5.2   Relaxed One-out-of-many Proof

Our one-out-of-many proof has the same structure as in [14], which combines ideas from [7,16]. The main differences of our proof from that in [14] are the use of an exponentially large challenge set, enabling one-shot proofs, the relation the verifier is convinced of and some tweaks to the rejection sampling. The challenging part here is the soundness proof of the protocol. We use our new tools, namely Lemmas 3, 5 and 6, from Sect. 3 for the soundness proof.

Let $L = \{P_0, \ldots, P_{N-1}\}$ be a set of public commitments for some $N \geq 1$. The prover's goal is to show that he knows an opening of one of these P_i's. In common with the previous works [7,14,16], we assume that $N = \beta^k$, which can be easily satisfied by adding dummy values to L when needed. Suppose that the prover's commitment is P_ℓ for some $0 \leq \ell < N$. Observe that $\sum_{i=0}^{N-1} \delta_{\ell,i} P_i = P_\ell$. The idea for the proof is then to prove knowledge of the index ℓ with $\sum_{i=0}^{N-1} \delta_{\ell,i} P_i$ being a commitment to zero. Writing $\ell = (\ell_0, \ldots, \ell_{k-1})$ and $i = (i_0, \ldots, i_{k-1})$ as the representations in base β, we have $\delta_{\ell,i} = \prod_{j=0}^{k-1} \delta_{\ell_j, i_j}$. The prover first commits to the sequences $(\delta_{\ell_j,0}, \ldots, \delta_{\ell_j, \beta-1})$ for all $0 \leq j \leq k-1$, and then uses Protocol Bin to show that they are well-formed (i.e., they construct an index in the range $[0, N)$ as in the range proof). Let us define the proved relations next.

Definition 6. *The following defines the relations for Protocol 3 for $T, \hat{T} \in \mathbb{R}^+$.*

$$\mathcal{R}_{1/N}(T) = \left\{ \begin{array}{c} ((ck, (P_0, \ldots, P_{N-1})), (\ell, r)) : \\ \ell \in [0, N) \wedge \|r\| \leq T \wedge P_\ell = \mathrm{Com}_{ck}(0; r) \end{array} \right\},$$

$$\mathcal{R}'_{1/N}(\hat{T}) = \left\{ \begin{array}{c} ((ck, (P_0, \ldots, P_{N-1})), (y, \ell, \hat{r})) : \ell \in [0, N) \wedge \|\hat{r}\| \leq \hat{T} \wedge \\ y P_\ell = \mathrm{Com}_{ck}(0; \hat{r}) \wedge y \text{ is a product of elements in } \Delta\mathcal{C}_{w,p}^d \end{array} \right\}.$$

From Protocol Bin, the prover's response contains $f_{j,i} = x\delta_{\ell_j,i} + a_{j,i}$ for a challenge x. Considering the product $p_i(x) := \prod_{j=0}^{k-1} f_{j,i_j}$, we see, for all $i \in [0, N-1]$,

$$p_i(x) = \prod_{j=0}^{k-1} \left(x\delta_{\ell_j,i_j} + a_{j,i_j} \right) = \prod_{j=0}^{k-1} x \cdot \delta_{\ell_j,i_j} + \sum_{j=0}^{k-1} p_{i,j} x^j = \delta_{\ell,i} x^k + \sum_{j=0}^{k-1} p_{i,j} x^j, \quad (28)$$

for some ring element $p_{i,j}$'s as a function of ℓ and $a_{j,i}$'s (independent of the challenge x). Since ℓ and $a_{j,i}$'s are known to the prover before receiving a challenge, he can compute $p_{i,j}$'s prior to sending the initial commitment. Since p_ℓ is the only such polynomial of degree k, in his first move, the prover sends some E_j's that are tailored to cancel out the coefficients of the terms $1, x, \ldots, x^{k-1}$, and the coefficient of x^k is set to the prover's commitment P_ℓ using $\sum_{i=0}^{N-1} \delta_{\ell,i} P_i$. The full description is given in Protocol 3. In the full version [13], we show how our one-out-of-many proof can be extended to a set membership proof.

Theorem 3. *Let $\gamma_{1/N} = (k+1)2^{\kappa'+2}\sqrt{3}\phi_2 \mathcal{B}md^2 w^\kappa p^{\kappa+1}$ for $\kappa' = k(k-1)/2$ and $\kappa = k(k+1)/2$. Assume $d \geq 128$, $q > 2^7\phi_1^2 p^5 w^3 d^2 k\beta$ and HMC is hiding and γ-binding for $\gamma = \max\{\gamma_{bin}, \gamma_{1/N}\}$. For $\mu(\cdot)$ as in Theorem 1, Protocol 3 is a $(k'+1)$-special sound Σ-protocol (as in Definition 3) for the relations $\mathcal{R}_{1/N}(\mathcal{B}\sqrt{md})$ and $\mathcal{R}'_{1/N}(\gamma_{1/N})$ with a completeness error $1 - 1/(\mu(\phi_1)\mu(\phi_2))$ where $k' = \max\{2, k\}$.*

Proof (Theorem 3). Completeness and SHVZK proofs are in the full version. $(k'+1)$-**special soundness:** Assume that $k > 1$. Given $(k+1)$ distinct challenges

$\mathcal{P}_{1/\mathrm{N}}((ck,(P_0,\ldots,P_{N-1})),(\ell,\boldsymbol{r}))$	$\mathcal{V}_{1/\mathrm{N}}(ck,(P_0,\ldots,P_{N-1}))$

1: $\boldsymbol{r}_b \leftarrow \{-\mathcal{B},\ldots,\mathcal{B}\}^{md}$

2: $\boldsymbol{\delta} = (\delta_{\ell_0,0},\ldots,\delta_{\ell_{k-1},\beta-1})$

3: $B = \mathrm{Com}_{ck}(\boldsymbol{\delta}; \boldsymbol{r}_b)$

4: $A,C,D \leftarrow \mathcal{P}_{\mathrm{bin}}((ck,B),(\boldsymbol{\delta},\boldsymbol{r}_b))$

5: $\boldsymbol{\rho}_0 \leftarrow D_{\phi_2 T_2}^{md}$ for $T_2 = \mathcal{B}p^k w^k \sqrt{3md}$

6: for $j = 0,\ldots,k-1$ do

7: $\boldsymbol{\rho}_j \leftarrow \{-\mathcal{B},\ldots,\mathcal{B}\}^{md}$ if $j \neq 0$

8: $E_j = \displaystyle\sum_{i=0}^{N-1} p_{i,j} P_i + \mathrm{Com}_{ck}(\boldsymbol{0}; \boldsymbol{\rho}_j)$

using $p_{i,j}$'s from (28) $\xrightarrow{\quad A,B,C,D,E_0,\ldots,E_{k-1} \quad}$

$\xleftarrow{\qquad\qquad x \qquad\qquad}$ $x \leftarrow \mathcal{C}_{w,p}^d$

9: $\boldsymbol{f}_1,\boldsymbol{z}_b,\boldsymbol{z}_c \leftarrow \mathcal{P}_{\mathrm{bin}}(x)$

10: $\mathrm{Rej}(\boldsymbol{f}_1, x\boldsymbol{\delta}_1, \phi_1, p\sqrt{kw})$ for $\boldsymbol{\delta}_1 := (\delta_{\ell_0,1},\ldots,\delta_{\ell_{k-1},\beta-1})$

11: $\boldsymbol{z} = x^k \boldsymbol{r} - \displaystyle\sum_{j=0}^{k-1} x^j \boldsymbol{\rho}_j$

12: $\mathrm{Rej}((\boldsymbol{z}_b,\boldsymbol{z}_c,\boldsymbol{z}),(x\boldsymbol{r}_b,x\boldsymbol{r}_c,x^k\boldsymbol{r}-\displaystyle\sum_{j=1}^{k-1}x^j\boldsymbol{\rho}_j),\phi_2,T_2)$

If aborted, return $\perp$. $\xrightarrow{\quad \boldsymbol{f}_1,\boldsymbol{z}_b,\boldsymbol{z}_c,\boldsymbol{z} \quad}$

1: $\mathcal{V}_{\mathrm{bin}}(ck, B, x, A, C, D, \boldsymbol{f}_1, \boldsymbol{z}_b, \boldsymbol{z}_c) \overset{?}{=} 1$

2: $\|\boldsymbol{z}\|, \|\boldsymbol{z}_b\|, \|\boldsymbol{z}_c\| \overset{?}{\leq} 2\sqrt{3}\phi_2 \mathcal{B}mdp^k w^k$

3: $\displaystyle\sum_{i=0}^{N-1}\left(\prod_{j=0}^{k-1} f_{j,i_j}\right)P_i - \sum_{j=0}^{k-1} E_j x^j \overset{?}{=} \mathrm{Com}_{ck}(\boldsymbol{0}; \boldsymbol{z})$

Protocol 3. Σ-protocol for $\mathcal{R}_{1/\mathrm{N}}$ and $\mathcal{R}'_{1/\mathrm{N}}$. $\mathcal{P}_{\mathrm{bin}}$ in Steps 4 and 9 refers to the commitment and response algorithms of Protocol Bin's prover, respectively, and $\mathcal{V}_{\mathrm{bin}}$ refers to Protocol Bin's verifier algorithm. The norm checks on $\boldsymbol{z}_b, \boldsymbol{z}_c$ in Protocol Bin are skipped when $\mathcal{V}_{\mathrm{bin}}(ck, B, x, A, C, D, \boldsymbol{f}_1, \boldsymbol{z}_b, \boldsymbol{z}_c)$ is run.

$x_0,\ldots,x_k$, we have $(k+1)$ accepting responses with the same $(A, B, C, D, E_0, \ldots, E_{k-1})$. Let $(\boldsymbol{f}_1^{(0)}, \boldsymbol{z}^{(0)}), \ldots, (\boldsymbol{f}_1^{(k)}, \boldsymbol{z}^{(k)})$ be part of the responses with respect to challenges $x_0, \ldots, x_k$, respectively. Setting $y = x_1 - x_0$, we first use 3-special soundness of Protocol Bin to extract exact valid message openings $\hat{b}_{j,i}$ and $\hat{a}_{j,i}$ of yB and yA, respectively. We know that $\hat{b}_{j,i} = yb_{j,i}$ for $b_{j,i} \in \{0,1\}$ and only a single one of $\{b_{j,0}, \ldots, b_{j,\beta-1}\}$ is 1 for each $j \in \{0, \ldots, k-1\}$. Now, we construct the representation of ℓ in base β as follows. For each $0 \leq j \leq k - 1$, the j-th digit ℓ_j is the integer c such that $b_{j,c} = 1$. It is easy to construct the index ℓ from here using its digit ℓ_j's.

From the soundness proof of Protocol Bin that use γ_{bin}-binding property of the commitment scheme, we have, for all $0 \leq \eta \leq k - 1$, $y f_{j,i}^{(\eta)} = x_\eta \hat{b}_{j,i} + \hat{a}_{j,i} = x_\eta \cdot y b_{j,i} + \hat{a}_{j,i}$. Now compute $\hat{p}_i(x_\eta) = y^k \prod_{j=0}^{k-1} f_{j,i_j}^{(\eta)} = \prod_{j=0}^{k-1} y f_{j,i_j}^{(\eta)} = \prod_{j=0}^{k-1} \left(y x_\eta b_{j,i_j} + \hat{a}_{j,i_j} \right)$ for each $i = 0, \ldots, N-1$. By the construction of ℓ, $\hat{p}_\ell(x_\eta)$ is the only polynomial of degree k in x_η for all $0 \leq \eta \leq k - 1$. Then, we can multiply the both sides of the last verification step by y^k and re-write it as below

$$\sum_{i=0}^{N-1} \hat{p}_i(x_\eta) P_i - \sum_{j=0}^{k-1} y^k E_j x_\eta^j = x_\eta^k \cdot y^k P_\ell + \sum_{j=0}^{k-1} \tilde{E}_j x_\eta^j = \mathrm{Com}_{ck}(\mathbf{0}; y^k \mathbf{z}^{(\eta)}), \quad (29)$$

where $\tilde{E}_j$'s are the terms multiplied by the monomials x_η^j's of degree at most $k - 1$ and are independent of x_η. Equation (29) is exactly the case described in (9) and the verification of Protocol 1 in Sect. 3 with $C_k = y^k P_\ell$. By the discussion in Sect. 3, we obtain exact openings of $\det(\mathbf{V}) y^k P_\ell$ as $(\mathbf{0}, y^k \hat{\mathbf{r}})$ where $\hat{\mathbf{r}} = \sum_{i=0}^{k} \Gamma_i \mathbf{z}^{(i)}$ for $\Gamma_i = (-1)^{i+k} \prod_{0 \leq l < j \leq k \wedge j, l \neq i} (x_j - x_l)$, i.e., we have

$$\det(\mathbf{V}) y^k P_\ell = \mathrm{Com}_{ck}(\mathbf{0}; y^k \hat{\mathbf{r}}) \implies y^k \cdot (\det(\mathbf{V}) P_\ell - \mathrm{Com}_{ck}(\mathbf{0}; \hat{\mathbf{r}})) = 0$$

$$(\text{by Lemma 6}) \implies y \cdot (\det(\mathbf{V}) P_\ell - \mathrm{Com}_{ck}(\mathbf{0}; \hat{\mathbf{r}})) = 0$$

$$\implies \det(\mathbf{V}) y P_\ell = \mathrm{Com}_{ck}(\mathbf{0}; y \hat{\mathbf{r}}). \quad (30)$$

In the end, we have an exact opening of $\det(\mathbf{V}) y P_\ell$ as $(\mathbf{0}, y \hat{\mathbf{r}})$. This randomness opening is a factor $y \in \Delta \mathcal{C}_{w,p}^d$ larger than what we have in Lemma 5. Thus, using Lemma 3 and Lemma 5, we conclude, for $\kappa' = k(k-1)/2$ and $\kappa = k(k+1)/2$,

$$\|y \hat{\mathbf{r}}\| \leq (k+1) d (2p)^{\kappa'+1} w^{\kappa'} \max_i \|\mathbf{z}^{(i)}\| \leq (k+1) d (2p)^{\kappa'+1} w^{\kappa'} \cdot 2\sqrt{3} \phi_2 \mathcal{B} m d w^k p^k$$

$$\leq (k+1) 2^{\kappa'+2} \sqrt{3} \phi_2 \mathcal{B} m d^2 w^\kappa p^{\kappa+1}.$$

Recall that we assumed $k > 1$. When $k = 1$, Protocol Bin still needs 3 challenges for its soundness property. Hence, Protocol 3 is at least 3-special sound. $\square$

6   Applications of Relaxed ZKPs to Advanced Tools

The relaxed range proof combined with a relaxed proof of knowledge results in a form of efficient anonymous credentials as detailed in the full version of the manuscript [13]. To prove relations on a set of attributes, a single use of our range proof is sufficient and we show how the relaxation is handled. Our second construction is a ring signature that builds on the relaxed one-out-of-many proof.

Ring Signature. The construction of ring signature from one-out-of-many proof follows the same strategy as in [7,14,16]. The users commit to their secret keys and these commitments represent the public keys. A set of public keys is then

Table 4. Parameter setting of our ring signature with a root Hermite factor ≤ 1.0045 for both M-LWE and M-SIS. $\mathcal{B} = 1, \phi_1 = \phi_2 = 15$ for all cases.

N	2	8	64	2^{12}	2^{21}
(d, w, p)	$(256, 60, 1)$	$(256, 60, 1)$	$(128, 66, 2)$	$(128, 66, 2)$	$(128, 66, 2)$
(n, m)	$(4, 12)$	$(4, 13)$	$(10, 28)$	$(13, 32)$	$(22, 46)$
(k, β)	$(1, 2)$	$(1, 8)$	$(1, 64)$	$(2, 64)$	$(3, 128)$
q	$\approx 2^{53}$	$\approx 2^{58}$	$\approx 2^{59}$	$\approx 2^{60}$	$\approx 2^{77}$
Signature Length (KB)	36	41	58	103	256
Public Key Length (KB)	6.63	7.25	9.22	12.19	26.47
Secret Key Length (KB)	0.38	0.41	0.44	0.50	0.72

used as the set of public commitments in one-out-of-many proof. The prover proves knowledge of an opening of one of the commitments (i.e., knowledge of a secret key corresponding to one of the public keys of the ring signature). The main difference from [7,14,16] is that we show that our relaxed proof is still sufficient (see the full version [13] for details). In Table 4, we give the concrete instantiation of the parameters.

Acknowledgement. Ron Steinfeld and Joseph K. Liu were supported in part by ARC Discovery Project grant DP180102199.

References

1. Albrecht, M.R., Rechberger, C., Schneider, T., Tiessen, T., Zohner, M.: Ciphers for MPC and FHE. In: Oswald, E., Fischlin, M. (eds.) EUROCRYPT 2015. LNCS, vol. 9056, pp. 430–454. Springer, Heidelberg (2015). https://doi.org/10.1007/978-3-662-46800-5_17

2. Baum, C., Bootle, J., Cerulli, A., del Pino, R., Groth, J., Lyubashevsky, V.: Sublinear lattice-based zero-knowledge arguments for arithmetic circuits. In: Shacham, H., Boldyreva, A. (eds.) CRYPTO 2018. LNCS, vol. 10992, pp. 669–699. Springer, Cham (2018). https://doi.org/10.1007/978-3-319-96881-0_23

3. Baum, C., Damgård, I., Lyubashevsky, V., Oechsner, S., Peikert, C.: More efficient commitments from structured lattice assumptions. In: Catalano, D., De Prisco, R. (eds.) SCN 2018. LNCS, vol. 11035, pp. 368–385. Springer, Cham (2018). https://doi.org/10.1007/978-3-319-98113-0_20

4. Baum, C., Lin, H., Oechsner, S.: Towards practical lattice-based one-time linkable ring signatures. In: Naccache, D., Xu, S., Qing, S., Samarati, P., Blanc, G., Lu, R., Zhang, Z., Meddahi, A. (eds.) ICICS 2018. LNCS, vol. 11149, pp. 303–322. Springer, Cham (2018). https://doi.org/10.1007/978-3-030-01950-1_18

5. Benhamouda, F., Camenisch, J., Krenn, S., Lyubashevsky, V., Neven, G.: Better zero-knowledge proofs for lattice encryption and their application to group signatures. In: Sarkar, P., Iwata, T. (eds.) ASIACRYPT 2014. LNCS, vol. 8873, pp. 551–572. Springer, Heidelberg (2014). https://doi.org/10.1007/978-3-662-45611-8_29

6. Benhamouda, F., Krenn, S., Lyubashevsky, V., Pietrzak, K.: Efficient zero-knowledge proofs for commitments from learning with errors over rings. In: Pernul, G., Ryan, P.Y.A., Weippl, E. (eds.) ESORICS 2015. LNCS, vol. 9326, pp. 305–325. Springer, Cham (2015). https://doi.org/10.1007/978-3-319-24174-6_16
7. Bootle, J., Cerulli, A., Chaidos, P., Ghadafi, E., Groth, J., Petit, C.: Short accountable ring signatures based on DDH. In: Pernul, G., Ryan, P.Y.A., Weippl, E. (eds.) ESORICS 2015. LNCS, vol. 9326, pp. 243–265. Springer, Cham (2015). https://doi.org/10.1007/978-3-319-24174-6_13
8. Bootle, J., Cerulli, A., Chaidos, P., Groth, J., Petit, C.: Efficient zero-knowledge arguments for arithmetic circuits in the discrete log setting. In: Fischlin, M., Coron, J.-S. (eds.) EUROCRYPT 2016. LNCS, vol. 9666, pp. 327–357. Springer, Heidelberg (2016). https://doi.org/10.1007/978-3-662-49896-5_12
9. Bünz, B., Bootle, J., Boneh, D., Poelstra, A., Wuille, P., Maxwell, G.: Bulletproofs: short proofs for confidential transactions and more. In: IEEE Symposium on Security and Privacy, pp. 315–334. IEEE (2018)
10. Chaum, D.: Security without identification: transaction systems to make big brother obsolete. Commun. ACM **28**(10), 1030–1044 (1985)
11. del Pino, R., Lyubashevsky, V., Seiler, G.: Lattice-based group signatures and zero-knowledge proofs of automorphism stability. In: ACM CCS, pp. 574–591. ACM (2018)
12. Derler, D., Ramacher, S., Slamanig, D.: Post-quantum zero-knowledge proofs for accumulators with applications to ring signatures from symmetric-key primitives. In: Lange, T., Steinwandt, R. (eds.) PQCrypto 2018. LNCS, vol. 10786, pp. 419–440. Springer, Cham (2018). https://doi.org/10.1007/978-3-319-79063-3_20. Extended version at https://eprint.iacr.org/2017/1154
13. Esgin, M.F., Steinfeld, R., Liu, J.K., Liu, D.: Lattice-based zero-knowledge proofs: new techniques for shorter and faster constructions and applications. Cryptology ePrint Archive, Report 2019/445 (2019). https://eprint.iacr.org/2019/445
14. Esgin, M.F., Steinfeld, R., Sakzad, A., Liu, J.K., Liu, D.: Short lattice-based one-out-of-many proofs and applications to ring signatures. Cryptology ePrint Archive, Report 2018/773 (2018). To appear in ACNS 2019. https://eprint.iacr.org/2018/773, https://dblp.uni-trier.de/rec/bibtex1/conf/acns/EsginSSLL19
15. Gentry, C., Halevi, S., Smart, N.P.: Fully homomorphic encryption with polylog overhead. In: Pointcheval, D., Johansson, T. (eds.) EUROCRYPT 2012. LNCS, vol. 7237, pp. 465–482. Springer, Heidelberg (2012). https://doi.org/10.1007/978-3-642-29011-4_28
16. Groth, J., Kohlweiss, M.: One-out-of-many proofs: or how to leak a secret and spend a coin. In: Oswald, E., Fischlin, M. (eds.) EUROCRYPT 2015. LNCS, vol. 9057, pp. 253–280. Springer, Heidelberg (2015). https://doi.org/10.1007/978-3-662-46803-6_9
17. Horn, R.A., Horn, R.A., Johnson, C.R.: Matrix Analysis. Cambridge University Press, New York (1990)
18. Katz, J., Kolesnikov, V., Wang, X.: Improved non-interactive zero knowledge with applications to post-quantum signatures. In: ACM CCS, pp. 525–537. ACM (2018)
19. Langlois, A., Stehlé, D.: Worst-case to average-case reductions for module lattices. Des. Codes Crypt. **75**(3), 565–599 (2015)
20. Libert, B., Ling, S., Nguyen, K., Wang, H.: Zero-knowledge arguments for lattice-based accumulators: logarithmic-size ring signatures and group signatures without trapdoors. In: Fischlin, M., Coron, J.-S. (eds.) EUROCRYPT 2016. LNCS, vol. 9666, pp. 1–31. Springer, Heidelberg (2016). https://doi.org/10.1007/978-3-662-49896-5_1

21. Lu, X., Au, M.H., Zhang, Z.: Raptor: a practical lattice-based (linkable) ring signature. Cryptology ePrint Archive, Report 2018/857 (2018). To appear in ACNS 2019. https://dblp.uni-trier.de/rec/bibtex1/conf/acns/LuAZ19

22. Lyubashevsky, V.: Fiat-Shamir with aborts: applications to lattice and factoring-based signatures. In: Matsui, M. (ed.) ASIACRYPT 2009. LNCS, vol. 5912, pp. 598–616. Springer, Heidelberg (2009). https://doi.org/10.1007/978-3-642-10366-7_35

23. Lyubashevsky, V.: Lattice signatures without trapdoors. In: Pointcheval, D., Johansson, T. (eds.) EUROCRYPT 2012. LNCS, vol. 7237, pp. 738–755. Springer, Heidelberg (2012). https://doi.org/10.1007/978-3-642-29011-4_43

24. Lyubashevsky, V., Neven, G.: One-shot verifiable encryption from lattices. In: Coron, J.-S., Nielsen, J.B. (eds.) EUROCRYPT 2017. LNCS, vol. 10210, pp. 293–323. Springer, Cham (2017). https://doi.org/10.1007/978-3-319-56620-7_11

25. Lyubashevsky, V., Seiler, G.: Short, invertible elements in partially splitting cyclotomic rings and applications to lattice-based zero-knowledge proofs. In: Nielsen, J.B., Rijmen, V. (eds.) EUROCRYPT 2018. LNCS, vol. 10820, pp. 204–224. Springer, Cham (2018). https://doi.org/10.1007/978-3-319-78381-9_8

26. Rivest, R.L., Shamir, A., Tauman, Y.: How to leak a secret. In: Boyd, C. (ed.) ASIACRYPT 2001. LNCS, vol. 2248, pp. 552–565. Springer, Heidelberg (2001). https://doi.org/10.1007/3-540-45682-1_32

27. Smart, N.P., Vercauteren, F.: Fully homomorphic SIMD operations. Des. Codes Crypt. **71**(1), 57–81 (2014)

28. Stehlé, D., Steinfeld, R., Tanaka, K., Xagawa, K.: Efficient public key encryption based on ideal lattices. In: Matsui, M. (ed.) ASIACRYPT 2009. LNCS, vol. 5912, pp. 617–635. Springer, Heidelberg (2009). https://doi.org/10.1007/978-3-642-10366-7_36

29. Stern, J.: A new paradigm for public key identification. IEEE Trans. Inf. Theory **42**(6), 1757–1768 (1996)

30. Alberto Torres, W.A., et al.: Post-quantum one-time linkable ring signature and application to ring confidential transactions in blockchain (Lattice RingCT v1.0). In: Susilo, W., Yang, G. (eds.) ACISP 2018. LNCS, vol. 10946, pp. 558–576. Springer, Cham (2018). https://doi.org/10.1007/978-3-319-93638-3_32

Efficient Lattice-Based Zero-Knowledge Arguments with Standard Soundness: Construction and Applications

Rupeng Yang[1,2], Man Ho Au[2(✉)], Zhenfei Zhang[3], Qiuliang Xu[4(✉)], Zuoxia Yu[2], and William Whyte[5]

[1] School of Computer Science and Technology, Shandong University, Jinan 250101, China
orbbyrp@gmail.com
[2] Department of Computing, The Hong Kong Polytechnic University, Hung Hom, Hong Kong
csallen@comp.polyu.edu.hk, zuoxia.yu@gmail.com
[3] Algorand, Boston, USA
zhenfei@algorand.com
[4] School of Software, Shandong University, Jinan 250101, China
xql@sdu.edu.cn
[5] Qualcomm Technologies Incorporated, Boxborough, MA, USA
wwhyte@qti.qualcomm.com

Abstract. We provide new zero-knowledge argument of knowledge systems that work directly for a wide class of language, namely, ones involving the satisfiability of matrix-vector relations and integer relations commonly found in constructions of lattice-based cryptography. Prior to this work, practical arguments for lattice-based relations either have a constant soundness error $(2/3)$, or consider a weaker form of soundness, namely, extraction only guarantees that the prover is in possession of a witness that "approximates" the actual witness. Our systems do not suffer from these limitations.

The core of our new argument systems is an efficient zero-knowledge argument of knowledge of a solution to a system of linear equations, where variables of this solution satisfy a set of quadratic constraints. This argument enjoys standard soundness, a small soundness error $(1/poly)$, and a complexity linear in the size of the solution. Using our core argument system, we construct highly efficient argument systems for a variety of statements relevant to lattices, including linear equations with short solutions and matrix-vector relations with hidden matrices.

Based on our argument systems, we present several new constructions of common privacy-preserving primitives in the *standard lattice* setting, including a group signature, a ring signature, an electronic cash system, and a range proof protocol. Our new constructions are one to three orders of magnitude more efficient than the state of the art (in standard lattice). This illustrates the efficiency and expressiveness of our argument system.

A. Boldyreva and D. Micciancio (Eds.): CRYPTO 2019, LNCS 11692, pp. 147–175, 2019.
https://doi.org/10.1007/978-3-030-26948-7_6

1   Introduction

Traditional cryptographic schemes based on number theoretic assumptions are at risk due to possible attacks from quantum computers. Among all alternatives, the lattice-based ones appear to be the most promising. To date, we have good candidates to fundamental cryptographic primitives such as public key encryption schemes (c.g., [3, 10, 11, 29]) and signature schemes (e.g., [9, 18, 21, 46]). However, lattice-based privacy-preserving primitives, such as group signatures [16], ring signatures [56], electronic cash (E-cash) [15], etc., are still significantly less efficient than their traditional counterparts, partially due to the lack of suitable lattice-based zero-knowledge proofs. Specifically, current zero-knowledge proofs for lattice-based relations either have a poor efficiency or have great restrictions when employed in constructing advanced applications.

The study of lattice-based zero-knowledge proofs is initialized by Goldreich and Goldwasser in [23]. Goldreich and Goldwasser's proof system, as well as proof systems developed in subsequent works [2, 28, 50, 54], are mainly of theoretical interest. While one can construct applications such as verifiable encryption [25] and group signature [14, 26] from these protocols, their lack of efficiency prevents them from being employed in practice.

For practical lattice-based zero-knowledge proofs, there are two main approaches in current literature.

Stern-type Protocol. One approach, which follows techniques in [31, 57], is proposed by Ling et al. in [40]. They construct an efficient zero-knowledge argument of knowledge (ZKAoK) for the basic Inhomogeneous Short Integer Solution (ISIS) relation $\mathcal{R}_{ISIS} = \{(A, y), x : A \cdot x = y \wedge \|x\| \leq \beta\}$. Focusing on arguing additional relations over witnesses, ZKAoKs for a wider class of lattice-based relations are constructed in subsequent works. This gives rise to various applications, such as verifiable encryption [40], group signature [33, 34, 36, 41, 43], ring signature [36], group encryption [35] and E-cash [37].

The major issue for Stern-type protocols is their inherent *large soundness error*. More precisely, a single round Stern-type protocol has a soundness error of $2/3$, i.e., a cheating prover is able to convince an honest verifier with probability $2/3$ even if it does not possess any valid witness. Thus, to achieve a negligible soundness error, the protocol is required to repeat for many (e.g., 219) times, and the final proof consists of proofs generated in all iterations. Consequently, its proof size is usually on the order of tens of megabytes to terabytes.

Fiat-Shamir with Abort. Another line of research follows the identification schemes from [44–46]. Early works in this direction [32, 51] consider ZKAoK protocols with binary challenges, which leads to a soundness error of $1/2$ for a single iteration. Thus, multiple (e.g., 128) repetitions are needed to achieve a negligible soundness error. Subsequently, ZKAoKs with larger challenge spaces are adopted to reduce the number of rounds required. This results in one-round protocols with inverse-polynomial/negligible soundness error. Thus, we only need to run them a few (e.g., 10 or even 1) time(s) to achieve a negligible soundness error. Consequently, the proof size is usually a few megabytes or less.

We have seen some applications, such as verifiable encryption [7,47], group signature [12,13,17] and ring signature [19] from Fiat-Shamir with abort (FSwA) protocols (with large challenge space). However, it is a complex task to design cryptographic protocols using FSwA. This is mainly due to the so-called *soundness gap*. For instance, for the ISIS relation $\mathcal{R}_{ISIS}$, the FSwA proof only attests the fact that the prover knows a witness for $\mathcal{R}'_{ISIS} = \{(\boldsymbol{A}, \boldsymbol{y}), \boldsymbol{x} : \boldsymbol{A} \cdot \boldsymbol{x} = c \cdot \boldsymbol{y} \wedge \|\boldsymbol{x}\| \leq \beta'\}$, where $\beta' > \beta$ and $c > 1$. Thus, to construct advanced applications from them, we have to use cryptographic primitives that are compatible with such relaxed soundness, e.g., encryption schemes with a relaxed decryption [7,47], commitment schemes with a relaxed opening [6,8] and signature schemes with a relaxed verification [13]. Unfortunately, it is usually hard or even impossible to construct primitives with such property. Meanwhile, general frameworks in the literature for advanced applications may not work when we use relaxed versions as building blocks. Thus, the construction and security analysis has to be conducted from scratch. Additionally, we do not have a simple manner to prove the relations over witnesses using Fiat-Shamir with abort protocols. Ad-hoc techniques are used to circumvent this requirement, which introduce additional complexity.

To summarize, we have some "user-friendly" lattice-based ZKAoKs that are less efficient; and some efficient ZKAoKs that are very complicated for advanced applications. The goal of this paper is, therefore, to construct ZKAoKs that are both efficient and easy to use.

On the Difficulty of Achieving Standard Soundness and Small Soundness Error. Before presenting our main results, we would like to discuss why previous works cannot achieve the standard soundness and a small soundness error simultaneously. First, for most (if not all) lattice-based relations, we need to prove that (parts of) the witnesses are small integers. This can be done in two approaches,

1. In a Stern-type protocol, a short integer is decomposed into a binary vector of bounded length. Then the prover proves that the decomposition outputs are correct via a standard Stern protocol, which asks the prover to open 2 out of 3 commitments in the challenge phase. Therefore, the soundness error $2/3$ is inherent for a Stern-type protocol.
2. In a Fiat-Shamir with abort protocol, the prover and the verifier run a Schnorr-type protocol with some tweaks for arguing shortness of the witness. However, the standard extraction procedure for the Schnorr protocol does not work here. This is because the extracted witnesses will be scaled by some large number (more accurately, the inverse of the difference of two challenges) and may be large. To circumvent this problem, the extraction procedure avoids multiplication of inverses. Correspondingly, the definition of soundness is relaxed in the sense that the extracted witness does not necessarily satisfy the original relation.

1.1   Our Results

In this work, we present a new approach for constructing efficient zero-knowledge arguments of knowledge for a large class of lattice-based relations. The core component of our methodology is an efficient ZKAoK for linear equations with additional quadratic constraints over the witnesses.

More concretely, let m, n, and ℓ be positive integers, and q be a large enough integer that is *a power-of-prime*. The ZKAoK protocol proves the following relation $\mathcal{R}^*$ in Eq.(1)[1]:

$$\mathcal{R}^* = \{(\boldsymbol{A}, \boldsymbol{y}, \mathcal{M}), (\boldsymbol{x}) \in (\mathbb{Z}_q^{m \times n} \times \mathbb{Z}_q^m \times ([1, n]^3)^\ell) \times (\mathbb{Z}_q^n) :$$
$$\boldsymbol{A} \cdot \boldsymbol{x} = \boldsymbol{y} \ \wedge \forall (h, i, j) \in \mathcal{M}, \boldsymbol{x}[h] = \boldsymbol{x}[i] \cdot \boldsymbol{x}[j]\} \qquad (1)$$

where $\mathcal{M}$ is a set of ℓ triples that defines quadratic constraints over $\boldsymbol{x}$. Usually, ℓ will be linear in n and in any case, we have $\ell \le n^3$.

Building upon our main protocol, we present a variety of ZKAoKs for some concrete lattice-based relations. The constructed ZKAoKs have standard soundness, yet achieving an inverse polynomial soundness error. We summarize the differences between our approaches and previous results in Table 1.

Table 1. Comparison of approaches for lattice-based ZKAoKs.

	Standard Soundness	Soundness Error
Stern-Style	✓	2/3
FSwA	✗	$1/poly$ or $negl$
This work	✓	$1/poly$

To further demonstrate the usefulness of our methodology, we develop several privacy-preserving primitives from these ZKAoKs. We illustrate the roadmap to these applications in Fig. 1.

In addition, we also examine the concrete efficiency (particularly, communication cost) of our applications. We highlight some of the results in Table 2. For more details, see the full version of this work.

We remark that the applications (and the performance data thereof) are to illustrate the usefulness of our framework. They are by no means exhaustive nor optimal. One may extend our results to other privacy-preserving primitives such as anonymous credential, decentralized anonymous credential, group encryption, traceable signature, linkable ring signature, CryptoNote protocol (and thus Monero), k-times anonymous authentication, blacklistable anonymous credential, Zerocoin, etc. Also, one can improve the results of this work via utilizing structured lattices (such as ideal lattices or NTRU lattices) and application-specific optimizations. Those extensions and optimizations are beyond the scope of this paper.

---

[1] In this paper, operations over group elements in $\mathbb{Z}_q$ are modulo q unless otherwise specified.

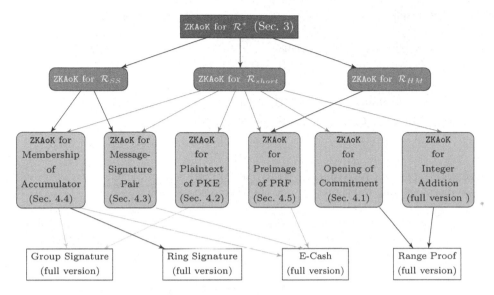

Fig. 1. The Roadmap for our ZKAoKs and their Applications. The starting point is our core ZKAoK for $\mathcal{R}^*$. It is then used to construct ZKAoKs for some elementary relations, namely, $\mathcal{R}_{short}$, $\mathcal{R}_{SS}$, and $\mathcal{R}_{HM}$ (we define these elementary relations and explain how to develop ZKAoKs for them in Sect. 1.2). Based on these elementary ZKAoKs, we further construct ZKAoKs for cryptographic schemes. Finally, we construct privacy-preserving primitives from these ZKAoKs.

Comparisons. Next, we give a brief comparison between the communication cost of applications in this work and that of previous results. Our examples in this section target 80 bits security unless otherwise specified.

We summarize the results in Table 2. Generally, for applications where solutions were only available through Stern-type protocols, our constructions are (much) more efficient than the state of the art. For applications where solutions were also available through Fiat-Shamir with abort protocols, our constructions are less efficient. Note that constructions utilizing Fiat-Shamir with abort are designed from scratch and these state-of-the-art constructions are optimized through the use of structured lattices (ideal lattices); while our solutions are built on standard lattices, which are believed to offer better security.

We stress again that the main advantage of our framework is that it provides a fairly good efficiency yet keeping its user-friendliness. Optimizing toward individual application, as stated earlier, is beyond the scope of this paper.

Ring Signatures. Following the framework of [36], a ring signature scheme can be obtained with our ZKAoK. The signature size of [36] is estimated by [19] at 47.3 MB, for a ring of 2^{10} users. In contrast, the signature size of our ring signature scheme is 4.24 MB in the same setting.

To the best of our knowledge, the most efficient ring signature scheme is from [19], using Fiat-Shamir with abort protocols. For the same number (i.e., 2^{10}) of

Table 2. Comparison of communication cost for applications from different ZKAoKs.

Application	This paper	Stern-type	FSwA (ideal lattice)
Ring Signature	4.24 MB	47.3 MB [36]	**1.41 MB** [19]
Group Signature	6.94 MB	61.5 MB [36]	**0.58 MB** [17]
Range Proof	**1.21 MB**	3.54 MB [38]	N/A
Electronic Cash	**262 MB**	≈720 TB [37]	N/A

users, its signature size is about 1.41 MB at 100 bits security level. Using a similar parameter setting, the signature size of our solution is 3.05 MB.[2]

Group Signatures. A group signature can also be obtained following a similar approach in [36] using our ZKAoK. The signature size of [36] is 61.5 MB for a group of 2^{10} users. In contrast, the signature size of our solution is 6.94 MB in the same setting.

The most efficient group signature scheme to date is from [17], achieving a signature size of less than 1 MB. Nonetheless, our approach can achieve additional features. For example, one can convert our group signature scheme into a fully dynamic one via the techniques in [42], without increasing its signature size.

Electronic Cash. To the best of our knowledge, the only lattice-based (compact) electronic cash system is from [37], but no concrete estimation of its performance is provided. In the full version of this work, we provide a rough estimation for the communication cost of their spend protocol, for a wallet of 2^{10} coins. The estimation shows that the communication cost of their spend protocol is at least several terabytes while our spend protocol can achieve a communication cost of 262 MB in the same setting.

There is no E-cash system from Fiat-Shamir with abort protocols in the literature. This is due to the following technical barriers. First, in an E-cash system, we need an argument of correct evaluation for pseudorandom function (PRF). This requires an argument for the learning with rounding (LWR) relation, i.e., proving the (rounded) error terms lie *exactly* in an interval. Due to the aforementioned soundness gap, it is not known how this proof can be done from Fiat-Shamir with abort protocols. Moreover, we also need an adaptively secure signature scheme and an argument of knowledge of a valid message/signature pair for it. To date, signature schemes that admit an argument from Fiat-Shamir with abort protocols can only achieve selective security. Complexity leveraging trick that converts a selectively secure scheme into an adaptively secure one does not work here either, since the message space, which contains all possible PRF keys, are exponentially large.

---

[2] In [19], parameters are set in a slightly mild way, so, the signature size is smaller if we use their criterion to select parameters.

Range Proof. Prior to our work, the most efficient lattice-based range proof is from [38]. When arguing knowledge of a 1000-bits committed value in a given range, its proof size is 3.54 MB. In contrast, the proof led by our solution is only 1.21 MB in the same setting.

1.2 Technical Overview

Warm-Up: An Argument for $\mathcal{R}_{ISIS}$. Before explaining the idea of our approach, we would like to give a simple intuition on how one can argue the ISIS relation, with standard soundness and small soundness error simultaneously. Our solution can be viewed as a somewhat mix of the Stern-type protocol and the Fiat-Shamir with abort protocol. In particular, we will first use the bit-decomposition technique to deal with small integers. Then we prove that the decomposition outputs are binary via proving some quadratic constraint over them (i.e., arguing $x = x^2$ for each bit x of the output). As shown in [27] (and its lattice variant [19]), this can be proved via arguing linear relations over commitments and thus can be instantiated with known commitment with a relaxed opening and Fiat-Shamir with abort protocols. Since we do not argue shortness of witnesses explicitly in the latter argument, soundness gap is not introduced.[3] Surprisingly, this simple strategy can produce much more than merely arguing shortness of witnesses. We elaborate this next.

Building ZKAoK for $\mathcal{R}^*$. We start with a protocol that proves

$$\mathcal{R}_0 = \{(\boldsymbol{A}, \boldsymbol{y}), (\boldsymbol{x}) \in (\mathbb{Z}_q^{m \times n} \times \mathbb{Z}_q^m) \times (\mathbb{Z}_q^n) : \boldsymbol{A} \cdot \boldsymbol{x} = \boldsymbol{y}\} \tag{2}$$

which is the linear equation part of $\mathcal{R}^*$. The protocol can be viewed as an extension of the Schnorr protocol to the linear algebra setting. It proceeds as follows:

1. The prover samples a vector $\boldsymbol{r} \xleftarrow{\$} \mathbb{Z}_q^n$ and sends $\boldsymbol{t} = \boldsymbol{A} \cdot \boldsymbol{r}$ to the verifier.
2. The verifier samples a challenge $\alpha \in \mathcal{C}$ and sends it to the prover. Here $\mathcal{C} \subset \mathbb{Z}$ is the challenge space of the protocol and will be specified later.
3. The prover sends $\boldsymbol{z} = \alpha \cdot \boldsymbol{x} + \boldsymbol{r}$ to the verifier.
4. The verifier accepts the proof iff $\boldsymbol{A} \cdot \boldsymbol{z} = \alpha \cdot \boldsymbol{y} + \boldsymbol{t}$.

Given two valid transcripts with distinct challenges, i.e., $(\boldsymbol{t}, \alpha, \boldsymbol{z})$ and $(\boldsymbol{t}, \alpha', \boldsymbol{z}')$, one can extract a vector $\bar{\boldsymbol{x}} = (\alpha - \alpha')^{-1} \cdot (\boldsymbol{z} - \boldsymbol{z}')$ that satisfies Eq. (2). In the meantime, a cheating prover cannot pass the verification unless it successfully guesses the challenge α. Thus, the protocol achieves a soundness error of $1/\|\mathcal{C}\|$. Hence, we can obtain an inverse-polynomial soundness error if $\mathcal{C}$ contains polynomial many distinct challenges.

In the remaining part of this section, we explain how to additionally prove the quadratic constraints over the witnesses.

---

[3] There exists a soundness gap in the proof, but it will not affect the proved argument due to the commitment with a relaxed opening.

Let (h, i, j) be an item in $\mathcal{M}$, our goal is to prove that $\boldsymbol{x}[h] = \boldsymbol{x}[i] \cdot \boldsymbol{x}[j]$. First, from the response $\boldsymbol{z} = \alpha \cdot \boldsymbol{x} + \boldsymbol{r}$, the verifier can compute

$$
\begin{aligned}
d &= \alpha \cdot \boldsymbol{z}[h] - \boldsymbol{z}[i] \cdot \boldsymbol{z}[j] \\
&= (\boldsymbol{x}[h] - \boldsymbol{x}[i] \cdot \boldsymbol{x}[j]) \cdot \alpha^2 + (\boldsymbol{r}[h] - \boldsymbol{r}[i] \cdot \boldsymbol{x}[j] - \boldsymbol{r}[j] \cdot \boldsymbol{x}[i]) \cdot \alpha - \boldsymbol{r}[i] \cdot \boldsymbol{r}[j] \\
&:= (\boldsymbol{x}[h] - \boldsymbol{x}[i] \cdot \boldsymbol{x}[j]) \cdot \alpha^2 + a \cdot \alpha - b
\end{aligned}
$$

where $a = \boldsymbol{r}[h] - \boldsymbol{r}[i] \cdot \boldsymbol{x}[j] - \boldsymbol{r}[j] \cdot \boldsymbol{x}[i]$ and $b = \boldsymbol{r}[i] \cdot \boldsymbol{r}[j]$. Note that $\boldsymbol{x}[h] = \boldsymbol{x}[i] \cdot \boldsymbol{x}[j]$ iff d is linear in α. Therefore, the main task is reduced to proving that the quadratic polynomial d is indeed linear in α, or alternatively $d - a \cdot \alpha + b$ is a *zero polynomial*.

To prove this, we can ask the prover to additionally send a and b in Step 1. Correspondingly, in Step 4, the verifier computes d and further checks if $d = a \cdot \alpha - b$. Since the prover does not know α in advance, a and b must be independent from α. Therefore, if the verification is successful, d is linear in α.

However, sending a and b in plaintext may leak information about the witness. To solve this problem, we adopt a homomorphic commitment scheme $\texttt{Commit}(m; r) \mapsto c$ that commits a message m to a commitment c using randomness r. More precisely, in Step 1, the prover generates $C_a = \texttt{Commit}(a; s_a)$ and $C_b = \texttt{Commit}(b; s_b)$ for some s_a and s_b, and send them to the verifier. In Step 3, the prover also computes $s = \alpha \cdot s_a - s_b$ and send s to the verifier. The verifier then checks if $\texttt{Commit}(d; s) = \alpha \cdot C_a - C_b$.

Remark 1.1. In this work, we will use the commitment scheme in [6], which is both additive homomorphic and supports multiplication by small constants. Therefore, we require the challenge space $\mathcal{C}$ to be a set of polynomially-many small integers. The commitment scheme also requires the randomness to be drawn from some distributions with bounded norm. Here, we instantiate it with the Gaussian distribution.

Since new variables C_a, C_b and s are introduced in the proof, we also need to make sure that they will not compromise the privacy of a and b. First, C_b is determined by α, d, s and C_a, thus, we only need to consider s and C_a in the analysis. Recall that both s_a and s_b are drawn from the Gaussian distributions. According to the rejection sampling lemma [46], we can use s_b to mask $\alpha \cdot s_a$, and enforce the output s to follow a specific distribution that is independent from s_a. Then, by the hiding property of the commitment scheme, C_a reveals nothing about a. As a result, the commitments C_a, C_b and the randomness s do not leak additional information to the verifier.

There is an additional subtlety that we need to deal with. Note that in the aforementioned protocol, we try to argue that the quadratic polynomial $d - a \cdot \alpha - b$ is a zero polynomial. Thus, in the proof for soundness, we need three valid transcripts with distinct challenges after rewinding (note that a quadratic polynomial with three distinct roots must be a zero polynomial). So, to fix the extracted witnesses from these transcripts, the prover should also commit the witness $\boldsymbol{x}$ and proves that the witness is properly committed (using a Fiat-Shamir with abort protocol).

In summary, our ZKAoK protocol contains three parts.

1. A Schnorr-type protocol that proves possession of a witness for $\mathcal{R}_0$.
2. A commitment of witness $\boldsymbol{x}$ and a Fiat-Shamir with abort protocol proving that the committed value is actually $\boldsymbol{x}$.
3. A proof for the quadratic constraints over the witnesses.

Building ZKAoK for More Relations. Next, we show how to develop ZKAoKs for relations relevant to lattice-based cryptographic schemes. As we illustrated in Fig. 1, such relations can be viewed as combinations of some elementary relations, namely, linear equations with short solutions ($\mathcal{R}_{short}$), subset sum of linear equations ($\mathcal{R}_{SS}$), and linear equations with hidden matrices ($\mathcal{R}_{HM}$). Thus, here we focus on how to deal with these elementary relations.[4]

Linear Equation with Short Solution. This is a primary lattice-based relation and appears in (almost) all applications. Concretely, let m, n, and k be positive integers, q be a large enough power-of-prime, and $\beta = 2^k - 1$. The relation $\mathcal{R}_{short}$ is given as

$$\mathcal{R}_{short} = \{(\boldsymbol{P}, \boldsymbol{v}), (\boldsymbol{w}) \in (\mathbb{Z}_q^{m \times n} \times \mathbb{Z}_q^m) \times ([0, \beta]^n) : \boldsymbol{P} \cdot \boldsymbol{w} = \boldsymbol{v}\}$$

The reduction from $\mathcal{R}_{short}$ to $\mathcal{R}^*$ takes the following steps:

- set a new witness $\boldsymbol{x}$ as the binary decomposition of the original witness $\boldsymbol{w}$, i.e., each element w in $\boldsymbol{w}$ is decomposed into k bits $x_1, \ldots, x_k$ such that $w = \sum_{i=1}^k x_i \cdot 2^{i-1}$ (note that a positive integer can be decomposed into k bits iff it is in $[0, 2^k - 1]$);
- set $\boldsymbol{A} = \boldsymbol{P} \cdot \boldsymbol{G}$ where the gadget matrix $\boldsymbol{G} := \boldsymbol{I}_n \otimes (1 \quad 2 \quad 4 \ldots 2^{k-1})$ (thus, we have $\boldsymbol{G} \cdot \boldsymbol{x} = \boldsymbol{w}$);
- set $\boldsymbol{y} = \boldsymbol{v}$;
- set $\mathcal{M} = \{(i, i, i)\}_{i \in [1, nk]}$;

In doing so, we obtain a new relation in the form of $\mathcal{R}^*$ where both the length of witness and the size of $\mathcal{M}$ are nk.

Note that since q is a power-of-prime, for any $x \in \mathbb{Z}_q$, $x^2 = x$ iff $x = 0$ or $x = 1$. Thus, the new relation is equivalent to the original relation $\mathcal{R}_{short}$.

There are two common variants to $\mathcal{R}_{short}$. First, for simplicity, we have set $\beta+1$ to be a power-of-2. The first variant removes this unnecessary constraint and deals with arbitrary positive integer β. This is achieved by applying the refined decomposition technique proposed in [40] and the length of the decomposed witness is $n \cdot (\lfloor \log \beta \rfloor + 1)$.

The second variant is to argue knowledge of a witness $\boldsymbol{w} \in [-\beta, \beta]^n$ that satisfies a linear equation. This can be reduced to the relation $\mathcal{R}_{short}$ via adding β to each element of $\boldsymbol{w}$. Note that the linear equation will also need to be modified accordingly.

---

[4] Detailed constructions of ZKAoKs for elementary relations can be found in Sect. 4, e.g, the ZKAoK for lattice-based PKE is in fact a ZKAoK for a variant of $\mathcal{R}_{short}$.

Optimized arguments for Linear Equation with Short Solution. In some cases, it is desirable to prove a relation $\mathcal{R}_{short}$ with a large n, which makes it inefficient to decompose all elements in $\boldsymbol{x}$. We propose an alternative relation, given by Eq. (3), to argue equations with short solutions more efficiently in this case, at a cost of re-introducing some soundness gap for the argument. More precisely, to argue a linear equation $\boldsymbol{P}\boldsymbol{w} = \boldsymbol{v}$ with β-bounded solution $\boldsymbol{w}$, the argument can only guarantee that the prover possesses a $n \cdot \beta$-bounded solution $\boldsymbol{w}'$ that satisfies $\boldsymbol{P}\boldsymbol{w}' = \boldsymbol{v}$.

$$
\begin{aligned}
\mathcal{R}'_{short} = \{ & (\boldsymbol{P}, \boldsymbol{v}, \boldsymbol{H}, \boldsymbol{c}), (\boldsymbol{w}, \boldsymbol{u}, \boldsymbol{r}) \in \\
& (\mathbb{Z}_q^{m \times n} \times \mathbb{Z}_q^m \times [0,1]^{\lambda \times n} \times \mathsf{C}) \times (\mathbb{Z}_q^n \times [0, n \cdot \beta]^{\lambda} \times \mathsf{R}) : \\
& \boldsymbol{P} \cdot \boldsymbol{w} = \boldsymbol{v} \ \wedge \ \boldsymbol{H} \cdot \boldsymbol{w} - \boldsymbol{u} = 0 \ \wedge \ \boldsymbol{c} = \mathtt{Commit}(\boldsymbol{w}; \boldsymbol{r}) \}
\end{aligned}
\tag{3}
$$

where

- $\mathtt{Commit}$ is a commitment scheme and $\boldsymbol{c} = \mathtt{Commit}(\boldsymbol{w}; \boldsymbol{r})$ is the commitment;
- C and R are the output space and the randomness space of $\mathtt{Commit}$;
- $\boldsymbol{H} \leftarrow H(\boldsymbol{c}) \in [0,1]^{\lambda \times n}$, where λ is the security parameter and H is modeled as a random oracle.

To see why $\mathcal{R}'_{short}$ could guarantee that all elements in $\boldsymbol{w}$ are in $[0, n \cdot \beta]$, assume there exists $i \in [n]$ such that $|\ \boldsymbol{w}[i]\ | > n \cdot \beta$. Let $\boldsymbol{h}_1$ and $\boldsymbol{h}_2$ be two n-dimension binary vectors that are identical in all positions except that $\boldsymbol{h}_1[i] \neq \boldsymbol{h}_2[i]$. Then we have $|\ \boldsymbol{h}_1^{\mathsf{T}} \cdot \boldsymbol{w} - \boldsymbol{h}_2^{\mathsf{T}} \cdot \boldsymbol{w}\ | = |\ \boldsymbol{w}[i]\ | > n \cdot \beta$. Thus, either $\boldsymbol{h}_1^{\mathsf{T}} \cdot \boldsymbol{w}$ or $\boldsymbol{h}_2^{\mathsf{T}} \cdot \boldsymbol{w}$ must be outside the interval $[0, n \cdot \beta]$. Therefore, for a vector $\boldsymbol{h}$ sampled uniformly from $[0,1]^n$, with a probability of at least $1/2$, $\boldsymbol{h}^{\mathsf{T}} \cdot \boldsymbol{w} > n \cdot \beta$. Therefore, the probability that all elements in $\boldsymbol{H} \cdot \boldsymbol{w}$ are in $[0, n \cdot \beta]$ is negligible.

It remains to show how to argue the relation $\mathcal{R}'_{short}$. Our strategy is to reduce the relation to an instance of relation $\mathcal{R}^*$ and then argue the instance via our main protocol. Looking ahead, in our main protocol, the prover also generates a commitment of the witness in the first step and will argue that the witness is properly committed during the proof. In addition, the commitment scheme allows one to commit part of the witness first, and then commit the remaining part later, where the partial commitment generated in the first stage is also included in the complete commitment. Consequently, the commitment and the argument for the opening of the commitment are free[5]. The remaining part of relation $\mathcal{R}'_{short}$ are equations with short solutions, and thus can be straightforwardly reduced to $\mathcal{R}^*$.

In more detail, to argue $\mathcal{R}'_{short}$, the prover first generates the commitment $\boldsymbol{c} = \mathtt{Commit}(\boldsymbol{w})$ and computes the matrix $\boldsymbol{H} = H(\boldsymbol{c})$ and $\boldsymbol{u} = \boldsymbol{H}\boldsymbol{w}$. Then, it commits $\boldsymbol{u}$ and appends the commitment to $\boldsymbol{c}$. Finally, it runs the remaining part of our main protocol, arguing that there exists a small vector $\boldsymbol{u}$ and a vector $\boldsymbol{w}$ that satisfies $\boldsymbol{u} = H(\boldsymbol{c})\boldsymbol{w}$ and $\boldsymbol{v} = \boldsymbol{P}\boldsymbol{w}$.

---

[5] In fact, we only obtain a relaxed argument for the opening of the commitment. This is sufficient for our purpose.

To summarize, we can prove equations with short solutions via our main protocol on $\mathcal{R}^*$, where the length of the witness is $n + \lambda \cdot (\lfloor \log(n \cdot \beta) \rfloor + 1)$ and the size of $\mathcal{M}$ is $\lambda \cdot (\lfloor \log(n \cdot \beta) \rfloor + 1)$.

Subset Sum of Linear Equations. Let m, n and l be positive integers and q be a large power-of-prime. The relation is given as

$$\mathcal{R}_{SS} = \{(\{\boldsymbol{P}_i\}_{i \in [1,l]}, \boldsymbol{v}), (\{\boldsymbol{w}\}_{i \in [1,l]}, \{b_i\}_{i \in [1,l]}) \in$$

$$((\mathbb{Z}_q^{m \times n})^l \times \mathbb{Z}_q^m) \times ((\mathbb{Z}_q^n)^l \times \{0,1\}^l) : \sum_{i=1}^{l} b_i \cdot \boldsymbol{P}_i \cdot \boldsymbol{w}_i = \boldsymbol{v}\}$$

To reduce $\mathcal{R}_{SS}$ to $\mathcal{R}^*$, we first compute $\boldsymbol{v}_i = \boldsymbol{P}_i \cdot \boldsymbol{w}_i$ and $\boldsymbol{v}_i' = b_i \cdot \boldsymbol{v}_i$ for $i \in [1,l]$. Then we set the new witness vector $\boldsymbol{x} = (b_1, \ldots, b_l, \boldsymbol{v}_1', \ldots, \boldsymbol{v}_l', \boldsymbol{v}_1, \ldots, \boldsymbol{v}_l, \boldsymbol{w}_1, \ldots, \boldsymbol{w}_l)$ and set

$$\boldsymbol{A} = \begin{pmatrix} 0 & 0 & -\boldsymbol{I}_{ml} & \boldsymbol{P} \\ 0 & \boldsymbol{J} & 0 & 0 \end{pmatrix} \text{ and } \boldsymbol{y} = \begin{pmatrix} 0 \\ \boldsymbol{v} \end{pmatrix}$$

where

$$\boldsymbol{P} = \begin{pmatrix} \boldsymbol{P}_1 & & & \\ & \boldsymbol{P}_2 & & \\ & & \ddots & \\ & & & \boldsymbol{P}_l \end{pmatrix} \text{ and } \boldsymbol{J} = \begin{pmatrix} \boldsymbol{I}_m & \boldsymbol{I}_m & \cdots & \boldsymbol{I}_m \end{pmatrix}.$$

Here, the first part of the equation $\boldsymbol{A}\boldsymbol{x} = \boldsymbol{y}$ (specified by the first "row" of $\boldsymbol{A}$) indicates that $\boldsymbol{v}_i = \boldsymbol{P}_i \cdot \boldsymbol{w}_i$ for $i \in [1,l]$ and its second part indicates that the sum of all $\boldsymbol{v}_i'$ are $\boldsymbol{v}$.

Finally, we set

$$\mathcal{M} = \{(i,i,i)\}_{i \in [1,l]} \cup \{(l + m \cdot (i-1) + j, l + ml + m \cdot (i-1) + j, i)\}_{i \in [1,l], j \in [1,m]}$$

where $\{(i,i,i)\}_{i \in [1,l]}$ indicates that b_i is binary and the rest indicates that $\boldsymbol{v}_i' = b_i \cdot \boldsymbol{v}_i$. This gives us an $\mathcal{R}^*$ statement where the length of witness becomes $(nl + 2ml + l)$ and the size of $\mathcal{M}$ is $ml + l$.

Linear Equation with Hidden Matrix. Let m and n be positive integers and q be a large power-of-prime, the relation is defined as follows:

$$\mathcal{R}_{HM} = \{(\boldsymbol{v}), (\boldsymbol{P}, \boldsymbol{w}) \in (\mathbb{Z}_q^m) \times (\mathbb{Z}_q^{m \times n} \times \mathbb{Z}_q^n) : \boldsymbol{P} \cdot \boldsymbol{w} = \boldsymbol{v}\}$$

To reduce $\mathcal{R}_{HM}$ to $\mathcal{R}^*$, we first obtain a new witness vector $\boldsymbol{x} = (\boldsymbol{x}_0, \ldots, \boldsymbol{x}_{2m})$ as follows:

- $\boldsymbol{x}_0 = \boldsymbol{w}$;
- for $i \in [1,m]$, $\boldsymbol{x}_i$ is the i-th row of $\boldsymbol{P}$;
- for $i \in [1,m]$, $\boldsymbol{x}_{m+i}$ is the Hadamard product between the i-th row of $\boldsymbol{P}$ and $\boldsymbol{w}$ (i.e., $\boldsymbol{x}_{m+i}[j] = \boldsymbol{x}_i[j] \cdot \boldsymbol{w}[j]$).

Then we set $\boldsymbol{A} = \begin{pmatrix} \mathbf{0}^{m \times n} & \mathbf{0}^{m \times mn} & \boldsymbol{M} \end{pmatrix}$ and $\boldsymbol{y} = \boldsymbol{v}$ where $\boldsymbol{M} = \boldsymbol{I}_m \otimes$ $\begin{pmatrix} 1 & 1 & \cdots & 1 \end{pmatrix} \in \mathbb{Z}_q^{m \times mn}$.

Finally, we set $\mathcal{M} = \{((m+i) \cdot n + j, i \cdot n + j, j)\}_{i \in [1,m], j \in [1,n]}$, which indicates that $\boldsymbol{x}_{m+i}[j] = \boldsymbol{x}_i[j] \cdot \boldsymbol{w}[j]$. In this way, we obtain a new relation in the form of $\mathcal{R}^*$, where the length of witness is $(2m+1) \cdot n$ and the size of $\mathcal{M}$ is mn.

2   Preliminaries

Notations. In this paper, we will use bold lower-case letters (e.g., $\boldsymbol{v}$) to denote vectors, and use bold upper-case letters (e.g., $\boldsymbol{A}$) to denote matrices. All elements in vectors and matrices are integers unless otherwise specified. For a vector $\boldsymbol{v}$ of length n, we use $\boldsymbol{v}[i]$ to denote the ith element of $\boldsymbol{v}$ for $i \in [1, n]$ and for an m-by-n matrix $\boldsymbol{A}$, we use $\boldsymbol{A}[i, j]$ to denote the element on the i-th row and the j-th column of $\boldsymbol{A}$ for $i \in [1, m]$ and $j \in [1, n]$. For a vector $\boldsymbol{v}$, we use $\mathtt{bin}(\boldsymbol{v})$ to denote the binary decomposition of $\boldsymbol{v}$, i.e., $\boldsymbol{v}[i] = \sum_{j=1}^{k} 2^{j-1} \cdot \bar{\boldsymbol{v}}[(i-1) \cdot k + j]$, where $\bar{\boldsymbol{v}} = \mathtt{bin}(\boldsymbol{v})$ and $k = \lceil \log(\|\boldsymbol{v}\|_\infty) \rceil$. We use $\boldsymbol{I}_n$ to denote an n-by-n identity matrix. We use $\otimes$ to denote the Kronecker product of two matrices.

For a string a, we use $\|a\|$ to denote the length of a. For a finite set $\mathcal{S}$, we use $\|\mathcal{S}\|$ to denote the size of $\mathcal{S}$ and use $s \xleftarrow{\$} \mathcal{S}$ to denote sampling an element s uniformly from set $\mathcal{S}$. For a distribution $\mathcal{D}$, we use $d \leftarrow \mathcal{D}$ to denote sampling d according to $\mathcal{D}$.

For integers $a \leq b$, we write $[a, b]$ to denote all integers from a to b. We write $negl(\cdot)$ to denote a negligible function and write $poly(\cdot)$ to denote a polynomial.

2.1   Discrete Gaussian Distribution

We recall the discrete Gaussian distribution and some results from [46].

Definition 2.1 (Discrete Gaussian Distribution). *The continuous Gaussian distribution over $\mathbb{R}^m$ centered at $\boldsymbol{v} \in \mathbb{R}^m$ with standard deviation σ is defined by the function $\rho_{v,\sigma}^m(\boldsymbol{x}) = (\frac{1}{\sqrt{2\pi\sigma^2}})^m e^{\frac{-\|\boldsymbol{x} - \boldsymbol{v}\|^2}{2\sigma^2}}$.*

The discrete Gaussian distribution over $\mathbb{Z}^m$ centered at $\boldsymbol{v} \in \mathbb{Z}^m$ with standard deviation σ is defined as $D_{v,\sigma}^m(\boldsymbol{x}) = \rho_{v,\sigma}^m(\boldsymbol{x})/\rho_\sigma^m(\mathbb{Z}^m)$, where $\rho_\sigma^m(\mathbb{Z}^m) = \sum_{\boldsymbol{x} \in \mathbb{Z}^m} \rho_\sigma^m(\boldsymbol{x})$.

We write $D_\sigma^m(\boldsymbol{x}) = D_{\mathbf{0},\sigma}^m(\boldsymbol{x})$ for short.

Lemma 2.1 ([46, Full Version, Lemma 4.4])

1. *For any $k > 0$, $\Pr[\|z\| > k\sigma : z \leftarrow D_\sigma^1] \leq 2e^{\frac{-k^2}{2}}$.*
2. *For any $\boldsymbol{z} \in \mathbb{Z}^m$, and $\sigma \geq 3/\sqrt{2\pi}$, $D_\sigma^m(\boldsymbol{z}) \leq 2^{-m}$.*
3. *For any $k > 1$, $\Pr[\|\boldsymbol{z}\| > k\sigma\sqrt{m} : \boldsymbol{z} \leftarrow D_\sigma^m] < k^m e^{\frac{m}{2}(1-k^2)}$.*

2.2 Rejection Sampling

In this work, we will also use the celebrated "rejection sampling lemma" from [45,46] to argue the zero-knowledge property of our protocol.

Lemma 2.2 ([46, **Full Version, Theorem 4.6**]). *Let $\mathcal{V}$ be a subset of $\mathbb{Z}^m$ in which all elements have norms less than T. Let h be a probability distribution over $\mathcal{V}$. Let σ be a real number that $\sigma = \omega(T\sqrt{\log m})$. Then there exists a constant M such that the distribution of the following algorithm $\mathcal{A}$ and that of the following algorithm $\mathcal{F}$ are within statistical distance $\frac{2^{-\omega(\log m)}}{M}$.*

$\mathcal{A}$:

1. $\boldsymbol{v} \leftarrow h$
2. $\boldsymbol{z} \leftarrow D^m_{\boldsymbol{v},\sigma}$
3. *Output* $(\boldsymbol{v}, \boldsymbol{z})$ *with probability*
   $\min(1, \frac{D^m_\sigma(\boldsymbol{z})}{M D^m_{\boldsymbol{v},\sigma}(\boldsymbol{z})})$

$\mathcal{F}$:

1. $\boldsymbol{v} \leftarrow h$
2. $\boldsymbol{z} \leftarrow D^m_\sigma$
3. *Output* $(\boldsymbol{v}, \boldsymbol{z})$ *with probability*
   $\frac{1}{M}$

Moreover, the probability that $\mathcal{A}$ outputs something is at least $\frac{1-2^{-\omega(\log m)}}{M}$.

As a concrete example (suggested in [30]), if $\sigma = \alpha T$ for some positive α, then $M = e^{13.3/\alpha + 1/(2\alpha^2)}$, the output of algorithm $\mathcal{A}$ is within statistical distance $\frac{2^{-128}}{M}$ of the output of $\mathcal{F}$, and the probability that $\mathcal{A}$ outputs something is at least $\frac{1-2^{-128}}{M}$.

2.3 Hardness Assumptions

The security of our main protocol relies on the short integer solution (SIS) assumption and the learning with errors (LWE) assumption. For both assumptions, we will use the normal form (as defined in [53]).

Definition 2.2 ($\mathrm{SIS}_{n,m,q,\beta}$, Normal Form). *Given a random matrix $\boldsymbol{A} \in \mathbb{Z}_q^{n \times (m-n)}$, find a nonzero integer vector $\boldsymbol{z} \in \mathbb{Z}^m$ such that $\|\boldsymbol{z}\| \leq \beta$ and $[\boldsymbol{I}_n \mid \boldsymbol{A}] \cdot \boldsymbol{z} = 0$.*

As hardness of the SIS assumption usually depends only on n, q, β (assuming m is large enough), in this work, we write $\mathrm{SIS}_{n,m,q,\beta}$ as $\mathrm{SIS}_{n,q,\beta}$ for short.

Lemma 2.3 ([1,22,48,49,53]). *For any $m = poly(n)$, any $\beta > 0$, and any sufficiently large $q \geq \beta \cdot \tilde{O}(\sqrt{n})$, solving (normal form) $\mathrm{SIS}_{n,m,q,\beta}$ with non-negligible probability is at least as hard as solving the decisional approximate shortest vector problem $GapSVP_\gamma$ and the approximate shortest independent vectors problems $SIVP_\gamma$ (among others) on arbitrary n-dimensional lattices (i.e., in the worst case) with overwhelming probability, for some $\gamma = \beta \cdot \tilde{O}(\sqrt{n})$.*

Definition 2.3 (Decision-$\mathrm{LWE}_{n,m,q,\chi}$, Normal Form). *Given a random matrix $\boldsymbol{A} \in \mathbb{Z}_q^{(m-n) \times n}$, and a vector $\boldsymbol{b} \in \mathbb{Z}_q^{m-n}$, where $\boldsymbol{b}$ is generated according to either of the following two cases:*

1. $\boldsymbol{b} = \boldsymbol{A} \cdot \boldsymbol{s} + \boldsymbol{e}$, where $\boldsymbol{s} \leftarrow \chi^n$ and $\boldsymbol{e} \leftarrow \chi^{m-n}$
2. $\boldsymbol{b} \xleftarrow{\$} \mathbb{Z}_q^{m-n}$

distinguish which is the case with non-negligible advantage.

If χ is a discrete Gaussian distribution with standard deviation σ, we write the problem as $LWE_{n,m,q,\alpha}$ where $\alpha = \sigma \cdot \sqrt{2\pi}/q$. Also, as the hardness of the LWE assumption usually depends only on n, q, α (assuming m is large enough), in this work, we write $LWE_{n,m,q,\alpha}$ as $LWE_{n,q,\alpha}$ for short.

Lemma 2.4 ([4,53,55]). *For any $m = poly(n)$, any modulus $q \leq 2^{poly(n)}$, and any (discrete) Gaussian error distribution χ with standard deviation σ (i.e., $\chi = D_\sigma$), where $\sigma = \alpha q/\sqrt{2\pi} \geq \sqrt{2n/\pi}$ and $0 < \alpha < 1$, solving the (normal form) decision-$LWE_{n,m,q,\chi}$ problem is at least as hard as (quantumly) solving $GapSVP_\gamma$ and $SIVP_\gamma$ on arbitrary n-dimensional lattices, for some $\gamma = \tilde{O}(n/\alpha)$.*

2.4 Zero-Knowledge Arguments of Knowledge

In a zero-knowledge argument of knowledge system [24], a prover proves to a verifier that he possesses the witness for a statement without revealing any additional information.

More formally, let $\mathsf{R} = \{(x,w)\} \in \{0,1\}^* \times \{0,1\}^*$ be a statements-witnesses set for an NP relation. The ZKAoK for R is an interactive protocol $\langle \mathcal{P}, \mathcal{V} \rangle$ run between a prover $\mathcal{P}$ and a verifier $\mathcal{V}$ that satisfies:

- **Completeness.** For any $(x,w) \in \mathsf{R}$, $\Pr[\langle \mathcal{P}(x,w), \mathcal{V}(x)\rangle \neq 1] \leq \delta_c$.
- **Proof of Knowledge.** There exists an extractor $\mathcal{E}$ that for any x, for any probabilistic polynomial time (PPT) cheating prover $\hat{\mathcal{P}}$, if $\Pr[\langle \hat{\mathcal{P}}, \mathcal{V}(x)\rangle = 1] > \delta_s + \epsilon$ for some non-negligible ϵ, then $\mathcal{E}$ can extract in polynomial time a witness w such that $(x,w) \in \mathsf{R}$ via accessing $\hat{P}$ in a black-box manner.
- **(Honest-Verifier) Zero-Knowledge.** There exists a simulator $\mathcal{S}$ that for any $(x,w) \in \mathsf{R}$, the two distributions are computationally indistinguishable:
  1. The view of an honest verifier $\mathcal{V}$ in an interaction $\langle \mathcal{P}(x,w), \mathcal{V}(x)\rangle$.
  2. The output of $\mathcal{S}(x)$.

where δ_c is the completeness error and δ_s is the soundness error.

In this work, we also consider non-interactive ZKAoKs (NIZKAoK). They can be obtained by applying the Fiat-Shamir heuristic [20] to public coin ZKAoKs. One advantage led by the Fiat-Shamir transform is that the transformed NIZKAoKs additionally admit a message as input, thus it is also called signature proof of knowledge (SPK), and is usually written as $SPK\{(x,w) : (x,w) \in \mathsf{R}\}[m]$, where m is the additional message.

2.5 Commitment with a Relaxed Opening

In our main construction, we will employ the commitment scheme presented in [6][6], which admits a relaxed opening.

---

[6] In fact, we will use its variant in the standard lattice setting. For completeness, we will restate its security in the security proof of our main construction.

Let λ be the security parameter. Let l_1 and l_2 be positive integers that are polynomials in the security parameter λ. Let σ be a small positive integer that satisfies $\sigma \geq \sqrt{2l_2/\pi}$. Also, let n be the length of the committed vector. The public parameter of the commitment scheme is a matrix $B \in \mathbb{Z}_q^{(l_1+n) \times (l_1+n+l_2)}$ defined as follows:

$$B = \left(\begin{array}{c|cc} I_{l_1} & B_1 & \\ \hline 0^{n \times l_1} & I_n & B_2 \end{array} \right)$$

where B_1 and B_2 are random matrices sampled from $\mathbb{Z}_q^{l_1 \times (l_2+n)}$ and $\mathbb{Z}_q^{n \times l_2}$ respectively.

To commit to a message $m \in \{0,1\}^n$, the commit algorithm first samples $s \in D_\sigma^{l_1+n+l_2}$. Then it outputs a commitment $c = B \cdot s + (0^\mathsf{T} \| m^\mathsf{T})^\mathsf{T}$ and the opening s.

The open algorithm outputs 1 on input B, m, c, s iff $c = B \cdot s + (0^\mathsf{T} \| m^\mathsf{T})^\mathsf{T}$ and s is small. Besides, it admits a relaxed opening, where the input of the algorithm includes B, m, c, s and a small integer f, and the algorithm outputs 1 iff $f \cdot c = B \cdot s + f \cdot (0^\mathsf{T} \| m^\mathsf{T})^\mathsf{T}$ and s, f are small.

3   Main Construction

In this section, we present our main construction, namely, an efficient zero-knowledge argument of knowledge for linear equations with quadratic constraints over the witness.

More concretely, let m, n, ℓ be positive integers, q be a large enough integer that is a *power-of-prime*, i.e., $q = q_0^e$ for some prime q_0 and some positive integer e. Also, let A be a matrix in $\mathbb{Z}_q^{m \times n}$, x and y be vectors in $\mathbb{Z}_q^n$ and $\mathbb{Z}_q^m$ respectively, and $\mathcal{M}$ be a set of ℓ 3-tuples, each of which consists of 3 integers in $[1, n]$. We will construct a ZKAoK for the following relation:

$$\mathcal{R}^* = \{(A, y, \mathcal{M}), (x) : A \cdot x = y \ \wedge \forall (h, i, j) \in \mathcal{M}, x[h] = x[i] \cdot x[j]\} \quad (4)$$

Specifically, in Sect. 3.1, we give a basic version of the ZKAoK protocol for $\mathcal{R}^*$ as defined in Eq. (4). This protocol achieves an inverse polynomial soundness error and a constant completeness error. Then, in Sect. 3.2, we transform the basic protocol into a NIZKAoK with negligible soundness error and completeness error.

3.1   The Basic Protocol

Let aCommit be an auxiliary bit commitment scheme with randomness space $\{0,1\}^\kappa$ and a suitable message space. As no additional requirement is desired for aCommit, we can safely assume it to be a random oracle G, i.e., given an input x and a random string ρ as randomness, the commitment is $G(x \| \rho)$. Nonetheless, aCommit can be instantiated by any secure commitment scheme.

Let λ be the security parameter. Let l_1 and l_2 be positive integers that are polynomials in the security parameter λ. Let $\boldsymbol{B}_{1,1}$, $\boldsymbol{B}_{1,2}$, $\boldsymbol{B}_{2,1}$ and $\boldsymbol{B}_{2,2}$ be random matrices sampled from $\mathbb{Z}_q^{l_1\times(l_2+n)}$, $\mathbb{Z}_q^{n\times l_2}$, $\mathbb{Z}_q^{l_1\times(l_2+\ell)}$ and $\mathbb{Z}_q^{\ell\times l_2}$ respectively. Also let

$$
\boldsymbol{B}_1 = \left(\begin{array}{c|cc} \boldsymbol{I}_{l_1} & \boldsymbol{B}_{1,1} \\ \hline 0^{n\times l_1} & \boldsymbol{I}_n & \boldsymbol{B}_{1,2} \end{array}\right), \qquad \boldsymbol{B}_2 = \left(\begin{array}{c|cc} \boldsymbol{I}_{l_1} & \boldsymbol{B}_{2,1} \\ \hline 0^{\ell\times l_1} & \boldsymbol{I}_\ell & \boldsymbol{B}_{2,2} \end{array}\right)
$$

Here $\boldsymbol{B}_1$ and $\boldsymbol{B}_2$ are public parameters of the underlying homomorphic commitment scheme, and we assume that they are honestly generated (via some public coin) and are shared by all parties in the protocol.

Let σ_1 be small positive integer that satisfies $\sigma_1 \geq \sqrt{2l_2/\pi}$. Let p be small positive integer that is polynomial in λ. Let $l = 2l_1 + 2l_2 + n + \ell$. Let $\sigma_2 = 2p \cdot \sqrt{l} \cdot \log l \cdot \sigma_1$. Let $M = e^{13.3/\log l + 1/(2\log^2 l)}$. For any l-dimension vectors $\boldsymbol{v}$ and $\boldsymbol{z}$, let $\mathfrak{p}(\boldsymbol{v}, \boldsymbol{z}) = \min(1, \frac{D_{\sigma_2}^l(\boldsymbol{z})}{M D_{\boldsymbol{v},\sigma_2}^l(\boldsymbol{z})})$.

The basic protocol P_1 for $\mathcal{R}^*$ is described in Fig. 2.

Theorem 3.1. *Assume the worst-case hardness of $GapSVP_\gamma$ (or $SIVP_\gamma$) for some polynomial γ, if $q \geq 16p \cdot \max(\sqrt{l_1+l_2+n}, \sqrt{l_1+l_2+\ell}) \cdot (\sigma_2 + p \cdot \sigma_1) \cdot \tilde{O}(\sqrt{l_1})$, q/σ_1 is a polynomial, $q_0 > 2p$, and $\mathsf{aCommit}$ is a secure bit commitment scheme, then the protocol P_1, which is described in Fig. 2, is a secure zero-knowledge argument of knowledge with completeness error $1 - 1/M$ and soundness error $2/(2p+1)$.*

We give the detailed proof for Theorem 3.1 in the full version.

3.2   NIZKAoK for $\mathcal{R}^*$

In this section, we show how to transform our basic protocol in Sect. 3.1 into a non-interactive zero-knowledge arguments of knowledge with negligible soundness error and completeness error. Generally, this can be done via some standard techniques such as repetition and Fiat-Shamir transform. Nonetheless, we will employ a few tricks (developed in previous works) to reduce the efficiency loss in the transformations. In particular, to minimize the number of repetitions, we will employ the tweaks in [19] when repeating the basic protocol. In a nutshell, it applies one rejection sampling on all (repeated) instances simultaneously, which avoids completeness error increasing caused by repetition.

The Construction. Let $\mathsf{aCommit}$, λ, l_1, l_2, $\boldsymbol{B}_{1,1}$, $\boldsymbol{B}_{1,2}$, $\boldsymbol{B}_{2,1}$ and $\boldsymbol{B}_{2,2}$, σ_1, p, l and M be identical to those of P_1. We highlight the differences.

In the new scheme, a proof is generated by repeating the basic protocol $N = \lambda/\log p$ times. Then we set $\sigma_2 = 2p \cdot \sqrt{N \cdot l} \cdot \log(N \cdot l) \cdot \sigma_1$, and for any $N \cdot l$-dimension vectors $\boldsymbol{v}$ and $\boldsymbol{z}$, we set $\mathfrak{p}(\boldsymbol{v}, \boldsymbol{z}) = \min(1, \frac{D_{\sigma_2}^{N\cdot l}(\boldsymbol{z})}{M D_{\boldsymbol{v},\sigma_2}^{N\cdot l}(\boldsymbol{z})})$. We will additionally use a hash function H with output space $[-p, p]^N$, which is modelled

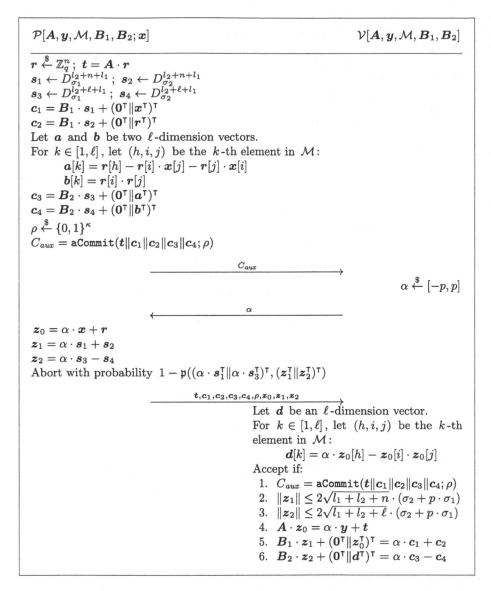

Fig. 2. The Basic Protocol P_1: A Zero-Knowledge Arguments of Knowledge for $\mathcal{R}^*$ with Inverse Polynomial Soundness Error and Constant Completeness Error.

as a random oracle. Also, let AUX be some application-dependent auxiliary information (e.g., the signed message in a group signature) that is specified as an input to H.

The prove algorithm and the verify algorithm of the NIZKAoK P_2 for $\mathcal{R}^*$ is described in Figs. 3 and 4 respectively.

$$\mathtt{Prove}(\boldsymbol{A}, \boldsymbol{x}, \boldsymbol{y}, \mathcal{M}, \boldsymbol{B}_1, \boldsymbol{B}_2, AUX):$$

For $\jmath \in [1, \lambda]$:

1. $\boldsymbol{s}_1 \leftarrow D_{\sigma_1}^{l_2+n+l_1}$, $\boldsymbol{c}_1 = \boldsymbol{B}_1 \cdot \boldsymbol{s}_1 + (\boldsymbol{0}^{\mathsf{T}} \| \boldsymbol{x}^{\mathsf{T}})^{\mathsf{T}}$

2. For $\imath \in [1, N]$:

   (a) $\boldsymbol{r}_\imath \xleftarrow{\$} \mathbb{Z}_q^n$, $\boldsymbol{t}_\imath = \boldsymbol{A} \cdot \boldsymbol{r}_\imath$

   (b) $\boldsymbol{s}_{2,\imath} \leftarrow D_{\sigma_2}^{l_2+n+l_1}$, $\boldsymbol{s}_{3,\imath} \leftarrow D_{\sigma_1}^{l_2+\ell+l_1}$, $\boldsymbol{s}_{4,\imath} \leftarrow D_{\sigma_2}^{l_2+\ell+l_1}$

   (c) $\boldsymbol{c}_{2,\imath} = \boldsymbol{B}_1 \cdot \boldsymbol{s}_{2,\imath} + (\boldsymbol{0}^{\mathsf{T}} \| \boldsymbol{r}_\imath^{\mathsf{T}})^{\mathsf{T}}$

   (d) Let $\boldsymbol{a}_\imath$ and $\boldsymbol{b}_\imath$ be two ℓ-dimension vectors and for $k \in [1, \ell]$, let (h, i, j) be the k-th element in $\mathcal{M}$:

      i. $\boldsymbol{a}_\imath[k] = \boldsymbol{r}_\imath[h] - \boldsymbol{r}_\imath[i] \cdot \boldsymbol{x}[j] - \boldsymbol{r}_\imath[j] \cdot \boldsymbol{x}[i]$

      ii. $\boldsymbol{b}_\imath[k] = \boldsymbol{r}_\imath[i] \cdot \boldsymbol{r}_\imath[j]$

   (e) $\boldsymbol{c}_{3,\imath} = \boldsymbol{B}_2 \cdot \boldsymbol{s}_{3,\imath} + (\boldsymbol{0}^{\mathsf{T}} \| \boldsymbol{a}_\imath^{\mathsf{T}})^{\mathsf{T}}$, $\boldsymbol{c}_{4,\imath} = \boldsymbol{B}_2 \cdot \boldsymbol{s}_{4,\imath} + (\boldsymbol{0}^{\mathsf{T}} \| \boldsymbol{b}_\imath^{\mathsf{T}})^{\mathsf{T}}$

   (f) $\rho_\imath \xleftarrow{\$} \{0, 1\}^\kappa$

   (g) $C_{aux,\imath} = \mathtt{aCommit}(\boldsymbol{t}_\imath \| \boldsymbol{c}_1 \| \boldsymbol{c}_{2,\imath} \| \boldsymbol{c}_{3,\imath} \| \boldsymbol{c}_{4,\imath}; \rho_\imath)$

3. $\{\alpha_\imath\}_{\imath \in [1,N]} = H(\boldsymbol{A}, \boldsymbol{y}, \mathcal{M}, \{C_{aux,\imath}\}_{\imath \in [1,N]}, AUX)$

4. For $\imath \in [1, N]$:

   (a) $\boldsymbol{z}_{0,\imath} = \alpha_\imath \cdot \boldsymbol{x} + \boldsymbol{r}_\imath$, $\boldsymbol{z}_{1,\imath} = \alpha_\imath \cdot \boldsymbol{s}_1 + \boldsymbol{s}_{2,\imath}$, $\boldsymbol{z}_{2,\imath} = \alpha_\imath \cdot \boldsymbol{s}_{3,\imath} - \boldsymbol{s}_{4,\imath}$

5. Smaple a real number $\tau \xleftarrow{\$} [0, 1]$ (Here, we use $[0, 1]$ to denote all real numbers between 0 and 1)

6. If $\tau < \mathfrak{p}((\alpha_1 \cdot \boldsymbol{s}_1^{\mathsf{T}} \| \dots \| \alpha_N \cdot \boldsymbol{s}_1^{\mathsf{T}} \| \alpha_1 \cdot \boldsymbol{s}_{3,1}^{\mathsf{T}} \| \dots \| \alpha_N \cdot \boldsymbol{s}_{3,N}^{\mathsf{T}})^{\mathsf{T}}, (\boldsymbol{z}_{1,1}^{\mathsf{T}} \| \dots \| \boldsymbol{z}_{1,N}^{\mathsf{T}} \| \boldsymbol{z}_{2,1}^{\mathsf{T}} \| \dots \| \boldsymbol{z}_{2,N}^{\mathsf{T}})^{\mathsf{T}})$:

   (a) Abort the algorithm with output $\pi = (\boldsymbol{c}_1, \{\alpha_\imath, \rho_\imath, \boldsymbol{c}_{3,\imath}, \boldsymbol{z}_{0,\imath}, \boldsymbol{z}_{1,\imath}, \boldsymbol{z}_{2,\imath}\}_{\imath \in [1,N]})$

Output $\perp$ if the algorithm does not abort in the loop above.

Fig. 3. The $\mathtt{Prove}$ Algorithm of P_2.

$$\mathtt{Verify}(\boldsymbol{A}, \boldsymbol{y}, \mathcal{M}, \boldsymbol{B}_1, \boldsymbol{B}_2, AUX, \pi = (\boldsymbol{c}_1, \{\alpha_\imath, \rho_\imath, \boldsymbol{c}_{3,\imath}, \boldsymbol{z}_{0,\imath}, \boldsymbol{z}_{1,\imath}, \boldsymbol{z}_{2,\imath}\}_{\imath \in [1,N]})):$$

For $\imath \in [1, N]$:

1. Let $\boldsymbol{d}_\imath$ be an ℓ-dimension vector and for $k \in [1, \ell]$, let (h, i, j) be the k-th element in $\mathcal{M}$:

   (a) $\boldsymbol{d}_\imath[k] = \alpha_\imath \cdot \boldsymbol{z}_{0,\imath}[h] - \boldsymbol{z}_{0,\imath}[i] \cdot \boldsymbol{z}_{0,\imath}[j]$

2. $\boldsymbol{t}_\imath = \boldsymbol{A} \cdot \boldsymbol{z}_{0,\imath} - \alpha_\imath \cdot \boldsymbol{y}$

3. $\boldsymbol{c}_{2,\imath} = \boldsymbol{B}_1 \cdot \boldsymbol{z}_{1,\imath} + (\boldsymbol{0}^{\mathsf{T}} \| \boldsymbol{z}_{0,\imath}^{\mathsf{T}})^{\mathsf{T}} - \alpha_\imath \cdot \boldsymbol{c}_1$

4. $\boldsymbol{c}_{4,\imath} = \alpha_\imath \cdot \boldsymbol{c}_{3,\imath} - \boldsymbol{B}_2 \cdot \boldsymbol{z}_{2,\imath} - (\boldsymbol{0}^{\mathsf{T}} \| \boldsymbol{d}_\imath^{\mathsf{T}})^{\mathsf{T}}$

5. $C_{aux,\imath} = \mathtt{aCommit}(\boldsymbol{t}_\imath \| \boldsymbol{c}_1 \| \boldsymbol{c}_{2,\imath} \| \boldsymbol{c}_{3,\imath} \| \boldsymbol{c}_{4,\imath}; \rho_\imath)$

6. If $\|\boldsymbol{z}_{1,\imath}\| > 2\sqrt{l_1 + l_2 + n} \cdot (\sigma_2 + p \cdot \sigma_1) \vee \|\boldsymbol{z}_{2,\imath}\| > 2\sqrt{l_1 + l_2 + \ell} \cdot (\sigma_2 + p \cdot \sigma_1)$:

   (a) Abort the algorithm with output "Reject"

Output "Accept" if $\{\alpha_\imath\}_{\imath \in [1,N]} = H(\boldsymbol{A}, \boldsymbol{y}, \mathcal{M}, \{C_{aux,\imath}\}_{\imath \in [1,N]}, AUX)$:

Fig. 4. The $\mathtt{Verify}$ Algorithm of P_2.

Theorem 3.2. *Assume the worst-case hardness of $GapSVP_\gamma$ (or $SIVP_\gamma$) for some polynomial γ, if $q \geq 16p \cdot \max(\sqrt{l_1 + l_2 + n}, \sqrt{l_1 + l_2 + \ell}) \cdot (\sigma_2 + p \cdot \sigma_1) \cdot \tilde{O}(\sqrt{l_1})$, q/σ_1 is a polynomial, $q_0 > 2p$, $\mathtt{aCommit}$ is a secure bit commitment* *scheme, and H is modelled as a random oracle, then the scheme* $\mathsf{P_2}$ *is a secure non-interactive zero-knowledge argument of knowledge with negligible completeness error and soundness error.*

Proof of Theorem 3.2 follows proof of Theorem 3.1 and well-known results, we omit the details here.

Efficiency. In $\mathsf{P_2}$, a proof π contains a commitment and a set of N elements, where each element consists of a challenge, a κ-bit string, a commitment and three vectors. Thus, we have

$$\|\pi\| = (\log{(2p+1)} + \kappa + (3l_1 + 2l_2 + 2n + 2\ell) \cdot \log q) \cdot N + (l_1 + n) \cdot \log q$$

4   ZKAoKs for Various Cryptographic Schemes

In this section, we build several tools that are useful for constructing privacy-preserving primitives. This includes an argument of knowledge of committed value, an argument of knowledge of plaintext, an argument of knowledge of signature, an argument for cryptographic accumulator and an argument for pseudorandom function.

4.1   ZKAoK of Committed Value

We start with an argument of knowledge of the committed value for the commitment scheme in [31].

Let l_1, l_2, L be positive integers and q be a power-of-prime. We propose a ZKAoK for the following relation:

$$\mathcal{R}_{com} = \{(\boldsymbol{B_1}, \boldsymbol{B_2}, \boldsymbol{c}), (\boldsymbol{r}, \boldsymbol{w}) \in$$
$$(\mathbb{Z}_q^{l_1 \times l_2} \times \mathbb{Z}_q^{l_1 \times L} \times \mathbb{Z}_q^{l_1}) \times (\{0,1\}^{l_2} \times \{0,1\}^L) : \boldsymbol{B_1} \cdot \boldsymbol{r} + \boldsymbol{B_2} \cdot \boldsymbol{w} = \boldsymbol{c}\}$$

$\mathcal{R}_{com}$ contains linear equations with binary witness. We construct the argument via reducing $\mathcal{R}_{com}$ to an instance of $\mathcal{R}^*$ through the following steps:

1. Set the new witness $\boldsymbol{x} = (\boldsymbol{r}^\mathsf{T} \| \boldsymbol{w}^\mathsf{T})^\mathsf{T}$;
2. Set $\boldsymbol{A} = (\boldsymbol{B_1} \| \boldsymbol{B_2})$ and $\boldsymbol{y} = \boldsymbol{c}$;
3. Set $\mathcal{M} = (i, i, i)_{i \in [1, l_2 + L]}$.

Note that since q is a power of prime, for any $x \in \mathbb{Z}_q$, $x^2 = x$ iff $x = 0$ or $x = 1$. Thus, the new relation $\mathcal{R}^*$ over $(\boldsymbol{A}, \boldsymbol{y}, \mathcal{M})$, $(\boldsymbol{x})$ is equivalent to the original relation $\mathcal{R}_{com}$. Also, both $\|\boldsymbol{x}\|$ and $\|\mathcal{M}\|$ are $l_2 + L$ for $\mathcal{R}^*$.

4.2   ZKAoK of Plaintext

Next, we give an argument of knowledge of the plaintext for the encryption scheme proposed in [39].

More precisely, let l_1, l_2, L and β be positive integers and q be a power-of-prime, we propose a ZKAoK for the following relation:

$$
\begin{aligned}
\mathcal{R}_{enc} = \{ & (\boldsymbol{B}_1, \boldsymbol{B}_2, \boldsymbol{c}_1, \boldsymbol{c}_2), (\boldsymbol{r}, \boldsymbol{e}_1, \boldsymbol{e}_2, \boldsymbol{w}) \in \\
& (\mathbb{Z}_q^{l_1 \times l_2} \times \mathbb{Z}_q^{L \times l_2} \times \mathbb{Z}_q^{l_1} \times \mathbb{Z}_q^{L}) \times (\mathbb{Z}_q^{l_2} \times \mathbb{Z}_q^{l_1} \times \mathbb{Z}_q^{L} \times \{0,1\}^L) : \\
& \|\boldsymbol{r}\|_\infty \le \beta \wedge \|\boldsymbol{e}_1\|_\infty \le \beta \wedge \|\boldsymbol{e}_2\|_\infty \le \beta \wedge \\
& \boldsymbol{B}_1 \cdot \boldsymbol{r} + \boldsymbol{e}_1 = \boldsymbol{c}_1 \wedge \boldsymbol{B}_2 \cdot \boldsymbol{r} + \boldsymbol{e}_2 + \lceil \tfrac{q}{2} \rceil \cdot \boldsymbol{w} = \boldsymbol{c}_2 \}
\end{aligned}
$$

We construct the argument via reducing the relation $\mathcal{R}_{enc}$, which contains linear equations with short solutions, to an instance of the relation $\mathcal{R}^*$.

First, we define vectors $\boldsymbol{\beta}_1 = (\beta \quad \beta \dots \beta)^{\mathsf{T}} \in \mathbb{Z}_q^{l_2}$, $\boldsymbol{\beta}_2 = (\beta \quad \beta \dots \beta)^{\mathsf{T}} \in \mathbb{Z}_q^{l_1}$, $\boldsymbol{\beta}_3 = (\beta \quad \beta \dots \beta)^{\mathsf{T}} \in \mathbb{Z}_q^{L}$ and define $\boldsymbol{r}' = \boldsymbol{r} + \boldsymbol{\beta}_1$, $\boldsymbol{e}_1' = \boldsymbol{e}_1 + \boldsymbol{\beta}_2$ and $\boldsymbol{e}_2' = \boldsymbol{e}_2 + \boldsymbol{\beta}_3$.

Then, we decompose vectors $\boldsymbol{r}'$, $\boldsymbol{e}_1'$ and $\boldsymbol{e}_2'$ into binary vectors $\bar{\boldsymbol{r}}$, $\bar{\boldsymbol{e}}_1$ and $\bar{\boldsymbol{e}}_2$ using the decomposition technique proposed in [40]. More precisely, let $k = \lfloor \log 2\beta \rfloor + 1$ and let $\boldsymbol{g} = (\lfloor (2\beta + 1)/2 \rfloor \| \lfloor (2\beta + 2)/4 \rfloor \| \dots \| \lfloor (2\beta + 2^{i-1})/2^i \rfloor \| \dots \| \lfloor (2\beta + 2^{k-1})/2^k \rfloor)$ be a row vector. It is claimed in [40] that (1) an integer $a \in [0, 2\beta]$ iff there exists a binary vector $\boldsymbol{a} \in \{0,1\}^k$ that $\boldsymbol{g} \cdot \boldsymbol{a} = a$; (2) one can decompose the integer $a \in [0, 2\beta]$ into the k-dimension binary vector $\boldsymbol{a}$ efficiently.

Next, we define the gadget matrix $\boldsymbol{G}_1 = \boldsymbol{I}_{l_2} \otimes \boldsymbol{g}$, $\boldsymbol{G}_2 = \boldsymbol{I}_{l_1} \otimes \boldsymbol{g}$, $\boldsymbol{G}_3 = \boldsymbol{I}_L \otimes \boldsymbol{g}$ and they satisfy that $\boldsymbol{G}_1 \cdot \bar{\boldsymbol{r}} = \boldsymbol{r}'$, $\boldsymbol{G}_2 \cdot \bar{\boldsymbol{e}}_1 = \boldsymbol{e}_1'$ and $\boldsymbol{G}_3 \cdot \bar{\boldsymbol{e}}_2 = \boldsymbol{e}_2'$.

Finally, we set

$$
\boldsymbol{A} = \begin{pmatrix} \boldsymbol{B}_1 \cdot \boldsymbol{G}_1 & \boldsymbol{G}_2 & \boldsymbol{0} & \boldsymbol{0} \\ \boldsymbol{B}_2 \cdot \boldsymbol{G}_1 & \boldsymbol{0} & \boldsymbol{G}_3 & \lceil \tfrac{q}{2} \rceil \cdot \boldsymbol{I}_L \end{pmatrix}
$$

$$
\boldsymbol{x} = (\bar{\boldsymbol{r}}^{\mathsf{T}} \quad \bar{\boldsymbol{e}}_1^{\mathsf{T}} \quad \bar{\boldsymbol{e}}_2^{\mathsf{T}} \quad \boldsymbol{w}^{\mathsf{T}})^{\mathsf{T}}, \quad \boldsymbol{y} = \begin{pmatrix} \boldsymbol{c}_1 + \boldsymbol{B}_1 \cdot \boldsymbol{\beta}_1 + \boldsymbol{\beta}_2 \\ \boldsymbol{c}_2 + \boldsymbol{B}_2 \cdot \boldsymbol{\beta}_1 + \boldsymbol{\beta}_3 \end{pmatrix}
$$

and set $\mathcal{M} = (i, i, i)_{i \in [1, (l_1 + l_2 + L) \cdot k + L]}$. Here, both $\|\boldsymbol{x}\|$ and $\|\mathcal{M}\|$ are $(l_1 + l_2 + L) \cdot k + L$.

One common variant of the encryption scheme in [39] is to use binary secrets and errors rather than sampling them from β bounded distributions. To generate arguments of knowledge of plaintexts for this variant, we can use an almost identical construction as above, except that we do not need to decompose the vectors $\boldsymbol{r}$, $\boldsymbol{e}_1$ and $\boldsymbol{e}_2$. Thus, when reducing the relation to $\mathcal{R}^*$ in this case, both $\|\boldsymbol{x}\|$ and $\|\mathcal{M}\|$ will be $l_1 + l_2 + 2L$.

4.3 ZKAoK of Message-Signature Pair

Next, we give an argument of knowledge of a valid message/signature pair for the signature scheme proposed in [37].

Let l_1, l_2, l_3, L, and β be positive integers and q be a power-of-prime. Also let $k_q = \lceil \log q \rceil$. We propose a ZKAoK that proves knowledge of

$$\begin{cases} \{\tau_i\}_{i \in [1,l_3]} \in \{0,1\}^{l_3}; \boldsymbol{v}_1 \in \mathbb{Z}_q^{l_2}; \boldsymbol{v}_2 \in \mathbb{Z}_q^{l_2}; \\ \boldsymbol{w} \in \{0,1\}^{k_q l_1}; \boldsymbol{s} \in \mathbb{Z}_q^{2l_2}; \boldsymbol{m} \in \{0,1\}^L \end{cases}$$

that satisfies

$$\begin{cases} \boldsymbol{B} \cdot \boldsymbol{v}_1 + \left(\boldsymbol{B}_0 + \sum_{i=1}^{l_3} \tau_i \cdot \boldsymbol{B}_i\right) \cdot \boldsymbol{v}_2 = \boldsymbol{u} + \boldsymbol{D} \cdot \boldsymbol{w} \\ \boldsymbol{H} \cdot \boldsymbol{w} = \boldsymbol{D}_0 \cdot \boldsymbol{s} + \boldsymbol{D}_1 \cdot \boldsymbol{m} \\ \|\boldsymbol{v}_1\|_\infty \leq \beta; \|\boldsymbol{v}_2\|_\infty \leq \beta; \|\boldsymbol{s}\|_\infty \leq \beta \end{cases}$$

for public

$$\begin{cases} \boldsymbol{B} \in \mathbb{Z}_q^{l_1 \times l_2}; \{\boldsymbol{B}_i\}_{i \in [0,l_3]} \in (\mathbb{Z}_q^{l_1 \times l_2})^{l_3+1}; \boldsymbol{u} \in \mathbb{Z}_q^{l_1} \\ \boldsymbol{D} \in \mathbb{Z}_q^{l_1 \times k_q l_1}; \boldsymbol{D}_0 \in \mathbb{Z}_q^{l_1 \times 2l_2}; \boldsymbol{D}_1 \in \mathbb{Z}_q^{l_1 \times L} \end{cases}$$

where $\boldsymbol{H} = \boldsymbol{I}_{l_1} \otimes (1 \quad 2 \quad 4 \dots 2^{k_q-1})$.

Again, we construct the argument via reducing the relation, which contains a subset sum of linear equations and linear equations with short solutions, to an instance of the relation $\mathcal{R}^*$.

First, we define vectors $\boldsymbol{\beta}_1 = (\beta \quad \beta \dots \beta)^\mathsf{T} \in \mathbb{Z}_q^{l_2}$, $\boldsymbol{\beta}_2 = (\beta \quad \beta \dots \beta)^\mathsf{T} \in \mathbb{Z}_q^{2l_2}$, and define $\boldsymbol{v}_1' = \boldsymbol{v}_1 + \boldsymbol{\beta}_1$, $\boldsymbol{v}_2' = \boldsymbol{v}_2 + \boldsymbol{\beta}_1$ and $\boldsymbol{s}' = \boldsymbol{s} + \boldsymbol{\beta}_2$.

Then, we decompose vectors $\boldsymbol{v}_1'$, $\boldsymbol{v}_2'$ and $\boldsymbol{s}'$ into binary vectors $\bar{\boldsymbol{v}}_1$, $\bar{\boldsymbol{v}}_2$, and $\bar{\boldsymbol{s}}$ using the decomposition technique proposed in [40]. Let $k = \lfloor \log 2\beta \rfloor + 1$, then the vectors $\bar{\boldsymbol{v}}_1$, $\bar{\boldsymbol{v}}_2$ and $\bar{\boldsymbol{s}}$ are of length kl_2, kl_2 and $2kl_2$ respectively.

Also, let $\boldsymbol{g} = (\lfloor (2\beta+1)/2 \rfloor \| \dots \| \lfloor (2\beta + 2^{i-1})/2^i \rfloor \| \dots \| \lfloor (2\beta + 2^{k-1})/2^k \rfloor)$ be a row vector. Then, we define the gadget matrix $\boldsymbol{G}_1 = \boldsymbol{I}_{l_2} \otimes \boldsymbol{g}$, $\boldsymbol{G}_2 = \boldsymbol{I}_{2l_2} \otimes \boldsymbol{g}$, and they satisfy that $\boldsymbol{G}_1 \cdot \bar{\boldsymbol{v}}_1 = \boldsymbol{v}_1'$, $\boldsymbol{G}_1 \cdot \bar{\boldsymbol{v}}_2 = \boldsymbol{v}_2'$ and $\boldsymbol{G}_2 \cdot \bar{\boldsymbol{s}} = \boldsymbol{s}'$.

Next, for $i \in [1,l_3]$, let $\boldsymbol{u}_i = \boldsymbol{B}_i \cdot \boldsymbol{v}_2$ and let $\boldsymbol{u}_i' = \tau_i \cdot \boldsymbol{u}_i$. Also, we define $\hat{\boldsymbol{u}} = (\boldsymbol{u}_1^\mathsf{T} \| \boldsymbol{u}_2^\mathsf{T} \| \dots \| \boldsymbol{u}_{l_3}^\mathsf{T})^\mathsf{T}$ and $\hat{\boldsymbol{u}}' = (\boldsymbol{u}_1'^\mathsf{T} \| \boldsymbol{u}_2'^\mathsf{T} \| \dots \| \boldsymbol{u}_{l_3}'^\mathsf{T})^\mathsf{T}$. Moreover, define $\boldsymbol{\tau} = (\tau_1 \quad \tau_2 \dots \tau_{l_3})^\mathsf{T}$.

Finally, we set

$$A = \begin{pmatrix} 0 & 0 & -\boldsymbol{I}_{l_1 l_3} & \bar{\boldsymbol{B}} \cdot \boldsymbol{G}_1 & 0 & 0 & 0 & 0 \\ 0 & \boldsymbol{J} & 0 & \boldsymbol{B}_0 \cdot \boldsymbol{G}_1 & \boldsymbol{B} \cdot \boldsymbol{G}_1 & -\boldsymbol{D} & 0 & 0 \\ 0 & 0 & 0 & 0 & 0 & -\boldsymbol{H} & \boldsymbol{D}_0 \cdot \boldsymbol{G}_2 & \boldsymbol{D}_1 \end{pmatrix}$$

$$\boldsymbol{x} = (\boldsymbol{\tau}^\mathsf{T} \quad \hat{\boldsymbol{u}}'^\mathsf{T} \quad \hat{\boldsymbol{u}}^\mathsf{T} \quad \bar{\boldsymbol{v}}_2^\mathsf{T} \quad \bar{\boldsymbol{v}}_1^\mathsf{T} \quad \boldsymbol{w}^\mathsf{T} \quad \bar{\boldsymbol{s}}^\mathsf{T} \quad \boldsymbol{m}^\mathsf{T})^\mathsf{T}, \quad \boldsymbol{y} = \begin{pmatrix} \bar{\boldsymbol{B}} \cdot \boldsymbol{\beta}_1 \\ \boldsymbol{u} + \boldsymbol{B}_0 \cdot \boldsymbol{\beta}_1 + \boldsymbol{B} \cdot \boldsymbol{\beta}_1 \\ \boldsymbol{D}_0 \cdot \boldsymbol{\beta}_2 \end{pmatrix}$$

where

$$\bar{B} = \begin{pmatrix} B_1 \\ \vdots \\ B_{l_3} \end{pmatrix}, \quad J = (I_{l_1} \quad I_{l_1} \quad \cdots \quad I_{l_1})$$

Besides, let $N = l_3 + 2l_1 l_3 + 2kl_2 + k_q l_1 + 2kl_2 + L$, we define

$$\begin{cases} \mathcal{M}_1 = \{(i,i,i)\}_{i \in [1,l_3]} \\ \mathcal{M}_2 = \{(i,i,i)\}_{i \in [l_3 + 2l_1 l_3 + 1, N]} \\ \mathcal{M}_3 = \{(l_3 + l_1 \cdot (i-1) + j, i, l_3 + l_1 l_3 + l_1 \cdot (i-1) + j)\}_{i \in [1,l_3], j \in [1,l_1]} \end{cases}$$

where $\mathcal{M}_1$ indicates that each τ_i is binary, $\mathcal{M}_2$ indicates that $\bar{v}_2, \bar{v}_1, w, \bar{s}, m$ are binary vectors, and $\mathcal{M}_3$ indicates that $u_i' = \tau_i \cdot u_i$ for $i \in [1, l_3]$. Then we set $\mathcal{M} = \mathcal{M}_1 \cup \mathcal{M}_2 \cup \mathcal{M}_3$. In the new relation, the length of the witness is N and the size of $\mathcal{M}$ is $N - l_1 l_3$.

We can also use the fast mode (mentioned in Sect. 1.2) to argue that v_1, v_2 and s are short. This will lead to an instance of $\mathcal{R}^*$, where the length of the witness is $l_3 + 2l_1 l_3 + 4l_2 + k_q l_1 + L + \lambda \cdot (\lfloor \log (2 \cdot 4l_2 \cdot \beta) \rfloor + 1)$, and the size of $\mathcal{M}$ is $l_3 + l_1 l_3 + k_q l_1 + L + \lambda \cdot (\lfloor \log (2 \cdot 4l_2 \cdot \beta) \rfloor + 1)$.

4.4   ZKAoK of Accumulated Value

In this section, we give an argument of knowledge of an accumulated value for the accumulator scheme presented in [36].

More precisely, let l_1, L be positive integers and q be a power-of-prime. Also, let $k_q = \lceil \log q \rceil$ and $l_2 = l_1 k_q$. We propose a zero knowledge argument of knowledge that proves knowledge of

$$\{\{\tau_i\}_{i \in [1,L]} \in \{0,1\}^L; \{v_i\}_{i \in [1,L]} \in ([0,1]^{l_2})^L; \{w_i\}_{i \in [1,L]} \in ([0,1]^{l_2})^L; \}$$

that satisfies

$$\begin{cases} B_{1+\tau_1} \cdot v_1 + B_{2-\tau_1} \cdot w_1 = H \cdot u \\ \forall i \in [2, L], B_{1+\tau_i} \cdot v_i + B_{2-\tau_i} \cdot w_i = H \cdot v_{i-1} \end{cases}$$

for public

$$\{B_1 \in \mathbb{Z}_q^{l_1 \times l_2}; B_2 \in \mathbb{Z}_q^{l_1 \times l_2}; u \in [0,1]^{l_1 k_q}\}$$

where $H = I_{l_1} \otimes (1 \quad 2 \quad 4 \ldots 2^{k_q - 1})$.

We construct the argument via reducing the relation to an instance of the relation $\mathcal{R}^*$. Note that the relation contains L parts, each of which is a disjunction of two equations, namely, $B_1 \cdot v_i + B_2 \cdot w_i = H \cdot v_{i-1}$ and $B_1 \cdot w_i + B_2 \cdot v_i = H \cdot v_{i-1}$ (here, we define $v_0 = u$). As shown in [36], each part can be transformed into a subset sum of these two equations via setting the coefficients as $(1 - \tau_i, \tau_i)$. Next, we describe the reduction in more details.

First, for $i \in [2, L]$, we define $z_{i,0} = B_1 \cdot v_i + B_2 \cdot w_i - H \cdot v_{i-1}$, $z_{i,1} = B_1 \cdot w_i + B_2 \cdot v_i - H \cdot v_{i-1}$, $z_{i,0}' = (1 - \tau_i) \cdot z_{i,0}$ and $z_{i,1}' = \tau_i \cdot z_{i,1}$. Moreover,

we set $z_{1,0} = B_1 \cdot v_1 + B_2 \cdot w_1$, $z_{1,1} = B_1 \cdot w_1 + B_2 \cdot v_1$, $z'_{1,0} = (1 - \tau_1) \cdot z_{1,0}$
and $z'_{1,1} = \tau_1 \cdot z_{1,1}$.

Then, we set $\tau_0 = (1 - \tau_1 \quad 1 - \tau_2 \ldots 1 - \tau_L)^\mathsf{T}$ and $\tau_1 = (\tau_1 \quad \tau_2 \ldots \tau_L)^\mathsf{T}$.
Also, we define $\hat{z}'_0 = (z'^\mathsf{T}_{1,0} \| z'^\mathsf{T}_{2,0} \| \ldots \| z'^\mathsf{T}_{L,0})^\mathsf{T}$, $\hat{z}'_1 = (z'^\mathsf{T}_{1,1} \| z'^\mathsf{T}_{2,1} \| \ldots \| z'^\mathsf{T}_{L,1})^\mathsf{T}$, $\hat{z}_0 = (z^\mathsf{T}_{1,0} \| z^\mathsf{T}_{2,0} \| \ldots \| z^\mathsf{T}_{L,0})^\mathsf{T}$, $\hat{z}_1 = (z^\mathsf{T}_{1,1} \| z^\mathsf{T}_{2,1} \| \ldots \| z^\mathsf{T}_{L,1})^\mathsf{T}$, $\hat{v} = (v^\mathsf{T}_1 \| v^\mathsf{T}_2 \| \ldots \| v^\mathsf{T}_L)^\mathsf{T}$, $\hat{w} = (w^\mathsf{T}_1 \| w^\mathsf{T}_2 \| \ldots \| w^\mathsf{T}_L)^\mathsf{T}$. Besides, we define $\hat{u} = ((H \cdot u)^\mathsf{T} \| 0^{1 \times (L-1) \cdot l_1})^\mathsf{T}$.

Finally, we set

$$
A = \begin{pmatrix}
I_L & I_L & 0 & 0 & 0 & 0 & 0 & 0 \\
0 & 0 & I_{l_1 L} & I_{l_1 L} & 0 & 0 & 0 & 0 \\
0 & 0 & 0 & 0 & I_{l_1 L} & 0 & M_1 & N_2 \\
0 & 0 & 0 & 0 & 0 & I_{l_1 L} & M_2 & N_1
\end{pmatrix}
$$

$$
x = \begin{pmatrix} \tau_0^\mathsf{T} & \tau_1^\mathsf{T} & \hat{z}'^\mathsf{T}_0 & \hat{z}'^\mathsf{T}_1 & \hat{z}^\mathsf{T}_0 & \hat{z}^\mathsf{T}_1 & \hat{v}^\mathsf{T} & \hat{w}^\mathsf{T} \end{pmatrix}^\mathsf{T}, \quad y = \begin{pmatrix} 1^L & \hat{u}^\mathsf{T} & 0 & 0 \end{pmatrix}^\mathsf{T}
$$

where

$$
M_1 = \begin{pmatrix} -B_1 & & & \\ H & -B_1 & & \\ & \ddots & \ddots & \\ & & H & -B_1 \end{pmatrix}, \quad M_2 = \begin{pmatrix} -B_2 & & & \\ H & -B_2 & & \\ & \ddots & \ddots & \\ & & H & -B_2 \end{pmatrix}
$$

$$
N_1 = -I_L \otimes B_1, \quad N_2 = -I_L \otimes B_2
$$

Besides, we define

$$
\begin{cases}
\mathcal{M}_1 = \{(i, i, i)\}_{i \in [1,L]} \\
\mathcal{M}_2 = \{(i, i, i)\}_{i \in [2L + 4l_1 L + 1, 2L + 4l_1 L + 2l_2 L]} \\
\mathcal{M}_3 = \{(2L + l_1 \cdot (i - 1) + j, 2L + 2l_1 L + l_1 \cdot (i - 1) + j, i)\}_{i \in [1,L], j \in [1, l_1]} \\
\mathcal{M}_4 = \{(2L + l_1 L + l_1 \cdot (i - 1) + j, 2L + 3l_1 L + l_1 \cdot (i - 1) + j, L + i)\}_{i \in [1,L], j \in [1, l_1]}
\end{cases}
$$

where $\mathcal{M}_1$ indicates that τ_0 is a binary vector, $\mathcal{M}_2$ indicates that $\bar{v}$ and $\bar{w}$ are binary vectors, $\mathcal{M}_3$ and $\mathcal{M}_4$ indicate $z'_{i,0} = (1 - \tau_i) \cdot z_{i,0}$ and $z'_{i,1} = \tau_i \cdot z_{i,1}$ for $i \in [1, L]$ respectively. Then we set $\mathcal{M} = \mathcal{M}_1 \cup \mathcal{M}_2 \cup \mathcal{M}_3 \cup \mathcal{M}_4$. Note that as in the linear equation $A \cdot x = y$, it is proved that $\tau_0[i] + \tau_1[i] = 1$ for $i \in [1, L]$, the fact that $\tau_0[i]$ is binary implies that $\tau_1[i]$ is also binary. In the new relation, the length of the witness is $2L + 4l_1 L + 2l_2 L$ and the size of $\mathcal{M}$ is $L + 2l_1 L + 2l_2 L$.

4.5 ZKAoK of PRF Preimage

In this section, we give an argument for the weak pseudorandom function constructed implicitly in [5]. In particular, the argument claims knowledge of a key/input pair that evaluates to a public output.

More precisely, let l_1, l_2 be positive integers, q_0 be a prime and $p = q_0^{e_1}$, $q = q_0^{e_2}$, where $1 \leq e_1 < e_2$, we propose a ZKAoK for the following relation:

$$\mathcal{R}_{PRF} = \{(c), (B, k) \in (\mathbb{Z}_p^{l_1}) \times (\mathbb{Z}_q^{l_1 \times l_2} \times \mathbb{Z}_q^{l_2}) : c = \lfloor B \cdot k \rfloor_p \mod p\}$$

We construct the argument via reducing the relation $\mathcal{R}_{PRF}$ to an instance of the relation $\mathcal{R}^*$. First, we rewrite the equation $c = \lfloor B \cdot k \rfloor_p \mod p$ as follows:

$$\begin{cases} B \cdot k = u \mod q \\ \lfloor \dfrac{p}{q} \cdot u \rfloor = c \mod p \end{cases}$$

The first equation is a linear equation with hidden matrix. The second equation, as shown in [37,58], holds iff each element of the vector $u - \frac{q}{p}c$ is in $[0, \frac{q}{p})$, and thus can be transformed into a linear equation with short solution. Next, we describe the reduction in more details. We remark that in the remaining part of this section, all arithmetic operations are under the modulus q, so we omit the moduli in the remaining part of this section.

First, for $i \in [1, l_1]$, we define b_i as the i-th row of B and define v_i as the Hadamard product between b_i and k, i.e., $v_i[j] = b_i[j] \cdot k[j]$ for $j \in [1, l_2]$.

Let $e = u - \frac{q}{p}c$, then we decompose the vector e into a binary vector $\bar{e}$ using the decomposition technique proposed in [40]. Let $\gamma = \frac{q}{p} - 1$ and $k = \lfloor \log \gamma \rfloor + 1$, then the length of $\bar{e}$ is $k \cdot l_1$.

Also, let $g = (\lfloor (\gamma + 1)/2 \rfloor \| \ldots \| \lfloor (\gamma + 2^{i-1})/2^i \rfloor \| \ldots \| \lfloor (\gamma + 2^{k-1})/2^k \rfloor)$ be a row vector. Then, we define the gadget matrix $G = I_{l_1} \otimes g$, and it satisfies that $G \cdot \bar{e} = e$.

Next, we define $b = (b_1^\mathsf{T} \| \ldots \| b_{l_1}^\mathsf{T})^\mathsf{T} \in \mathbb{Z}_q^{l_1 \cdot l_2}$ and define $v = (v_1^\mathsf{T} \| \ldots \| v_{l_1}^\mathsf{T})^\mathsf{T} \in \mathbb{Z}_q^{l_1 \cdot l_2}$.

Finally, we set

$$A = \begin{pmatrix} 0 & 0 & M & -I_{l_1} & 0 \\ 0 & 0 & 0 & I_l & -G \end{pmatrix}$$

$$x = (k^\mathsf{T} \quad b^\mathsf{T} \quad v^\mathsf{T} \quad u^\mathsf{T} \quad \bar{e}^\mathsf{T})^\mathsf{T}, \quad y = \left(0 \quad \frac{q}{p} \cdot c^\mathsf{T}\right)^\mathsf{T}$$

where $M = I_{l_1} \otimes (1 \ 1 \ldots 1) \in \mathbb{Z}_q^{l_1 \times l_1 \cdot l_2}$.

Besides, we define

$$\begin{cases} \mathcal{M}_1 = \{(i, i, i)\}_{i \in [l_2 + 2l_1 l_2 + l_1 + 1, l_2 + 2l_1 l_2 + l_1 + kl_1]} \\ \mathcal{M}_2 = \{(l_2 + l_1 l_2 + (i - 1) \cdot l_2 + j, l_2 + (i - 1) \cdot l_2 + j, j)\}_{i \in [1, l_1], j \in [1, l_2]} \end{cases}$$

where $\mathcal{M}_1$ indicates that $\bar{e}$ is a binary vector and $\mathcal{M}_2$ indicates that v_i is the Hadamard product between b_i and k. Then we set $\mathcal{M} = \mathcal{M}_1 \cup \mathcal{M}_2$. In the new relation, the length of the witness is $l_2 + 2l_1 l_2 + l_1 + kl_1$, and the size of $\mathcal{M}$ is $kl_1 + l_1 l_2$.

Remark 4.1. We remark that besides privacy-preserving primitives, our ZKAoK for weak PRF also implies a lattice-based verifiable random function (VRF) with trusted uniqueness (as formally defined in [52]).

More precisely, let λ be the security parameter. Let m, n, p, q be positive integers that are polynomial in λ, where $m \geq n(\log q + 1)/(\log p - 1)$. Let A be a random matrix in $\mathbb{Z}_q^{m \times n}$ and serves as a public parameter. The secret key of the VRF is a random vector $s \in \mathbb{Z}_q^n$ and the public key is a vector $b = \lfloor A \cdot s \rfloor_p$ mod p. The evaluation algorithm outputs $y = \lfloor H(x) \cdot s \rfloor_p$ mod p on input a bitstring x, where H is a hash function that maps an arbitrary-length bitstrings onto a matrix in $\mathbb{Z}_q^{m \times n}$ and is modeled as a random oracle. The proof for the correct evaluation of the VRF on an input x is a ZKAoK that argues knowledge of a secret key s s.t. $b = \lfloor A \cdot s \rfloor_p \wedge y = \lfloor B \cdot s \rfloor_p$, where $B = H(x)$ (Note that, we do not need to hide the matrices in this argument.).

First, as proved in [58], with all but negligible probability over the choice of A, the secret key and the public key are bijective. Then the trusted uniqueness of the VRF follows directly from the soundness of the underlying arguments.

Acknowledgement. We appreciate the anonymous reviewers for their valuable suggestions. Part of this work was supported by the National Natural Science Foundation of China (Grant No. 61602396, 61572294, 61632020), Early Career Scheme research grant (ECS Grant No. 25206317) from the Research Grant Council of Hong Kong, the Innovation and Technology Support Programme of Innovation and Technology Fund of Hong Kong (Grant No. ITS/356/17), and the MonashU-PolyU-Collinstar Capital Joint Lab on Blockchain.

References

1. Ajtai, M.: Generating hard instances of lattice problems. In: STOC, pp. 99–108. ACM (1996)
2. Alamati, N., Peikert, C., Stephens-Davidowitz, N.: New (and old) proof systems for lattice problems. In: Abdalla, M., Dahab, R. (eds.) PKC 2018, Part II. LNCS, vol. 10770, pp. 619–643. Springer, Cham (2018). https://doi.org/10.1007/978-3-319-76581-5_21
3. Alkim, E., Ducas, L., Pöppelmann, T., Schwabe, P.: Post-quantum key exchange-a new hope. In: USENIX Security Symposium, vol. 2016 (2016)
4. Applebaum, B., Cash, D., Peikert, C., Sahai, A.: Fast cryptographic primitives and circular-secure encryption based on hard learning problems. In: Halevi, S. (ed.) CRYPTO 2009. LNCS, vol. 5677, pp. 595–618. Springer, Heidelberg (2009). https://doi.org/10.1007/978-3-642-03356-8_35
5. Banerjee, A., Peikert, C., Rosen, A.: Pseudorandom functions and lattices. In: Pointcheval, D., Johansson, T. (eds.) EUROCRYPT 2012. LNCS, vol. 7237, pp. 719–737. Springer, Heidelberg (2012). https://doi.org/10.1007/978-3-642-29011-4_42
6. Baum, C., Damgård, I., Lyubashevsky, V., Oechsner, S., Peikert, C.: More efficient commitments from structured lattice assumptions. In: Catalano, D., De Prisco, R. (eds.) SCN 2018. LNCS, vol. 11035, pp. 368–385. Springer, Cham (2018). https://doi.org/10.1007/978-3-319-98113-0_20

7. Benhamouda, F., Camenisch, J., Krenn, S., Lyubashevsky, V., Neven, G.: Better zero-knowledge proofs for lattice encryption and their application to group signatures. In: Sarkar, P., Iwata, T. (eds.) ASIACRYPT 2014, Part I. LNCS, vol. 8873, pp. 551–572. Springer, Heidelberg (2014). https://doi.org/10.1007/978-3-662-45611-8_29

8. Benhamouda, F., Krenn, S., Lyubashevsky, V., Pietrzak, K.: Efficient zero-knowledge proofs for commitments from learning with errors over rings. In: Pernul, G., Ryan, P.Y.A., Weippl, E. (eds.) ESORICS 2015, Part I. LNCS, vol. 9326, pp. 305–325. Springer, Cham (2015). https://doi.org/10.1007/978-3-319-24174-6_16

9. Bindel, N., et al.: qTESLA. Submission to the NIST's post-quantum cryptography standardization process (2018)

10. Bos, J., et al.: Frodo: take off the ring! practical, quantum-secure key exchange from LWE. In: CCS, pp. 1006–1018. ACM (2016)

11. Bos, J., et al.: CRYSTALS-Kyber: a CCA-secure module-lattice-based KEM. In: EuroS&P, pp. 353–367. IEEE (2018)

12. Boschini, C., Camenisch, J., Neven, G.: Floppy-sized group signatures from lattices. In: Preneel, B., Vercauteren, F. (eds.) ACNS 2018. LNCS, vol. 10892, pp. 163–182. Springer, Cham (2018). https://doi.org/10.1007/978-3-319-93387-0_9

13. Boschini, C., Camenisch, J., Neven, G.: Relaxed lattice-based signatures with short zero-knowledge proofs. In: Chen, L., Manulis, M., Schneider, S. (eds.) ISC 2018. LNCS, vol. 11060, pp. 3–22. Springer, Cham (2018). https://doi.org/10.1007/978-3-319-99136-8_1

14. Camenisch, J., Neven, G., Rückert, M.: Fully anonymous attribute tokens from lattices. In: Visconti, I., De Prisco, R. (eds.) SCN 2012. LNCS, vol. 7485, pp. 57–75. Springer, Heidelberg (2012). https://doi.org/10.1007/978-3-642-32928-9_4

15. Chaum, D.: Blind signatures for untraceable payments. In: Chaum, D., Rivest, R.L., Sherman, A.T. (eds.) Advances in Cryptology, pp. 199–203. Springer, Boston (1983). https://doi.org/10.1007/978-1-4757-0602-4_18

16. Chaum, D., van Heyst, E.: Group signatures. In: Davies, D.W. (ed.) EUROCRYPT 1991. LNCS, vol. 547, pp. 257–265. Springer, Heidelberg (1991). https://doi.org/10.1007/3-540-46416-6_22

17. del Pino, R., Lyubashevsky, V., Seiler, G.: Lattice-based group signatures and zero-knowledge proofs of automorphism stability. In: CCS, pp. 574–591. ACM (2018)

18. Ducas, L., Durmus, A., Lepoint, T., Lyubashevsky, V.: Lattice signatures and bimodal Gaussians. In: Canetti, R., Garay, J.A. (eds.) CRYPTO 2013, Part I. LNCS, vol. 8042, pp. 40–56. Springer, Heidelberg (2013). https://doi.org/10.1007/978-3-642-40041-4_3

19. Esgin, M.F., Steinfeld, R., Sakzad, A., Liu, J.K., Liu, D.: Short lattice-based one-out-of-many proofs and applications to ring signatures. Cryptology ePrint Archive, Report 2018/773 (2018). https://eprint.iacr.org/2018/773

20. Fiat, A., Shamir, A.: How to prove yourself: practical solutions to identification and signature problems. In: Odlyzko, A.M. (ed.) CRYPTO 1986. LNCS, vol. 263, pp. 186–194. Springer, Heidelberg (1987). https://doi.org/10.1007/3-540-47721-7_12

21. Fouque, P.-A., et al.: Falcon: fast-fourier lattice-based compact signatures over NTRU. Submission to the NIST's post-quantum cryptography standardization process (2018)

22. Gentry, C., Peikert, C., Vaikuntanathan, V.: Trapdoors for hard lattices and new cryptographic constructions. In: STOC, pp. 197–206. ACM (2008)

23. Goldreich, O., Goldwasser, S.: On the limits of non-approximability of lattice problems. In: STOC, pp. 1–9. ACM (1998)

24. Goldwasser, S., Micali, S., Rackoff, C.: The knowledge complexity of interactive proof-systems. In: STOC, pp. 291–304. ACM (1985)
25. Goldwasser, S., Kharchenko, D.: Proof of plaintext knowledge for the Ajtai-Dwork cryptosystem. In: Kilian, J. (ed.) TCC 2005. LNCS, vol. 3378, pp. 529–555. Springer, Heidelberg (2005). https://doi.org/10.1007/978-3-540-30576-7_29
26. Gordon, S.D., Katz, J., Vaikuntanathan, V.: A group signature scheme from lattice assumptions. In: Abe, M. (ed.) ASIACRYPT 2010. LNCS, vol. 6477, pp. 395–412. Springer, Heidelberg (2010). https://doi.org/10.1007/978-3-642-17373-8_23
27. Groth, J., Kohlweiss, M.: One-out-of-many proofs: or how to leak a secret and spend a coin. In: Oswald, E., Fischlin, M. (eds.) EUROCRYPT 2015, Part II. LNCS, vol. 9057, pp. 253–280. Springer, Heidelberg (2015). https://doi.org/10.1007/978-3-662-46803-6_9
28. Guruswami, V., Micciancio, D., Regev, O.: The complexity of the covering radius problem. Comput. Complex. **14**(2), 90–121 (2005)
29. Hoffstein, J., Pipher, J., Silverman, J.H.: NTRU: a ring-based public key cryptosystem. In: Buhler, J.P. (ed.) ANTS 1998. LNCS, vol. 1423, pp. 267–288. Springer, Heidelberg (1998). https://doi.org/10.1007/BFb0054868
30. Hoffstein, J., Pipher, J., Whyte, W., Zhang, Z.: A signature scheme from learning with truncation. Cryptology ePrint Archive, Report 2017/995 (2017). https://eprint.iacr.org/2017/995
31. Kawachi, A., Tanaka, K., Xagawa, K.: Concurrently secure identification schemes based on the worst-case hardness of lattice problems. In: Pieprzyk, J. (ed.) ASIACRYPT 2008. LNCS, vol. 5350, pp. 372–389. Springer, Heidelberg (2008). https://doi.org/10.1007/978-3-540-89255-7_23
32. Laguillaumie, F., Langlois, A., Libert, B., Stehlé, D.: Lattice-based group signatures with logarithmic signature size. In: Sako, K., Sarkar, P. (eds.) ASIACRYPT 2013, Part II. LNCS, vol. 8270, pp. 41–61. Springer, Heidelberg (2013). https://doi.org/10.1007/978-3-642-42045-0_3
33. Langlois, A., Ling, S., Nguyen, K., Wang, H.: Lattice-based group signature scheme with verifier-local revocation. In: Krawczyk, H. (ed.) PKC 2014. LNCS, vol. 8383, pp. 345–361. Springer, Heidelberg (2014). https://doi.org/10.1007/978-3-642-54631-0_20
34. Libert, B., Ling, S., Mouhartem, F., Nguyen, K., Wang, H.: Signature schemes with efficient protocols and dynamic group signatures from lattice assumptions. In: Cheon, J.H., Takagi, T. (eds.) ASIACRYPT 2016, Part II. LNCS, vol. 10032, pp. 373–403. Springer, Heidelberg (2016). https://doi.org/10.1007/978-3-662-53890-6_13
35. Libert, B., Ling, S., Mouhartem, F., Nguyen, K., Wang, H.: Zero-knowledge arguments for matrix-vector relations and lattice-based group encryption. In: Cheon, J.H., Takagi, T. (eds.) ASIACRYPT 2016, Part II. LNCS, vol. 10032, pp. 101–131. Springer, Heidelberg (2016). https://doi.org/10.1007/978-3-662-53890-6_4
36. Libert, B., Ling, S., Nguyen, K., Wang, H.: Zero-knowledge arguments for lattice-based accumulators: logarithmic-size ring signatures and group signatures without trapdoors. In: Fischlin, M., Coron, J.-S. (eds.) EUROCRYPT 2016, Part II. LNCS, vol. 9666, pp. 1–31. Springer, Heidelberg (2016). https://doi.org/10.1007/978-3-662-49896-5_1
37. Libert, B., Ling, S., Nguyen, K., Wang, H.: Zero-knowledge arguments for lattice-based PRFs and applications to e-cash. In: Takagi, T., Peyrin, T. (eds.) ASIACRYPT 2017, Part III. LNCS, vol. 10626, pp. 304–335. Springer, Cham (2017). https://doi.org/10.1007/978-3-319-70700-6_11

38. Libert, B., Ling, S., Nguyen, K., Wang, H.: Lattice-based zero-knowledge arguments for integer relations. In: Shacham, H., Boldyreva, A. (eds.) CRYPTO 2018, Part II. LNCS, vol. 10992, pp. 700–732. Springer, Cham (2018). https://doi.org/10.1007/978-3-319-96881-0_24

39. Lindner, R., Peikert, C.: Better key sizes (and attacks) for LWE-based encryption. In: Kiayias, A. (ed.) CT-RSA 2011. LNCS, vol. 6558, pp. 319–339. Springer, Heidelberg (2011). https://doi.org/10.1007/978-3-642-19074-2_21

40. Ling, S., Nguyen, K., Stchlć, D., Wang, H.: Improved zero-knowledge proofs of knowledge for the ISIS problem, and applications. In: Kurosawa, K., Hanaoka, G. (eds.) PKC 2013. LNCS, vol. 7778, pp. 107–124. Springer, Heidelberg (2013). https://doi.org/10.1007/978-3-642-36362-7_8

41. Ling, S., Nguyen, K., Wang, H.: Group signatures from lattices: simpler, tighter, shorter, ring-based. In: Katz, J. (ed.) PKC 2015. LNCS, vol. 9020, pp. 427–449. Springer, Heidelberg (2015). https://doi.org/10.1007/978-3-662-46447-2_19

42. Ling, S., Nguyen, K., Wang, H., Xu, Y.: Lattice-based group signatures: achieving full dynamicity with ease. In: Gollmann, D., Miyaji, A., Kikuchi, H. (eds.) ACNS 2017. LNCS, vol. 10355, pp. 293–312. Springer, Cham (2017). https://doi.org/10.1007/978-3-319-61204-1_15

43. Ling, S., Nguyen, K., Wang, H., Xu, Y.: Constant-size group signatures from lattices. In: Abdalla, M., Dahab, R. (eds.) PKC 2018, Part II. LNCS, vol. 10770, pp. 58–88. Springer, Cham (2018). https://doi.org/10.1007/978-3-319-76581-5_3

44. Lyubashevsky, V.: Lattice-based identification schemes secure under active attacks. In: Cramer, R. (ed.) PKC 2008. LNCS, vol. 4939, pp. 162–179. Springer, Heidelberg (2008). https://doi.org/10.1007/978-3-540-78440-1_10

45. Lyubashevsky, V.: Fiat-Shamir with aborts: applications to lattice and factoring-based signatures. In: Matsui, M. (ed.) ASIACRYPT 2009. LNCS, vol. 5912, pp. 598–616. Springer, Heidelberg (2009). https://doi.org/10.1007/978-3-642-10366-7_35

46. Lyubashevsky, V.: Lattice signatures without trapdoors. In: Pointcheval, D., Johansson, T. (eds.) EUROCRYPT 2012. LNCS, vol. 7237, pp. 738–755. Springer, Heidelberg (2012). https://doi.org/10.1007/978-3-642-29011-4_43

47. Lyubashevsky, V., Neven, G.: One-shot verifiable encryption from lattices. In: Coron, J.-S., Nielsen, J.B. (eds.) EUROCRYPT 2017, Part I. LNCS, vol. 10210, pp. 293–323. Springer, Cham (2017). https://doi.org/10.1007/978-3-319-56620-7_11

48. Micciancio, D., Regev, O.: Worst-case to average-case reductions based on Gaussian measures. In: FOCS, pp. 372–381. IEEE (2004)

49. Micciancio, D., Peikert, C.: Hardness of SIS and LWE with small parameters. In: Canetti, R., Garay, J.A. (eds.) CRYPTO 2013, Part I. LNCS, vol. 8042, pp. 21–39. Springer, Heidelberg (2013). https://doi.org/10.1007/978-3-642-40041-4_2

50. Micciancio, D., Vadhan, S.P.: Statistical zero-knowledge proofs with efficient provers: lattice problems and more. In: Boneh, D. (ed.) CRYPTO 2003. LNCS, vol. 2729, pp. 282–298. Springer, Heidelberg (2003). https://doi.org/10.1007/978-3-540-45146-4_17

51. Nguyen, P.Q., Zhang, J., Zhang, Z.: Simpler efficient group signatures from lattices. In: Katz, J. (ed.) PKC 2015. LNCS, vol. 9020, pp. 401–426. Springer, Heidelberg (2015). https://doi.org/10.1007/978-3-662-46447-2_18

52. Papadopoulos, D., et al.: Making NSEC5 practical for DNSSEC. Cryptology ePrint Archive, Report 2017/099 (2017). https://eprint.iacr.org/2017/099

53. Peikert, C.: A decade of lattice cryptography. Found. Trends® Theor. Comput. Sci. **10**(4), 283–424 (2016)

54. Peikert, C., Vaikuntanathan, V.: Noninteractive statistical zero-knowledge proofs for lattice problems. In: Wagner, D. (ed.) CRYPTO 2008. LNCS, vol. 5157, pp. 536–553. Springer, Heidelberg (2008). https://doi.org/10.1007/978-3-540-85174-5_30
55. Regev, O.: On lattices, learning with errors, random linear codes, and cryptography. In: STOC, pp. 84–93. ACM (2005)
56. Rivest, R.L., Shamir, A., Tauman, Y.: How to leak a secret. In: Boyd, C. (ed.) ASIACRYPT 2001. LNCS, vol. 2248, pp. 552–565. Springer, Heidelberg (2001). https://doi.org/10.1007/3-540-45682-1_32
57. Stern, J.: A new identification scheme based on syndrome decoding. In: Stinson, D.R. (ed.) CRYPTO 1993. LNCS, vol. 773, pp. 13–21. Springer, Heidelberg (1994). https://doi.org/10.1007/3-540-48329-2_2
58. Yang, R., Au, M.H., Lai, J., Xu, Q., Yu, Z.: Lattice-based techniques for accountable anonymity: composition of abstract stern's protocols and weak PRF with efficient protocols from LWR. Cryptology ePrint Archive, Report 2017/781 (2017). http://eprint.iacr.org/2017/781

Algebraic Techniques for Short(er) Exact Lattice-Based Zero-Knowledge Proofs

Jonathan Bootle[1(✉)], Vadim Lyubashevsky[1(✉)], and Gregor Seiler[1,2]

[1] IBM Research – Zurich, Rüschlikon, Switzerland
{jbt,vad}@zurich.ibm.com
[2] ETH Zurich, Zurich, Switzerland

Abstract. A key component of many lattice-based protocols is a zero-knowledge proof of knowledge of a vector $\vec{s}$ with small coefficients satisfying $A\vec{s} = \vec{u} \bmod q$. While there exist fairly efficient proofs for a relaxed version of this equation which prove the knowledge of $\vec{s}'$ and c satisfying $A\vec{s}' = \vec{u}c$ where $\|\vec{s}'\| \gg \|\vec{s}\|$ and c is some small element in the ring over which the proof is performed, the proofs for the exact version of the equation are considerably less practical. The best such proof technique is an adaptation of Stern's protocol (Crypto '93), for proving knowledge of nearby codewords, to larger moduli. The scheme is a Σ-protocol, each of whose iterations has soundness error $2/3$, and thus requires over 200 repetitions to obtain soundness error of 2^{-128}, which is the main culprit behind the large size of the proofs produced.

In this paper, we propose the first lattice-based proof system that significantly outperforms Stern-type proofs for proving knowledge of a short $\vec{s}$ satisfying $A\vec{s} = \vec{u} \bmod q$. Unlike Stern's proof, which is combinatorial in nature, our proof is more algebraic and uses various relaxed zero-knowledge proofs as sub-routines. The main savings in our proof system comes from the fact that each round has soundness error of $1/n$, where n is the number of columns of A. For typical applications, n is a few thousand, and therefore our proof needs to be repeated around 10 times to achieve a soundness error of 2^{-128}. For concrete parameters, it produces proofs that are around an order of magnitude smaller than those produced using Stern's approach.

Keywords: Lattices · Zero-knowledge proofs · Commitments

1 Introduction

Lattice based cryptography is viewed as one of the most promising post-quantum replacements for traditional public key cryptography because the most crucial cryptographic primitives, such as public key encryption and digital signatures, can be efficiently constructed from lattice assumptions. Furthermore, there exist cryptographic primitives (e.g. FHE [Gen09]) whose only current realization stems from lattice assumptions.

© International Association for Cryptologic Research 2019
A. Boldyreva and D. Micciancio (Eds.): CRYPTO 2019, LNCS 11692, pp. 176–202, 2019.
https://doi.org/10.1007/978-3-030-26948-7_7

1.1   Lattice-Based Zero-Knowledge Proofs

A central part of many lattice protocols is a zero-knowledge proof of a vector $\vec{s}$ satisfying

$$A\vec{s} = \vec{u} \bmod q \tag{1}$$

for public $A \in \mathbb{Z}_q^{m \times n}$ and $\vec{u} \in \mathbb{Z}_q^m$. Current lattice-based zero-knowledge proofs for the above equation come in several varieties. The most direct approach proves exactly the knowledge of $\vec{s}$ satisfying (1) that the prover uses to generate the proof. This proof system [KTX08, LNSW13] is an adaptation of Stern's protocol [Ste93], which proves knowledge of nearby codewords, to larger moduli. Its main weakness is that each iteration of the proof has soundness error $2/3$ and it therefore needs to be repeated 219 times to achieve soundness error 2^{-128}. For typical applications where the modulus is $q \approx 2^{30}$, the size of such a proof is several megabytes long.

There are other protocols that give "relaxed" proofs of (1), which may be useful in some situations. The Fiat-Shamir-with-Aborts [Lyu09, Gro10, Lyu12] approach proves knowledge of an $\vec{s}'$ and c satisfying $A\vec{s}' = c\vec{u} \bmod q$. Despite the fact that $\|\vec{s}'\| > \|\vec{s}\|$ and the presence of an extra factor c, this technique is useful for producing short lattice-based primitives, such as digital signatures, when performed over polynomial rings. The reason that these protocols are so efficient is that each run of the protocol has negligible soundness error and so only needs to be performed once. Another approach [BCK+14] proves the knowledge of $\vec{s}'$ satisfying $A\vec{s}' = 2\vec{u} \bmod q$ for $\|\vec{s}'\| > \|\vec{s}\|$. When performed over polynomial rings, the soundness error of this protocol $1/2d$, where d is the dimension of the ring. In the case where one has many equations as in (1) for the same A, but different $\vec{s}_i$ and $\vec{u}_i$, there are even sub-linear size proofs [BBC+18] showing that $A\vec{s}_i' = \vec{u}_i$, where $\|\vec{s}_i'\| > \|\vec{s}_i\|$.

The main downside in all of the aforementioned efficient proofs is that even though they are more efficient than Stern-type proofs, they always prove knowledge of an $\vec{s}'$ which is larger than the $\vec{s}$ that the prover knows. Other than the Stern-type proofs mentioned above, the only other known proof system that exactly proves knowledge of the $\vec{s}$ in (1) is based on the hardness of the discrete logarithm problem [dPLS19] using the "Bulletproofs" [BCC+16, BBB+18] approach which results in short proofs, but long running times (in addition to requiring the discrete logarithm assumption).[1] The disadvantage of proofs that prove knowledge of a larger $\vec{s}'$ is that, for security reasons, they force the modulus q to be larger. When the zero-knowledge proof is the main part of the protocol one is building (e.g. group signatures [LNWX18, dPLS18]), this trade-off may be worthwhile. On the other hand, if one would like to use a zero-knowledge proof to prove something about a relation used in a different protocol (e.g. proving that the public key of a lattice based encryption scheme is well-formed), then

---

[1] Since the submission of this paper, independently achieved results (some using very different techniques) appeared for solving versions of this problem [Beu19, BN19, YAZ+19].

one may not want to increase the parameters of the scheme just to make the zero-knowledge proof more efficient.

In this paper, we present a new proof technique for exactly proving (1) which is different from the "combinatorial" approach of Stern-like proofs. The proof crucially uses the connection between the coefficient and the NTT (i.e. FFT) representation in polynomial rings, invokes a "relaxed" lattice-based commitment scheme as a sub-routine, and uses some "tricks" present in certain discrete-log based proofs (e.g. [GK15]).

1.2   Our Approach

The basic building block of our zero-knowledge proof system is a proof of knowledge of an $\vec{s}$ with coefficients in $\{0, 1, 2\}$ satisfying (1). One can easily transform this into a proof system where $\vec{s}$ comes from the more typical space of $\{-1, 0, 1\}$ and also extend it into a proof system where $\vec{s}$ has coefficients in the set $\{-S \ldots, S\}$. The former is trivial, whereas the latter involves rewriting $\vec{s} = G\vec{s}'$, where $\vec{s}'$ has coefficients in $\{0, 1, 2\}$ for some public matrix G, and then proving knowledge of an $\vec{s}'$ such that $A'\vec{s}' = \vec{u}$ for $A' = AG$.

Notice that in the above transformation from a basic proof to a general one, the larger the size of the basic set is, the fewer columns A' will have – which is good for keeping the proof size small. On the other hand, as we'll see below, the larger the basic set is, the larger the proof will be for the fact that each coefficient of $\vec{s}'$ is in the basic set. When picking the size of the basic set, it is thus important to balance these two conditions to obtain the optimally minimal proof size. It turns out that choosing the basic set to be $\{0, 1, 2\}$ is very close to the optimal choice. Furthermore, $\{0, 1, 2\}$ (which is equivalent to $\{-1, 0, 1\}$) is often the actual set in which we want to prove that the coefficients of the solution lie. We therefore choose to work with this set for the remainder of the paper.

If $\vec{1}$ and $\vec{2}$ are n-dimensional vectors consisting of 1's and 2's, then proving that the coefficients are all in the set $\{0, 1, 2\}$ is equivalent to showing that

$$\vec{s} \circ (\vec{s} - \vec{1}) \circ (\vec{s} - \vec{2}) = \vec{0} \bmod q,$$

where $\circ$ denotes component-wise multiplication. Let us now consider a polynomial ring $\mathcal{R} = \mathbb{Z}_q[X]/(f(X))$ where $f(X)$ is a polynomial of degree n that splits into linear factors modulo q. For example, if n is a power of 2 and $q \equiv 1$ (mod $2n$), then $f(X) = X^n + 1$ is a good polynomial to use. If $\mathbf{s} \in \mathcal{R}$ satisfies $\mathbf{s}(\mathbf{s} - 1)(\mathbf{s} - 2) = \mathbf{0}$, then it also holds that $\hat{\mathbf{s}} \circ (\hat{\mathbf{s}} - \hat{\mathbf{1}}) \circ (\hat{\mathbf{s}} - \hat{\mathbf{2}}) = \hat{\mathbf{0}} \bmod q$, where $\hat{\mathbf{s}}$ is the NTT (or FFT) representation of $\mathbf{s}$. Since the we chose our ring so that $f(X)$ fully splits, $\hat{\mathbf{s}}$ is a vector of dimension n and so $\hat{\mathbf{1}}$ and $\hat{\mathbf{2}}$ are n-dimensional vectors consisting entirely of 1's and 2's. We can now rephrase what we're trying to prove in terms of polynomials and their NTT representations. Proving the knowledge of a polynomial $\mathbf{s} \in \mathcal{R}$ such that

$$\mathbf{s}(\mathbf{s} - 1)(\mathbf{s} - 2) = \mathbf{0} \text{ and } A\hat{\mathbf{s}} = \vec{u} \bmod q \tag{2}$$

is equivalent to proving the knowledge of $\vec{s}$ with coefficients in $\{0,1,2\}$ satisfying (1).

Our proof of knowledge of (2) begins with the prover picking a random masking polynomial $\mathbf{y} \in R$ and producing a $\vec{w} = A\hat{\mathbf{y}} \bmod q$. For a challenge $c \in \mathbb{Z}_q \subset R$, if the prover outputs $\mathbf{z} = \mathbf{y} + c\mathbf{s}$, then this can be rewritten as $\hat{\mathbf{z}} = \hat{\mathbf{y}} + c\hat{\mathbf{s}}$, and therefore the verifier can check the equation

$$A\hat{\mathbf{z}} = \vec{w} + c\vec{u}. \tag{3}$$

Notice that in order for $\mathbf{z} = \mathbf{y} + c\mathbf{s}$ to imply (3), it is crucial that $c \in \mathbb{Z}_q$, since this is the only way that all the coefficients of $\hat{c}$ can be identical. By rewinding, we can obtain another equation $A\hat{\mathbf{z}}' = \vec{w} + c'\vec{u}$, for a $c' \neq c$ and combining the two we get

$$A(\hat{\mathbf{z}} - \hat{\mathbf{z}}') = (c - c')\vec{u}. \tag{4}$$

The above does not really prove (1) since we still do not know that the coefficients of $(\hat{\mathbf{z}} - \hat{\mathbf{z}})$ are in $\{0, 1, 2\}$ and there is the term $(c - c') \in \mathbb{Z}_q$ which is not necessarily 1. Let us first describe how the latter problem is handled. In the first step, the prover additionally makes commitments $\mathrm{Com}(\mathbf{y})$ and $\mathrm{Com}(\mathbf{s})$ to $\mathbf{y}$ and $\mathbf{s}$ using the commitment scheme from [BDL+18] which has the property that for any $c \in R$

$$\mathrm{Com}(\mathbf{y}) + c \cdot \mathrm{Com}(\mathbf{s}) = \mathrm{Com}(\mathbf{y} + c\mathbf{s}).$$

After receiving the challenge c, the prover will prove that $\mathrm{Com}(\mathbf{y}) + c \cdot \mathrm{Com}(\mathbf{s})$ is a commitment to $\mathbf{z}$, which implies that $\mathbf{y} + c\mathbf{s} = \mathbf{z}$, and therefore after rewinding, $(c - c')\mathbf{s} = \mathbf{z} - \mathbf{z}'$. Plugging this into (4) implies that $A(c - c')\hat{\mathbf{s}} = (c - c')\vec{u}$, and since $c \neq c'$ and q is prime, we can divide out by $(c - c')$ to obtain

$$A\hat{\mathbf{s}} = \vec{u}. \tag{5}$$

What we still have not proved is that the coefficients of $\hat{\mathbf{s}}$ (or more precisely, the NTT coefficients of the message that was committed to in $\mathrm{Com}(\mathbf{s})$) are in $\{0, 1, 2\}$. For this proof, we make the observation that

$$\mathbf{z}(\mathbf{z} - c)(\mathbf{z} - 2c) = \mathbf{y}^3 + 3\mathbf{y}^2(\mathbf{s} - 1)c + \mathbf{y}(3\mathbf{s}^2 - 6\mathbf{s} + 2)c^2 + \mathbf{s}(\mathbf{s} - 1)(\mathbf{s} - 2)c^3. \tag{6}$$

In particular, the last coefficient of the above polynomial is exactly what we would like to prove equals to $\mathbf{0}$. In the first step of the protocol, the prover will also commit to

$$\mathbf{t}_0 = \mathrm{Com}(\mathbf{y}^3)$$
$$\mathbf{t}_1 = \mathrm{Com}(3\mathbf{y}^2(\mathbf{s} - 1))$$
$$\mathbf{t}_2 = \mathrm{Com}(\mathbf{y}(3\mathbf{s}^2 - 6\mathbf{s} + 2))$$

and after receiving the challenge c, he will again use the linearity of the commitment scheme to show that

$$\mathrm{Com}(\mathbf{z}(\mathbf{z} - c)(\mathbf{z} - 2c)) = \mathbf{t}_0 + c\mathbf{t}_1 + c^2\mathbf{t}_2 \tag{7}$$

Intuitively (by an argument similar to the Schwartz-Zippel Lemma) this implies that $\mathbf{z}(\mathbf{z} - c)(\mathbf{z} - 2c)$ as written in (6) is indeed a polynomial that is quadratic in c and therefore the last term of (6) is $\mathbf{0}$ as we wanted.

The one thing that is still left to do is show that all the commitments that we made are valid. For this we use the proof from [BDL+18], paying careful attention to the fact that the challenges have to come from a set whose differences are all invertible. To make this set large, [BDL+18] proposed the use of a polynomial ring $\mathcal{R}$ such that the underlying polynomial $f(X)$ splits into a few high-degree irreducible terms. But in our proof, we crucially need $f(X)$ to fully split, and so the largest set that we can use is $\{0, \pm X^i\}$, for $0 \leq i < n$, which is of size $2n + 1$. Thus the commitment validity proof needs to be repeated $128/\log 2n$ times.

Decreasing the soundness error. Looking at the number of repetitions, the challenge c comes from the set $\mathbb{Z}_q$ and therefore one would need $128/\log q$ such challenges for achieving 128-bit security. Since we mentioned above that the challenges for proving the commitments are valid come from a set of size $2n$, one may naïvely assume that $(128/\log q) \cdot (128/\log 2n)$ (parallel) repetitions of the protocol will be necessary – but this would be an overestimate. The prover does not have to convince the verifier that each commitment is correct with overwhelming probability. Intuitively, the probability of the verifier cheating is if he can guess the challenge c (which is $\frac{1}{q}$) or he can create an invalid commitment and not get caught. If the latter probability is ρ, then the probability of the verifier cheating is less than $\frac{1}{q} + \rho$. It is therefore not very useful to decrease ρ below $\frac{1}{q}$. Thus the commitment validity proof will need to be repeated (in parallel) a total of $128/\log 2n$ times (for the whole protocol) and the number proofs of (1) that will need to be made, conditioned on the commitment being valid, is $128/\log q$.

Observations. One interesting observation is that our proof crucially uses polynomial rings and the security of the commitment scheme in [BDL+18] based on problems in polynomial rings, but the original problem instance in (1) is only viewed as a linear equation over $\mathbb{Z}_q$. One could, of course, have (1) represent an equation over some ring $\mathcal{R}'$ (which is not the same as the ring $\mathcal{R}$ that we did the proof over!) by having the matrix A be "structured". For example if A consists of concatenations of rotation matrices, then (1) is a polynomial equation over $\mathbb{Z}_q[X]/(X^m - 1)$. So our proof can also be seen as a way to give a more efficient proof (of any kind, even relaxed) of a linear equation over $\mathbb{Z}_q$, though relying on the hardness of problems over polynomial rings.

While the beginning of our proof may have some similarity to proofs of a relaxed version of (1) (e.g. [Lyu09, Lyu12]), we believe that the resemblance is only superficial. Ignoring the NTT step (which is not present in other protocols), the extracted values of $\hat{\mathbf{z}}$ and c in (4) somewhat resemble what one obtains in the final step of the aforementioned protocols. In those protocols, the values of $\hat{\mathbf{z}}$ are constructed to be small (but still larger than $\hat{\mathbf{s}}$) by choosing the $\hat{\mathbf{y}}$ from a particular narrow distribution and using rejection sampling to keep the $\hat{\mathbf{z}}$ small. In the current proof, however, the $\hat{\mathbf{z}}$ are not small and everything about the size of the secret $\hat{\mathbf{s}}$ is proved elsewhere in the protocol by showing that the c^3 term of (6) is $\mathbf{0}$.

2   Preliminaries

2.1   Notation

The following Table summarizes the notation and parameters that will appear in this paper (Table 1).

Table 1. Overview of parameters and notation

Parameter	Explanation
$q \equiv 1 \pmod{l}$	Prime modulus that splits completely in $\mathcal{R}$
$\mathbb{Z}_q = \mathbb{Z}/q\mathbb{Z}$	The field over which the linear system is defined
$m \in \mathbb{Z}$	The number of rows in the linear system
$n \in \mathbb{Z}$	The number of columns in the linear system and the rank of $\mathcal{R}$
$\Phi_l \in \mathbb{Z}[X]$	The l-th cyclotomic polynomial of degree $n = \varphi(l)$
$\mathcal{R} = \mathbb{Z}[X]/(\Phi_l)$	The ring of integers in the l-th cyclotomic number field
$\mathcal{R}_q = \mathbb{Z}_q[X]/(\Phi_l)$	The ring of integers $\mathcal{R}$ modulo the fully splitting rational prime q
$\mathcal{C} \subset \mathcal{R}$	A set of low-weight challenge polynomials
$\bar{\mathcal{C}} = (\mathcal{C} - \mathcal{C}) \setminus \{0\}$	The set of challenge differences excluding $\mathbf{0}$
T	Bound for honest prover's $\mathbf{f}\vec{r}$ in embedding norm
$\sigma = 5T$	Standard deviation for sampling $\vec{\mathbf{y}}'$
$B = \sigma\sqrt{12n}$	Bound for honest prover's $\vec{\mathbf{z}}'$ in embedding norm
β^n	Error distribution on $\mathcal{R}$ in the RLWE problem
D_σ^n	Discrete Gaussian distribution on $\mathcal{R}$ with standard deviation σ

We use bold letters $\mathbf{f}$ for polynomials in $\mathcal{R}$, arrows as in $\vec{v}$ for integer vectors $\vec{v} \in \mathbb{Z}^k$, bold letters with arrows $\vec{\mathbf{v}}$ for vectors of polynomials $\vec{\mathbf{v}} \in \mathcal{R}^k$ and capital letters A and $\mathbf{A}$ for integer and polynomial matrices, respectively. We write $x \xleftarrow{\$} S$ when $x \in S$ is sampled uniformly at random from the set S and similarly $x \xleftarrow{\$} \rho$ when x is sampled according to the distribution ρ.

As is often the case in ring-based lattice cryptography, computation will be performed in the quotient ring $\mathcal{R}_q$ modulo q of the ring of integers $\mathcal{R}$ of the l-th cyclotomic number field. The geometry on $\mathcal{R}$ is inherited by embedding $\mathcal{R}$ into the Minkowski space, an n-dimensional real subspace of $\mathbb{C}^n$. Concretely, for $\mathbf{f}, \mathbf{g} \in \mathcal{R}$, we have the scalar product and its induced norm

$$\langle \mathbf{f}, \mathbf{g} \rangle = \sum_{j \in \mathbb{Z}_l^\times} f(\zeta^j)\overline{g(\zeta^j)} \quad \text{and}$$

$$\|\mathbf{f}\|_2 = \left(\sum_{j \in \mathbb{Z}_l^\times} |f(\zeta^j)|^2 \right)^{\frac{1}{2}},$$

where ζ is the primitive l-th complex root of unity $\zeta = e^{2\pi i/l}$. In the special case where $\mathcal{R}$ is a power-of-two cyclotomic ring, i.e. $l = 2^r$, the norm of $\mathbf{f} = f_0 + \cdots + f_{n-1}X^{n-1}$ is identical, up to a scaling factor, to the ℓ_2-norm of the coefficient vector $\vec{f} = (f_0, \ldots, f_{n-1}) \in \mathbb{Z}^n$; that is,

$$\|\mathbf{f}\|_2 = \sqrt{n} \left(\sum_{i=1}^{n} |f_i|^2 \right)^{\frac{1}{2}} = \sqrt{n} \|\vec{f}\|_2.$$

The scalar product and norm are extended to vectors $\vec{\mathbf{v}} = (\mathbf{v}_1, \ldots, \mathbf{v}_k), \vec{\mathbf{w}} = (\mathbf{w}_1, \ldots, \mathbf{w}_k) \in \mathcal{R}^k$ of polynomials in the natural way,

$$\langle \vec{\mathbf{v}}, \vec{\mathbf{w}} \rangle = \sum_{i=1}^{k} \langle \mathbf{v}_i, \mathbf{w}_i \rangle,$$

$$\|\vec{\mathbf{v}}\|_2 = \left(\sum_{i=1}^{k} \|\mathbf{v}_i\|_2^2 \right)^{\frac{1}{2}}.$$

2.2 Fully Splitting Primes and the Number Theoretic Transform

Our prime modulus q needs to be such that q splits completely in $\mathcal{R}$; that is, the cyclotomic polynomial Φ_l needs to factor into linear polynomials modulo q. This is the case if and only if there exists a primitive l-th root of unity modulo q, which in turn is equivalent to the condition $q - 1 \equiv 0 \pmod{l}$.

Then, by the Chinese remainder theorem, we have that $\mathcal{R}_q = \mathbb{Z}_q[X]/\Phi_l$ is isomorphic $\mathbb{Z}_q^n$. Concretely,

$$\mathbb{Z}_q[X]/(\Phi_l) \cong \mathbb{Z}_q[X]/(X - \zeta_1) \times \cdots \times \mathbb{Z}_q[X]/(X - \zeta_n)$$

where $\zeta_1, \ldots, \zeta_n$ are the primitive l-th roots of unity modulo q. The isomorphism is given by reduction modulo $X - \zeta_i$. We write $\hat{\mathbf{f}}$ for the image of $\mathbf{f} \in \mathcal{R}_q$ under the isomorphism and call it the *Number Theoretic Transform* (NTT) of $\mathbf{f}$.

When l is a product of powers of small primes then the NTT (and its inverse) can be computed very efficiently in a divide an conquer fashion. Especially popular is the optimal case where l is a power of two and indeed many schemes in lattice cryptography are instantiated over such a ring.

The existence of a fast NTT algorithm for computing the isomorphism speeds-up and simplifies computation but is not crucial for our results. Therefore we do not go into more details here.

2.3 Challenge Space

We define the challenge space $\mathcal{C} \subset \mathcal{R}$ as

$$\mathcal{C} = \{0, X^i \mid 0 \leq i < l\}.$$

The crucial property of this set is that the difference of any two members is invertible in $\mathcal{R}$ and the multiplication of any element in $\mathcal{R}$ by any member of the set does not increase the norm of the element.

In the area of lattice-based zero-knowledge proofs, when $\mathcal{R}$ is a power of two cyclotomic ring, there is a sometimes-used stronger result stating that $2(X^i - X^j)^{-1}$ exists and has ternary coefficients in $\{-1, 0, 1\}$; c.f. [BCK+14, Lemma 3.1]. In our application we do not need any condition on the smallness of the inverse of a difference of challenges and hence we will not be concerned with this property.

Lemma 2.1. *The polynomials $X^i - X^j \in \mathcal{R}_q$ for $i \not\equiv j \pmod{l}$ are invertible.*

Proof. Let $\zeta \in \mathbb{Z}_q$ be one of the primitive l-th roots of unity. Then $X^i - X^j \mod X - \zeta = \zeta^i - \zeta^j$. The latter is zero in $\mathbb{Z}_q$ if and only if $i \equiv j \pmod{l}$. $\square$

2.4   Error Distribution, Discrete Gaussians and Rejection Sampling

For sampling randomness in the commitment scheme that we use, and to define a variant of the Ring Learning with Errors problem, we need to define an error distribution β^n on $\mathcal{R}$. For general cyclotomic rings one has to be careful when sampling error polynomials as one has to do it over the Minkowski space [LPR13].

For power-of-two cyclotomics, however, it is secure and much easier to directly sample the polynomial coefficients. Moreover, we will need to bound the norm of error polynomials and these bounds turn out to be slightly better when sampling the coefficients using a uniform or binomial distribution on a small interval instead of a small one-dimensional (discrete) Gaussian. Also this is much easier to implement in practice. Therefore, in the power-of-two case we sample the coefficients of the random polynomials in the commitment scheme using the distribution β_2 on $\{-1, 0, 1\}$ where ± 1 both have probability $5/16$ and 0 has probability $6/16$. This distribution is chosen (rather than the more "natural" uniform one) because it is easy to sample given a random bitstring by computing $a_1 + a_2 - b_1 - b_2 \mod 3$ with uniformly random bits a_i, b_i. Now if $\vec{v} \xleftarrow{\$} \beta_2^n$ then we have the Chernov bound for $0 < \delta \leq 1$ given by

$$\Pr\left[\|\vec{v}\|_2 < \sqrt{(1 + \delta)\frac{10}{16}n}\right] \geq 1 - \exp\left(-\frac{\delta^2}{3}\frac{10}{16}n\right). \tag{8}$$

In our zero-knowledge proof, the prover will want to output a vector $\vec{z}$ whose distribution should be independent of a secret randomness vector $\vec{r}$, so that $\vec{z}$ cannot be used to gain any information on the prover's secret. During the protocol, the prover computes $\vec{z} = \vec{y} + \mathbf{f}\vec{r}$ where $\vec{r}$ is the randomness used to commit to the prover's secret, $\mathbf{f} \leftarrow \mathcal{C}$ is a challenge polynomial, and $\vec{y}$ is a "masking" vector. To remove the dependency of $\vec{z}$ on $\vec{r}$, we use the rejection sampling technique by Lyubashevsky [Lyu09, Lyu12]. In the two variants of this technique the masking vector is either sampled uniformly from some bounded region or using a discrete Gaussian distribution. In the high dimensions we will encounter, the

Gaussian variant is far superior as it gives acceptable rejection probabilities for much narrower distributions. We first define the discrete Gaussian distribution and then state the rejection sampling algorithm in Fig. 1, which plays a central role in Lemma 2.4.

Definition 2.2. *The* discrete Gaussian distribution *on* $\mathcal{R}^k$ *centered around* $\vec{\mathbf{v}} \in \mathcal{R}^k$ *with standard deviation* $\sigma > 0$ *is given by*

$$D_{\vec{\mathbf{v}},\sigma}^{kn}(\vec{\mathbf{z}}) = \frac{e^{-\|\vec{\mathbf{z}}-\vec{\mathbf{v}}\|_2^2/2\sigma^2}}{\sum_{\vec{\mathbf{z}}' \in \mathcal{R}^k} e^{-\|\vec{\mathbf{z}}'\|_2^2/2\sigma^2}}.$$

When it is centered around $\vec{\mathbf{0}} \in \mathcal{R}^k$ *we write* $D_\sigma^{kn} = D_{\vec{\mathbf{0}},\sigma}^{kn}$

We will use the following tail bound, which follows from [Ban93, Lemma 1.5(i)].

Lemma 2.3. *Let* $\vec{\mathbf{z}} \xleftarrow{\$} D_\sigma^{kn}$. *Then*

$$\Pr\left[\|\vec{\mathbf{z}}\|_2 \le \sigma\sqrt{2kn}\right] \ge 1 - 2^{-\log(e/2)kn/4}.$$

Algorithm 1. $\mathrm{Rej}\,(\vec{\mathbf{z}}, \vec{\mathbf{v}}, \sigma)$

$u \xleftarrow{\$} [0,1)$
if $u < \frac{1}{12} \cdot \exp\left(\frac{-2\langle\vec{\mathbf{z}},\vec{\mathbf{v}}\rangle + \|\vec{\mathbf{v}}\|_2}{2\sigma^2}\right)$ **then**
   return 0
else
   return 1
end if

Lemma 2.4. *Let* $\rho\colon \mathcal{R}^k \to [0,1]$ *be a probability distribution such that, for some* $T > 0$, $\rho(\{\vec{\mathbf{v}} \in \mathcal{R}^k \mid \|\vec{\mathbf{v}}\|_2 \le T\}) \ge 1 - 2^{-101}$ *and let* $\sigma \ge 5T$. *Sample* $\vec{\mathbf{v}} \xleftarrow{\$} \rho$ *and* $\vec{\mathbf{y}} \xleftarrow{\$} D_\sigma^{kn}$, *set* $\vec{\mathbf{z}} = \vec{\mathbf{y}} + \vec{\mathbf{v}}$, *and run* $b \leftarrow \mathrm{Rej}\,(\vec{\mathbf{z}}, \vec{\mathbf{v}}, \sigma)$. *Then, the probability that* $b = 0$ *is at least* $1/12 - 2^{-104}$ *and the distribution of* $(\vec{\mathbf{v}}, \vec{\mathbf{z}})$, *conditioned on* $b = 0$, *is within statistical distance of* 2^{-100} *of the product distribution* $\rho \times D_\sigma^{kn}$.

The proof is essentially the same as in [Lyu12, Theorem 4.6], but we include it here for the sake of completeness since the statement in [Lyu12] is slightly different.

Proof. For every $\vec{\mathbf{v}}' \in \mathcal{R}^k$ let $S_{\vec{\mathbf{v}}'} \subset \mathcal{R}^k$ be the set of vectors $\vec{\mathbf{z}}'$ such that

$$\frac{D_\sigma^{kn}(\vec{\mathbf{z}}')}{D_{\vec{\mathbf{v}}',\sigma}^{kn}(\vec{\mathbf{z}}')} \le 12.$$

By a simple variant of [Lyu12, Lemma 4.5] it follows that for all $\vec{v}'$ such that $\|\vec{v}'\|_2 \leq T$,

$$D_\sigma^{kn}(S_{\vec{v}'}) \geq 1 - 2^{-102}.$$

Then,

$$\Pr\left[b = 0\right] = \sum_{\vec{v}' \in \mathcal{R}^k} \rho(\vec{v}') \sum_{\vec{z}' \in \mathcal{R}^k} D_{\vec{v}',\sigma}^{kn}(\vec{z}') \min\left(\frac{1}{12} \frac{D_\sigma^{kn}(\vec{z}')}{D_{\vec{v}',\sigma}^{kn}(\vec{z}')}, 1\right)$$

$$\geq \sum_{\|\vec{v}'\|_2 \leq T} \rho(\vec{v}') \sum_{\vec{z}' \in S_{\vec{v}'}} \frac{1}{12} D_\sigma^{kn}(\vec{z}')$$

$$\geq \frac{1}{12}(1 - 2^{-101})(1 - 2^{-102}) > \frac{1}{12} - 2^{-104}.$$

And on the other hand,

$$\Pr\left[b = 0\right] \leq \frac{1}{12} \sum_{\vec{v} \in \mathcal{R}^k} \rho(\vec{v}') \sum_{\vec{z}' \in S_{\vec{v}'}} D_\sigma^{kn}(\vec{z}') + \sum_{\vec{v} \in \mathcal{R}^k} \rho(\vec{v}') \sum_{\vec{z}' \notin S_{\vec{v}'}} D_{\vec{v}',\sigma}^{kn}(\vec{z}')$$

$$\leq \frac{1}{12} + \frac{1}{12} \sum_{\|\vec{v}\|_2 \leq T} \rho(\vec{v}') \sum_{\vec{z}' \notin S_{\vec{v}'}} D_\sigma^{kn}(\vec{z}')$$

$$+ \frac{1}{12} \sum_{\|\vec{v}\|_2 > T} \rho(\vec{v}') \sum_{\vec{z}' \notin S_{\vec{v}'}} D_\sigma^{kn}(\vec{z}')$$

$$\leq \frac{1 + 2^{-102} + 2^{-101}}{12} = \frac{1}{12} + 2^{-104}.$$

Therefore, we find for the statistical distance between the conditional distribution of $(\vec{v}, \vec{z})$ and the product distribution $\rho \times D_\sigma$,

$$\frac{1}{2} \sum_{\vec{v}' \in \mathcal{R}^k} \sum_{\vec{z}' \in \mathcal{R}^k} \left|\Pr\left[\vec{v} = \vec{v}' \wedge \vec{z} = \vec{z}' \mid b = 0\right] - \rho(\vec{v}')D_\sigma^{kn}(\vec{z}')\right|$$

$$= \frac{1}{2} \sum_{\vec{v}' \in \mathcal{R}^k} \sum_{\vec{z}' \in S_{\vec{v}'}} \left|\frac{\rho(\vec{v}')D_\sigma^{kn}(\vec{z}')}{12\Pr\left[b = 0\right]} - \rho(\vec{v}')D_\sigma^{kn}(\vec{z}')\right|$$

$$+ \frac{1}{2} \sum_{\vec{v}' \in \mathcal{R}^k} \sum_{\vec{z}' \notin S_{\vec{v}'}} \left|\frac{\rho(\vec{v}')D_{\vec{v}',\sigma}^{kn}(\vec{z}')}{\Pr\left[b = 0\right]} - \rho(\vec{v}')D_\sigma^{kn}(\vec{z}')\right|$$

$$\leq \frac{1}{2} \left|\frac{1}{12\Pr\left[b = 0\right]} - 1\right| \sum_{\vec{v}' \in \mathcal{R}^k} \rho(\vec{v}') \sum_{\vec{z}' \in \mathcal{R}^k} D_\sigma^{kn}(\vec{z}')$$

$$+ \frac{1}{2} \sum_{\vec{v}' \in \mathcal{R}^k} \rho(\vec{v}') \sum_{\vec{z}' \notin S_{\vec{v}'}} D_\sigma^{kn}(\vec{z}')$$

$$\leq \frac{1}{2} \left|\frac{1}{12\Pr\left[b = 0\right]} - 1\right| + 3 \cdot 2^{-103} \leq 2^{-100} \qquad \square$$

2.5   Lattice Problems

We will use the commitment scheme from [BDL+18] whose security can be based on variants of the following two standard lattice problems.

Definition 2.5. *The* Ring Short Integer Solution *problem* $\text{RSIS}_{k,B}$ *with parameters* $k \geq 1$ *and* $B > 0$ *is solved by finding a short, non-zero vector* $\vec{s} \in \mathcal{R}^{k+1}$ *such that* $(\mathbf{1}, \vec{\mathbf{a}}^T) \cdot \vec{s} = \mathbf{0}$ *over* $\mathcal{R}_q$. *We say that an algorithm* $\mathcal{A}$ *has advantage* ε *in solving the* $\text{RSIS}_{k,B}$ *problem if*

$$\Pr\left[\|\vec{s}\|_2 \leq B \,\wedge\, (\mathbf{1}, \vec{\mathbf{a}}^T) \cdot \vec{s} = \mathbf{0} \,\wedge\, \vec{s} \neq \vec{\mathbf{0}}^{k+1} \,\middle|\, \vec{\mathbf{a}} \xleftarrow{\$} \mathcal{R}_q^k; \; \vec{s} \leftarrow \mathcal{A}(\vec{\mathbf{a}})\right] \geq \varepsilon$$

Definition 2.6. *In the* Ring Learning with Errors *problem* RLWE_m *with parameter* $m \geq 1$, *an adversary* $\mathcal{A}$ *tries to distinguish* $(\vec{\mathbf{a}}, \vec{\mathbf{b}}) \xleftarrow{\$} \mathcal{R}_q^m \times \mathcal{R}_q^m$ *from* $(\vec{\mathbf{a}}, \vec{\mathbf{a}}s + \vec{\mathbf{e}})$ *with* $\vec{\mathbf{a}} \xleftarrow{\$} \mathcal{R}_q^m$ *and secret short* $s \xleftarrow{\$} \beta^n$, $\vec{\mathbf{e}} \xleftarrow{\$} \beta^{mn}$. *We say that an algorithm* $\mathcal{A}$ *has advantage* ε *in solving the* RLWE_m *problem if*

$$\left| \Pr\left[b = 1 \,\middle|\, \vec{\mathbf{a}} \xleftarrow{\$} \mathcal{R}_q^m \; ; \; s \xleftarrow{\$} \beta^n \; ; \; \vec{\mathbf{e}} \xleftarrow{\$} \beta^{mn} \; ; \; b \leftarrow \mathcal{A}(\vec{\mathbf{a}}, \vec{\mathbf{a}}s + \vec{\mathbf{e}})\right] \right.$$
$$\left. - \Pr\left[b = 1 \,\middle|\, \vec{\mathbf{a}} \xleftarrow{\$} \mathcal{R}_q^m \; ; \; \vec{\mathbf{b}} \xleftarrow{\$} \mathcal{R}_q^m \; ; \; b \leftarrow \mathcal{A}(\vec{\mathbf{a}}, \vec{\mathbf{b}})\right] \right| \geq \varepsilon$$

2.6   Commitment Scheme

A commitment scheme consists of a triple of algorithms (KeyGen, Com, Open) which work as follows.

$\text{KeyGen}(1^\lambda) \to \text{pp}$ is a probabilistic polynomial-time algorithm that produces the public parameters pp for the commitment scheme, defines the message space M, randomness space R and commitment space C, and implicitly includes the security parameter λ.

$\text{Com}(\text{pp}, m) \to (c, r)$ is a probabilistic polynomial-time algorithm that takes a message m and the public parameters pp as input and produces a commitment $c \in C$ and some randomness $r \in R$ used to compute and open c.

$\text{Open}(\text{pp}, m, c, r) \to b$ is a deterministic polynomial-time algorithm that takes the public parameters pp, a message m, randomness r, and a commitment c as input, and produces a bit $b \in \{0, 1\}$ as output.

A commitment scheme should be *hiding* and *binding*.

Definition 2.7 (Hiding). *A commitment scheme is* ε-hiding *if for all algorithms* $\mathcal{A}$

$$\Pr\left[b = b' \,\middle|\, \begin{array}{l} \text{pp} \leftarrow \text{Keygen}(1^\lambda), \; (m_0, m_1) \leftarrow \mathcal{A}(\text{pp}) \\ b \leftarrow \{0, 1\}, \; (c, r) \leftarrow \text{Com}(\text{pp}, m_b) \\ b' \leftarrow \mathcal{A}(\text{pp}, c) \end{array}\right] < \varepsilon$$

where the probability is taken over the randomness of KeyGen, Com *and* $\mathcal{A}$.

Definition 2.8 (Binding). *A commitment scheme is ε-binding if for all algorithms $\mathcal{A}$*

$$\Pr\left[\begin{array}{c|c} m \neq m' \text{ and} & \mathrm{pp} \leftarrow \mathrm{KeyGen}(1^\lambda), \\ \mathrm{Open}(\mathrm{pp}, m, c, r) = \mathrm{Open}(\mathrm{pp}, m', c, r) & (m, m', r, r', c) \leftarrow \mathcal{A}(\mathrm{pp}) \end{array}\right] < \varepsilon$$

where the probability is taken over the randomness of KeyGen *and* $\mathcal{A}$.

If we restrict the algorithms $\mathcal{A}$ to probabilistic polynomial time algorithms in the definition of the hiding or binding properties, then we say that the property is computational. If we allow for arbitrarily powerful algorithms, then the property is statistical.

In our protocol, we use a variant of the commitment scheme from [BDL+18] which splits the message space into different components. This allows useful manipulations on the different components as part of our zero-knowledge proof.

We will create public parameters that can be used to commit to messages $\vec{\mathbf{m}} \in \mathcal{R}_q^4$. Define the matrix $\mathbf{B} \in \mathcal{R}_q^{5 \times 6}$ (with row vectors $\vec{\mathbf{b}}_1^T, \ldots, \vec{\mathbf{b}}_5^T$).

$$\mathbf{B} = \begin{pmatrix} \vec{\mathbf{b}}_1^T \\ \vec{\mathbf{b}}_2^T \\ \vec{\mathbf{b}}_3^T \\ \vec{\mathbf{b}}_4^T \\ \vec{\mathbf{b}}_5^T \end{pmatrix} = \begin{pmatrix} 1 & \mathbf{b}_{1,2} & \mathbf{b}_{1,3} & \mathbf{b}_{1,4} & \mathbf{b}_{1,5} & \mathbf{b}_{1,6} \\ 0 & 1 & 0 & 0 & 0 & \mathbf{b}_{2,6} \\ 0 & 0 & 1 & 0 & 0 & \mathbf{b}_{3,6} \\ 0 & 0 & 0 & 1 & 0 & \mathbf{b}_{4,6} \\ 0 & 0 & 0 & 0 & 1 & \mathbf{b}_{5,6} \end{pmatrix}$$

where the polynomials $\mathbf{b}_{i,j} \in \mathcal{R}_q$ are chosen uniformly at random.

To commit to $\vec{\mathbf{m}} = (\mathbf{m}_2, \mathbf{m}_3, \mathbf{m}_4, \mathbf{m}_5)^T \in \mathcal{R}_q^4$, we choose a random polynomial vector $\vec{\mathbf{r}} \xleftarrow{\$} \beta^{6n}$ from the error distribution and output the commitment

$$\mathrm{Com}(\vec{\mathbf{m}}; \vec{\mathbf{r}}) = \vec{\mathbf{t}} = \begin{pmatrix} \mathbf{t}_1 \\ \mathbf{t}_2 \\ \mathbf{t}_3 \\ \mathbf{t}_4 \\ \mathbf{t}_5 \end{pmatrix} = \mathbf{B} \cdot \vec{\mathbf{r}} + \begin{pmatrix} 0 \\ \mathbf{m}_2 \\ \mathbf{m}_3 \\ \mathbf{m}_4 \\ \mathbf{m}_5 \end{pmatrix}$$

A valid (relaxed) opening of such a commitment $\vec{\mathbf{t}}$ consists of a message vector $\vec{\mathbf{m}} \in \mathcal{R}_q^4$, a short vector $\vec{\mathbf{r}} \in \mathcal{R}_q^6$ with $\|\vec{\mathbf{r}}\|_2 \leq 2B$ and a challenge difference $\bar{\mathbf{f}} \in \bar{\mathcal{C}}$ or $\bar{\mathbf{f}} = 1$. The verifier checks that

$$\bar{\mathbf{f}}\vec{\mathbf{t}} = \mathbf{B}\vec{\mathbf{r}} + \bar{\mathbf{f}}\begin{pmatrix} 0 \\ \vec{\mathbf{m}} \end{pmatrix}$$

and that $\|\vec{\mathbf{r}}\|_2 \leq 2B$.

Remark. Although the commitment scheme allows relaxed openings to a multiple of the original commitment, it is used incidentally in our protocol. We would like to stress that our zero-knowledge proof shows that the prover knows an *exact* solution to a system of linear equations.

Lemma 2.9. *C.f. [BDL+18, Lemma 6] For every algorithm $\mathcal{A}$ that has advantage ε in breaking the* hiding *property of the commitment scheme, there exists another algorithm $\mathcal{A}'$ that runs in the same time and has advantage ε in distinguishing* RLWE_5.

Lemma 2.10. *C.f. [BDL+18, Lemma 7] For every algorithm $\mathcal{A}$ that succeeds with probability ε in breaking the* binding *property of the commitment scheme, there exists another algorithm $\mathcal{A}'$ that runs in the same time and solves* $\mathrm{RSIS}_{5,8B}$ *with probability ε.*

3 The Main Protocol

We want to prove knowledge of a short integer vector $\vec{s}$ that is a solution to a linear equation $A\vec{s} = \vec{u}$ over $\mathbb{Z}_q$ with public matrix A and vector $\vec{u}$. We now describe our protocol for this task. In the introduction, we made various simplifications to make the key ideas easier to understand. We now give more precise details.

Concretely, let A be an $m \times n$ matrix over $\mathbb{Z}_q$ and $\vec{s}$ have coefficients in $\{-S, \ldots, S\}$. First we transform the equation to an equation with vector $\vec{s}'$ having coefficients in $\{0, 1, 2\}$. The easiest way to achieve this is simply to write the coefficients $s_1, \ldots, s_n$ of $\vec{s}$ as

$$s_i = s'_{i,0} + 3s'_{i,1} + \cdots + 3^{r-1}s'_{i,r-1} - 3^r s'_{i,r} = \vec{g}^T \vec{s}'_i$$

where $r = \lfloor \log_3 S + 1 \rfloor$, the coefficients $s'_{i,j}$ of $\vec{s}'_i$ are in $\{0, 1, 2\}$, and $\vec{g}^T$ is the gadget row vector $\vec{g}^T = (1, 3, \ldots, 3^{r-1}, -3^r)^T$. Then we have $\vec{s} = (I_n \otimes \vec{g}^T)\vec{s}'$ and hence

$$A'\vec{s}' = A(I_n \otimes \vec{g}^T)\vec{s}' = A\vec{s} = \vec{u}$$

when we write $A' = A(I_n \otimes \vec{g}^T) \in \mathbb{Z}_q^{m \times rn}$.

As discussed in the introduction, our high level strategy is for the prover to send the masked opening $\mathbf{z} = \mathbf{y} + \mathbf{cs}$, and use commitments to $\mathbf{y}$ and $\mathbf{s}$ to show that $\mathbf{z}$ was correctly formed. Then, the prover and verifier can use this masked opening $\mathbf{z}$, along with some extra commitments, to prove that the following polynomial expression is a polynomial of degree 2, and not degree 3.

$$\mathbf{z}(\mathbf{z} - \mathbf{c})(\mathbf{z} - 2\mathbf{c}) = \mathbf{y}^3 + 3\mathbf{y}^2(\mathbf{s} - 1)\mathbf{c} + \mathbf{y}(3\mathbf{s}^2 - 6\mathbf{s} + 2)\mathbf{c}^2 + \mathbf{s}(\mathbf{s} - 1)(\mathbf{s} - 2)\mathbf{c}^3. \quad (9)$$

The simplest way to do this would be to make 5 commitments, and check Eq. 9 in committed form, i.e.

$$\mathbf{t}_1 = \mathrm{Com}(\mathbf{y}) \qquad\qquad\qquad \mathbf{t}_2 = \mathrm{Com}(\mathbf{s})$$

$$\mathbf{t}_3 = \mathrm{Com}(\mathbf{y}^3) \qquad\qquad \mathbf{t}_4 = \mathrm{Com}(3\mathbf{y}^2(\mathbf{s} - 1))$$

$$\mathbf{t}_5 = \mathrm{Com}(\mathbf{y}(3\mathbf{s}^2 - 6\mathbf{s} + 2))$$

$$\mathrm{Com}(\mathbf{z}) \stackrel{?}{=} \mathbf{t}_1 + \mathbf{c}\mathbf{t}_2 \qquad\qquad \mathrm{Com}(\mathbf{z}(\mathbf{z} - \mathbf{c})(\mathbf{z} - 2\mathbf{c})) \stackrel{?}{=} \mathbf{t}_3 + \mathbf{t}_4\mathbf{c} + \mathbf{t}_5\mathbf{c}^2$$

In our protocol, we optimize the procedure so that the prover needs only commit to 4 polynomials, instead of 5. Given that we will send $\mathbf{z}$, and check that it was correctly computed as $\mathbf{y} + \mathbf{cs}$, we can use $\mathbf{z}$ to help evaluate the left-hand side of Eq. 9, and use the commitment to $\mathbf{s}$ to simplify the right hand side. After these optimisations, our proof uses the following alternative expression.

$$(\mathbf{z} - \mathbf{c})(\mathbf{z} - 2\mathbf{c})\mathbf{s} = \mathbf{z}\mathbf{y}(2\mathbf{s} - 3) - \mathbf{y}^2(\mathbf{s} - 3) + \mathbf{s}(\mathbf{s} - 1)(\mathbf{s} - 2)\mathbf{c}^2. \tag{10}$$

Our protocol is based around making 4 commitments and checking (10) in committed form.

$$\mathbf{t}_2 = \mathrm{Com}(\mathbf{y}) \qquad\qquad \mathbf{t}_3 = \mathrm{Com}(\mathbf{s})$$
$$\mathbf{t}_4 = \mathrm{Com}(\mathbf{y}(2\mathbf{s} - 3)) \qquad\qquad \mathbf{t}_5 = \mathrm{Com}(\mathbf{y}^2(\mathbf{s} - 3))$$

$$\mathrm{Com}(\mathbf{z}) \stackrel{?}{=} \mathbf{t}_1 + \mathbf{c}\mathbf{t}_2 \qquad\qquad \mathrm{Com}(\mathbf{0}) \stackrel{?}{=} (\mathbf{z} - \mathbf{c})(\mathbf{z} - 2\mathbf{c})\mathbf{t}_3 - \mathbf{z}\mathbf{t}_4 + \mathbf{t}_5$$

This is still a slight simplification of what takes place in the protocol, as the commitment scheme given in Sect. 2.6 will actually commit to all four messages at the same time, but fortunately, the commitment scheme nevertheless allows us to manipulate the individual components and check the given equations.

The protocol uses two challenges, $c \in \mathbb{Z}_q$, and $\mathbf{f} \in \mathcal{C}$. The first challenge c is used to embed $\mathbf{s}$ into a masked value, which is used to show that $A\hat{\mathbf{s}} = \vec{u}$. The second challenge $\mathbf{f}$ is used to embed the commitment randomness into a masked value, which will help us to check important equations in committed form. Of course, we cannot allow the verifier to see the commitment randomness without any random masking, as this would leak information about the committed secret $\mathbf{s}$. This leads to two more extra terms when checking the equations, which are given by $\mathbf{x}_1$ and $\mathbf{x}_2$ in the protocol.

We now discuss each step of the protocol, describing the actions of the prover and verifier.

In the first move, the prover samples a random masking value $\mathbf{y}$, which will later be used to hide the secret $\mathbf{s}$. Then they sample the randomness $\vec{r}$ used to commit to the four ring elements given in the polynomial equations above. They also fix the random masking value $\hat{\mathbf{y}}$ by computing $\vec{w} = A\hat{\mathbf{y}}$. The value $\hat{\mathbf{y}}$ will be used to help verify that $A\hat{\mathbf{s}} = \vec{u}$ later on. The prover sends these to the verifier.

Next, the verifier sends a random challenge $c \in \mathbb{Z}_q$ to the prover. As we have seen, the challenge c is used to embed the secret $\mathbf{s}$ into $\mathbf{z}$. The prover samples a new masking value $\vec{y}'$ which will be used to hide the commitment randomness $\vec{r}$. They also compute the values $\mathbf{x}_1$ and $\mathbf{x}_2$, which will later allow the verifier to check Eq. (10) in committed form using a masked version of $\vec{r}$. They send these values to the verifier.

Next, the verifier sends a random challenge $\mathbf{f} \in \mathcal{C}$ to the prover. The prover computes $\vec{z}'$, a masked version of the commitment randomness, and applies a rejection sampling algorithm to make sure that this value does not leak any information about $\mathbf{r}$.

Finally, the verifier checks a blinded version of the equation $A\hat{s} = \vec{u}$, and blinded versions of the Eq. (10) and $\mathbf{z} = \mathbf{y} + c\mathbf{s}$ written in committed form, using the extra terms which the prover sent earlier.

The full protocol is given in Fig. 1.

3.1 Security Analysis

Theorem 3.1. *The protocol in Fig. 1 is complete, computational honest verifier zero-knowledge if RLWE_5 is hard and generalized special sound if $\mathrm{RSIS}_{5,8B}$ is hard.*

More precisely, the honest prover $\mathcal{P}$ convinces the honest verifier $\mathcal{V}$ with probability $\varepsilon \approx 1/12$.

For zero-knowledge, there exists a simulator $\mathcal{S}$, that, without access to secret information, outputs a simulation of a non-aborting transcript of the protocol between $\mathcal{P}$ and $\mathcal{V}$. Then for every algorithm $\mathcal{A}$ that has advantage ε in distinguishing the simulated transcript from an actual transcript, there is an algorithm $\mathcal{A}'$ with the same running time that has advantage $\varepsilon - 2^{-100}$ in distinguishing RLWE_5.

For knowledge-soundness, there is an extractor $\mathcal{E}$ with the following properties. When given rewindable black-box access to a deterministic prover $\mathcal{P}^*$ that convinces $\mathcal{V}$ with probability $\varepsilon > 2/q + 2/l$, $\mathcal{E}$ either outputs a solution $\vec{s}^* \in \{0,1,2\}^n$ to $A\vec{s}^* = \vec{u}$, or a $\mathrm{RSIS}_{5,8B}$ solution for $\vec{\mathbf{b}}_1^T$ in expected time at most $144/(\varepsilon - 2/q - 2/l)$ when running $\mathcal{P}^*$ once is assumed to take unit time.

Notice that we only require the simulator $\mathcal{S}$ to simulate non-aborting transcripts, i.e. the interaction between $\mathcal{P}$ and $\mathcal{V}$ conditioned on the prover not aborting. The rationale behind this is that in the non-interactive version that is relevant in practice one never gets to see the aborting proofs. In any case, there is a standard technique which makes it possible to simulate the aborting transcripts too, whereby the prover commits to the binding quantities $\mathbf{w}'$, $\mathbf{x}_1$ and $\mathbf{x}_2$ and only opens the commitments if he does not abort.

Proof. Completeness. It follows directly from Lemma 2.4 that the honest prover $\mathcal{P}$ does not abort with probability at least $1/12 - 2^{-100}$. Moreover, in this case the distribution of the vector $\vec{z}'$ sent by $\mathcal{P}$ has statistical distance at most 2^{-100} from D_σ^{6n}, and Lemma 2.3 implies that the bound $\|\vec{z}'\|_2 \le B = \sigma\sqrt{12n}$ is true with probability at least $1 - 2^{-0.66n} - 2^{-100}$. It is easy to see that all of the other verification equations are always true for the messages sent by $\mathcal{P}$. Therefore, the honest prover convinces the honest verifier with probability $\varepsilon \approx 1/12$.

Soundness. The extractor $\mathcal{E}$ needs to obtain accepting transcripts from $\mathcal{P}^*$ for 3 different first challenges $c_1, c_2, c_3 \in \mathbb{Z}_q$. Moreover, for each of the 3 c_i, $\mathcal{E}$ needs 2 accepting transcripts with first challenge c_i and two different second challenges $\mathbf{f}_{i,1} \ne \mathbf{f}_{i,2}$. So in total $\mathcal{E}$ needs 6 transcripts. To this end, he runs $\mathcal{P}^*$, sends uniformly random challenges c_1 and $\mathbf{f}_{1,1}$ and repeats until he obtains a first accepting transcript. This takes expected time $1/\varepsilon$. Then, by a standard heavy rows argument, with probability at least $1/2$, the probability of obtaining an

Prover $\mathcal{P}$ Verifier $\mathcal{V}$

Inputs:

$A \in \mathbb{Z}_q^{m \times n}, \hat{s} \in \{0,1,2\}^n$ $A, \vec{u}, \vec{b}_1, \ldots, \vec{b}_5$

$\vec{u} = A\hat{s} \in \mathbb{Z}_q^m$

$\vec{b}_1, \ldots, \vec{b}_5 \in \mathcal{R}_q^6$

$\mathbf{y} \xleftarrow{\$} \mathcal{R}_q$

$\vec{r} \xleftarrow{\$} \beta^{6n}$

$$\vec{t} = \begin{pmatrix} \vec{b}_1^T \\ \vec{b}_2^T \\ \vec{b}_3^T \\ \vec{b}_4^T \\ \vec{b}_5^T \end{pmatrix} \vec{r} + \begin{pmatrix} \mathbf{0} \\ \mathbf{y} \\ \mathbf{s} \\ \mathbf{y}(2\mathbf{s}-3) \\ \mathbf{y}^2(\mathbf{s}-3) \end{pmatrix}$$

$\vec{w} = A\hat{y}$

                 $\xrightarrow{\vec{t}, \vec{w}}$

                 $\xleftarrow{c}$ $c \xleftarrow{\$} \mathbb{Z}_q$

$\mathbf{z} = \mathbf{y} + c\mathbf{s}$

$\vec{y}' \xleftarrow{\$} D_\sigma^{6n}$

$\mathbf{w}' = \vec{b}_1^T \vec{y}'$

$\mathbf{x}_1 = \left(\vec{b}_2^T + c\vec{b}_3^T \right) \vec{y}'$

$\mathbf{x}_2 = \left((\mathbf{z}-c)(\mathbf{z}-2c)\vec{b}_3^T - \mathbf{z}\vec{b}_4^T + \vec{b}_5^T \right) \vec{y}'$ $\xrightarrow{\mathbf{z}, \mathbf{w}', \mathbf{x}_1, \mathbf{x}_2}$

                 $\xleftarrow{\mathbf{f}}$ $\mathbf{f} \xleftarrow{\$} \mathcal{C}$

$\vec{z}' = \vec{y}' + \mathbf{f}\vec{r}$

If Rej $\left(\vec{z}', \mathbf{f}\vec{r}, \sigma \right) = 1$, abort $\xrightarrow{\vec{z}'}$

                         $\|\vec{z}'\| \leq B = \sigma\sqrt{12n}$

                         $A\hat{z} \overset{?}{=} \vec{w} + c\vec{u}$

                         $\vec{b}_1^T \vec{z}' \overset{?}{=} \mathbf{w}' + \mathbf{f}\mathbf{t}_1$

                         $\left(\vec{b}_2^T + c\vec{b}_3^T \right) \vec{z}' + \mathbf{f}\mathbf{z}$

                           $\overset{?}{=} \mathbf{x}_1 + \mathbf{f}(\mathbf{t}_2 + c\mathbf{t}_3)$

                         $\left((\mathbf{z}-c)(\mathbf{z}-2c)\vec{b}_3^T - \mathbf{z}\vec{b}_4^T + \vec{b}_5^T \right) \vec{z}'$

                           $\overset{?}{=} \mathbf{x}_2 + \mathbf{f}((\mathbf{z}-c)(\mathbf{z}-2c)\mathbf{t}_3 - \mathbf{z}\mathbf{t}_4 + \mathbf{t}_5)$

Fig. 1. Lattice-based proof of knowledge of a ternary solution to a linear equation over $\mathbb{Z}_q$.

accepting transcript conditioned fixing the first challenge c_1, but with uniformly random second challenge, is at least $\varepsilon/2$. So conditioned on c_1, the extractor obtains a second accepting transcript with challenges c_1 and $\mathbf{f}_{1,2} \neq \mathbf{f}_{1,1}$ with probability at least $\varepsilon/2 - 1/l$, and he succeeds in getting such a transcript in expected time at most $(\varepsilon/2 - 1/l)^{-1}$. For the third transcript he sends uniformly random $c_2 \neq c_1$ and $\mathbf{f}_{2,1}$ and succeeds in expected time at most $(\varepsilon - 1/q)^{-1}$. Then, using the heavy rows argument again, we can assume that the acceptance probability for fixed first challenge c_2 is at least $\varepsilon/2 - 1/(2q)$, which is true with probability at least $1/2$. Therefore, in conditioned expected time $(\varepsilon/2 - 1/(2q) - 1/l)^{-1}$, the extractor receives the 4-th transcript with challenges c_2 and $\mathbf{f}_{2,2} \neq \mathbf{f}_{2,1}$. Continuing in the same way, the last two transcripts are obtained in conditioned expected time at most $3/(\varepsilon - 2/q - 2/l)$.

In summary, with probability $1/8$, the total expected time needed to obtain the 6 transcripts is less than

$$T = \frac{9}{\varepsilon - 2/q - 2/l}.$$

With probability $7/8$ the extractor is not so lucky and might run for a long time or not terminate at all. We cope with this by limiting the runtime of $\mathcal{E}$ to $2T$. Then, by Markov's inequality, the extractor gets hold of the 6 accepting transcripts in time at most $2T$ with probability at least $1/16$. By restarting in case of failure we finally conclude that in expected time $16T$ the extractor indeed has the 6 accepting transcripts needed.

Let us now see how to use the transcripts. Let $\vec{\mathbf{z}}'_{i,j}$, $i = 1, 2, 3$, $j = 1, 2$, be the last messages from $\mathcal{P}^*$. Write $\vec{\mathbf{z}}'_i = \vec{\mathbf{z}}'_{i,1} - \vec{\mathbf{z}}'_{i,2}$ and $\bar{\mathbf{f}}_i = \mathbf{f}_{i,1} - \mathbf{f}_{i,2}$ for the difference of these messages in the transcripts with the same first challenge and the difference of the corresponding second challenges, respectively. The verification equation $\vec{\mathbf{b}}_1^T \vec{\mathbf{z}}'_{i,j} = \mathbf{w}' + \mathbf{f}_{i,j} \mathbf{t}_1$ yields approximate solutions to the first equation of the commitment $\vec{\mathbf{t}}$ by subtracting,

$$\vec{\mathbf{b}}_1^T \vec{\mathbf{z}}'_i = \bar{\mathbf{f}}_i \mathbf{t}_1.$$

Then we can compute openings $\mathbf{m}_2 = \mathbf{y}^*$, $\mathbf{m}_3 = \mathbf{s}^*$, $\mathbf{m}_4$ and $\mathbf{m}_5$ of $\vec{\mathbf{t}}$. For instance,

$$\mathbf{m}_k = \mathbf{t}_k - \vec{\mathbf{b}}_k^T \frac{\vec{\mathbf{z}}'_1}{\bar{\mathbf{f}}_1}.$$

Note these openings are valid relaxed openings of our commitment scheme with $\|\vec{\mathbf{z}}'_1\|_2 \leq 2B$. Therefore, when using $\vec{\mathbf{z}}'_2$ and $\bar{\mathbf{f}}_2$ or $\vec{\mathbf{z}}'_3$ and $\bar{\mathbf{f}}_3$ to compute openings we either get the same $\mathbf{m}_k$ or break the binding property of the commitment scheme. The latter would translate to a $\mathrm{RSIS}_{5,8B}$ solution; c.f. Lemma 2.10. Concretely, if

$$\mathbf{m}_k \neq \mathbf{m}'_k = \mathbf{t}_k - \vec{\mathbf{b}}_2^T \frac{\vec{\mathbf{z}}'_2}{\bar{\mathbf{f}}_2},$$

then $\bar{\mathbf{f}}_2 \vec{\mathbf{z}}'_1 - \bar{\mathbf{f}}_1 \vec{\mathbf{z}}'_2 \neq 0$ and we get the $\mathrm{RSIS}_{5,8B}$ solution

$$\vec{\mathbf{b}}_1^T \left(\bar{\mathbf{f}}_2 \vec{\mathbf{z}}'_1 - \bar{\mathbf{f}}_1 \vec{\mathbf{z}}'_2 \right) = \mathbf{0}.$$

Here we have used the fact that $\|\vec{\mathbf{z}}'_i\|_2 \leq 2B$, which implies $\|\bar{\mathbf{f}}_i \vec{\mathbf{z}}'_i\|_2 \leq 2\|\vec{\mathbf{z}}'_i\|_2 \leq 4B$ and $\|\bar{\mathbf{f}}_2 \vec{\mathbf{z}}'_1 - \bar{\mathbf{f}}_1 \vec{\mathbf{z}}'_2\|_2 \leq 8B$.

Assume we did not break the commitment scheme and write $\mathbf{z}_i$ for the message $\mathbf{z}$ sent by the prover in the $(2i-1)$-th and $(2i)$-th transcript, which is equal in the two transcripts. Consider the verification equations

$$\left(\vec{\mathbf{b}}_2^T + c_i \vec{\mathbf{b}}_3^T\right) \vec{\mathbf{z}}'_{i,j} + \mathbf{f}_{i,j} \mathbf{z}_i = \mathbf{x}_{1,i} + \mathbf{f}_{i,j}\left(\mathbf{t}_2 + c_i \mathbf{t}_3\right).$$

Subtract the equations with $j = 1, 2$ and the same i to obtain

$$\left(\vec{\mathbf{b}}_2^T + c_i \vec{\mathbf{b}}_3^T\right) \frac{\vec{\mathbf{z}}'_i}{\vec{\mathbf{f}}_i} + \mathbf{z}_i = \mathbf{t}_2 + c_i \mathbf{t}_3.$$

Now substitute the opening

$$\mathbf{y}^* + c_i \mathbf{s}^* = \mathbf{m}_2 + c_i \mathbf{m}_3 = \mathbf{t}_2 + c_i \mathbf{t}_3 - \left(\vec{\mathbf{b}}_2^T + c_i \vec{\mathbf{b}}_3^T\right) \frac{\vec{\mathbf{z}}'_i}{\vec{\mathbf{f}}_i}$$

corresponding to $\mathbf{t}_2 + c_i \mathbf{t}_3$. This gives

$$\mathbf{z}_i = \mathbf{y}^* + c_i \mathbf{s}^*. \tag{11}$$

So we see that the messages $\mathbf{z}_i$ are of the expected form with constant polynomials $\mathbf{y}^*$ and $\mathbf{s}^*$ that are independent of the challenges c_i. Next from the verification equations

$$\left((\mathbf{z}_i - c_i)(\mathbf{z}_i - 2c_i)\vec{\mathbf{b}}_3^T - \mathbf{z}_i \vec{\mathbf{b}}_4^T + \vec{\mathbf{b}}_5^T\right) \vec{\mathbf{z}}'_{i,j}$$
$$= \mathbf{x}_{2,i} + \mathbf{f}_{i,j}\left((\mathbf{z}_i - c_i)(\mathbf{z}_i - 2c_i)\mathbf{t}_3 - \mathbf{z}_i \mathbf{t}_4 + \mathbf{t}_5\right)$$

we find by using the opening $(\mathbf{z}_i - c_i)(\mathbf{z}_i - 2c_i)\mathbf{s}^* - \mathbf{z}_i \mathbf{m}_4 + \mathbf{m}_5$ corresponding to $(\mathbf{z}_i - c_i)(\mathbf{z}_i - 2c_i)\mathbf{t}_2 - \mathbf{z}_i \mathbf{t}_4 + \mathbf{t}_5$ and Eq. (11),

$$(\mathbf{z}_i - c_i)(\mathbf{z}_i - 2c_i)\mathbf{s}^* - \mathbf{z}_i \mathbf{m}_4 + \mathbf{m}_5$$
$$= \left(\mathbf{y}^* + c_i(\mathbf{s}^* - 1)\right)\left(\mathbf{y}^* + c_i(\mathbf{s}^* - 2)\right)\mathbf{s}^* - \mathbf{y}^* \mathbf{m}_4 - c_i \mathbf{s}^* \mathbf{m}_4 + \mathbf{m}_5$$
$$= \left((\mathbf{y}^*)^2 \mathbf{s}^* - \mathbf{y}^* \mathbf{m}_4 + \mathbf{m}_5\right) + \left(\mathbf{y}^*(2\mathbf{s}^* - 3) - \mathbf{m}_4\right)\mathbf{s}^* c_i + (\mathbf{s}^* - 1)(\mathbf{s}^* - 2)\mathbf{s}^* c_i^2$$
$$= \mathbf{0}.$$

So we have a polynomial of degree 2 over $\mathcal{R}_q$ that evaluates to zero at the 3 points c_1, c_2 and c_3. We can write this as a matrix-vector equation over $\mathcal{R}_q$,

$$\begin{pmatrix} 1 & c_1 & c_1^2 \\ 1 & c_2 & c_2^2 \\ 1 & c_3 & c_3^2 \end{pmatrix} \begin{pmatrix} (\mathbf{y}^*)^2 \mathbf{s}^* - \mathbf{y}^* \mathbf{m}_4 + \mathbf{m}_5 \\ (\mathbf{y}^*(2\mathbf{s}^* - 3) - \mathbf{m}_4)\mathbf{s}^* \\ (\mathbf{s}^* - 1)(\mathbf{s}^* - 2)\mathbf{s}^* \end{pmatrix} = \begin{pmatrix} 0 \\ 0 \\ 0 \end{pmatrix}.$$

The determinant of this well-known Vandermonde matrix is equal to $(c_1 - c_2)(c_1 - c_3)(c_2 - c_3) \in \mathbb{Z}_q^\times \subset \mathcal{R}_q^\times$ and hence the matrix is invertible over $\mathcal{R}_q$. Therefore, $\mathbf{s}^*(\mathbf{s}^* - 1)(\mathbf{s}^* - 2) = \mathbf{0}$. Applying the NTT to this last equation implies

$$\hat{\mathbf{s}}^* \circ (\hat{\mathbf{s}}^* - \vec{1}) \circ (\hat{\mathbf{s}}^* - \vec{2}) = \vec{0}$$

in $\mathbb{Z}_q^n$. So the coefficients of $\hat{s}^*$ are all in $\{0, 1, 2\}$. Finally, by subtracting copies of the second verification equation from on another, we get $A(\hat{z}_1 - \hat{z}_2) = (c_1 - c_2)\vec{u}$. But we know that

$$\frac{\hat{z}_1 - \hat{z}_2}{c_1 - c_2} = \hat{s}^*$$

has only coefficients in $\{0, 1, 2\}$ and is the solution to the linear equation with matrix A that we wanted to find.

Zero-Knowledge. We can simulate a non-aborting transcript between the honest prover and the honest verifier in the following way. First, note that in such a transcript $\mathbf{z} = \mathbf{y} + c\mathbf{s}$ is uniformly random because the honest prover samples $\mathbf{y}$ uniformly at random. Moreover, $\vec{z}'$ is statistically close to D_σ^{6n} by Lemma 2.4. So the simulator can just pick $\mathbf{z} \xleftarrow{\$} \mathcal{R}_q$ and $\vec{z}' \leftarrow D_\sigma^{6n}$. Next, by Lemma 2.4 again, we know that $\mathbf{f}\vec{r}$ is independent of $\vec{z}'$, and hence that $\mathbf{f}$ is independent of $\vec{z}'$. The two challenges c and $\mathbf{f}$ are uniformly random since the honest verifier chooses them in this way. Therefore, the simulator picks $c \xleftarrow{\$} \mathbb{Z}_q$ and $\mathbf{f} \xleftarrow{\$} \mathcal{C}$. The commitment $\vec{t}$ is computationally indistinguishable from a dummy commitment if RLWE_5 is hard (c.f. Lemma 2.9. In fact, the construction of the commitment scheme is such that $\vec{t}$ contains an additive term that is precisely a RLWE_5 sample. So the simulator can just take a uniformly random $\vec{t} \xleftarrow{\$} \mathcal{R}_q^5$. Now, in an honest transcript, the remaining messages $\vec{w}$, $\mathbf{w}'$, $\mathbf{x}_1$ and $\mathbf{x}_2$ are all uniquely determined by the verification equations because of completeness. We see that if the simulator computes these messages so that the verification equations become true, then the resulting transcript is indistinguishable from the honest transcript. More precisely, a simulated transcript has statistical distance at most 2^{-100} from a distribution which differs from the actual transcripts only in that $\vec{t}$ is distributed differently. Therefore, if there is an algorithm $\mathcal{A}$ that has advantage ε in distinguishing a simulated transcript from an actual transcript, then this algorithm must be able to distinguish RLWE_5 samples from random with advantage $\varepsilon - 2^{-100}$.

3.2 Repeating the Proof

For the moduli q and the dimensions $n = \varphi(l)$ that occur when proving equations from lattice-based cryptographic schemes, our proof does not have sufficiently low soundness error as $\varepsilon_0 = 2/q + 2/l$ will be much larger than 2^{-128}. Therefore the proof needs to be repeated multiple times. If for t repetitions, every single repetition succeeds with probability $\varepsilon > (\varepsilon_0)^t$, then it cannot be that each of them has success probability less than ε_0. Otherwise we would have $\varepsilon < (\varepsilon_0)^t$. So one of the proofs will be extractable. Since $l < q$, the number of repetitions necessary is determined by l. If l is considerably smaller than q then it is worth repeating the lower half of the proof with challenge $\mathbf{f}$ a couple of times for a single execution of the upper half with challenge c. The lower part of the proof demonstrates knowledge of an opening of the commitment $\vec{t}$. Recall that the extractor needs successful transcripts of the full protocol with the same challenge c and two different challenges $\mathbf{f}_1$ and $\mathbf{f}_2$. He gets these by obtaining a first successful transcript and then running the prover with fixed challenge c and random $\mathbf{f}_2 \neq \mathbf{f}_1$. So if the lower part is repeated twice then the first successful execution will have challenges c and $(\mathbf{f}_1, \mathbf{f}_1')$ and the extractor can choose fresh challenges $(\mathbf{f}_2, \mathbf{f}_2')$ from the set $\mathcal{C}^2$ of size l^2 and only needs that one of the two $\mathbf{f}_2$ and $\mathbf{f}_2'$ is different from the corresponding $\mathbf{f}_1$ or $\mathbf{f}_1'$, i.e. that $(\mathbf{f}_1, \mathbf{f}_1') \neq (\mathbf{f}_2, \mathbf{f}_2')$. Hence we see that the proof with two repetitions of the lower part will have soundness error $\varepsilon_0 = 2/q + 2/l^2$.

3.3 Non-interactive Proof

In practice, the interactive protocol given in Fig. 1 is usually converted to a non-interactive protocol by using the Fiat-Shamir heuristic. So the two challenges $c \in \mathbb{Z}_q$ and $\mathbf{f} \in \mathcal{C}$ are computed by the prover from a hash of public information and all previous messages, where the hash function is modelled as a random oracle. Since our protocol does not have sufficiently low soundness error, it needs to be repeated multiple times to be secure. In the non-interactive version this is done by computing multiple proofs in parallel where all messages of all parallel proofs are put into the hash function to derive the various challenges for the parallel executions of the protocol. Here we allow for the lower half to be repeated multiple times for each repetition of the upper half, as explained in Sect. 3.2. Concretely, we repeat the upper half t times with challenges c_i, $i = 1, \ldots, t$, and for each of the repetitions we perform the lower part t' times with challenges $\mathbf{f}_j$, $j = t'(i-1) + 1, \ldots, t'(i-1) + t'$.

If the rejection sampling on the vectors $\vec{z}_j'$ in the parallel proofs was performed individually, the whole proof would need to be restarted if only one of the $\vec{z}_j'$ was rejected, which would happen with probability about $1 - (1/12)^{tt'}$. Therefore, the runtime of the non-interactive prover would be very long. Instead, we mask the concatenation of the t secret vectors $\mathbf{f}_j \vec{r}_i$ for $i = 1, \ldots, t$ and $j = (i-1)t' + k$ with the same k by sampling the masking vectors $\vec{y}_j'$ with a standard deviation that is equal to $5T'$, where T' is a bound on the concatenation of those secret vectors. Then we do rejection sampling on all of the corresponding $\vec{z}_j'$ at once. The downside of this is that the bound T' and hence the standard deviation of the discrete Gaussian distribution for the $\vec{y}_j'$ increases by a factor of $\sqrt{t}$. We could also perform rejection sampling on all of the tt' masking vectors at once with another increase of the standard deviation by a factor of $\sqrt{t'}$. But usually t' is at most two or three and hence the increase in prover time from not including this optimisation this does not pose a problem.

As another improvement we make use of the fact that it is not necessary to recommit to the constant secret polynomial $\mathbf{s}$ in all of the parallel executions of the proof. Instead it is actually enough to recommit to all of the other messages by sampling fresh RLWE errors $\mathbf{r}_1, \mathbf{r}_2, \mathbf{r}_4, \mathbf{r}_5$ for them and the first row of the commitment. In this way, we actually give out $1 + 4t$ RLWE samples and require RLWE_{1+4t} to be a hard problem. The complete non-interactive prover algorithm is given in Algorithm 2 and the corresponding verifier in Algorithm 3.

Apart from the improvements described, the non-interactive algorithms also make use of the standard technique of sending the challenges c_i and $\mathbf{f}_j$ instead of the large binding quantities $\vec{w}_i$, $\mathbf{w}'_j$, $\mathbf{x}_{1,j}$ and $\mathbf{x}_{2,j}$. The verifier computes these as the only missing terms in the verification equations, which allows him to check the challenges. The functions $G(\cdot)$ and $H(\cdot)$ are the two hash functions, modelled as random oracles, for sampling the challenges.

Algorithm 2. Non-Interactive Prover

1: **Input:** $A, \vec{u}, \hat{\mathbf{s}}$
2: **Output:** $(\vec{\mathbf{t}}_i)_{i \in [t]}, (c_i)_{i \in [t]}, (\mathbf{z}_i)_{i \in [t]}, (\mathbf{f}_j)_{j \in [tt']}, (\vec{\mathbf{z}}'_j)_{j \in [tt']}$
3: $\mathbf{r}_3, \mathbf{r}_6 \overset{\$}{\leftarrow} \beta^n$
4: $\mathbf{t}_3 = \mathbf{b}_{3,6}\mathbf{r}_6 + \mathbf{r}_3 + \mathbf{s}$
5: **for** $i = 1, \ldots, t$ **do**
6:     $\mathbf{y}_i \overset{\$}{\leftarrow} \mathcal{R}_q$
7:     $\vec{w}_i = A\hat{\mathbf{y}}_i$
8:     $\mathbf{r}_{i,1}, \mathbf{r}_{i,2}, \mathbf{r}_{i,4}, \mathbf{r}_{i,5} \overset{\$}{\leftarrow} \beta^n$
9:     $\vec{\mathbf{r}}_i = (\mathbf{r}_{i,1}, \mathbf{r}_{i,2}, \mathbf{r}_3, \mathbf{r}_{i,4}, \mathbf{r}_{i,5}, \mathbf{r}_6)^T$
10:    $\mathbf{t}_{i,1} = \vec{\mathbf{b}}_1^T \vec{\mathbf{r}}_i$
11:    $\mathbf{t}_{i,2} = \vec{\mathbf{b}}_2^T \vec{\mathbf{r}}_i + \mathbf{y}_i$
12:    $\mathbf{t}_{i,4} = \vec{\mathbf{b}}_4^T \vec{\mathbf{r}}_i + \mathbf{y}_i(2\mathbf{s} - 3)$
13:    $\mathbf{t}_{i,5} = \vec{\mathbf{b}}_5^T \vec{\mathbf{r}}_i + \mathbf{y}_i^2(\mathbf{s} - 3)$
14:    $\vec{\mathbf{t}}_i = (\mathbf{t}_{i,1}, \mathbf{t}_{i,2}, \mathbf{t}_3, \mathbf{t}_{i,4}, \mathbf{t}_{i,5})^T$
15: **end for**
16: $(c_i)_{i \in [t]} = H(A, \vec{u}, (\vec{\mathbf{t}}_i)_i, (\vec{w}_i)_i)$
17: **for** $i = 1, \ldots, t$ **do**
18:    $\mathbf{z}_i = \mathbf{y}_i + c_i\mathbf{s}$
19:    **for** $j = (i-1)t' + 1, \ldots, (i-1)t' + t'$ **do**
20:        $\vec{\mathbf{y}}'_j \overset{\$}{\leftarrow} D_\sigma^{6n}$
21:        $\mathbf{w}'_j = \vec{\mathbf{b}}_1^T \vec{\mathbf{y}}'_j$
22:        $\mathbf{x}_{1,j} = (\vec{\mathbf{b}}_2^T + c_i\vec{\mathbf{b}}_3^T)\vec{\mathbf{y}}'_j$
23:        $\mathbf{x}_{2,j} = ((\mathbf{z}_i - c_i)(\mathbf{z}_i - 2c_i)\vec{\mathbf{b}}_3^T - \mathbf{z}_i\vec{\mathbf{b}}_4^T + \vec{\mathbf{b}}_5^T)\vec{\mathbf{y}}'_j$
24:    **end for**
25: **end for**
26: $(\mathbf{f}_j)_{j \in [tt']} = G((c_i)_i, (\mathbf{z}_i)_i, (\mathbf{w}'_j)_j, (\mathbf{x}_{1,j})_j, (\mathbf{x}_{2,j})_j)$
27: **for** $j = 1, \ldots, tt'$ **do**
28:    $\vec{\mathbf{z}}'_j = \vec{\mathbf{y}}'_j + \mathbf{f}_j\vec{\mathbf{r}}_{\lceil j/t' \rceil}$
29: **end for**
30: **for** $k = 1, \ldots, t'$ **do**
31:    **if** Rej $\left((\vec{\mathbf{z}}'_j)_{j=k,\ldots,(t-1)t'+k}, (\mathbf{f}_{(i-1)t'+k}\vec{\mathbf{r}}_i)_i, \sigma\right) = 1$ or $\left\| (\vec{\mathbf{z}}'_j)_j \right\|_\infty > 6\sigma$ **then**
32:        **goto** 3
33:    **end if**
34: **end for**

Algorithm 3. Non-Interactive Verifier

1: **Input:** $A, \vec{u}, (\vec{\mathbf{t}}_i)_{i \in [t]}, (c_i)_{i \in [t]}, (\mathbf{z}_i)_{i \in [t]}, (\mathbf{f}_j)_{j \in [tt']}, (\vec{\mathbf{z}}'_j)_{j \in [tt']}$
2: **Output:** $b \in \{0, 1\}$
3: **for** $i = 1, \dots, t$ **do**
4:     $\vec{w}_i = A\hat{\mathbf{z}}_i - c_i \vec{u}$
5:     **for** $j = (i-1)t' + 1, \dots, (i-1)t' + t'$ **do**
6:         $\mathbf{w}'_j = \vec{\mathbf{b}}_1^T \vec{\mathbf{z}}'_j - \mathbf{f}_j \mathbf{t}_{i,1}$
7:         $\mathbf{x}_{1,j} = (\vec{\mathbf{b}}_2^T + c_i \vec{\mathbf{b}}_3^T)\vec{\mathbf{z}}'_j + \mathbf{f}_j \mathbf{z}_i - \mathbf{f}_j(\mathbf{t}_{i,2} + c_i \mathbf{t}_{i,3})$
8:         $\mathbf{x}_{2,j} = ((\mathbf{z}_i - c_i)(\mathbf{z}_i - 2c_i)\vec{\mathbf{b}}_3^T - \mathbf{z}_i \vec{\mathbf{b}}_4^T + \vec{\mathbf{b}}_5^T)\vec{\mathbf{z}}'_j$
9:                 $- \mathbf{f}_j((\mathbf{z}_i - c_i)(\mathbf{z}_i - 2c_i)\mathbf{t}_{i,3} - \mathbf{z}_i \mathbf{t}_{i,4} + \mathbf{t}_{i,5})$
10:     **end for**
11: **end for**
12: $(c'_i)_{i \in [t]} = \mathrm{H}(A, \vec{u}, (\vec{\mathbf{t}}_i)_i, (\vec{w}_i)_i)$
13: $(\mathbf{f}'_j)_{j \in [tt']} = \mathrm{G}((c_i)_i, (\mathbf{z}_i)_i, (\mathbf{w}'_j)_j, (\mathbf{x}_{1,j})_j, (\mathbf{x}_{2,j})_j)$
14: **if** $\|\vec{\mathbf{z}}'_j\|_2 \le B \wedge c'_i = c_i \wedge \mathbf{f}'_j = \mathbf{f}_j$ **then**
15:     **return** 1
16: **else**
17:     **return** 0
18: **end if**

3.4   Proof Size

We want to compute the size of the non-interactive proofs that are produced by Algorithm 2. Each of the t polynomial vectors $\vec{\mathbf{t}}_i$ consists of 5 uniformly random polynomials $\mathbf{t}_{i,\nu} \in \mathcal{R}_q$ of which one of them, namely $\mathbf{t}_{i,3}$, is the same in all $\vec{\mathbf{t}}_i$ and only needs to be transmitted once. The polynomials $\mathbf{z}_i$ are also uniformly random. So we need

$$(1 + 5t)n\lceil \log q \rceil / 8$$

bytes for $(\vec{\mathbf{t}}_i)_i$ and $(\mathbf{z}_i)_i$. By contrast the vectors $\vec{\mathbf{z}}'_j$ sampled from discrete Gaussian distributions with standard deviation $\sigma = 5T'$ where T' is a bound on the vector $(\mathbf{f}_{(i-1)t'+k}\vec{\mathbf{r}}_i)_i$ in dimension $6tn$. Note that the embedding norm is invariant under multiplication by the monomials $\mathbf{f}_j$ and we do not need to take them into account. The coefficients of a discrete Gaussian are smaller in absolute value than 6σ with probability at least $1 - 2^{-24}$, c.f. [Lyu12, Lemma 4.4], and our non-interactive prover enforces this. So the transmission of $(\vec{\mathbf{z}}'_j)_j$ requires

$$6tt'n\lceil \log(12\sigma) \rceil / 8$$

bytes; that is, $\lceil \log(6\sigma) \rceil$ bits per coefficient for the absolute value and one sign bit per coefficient. This does not make use of the fact that the coefficients of $\vec{\mathbf{z}}_j$ are distributed according to a (truncated) discrete Gaussian with known standard deviation, which has less entropy than the uniform distribution. So to get slightly smaller proof sizes one can encode the $\vec{\mathbf{z}}_j$ using a Huffman code, for instance.

Finally, the challenge polynomials $(c_i)_i$ and $(\mathbf{f}_j)_j$ together require

$$t(\lceil \log q \rceil + t' \lceil \log l \rceil)/8$$

bytes.

4   Efficiency Comparison

The simplest application of our proof protocol is to prove knowledge of the secret in LWE samples over $\mathbb{Z}_q$. Let's consider the case of ternary error, modulus q below 2^{32} such that $4096 \mid q - 1$, and dimension $d = 1024$. Moduli of around this size are used in FHE schemes and group signature schemes following the hash-and-sign paradigm with Boyen [Boy10] or Ducas-Micciancio standard-model signatures [DM14], for example. Now m such LWE samples $\vec{u}$ are of the form

$$\vec{u} = A'\vec{s}' + \vec{e}$$

with $A' \in \mathbb{Z}_q^{m \times d}$ public and chosen uniformly at random, and $\vec{s}' \in \{-1, 0, 1\}^d$ and $\vec{e} \in \{-1, 0, 1\}^m$ secret. We can write $A = (A', I_m)$ and then the above LWE equation as $\vec{u} = A(\vec{s}' \parallel \vec{e})$, which is of the form suitable for our proof system. So let $\mathcal{R} = \mathbb{Z}[X]/(X^n + 1)$ with $n = 2d = 2048$ and define $\mathbf{s} \in \mathcal{R}_q$ to be the polynomial whose NTT $\hat{\mathbf{s}}$ is given by the concatenation of the vectors $\vec{s}'$ and $\vec{e}$.

4.1   Our Proof System

With $t' = 3$ lower repetitions, the protocol has soundness error $2/q + 2/l^3$ which is approximately 2^{-31}. So we make $t = 4$ upper repetitions of the protocol to reach the 128 bit security level.

As we are in the power-of-two case recall that we are sampling the randomness vectors $\vec{r}_i \in \mathcal{R}^6$ using the binomial distribution β_2 independently for each coefficient. By the Chernov bound (8) it follows that $T' = \sqrt{1.1 \cdot 0.625 \cdot 6tn} = 183.83$ with probability at least $1 - 2^{-102}$. So we sample the vectors $\vec{y}'_j$ with $\sigma = 5T' = 919.13$.

Hardness. The security of the above instantiation of our protocol is based on the hardness of the $\mathrm{RSIS}_{5,8B}$ and RLWE_{1+4t} problems over the ring $\mathbb{Z}_q[X]/(X^{2048} + 1)$ with $q \approx 2^{32}$. We analyze known attacks against these problems and start with the Ring SIS problem. Here one needs to find a short vector in the $k = 6n$-dimensional lattice

$$\Lambda^{\perp}(\vec{\mathbf{b}}_1^T) = \left\{ \vec{\mathbf{x}} \in \mathcal{R}^6 \mid \vec{\mathbf{b}}_1^T \vec{\mathbf{x}} \equiv 0 \pmod{q\mathcal{R}} \right\}.$$

It has volume q^n, as one can easily see by writing down a basis. By applying a reduction algorithm to the basis that achieves a root Hermite factor δ_0 we find a short vector of length $q^{n/k}\delta_0^k$. But it is actually sufficient to find a short vector in a sublattice by omitting some of the columns of the matrix corresponding to $\vec{\mathbf{b}}_1^T$.

It turns out that the optimal dimension is $k = 6509$. There a root Hermite factor of 1.0011 would be needed to find a vector of length $8B$. This is out of reach for current reduction algorithms.

For the Ring LWE problem RLWE_{1+4t} we study the primal attack and use the fact that the lattice

$$\Lambda^\perp = \left\{ \vec{x} \in \mathcal{R}^{3+4t} \mid \left(\vec{a} \, I_{1+4t} \, \vec{t} \right) \vec{x} \equiv \vec{0} \pmod{q\mathcal{R}} \right\}$$

of volume $q^{(1+4t)n}$ contains the unusually short vector $(s, \vec{e}^T, -1)^T$ of expected length about $\sqrt{(2 + 4t)n10/16}$. Here we do not need to use all of the LWE samples and can instead search for an unusually short vector in a lattice of dimension $k = (i + 1)n + 1$ that we get from considering i samples, $1 \le i \le 1 + 4t$. Lattice reduction will succeed in finding the unusually short vector if $\lambda_2/\lambda_1 \ge 0.3\delta_0^k$ where we assume that there is no other very short vector and hence, by the Gaussian heuristic,

$$\lambda_2 = \sqrt{\frac{k}{2\pi e}} q^{in/k}.$$

It follows that in our case we would need to achieve a root Hermite factor of about $\delta_0 = 1.0027$, which is impossible.

Size. It follows from the formulas in Sect. 3.4 that the total size of the proof is $384.03\,\text{KB}$. Here we have not used the trivial encoding for the vectors $\vec{z}_j$ using $\lceil \log(12\sigma) \rceil = 14$ bits per coefficient. Instead we have computed the entropy of the discrete Gaussian distribution with $\sigma = 919.13$, truncated to $\{-6\sigma, \ldots, 6\sigma\}$, which is below 12 bits. So using a Huffman code the vectors $\vec{z}_j$ can be encoded using 12 bits per coefficient on average.

4.2   Stern-Like Proofs

We compare our result against the Stern-type protocol presented in [KTX08, LNSW13], as it is the only other lattice-based zero-knowledge protocol capable of proving that a prover knows an exact solution to a system of linear equations, rather than a solution to a related system.

The protocol of [LNSW13] proves knowledge of $\vec{s} \in \mathbb{Z}^n$ with coefficients in $\{-S, \ldots, S\}$, such that $A\vec{s} = \vec{u}$, where A is an $m \times n$ matrix over $\mathbb{Z}_q$. For the analysis, we closely follow [LNSW13, Figure 1].

Set $k = \lfloor \log S \rfloor + 1$. The protocol decomposes $\vec{s}$ into k vectors $\vec{s}_j$ with coefficients in $\{-1, 0, 1\}$ using a type of binary decomposition, and extends each $\vec{s}_j$ to a longer vector $\tilde{\vec{s}}_j$ with a constant number of 0, 1 and -1 entries. The protocol also uses a matrix A' which is derived from A. Then, the protocol proves that that all of the coefficients of the extended vectors do indeed lie in $\{-1, 0, 1\}$ and that $A' \sum_{j=0}^{k-1} \tilde{\vec{s}}_j$ is equal to $\vec{u}$, which implies a short solution to the original system using A.

The protocol involves choosing a random permutation, choosing random masking vectors $\vec{r}_j$ for the $\tilde{\vec{s}}_j$, and making three commitments.

- The first commitment is a commitment to a random permutation and a matrix-vector product involving A' and the $\vec{r}_j$. The random permutation can be generated from a short seed of using a PRG. The result of the matrix-vector product is $n \log q$ elements, but this value itself is never revealed.
- The second commitment is a commitment to permutations of the $\vec{r}_j$. The $\vec{r}_j$ can also be generated using a PRG.
- The third commitment is a commitment to permutations of the vectors $\tilde{\vec{s}}_j + \vec{r}_j$.

The prover sends these three commitments to the verifier. Using a simple commitment scheme which commits by hashing and is secure in the random oracle model, each of these commitments has size 256 bits.

The protocol uses challenges from the set $\{1, 2, 3\}$. As for the prover's responses to challenges, when the challenge is equal to 1, the prover sends the permuted $\vec{r}_j$ and $\tilde{\vec{s}}_j$ to the verifier. This means sending $6kn + 3kn\lceil \log q \rceil$ bits. When the challenge is equal to 2, the prover sends the permutation seed and the permuted $\tilde{\vec{s}}_j + \vec{r}_j$ to the verifier. This means sending $256 + 3kn\lceil \log q \rceil$ bits. When the challenge is equal to 3, the prover sends the permutation seed and the permuted $\vec{r}_j$ to the verifier. This means sending 512 bits, as it is sufficient to send the random seed for the $\vec{r}_j$ alongside the permutation seed.

Summing up the challenge responses, dividing by 3, and adding the sizes of the 3 commitments, a single execution of the protocol has an expected proof size of $1024 + kn(2\lceil \log q \rceil + 1)$ bits. A single execution has a soundness error of $2/3$. For a soundness error of λ bits, this means repeating the protocol $t = \lceil \lambda/(\log 3 - 1) \rceil$ times, for a total proof size of $1024t + knt(2\lceil \log q \rceil + 2)$ bits.

For the application above, with $\lambda = 124$ and $k = 1$, the result is a proof size of 3.44 MB.

References

[Ban93]   Banaszczyk, W.: New bounds in some transference theorems in the geometry of numbers. Math. Ann. **296**, 625–635 (1993)

[BBB+18] Bünz, B., Bootle, J., Boneh, D., Poelstra, A., Wuille, P., Maxwell, G.: Bulletproofs: short proofs for confidential transactions and more. In: IEEE Symposium on Security and Privacy, pp. 315–334 (2018)

[BBC+18] Baum, C., Bootle, J., Cerulli, A., del Pino, R., Groth, J., Lyubashevsky, V.: Sub-linear lattice-based zero-knowledge arguments for arithmetic circuits. In: Shacham, H., Boldyreva, A. (eds.) CRYPTO 2018. LNCS, vol. 10992, pp. 669–699. Springer, Cham (2018). https://doi.org/10.1007/978-3-319-96881-0_23

[BCC+16] Bootle, J., Cerulli, A., Chaidos, P., Groth, J., Petit, C.: Efficient zero-knowledge arguments for arithmetic circuits in the discrete log setting. In: Fischlin, M., Coron, J.-S. (eds.) EUROCRYPT 2016. LNCS, vol. 9666, pp. 327–357. Springer, Heidelberg (2016). https://doi.org/10.1007/978-3-662-49896-5_12

[BCK+14] Benhamouda, F., Camenisch, J., Krenn, S., Lyubashevsky, V., Neven, G.: Better zero-knowledge proofs for lattice encryption and their application to group signatures. In: Sarkar, P., Iwata, T. (eds.) ASIACRYPT 2014. LNCS, vol. 8873, pp. 551–572. Springer, Heidelberg (2014). https://doi.org/10.1007/978-3-662-45611-8_29

[BDL+18] Baum, C., Damgård, I., Lyubashevsky, V., Oechsner, S., Peikert, C.: More efficient commitments from structured lattice assumptions. In: Catalano, D., De Prisco, R. (eds.) SCN 2018. LNCS, vol. 11035, pp. 368–385. Springer, Cham (2018). https://doi.org/10.1007/978-3-319-98113-0_20

[Beu19] Beullens, W.: On sigma protocols with helper for MQ and PKP, fishy signature schemes and more. Cryptology ePrint Archive, Report 2019/490 (2019). https://eprint.iacr.org/2019/490

[BN19] Baum, C., Nof, A.: Concretely-efficient zero-knowledge arguments for arithmetic circuits and their application to lattice-based cryptography. Cryptology ePrint Archive, Report 2019/532 (2019). https://eprint.iacr.org/2019/532

[Boy10] Boyen, X.: Lattice mixing and vanishing trapdoors: a framework for fully secure short signatures and more. In: Nguyen, P.Q., Pointcheval, D. (eds.) PKC 2010. LNCS, vol. 6056, pp. 499–517. Springer, Heidelberg (2010). https://doi.org/10.1007/978-3-642-13013-7_29

[DM14] Ducas, L., Micciancio, D.: Improved short lattice signatures in the standard model. In: Garay, J.A., Gennaro, R. (eds.) CRYPTO 2014. LNCS, vol. 8616, pp. 335–352. Springer, Heidelberg (2014). https://doi.org/10.1007/978-3-662-44371-2_19

[dPLS18] del Pino, R., Lyubashevsky, V., Seiler, G.: Lattice-based group signatures and zero-knowledge proofs of automorphism stability. In: CCS, pp. 574–591 (2018)

[dPLS19] del Pino, R., Lyubashevsky, V., Seiler, G.: Short discrete log proofs for FHE and Ring-LWE ciphertexts. In: Lin, D., Sako, K. (eds.) PKC 2019. LNCS, vol. 11442, pp. 344–373. Springer, Cham (2019). https://doi.org/10.1007/978-3-030-17253-4_12

[Gen09] Gentry, C.: Fully homomorphic encryption using ideal lattices. In: STOC, pp. 169–178 (2009)

[GK15] Groth, J., Kohlweiss, M.: One-out-of-many proofs: or how to leak a secret and spend a coin. In: Oswald, E., Fischlin, M. (eds.) EUROCRYPT 2015. LNCS, vol. 9057, pp. 253–280. Springer, Heidelberg (2015). https://doi.org/10.1007/978-3-662-46803-6_9

[Gro10] Groth, J.: A verifiable secret shuffle of homomorphic encryptions. J. Cryptol. **23**(4), 546–579 (2010)

[KTX08] Kawachi, A., Tanaka, K., Xagawa, K.: Concurrently secure identification schemes based on the worst-case hardness of lattice problems. In: Pieprzyk, J. (ed.) ASIACRYPT 2008. LNCS, vol. 5350, pp. 372–389. Springer, Heidelberg (2008). https://doi.org/10.1007/978-3-540-89255-7_23

[LNSW13] Ling, S., Nguyen, K., Stehlé, D., Wang, H.: Improved zero-knowledge proofs of knowledge for the ISIS problem, and applications. In: Kurosawa, K., Hanaoka, G. (eds.) PKC 2013. LNCS, vol. 7778, pp. 107–124. Springer, Heidelberg (2013). https://doi.org/10.1007/978-3-642-36362-7_8

[LNWX18] Ling, S., Nguyen, K., Wang, H., Xu, Y.: Constant-size group signatures from lattices. In: Abdalla, M., Dahab, R. (eds.) PKC 2018. LNCS, vol. 10770, pp. 58–88. Springer, Cham (2018). https://doi.org/10.1007/978-3-319-76581-5_3

[LPR13] Lyubashevsky, V., Peikert, C., Regev, O.: A toolkit for Ring-LWE cryptography. In: Johansson, T., Nguyen, P.Q. (eds.) EUROCRYPT 2013. LNCS, vol. 7881, pp. 35–54. Springer, Heidelberg (2013). https://doi.org/10.1007/978-3-642-38348-9_3

[Lyu09] Lyubashevsky, V.: Fiat-Shamir with aborts: applications to lattice and factoring-based signatures. In: Matsui, M. (ed.) ASIACRYPT 2009. LNCS, vol. 5912, pp. 598–616. Springer, Heidelberg (2009). https://doi.org/10.1007/978-3-642-10366-7_35

[Lyu12] Lyubashevsky, V.: Lattice signatures without trapdoors. In: Pointcheval, D., Johansson, T. (eds.) EUROCRYPT 2012. LNCS, vol. 7237, pp. 738–755. Springer, Heidelberg (2012). https://doi.org/10.1007/978-3-642-29011-4_43

[Ste93] Stern, J.: A new identification scheme based on syndrome decoding. In: Stinson, D.R. (ed.) CRYPTO 1993. LNCS, vol. 773, pp. 13–21. Springer, Heidelberg (1994). https://doi.org/10.1007/3-540-48329-2_2

[YAZ+19] Yang, R., Au, M.H., Zhang, Z., Xu, Q., Yu, Z., Whyte, W.: Efficient lattice-based zero-knowledge arguments with standard soundness: construction and applications. In: Boldyreva, A., Micciancio, D. (eds.) CRYPTO 2019. LNCS, vol. 11692, pp. 147–175. Springer, Cham (2019)

Symmetric Cryptography

Seedless Fruit Is the Sweetest: Random Number Generation, Revisited

Sandro Coretti[1][(✉)], Yevgeniy Dodis[2][(✉)], Harish Karthikeyan[2],
and Stefano Tessaro[3]

[1] IOHK, Zurich, Switzerland
corettis@gmail.com
[2] New York University, New York, USA
{dodis,karthik}@cs.nyu.edu
[3] University of Washington, Seattle, WA, USA
tessaro@cs.washington.edu

Abstract. The need for high-quality randomness in cryptography makes random-number generation one of its most fundamental tasks.

A recent important line of work (initiated by Dodis et al., CCS '13) focuses on the notion of *robustness* for *pseudorandom number generators (PRNGs) with inputs*. These are primitives that use various sources to accumulate sufficient entropy into a state, from which pseudorandom bits are extracted. Robustness ensures that PRNGs remain secure even under state compromise and adversarial control of entropy sources. However, the achievability of robustness inherently depends on a *seed*, or, alternatively, on an ideal primitive (e.g., a random oracle), independent of the source of entropy. Both assumptions are problematic: seed generation requires randomness to start with, and it is arguable whether the seed or the ideal primitive can be kept independent of the source.

This paper resolves this dilemma by putting forward new notions of robustness which enable both (1) *seedless* PRNGs and (2) *primitive-dependent* adversarial sources of entropy. To bypass obvious impossibility results, we make a realistic compromise by requiring that the source produce sufficient entropy *even* given its evaluations of the underlying primitive. We also provide natural, practical, and provably secure constructions based on hash-function designs from compression functions, block ciphers, and permutations. Our constructions can be instantiated with minimal changes to industry-standard hash functions SHA-2 and SHA-3, or key derivation function HKDF, and can be downgraded to *(online) seedless randomness extractors*, which are of independent interest.

On the way we consider both a *computational* variant of robustness, where attackers only make a bounded number of queries to the ideal primitive, as well as a new *information-theoretic* variant, which dispenses with

S. Coretti—Work done while at NYU. Supported by NSF grants 1314568 and 1619158.
Y. Dodis—Partially supported by gifts from VMware Labs, Facebook and Google, and NSF grants 1314568, 1619158, 1815546.
H. Karthikeyan—Supported by NSF grant 1619158.
S. Tessaro—Partially supported by NSF grants CNS-1553758 (CAREER), CNS-1719146, CNS-1528178, and IIS-1528041, and by a Sloan Research Fellowship.

A. Boldyreva and D. Micciancio (Eds.): CRYPTO 2019, LNCS 11692, pp. 205–234, 2019.
https://doi.org/10.1007/978-3-030-26948-7_8

this assumption to a certain extent, at the price of requiring a high rate of injected weak randomness (as it is, e.g., plausible on Intel's on-chip RNG). The latter notion enables applications such as everlasting security. Finally, we show that the CBC extractor, used by Intel's on-chip RNG, is provably insecure in our model.

Keywords: Provable security · Pseudorandom number generation · Symmetric cryptography

1   Introduction

Good random number generation is essential for cryptography and beyond. In practice, this difficult task is solved by a primitive called *pseudorandom number generator with input (PRNG)*, whose aim is to quickly accumulate entropy from various physical sources in the environment (such as keyboard presses, timing of interrupts, etc.) into the state of the PRNG and then convert this high-entropy state into (pseudo) random bits. In particular, entropy accumulation should never stop since one may need to recover from occasional compromises of the PRNG state. PRNGs are ubiquitous and have extensive applications. For example, virtually all operating systems come equipped with a PRNG; e.g., /dev/random [48] for Linux, Yarrow [34] for MacOs/iOS/FreeBSD, and Fortuna [24] for Windows [23], where the latter two make use of standard cryptographic primitives as part of their design. Still, as we will argue below in a much broader context, even these widely used PRNGs lack adequate theoretical understanding and analysis, which are critical if such PRNGs or their future tweaks continue to be used ubiquitously.

The situation is not better in terms of standardization efforts, where existing PRNG standards [5, 22, 32, 35] are less mature than those for most other cryptographic primitives. For starters, there has not been any rigorous competition soliciting PNRG designs, and big parts of the existing standards concentrate on the difficult (ad-hoc and non-cryptographic) problem of entropy estimation rather than entropy accumulation and extraction. More importantly, standardized cryptographic PRNG constructions are rather ad-hoc, have no clear security definition/model, often have confusing syntax, and sometimes have been broken by subsequent analyses of the cryptographic community. The most widely known example is the DualEC PRNG, which appeared in the first version of the NIST SP 800-90A standard [5] in 2005 and remained there for years—despite early warnings by [42,44] and allowing potential exploitation [12]—until Snowden's revelations finally led to its deprecation. Recent work [49] identified a lot of gaps and imprecision (sometimes leading to attacks or security concerns) in the existing analyses and deployment for the other 3 PRNGs from the NIST SP 800-90A standard. In a similar vein, [43] found several gaps and misconceptions in previous analyses and security justifications for the popular Intel Secure Key Hardware PRNG introduced in 2011.

One of the main goals of this work is to reverse this poor state of affairs and to design a rigorous, theoretically sound model of PRNGs. This model should be general enough to incorporate practical entropy sources available in the real world, as well as to formally prove security of "good," widely used PRNGs against realistic attackers.

1.1   Previous Theoretical Models for PRNGs: Seeds

In view of their practical importance, we are certainly not the first to formally study PRNGs through a theoretical lens. Indeed, several theoretical models and analyses of PRNGs have appeared in the literature [1,19,21,26,28,43]. While differing in various details, these important works share two key principles:

(a) The PRNG should work even against *adversarial* entropy sources, as long as such sources eventually provide enough entropy (such sources are called "legitimate" [19]);
(b) assuming more structure beyond entropy is undesirable and brittle,[1] as this requires a rather detailed understanding of one's entropy sources.

However, while such extremely minimalist assumptions make these PRNG models applicable to a wide variety of entropy sources, they also come with a subtle, but very important caveat: the randomness extraction module *cannot* be deterministic, as deterministic extraction from *general* entropy sources is impossible [15]. As a result, the PRNGs studied by these works are *seeded* (with the seed somehow chosen at initialization), but the entropy sources are assumed to be *independent of the seed*. This modeling is inherited from the underlying problem of randomness extraction, where *seeded extractors* [40] indeed overcome the impossibility of deterministic (or "seedless") extraction from general entropy sources.

While natural and sufficient for some applications of extractors, we argue that the need for a seed seems rather problematic in the deployment of PRNGs. First, if the reason for random number generation is the lack of access to high-quality random bits, then we may not have any way to generate the seed. More importantly, even if we *can* generate a uniformly random seed, it is crucial for the analysis that (potentially adversarial) entropy sources remain *independent* of the seed, for otherwise the extractor guarantees are lost. For example, if physical entropy sources inside the computer are used, these sources may be affected by the internal computations of the PRNG itself, and thus there may be correlations between the seed and the sources. Moreover, for many seeded PRNGs, the attacker could obtain information about the seed by either directly reading it from memory, or indirectly when the recently compromised or rebooted RNG is called on "low-entropy" inputs (so the output is no longer random and leaks information about the seed; this is called "premature next" attack by [21]).

This means that it is certainly an issue if the seed is just generated once and for all (perhaps using an expensive source of randomness) and hard-coded within implementations to be used for all future randomness extractions. Moreover, if multiple entropy sources are used, it is natural that some of these sources are

---

[1] We do, however, later discuss an interesting approach suggested by [3].

adversarial and could depend on the seed (which is hard to protect against with a dedicated attacker). Somewhat paradoxically (considering the common belief that "more entropy cannot hurt"), the mixing of such seed-dependent sources once again invalidates all the provable guarantees of seeded PRNGs, even if all the entropy is obtained from other, seed-independent sources.

We thus face a dilemma:

> *We want to support general entropy sources, for which seedless extraction is impossible, and seeded extraction is only possible under very dangerous and hard-to-ensure independence assumptions, which we would rather avoid.*

The goal of this work is to provide a meaningful solution to this dilemma, by keeping the PRNG design *seedless* while respecting properties (a) and (b) mentioned above.

1.2 *Seedless* PRNGs and Extractors from Cryptographic Hashing

We will achieve this goal by using popular *cryptographic hash functions (CHF)* as our technical tool, and by carefully defining the notion of entropy in the setting when certain components of these CHFs are assumed idealized.

WHY CRYPTOGRAPHIC HASHING? Before describing our solution in more detail, we explain why using CHFs appears essential for the design of *seedless*[2] PRNGs. For starters, all general-purpose software PRNGs used today, as well as all recommendations in existing PRNG standards, are based on CHFs. Hence, this setting must definitely be understood in order to provide results useful in the real world.

However, there is a more glaring theoretical reason as well. The key component of any PRNG is the shrinking function refresh which takes the current PRNG state S as well as a new entropic input X and produces a new state $S' \leftarrow \mathsf{refresh}(S, X)$. The goal of this function is to absorb the potential entropy of X into the PRNG state S, in which case the entropy of S' should be higher than the original entropy of S. In the extraction literature, this property is called *condensing*. If one uses a seed, building such condensers is easy to accomplish information-theoretically. For example, in the PRNG design of [19], the refresh function is linear: $S' = aS + X$, where a is a seed independent of X.

In the seedless/seed-dependent setting, it is not hard to see [20] that condensers must be built cryptographically, as they require at least some form of preimage- and collision-resistance.[3] For example, when used in iteration, the simple $aS+X$ condenser function above—which yields (together with other building blocks) a provably secure seeded PRNG construction [19]—can be broken *in a catastrophic way* if the distribution of the input blocks $X_1, X_2, \ldots$ could depend

---

[2] Or, in the non-uniform setting, "seed-dependent".

[3] For example, the ability to compute a random preimage of a given element, which is known to imply one-way functions [31], allows the attacker to produce entropic inputs whose entropy is completely lost by the refresh procedure.

on the constant a: it is not hard to see that an attacker knowing a can rather easily produce *high-entropy inputs* such that if the condenser is applied to it, the resulting would have no entropy at all. In practice, one cannot imagine a PRNG system which would risk such a catastrophic failure by critically depending on the fact that the constant a must remain hidden for the lifetime of the PRNG. Therefore, not surprisingly, all real-world PRNG designs—including those used by Windows, MacOS, and FreeBSD—critically rely on CHFs, despite lacking adequate theoretical justification.

Cryptographically secure condensers, which at an absolute minimum seedless PRNGs have to be, can be built using a (very strong form of) collision-resistance [20]. However, the types of condensers needed for applications, called average-case seedless condensers, seem to require non-standard cryptographic assumptions. For example, a relatively weak form of such average-case condensers (called "condensers for leaky sources") are already sufficient for instantiating the Fiat-Shamir heuristic for public-coin proof systems [20]—and it is a major open problem to provide such an instantiation under standard cryptographic assumptions.

To put it differently, even ignoring the fact that we want our PRNGs to be full-blown *seedless extractors*—a problem we will address next—just achieving provably secure entropy accumulation appears to require the use of CHFs as well as either (1) non-standard cryptographic assumptions (making the results appear somewhat tautologous) or (2) some supporting justification argument in an idealized model of computation, which is the approach taken by this work.

OUR APPROACH: NEW MIN-ENTROPY NOTION. To describe our approach, it is instructive to recall the basic impossibility of seedless extraction for general entropy sources. Given any candidate (seedless) extractor G, an adversary can perform a so-called *extractor-fixing attack* by sampling a random input X several times until the first bit of $G(X)$ is 0. The resulting distribution X has very high entropy, but $G(X)$ is clearly not uniformly random. Observe that with a strong enough CHF G, one might be able to formally argue that the extractor-fixing attack is the "most damaging" attack possible; for example by showing, that $G(X)$ has almost full entropy (i.e., is a good condenser) for any efficiently samplable source X, as was done by [20]. In other words, using CHFs will protect against the completely devastating attacks possible with information-theoretic extractors.

However, our goal is to have a meaningful model where real randomness *extraction* is possible, so that we can later extend it all the way to the full PRNG system. Our solution will be to define a elegant and practically motivated refinement of general min-entropy *in settings where CHFs exist*, so that:

(a) somewhat artificial sources resulting from intentionally performing extractor-fixing will not have much entropy according to our notion (meaning they are no longer "legitimate"); in fact, seedless extraction will become *possible* for our notion of min-entropy;

(b) most natural entropy sources, including those used by major operating systems, will likely have good entropy according to our new measure.

While our final constructions and interpretation of our security analyses will apply to real-world CHFs, such as those derived from SHA-2, SHA-3, HMAC or HKDF, at present the only rigorous way we know how to achieve our ambitious goals (a) and (b) will be by going to the idealized models of computation, such as the random oracle, the ideal cipher or the random permutation model. This is quite standard for many areas of symmetric-key cryptography, and we already indicated that doing provably secure (non-tautologous) seedless PRNG constructions in the "standard model" appears beyond our current capabilities, even for much simpler building blocks, such as (average-case) seedless condensers.

1.3   Toy Case: Monolithic Seedless Extraction from Oracle-Dependent Sources

We start by presenting our new entropy notion for the simpler problem of "monolithic randomness extraction," where the entropy source X is assumed to come in one piece (rather than slowly accumulated using a fixed-length PRNG state), and a monolithic CHF G—modeled as a monolithic random oracle—is used to output the value $R = G(X)$ (so that we temporarily ignore any find-grained structure inside G, such as Merkle-Damgård or Sponge [8] iteration).

At first, it appears that we solved our problem in a totally trivial (and uninteresting) way, even without refining standard min-entropy. Namely, in the random oracle model, the following folklore proof (see [18]) appears to show that a (seedless) random oracle G is a good extractor: For any min-entropy γ^* source X, the probability the distinguisher D can distinguish $G(X)$ is upper bounded by the probability D queries G on X, which is at most $q \cdot 2^{-\gamma^*}$, where q is the number of random oracle queries allowed to $\mathcal{A}$.[4]

Implicit in this simple proof, however, is the key assumption that the distribution X is independent of the random oracle G, meaning that our (potentially adversarial) sampler producing X is not allowed to call the random oracle G. Thus, modeling G as a random oracle is but a fancy way of introducing an exponentially long seed that is independent of the source, making extraction trivial.[5] Indeed, to capture PRNG sources X arising in the real world, we must allow the source X to depend on the ideal primitive G. For example, if the timing of computer interrupts is used as our entropy source X—which is the most common source of randomness in software PRNGs—it seems unreasonable to assume that none of these interrupts could be affected by frequent hash function computations done inside and outside the operating system.

---

[4] In fact, if the length of $G(X)$ is slightly less than γ^*, we can even let $\mathcal{A}$ query all of G and use leftover-hash lemma [30] to get information-theoretic security.

[5] Prior to our work, the above modeling of sources as being independent of the ideal primitive, was the only way to overcome extractor-fixing attacks. Examples of this approach include [18,36,49] and many others. While these results are non-trivial due to the "non-monolithic" structure of their extractors G, none of these works model the setting where *the source could depend on the ideal primitive*.

ORACLE-DEPENDENT SOURCES. To fix this problem, in Sect. 3 we will explicitly model our source as part of the attacker $\mathcal{A}$, so that $\mathcal{A}^G = (\mathcal{A}_1^G, \mathcal{A}_2^G)$, where $\mathcal{A}_1^G$ outputs the *oracle-dependent* source X and passes state Σ to the second state attacker $\mathcal{A}_2^G(\Sigma)$, whose goal is to distinguish $R = G(X)$ from uniform. Of course, for this definition to make sense, we must require that X is "legitimate," meaning it has entropy at least γ^* given the state information Σ (for some parameter γ^*). In the standard model, this could be formalized by requiring $\mathrm{H}_\infty(X|\Sigma) \geq \gamma^*$ (see Sect. 2). But this is too weak, as this still allows for extractor-fixing attacks, by sampling a long random X and remembering a few bits of $G(X)$ in the leakage Σ. In fact, this extractor-fixing attack still works even if we condition on the entire random oracle G (i.e., require $\mathrm{H}_\infty(X|\Sigma, G) \geq \gamma^*$). This leads to a central question of this work:

> *What is the "right" notion of entropy for oracle-dependent sources X?*

The key insight of our work comes from the fact that while it is reasonable to assume that the source X could *depend* on the random oracle G, the natural sources of entropy we want to extract from do not natively evaluate cryptographic hash functions, but somehow add extra entropy *in addition* to all hash function evaluations around them. For example, it is unreasonable to assume that the timing of interrupts could not depend, even slightly, on various hash function evaluations inside the computer. However, it seems that the real entropy of interrupt timings comes from the fact that the attacker cannot perfectly predict the exact lower order bits of the timing measurements, *even if the attacker knew all the hash function evaluations*. Indeed, instead of only requiring that $\mathrm{H}_\infty(X|\Sigma, G) \geq \gamma^*$, our approach will make a stronger requirement that

$$\mathrm{H}_\infty(X|(\Sigma, \mathcal{L})) \geq \gamma^* \,, \tag{1}$$

where $\mathcal{L}$ is the *input-output list of random oracle queries made by the sampler* $\mathcal{A}_1$ to the random oracle. Another, equivalent way to interpret this legitimacy condition is to mandate that $\mathcal{A}_1$ cannot "forget" any of its random oracle queries when passing its state Σ to $\mathcal{A}_2$, but must forget some other useful information about X, to ensure that X has entropy conditioned on Σ *and* $\mathcal{L}$.

Notice, our solution places a more stringent requirement than conditioning on the entire G, as $\mathcal{A}_1$ did not touch anything outside $\mathcal{L}$, so these un-queried values do not reduce entropy of X beyond what is done by $\mathcal{L}$. Also, when the number of queries q is not too large, the extractor-fixing is no longer a legitimate attack, since X will not have much entropy when conditioned on $\mathcal{L}$ (which contains the pair $(X, G(X))$). In fact, we can easily show *full extraction* (see Theorems 1 and 2), along the lines of the folklore proof for oracle-independent sources mentioned above. The basic intuition comes from the fact that our conditioning on the list $\mathcal{L}$ ensures that with overwhelming probability the sampler $\mathcal{A}_1$ did not himself evaluate $G(X)$, which is essential for the extractor-fixing attack to succeed.

DID WE GO TOO FAR? Of course, the main question is whether the legitimacy requirement $H_\infty(X|(\Sigma, \mathcal{L})) \geq \gamma^*$ does not overly limit the class of high-entropy sources from which we want to extract. We believe the answer is negative. First, in the restrictive "folklore case" when X is independent of G (meaning $\mathcal{L} = \emptyset$), we get the best-possible min-entropy condition $H_\infty(X|\Sigma) \geq \gamma^*$ we had in the standard (non-random-oracle) model. Namely, our notion of min-entropy relative to G includes all general min-entropy sources.[6]

Second, while we certainly allow the source X to substantially depend on G, we ensure that non-trivial bulk of entropy must come from *outside* of the actual oracle evaluation queries. In other words, while "nature," who outputs X, could conceivably be influenced by a couple of hash function evaluations, it should generate some intrinsic entropy *in addition to* (but possibly dependent on!) these evaluations. We feel that all practically used physical sources (timing of interrupts, temperature, keystroke dynamics, etc.) have very little to do with hash functions, and should easily satisfy this requirement.

Thus, we believe that our technical restriction on the legitimacy for extraction using CHFs—by conditioning min-entropy on the list of hash function evaluations—strikes the right balance between allowing for seedless extraction, and yet keeping the family of high-entropy sources large and realistic for applications.

1.4 Our Results

While the above toy example (analyzed in Sect. 3.2) illustrated the key technical insight behind our approach, in practice it is uncommon to assume access to a monolithic random oracle G. Instead, practical hash functions are usually built from (public) compression functions, ciphers, or permutations. These underlying primitives P have limited input length and will therefore not be able to process inputs of arbitrary length m. Therefore, extractors and PRNGs should be designed in such a way that they can process short m-bit input blocks (e.g., $m = 256, 512, 1600$) and accumulate their entropy in the internal state.

ONLINE EXTRACTORS AND INSECURITY OF CBC. Thus, in Sect. 3.3 we formalize the more realistic notion of *online (seedless) extractors*, which slowly accumulate their long input into a fixed-length state (using access to a P), and then finalize their output once the whole input is processed. We also define both computational and information-theoretic (IT) notions of online extractor security, where in the latter notion the attacker is allowed to read the entire ideal primitive P after it finished generating the oracle-dependent source X.

Turning to natural and widely used examples of such online extractors, we show that the popular CBC mode of operation is insecure as a seedless extractor in our framework. The details of our attack are given in Sect. 3.4, but the result is a somewhat unexpected, since CBC is used as the extractor underlying the CTR_DRBG construction in the NIST PRNG standard NIST SP 800-90A Rev. 1 [4],

---

[6] Of course, when we instantiate G with a real-world hash function, this is no longer the case, as we discuss below.

and also as the extractor for Intel's on-chip RNG [38]. Moreover, its security was formally shown by Dodis et al. [18], but in the setting where the entropy source X was *independent* of the random permutation π. In contrast, we show that once the latter assumption is relaxed to our oracle-dependent sources, the CBC extractor is no longer secure (unless one generalizes it to the Sponge construction in Sect. 5.3, where the input is only XORed to *part* of the state). Of course, our attack is somewhat theoretical, and does not directly translate to attacking the Intel on-chip RNG, for example. However, coupled with our positive results, we feel our attack suggests using a different online extractor, if possible.

On a positive side, in the full version [17], we show several other (both computational and information-theoretic) online extractors based on popular modes of operations used inside hash functions SHA-2 and SHA-3, which are provably secure in our framework: from Merkle-Damgård with a random compression function, from Merkle-Damgård with the Davies-Meyer compression function, and from Sponges. Hence, for the first time practitioners can use seedless extractors which are both practical and have firm theoretical foundation. The security of these natural online extractors follows as special cases of more general PRNG security results, which we describe next.

FULL-SCALE SEEDLESS PRNGS. Finally, we take all our ideas together to solve our main problem: defining and building practical, yet provably secure seedless PRNGs. In Sect. 4 we introduce a novel security definition for PRNGs that differs from previous notions [1,19,26] in several crucial ways. The detailed comparison appears in the full version, but we present the highlights here.

First and foremost, our design is seedless. This is accomplished by carefully defining the legitimacy condition (relative to the fixed-length ideal primitive P), by conditioning our entropy notion on the list $\mathcal{L}$ of the queries to P made by the attacker. Second, our seedless design allows us to merge the "distribution sampler" and the distinguisher used by [19,26] into a single attacker $\mathcal{A}$,[7] making our notion much simpler to describe. Third, the works of [19,26] used a much weaker notion of worst-case min-entropy; moreover, the final entropy of the source X was defined as sum of individual worst-case min-entropies of the individual blocks of X conditioned on all the other blocks (before and after). In contrast, we use a much better notion of *average-case* min-entropy, and only look at the global average-case min-entropy of the entire (long) vector X. Thus, our notion of entropy is much less conservative: realistic entropy sources are likely to have *much higher* entropy according to our definition, even when conditioning on the list $\mathcal{L}$. Fourth, the notion of [19,26] had explicit "entropy estimates" that the attacker had to provide. Our notion gets rid of these estimates. Finally, and somewhat surprisingly, we still managed to define our notion of legitimacy of the entropy source in a manner which is *construction-independent*. This means that one can potentially study the entropy properties of the source in a manner independent of the PRNG used on this source.

---

[7] Since we no longer need to hide the seed from the distribution sampler, forcing us to separate it from the attacker.

We also define both computational and information-theoretic (IT) notions of PRNG security. As with on-line extractors, for IT-PRNGs the attacker is allowed to read the entire ideal primitive P after it finished generating the last block of it's oracle-dependent source X used for extraction. Such a notion is important for applications where privacy must hold well after the PRNG is finished its operations, or where information-theoretic security is important.

OUR PRNG CONSTRUCTIONS. In Sect. 5 we then present three main PRNGs which are provably secure in our framework: based on Merkle-Damgård with a random compression function (see Fig. 2), based on Merkle-Damgård with the Davies-Meyer compression function (see Fig. 3), and based on Sponges (see Fig. 4). All these constructions are extremely natural and practical, as Merkle-Damgård-based functions abstract SHA-2, while Sponges abstract SHA-3—two most widely used cryptographic hash functions. Thus, our work (including new notion of oracle-dependent entropy) could be used as theoretical justifications why these popular hash functions yield good *seedless* PRNGs (as well as online randomness extractors) even for a wide class of oracle-dependent entropy sources.

Moreover, for Merkle-Damgård based variants we also proved the security for the information-theoretic variant (the Sponge case is open, although we defined the variant which we conjecture is IT-secure). Our three computational proofs heavily use the "coefficient-H" technique [13,41], while our two information-theoretic proofs extend the framework of so-called "graph-counting" proofs [7,18,25] to bound the collision probability of iterated hash constructions. One novel challenge we had to solve here comes from the fact that the input source could depend on the list $\mathcal{L}$ of the ideal primitive queries, which breaks the "source-primitive" independence assumption crucially used in these already subtle proofs.

We also showed numeric examples of how we propose to use our constructions. Overall, we believe all of them are deployment ready, and we hope this work will start influencing future PRNG deployments, and will be incorporated into next RNG standards.

IMPLICATIONS TO STANDARD MODEL. To overcome the impossibility of seedless extraction, our entropy notion is defined relative to the ideal primitive P. As we argued in detail in Sect. 1.2, working in the idealized model seems somewhat inherent to our approach, provided we wish to avoid highly non-standard, and likely tautological, cryptographic assumptions about the CHF we are using in the standard model. Still, it is good to ask what one might expect from our extractor and PRNG constructions with real-world CHFs, such as those based on SHA-2, SHA-3, HKDF, etc. As we already mentioned, we believe these constructions are secure for real-world entropy sources, because our idealized notion of entropy informally corresponds to sources which have fresh entropy, even given all the hash function evaluations happening around the source. To state the counter-positive, we believe that any real-world attack against our constructions with existing hash functions will either require a highly artificial entropy source, or will find a surprising weakness in the corresponding CHF.

1.5 Other Related Work

We mention some important categories of related works, in particular with respect to seedless extraction, PRNGs, and their security.

SEEDED EXTRACTORS AND PRNGS. We already mentioned the extensive work on seeded extractors started by the seminal paper of Nisan and Zuckerman [39], and why they are problematic in our context. In the context of PRNGs, the first seeded PRNG notion was defined and constructed by Dodis et al. [19], who extended the prior "monolithic PRNG" definition of Barak and Halevi [1] (which did not explicitly talk about the seed, assuming the extraction module is "good enough" for the class of distributions produced by the entropy source). This line of work was extended in various ways by [21,26,29], where the latter two works were also analyzed in the random permutation model (in addition to the seed). However, none of these works considered a seedless setting for general entropy sources.

EXTRACTORS AND PRNGS IN IDEAL MODELS. Extractors and PRNGs were also studied in the ideal models by several works [9,18,43,49]. While not having explicit seeds, these works nevertheless modeled the *entropy source as being independent of the ideal primitive*. As we argued above, such oracle-independent modeling seems to be too restrictive for many realistic scenarios. Also, from a theory point of view, it effectively allows an exponentially long seed (the randomness used to sample the corresponding ideal primitive), making the positive results less interesting theoretically than the above-mentioned work on seeded extractors and PRNGs.

Indeed, the main motivation of all these papers was not to design theoretically optimal extractors and PRNGs, but to analyze the heuristic use of various cryptographic hash functions and popular modes of operations (such as CBC, HMAC, etc.) for randomness generation and extraction—a task these objects were not natively designed for. From this perspective, and given their widespread use, analyzing their extraction properties was an important first step in understanding their security, even under the restrictive oracle-independence assumption. Our work could be viewed as making a critical leap forward, by dropping—for the first time—the oracle-independence assumption, but instead carefully modeling what constitutes entropy in the much more realistic, oracle-dependent setting.

RESTRICTING THE CLASS OF ENTROPY SOURCES. This line of work has primarily focused on the question of extraction, by assuming that the source X has more structure beyond entropy. Early examples [10,14,16,37,47] include various bit-fixing and limited dependence sources, culminating with the question of extracting from several independent sources [2,11]. While mathematically very elegant, the types of sources studied by these works appear "too structured" to be realistic in the PRNGs scenario.

A different kind of restriction on the entropy source was studied by Barak et al. [3]. Rather than restrict sources by some property of their distribution, the work of [3] allows for arbitrary min-entropy sources, but assumes they come from an a-priori bounded number of distributions. While potentially promising for the setting of PRNGs, there are two disadvantages of the work of [3] as compared to this work. First, the work of [3] concentrated on the "monolithic" extraction setting, and did not address the question of entropy accumulation, where the entropy in X might come slowly from a large number of samples, and has to be accumulated into bounded state. In particular, it is unclear how to extend their constructions to address entropy accumulation with a fixed-length state. Second, the particular solutions offers by [3] used so called t-wise independent hash functions for a large values of t (at least as large as the overall source length). These functions are quite inefficient, and might not be fast enough for general purpose PRNGs.

We note that our work could also be viewed as overcoming impossibility of extraction by restricting the type of the source. However, we feel that our modeling is more natural for (and, thus, applicable to) the existing entropy sources, as used by the current PRNGs.

LOW-COMPLEXITY SAMPLERS. Introduced by Trevisan and Vadhan [46] and later extended by [33], here one assumes that the entropy source producing input X is unable to run the extractor/PRNG even once, thus making it impossible to do extractor-fixing. While this might be useful for situations where the entropy source is extremely simple, it is too restrictive for most applications, such as general purpose PRNG design studied in this work. In contrast, in this work the entropy source can easily run the extractor, but the legitimacy condition is defined in a way that doing the trivial extractor-fixing attack—by running the extractor—will result in a low-entropy, "illegitimate" source.

RANDOMNESS CONDENSERS. This approach, formalized by Dodis, Ristenpart and Vadhan [20], relaxes the security guarantees of the randomness extractor to only ensure that the output of the (seedless or "source-dependent-on-seed") condenser is almost full entropy, despite not being perfectly uniform. Indeed, this weaker security turns out to be sufficient for several applications, such as key derivation schemes for signature schemes. Unfortunately, if we want an extractor rather than a condenser—which is essential for general purpose PRNGs—this approach is not sufficient.

UCEs AND PUBLIC-SEED PSEUDORANDOMNESS. The notion of universal computational extractors (UCEs) [6], and its generalizations [45], study a complementary problem to the one studies here: how to extract from any entropy source which is only *computationally*-hard-to-predict, so it only has "computational entropy". On a positive, and similar to this work, when instantiated with constructions from an ideal primitive P, a UCE hash function yields a good extractor even if the inputs to it (the actual source) can be sampled depending on the ideal primitive. The issue, however, is that the current UCE notion inherently *requires a seed*, making in inapplicable for the PRNG scenario. An interesting direction for future research could be to extend our work to deal with computational entropy, by defining and constructing *seedless* UCEs in idealized models, and possibly extending them to full-blown seedless PRNGs for computational entropy.

2   Preliminaries

2.1   Statistical Distance and Min-Entropy

The *statistical distance* of two random variables X and Y is $\mathsf{SD}(X, Y) = \frac{1}{2} \sum_x |\mathsf{P}[X = x] - \mathsf{P}[Y = x]|$. The *prediction probability* of a random variable X is $\mathsf{Pred}(X) := \max_x \mathsf{P}[X = x]$, and we also denote $\mathsf{Pred}(X|y) := \max_x \mathsf{P}[X = x|Y = y]$. The conditional version of prediction probability is defined as

$$\mathsf{Pred}(X|Y) := \mathbf{E}_{y \leftarrow Y}\left[\mathsf{Pred}(X|y)\right].$$

The *(average-case) conditional min-entropy* is $\mathsf{H}_\infty(X|Y) = -\log(\mathsf{Pred}(X|Y))$.

2.2   Security Games

All of the security properties considered in this paper are captured by considering a game between a challenger and an attacker $\mathcal{A}$, both of which may have access to an ideal primitive P. The goal of the attacker is to guess a random bit b chosen by the challenger, who offers a set of oracles to the attacker to aid with this task. The *advantage* of $\mathcal{A}$ is defined as

$$2 \cdot \left| \mathsf{P}[\mathcal{A} \text{ wins}] - 1/2 \right|,$$

where the probability is over the randomness of $\mathcal{A}$, of the challenger, and of the ideal primitive. The cases where $b = 0$ and $b = 1$ are referred to as the *real world* and the *ideal world*, respectively. One may equivalently consider $\mathcal{A}$'s advantage at telling these two worlds apart, i.e.,

$$\left| \mathsf{P}[\mathcal{A} = 1|b = 0] - \mathsf{P}[\mathcal{A} = 1|b = 1] \right|.$$

3   Seedless Extraction

As a warm-up for full-fledged seedless PRNGs, this section considers the simpler property of *extraction*, i.e., producing uniformly random bits from weak high-entropy sources. Extraction can be seen as corresponding to the post-compromise security of PRNGs, and as such it will be implied by PRNG *robustness* (as defined in Sect. 4.2).

The definition of extraction security in Sect. 3.1 considers the entropy of the attacker's input to the extractor conditioned on the attackers *state* and the *queries* made to an ideal primitive P. A definition is provided for *computational* or *information-theoretic* security. IT extractors differ from computational ones in that the output of the extractor remains random even if the attacker, *after providing the input*, is given the entire function table of the underlying ideal primitive. That is, IT extractors achieve so-called *everlasting security* (cf. works in the hybrid bounded-storage model by Harnik and Naor [27]).

Section 3.2 considers extracting with a *monolithic random oracle*. The corresponding security proofs (for the computational and IT cases) are instructive for understanding the actual PRNG constructions provided in Sect. 5. Since considering a monolithic oracle is not motivated by any hash function used in practice, Sect. 3.3 introduces the concept of *online* extraction. An online extractor accumulates the entropy of its inputs in an internal state, from which uniform randomness can be produced. Finally, in order to illustrate the non-triviality of online extraction, Sect. 3.4 shows that extractors based on the popular CBC mode are not suitable for extraction.

3.1 Definition

In a model with idealized primitive P (chosen from some set $\mathcal{P}$), seedless extractors are algorithms $\mathsf{ext}^P : \mathcal{X} \to \mathcal{Y}$ with oracle access to P. The security definition for such extractors considers a two-stage attacker $\mathcal{A} = (\mathcal{A}_1, \mathcal{A}_2)$, where both parts have access to P. The first stage $\mathcal{A}_1$ outputs a value x and some state information σ for $\mathcal{A}_2$. The second stage takes an input $y \in \mathcal{Y}$ and outputs a single bit (i.e., it acts as a distinguisher).

For an attacker $\mathcal{A}$, denote by $\mathcal{L}_1$ and $\mathcal{L}_2$ the (random variables corresponding to) the lists of the P-queries made by $\mathcal{A}_1$ and $\mathcal{A}_2$, respectively.

Definition 1. *An attacker $\mathcal{A} = (\mathcal{A}_1, \mathcal{A}_2)$ is called a q-attacker if $|\mathcal{L}_1 \cup \mathcal{L}_2| \le q$ always; it is called a q-IT-attacker if $|\mathcal{L}_1| \le q$ always.*

That is, for IT-attackers the second stage $\mathcal{A}_2$ may make an arbitrary number of queries to P. Equivalently, $\mathcal{A}_2$ can be thought of as being given the entire function table of P.

The security game for seedless extractors in the P-model roughly requires that if the extractor is given a high-entropy input by $\mathcal{A}_1$, then $\mathcal{A}_2$ cannot tell the extractor output apart from a random value in $\mathcal{Y}$, even given the state information σ and access to P. Formally, it proceeds as follows:

1. The challenger chooses $b \leftarrow \{0,1\}$ and $P \leftarrow \mathcal{P}$ uniformly at random.
2. $\mathcal{A}_1$ gets access to P and produces $(\sigma, x) \leftarrow \mathcal{A}_1^P$.
3. The output of the extractor is computed as $y_0 \leftarrow \mathsf{ext}^P(x)$. Moreover, the challenger picks a value $y_1 \leftarrow \mathcal{Y}$ uniformly at random.
4. The second-stage attacker $\mathcal{A}_2$ is given σ and y_b and outputs a decision bit $b' \leftarrow \mathcal{A}_2^P(\sigma, y_b)$. The attacker wins if and only if $b' = b$.

The advantage of $\mathcal{A}$ in this extraction game is denoted by $\mathsf{Adv}_{\mathsf{ext}}^{\mathsf{ext},P}(\mathcal{A})$.

An attacker has to satisfy a legitimacy condition. Intuitively, this condition requires that the output X of $\mathcal{A}_1$ have high min-entropy even conditioned on the state information Σ and the list of queries $\mathcal{L}_1$.[8]

Definition 2. *An attacker $\mathcal{A} = (\mathcal{A}_1, \mathcal{A}_2)$ is said to be γ^*-legitimate if, in the extraction game above,*

$$\mathrm{H}_\infty(X | \Sigma \mathcal{L}_1) \ge \gamma^* .$$

---

[8] Note, in the extraction game the definition of $\mathcal{L}_1$ is the same in the real and the ideal worlds. For our future definitions of PRNGs, however, it will be important that the notion of legitimacy is defined in the ideal world (i.e., conditioned on $b = 1$).

The above finally leads to the following definition of seedless extractor in the P-model:

Definition 3. *An algorithm* $\mathsf{ext}^P : \mathcal{X} \to \mathcal{Y}$ *with oracle access to P is an $(\gamma^*, q, \varepsilon)$-(IT-)extractor in the P-model if for every γ^*-legitimate q-(IT-)attacker $\mathcal{A}$,*

$$\mathrm{Adv}_{\mathsf{ext}}^{\mathsf{ext}, P}(\mathcal{A}) \leq \varepsilon .$$

3.2   Seedless Extraction with a Monolithic Random Oracle

For instructive purposes it is useful to consider monolithic extraction, i.e., the case where the ideal primitive P itself is used as an extractor. To exemplify this, assume P is a random oracle, i.e., a function $G : \{0,1\}^m \to \{0,1\}^n$ chosen uniformly at random. Then, the monolithic extractor is defined as follows:

Construction 1 (Monolithic extractor). *The monolithic seedless extractor* $\mathsf{mono}^G : \{0,1\}^m \to \{0,1\}^n$ *using a random oracle* $G : \{0,1\}^m \to \{0,1\}^n$ *is defined by*

$$\mathsf{mono}^G(x) := G(x) .$$

Theorem 1 (Monolithic seedless extraction).   *Construction* mono *is a $(\gamma^*, q, \varepsilon)$-extractor in the G-model for*

$$\varepsilon \leq \frac{q}{2^{\gamma^*}} .$$

The proof of Theorem 1 is a straight-forward application of the H-coefficient technique. The idea is to first show that unless $\mathcal{A}_1$ or $\mathcal{A}_2$ queries the input x provided by $\mathcal{A}_1$, the real and ideal worlds (i.e., the cases where $b = 0$ and $b = 1$, respectively) are indistinguishable. That is, the corresponding ratio of transcript probabilities is 1. Transcripts where x is in the query list are defined to be *bad* transcripts, and the second part of the proof shows that bad transcripts are unlikely to occur due to the legitimacy of $\mathcal{A}$. The latter proof crucially relies on the fact that the H-coefficient technique enables performing the bad-event analysis in the *ideal* world. The proof of the following theorem is deferred and can be found in the full version.

Theorem 2 (Monolithic seedless IT-extraction).   *Construction* mono *is a $(\gamma^*, q, \varepsilon)$-IT-extractor in the G-model for*

$$\varepsilon \leq \frac{1}{2}\sqrt{\frac{2^{-(\gamma^* - n)}}{1 - \rho}} + \rho ,$$

where $\rho = q/2^{\gamma^*}$.

The proof of Theorem 2 proceeds by bounding the statistical distance of $\mathcal{A}_2$'s views in the real and ideal experiments via the corresponding collision probabilities (as done in the proof of the left-over hash lemma). In the proofs of the actual PRNG constructions in the following sections, bounding said collision probabilities constitutes the bulk of the proof and is quite involved. The formal proof is deferred and can be found in the full version.

PARAMETER CHOICES. In terms of concrete parameters, observe the following for the constructions towards monolithic seedless extraction from above:

- *Computational:* If we let $n = 512$ and $q = 2^{80}$. We would need $\gamma^* \approx 160$ to get 80 bits of security.
- *Information Theoretic:* We let $n = 512$. We also approximate $1/(1 - \rho) \leq 2$, very generously Then, if we set for example $q = 2^{80}$. We would need the entropy loss, i.e., $\gamma^* = 160$ for 80 bits of security.

3.3 Online Extraction

An "accumulating" extractor ext satisfies the same security Definition 3, but its syntax can be thought of as two algorithms ext = (refresh, finalize), where refresh accumulates entropy in an internal state and finalize produces the extractor output from the current state.

Definition 4. *An* online extractor construction *consists of two algorithms* ext = (refresh, finalize), *where*

- refresh *takes a state* s *and an input* $x \in \{0,1\}^m$ *and produces a new state* $s' \leftarrow \text{refresh}^P(s, x)$, *and*
- finalize *takes a state* s *and produces an output* $y \in \{0,1\}^r$, *i.e.,* $y \leftarrow \text{finalize}^P(s)$.

An online extractor processing m-bit inputs and producing r-bit output is called a (m, r)-online extractor.

The security definition for online extractors additionally considers the number ℓ of times refresh is called by the attacker, i.e., it considers (q, ℓ)-attackers.

Definition 5. *An algorithm* $\text{ext}^P : \mathcal{X} \rightarrow \mathcal{Y}$ *defined by two algorithms* ext = (refresh, finalize) *with oracle access to P is an $(\gamma^*, q, \ell, \varepsilon)$-(IT-)online extractor in the P-model if for every γ^*-legitimate (q, ℓ)-(IT-)attacker $\mathcal{A}$,*

$$\text{Adv}_{\text{ext}}^{\text{ext}, P}(\mathcal{A}) \leq \varepsilon .$$

Online extractors can be built just like the PRNG constructions in Sect. 5, and, in fact, the corresponding security results follow as a special case of PRNG security. Correspondingly, their treatment is deferred until Sect. 5, where such online extractors (and, in fact, full-fledged PRNGs) can be obtained from Merkle-Damgård with a random compression function, from Merkle-Damgård with the

Davies-Meyer compression function, and from Sponges. For the reader's convenience, the full version of this paper [17] contains the online extractor constructions along with the security bounds—for applications where extraction is sufficient.

In contrast to Merkle-Damgård and Sponges, as shown in the next section, using the CBC paradigm (which can be thought of as an "extreme sponge") will not lead to a secure online extractor.

3.4 CBC-Based Extractors Are Insecure

A natural candidate for an online seedless extractor is using a permutation in CBC mode. A CBC-based extractor construction uses a permutation $\pi :\{0,1\}^n \to \{0,1\}^n$ to absorb n-bit inputs. Its refresh function is defined as

$$\mathsf{refresh}^\pi(s,x) \;=\; \pi(s \oplus x) \;.$$

However, it turns out that this approach does not lead to a secure extractor. This section presents a simple attack against CBC-based extractors. The attack works irrespective of how the finalization function is defined.

Theorem 3 (Attack against CBC Extractors). *Let* refresh *as defined above. There exists an ℓ-legitimate q-attacker $\mathcal{A}$ with black-box access to a function* finalize, *such that for all* CBC = (refresh, finalize)

$$\mathrm{Adv}_{\mathsf{CBC}}^{\mathrm{ext},\pi}(\mathcal{A}) \;=\; 1 - 2^{-(r-1)} \;,$$

where r is the output length of the extractor, $q = 2\ell + 2\alpha$, and α is the query complexity of finalize.

The idea of the attack is to have the attacker create the ith input block as either $\pi^i(0^n) \oplus \pi^i(1^n)$ or 0, each with probability $1/2$.[9] After ℓ such steps, the attacker will have provided ℓ bits of entropy (even conditioned on its π-queries), but only a single bit will have accumulated in the state, which will be $\pi^i(0^n)$ or $\pi^i(1^n)$, each with probability $1/2$.

The proof can be found in the full version of this paper [17].

4 Pseudorandom Number Generators with Input

A *pseudorandom number generator with input (PRNG)* is a stateful cryptographic primitive. It gradually accumulates entropy in its state by absorbing inputs and can be used to output pseudorandom bits once the entropy of the state is sufficiently high. Moreover, it is both forward and backward secure, i.e., past outputs remain random upon future state compromise, and, by absorbing sufficient amounts of entropy, a PRNG can recover from state compromise.

---

[9] Here, π^i denotes the i-fold application of π.

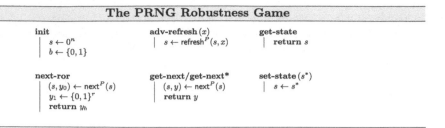

Fig. 1. Oracles for the PRNG robustness game.

This section introduces a novel security definition for PRNGs that differs from previous notions in several crucial ways. Specifically, a comparison to the original *robustness* notion by Dodis et al. [19], based on work by Barak and Halevi [1], as well as to an adaptation of it by Gaži and Tessaro [26] for idealized models is provided in the full version which is available on ePrint.

This paper considers two notions of PRNGs: computational PRNGs and information-theoretically secure (IT) PRNGs. IT PRNGs differ from computational PRNGs in that once the attacker stops interacting with the PRNG, the output of the PRNG remains random even if the attacker is given the entire function table of the underlying ideal primitive. That is, IT PRNGs achieve so-called *everlasting security* (cf. works in the hybrid bounded-storage model by Harnik and Naor [27]). This distinction is analogous to that between seedless extractors and IT seedless extractors (cf. Sect. 3).

4.1 Syntax

A PRNG consists of two algorithms: one for absorbing new inputs and one for producing pseudorandom outputs. Formally, it is defined as follows:

Definition 6 (Syntax of PRNGs). *A pseudorandom number generator with input (PRNG) is a pair of algorithms* PRNG = (refresh, next) *having access to an ideal primitive P and sharing an n-bit state s, where*

- refresh *takes a state s and an input* $x \in \{0,1\}^m$ *and produces a new state* $s' \leftarrow \text{refresh}^P(s, x)$, *and*
- next *takes a state s and produces a new state and an output* $y \in \{0,1\}^r$, *i.e.,* $(s', y) \leftarrow \text{next}^P(s)$.

A PRNG processing m-bit inputs and producing r-bit output is called a (m, r)-PRNG.

4.2 Security Game

ROBUSTNESS GAME. PRNGs are expected to satisfy the so-called *robustness* property, which captures the properties discussed at the beginning of Sect. 4. The corresponding security game is depicted in Fig. 1. The game initially chooses a random bit b and initializes the state of the PRNG to 0^n. Subsequently, it offers the following oracles to $\mathcal{A}$:

- **adv-refresh**(x) calls the refresh procedure to absorb $x \in \{0,1\}^n$ into the internal state of the PRNG;
- **get-next** and **get-next*** allow the attacker to get pseudorandom outputs by calling the next procedure on the current state and returning the output y. The difference between the two oracles is that **get-next** is supposed to be called only when the state has high entropy, whereas **get-next*** can be called *prematurely*, i.e., before the state has absorbed enough randomness for the next function to output pseudorandom values (cf. definition of legitimate attackers below).
- **next-ror** works like the **get-next**-oracle, except that it creates a challenge, i.e., if $b = 1$, it outputs a uniform random value $y_1 \in \{0,1\}^r$ instead of the PRNG output y_0.
- **get-state** and **set-state** model state compromises by letting the attacker learn the current state or set it to an arbitrary value, respectively.

The advantage of $\mathcal{A}$ in the robustness game is denoted by $\mathrm{Adv}_{\mathsf{PRNG}}^{\mathrm{rob},P}(\mathcal{A})$.

CANONICAL ATTACKERS. It will be useful to define to following notion of canonical attackers: Consider the interaction of an attacker $\mathcal{A}$ with the robustness game. The following events are called *entropy drains*:

- the beginning of the game,
- calls to **get-state** or **set-state**, and
- calls to **get-next***.

In other words, entropy drains are the events that cause the PRNG state to lose its entropy, which includes premature calls to next. An attacker $\mathcal{A}$ is said to be *canonical* if it does not make **get-next*** queries nor the following query pattern: an entropy drain followed by one or more **adv-refresh** queries, followed by a **get-state** query.

Considering canonical attackers only is without loss of generality. This is because the above sequence of queries can be simulated by the attacker by making a **get-state** query right away and computing the output of **get-state** or **get-next*** itself. In particular, for every attacker $\mathcal{A}$, there exists a canonical attacker $\mathcal{A}$ with the same advantage. All attackers in the remainder of this work are therefore assumed to be canonical.

LEGITIMATE ATTACKERS. In order to obtain a sensible definition devoid of trivial attacks, attackers must satisfy a "legitimacy" condition. The condition roughly requires that an attacker only ask for challenges when it has sufficient amount of uncertainty about the PRNG's internal state.

Towards formalizing the legitimacy condition, consider the interaction of $\mathcal{A}$ with a *variant* of the robustness game defined as follows: Whenever oracles **next-ror** or **get-next** are called, instead of evaluating next, the game simply uses two uniformly random and independent values (s, y) as the output of next.

Observe that this variant of the robustness game, called the *legitimacy game* corresponds to an interaction between $\mathcal{A}$ and an *ideal* PRNG, which produces perfect randomness. Moreover, the legitimacy game is *construction-independent*.

In the legitimacy game, define now the following random variables immediately before $\mathcal{A}$ makes the ith call to oracle **get-next** or **next-ror**:

- $\mathcal{L}_i$: the list of P-queries by $\mathcal{A}$ and the corresponding answers;
- Σ_i: the state of $\mathcal{A}$;
- $\overline{X}_i$: vector of inputs provided by $\mathcal{A}$ since the *the most recent entropy drain (MRED)*; and
- S_i: the state of the PRNG immediately after the MRED.

The legitimacy condition requires that $\mathcal{A}$ provide inputs that have high min-entropy even conditioned on its current state, the queries so far, and the state of the PRNG after the MRED.

Definition 7 (Legitimate attackers). *An attacker $\mathcal{A}$ is said to be γ^*-legitimate if for all i,*
$$\mathrm{H}_\infty(\overline{X}_i | \Sigma_i \mathcal{L}_i S_i) \geq \gamma^* ,$$
where MREDs are defined as above.

In order to capture IT-legitimate attackers (against IT PRNGs), the set of entropy drains is extended to include

- calls to **get-next** and **next-ror**.

With this definition of MRED and notation analogous to that in the previous definition, IT-legitimate attackers are defined as follows:

Definition 8 (Legitimate IT attackers). *An attacker $\mathcal{A}$ is said to be γ^*-IT-legitimate if for all i,*
$$\mathrm{H}_\infty(\overline{X}_i | \Sigma_i \mathcal{L}_i S_i) \geq \gamma^* ,$$
w.r.t. the extended definition of MRED.

ROBUST PRNGS. We are now ready to quantify the efficiency of attacker $\mathcal{A}$, and to define our final notion of PRNG robustness.

Definition 9 (Attacker efficiency). *An attacker is called a (q, t, ℓ)-attacker if*

- *q is the maximum number of P-queries it makes,*
- *ℓ is the maximum number of **adv-refresh** calls between any entropy drain and successive call to either **next-ror** or **get-next**, and*
- *t is the maximum total number of calls to any oracle in the robustness game other than **adv-refresh**.*

An attacker is called a (q, t, ℓ)-IT-attacker if it satisfies the above conditions but makes an arbitrary number of queries to P after the interaction with the challenger ends.

Definition 10 (Robustness of PRNGs). *A PRNG construction* PRNG = (refresh, next) *with oracle access an ideal primitive P is* $(\gamma^*, q, t, \ell, \varepsilon)$ *-(IT-)robust in the P-model if for every* γ^**-(IT-)legitimate* (q, t, ℓ)*-(IT-)attacker,*

$$\mathrm{Adv}_{\mathsf{PRNG}}^{\mathrm{rob}, P}(\mathcal{A}) \leq \varepsilon .$$

Observe that online extractors (cf. Definition 4) are a special case of robust PRNGs. In terms of construction, the PRNG next algorithm can be replaced by finalize, which simply discards the state output by next. If then the PRNG robustness game is relaxed such that the only queries the attacker can make are (a) arbitrarily many queries to **adv-refresh** followed by (b) $t = 1$ query to **next-ror**, one obtains a notion equivalent to Definition 3.

5 Constructions of PRNGs

This section presents three simple, intuitive, and—most importantly—practical PRNG constructions:

- a construction based on the *Merkle-Damgård paradigm* using a public *fixed-length compression function*;
- a construction based on the *Merkle-Damgård paradigm* using the *Davies-Meyer compression function* (as in SHA-2), which is built from any public block cipher; and
- a construction based on the *Sponge paradigm* (as in SHA-3), which uses a public permutation.

For each paradigm, there are in fact two constructions: one achieving normal, computational PRNG security and one achieving information-theoretic (IT) security. The security analyses of these constructions can be found in the full version of this paper, available online.

5.1 PRNGs from Merkle-Damgård

A PRNG can be obtained from a compression function F as follows (cf. Fig. 2):[10]

Construction 2 (PRNG from Merkle-Damgård). *The* (m, r)*-PRNG construction* MD = (refresh, next) *based on Merkle-Damgård with a compression function* $F : \{0, 1\}^n \times \{0, 1\}^m \to \{0, 1\}^n$ *is defined as follows:*[11]

- $\mathsf{refresh}^F(s, x) = F(s, x)$, *and*
- $\mathsf{next}^F(s) = (F(s, 0), F(s, 1) \| \cdots \| F(s, r/n))$.

---

[10] To reduce notational clutter, the algorithms refresh and next of the PRNG constructions are not "branded" with the design name. There will be no ambiguity as to which construction is meant in any place in this paper.

[11] The integer arguments to the compression function are to be naturally mapped to $\{0, 1\}^n$.

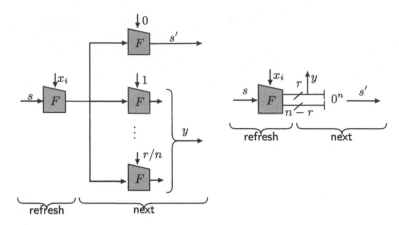

Fig. 2. Procedures refresh (processing a single-block input x_i) and next of Merkle-Damgård PRNG constructions with compression function F. Left: Computationally secure Construction 2; right: IT secure Construction 3.

The security of Construction 2 is proved in the F-model, where F is a uniformly random function.

Theorem 4 (Robustness of Merkle-Damgård PRNGs). *Construction 2 is a $(\gamma^*, q, t, \ell, \varepsilon_{\mathrm{rob}})$-robust PRNG in the F-model for*

$$\varepsilon_{\mathrm{rob}} \leq 2t \cdot \left(\frac{\tilde{q}^2 + \tilde{q}\ell + \ell^2}{2^n} + \frac{\tilde{q}}{2^{\gamma^*}} \right),$$

where $\tilde{q} = q + r/n + 1$.

An IT-robust PRNG based on Merkle-Damgård can be obtained if the next function simply outputs the truncated state (and outputs 0^n as the new state):

Construction 3 (IT-PRNG from Merkle-Damgård). *The (m, r)-PRNG construction $\mathsf{MD}_r = (\mathsf{refresh}, \mathsf{next})$ based on Merkle-Damgård with a compression function $F : \{0,1\}^n \times \{0,1\}^m \to \{0,1\}^n$ is defined as follows:*

- *$\mathsf{refresh}^F(s, x) = F(s, x)$, and*
- *$\mathsf{next}^F(s) = (0^n, s[1..r])$.*

The security of Construction 3 is proved in the F-model, where F is a uniformly random function. To state the theorem for the IT construction, for an integer ℓ, let

$$d'(\ell) = \max_{\ell' \in \{1, \ldots, \ell\}} |\{d \in \mathbb{N} : d|\ell'\}|.$$

Observe that, asymptotically, $d'(\ell)$ grows very slowly, i.e., as $\ell^{o(1)}$. Furthermore, let F be a random compression function.

Theorem 5 (IT-Robustness of Merkle-Damgård PRNGs). *Construction 3 is a $(\gamma^*, q, t, \ell, \varepsilon_{\mathrm{rob}})$-IT-robust PRNG in the F-model, where*

$$\varepsilon_{\mathrm{rob\text{-}it}} \leq \frac{t}{2}\sqrt{\frac{2^{r-\gamma^*}}{(1-\rho)} + \ell \cdot d'(\ell) \cdot \frac{2^r}{2^n} + 64\ell^4 \cdot \frac{2^r}{2^{2n}} + 16\ell^2 \cdot \frac{\tilde{q}^2 2^r}{2^{2n}}} + t\rho \ ,$$

for $\rho = \frac{\tilde{q}^2}{2^r}$ where $\tilde{q} = q + t\ell$.

PARAMETER CHOICES. In terms of concrete parameters, observe the following for the Merkle-Damgård constructions above:

– *Computational PRNG:* If one were to use SHA-512 as compression function with $n = 512$, and, moreover, choose $r = n$. We let $t = 1, q = 2^{80}$ and let $\gamma^* = \ell$. This assumes that we get at least one bit of entropy from each block. We would need $\gamma^* \approx 160$ to get 80 bits of security.
– *IT PRNG:* For example, assume SHA-512's compression function is used, i.e., $n = 512$. If we let $r = 256$, then we get (we also approximate $1/(1 - \rho) \leq 2$, very generously)

$$\varepsilon_{\mathrm{rob\text{-}it}} \leq \frac{t}{2}\sqrt{2^{257-\gamma^*} + \frac{\ell \cdot d'(\ell)}{2^{256}}} + t\frac{q^2}{2^{256}} \ ,$$

We let $\ell = \gamma^*$. Then, if we set for example $q = 2^{80}$. We would need the entropy loss, i.e., $\gamma^* - r = 162$ for 80 bits of security.

5.2 PRNGs from Merkle-Damgård with Davies-Meyer

The Davies-Meyer compression function maps two inputs $a \in \{0,1\}^m$ and $b \in \{0,1\}^n$ to an n-bit string

$$E(b, a) \oplus a \ ,$$

where E is an arbitrary block cipher (where b is the key and a the input).[12] Correspondingly, a PRNG can be obtained from E as follows (cf. Fig. 3):

Construction 4 (PRNG from MD-DM). *The (n, r)-PRNG construction DM = (refresh, next) based on Merkle-Damgård with Davies-Meyer (MD-DM) uses a cipher $E : \{0,1\}^k \times \{0,1\}^n \to \{0,1\}^n$ and is defined as follows:[13]*

– refresh$^E(s, x) = E(x, s) \oplus s$, *and*
– next$^E(s) = (E(0, s) \oplus s, E(1, s) \oplus s \| \cdots \| E(r/n, s) \oplus s)$.

The security of Construction 4 is proved in the E-model, where E is a cipher chosen uniformly at random from the set of all ciphers and can be queried in both the forward and backward direction.

---

[12] A (block) cipher is an efficiently computable and invertible permutation $E(k, \cdot) : \{0,1\}^n \to \{0,1\}^n$ for every key $k \in \{0,1\}^n$.
[13] The integer arguments to the cipher are to be naturally mapped to $\{0,1\}^n$.

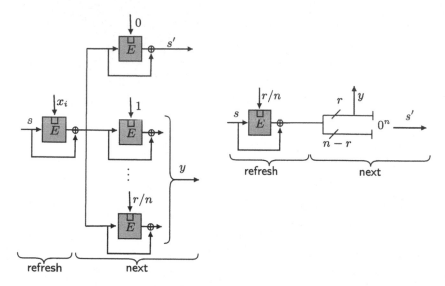

Fig. 3. Procedures refresh (processing a single-block input x_i) and next of Merkle-Damgård PRNG constructions with the Davies-Meyer compression function based on a block cipher E. Left: Computationally secure Construction 4; right: IT secure Construction 5.

Theorem 6 (Robustness of MD-DM PRNGs). *Construction 4 is a* $(\gamma^*, q, t, \ell, \varepsilon_{\text{rob}})$-*robust PRNG in the E-model for*

$$\varepsilon_{\text{rob}} \leq 4t \cdot \left(\frac{\tilde{q}^2 + \tilde{q}\ell + \ell^2}{2^n} + \frac{\tilde{q}}{2^{\gamma^*}} \right),$$

where $\tilde{q} = q + r/n + 1$.

In the IT-secure variant of the MD-DM construction, refresh remains the same, but next will truncate the input state to r bits, which it outputs, and then zero out the state.

Construction 5 (IT-PRNG from MD-DM). *The* (n, r)-*PRNG construction* $\mathsf{DM}_r = (\mathsf{refresh}, \mathsf{next})$ *using Merkle-Damgård with Davies-Meyer (MD-DM) uses a block cipher* $E : \{0,1\}^k \times \{0,1\}^n \to \{0,1\}^n$ *and is defined as follows:*

- refresh$^E(s, x) = E(x, s) \oplus s$, *and*
- next$^E(s) = (0^n, s[1..r])$.

The security of Construction 5 is proved in the E-model, where E is a cipher chosen uniformly at random from the set of all ciphers and can be queried in both the forward and backward direction. Let $d'(\ell)$ be defined as in Sect. 5.1.

Theorem 7 (IT-Robustness of MD-DM PRNGs). *Construction 5 is a* $(\gamma^*, q, t, \ell, \varepsilon_{\text{rob}})$*-IT-robust PRNG in the E-model, where*

$$\varepsilon_{\text{rob-it}} \leq \frac{t}{2}\sqrt{\frac{2^{r-\gamma^*}}{(1-\rho)} + \ell \cdot d'(\ell)\frac{2^r}{2^{n-1}} + 64\ell^4 \cdot \frac{2^r}{2^{2n-2}} + 16\ell^2\tilde{q}^2 \cdot \frac{2^r}{2^{2n-2}}} + t\rho ,$$

for $\rho = \frac{\tilde{q}^2}{2^r}$ *where* $\tilde{q} = q + t\ell$.

PARAMETER CHOICES. In terms of concrete parameters, observe the following for the PRNG constructions from Merkle-Damgård with Davies-Meyer above:

- *Computational PRNG:* SHA-512 is a 512-bit block cipher algorithm that encrypts 512 bit hash value using the input as key. Therefore, we let $n = 512$ and set $r = n$. We let $t = 1, q = 2^{80}$ and let $\ell = \gamma^*$. This assumes that we get at least one bit of entropy from each block. We would need $\gamma^* \approx 163$ to get 80 bits of security.
- *IT PRNG:* We again let $n = 512$. If we let $r = 256$, then we get (we also approximate $1/(1-\rho) \leq 2$, very generously)

$$\varepsilon_{\text{rob-it}} \leq \frac{t}{2}\sqrt{2^{129-\gamma^*} + \frac{\ell \cdot d'(\ell)}{2^{127}} + t\frac{q^2}{2^{128}}} ,$$

We let $\ell = \gamma^*$. Then, if we set for example $q = 2^{80}$. We would need the entropy loss, i.e., $\gamma^* - r = 162$ for 80 bits of security.

5.3 PRNGs from Sponges

Let $n \in \mathbb{N}$ and $n = r + c$. In the following, for an n-bit string s, let $s = s^{(r)}\|s^{(c)}$ be decomposition of s into an r-bit and c-bit string. A PRNG using the Sponge paradigm can be obtained from a permutation π as follows (cf. Fig. 4):

Construction 6 (PRNG from Sponges). *The Sponge-based PRNG construction* Spg $= (\text{refresh}, \text{next})$ *uses a permutation* $\pi : \{0,1\}^n \rightarrow \{0,1\}^n$ *to absorb and produce* r*-bit inputs and outputs, respectively, and is defined as follows:*

- $\text{refresh}^\pi(s, x) = \pi(s \oplus x\|0^c)$, *and*
- $\text{next}^\pi(s) = (\pi(s) \oplus 0^r\|s^{(c)}, s^{(r)})$.

The next function design is due to Hutchinson [28], who simplified a proposal by Gaži and Tessaro [26]. Recall that the Merkle-Damgård constructions have a "parallel" next function in order to produce r/n blocks of random output with $r/n+1$ calls to the ideal primitive, where the additional call is used to produce a new state. Were it not for this optimization, on order to obtain r bits of output, one would have to apply the next function r/n times in a row, which would results in twice the number of ideal-primitive calls.

The next function for Sponges, on the other hand, only makes a single call to the ideal primitive to produce both a new state and the random output. Therefore, no parallel next function is provided for the Sponge-based PRNG.

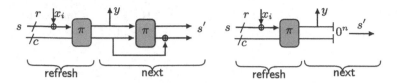

Fig. 4. Procedures refresh (processing a single-block input x_i) and next of Merkle-Damgård PRNG constructions with compression function F. Left: Computationally secure Construction 2; right: IT candidate Construction 3.

The security of Construction 6 is proved in the π-model, where π is a uniformly random permutation, which can be queried in both the forward and backward direction.

Theorem 8 (Robustness of Sponge PRNGs). *Construction 6 is a* $(\gamma^*, q, t, \ell, \varepsilon_{\mathrm{rob}})$*-robust PRNG in the π-model for*

$$
\varepsilon_{\mathrm{rob}} \leq 4t \cdot \left(\frac{\tilde{q}^2 + \tilde{q}\ell + \ell^2}{2^n} + \frac{\tilde{q}}{2^{\gamma^*}} + \frac{\tilde{q}^2}{2^c} \right),
$$

where $\tilde{q} = q + r/n + 1$.

Observe that the bound in Theorem 8 is only reasonable when c is large enough, which matches the fact that CBC-based PRNGs—which correspond to the case $c = 0$, are not secure.

In the IT variant of the Sponge construction, refresh remains the same, but next will truncate the input state to r bits, which it outputs, and then zero out the state.

Construction 7 (IT-PRNG from Sponges). *The Sponge-based PRNG construction* $\mathsf{Spg}_r = (\mathsf{refresh}, \mathsf{next})$ *uses a permutation* $\pi : \{0,1\}^n \to \{0,1\}^n$ *to absorb and produce r-bit inputs and outputs, respectively, and is defined as follows:*

- $\mathsf{refresh}^\pi(s, x) = \pi(s \oplus x \| 0^c)$, *and*
- $\mathsf{next}^\pi(s) = (0^n, s[1..r])$.

Theorem 9 (IT-Robustness of Sponge PRNGs). *Construction 7 is a* $(\gamma^*, q, t, \ell, \varepsilon_{\mathrm{rob}})$*-IT-robust PRNG in the π-model for*

$$
\varepsilon_{\mathrm{rob\text{-}it}} \leq \frac{t}{2} \sqrt{\frac{2^{r-\gamma^*}}{(1-\rho)} + \frac{\ell \cdot (\ell + \tilde{q})}{2^{c-1}}} + t\rho ,
$$

for $\rho = \frac{\tilde{q}^2}{2^c}$ *where* $\tilde{q} = q + t\ell$.

PARAMETER CHOICES. In terms of concrete parameters, observe the following for the PRNG constructions from Sponges above: above:

- *Computational PRNG:* SHA-3 like parameters have $n = 1600$ and $c = 1024$. We let $t = 1, q = 2^{80}$ and let $\ell = \gamma^*$. This assumes that we get at least one bit of entropy from each block. We would need $\gamma^* \approx 163$ to get 80 bits of security.
- *IT PRNG:* We let $n = 1600$ and $c = 1024$. In addition, we let $t = 1$ and $q = 2^{80}$. We also let $\ell = \gamma^*$. Therefore, we incur an entropy loss of 160 bits to get 80 bits of security.

6   Overview of Our Techniques

Due to paucity of space we defer the proofs of the various constructions to the appendix. Due to paucity of space, the proofs have been deferred to the full version of the paper which is now available on ePrint [17]. The proofs appear in separate sections for the computational PRNG constructions and the IT constructions. In this section we give a brief overview of our techniques.

COMPUTATIONAL PRNGs PROVING TECHNIQUES. The main technique we use in all the proofs is the "H-Coefficient" technique. In addition, it is instructive to view the robustness game through the lens of simpler intermediate security notions. We define two properties - *recovering* and *preserving*. The former requires that the PRNG, after accumulating enough entropy after a drain, has the output of the next function looking random. The latter defines the property that when the start state is random, even after absorbing adversarially controlled inputs, the output of next is still random. A formal proof showing how they generically imply robustness can be found in the full version.

Further, we define the ideas of *extraction security, maintaining security* and *next security*. The first of the three requires that the *state* of the PRNG is indistinguishable from random when sufficient entropy has been absorbed. Maintaining security requires that the PRNG *state* is indistinguishable from random even in the face of adversarially chosen inputs, provided the initial state itself was random. Next security requires that the output of next is indistinguishable from random if the input itself was random. It is easy to see how these ideas would imply the larger properties of recovering and preserving.

IT PRNGs PROVING TECHNIQUES. The crux of our proofs is the idea of reducing the robustness game to online extraction. We then employ a graph counting argument to bound the collision probability. The bound for the collision probability is then used to compute an upper bound for the statistical distance of our distribution from uniform. To this end, we use three propositions to achieve the final bound. Indeed, similar to the intermediate security notion for robustness of computational PRNGs, we define a notion of *recovering security*. This requires that, after an entropy drain, the IT-PRNG can accumulate enough entropy thereby making the output of next indistinguishable from $(0^n, U_r)$. It is easy to see that this constraint is a relaxation of the requirement posed by its computational counterpart.

References

1. Barak, B., Halevi, S.: A model and architecture for pseudo-random generation with applications to /dev/random. In: Atluri, V., Meadows, C., Juels, A. (eds.) ACM CCS 2005, Alexandria, Virginia, USA, 7–11 November 2005, pp. 203–212. ACM Press (2005)
2. Barak, B., Impagliazzo, R., Wigderson, A.: Extracting randomness using few independent sources. In: 45th FOCS, Rome, Italy, 17–19 October 2004, pp. 384–393. IEEE Computer Society Press (2004)
3. Barak, B., Shaltiel, R., Tromer, E.: True random number generators secure in a changing environment. In: Walter, C.D., Koç, Ç.K., Paar, C. (eds.) CHES 2003. LNCS, vol. 2779, pp. 166–180. Springer, Heidelberg (2003). https://doi.org/10.1007/978-3-540-45238-6_14
4. Barker, E., Kelsey, J.: NIST Special Publication 800–90A (A revision of SP 800–90) Recommendation for random number generation using deterministic random bit generators (2012). https://csrc.nist.gov/publications/detail/sp/800-90a/rev-1/final
5. Barker, E., Kelsey, J.: Recommendation for random number generation using deterministic random bit generators. NIST Special Publication 800–90A (2012)
6. Bellare, M., Hoang, V.T., Keelveedhi, S.: Instantiating random oracles via UCEs. In: Canetti, R., Garay, J.A. (eds.) CRYPTO 2013, Part II. LNCS, vol. 8043, pp. 398–415. Springer, Heidelberg (2013). https://doi.org/10.1007/978-3-642-40084-1_23
7. Bellare, M., Pietrzak, K., Rogaway, P.: Improved security analyses for CBC MACs. In: Shoup, V. (ed.) CRYPTO 2005. LNCS, vol. 3621, pp. 527–545. Springer, Heidelberg (2005). https://doi.org/10.1007/11535218_32
8. Bertoni, G., Daemen, J., Peeters, M., Van Assche, G.: On the indifferentiability of the sponge construction. In: Smart, N. (ed.) EUROCRYPT 2008. LNCS, vol. 4965, pp. 181–197. Springer, Heidelberg (2008). https://doi.org/10.1007/978-3-540-78967-3_11
9. Bertoni, G., Daemen, J., Peeters, M., Van Assche, G.: Sponge-based pseudo-random number generators. In: Mangard, S., Standaert, F.-X. (eds.) CHES 2010. LNCS, vol. 6225, pp. 33–47. Springer, Heidelberg (2010). https://doi.org/10.1007/978-3-642-15031-9_3
10. Blum, M.: Independent unbiased coin flips from a correlated biased source-a finite stae Markov chain. Combinatorica 6(2), 97–108 (1986)
11. Chattopadhyay, E., Zuckerman, D.: Explicit two-source extractors and resilient functions. In: Wichs, D., Mansour, Y. (eds.) 48th ACM STOC, Cambridge, MA, USA, 18–21 June 2016, pp. 670–683. ACM Press (2016)
12. Checkoway, S., et al.: On the practical exploitability of dual EC in TLS implementations. In: Proceedings of the 23rd USENIX Security Symposium, San Diego, CA, USA, 20–22 August 2014, pp. 319–335 (2014)
13. Chen, S., Steinberger, J.: Tight security bounds for key-alternating ciphers. In: Nguyen, P.Q., Oswald, E. (eds.) EUROCRYPT 2014. LNCS, vol. 8441, pp. 327–350. Springer, Heidelberg (2014). https://doi.org/10.1007/978-3-642-55220-5_19
14. Chor, B., Goldreich, O.: Unbiased bits from sources of weak randomness and probabilistic communication complexity (extended abstract). In: 26th FOCS, Portland, Oregon, 21–23 October 1985, pp. 429–442. IEEE Computer Society Press (1985)
15. Chor, B., Goldreich, O.: Unbiased bits from sources of weak randomness and probabilistic communication complexity. SIAM J. Comput. 17(2), 230–261 (1988)

16. Chor, B., Goldreich, O., Håstad, J., Friedman, J., Rudich, S., Smolensky, R.: The bit extraction problem of t-resilient functions (preliminary version). In: 26th FOCS, Portland, Oregon, 21–23 October 1985, pp. 396–407. IEEE Computer Society Press (1985)
17. Coretti, S., Dodis, Y., Karthikeyan, H., Tessaro, S.: Seedless fruit is the sweetest: random number generation, revisited. Cryptology ePrint Archive, Report 2019/198 (2019). https://eprint.iacr.org/2019/198
18. Dodis, Y., Gennaro, R., Håstad, J., Krawczyk, H., Rabin, T.: Randomness extraction and key derivation using the CBC, cascade and HMAC modes. In: Franklin, M. (ed.) CRYPTO 2004. LNCS, vol. 3152, pp. 494–510. Springer, Heidelberg (2004). https://doi.org/10.1007/978-3-540-28628-8_30
19. Dodis, Y., Pointcheval, D., Ruhault, S., Vergnaud, D., Wichs, D.: Security analysis of pseudo-random number generators with input: /dev/random is not robust. In: Sadeghi, A.-R., Gligor, V.D., Yung, M. (eds.) ACM CCS 2013, Berlin, Germany, 4–8 November 2013, pp. 647–658. ACM Press (2013)
20. Dodis, Y., Ristenpart, T., Vadhan, S.: Randomness condensers for efficiently samplable, seed-dependent sources. In: Cramer, R. (ed.) TCC 2012. LNCS, vol. 7194, pp. 618–635. Springer, Heidelberg (2012). https://doi.org/10.1007/978-3-642-28914-9_35
21. Dodis, Y., Shamir, A., Stephens-Davidowitz, N., Wichs, D.: How to eat your entropy and have it too – optimal recovery strategies for compromised RNGs. In: Garay, J.A., Gennaro, R. (eds.) CRYPTO 2014, Part II. LNCS, vol. 8617, pp. 37–54. Springer, Heidelberg (2014). https://doi.org/10.1007/978-3-662-44381-1_3
22. Eastlake, D., Schiller, J., Crocker, S.: RFC 4086 - Randomness Requirements for Security, June 2005
23. Ferguson, N.: Private communication (2013)
24. Ferguson, N., Schneier, B.: Practical Cryptography, 1st edn. Wiley, New York (2003)
25. Gaži, P., Pietrzak, K., Rybár, M.: The exact PRF-security of NMAC and HMAC. In: Garay, J.A., Gennaro, R. (eds.) CRYPTO 2014, Part I. LNCS, vol. 8616, pp. 113–130. Springer, Heidelberg (2014). https://doi.org/10.1007/978-3-662-44371-2_7
26. Gaži, P., Tessaro, S.: Provably robust sponge-based PRNGs and KDFs. In: Fischlin, M., Coron, J.-S. (eds.) EUROCRYPT 2016, Part I. LNCS, vol. 9665, pp. 87–116. Springer, Heidelberg (2016). https://doi.org/10.1007/978-3-662-49890-3_4
27. Harnik, D., Naor, M.: On everlasting security in the *hybrid* bounded storage model. In: Bugliesi, M., Preneel, B., Sassone, V., Wegener, I. (eds.) ICALP 2006, Part II. LNCS, vol. 4052, pp. 192–203. Springer, Heidelberg (2006). https://doi.org/10.1007/11787006_17
28. Hutchinson, D.: A robust and sponge-like PRNG with improved efficiency. In: Avanzi, R., Heys, H. (eds.) SAC 2016. LNCS, vol. 10532, pp. 381–398. Springer, Cham (2017). https://doi.org/10.1007/978-3-319-69453-5_21
29. Hutchinson, D.: A robust and sponge-like PRNG with improved efficiency. Cryptology ePrint Archive, Report 2016/886 (2016). http://eprint.iacr.org/2016/886
30. Impagliazzo, R., Levin, L.A., Luby, M.: Pseudo-random generation from one-way functions (extended abstracts). In: 21st ACM STOC, Seattle, WA, USA, 15–17 May 1989, pp. 12–24. ACM Press (1989)
31. Impagliazzo, R., Luby, M.: One-way functions are essential for complexity based cryptography (extended abstract). In: 30th FOCS, Research Triangle Park, North Carolina, 30 October–1 November 1989, pp. 230–235. IEEE Computer Society Press (1989)

32. Information technology - Security techniques - Random bit generation. ISO/IEC18031:2011 (2011)
33. Kamp, J., Rao, A., Vadhan, S.P., Zuckerman, D.: Deterministic extractors for small-space sources. J. Comput. Syst. Sci. **77**(1), 191–220 (2011)
34. Kelsey, J., Schneier, B., Ferguson, N.: Yarrow-160: notes on the design and analysis of the yarrow cryptographic pseudorandom number generator. In: Heys, H., Adams, C. (eds.) SAC 1999. LNCS, vol. 1758, pp. 13–33. Springer, Heidelberg (2000). https://doi.org/10.1007/3-540-46513-8_2
35. Killmann, W., Schindler, W.: A proposal for: functionality classes for random number generators. AIS 20/AIS31 (2011)
36. Krawczyk, H.: Cryptographic extraction and key derivation: the HKDF scheme. In: Rabin, T. (ed.) CRYPTO 2010. LNCS, vol. 6223, pp. 631–648. Springer, Heidelberg (2010). https://doi.org/10.1007/978-3-642-14623-7_34
37. Lichtenstein, D., Linial, N., Saks, M.E.: Some extremal problems arising form discrete control processes. Combinatorica **9**(3), 269–287 (1989)
38. John, M.: Intel digital random number generator (DRNG) software implementation guide (2014). https://software.intel.com/en-us/articles/intel-digital-random-number-generator-drng-software-implementation-guide
39. Nisan, N., Zuckerman, D.: More deterministic simulation in logspace. In: Proceedings of the Twenty-Fifth Annual ACM Symposium on Theory of Computing, San Diego, CA, USA, 16–18 May 1993, pp. 235–244 (1993)
40. Nisan, N., Zuckerman, D.: Randomness is linear in space. J. Comput. Syst. Sci. **52**(1), 43–52 (1996)
41. Patarin, J.: The "coefficients H" technique. In: Avanzi, R.M., Keliher, L., Sica, F. (eds.) SAC 2008. LNCS, vol. 5381, pp. 328–345. Springer, Heidelberg (2009). https://doi.org/10.1007/978-3-642-04159-4_21
42. Schoenmakers, B., Sidorenko, A.: Cryptanalysis of the dual elliptic curve pseudorandom generator. Cryptology ePrint Archive, Report 2006/190 (2006). http://eprint.iacr.org/2006/190
43. Shrimpton, T., Terashima, R.S.: A provable-security analysis of Intel's secure key RNG. In: Oswald, E., Fischlin, M. (eds.) EUROCRYPT 2015, Part I. LNCS, vol. 9056, pp. 77–100. Springer, Heidelberg (2015). https://doi.org/10.1007/978-3-662-46800-5_4
44. Shumow, D., Ferguson, N.: On the possibility of a back door in the NIST SP800-90 Dual Ec PRNG. CRYPTO Rump Session (2007)
45. Soni, P., Tessaro, S.: Public-seed pseudorandom permutations. In: Coron, J.-S., Nielsen, J.B. (eds.) EUROCRYPT 2017, Part II. LNCS, vol. 10211, pp. 412–441. Springer, Cham (2017). https://doi.org/10.1007/978-3-319-56614-6_14
46. Trevisan, L., Vadhan, S.P.: Extracting randomness from samplable distributions. In: 41st FOCS, Redondo Beach, CA, USA, 12–14 November 2000, pp. 32–42. IEEE Computer Society Press (2000)
47. von Neumann, J.: Various techniques used in connection with random digits. In: Householder, A.S., Forsythe, G.E., Germond, H.H. (eds.) Monte Carlo Method. National Bureau of Standards Applied Mathematics Series, vol. 12, pp. 36–38. U.S. Government Printing Office, Washington, D.C. (1951)
48. Wikipedia: /dev/random (2004). http://en.wikipedia.org/wiki//dev/random. Accessed 09 Feb 2014
49. Woodage, J., Shumow, D.: An analysis of NIST SP 800-90A. In: Ishai, Y., Rijmen, V. (eds.) EUROCRYPT 2019. LNCS, vol. 11477, pp. 151–180. Springer, Cham (2019). https://doi.org/10.1007/978-3-030-17656-3_6

Nonces Are Noticed: AEAD Revisited

Mihir Bellare[1]([✉]), Ruth Ng[1], and Björn Tackmann[2]

[1] Department of Computer Science and Engineering,
University of California San Diego, San Diego, USA
{mihir,ring}@eng.ucsd.edu
[2] IBM Research – Zurich, Rüschlikon, Switzerland
bta@zurich.ibm.com

Abstract. We draw attention to a gap between theory and usage of nonce-based symmetric encryption, under which the way the former treats nonces can result in violation of privacy in the latter. We bridge the gap with a new treatment of nonce-based symmetric encryption that modifies the syntax (decryption no longer takes a nonce), upgrades the security goal (asking that not just messages, but also nonces, be hidden) and gives simple, efficient schemes conforming to the new definitions. We investigate both basic security (holding when nonces are not reused) and advanced security (misuse resistance, providing best-possible guarantees when nonces are reused).

1 Introduction

This paper revisits nonce-based symmetric encryption, raising some concerns, and then addressing them, via a new syntax, a new framework of security definitions, and schemes that offer both usability and security benefits.

Background. As the applications and usage of symmetric encryption have evolved and grown, so has a theory that seeks to support and guide them. A definition of symmetric encryption (as with any other primitive) involves a *syntax* and then, for this syntax, definitions of *security*. In the first modern treatment [10], the syntax asked the encryption algorithm to be randomized or stateful. Security for these syntaxes evolved from asking for various forms of privacy [10] to asking for both privacy and authenticity [11,14,33], inaugurating authenticated encryption (AE). The idea that encryption be a deterministic algorithm taking as additional input a non-repeating quantity called a nonce seems to originate in [50] and reached its current form with Rogaway [46,48].

NBE1 and AE1-security. We refer to the syntax of this current form of nonce-based symmetric encryption [46,48] as NBE1. An NBE1 scheme SE1 specifies a *deterministic* encryption algorithm SE1.Enc that takes the key K, a nonce N, message M and a header (also called associated data) H to return what we call a core ciphertext C_1. Deterministic decryption algorithm SE1.Dec takes K, N, C_1, H to return either a message or $\perp$.

© International Association for Cryptologic Research 2019
A. Boldyreva and D. Micciancio (Eds.): CRYPTO 2019, LNCS 11692, pp. 235–265, 2019.
https://doi.org/10.1007/978-3-030-26948-7_9

Security asks for privacy of M and integrity of both M and H *as long as nonces are unique*, meaning not re-used. Rogaway's formalization [46] asks that an adversary given oracles for encryption (taking nonce, message and header) and decryption (taking nonce, core ciphertext and header) be unable to distinguish between the case where they perform their prescribed tasks under a hidden key, and the case where the former returns random strings and the latter returns $\bot$, as long as the adversary does not repeat a nonce across its encryption queries. We will refer to this as basic AE1-security.

NBE1 providing basic AE1-security has been the goal of recent schemes, standards and proposed standards, as witnessed by GCM [22,40] (used in TLS), OCB [35,47,50], CAESAR candidates [17] and RFC 5116 [39]. The security of NBE1, which we revisit, is thus of some applied interest.

The gap. Our concern is a gap between theory and usage that can result in privacy vulnerabilities in the latter. Recall that the decryption algorithm SE1.Dec, to be run by the receiver, takes as input not just the key K, core ciphertext C_1 and header H, but *also the nonce N*. The theory says that how the receiver gets the nonce is "outside of the model" [46] or that it is assumed to be communicated "out-of-band" [48]. Usage cannot so dismiss it, and must find a way to convey the nonce to the receiver. The prevailing understanding, reflected in the following quote from RBBK [50], is that this is a simple matter—if the receiver does not already have the nonce N, just send it in the clear along with the core ciphertext C_1:

> The nonce N is needed both to encrypt and to decrypt. Typically it would be communicated, in the clear, along with the (core) ciphertext.

RFC 5116 is a draft standard for an interface for authenticated encryption [39]. It also considers it fine to send the nonce in the clear:

> ... there is no need to coordinate the details of the nonce format between the encrypter and the decrypter, as long *the entire nonce is sent* or stored with the ciphertext and is thus available to the decrypter ... the nonce MAY be stored *or transported* with the ciphertext ...

To repeat and summarize, the literature and proposed standards suggest transmitting what we call the "full" ciphertext, consisting of the nonce and the core ciphertext. Yet, as we now explain, this can be wrong.

Nonces can compromise privacy. We point out that communicating a nonce in the clear with the ciphertext can damage, or even destroy, message privacy. One simple example is a nonce $N = F(M)$ that is a hash—under some public, collision-resistant hash function F—of a low-entropy message M, meaning one, like a password, which the attacker knows is likely to fall in some small set or dictionary D. Given a (full) ciphertext $C_2 = (N, C_1)$ consisting of the core ciphertext $C_1 = \mathsf{SE1.Enc}(K, N, M, H)$ together with the nonce $N = F(M)$, the attacker can recover M via "For $M' \in D$ do: If $F(M') = N$ then return M'." To take a more extreme case, consider that the nonce is some part of the message, or even the entire message, in which case the full ciphertext clearly reveals information about the message.

The concern that (adversary-visible) nonces compromise privacy, once identified, goes much further. Nonces are effectively meta-data. Even recommended and innocuous-seeming choices like counters, device identities, disk-sector numbers or packet headers reveal information about the system and identity of the sender. For example, the claim that basic-AE1-secure NBE1 provides anonymity—according to [49, Slide 19/40], this is a dividend of the requirement that core ciphertexts be indistinguishable from random strings—is moot when the nonce includes sender identity. Yet the latter is not only possible but explicitly recommended in RFC 5116 [39], which says: "When there are multiple devices performing encryption ... use a nonce format that contains a field that is distinct for each one of the devices." As another concrete example, counters are *not* a good choice of nonce from a user privacy perspective, as indicated in the ECRYPT-CSA *Challenges in Authenticated Encryption* report [5].

The above issues apply to all NBE1 schemes and do not contradict their (often, proven) AE1-security. They are not excluded by the unique nonce requirement or by asking for misuse resistance [51], arising in particular for the encryption of a single message with a single corresponding nonce.

A natural critique is that the privacy losses we have illustrated occur only for "pathological" choices of nonces, and choices made in practice, such as random numbers or counters, are "fine." This fails, first, to recognize the definitional gap that allows the "pathological" choices. With regard to usage, part of the selling point of NBE1 was exactly that *any* (non-repeating, unique) nonce is fine, and neither existing formalisms [46] nor existing standards [39] preclude nonce choices of the "pathological" type. Also, application designers and users cannot, and should not, carry the burden of deciding which nonces are "pathological" and which are "fine," a decision that may not be easy. (And as discussed above, for example, counters may *not* be fine.) Finally, Sect. 8 indicates that poor choices can in fact arise in practice.

Our perspective is that the above issues reflect a gap between the NBE1 formalism and the privacy provided by NBE1 in usage. Having pointed out this gap, we will also bridge it.

Contributions in brief. The first contribution of this paper is to suggest that the way NBE1 treats nonces can result (as explained above) in compromise of privacy of messages or users. The second contribution is to address these concerns. We give a modified syntax for nonce-based encryption, called NBE2, in which decryption does not get the nonce, a corresponding framework of security definitions called AE2 that guarantee nonce privacy in addition to authenticity and message privacy, and simple ways to turn NBE1 AE1-secure schemes into NBE2 AE2-secure schemes.

AE2-secure NBE2 obviates application designers and users from the need to worry about privacy implications of their nonce choices, simplifying design and usage. With AE2-secure NBE2, one can use any nonce, even a message-dependent one such as a hash of the message, without compromising privacy of the message. And the nonces themselves are hidden just as well as messages, so user-identifying information in nonces doesn't actually identify users.

Our NBE2 syntax. In an NBE2 scheme SE2, the inputs to the deterministic encryption algorithm SE2.Enc continue to be key K, nonce N, message M and header H, the output C_2 now called a ciphertext rather than a core ciphertext. The deterministic decryption algorithm SE2.Dec *no longer gets a nonce*, taking just key K, ciphertext C_2 and header H to return either a message M or $\bot$.

Just as an interface, NBE2 already benefits application designers and users, absolving them of the burden they had, under NBE1, of figuring out and architecting a way to communicate the nonce from sender to receiver. The NBE2 receiver, in fact, is nonce-oblivious, not needing to care, or even know, that something called a nonce was used by the sender. By reducing choice (how to communicate the nonce), NBE2 reduces error and misuse.

We associate to a given NBE1 scheme SE1 the NBE2 scheme $SE2 = \mathbf{TN}[SE1]$ that sets the ciphertext to the nonce plus the core ciphertext: $SE2.\mathsf{Enc}(K, N, M, H) = (N, SE1.\mathsf{Enc}(K, N, M, H))$ and $SE2.\mathsf{Dec}(K, (N, C_1), H) = SE1.\mathsf{Dec}(K, N, C_1, H)$. We refer to $\mathbf{TN}$ as the Transmit Nonce transform. This is worth defining because it will allow us, in Sect. 4, to formalize the above-discussed usage weaknesses in NBE1, but $SE2 = \mathbf{TN}[SE1]$ is certainly not nonce hiding and will fail to meet the definitions we discuss next.

Our AE2-security framework. Our AE2 game gives the adversary an encryption oracle ENC (taking nonce N, message M and header H to return a ciphertext C_2) and decryption oracle DEC (as per the NBE2 syntax, taking ciphertext C_2 and header H but no nonce, to return either a message M or $\bot$). When the challenge bit is $b = 1$, these oracles reply as per the encryption algorithm SE2.Enc and decryption algorithm SE2.Dec of the scheme, respectively, using a key chosen by the game. When the challenge bit is $b = 0$, oracle ENC returns a ciphertext that is drawn at random from a space $SE2.\mathsf{CS}(|N|, |M|, |H|)$ that is prescribed by the scheme SE2 and that depends only on the lengths of the nonce, message and header, which guarantees privacy of both the nonce and message. (This space may be, but unlike for AE1 need not be, the set of all strings of some length, because NBE2 ciphertexts, unlike NBE1 core ciphertexts, may have some structure.) In the $b = 0$ case, decryption oracle DEC returns $\bot$ on any non-trivial query. The adversary eventually outputs a guess b' as to the value of b, and its advantage is $2 \Pr[b = b'] - 1$.

We say that SE2 is AE2[$\mathcal{A}$]-secure if practical adversaries in the class $\mathcal{A}$ have low advantage. Let $\mathcal{A}_{\mathrm{u-n}}^{\mathrm{ae2}}$ be the class of unique-nonce adversaries, meaning ones that do not reuse a nonce across their ENC queries. We refer to AE2[$\mathcal{A}_{\mathrm{u-n}}^{\mathrm{ae2}}$]-security as basic AE2-security. As the nonce-hiding analogue of basic AE1-security, it will be our first and foremost target.

Before moving to schemes, we make two remarks. First that above, for simplicity, we described our definitions in the single-user setting, but the definitions and results in the body of the paper are in the multi-user setting. Second, the framework of a single game with different notions captured via different adversary classes allows us to unify, and compactly present, many variant definitions, including basic, advanced (misuse resistance), privacy-only and random-nonce security, and in Sect. 3 we give such a framework not just for AE2 but also for AE1.

Our transforms. In the presence of a portfolio of efficient AE1-secure NBE1 schemes supported by proofs of security with good concrete bounds [17,18,25,26, 30,31,35,40,43,50,53], designing AE2-secure NBE2 schemes from scratch seems a step backwards. Instead we give simple, cheap ways to transform AE1-secure NBE1 schemes into AE2-secure NBE2 schemes, obtaining a corresponding portfolio of AE2-secure NBE2 schemes and also allowing implementors to more easily upgrade deployed AE1-secure NBE1 to AE2-secure NBE2.

Since NBE2 schemes effectively take care of nonce communication, we expect ciphertext length to grow by at least SE1.nl, the nonce length of the base NBE1 scheme. The *ciphertext overhead* is defined as the difference between the ciphertext length and the sum of plaintext length and SE1.nl. *All our transforms have zero ciphertext overhead.* One challenge in achieving this is that nonce lengths like SE1.nl = 96 are widely-used but short of the block length 128 of many blockciphers, precluding inclusion of an extra blockcipher output in the ciphertext. With regard to computational overhead, the challenge is that it should be constant, meaning independent of the lengths of the message and header for encryption, and of the ciphertext and header for decryption. *All our transforms have constant computational overhead.* Note that all overhead is in comparison to transmitting the nonce in the clear (i.e. the **TN** transform).

The following discussion first considers achieving basic security and then advanced security. Security attributes of our corresponding "Hide-Nonce (HN)" transforms are summarized in Fig. 1.

Basic HN transforms. We prove that all the following transforms turn a basic-AE1-secure NBE1 scheme SE1 into a basic-AE2-secure NBE2 scheme SE2. (Recall basic means nonces are unique, never reused across encryption queries.) Pseudocode and pictures for the transforms are in Fig. 4.

Having first produced a core ciphertext C_1 under SE1, the idea of scheme SE2 = **HN1**[SE1, F] is to use C_1 itself as a nonce to encrypt the actual nonce in counter mode under PRF F. A drawback is that this requires the minimal core-ciphertext length SE1.mccl to be non-trivial, like at least 128, which is not true for all SE1. Scheme SE2 = **HN2**[SE1, ℓ, E, Spl] turns to the perhaps more obvious idea of enciphering the nonce with a PRF-secure blockcipher E. The difficulty is the typicality of 96-bit nonces and 128-bit blockciphers, under which naïve enciphering would add a 32-bit ciphertext overhead, which we resolve by ciphertext stealing, ℓ representing the number of stolen bits (32 in our example) and Spl an ability to choose how the splitting is done. Scheme SE2 = **HN3**[SE1, F] uses the result of PRF F on the actual nonce as a derived nonce under which to run SE1. This is similar to SIV [43,51]; the difference is to achieve AE2 rather than AE1 and to apply the PRF only to the nonce (rather than nonce, message and header) to have constant computational overhead.

NBE2 scheme	AE2-security provided	
	Basic	Advanced
HN1[SE1, F]	Yes	Yes
HN2[SE1, ℓ, E, Spl]	Yes	Yes if $\ell \geq 128$
HN3[SE1, F]	Yes	No
HN4[SE1, ℓ, F]		Yes
HN5[TE, ℓ, ℓ_t]		Yes

Fig. 1. Security attributes of the NBE2 schemes defined by our Hide-Nonce (HN) transforms. In the table SE1 denotes an NBE1 scheme, F a PRF, E a block cipher, and TE a variable-length tweakable block cipher. Spl is a splitting function, and ℓ, ℓ_t are non-negative integer parameters. A blank entry in the Basic column means the transform is not for that purpose. Note that **HN1**'s advanced security only holds when ciphertexts have sufficiently large (e.g. 128 bits) minimum length, and **HN2**'s depends on the length of the stolen ciphertext.

Advanced HN transforms. Unique nonces are easier to mandate in theory than assure in practice, where nonces may repeat due to errors, system resets, or replication. In that case (returning here to NBE1), not only does basic AE1-security give no security guarantees, but also damaging attacks are possible for schemes including CCM and GCM [32,52]. Rogaway and Shrimpton's misuse resistant NBE1, which we refer to as advanced-AE1-secure NBE1, minimizes the damage from reused nonces, retaining AE1-security as long as no nonce, message, header triple is re-encrypted [51]. This still being for the NBE1 syntax, however, the concerns with adversary-visible nonces compromising message and user privacy are unchanged. We seek the NBE2 analogue, correspondingly defining and achieving advanced-AE2-secure NBE2 to provide protection against reused nonces while also hiding them.

With our framework, the definition is easy, calling for no new games; the goal is simply AE2[$\mathcal{A}^{ae2}_{u\text{-}nmh}$]-security where $\mathcal{A}^{ae2}_{u\text{-}nmh}$ is the class of <u>u</u>nique-<u>n</u>once, <u>m</u>essage, <u>h</u>eader adversaries, meaning ones that do not repeat a query to their ENC oracle. The presence of well-analyzed advanced-AE1-secure NBE1 schemes [18,25,26,28,51] again motivates transforms rather than from-scratch designs.

We start by revisiting our basic-security preserving transforms, asking whether they also preserve advanced security, meaning, if the starting NBE1 scheme is advanced-AE1-secure, is the transformed NBE2 scheme advanced-AE2-secure? We show that for **HN1**, the answer is YES. We then show that it is YES also for **HN2** as long as the amount ℓ of stolen ciphertext is large enough. (In practical terms, at least 128.) For **HN3**, the answer is NO.

That **HN1** and **HN2** have these properties is good, but we would like to do better. (Limitations of the above are that **HN1** puts a lower bound on SE1.mccl that is not always met, and setting $\ell = 128$ in **HN2** with typical 96-bit nonces will call for a 224-bit blockcipher.) We offer **HN4** and **HN5**, showing they provide advanced AE2-security. Pseudocode and pictures are in Fig. 5.

Scheme SE2 = **HN4**[SE1, ℓ, F] uses the result of PRF F on the actual nonce, message and header as a derived nonce for SE1. The difference with SIV [43,51] is that what is encrypted under SE1 includes the actual nonce in order to hide it. The computational overhead stays constant because SE1 need provide only privacy, which it can do in one pass. Scheme SE2 = **HN5**[TE, ℓ, ℓ_t] is different, using the encode-then-encipher paradigm [14] to set the ciphertext to an enciphering, under an arbitrary-input-length, tweakable cipher TE, of the nonce, message and ℓ_t-bits of redundancy, with the header as tweak. Instantiating TE via the very fast AEZ tweakable block cipher [28] yields correspondingly fast, advanced-AE2-secure NBE2.

Dedicated transforms. While our generic transforms are already able, with low overhead, to immunize GCM [22,40]—by this we mean turn this basic-AE1-secure NBE1 scheme into a basic-AE2-secure NBE2 scheme—we ask if a dedicated transform—ones that exploit the structure of GCM—can do even better. The goal is not just even lower overhead, but minimization of software changes. We show that simply pre-pending a block of 0s to the message and then GCM-encrypting provides basic-AE2-security, so neither the key nor the encryption software need be changed. Decryption software however does need a change, and, unlike with our generic transforms, we incur 32 bits of ciphertext overhead.

Related work. As a technical step in achieving security against release of unverified plaintext (RUP), Ashur, Dunkelman and Luykx (ADL) [4] use a syntax identical to NBE2, and their techniques bear some similarities with ours that we discuss further in Sect. 7.

The CAESAR competition's call for authenticated encryption schemes describes a syntax where encryption receives, in place of a nonce, a public message number (PMN) and a secret message number (SMN), decryption taking only the former [19]. The formalization of Namprempre, Rogaway and Shrimpton (NRS) [44] dubs this "AE5." In this light, an NBE1 scheme is a AE5 scheme without a SMN and an NBE2 scheme is an AE5 scheme without a PMN.

Possible future work. The concerns we have raised with regard to a gap between theory and usage, and privacy vulnerabilities created by adversary-visible nonces in the latter, arise fundamentally from the choice of *syntax* represented by NBE1, and as such hold also in other contexts where an NBE1-style syntax is used. This includes AE secure under release of unverified plaintext [3], robust AE [28], online AE [23,29], committing AE [21,24], indifferentiable AE [6], leakage-resilient AE [7] and MiniAE [42]. A direction for future work is to treat these with an NBE2-style syntax (decryption does not get the nonce) to provide nonce hiding.

While our transforms can be applied to promote the advanced-AE1-secure AES-GCM-SIV NBE1 scheme [25] to an advanced-AE2-secure NBE2 scheme, the bounds we get are inferior to those of [18]. Bridging this gap to get advanced-AE2-secure NBE2 with security bounds like [18] is a direction for future work. Similarly, while we have many ways to turn GCM into a basic-AE2-secure NBE2 scheme with little overhead, one that matches the bounds of [30,38] would be desirable.

2   Preliminaries

Notation and terminology. By ε we denote the empty string. By $|Z|$ we denote the length of a string Z. If Z is a string then $Z[i..j]$ is bits i through j of Z if $1 \leq i \leq j \leq |Z|$, and otherwise is ε. By $x\|y$ we denote the concatenation of strings x, y. If x, y are equal-length strings then $x \oplus y$ denotes their bitwise xor. If i is an integer in the range $0 \leq i < 2^n$ then $\langle i \rangle_n \in \{0,1\}^n$ denotes the representation of i as a string of (exactly) n bits. (For example, $\langle 3 \rangle_4 = 0011$.) If S is a finite set, then $|S|$ denotes it size. We say that a set S is *length-closed* if, for any $x \in S$ it is the case that $\{0,1\}^{|x|} \subseteq S$. (This will be a requirement for message, header and nonce spaces.) If D, R are sets and $f : D \to R$ is a function then its image is $\text{Im}(f) = \{ f(x) : x \in D \} \subseteq R$.

If X is a finite set, we let $x \leftarrow\!\!\text{\$}\; X$ denote picking an element of X uniformly at random and assigning it to x. Algorithms may be randomized unless otherwise indicated. If A is an algorithm, we let $y \leftarrow A^{O_1,\cdots}(x_1,\ldots;\omega)$ denote running A on inputs $x_1,\ldots$ and coins ω, with oracle access to $O_1,\ldots$, and assigning the output to y. By $y \leftarrow\!\!\text{\$}\; A^{O_1,\cdots}(x_1,\ldots)$ we denote picking ω at random and letting $y \leftarrow A^{O_1,\cdots}(x_1,\ldots;\omega)$. We let $[A^{O_1,\cdots}(x_1,\ldots)]$ denote the set of all possible outputs of A when run on inputs $x_1,\ldots$ and with oracle access to $O_1,\ldots$. An adversary is an algorithm. Running time is worst case, which for an algorithm with access to oracles means across all possible replies from the oracles. We use $\perp$ (bot) as a special symbol to denote rejection, and it is assumed to not be in $\{0,1\}^*$.

Games. We use the code-based game-playing framework of BR [15]. A game G (see Fig. 2 for an example) starts with an optional INITIALIZE procedure, followed by a non-negative number of additional procedures called oracles, and ends with a FINALIZE procedure. If FINALIZE is omitted, it is understood to be the trivial procedure that simply returns (outputs) its input. Execution of adversary A with game G consists of running A with oracle access to the game procedures, with the restrictions that A's first call must be to INITIALIZE (if present), its last call must be to FINALIZE, and it can call these procedures at most once. The output of the execution is the output of FINALIZE. By $\Pr[G(A)]$ we denote the probability that the execution of game G with adversary A results in this output being the boolean **true**. In games, integer variables, set variables boolean variables and string variables are assumed initialized, respectively, to 0, the empty set $\emptyset$, the boolean **false** and $\perp$.

Multi-user security. There is growing recognition that security should be considered in the multi-user (mu) setting [8] rather than the traditional single-user (su) one. Our main definitions are in the mu setting. The games provide the adversary a NEW oracle, calling which results in a new user being initialized, with a fresh key. Other oracles are enhanced (relative to the su setting) to take an additional argument i indicating the user (key). We assume that adversaries do not make oracle queries to users (also called sessions) they have not initialized.

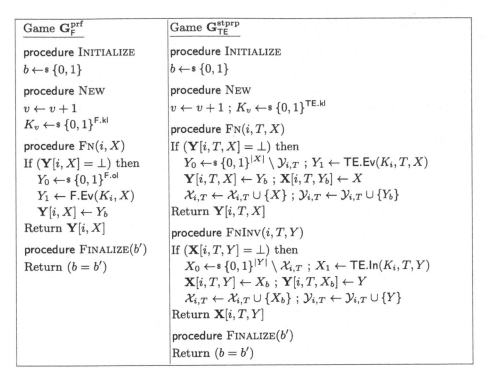

Fig. 2. Left: Games defining multi-user PRF security for function family F. Right: Game defining multi-user stPRP security for tweakable cipher TE.

Function families. A function family F specifies a deterministic evaluation algorithm $\text{F.Ev} : \{0,1\}^{\text{F.kl}} \times \text{F.D} \to \{0,1\}^{\text{F.ol}}$ that takes a key K and input x to return output $\text{F.Ev}(K, x)$, where F.kl is the key length, F.D is the domain and F.ol is the output length. We say that F is invertible if there is an inversion algorithm $\text{F.In} : \{0,1\}^{\text{F.kl}} \times \{0,1\}^{\text{F.ol}} \to \text{F.D} \cup \{\bot\}$ such that for all $K \in \{0,1\}^{\text{F.kl}}$ we have (1) $\text{F.In}(K, \text{F.Ev}(K, x)) = x$ for all $x \in \text{F.D}$, and (2) $\text{F.In}(K, y) = \bot$ for all $y \notin \text{Im}(\text{F.Ev}(K, \cdot))$. We say that F is a permutation family if it is invertible and $\text{F.D} = \{0,1\}^{\text{F.ol}}$. In that case, we also refer to F as a block cipher and to F.ol as the block length of F, which we may denote F.bl.

PRF security. We define multi-user PRF security [9] for a function family F and adversary A via the game $\mathbf{G}_{\text{F}}^{\text{prf}}(A)$ in Fig. 2. Here b is the challenge bit and $\mathbf{Y}[\cdot, \cdot]$ is a table, all of whose entries are assumed to initially be $\bot$. It is required that any $\text{FN}(i, X)$ query of A satisfies $i \le v$ and $X \in \text{F.D}$. The multi-user PRF advantage of adversary A is $\mathbf{Adv}_{\text{F}}^{\text{prf}}(A) = 2\Pr[\mathbf{G}_{\text{F}}^{\text{prf}}(A)] - 1$.

Tweakable ciphers. A tweakable cipher TE [28,37] specifies a deterministic evaluation algorithm $\text{TE.Ev} : \{0,1\}^{\text{TE.kl}} \times \text{TE.TS} \times \{0,1\}^* \to \{0,1\}^*$ and a deterministic inversion algorithm $\text{TE.In} : \{0,1\}^{\text{TE.kl}} \times \text{TE.TS} \times \{0,1\}^* \to \{0,1\}^*$.

Here, TE.kl is the key length and TE.TS is the tweak space. We require that for all $K \in \{0,1\}^{\mathsf{TE.kl}}$, $T \in \mathsf{TE.TS}$ and $X \in \{0,1\}^*$ we have $|\mathsf{TE.Ev}(K,T,X)| = |X|$ and $\mathsf{TE.In}(K,T,\mathsf{TE.Ev}(K,T,X)) = X$.

stPRP security. We define multi-user stPRP (strong tweakable PRP) security [37] for tweakable cipher TE and adversary A via the game $\mathbf{G}_{\mathsf{TE}}^{\mathrm{stprp}}(A)$ in Fig. 2. In the game, b is the challenge bit and $\mathbf{X}[\cdot,\cdot,\cdot]$, $\mathbf{Y}[\cdot,\cdot,\cdot]$ are tables whose entries are assumed initialized to $\bot$. In this game, the adversary has access to an evaluation oracle FN and an inversion oracle FNINV. When $b = 0$, they sample without replacement (within each session) from the set of strings of the same length as the input. If $b = 1$ they evaluate TE.Ev and TE.In under game-chosen keys. It is required that any $\mathrm{FN}(i,T,X)$ or $\mathrm{FNINV}(i,T,Y)$ query of A satisfies $i \leq v$, $T \in \mathsf{TE.TS}$ and $X, Y \in \{0,1\}^*$. The multi-user stPRP advantage of adversary A is $\mathbf{Adv}_{\mathsf{TE}}^{\mathrm{stprp}}(A) = 2\Pr[\mathbf{G}_{\mathsf{TE}}^{\mathrm{stprp}}(A)] - 1$.

3   Two Frameworks for Nonce-Based Encryption

We give definitions for both AE1-secure NBE1—current nonce-based encryption [46, 48, 50]—and AE2-secure NBE2—our new nonce-based encryption. In each case there is a single security game, different variant definitions then being captured by different adversary classes. This allows a unified and compact treatment.

NBE1. An NBE1 scheme SE1 specifies several algorithms and related quantities, as follows. Deterministic encryption algorithm $\mathsf{SE1.Enc} : \mathsf{SE1.KS} \times \mathsf{SE1.NS} \times \mathsf{SE1.MS} \times \mathsf{SE1.HS} \to \{0,1\}^*$ takes a key K in the (finite) key-space SE1.KS, a nonce N in the nonce-space SE1.NS, a message M in the message space SE1.MS and a header H in the header space SE1.HS to return what we call a core cipher-text C_1. This is a string of length $\mathsf{SE1.ccl}(|N|,|M|,|H|)$, where SE1.ccl is the core-ciphertext length function. SE1 also specifies a deterministic decryption algorithm $\mathsf{SE1.Dec} : \mathsf{SE1.KS} \times \mathsf{SE1.NS} \times \{0,1\}^* \times \mathsf{SE1.HS} \to \mathsf{SE1.MS} \cup \{\bot\}$ that takes key K, nonce N, core ciphertext C_1 and header H to return an output that is either a message $M \in \mathsf{SE1.MS}$, or $\bot$. It is required that SE1.NS, SE1.MS, SE1.HS are length-closed sets as defined in Sect. 2. Most often nonces are of a fixed length denoted SE1.nl, meaning $\mathsf{SE1.NS} = \{0,1\}^{\mathsf{SE1.nl}}$. Decryption correctness requires that $\mathsf{SE1.Dec}(K,N,\mathsf{SE1.Enc}(K,N,M,H),H) = M$ for all $K \in \mathsf{SE1.KS}$, $N \in \mathsf{SE1.NS}$, $M \in \mathsf{SE1.MS}$ and $H \in \mathsf{SE1.HS}$.

AE1 game and advantage. Let SE1 be an NBE1 scheme and A an adversary. We associate to them the game $\mathbf{G}_{\mathsf{SE1}}^{\mathrm{ae1}}(A)$ shown on the top left of Fig. 3. (We use the name "AE1" to associate the game with the NBE1 syntax). The AE1-advantage of adversary A is $\mathbf{Adv}_{\mathsf{SE1}}^{\mathrm{ae1}}(A) = 2\Pr[\mathbf{G}_{\mathsf{SE1}}^{\mathrm{ae1}}(A)] - 1$. The game is in the multi-user setting, oracle NEW allowing the adversary to initialize a new user with a fresh key. It is required that any $\mathrm{ENC}(i,N,M,H)$ query of A satisfy $1 \leq i \leq v$, $N \in \mathsf{SE1.NS}$, $M \in \mathsf{SE1.MS}$ and $H \in \mathsf{SE1.HS}$. When the challenge bit b is 1, the encryption oracle will return a core ciphertext as stipulated by SE1.Enc, using the key for the

Game $\mathbf{G}^{\text{ae1}}_{\text{SE1}}$	Game $\mathbf{G}^{\text{ae2}}_{\text{SE2}}$
procedure INITIALIZE $b \leftarrow\!\!\text{\$} \{0, 1\}$	procedure INITIALIZE $b \leftarrow\!\!\text{\$} \{0, 1\}$
procedure NEW $v \leftarrow v + 1$; $K_v \leftarrow\!\!\text{\$}$ SE1.KS	procedure NEW $v \leftarrow v + 1$; $K_v \leftarrow\!\!\text{\$}$ SE2.KS
procedure ENC(i, N, M, H) If $(b = 1)$ then $\quad C_1 \leftarrow$ SE1.Enc(K_i, N, M, H) $\quad$Else $C_1 \leftarrow\!\!\text{\$} \{0, 1\}^{\text{SE1.ccl}(\lvert N\rvert, \lvert M\rvert, \lvert H\rvert)}$ $\mathbf{M}[i, N, C_1, H] \leftarrow M$; Return C_1	procedure ENC(i, N, M, H) If $(b = 1)$ then $\quad C_2 \leftarrow$ SE2.Enc(K_i, N, M, H) $\quad$Else $C_2 \leftarrow\!\!\text{\$}$ SE2.CS$(\lvert N\rvert, \lvert M\rvert, \lvert H\rvert)$ $\mathbf{M}[i, C_2, H] \leftarrow M$; Return C_2
procedure DEC(i, N, C_1, H) If $(\mathbf{M}[i, N, C_1, H] \neq \perp)$ then $\quad$Return $\mathbf{M}[i, N, C_1, H]$ If $(b = 0)$ then $M \leftarrow \perp$ $\quad$Else $M \leftarrow$ SE1.Dec(K_i, N, C_1, H) Return M	procedure DEC(i, C_2, H) If $(\mathbf{M}[i, C_2, H] \neq \perp)$ then $\quad$Return $\mathbf{M}[i, C_2, H]$ If $(b = 0)$ then $M \leftarrow \perp$ $\quad$Else $M \leftarrow$ SE2.Dec(K_i, C_2, H) Return M
procedure FINALIZE(b') Return $(b = b')$	procedure FINALIZE(b') Return $(b = b')$

$\mathcal{A}^{\text{x}}_{\text{u-n}}$	Unique nonce adversaries — $A \in \mathcal{A}^{\text{x}}_{\text{u-n}}$ does not repeat a user-nonce pair i, N across its ENC queries
$\mathcal{A}^{\text{x}}_{\text{u-nmh}}$	Unique nonce-message-header adversaries — $A \in \mathcal{A}^{\text{x}}_{\text{u-nmh}}$ does not repeat a query to ENC
$\mathcal{A}^{\text{x}}_{\text{priv}}$	Privacy adversaries — $A \in \mathcal{A}^{\text{x}}_{\text{priv}}$ makes no DEC queries
$\mathcal{A}^{\text{x}}_1$	Single-user adversaries — $A \in \mathcal{A}^{\text{x}}_1$ makes only one NEW query
$\mathcal{A}^{\text{x}}_{\text{r-n}}$	Random-nonce adversaries — The nonces in the ENC queries of $A \in \mathcal{A}^{\text{x}}_{\text{r-n}}$ are distributed uniformly and independently at random

Fig. 3. Top Left: Game defining AE1-security of NBE1 scheme SE1. **Top Right:** Game defining AE2-security of NBE2 scheme SE2. **Bottom:** Some classes of adversaries, leading to different security notions, where x $\in \{\text{ae1}, \text{ae2}\}$.

indicated user i. In the $b = 0$ case, ENC will return a random string of length SE1.ccl$(\lvert N\rvert, \lvert M\rvert, \lvert H\rvert)$. The array $\mathbf{M}$ is assumed to initially be $\perp$ everywhere, and holds core ciphertexts returned by ENC. It is required that any DEC(i, N, C_1, H) query of A satisfy $1 \leq i \leq v$, $N \in$ SE1.NS and $H \in$ SE1.HS. When the challenge bit b is 1, the decryption oracle will perform decryption as stipulated by SE1.Dec, using the key for the indicated user i. In the $b = 0$ case, DEC will return $\perp$ on any core ciphertext not previously returned by the encryption oracle.

AE1 security metrics. AE1-security is clearly not achievable without restrictions on the adversary. For example, if A repeats a query i, N, M, H to ENC, then, when $b = 1$ it gets back the same reply both times, while if $b = 0$ it likely does not, allowing it to determine b with high probability. We define different classes of adversaries, summarized by the table at the bottom of Fig. 3, with the superscript "x" here being ael. We say that NBE1 scheme SE1 is AE1[$\mathcal{A}$]-secure if adversaries in $\mathcal{A}$ have low AE1-advantage. The definition is in the multi-user setting, but restricting attention to adversaries in the class $\mathcal{A}_1^{\mathrm{ael}}$ allows us to recover the single-user setting. Different security notions in the literature are then captured as AE1[$\mathcal{A}$]-security for different classes of adversaries $\mathcal{A}$, as we illustrate below:

- $\mathcal{A}_{\mathrm{u\text{-}n}}^{\mathrm{ael}}$ is the class of adversaries whose ENC queries never repeat a user-nonce pair. AE1[$\mathcal{A}_{\mathrm{u\text{-}n}}^{\mathrm{ael}} \cap \mathcal{A}_1^{\mathrm{ael}}$]-security is thus AEAD as defined in [46, 48].
- AE1[$\mathcal{A}_{\mathrm{u\text{-}n}}^{\mathrm{ael}}$]-security is the extension of this to the multi-user setting as defined in [16], which we have referred to as basic AE1-security in Sect. 1.
- Adversaries in $\mathcal{A}_{\mathrm{u\text{-}nmh}}^{\mathrm{ael}} \supseteq \mathcal{A}_{\mathrm{u\text{-}n}}^{\mathrm{ael}}$ are allowed to re-use a user-nonce pair across ENC queries as long as they never repeat an entire query. AE1[$\mathcal{A}_{\mathrm{u\text{-}nmh}}^{\mathrm{ael}} \cap \mathcal{A}_1^{\mathrm{ael}}$]-security is misuse resistant AE [51].
- AE1[$\mathcal{A}_{\mathrm{u\text{-}nmh}}^{\mathrm{ael}}$]-security is the extension of this to the multi-user setting [18], which we have referred to as advanced-AE1-security in Sect. 1.
- Adversaries in $\mathcal{A}_{\mathrm{r\text{-}n}}^{\mathrm{ael}}$ pick the nonces in their ENC queries uniformly and independently at random from SE1.NS. (While the intent here is likely understandable, what precisely it means for an adversary to be in this class does actually need a careful definition, which is given in [12].) No restriction is placed on how the adversary picks nonces in DEC queries. AE1[$\mathcal{A}_{\mathrm{r\text{-}n}}^{\mathrm{ael}} \cap \mathcal{A}_1^{\mathrm{ael}}$]-security is thus classical randomized AE [11] for schemes which make encryption randomness public, which is the norm.
- Sometimes, in the unique-nonce setting, we consider schemes that provide only privacy, not authenticity, and, rather than giving a separate game, can capture this as AE1[$\mathcal{A}_{\mathrm{priv}}^{\mathrm{ael}} \cap \mathcal{A}_{\mathrm{u\text{-}n}}^{\mathrm{ael}}$]-security. AE1[$\mathcal{A}_{\mathrm{priv}}^{\mathrm{ael}} \cap \mathcal{A}_{\mathrm{u\text{-}n}}^{\mathrm{ael}} \cap \mathcal{A}_1^{\mathrm{ael}}$]-security is IND\$-CPA security, as defined in [46].

Further adversary classes can be defined to capture limited nonce reuse [18] or other resource restrictions.

The following says that AE1[$\mathcal{A}_{\mathrm{u\text{-}n}}^{\mathrm{ael}}$]-security implies AE1[$\mathcal{A}_{\mathrm{r\text{-}n}}^{\mathrm{ael}}$]-security with a degradation in advantage corresponding to the probability that a nonce repeats for some user. We will refer to this later. We omit the (obvious) proof.

Proposition 1. *Let* SE1 *be an NBE1 scheme. Given adversary* $A_{\mathrm{rn}} \in \mathcal{A}_{\mathrm{r\text{-}n}}^{\mathrm{ael}}$ *making at most* u NEW *queries and at most* q ENC *queries per user, we construct adversary* $A_{\mathrm{un}} \in \mathcal{A}_{\mathrm{u\text{-}n}}^{\mathrm{ael}}$ *such that*

$$\mathbf{Adv}_{\mathsf{SE1}}^{\mathrm{ael}}(A_{\mathrm{rn}}) \leq \mathbf{Adv}_{\mathsf{SE1}}^{\mathrm{ael}}(A_{\mathrm{un}}) + \frac{uq(q-1)}{2^{\mathsf{SE1.nl}}} \,.$$

Adversary A_{un} *preserves the resources of* A_{rn}.

Saying A_{un} preserves the resources of A_{rn} means that the number of queries to all oracles are the same for both.

We believe our (above) AE1 framework (single game, many adversary classes) is of independent interest, as a way to unify, better understand and compactly present existing and new notions of security for NBE1 schemes. We give a similar framework for AE2 next.

NBE2 syntax. An NBE2 scheme SE2 specifies several algorithms and related quantities, as follows. Deterministic encryption algorithm SE2.Enc : SE2.KS $\times$ SE2.NS $\times$ SE2.MS $\times$ SE2.HS $\rightarrow \{0,1\}^*$, just like for NBE1, takes a key K in the (finite) key-space SE2.KS, a nonce N in the nonce-space SE2.NS, a message M in the message space SE2.MS and a header H in the header space SE2.HS to return a ciphertext C_2 that is in the ciphertext space SE2.CS($|N|, |M|, |H|$). SE2 also specifies a deterministic decryption algorithm SE2.Dec : SE2.KS $\times \{0,1\}^* \times$ SE2.HS $\rightarrow$ SE2.MS $\cup \{\bot\}$ that takes key K, ciphertext C_2 and header H to return an output that is either a message $M \in$ SE2.MS, or $\bot$. (Unlike in NBE1, it does *not* take a nonce input.) It is required that SE2.NS, SE2.MS, SE2.HS are length-closed sets as defined in Sect. 2. Most often nonces are of a fixed length denoted SE2.nl, meaning SE2.NS $= \{0,1\}^{\mathsf{SE2.nl}}$. Decryption correctness requires that SE2.Dec(K, SE2.Enc(K, N, M, H), H) $= M$ for all $K \in$ SE2.KS, $N \in$ SE2.NS, $M \in$ SE2.MS and $H \in$ SE2.HS.

AE2 game and advantage. Let SE2 be an NBE2 scheme and A an adversary. We associate to them the game $\mathbf{G}_{\mathsf{SE2}}^{\mathrm{ae2}}(A)$ shown on the top right of Fig. 3. (We use the name "AE2" to associate the game with the NBE2 syntax). The AE2-advantage of adversary A is $\mathbf{Adv}_{\mathsf{SE2}}^{\mathrm{ae2}}(A) = 2\Pr[\mathbf{G}_{\mathsf{SE2}}^{\mathrm{ae2}}(A)] - 1$. The game is in the multi-user setting, oracle NEW allowing the adversary to initialize a new user with a fresh key. It is required that any ENC(i, N, M, H) query of A satisfy $1 \le i \le v$, $N \in$ SE2.NS, $M \in$ SE2.MS and $H \in$ SE2.HS. When the challenge bit b is 1, the encryption oracle will return a ciphertext as stipulated by SE2.Enc, using the key for the indicated user i. When $b = 0$, ENC will return a random element of the ciphertext space SE2.CS($|N|, |M|, |H|$). The array $\mathbf{M}$ is assumed to initially be $\bot$ everywhere, and holds ciphertexts returned by ENC. It is required that any DEC(i, C_2, H) query of A satisfy $1 \le i \le v$ and $H \in$ SE2.HS. When the challenge bit b is 1, the decryption oracle will perform decryption as stipulated by SE2.Dec, using the key for the indicated user i. When $b = 0$, DEC will return $\bot$ on any ciphertext not previously returned by the encryption oracle.

AE2 security metrics. As with AE1-security, restrictions must be placed on the adversary to achieve AE2-security, and we use adversary classes to capture restrictions corresponding to different notions of interest. The classes are summarized by the table at the bottom of Fig. 3, with the superscript "x" now being ae2. The classes and resulting notions are analogous to those for AE1. Thus, AE2[$\mathcal{A}_1^{\mathrm{ae2}}$]-security recovers the single-user setting. $\mathcal{A}_{\mathrm{u-n}}^{\mathrm{ae2}}$ is the class of adversaries whose ENC queries never repeat a user-nonce pair, so AE2[$\mathcal{A}_{\mathrm{u-n}}^{\mathrm{ae2}}$]-security is what we have referred to as basic AE2-security in Sect. 1. Adversaries in $\mathcal{A}^{\mathrm{ae2}}_{\mathrm{u\text{-}nmh}} \supseteq \mathcal{A}^{\mathrm{ae2}}_{\mathrm{u\text{-}n}}$ are allowed to re-use a user-nonce pair across ENC queries as long as they never repeat an entire query, so $\mathrm{AE2}[\mathcal{A}^{\mathrm{ae2}}_{\mathrm{u\text{-}nmh}}]$-security is what we have referred to as advanced AE2-security in Sect. 1. Adversaries in $\mathcal{A}^{\mathrm{ae2}}_{\mathrm{r\text{-}n}}$ pick the nonces in their ENC queries uniformly and independently at random from SE2.NS. $\mathrm{AE2}[\mathcal{A}^{\mathrm{ae2}}_{\mathrm{priv}}]$-security is privacy only.

Discussion. The main (small but important) change in the syntax from NBE1 to NBE2 is that in the latter, the decryption algorithm no longer gets the nonce as input. It is up to encryption to ensure that the ciphertext contains everything (beyond key and header) needed to decrypt. Nonces are thus no longer magically communicated, making the interface, and the task of application designers, simpler and less error-prone, reducing the possibility of loss of privacy from poor choices of nonces and opening the door to nonce-hiding security as captured by AE2. Another change is that, rather than a ciphertext length function, an NBE2 scheme specifies a ciphertext space. The reason is that a ciphertext might have some structure, like being a pair (C, C'). Ciphertexts like this cannot be indistinguishable from random strings, but they can be indistinguishable from pairs of random strings, which is captured by defining the ciphertext space correspondingly. This follows [24], in whose committing AE definition the same issue arose.

Nonce-Recovering NBE2. A natural subclass of NBE2 schemes are those which recover the nonce explicitly during decryption. We provide definitions to capture such schemes. We say that an NBE2 scheme SE2 is nonce-recovering if there exists a deterministic nonce-plus-message recovery algorithm SE2.NMR such that for any $(K, C_2, H) \in \mathrm{SE2.KS} \times \{0, 1\}^* \times \mathrm{SE2.HS}$, if $\mathrm{SE2.NMR}(K, C_2, H) \neq \bot$ then it parses as a pair $(M, N) \in \mathrm{SE2.MS} \times \mathrm{SE2.NS}$ satisfying $\mathrm{SE2.Dec}(K, C_2, H) = M$ and $\mathrm{SE2.Enc}(K, N, M, H) = C_2$. Most of our transforms from NBE1 scheme to NBE2 schemes yield nonce-recovering NBE2 schemes.

4   Usage of NBE1: The Transmit-Nonce Transform

With AE1-secure NBE1, the nonce is needed for decryption. But how does the decryptor get it? This is a question about usage not addressed in the formalism. The understanding, however, is that the nonce can be communicated in the clear, with the core ciphertext. One might argue this is fine because, in the AE1-formalism, the adversary picks the nonce, so seeing the nonce again in the ciphertext cannot give the adversary an advantage.

We have discussed in the introduction why this fails to model cases where the nonce is chosen by the user, and why, at least in general, nonce transmission may violate message privacy. But the claim, so far, was informal. The reason was that transmitting the nonce represents a *usage* of NBE1 and we had no definitions to capture this. With AE2-secure NBE2, that gap is filled and we are in a position to formalize the claim of usage insecurity.

Some readers may see this is unnecessary, belaboring an obvious point. Indeed, the intuition is clear enough. But formalizing it serves also as an introduction to exercising our framework. We capture the usage in question as an NBE2 scheme $SE_{TN} = TN[SE1]$ built from a given NBE1 scheme SE1 by what we call the transmit-nonce transform TN. We detail the (rather obvious) claim that SE_{TN} fails to meet AE2-security, and discuss how it will also fail to meet other, weaker privacy goals.

The TN transform. Our TN ($\underline{T}$ransmit $\underline{N}$once) transform takes an NBE1 scheme SE1 and returns the NBE2 scheme $SE_{TN} = TN[SE1]$, that, as the name suggests, transmits the nonce in the clear, meaning the SE_{TN} ciphertext is the nonce together with the SE1 core ciphertext. In more detail, encryption algorithm $SE_{TN}.Enc(K, N, M, H)$ lets $C_1 \leftarrow SE1.Enc(K, N, M, H)$ and returns ciphertext $C_2 \leftarrow (N, C_1)$. Decryption algorithm $SE_{TN}.Dec(K, C_2, H)$ parses C_2 as a pair (N, C_1) with $N \in SE1.NS$—we write this as $(N, C_1) \leftarrow C_2$—returning $\perp$ if the parsing fails, and else returning $M \leftarrow SE1.Dec(K, N, C_1, H)$. NBE2 scheme SE_{TN} has the same key space, message space and header space as SE1, and we define its ciphertext space via $SE_{TN}.CS(\ell_n, \ell_m, \ell_h) = SE1.NS \times \{0,1\}^{SE1.ccl(\ell_n, \ell_m, \ell_h)}$ for all $\ell_n, \ell_m, \ell_h \geq 0$. Usage of SE1 in which the nonce is sent in the clear (along with the core ciphertext) can now be formally modeled by asking what formal security notions for NBE2 schemes are met by $SE_{TN} = TN[SE1]$.

Insecurity of TN[SE1]. Let SE1 be *any* NBE1 scheme. It might, like GCM, be $AE1[\mathcal{A}_{u\text{-}n}^{ae1}]$-secure, or it might even be $AE1[\mathcal{A}_{u\text{-}nmh}^{ae1}]$-secure. Regardless, we claim that NBE2 scheme $SE_{TN} = TN[SE1]$ fails to be $AE2[\mathcal{A}_{priv}^{ae2} \cap \mathcal{A}_{u\text{-}n}^{ae2}]$-secure, meaning fails to provide privacy even for adversaries that do not reuse a nonce. This is quite obvious, since the adversary can test whether the nonce in its ENC query matches the one returned in the ciphertext. In detail:

Adversary A

INITIALIZE
Pick some $(N, M, H) \in SE1.NS \times SE1.MS \times SE1.HS$ with $|N| \geq 1$
NEW // Initialize one user
$(N^*, C_1) \leftarrow_\$ ENC(1, N, M, H)$ // Ciphertext returned is a pair
If $(N^* = N)$ then $b' \leftarrow 1$ else $b' \leftarrow 0$
FINALIZE(b')

This adversary has advantage $\mathbf{Adv}_{SE_{TN}}^{ae2}(A) \geq 1 - 1/2 = 1/2$, so represents a violation of $AE2[\mathcal{A}_{priv}^{ae2} \cap \mathcal{A}_{u\text{-}n}^{ae2}]$-security.

Discussion. The attack above may be difficult to reconcile with SE1 being $AE1[\mathcal{A}_{u\text{-}n}^{ae1}]$-secure, the question being that, in the AE1 game, the adversary picks the nonce, and thus already knows it, so why should seeing it again in the ciphertext give the adversary extra information? The answer is that in usage the adversary does not know the nonce *a priori* and seeing may provide additional information. This is not modeled in AE1 but is modeled in AE2. To be clear, the above violation of AE2 security does *not* contradict the assumed AE1-security of SE1.

One might (correctly) argue that AE2 is a strong requirement so failing it does not represent a concerning violation of security, but it is clear that $\mathsf{SE}_{\mathsf{TN}}$ will fail to meet even much weaker notions of privacy for NBE2 schemes that one could formalize in natural ways, such as message recovery security or semantic security. (The nonce could be message dependent, in the extreme equal to the message.) One might also suggest that the losses of privacy occur for pathological choices of nonces, and nonce transmission is just fine if the nonce is a random number or counter, to which there are two responses. (1) The pitch and promise of $\mathsf{AE1}[\mathcal{A}^{\mathrm{ae1}}_{\mathrm{u\text{-}n}}]$-secure NBE1 is that *any* (non-repeating) nonce is fine. For example RBBK [50] says "The entity that encrypts chooses a new nonce for every message with the *only* restriction that no nonce is used twice," and RFC 5116 says "Applications SHOULD use the nonce formation method defined in Sect. 3.2, and MAY use any other method that meets the uniqueness requirement." It is important to know (both to prevent misuse and for our understanding) that in usage of NBE1, security requires more than just uniqueness of nonces; one must be concerned with how they are conveyed to the receiver. (2) A counter nonce can lead to loss of user privacy, for example revealing identity information, that is resolved by moving to $\mathsf{AE2}[\mathcal{A}^{\mathrm{ae2}}_{\mathrm{u\text{-}n}}]$-secure NBE2, which is nonce hiding.

5   Basic Transforms

We have explained that AE2-secure NBE2 offers valuable security and usability benefits over current encryption. So we now turn to achieving it. We follow the development path of NBE1, first, in this section, targeting basic AE2-security—no user reuses a nonce, which in our framework corresponds to adversaries in the class $\mathcal{A}^{\mathrm{ae2}}_{\mathrm{u\text{-}n}}$—and then, in Sect. 6, targeting advanced AE2-security—misuse resistance, where nonce-reuse is allowed, which in our framework corresponds to adversaries in the class $\mathcal{A}^{\mathrm{ae2}}_{\mathrm{u\text{-}nmh}}$.

Significant effort has gone into the design and analysis of basic-AE1-secure NBE1 schemes. We want to leverage rather than discard this. Accordingly, rather than from-scratch designs, we seek *transforms* of basic-AE1-secure NBE1 schemes into basic-AE2-secure NBE2 ones. This section gives three transforms that are simple and efficient and minimize quantitative security loss.

Preliminaries. We assume for simplicity that the NBE1 schemes provided as input to our transforms have nonces of a fixed length, meaning that $\mathsf{SE1.NS} = \{0,1\}^{\mathsf{SE1.nl}}$. This holds for most real-world AE1-secure NBE1 schemes. All our transforms can be adapted to allow variable-length nonces.

Core ciphertexts in practical NBE1 schemes tend to be no shorter than a certain minimal value, for example 96 bits for typical usage of GCM with AES [22]. We refer to this value as the minimal core-ciphertext length of the scheme $\mathsf{SE1}$, formally defining $\mathsf{SE1.mccl} = \min_{N,M,H}\{\mathsf{SE1.ccl}(|N|,|M|,|H|)\}$ where the minimum is over all $(N, M, H) \in \mathsf{SE1.NS} \times \mathsf{SE1.MS} \times \mathsf{SE1.HS}$. This is relevant because some of our transforms need $\mathsf{SE1.mccl}$ to be non-trivial to provide security.

All transforms here use two keys, meaning the key for the constructed NBE2 scheme SE2 is a pair consisting of a key for a PRF and a key for SE1. An implementation can, starting from a single overlying key, derive these sub-keys and store them, so that neither key size nor computational cost increase. This is well understood and is done as part of OCB, GCM and many other designs.

The ciphertext overhead is the bandwidth cost of the transform. We now discuss how to measure it. In the NBE2 scheme SE2 constructed by any of our transforms from an NBE1 scheme SE1, the ciphertext space is the set of strings of some length, $\mathsf{SE2.CS}(\ell_n, \ell_m, \ell_h) = \{0,1\}^{\mathsf{SE2.cl}(\ell_n, \ell_m, \ell_h)}$. Since NBE1 decryption gets the nonce for free while NBE2 decryption must, effectively, communicate it via the ciphertext, the "fair" definition of the ciphertext overhead of the transform is the maximum, over all possible choices of ℓ_n, ℓ_m, ℓ_h, of

$$\mathsf{SE2.cl}(\ell_n, \ell_m, \ell_h) - \mathsf{SE2.ccl}(\ell_n, \ell_m, \ell_h) - \mathsf{SE1.nl}\,.$$

Another way to put it is that the ciphertext overhead is how much longer ciphertexts are in SE2 than in $\mathbf{TN}[\mathsf{SE1}]$. All our transforms have ciphertext overhead zero, meaning are optimal in terms of bandwidth usage.

The **HN1** *transform.* The idea of our first transform is that a piece of the core ciphertext may be used as a nonce under which to encrypt the actual nonce. Let SE1 be an NBE1 scheme and F a function family with $\mathsf{F.ol} = \mathsf{SE1.nl}$, so that outputs of F.Ev can be used to mask nonces for SE1. Assume $\mathsf{SE1.mccl} \geq \mathsf{F.il}$, so that an F.il-bit prefix of a core ciphertext can be used as an input to F.Ev. Invertibility of F is not required, so it can, but need not, be a blockcipher. Our **HN1** transform defines NBE2 scheme $\mathsf{SE}_{\mathsf{HN1}} = \mathbf{HN1}[\mathsf{SE1}, \mathsf{F}]$ whose encryption and decryption algorithms are shown in Fig. 4. A key (K_{F}, K_1) for $\mathsf{SE}_{\mathsf{HN1}}$ is a pair consisting of a key K_{F} for F and a key K_1 for SE1, so that the key space is $\mathsf{SE}_{\mathsf{HN1}}.\mathsf{KS} = \{0,1\}^{\mathsf{F.kl}} \times \mathsf{SE1.KS}$. The message, header and nonce spaces are unchanged. The parsing $Y \| C_1 \leftarrow C_2$ in the second line of the decryption algorithm $\mathsf{SE}_{\mathsf{HN1}}$ is such that $|Y| = \mathsf{SE1.nl}$. The ciphertext overhead is zero. The computational overhead is one call to F.Ev for each of encryption or decryption. The following says that if the starting NBE1 scheme SE1 is basic-AE1-secure and F is a PRF then the NBE2 scheme $\mathsf{SE}_{\mathsf{HN1}}$ returned by the transform is basic-AE2-secure. The proof is in the full version.

Theorem 2. *Let* $\mathsf{SE}_{\mathsf{HN1}} = \mathbf{HN1}[\mathsf{SE1}, \mathsf{F}]$ *be obtained as above. Then, given adversary* $A_2 \in \mathcal{A}_{\text{u-n}}^{\text{ae2}}$, *making* q_n *queries to its* NEW *oracle,* q_e *queries per user to its* ENC *oracle, and* q_d *queries per user to its* DEC *oracle, we construct adversaries* $A_1 \in \mathcal{A}_{\text{u-n}}^{\text{ae1}}$ *and* B *such that*

$$\mathbf{Adv}_{\mathsf{SE}_{\mathsf{HN1}}}^{\text{ae2}}(A_2) \leq \mathbf{Adv}_{\mathsf{SE1}}^{\text{ae1}}(A_1) + \mathbf{Adv}_{\mathsf{F}}^{\text{prf}}(B) + \frac{q_n(q_e + q_d)(q_e + q_d - 1)}{2^{\mathsf{F.il}+1}}\,.$$

Adversary A_1 *preserves the resources of* A_2. *Adversary* B *makes* q_n *queries to its* NEW *oracle and* $q_e + q_d$ *queries per user to its* FN *oracle. Adversary* B *has about the same running time as* A_2.

Splitting. Our next transform employs ciphertext stealing [41] to get zero ciphertext overhead. There are many choices with regard to how to implement stealing, for example whether one steals from the first part of the core ciphertext or the last, and implementations may have different preferences. Accordingly, we do not pin down a choice but instead parameterize the transform by a splitting algorithm responsible for splitting a given string X (the core ciphertext) into segments x (the stolen part, of a prescribed length ℓ) and y (the rest). Formally, splitting scheme Spl specifies a deterministic algorithm Spl.Ev that takes an integer $\ell \geq 0$ and a string X with $|X| \geq \ell$, and returns a pair of strings $(x, y) \leftarrow$ Spl.Ev(ℓ, X) with $|x| = \ell$. If $(x, y) \in \text{Im}(\text{Spl.Ev}(|x|, \cdot))$—the image of a function was defined in Sect. 2—then $X \leftarrow$ Spl.In(x, y) recovers the unique X such that Spl.Ev$(|x|, X) = (x, y)$, and otherwise returns $X = \bot$.

This isn't enough because for security we want that if X is random then so are x, y. A simple way to ensure this is to require that the split sets x to some bit positions of X and y to the rest, *with the choice of positions depending only on $|X|$.* Formally, we require that there is a (deterministic) function Spl.St that given integers ℓ, n with $n \geq \ell \geq 0$ returns a starting index $s = $ Spl.St(ℓ, n) in the range $1 \leq s \leq n - \ell + 1$, and Spl.Ev$(\ell, X)$ returns $x = X[s..(s + \ell - 1)]$ and $y = X[1..(s - 1)] \| X[(s + \ell)..|X|]$ for $s = $ Spl.St$(\ell, |X|)$. The most common choices are that Spl.St$(\ell, n) = 1$, so that $x = X[1..\ell]$ is the ℓ-bit prefix of X and $y = X[(\ell + 1)..|X|]$ is the rest (corresponding to stealing from the first part of X), or Spl.St$(\ell, n) = n - \ell + 1$, so that $x = X[(|X| - \ell + 1)..|X|]$ is the ℓ-bit suffix of X and $y = X[1..(|X| - \ell)]$ is the rest (corresponding to stealing from the last part of X), but other choices are possible.

The **HN2** *transform.* The starting idea of this transform is that our NBE2 scheme can encrypt under the given NBE1 scheme and then also include in the ciphertext an enciphering, under a blockcipher E, of the nonce. We enhance this to encipher, along with the nonce, ℓ bits stolen from the core ciphertext. The stealing has two dividends. First, nonces are often shorter than the block length of E—for example SE1.nl $= 96$ and E.bl $= 128$ for AES-GCM and OCB [35, 50]—so in the absence of stealing, the nonce would be padded before enciphering, leading to ciphertext overhead. Second, while we show here (Theorem 3) that the scheme preserves basic security regardless of the amount ℓ stolen, we show later (Theorem 6) that it preserves even advanced security if ℓ is non-trivial (128 bits or more). We now proceed to the full description.

Let SE1 be an NBE1 scheme, Spl a splitting scheme and $\ell \geq 0$ the prescribed length of the stolen segment of the core ciphertext. We assume the minimal core-ciphertext length of SE1 satisfies SE1.mccl $\geq \ell$, which ensures that core ciphertexts are long enough to allow the desired splitting. Let E be a blockcipher with block length E.bl $=$ SE1.nl $+ \ell$. Our **HN2** transform defines NBE2 scheme $\text{SE}_{\text{HN2}} = $ **HN2**$[\text{SE1}, \ell, \text{E}, \text{Spl}]$ whose encryption and decryption algorithms are shown in Fig. 4. The parsing in the second line of the decryption algorithm SE_{HN2} is such that $|N| = $ SE1.nl. A key (K_{E}, K_1) for SE_{HN2} is a pair consisting of a key K_{E} for E and a key K_1 for SE1, so that the key space is $\text{SE}_{\text{HN2}}.\text{KS} = \{0, 1\}^{\text{E.kl}} \times \text{SE1.KS}$. The nonce, message and header spaces are unchanged.

$\mathsf{SE}_{\mathsf{HN1}}.\mathsf{Enc}((K_\mathsf{F}, K_1), N, M, H)$	$\mathsf{SE}_{\mathsf{HN1}}.\mathsf{Dec}((K_\mathsf{F}, K_1), C_2, H)$
$C_1 \leftarrow \mathsf{SE1}.\mathsf{Enc}(K_1, N, M, H)$	If $(|C_2| < \mathsf{SE1.nl} + \mathsf{F.il})$ then return $\perp$
$x \leftarrow C_1[1..\mathsf{F.il}]$; $P \leftarrow \mathsf{F}(K_\mathsf{F}, x)$	$Y \| C_1 \leftarrow C_2$; $x \leftarrow C_1[1..\mathsf{F.il}]$; $P \leftarrow \mathsf{F}(K_\mathsf{F}, x)$
$Y \leftarrow P \oplus N$; $C_2 \leftarrow Y \| C_1$	$N \leftarrow P \oplus Y$; $M \leftarrow \mathsf{SE1}.\mathsf{Dec}(K_1, N, C_1, H)$
Return C_2	Return M
$\mathsf{SE}_{\mathsf{HN2}}.\mathsf{Enc}((K_\mathsf{E}, K_1), N, M, H)$	$\mathsf{SE}_{\mathsf{HN2}}.\mathsf{Dec}((K_\mathsf{E}, K_1), C_2, H)$
$C_1 \leftarrow \mathsf{SE1}.\mathsf{Enc}(K_1, N, M, H)$	If $(|C_2| < \mathsf{E.bl})$ then return $\perp$
$(x, y) \leftarrow \mathsf{Spl}.\mathsf{Ev}(\ell, C_1)$	$N \| x \leftarrow \mathsf{E.In}(K_\mathsf{E}, C_2[1..\mathsf{E.bl}])$
$C_{2,1} \leftarrow \mathsf{E}.\mathsf{Ev}(K_\mathsf{E}, N \| x)$	$y \leftarrow C_2[\mathsf{E.bl} + 1..|C_2|]$; $C_1 \leftarrow \mathsf{Spl}.\mathsf{In}(x, y)$
$C_2 \leftarrow C_{2,1} \| y$	If $(C_1 = \perp)$ then return $\perp$
Return C_2	$M \leftarrow \mathsf{SE1}.\mathsf{Dec}(K_1, N, C_1, H)$; Return M
$\mathsf{SE}_{\mathsf{HN3}}.\mathsf{Enc}((K_\mathsf{F}, K_1), N, M, H)$	$\mathsf{SE}_{\mathsf{HN3}}.\mathsf{Dec}((K_\mathsf{F}, K_1), C_2, H)$
$N_1 \leftarrow \mathsf{F}.\mathsf{Ev}(K_\mathsf{F}, N)$	If $(|C_2| < \mathsf{F.ol})$ then return $\perp$
$C_1 \leftarrow \mathsf{SE1}.\mathsf{Enc}(K_1, N_1, M, H)$	$N_1 \| C_1 \leftarrow C_2$; $M \leftarrow \mathsf{SE1}.\mathsf{Dec}(K_1, N_1, C_1, H)$
$C_2 \leftarrow N_1 \| C_1$; Return C_2	Return M

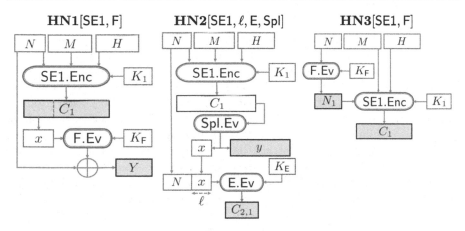

Fig. 4. Top: Encryption and decryption algorithms of the NBE2 schemes constructed by our basic transforms. From top to bottom: $\mathsf{SE}_{\mathsf{HN1}} = \mathsf{HN1}[\mathsf{SE1}, \mathsf{F}]$, $\mathsf{SE}_{\mathsf{HN2}} = \mathsf{HN2}[\mathsf{SE1}, \ell, \mathsf{E}, \mathsf{Spl}]$ and $\mathsf{SE}_{\mathsf{HN3}} = \mathsf{HN3}[\mathsf{SE1}, \mathsf{F}]$. Bottom: Diagrams illustrating the encryption algorithms of the constructed schemes.

The length of ciphertext C_2 is $\mathsf{E.bl} + |C_1| - \ell = |C_1| + \mathsf{SE1.nl}$, so the ciphertext space is $\mathsf{SE}_{\mathsf{HN2}}.\mathsf{CS}(\ell_n, \ell_m, \ell_h) = \{0, 1\}^{\mathsf{SE1.nl} + \mathsf{SE1.ccl}(\ell_n, \ell_m, \ell_h)}$. The ciphertext overhead is zero. The computational overhead is an extra blockcipher call for encryption and a blockcipher inverse for decryption.

A typical instantiation for basic security is $\mathsf{E} = \mathsf{AES}$, so that $\mathsf{E.bl} = 128$. Nonces would have length $\mathsf{SE1.nl} = 96$. We then set $\ell = 32$ and $\mathsf{Spl}.\mathsf{St}(\ell, n) = 1$ for all n. This means $\mathsf{SE1.mccl}$ must be at least 32, which is true for all real-world schemes we know. This reduction in the required value of $\mathsf{SE1.mccl}$ for security is the benefit that **HN2** offers over **HN1**. Recall the latter needs F.il $\geq$ SE1.mccl, and hence by Theorem 2 needs SE1.mccl $\geq$ 128, for the same security that **HN2** can offer with SE1.mccl $\geq$ 32.

The following says that if the starting NBE1 scheme SE1 is basic-AE1-secure and E is a PRF, then the NBE2 scheme SE_{HN2} returned by the transform is basic-AE2-secure. This holds regardless of the value of ℓ. The proof is in the full version of this paper [12].

Theorem 3. *Let* $SE_{HN2} = \textbf{HN2}[SE1, \ell, E, Spl]$ *be obtained as above. Then, given adversary* $A_2 \in \mathcal{A}_{u\text{-}n}^{ae2}$, *making* q_n *queries to its* NEW *oracle,* q_e *queries per user to its* ENC *oracle, and* q_d *queries per user to its* DEC *oracle, we construct adversaries* $A_1 \in \mathcal{A}_{u\text{-}n}^{ae1}$ *and* B *such that*

$$\mathbf{Adv}_{SE_{HN2}}^{ae2}(A_2) \leq \mathbf{Adv}_{SE1}^{ae1}(A_1) + \mathbf{Adv}_E^{prf}(B). \tag{1}$$

Adversary A_1 *preserves the resources of* A_2. *Adversary* B *makes* q_n *queries to its* NEW *oracle and* q_e *queries per user to its* FN *oracle. Adversary* B *has about the same running time as* A_2.

The **HN3** *transform.* Our third transform uses what we call nonce-based nonce-derivation, in which encryption is performed under SE1 using as nonce the result $N_1 = F(K_F, N)$ of a PRF F on the actual nonce N. The idea comes from SIV [51] but differences include that: (1) SIV constructs an AE1-secure NBE1 scheme while we construct an AE2-secure NBE2 scheme. (2) SIV decryption needs to have the original nonce. (3) Our synthetic nonce N_1 is a function only of the actual nonce while the one in SIV is also a function of the message and header.

Proceeding to the details, let SE1 be an NBE1 scheme. Let F be a function family with F.ol = SE1.nl, meaning outputs of F.Ev can be used as nonces for SE1. Invertibility of F is not required, so it can, but need not, be a blockcipher. Our **HN3** transform defines NBE2 scheme $SE_{HN3} = \textbf{HN3}[SE1, F]$ whose encryption and decryption algorithms are shown in Fig. 4. A key (K_F, K_1) for SE_{HN3} is a pair consisting of a key K_F for F and a key K_1 for SE1, so that the key space is $SE_{HN3}.KS = \{0,1\}^{F.kl} \times SE1.KS$. The message and header spaces are unchanged, and the nonce space is $SE_{HN3}.NS = \{0,1\}^{F.il}$, meaning inputs to F are nonces for SE2. The parsing in the second line of the decryption algorithm SE_{HN3} of Fig. 4 is such that $|N_1| = SE1.nl$. Note that the decryption algorithm does not use F or K_F.

As with **HN1** and **HN2**, the **HN3** transform has zero ciphertext overhead. The computational overhead for encryption is one invocation of F. Advantages emerge with decryption, where there is now *no* computational overhead. Indeed decryption in SE_{HN3} is effectively the same as in SE1. In particular, in the typical case that F is a blockcipher on which SE1 is itself based, decryption (unlike with **HN2**) no longer needs to implement its inverse, which can be a benefit in hardware and for reducing code size.

It is natural and convenient here to assume SE1 is $AE1[\mathcal{A}_{r\text{-}n}^{ae1}]$-secure. (Recall this is AE1-security for the class of adversaries that pick the nonce at random.)

By Proposition 1 this is implied by its being $\text{AE1}[\mathcal{A}^{\text{ae1}}_{\text{u-n}}]$-secure (that is, basic-AE1-secure). Assuming additionally that F is a PRF, the following says that $\textbf{HN3}[\text{SE1}, \text{F}]$ is $\text{AE2}[\mathcal{A}^{\text{ae2}}_{\text{u-n}}]$-secure (that is, basic-AE2-secure). The proof is in the full version.

Theorem 4. *Let* $\text{SE}_{\text{HN3}} = \textbf{HN3}[\text{SE1}, \text{F}]$ *be obtained as above. Then, given adversary* $A_2 \in \mathcal{A}^{\text{ae2}}_{\text{u-n}}$ *that makes* q_n *queries to its* NEW *oracle,* q_e *queries to its* ENC *oracle, and* q_d *queries to its* DEC *oracle, we construct adversaries* $A_1 \in \mathcal{A}^{\text{ae1}}_{\text{r-n}}$ *and* B *such that*

$$\textbf{Adv}^{\text{ae2}}_{\text{SE2}}(A_2) \leq \textbf{Adv}^{\text{ae1}}_{\text{SE1}}(A_1) + \textbf{Adv}^{\text{prf}}_{\text{F}}(B) .$$

Adversary A_1 *preserves the resources of* A_2. *Adversary* B *makes* q_n *queries to its* NEW *oracle and* q_e *queries to its* FN *oracle, respectively. Adversary* B *has about the same running time as* A_2.

6   Advanced Transforms

We now turn to achieving AE2-security in the nonce-misuse setting, which we formalized as $\text{AE2}[\mathcal{A}^{\text{ae2}}_{\text{u-nmh}}]$-security. We discuss various transforms for this purpose.

Advanced security of **HN1**. We showed in Theorem 2 that **HN1** preserves basic security. It turns out that it also preserves advanced security. The following says that if the starting NBE1 scheme SE1 is advanced-AE1-secure and F is a PRF then the NBE2 scheme SE_{HN1} returned by the transform is advanced-AE2-secure. The proof is in the full version.

Theorem 5. *Let* $\text{SE}_{\text{HN1}} = \textbf{HN1}[\text{SE1}, \text{F}]$ *be obtained as above. Then, given adversary* $A_2 \in \mathcal{A}^{\text{ae2}}_{\text{u-nmh}}$, *making* q_n *queries to its* NEW *oracle,* q_e *queries per user to its* ENC *oracle, and* q_d *queries per user to its* DEC *oracle, we construct adversaries* $A_1 \in \mathcal{A}^{\text{ae1}}_{\text{u-nmh}}$ *and* B *such that*

$$\textbf{Adv}^{\text{ae2}}_{\text{SE}_{\text{HN2}}}(A_2) \leq \textbf{Adv}^{\text{ae1}}_{\text{SE1}}(A_1) + \textbf{Adv}^{\text{prf}}_{\text{F}}(B) + \frac{q_n(q_e + q_d)(q_e + q_d - 1)}{2^{\text{F.il}+1}} . \quad (2)$$

Adversary A_1 *preserves the resources of* A_2. *Adversary* B *makes* q_n *queries to its* NEW *oracle and* $q_e + q_d$ *queries per user to its* FN *oracle. Adversary* B *has about the same running time as* A_2.

Advanced security of **HN2**. We showed in Theorem 3 that **HN2** preserves basic security regardless of the amount ℓ of stolen core-ciphertext—even if $\ell = 0$. For small ℓ, **HN2** may, however, leak information about the nonce in the advanced (misuse resistance) setting. The transformation does therefore not provide $\text{AE2}[\mathcal{A}^{\text{ae2}}_{\text{u-nmh}}]$-security. This is easy to see when $\ell = 0$, in which case if two different message-header pairs are encrypted with the same nonce, then the first

$\mathsf{SE}_{\mathsf{HN4}}.\mathsf{Enc}((K_{\mathsf{F}}, K_1), N, M, H)$	$\mathsf{SE}_{\mathsf{HN4}}.\mathsf{Dec}((K_{\mathsf{F}}, K_1), C_2, H)$
$N_1 \leftarrow \mathsf{F}.\mathsf{Ev}(K_{\mathsf{F}}, (N, M, H))$	If $(|C_2| < \mathsf{F}.\mathsf{ol})$ then return $\perp$
$C_1 \leftarrow \mathsf{SE1}.\mathsf{Enc}(K_1, N_1, N\|M, H)$	$N_1 \| C_1 \leftarrow C_2$; $X \leftarrow \mathsf{SE1}.\mathsf{Dec}(K_1, N_1, C_1, H)$
$C_2 \leftarrow N_1 \| C_1$	If $(X = \perp)$ then return $\perp$
Return C_2	$N \| M \leftarrow X$; $T \leftarrow \mathsf{F}.\mathsf{Ev}(K_{\mathsf{F}}, (N, M, H))$
	If $(T = N_1)$ then return M else return $\perp$

$\mathsf{SE}_{\mathsf{HN5}}.\mathsf{Enc}(K_{\mathsf{TE}}, N, M, H)$	$\mathsf{SE}_{\mathsf{HN5}}.\mathsf{Dec}(K_{\mathsf{TF}}, C_2, H)$
$C_2 \leftarrow \mathsf{TE}.\mathsf{Ev}(K_{\mathsf{TE}}, H, 0^{\ell_t}\|N\|M)$	$X \leftarrow \mathsf{TE}.\mathsf{In}(K_{\mathsf{TE}}, H, C_2)$
Return C_2	If $X[1..\ell_t] \neq 0^{\ell_t}$ then return $\perp$
	$N\|M \leftarrow X[(\ell_t + 1)..|X|]$; Return M

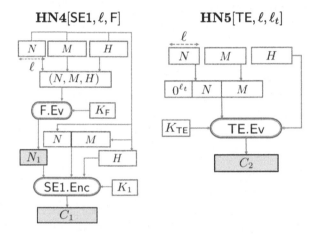

HN4$[\mathsf{SE1}, \ell, \mathsf{F}]$ **HN5**$[\mathsf{TE}, \ell, \ell_t]$

Fig. 5. Top: Encryption and decryption algorithms of the NBE2 schemes constructed by our advanced transforms. From top to bottom: $\mathsf{SE}_{\mathsf{HN4}} = $ **HN4**$[\mathsf{SE1}, \ell, \mathsf{F}]$ and $\mathsf{SE}_{\mathsf{HN5}} = $ **HN5**$[\mathsf{TE}, \ell, \ell_t]$. Bottom: Diagrams illustrating the encryption algorithms of the constructed schemes.

part of the ciphertext is the same, leading to an $\mathcal{A}_{\text{u-nmh}}^{\text{ae2}}$-adversary with advantage $1 - 2^{-\mathsf{E.bl}}$. The advantage of this attack however decreases (exponentially) as ℓ increases. The following theorem says that once ℓ is non-trivial (say, 128 bits or more), the transform actually preserves advanced security as well. In the full version of this paper, we prove this theorem and describe the attack alluded to above in detail, showing that the bound in Theorem 6 is tight [12].

Theorem 6. *Let* $\mathsf{SE}_{\mathsf{HN2}} = $ **HN2**$[\mathsf{SE1}, \ell, \mathsf{E}, \mathsf{Spl}]$ *be obtained as above. Then, given adversary* $A_2 \in \mathcal{A}_{\text{u-nmh}}^{\text{ae2}}$, *making* q_n *queries to its* NEW *oracle and* q_e *queries per user to its* ENC *oracle, we construct adversaries* $A_1 \in \mathcal{A}_{\text{u-nmh}}^{\text{ae1}}$ *and* B *such that*

$$\mathbf{Adv}_{\mathsf{SE}_{\mathsf{HN2}}}^{\text{ae2}}(A_2) \leq \mathbf{Adv}_{\mathsf{SE1}}^{\text{ae1}}(A_1) + \mathbf{Adv}_{\mathsf{E}}^{\text{prf}}(B) + \frac{q_n q_e (q_e - 1)}{2^{\ell+1}} . \tag{3}$$

Adversary A_1 preserves the resources of A_2. Adversary B makes q_n queries to its NEW *oracle and q_e queries per user to its* FN *oracle. Adversary B has about the same running time as A_2.*

This however is not ideal because security would need $\ell = 128$, which requires SE1.mccl ≥ 128 (not always true) and also, assuming 96-bit nonces, would require that the blockcipher E have block length $128 + 96 = 224$, which precludes AES. We now give further transforms that do better.

The **HN4** *transform.* The **HN3** transform clearly does *not* provide advanced-AE2-security because, if a nonce is repeated, the resulting ciphertexts have the same synthetic nonce, and hence the same first parts, which an adversary can notice. The starting idea for **HN4** is to obtain the synthetic nonce N_1 by applying the PRF F, not just to the actual nonce N as in **HN3**, but, as in SIV [51], to (N, M, H). If we now encrypt with N_1 under an NBE1 scheme SE1, we can indeed show that $\mathrm{AE2}[\mathcal{A}_{\mathrm{u\text{-}nmh}}^{\mathrm{ae2}}]$-security is achieved, assuming SE1 is $\mathrm{AE1}[\mathcal{A}_{\mathrm{u\text{-}nmh}}^{\mathrm{ae1}}]$-secure. The latter assumption, however, is not satisfactory here because $\mathrm{AE1}[\mathcal{A}_{\mathrm{u\text{-}nmh}}^{\mathrm{ae1}}]$-security (typically achieved via SIV itself) already requires two passes through the entire input, so our computation of N_1 adds another entire pass, resulting in significant (non-constant) computational overhead. To avoid this we ask whether it would be enough for SE1 to provide only privacy, meaning be $\mathrm{AE1}[\mathcal{A}_{\mathrm{r\text{-}n}}^{\mathrm{ae1}} \cap \mathcal{A}_{\mathrm{priv}}^{\mathrm{ae1}}]$-secure, because this can be achieved in one pass. Indeed, this is what SIV assumes, but the difficulty is that SIV decryption makes crucial use of the original nonce N to provide authenticity, recomputing it and checking that it matches the one in the ciphertext. But to be nonce hiding, we cannot transmit N. We resolve this by including N as part of the message encrypted under SE1.

Proceeding to the details, let SE1 be an NBE1 scheme. Let F be a function family with F.ol = SE1.nl, meaning outputs of F.Ev can be used as nonces for SE1, and also with SE1.NS × SE1.MS × SE1.HS ⊆ F.D, meaning triples (N, M, H) can be used as inputs to F. Let $\ell \geq 1$ be an integer prescribing the nonce length of the constructed scheme. Our **HN4** transform defines NBE2 scheme $\mathrm{SE}_{\mathrm{HN4}} = \mathbf{HN4}[\mathrm{SE1}, \ell, \mathrm{F}]$ whose encryption and decryption algorithms are shown in Fig. 5. A key (K_F, K_1) for $\mathrm{SE}_{\mathrm{HN4}}$ is a pair consisting of a key K_F for F and a key K_1 for SE1, so that the key space is $\mathrm{SE}_{\mathrm{HN4}}.\mathrm{KS} = \{0,1\}^{\mathrm{F.kl}} \times \mathrm{SE1.KS}$. The message and header spaces are unchanged, and the nonce space is $\mathrm{SE}_{\mathrm{HN4}}.\mathrm{NS} = \{0,1\}^{\ell}$. The parsing in the second line of the decryption algorithm $\mathrm{SE}_{\mathrm{HN4}}$ of Fig. 4 is such that $|N_1| = \mathrm{SE1.nl}$. The ciphertext overhead is zero, and if SE1 is a standard one-pass privacy only scheme like counter-mode, then the computational overhead is constant.

Security, as with SIV, requires that SE1 satisfies tidiness [43]. Formally, for all K, N, C_1, H, if SE1.Dec$(K, N, C_1, H) = M \neq \bot$ then SE1.Enc$(K, N, M, H) = C_1$. We capture the assumption that SE1 provides only privacy in the nonce respecting setting, and it continues to be convenient for this to be for adversaries that pick the nonce at random, so our assumption for SE1 is $\mathrm{AE1}[\mathcal{A}_{\mathrm{r\text{-}n}}^{\mathrm{ae1}} \cap \mathcal{A}_{\mathrm{priv}}^{\mathrm{ae1}}]$-security. By Proposition 1 this is implied by its being $\mathrm{AE1}[\mathcal{A}_{\mathrm{u\text{-}n}}^{\mathrm{ae1}} \cap \mathcal{A}_{\mathrm{priv}}^{\mathrm{ae1}}]$-secure.

Assuming additionally that F is a PRF, the following says that $\mathbf{HN4}[\mathsf{SE1}, \ell, \mathsf{F}]$ is $\mathsf{AE2}[\mathcal{A}^{\text{ae2}}_{\text{u-nmh}}]$-secure. The proof is in the full version [12].

Theorem 7. *Let* $\mathsf{SE}_{\text{HN4}} = \mathbf{HN4}[\mathsf{SE1}, \ell, \mathsf{F}]$ *be obtained as above, and let* $\mathsf{SE1}$ *satisfy tidiness. Then, given adversary* $A_2 \in \mathcal{A}^{\text{ae2}}_{\text{u-nmh}}$ *making* q_n *queries to its* NEW *oracle and* q_e, q_d *encryption and decryption queries for each user, respectively, we construct adversaries* $A_1 \in \mathcal{A}^{\text{ae1}}_{\text{r-n}} \cap \mathcal{A}^{\text{ae1}}_{\text{priv}}$ *and* B *such that*

$$\mathbf{Adv}^{\text{ae2}}_{\mathsf{SE2}}(A_2) \leq \mathbf{Adv}^{\text{ae1}}_{\mathsf{SE1}}(A_1) + \mathbf{Adv}^{\text{prf}}_{\mathsf{F}}(B) + \frac{q_n q_d}{2^{\mathsf{SE1.nl}}} \, .$$

Adversary A_1 *makes* q_n *queries to its* NEW *oracle,* q_e *queries to its* ENC *oracle per user, and no queries to its* DEC *oracle.* B *makes* q_n *queries to its* NEW *oracle, and* $q_e + q_d$ *queries to its* FN *oracle per user. Adversaries* A_1 *and* B *both have about the same running time as* A_2.

Our final transform **HN5** is different. It does not start from an NBE1 scheme but rather from a (arbitrary-input-length) tweakable cipher, extending the encode-then-encipher paradigm [14] to provide advanced-AE2-security. Instantiation via a fast tweakable cipher like AEZ [28] results in correspondingly fast advanced-AE2-secure NBE2.

The **HN5** *transform.* We encipher the nonce, message and some redundancy, using the header as the tweak. The change from [28] is to move the nonce from tweak to an input so as to hide it, which we will show is enough to confer AE2-security.

Proceeding to the details, let TE be a tweakable cipher as defined in Sect. 2. Let $\ell \geq 1$ be an integer prescribing the nonce length of the constructed scheme. Let $\ell_z \geq 0$ be the number of bits of redundancy we introduce to provide authenticity [14]. Our transform defines NBE2 scheme $\mathsf{SE}_{\text{HN5}} = \mathbf{HN5}[\mathsf{TE}, \ell, \ell_z]$ whose encryption and decryption algorithms are shown in Fig. 5. The key space of SE_{HN5} is the key space of TE. The message space is $\{0,1\}^*$. The header space $\mathsf{SE}_{\text{HN5}}.\mathsf{HS}$ is set to the tweak space $\mathsf{TE.TS}$ of TE. The nonce space is $\mathsf{SE}_{\text{HN5}}.\mathsf{NS} = \{0,1\}^\ell$. The length of ciphertext $\mathsf{SE}_{\text{HN5}}.\mathsf{Enc}(K, N, M, H)$ is $\ell_z + |N| + |M|$, so $\mathsf{SE}_{\text{HN5}}.\mathsf{CS}(\ell_n, \ell_m, \ell_h) = \{0,1\}^{\ell_z + \ell + \ell_m}$. Ciphertext overhead, in this case, is not relative to an underlying NBE1 scheme, since there isn't any, but we see that ciphertexts are longer than message plus nonce by just ℓ_z bits, which is effectively optimal [28].

The following theorem shows that SE_{HN5} is advanced-AE2-secure if tweakable cipher TE is an stPRP (as defined in Sect. 2) and ℓ_z is sufficiently large.

Theorem 8. *Let* $\mathsf{SE}_{\text{HN5}} = \mathbf{HN5}[\mathsf{TE}, \ell, \ell_z]$ *be obtained as above. Let* $A \in \mathcal{A}^{\text{ae2}}_{\text{u-nmh}}$ *be an adversary making* q_n *queries to its* NEW *oracle,* q_e *queries per user to its* ENC *oracle with minimum message length* ℓ_1, *and* q_d *queries with minimum ciphertext length* $\ell_2 \geq \ell_z$ *per user to its* DEC *oracle. We construct adversary* B *such that*

$$\mathbf{Adv}^{\text{ae2}}_{\mathsf{SE}_{\text{HN5}}}(A) \leq \mathbf{Adv}^{\text{stprp}}_{\mathsf{TE}}(B) + \frac{q_n q_e(q_e+1)}{2^{\ell_z + \ell + \ell_1 + 1}} + \frac{q_n q_d(q_d+1)}{2^{\ell_2+1}} + \frac{q_n q_d}{2^{\ell_z}} \, .$$

Adversary B makes q_n queries to its NEW *oracle, q_e queries per user to its* FN *oracle, and q_d queries per user to its* FNINV *oracle.*

7   Dedicated Transform for GCM

We have shown that our generic transforms allow us to immunize NBE1 schemes with low overhead. We now present a transform specific to a real-world NBE1 scheme: GCM. Our transform takes advantage of the underlying structure of GCM to further minimize overhead. Crucially, we also minimize changes to the scheme so that existing hardware and software can easily adapt.

Generalizing GCM to CAU1. Following Bellare and Tackmann [16], we generalize GCM via a transform CAU1. (We add the "1" to indicate that it is an NBE1 scheme.)

Let E be a block cipher, H be a function family and $\ell \geq 1$ be an integer indicating the desired nonce-length. Then CAU1 = **CAU1**[E, H, ℓ] is an NBE1 scheme. E.bl($2^{\text{E.bl}-\ell} - 2$) is the maximum message length for CAU1 so we require that $1 \leq \ell < $ E.bl. Core ciphertexts returned by CAU1.Enc take the form $\tau \| C$, where τ is a tag of length E.bl. CAU1's keys are keys to its underlying block cipher E, meaning that CAU1.kl = E.kl. We use function family H to compute the tag τ. H takes input of the form (C, H) and returns an output of length E.bl. It uses a key which is generated by enciphering $0^{\text{E.bl}}$ using E. This means that we require that H.D = $\{0, 1\}^* \times$ CAU1.HS and H.ol = H.kl = E.bl. The full description of CAU1.Enc and CAU1.Dec is in the full version [12].

AES-GCM, as proposed by McGrew and Viega [40] and standardized by NIST [22], is obtained by instantiating E = AES (so E.bl = 128), H = GHASH and $\ell = 96$. It is widely used in practice and achieves basic AE1-security (i.e. AE1[$\mathcal{A}_{\text{u-n}}^{\text{ae2}}$]-security). CAU1 has a fixed-length nonce, reflecting the standardized version of GCM, but a variant with variable-length nonces can be obtained by pre-processing the nonce, as discussed in [40].

AE2-secure CAU2. We exploit a feature of GCM, that the nonce can be derived from the authentication tag τ. In particular, if $\tau \| C \leftarrow$ CAU1.Enc(K, N, M, H), then $\tau = $ H.Ev(E.Ev($K, 0^{\text{E.bl}}$), (C, H))$\oplus$E.Ev($K, N\|\langle 1\rangle_{\text{E.bl}-\ell}$). (Recall that, as defined in Sect. 2, $\langle i\rangle_n$ is the n-bit representation of integer i.) Therefore, in constructing our NBE2 variant CAU2, we make use of the fact that the sender does not need to communicate the nonce—the receiver uses the tag to recover it. In other words, we exploit the "parsimoniousness" of **TN**[CAU1] [13].

Unfortunately, the recovery procedure will succeed for any given ciphertext with probability $2^{-\text{E.bl}+\ell}$, since this is the probability that *some* nonce with suffix $\langle 1\rangle_{\text{E.bl}-\ell}$ is recovered. This would be unacceptable in GCM since an adversary would be able to forge valid tags with probability 2^{-32}.

So in order to make the scheme work, we add redundancy to the scheme by prepending the message with 0^ℓ. CAU2 decryption will check that the message returned by CAU1.Dec indeed starts with such a string; this check works because

CAU2.Enc(K, N, M, H)	CAU2.Dec(K, C_2, H)
$C_2 \leftarrow$ CAU1.Enc$(K, N, 0^\ell \| M, H)$	$\tau \| C \leftarrow C_2$; $h \leftarrow$ H.Ev(E.Ev$(K, 0^{\mathsf{E.bl}}), (C, H))$
Return C_2	$y \leftarrow$ E.In$(K, \tau \oplus h)$; $N \leftarrow y[1..\ell]$
	If $(y[(\ell + 1)..\mathsf{E.bl}] \neq \langle 1 \rangle_{\mathsf{E.bl}-\ell})$ then return $\bot$
	$M^* \leftarrow$ CAU1.Dec(K, N, C_2, H)
	If $(M^* = \bot)$ then return $\bot$
	$x \| M \leftarrow M^*$
	If $(x \neq 0^\ell)$ then return $\bot$ else return M

Fig. 6. Encryption and decryption algorithms of NBE2 scheme CAU2 = **CAU2**[E, H, ℓ], a special case of which is an AE2[$\mathcal{A}_{\mathsf{u-n}}^{\mathsf{ae2}}$]-secure variant of GCM.

a decryption with a "wrong" nonce leads to a random ciphertext. (For this reason, the maximum message length of CAU2 is ℓ bits shorter than CAU1.) A similar technique is used by ADL [4] in their scheme, GCM-RUP, but for a slightly different variant of GCM.

More formally, the transform **CAU2** defines an NBE2 scheme CAU2 = **CAU2**[E, H, ℓ] whose encryption and decryption algorithms are shown in Fig. 6. The parsing in the first and sixth line of CAU2.Dec is such that $|\tau| =$ E.bl and $|x| = \ell$. If either parsing fails, CAU2.Dec will return $\bot$.

The theorem below demonstrates that CAU2 achieves basic security assuming that E is an sPRP and H is an (ϵ_1, ϵ_2)-AXU function family (as defined in [2, 16, 34, 36] and others). We refer the reader to the full version of this paper for a description of these notions of security [12].

Theorem 9. *Let* CAU2 = **CAU2**[E, H, ℓ] *be the NBE2 scheme defined above where* H *is an* (ϵ_1, ϵ_2)-*AXU function family. Let* $A \in \mathcal{A}_{\mathsf{u-n}}^{\mathsf{ae2}}$ *be an adversary making* q_n *calls to its* NEW *oracle,* q_e *calls to its* ENC *oracle per session and* q_d *calls to its* DEC *oracle per session. The total number of message blocks passed to the encryption oracle by* A *for any single session does not exceed* Q' *and the lengths of* C_2, H *passed to the decryption oracle by* A *do not exceed* ℓ_1', ℓ_2, *respectively. Let* $Q = Q' + q_e$ *and* $\ell_1 = \ell_1' +$ E.bl. *Then we can construct adversary* B *such that:*

$$\mathbf{Adv}_{\mathsf{CAU2}}^{\mathsf{ae2}}(A) \leq 2\mathbf{Adv}_{\mathsf{E}}^{\mathsf{sprp}}(B) + q_n(q_e q_d + q_d^2) \cdot \epsilon_1(\ell_1, \ell_2) + q_n(q_d^2 - q_d) \cdot \epsilon_2(\ell_1, \ell_2)$$
$$+ q_n \left(\frac{2Q^2 + 2Q + q_d^2 + 4q_d Q + 3q_d + 2}{2^{\mathsf{E.bl}+1}} + \frac{q_d^2 + q_d + 2q_e q_d}{2^{\ell+1}} \right)$$

B *makes* q_n *queries to its* NEW *oracle, no more than* $Q + 1$ *queries to its* FN *oracle for each user and no more than* q_d *queries to its* DEC *oracle for each user.*

The proof of the theorem is in the full version of this paper. Future work can apply the techniques used in recent work to improve upon this bound [16, 30, 38].

CAU2 has some advantages over the schemes obtained through our basic transforms described in Sect. 5. CAU2 only makes use of the same keys and (often extensively optimized) primitives already existing in CAU1. This allows for code reuse, making it easy for existing hardware and software to adapt. In contrast to the generic transforms, CAU2 has a (E.bl − ℓ)-bit ciphertext overhead (for reference, in AES-GCM this is 32-bits), but lower or comparable computational overhead—a single block cipher call in both encryption and decryption.

8   A Real-World Perspective

In addition to bridging the gap between theory and usage, our framework allows us to formalize weaknesses of real-world schemes which communicate nonces in the clear.

First, it allows us to formalize an intuitive fact: pathologically chosen nonces cannot be communicated in the clear. It may seem obvious that message or key-dependent nonces violate security but such pathological nonce choices have occurred in the wild. For instance, CakePHP, a web framework, used the key as the nonce [1] when encrypting data. The use of a hash of a message has also been proposed, and subsequently argued as insecure, in an Internet forum [45].

Second, it disallows metadata leakage through the nonce. Implicit nonces with a device specific field, such as those recommended in RFC 5116 [39] enable an adversary to distinguish between different user sessions. Even the "standard" nonce choices are not safe against these adversaries. A counter will allow an adversary distinguish between sessions with high traffic and low traffic, and a randomly chosen nonce can detect devices with poor entropy (RSA public keys were used to a similar end by HDWH [27]).

Acknowledgements. We thank the anonymous reviewers for their feedback and suggestions. Bellare was supported in part by NSF grants CNS-1526801 and CNS-1717640, ERC Project ERCC FP7/615074 and a gift from Microsoft. Ng was supported by DSO National Labs. Tackmann was supported in part by the Swiss National Science Foundation (SNF) via Fellowship No. P2EZP2_155566 and NSF grant CNS-1228890.

References

1. CakePHP: Using the IV as the key. http://www.cryptofails.com/post/70059594911/cakephp-using-the-iv-as-the-key. Accessed 12 Feb 2019
2. Abed, F., et al.: Pipelineable on-line encryption. In: Cid, C., Rechberger, C. (eds.) FSE 2014. LNCS, vol. 8540, pp. 205–223. Springer, Heidelberg (2015). https://doi.org/10.1007/978-3-662-46706-0_11
3. Andreeva, E., Bogdanov, A., Luykx, A., Mennink, B., Mouha, N., Yasuda, K.: How to securely release unverified plaintext in authenticated encryption. In: Sarkar, P., Iwata, T. (eds.) ASIACRYPT 2014, Part I. LNCS, vol. 8873, pp. 105–125. Springer, Heidelberg (2014). https://doi.org/10.1007/978-3-662-45611-8_6
4. Ashur, T., Dunkelman, O., Luykx, A.: Boosting authenticated encryption robustness with minimal modifications. In: Katz, J., Shacham, H. (eds.) CRYPTO 2017, Part III. LNCS, vol. 10403, pp. 3–33. Springer, Cham (2017). https://doi.org/10.1007/978-3-319-63697-9_1

5. Aumasson, J., et al.: CHAE: challenges in authenticated encryption. ECRYPT-CSA D1.1, Revision 1.05, March 2017. https://chae.cr.yp.to/whitepaper.html
6. Barbosa, M., Farshim, P.: Indifferentiable authenticated encryption. In: Shacham, H., Boldyreva, A. (eds.) CRYPTO 2018, Part I. LNCS, vol. 10991, pp. 187–220. Springer, Cham (2018). https://doi.org/10.1007/978-3-319-96884-1_7
7. Barwell, G., Martin, D.P., Oswald, E., Stam, M.: Authenticated encryption in the face of protocol and side channel leakage. In: Takagi, T., Peyrin, T. (eds.) ASIACRYPT 2017, Part I. LNCS, vol. 10624, pp. 693–723. Springer, Cham (2017). https://doi.org/10.1007/978-3-319-70694-8_24
8. Bellare, M., Boldyreva, A., Micali, S.: Public-key encryption in a multi-user setting: security proofs and improvements. In: Preneel, B. (ed.) EUROCRYPT 2000. LNCS, vol. 1807, pp. 259–274. Springer, Heidelberg (2000). https://doi.org/10.1007/3-540-45539-6_18
9. Bellare, M., Canetti, R., Krawczyk, H.: Pseudorandom functions revisited: the cascade construction and its concrete security. In: 37th FOCS. IEEE Computer Society Press, October 1996
10. Bellare, M., Desai, A., Jokipii, E., Rogaway, P.: A concrete security treatment of symmetric encryption. In: 38th FOCS. IEEE Computer Society Press, October 1997
11. Bellare, M., Namprempre, C.: Authenticated encryption: relations among notions and analysis of the generic composition paradigm. In: Okamoto, T. (ed.) ASIACRYPT 2000. LNCS, vol. 1976, pp. 531–545. Springer, Heidelberg (2000). https://doi.org/10.1007/3-540-44448-3_41
12. Bellare, M., Ng, R., Tackmann, B.: Nonces are noticed: AEAD revisited. Cryptology ePrint Archive Report 2019/624 (2019). http://eprint.iacr.org/2019/624
13. Bellare, M., Rogaway, P.: On the construction of variable-input-length ciphers. In: Knudsen, L. (ed.) FSE 1999. LNCS, vol. 1636, pp. 231–244. Springer, Heidelberg (1999). https://doi.org/10.1007/3-540-48519-8_17
14. Bellare, M., Rogaway, P.: Encode-then-encipher encryption: how to exploit nonces or redundancy in plaintexts for efficient cryptography. In: Okamoto, T. (ed.) ASIACRYPT 2000. LNCS, vol. 1976, pp. 317–330. Springer, Heidelberg (2000). https://doi.org/10.1007/3-540-44448-3_24
15. Bellare, M., Rogaway, P.: The security of triple encryption and a framework for code-based game-playing proofs. In: Vaudenay, S. (ed.) EUROCRYPT 2006. LNCS, vol. 4004, pp. 409–426. Springer, Heidelberg (2006). https://doi.org/10.1007/11761679_25
16. Bellare, M., Tackmann, B.: The multi-user security of authenticated encryption: AES-GCM in TLS 1.3. In: Robshaw, M., Katz, J. (eds.) CRYPTO 2016, Part I. LNCS, vol. 9814, pp. 247–276. Springer, Heidelberg (2016). https://doi.org/10.1007/978-3-662-53018-4_10
17. Bernstein, D.: CAESAR call for submissions, final, 27 January 2014. https://competitions.cr.yp.to/caesar-call.html
18. Bose, P., Hoang, V.T., Tessaro, S.: Revisiting AES-GCM-SIV: multi-user security, faster key derivation, and better bounds. In: Nielsen, J.B., Rijmen, V. (eds.) EUROCRYPT 2018, Part I. LNCS, vol. 10820, pp. 468–499. Springer, Cham (2018). https://doi.org/10.1007/978-3-319-78381-9_18
19. CAESAR Committee: Cryptographic competitions: Caesar call for submissions, final, 27 January 2014. https://competitions.cr.yp.to/caesar-call.html. Accessed 23 July 2018

20. Checkoway, S., et al.: A systematic analysis of the juniper dual EC incident. In: Weippl, E.R., Katzenbeisser, S., Kruegel, C., Myers, A.C., Halevi, S. (eds.) ACM CCS (2016)
21. Dodis, Y., Grubbs, P., Ristenpart, T., Woodage, J.: Fast message franking: from invisible salamanders to encryptment. In: Shacham, H., Boldyreva, A. (eds.) CRYPTO 2018, Part I. LNCS, vol. 10991, pp. 155–186. Springer, Cham (2018). https://doi.org/10.1007/978-3-319-96884-1_6
22. Dworkin, M.: Recommendation for block cipher modes of operation: Galois/Counter Mode (GCM) and GMAC. NIST Special Publication 800–38D, November 2007
23. Fleischmann, E., Forler, C., Lucks, S.: McOE: a family of almost foolproof on-line authenticated encryption schemes. In: Canteaut, A. (ed.) FSE 2012. LNCS, vol. 7549, pp. 196–215. Springer, Heidelberg (2012). https://doi.org/10.1007/978-3-642-34047-5_12
24. Grubbs, P., Lu, J., Ristenpart, T.: Message franking via committing authenticated encryption. In: Katz, J., Shacham, H. (eds.) CRYPTO 2017, Part III. LNCS, vol. 10403, pp. 66–97. Springer, Cham (2017). https://doi.org/10.1007/978-3-319-63697-9_3
25. Gueron, S., Langley, A., Lindell, Y.: AES-GCM-SIV: specification and analysis. Cryptology ePrint Archive, Report 2017/168 (2017). http://eprint.iacr.org/2017/168
26. Gueron, S., Lindell, Y.: GCM-SIV: full nonce misuse-resistant authenticated encryption at under one cycle per byte. In: Ray, I., Li, N., Kruegel, C. (eds.) ACM CCS (2015)
27. Heninger, N., Durumeric, Z., Wustrow, E., Halderman, J.A.: Mining your Ps and Qs: detection of widespread weak keys in network devices. In: USENIX Security Symposium, vol. 8, p. 1 (2012)
28. Hoang, V.T., Krovetz, T., Rogaway, P.: Robust authenticated-encryption AEZ and the problem that it solves. In: Oswald, E., Fischlin, M. (eds.) EUROCRYPT 2015, Part I. LNCS, vol. 9056, pp. 15–44. Springer, Heidelberg (2015). https://doi.org/10.1007/978-3-662-46800-5_2
29. Hoang, V.T., Reyhanitabar, R., Rogaway, P., Vizár, D.: Online authenticated-encryption and its nonce-reuse misuse-resistance. In: Gennaro, R., Robshaw, M. (eds.) CRYPTO 2015, Part I. LNCS, vol. 9215, pp. 493–517. Springer, Heidelberg (2015). https://doi.org/10.1007/978-3-662-47989-6_24
30. Hoang, V.T., Tessaro, S., Thiruvengadam, A.: The multi-user security of GCM, revisited: tight bounds for nonce randomization. In: Lie, D., Mannan, M., Backes, M., Wang, X. (eds.) ACM CCS (2018)
31. Iwata, T., Ohashi, K., Minematsu, K.: Breaking and repairing GCM security proofs. In: Safavi-Naini, R., Canetti, R. (eds.) CRYPTO 2012. LNCS, vol. 7417, pp. 31–49. Springer, Heidelberg (2012). https://doi.org/10.1007/978-3-642-32009-5_3
32. Joux, A.: Authentication failures in NIST version of GCM (2006). Comments submitted to NIST modes of operation process. https://csrc.nist.gov/csrc/media/projects/block-cipher-techniques/documents/bcm/comments/800-38-series-drafts/gcm/joux_comments.pdf
33. Katz, J., Yung, M.: Unforgeable encryption and chosen ciphertext secure modes of operation. In: Goos, G., Hartmanis, J., van Leeuwen, J., Schneier, B. (eds.) FSE 2000. LNCS, vol. 1978, pp. 284–299. Springer, Heidelberg (2001). https://doi.org/10.1007/3-540-44706-7_20

34. Krawczyk, H.: LFSR-based hashing and authentication. In: Desmedt, Y.G. (ed.) CRYPTO 1994. LNCS, vol. 839, pp. 129–139. Springer, Heidelberg (1994). https://doi.org/10.1007/3-540-48658-5_15

35. Krovetz, T., Rogaway, P.: The software performance of authenticated-encryption modes. In: Joux, A. (ed.) FSE 2011. LNCS, vol. 6733, pp. 306–327. Springer, Heidelberg (2011). https://doi.org/10.1007/978-3-642-21702-9_18

36. Kurosawa, K., Iwata, T.: TMAC: two-key CBC MAC. In: Joye, M. (ed.) CT-RSA 2003. LNCS, vol. 2612, pp. 33–49. Springer, Heidelberg (2003). https://doi.org/10.1007/3-540-36563-X_3

37. Liskov, M., Rivest, R.L., Wagner, D.: Tweakable block ciphers. J. Cryptol. 24(3), 588–613 (2011)

38. Luykx, A., Mennink, B., Paterson, K.G.: Analyzing multi-key security degradation. In: Takagi, T., Peyrin, T. (eds.) ASIACRYPT 2017, Part II. LNCS, vol. 10625, pp. 575–605. Springer, Cham (2017). https://doi.org/10.1007/978-3-319-70697-9_20

39. McGrew, D.: An interface and algorithms for authenticated encryption. IETF Network Working Group, RFC 5116, January 2008

40. McGrew, D.A., Viega, J.: The security and performance of the Galois/Counter Mode (GCM) of operation. In: Canteaut, A., Viswanathan, K. (eds.) INDOCRYPT 2004. LNCS, vol. 3348, pp. 343–355. Springer, Heidelberg (2004). https://doi.org/10.1007/978-3-540-30556-9_27

41. Meyer, C.H., Matyas, S.M.: CRYPTOGRAPHY: A New Dimension in Computer Data Security: A Guide for the Design and Implementation of Secure Systems. Wiley, New York (1982)

42. Minematsu, K.: Authenticated encryption with small stretch (or, how to accelerate AERO). In: Liu, J.K., Steinfeld, R. (eds.) ACISP 2016, Part II. LNCS, vol. 9723, pp. 347–362. Springer, Cham (2016). https://doi.org/10.1007/978-3-319-40367-0_22

43. Namprempre, C., Rogaway, P., Shrimpton, T.: Reconsidering generic composition. In: Nguyen, P.Q., Oswald, E. (eds.) EUROCRYPT 2014. LNCS, vol. 8441, pp. 257–274. Springer, Heidelberg (2014). https://doi.org/10.1007/978-3-642-55220-5_15

44. Namprempre, C., Rogaway, P., Shrimpton, T.: AE5 security notions: definitions implicit in the CAESAR call. Cryptology ePrint Archive, Report 2013/242 (2013). http://eprint.iacr.org/2013/242

45. Reddit: Hash of message as nonce? (2015). https://redd.it/3c504m

46. Rogaway, P.: Authenticated-encryption with associated-data. In: Atluri, V. (ed.) ACM CCS (2002)

47. Rogaway, P.: Efficient instantiations of tweakable blockciphers and refinements to modes OCB and PMAC. In: Lee, P.J. (ed.) ASIACRYPT 2004. LNCS, vol. 3329, pp. 16–31. Springer, Heidelberg (2004). https://doi.org/10.1007/978-3-540-30539-2_2

48. Rogaway, P.: Nonce-based symmetric encryption. In: Roy, B., Meier, W. (eds.) FSE 2004. LNCS, vol. 3017, pp. 348–358. Springer, Heidelberg (2004). https://doi.org/10.1007/978-3-540-25937-4_22

49. Rogaway, P.: The evolution of authenticated encryption. Real World Cryptography Workshop, Stanford, January 2013. https://crypto.stanford.edu/RealWorldCrypto/slides/phil.pdf

50. Rogaway, P., Bellare, M., Black, J., Krovetz, T.: OCB: a block-cipher mode of operation for efficient authenticated encryption. In: Reiter, M.K., Samarati, P. (eds.) ACM CCS (2001)

51. Rogaway, P., Shrimpton, T.: A provable-security treatment of the key-wrap problem. In: Vaudenay, S. (ed.) EUROCRYPT 2006. LNCS, vol. 4004, pp. 373–390. Springer, Heidelberg (2006). https://doi.org/10.1007/11761679_23

52. Vaudenay, S., Vizár, D.: Under pressure: security of Caesar candidates beyond their guarantees. Cryptology ePrint Archive, Report 2017/1147 (2017). https://eprint.iacr.org/2017/1147
53. Wu, H., Preneel, B.: AEGIS: a fast authenticated encryption algorithm. In: Lange, T., Lauter, K., Lisoněk, P. (eds.) SAC 2013. LNCS, vol. 8282, pp. 185–201. Springer, Heidelberg (2014). https://doi.org/10.1007/978-3-662-43414-7_10

How to Build Pseudorandom Functions from Public Random Permutations

Yu Long Chen[1](✉), Eran Lambooij[2](✉), and Bart Mennink[3]

[1] imec-COSIC, KU Leuven, Leuven, Belgium
yulong.chen@kuleuven.be
[2] University of Haifa, Haifa, Israel
eranlambooij@gmail.com
[3] Digital Security Group, Radboud University, Nijmegen, The Netherlands
b.mennink@cs.ru.nl

Abstract. Pseudorandom functions are traditionally built upon block ciphers, but with the trend of permutation based cryptography, it is a natural question to investigate the design of pseudorandom functions from random permutations. We present a generic study of how to build beyond birthday bound secure pseudorandom functions from public random permutations. We first show that a pseudorandom function based on a single permutation call cannot be secure beyond the $2^{n/2}$ birthday bound, where n is the state size of the function. We next consider the Sum of Even-Mansour (SoEM) construction, that instantiates the sum of permutations with the Even-Mansour construction. We prove that SoEM achieves tight $2n/3$-bit security if it is constructed from two independent permutations and two randomly drawn keys. We also demonstrate a birthday bound attack if either the permutations or the keys are identical. Finally, we present the Sum of Key Alternating Ciphers (SoKAC) construction, a translation of Encrypted Davies-Meyer Dual to a public permutation based setting, and show that SoKAC achieves tight $2n/3$-bit security even when a single key is used.

Keywords: RP-to-PRF · SoEM · SoKAC · Beyond the birthday bound

1 Introduction

In the seminal work of Luby and Rackoff [47], a paradigm of constructing a pseudorandom permutation (PRP) from a pseudorandom function (PRF) was introduced. Their work, motivated by the DES block cipher, consists of an r-round Feistel construction involving independent invocations of a PRF. Soon people realized that they actually needed the opposite construction, i.e., constructing a PRF from a PRP. The reason for this is two-fold: (i) PRPs are easier to design than PRFs and (ii) many cryptographic schemes, such as counter mode, are better off if instantiated with a PRF.

The classical PRP-PRF switch [6,8,19,38,41], which consists of taking an n-bit block cipher E_K as a PRF, is only secure up to the birthday bound: an attacker that

© International Association for Cryptologic Research 2019
A. Boldyreva and D. Micciancio (Eds.): CRYPTO 2019, LNCS 11692, pp. 266–293, 2019.
https://doi.org/10.1007/978-3-030-26948-7_10

can learn around $2^{n/2}$ evaluations of E_K can distinguish it from random. Although this bound is acceptable for large enough n, in light of the rise of lightweight block ciphers [3,4,16,18,30,36,40,46,62,67] this bound is on the edge for certain applications. For example, for a 64-bit block cipher, breaking security requires approximately $2^{32} \cdot 64$ bits of data, which is approximately 35GB. Of a similar kind, Bhargavan and Leurent [13] performed practical attacks on TLS and OpenVPN when a 64-bit block cipher is used.

Various approaches of turning a PRP into a PRF with beyond birthday bound security have been introduced. Hall et al. [38] suggested truncation: $\mathrm{trunc}_m(E_K(M))$, an approach that was later proven to be secure up to around $2^{n-m/2}$ queries [5,35]. Bellare et al. [7] proposed the sum of permutations (SoP),

$$E_{K_1}(M) \oplus E_{K_2}(M), \tag{1}$$

a construction that is known to achieve $q/2^n$ security [5,28,48,57]. Cogliati and Seurin [24] introduced the Encrypted Davies-Meyer (EDM) construction, $E_{K_2}(E_{K_1}(M) \oplus M)$, and proved that it is $2^{2n/3}$ secure. Mennink and Neves [50] improved the security to be 2^n using Patarin's mirror theory [53,55,57,58]. They also introduced the dual: $E_{K_2}(E_{K_1}(M)) \oplus E_{K_1}(M)$, called Encrypted Davies-Mayer Dual (EDMD), and showed that its security is implied by that of the sum of permutations.

All constructions, however, are yet based on block ciphers. Even stronger, they only evaluate E_K in the forward direction. As block ciphers are designed to be efficient in both the forward and inverse direction, these are thus over-engineered primitives for this purpose. This is in contrast with the modern trend in cryptography, namely that of permutation based cryptography, where the underlying permutations are particularly developed to be fast in the forward direction, but not necessarily in the inverse direction. Examples of cryptographic permutations include Keccak [12], Gimli [9], and SPONGENT [15].

So what we really need is a PRF designed from public permutations, but the state of the art in this direction is scarce. To our knowledge, the only notable approach in this direction are the keyed sponge [1,11,52] and Farfalle [10], however these constructions have been developed with different incentives in mind. Most importantly, they are variable-length, and for small fixed length messages better solutions may be possible.

Acknowledgedly, the state size of a permutation is typically larger than the block size n of a message: whereas AES has a block size of 128 bits, making the naive birthday bound PRP-PRF switch on the edge, the SHA-3 permutation is of size 1600 bits, and a simple Even-Mansour [32] construction on top of it would give a PRP that behaves like a PRF up to an attack complexity of 2^{800}. However, this example permutation is on the extreme end: lightweight permutations such as SPONGENT [15] and PHOTON [37] go as low as 88 and 100 bits, respectively. For these types of permutations, birthday bound solutions are inadequate.

1.1   Towards Birthday Bound Security

Suppose we take the sum of permutations (1), and want to turn it into a PRF conversion function for a public random permutation. Recall that the sum of permutations is secure up to complexity 2^n as long as the underlying block ciphers are secure. A naive way of proceeding is to plug the Even-Mansour block cipher construction

$$EM_K(M) = \pi(M \oplus K) \oplus K,$$

where π is an n-bit permutation, into the sum of permutations. However, the Even-Mansour construction is known to be tightly $2^{n/2}$ birthday bound secure. A simple modular reasoning, in turn, leaves us with an unsatisfiable birthday bound security level.

One way to resolve this is by eschewing the Even-Mansour construction in favor of multiple-round Even-Mansour. For example, 2-round Even-Mansour is secure up to complexity around $2^{2n/3}$, and the generic composition of the sum of permutation with this construction guarantees security up to the same level as well. On the other hand, the scheme has become twice as expensive in the number of primitive evaluations: it is based on four permutation calls. Fortunately, the poor bound of the composition of the sum of permutations with Even-Mansour is not inherent to the scheme, but rather, it is due to a lossy composition. A dedicated analysis can render an improved bound.

1.2   Our Contribution

We tackle the problem of designing a PRF from a public random permutation from a generalized perspective. First, we consider the general design of a PRF based on one and only one public permutation that is preceded and followed by linear mappings, and demonstrate that such construction cannot be secure beyond the birthday bound. The proof consists of considering different types of linear mappings, and deriving attacks in the birthday bound (or faster) for all variants. The result is given in Sect. 3.

Our second and main contribution centers around the sum of permutations instantiated with Even-Mansour, a construction which we dub SoEM: (Sum of Even Mansour). It is based on two permutations π_1, π_2, and it either takes two keys K_1, K_2 (one before and after each permutation) or it takes a single key K (added before each permutation, and to the final sum). We derive the following results in Sect. 4:

(i) If $\pi_1 = \pi_2$, so if both Even-Mansour constructions are instantiated using the same permutation, SoEM can be broken in complexity around $2^{n/2}$;

(ii) If π_1 and π_2 are independent, and the construction takes a single key K, SoEM can again be broken in complexity around $2^{n/2}$;

(iii) If π_1 and π_2 are independent, and so are K_1 and K_2, the resulting construction is tightly secure up to complexity $2^{2n/3}$.

The proof of (iii) is performed in the ideal permutation model, using Patarin's H-coefficient technique [21,54,56]. It resembles ideas of the first iteration in Patarin's mirror theory [57], but difficulties appear in the fact that the permutations π_1, π_2 can be queried by the distinguisher.

The result sparks curiosity on whether $2n/3$-security is also achievable by a construction based on a single key. We answer this question positively by introducing SoKAC (Sum of Key Alternating Ciphers) in Sect. 5. SoKAC reminds of EDMD instantiated with Even-Mansour, barring subtle differences, but it can likewise be seen as adding a 1-round Key Alternating Cipher (KAC) [17] to a 2-round one. By putting the first permutation equal in both KACs, the construction makes in total two permutation calls per evaluation. Whereas the scheme is only birthday bound secure if the permutations are identical, i.e. if $\pi_1 = \pi_2$, for the case of independent permutations the construction achieves $2n/3$-security even though it only relies on a single n-bit key. The proof is based on the sum-capture lemma [2,20,25,51,63].

1.3 Our Contribution in Bigger Perspective

Conversion from public or secret permutations to public or secret functions and vice versa is a fundamental problem in symmetric key cryptography, and our work fills the last remaining notable gap in the picture.

We already discussed the issue of PRF-to-PRP conversion: Luby and Rackoff [47] described the Feistel network, a method still used to design block ciphers. Reversely, PRP-to-PRF conversion was covered by SoP [7], EDM [24], and EDMD [50].

One can consider similar techniques for conversion between public random permutations (RPs) and public random functions (RFs). In this setting, the functions are keyless, and one assumes ideality of the underlying primitives in order to prove security in the indifferentiability framework [49]. The Feistel construction has seen notable indifferentiability analysis [26,27,29], and so has the sum of permutation construction [14,23,51].

Note that there is little incentive to investigate conversion from PRP/PRF to RP/RF. The Even-Mansour construction [32] transforms an RP to a PRP; it has been generalized in [17,21,31,39,44,64]. Gentry and Ramzan [34] proposed the idea of combining the Feistel construction and the Even-Mansour cipher, which was later named the Key Alternating Feistel (KAF) cipher by Lampe and Seurin [45]. In the work of Gazi and Tessaro [33], a construction that turns RFs into PRF has been introduced. Moreover, the Whitened Swap-or-Not construction by Tessaro [65] provides another way of building nearly optimal n-bits secure PRP from RPs or RFs.

This leaves the problem of RP-to-PRF conversion, i.e. the problem considered in this work. The full picture of example conversion techniques is given in Fig. 1.

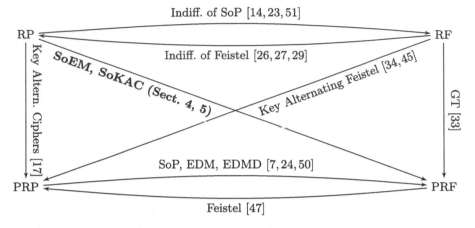

Fig. 1. Conversion among PRP, PRF, RP, and RF. The given example constructions are not exhaustive.

2   Preliminaries

For $n \in \mathbb{N}$, we denote by $\{0,1\}^n$ the set of bit strings of length n. For two bit strings $X, Y \in \{0,1\}^n$, we denote their bitwise addition as $X \oplus Y$. For a value Z, we denote by $A \leftarrow Z$ the assignment of Z to the variable A. For a finite set $\mathcal{S}$, we denote by $S \xleftarrow{\$} \mathcal{S}$ the uniformly random selection of S from $\mathcal{S}$. We denote by $\mathrm{Func}(n)$ the set of all functions on $\{0,1\}^n$ and by $\mathrm{Perm}(n)$ the set of all permutations on $\{0,1\}^n$. We denote by $\langle t \rangle_n$ the encoding of a value $t \in \{0, \ldots, 2^n - 1\}$ as an n-bit string.

For $k, n, r \in \mathbb{N}$, let $F \colon \{0,1\}^k \times \{0,1\}^n \to \{0,1\}^n$ be a function that is based on r n-bit permutations $\pi_1, \ldots, \pi_r$. We will consider pseudorandom function security of F, where we assume that $\pi_1, \ldots, \pi_r \xleftarrow{\$} \mathrm{Perm}(n)$, and where the distinguisher $\mathcal{D}$ is given access to either $(F_K^{\pi_1, \ldots, \pi_r}, \pi_1^\pm, \ldots, \pi_r^\pm)$ for secret key $K \xleftarrow{\$} \{0,1\}^k$ or $(\varphi, \pi_1^\pm, \ldots, \pi_r^\pm)$ for $\varphi \xleftarrow{\$} \mathrm{Func}(n)$, where the superscript $\pm$ for the π_i's indicates that the distinguisher has bi-directional access. Its goal is to determine which oracle it is given access to:

$$\mathbf{Adv}_F^{\mathrm{prf}}(\mathcal{D}) = \left| \Pr\left[\mathcal{D}^{F_K^{\pi_1, \ldots, \pi_r}, \pi_1^\pm, \ldots, \pi_r^\pm} = 1 \right] - \Pr\left[\mathcal{D}^{\varphi, \pi_1^\pm, \ldots, \pi_r^\pm} = 1 \right] \right|, \quad (2)$$

for $K \xleftarrow{\$} \{0,1\}^k$, $\pi_1, \ldots, \pi_r \xleftarrow{\$} \mathrm{Perm}(n)$, and $\varphi \xleftarrow{\$} \mathrm{Func}(n)$.

In the remainder of this work, we will focus on keys of size n or $2n$ bits.

3   Pseudorandom Functions with One Permutation Call

We will show that any pseudorandom function F that makes only one permutation call and has linear pre- and post-processing functions cannot achieve security beyond the birthday bound. Let $n \in \mathbb{N}$, and let $\pi \in \mathrm{Perm}(n)$.

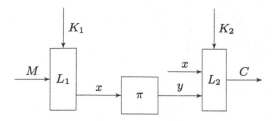

Fig. 2. Function $F1$ based on two keys K_1 and K_2, and making one public random permutations evaluation.

Let $L_1\colon \{0,1\}^n \times \{0,1\}^n \to \{0,1\}^n$ and $L_2\colon \{0,1\}^n \times \{0,1\}^n \times \{0,1\}^n \to \{0,1\}^n$ be any two linear mappings (that only consist of modular addition and scalar multiplication). Let $F1\colon \{0,1\}^{2n} \times \{0,1\}^n \to \{0,1\}^n$ be the function of Fig. 2. We will show that for independent K_1, K_2, there exists a distinguisher that can distinguish any such function from random using at most $3 \cdot 2^{n/2}$ construction queries and at most $3 \cdot 2^{n/2}$ primitive queries. Note that modular addition of the input M to the output C does not influence the security of $F1$, as the distinguisher knows the exact value of M.

Proposition 1. *Let $n \in \mathbb{N}$, and consider the function $F1\colon \{0,1\}^{2n} \times \{0,1\}^n \to \{0,1\}^n$ of Fig. 2 based on permutation $\pi \xleftarrow{\$} \mathrm{Perm}(n)$ and two keys $K_1, K_2 \xleftarrow{\$} \{0,1\}^n$, for any linear L_1, L_2. There exists a distinguisher $\mathcal{D}$ making at most $3 \cdot 2^{n/2}$ construction queries and at most $3 \cdot 2^{n/2}$ primitive queries such that*

$$\mathbf{Adv}_{F1}^{\mathrm{prf}}(\mathcal{D}) \geq 1 - \frac{1}{e}. \tag{3}$$

Proof. As the mixing functions L_1, L_2 are linear, we can represent these as

$$L_1 = \big(l_{11}\ l_{12}\big)$$
$$L_2 = \big(l_{21}\ l_{22}\ l_{23}\big)\,,$$

where L_1, L_2 are evaluated on (K_1, M) and (K_2, x, y), respectively.
    The distinguisher's advantage satisfies

$$\mathbf{Adv}_{F1}^{\mathrm{prf}}(\mathcal{D}) = \left| \Pr\left[\mathcal{D}^{F1^\pi, \pi^\pm} = 1\right] - \Pr\left[\mathcal{D}^{\varphi, \pi^\pm} = 1\right] \right|.$$

Subcase $l_{12} = 0 \vee l_{23} = 0$. In this case, the input to or the output of the permutation π is not related to M or C. When $l_{12} = 0$, the distinguisher selects arbitrary M, M' to obtain C, C'. If the event $C = C'$ happens, then output 1; otherwise, output 0. This gives a distinguisher in two construction queries with a success probability of $1 - 1/2^n$. Similar for $l_{23} = 0$.

Subcase $l_{11} = 0 \lor l_{21} = 0$. In this case, the input to or the output of the permutation π is independent of the keys. When $l_{11} = 0$, the distinguisher selects arbitrary x, x' to obtain y, y'. Then, it puts $M = l_{12}^{-1}x$ and $M' = l_{12}^{-1}x'$ to obtain C and C'. If the event A happens, then output 1; otherwise, output 0:

$$A = \begin{cases} C \oplus C' = l_{23}y \oplus l_{23}y' & \text{if } l_{22} = 0 , \\ C \oplus C' = l_{23}y \oplus l_{23}y' \oplus l_{22}x \oplus l_{22}x' & \text{if } l_{22} \neq 0 . \end{cases}$$

This gives a distinguisher in two construction and two primitive queries with a success probability of $1 - 1/2^n$. Similar for $l_{21} = 0$.

Subcase $l_{22} = 0$. In this case, the construction is a generalization of the Even-Mansour cipher. We will construct a distinguisher $\mathcal{D}$ distinguishing the real world oracle $(F1^\pi, \pi)$ from the ideal world oracle (φ, π) with significant probability. $\mathcal{D}$ makes $2^{n/2}$ construction queries and no primitive queries and operates as follows. For $j = 1, \ldots, 2^{n/2}$, the distinguisher selects arbitrary $M^{(j)}$'s to obtain $C^{(j)}$. If we have $C^{(j)} \neq C^{(j')}$ for all query indices $j \neq j'$, then output 1; otherwise, output 0.

In the real world, $F1$ behaves as a PRP, and thus $\Pr\left[\mathcal{D}^{F1^\pi, \pi^\pm} = 1\right] = 1$. For the ideal world, we have

$$\Pr\left[\mathcal{D}^{\varphi, \pi^\pm} = 1\right] = \Pr\left[\cap_{j, j'} C^{(j)} \neq C^{(j')}\right] \leq 1 - \left(1 - e^{-\binom{q}{2}\frac{1}{2^n}}\right) = e^{-\binom{q}{2}\frac{1}{2^n}},$$

where $q = 2^{n/2}$.

Subcase $l_{11}, l_{12}, l_{21}, l_{22}, l_{23} \neq 0$. This is the most general subcase. We will construct a distinguisher $\mathcal{D}$ distinguishing the real world oracle $(F1^\pi, \pi)$ from the ideal world oracle (φ, π) with significant probability. The distinguisher $\mathcal{D}$ returns 1 if it guesses that it is interacting with the real world oracle and returns 0 otherwise. $\mathcal{D}$ makes $3 \cdot 2^{n/2}$ construction queries, and $3 \cdot 2^{n/2}$ primitive queries to π in total and operates as follows.

(i) For $j = 1, \ldots, 2^{n/2}$, query $M^{(j)} = l_{12}^{-1}(\langle j \rangle_{n/2} \parallel 0^{n/2})$ to obtain $C^{(j)}$, query $M^{*(j)} = l_{12}^{-1}(\langle j \rangle_{n/2} \parallel 0^{n/2-1}1)$ to obtain $C^{*(j)}$, and $M^{**(j)} = l_{12}^{-1}(\langle j \rangle_{n/2} \parallel 0^{n/2-2}10)$ to obtain $C^{**(j)}$;

(ii) For $i = 1, \ldots, 2^{n/2}$, query $x^{(i)} = 0^{n/2} \parallel \langle i \rangle_{n/2}$ to obtain $y^{(i)}$. Define $(x^{*(i)}, y^{*(i)})$ and $(x^{**(i)}, y^{**(i)})$ as the tuples that satisfy $x^{*(i)} = x^{(i)} \oplus 0^{n-1}1$ and $x^{**(i)} = x^{(i)} \oplus 0^{n-2}10$, respectively;

(iii) If there are two query indices $\bar{j}, \bar{i}$ such that $C^{(\bar{j})} \oplus C^{*(\bar{j})} = l_{22}(x^{(\bar{i})} \oplus x^{*(\bar{i})}) \oplus l_{23}(y^{(\bar{i})} \oplus y^{*(\bar{i})})$ and $C^{(\bar{j})} \oplus C^{**(\bar{j})} = l_{22}(x^{(\bar{i})} \oplus x^{**(\bar{i})}) \oplus l_{23}(y^{(\bar{i})} \oplus y^{**(\bar{i})})$, then output 1; otherwise, output 0.

In the real world, there is exactly one $(\bar{j}, \bar{i})$ such that $l_{11}^{-1}(l_{12}M^{(\bar{j})} \oplus x^{(\bar{i})}) = K_1$, leading to

$$C^{(\bar{j})} = l_{22}x^{(\bar{i})} \oplus l_{23}y^{(\bar{i})} \oplus l_{21}K_2 .$$

In addition, also $l_{11}^{-1}(l_{12}M^{*(\bar{j})} \oplus x^{*(\bar{i})}) = K_1$ and $l_{11}^{-1}(l_{12}M^{**(\bar{j})} \oplus x^{**(\bar{i})}) = K_1$, leading to

$$C^{*(\bar{j})} = l_{22}x^{*(\bar{i})} \oplus l_{23}y^{*(\bar{i})} \oplus l_{21}K_2 \,,$$
$$C^{**(\bar{j})} = l_{22}x^{**(\bar{i})} \oplus l_{23}y^{**(\bar{i})} \oplus l_{21}K_2 \,.$$

The equations imply that

$$A_{\bar{j},\bar{i}} \colon C^{(\bar{j})} \oplus C^{*(\bar{j})} = l_{22}(x^{(\bar{i})} \oplus x^{*(\bar{i})}) \oplus l_{23}(y^{(\bar{i})} \oplus y^{*(\bar{i})}) \,,$$
$$B_{\bar{j},\bar{i}} \colon C^{(\bar{j})} \oplus C^{**(\bar{j})} = l_{22}(x^{(\bar{i})} \oplus x^{**(\bar{i})}) \oplus l_{23}(y^{(\bar{i})} \oplus y^{**(\bar{i})}) \,,$$

and thus that $\Pr\left[\mathcal{D}^{F1^\pi,\pi^\pm} = 1\right] = 1$.

For the ideal world, we have

$$\Pr\left[\mathcal{D}^{\varphi,\pi^\pm} = 1\right] = \Pr\left[\cup_{j,i} A_{j,i} \wedge B_{j,i}\right] \leq \frac{qp}{2^{2n}} \,,$$

where $q = p = 2^{n/2}$. $\qquad\qquad\qquad\qquad\qquad\qquad\qquad\qquad\qquad\qquad\square$

4   Sum of Even-Mansour

We consider the *Sum of Even-Mansour* construction, called SoEM, that combines the sum of permutations of Bellare et al. [7] with the Even-Mansour cipher [32]. Let $n \in \mathbb{N}$, and let $\pi_1, \pi_2 \in \mathrm{Perm}(n)$. One can consider a generic construction SoEM: $\{0,1\}^{2n} \times \{0,1\}^n \to \{0,1\}^n$ as

$$\mathrm{SoEM}(K_1, K_2, M) = \pi_1(M \oplus K_1) \oplus K_1 \oplus \pi_2(M \oplus K_2) \oplus K_2 \,. \tag{4}$$

See also Fig. 3. We will consider the construction for three variants: SoEM1 for the case where π_1 and π_2 are identical in Sect. 4.1, SoEM21 for the case where π_1, π_2 are independent but K_1 and K_2 are identical (so the key space is n bits) in Sect. 4.2, and SoEM22 for the case where π_1, π_2 are independent and K_1, K_2 are independent in Sect. 4.3. Note that for SoEM21, we will have to make a slight adjustment, because by simply putting $K_1 = K_2$ in above equation, the addition of the keys at the end of the permutation calls will cancel out. We will detail this in Sect. 4.2.

4.1   One Permutation

We show that SoEM1, where $\pi_1 = \pi_2$ (but no a priori restriction on K_1, K_2 is imposed) cannot achieve security beyond the birthday bound.

Proposition 2. *Let* $n \in \mathbb{N}$*, and consider* SoEM1: $\{0,1\}^{2n} \times \{0,1\}^n \to \{0,1\}^n$ *based on permutation* $\pi \xleftarrow{\$} \mathrm{Perm}(n)$ *and two keys* $K_1, K_2 \xleftarrow{\$} \{0,1\}^n$*. There exists a distinguisher* $\mathcal{D}$ *making* $4 \cdot 2^{n/2}$ *construction queries such that*

$$\mathbf{Adv}^{\mathrm{prf}}_{\mathrm{SoEM1}}(\mathcal{D}) \geq 1 - \frac{1}{2^n} \,. \tag{5}$$

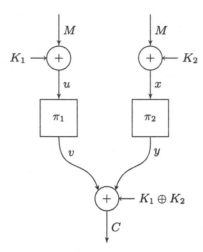

Fig. 3. Encryption of SoEM based on two keys K_1 and K_2, and with π_1 and π_2 two public random permutations.

Proof. We will construct a distinguisher $\mathcal{D}$ distinguishing the real world oracle $(\text{SoEM1}^\pi, \pi^\pm)$ from the ideal world oracle $(\varphi, \pi^\pm)$ with significant probability. The distinguisher $\mathcal{D}$ returns 1 if it guesses that it is interacting with the real world oracle and returns 0 otherwise. $\mathcal{D}$ makes $4 \cdot 2^{n/2}$ construction queries and no primitive queries and operates as follows.

(i) For $j = 1, \ldots, 2^{n/2}$, query $M^{(j)} = \langle j \rangle_{n/2} \parallel 0^{n/2}$ to obtain $C^{(j)}$, and query $M^{*(j)} = M^{(j)} \oplus 0^{n-1}1$ to obtain $C^{*(j)}$;

(ii) For $j' = 1, \ldots, 2^{n/2}$, query $M^{(j')} = 0^{n/2} \parallel \langle j' \rangle_{n/2}$ to obtain $C^{(j')}$. Define $(M^{*(j')}, C^{*(j')})$ as the tuple that satisfies $M^{*(j')} = M^{(j')} \oplus 0^{n-1}1$;

(iii) If there are two query indices $\bar{j}, \bar{j}'$ such that $C^{(\bar{j})} = C^{(\bar{j}')}$ and $C^{*(\bar{j})} = C^{*(\bar{j}')}$, then output 1; otherwise, output 0.

The distinguisher's advantage satisfies

$$\mathbf{Adv}^{\text{prf}}_{\text{SoEM1}}(\mathcal{D}) = \left| \Pr\left[\mathcal{D}^{\text{SoEM1}^\pi_{K_1,K_2},\pi^\pm} = 1 \right] - \Pr\left[\mathcal{D}^{\varphi,\pi^\pm} = 1 \right] \right|.$$

In the real world, there is exactly one $(\bar{j}, \bar{j}')$ such that $M^{(\bar{j})} \oplus M^{(\bar{j}')} = K_1 \oplus K_2$, leading to $C^{(\bar{j})} = C^{(\bar{j}')}$ in the real world. In addition, also $M^{*(\bar{j})} \oplus M^{*(\bar{j}')} = K_1 \oplus K_2$, and $C^{*(\bar{j})} = C^{*(\bar{j}')}$ as well. Thus, $\Pr\left[\mathcal{D}^{\text{SoEM1}^\pi_{K_1,K_2},\pi^\pm} = 1 \right] = 1$.

For the ideal world, we have

$$\Pr\left[\mathcal{D}^{\varphi,\pi^\pm} = 1 \right] = \Pr\left[\cup_{j,j'} C^{(j)} = C^{(j')} \wedge C^{*(j)} = C^{*(j')} \right] \leq \frac{q^2}{2^{2n}},$$

where $q = 2^{n/2}$. □

Note that the cost of step (i) in the attack can be reduced by only querying $M^{*(j)}$ for $j = \bar{j}$, but this would complicate the simple description of the distinguisher.

4.2 Two Permutations, One Key

Let $n \in \mathbb{N}$. Let $\pi_1, \pi_2 : \{0,1\}^n \to \{0,1\}^n$ be two independent random permutations. We define SoEM construction based on π_1, π_2 and using a single key K as follows:

$$\mathrm{SoEM21}^{\pi_1,\pi_2}(K, M) = \pi_1(M \oplus K) \oplus \pi_2(M \oplus K) \oplus K, \tag{6}$$

and we show that SoEM21 cannot achieve beyond the birthday bound security.

Proposition 3. *Let $n \in \mathbb{N}$, and consider* SoEM21$: \{0,1\}^n \times \{0,1\}^n \to \{0,1\}^n$ *based on two permutations $\pi_1, \pi_2 \xleftarrow{\$} \mathrm{Perm}(n)$ and one key $K \xleftarrow{\$} \{0,1\}^n$. There exists a distinguisher $\mathcal{D}$ making $3 \cdot 2^{n/2}$ construction queries, $3 \cdot 2^{n/2}$ primitive queries to π_1, and $3 \cdot 2^{n/2}$ primitive queries to π_2 such that*

$$\mathbf{Adv}^{\mathrm{prf}}_{\mathrm{SoEM21}}(\mathcal{D}) \geq 1 - \frac{1}{2^n}. \tag{7}$$

Proof. We will construct a distinguisher $\mathcal{D}$ distinguishing the real world oracle $(\mathrm{SoEM21}^{\pi_1,\pi_2}_K, \pi_1^{\pm}, \pi_2^{\pm})$ from the ideal world oracle $(\varphi, \pi_1^{\pm}, \pi_2^{\pm})$ with significant probability. The distinguisher $\mathcal{D}$ returns 1 if it guesses that it is interacting with the real world oracle and returns 0 otherwise. $\mathcal{D}$ makes $3 \cdot 2^{n/2}$ construction queries, $3 \cdot 2^{n/2}$ primitive queries to π_1, and $3 \cdot 2^{n/2}$ primitive query to π_2 in total and operates as follows.

(i) For $j = 1, \ldots, 2^{n/2}$, query $M^{(j)} = \langle j \rangle_{n/2} \parallel 0^{n/2}$ to obtain $C^{(j)}$, query $M^{*(j)} = \langle j \rangle_{n/2} \parallel 0^{n/2-1}1$ to obtain $C^{*(j)}$, and query $M^{**(j)} = \langle j \rangle_{n/2} \parallel 0^{n/2-2}10$ to obtain $C^{**(j)}$;

(ii) For $i = 1, \ldots, 2^{n/2}$, query $x^{(i)} = 0^{n/2} \parallel \langle i \rangle_{n/2}$ to π_1 and π_2 to obtain $y_1^{(i)}$ and $y_2^{(i)}$. Define $(x^{*(i)}, y_1^{*(i)})$ and $(x^{**(i)}, y_1^{**(i)})$ as the tuples that satisfy $x^{*(i)} = x^{(i)} \oplus 0^{n-1}1$ and $x^{**(i)} = x^{(i)} \oplus 0^{n-2}10$, respectively, and similarly for the queries to π_2;

(iii) If there are two query indices $\bar{j}, \bar{i}$ such that $C^{(\bar{j})} \oplus C^{*(\bar{j})} = y_1^{(\bar{i})} \oplus y_1^{*(\bar{i})} \oplus y_2^{(\bar{i})} \oplus y_2^{*(\bar{i})}$ and $C^{(\bar{j})} \oplus C^{**(\bar{j})} = y_1^{(\bar{i})} \oplus y_1^{**(\bar{i})} \oplus y_2^{(\bar{i})} \oplus y_2^{**(\bar{i})}$, then output 1; otherwise, output 0.

The distinguisher's advantage satisfies

$$\mathbf{Adv}^{\mathrm{prf}}_{\mathrm{SoEM21}}(\mathcal{D}) = \left| \Pr\left[\mathcal{D}^{\mathrm{SoEM21}^{\pi_1,\pi_2}, \pi_1^{\pm}, \pi_2^{\pm}} = 1 \right] - \Pr\left[\mathcal{D}^{\varphi, \pi_1^{\pm}, \pi_2^{\pm}} = 1 \right] \right|.$$

In the real world, there is exactly one $(\bar{j}, \bar{i})$ such that $M^{(\bar{j})} \oplus x^{(\bar{i})} = K$, leading to

$$C^{(\bar{j})} = y_1^{(\bar{i})} \oplus y_2^{(\bar{i})} \oplus K.$$

In addition, also $M^{*(\bar{j})} \oplus x^{*(\bar{i})} = K$ and $M^{**(\bar{j})} \oplus x^{**(\bar{i})} = K$, leading to

$$C^{*(\bar{j})} = y_1^{*(\bar{i})} \oplus y_2^{*(\bar{i})} \oplus K,$$
$$C^{**(\bar{j})} = y_1^{**(\bar{i})} \oplus y_2^{**(\bar{i})} \oplus K.$$

The equations imply that

$$A_{\bar{j},\bar{i}}\colon C^{(\bar{j})}\oplus C^{*(\bar{j})}=y_1^{(\bar{i})}\oplus y_1^{*(\bar{i})}\oplus y_2^{(\bar{i})}\oplus y_2^{*(\bar{i})}\,,$$
$$B_{\bar{j},\bar{i}}\colon C^{(\bar{j})}\oplus C^{**(\bar{j})}=y_1^{(\bar{i})}\oplus y_1^{**(\bar{i})}\oplus y_2^{(\bar{i})}\oplus y_2^{**(\bar{i})}\,,$$

and thus that $\Pr\left[\mathcal{D}^{\mathrm{SoEM21}^{\pi_1,\pi_2},\pi_1^{\pm},\pi_2^{\pm}}=1\right]=1$.

For the ideal world, we have

$$\Pr\left[\mathcal{D}^{\varphi,\pi_1^{\pm},\pi_2^{\pm}}=1\right]=\Pr\left[\cup_{j,i}\,A_{j,i}\wedge B_{j,i}\right]\le\frac{qp}{2^{2n}}\,,$$

where $q=p=2^{n/2}$. $\qquad\qquad\qquad\qquad\qquad\qquad\qquad\qquad\Box$

4.3   Two Permutations, Two Keys

We prove that SoEM22 for independent π_1,π_2 and independent K_1,K_2 is secure up to attack complexity $2^{2n/3}$. We also demonstrate an attack matching this bound.

Theorem 1. *Let $n\in\mathbb{N}$, and consider SoEM22: $\{0,1\}^{2n}\times\{0,1\}^n\to\{0,1\}^n$ based on two permutations $\pi_1,\pi_2\xleftarrow{\$}\mathrm{Perm}(n)$ and two keys $K_1,K_2\xleftarrow{\$}\{0,1\}^n$. For any distinguisher $\mathcal{D}$ making at most q construction queries, at most p primitive queries to $\pi_1^{\pm}$ and p primitive queries to $\pi_2^{\pm}$, we have*

$$\mathbf{Adv}_{\mathrm{SoEM22}}^{\mathrm{prf}}(\mathcal{D})\le\frac{q(p+q)^2}{2^{2n}}+\frac{3qp^2}{2^{2n}}\,. \qquad (8)$$

The proof is given in Sect. 6.3.

Proposition 4. *Let $n\in\mathbb{N}$, and consider SoEM22: $\{0,1\}^{2n}\times\{0,1\}^n\to\{0,1\}^n$ based on two permutations $\pi_1,\pi_2\xleftarrow{\$}\mathrm{Perm}(n)$ and two keys $K_1,K_2\xleftarrow{\$}\{0,1\}^n$. There exists a distinguisher $\mathcal{D}$ making $4\cdot2^{2n/3}$ construction queries, and $4\cdot2^{2n/3}$ primitive queries to π_1 and $4\cdot2^{2n/3}$ primitive queries to π_2 such that*

$$\mathbf{Adv}_{\mathrm{SoEM22}}^{\mathrm{prf}}(\mathcal{D})\ge1-\frac{1}{e}-\frac{1}{2^n}\,. \qquad (9)$$

Proof. We will construct a distinguisher $\mathcal{D}$ distinguishing the real world oracle $(\mathrm{SoEM22}_{K_1,K_2}^{\pi_1,\pi_2},\pi_1^{\pm},\pi_2^{\pm})$ from the ideal world oracle $(\varphi,\pi_1^{\pm},\pi_2^{\pm})$ with significant probability. The distinguisher $\mathcal{D}$ returns 1 if it guesses that it is interacting with the real world oracle and returns 0 otherwise. $\mathcal{D}$ makes $4\cdot2^{2n/3}$ construction queries, $4\cdot2^{2n/3}$ primitive queries to π_1, and $4\cdot2^{2n/3}$ primitive query to π_2 in total and operates as follows.

(i) For $j=1,\ldots,2^{2n/3}$, query $M^{(j)}=\langle j\rangle_{2n/3}\parallel0^{n/3}$ to obtain $C^{(j)}$, query $M^{*(j)}=\langle j\rangle_{2n/3}\parallel0^{n/3-1}1$ to obtain $C^{*(j)}$, query $M^{**(j)}=\langle j\rangle_{2n/3}\parallel0^{n/3-2}10$ to obtain $C^{**(j)}$, and query $M^{***(j)}=\langle j\rangle_{2n/3}\parallel0^{n/3-2}11$ to obtain $C^{***(j)}$;

(ii) For $i = 1, \ldots, 2^{2n/3}$, query $u^{(i)} = 0^{n/3} \parallel \langle i \rangle_{2n/3}$ to π_1 to obtain $v^{(i)}$. Define $(u^{*(i)}, v^{*(i)})$, $(u^{**(i)}, v^{**(i)})$, and $(u^{***(i)}, v^{***(i)})$ as the tuples that satisfy $u^{*(i)} = u^{(i)} \oplus 0^{n-1}1$, $u^{**(i)} = u^{(i)} \oplus 0^{n-2}10$, and $u^{***(i)} = u^{(i)} \oplus 0^{n-2}11$, respectively;

(iii) For $i' = 1, \ldots, 2^{2n/3}$, query $x^{(i')}$ at random to obtain $y^{(i')}$, query $x^{*(i')} = x^{(i')} \oplus 0^{n-1}1$ to obtain $y^{*(i')}$, query $x^{**(i')} = x^{(i')} \oplus 0^{n-2}10$ to obtain $y^{**(i')}$, and query $x^{***(i')} = x^{(i')} \oplus 0^{n-2}11$ to obtain $y^{***(i')}$;

(iv) If there are three query indices $\bar{j}, \bar{i}, \bar{i}'$ such that $C^{(\bar{j})} \oplus C^{*(\bar{j})} = v^{(\bar{i})} \oplus v^{*(\bar{i})} \oplus y^{(\bar{i}')} \oplus y^{*(\bar{i}')}$, $C^{(\bar{j})} \oplus C^{**(\bar{j})} = v^{(\bar{i})} \oplus v^{**(\bar{i})} \oplus y^{(\bar{i}')} \oplus y^{**(\bar{i}')}$ and $C^{(\bar{j})} \oplus C^{***(\bar{j})} = v^{(\bar{i})} \oplus v^{***(\bar{i})} \oplus y^{(\bar{i}')} \oplus y^{***(\bar{i}')}$, then output 1; otherwise, output 0.

The distinguisher's advantage satisfies

$$\mathbf{Adv}^{\mathrm{prf}}_{\mathrm{SoEM22}}(\mathcal{D}) = \left| \Pr\left[\mathcal{D}^{\mathrm{SoEM22}^{\pi_1, \pi_2}, \pi_1^{\pm}, \pi_2^{\pm}} = 1 \right] - \Pr\left[\mathcal{D}^{\varphi, \pi_1^{\pm}, \pi_2^{\pm}} = 1 \right] \right|.$$

Put $q = p = 2^{2n/3}$. First consider the real world. Define $I_{K_1} = \{(j, i) \colon M^{(j)} \oplus u^{(i)} = K_1\}$, and note that $|I_{K_1}| = 2^{n/3}$. We denote by $E_{j,i'}$ the event that $M^{(j)} \oplus x^{(i')} = K_2$, for fixed j, i' where $(j, \cdot) \in I_{K_1}$. For each j, i', we have $\Pr[E_{j,i'}] = 1/2^n$, and we obtain from the union bound:

$$\Pr\left[\cup_{j,i'} E_{j,i'} \right] \le \frac{2^{n/3}p}{2^n}. \tag{10}$$

For the lower bound, we denote by D_j the event that a fixed j with $(j, \cdot) \in I_{K_1}$ satisfies $M^{(j)} \oplus x^{(i')} \ne K_2$ for all i'. Note that the D_j's are mutually independent for different j, and the probability of any D_j is

$$\Pr[D_j] = \frac{2^n - p}{2^n} = 1 - \frac{p}{2^n}.$$

The probability of $M^{(j)} \oplus x^{(i')} \ne K_2$ for all j, i' can now be computed as

$$1 - \Pr\left[\cup_{j,i'} E_{j,i'} \right] = \prod_{j=1}^{2^{n/3}} \Pr[D_j] = \prod_{j=1}^{2^{n/3}} \left(1 - \frac{p}{2^n} \right).$$

As $p/2^n \le 1$, we can use the inequality $1 - x \le e^{-x}$ for each term of above expression, and find an upper bound

$$\prod_{j=1}^{2^{n/3}} e^{-\frac{p}{2^n}} = e^{-\frac{2^{n/3}p}{2^n}}.$$

Putting all this together we get the lower bound

$$\Pr\left[\cup_{j,i'} E_{j,i'} \right] \ge 1 - e^{-\frac{2^{n/3}p}{2^n}}. \tag{11}$$

Note that if there exist $(\bar{j}, \bar{i}) \in I_{K_1}$ and $\bar{i}'$ such that $M^{(\bar{j})} \oplus x^{(\bar{i}')} = K_2$, we also have that

$$C^{(\bar{j})} \oplus v^{(\bar{i})} \oplus y^{(\bar{i}')} = K_1 \oplus K_2. \tag{12}$$

We in addition have that $(M^{(\bar{j})} \oplus \Delta) \oplus (u^{(\bar{i})} \oplus \Delta) = K_1$ and that $(M^{(\bar{j})} \oplus \Delta) \oplus (x^{(\bar{i}')} \oplus \Delta) = K_2$ for any $\Delta \in \{0,1\}^n$. Due to our definition of $M^{**(\bar{j})}$, $M^{***(\bar{j})}$, $u^{**(\bar{j})}$, $u^{***(\bar{j})}$, $x^{**(\bar{j})}$, and $x^{***(\bar{j})}$,, we thus obtain that also

$$C^{*(\bar{j})} \oplus v^{*(\bar{i})} \oplus y^{*(\bar{i}')} = K_1 \oplus K_2,$$

$$C^{**(\bar{j})} \oplus v^{**(\bar{i})} \oplus y^{**(\bar{i}')} = K_1 \oplus K_2,$$

$$C^{***(\bar{j})} \oplus v^{***(\bar{i})} \oplus y^{***(\bar{i}')} = K_1 \oplus K_2.$$

Combining these three equations with (12), we can conclude that under the premise that (12) holds, the following three events

$$A_{\bar{j},\bar{i},\bar{i}'} : C^{(\bar{j})} \oplus C^{*(\bar{j})} = v^{(\bar{i})} \oplus v_1^{*(\bar{i})} \oplus y^{(\bar{i}')} \oplus y^{*(\bar{i}')},$$

$$B_{\bar{j},\bar{i},\bar{i}'} : C^{(\bar{j})} \oplus C^{**(\bar{j})} = v^{(\bar{i})} \oplus v^{**(\bar{i})} \oplus y^{(\bar{i}')} \oplus y^{**(\bar{i}')},$$

$$C_{\bar{j},\bar{i},\bar{i}'} : C^{(\bar{j})} \oplus C^{***(\bar{j})} = v^{(\bar{i})} \oplus v^{***(\bar{i})} \oplus y^{(\bar{i}')} \oplus y^{***(\bar{i}')},$$

are satisfied in the real world. Therefore, for the real world, we can conclude the following:

$$\Pr\left[\mathcal{D}^{\text{SoEM22}^{\pi_1,\pi_2},\pi_1^{\pm},\pi_2^{\pm}} = 1\right]$$

$$= \Pr\left[\cup_{j,i'} E_{j,i'}\right] + \Pr\left[\cup_{j,i,i'} A_{j,i,i'} \wedge B_{j,i,i'} \wedge C_{j,i,i'} \mid \cap_{j,i'} \neg E_{j,i'}\right] \cdot \Pr\left[\cap_{j,i'} \neg E_{j,i'}\right].$$

From (10) and (11), we obtain

$$\Pr\left[\mathcal{D}^{\text{SoEM22}^{\pi_1,\pi_2},\pi_1^{\pm},\pi_2^{\pm}} = 1\right] \geq 1 - e^{-\frac{2^{n/3}p}{2^n}} + \frac{qp^2}{2^{3n}}\left(1 - \frac{2^{n/3}p}{2^n}\right)$$

$$= 1 - e^{-\frac{2^{n/3}p}{2^n}},$$

where $p = 2^{2n/3}$.

For the ideal world, we have

$$\Pr\left[\mathcal{D}^{\varphi,\pi_1^{\pm},\pi_2^{\pm}} = 1\right] = \Pr\left[\cup_{j,i,i'} A_{j,i,i'} \wedge B_{j,i,i'} \wedge C_{j,i,i'}\right] \leq \frac{qp^2}{2^{3n}},$$

where $q = p = 2^{2n/3}$. $\square$

5 Sum of Key Alternating Ciphers

Inspired by the result on SoEM22, we consider a sequential evaluation, which we call the *Sum of Key Alternating Ciphers* (SoKAC). It reminds of the EDMD construction of Mennink and Neves [50] instantiated with Even-Mansour, but it is not quite the same. Let $n \in \mathbb{N}$, and let $\pi_1, \pi_2 \in \mathrm{Perm}(n)$. We define the generic construction SoKAC: $\{0,1\}^{2n} \times \{0,1\}^n \to \{0,1\}^n$ as

$$\mathrm{SoKAC}(K_1, K_2, M) = \pi_2(\pi_1(M \oplus K_1) \oplus K_2) \oplus K_1 \oplus \pi_1(M \oplus K_1) \oplus K_2, \quad (13)$$

See also Fig. 4. We will consider the construction for two variants: SoKAC1 for the case where $\pi_1 = \pi_2$ are identical in Sect. 5.1, and SoKAC21 for the case where π_1, π_2 are independent but $K_1 = K_2$ are identical (so the key space is n bits) in Sect. 5.2. As before, for SoKAC21, we will have to make a slight adjustment, because by simply putting $K_1 = K_2$ in above equation, the addition of the keys at the end of the permutation calls will cancel out. We will detail this in Sect. 5.2.

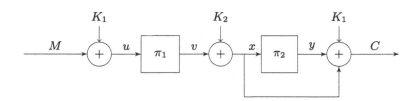

Fig. 4. Encryption of SoKAC based on two keys K_1 and K_2, and with π_1 and π_2 two public random permutations.

5.1   One Permutation

We show that SoKAC1, where $\pi_1 = \pi_2$ (but no a priori restriction on K_1, K_2 is imposed), cannot achieve security beyond the birthday bound.

Proposition 5. *Let $n \in \mathbb{N}$, and consider* SoKAC1 : $\{0,1\}^{2n} \times \{0,1\}^n \to \{0,1\}^n$ *based on permutation $\pi \xleftarrow{\$} \mathrm{Perm}(n)$ and two keys $K_1, K_2 \xleftarrow{\$} \{0,1\}^n$. There exists a distinguisher $\mathcal{D}$ making $3 \cdot 2^{n/2}$ construction queries such that*

$$\mathbf{Adv}^{\mathrm{prf}}_{\mathrm{SoKAC1}}(\mathcal{D}) \geq 1 - \frac{1}{2^n}. \quad (14)$$

Proof. The attack is identical to that of SoEM1 of Proposition 2, and henceforth omitted. □

5.2   Two Permutations, One Key

Let $n \in \mathbb{N}$. Let $\pi_1, \pi_2 : \{0,1\}^n \to \{0,1\}^n$ be two independent random permutations. We define SoKAC construction based on π_1, π_2 and using a single key K as follows:

$$\mathrm{SoKAC21}^{\pi_1, \pi_2}(K, M) = \pi_2(\pi_1(M \oplus K) \oplus K) \oplus \pi_1(M \oplus K) \oplus K, \quad (15)$$

and we show that SoKAC21 is secure up to attack complexity $2^{2n/3}$. We also demonstrate an attack matching this bound.

Theorem 2. *Let* $n \in \mathbb{N}$, *and consider* SoKAC21: $\{0,1\}^n \times \{0,1\}^n \to \{0,1\}^n$ *based on two permutations* $\pi_1, \pi_2 \xleftarrow{\$} \mathrm{Perm}(n)$ *and one key* $K \xleftarrow{\$} \{0,1\}^n$. *For any distinguisher* $\mathcal{D}$ *making at most* q *construction queries, at most* p *primitive queries to* $\pi_1^{\pm}$ *and* p *primitive queries to* $\pi_2^{\pm}$, *we have*

$$\mathbf{Adv}_{\mathrm{SoKAC21}}^{\mathrm{prf}}(\mathcal{D}) \leq \frac{q(p+q)^2}{2^{2n}} + \frac{2}{2^n} + \frac{qp^2}{2^{2n}} + \frac{2p^2\sqrt{qp}}{2^{2n}} + \frac{3\sqrt{nqp^2}}{2^n} + \frac{4\sqrt{qp^2}}{2^n}. \tag{16}$$

The proof is given in Sect. 6.4.

Proposition 6. *Let* $n \in \mathbb{N}$, *and consider* SoKAC21: $\{0,1\}^n \times \{0,1\}^n \to \{0,1\}^n$ *based on two permutations* $\pi_1, \pi_2 \xleftarrow{\$} \mathrm{Perm}(n)$ *and one key* $K \xleftarrow{\$} \{0,1\}^n$. *There exists a distinguisher* $\mathcal{D}$ *making* $4 \cdot 2^{2n/3}$ *construction queries, and* $4 \cdot 2^{2n/3}$ *primitive queries to* π_1 *and* $4 \cdot 2^{2n/3}$ *primitive queries to* π_2 *such that*

$$\mathbf{Adv}_{\mathrm{SoKAC21}}^{\mathrm{prf}}(\mathcal{D}) \geq 1 - \frac{1}{e} - \frac{1}{2^n}. \tag{17}$$

Proof. The attack is identical to that of SoEM22 of Proposition 4, and henceforth omitted. □

6   Security Proofs

The security proofs of SoEM22 and SoKAC21 are given in Sects. 6.3 and 6.4. The proofs are performed using Patarin's H-coefficient technique, which we will recap in Sect. 6.1. The proof of SoKAC21 relies on the sum-capture lemma, which we revisit in Sect. 6.2. The analysis for good transcripts resembles ideas of the first iteration in Patarin's mirror theory, but difficulties appear in the fact that the distinguisher can make direct queries to the permutations π_1 and π_2.

6.1   Patarin's H-Coefficient Technique

In this work, we use the H-coefficient technique by Patarin [54,56], but we will follow the modernization of Chen and Steinberger [21].

Let $\pi_1, \pi_2, \ldots, \pi_r \xleftarrow{\$} \mathrm{Perm}(n)$, and $\varphi \xleftarrow{\$} \mathrm{Func}(n)$. Let $K \xleftarrow{\$} \{0,1\}^k$, and $F \colon \{0,1\}^k \times \{0,1\}^n \to \{0,1\}^n$ be a pseudorandom function based on public random permutations $\pi_1, \pi_2, \ldots, \pi_r$. We consider a deterministic distinguisher $\mathcal{D}$ that has query access to either the real world oracle $\mathcal{O} = (F_K^{\pi_1, \ldots, \pi_r}, \pi_1^{\pm}, , \ldots, \pi_r^{\pm})$ or the ideal world oracle $\mathcal{P} = (\varphi, \pi_1^{\pm}, \ldots, \pi_r^{\pm})$. The distinguisher's goal is to distinguish both worlds and we denote by

$$\mathbf{Adv}(\mathcal{D}) = \left| \Pr\left[\mathcal{D}^{\mathcal{O}} = 1 \right] - \Pr\left[\mathcal{D}^{\mathcal{P}} = 1 \right] \right|$$

its advantage. We summarize all query-response tuples learned by $\mathcal{D}$ during its interaction with its oracle $\mathcal{O}$ or $\mathcal{P}$ in a transcript τ. We denote by $X_{\mathcal{O}}$ (resp. $X_{\mathcal{P}}$) the probability distribution of transcripts when interacting with $\mathcal{O}$ (resp. $\mathcal{P}$). We call a transcript $\tau \in \mathcal{T}$ attainable if $Pr[X_{\mathcal{P}} = \tau] > 0$, or in other words if the transcript τ can be obtained from an interaction with $\mathcal{P}$.

Lemma 1 (H-coefficient Technique). *Consider a deterministic distinguisher* $\mathcal{D}$. *Define a partition* $\mathcal{T} = \mathcal{T}_{\mathrm{good}} \cup \mathcal{T}_{\mathrm{bad}}$, *where* $\mathcal{T}_{\mathrm{good}}$ *is the subset of* $\mathcal{T}$ *which contains all the "good" transcripts and* $\mathcal{T}_{\mathrm{bad}}$ *is the subset with all the "bad" transcripts. Let* $0 \leq \epsilon \leq 1$ *be such that for all* $\tau \in \mathcal{T}_{\mathrm{good}}$:

$$\frac{Pr(X_{\mathcal{O}} = \tau)}{Pr(X_{\mathcal{P}} = \tau)} \geq 1 - \epsilon. \tag{18}$$

Then, we have $\mathbf{Adv}(\mathcal{D}) \leq \epsilon + \Pr[X_{\mathcal{P}} \in \mathcal{T}_{\mathrm{bad}}]$.

6.2   Sum-Capture Lemma

We use the sum-capture lemma [20,25,51], which is built upon the work of Babai [2] and Steinberger [63]. Such results typically state that for a random subset Z of $\{0,1\}^n$ of size p, the quantity

$$\mu(Z, A, B) = |\{(z, a, b) \in Z \times A \times B : z = a \oplus b\}|$$

is at most around $p \cdot |A| \cdot |B| / 2^n$ for any possible choice of A and B, except with negligible probability. In our setting, Z will consist of query-response tuples from a permutation, i.e., Z consists of values $u^{(i)} \oplus v^{(i)}$ where $\{(u^{(1)}, v^{(1)}), \ldots, (u^{(p)}, v^{(p)})\}$ is a permutation transcript. We will appeal to the sum-capture theorem by Chen et al. [20].

Lemma 2 (Sum-Capture Lemma). *Let* $n, p \in \mathbb{N}$ *such that* $9n \leq p \leq 2^{n-1}$. *Let* $\pi \xleftarrow{\$} \mathrm{Perm}(n)$, *let* $\{(u^{(1)}, v^{(1)}), \ldots, (u^{(p)}, v^{(p)})\}$ *be* p *tuples of* π, *and let* $Z = \{(u^{(1)} \oplus v^{(1)}), \ldots, (u^{(p)} \oplus v^{(p)})\}$. *For any two subsets* $A, B \subseteq \{0,1\}^n$, *we have*

$$\Pr\left[\mu(Z, A, B) \geq \frac{p|A||B|}{2^n} + \frac{2p^2\sqrt{|A||B|}}{2^n} + 3\sqrt{np|A||B|}\right] \leq \frac{2}{2^n}.$$

6.3   Proof of Theorem 1 on SoEM22

Let $K = (K_1, K_2) \xleftarrow{\$} \{0,1\}^{2n}$, $\pi_1, \pi_2 \xleftarrow{\$} \mathrm{Perm}(n)$, and $\varphi \xleftarrow{\$} \mathrm{Func}(n)$. Consider any distinguisher $\mathcal{D}$ that has access to three oracles: $(\mathrm{SoEM22}_K^{\pi_1, \pi_2}, \pi_1^{\pm}, \pi_2^{\pm})$ in the real world or $(\varphi, \pi_1^{\pm}, \pi_2^{\pm})$ in the ideal world. We assume $\mathcal{D}$ is computational unbounded and deterministic. The distinguisher makes q construction queries to $\mathcal{O}_0 \in \{\mathrm{SoEM22}_K^{\pi_1, \pi_2}, \varphi\}$, and these are summarized in a transcript of the form $\tau_0 = \{(M^{(1)}, C^{(1)}), \ldots, (M^{(q)}, C^{(q)})\}$. It also makes p primitive queries to $\mathcal{O}_1 = \pi_1^{\pm}$ and p primitive queries to $\mathcal{O}_2 = \pi_2^{\pm}$, and like before, these are respectively summarized in transcripts $\tau_1 = \{(u^{(1)}, v^{(1)}), \ldots, (u^{(p)}, v^{(p)})\}$ and $\tau_2 = \{(x^{(1)}, y^{(1)}), \ldots, (x^{(p)}, y^{(p)})\}$. We assume that τ_0, τ_1, and τ_2 do not contain duplicate elements. After $\mathcal{D}$'s interaction with the oracles, but before it outputs its decision, we disclose the keys K_1, K_2 to the distinguisher. In real world, these are the keys used in the construction. In the ideal world K_1, K_2 are dummy keys that are drawn uniformly at random. The complete view is denoted $\tau = (\tau_0, \tau_1, \tau_2, K_1, K_2)$.

Bad Events. We say that $\tau \in \mathcal{T}_{\text{bad}}$ if and only if there exists a construction query $(M^{(j)}, C^{(j)}) \in \tau_0$ and primitive queries $(u^{(i)}, v^{(i)}) \in \tau_1$ and $(x^{(i')}, y^{(i')}) \in \tau_2$ such that one of the following conditions holds:

$$\text{bad}_1 : M^{(j)} \oplus u^{(i)} = K_1 \wedge M^{(j)} \oplus x^{(i')} = K_2, \tag{19}$$

$$\text{bad}_2 : M^{(j)} \oplus u^{(i)} = K_1 \wedge C^{(j)} \oplus v^{(i)} \oplus y^{(i')} = K_1 \oplus K_2, \tag{20}$$

$$\text{bad}_3 : M^{(j)} \oplus x^{(i')} = K_2 \wedge C^{(j)} \oplus v^{(i)} \oplus y^{(i')} = K_1 \oplus K_2. \tag{21}$$

Note that any attainable transcript τ for which $\tau \notin \mathcal{T}_{\text{bad}}$, implies that τ is a good transcript.

We give an informal explanation of the definition of the bad event. In the real world, every construction query j induces *exactly one* evaluation $(u^{(j)}, v^{(j)})$ of the underlying public permutation π_1, and *exactly one* evaluation $(x^{(j)}, y^{(j)})$ of the underlying public permutation π_2. These two queries naturally satisfy

$$M^{(j)} \oplus u^{(j)} = K_1,$$
$$M^{(j)} \oplus x^{(j)} = K_2,$$
$$C^{(j)} \oplus v^{(j)} \oplus y^{(j)} = K_1 \oplus K_2.$$

Clearly, $u^{(j)}$ and $x^{(j)}$ are fixed by $M^{(j)}$, K_1, and K_2, but there is "freedom" in the value $v^{(j)} \oplus y^{(j)}$. If it happens to be that the distinguisher queried $u^{(j)}$, i.e., that $(u^{(j)}, v^{(j)}) \in \tau_1$, it consequently fixes the tuple $(x^{(j)}, y^{(j)})$ for π_2. However, in the ideal world, there is no such dependency. This means that if the adversary had queried $u^{(j)} = M^{(j)} \oplus K_1$ to π_1 and $x^{(j)} = M^{(j)} \oplus K_2$ to π_2, with high probability the third equation would not hold. An identical reasoning applies for the case where the distinguisher happened to have set any other two out of three equations.

$\Pr[X_{\mathcal{P}} \in \mathcal{T}_{\text{bad}}]$. We want to bound the probability that an ideal world transcript τ satisfies either of (19)–(21). Therefore, the probability that $\tau \in \mathcal{T}_{\text{bad}}$ is given by

$$\Pr[\tau \in \mathcal{T}_{\text{bad}}] \leq \Pr[\text{bad}_1] + \Pr[\text{bad}_2] + \Pr[\text{bad}_3].$$

We consider the first bad event bad_1. For any possible construction query $(M^{(j)}, C^{(j)}) \in \tau_0$, any possible π_1 primitive query $(u^{(i)}, v^{(i)})$, and any possible π_2 primitive query $(x^{(i')}, y^{(i')})$, the only randomness in the first equation is K_1 and the only randomness in the second equation is K_2. This means that the probabilities that each of the equation holds in bad_1 are independent of each other. By the fact that the keys $K = (K_1, K_2) \xleftarrow{\$} \{0,1\}^{2n}$ are dummy keys generated independently of τ_0, τ_1 and τ_2, the probability that bad_1 holds for fixed j, i, i' is $1/2^{2n}$. Summed over all q possible construction queries, p possible π_1 primitive queries, and p possible π_2 primitive queries, we have

$$\Pr[\text{bad}_1] \leq \frac{qp^2}{2^{2n}}.$$

For the second bad event bad_2, note that we can replace K_1 in the second equation by $M^{(j)} \oplus u^{(i)}$. Hereby, the only randomness in the first equation is K_1 and the only randomness in the second equation is K_2. The probabilities that each of the equation holds in bad_2 are independent of each other. Again, summing over all the construction and the primitive queries, we have

$$\Pr[\text{bad}_2] \leq \frac{qp^2}{2^{2n}} \,.$$

The same reasoning applies for bad_3. Summing the three probabilities, we get

$$\Pr[\tau \in \mathcal{T}_{\text{bad}}] \leq \frac{3qp^2}{2^{2n}} \,. \tag{22}$$

$\mathbf{\Pr[X_{\mathcal{O}} = \tau] / \Pr[X_{\mathcal{P}} = \tau]}$. Consider an attainable transcript $\tau \in \mathcal{T}_{\text{good}}$. To compute $\Pr[X_{\mathcal{O}} = \tau]$ and $\Pr[X_{\mathcal{P}} = \tau]$, it suffices to compute the probability of oracles that could result in view τ. Denote by $all_{\mathcal{O}}$ the set of all oracles in the real world, and by $comp_{\mathcal{O}}(\tau)$ the fraction of them compatible with τ, we see that $\Pr[X_{\mathcal{O}} = \tau] = |comp_{\mathcal{O}}(\tau)| / |all_{\mathcal{O}}|$. Similarly we have $all_{\mathcal{P}}$ and $comp_{\mathcal{P}}(\tau)$ for the ideal world. We obtain

$$\frac{\Pr[X_{\mathcal{O}} = \tau]}{\Pr[X_{\mathcal{P}} = \tau]} = \frac{|comp_{\mathcal{O}}(\tau)| \cdot |all_{\mathcal{P}}|}{|all_{\mathcal{O}}| \cdot |comp_{\mathcal{P}}(\tau)|} \,. \tag{23}$$

For the real world $\mathcal{O}$, we have $|all_{\mathcal{O}}| = 2^{2n} \cdot (2^n!)^2$, which is equal to the number of possible keys $K = (K_1, K_2)$ times the number of possible public random permutations π_1 and π_2. Similarly, for the ideal world $\mathcal{P}$, we have $|all_{\mathcal{P}}| = 2^{2n} \cdot 2^{n2^n}(2^n!)^2$. The first term corresponds to the number of randomly drawn keys, the second term is the number of possible random functions $\varphi \in \text{Func}(n)$, and the last term the number of possible public random permutations π_1 and π_2. For the computation of the number of oracles compatible with τ in the ideal world, we see that there are $2^{n(2^n - q)}$ random functions $\varphi \in \text{Func}(n)$ compliant with τ_0, $(2^n - p)!$ public random permutations π_1 compliant with τ_1, and $(2^n - p)!$ public random permutations π_2 compliant with τ_2. We find

$$|comp_{\mathcal{P}}(\tau)| = 2^{n(2^n - q)} \cdot (2^n - p)!^2 \,.$$

From (23), we have

$$\frac{\Pr[X_{\mathcal{O}} = \tau]}{\Pr[X_{\mathcal{P}} = \tau]} = \frac{|comp_{\mathcal{O}}(\tau)| \cdot 2^{2n} 2^{n2^n} (2^n!)^2}{2^{2n}(2^n!)^2 \cdot (2^{n(2^n - q)})(2^n - p)!^2} = \frac{|comp_{\mathcal{O}}(\tau)| \cdot 2^{nq}}{(2^n - p)!^2} \,. \tag{24}$$

What remains is the computation of the number of oracles compatible with τ in the real world. As defined by the bad events, a transcript τ is bad if we get both the same input or output to π_1, and the same input or output to π_2. This means that for any $\tau \in \mathcal{T}_{\text{good}}$, a construction query collides with at most one query in $\tau_1 \cup \tau_2$. We conclude this fact in the following claim:

Claim. For $\tau \in \mathcal{T}_{\text{good}}$, any construction query $(M^{(j)}, C^{(j)}) \in \tau_0$ collides with at most one primitive query $(u^{(i)}, v^{(i)}) \in \tau_1$ and at most one primitive query $(x^{(i')}, y^{(i')}) \in \tau_2$, but never with both a τ_1 and τ_2 query.

We will use this claim to re-group the transcripts τ_0, τ_1, and τ_2 into three new transcripts τ_0^{new}, τ_1^{new}, and τ_2^{new}. We initially define $\tau_0^{\text{new}} = \tau_0$, $\tau_1^{\text{new}} = \tau_1$ and $\tau_2^{\text{new}} = \tau_2$. The trick will be to consider each individual construction query $(M^{(j)}, C^{(j)})$, and to operate as follows:

- if $M^{(j)} \oplus K_1 = u^{(i)}$ for some i, then remove $(M^{(j)}, C^{(j)})$ from τ_0^{new}, and add $(x, y) = (M^{(j)} \oplus K_2, C^{(j)} \oplus v^{(i)} \oplus K_1 \oplus K_2)$ to τ_2^{new};
- if $M^{(j)} \oplus K_2 = x^{(i')}$ for some i', then remove $(M^{(j)}, C^{(j)})$ from τ_0^{new}, and add $(u, v) = (M^{(j)} \oplus K_1, C^{(j)} \oplus y^{(i')} \oplus K_1 \oplus K_2)$ to τ_1^{new}.

Note that any good transcript will have to meet $\neg\text{bad}_1 \wedge \neg\text{bad}_2 \wedge \neg\text{bad}_3$. We know that if a construction query $(M^{(j)}, C^{(j)})$ collides with $(u^{(i)}, v^{(i)}) \in \tau_1$, then $M^{(j)} \oplus K_2$ cannot be a valid $x^{(i')}$ value because of $\neg\text{bad}_1$, and $C^{(j)} \oplus v^{(i)} \oplus K_1 \oplus K_2$ cannot be a valid $y^{(i')}$ value because of $\neg\text{bad}_2$, for any $(x^{(i')}, y^{(i')}) \in \tau_2$. Similarly for τ_1^{new}. This way, we will end up with soundly defined τ_1^{new} and τ_2^{new} for π_1 and π_2, and a set of construction queries τ_0^{new} that does not collide with any tuple in τ_1^{new} or τ_2^{new}. Let $s_2, s_1 \leq p$ be the number of construction queries that collides with $(u^{(i)}, v^{(i)}) \in \tau_1$ resp. $(x^{(i')}, y^{(i')}) \in \tau_2$. The number of elements in the new transcripts τ_1^{new} and τ_2^{new} are equal to $p + s_2$ resp. $p + s_1$, and the number of construction queries that remains in τ_0^{new} is equal to $q' = q - s_1 - s_2$.

The two sets of transcripts, τ_1^{new} and τ_2^{new}, define *exactly* $p + s_2$ input-output tuples for π_1 and *exactly* $p + s_1$ input-output tuples for π_2. What remains is the counting of the number of permutations π_1, π_2 that satisfy these $p + s_2$ resp. $p + s_1$ tuples, and that could give the remaining transcript τ_0^{new}.

For a given transcript τ_0^{new} of q' elements, our goal is to count the number of n-bit permutations $\pi_1 \colon \mathcal{D}_1 \to \mathcal{R}_1$ with $|\mathcal{D}_1| = |\mathcal{R}_1| = 2^n - p - s_2$, and the number of n-bit permutations $\pi_2 \colon \mathcal{D}_2 \to \mathcal{R}_2$ with $|\mathcal{D}_2| = |\mathcal{R}_2| = 2^n - p - s_1$. We define $V_{\text{out}} = \{0,1\}^n \backslash \mathcal{R}_1$ as the set of range values of π_1 that are not permitted (basically these are the v values from $\tau_1^{\text{new}}, \tau_2^{\text{new}}$) and similarly for Y_{out}.

For $\alpha = 0, \ldots, q' - 1$, define $\lambda_{\alpha+1}$ as the number of solutions

$$\{v^{(1)}, \ldots, v^{(\alpha+1)}; y^{(1)}, \ldots, y^{(\alpha+1)}\}$$

that satisfy:

(1) $\{v^{(1)}, \ldots, v^{(\alpha)}; y^{(1)}, \ldots, y^{(\alpha)}\}$ satisfy λ_α;
(2) $v^{(\alpha+1)} \oplus y^{(\alpha+1)} = C^{(\alpha+1)} \oplus K_1 \oplus K_2$;
(3) $v^{(\alpha+1)} \notin \{v^{(1)}, \ldots, v^{(\alpha)}\} \cup V_{\text{out}}$;
(4) $y^{(\alpha+1)} \notin \{y^{(1)}, \ldots, y^{(\alpha)}\} \cup Y_{\text{out}}$.

Our goal is to derive a recursive formula for $\lambda_{\alpha+1}$ that depends on λ_α, such that a lower bound can be found for the expression $\lambda_{\alpha+1}/\lambda_\alpha$. Note that, by definition,

$$|comp_{\mathcal{O}}(\tau)| = \lambda_{q'}(2^n - p - s_2 - q')!(2^n - p - s_1 - q')!. \tag{25}$$

Processing from (24), we obtain

$$\frac{\Pr[X_{\mathcal{O}} = \tau]}{\Pr[X_{\mathcal{P}} = \tau]} = \frac{\lambda_{q'}(2^n - p - s_2 - q')!(2^n - p - s_1 - q')! \cdot 2^{nq}}{(2^n - p)!^2}. \tag{26}$$

We will derive a lower bound for $\lambda_{\alpha+1}/\lambda_\alpha$. Define by $B_{(1,2)}$ the set of solutions that only comply with (1) and (2), with no side condition from (3) and (4). Define by $B_{(3:i)}$ the set of solutions that comply with (1) and (2) of above, and satisfy $\neg(3:i)$ for $i = 1, \ldots, \alpha + |V_{\text{out}}|$. It means that any solution in this case satisfies (1) and (2), and $v^{(\alpha+1)} \in \{v^{(1)}, \ldots, v^{(\alpha)}\} \cup V_{\text{out}}$ (nothing is said about $y^{(\alpha+1)}$ except for property (2)). Similarly for $B(4:i)$. By the principle of inclusion-exclusion, we obtain

$$\lambda_{\alpha+1} = \left|B_{(1,2)}\right| - \left| \bigcup_{i=1}^{\alpha+|V_{\text{out}}|} B_{(3:i)} \cup \bigcup_{i=1}^{\alpha+|Y_{\text{out}}|} B_{(4:i')} \right|$$

$$\geq \left|B_{(1,2)}\right| - \sum_{i=1}^{\alpha+|V_{\text{out}}|} \left|B_{(3:i)}\right| - \sum_{i=1}^{\alpha+|Y_{\text{out}}|} \left|B_{(4:i)}\right| + \sum_{i'=1}^{\alpha+|Y_{\text{out}}|} \sum_{i=1}^{\alpha+|V_{\text{out}}|} \left|B_{(3:i)} \cap B_{(4:i')}\right|$$

$$\geq 2^n \cdot \lambda_\alpha - \sum_{i=1}^{\alpha+|V_{\text{out}}|} \lambda_\alpha - \sum_{i=1}^{\alpha+|Y_{\text{out}}|} \lambda_\alpha + \sum_{i'=1}^{\alpha+|Y_{\text{out}}|} \sum_{i=1}^{\alpha+|V_{\text{out}}|} \left|B_{(3:i)} \cap B_{(4:i')}\right| .$$

By the fact that

$$\sum_{i'=1}^{\alpha+|Y_{\text{out}}|} \sum_{i=1}^{\alpha+|V_{\text{out}}|} \left|B_{(3:i)} \cap B_{(4:i')}\right| \geq 0 ,$$

we get

$$\lambda_{\alpha+1} \geq 2^n \lambda_\alpha - (\alpha + p + s_2)\lambda_\alpha - (\alpha + p + s_1)\lambda_\alpha .$$

Thus, we have obtained

$$\frac{\lambda_{\alpha+1}}{\lambda_\alpha} \geq 2^n - 2\alpha - 2p - s_1 - s_2 , \tag{27}$$

with $\lambda_0 = 1$.

Processing from (26), we obtain

$$(26) = \prod_{i=1}^{s_1-1} \frac{2^n}{(2^n - p - i)} \cdot \prod_{i=1}^{s_2-1} \frac{2^n}{(2^n - p - i)}$$

$$\cdot \prod_{i=0}^{q'-1} \frac{\lambda_{i+1}}{\lambda_i} \cdot \frac{2^n}{(2^n - p - s_2 - i)(2^n - p - s_1 - i)} . \tag{28}$$

Using that $p, s_1, s_2 \leq 2^n$, and combining (27) with (28), we obtain

$$(28) \geq \prod_{i=0}^{q'-1} \frac{\lambda_{i+1}}{\lambda_i} \cdot \frac{2^n}{(2^n - p - s_2 - i)(2^n - p - s_1 - i)}$$

$$\geq \prod_{i=0}^{q'-1} \frac{(2^n - 2i - 2p - s_1 - s_2)2^n}{(2^n - p \quad s_2 - i)(2^n - p - s_1 - i)}$$

$$= \prod_{i=0}^{q'-1} \left(1 - \frac{(p + s_2 + p)(p + s_1 + p)}{(2^n - p - s_2 - p)(2^n - p - s_1 - p)}\right)$$

$$\geq \prod_{i=0}^{q'-1} \left(1 - \frac{(p + s_2 + q')(p + s_1 + q')}{(2^n - p - s_2 - q')(2^n - p - s_1 - q')}\right)$$

$$\geq \prod_{i=0}^{q'-1} \left(1 - \frac{(p + s_2 + q')(p + s_1 + q')}{2^{2n}}\right)$$

$$= \left(1 - \frac{(p + s_2 + q')(p + s_1 + q')}{2^{2n}}\right)^{q'}$$

$$\geq 1 - \frac{q'(p + s_2 + q')(p + s_1 + q')}{2^{2n}}$$

$$\geq 1 - \frac{q(p + q)^2}{2^{2n}}. \tag{29}$$

where we use that $(1 - x)^y \geq 1 - xy$ and $q' + s_1 + s_2 = q$. We conclude from (28) and (29) that

$$\frac{\Pr[X_{\mathcal{O}} = \tau]}{\Pr[X_{\mathcal{P}} = \tau]} \geq 1 - \frac{q(p + q)^2}{2^{2n}} =: 1 - \epsilon.$$

Conclusion. Using Patarin's H-Coefficient technique (Lemma 1), we obtain

$$\mathbf{Adv}_{\mathrm{SoEM22}}^{\mathrm{prf}}(\mathcal{D}) \leq \frac{q(p + q)^2}{2^{2n}} + \frac{3qp^2}{2^{2n}}.$$

6.4   Proof of Theorem 2 on SoKAC21

The proof is similar to the one of Theorem 1 (Sect. 6.3). Let $K \xleftarrow{\$} \{0,1\}^n$, $\pi_1, \pi_2 \xleftarrow{\$} \mathrm{Perm}(n)$, and $\varphi \xleftarrow{\$} \mathrm{Func}(n)$. Consider any distinguisher $\mathcal{D}$ that has access to three oracles: $(\mathrm{SoKAC21}_K^{\pi_1, \pi_2}, \pi_1^{\pm}, \pi_2^{\pm})$ in the real world or $(\varphi, \pi_1^{\pm}, \pi_2^{\pm})$ in the ideal world. We assume $\mathcal{D}$ is computational unbounded and deterministic. The distinguisher makes q construction queries to $\mathcal{O}_0 \in \{\mathrm{SoKAC21}_K^{\pi_1, \pi_2}, \varphi\}$, and these are summarized in a transcript of the form $\tau_0 = \{(M^{(1)}, C^{(1)}), \dots, (M^{(q)}, C^{(q)})\}$. It also makes p primitive queries to $\mathcal{O}_1 = \pi_1^{\pm}$ and p primitive queries to $\mathcal{O}_2 = \pi_2^{\pm}$, and like before, these are respectively summarized in transcripts $\tau_1 = \{(u^{(1)}, v^{(1)}), \dots, (u^{(p)}, v^{(p)})\}$ and

$\tau_2 = \{(x^{(1)}, y^{(1)}), \ldots, (x^{(p)}, y^{(p)})\}$. We assume that τ_0, τ_1, and τ_2 do not contain duplicate elements. After $\mathcal{D}$'s interaction with the oracles, but before it outputs its decision, we disclose the key K to the distinguisher. In real world, this is the key used in the construction. In the ideal world K is a dummy key that is drawn uniformly at random. The complete view is denoted $\tau = (\tau_0, \tau_1, \tau_2, K)$.

Bad Events. We say that $\tau \in \mathcal{T}_{\text{bad}}$ if and only if there exists a construction query $(M^{(j)}, C^{(j)}) \in \tau_0$ and primitive queries $(u^{(i)}, v^{(i)}) \in \tau_1$ and $(x^{(i')}, y^{(i')}) \in \tau_2$ such that one of the following conditions holds:

$$\text{bad}_1 : K = M^{(j)} \oplus u^{(i)} = v^{(i)} \oplus x^{(i')}, \tag{30}$$

$$\text{bad}_2 : K = M^{(j)} \oplus u^{(i)} = C^{(j)} \oplus v^{(i)} \oplus y^{(i')}, \tag{31}$$

$$\text{bad}_3 : K = v^{(i)} \oplus x^{(i')} = C^{(j)} \oplus v^{(i)} \oplus y^{(i')}. \tag{32}$$

Note that any attainable transcript τ for which $\tau \notin \mathcal{T}_{\text{bad}}$, implies that τ is a good transcript.

The bad events (30–32) match those of SoEM22, (19–21), with the difference that one single key K is used instead of two different keys K_1, K_2. Indeed, in SoKAC21$_K^{\pi_1, \pi_2}$, every construction query j induces *exactly one* evaluation $(u^{(j)}, v^{(j)})$ of the underlying public permutation π_1, and *exactly one* evaluation $(x^{(j)}, y^{(j)})$ of the underlying public permutation π_2, and these two queries satisfy

$$M^{(j)} \oplus u^{(j)} = K,$$

$$v^{(j)} \oplus x^{(j)} = K,$$

$$C^{(j)} \oplus v^{(j)} \oplus y^{(j)} = K.$$

As before, $(M^{(j)}, C^{(j)})$ and K fix the value $u^{(j)}$, but there is "freedom" in the values $v^{(j)} \oplus x^{(j)}$ and $v^{(j)} \oplus y^{(j)}$. As before, if it happens to be that the distinguisher queried $u^{(j)}$, this would fix the tuple $(x^{(j)}, y^{(j)})$ for π_2. If the distinguisher also happened to have queried this one, in the real world it would match but in the ideal world it would mismatch with high probability.

$\mathbf{Pr[X_{\mathcal{P}} \in \mathcal{T}_{\text{bad}}]}$. We want to bound the probability that an ideal world transcript τ satisfies either of (30)–(32). Therefore, the probability that $\tau \in \mathcal{T}_{\text{bad}}$ is given by

$$\text{Pr}[\tau \in \mathcal{T}_{\text{bad}}] \leq \text{Pr}[\text{bad}_1] + \text{Pr}[\text{bad}_2] + \text{Pr}[\text{bad}_3].$$

We denote

$$\Omega_1 = \left| \left\{ (j, i, i') \mid u^{(i)} \oplus v^{(i)} = M^{(j)} \oplus x^{(i')} \right\} \right|,$$

$$\Omega_2 = \left| \left\{ (j, i, i') \mid M^{(j)} \oplus C^{(j)} = u^{(i)} \oplus v^{(i)} \oplus y^{(i')} \right\} \right|,$$

$$\Omega_3 = \left| \left\{ (j, i, i') \mid C^{(j)} = x^{(i')} \oplus y^{(i')} \right\} \right|.$$

Clearly, as $K \xleftarrow{\$} \{0,1\}^n$, for any $i \in \{1, 2, 3\}$ and $A_i \in \mathbb{N}$, we have

$$\text{Pr}[\text{bad}_i] \leq \text{Pr}[\Omega_i \geq A_i] + \frac{A_i}{2^n}.$$

For $i = 1$, we will use the sum-capture lemma of Sect. 6.2. Define

$$Z = \{u^{(i)} \oplus v^{(i)} : (u^{(i)}, v^{(i)}) \in \tau_1\},$$
$$A = \{M^{(j)} : (M^{(j)}, C^{(j)}) \in \tau_0\},$$
$$B = \{x^{(i')} : (x^{(i')}, y^{(i')}) \in \tau_2\}.$$

Then, by Lemma 2 with $\Omega_1 = \mu(Z, A, B)$,

$$\Pr\left[\mu(Z, A, B) \geq \frac{qp^2}{2^n} + \frac{2p^2\sqrt{qp}}{2^n} + 3\sqrt{nqp^2}\right] \leq \frac{2}{2^n}.$$

We thus set $A_1 = \frac{qp^2}{2^n} + \frac{2p^2\sqrt{qp}}{2^n} + 3\sqrt{nqp^2}$ and obtain

$$\Pr[\text{bad}_1] \leq \frac{2}{2^n} + \frac{qp^2}{2^{2n}} + \frac{2p^2\sqrt{qp}}{2^{2n}} + \frac{3\sqrt{nqp^2}}{2^n}.$$

For $i = 2$, the equation in Ω_2 involves two random values ($C^{(j)}$ and $u^{(i)} \oplus v^{(i)}$), and we resort to a simple Markov bound:

$$\Pr[\Omega_2 \geq A_2] \leq \frac{qp^2}{2^n A_2},$$

and obtain by setting $A_2 = \sqrt{qp^2}$:

$$\Pr[\text{bad}_2] \leq \frac{2\sqrt{qp^2}}{2^n}.$$

For $i = 3$, $\Omega_3 \geq A_3$ means that

$$\Omega_3' = \left|\left\{(j, i') \mid C^{(j)} = x^{(i')} \oplus y^{(i')}\right\}\right| \geq A_3/p.$$

By a simple Markov bound,

$$\Pr[\Omega_3' \geq A_3/p] \leq \frac{qp^2}{2^n A_3},$$

and we obtain by setting $A_3 = \sqrt{qp^2}$:

$$\Pr[\text{bad}_3] \leq \frac{2\sqrt{qp^2}}{2^n}.$$

Summing the three probabilities, we get

$$\Pr[\tau \in \mathcal{T}_{\text{bad}}] \leq \frac{2}{2^n} + \frac{qp^2}{2^{2n}} + \frac{2p^2\sqrt{qp}}{2^{2n}} + \frac{3\sqrt{nqp^2}}{2^n} + \frac{4\sqrt{qp^2}}{2^n}. \tag{33}$$

$\Pr[X_{\mathcal{O}} = \tau]/\Pr[X_{\mathcal{P}} = \tau]$. The analysis of good transcripts of Theorem 1 (Sect. 6.3) carries over verbatim with the difference that we generate the transcripts τ_0^{new}, τ_1^{new} and τ_2^{new} in the following way. Consider each individual construction query $(M^{(j)}, C^{(j)})$, if $M^{(j)} \oplus K = u^{(i)}$ for some i, then remove $(M^{(j)}, C^{(j)})$ from τ_0^{new} and add $(x, y) = (v^{(i)} \oplus K, C^{(j)} \oplus v^{(i)} \oplus K)$ to τ_2^{new}. We know that if a construction query $(M^{(j)}, C^{(j)})$ collides with $(u^{(i)}, v^{(i)}) \in \tau_1$, then $v^{(i)} \oplus K$ cannot be a valid $x^{(i')}$ value because of $\neg \text{bad}_1$, and $C^{(j)} \oplus v^{(i)} \oplus K$ cannot be a valid $y^{(i')}$ value because of $\neg \text{bad}_2$, for any $(x^{(i')}, y^{(i')}) \in \tau_2$. Similarly for τ_1^{new}.

Conclusion. Using Patarin's H-Coefficient technique (Lemma 1), we obtain

$$\mathbf{Adv}_{\text{SoKAC21}}^{\text{prf}}(\mathcal{D}) \leq \frac{q(p+q)^2}{2^{2n}} + \frac{2}{2^n} + \frac{qp^2}{2^{2n}} + \frac{2p^2\sqrt{qp}}{2^{2n}} + \frac{3\sqrt{nqp^2}}{2^n} + \frac{4\sqrt{qp^2}}{2^n}.$$

Acknowledgments. This work was supported in part by the Research Council KU Leuven: GOA TENSE (C16/15/058). Yu Long Chen is supported by a Ph.D. Fellowship from the Research Foundation - Flanders (FWO). Bart Mennink is supported by a postdoctoral fellowship from the Netherlands Organisation for Scientific Research (NWO) under Veni grant 016.Veni.173.017. The authors would like to thank the anonymous reviewers of CRYPTO 2019 for their comments and suggestions.

References

1. Andreeva, E., Daemen, J., Mennink, B., Van Assche, G.: Security of keyed sponge constructions using a modular proof approach. In: Leander, G. (ed.) FSE 2015. LNCS, vol. 9054, pp. 364–384. Springer, Heidelberg (2015). https://doi.org/10.1007/978-3-662-48116-5_18

2. Babai, L.: The Fourier transform and equations over finite Abelian groups (Lecture Notes, version 1.3) (2002). http://people.cs.uchicago.edu/~laci/reu02/fourier.pdf

3. Beaulieu, R., Shors, D., Smith, J., Treatman-Clark, S., Weeks, B., Wingers, L.: The SIMON and SPECK families of lightweight block ciphers. Cryptology ePrint Archive, Report 2013/404 (2013)

4. Beierle, C., et al.: The SKINNY family of block ciphers and its low-latency variant MANTIS. In: Robshaw, M., Katz, J. (eds.) CRYPTO 2016, Part II. LNCS, vol. 9815, pp. 123–153. Springer, Heidelberg (2016). https://doi.org/10.1007/978-3-662-53008-5_5

5. Bellare, M., Impagliazzo, R.: A tool for obtaining tighter security analyses of pseudorandom function based constructions, with applications to PRP to PRF conversion. Cryptology ePrint Archive, Report 1999/024 (1999)

6. Bellare, M., Kilian, J., Rogaway, P.: The security of cipher block chaining. In: Desmedt, Y.G. (ed.) CRYPTO 1994. LNCS, vol. 839, pp. 341–358. Springer, Heidelberg (1994). https://doi.org/10.1007/3-540-48658-5_32

7. Bellare, M., Krovetz, T., Rogaway, P.: Luby-Rackoff backwards: increasing security by making block ciphers non-invertible. In: Nyberg, K. (ed.) EUROCRYPT 1998. LNCS, vol. 1403, pp. 266–280. Springer, Heidelberg (1998). https://doi.org/10.1007/BFb0054132

8. Bellare, M., Rogaway, P.: The security of triple encryption and a framework for code-based game playing proofs. In: Vaudenay, S. (ed.) EUROCRYPT 2006. LNCS, vol. 4004, pp. 409–426. Springer, Heidelberg (2006). https://doi.org/10.1007/11761679_25

9. Bernstein, D.J., et al.: GIMLI: a cross-platform permutation. In: Fischer, W., Homma, N. (eds.) CHES 2017. LNCS, vol. 10529, pp. 299–320. Springer, Cham (2017). https://doi.org/10.1007/978-3-319-66787-4_15

10. Bertoni, G., Daemen, J., Hoffert, S., Peeters, M., Van Assche, G., Van Keer, R.: Farfalle: parallel permutation-based cryptography. IACR Trans. Symmetric Cryptol. **2017**(4), 1–38 (2017)

11. Bertoni, G., Daemen, J., Peeters, M., Van Assche, G.: On the security of the keyed sponge construction. In: Symmetric Key Encryption Workshop, February 2011

12. Bertoni, G., Daemen, J., Peeters, M., Van Assche, G.: The Keccak SHA-3 submission. Submission to NIST (Round 3), vol. 6, no. 7, p. 16 (2011)

13. Bhargavan, K., Leurent, G.: On the practical (in-)security of 64-bit block ciphers: collision attacks on HTTP over TLS and OpenVPN. In: Weippl, E.R., Katzenbeisser, S., Kruegel, C., Myers, A.C., Halevi, S. (eds.) ACM SIGSAC, pp. 456–467. ACM (2016)

14. Bhattacharya, S., Nandi, M.: Full indifferentiable security of the XOR of two or more random permutations using the χ^2 method. In: Nielsen, J.B., Rijmen, V. (eds.) EUROCRYPT 2018, Part I. LNCS, vol. 10820, pp. 387–412. Springer, Cham (2018). https://doi.org/10.1007/978-3-319-78381-9_15

15. Bogdanov, A., Knezevic, M., Leander, G., Toz, D., Varici, K., Verbauwhede, I.: SPONGENT: a lightweight hash function. In: Preneel and Takagi [60], pp. 312–325

16. Bogdanov, A., et al.: PRESENT: an ultra-lightweight block cipher. In: Paillier, P., Verbauwhede, I. (eds.) CHES 2007. LNCS, vol. 4727, pp. 450–466. Springer, Heidelberg (2007). https://doi.org/10.1007/978-3-540-74735-2_31

17. Bogdanov, A., Knudsen, L.R., Leander, G., Standaert, F., Steinberger, J.P., Tischhauser, E.: Key-alternating ciphers in a provable setting: encryption using a small number of public permutations - (extended abstract). In: Pointcheval and Johansson [59], pp. 45–62

18. Borghoff, J., et al.: PRINCE - a low-latency block cipher for pervasive computing applications - extended abstract. In: Wang and Sako [66], pp. 208–225

19. Chang, D., Nandi, M.: A short proof of the PRP/PRF switching lemma. Cryptology ePrint Archive, Report 2008/078 (2008)

20. Chen, S., Lampe, R., Lee, J., Seurin, Y., Steinberger, J.: Minimizing the two-round Even-Mansour cipher. In: Garay, J.A., Gennaro, R. (eds.) CRYPTO 2014, Part I. LNCS, vol. 8616, pp. 39–56. Springer, Heidelberg (2014). https://doi.org/10.1007/978-3-662-44371-2_3

21. Chen, S., Steinberger, J.: Tight security bounds for key-alternating ciphers. In: Nguyen, P.Q., Oswald, E. (eds.) EUROCRYPT 2014. LNCS, vol. 8441, pp. 327–350. Springer, Heidelberg (2014). https://doi.org/10.1007/978-3-642-55220-5_19

22. Cid, C., Rechberger, C. (eds.): FSE 2014. LNCS, vol. 8540, pp. 285–302. Springer, Heidelberg (2015). https://doi.org/10.1007/978-3-662-46706-0

23. Cogliati, B., Lampe, R., Patarin, J.: The indistinguishability of the XOR of k permutations. In: Cid and Rechberger [22], pp. 285–302

24. Cogliati, B., Seurin, Y.: EWCDM: an efficient, beyond-birthday secure, nonce-misuse resistant MAC. In: Robshaw and Katz [61], pp. 121–149

25. Cogliati, B., Seurin, Y.: Analysis of the single-permutation encrypted Davies-Meyer construction. Des. Codes Crypt. **86**(12), 2703–2723 (2018)

26. Coron, J., Holenstein, T., Künzler, R., Patarin, J., Seurin, Y., Tessaro, S.: How to build an ideal cipher: the indifferentiability of the Feistel construction. J. Cryptol. **29**(1), 61–114 (2016)

27. Dachman-Soled, D., Katz, J., Thiruvengadam, A.: 10-round Feistel is indifferentiable from an ideal cipher. In: Fischlin, M., Coron, J.-S. (eds.) EUROCRYPT 2016, Part II. LNCS, vol. 9666, pp. 649–678. Springer, Heidelberg (2016). https://doi.org/10.1007/978-3-662-49896-5_23
28. Dai, W., Hoang, V.T., Tessaro, S.: Information-theoretic indistinguishability via the Chi-squared method. In: Katz and Shacham [43], pp. 497–523
29. Dai, Y., Steinberger, J.P.: Indifferentiability of 8-round Feistel networks. In: Robshaw and Katz [61], pp. 95–120
30. De Cannière, C., Dunkelman, O., Knežević, M.: KATAN and KTANTAN — a family of small and efficient hardware-oriented block ciphers. In: Clavier, C., Gaj, K. (eds.) CHES 2009. LNCS, vol. 5747, pp. 272–288. Springer, Heidelberg (2009). https://doi.org/10.1007/978-3-642-04138-9_20
31. Dunkelman, O., Keller, N., Shamir, A.: Minimalism in cryptography: the Even-Mansour scheme revisited. In: Pointcheval and Johansson [59], pp. 336–354
32. Even, S., Mansour, Y.: A construction of a cipher from a single pseudorandom permutation. In: Imai, H., Rivest, R.L., Matsumoto, T. (eds.) ASIACRYPT 1991. LNCS, vol. 739, pp. 210–224. Springer, Heidelberg (1993). https://doi.org/10.1007/3-540-57332-1_17
33. Gazi, P., Tessaro, S.: Secret-key cryptography from ideal primitives: a systematic overview. In: 2015 IEEE Information Theory Workshop, ITW 2015, Jerusalem, 26 April–1 May 2015, pp. 1–5. IEEE (2015)
34. Gentry, C., Ramzan, Z.: Eliminating random permutation oracles in the Even-Mansour cipher. In: Lee, P.J. (ed.) ASIACRYPT 2004. LNCS, vol. 3329, pp. 32–47. Springer, Heidelberg (2004). https://doi.org/10.1007/978-3-540-30539-2_3
35. Gilboa, S., Gueron, S.: The advantage of truncated permutations. CoRR abs/1610.02518 (2016)
36. Gong, Z., Nikova, S., Law, Y.W.: KLEIN: a new family of lightweight block ciphers. In: Juels, A., Paar, C. (eds.) RFIDSec 2011. LNCS, vol. 7055, pp. 1–18. Springer, Heidelberg (2012). https://doi.org/10.1007/978-3-642-25286-0_1
37. Guo, J., Peyrin, T., Poschmann, A.: The PHOTON family of lightweight hash functions. In: Rogaway, P. (ed.) CRYPTO 2011. LNCS, vol. 6841, pp. 222–239. Springer, Heidelberg (2011). https://doi.org/10.1007/978-3-642-22792-9_13
38. Hall, C., Wagner, D., Kelsey, J., Schneier, B.: Building PRFs from PRPs. In: Krawczyk, H. (ed.) CRYPTO 1998. LNCS, vol. 1462, pp. 370–389. Springer, Heidelberg (1998). https://doi.org/10.1007/BFb0055742
39. Hoang, V.T., Tessaro, S.: Key-alternating ciphers and key-length extension: exact bounds and multi-user security. In: Robshaw and Katz [61], pp. 3–32
40. Hong, D., et al.: HIGHT: a new block cipher suitable for low-resource device. In: Goubin, L., Matsui, M. (eds.) CHES 2006. LNCS, vol. 4249, pp. 46–59. Springer, Heidelberg (2006). https://doi.org/10.1007/11894063_4
41. Impagliazzo, R., Rudich, S.: Limits on the provable consequences of one-way permutations. In: Goldwasser, S. (ed.) CRYPTO 1988. LNCS, vol. 403, pp. 8–26. Springer, New York (1990). https://doi.org/10.1007/0-387-34799-2_2
42. Iwata, T., Cheon, J.H. (eds.): ASIACRYPT 2015, Part II. LNCS, vol. 9453, pp. 465–489. Springer, Heidelberg (2015). https://doi.org/10.1007/978-3-662-48800-3
43. Katz, J., Shacham, H. (eds.): CRYPTO 2017, Part III. LNCS, vol. 10403, pp. 497–523. Springer, Cham (2017). https://doi.org/10.1007/978-3-319-63697-9
44. Lampe, R., Patarin, J., Seurin, Y.: An asymptotically tight security analysis of the iterated Even-Mansour cipher. In: Wang and Sako [66], pp. 278–295
45. Lampe, R., Seurin, Y.: Security analysis of key-alternating Feistel ciphers. In: Cid and Rechberger [22], pp. 243–264

46. Lim, C.H., Korkishko, T.: mCrypton – a lightweight block cipher for security of low-cost RFID tags and sensors. In: Song, J.-S., Kwon, T., Yung, M. (eds.) WISA 2005. LNCS, vol. 3786, pp. 243–258. Springer, Heidelberg (2006). https://doi.org/10.1007/11604938_19

47. Luby, M., Rackoff, C.: How to construct pseudorandom permutations from pseudorandom functions. SIAM J. Comput. **17**(2), 373–386 (1988)

48. Lucks, S.: The sum of PRPs is a secure PRF. In: Preneel, B. (ed.) EUROCRYPT 2000. LNCS, vol. 1807, pp. 470–484. Springer, Heidelberg (2000). https://doi.org/10.1007/3-540-45539-6_34

49. Maurer, U., Renner, R., Holenstein, C.: Indifferentiability, impossibility results on reductions, and applications to the random oracle methodology. In: Naor, M. (ed.) TCC 2004. LNCS, vol. 2951, pp. 21–39. Springer, Heidelberg (2004). https://doi.org/10.1007/978-3-540-24638-1_2

50. Mennink, B., Neves, S.: Encrypted Davies-Meyer and its dual: towards optimal security using mirror theory. In: Katz and Shacham [43], pp. 556–583

51. Mennink, B., Preneel, B.: On the XOR of multiple random permutations. In: Malkin, T., Kolesnikov, V., Lewko, A.B., Polychronakis, M. (eds.) ACNS 2015. LNCS, vol. 9092, pp. 619–634. Springer, Cham (2015). https://doi.org/10.1007/978-3-319-28166-7_30

52. Mennink, B., Reyhanitabar, R., Vizár, D.: Security of full-state keyed sponge and duplex: applications to authenticated encryption. In: Iwata and Cheon [42], pp. 465–489

53. Nachef, V., Patarin, J., Volte, E.: Feistel Ciphers - Security Proofs and Cryptanalysis. Springer, Cham (2017). https://doi.org/10.1007/978-3-319-49530-9

54. Patarin, J.: Étude des Générateurs de Permutations Basés sur le Schéma du D.E.S. Ph.D. thesis, Université Paris 6, Paris, November 1991

55. Patarin, J.: On linear systems of equations with distinct variables and small block size. In: Won, D.H., Kim, S. (eds.) ICISC 2005. LNCS, vol. 3935, pp. 299–321. Springer, Heidelberg (2006). https://doi.org/10.1007/11734727_25

56. Patarin, J.: The "Coefficients H" technique. In: Avanzi, R.M., Keliher, L., Sica, F. (eds.) SAC 2008. LNCS, vol. 5381, pp. 328–345. Springer, Heidelberg (2009). https://doi.org/10.1007/978-3-642-04159-4_21

57. Patarin, J.: Introduction to mirror theory: analysis of systems of linear equalities and linear non equalities for cryptography. Cryptology ePrint Archive, Report 2010/287 (2010)

58. Patarin, J.: Mirror theory and cryptography. Cryptology ePrint Archive, Report 2016/702 (2016)

59. Pointcheval, D., Johansson, T. (eds.): EUROCRYPT 2012. LNCS, vol. 7237, pp. 336–354. Springer, Heidelberg (2012). https://doi.org/10.1007/978-3-642-29011-4

60. Preneel, B., Takagi, T. (eds.): CHES 2011. LNCS, vol. 6917. Springer, Heidelberg (2011). https://doi.org/10.1007/978-3-642-23951-9

61. Robshaw, M., Katz, J. (eds.): CRYPTO 2016, Part I. LNCS, vol. 9814. Springer, Heidelberg (2016). https://doi.org/10.1007/978-3-662-53018-4

62. Shibutani, K., Isobe, T., Hiwatari, H., Mitsuda, A., Akishita, T., Shirai, T.: Piccolo: an ultra-lightweight blockcipher. In: Preneel and Takagi [60], pp. 342–357

63. Steinberger, J.: The sum-capture problem for Abelian groups (2014). http://arxiv.org/abs/1309.5582

64. Steinberger, J.P.: Improved security bounds for key-alternating ciphers via Hellinger distance. Cryptology ePrint Archive, Report 2012/481 (2012)

65. Tessaro, S.: Optimally secure block ciphers from ideal primitives. In: Iwata and Cheon [42], pp. 437–462

66. Wang, X., Sako, K. (eds.): ASIACRYPT 2012. LNCS, vol. 7658, pp. 278–295. Springer, Heidelberg (2012). https://doi.org/10.1007/978-3-642-34961-4
67. Wu, W., Zhang, L.: LBlock: a lightweight block cipher. In: Lopez, J., Tsudik, G. (eds.) ACNS 2011. LNCS, vol. 6715, pp. 327–344. Springer, Heidelberg (2011). https://doi.org/10.1007/978-3-642-21554-4_19

Mathematical Cryptanalysis

New Results on Modular Inversion Hidden Number Problem and Inversive Congruential Generator

Jun Xu[1,2]($\boxtimes$), Santanu Sarkar[3], Lei Hu[1,2,6], Huaxiong Wang[4], and Yanbin Pan[5]

[1] State Key Laboratory of Information Security, Institute of Information Engineering, Chinese Academy of Sciences, Beijing 100093, China
{xujun,hulei}@iie.ac.cn
[2] Data Assurance and Communications Security Research Center, Chinese Academy of Sciences, Beijing 100093, China
[3] Department of Mathematics, Indian Institute of Technology Madras, Sardar Patel Road, Chennai 600036, India
sarkar.santanu.bir@gmail.com
[4] Division of Mathematical Sciences, School of Physical and Mathematical Sciences, Nanyang Technological University Singapore, Singapore, Singapore
HXWang@ntu.edu.sg
[5] Key Laboratory of Mathematics Mechanization, NCMIS, Academy of Mathematics and Systems Science, Chinese Academy of Sciences, Beijing 100190, China
[6] School of Cyber Security, University of Chinese Academy of Sciences, Beijing 100049, China

Abstract. The Modular Inversion Hidden Number Problem (MIHNP), introduced by Boneh, Halevi and Howgrave-Graham in Asiacrypt 2001, is briefly described as follows: Let $\mathrm{MSB}_\delta(z)$ refer to the δ most significant bits of z. Given many samples $\left(t_i, \mathrm{MSB}_\delta((\alpha + t_i)^{-1} \bmod p)\right)$ for random $t_i \in \mathbb{Z}_p$, the goal is to recover the hidden number $\alpha \in \mathbb{Z}_p$. MIHNP is an important class of Hidden Number Problem.

In this paper, we revisit the Coppersmith technique for solving a class of modular polynomial equations, which is respectively derived from the recovering problem of the hidden number α in MIHNP. For any positive integer constant d, let integer $n = d^{3+o(1)}$. Given a sufficiently large modulus p, $n + 1$ samples of MIHNP, we present a heuristic algorithm to recover the hidden number α with a probability close to 1 when $\delta/\log_2 p > \frac{1}{d+1} + o(\frac{1}{d})$. The overall time complexity of attack is polynomial in $\log_2 p$, where the complexity of the LLL algorithm grows as $d^{\mathcal{O}(d)}$ and the complexity of the Gröbner basis computation grows as $(2d)^{\mathcal{O}(n^2)}$. When $d > 2$, this asymptotic bound outperforms $\delta/\log_2 p > \frac{1}{3}$ which is the asymptotic bound proposed by Boneh, Halevi and Howgrave-Graham in Asiacrypt 2001. It is the first time that a better bound for solving MIHNP is given, which implies that the conjecture that MIHNP is hard whenever $\delta/\log_2 p < \frac{1}{3}$ is broken. Moreover, we also get the best result for attacking the Inversive Congruential Generator (ICG) up to now.

Keywords: Modular Inversion Hidden Number Problem ·
Inversive Congruential Generator · Lattice · LLL algorithm ·
The Coppersmith technique

© International Association for Cryptologic Research 2019
A. Boldyreva and D. Micciancio (Eds.): CRYPTO 2019, LNCS 11692, pp. 297–321, 2019.
https://doi.org/10.1007/978-3-030-26948-7_11

1   Introduction

1.1   Background

In cryptography research, one focuses on whether a mathematical problem is computationally hard, as the hard mathematical problem is the foundation of constructing cryptographic secure schemes. In [4], Boneh, Halevi and Howgrave-Graham introduced an algebraic complexity assumption called the Modular Inversion Hidden Number Problem (MIHNP) in order to design a pseudorandom number generator and message authentication code.

Definition 1 (Modular Inversion Hidden Number Problem(MIHNP)). *For a given prime p, consider a secret $\alpha \in \mathbb{Z}_p$ and $n + 1$ elements $t_0, t_1, \ldots, t_n$ $\in \mathbb{Z}_p \backslash \{-\alpha\}$, chosen independently and uniformly at random. Given $n+1$ samples*

$$\left\{ \left(t_i, \mathrm{MSB}_\delta((\alpha + t_i)^{-1} \bmod p)\right) \right\}_{i=0}^n$$

where $\mathrm{MSB}_\delta(z)$ refers to the δ most significant bits of z, the goal is to recover the hidden number α.

MIHNP is closely related to Hidden Number Problem (HNP), which was introduced in [5] by Boneh and Venkatesan to prove the bit security of the Diffie-Hellman key-exchange in $\mathbb{Z}_p$. Shparlinski [28] revealed that the primary motivation of studying MIHNP is to expect the bit security result of the Elliptic Curve Diffie-Hellman key-exchange. In PKC 2017, Shani [27] used ideas [4,20] of solving MIHNP to get the first rigorous result about the bit security of the Elliptic Curve Diffie-Hellman key-exchange.

1.2   Cryptanalysis

In Asiacrypt 2001, Boneh, Halevi and Howgrave-Graham gave two heuristic lattice methods to solve MIHNP [4]. Let δ denote the given number of most significant bits of $(\alpha + t_i)^{-1} \bmod p$'s. The first method works if $\delta > \frac{2}{3} \log_2 p$. The second method solves MIHNP if $\delta > \frac{1}{3} \log_2 p$, i.e., the knowledge of significantly fewer bits is needed. Moreover, *Boneh, Halevi and Howgrave-Graham* [4] *conjectured that MIHNP is hard whenever $\delta < \frac{1}{3} \log_2 p$.* In 2012, Ling et al. presented a rigorous polynomial time algorithm for solving MIHNP [20]. The obtained asymptotic result is $\delta > \frac{2}{3} \log_2 p$, which is the same as that of the first method in [4]. In 2014, Xu et al. [34] gave a heuristic lattice approach based on the Coppersmith technique, which has certain advantages when the number of samples is sufficiently small. However, the corresponding asymptotic result is $\delta > \frac{1}{2} \log_2 p$ which is still weaker than the second method in [4]. On the other hand, recently Xu et al. [35] obtained the explicit lattice construction of the second method in [4] and achieved the same asymptotic result $\delta > \frac{1}{3} \log_2 p$.

1.3   Our Contribution

We revisit the Coppersmith technique to solve the following system of multivariate modular polynomial equations

$$f_{0j}(x_0, x_j) := a_{0j} + b_{0j}x_0 + c_{0j}x_j + x_0x_j = 0 \pmod{p} \text{ for } 1 \le j \le n,$$

which is obtained from the recovering problem of the hidden number in MIHNP [35]. In the polynomial selection strategy for the Coppersmith lattice, we use the idea on *helpful polynomials* in [21,29] (see Sect. 2.2). The diagonals of helpful polynomials in the basis matrix are smaller than the involved modulo. This criterion enables helpful polynomials to facilitate the solution of modular equations. Therefore, we should try our best to add helpful polynomials into the involved lattice.

Based on the lattice construction of [4,35], we find that new linearly independent polynomials can still be added into the lattice by making full use of the linear combination of multiplies of several $f_{0j}(x_0, x_j)$ with common monomials. These newly added polynomials are helpful because their diagonal elements are smaller than modulo. Because the number of newly added helpful polynomials dominates the number of all the selected polynomials, it makes the Coppersmith technique search the desired small roots much efficiently.

In this paper, we obtain the following results. For any positive integer constant d, let integer $n = d^{3+o(1)}$. For a given sufficiently large modulus $p = 2^{\omega(d^{3d+2})}$, and $n + 1$ given samples of MIHNP, we present a heuristic algorithm to recover the hidden number α with a probability close to 1 when $\delta/\log_2 p > \frac{1}{d+1} + o(\frac{1}{d})$. The overall time complexity of attack is polynomial in $\log_2 p$, where the complexity of the LLL algorithm grows as $d^{\mathcal{O}(d)}$ and the complexity of the Gröbner basis computation grows as $(2d)^{\mathcal{O}(n^2)}$. When $d = 2$, our asymptotic result of $\delta/\log_2 p$ is equal to $\frac{1}{3}$, which is same as the previous best result [4,35]. When $d > 2$, the corresponding asymptotic bound is $\frac{1}{d+1} < \frac{1}{3}$. This implies that our result is beyond the bound given by the second method in [4]. Hence, we disprove the conjecture proposed by Boneh, Halevi and Howgrave-Graham in [4]. This attack also applies to ICG, as in prior work [35].

In Table 1, we compare new bound of $\delta/\log_2 p$ and the corresponding time complexity with the existing works (see Appendix A and Remark 4). Our results show that new bound of $\delta/\log_2 p$ is equal to 0 in the asymptotic sense. This is to say that MIHNP can be heuristically solved in polynomial time when δ is a constant fraction of $\log_2 p$. However, for the practical solutions, it requires a huge lattice dimension $\mathcal{O}\left((\frac{\log_2 p}{\delta})^{\mathcal{O}(\frac{\log_2 p}{\delta})}\right)$ in order to ensure that $\delta/\log_2 p$ is close to 0.

1.4   Organization of the Paper

The rest of this paper is organized as follows. In Sect. 2, we recall some terminologies and preliminaries. In Sect. 3, we present a strategy for solving modular polynomial equations and give the result for attacking MIHNP. Section 4 presents the proof of triangle basis matrix. Section 5 gives the experimental result. Section 6 concludes the paper. In Appendices, we respectively give asymptotic time complexities in previous works, the computation of lattice determinant and the analysis of bound of the desired small root.

Table 1. Comparison of lower bounds of $\delta/\log_2 p$ and corresponding time complexities, where $\rho := \delta/\log_2 p$ and $k := \log_2 p$.

MIHNP ICG	Lower Bound of $\delta/\log_2 p$	Asymptotic Time Complexities		
		LLL	Gröbner basis	SVP
[3]	**3/4**	—	—	$k^{O(1)}$
[20]	**2/3**	—	—	$k^{O(1)}2^{O\left(\frac{1}{\rho-\frac{2}{3}}\right)}$
[1]	**1/2**	$O\left(k^{O(1)}\left(\log_2 \frac{1}{\rho-\frac{1}{2}}\right)^{O\left(\log_2 \frac{1}{\rho-\frac{1}{2}}\right)}\right)$	$\left(\log_2 \frac{1}{\rho-\frac{1}{2}}\right)^{O\left(\left(\log_2 \frac{1}{\rho-\frac{1}{2}}\right)^2\right)}$	—
[34]	**1/2**	$O\left(k^{O(1)}\left(\frac{1}{\rho-\frac{1}{2}}\right)^{O(1)}\right)$	$\left(\frac{1}{\rho-\frac{1}{2}}\right)^{O\left(\log_2 \frac{1}{\rho-\frac{1}{2}}\right)}$	—
[4]	**1/3**	—	—	$k^{O(1)}2^{O\left(\left(\frac{2}{3\rho-1}\right)^{O\left(\frac{1}{\rho-\frac{1}{3}}\right)}\right)}$
[35]	**1/3**	$O\left(k^{O(1)}\left(\frac{2}{3\rho-1}\right)^{O\left(\frac{1}{\rho-\frac{1}{3}}\right)}\right)$	$\left(\frac{4}{3\rho-1}\right)^{O\left(\left(\frac{1}{\rho-\frac{1}{3}}\right)^{O(1)}\right)}$	—
This paper	**0**	$O\left(k^{O(1)}\left(\frac{1}{\rho}\right)^{O\left(\frac{1}{\rho}\right)}\right)$	$\left(\frac{2}{\rho}\right)^{O\left(\left(\frac{1}{\rho}\right)^{O(1)}\right)}$	—

2 Preliminaries

2.1 Lattices

Let vectors $\mathbf{b}_1, \ldots, \mathbf{b}_w$ be linearly independent in $\mathbb{R}^n$. The set

$$\mathcal{L} = \Big\{ \sum_{i=1}^{w} k_i \mathbf{b}_i, k_i \in \mathbb{Z} \Big\}$$

is called a lattice with basis vectors $\mathbf{b}_1, \cdots, \mathbf{b}_w$. In this paper, the basis vectors involved are row vectors. The dimension and determinant of $\mathcal{L}$ are respectively $\dim(\mathcal{L}) = w$, $\det(\mathcal{L}) = \sqrt{\det(BB^T)}$, where $B = [\mathbf{b}_1^T, \cdots, \mathbf{b}_w^T]^T$ is a basis matrix. If B is a square matrix, then $\det(\mathcal{L}) = |\det(B)|$.

In 1982, Lenstra, Lenstra and Lovász presented a deterministic polynomial-time algorithm [19] in order to find a reduced basis of the lattice.

Lemma 1 ([19]). *Let $\mathcal{L}$ be a lattice. Within polynomial time, the LLL algorithm outputs reduced basis vectors $\mathbf{v}_1, \ldots, \mathbf{v}_w$ that satisfy*

$$\|\mathbf{v}_1\| \leq \|\mathbf{v}_2\| \leq \cdots \leq \|\mathbf{v}_i\| \leq 2^{\frac{w(w-1)}{4(w+1-i)}} \det(\mathcal{L})^{\frac{1}{w+1-i}}, 1 \leq i \leq w.$$

2.2 The Coppersmith Technique

In 1996, Coppersmith proposed lattice-based techniques [7–9] for finding the small solution of univariate modular polynomials and bivariate integer polynomials. In 2006, May et al. presented heuristic strategies for solving multivariate polynomials [15]. The Coppersmith technique has been widely used in the field of cryptanalysis such as attacking RSA and its variants (see the survey [21] and recent results such as [16,25,30,31]) and analyzing pseudorandom number generators as well as computationally hard mathematical problems such as [1,2,6,11,12,14,32,35].

We explain briefly how one can utilize the idea of the Coppersmith technique to solve multivariate modular polynomials.

Definition of the Problem. Let $f_1(x_0, x_1, \cdots, x_n), \cdots, f_m(x_0, x_1, \cdots, x_n)$ be m irreducible multivariate polynomials defined over $\mathbb{Z}$, which have a common root $(\widetilde{x}_0, \widetilde{x}_1, \cdots, \widetilde{x}_n)$ modulo a known integer p such that $|\widetilde{x}_0| < X_0, \cdots, |\widetilde{x}_n| < X_n$. The question is to recover the desired root $(\widetilde{x}_0, \widetilde{x}_1, \cdots, \widetilde{x}_n)$ in polynomial time. The analysis needs to establish bounds X_i's to ensure recovery.

Step 1: Collection of Polynomials. One generates a collection of polynomials $g_1(x_0, x_1, \cdots, x_n), \cdots, g_w(x_0, x_1, \cdots, x_n)$ such that $(\widetilde{x}_0, \widetilde{x}_1, \cdots, \widetilde{x}_n)$ is a common modular root. For example, g_i's can be constructed as follows: $g_i(x_0, x_1, \ldots, x_n) = p^{d-(\beta_1^i + \cdots + \beta_m^i)} x_0^{\alpha_0^i} x_1^{\alpha_1^i} \cdots x_n^{\alpha_n^i} f_1^{\beta_1^i} \cdots f_m^{\beta_m^i}$ for $i = 1, \cdots, w$, where $d \in \mathbb{Z}^+$, $\alpha_0^i, \alpha_1^i, \cdots, \alpha_n^i$, $\beta_1^i, \cdots, \beta_m^i$ are nonnegative integers and $0 \leq \beta_1^i + \cdots + \beta_m^i \leq d$. It is easy to see that $g_i(\widetilde{x}_0, \widetilde{x}_1, \cdots, \widetilde{x}_n) \equiv 0 \bmod p^d$ for every $i \in [1, \cdots, w]$.

Step 2: Construction of Lattice. Let $\mathbf{b}_i$ be the coefficient vector of the polynomial $g_i(x_0 X_0, x_1 X_1, \ldots, x_n X_n)$ for all $1 \le i \le w$. Then one generates the lattice $\mathcal{L} = \left\{ \sum_{i=1}^{w} k_i \mathbf{b}_i, k_i \in \mathbb{Z} \right\}$.

Step 3: Generation of Reduced Basis. One runs a lattice reduction algorithm, such as LLL algorithm, to obtain the $n + 1$ reduced basis vectors $\mathbf{v}_1, \ldots, \mathbf{v}_{n+1}$ such that the corresponding polynomials $h_1(x_0, x_1, \cdots, x_n), \cdots, h_{n+1}(x_0, x_1, \cdots, x_n)$ have the desired common root $(\widetilde{x}_0, \widetilde{x}_1, \ldots, \widetilde{x}_n)$ over $\mathbb{Z}$, where $\mathbf{v}_i$ is the coefficient vector of the polynomial $h_i(x_0 X_0, x_1 X_1, \ldots, x_n X_n)$ for $i = 1, \cdots, n + 1$. Note that $h_i(x_0, x_1, \ldots, x_n)$ is a linear combination of $g_1(x_0, x_1, \ldots, x_n), \cdots, g_w(x_0, x_1, \ldots, x_n)$. Hence, we have $h_i(\widetilde{x}_0, \widetilde{x}_1, \cdots, \widetilde{x}_n) = 0$ (mod p^d) for every $i \in [1, \cdots, n + 1]$. In order to obtain $h_i(\widetilde{x}_0, \widetilde{x}_1, \cdots, \widetilde{x}_n) = 0$ for all $1 \le i \le n$, we need the following lemma in this process.

Lemma 2 ([13]). *Let $h(x_0, x_1, \ldots, x_n)$ be an integer polynomial that consists of at most w monomials. Let d be a positive integer and the integers X_i be the upper bound of $|\widetilde{x}_i|$ for $i = 0, 1, \cdots, n$. Let $\|h(x_0 X_0, x_1 X_1, \ldots, x_n X_n)\|$ be the Euclidean norm of the coefficient vector of the polynomial $h(x_0 X_0, x_1 X_1, \ldots, x_n X_n)$ with variables $x_0, x_1, \ldots, x_n$. Suppose that*

1. $h(\widetilde{x}_0, \widetilde{x}_1, \cdots, \widetilde{x}_n) = 0$ (mod p^d),
2. $\|h(x_0 X_0, x_1 X_1, \ldots, x_n X_n)\| < \frac{p^d}{\sqrt{w}}$,

then $h(\widetilde{x}_0, \widetilde{x}_1, \cdots, \widetilde{x}_n) = 0$ holds over $\mathbb{Z}$.

To get the above $n + 1$ polynomials $h_1(x_0, x_1, \cdots, x_n), \cdots h_{n+1}(x_0, x_1, \cdots, x_n)$, from Lemmas 1 and 2, one needs the Euclidean lengths of the $n + 1$ reduced basis vectors $\mathbf{v}_1, \ldots, \mathbf{v}_{n+1}$ satisfy the condition

$$2^{\frac{w(w-1)}{4(w-n)}} \cdot \left(\det(\mathcal{L}) \right)^{\frac{1}{w-n}} < \frac{p^d}{\sqrt{w}}, \tag{1}$$

where $w = \dim(\mathcal{L})$.

Based on Condition (1), one can determine the bounds X_i for $i = 0, \cdots, n$. In order to make the bounds X_i as large as possible, the polynomials $g_1(x_0, x_1, \cdots, x_n), \cdots, g_w(x_0, x_1, \cdots, x_n)$ in Step 1 need to be constructed carefully. It is a difficult step in the Coppersmith technique.

The strategy of choosing polynomials for our lattice construction is based on the idea of *helpful polynomials* [21,29]. Neglecting low-order terms in (1), we can rewrite condition (1) and obtain the simplified condition as follows:

$$(\det(\mathcal{L}))^{\frac{1}{w}} < p^d.$$

For a triangular basis matrix, the left side of this simplified condition is regarded as the geometric mean of all diagonals of the basis matrix. The polynomials whose diagonals are less than p^d are called *helpful polynomials*. For a polynomial, for example, $h(x_0, \cdots, x_n)$, the diagonal of $h(x_0, \cdots, x_n)$ means the leading coefficient of $h(x_0 X_0, \cdots, x_n X_n)$. A helpful polynomial contributes to the determinant with a factor less than p^d. The more helpful polynomials are added to the lattice, the better the condition for solving modular equations becomes. This means that the Coppersmith technique of finding the wanted small root becomes more and more effective, and the above bounds X_i become larger and larger. Therefore, we should choose as many helpful polynomials as possible. In this paper, our method can significantly improve previous results because the number of helpful polynomials dominates the number of all selected polynomials.

Step 4: Recovering the Desired Root. We have no assurance that the $n+1$ obtained polynomials $h_1, \cdots, h_{n+1}$ are algebraically independent. Under the following heuristic assumption that the $n+1$ polynomials define an algebraic variety of dimension zero, the corresponding equations can be solved using elimination techniques such as the Gröbner basis computation, and then the desired root $(\widetilde{x}_0, \widetilde{x}_1, \cdots, \widetilde{x}_n)$ is recovered. In this paper, we justify the validity of our heuristic attack by computer experiments.

Assumption 1. *Let* $h_1, \cdots, h_{n+1} \in \mathbb{Z}[x_0, x_1, \cdots, x_n]$ *be the polynomials that are found by the Coppersmith technique. Then the ideal generated by the polynomial equations* $h_1(x_0, x_1, \cdots, x_n) = 0, \cdots, h_{n+1}(x_0, x_1, \cdots, x_n) = 0$ *has dimension zero.*

2.3 A Class of Modular Polynomial Equations

In this subsection, we translate the problem of recovering the hidden number in MIHNP into solving modular polynomial equations with small root.

   For a given prime p, *consider a hidden number* $\alpha \in \mathbb{Z}_p$ *and* $n+1$ *elements* $t_0, t_1, \ldots, t_n \in \mathbb{Z}_p \setminus \{-\alpha\}$, *chosen independently and uniformly at random. The goal is to recover* α, *given* $n+1$ *samples* $\left(t_i, \mathrm{MSB}_\delta((\alpha + t_i)^{-1} \bmod p)\right)$.

   Denote $u_i = \mathrm{MSB}_\delta\left((\alpha + t_i)^{-1} \bmod p)\right)$ and $\widetilde{x}_i = \left((\alpha + t_i)^{-1} \bmod p\right) - u_i$, where unknown $\widetilde{x}_i$ satisfies $0 \leq \widetilde{x}_i \leq \frac{p}{2^\delta}$ for all $0 \leq i \leq n$. Hence, we obtain $(\alpha + t_i)(u_i + \widetilde{x}_i) = 1 \bmod p$, eliminate α from these equations and get the following relations

$$a_{0i} + b_{0i}\widetilde{x}_0 + c_{0i}\widetilde{x}_i + \widetilde{x}_0\widetilde{x}_i = 0 \bmod p, 1 \leq i \leq n, \tag{2}$$

where

$$\begin{aligned} a_{0i} &= u_0 u_i + (u_0 - u_i)(t_0 - t_i)^{-1} \bmod p, \\ b_{0i} &= u_i + (t_0 - t_i)^{-1} \bmod p, \\ c_{0i} &= u_0 - (t_0 - t_i)^{-1} \bmod p. \end{aligned} \tag{3}$$

If the corresponding $\widetilde{x}_0, \widetilde{x}_1, \cdots, \widetilde{x}_n$ are found out, then the hidden number α can be recovered. Hence, our goal is to find the desired root $(\widetilde{x}_0, \widetilde{x}_1, \cdots, \widetilde{x}_n)$ of the following modular polynomial equations

$$f_{0i}(x_0, x_i) := a_{0i} + b_{0i}x_0 + c_{0i}x_i + x_0 x_i = 0 \bmod p, 1 \leq i \leq n, \tag{4}$$

where $n < p$ and $|\widetilde{x}_0|, |\widetilde{x}_1|, \cdots, |\widetilde{x}_n|$ are bounded by X. We take $X = \frac{p}{2^\delta}$ where δ is the number of known MSBs. Moreover, in the following analysis, we need that all $c_{01}, \cdots, c_{0n} \in \mathbb{Z}_p$ are distinct.

According to (3), we get $c_{0i} = u_0 - (t_0 - t_i)^{-1} \bmod p$ for $i = 1, \cdots, n$. Note that elements $t_0, t_1, \ldots, t_n \in \mathbb{Z}_p \setminus \{-\alpha\}$, chosen independently and uniformly, where α is the hidden number. The probability that all c_{0i} are distinct is equal to $\prod_{k=1}^{n-1} (1 - \frac{k}{p}) \approx e^{-\sum_{k=1}^{n-1} \frac{k}{p}} = e^{-\frac{n(n-1)}{2p}} \approx 1 - \frac{n^2 - n}{2p}$, which is close to 1 for a sufficiently large p.

2.4   Order of Monomials

First, we describe reverse lexicographic order and graded lexicographic reverse order respectively. Please refer to [33, Section 21.2] for more details of these orders. Let $(i_1, \cdots, i_n)$ and $(i'_1, \cdots, i'_n)$ be integer vectors, where $i_m \geq 0, i'_m \geq 0$ for all $1 \leq m \leq n$.

Reverse Lexicographic Order: $(i'_1, \cdots, i'_n) \prec_{revlex} (i_1, \cdots, i_n) \Leftrightarrow$ the rightmost nonzero entry in $(i'_1 - i_1, \cdots, i'_n - i_n)$ is negative.

Graded Reverse Lexicographic Order: $(i'_1, \cdots, i'_n) \prec_{grevlex} (i_1, \cdots, i_n) \Leftrightarrow$
$$\sum_{m=1}^{n} i'_m < \sum_{m=1}^{n} i_m \text{ or } \left(\sum_{m=1}^{n} i'_m = \sum_{m=1}^{n} i_m \text{ and } (i'_1, \cdots, i'_n) \prec_{revlex} (i_1, \cdots, i_n) \right).$$

Next, we consider the following order of monomials.

$$x_0^{i'_0} x_1^{i'_1} \cdots x_n^{i'_n} \prec x_0^{i_0} x_1^{i_1} \cdots x_n^{i_n} \Leftrightarrow$$
$$(i'_1, \cdots, i'_n) \prec_{grevlex} (i_1, \cdots, i_n) \text{ or } ((i'_1, \cdots, i'_n) = (i_1, \cdots, i_n) \text{ and } i'_0 < i_0). \tag{5}$$

It is worth noting that we treat i_0 differently than $i_1, \cdots, i_n$ for vector $(i_0, i_1, \cdots, i_n)$.

2.5   Elementary Symmetric Polynomials and Matrix

In this section, we first describe the definition of elementary symmetric polynomials. Please refer to [26, Section 3.1] for more details.

The elementary symmetric polynomials on m variables $\{y_1, \cdots, y_m\}$, written as $\sigma_k(y_1, \cdots, y_m)$ for $k = 0, 1, \cdots, m$, are defined by

$$\begin{cases} \sigma_0(y_1, \cdots, y_m) = 1, \\ \sigma_1(y_1, \cdots, y_m) = \sum_{1 \leq i \leq m} y_i, \\ \sigma_2(y_1, \cdots, y_m) = \sum_{1 \leq i < j \leq m} y_i y_j, \\ \sigma_3(y_1, \cdots, y_m) = \sum_{1 \leq i < j < k \leq m} y_i y_j y_k, \\ \quad \vdots \\ \sigma_m(y_1, \cdots, y_m) = \prod_{1 \leq i \leq m} y_i. \end{cases}$$

From the above formulas, we can see that $\sigma_k(y_1, \cdots, y_m)$ is the sum of all products of exactly k distinct y_i's.

Next, we define the following $s \times s$ matrix whose entries depend on elementary symmetric polynomials, which will be used in Sects. 3 and 4. Consider the matrix

$$M_{j_1,\cdots,j_s} := \begin{pmatrix} \sigma_{s-1}(\wedge_0) & \cdots & \sigma_1(\wedge_0) & \sigma_0(\wedge_0) \\ \sigma_{s-1}(\wedge_1) & \cdots & \sigma_1(\wedge_1) & \sigma_0(\wedge_1) \\ & \cdots & & \\ \sigma_{s-1}(\wedge_{s-1}) & \cdots & \sigma_1(\wedge_{s-1}) & \sigma_0(\wedge_{s-1}) \end{pmatrix},$$

where $\sigma_i(\wedge_l)$ is the i-th elementary symmetric polynomial on

$$\wedge_l := \{c_{0,j_1}, \cdots, c_{0,j_s}\} \setminus \{c_{0,j_{l+1}}\} \text{ with } 0 \le i \le s-1, \ 0 \le l \le s-1.$$

Here $1 \le j_1 < \cdots < j_s \le n$ and $c_{0,j_{l+1}}$ is the coefficient of variable $x_{j_{l+1}}$ in the polynomial $f_{0,j_{l+1}}$ in (4).

For indexes $j_1, \cdots, j_s$, row u and column v of matrix $M_{j_1,\cdots,j_s}$ is the evaluation of σ_{s-v} on all the variables c_{0,j_i} except c_{0,j_u}, where $1 \le u, v \le s$. From another perspective, we first let polynomials

$$G_u(x) := (x + c_{0,j_1}) \cdots (x + c_{0,j_{u-1}})(x + c_{0,j_{u+1}}) \cdots (x + c_{0,j_s}) \text{ for all } 1 \le u \le s.$$

For $1 \le v \le s$, we have that the coefficient of $G_u(x)$ on monomial x^{s-v} is the evaluation of σ_{s-v} on all the variables c_{0,j_i} except c_{0,j_u}. In other words, row u and column v of matrix $M_{j_1,\cdots,j_s}$ is the coefficient of $G_u(x)$ on monomial x^{s-v}.

Lemma 3. *For a given prime p and any integer $s \ge 2$, define matrix $M_{j_1,\cdots,j_s}$ as above. Then $M_{j_1,\cdots,j_s}$ is invertible over $\mathbb{Z}_{p^{s-1}}$ if $c_{0,j_1}, \cdots, c_{0,j_s}$ are distinct in $\mathbb{Z}_p$.*

Proof. Since p is a prime number, we get that $M_{j_1,\cdots,j_s}$ is invertible over $\mathbb{Z}_{p^{s-1}}$ if and only if $M_{j_1,\cdots,j_s}$ is invertible over $\mathbb{Z}_p$. Note that row u of matrix $M_{j_1,\cdots,j_s}$ is the coefficient vector of polynomial $G_u(x)$ on the basis $(1, x, \cdots, x^{s-1})$ for all $1 \le u \le s$. Hence, $M_{j_1,\cdots,j_s}$ is invertible over $\mathbb{Z}_p$ if and only if polynomials $G_1(x), \cdots, G_s(x)$ are linearly independent over $\mathbb{Z}_p$.

Suppose that there exist integers $c_1, \cdots, c_s$ satisfying

$$c_1 G_1(x) + \cdots + c_s G_s(x) = 0. \tag{6}$$

Note that $G_u(x) = (x + c_{0,j_1}) \cdots (x + c_{0,j_{u-1}})(x + c_{0,j_{u+1}}) \cdots (x + c_{0,j_s})$ for $1 \le u \le s$. Taking modulo $x + c_{0,j_u}$ on both sides of (6), we obtain that

$$c_u G_u(x) \equiv 0 \bmod (x + c_{0,j_u}) \text{ for } u = 1, \cdots, s.$$

If $c_{0,j_1}, \cdots, c_{0,j_s}$ are distinct in $\mathbb{Z}_p$, then the polynomials $x + c_{0,j_1}, \cdots, x + c_{0,j_s}$ are pairwise coprime. Furthermore, we have $\gcd(x + c_{0,j_u}, G_u(x)) = 1$. Combining this relation with the above equations, we deduce that $c_1 = \cdots = c_s = 0$. Based on (6), we have that the polynomials $G_1(x), \cdots, G_s(x)$ are linearly independent over $\mathbb{Z}_p$. In other words, $M_{j_1,\cdots,j_s}$ is invertible over $\mathbb{Z}_{p^{s-1}}$ if $c_{0,j_1}, \cdots, c_{0,j_s}$ are distinct in $\mathbb{Z}_p$. $\square$

Note that the indexes $j_1, \cdots, j_s$ satisfy $1 \le j_1 < \cdots < j_s \le n$. We always have that elements $c_{0,j_1}, \cdots, c_{0,j_s}$ are from $c_{01}, \cdots, c_{0n}$. According to the analysis of Sect. 2.3, we know that $c_{01}, \cdots, c_{0n}$ are distinct with a probability close to 1 for a sufficiently large p. Hence, from Lemma 3, matrix $M_{j_1,\cdots,j_s}$ is invertible over $\mathbb{Z}_{p^{s-1}}$ with a probability close to 1 for a sufficiently large p.

3   The Strategy for Solving a Class of Modular Polynomial Equations

In this section, we first present theorems to solve the equation system (4), and then give the corresponding results for solving MIHNP.

Theorem 1. *For any given positive integer d, take positive integer $n = d^{3+o(1)}$. Given a sufficiently large prime $p = 2^{\omega(d^{3d+2})}$, and polynomials $f_{0j}(x_0, x_j)$ with $1 \leq j \leq n$ in (4), under Assumption 1, one can compute the desired root $(\tilde{x}_0, \tilde{x}_1, \cdots, \tilde{x}_n)$ with a probability close to 1, if the bound X of $|\tilde{x}_0|, |\tilde{x}_1|, \cdots, |\tilde{x}_n|$ satisfies*

$$X < p^{1 - \frac{1}{d+1} - o(\frac{1}{d})}. \tag{7}$$

The corresponding time complexity is polynomial in $\log_2 p$ for any constant d, where the complexity of the LLL algorithm grows as $d^{\mathcal{O}(d)}$ and the complexity of the Gröbner basis computation grows as $(2d)^{\mathcal{O}(n^2)}$.

Proof. For any given positive integer d, and integers n, t satisfying $n \geq d + 1$, $0 \leq t \leq d$, we first construct the polynomials $F_{i_0, i_1, \ldots, i_n}(x_0, x_1, \cdots, x_n)$ for all vectors $(i_0, i_1, \cdots, i_n) \in I(n, d, t)$, where

$$I(n, d, t) = \{(i_0, i_1, \cdots, i_n) \mid 0 \leq i_0 \leq d, 0 \leq i_1, \cdots, i_n \leq 1, 0 \leq i_1 + \cdots + i_n \leq d\}$$
$$\cup \{(i_0, i_1, \cdots, i_n) \mid 0 \leq i_0 \leq t, 0 \leq i_1, \cdots, i_n \leq 1, i_1 + \cdots + i_n = d + 1\}.$$

We will optimize integers n, t later. Denote the level $s := i_1 + \cdots + i_n$, where $0 \leq s \leq d + 1$.

When $s = 0$, we construct $F_{i_0, i_1, \ldots, i_n}(x_0, x_1, \cdots, x_n) = p^d x_0^{i_0}$ for $i_0 = 0, 1, \cdots, d$.
When $s = 1$, we construct

$$F_{i_0, i_1, \ldots, i_n}(x_0, x_1, \cdots, x_n) = \begin{cases} p^d x_1^{i_1} \cdots x_n^{i_n} & \text{for } i_0 = 0, \\ p^{d-1} x_0^{i_0 - 1} f_{01}^{i_1} \cdots f_{0n}^{i_n} & \text{for } 1 \leq i_0 \leq d. \end{cases}$$

When $2 \leq s \leq d + 1$, if $s \leq i_0 \leq d$, we construct the polynomials

$$F_{i_0, i_1, \ldots, i_n}(x_0, x_1, \cdots, x_n) = p^{d-s} x_0^{i_0 - s} f_{01}^{i_1} \cdots f_{0n}^{i_n}.$$

If $0 \leq i_0 < s$, we construct the polynomials $F_{i_0, i_1, \ldots, i_n}(x_0, x_1, \cdots, x_n)$ as follows.
Notice that all integers $i_1, \cdots, i_n$ are equal to 0 or 1. We can rewrite $f_{01}^{i_1} \cdots f_{0n}^{i_n} = f_{0, j_1} \cdots f_{0, j_s}$, where $j_1, \cdots, j_s$ are some integers satisfying $1 \leq j_1 < \cdots < j_s \leq n$. Define $M_{j_1, \cdots, j_s}$ as Sect. 2.5. Based on Lemma 3, we have that $M_{j_1, \cdots, j_s}$ is invertible in $\mathbb{Z}_{p^{s-1}}$ with a probability close to 1 for a sufficiently large p. Let $M_{j_1, \cdots, j_s}^{-1}$ be the inverse of $M_{j_1, \cdots, j_s}$ modulo p^{s-1}. Then we generate s polynomials $g_0(x_0, x_{j_1}, \ldots, x_{j_s}), g_1(x_0, x_{j_1}, \ldots, x_{j_s}), \cdots, g_{s-1}(x_0, x_{j_1}, \ldots, x_{j_s})$ according to the following way:

$$\begin{pmatrix} g_0(x_0, x_{j_1}, \ldots, x_{j_s}) \\ g_1(x_0, x_{j_1}, \ldots, x_{j_s}) \\ \vdots \\ g_{s-1}(x_0, x_{j_1}, \ldots, x_{j_s}) \end{pmatrix} = M_{j_1, \cdots, j_s}^{-1} \cdot \begin{pmatrix} x_{j_1} f_{0, j_2} \cdots f_{0, j_s} \\ f_{0, j_1} x_{j_2} \cdots f_{0, j_s} \\ \vdots \\ f_{0, j_1} \cdots f_{0, j_{s-1}} x_{j_s} \end{pmatrix} \mod p^{s-1}. \tag{8}$$

Here, $g_0(x_0, x_{j_1}, \ldots, x_{j_s})$, $g_1(x_0, x_{j_1}, \ldots, x_{j_s})$, $\cdots$, $g_{s-1}(x_0, x_{j_1}, \ldots, x_{j_s})$ are treated as the corresponding polynomials over $\mathbb{Z}$.

Further, we define

$$F_{i_0, i_1, \ldots, i_n}(x_0, x_1, \cdots, x_n) = p^{d+1-s} \cdot g_{i_0}(x_0, x_{j_1}, \ldots, x_{j_s}), \tag{9}$$

where

$$\begin{cases} 0 \leq i_0 \leq s-1 & \text{for } 0 \leq s \leq d, \\ 0 \leq i_0 \leq t & \text{for } s = d+1. \end{cases}$$

Note that $g_{i_0}(\widetilde{x}_0, \widetilde{x}_1, \cdots, \widetilde{x}_n) = 0 \bmod p^{s-1}$. The corresponding

$$F_{i_0, i_1, \cdots, i_n}(\widetilde{x}_0, \widetilde{x}_1, \cdots, \widetilde{x}_n) = 0 \bmod p^d.$$

In fact, for all tuples $(i_0, i_1, \cdots, i_n) \in I(n, d, t)$, we always get

$$F_{i_0, i_1, \cdots, i_n}(\widetilde{x}_0, \widetilde{x}_1, \cdots, \widetilde{x}_n) = 0 \bmod p^d.$$

Next, we present the following lemma in order to construct a triangular lattice basis matrix. The corresponding proof is given in Sect. 4.

Lemma 4. *Define polynomials $F_{i_0, i_1, \ldots, i_n}(x_0, x_1, \cdots, x_n)$ as above, where the corresponding monomials are arranged according to the order (5). Let $\mathcal{L}(n, d, t)$ be a lattice spanned by the coefficient vectors of polynomials*

$$F_{i_0, i_1, \cdots, i_n}(x_0 X, x_1 X, \cdots, x_n X),$$

for all $(i_0, i_1, \cdots, i_n) \in I(n, d, t)$. Then the basis matrix becomes triangular if these coefficient vectors are arranged according to the leading monomial of the corresponding $F_{i_0, i_1, \cdots, i_n}(x_0, x_1, \cdots, x_n)$ from low to high. Moreover, diagonal elements of the triangular basis matrix of $\mathcal{L}(n, d, t)$ are as follows:

$$\begin{cases} p^{d-s} X^{i_0+s} & \text{for } i_0 \geq s, \\ p^{d+1-s} X^{i_0+s} & \text{for } i_0 < s, \end{cases} \tag{10}$$

where $s = i_1 + \cdots + i_n$.

We will provide an example for lattice $\mathcal{L}(n, d, t)$ in full version. It is easy to see that the dimension of $\mathcal{L}(n, d, t)$ is equal to

$$\dim(\mathcal{L}(n, d, t)) = (d+1) \sum_{s=0}^{d} \binom{n}{s} + (t+1) \binom{n}{d+1}. \tag{11}$$

We compute the determinant of $\mathcal{L}(n, d, t)$ as

$$\det(\mathcal{L}(n, d, t)) = p^{\alpha(n,d)} \cdot X^{\beta(n,d,t)}, \tag{12}$$

where

$$\alpha(n, d) = d(d+1) \sum_{s=0}^{d} \binom{n}{s} - d \sum_{s=0}^{d} s \binom{n}{s},$$

$$\beta(n, d, t) = \frac{d(d+1)}{2} \sum_{s=0}^{d} \binom{n}{s} + (d+1) \sum_{s=0}^{d} s \binom{n}{s} + \frac{(2d+t+2)(t+1)}{2} \binom{n}{d+1}.$$

The detailed computation is left in Appendix B. By the property of LLL algorithm and Howgrave-Graham's lemma, if Condition (1) is satisfied, namely,

$$2^{\frac{w(w-1)}{4(w-n)}} \cdot \det(\mathcal{L}(n,d,t))^{\frac{1}{w-n}} < \frac{p^d}{\sqrt{w}},\tag{13}$$

where $w = \dim(\mathcal{L}(n,d,t))$, after reduction of lattice we get $n+1$ polynomials which contain the root $(\tilde{x}_0, \tilde{x}_1, \cdots, \tilde{x}_n)$ over integers. Under Assumption 1, we can find $\tilde{x}_0, \tilde{x}_1, \cdots, \tilde{x}_n$.

Plugging (11) and (12) into (13), we obtain the condition

$$X < \left(2^{-\frac{w(w-1)}{4\beta(n,d,t)}} w^{-\frac{w-n}{2\beta(n,d,t)}}\right) \cdot p^{\lambda(n,d,t)},\tag{14}$$

where

$$\lambda(n,d,t) := \frac{d(w-n) - \alpha(n,d)}{\beta(n,d,t)} = \frac{2d(t+1)\binom{n}{d+1} + 2d\sum_{s=2}^{d} s\binom{n}{s}}{(2d+2+t)(t+1)\binom{n}{d+1} + d(d+1)\sum_{s=0}^{d}\binom{n}{s} + 2(d+1)\sum_{s=0}^{d} s\binom{n}{s}}.$$

For a sufficiently large $p = 2^{\omega(d^{3d+2})}$, the above condition reduces to $X < p^{\lambda(n,d,t)}$. By taking the optimal $t = 0$ and $n = d^{3+o(1)}$, this condition further becomes

$$X < p^{1 - \frac{1}{d+1} - o(\frac{1}{d})}.$$

The detailed analysis is presented in Appendix C.

Finally, we analyze the time complexity of our algorithm. Note that the running time of the LLL algorithm depends on the dimension and the maximal bit size of input basis matrix. For the optimal case that $t = 0$ and $n = d^{3+o(1)}$, the dimension of $\mathcal{L}(n,d,0)$ is

$$(d+1)\sum_{s=0}^{d}\binom{n}{s} + \binom{n}{d+1} = \mathcal{O}(n^{d+1}) = \mathcal{O}(d^{\mathcal{O}(d)}).$$

The bit size of the entries in the basis matrix can be bounded by $2d\log_2 p$ based on (10). Hence, according to [24], the time complexity of the LLL algorithm is equal to

$$\text{poly}\left(2d\log_2 p, \mathcal{O}(d^{\mathcal{O}(d)})\right) = \mathcal{O}((\log_2 p)^{\mathcal{O}(1)} d^{\mathcal{O}(d)}).\tag{15}$$

Moreover, we use the Gröbner basis computation to solve the polynomials obtained from the LLL algorithm. The running time of the Gröbner basis computation relies on degrees of the polynomials in the Gröbner basis and the number of variables in these polynomials [10,18]. Under Assumption 1, these polynomials generate a zero-dimensional ideal. Note that the maximal degree is $2d$ and the number of variables is $n+1$. Based on [10], we get that the time complexity of the Gröbner basis computation is

$$\text{poly}((2d)^{(n+1)^2}) = (2d)^{\mathcal{O}(n^2)}.\tag{16}$$

Therefore, the overall time complexity is equal to $\mathcal{O}((\log_2 p)^{\mathcal{O}(1)} d^{\mathcal{O}(d)}) + (2d)^{\mathcal{O}(n^2)}$, which is polynomial in $\log_2 p$ for any constant d, where the complexity of the LLL algorithm grows as $d^{\mathcal{O}(d)}$ and the complexity of the Gröbner basis computation grows as $(2d)^{\mathcal{O}(n^2)}$.   □

Remark 1. Similar to [4,35], we choose the same polynomials $F_{i_0,i_1,\ldots,i_n}$ $(x_0, x_1, \cdots, x_n)$ where any $(i_0, i_1, \cdots, i_n)$ lies in the set $\{(i_0, i_1, \cdots, i_n) \mid 0 \le i_0 \le d, 0 \le i_1, \cdots, i_n \le 1, 0 \le i_1 + \cdots + i_n \le d\}$. The difference from [4,35] is that we add new polynomials $F_{i_0,i_1,\ldots,i_n}(x_0, x_1, \cdots, x_n)$ where any $(i_0, i_1, \cdots, i_n)$ belongs to the set $\{(i_0, i_1, \cdots, i_n) \mid 0 \le i_0 \le t, 0 \le i_1, \cdots, i_n \le 1, i_1 + \cdots + i_n = d + 1\}$, where $0 \le t \le d$. This corresponds to the case of $s = d+1$ in the proof of Theorem 1. When $t = 0$, the involved lattice $\mathcal{L}(n, d, t)$ is optimized.

According to (8) and (9), we get that newly added polynomials $F_{i_0,i_1,\ldots,i_n}(x_0, x_1, \cdots, x_n)$ are linear combinations of $d+1$ polynomials $x_{j_1} f_{0,j_2} \cdots f_{0,j_{d+1}}$, $f_{0,j_1} x_{j_2} \cdots f_{0,j_{d+1}}$, $\cdots$, $f_{0,j_1} \cdots f_{0,j_d} x_{j_{d+1}}$, which have common monomials. Concretely speaking,

$$F_{i_0,i_1,\ldots,i_n}(x_0, x_1, \cdots, x_n) = g_{i_0}(x_0, x_{j_1}, \ldots, x_{j_{d+1}}),$$

where $1 \le j_1, \cdots, j_{d+1} \le n$ satisfying $x_1^{i_1} \cdots x_n^{i_n} = x_{j_1} \cdots x_{j_{d+1}}$. These newly added polynomials $F_{i_0,i_1,\ldots,i_n}(x_0, x_1, \cdots, x_n)$ are linearly independent of previous $F_{i_0,i_1,\ldots,i_n}(x_0, x_1, \cdots, x_n)$ according to the analysis of Lemma 4.

Finally, we explain why this method can work efficiently. Consider the optimized case of $t = 0$, we have $i_0 = 0$ according to $0 \le i_0 \le t$. Note that $i_1, \cdots, i_n$ satisfy $0 \le i_1, \cdots, i_n \le 1, i_1 + \cdots + i_n = d + 1$. It implies that we added $\binom{n}{d+1}$ such polynomials $F_{i_0,i_1,\ldots,i_n}(x_0, x_1, \cdots, x_n)$ into the involved lattice $\mathcal{L}(n, d, t)$. Based on (7) and (10), we get that every newly added polynomial $F_{i_0,i_1,\ldots,i_n}(x_0, x_1, \cdots, x_n)$ contributes to a diagonal element X^{d+1} ($i_1 = 0$ and $s = d + 1$ in (10)), which is smaller than modulo p^d. Such a $F_{i_0,i_1,\ldots,i_n}(x_0, x_1, \cdots, x_n)$ is called a *helpful polynomial* [21,29]. Hence, we have $\binom{n}{d+1}$ helpful polynomials for lattice $\mathcal{L}(n, d, t)$. Since $\dim(\mathcal{L}(n, d, t)) = \binom{n}{d+1}(1 + o(1))$ for the optimized case of $t = 0$, we get that the number of all selected polynomials for lattice $\mathcal{L}(n, d, t)$ is $\binom{n}{d+1}(1 + o(1))$. It implies that newly added $\binom{n}{d+1}$ helpful polynomials are dominant. This is the fundamental reason behind the effectiveness of our approach.

Since $X = \frac{p}{2^\delta}$ in the case of MIHNP, we give the following result.

Corollary 1. *For any given positive integer d, let positive integer $n = d^{3+o(1)}$. For a given sufficiently large prime $p = 2^{\omega(d^{3d+2})}$ and $n + 1$ given samples in MIHNP, the hidden number can be recovered with a probability close to 1 under Assumption 1 if the number δ of known MSBs satisfies*

$$\frac{\delta}{\log_2 p} \ge \frac{1}{d+1} + o(\frac{1}{d}). \tag{17}$$

The involved time complexity is polynomial in $\log_2 p$ for any constant d, where the complexity of the LLL algorithm grows as $d^{\mathcal{O}(d)}$ and the complexity of the Gröbner basis computation grows as $(2d)^{\mathcal{O}(n^2)}$.

Remark 2. The algorithm in Theorem 1 can be also applied to the attack case of ICG, as described in prior work [35].

Remark 3. Taking $d = 2$, the asymptotic result of $\delta/\log_2 p$ is equal to $\frac{1}{3}$, which is the same as the previous best result [4,35]. When $d > 2$, our asymptotic bound is $\frac{1}{d+1} < \frac{1}{3}$, resulting in the best asymptotic result known so far.

Remark 4. Similar to Appendix A, we also use notations $\rho = \delta/\log_2 p$ and $k = \log_2 p$, where $0 < \rho < 1$. According to (17), namely, $\rho \geq \frac{1}{d+1} + o(\frac{1}{d})$. In the asymptotic sense, we have $\rho > \frac{1}{d+1}$, i.e., $d > \frac{1}{\rho} - 1$. Hence, we can take $d = 1/\rho$ asymptotically. Then, (15) and (16) respectively become $\mathcal{O}\left(k^{\mathcal{O}(1)}(\frac{1}{\rho})^{\mathcal{O}(\frac{1}{\rho})}\right)$ and $\left(\frac{2}{\rho}\right)^{\mathcal{O}((\frac{1}{\rho})^{\mathcal{O}(1)})}$. Hence, the overall time complexity is polynomial in $\log_2 p$ for any constant ρ (i.e., δ is a constant fraction of $\log_2 p$). Note that $\rho = \delta/\log_2 p$ tends to 0 as d becomes large. It implies that the asymptotic lower bound of $\delta/\log_2 p$ is equal to 0. However, in order to ensure that $\delta/\log_2 p$ is close to 0, a huge lattice dimension is required, which is because that the dimension of the involved lattice is equal to $\mathcal{O}(d^{\mathcal{O}(d)}) = \mathcal{O}\left((\frac{1}{\rho})^{\mathcal{O}(\frac{1}{\rho})}\right) = \mathcal{O}\left((\frac{\log_2 p}{\delta})^{\mathcal{O}(\frac{\log_2 p}{\delta})}\right)$.

Figure 1 shows that the theoretical values of $\delta/\log_2 p$ for different lattice dimension, where the smallest dimension is calculated among different n, d, t for the fixed $\delta/\log_2 p$. One can achieve $\delta/\log_2 p < \frac{1}{3}$ by using a lattice of dimension 209899. Theoretical value of the involved $\lambda(n, d, t)$ in this case is 0.671. Corresponding parameters are $n = 45, d = 3, t = 0$.

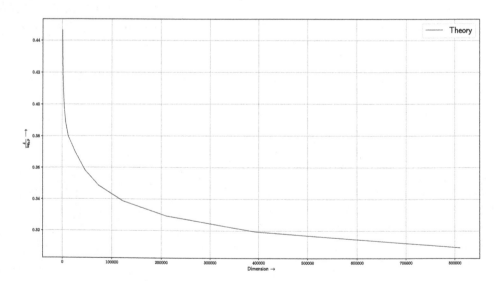

Fig. 1. Theoretical bound of $\delta/\log_2 p$ for different dimensions.

4   Proof of Lemma 4

Proof. First, we will show that the leading term of $F_{i_0,i_1,\cdots,i_n}(x_0, x_1, \cdots, x_n)$ according to the order (5) is as follows:

$$
\begin{aligned}
&- p^{d-s} x_0^{i_0} x_1^{i_1} \cdots x_n^{i_n} && i_0 \geq s, \\
&- p^{d+1-s} x_0^{i_0} x_1^{i_1} \cdots x_n^{i_n} && i_0 < s,
\end{aligned}
$$

where $s = i_1 + \cdots + i_n$.

For the case of $s = 0$, $F_{i_0,i_1,\cdots,i_n}(x_0, x_1, \cdots, x_n) = p^d x_0^{i_0}$ for $i_0 \geq 0$. Obviously, the corresponding leading term is $p^{d-s} x_0^{i_0} x_1^{i_1} \cdots x_n^{i_n}$ where $i_0 \geq s = 0$.

For the case of $s = 1$, we have

$$
F_{i_0,i_1,\ldots,i_n}(x_0, x_1, \cdots, x_n) =
\begin{cases}
p^d x_1^{i_1} \cdots x_n^{i_n} & \text{for } i_0 = 0, \\
p^{d-1} x_0^{i_0-1} f_{01}^{i_1} \cdots f_{0n}^{i_n} & \text{for } 1 \leq i_0 \leq d.
\end{cases}
$$

For $i_0 = 0$, the leading term of $F_{i_0,i_1,\ldots,i_n}(x_0, x_1, \cdots, x_n) = p^d x_1^{i_1} \cdots x_n^{i_n}$ can be rewritten as $p^{d+1-s} x_0^{i_0} x_1^{i_1} \cdots x_n^{i_n}$ since $s = 1$. For $i_0 \geq 1$, $F_{i_0,i_1,\ldots,i_n}(x_0, x_1, \cdots, x_n) = p^{d-1} x_0^{i_0-1} f_{01}^{i_1} \cdots f_{0n}^{i_n}$. We analyze its leading term as follows. Note that $f_{0j} = a_{0j} + b_{0j} x_0 + c_{0j} x_j + x_0 x_j$ for $1 \leq j \leq n$. Based on the order (5), we get

$$
1 \prec x_0 \prec x_j \prec x_0 x_j \text{ for } j = 1, \cdots, n.
$$

So the leading term of f_{0j} is $x_0 x_j$. Furthermore, the leading term of $F_{i_0,i_1,\ldots,i_n}(x_0, x_1, \cdots, x_n) = p^{d-1} x_0^{i_0-1} f_{01}^{i_1} \cdots f_{0n}^{i_n}$ is equal to

$$
p^{d-1} x_0^{i_0-1} (x_0 x_1)^{i_1} \cdots (x_0 x_n)^{i_n} = p^{d-s} x_0^{i_0} x_1^{i_1} \cdots x_n^{i_n},
$$

where $i_0 \geq s = 1$.

For the case of $2 \leq s \leq d+1$, if $s \leq i_0 \leq d$, we define

$$
F_{i_0,i_1,\ldots,i_n}(x_0, x_1, \cdots, x_n) = p^{d-s} x_0^{i_0-s} f_{01}^{i_1} \cdots f_{0n}^{i_n}.
$$

In this situation, the leading term of $F_{i_0,i_1,\ldots,i_n}(x_0, x_1, \cdots, x_n)$ is

$$
p^{d-s} x_0^{i_0-s} (x_0 x_1)^{i_1} \cdots (x_0 x_n)^{i_n} = p^{d-s} x_0^{i_0} x_1^{i_1} \cdots x_n^{i_n}.
$$

For the following situations

$$
\begin{cases}
0 \leq i_0 \leq s-1 & \text{for } 0 \leq s \leq d, \\
0 \leq i_0 \leq t & \text{for } s = d+1,
\end{cases}
$$

where $0 \leq t \leq d$, we define

$$
F_{i_0,i_1,\ldots,i_n}(x_0, x_1, \cdots, x_n) = p^{d+1-s} \cdot g_{i_0}(x_0, x_{j_1}, \ldots, x_{j_s}).
$$

Our goal is to show that $p^{d+1-s} x_0^{i_0} x_1^{i_1} \cdots x_n^{i_n}$ is the leading term of the corresponding polynomial $F_{i_0,i_1,\ldots,i_n}(x_0, x_1, \cdots, x_n)$. Note that $f_{01}^{i_1} \cdots f_{0n}^{i_n}$ is expressed as $f_{0,j_1} \cdots f_{0,j_s}$ in this situation. It is easy to deduce that $x_1^{i_1} \cdots x_n^{i_n} = x_{j_1} \cdots x_{j_s}$ by comparing terms of $f_{01}^{i_1} \cdots f_{0n}^{i_n}$ and $f_{0,j_1} \cdots f_{0,j_s}$. Hence we aim to prove that $x_0^{i_0} x_{j_1} \cdots x_{j_s}$ is the leading term of $g_{i_0}(x_0, x_{j_1}, \ldots, x_{j_s})$.

According to (8), i.e.,

$$
\begin{pmatrix} g_0(x_0, x_{j_1}, \ldots, x_{j_s}) \\ g_1(x_0, x_{j_1}, \ldots, x_{j_s}) \\ \vdots \\ g_{s-1}(x_0, x_{j_1}, \ldots, x_{j_s}) \end{pmatrix} = M_{j_1, \cdots, j_s}^{-1} \cdot \begin{pmatrix} x_{j_1} f_{0,j_2} \cdots f_{0,j_s} \\ f_{0,j_1} x_{j_2} \cdots f_{0,j_s} \\ \vdots \\ f_{0,j_1} \cdots f_{0,j_{s-1}} x_{j_s} \end{pmatrix} \bmod p^{s-1},
$$

we get that $g_{i_0}(x_0, x_{j_1}, \ldots, x_{j_s})$ is some linear combination of the following polynomials

$$
x_{j_1} f_{0,j_2} \cdots f_{0,j_s}, f_{0,j_1} x_{j_2} \cdots f_{0,j_s}, \cdots, f_{0,j_1} \cdots f_{0,j_{s-1}} x_{j_s}.
$$

Note that these polynomials have common monomials

$$
x_{j_1} \cdots x_{j_s}, x_0 x_{j_1} \cdots x_{j_s}, \cdots, x_0^{s-1} x_{j_1} \cdots x_{j_s}. \tag{18}
$$

Let the polynomial $g_l^*(x_0, x_{j_1}, \ldots, x_{j_s})$ $(0 \le l \le s-1)$ be composed of the terms in the polynomial $f_{0,j_1} \cdots f_{0,j_l} x_{j_{l+1}} f_{0,j_{l+2}} \cdots f_{0,j_s}$ except the corresponding terms of common monomials in (18). Then we can rewrite

$$
\begin{aligned}
f_{0,j_1} \cdots f_{0,j_l} x_{j_{l+1}} f_{0,j_{l+2}} \cdots f_{0,j_s} &= x_{j_{l+1}} \cdot \prod_{k \ne l+1} (c_{0,j_k} x_{j_k} + x_0 x_{j_k}) + g_l^*(x_0, x_{j_1}, \ldots, x_{j_s}) \\
&= (x_{j_1} \cdots x_{j_s}) \cdot \prod_{k \ne l+1} (x_0 + c_{0,j_k}) + g_l^*(x_0, x_{j_1}, \ldots, x_{j_s}) \\
&= (x_{j_1} \cdots x_{j_s}) \cdot \sum_{i=0}^{s-1} \left(\sigma_i(\wedge_l) \cdot x_0^{s-1-i} \right) + g_l^*(x_0, x_{j_1}, \ldots, x_{j_s}),
\end{aligned}
$$

where $\wedge_l = \{c_{0,j_1}, \cdots, c_{0,j_s}\} \setminus \{c_{0,j_{l+1}}\}$ and σ_i is the i-th elementary symmetric polynomial. Furthermore, we express the above equalities for all $0 \le l \le s-1$ by using the matrix equation as follows:

$$
\begin{pmatrix} x_{j_1} f_{0,j_2} \cdots f_{0,j_s} \\ f_{0,j_1} x_{j_2} \cdots f_{0,j_s} \\ \vdots \\ f_{0,j_1} \cdots f_{0,j_{s-1}} x_{j_s} \end{pmatrix} = M_{j_1, \cdots, j_s} \cdot \begin{pmatrix} x_{j_1} \cdots x_{j_s} \\ x_0 x_{j_1} \cdots x_{j_s} \\ \vdots \\ x_0^{s-1} x_{j_1} \cdots x_{j_s} \end{pmatrix} + \begin{pmatrix} g_0^*(x_0, x_{j_1}, \ldots, x_{j_s}) \\ g_1^*(x_0, x_{j_1}, \ldots, x_{j_s}) \\ \vdots \\ g_{s-1}^*(x_0, x_{j_1}, \ldots, x_{j_s}) \end{pmatrix}. \tag{19}
$$

Plugging (19) into (8), we obtain

$$
\begin{pmatrix} g_0(x_0, x_{j_1}, \ldots, x_{j_s}) \\ \vdots \\ g_{i_0}(x_0, x_{j_1}, \ldots, x_{j_s}) \\ \vdots \\ g_{s-1}(x_0, x_{j_1}, \ldots, x_{j_s}) \end{pmatrix} = \begin{pmatrix} x_{j_1} \cdots x_{j_s} \\ \vdots \\ x_0^{i_0} x_{j_1} \cdots x_{j_s} \\ \vdots \\ x_0^{s-1} x_{j_1} \cdots x_{j_s} \end{pmatrix} + M_{j_1, \cdots, j_s}^{-1} \begin{pmatrix} g_0^*(x_0, x_{j_1}, \ldots, x_{j_s}) \\ \vdots \\ g_{i_0}^*(x_0, x_{j_1}, \ldots, x_{j_s}) \\ \vdots \\ g_{s-1}^*(x_0, x_{j_1}, \ldots, x_{j_s}) \end{pmatrix} \tag{20}
$$

in the sense of modulo p^{s-1}. According to (20), in order to prove that $x_0^{i_0} x_{j_1} \cdots x_{j_s}$ is the leading monomial of $g_{i_0}(x_0, x_{j_1}, \ldots, x_{j_s})$, we need to analyze that all monomials from the following polynomials

$$g_0^*(x_0, x_{j_1}, \ldots, x_{j_s}), g_1^*(x_0, x_{j_1}, \ldots, x_{j_s}), \cdots, g_{s-1}^*(x_0, x_{j_1}, \ldots, x_{j_s})$$

are lower than $x_0^{i_0} x_{j_1} \cdots x_{j_s}$ based on the order (5).

From (19), we can deduce that the monomial set from these polynomials $g_0^*, g_1^*, \cdots, g_{s-1}^*$ is equal to

$$\left\{ x_0^{r_0} x_{k_1} \cdots x_{k_m} \mid 0 \leq r_0 \leq d, \{k_1, \cdots, k_m\} \subsetneqq \{j_1, \cdots, j_s\} \right\}.$$

It implies that for any monomial $x_0^{r_0} x_{k_1} \cdots x_{k_m}$ from the above monomial set, we have $m < s$. Therefore, we get $x_0^{r_0} x_{k_1} \cdots x_{k_m} \prec x_0^{i_0} x_{j_1} \cdots x_{j_s}$ according to the order (5). In other words, $x_0^{i_0} x_{j_1} \cdots x_{j_s}$ is the leading monomial of $g_{i_0}(x_0, x_{j_1}, \ldots, x_{j_s})$. Hence, $p^{d+1-s} x_0^{i_0} x_1^{i_1} \cdots x_n^{i_n}$ is the leading term of $F_{i_0, i_1, \ldots, i_n}(x_0, x_1, \cdots, x_n)$ in this situation.

Next, we will show that the basis matrix of $\mathcal{L}(n, d, t)$ is triangular based on the leading monomials of the polynomials $F_{i_0, i_1, \cdots, i_n}(x_0, x_1, \cdots, x_n)$ from low to high. Note that the basis matrix of $\mathcal{L}(n, d, t)$ consists of the coefficient vectors of the polynomials $F_{i_0, i_1, \cdots, i_n}(x_0 X, x_1 X, \cdots, x_n X)$. It is easy to see that there is a one-to-one correspondence between the polynomials $F_{i_0, i_1, \cdots, i_n}(x_0, x_1, \cdots, x_n)$ and $F_{i_0, i_1, \cdots, i_n}(x_0 X, x_1 X, \cdots, x_n X)$. So, our goal is to prove that all polynomials $F_{i_0, i_1, \cdots, i_n}(x_0, x_1, \cdots, x_n)$ form a triangular matrix according to the corresponding leading monomials from low to high.

For the case of $s = 0$, the corresponding polynomial $F_{i_0, i_1, \cdots, i_n}(x_0, x_1, \cdots, x_n)$ is equal to $p^d x_0^{i_0}$, where $i_0 = 0, 1, \cdots, d$. According to the order (5), we have $p^d \prec p^d x_0 \prec \cdots \prec p^d x_0^d$. It is obvious that all polynomials $F_{i_0, i_1, \cdots, i_n}(x_0, x_1, \cdots, x_n)$ for the case of $s = 0$ generate a triangular matrix. The remaining proof is inductive. Suppose that all $F_{i_0', i_1', \cdots, i_n'}(x_0, x_1, \cdots, x_n)$ satisfying $x_0^{i_0'} x_1^{i_1'} \cdots x_n^{i_n'} \prec x_0^{i_0} x_1^{i_1} \cdots x_n^{i_n}$ produce a triangular matrix as stated in Lemma 4. Then, we show that a matrix is still triangular with a new polynomial $F_{i_0, i_1, \cdots, i_n}(x_0, x_1, \cdots, x_n)$. According to the above analysis, we get that $x_0^{i_0} x_1^{i_1} \cdots x_n^{i_n}$ is the leading monomial of $F_{i_0, i_1, \cdots, i_n}(x_0, x_1, \cdots, x_n)$. Without loss of generality, let $x_0^{k_0} x_1^{k_1} \cdots x_n^{k_n}$ be any monomial of the polynomial $F_{i_0, i_1, \cdots, i_n}(x_0, x_1, \cdots, x_n)$ except its leading monomial $x_0^{i_0} x_1^{i_1} \cdots x_n^{i_n}$. Clearly, we have $x_0^{k_0} x_1^{k_1} \cdots x_n^{k_n} \prec x_0^{i_0} x_1^{i_1} \cdots x_n^{i_n}$. Note that $x_0^{k_0} x_1^{k_1} \cdots x_n^{k_n}$ is the leading monomial of the polynomial $F_{k_0, k_1, \cdots, k_n}(x_0, x_1, \cdots, x_n)$. It implies that these monomials except $x_0^{i_0} x_1^{i_1} \cdots x_n^{i_n}$ already appeared in the diagonals of a basis matrix. Hence, all polynomials $F_{i_0, i_1, \cdots, i_n}(x_0, x_1, \cdots, x_n)$ can produce a triangular matrix. In other words, the corresponding basis matrix of $\mathcal{L}(n, d, t)$ is triangular.

Since the leading term of $F_{i_0, i_1, \cdots, i_n}(x_0, x_1, \cdots, x_n)$ is as follows:

$$\begin{cases} p^{d-s} x_0^{i_0} x_1^{i_1} \cdots x_n^{i_n} & \text{for } i_0 \geq s, \\ p^{d+1-s} x_0^{i_0} x_1^{i_1} \cdots x_n^{i_n} & \text{for } i_0 < s, \end{cases}$$

where $s = i_1 + \cdots + i_n$, the diagonal elements of the triangular basis matrix of $\mathcal{L}(n, d, t)$ are as follows:

$$\begin{cases} p^{d-s} X^{i_0 + i_1 + \cdots + i_n} = p^{d-s} X^{i_0 + s} & \text{for } i_0 \geq s, \\ p^{d+1-s} X^{i_0 + i_1 + \cdots + i_n} = p^{d+1-s} X^{i_0 + s} & \text{for } i_0 < s. \end{cases}$$

$\square$

5   Experimental Results

We implemented our lattice-based algorithm in SAGE 8.2 on a desktop with Intel(R) Xeon(R) CPU E5-2670 v3 @ 2.30 GHz, 3 GB RAM and 3 MB Cache using the L^2 reduction algorithm [23] from Nguyen and Stehlé. We tested the algorithm up to lattice dimension 291. Table 2 shows the experimental results for MIHNP with 1000 bit prime p. To confirm the claim that experimental outcome is better than theoretical bound based on (14), 100 experiments each time have been carried out. We see that the success rate of each time is 100% for most cases. Total time means that sum of time for 100 experiments of LLL algorithm and Gröbner basis computation respectively.

Table 2. Experimental results on low bounds of $\delta/\log_2 p$ for 1000-bit p

n	d	t	Dimension	Low bounds of $\delta/\log_2 p$			Total Time (sec.)	
				Theory	Exp.	Success	LLL	Gröbner
3	2	1	23	0.712	0.595	100	11.01	1.22
6	1	0	29	0.699	0.575	100	29.42	13.36
4	2	0	37	0.660	0.560	100	190.41	10.65
4	2	1	41	0.638	0.550	99	636.12	54.36
5	2	0	58	0.614	0.530	100	2555.91	182.38
5	2	1	68	0.592	0.525	100	7889.82	809.49
6	2	0	86	0.582	0.505	100	18896.34	2185.73
6	2	1	106	0.564	0.505	100	33276.93	4974.75
7	2	0	122	0.558	0.495	100	175276.85	29248.29
7	2	1	157	0.546	0.490	100	312450.32	23893.45
8	2	0	167	0.540	0.475	100	872078.62	128818.90
6	3	0	183	0.547	0.485	100	897793.07	14371.18
9	2	0	222	0.528	0.460	100	5440027.10	858799.13
10	2	0	288	0.519	0.450	87	18250890.61	3415266.53
7	3	0	291	0.521	0.465	100	9223260.81	287510.60

We also perform one experiment for $n = 11, d = 2$ and $t = 0$. Corresponding lattice dimension is 366. Here theoretical bound of $\frac{\delta}{\log_2 p}$ is 0.514. As for other parameters, in this case also we get better experimental bound 0.445. Lattice reduction takes 336895.32 s and Gröbner computation takes 191821.33 s.

One may see Fig. 2 for a comparison between theoretical and experimental values of $\delta/\log_2 p$ for different dimensions. One can see from the figure that for smaller lattice dimensions, experimental values substantially outperform their theoretical values.

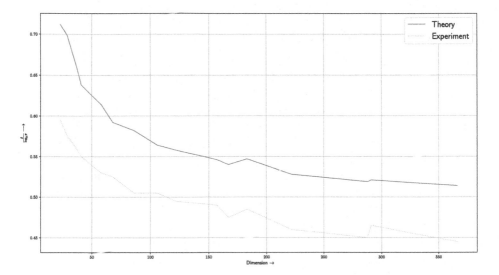

Fig. 2. Theoretical vs Experimental values of $\frac{\delta}{\log_2 p}$ for different dimensions.

6   Conclusion

We presented a heuristic polynomial time algorithm to find the hidden number in the modular inversion hidden number problem. After more than 15 years, we improved the bound for solving modular inversion hidden number problem for the first time. We also obtained the best attack result on the inversive congruential generator till now.

Acknowledgments. The authors would like to thank the reviewers of Eurocrypt 2019 and Crypto 2019 for their helpful comments and suggestions. The work of this paper was supported the National Natural Science Foundation of China (Grants 61732021, 61502488, 61572490 and 61702505). J. Xu is supported by China Scholarship Council (No. 201804910206). H. Wang is supported by the National Research Foundation, Prime Ministers Office, Singapore under its Strategic Capability Research Centres Funding Initiative and Singapore Ministry of Education under Research Grant MOE2016-T2-2-014(S). Y. Pan is supported by the National Center for Mathematics and Interdisciplinary Sciences, CAS.

A   Asymptotic Time Complexities in Previous Works

The running time functions for solving MIHNP or ICG are not fully presented explicitly in previous works. For the sake of comparison, we analyze the corresponding running time functions according to the following way. Let $\rho = \delta / \log_2 p$ and $k = \log_2 p$, where $0 < \rho < 1$.

In [3, Theorem 1], the bound $\rho > \frac{3}{4}$ is shown for solving ICG with known $\mathcal{F}$ based on the SVP assumption. Since the involved lattice is 4-dimensional, the time complexity of the SVP algorithm is $k^{\mathcal{O}(1)}$, which is deterministic polynomial in the bit size of a given basis of the lattice for the fixed dimension [17].

In [20, Corollary 1], the bound $\rho \geq \frac{2}{3} + \varepsilon$ is presented to solve MIHNP based on the SVP assumption. By taking $\varepsilon = \rho - \frac{2}{3}$, the time complexity using SVP algorithm becomes $k^{\mathcal{O}(1)} 2^{\mathcal{O}\left(\frac{1}{\rho - \frac{2}{3}}\right)}$ [22].

In [1, Section 3.4 and Theorem 2], the asymptotic bound $\rho \geq \frac{1}{2} + \frac{1}{2^{n+3}}$ is obtained to solve ICG with known $\mathcal{F}$ based on the Coppersmith technique, where $n + 2$ denotes the number of unknown variables. Let $m = n^{\mathcal{O}(1)}$. The involved lattice dimension can be expressed as $\mathcal{O}(m^n)$, and the bit size of lattice basis matrix is at most km. Hence, the time complexity of the LLL algorithm is $(\mathcal{O}(m^n))^{\mathcal{O}(1)} \cdot (km)^{\mathcal{O}(1)} = \mathcal{O}(k^{\mathcal{O}(1)} n^{\mathcal{O}(n)})$. For the Gröbner basis, the maximal degree of input polynomials is $2m$, and the number of unknown variables of input polynomials is $n + 2$. Under Assumption 1, these polynomials generate a zero-dimensional Gröbner basis. We have that the time complexity of Gröbner basis computation is $(n + 2)^{\mathcal{O}((2m)^2)} = n^{\mathcal{O}(n^2)}$ [10]. Based on the above bound $\rho \geq \frac{1}{2} + \frac{1}{2^{n+3}}$, we can take $n \approx \log_2 \left(\frac{1}{\rho - \frac{1}{2}}\right)$. Hence, time complexities of the LLL algorithm and the Gröbner basis computation are reduced to

$$\mathcal{O}\left(k^{\mathcal{O}(1)}\left(\log_2 \frac{1}{\rho - \frac{1}{2}}\right)^{\mathcal{O}\left(\log_2 \frac{1}{\rho - \frac{1}{2}}\right)}\right) \text{ and } \left(\log_2 \frac{1}{\rho - \frac{1}{2}}\right)^{\mathcal{O}\left((\log_2 \frac{1}{\rho - \frac{1}{2}})^2\right)} \text{ respectively.}$$

In [34, Theorem 1], the asymptotic bound $\rho \geq \frac{1}{2} + \frac{1}{(n+1)!}$ is obtained to solve MIHNP according to the Coppersmith technique, where n denotes the number of unknown variables. Similar to the above analysis, we can also get that time complexities of the LLL algorithm and Gröbner basis computation are $\mathcal{O}(k^{\mathcal{O}(1)} n^{\mathcal{O}(n)})$ and $n^{\mathcal{O}(n^2)}$ respectively. Further, from the above bound $\rho \geq \frac{1}{2} + \frac{1}{(n+1)!}$, we can take $n \log_2 n \approx \log_2 \left(\frac{1}{\rho - \frac{1}{2}}\right)$ by the Stirling formula. Therefore, time complexities of the LLL algorithm and the Gröbner basis computation are reduced to $\mathcal{O}\left(k^{\mathcal{O}(1)} \left(\frac{1}{\rho - \frac{1}{2}}\right)^{\mathcal{O}(1)}\right)$ and $\left(\frac{1}{\rho - \frac{1}{2}}\right)^{o\left(\log_2 \frac{1}{\rho - \frac{1}{2}}\right)}$ respectively.

In [4, Section 3.2], the asymptotic bound $\rho \geq \frac{1}{3} + \frac{2}{3d+3}$ is obtained to solve MIHNP based on the SVP assumption, where d is an integer satisfying some requirement. Note that the dimension of the involved lattice is equal to $\mathcal{O}(d^{\mathcal{O}(d)})$. Thus, the time complexity to solve MIHNP is $k^{\mathcal{O}(1)} 2^{\mathcal{O}(d^{\mathcal{O}(d)})}$ using the SVP algorithm, such as [22]. According to the above bound $\rho \geq \frac{1}{3} + \frac{2}{3d+3}$, we can take $d \approx \frac{2}{3\rho - 1}$. Then the above time complexity is reduced to $k^{\mathcal{O}(1)} 2^{\mathcal{O}\left(\left(\frac{2}{3\rho - 1}\right)^{\mathcal{O}\left(\frac{1}{\rho - \frac{1}{3}}\right)}\right)}$.

In [35, Remark 4], the asymptotic bound $\rho \geq \frac{1}{3} + \frac{2}{3d+3}$ is given for solving MIHNP and ICG based on the Coppersmith technique, where d is the same as that in [4]. Note that the dimension of the involved lattice is equal to $\mathcal{O}(d^{\mathcal{O}(d)})$ and the maximal bit size of lattice basis matrix is at most $2dk$. Hence, the time complexity of the LLL algorithm is $(\mathcal{O}(d^{\mathcal{O}(d)}))^{\mathcal{O}(1)} \cdot (2dk)^{\mathcal{O}(1)} = \mathcal{O}(k^{\mathcal{O}(1)} d^{\mathcal{O}(d)})$. For the Gröbner basis, the maximal degree of input polynomials is $2d$ and the number of variables is equal to $d^{\mathcal{O}(1)}$. Thus, under Assumption 1, the time complexity of the Gröbner basis computation is $(2d)^{\mathcal{O}(d^{\mathcal{O}(1)})}$ [10]. Based on the above bound $\rho \geq \frac{1}{3} + \frac{2}{3d+3}$, we can take $d \approx \frac{2}{3\rho-1}$. Then, time complexities of the LLL algorithm and Gröbner basis computation are reduced to $\mathcal{O}(k^{\mathcal{O}(1)} (\frac{2}{3\rho-1})^{\mathcal{O}((\frac{1}{\rho-\frac{1}{3}})})$ and $(\frac{4}{3\rho-1})^{\mathcal{O}((\frac{1}{\rho-\frac{1}{3}})^{\mathcal{O}(1)})}$ respectively.

B   Computation of the Determinant of $\mathcal{L}(n, d, t)$

Note that the determinant of $\mathcal{L}(n, d, t)$ is the product of the diagonal entries. We will consider the following two cases.

For the case of $i_0 \geq s$, the contribution of $F_{i_0, i_1, \cdots, i_n}(x_0 X, x_1 X, \cdots, x_n X)$ to the determinant of $\mathcal{L}(n, d, t)$ is

$$\prod_{s=0}^{d} \prod_{i_0=s}^{d} \left(p^{(d-s)\binom{n}{s}} \cdot X^{(i_0+s)\binom{n}{s}} \right).$$

For the case of $i_0 < s$, the contribution of $F_{i_0, i_1, \cdots, i_n}(x_0 X, x_1 X, \cdots, x_n X)$ is

$$\prod_{s=1}^{d} \prod_{i_0=0}^{s-1} \left(p^{(d+1-s)\binom{n}{s}} \cdot X^{(i_0+s)\binom{n}{s}} \right) \cdot \prod_{i_0=0}^{t} X^{(i_0+d+1)\binom{n}{d+1}}.$$

To sum up, we get

$$\det(\mathcal{L}(n, d, t)) = p^{\alpha(n,d)} \cdot X^{\beta(n,d,t)},$$

where

$$\alpha(n, d) = d(d+1) \sum_{s=0}^{d} \binom{n}{s} - d \sum_{s=0}^{d} s\binom{n}{s},$$

$$\beta(n, d, t) = \frac{d(d+1)}{2} \sum_{s=0}^{d} \binom{n}{s} + (d+1) \sum_{s=0}^{d} s\binom{n}{s} + \frac{(2d+t+2)(t+1)}{2}\binom{n}{d+1}.$$

C   Lower Bound in Theorem 1

Our goal is to derive a lower bound of

$$2^{-\frac{w(w-1)}{4\beta(n,d,t)}} w^{-\frac{w-n}{2\beta(n,d,t)}} p^{\lambda(n,d,t)},$$

where w is the dimension of $\mathcal{L}(n, d, t)$. We now analyze its first two terms. According to the expressions of w and $\beta(n, d, t)$, i.e.,

$$w = (t+1)\binom{n}{d+1} + (d+1)\sum_{s=0}^{d}\binom{n}{s},$$

$$\beta(n, d, t) = \frac{(2d+t+2)(t+1)}{2}\binom{n}{d+1} + \frac{d(d+1)}{2}\sum_{s=0}^{d}\binom{n}{s} + (d+1)\sum_{s=0}^{d}s\binom{n}{s},$$

it is easy to deduce $\frac{\beta(n,d,t)}{w} > \frac{d+2}{2}$. Then we have $2^{-\frac{w(w-1)}{4\beta(n,d,t)}} \geq 2^{-\frac{w}{2(d+2)}}$ and $w^{-\frac{w-n}{2\beta(n,d,t)}} \geq w^{-\frac{1}{d+2}}$. Furthermore, we obtain

$$2^{-\frac{w(w-1)}{4\beta(n,d,t)}}w^{-\frac{w-n}{2\beta(n,d,t)}}p^{\lambda(n,d,t)} \geq p^{\lambda(n,d,t)-\frac{w+2\log w}{2(d+2)\log_2 p}}.$$

Note that d and w are independent of the modulus p. For a sufficiently large p, the exponent term $-\frac{w+2\log w}{2(d+2)\log_2 p}$ is negligible. In this case, we only consider the exponent term $\lambda(n, d, t)$. In other words, the right-hand side of the above condition can be simplified as $p^{\lambda(n,d,t)}$ for a sufficiently large p.

Next, we further analyze the lower bound of $\lambda(n, d, t)$. We rewrite

$$\lambda(n, d, t) = \frac{2d(t+1)\binom{n}{d+1} + 2d\sum_{s=2}^{d}s\binom{n}{s}}{(2d+2+t)(t+1)\binom{n}{d+1} + d(d+1)\sum_{s=0}^{d}\binom{n}{s} + 2(d+1)\sum_{s=0}^{d}s\binom{n}{s}}$$

$$= \frac{2d}{2d+2+t}(1 - \epsilon(n, d, t)),$$

where

$$\epsilon(n, d, t) = \frac{d(d+1)\sum_{s=0}^{d}\binom{n}{s} - t\sum_{s=2}^{d}s\binom{n}{s} + 2(d+1)\binom{n}{1}}{(2d+2+t)(t+1)\binom{n}{d+1} + d(d+1)\sum_{s=0}^{d}\binom{n}{s} + 2(d+1)\sum_{s=0}^{d}s\binom{n}{s}}.$$

Note that we have

$$\epsilon(n, d, t) < \frac{d(d+1)}{(2d+2+t)(t+1)} \cdot \frac{\sum_{s=0}^{d}\binom{n}{s}}{\binom{n}{d+1}} + \frac{2(d+1)}{(2d+2+t)(t+1)} \cdot \frac{\binom{n}{1}}{\binom{n}{d+1}} < \frac{d}{2}\sum_{s=0}^{d}\frac{\binom{n}{s}}{\binom{n}{d+1}} + \frac{\binom{n}{1}}{\binom{n}{d+1}}.$$

For any $0 \leq s \leq d$, according to

$$\frac{\binom{n}{s}}{\binom{n}{d+1}} = \frac{(d+1)!(n-d-1)!}{s!(n-s)!} = \frac{d+1}{n-d} \cdot \frac{d}{n-d+1} \cdots \frac{s+1}{n-s} \leq \left(\frac{d+1}{n-d}\right)^{d-s+1},$$

we deduce that

$$\epsilon(n, d, t) < \left(\frac{d}{2}\sum_{s=0}^{d}\left(\frac{d+1}{n-d}\right)^{d-s+1}\right) + \left(\frac{d+1}{n-d}\right)^d = \frac{d(d+1)}{2(n-2d-1)}\left(1 - \left(\frac{d+1}{n-d}\right)^{d+1}\right) + \left(\frac{d+1}{n-d}\right)^d.$$

Then we obtain that

$$\lambda(n,d,t) = \tfrac{2d}{2d+2+t}(1 - \epsilon(n,d,t)) > \tfrac{2d}{2d+2+t}\Big(1 - \tfrac{d(d+1)}{2(n-2d-1)}\big(1 - (\tfrac{d+1}{n-d})^{d+1}\big) - (\tfrac{d+1}{n-d})^d\Big).$$

By taking the parameter $t = 0$, $\lambda(n,d,t)$ is optimized as

$$\lambda(n,d,0) > 1 - \frac{1}{d+1} - \Big(\frac{d^2}{2(n-2d-1)}\big(1 - (\frac{d+1}{n-d})^{d+1}\big) + \frac{d}{d+1}(\frac{d+1}{n-d})^d\Big).$$

Further, by taking the parameter $n = d^{3+o(1)}$, the above relation is expressed as

$$\lambda(n,d,0) > 1 - \frac{1}{d+1} - o\Big(\frac{1}{d}\Big).$$

Finally, we explicitly present how big the modulus p is in the asymptotic sense. Based on the above analysis, we need that the term $-\frac{w+2\log w}{2(d+2)\log_2 p}$ is negligible. For the case of $t = 0$ and $n = d^{3+o(1)}$, we have that the dimension of $L(n,d,t)$ is equal to $w = (d+1)\sum_{s=0}^{d}\binom{n}{s} + \binom{n}{d+1} = d^{3d+3}(1 + o(1))$. Hence, when $\log_2 p = \omega(d^{3d+2})$, i.e., $p = 2^{\omega(d^{3d+2})}$, the term $-\frac{w+2\log w}{2(d+2)\log_2 p}$ is negligible.

References

1. Bauer, A., Vergnaud, D., Zapalowicz, J.C.: Inferring sequences produced by nonlinear pseudorandom number generators using Coppersmith's methods. In: Fischlin, M., Buchmann, J., Manulis, M. (eds.) PKC 2012. LNCS, vol. 7293, pp. 609–626. Springer, Heidelberg (2012). https://doi.org/10.1007/978-3-642-30057-8_36
2. Bi, J., Coron, J., Faugère, J., Nguyen, P.Q., Renault, G., Zeitoun, R.: Rounding and chaining LLL: finding faster small roots of univariate polynomial congruences. In: Krawczyk, H. (ed.) PKC 2014. LNCS, vol. 8383, pp. 185–202. Springer, Heidelberg (2014). https://doi.org/10.1007/978-3-642-54631-0_11
3. Blackburn, S.R., Gomez-perez, D., Gutierrez, J., Shparlinski, I.E.: Predicting nonlinear pseudorandom number generators. Math. Comput. **74**, 2004 (2004)
4. Boneh, D., Halevi, S., Howgrave-Graham, N.: The modular inversion hidden number problem. In: Boyd, C. (ed.) ASIACRYPT 2001. LNCS, vol. 2248, pp. 36–51. Springer, Heidelberg (2001). https://doi.org/10.1007/3-540-45682-1_3
5. Boneh, D., Venkatesan, R.: Hardness of computing the most significant bits of secret keys in Diffie-Hellman and related schemes. In: Koblitz, N. (ed.) CRYPTO 1996. LNCS, vol. 1109, pp. 129–142. Springer, Heidelberg (1996). https://doi.org/10.1007/3-540-68697-5_11
6. Cohn, H., Heninger, N.: Approximate common divisors via lattices. Open Book Ser. **1**(1), 271–293 (2013)
7. Coppersmith, D.: Finding a small root of a bivariate integer equation; factoring with high bits known. In: Maurer, U. (ed.) EUROCRYPT 1996. LNCS, vol. 1070, pp. 178–189. Springer, Heidelberg (1996). https://doi.org/10.1007/3-540-68339-9_16
8. Coppersmith, D.: Finding a small root of a univariate modular equation. In: Maurer, U. (ed.) EUROCRYPT 1996. LNCS, vol. 1070, pp. 155–165. Springer, Heidelberg (1996). https://doi.org/10.1007/3-540-68339-9_14

9. Coppersmith, D.: Small solutions to polynomial equations, and low exponent RSA vulnerabilities. J. Cryptol. **10**(4), 233–260 (1997)

10. Faugère, J., Gianni, P.M., Lazard, D., Mora, T.: Efficient computation of zero-dimensional Gröbner bases by change of ordering. J. Symb. Comput. **16**(4), 329–344 (1993)

11. Herrmann, M., May, A.: Solving linear equations modulo divisors: on factoring given any bits. In: Pieprzyk, J. (ed.) ASIACRYPT 2008. LNCS, vol. 5350, pp. 406–424. Springer, Heidelberg (2008). https://doi.org/10.1007/978-3-540-89255-7_25

12. Herrmann, M., May, A.: Attacking power generators using unravelled linearization: when do we output too much? In: Matsui, M. (ed.) ASIACRYPT 2009. LNCS, vol. 5912, pp. 487–504. Springer, Heidelberg (2009). https://doi.org/10.1007/978-3-642-10366-7_29

13. Howgrave-Graham, N.: Finding small roots of univariate modular equations revisited. In: Darnell, M. (ed.) Cryptography and Coding 1997. LNCS, vol. 1355, pp. 131–142. Springer, Heidelberg (1997). https://doi.org/10.1007/BFb0024458

14. Howgrave-Graham, N.: Approximate integer common divisors. In: Silverman, J.H. (ed.) CaLC 2001. LNCS, vol. 2146, pp. 51–66. Springer, Heidelberg (2001). https://doi.org/10.1007/3-540-44670-2_6

15. Jochemsz, E., May, A.: A strategy for finding roots of multivariate polynomials with new applications in attacking RSA variants. In: Lai, X., Chen, K. (eds.) ASIACRYPT 2006. LNCS, vol. 4284, pp. 267–282. Springer, Heidelberg (2006). https://doi.org/10.1007/11935230_18

16. Kakvi, S.A., Kiltz, E., May, A.: Certifying RSA. In: Wang, X., Sako, K. (eds.) ASIACRYPT 2012. LNCS, vol. 7658, pp. 404–414. Springer, Heidelberg (2012). https://doi.org/10.1007/978-3-642-34961-4_25

17. Kannan, R.: Minkowski's convex body theorem and integer programming. Math. Oper. Res. **12**(3), 415–440 (1987)

18. Lazard, D.: Gröbner bases, Gaussian elimination and resolution of systems of algebraic equations. In: van Hulzen, J.A. (ed.) EUROCAL 1983. LNCS, vol. 162, pp. 146–156. Springer, Heidelberg (1983). https://doi.org/10.1007/3-540-12868-9_99

19. Lenstra, A.K., Lenstra, H.W., Lovász, L.: Factoring polynomials with rational coefficients. Math. Ann. **261**(4), 515–534 (1982)

20. Ling, S., Shparlinski, I.E., Steinfeld, R., Wang, H.: On the modular inversion hidden number problem. J. Symb. Comput. **47**(4), 358–367 (2012)

21. May, A.: Using LLL-reduction for solving RSA and factorization problems. In: Nguyen, P., Vallée, B. (eds.) The LLL Algorithm. Information Security and Cryptography, pp. 315–348. Springer, Heidelberg (2010). https://doi.org/10.1007/978-3-642-02295-1_10

22. Micciancio, D., Voulgaris, P.: A deterministic single exponential time algorithm for most lattice problems based on voronoi cell computations. Electron. Colloq. Comput. Complex. (ECCC) **17**, 14 (2010)

23. Nguyen, P.Q., Stehlé, D.: An LLL algorithm with quadratic complexity. SIAM J. Comput. **39**(3), 874–903 (2009)

24. Novocin, A., Stehlé, D., Villard, G.: An LLL-reduction algorithm with quasi-linear time complexity: extended abstract. In: Proceedings of the Forty-third Annual ACM Symposium on Theory of Computing, STOC 2011, pp. 403–412. ACM, New York (2011)

25. Peng, L., Hu, L., Lu, Y., Xu, J., Huang, Z.: Cryptanalysis of dual RSA. Des. Codes Cryptogr. **83**(1), 1–21 (2017)

26. Prasolov, V.V.: Polynomials. Algorithms and Computation in Mathematics, vol. 11. Springer, Heidelberg (2004). https://doi.org/10.1007/978-3-642-03980-5
27. Shani, B.: On the bit security of elliptic curve Diffie–Hellman. In: Fehr, S. (ed.) PKC 2017. LNCS, vol. 10174, pp. 361–387. Springer, Heidelberg (2017). https://doi.org/10.1007/978-3-662-54365-8_15
28. Shparlinski, I.E.: Playing hide-and-seek with numbers: the hidden number problem, lattices, and exponential sums. In: Proceeding of Symposia in Applied Mathematics, vol. 62, pp. 153–177 (2005)
29. Takayasu, A., Kunihiro, N.: Better lattice constructions for solving multivariate linear equations modulo unknown divisors. In: Boyd, C., Simpson, L. (eds.) ACISP 2013. LNCS, vol. 7959, pp. 118–135. Springer, Heidelberg (2013). https://doi.org/10.1007/978-3-642-39059-3_9
30. Takayasu, A., Kunihiro, N.: How to generalize RSA cryptanalyses. In: Cheng, C.-M., Chung, K.-M., Persiano, G., Yang, B.-Y. (eds.) PKC 2016. LNCS, vol. 9615, pp. 67–97. Springer, Heidelberg (2016). https://doi.org/10.1007/978-3-662-49387-8_4
31. Takayasu, A., Lu, Y., Peng, L.: Small CRT-exponent RSA revisited. In: Coron, J.-S., Nielsen, J.B. (eds.) EUROCRYPT 2017. LNCS, vol. 10211, pp. 130–159. Springer, Cham (2017). https://doi.org/10.1007/978-3-319-56614-6_5
32. Tosu, K., Kunihiro, N.: Optimal bounds for multi-prime Φ-hiding assumption. In: Information Security and Privacy - 17th Australasian Conference, ACISP 2012, Wollongong, NSW, Australia, 9–11 July 2012, Proceedings, pp. 1–14 (2012)
33. von zur Gathen, J., Gerhard, J.: Modern Computer Algebra, 3rd edn. Cambridge University Press, Cambridge (2013)
34. Xu, J., Hu, L., Huang, Z., Peng, L.: Modular inversion hidden number problem revisited. In: Huang, X., Zhou, J. (eds.) ISPEC 2014. LNCS, vol. 8434, pp. 537–551. Springer, Cham (2014). https://doi.org/10.1007/978-3-319-06320-1_39
35. Xu, J., Sarkar, S., Hu, L., Huang, Z., Peng, L.: Solving a class of modular polynomial equations and its relation to modular inversion hidden number problem and inversive congruential generator. Des. Codes Crypt. **86**(9), 1997–2033 (2018)

On the Shortness of Vectors to Be Found by the Ideal-SVP Quantum Algorithm

Léo Ducas[1]([⊠]), Maxime Plançon[2], and Benjamin Wesolowski[1]

[1] Cryptology Group, CWI, Amsterdam, The Netherlands
ducas@cwi.nl
[2] Ecole Normale Supérieure Paris-Saclay, Cachan, France

Abstract. The hardness of finding short vectors in ideals of cyclotomic number fields (hereafter, Ideal-SVP) can serve as a worst-case assumption for numerous efficient cryptosystems, via the average-case problems Ring-SIS and Ring-LWE. For a while, it could be assumed the Ideal-SVP problem was as hard as the analog problem for general lattices (SVP), even when considering quantum algorithms.

But in the last few years, a series of works has lead to a quantum algorithm for Ideal-SVP that outperforms what can be done for general SVP in certain regimes. More precisely, it was demonstrated (under certain hypotheses) that one can find in quantum polynomial time a vector longer by a factor at most $\alpha = \exp(\widetilde{O}(n^{1/2}))$ than the shortest non-zero vector in a cyclotomic ideal lattice, where n is the dimension.

In this work, we explore the constants hidden behind this asymptotic claim. While these algorithms have quantum steps, the steps that impact the approximation factor α are entirely classical, which allows us to estimate it experimentally using only classical computing. Moreover, we design heuristic improvements for those steps that significantly decrease the hidden factors in practice. Finally, we derive new provable effective lower bounds based on volumetric arguments.

This study allows to predict the crossover point with classical lattice reduction algorithms, and thereby determine the relevance of this quantum algorithm in any cryptanalytic context. For example we predict that this quantum algorithm provides shorter vectors than BKZ-300 (roughly the weakest security level of NIST lattice-based candidates) for cyclotomic rings of rank larger than about 24000.

Keywords: Quantum cryptanalysis · Cyclotomic ideal lattices

L. Ducas—Supported by a Veni Innovational Research Grant from NWO under project number 639.021.645 and by the European Union Horizon 2020 Research and Innovation Program Grant 780701.

M. Plançon—Part of this work was realized during an internship at the Cryptology Group, CWI, Amsterdam.

B. Wesolowski—Supported by the ERC Advanced Investigator Grant 740972 (ALGSTRONGCRYPTO).

A. Boldyreva and D. Micciancio (Eds.): CRYPTO 2019, LNCS 11692, pp. 322–351, 2019.
https://doi.org/10.1007/978-3-030-26948-7_12

1   Introduction

The shortest vector problem (hereafter, SVP), that is the problem of finding the shortest vector of a Euclidean lattice, is a central hard problem in complexity theory. An approximated version (approx-SIVP) can serve as a theoretical foundation for many cryptographic constructions thanks to the worst-case to average-case reductions of Ajtai [Ajt99]—a classical reduction from approx-SVP to the Short Integer Solution (SIS) problem—and Regev [Reg09]—a quantum reduction from approx-SIVP to Learning with Errors (LWE).

However, the efficiency of schemes based on plain SIS and LWE remains unsatisfactory, and one may prefer to rely on certain structured lattices, namely lattices that are also modules over certain rings, as done by the NTRU cryptosystem [HPS98], and more recently by many more cryptosystems based on Ring-SIS and Ring-LWE. The Ring-SIS and Ring-LWE problems also enjoy worst-case to average-case reductions from a variant of approx-SIVP[1] for lattices that are ideals in some ring [Mic07, SSTX09, LPR10, SS11, PRSD17]. The typical choice of ring is the integer ring of a cyclotomic number field $\mathbb{Q}(\omega_m)$, of degree $n = \varphi(m)$, where ω_m is a primitive m-th root of unity. One notable exception is the NTRU Prime cryptosystem [BCLvV17], which was designed to mitigate the potential cryptanalytic risk that we are about to discuss.

The assumption that approx-SIVP is as hard in ideal lattices as in general lattices was challenged by Campbell *et al.* [CGS14], who sketched a quantum polynomial-time attack against a few schemes using so-called *principal idcals* (Soliloquy, and the fully-homomorphic encryption scheme of [SV10]). Following the claims of Campbell *et al.*, Biasse and Song [BS16] proved that the Principal Ideal Problem could be efficiently solved using a quantum computer. In other words, given a principal ideal, one may recover an arbitrary generator in quantum polynomial time. Analyzing the geometry of cyclotomic units in the log-unit lattice, Cramer *et al.* [CDPR16] also confirmed that the secret key (a short generator) of the few aforementioned schemes could be recovered exactly, due to their specific distribution.

Furthermore, it is also proven in [CDPR16] that from an arbitrary generator, one could asymptotically recover a short one, with an approximation factor of $\alpha = \exp(\widetilde{O}(n^{1/2}))$. A generalization to all ideals (i.e., not necessarily principal) was provided in [CDW17]. They showed that by exploiting the Stickelberger class relations, one could efficiently find a sub-ideal $\mathfrak{b} \subset \mathfrak{a}$ (i.e., an integral multiple) such that $\mathfrak{b}$ is principal, and such that $|\mathfrak{b}/\mathfrak{a}| \leq \exp(\widetilde{O}(n^{3/2}))$ (i.e., the sub-ideal is not much sparser than the original lattice). Putting both results together leads to an approximation factor of $\alpha = \exp(\widetilde{O}(n^{1/2}))$ also for non-principal ideals.

Nevertheless, the work of [CDW17] still leaves two obstacles for cryptanalytic applications of their algorithm to the widespread hardness assumptions Ring-SIS, Ring-LWE and NTRU:

1. The approximation factor in the worst-case is asymptotically too large to affect any actual Ring-LWE based scheme, which typically rely on polynomial approximation factors $\alpha = \mathrm{poly}(n)$.

---

[1] For cyclotomic ideal lattices, approx-SVP and approx-SIVP are trivially equivalent.

2. Ring-SIS and Ring-LWE are known to be at least as hard as Ideal-SIVP [Mic07, SS11, LPR13] but not known to be equivalent. In fact, problems like Ring-SIS, Ring-LWE and NTRU, are naturally phrased as short vector problems in *module* lattices of rank $k \geq 2$. An approach for such a converse reduction would be to generalize LLL over other rings than $\mathbb{Z}$, but this seems to fail since only a few cyclotomic rings of small degree are Euclidean [Len75].

This work. In this work, we are interested in precisely quantifying the obstacle 1 above. It is proven in [CDPR16] that the short generator that can be recovered is asymptotically close to optimal, yet it is unclear how this asymptotic statement translates in practice. One could fear that the hidden factors in $\alpha = \exp(\widetilde{O}(n^{1/2}))$ make α small enough in practice to threaten concrete cryptosystems (assuming obstacle 2 can also be tackled). Or, on the contrary, one could doubt that this algorithm is ever to give better results than classical methods for reasonable dimensions, given how small the Hermite factor $\eta = 1.022^n$ of LLL [LLL82] already is in practice [NS06].[2]

After some preliminaries in Sect. 2, we recall in Sect. 3 the main steps for solving Ideal-SVP [CGS14, EHKS14, CDPR16, BS16, CDW17]. We discuss the slackness of the bounds derived in these works, and we identify the more meaningful quantities that should be studied to predict more precisely the Hermite factor achieved by the algorithm. We note that we do not need to resort to a quantum computer to experiment with those meaningful quantities, at least by making an informed assumption on the input distribution of the relevant steps (see Assumption 8 and the subsequent discussion). All working hypotheses are summarized in Sect. 3.4.

We then propose in Sect. 4 several heuristic techniques, designed to improve in practice the meaningful quantities determined above. First, we propose to exploit the knowledge of $\Theta(d^2)$ many short vectors of both the Stickelberger and log-unit lattices and go beyond what can be done with just a basis (where d is the dimension). To properly exploit a large number of short vectors, we propose to use an approximate Voronoi-cell-based algorithm [MV10, Laa16, DLdW19], adapted to our specific setting, where we wish to minimize some carefully determined meaningful quantities rather than the Euclidean distance.

In Sect. 5, we discuss our implementation, and report on the experimental behavior of both the original algorithm, and our heuristically improved variant. We observe that the experimental behavior asymptotically matches with the upper bound, and we experimentally determine the hidden constants. We also note that our heuristic variant indeed improves these hidden constants, especially for the Approx-CVP step in the log-unit lattice.

Finally, we study in Sect. 6 the volumetric lower-bounds for the CVP instances. We determine the effective asymptotic behaviour of those lower bounds (i.e., without hidden constants). We note that our bound for the log-unit lattice is not only effective, but also asymptotically better than the one of [CDPR16]. We also perform numerical experiments, which show that the convergence to the asymptotic behaviour is sufficiently fast to allow reliable use of the estimates.

---

[2] In the rest of this work, we prefer to use the so called Hermite factor η instead of the approximation factor α; this is justified in Remark 1.

We conclude in Sect. 7 with a summary of our effective asymptotic predictions. Combining these results, we compare the predicted performance with that of the classical lattice reduction algorithms LLL and BKZ, in Fig. 5. For a concrete example, we predict that the crossover point between the original algorithm and LLL happens for cyclotomic ideals of rank around 4000, and our heuristic improvement brings this crossover point down to rank 1000. We conclude our work by summarizing the limits of the conclusions that can be drawn from this work regarding cryptanalytic concerns.

Concurrent work. Recently, Pellet–Mary, Hanrot and Stehlé proposed [PMHS19] a heuristic algorithm that should reach even lower approximation factors than discussed above, but at the cost of a pre-computation using exponential time and memory, and a computation using sub-exponential time and memory. It also makes use of the approx-CVP algorithm of Laarhoven [Laa16, DLdW19, SD19], but in a different regime, and in a lattice with much less structure. In would be interesting to find an efficient simulation of their precomputation phase, so as to be able to run more extensive experiments and estimate the hidden constants, possibly using the heuristic improvements introduced in this paper.

2   Preliminaries

Vectors are to be read as column-vectors. Matrices are denoted by capital letters. We write a matrix B as $B = (b_1, \cdots, b_n)$ where b_i is the i-th column vector of B. We denote by $B^\star = (b_0^\star, \cdots, b_{n-1}^\star)$ the Gram-Schmidt orthogonalization of the matrix B.

2.1   Geometry

Norms, asymmetric norms, pseudo-norms. We will use the ℓ_1, ℓ_2 (Euclidean) and ℓ_∞ norms, respectively defined by $\|x\|_1 = \sum |x_i|$, $\|x\|_2 = \sqrt{\sum x_i^2}$ and $\|x\|_\infty = \max |x_i|$. Beware that, contrary to some of the literature, the notation $\| \cdot \|$ *does not* refer by default to the Euclidean norm, but is a place-holder for any norm, asymmetric norm or pseudo-norm (defined below).

We will make use of two weakened notions of norm during this paper. We recall that a norm $\| \cdot \| : V \to [0, +\infty)$ on a real vector space V is a function satisfying the three following axioms:

1. Sub-additivity: $\|x + y\| \leq \|x\| + \|y\|$ for all $x, y \in V$,
2. Absolute homogeneity: $\|ax\| = |a| \cdot \|x\|$ for all $a \in \mathbb{R}$, $x \in V$,
3. Positive definiteness: $\|x\| = 0 \Rightarrow x = 0$ for all $x \in V$.

An asymmetric norm $\| \cdot \| : V \to [0, +\infty)$ is a function verifying axioms 1 and 3 and the following positive homogeneity axiom:

4. Positive homogeneity: $\|ax\| = a \cdot \|x\|$ for all $a \geq 0$, $x \in V$.

Finally, in this article we will call a pseudo-norm a function $\|\cdot\| : V \to [0, +\infty)$ verifying the axiom 1 and the following linear monotonicity axiom:

5. Linear monotonicity: $\|ax\| \geq \|x\|$ for all $a \geq 1$.

Lattices. A lattice Λ is a discrete subgroup of a finite-dimensional Euclidean vector space $\mathbb{R}^n$ (or Hermitian vector space $\mathbb{C}^{n/2} \simeq \mathbb{R}^n$). A lattice admits a basis, that is a matrix $B \in \mathbb{R}^{d \times n}$ such that $\Lambda = B \cdot \mathbb{Z}^n$ for some $n \le d$; n is called the dimension of the lattice. Its volume is defined by $\mathrm{Vol}(L) = \sqrt{\det(B^t B)}$ for any basis B of Λ (this measure is independent of the choice of the basis).

To quantify the shortness of a vector $v \in \Lambda$, we use the so-called Hermite factor $\eta = \|v\|_2 / \mathrm{Vol}(\Lambda)^{1/n}$ (where $n = \dim(\Lambda)$) instead of the approximation factor $\alpha = \|v\|_2 / \lambda_1(\Lambda)$ (where $\lambda_1(\Lambda) = \min_{w \in \Lambda \setminus \{0\}} \|w\|_2$), as the minimal length of a lattice is typically not known exactly. Note that this choice does not affect the comparison of reduction performances between different algorithms.

Remark 1. While the latter approximation factor α is often preferred in worst-case complexity theory, the former Hermite factor η is typically more relevant and convenient for average-case cryptanalysis. Note that from Minkowski's theorem, we have $\lambda_1(\Lambda) \le (1 + O(1/n)) \sqrt{2n/\pi e}\, \mathrm{Vol}(\Lambda)^{1/n}$; moreover, for cyclotomic ideal lattices we also have $\lambda_1(\Lambda) \ge \mathrm{Vol}(\Lambda)^{1/n}$. Therefore, the ratio between both measure is reasonably well controlled: $\alpha/\eta \in [1, (1+O(1))\sqrt{2n/\pi e}]$. The extreme case $\alpha/\eta = 1$ is reached by orthogonal lattices, and for random lattices the Gaussian heuristic predicts $\alpha/\eta \approx \sqrt{n/2\pi e}$.

Close vector algorithm. We recall from [Bab86] two polynomial time algorithms RoundOff and NearestPlane (as Algorithms 1 and 2) for solving the close vector problem given a basis of short vectors. The output v is guaranteed to lie in the parallelepiped $t + \mathcal{P}(B)$ for RoundOff and $t + \mathcal{P}(B^\star)$ for NearestPlane, where

$$\mathcal{P}(B) = \left\{ \sum \alpha_i b_i \,\middle|\, \alpha_i \in [-1/2, 1/2) \right\}.$$

This allows to bound $\|v - t\|$, depending on the quality of the basis B, and of considered norm $\| \cdot \|$.

Algorithm 1. RoundOff(B, t)

Require: A basis B of a full-rank lattice $L \subset \mathbb{R}^n$, a target point $t \in \mathbb{R}^n$.
Ensure: A lattice vector $v \in L$ close to t: $v - t \in \mathcal{P}(B)$
  1: $x \leftarrow B^{-1} t$
  2: $y \leftarrow (\lfloor x_1 \rceil, \ldots, \lfloor x_n \rceil)$
  3: $v \leftarrow By$
  4: **return** v

2.2 Number Theory

Cyclotomic number fields. Throughout this paper, m denotes the power of a prime, ω_m is a primitive m-th root of unity, and $K = \mathbb{Q}(\omega_m)$ is the m-th cyclotomic number field. It is a number field of degree $n = \varphi(m) = \Theta(m)$.

Algorithm 2. NearestPlane(B, t)

Require: A basis B of a full-rank lattice $L \subset \mathbb{R}^n$, a target point $t \in \mathbb{R}^n$.
Ensure: A lattice vector $v \in L$ close to t: $v - t \in \mathcal{P}(B^\star)$
1: $f \leftarrow t$
2: $v \leftarrow 0$
3: **for** $i = n$ downto 1 **do**
4: $\quad y \leftarrow \langle t, b_i^\star \rangle / \|b_i^\star\|^2$
5: $\quad z_i = \lfloor y \rceil$
6: $\quad f \leftarrow f - z_i b_i$
7: $\quad v \leftarrow v + z_i b_i$
8: **end for**
9: **return** v

We denote by G its Galois group over $\mathbb{Q}$, while $\tau \in G$ denotes complex conjugation. We recall that $G \simeq (\mathbb{Z}/m\mathbb{Z})^\times$, by constructing the automorphism $\sigma_i \in G : \omega \mapsto \omega^i$ for any $i \in (\mathbb{Z}/m\mathbb{Z})^\times$. Complex conjugation corresponds to -1, i.e., $\tau = \sigma_{-1}$. The norm of an element $x \in K$ is given by $Nx = \prod_{\sigma \in G} \sigma(x)$, and it holds that $Nx \in \mathbb{Q}$ for any element $x \in K$.

We recall that the discriminant Δ_K of cyclotomic number fields K asymptotically satisfies $\log|\Delta_K| = O(n \log n)$ [Was12]. More specifically, for any prime power conductor $m = p^k$, the discriminant of $\mathbb{Q}(\omega_{p^k})$ is $\pm p^{p^{k-1}(pk-k-1)}$.

Ideals of $\mathcal{O}_K$. The ring of integers of K is denoted $\mathcal{O}_K = \mathbb{Z}[\omega_m]$. An integral ideal $\mathfrak{h} \subset \mathcal{O}_K$ is an additive subgroup closed under multiplication by any element of the ring; more precisely $\forall a \in \mathcal{O}_K$, $a\mathfrak{h} \subset \mathfrak{h}$. A fractional ideal $f \subset K$ is an ideal of the form $f = \frac{1}{s}\mathfrak{h}$ for some scalar $s \in \mathbb{Z}$. Unless specified to be integral, ideals will be considered to be fractional.

The elements $(g_1, ..., g_r)$ are generators of the ideal f when $f = \sum_i g_i \mathcal{O}_K$. In particular, when the ideal is generated by a single element, it is called principal. For an integral ideal $\mathfrak{h} \subset \mathcal{O}_K$, the quotient $\mathcal{O}_K/\mathfrak{h}$ is finite and $N\mathfrak{h} = |\mathcal{O}_K/\mathfrak{h}|$ is the norm of the ideal $\mathfrak{h}$. When $\mathfrak{h}$ is principal, there is an element h such that $\mathfrak{h} = h\mathcal{O}_K$, and the norm of $\mathfrak{h}$ coincides with the algebraic norm of h, i.e., $N\mathfrak{h} = Nh$.

Ideals as lattices. The field K is endowed with a canonical structure of Hermitian vector space via its Minkowski embedding. That is, letting $\zeta_m = \exp(2\imath\pi/m) \in \mathbb{C}$, and letting $\psi_i : K \to \mathbb{C}$ be the field morphism sending ω_m to ζ_m^i for each $i \in (\mathbb{Z}/m\mathbb{Z})^\times$ coprime to m, each elements $e \in K$ is identified with the vector $\psi(e) = (\psi_i(e))_{i \in (\mathbb{Z}/m\mathbb{Z})^\times} \in \mathbb{C}^n$. By abuse of notation, we often identify the elements e and $\psi(e)$; in particular, $\|e\|_\alpha$ refers to $\|\psi(e)\|_\alpha$ for $\alpha \in \{1, 2, \infty\}$.

Any ideal $\mathfrak{h}$ of $\mathcal{O}_K$ can be viewed as a Euclidean lattice via the above embedding. The volume of $\mathfrak{h}$ as a lattice relates to its algebraic norm via the equation $\text{Vol}(\mathfrak{h}) = \sqrt{|\Delta_K|}N\mathfrak{h}$.

Class group. The class group $\mathrm{Cl}_K = \mathcal{I}_K/\mathcal{P}_K$ of K is the quotient of the (abelian) multiplicative group of fractional ideals $\mathcal{I}_K$ by the subgroup of principal ideals. We denote by $[\mathfrak{h}]$ the class of the ideal $\mathfrak{h}$ in Cl_K. The trivial class $[\mathcal{O}_K]$ is the class of principal ideals. The class group is written multiplicatively. The minus-part Cl_K^- of the class group is defined as the kernel of the relative norm map $N_{K/K^+} : \mathrm{Cl}_K \to \mathrm{Cl}_{K^+}$, $[\mathfrak{h}] \mapsto [\mathfrak{h}\mathfrak{h}^\tau]$, where K^+ is the maximal real subfield of K, and $\mathfrak{h}^\tau$ denotes the complex conjugation of $\mathfrak{h}$.

The class number $h_m = |\mathrm{Cl}_K|$ is the order of the class group. Denoting $h_m^+ = |\mathrm{Cl}_{K^+}|$ and $h_m^- = |\mathrm{Cl}_K^-|$ we have $h_m = h_m^+ \cdot h_m^-$.

Galois group ring. The Galois group ring $R = \mathbb{Z}[G]$ is the set of formal linear combinations of elements of G with integral coefficients. The group operation of G is extended to a multiplication law in R, providing R with a ring structure. The ring R acts naturally on the ideals of $\mathcal{O}_K$ as follows: let $s = \sum_{\sigma \in G} s_\sigma \sigma \in R$ and let $\mathfrak{h}$ be an ideal of $\mathcal{O}_K$, then we define the action of s on $\mathfrak{h}$ as

$$\mathfrak{h}^s = \prod_{\sigma \in G} \sigma(\mathfrak{h})^{s_\sigma}.$$

2.3 Cyclotomic Log-Unit Lattice

We abusively call units of K the elements of the group $\mathcal{O}_K^\times$. The embeddings of K are all complex, and such that $\overline{\psi_i} = \psi_{-i}$, hence $|\psi_i| = |\psi_{-i}|$, so we define the set of indices $I = (\mathbb{Z}/m\mathbb{Z})^\times /\{\pm 1\}$. The logarithmic embedding

$$\mathrm{Log} : K^\times \to \mathbb{R}^{n/2}$$
$$x \longmapsto \mathbf{x} = (\log(|\psi_i(x)|))_{i \in I}$$

defines a group homomorphism. The Dirichlet Unit Theorem ensures that $\Lambda = \mathrm{Log}(\mathcal{O}_K^\times)$ is a lattice (called the log-unit lattice) of rank $n/2 - 1$. The projection of the log-embedding of an element x on the all-1 vector $\mathbf{1} = (1, \ldots, 1)$ directed line is proportional to the logarithm of its algebraic norm $\log(Nx)$. In particular, as the algebraic norm is multiplicative, the algebraic norm of a unit is ± 1 and $\Lambda \perp \mathrm{Span}(\mathbf{1})$. We denote by H the orthogonal complement of $\mathrm{Span}(\mathbf{1})$, the minimal vector space supporting the log-unit lattice Λ. Conversely, we define a reciprocal function to Log, that is

$$\mathrm{Exp} : \mathbb{R}^{n/2} \to \mathbb{R}^n$$
$$(x_1, \ldots, x_{n/2}) \mapsto (\exp(x_1), \exp(x_1), \ldots, \exp(x_{n/2}), \exp(x_{n/2}))$$

Up to reordering of coefficients, we have that $(|\psi_i(x)|)_{i \in (\mathbb{Z}/m\mathbb{Z})^\times} = \mathrm{Exp}(\mathrm{Log}(x))$, in particular $\|\mathrm{Exp}(\mathrm{Log}(x))\|_2 = \|x\|_2$.

Not only do we know the structure of the units of $\mathcal{O}_K$ by Dirichlet's Theorem, but in the case of cyclotomic fields of prime-power conductor we also have an explicit set of relatively short vectors (namely, the $\mathrm{Log}\, b_{ij}$'s defined below) which generate a finite index sublattice of the log-unit lattice Λ.

More precisely, with $\zeta \in K$ a primitive m-th root of unity, we define the multiplicative group V generated by $\pm\zeta$ and the elements $z_i = \zeta^i - 1$, for $1 \leq i \leq m - 1$. Then, the cyclotomic units are defined as $C = V \cap \mathcal{O}_K^\times$. The elements $b_{ij} = \frac{z_i}{z_j}$ (when only one index is given b_i, we refer to b_{i1}) are units of $\mathcal{O}_K$. Then, the sublattice $\mathrm{Log}\,C$ is generated by the vectors $(\mathrm{Log}\,b_i)_{i \in I \setminus \{1\}}$. The index $[\Lambda : \mathrm{Log}\,C]$ and the length of the vectors $\mathrm{Log}\,b_{ij}$ are controlled by the following results.

Theorem 1 (See [Was12] Thm. 8.2 and Exercise 8.5). *For any prime power $m > 2$, the index of the log-unit lattice Λ over $\mathrm{Log}\,C$ is*

$$[\Lambda : \mathrm{Log}\,C] = h_m^+ < \infty.$$

Corollary 2 (Corollary of [CDPR16], Lemma 6.7). *Let $m = p^k$ be a prime power. Then, $\|\mathrm{Log}\,b_{ij}\| = O(\sqrt{m})$.*

The two above statements allow to establish upper bounds on how well one can solve the close vector problem in this lattice Λ. Lower bounds can also be established by volumetric arguments, as done in [CDPR16]. In particular, they established that $\mathrm{Vol}(\Lambda)^{1/(n/2-1)} \geq \Omega(\sqrt{m}/\log m)$. We provide the following better estimate.

Theorem 3. *For prime powers m, we have $\mathrm{Vol}(\Lambda)^{\frac{1}{n/2-1}} \sim \sqrt{m}/2$.*

The proof is deferred to Appendix B.

2.4   Stickelberger Lattice

Let us define the Stickelberger lattice S as the $\mathbb{Z}[G]$-multiples in $\mathbb{Z}[G]$ of the Stickelberger element

$$\theta = \sum_{a \in (\mathbb{Z}/m\mathbb{Z})^\times} \left\{\frac{a}{m}\right\} \sigma_a^{-1} \in \mathbb{Q}[G],$$

where $\{x\}$ denotes the fractional part $x - \lfloor x \rfloor$ of the rational number x. In other words, $S = \mathbb{Z}[G] \cap \theta\mathbb{Z}[G]$.

Theorem 4 ([Was12]). *The Stickelberger ideal S is such that for any fractional ideal $\mathfrak{h}$ of $\mathcal{O}_K$, and for any $s \in S$, the ideal $\mathfrak{h}^s$ is principal. In other words, S annihilates the ideal class group of K.*

Similarly to the log-unit lattice, we know a generating set of relatively short vectors (namely, the w_i's defined below) of S. Let us define the vectors v_i, $2 \leq i \leq n + 1$ as $v_i = (a_i - \sigma_{a_i})\theta$. The aforementioned vectors w_i's, $2 \leq i \leq n + 1$ are defined by $w_{i+1} = v_{i+1} - v_i$, and we have the following inequality on their norms from [CDW17,Wes18].

Fact 5 ([Wes18]). *For any $2 \leq i \leq n + 1$, we have $\|w_i\|_2 \leq 2\sqrt{n}$.*

In the case of prime conductors m, Schoof established in [Sch10] that all the w_i's have ± 1 coefficients, in particular $\|w_i\|_2 = \sqrt{n}$.

3 Approx-SVP on Cyclotomic Ideals

3.1 Overview

Building upon [CGS14, EHKS14, CDPR16, BS16], the Approx-SVP algorithm for cyclotomic ideals of [CDW17] splits in the following 4 steps given below. A more detailed overview of these recent works is given in [Duc17]. Some details have been simplified by making use of several working hypotheses summarized at the end of this section.

Step 1 (quantum): Class-Group Discrete Logarithm. The first step consists in expressing the class $[\mathfrak{a}]$ of the input ideal $\mathfrak{a}$ in base $\mathfrak{B} = \{\mathfrak{p}^\sigma | \sigma \in G\}$ for some prime ideal $\mathfrak{p}$, using the quantum poly-time algorithm of [BS16]. Under Hypothesis 7, such a decomposition always exists. This algorithm is heavily based on the quantum algorithm for the Hidden Subgroup Problem over $\mathbb{R}^n$ from [EHKS14]. This provides an element $e \in \mathbb{Z}[G]$ such that $[\mathfrak{p}^e] = [\mathfrak{a}]$.

Step 2 (classical): Close Principal Multiple. The second step, introduced in [CDW17] consists in finding a *close principal multiple* of $\mathfrak{a}$, that is a principal ideal of the form $\mathfrak{b} = \mathfrak{a}\mathfrak{c}$ where $\mathfrak{c} \subset \mathcal{O}_K$ is an integral ideal of reasonably small norm $N\mathfrak{c} \leq F$. This will allow to focus the search of a short vector to the (principal) sublattice $\mathfrak{b} \subset \mathfrak{a}$.

This is done by finding a point $v \in S$ close to e. Setting $w = v - e$ gives a 'small' ideal $\mathfrak{c} = \mathfrak{p}^w$ such that $\mathfrak{b} = \mathfrak{a}\mathfrak{c}$ is principal. Indeed, $[\mathfrak{b}] = [\mathfrak{a}][\mathfrak{c}] = [\mathfrak{p}]^e[\mathfrak{p}]^{v-e} = [\mathfrak{p}]^v$, and $[\mathfrak{p}]^v = [\mathcal{O}_K]$ by Stickelberger's Theorem.

Yet $\mathfrak{c}$ is not necessarily integral as coefficients of $w \in \mathbb{Z}[G]$ can be negative. This is nevertheless easy to solve under Hypothesis 6, as it then holds that $[\mathfrak{p}^{-1}] = [\mathfrak{p}^\tau]$. This gives the desired $\mathfrak{b} \subset \mathcal{O}_K$ of bounded norm $N\mathfrak{b} \leq p^{\|w\|_1}$.

Using the NearestPlane algorithm and an explicit short basis of the augmented Stickelberger lattice $S' := S + (1 + \tau)$, it is shown in [CDW17] that one can find a close vector $v \in S$, at ℓ_1-distance at most B_2

$$\|w\|_1 = \|v - e\|_1 \leq B_2 = O(n^{3/2}). \tag{1}$$

Assuming $N\mathfrak{p} = \mathrm{poly}(n)$ leads to

$$N\mathfrak{b}/N\mathfrak{a} = (N\mathfrak{p})^{B_2} = \exp(\widetilde{O}(n^{3/2})). \tag{2}$$

Step 3 (quantum): Principal Ideal Problem. The next step consists of solving the Principal Ideal Problem (PIP) on the principal ideal $\mathfrak{b}$, that is, finding a generator h of it: $h\mathcal{O}_K = \mathfrak{b}$. As for the Class-Group Discrete Logarithm Problem, there is a quantum poly-time algorithm [BS16] for this task.

Step 4 (classical): Short Generator Problem. The last step consists in finding a unit $u \in \mathcal{O}_K^\times$ such that $g = uh$ (which also generates $\mathfrak{b}$) has small norm. As in Step 2, this again can be rephrased as a close-vector problem, this time in the log-unit lattice $\Lambda = \mathrm{Log}\,\mathcal{O}_K^\times$.

Using a randomized variant of the RoundOff Algorithm with the explicit short basis $\{\mathrm{Log}\,b_j, i \in I\}$ of the log-unit lattice, it is shown [CDPR16, Theorem 6.3] that for any target $H = \mathrm{Span}(\Lambda)$, one can find a logarithmic unit $l \in \Lambda$ at distance at most $B_4 = O(\sqrt{m \log m})$

$$\|l - t\|_\infty \leq B_4. \tag{3}$$

From any target $t \in H$. Setting t to be the orthogonal projection of $\mathrm{Log}\,h$ onto H, and u such that $l = \mathrm{Log}\,u$ leads to a short generator $h = gu$, of norm bounded by

$$\|h\|_\infty \leq (Ng)^{1/n} \cdot \exp(\|l - t\|_\infty) \leq (Ng)^{1/n} \cdot \exp(O(\sqrt{n \log n})). \tag{4}$$

Conclusion. In conclusion, we have found a vector $g \in \mathfrak{b} \subset \mathfrak{a}$ of norm at most:

$$\begin{aligned}
\|h\|_2 &\leq \sqrt{n}\|h\|_\infty \leq \sqrt{n} \cdot (Ng)^{1/n} \cdot \exp(B_4) \\
&\leq \sqrt{n} \cdot (N\mathfrak{a})^{1/n} \cdot p^{B_2/n} \cdot \exp(B_4) \\
&\leq \mathrm{Vol}(\mathfrak{a})^{1/n} \cdot \sqrt{n} \cdot \Delta_K^{-1/2n} \cdot p^{B_2/n} \cdot \exp(B_4) \\
&\leq \mathrm{Vol}(\mathfrak{a})^{1/n} \cdot \exp(\widetilde{O}(\sqrt{n})),
\end{aligned}$$

that is, we have solved approx-SVP on the cyclotomic ideal $\mathfrak{a}$ with an Hermite factor of $\eta = \exp(\widetilde{O}(\sqrt{n}))$.

3.2   Slackness of the Bounds of Step 4

Note that the 4th step from [CDPR16] makes use of a non-tight bound. Indeed the exact length of h can be written as

$$\|h\|_2 = (Ng)^{1/n} \cdot \|\mathrm{Exp}(l - t)\|_2,$$

and [CDPR16] simply considers

$$\|\mathrm{Exp}(l - t)\|_2 \leq \sqrt{n} \cdot \exp(\|l - t\|_\infty).$$

For our concrete analysis, it is therefore more relevant to define the pseudo-norm $\|\cdot\|_\wr : H \to [0, +\infty)$

$$\|x\|_\wr := \ln(\|\mathrm{Exp}(x)\|_2).$$

While it holds that $\|x\|_\wr \leq \|x\|_\infty + \ln(\sqrt{n})$, the slackness of this inequality is *not* only induced by the typical $\ell_2 - \ell_\infty$ slackness $\|x\|_\infty \leq \|x\|_2 \leq \sqrt{n}\|x\|_\infty$, in the sense that we can have $\|x\|_\wr \not\geq \|x\|_\infty$.

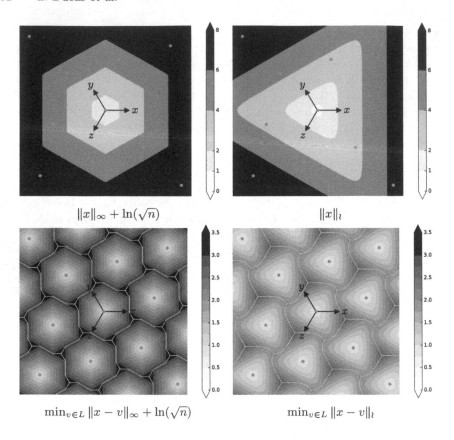

$$\|x\|_\infty + \ln(\sqrt{n}) \qquad\qquad \|x\|_\imath$$

$$\min_{v \in L} \|x - v\|_\infty + \ln(\sqrt{n}) \qquad\qquad \min_{v \in L} \|x - v\|_\imath$$

Fig. 1. Greyscale plots comparisons of $\|\cdot\|_\infty$ and $\|\cdot\|_\imath$ on the space H for $m = 7$ ($n = 6$, $\dim(H) = n/2 - 1 = 2$, $H \subset \mathbb{R}^{n/2}$). The black arrows represent the projection of the canonical axes of $\mathbb{R}^3$ onto H. The blue dots represent the points of the log-unit lattice $\Lambda = \mathrm{Log}\,\mathcal{O}_K^\times$. The red cells represent Voronoi partitions. (Color figure online)

Indeed, negative coefficients in x contribute very little to $\|x\|_\imath$. This is exemplified by having a pathologically negative coefficient: taking $x = \alpha(1 - n/2, 1, \ldots, 1) \in H$ where $\alpha > 0$ we have

$$\|x\|_\infty = \alpha(n/2 - 1)$$
$$\|x\|_\imath \leq \alpha + \ln(n).$$

To represent things more pictorially, let us assume $m = 7$, for which $n = \phi(m) = 6$: the space H has dimension $n/2 - 1 = 2$ and is embedded in $\mathbb{R}^3$: $H = \{(x, y, z) | x + y + z = 0\}$. A graphical comparison of $\|\cdot\|_\infty$ and $\|\cdot\|_\imath$ is provided in Fig. 1. As we can see, not only the $\|\cdot\|_\infty$ is pessimistic, but it can also lead to a wrong choice for the optimal solution: the Voronoi partitioning under $\|\cdot\|_\infty$ and $\|\cdot\|_\imath$ do differ.

3.3   Concrete Estimation of the Hermite Factor

At the time of writing, the authors do not possess a quantum computer sufficiently powerful to execute the full algorithm. Fortunately, it is nevertheless possible to simulate the behavior of the Hermite factor, since it depends only on the behavior of the classical steps 2 and 4. More precisely, assuming that $e \bmod S'$ and $t \bmod \Lambda$ are uniform and independent (Hypothesis 8), we can study experimentally the average behavior of the whole algorithm.

More precisely, having introduced the appropriate pseudo-norm $\|\cdot\|_{\iota}$, we can now write the exact value of the Hermite factor as a function of intermediate values $v - e$ and $l - t$ as follows:

$$\eta = \Delta_K^{-\frac{1}{2n}} \cdot \exp\left(\frac{\ln p}{n} \cdot \|v - e\|_1 + \|l - t\|_{\iota}\right). \tag{5}$$

Therefore, we can predict the behavior of η simply by measuring experimentally the distribution of $\|v - e\|_1$ and $\|l - t\|_{\iota}$. For comparison with LLL and BKZ, it is more convenient to consider the root Hermite factor $\delta = \eta^{1/n}$. For example, for LLL we have $\delta \approx 1.022$ according to [NS06], and for BKZ with blocksize $\beta \geq 50$, both heuristic arguments and experiments [CN11] give $\delta^{2(\beta-1)} \approx (\beta/(2\pi e))(\beta\pi)^{\frac{1}{\beta}}$.

3.4   Working Hypotheses

Restriction on the conductor. While the algorithm above has been initially studied for all prime-power conductors m in [CDW17, CDPR16], and even generalized to all conductors in [Wes18], the body of this paper will focus only on prime conductors m. This avoids numerous case by case discussions. One may prefer to directly study the case of power of 2 conductors, which is the most common in applications. However, powers of 2 are too sparse to allow for reasonable extrapolation. We therefore defer it to Appendix A, where we will compare it to the prime case.

Number-theoretic hypotheses. Two hypotheses are used in the works of [CDW17, CDPR16] concerning the structure of the class-group. The first is that the size of the *plus-part* of the class group h_m^+ (i.e. the size of the class group of the maximal real subfield) is only polynomial in the conductor m. The second is that one can construct (by random sampling) a small set of small-norm ideals that generate the class group as a $\mathbb{Z}[G]$-module.

While these assumptions are sufficient for asymptotic results, they are not precise enough for a more effective study such as ours. We will therefore, as a working hypotheses strengthen those assumptions.

Hypothesis 6. *The* plus-part *of the class group is trivial, i.e. $h_m^+ = 1$.*

Hypothesis 7. *The class group is generated by the ideals above the smallest totally split prime. That is, let $p \in \mathbb{Z}$ be the smallest prime such that $p \equiv 1 \bmod m$, and $\mathfrak{p} \subset \mathcal{O}_K$ such that $N\mathfrak{p} = p$. We assume that $[\mathfrak{p}]$ generates Cl_K as a $\mathbb{Z}[G]$-module, or equivalently that $\{[\mathfrak{p}^\sigma] | \sigma \in G\}$ generates Cl_K as a group.*

We will keep the notation p and $\mathfrak{p}$ as a function of m for the rest of this paper. For our final conclusion, we will need estimates on p. We note that for prime conductors m, we necessarily have $p \geq 2m+1$. On the other hand, prime density suggest that "on average" over m we have $p \approx m \ln m$.

Because of these strengthened hypotheses, our final claims should be interpreted as a best-case scenario for the efficiency of those algorithms. We remind that various computational results suggest that those assumptions are plausible for a substantial fraction of conductors m [Was12, Sch98, Sch03]. In any case, the failure of those two hypotheses would not invalidate our lower-bound.

Input distribution. In the light of the worst-case to average-case results of [Mic07, SSTX09, LPR10, SS11, PRSD17], it would be interesting to study the worst-case behavior of those algorithms. Alas, finding which input leads to the worst-case is most likely an intractable problem. We therefore instead assume that the inputs will be uniform modulo the respective lattices.

Hypothesis 8. *The input* $e \in \mathbb{Z}[G]$ *of step 2 is uniform in* $\mathbb{Z}[G]/(S + (1 + \tau)\mathbb{Z}[G])$, *and the target* t *in step 4 is uniform in* H/Λ.

Remark 2. The first part of the hypothesis essentially states that the class $[\mathfrak{a}]$ of the input ideal $\mathfrak{a}$ is uniform over $\mathrm{Cl} = \mathrm{Cl}^-$. Interestingly, the main theorem of [JW18] allows to randomize the input so as to ensure its uniformity in the class group, by randomly multiplying it by a few small prime ideals. This only affects its norm by a factor $\exp(\widetilde{O}(n))$, which asymptotically has a negligible impact on the final approximation factor. This implies that we can re-randomize any instance (even a worst-case one) to an average case one at a small cost.

The second part of the hypothesis can also be enforced by some randomization of t. A straightforward approach would be to simply add to t a (short) random vector r of H uniformly distributed in H/Λ. Reducing r with the good basis of Λ, this randomization has a limited impact on the final approximation factor. More precisely, we end up with $\|t - l\|_{l} \leq \|t + r - l\|_{l} + \|r\|_{l}$ where both $\|r\|_{l}$ and $\|t + r - l\|_{l}$ follow the average case distribution studied in this paper (yet are not independent). In particular, if the average case gives a solution of length less than B with probability greater than $2/3$, we can find solutions of length at most $2B$ in the worst-case, by randomizing on average 3 times.

This loss of a factor 2 should only be read as a preliminary conclusion concerning the worst case. Indeed, heuristically, randomizing the input ideal for the first step will also rerandomize the target of the second step. Making such a statement formal requires generalizing [JW18] to the Arakelov class group; this is beyond the scope of the present article and left as future work.

4   Heuristic Improvement for the Close Vector Steps

In this section, we consider potential heuristic improvements for solving the close vector problems relatively to the log-unit lattice and to the Stickelberger lattice. Indeed, we note that [CDPR16, CDW17] focus on proving worst-case bounds, and therefore apply simple and easy to analyse close-vector algorithms, namely NearestPlane and RoundOff. There are several reasons to think that this can be improved in practice, as discussed below.

4.1   More Short Vectors to Be Exploited

We note that the NearestPlane and RoundOff algorithms are restricted to use exactly d short vectors for a d-dimensional lattice, while in both cases, we actually know $\Theta(d^2)$ short vectors in these lattices. Indeed, for the log-unit lattice we know the following $n/2(n/2 - 1)$ short units:

$$\mathrm{Log}\, b_{ij} = \mathrm{Log}\left(\frac{1 - \zeta^i}{1 - \zeta^j}\right), i, j \in I, i \neq j.$$

Similarly, in the Stickelberger lattice, we know the following n^2 short class relations:

$$w_i \sigma, 2 \leq i \leq n + 1, \sigma \in G.$$

This extra knowledge can be exploited by using algorithms that can take advantage of many short vectors to solve CVP. In fact, if one knows the set V of all the *Voronoi relevants vector* of a lattice of dimension d, one can solve exact-CVP in $O(|V| \cdot \mathrm{poly}(d))$ arithmetic operations [MV10, DB15]. This is described as Algorithm 3 (VoronoiCVP). Unfortunately the size of V can be as large as $2^d - 2$, and the best known algorithm [MV10] to determine it takes time $O(4^d)$. Yet it remains possible to run this algorithm with an approximation of the set V'; this has been proposed and analyzed in [Laa16, DLdW19, SD19]. We cannot apply this analysis in our case because it uses heuristic arguments that are valid for random lattices, and those heuristics are most likely invalid for the lattices at hand which are somewhat close to orthogonal. Furthermore, this analysis is strongly restricted to the Euclidean norm, while we are here interested in other norms, or even pseudo-norms. But we can nevertheless apply a similar strategy and see how it behaves experimentally.

Algorithm 3. VoronoiCVP(V, t) ([MV10, Laa16, DLdW19])

$c \leftarrow 0$
while $\exists v \in \pm V$ such that $\|t - c - v\|_2 < \|t - c\|_2$ **do**
    $c \leftarrow c + v$
end while
return c

This algorithm can be viewed as a discrete gradient descent, and if V is indeed the set of Voronoi relevant vectors this descent will stop at an exact closest vector. Otherwise, the descent can get stuck in a discrete local minima, and therefore it was also proposed in [Laa16, DLdW19] to randomize the starting point $c = 0$ and to take the best results over several descents.

Rather than re-starting from scratch, in practice it seems preferable to continue the search nearby the current local minima: indeed the descent is done on a convex function, it is only because it is discretized that it can get stuck, and we expect the closest point to be not that far from the current point. Proceeding with such a strategy requires care to avoid looping over a cycle; this is easily prevented by keeping track of the points visited so far. At last, we also accelerate the descent by starting from either the NearestPlane or RoundOff approximation; this also ensures that its result will be at least as good as that of the original algorithm. The resulting algorithm is detailed in Algorithm 4 (HeuristicCVP), after the following final tweak.

4.2 Norm Inadequacy

Another source of inefficiency comes from the fact that NearestPlane, RoundOff and even the above VoronoiCVP are attempting to optimize the Euclidean distance, while for our application what we really want to optimize are the ℓ_1-distance $\| \cdot \|_1$ for Stickelberger lattice, and the pseudo-norm $\| \cdot \|_l$ for the log-unit lattice.

This inadequacy is easily addressed in practice simply by replacing the Euclidean norm $\| \cdot \|_2$ used in our HeuristicCVP algorithm by the desired (pseudo)-norm $\| \cdot \|_1$ or $\| \cdot \|_l$.

Algorithm 4. HeuristicCVP($B, V, t, S, \| \cdot \|$)

$c \leftarrow$ NearestPlane(B, t) or $c \leftarrow$ RoundOff(B, t)
$C \leftarrow \{c\}$
for $i \in \{1, \ldots, S\}$ **do**
    $c \leftarrow \operatorname{argmin}_{c'} \|c' - t\|$ where c' ranges over $(c + V) \setminus C$
    $C \leftarrow C \cup \{c\}$
end for
return $\operatorname{argmin}_{c'} \|c' - t\|$ where c' ranges over C

4.3 Dimension-Halving for Step 2

Because the Stickelberger ideal S is not full rank as a $\mathbb{Z}$-module in $\mathbb{Z}[G]$, the augmented ideal $S' = S + (1 + \tau)\mathbb{Z}[G]$ was introduced in [CDW17], which also annihilates the class group under the assumption that $h_m^+ = 1$. Alternatively, it is proposed in [Wes18] to instead project the lattice and the target down to the quotient ring $\mathbb{Z}[G]/(1 + \tau)$. More specifically, let $F \subset G$ be such that F and τF form a partition of G. We define a projection morphism

$$\pi : \mathbb{Z}[G] \to \mathbb{Z}^F$$
$$f \in F \mapsto f$$
$$f \in G \setminus F \mapsto -\tau f$$

where $\mathbb{Z}^F \simeq \mathbb{Z}^{n/2}$ is the $\mathbb{Z}$-module of formal integral sums of elements of F. We note that there is a reciprocal function $\hat{\pi}$ such that for all $x \in \mathbb{Z}^F$ it holds that $\pi(\hat{\pi}(x)) = x$, $\hat{\pi}(x)$ has positive coordinates, and $\|\hat{\pi}(x)\|_1 = \|x\|_1$: any $x \in \mathbb{Z}^F$ can be lifted back to a positive exponent in $\mathbb{Z}[G]$ with the same ℓ_1 norm, as needed to solve the Close Principal Multiple problem.

While this tweak from [Wes18] was originally mostly aesthetic as it didn't improve the asymptotic analysis, it effectively decreases the dimension of the problem from n to $n/2$; we note experimentally that this trick noticeably improved the average length of $\|v - e\|_1$.

Remark 3. We note during those experiments that the index $\mathrm{Vol}(S') = |\mathbb{Z}[G]/S'|$ (or equivalently the index $\mathrm{Vol}(\pi(S)) = |\mathbb{Z}^F/\pi(S)|$) is not equal to h_m^-, but rather to $2^{n/2-1} \cdot h_m^-$ (at least for all primes $m \leq 1000$): the representation of a class of Cl^- as an element of $\mathbb{Z}[G]/S'$ is not unique. And indeed, only a weaker statement is known, namely the theorem of Iwasawa [Sin80, Was12] stating that $|((1 - \tau)\mathbb{Z}[G])/((1 - \tau) \cap S)| = h_m^-$.

5 Implementation and Experiments

5.1 Implementation Details

Sources. Our implementation was realized in `python3`, and exploits the library `numpy`. It is provided in open-source for repeatability and review of our experiments at https://github.com/lducas/Cyclotomic-QISVP-Effective. The algorithms discussed above are implemented in `stickelberger.py` and `logunit.py`. The script `experiments.py` provides a convenient command line interface for running experiments. The script `verifications.py` provides sanity-checks, in particular with respect to the construction of the Stickelberger and log-unit lattices.

Optimizations. The critical computation regarding the performance of Algorithm 4 is the evaluation of the pseudo-norm $\|\cdot\|_?$ of $x + v$. In this loop, $x = c - t$ is fixed, while v varies over the set V, of size $\Theta(n^2)$.

Naively, the efficiency of evaluating the pseudo-norm is pretty terrible: not only does it requires $\Theta(n)$ calls to transcendental functions (log, exp), but it also requires to run the `for` $v \in V$ loop at the `python` level, inducing interpretation overheads. We note the following identity:

$$\exp(\|x + v\|_?^2) = \|\mathrm{Exp}(x + v)\|^2 = \sum e^{2x_i} \cdot e^{2v_i} = \langle \mathrm{Exp}(2x), \mathrm{Exp}(2v) \rangle.$$

Since $y \mapsto \exp(y^2)$ is monotonic over $[0, +\infty)$, this means that we can actually determine the minimizing v using a matrix-vector product $M \cdot \mathrm{Exp}(2x)$, where the rows of M are the row vectors $\{\mathrm{Exp}(-2v)^T | v \in V\}$. Having precomputed M, this step becomes very fast thanks to the optimized linear algebra library included in `numpy`.

Another optimization consists in using a custom hash function $\mathcal{H}$ for testing $c' \notin C$ in Algorithm 4. By making this function linear, we can accelerate the computation of $\mathcal{H}(c') = \mathcal{H}(c) + \mathcal{H}(v)$.

Numerical stability issues. In the experiment reported below, Fig. 2a has been truncated at dimension 800: after this point the behavior started being erratic. We strongly suspect that this is due to numerical stability issues during the Gram-Schmidt Orthogonalization algorithm. Unfortunately, increasing floating point precision seems difficult within our programming set-up, as `python/numpy` does not support more than double precision floats. Perhaps surprisingly, step 4 showed no such issue, at least up to dimension 3000. It may be that matrix inversion is more numerically stable than Gram-Schmidt, but also that the log-unit basis is better conditioned than the Stickelberger basis.

5.2   Experimental Results

We now report on the behavior of the original algorithms of [CDW17, CDPR16] and our heuristic improvements. Our experiments are depicted in Fig. 2. The data points are averaged over 100 samples per prime conductor m. For certain batches of experiments, we may have skipped some conductors so as to obtain data points for larger conductors in reasonable time. The computation ran for about a week, using 8 cores (Intel Xeon E5-2650v3 @2.3 GHz).

Deviation from average. Before commenting on the average behavior, we first note that, apart from the naive algorithms, the deviation from average was extremely small: the standard deviation is smaller than the average by a factor at least 20 for conductors $m \geq 200$, and the gap seems to grow further with the dimension. This may not entirely dismiss the possibility of rare outliers, but the bounds from Sect. 6 will control the probability of outliers.

Experimental effective asymptotics. Our first remark is that the upper bounds from [CDW17, CDPR16] $\|v - e\|_1 = O(n^{3/2})$ and $\|l - t\|_i = O(\sqrt{n \log n})$ seem to be reached in practice, i.e., it seems very plausible that $\|v - e\|_1 = \Theta(n^{3/2})$ and quite plausible $\|l - t\|_i = \Theta(\sqrt{n \log n})$. More precisely, for the original algorithms, for large ranks $n = \varphi(m)$ it seems to hold that:

$$\|v - e\|_1 \approx 0.039 \cdot n^{3/2}, \qquad \text{and} \quad \|l - t\|_i \approx 0.32 \cdot \sqrt{n \ln n}. \tag{6}$$

Our heuristically improved variant using HeuristicCVP with $n^{3/2}$ iterations yields

$$\|v - e\|_1 \approx 0.032 \cdot n^{3/2}, \qquad \text{and} \quad \|l - t\|_i \approx 0.117 \cdot \sqrt{n \ln n}. \tag{7}$$

Increased number of iterations for HeuristicCVP. Of course, one would ideally want to estimate how those constants evolve as the number of iterations for HeuristicCVP increases. However, such experiments become impractical as this number grows further than $n^{3/2}$.

From Fig. 2c, we note that increasing the number of iterations beyond n does not seem to provide significantly better solutions in the log-unit lattice. No such conclusion can be drawn for the Stickelberger lattice (Fig. 2a). Fortunately, the lower bound studied in Sect. 6.1, Fig. 3, will show that the solution found with $n^{3/2}$ iterations is already quite close to optimal.

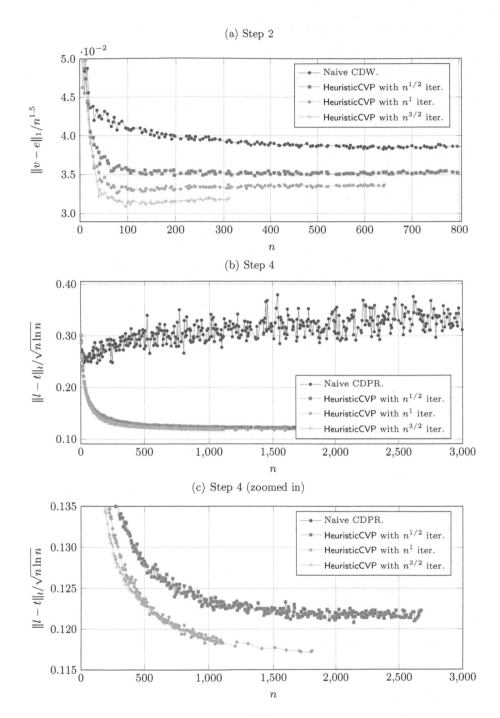

Fig. 2. Average distance given by various CVP algorithms for steps 2 & 4, for prime conductors m.

6   Volumetric Lower Bounds

In this section, we provide probabilistic lower bounds using volumetric arguments. More specifically, we compute a lower bound $r := r(L, \| \cdot \|)$ for the covering radius of a given lattice L under a given (asymmetric) norm $\| \cdot \|$. The following proposition states that most points are at a distance almost r from L.

Proposition 1. *Let L be a full-rank lattice in a euclidean vector space V of dimension d, and let $\mathcal{B} = \{x \in V \,|\, \|x\| < 1\}$ be the open unit ball associated to an (asymetric) norm $\| \cdot \|$. Let $r = (\mathrm{Vol}(L)/\mathrm{Vol}(\mathcal{B}))^{1/d}$.*
   Then, for any $\alpha \in [0,1]$, and for a random vector x such that $x \bmod L$ is uniformly distributed, the probability that

$$\|x - L\| := \min_{v \in L} \|x - v\| \le \alpha r$$

is less than α^d. In particular, there exists a vector $x \in V$ such that $\min_{v \in L} \|x - v\| \ge r$.

Proof. We work over the torus V/L, whose total measure is $\mathrm{Vol}(L)$. The probability that $\|x - L\| \le \alpha r$ is given by

$$P = \frac{\mathrm{Vol}(\alpha r \mathcal{B} \bmod L)}{\mathrm{Vol}(L)}.$$

Note that $\mathrm{Vol}(\alpha r \mathcal{B} \bmod L) \le \mathrm{Vol}(\alpha r \mathcal{B})$, with equality if and only if the union $\bigcup_{v \in L} v + \alpha r \mathcal{B}$ is disjoint. In particular

$$P \le \alpha^d r^d \, \mathrm{Vol}(\mathcal{B})/\mathrm{Vol}(L) = \alpha^d.$$

Remark 4. When comparing experimental results to those lower bounds, one should keep in mind that a gap does not necessarily imply that the algorithm fails to find the exact closest vector. Indeed, the above bound is tight only for lattices that are a perfect packing with respect to the considered balls.
   For example consider $\mathbb{Z}^n$, for which CVP is easy to solve in any ℓ_p norm. It is a perfect packing for the ℓ_∞ distance, and we have $r(\mathbb{Z}^n, \| \cdot \|_\infty) = 1/2$, while the average ℓ_∞ distance of a point to $\mathbb{Z}^n$ is $1/2 - o(1)$. Now, consider $\mathbb{Z}^n$ for the ℓ_1 distance, which is far from a perfect packing. We have $r(\mathbb{Z}^n, \| \cdot \|_1) = (n!/2^n)^{1/n} \approx n/2e \approx 0.184 \cdot n$, yet the average ℓ_1 distance is $n/4 = 0.25 \cdot n$.

6.1   Volumetric Bound for Step 2

Before we proceed, we must first discuss whether we should apply the lower bound with or without the dimension halving trick, i.e., whether we should apply it to the augmented Stickelberger lattice $S' = S + (1 + \tau)\mathbb{Z}[G]$, or to the projected one $\pi(S)$. While both have the same volume, the dimension of S' is twice the dimension of $\pi(S)$, which would give a smaller lower bound.

Yet, we note that π can only decrease ℓ_1 distances, so a lower bound for $\pi(S)$ will also apply to S'.

We have that $\dim(\pi(S)) = n/2 =: d$ and $\mathrm{Vol}(\pi(S)) = 2^{d-1}h_m^-$. The volume of the ℓ_1 unit ball in dimension d is given by $\mathrm{Vol}(\mathcal{B}_1) = 2^d/d!$. We need an estimation of h_m^-. Let

$$G(m) = 2m(m/4\pi^2)^{\varphi(m)/4}.$$

Kummer claimed, without publishing a proof, that for any prime m we have $h_m^- \sim G(m)$. Although this is now believed to be unlikely, Lepistö [Lep74] proved a weaker (but sufficient here) explicit bound of the form

$$\left| \log\left(\frac{h_m^-}{G(m)} \right) \right| = O(\log(m)).$$

We deduce that $h_m^- = G(m)e^{O(\log(m))}$, and therefore $h_m^{-1/d} \sim G(m)^{1/d}$. Such an approximation is numerically satisfied up to a 1% error for primes $m \in [100, 2000]$ by our script `verification.py`. Using Stirling's formula, and the facts that $d = n/2 \sim m/2$ (since m is prime) and $(2m)^{1/d} \sim 1$, we conclude that

$$r(\pi(S), \|\cdot\|_1) \sim \left(2^d \cdot m(m/4\pi^2)^{n/4} \Big/ (2e/d)^d \right)^{1/d}$$

$$\sim (m/4\pi^2)^{1/2} \cdot (d/e)$$

$$\sim \frac{1}{4e\pi} \cdot n^{3/2} \approx 0.02927 \cdot n^{3/2}$$

Adjusting to the integral input setting. While these bounds hold asymptotically, we note that our experiments violate them for dimensions below 200. The reason is that in Step 2, the input is an integral vector, uniform in $\mathbb{Z}^F/\pi(S)$, and not uniform in $\mathbb{R}^F/\pi(S)$ as required by Proposition 1. However, we can rather easily adjust to this setting, by counting integral points $N_{d,b} = |b\mathcal{B}_1 \cap \mathbb{Z}^d|$ in the ball of radius b. Using dynamic programming, $N_{d,b}$ is easily computed in polynomial time thanks to the following recursion:

$$N_{d,0} = 1, \qquad N_{1,b} = 2b + 1, \qquad N_{d,b} = N_{d-1,b} + 2\sum_{k=1}^{b} N_{d-1,b-k}.$$

For our concrete lower bound, we can therefore take r to be the largest integer such that $N_{d,r} \le |\mathbb{Z}^F/\pi(S)|$. This is depicted in Fig. 3, and compared to the performance of our algorithm HeuristicCVP. We note (as expected) that the asymptotic behavior is similar to our continuous volumetric analysis above.

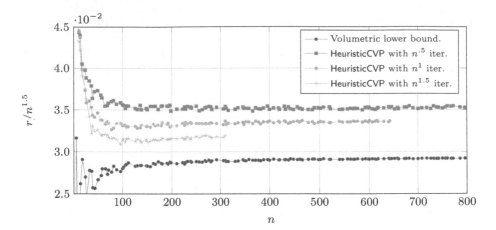

Fig. 3. Numerically computed volumetric lower bounds: maximal r such that $N_{d,r} \leq |\mathbb{Z}^F/\pi(S)|$, compared to the experimental behavior of HeuristicCVP.

Remark 5. In the above analysis, we have accounted for the factor $2^{n/2-1}$ that separates the lattice of (augmented) Stickelberger class relations from the full lattice of class relations (see Remark 3). While we are currently uncertain whether or not this factor is unavoidable, we note that its impact is asymptotically very simple: it contributes a factor 2 to our lower bound. Therefore, one may prefer the rely on a halved lower bound.

6.2   Volumetric Bound for Step 4

We start by noting that we cannot apply Proposition 1 directly to our pseudo-norm, the issue being the lack of homogeneity: $\{x \in H \mid \|x\|_\wr \leq r\} \neq r \cdot \{x \in H \mid \|x\|_\wr \leq 1\}$. Fortunately, there seems to be a reasonably close asymmetric norm $\|x\|_{+\infty} = \max_i x_i$ that can be used to bound the pseudo-norm $\|x\|_\wr$.[3] Note that, on the space H, it differs from the usual ℓ_∞ norm by ignoring negative coefficients. For any $x \in H$, we have the inequalities

$$\|x\|_{+\infty} + \ln(\sqrt{n}) \geq \|x\|_\wr \geq \|x\|_{+\infty} + \ln(\sqrt{2}) \tag{8}$$

The asymmetric unit ball $\mathcal{B}_{+\infty}$ for the $\|\cdot\|_{+\infty}$ asymmetric norm is the $(d-1)$-simplex whose d vertices that are a permutation of $(1, \ldots, 1, 1-d)$. Its volume is given by $\mathrm{Vol}(\mathcal{B}_{+\infty}) = d^{d-1/2}/(d-1)!$, and we have $\mathrm{Vol}(\mathcal{B}_{+\infty})^{1/(d-1)} \to e$.

On the other hand, According to Theorem 3, the root volume of the log-unit lattice satisfies $\mathrm{Vol}(\Lambda)^{1/(d-1)} \sim \sqrt{n}/2$ for any prime conductors m. Such an approximation is numerically satisfied up to a 1% error for primes

---

[3] To verify that $\|\cdot\|_{+\infty}$ is indeed an asymmetric norm over H, we recall that vector space H is $\{x \in \mathbb{R}^d \mid \sum x_i = 0\}$: there is always one coordinate that is positive.

$m \in [100, 2000]$, as can be verified with the script `verification.py`. We therefore conclude that:

$$r(\Lambda, \| \cdot \|_{+\infty}) \sim \frac{\sqrt{n}}{2e} \approx 0.1839 \cdot \sqrt{n} \tag{9}$$

Remark 6. We note that our concrete lower bound is also asymptotically better than the one given in [CDPR16]. The reason is that it is based on Theorem 3 stating that $\mathrm{Vol}(\Lambda)^{1/(d-1)} \sim \sqrt{n}/2$, while [CDPR16] relied on the inequality $\mathrm{Vol}(\Lambda)^{1/(d-1)} \geq \Omega(\sqrt{n}/\log n)$. This $1/\log(n)$ factor comes from cumulating the approximation factors from Landau's estimate for L-functions at 1 [Lan27] over all non-trivial character. Our Theorem 3 shows that Landau's approximations essentially cancel out under geometric average over all characters.

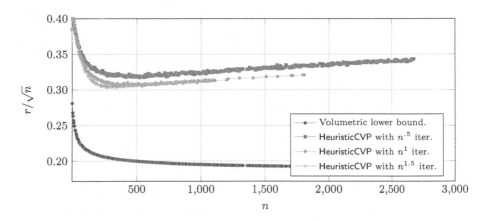

Fig. 4. Numerically computed lower bound $r := r(\Lambda, \| \cdot \|_{+\infty}) + \ln(\sqrt{2})$, compared to the experimental behavior of HeuristicCVP.

7   Conclusion

7.1   Summary

In Table 1 we summarize the asymptotic behavior of the algorithms and lower bounds studied in the previous sections.

Recall from formula (5) that the Hermite factor is

$$\eta = \Delta_K^{-\frac{1}{2n}} \cdot \exp\left(\frac{\ln p}{n} \cdot \|v - e\|_1 + \|l - t\|_i\right),$$

where p is the smallest prime such that $p \equiv 1 \bmod m$. We can now predict the concrete Hermite factor of the quantum algorithms for Ideal-SVP.

Table 1. Asymptotic summary.

	Step 2 $\|v - e\|_1$	Step 4 $\|l - t\|_2$
Naive algorithms from [CDW17,CDPR16]	$0.039 \cdot n^{3/2}$	$0.32 \cdot \sqrt{n \ln n}$
HeuristicCVP with $n^{3/2}$ iterations	$0.032 \cdot n^{3/2}$	$0.117 \cdot \sqrt{n \ln n}$
Volumetric lower bound	$0.02927 \cdot n^{3/2}$	$0.1839 \cdot \sqrt{n}$
Halved volumetric lower bound (Remark 5)	$0.01463 \cdot n^{3/2}$	N/A

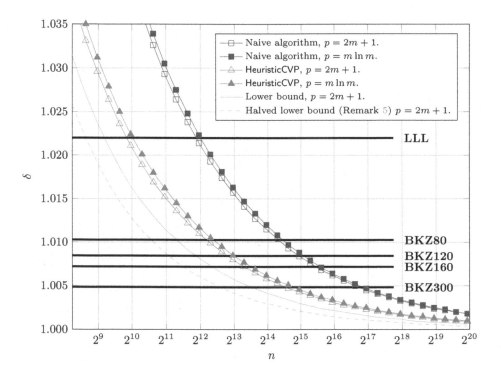

Fig. 5. Quality of Quantum Ideal-SVP vs. LLL and BKZ.

7.2 Comparison with Classical Algorithms

We now compare our prediction to the classical algorithms LLL and BKZ. For this comparison, we will consider the smallest possible value for $p = 2m + 1$ and the expected value $p = m \ln m$ derived from prime density. This comparison is provided in Fig. 5, using the root Hermite factor $\delta = \eta^{1/n}$.

We provide the reference root Hermite factors for LLL and BKZ with block-sizes $\beta \in \{80, 120, 160, 300\}$. The LLL algorithm is the cheapest lattice reduction available, and it should be noted that the quantum steps [EHKS14] 1 and 3 also make several quantum calls to LLL: the computational cost of the quantum algorithm is therefore bounded below by the cost of LLL.[4] The cost of BKZ grows exponentially or even super-exponentially with β, depending on the choice of algorithm. Nevertheless, BKZ-80 remains a reasonably easy computation (say, about $8m$ core-minutes), while BKZ-120 is to be considered doable ($8m$ core-days). Running BKZ-160 is on the borderline of feasible: to this date, computational records almost correspond to one out of the $\approx 8m$ steps of such a lattice reduction [ADH+19, SG10]. Finally, BKZ-300 is roughly what is required to break the weakest lattice-based candidates to the NIST post-quantum standardization [ACD+18].

7.3 Conclusion

Our first conclusion is that the naive version of the quantum algorithm is not relevant for rings of ranks considered practical for use in cryptography, as it does not outperform classically feasible computation (BKZ-120) before prime conductor $m \approx 32000$. Nevertheless, our heuristic improvements allow to decrease this cross-over point down to $m \approx 6000$. Such a dimension is still one order of magnitude larger than what is used for NIST post-quantum standardization candidates, but is within the range of what is used by certain concrete Fully Homomorphic Encryption schemes, for example [HS15].

Finally, one may fear that further tricks could improve the heuristic CVP steps within [CDPR16, CDW17], and maybe reach the lower bound.[5] The conclusion is somewhat reassuring for NIST candidates, as the cross-over point with BKZ-300 should not happen before ring rank $n \approx 6000$, even given a perfect CVP oracle for the Log-unit lattice and the Stickelberger lattice: NIST candidates use cyclotomic rings of rank at most $n = 1024$.

While the body of this article is focused on prime conductors m, we also considered the powers of 2 conductors, and found that both the experimental behavior and the numerical lower bounds were slightly worse in the powers of 2 case. This is reported in Appendix A.

7.4 Limitations

To avoid any over-interpretation of our results, we summarize here the limits of what can be concluded from the present work.

---

[4] Unfortunately, while proved polynomial time, the algorithms of [EHKS14, BS16] have, to our knowledge not been the subject of refined complexity analysis. But already, one can note that the lower bound we suggest is far from tight, considering the overheads of running LLL quantumly rather than classically, and this, many times.

[5] We recall that this bound is plausibly not tight, that is, even a perfect CVP oracle may not be able to reach it; see Remark 4.

Limitation of the lower bounds. We first remind that this lower-bound is only probabilistic, i.e., Proposition 1 states that the probability that a target falls closer to the lattice by a factor $\alpha < 1$ is at most α^d. That is, it may not be impossible to rerandomize the input to bruteforce a better solution, but it will raise the cost of the algorithm to exponential time.

Moreover, it should be noted that these lower bounds apply only to algorithms that are slight variations of [CDPR16, CDW17]. It has been proved that ideas beyond this framework make it asymptotically possible to go below those lower bounds [PMHS19], but at the cost of a sub-exponential running time, together with an exponential amount of precomputation.

Limitation of the cryptanalytic impact. On the other hand, we also remind the reader that we have made several working assumptions for the sake of simplicity, putting ourselves in the most favorable set-up. In particular, if one were to need not 1 but 2 ideals to generate the class group, this would asymptotically double the constant for Step 2.

Most importantly, we also recall that this work only studies the concreteness of the first obstacle discussed in our introduction, while the second obstacle remains unsolved. That is, these results concern only Ideal-SVP, and it remains unclear how they could be generalized to Ring-SIS, Ring-LWE, or NTRU.

A   The Power of 2 Case

In this section we compare the power of 2 case to the prime case. The experimental behavior and lower bounds for step 2 and step 4 are given in Fig. 6. We see that the asymptotic lower bounds for the power of 2 case is similar to the prime case, yet for both step 2 and 4, the experimental behavior is slightly worse for the power of 2 case.

We also need to account for the inverse root discriminant, which is also a factor in final Hermite factor η given by Formula (5). A quick calculation shows that this factor is a similar function of the rank n in both cases. Indeed, when m is prime, the inverse root discriminant $|\Delta_K|^{-1/2n}$ appearing in the formula for the root Hermite factor (5) is given by

$$|\Delta_K|^{-1/2n} = m^{-(n-1)/2n} \sim 1/\sqrt{m} \sim 1/\sqrt{n}.$$

On the other hand for $m = 2^k$ we have

$$|\Delta_K|^{-1/2n} = 2^{-n(k-1)/2n} = 2^{(1-k)/2} = \sqrt{2/m} = 1/\sqrt{n}.$$

In conclusion, we expect that the quantum algorithm for Ideal-SVP at hand provides vectors slightly longer for power of 2 conductors than for prime conductors.

B   Estimation of the Regulator

In this appendix we prove Theorem 3, which states that for any prime power $m = p^k$, we have $(\mathrm{Vol}(\Lambda)/h^+)^{\frac{1}{n/2-1}} \sim \sqrt{m}/2$. First, we recall that the volume of

(a) Step 2: behavior of $\|v - e\|_1$

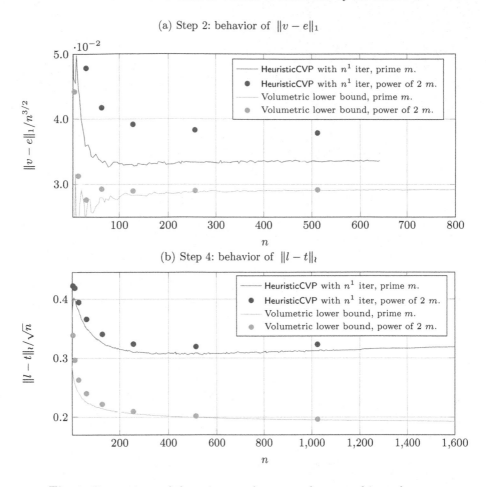

(b) Step 4: behavior of $\|l - t\|_l$

Fig. 6. Comparison of the prime conductors and power of 2 conductor.

the log-unit lattice is related to the so-called *regulator* R of K by the formula[6]

$$\mathrm{Vol}(\Lambda) = \frac{R\sqrt{n/2}}{2^{n/2-1}}.$$

Therefore $\mathrm{Vol}(\Lambda)^{\frac{1}{n/2-1}} \sim R^{\frac{1}{n/2-1}}/2$, and it remains to estimate Rh^+. Let Δ_{K^+} denote the discriminant of K^+, the maximal real subfield of K. We have that $|\Delta_{K^+}| = |\Delta_K/p|^{1/2}$ when m is a power of $p \neq 2$ (for $p = 2$, the following results should adjust for the fact that $|\Delta_{K^+}| = |\Delta_K/4|^{1/2}$). From [Was12, p. 42],

---

[6] The denominator $2^{n/2-1}$ may not be standard in the litterature, and is due to our definition of the logarithmic embedding. Indeed since the field at hand is totally complex, we only use one embedding from each pair of conjugate embeddings.

we get

$$Rh^+ = |\Delta_K/p|^{1/4} \prod_{\chi \neq 1 \text{ even}} L(1, \chi),$$

where the product is over all non-trivial even Dirichlet characters modulo m. We have

$$\log\left(\prod_{\chi \neq 1 \text{ even}} L(1, \chi)\right) = -\sum_\chi \sum_q \log\left(1 - \frac{\chi(q)}{q}\right)$$

$$= \sum_\chi \sum_q \sum_{i=1}^\infty \frac{\chi(q^i)}{iq^i}$$

$$= \sum_q \sum_{i=1}^\infty \frac{1}{iq^i} \sum_\chi \chi(q^i).$$

Since

$$\sum_\chi \chi(a) = \begin{cases} n/2 - 1 & \text{if } a \equiv \pm 1 \mod m, \\ -1 & \text{otherwise,} \end{cases}$$

we deduce that

$$\log\left(\prod_{\chi \neq 1 \text{ even}} L(1, \chi)\right) = \lim_{x \to \infty} \left(\frac{n-2}{2} \sum_{\substack{q^i \leq x \\ q^i \equiv \pm 1 \mod m}} \frac{1}{iq^i} - \sum_{\substack{q^i \leq x \\ q^i \not\equiv \pm 1 \mod m}} \frac{1}{iq^i}\right).$$

Let us first deal with the terms where $i = 1$. From [Pom77], for any a such that $(a, m) = 1$, we have

$$\sum_{\substack{q \leq x \\ q \equiv a \mod m}} \frac{1}{q} = \frac{\log\log(x)}{n} + \frac{1}{P(m, a)} + O\left(\frac{\log(m)}{n}\right),$$

where $P(m, a)$ is the first prime q such that $q \equiv a \mod m$. We get

$$\lim_{x \to \infty} \left(\frac{n-2}{2} \sum_{\substack{q \leq x \\ q \equiv 1 \mod m}} \frac{1}{q} - \sum_{\substack{q \leq x \\ q \not\equiv \pm 1 \mod m}} \frac{1}{q}\right)$$

$$= \frac{n-2}{2P(m, 1)} + \frac{n-2}{2P(m, -1)} - \sum_{\substack{a \in \{2, \dots, m-2\} \\ (a, m) = 1}} \frac{1}{P(m, a)} + O(\log(m))$$

$$= O(\log(m)).$$

For the terms where $i \geq 2$, we have from [AC49] that

$$\sum_{i \geq 2} \sum_{\substack{q^i \leq x \\ q^i \equiv \pm 1 \mod m}} \frac{1}{iq^i} = O(1/m).$$

The proof in [AC49] is given for m prime, but is easily adapted to powers of primes. We deduce that

$$\log \left(\prod_{\chi \neq 1 \text{ even}} L(1, \chi) \right) = O(\log(m)).$$

We get the estimate

$$\left(R h^+ \right)^{\frac{1}{n/2-1}} = p^{\frac{p^{k-1}(pk-k-1)-1}{2(n-2)}} e^{O\left(\frac{\log(m)}{n} \right)} = m^{\frac{1}{2}+o(1)},$$

from which we conclude that $(\mathrm{Vol}(\Lambda)/h^+)^{\frac{1}{n/2-1}} \sim \sqrt{m}/2$.

References

[AC49] Ankeny, N.C., Chowla, S.: The class number of the cyclotomic field. Proc. Natl. Acad. Sci. **35**(9), 529–532 (1949)

[ACD+18] Albrecht, M.R., et al.: Estimate all the {LWE, NTRU} schemes! (2018). https://doi.org/10.1007/978-3-319-98113-0_19

[ADH+19] Albrecht, M.R., Ducas, L., Herold, G., Kirshanova, E., Postlethwaite, E.W., Stevens, M.: The general sieve kernel and new records in lattice reduction. Cryptology ePrint Archive, Report 2019/089 (2019). https://eprint.iacr.org/2019/089, https://doi.org/10.1007/978-3-030-17656-3_25

[Ajt99] Ajtai, M.: Generating hard instances of the short basis problem. In: Wiedermann, J., van Emde Boas, P., Nielsen, M. (eds.) ICALP 1999. LNCS, vol. 1644, pp. 1–9. Springer, Heidelberg (1999). https://doi.org/10.1007/3-540-48523-6_1

[Bab86] Babai, L.: On Lovász' lattice reduction and the nearest lattice point problem. Combinatorica **6**(1), 1–13 (1986). Preliminary version in STACS 1985

[BCLvV17] Bernstein, D.J., Chuengsatiansup, C., Lange, T., van Vredendaal, C.: NTRU prime: reducing attack surface at low cost. In: Adams, C., Camenisch, J. (eds.) SAC 2017. LNCS, vol. 10719, pp. 235–260. Springer, Cham (2018). https://doi.org/10.1007/978-3-319-72565-9_12

[BS16] Biasse, J.-F., Song, F.: Efficient quantum algorithms for computing class groups and solving the principal ideal problem in arbitrary degree number fields. In: Proceedings of the Twenty-Seventh Annual ACM-SIAM Symposium on Discrete Algorithms, pp. 893–902. SIAM (2016)

[CDPR16] Cramer, R., Ducas, L., Peikert, C., Regev, O.: Recovering short generators of principal ideals in cyclotomic rings. In: Fischlin, M., Coron, J.-S. (eds.) EUROCRYPT 2016. LNCS, vol. 9666, pp. 559–585. Springer, Heidelberg (2016). https://doi.org/10.1007/978-3-662-49896-5_20

[CDW17] Cramer, R., Ducas, L., Wesolowski, B.: Short Stickelberger class relations and application to ideal-SVP. In: Coron, J.-S., Nielsen, J.B. (eds.) EUROCRYPT 2017. LNCS, vol. 10210, pp. 324–348. Springer, Cham (2017). https://doi.org/10.1007/978-3-319-56620-7_12

[CGS14] Campbell, P., Groves, M., Shepherd, D.: Soliloquy: a cautionary tale. In: ETSI 2nd Quantum-Safe Crypto Workshop (2014). http://docbox.etsi. org/Workshop/2014/201410_CRYPTO/S07_Systems_and_Attacks/ S07_Groves_Annex.pdf

[CN11] Chen, Y., Nguyen, P.Q.: BKZ 2.0: better lattice security estimates. In: Lee, D.H., Wang, X. (eds.) ASIACRYPT 2011. LNCS, vol. 7073, pp. 1–20. Springer, Heidelberg (2011). https://doi.org/10.1007/978-3-642-25385-0_1

[DB15] Dadush, D., Bonifas, N.: Short paths on the Voronoi graph and closest vector problem with preprocessing. In: Proceedings of the Twenty-Sixth Annual ACM-SIAM Symposium on Discrete Algorithms, pp. 295–314. Society for Industrial and Applied Mathematics (2015)

[DLdW19] Doulgerakis, E., Laarhoven, T., de Weger, B.: Finding closest lattice vectors using approximate Voronoi cells. In: Ding, J., Steinwandt, R. (eds.) PQCrypto 2019. LNCS, vol. 11505, pp. 3–22. Springer, Cham (2019). https://eprint.iacr.org/2016/888

[Duc17] Ducas, L.: Advances on quantum cryptanalysis of ideal lattices. Nieuw Archief voor Wiskunde **5**, 184–189 (2017)

[EHKS14] Eisenträger, K., Hallgren, S., Kitaev, A., Song, F.: A quantum algorithm for computing the unit group of an arbitrary degree number field. In: STOC, pp. 293–302. ACM (2014)

[HPS98] Hoffstein, J., Pipher, J., Silverman, J.H.: NTRU: a ring-based public key cryptosystem. In: Buhler, J.P. (ed.) ANTS 1998. LNCS, vol. 1423, pp. 267–288. Springer, Heidelberg (1998). https://doi.org/10.1007/BFb0054868

[HS15] Halevi, S., Shoup, V.: Bootstrapping for HElib. In: Oswald, E., Fischlin, M. (eds.) EUROCRYPT 2015. LNCS, vol. 9056, pp. 641–670. Springer, Heidelberg (2015). https://doi.org/10.1007/978-3-662-46800-5_25

[JW18] Jetchev, D., Wesolowski, B.P.C.: Horizontal isogeny graphs of ordinary abelian varieties and the discrete logarithm problem. Acta Arithmetica (2018, in press)

[Laa16] Laarhoven, T.: Finding closest lattice vectors using approximate Voronoi cells. In: Published at SAC 2016 (2016). https://eprint.iacr.org/2016/888/ 20161219:141310

[Lan27] Landau, E.: Über Dirichletsche Reihen mit komplexen Charakteren. Journal für die reine und angewandte Mathematik **157**, 26–32 (1927)

[Len75] Lenstra Jr., H.W.: Euclid's algorithm in cyclotomic fields. J. London Math. Soc. **10**, 457–465 (1975)

[Lep74] Lepistö, T.: On the growth of the first factor of the class number of the prime cyclotomic field. Ann. Acad. Sci. Fenn. Ser. **577**(Ser. A I), 1–21 (1974)

[LLL82] Lenstra, A.K., Lenstra Jr., H.W., Lovász, L.: Factoring polynomials with rational coefficients. Math. Ann. **261**(4), 515–534 (1982)

[LPR10] Lyubashevsky, V., Peikert, C., Regev, O.: On ideal lattices and learning with errors over rings. In: Gilbert, H. (ed.) EUROCRYPT 2010. LNCS, vol. 6110, pp. 1–23. Springer, Heidelberg (2010). https://doi.org/10.1007/ 978-3-642-13190-5_1

[LPR13] Lyubashevsky, V., Peikert, C., Regev, O.: On ideal lattices and learning with errors over rings. J. ACM **60**(6), 43:1–43:35 (2013). Preliminary version in Eurocrypt 2010

[Mic07] Micciancio, D.: Generalized compact knapsacks, cyclic lattices, and effi-
         cient one-way functions. Comput. Complex. **16**(4), 365–411 (2007). Pre-
         liminary version in FOCS 2002
[MV10]   Micciancio, D., Voulgaris, P.: A deterministic single exponential time algo-
         rithm for most lattice problems based on Voronoi cell computations. In:
         STOC, pp. 351–358 (2010)
[NS06]   Nguyen, P.Q., Stehlé, D.: LLL on the average. In: Hess, F., Pauli, S., Pohst,
         M. (eds.) ANTS 2006. LNCS, vol. 4076, pp. 238–256. Springer, Heidelberg
         (2006). https://doi.org/10.1007/11792086_18
[PMHS19] Pellet-Mary, A., Hanrot, G., Stehlé, D.: Approx-SVP in ideal lat-
         tices with pre-processing. Cryptology ePrint Archive, Report 2019/215
         (2019). https://eprint.iacr.org/2019/215. To appear at EUROCRYPT
         2019. https://doi.org/10.1007/978-3-030-17656-3_24
[Pom77] Pomerance, C.: On the distribution of amicable numbers. J. Reine Angew.
         Math. **293**(294), 217–222 (1977)
[PRSD17] Peikert, C., Regev, O., Stephens-Davidowitz, N.: Pseudorandomness of
         ring-LWE for any ring and modulus. In: Proceedings of the 49th Annual
         ACM SIGACT Symposium on Theory of Computing, pp. 461–473. ACM
         (2017)
[Reg09] Regev, O.: On lattices, learning with errors, random linear codes, and
         cryptography. J. ACM **56**(6), 1–40 (2009). Preliminary version in STOC
         2005
[Sch98] Schoof, R.: Minus class groups of the fields of the l-th roots of unity. Math.
         Comput. Am. Math. Soc. **67**(223), 1225–1245 (1998)
[Sch03] Schoof, R.: Class numbers of real cyclotomic fields of prime conductor.
         Math. Comput. **72**(242), 913–937 (2003)
[Sch10] Schoof, R.: Catalan's Conjecture. Springer, London (2010). https://doi.
         org/10.1007/978-1-84800-185-5
[SD19]   Stephens-Davidowitz, N.: A time-distance trade-off for GDD with
         preprocessing—instantiating the DLW heuristic. arXiv (2019). https://
         arxiv.org/abs/1902.08340
[SG10]   Schneider, M., Gama, N.: Darmstadt SVP challenges (2010). https://www.
         latticechallenge.org/svp-challenge/index.php. Accessed 02 Feb 2019
[Sin80] Sinnott, W.: On the Stickelberger ideal and the circular units of an abelian
         field. Inventiones Math. **62**, 181–234 (1980)
[SS11]   Stehlé, D., Steinfeld, R.: Making NTRU as secure as worst-case problems
         over ideal lattices. In: Paterson, K.G. (ed.) EUROCRYPT 2011. LNCS,
         vol. 6632, pp. 27–47. Springer, Heidelberg (2011). https://doi.org/10.1007/
         978-3-642-20465-4_4
[SSTX09] Stehlé, D., Steinfeld, R., Tanaka, K., Xagawa, K.: Efficient public key
         encryption based on ideal lattices. In: Matsui, M. (ed.) ASIACRYPT 2009.
         LNCS, vol. 5912, pp. 617–635. Springer, Heidelberg (2009). https://doi.
         org/10.1007/978-3-642-10366-7_36
[SV10]   Smart, N.P., Vercauteren, F.: Fully homomorphic encryption with rela-
         tively small key and ciphertext sizes. In: Nguyen, P.Q., Pointcheval, D.
         (eds.) PKC 2010. LNCS, vol. 6056, pp. 420–443. Springer, Heidelberg
         (2010). https://doi.org/10.1007/978-3-642-13013-7_25
[Was12] Washington, L.C.: Introduction to Cyclotomic Fields, vol. 83. Springer,
         New York (2012)
[Wes18] Wesolowski, B.P.C.: Arithmetic and geometric structures in cryptography.
         Ph.D. thesis, EPFL (2018)

Proofs of Storage

Proofs of Replicated Storage
Without Timing Assumptions

Ivan Damgård, Chaya Ganesh[✉], and Claudio Orlandi[✉]

Computer Science Department, DIGIT, Aarhus University, Aarhus, Denmark
{ivan,ganesh,orlandi}@cs.au.dk

Abstract. In this paper we provide a formal treatment of *proof of replicated storage*, a novel cryptographic primitive recently proposed in the context of a novel cryptocurrency, namely Filecoin.

In a nutshell, proofs of replicated storage is a solution to the following problem: A user stores a file m on n different servers to ensure that the file will be available even if some of the servers fail. Using proof of retrievability, the user could check that every server is indeed storing the file. However, what if the servers collude and, in order to save on resources, decide to only store one copy of the file? A proof of replicated storage guarantees that, unless the (potentially colluding) servers are indeed reserving the space necessary to store n copies of the file, the user will not accept the proofs. While some candidate proofs of replicated storage have already been proposed, their soundness relies on timing assumptions i.e., the user must reject the proof if the prover does not reply within a certain time-bound.

In this paper we provide the first construction of a proof of replication which does not rely on any timing assumptions.

1 Introduction

Consider a scenario where a user A wants to use the cloud or some other decentralized network of servers to store and distribute some file m to other users. To make sure she and other users will be able to access the file later on, A stores several replicas of m in different locations. However, A suspects that the servers she is using are adversarial and may collude, for instance to save on costs by using less space than they are supposed to. So she will be interested in checking that indeed unique space has been dedicated to each replica, and it is natural to require that this can be verified, even if all servers are controlled by an adversary. We will call this *proof of replication*.

A first issue to note is that the well-known notions of proof of retrievability or proof of space (which we discuss in more detail below) do not solve the problem if

This work was supported by the: Protocol Labs RFP Program; Danish Independent Research Council under Grant-ID DFF-6108-00169 (FoCC); European Research Council (ERC) under the European Unions's Horizon 2020 research and innovation program under grant agreement No. 669255 (MPCPRO) and No. 803096 (SPEC); Concordium Blockchain Research Center, Aarhus University, Denmark.

A. Boldyreva and D. Micciancio (Eds.): CRYPTO 2019, LNCS 11692, pp. 355–380, 2019.
https://doi.org/10.1007/978-3-030-26948-7_13

each replica is simply a copy of m. Such proofs allow a user to check that a given file is retrievable from a server, much more efficiently than by simply retrieving the file. However, even if A asks for a proof of retrievability of m from each of the servers and all these proofs are successful, this may simply be because the user is actually talking to the adversary who stores only a single copy of m.

Another idea that comes to mind is that A could let each replica be an encryption of m under some key K, but with fresh randomness for each replica. If the encryption is IND-CPA secure, the adversary cannot distinguish this from encryptions of random independent messages, and hence it seems they are forced to store all replicas in order for them to be retrievable later. While this intuition can in fact be proved, this would not be a satisfactory solution: recall that we want that anyone, not just A, can retrieve the original file, so A would have to share K with other users. However, if any of these users collude with the adversary, the security breaks down. Besides, a solution that does not require A to store secret information for later is clearly more practical.

The idea of proof of replication was introduced in Filecoin [Lab17a, Lab17b], a decentralized storage network[1]. They articulate a list of properties that they desire from such a notion. They define a *Sybil attack* which is exactly what we discussed above: if an honest client wishes to store the same file m on n different servers, an adversary can store these using sybil identities (all servers are controlled by one adversary) and successfully pass the storage audit, while essentially storing only one copy of the file.

While the Filecoin paper does not give a formal treatment of proof of replication, they propose a construction for what they call a time-bounded proof of replication. In such a notion, the file to be stored is encoded so that the encoding process is slow: slow enough for a client to distinguish between honest proving time, and potentially adversarial proving time which includes the time to re-encode. Thus, the encoding process is, by design, distinguishably more expensive than honest proving time. This notion is realized by using a block-cipher and slowing it down by block chaining, and a time-bounded proof of replication is a proof of storage of a replica that is encoded in this way.

The basic problem with all time-bounded schemes is the handling of recomputing attack: the encoding has to be made so slow that even a powerful server cannot encode faster than the time a proof takes. This is harder than it may seem at first: even if we know for sure how many operations are needed to encode for a given value of security parameter, the actual time it takes depends on the hardware held by the adversarial parties, and so is beyond the control of honest users. This makes a concrete choice of parameters very difficult: should we compensate for the adversary being more powerful than we expect and choose a very slow encoding thus making life harder also for honest clients when they encode? Or should we choose parameters more aggressively and run a bigger risk of being cheated? It would clearly be better if we did not have to make such a choice.

---

[1] Other related notions in the context of data replication have been studied earlier in the cryptographic literature; we discuss the connection and differences in the related work section.

We ask if we can do better in all the above aspects: can we have a proof of replication scheme that provably resists sybil attacks, and is not time-bounded?

Our Results. We give a formal treatment of proofs of replication, by giving a definition that captures the desired properties as well as a construction which we prove secure according to the definition. The construction works in the random oracle model and can be instantiated from any one-way permutation. We concentrate on the case where the client doing the encoding is honest, as this seems to be the most important case in practice, and is in line with the definitions of proof of retrievability and storage.

Each replica of the file m to be stored in our construction has size $O(|m|+\kappa)$, where $|m|$ is the length of m and κ is the security parameter. To verify replication, the user conducts a proof of retrievability with each server. Any such proof can be used, so we inherit whatever communication complexity that proof has.

Very roughly speaking, the idea in our solution is that the adversary first receives each of the replicas to store, where each replica is a special encoding of m. The adversary may now store a state for later use, which in the honest case would contain all replicas. What we show is that, no matter how the adversary computes the state, if it is significantly smaller than the combined size of all replicas, then some of the proofs of retrievability will fail, unless the adversary breaks a computational assumption.

Let us consider what this exactly guarantees us. Since the proofs of retrievability are *extractable*, the above guarantees that the replicas cannot be compressed i.e., the adversary must reserve enough space to store all replicas, and this space must contain some data which is equivalent (up to polynomial time computation) to the replicas of the file. But is this the best we can do? Why don't we ask that the adversary in fact stores a concatenation of all the replicas? Unfortunately, this is impossible to achieve: even honest servers will most likely store the same information in different formats (think of *little-* vs. *big-endian* representation). So we certainly cannot expect that the adversary will store exactly the same data that was received from the client. However, this should not matter from a security point of view, as long as the original data can be efficiently recovered.

In conclusion: it is impossible to force the corrupted servers to store *exactly* the n replicas or n copies of the file. Therefore, the best we can hope for is what we do in this paper: no matter how the corrupted servers behave, it is possible to recover n distinct, incompressible encodings of the same file, thus the servers cannot pass the verification unless they reserve the necessary space for all replicas. Note, however, that in such a scenario, the corrupted servers have no incentive to do anything else than simply store the replicas.

The main difference between our work and previously proposed solutions to the problem, is that our solution does not require the use of *time*: while the original, informal definition of proof of replication states that it should be hard for the server to recompute the encodings of the file in the time it takes to verify the proof, our definition is much stronger as it rules out that any polynomially bounded attacker who uses less storage than claimed can pass the verification. As discussed above, this makes implementing proof of replications much easier, since one does not need to worry about finding an appropriate value for the verifier timeout.

To avoid misunderstandings, we emphasize that even if our definitions and proof work with a single adversary that handles all replicas, the actual use case includes several servers that each store one replica (if they are honest). Since it is clearly impossible to check if a server stores something without talking to that server, the communication complexity of our protocol must be proportional to the number of servers[2].

Finally, our main construction achieves public verifiability in the sense that if the encoder is honest, then anyone can interact with the servers and verify the proofs. At the end of the paper we discuss extensions which allow to cope with malicious encoders.

1.1 Related Work

Proofs of retrievability. A lot of user data today is outsourced for storage on the cloud both because of large volumes of data, and for reliability in case of failure of local storage. The problem with cloud storage is that of maintaining integrity of data and enforcing accountability of the storage provider. Proofs of retrievability, first formalized by Juels and Kaliski in [JK07] address this problem by allowing for audits. In a proof of retrievability, a client can store a file on the server, while storing (a short) verification string locally. In an audit protocol, the client acts as the verifier and the server proves that it possesses the client's file. The property that the server "possesses" a file is formalized by the existence of an extractor that retrieves the client's file from a server that makes a client accept in the audit protocol. Since their introduction, there have been several works [SW08, DVW09] constructing proof of retrievability schemes with a proof of security and efficient audit procedures. One property we prioritize in this work is *public verifiability* where any party can take the role of the verifier in the audit protocol, not just the client who originally stored the file. This means the client's state storing any verification information for the file should not contain any secrets. The construction of [SW08] gives a proof of retrievability scheme secure in the random oracle model that allows public verifiability.

Proofs of space. A proof of space is a protocol where a prover convinces a verifier that it has dedicated a significant amount of disk-space. Proofs of space were introduced in [DFKP15] as an alternative to proof of work (PoW), and further studied in [RD16, AAC+17]. There have been proposals based on proof of space like chia network [chi17] and Spacemint [PPK+15]. Very roughly, a proof of space gives the guarantee that it is more "expensive" for a malicious server that dedicates less space than an honest server to successfully pass an audit.

---

[2] Of course, if a single server would store all replicas, we can optimize the communication needed, this is also easy to see for our protocol, but this hardly seems like an interesting use case.

Data replication. Curtmola et al. [CKBA08] and Barsoum et al. [BH11] propose protocols that enable proofs of data replication in the private verifier model, where the client stores a secret key that is used for verification. The work of Hao and Yu [HY10] allows public verifiability but nevertheless requires the client to store a secret. The work of Etemad and Küpçü [EK13] studies replicated provable data possession, but does not formalize replicated storage, and the client need not be aware of any replication. Finally, the protocol of Armknecht et al. [ABBK16] is also in the private verification model, and in addition, uses RSA time-lock puzzles which results in a protocol with a time-bounded property that we elaborate on below.

Filecoin. Filecoin is a decentralized storage network [Lab17a]. Essentially this can be seen as a network of independent storage providers that offer verifiable file storage and retrieval services. In the Filecoin protocol, miners earn protocol tokens by providing data storage services.

To be used in the Filecoin context, a proof of replicated storage should satisfy several properties. First, the scheme should protect against Sybil attacks as described above e.g., a corrupt server should not be able to impersonate n different servers while storing a single copy of the file. Then, the scheme should be publicly verifiable, meaning that any user (not only the original encoder) should be able to verify the proof. It is also crucial that the security definition allows the adversary to choose the file m. This is because an adversary could request for m to be stored, and then prove that m was stored to collect network rewards. Finally, the scheme should be resilient against *generation attacks*, meaning that the adversary should not be able to reconstruct an encoding "on the fly" when a proof of storage is requested.

Our main construction cannot be directly used in the Filecoin context since the soundness of the proof relies on the encoder being honest. Thus, a malicious encoder colluding with malicious servers could perform a generation attack i.e., persuade other users that some servers are storing several copies of a file without reserving any space. At the end of the paper, we discuss how to extend our solution to handle malicious clients too.

Time-bounded Proofs of Replication. In a recent work by Pietrzak [Pie18], a construction for proof of replication based on proof of space is given. A proof of replication is not formally defined, and therefore it is not clear what is the replication property that the construction satisfies. In addition, since a proof of space is the starting point of the construction, it has the same "time-bounded" property as the Filecoin construction, since a malicious server can pass the audit by recomputing data. More recently, [FBBG18, BBBF18, CFMJ18, Fis18] construct proofs of replication based on slow encodings. They have the same time-bounded flavour of other recent works and is thus significantly different from ours.

Comparison with Hourglass scheme [VDJO+12]. We note that our construction and the construction of [VDJO+12] are reminiscent of each other; at a high level both involve repeated applications of inversion of a trapdoor permutation and a random permutation. However, there are differences in both the goals and the details of the constructions.

The difference between the goal of the present work and the Hourglass schemes can be summarized as follows: Hourglass only tries to guarantee incompressibility of a single encoding (such that the original file can be recovered), whereas the goal of our proof of replicated storage is to get different incompressible encodings to be stored on independent servers, such that the original file can be recovered interacting with a single server. Regarding the constructions, our work applies the random permutation over all blocks of the file and produces randomized and independent encodings to be stored on each server, which makes a notable difference in the our analysis[3].

1.2 Technical Overview

The existing time-bounded proofs use a public deterministic encoding function. The problem is that this always allow a malicious server to recompute encoded data and this may lead to a successful recomputation attack if the server has sufficient computational resources. Our observation is that one can instead make the encoding be probabilistic. Now the adversary will only see the encoded data but not the randomness that the client used to encode. One may therefore hope that recomputing an encoding is not only slow, but completely unfeasible. On the other hand, decoding must still be easy for anyone.

To illustrate the idea of our solution, we start with a toy example: we assume that we are given oracle access to a random permutation T, and its inverse[4], acting on strings $\{0,1\}^n$. As is well known (and discussed in detail later) we can instantiate such an oracle in the standard random oracle model. In order to create replicas of a file, A will generate an instance of a one-way trapdoor permutation $f : \{0,1\}^n \mapsto \{0,1\}^n$, with trapdoor t_f. For simplicity, we assume that the file m to store is an $(n - \log n)$-bit string. Then the i'th replica is defined to be $(f, f^{-1}(T(m||i)))$, where $||$ denotes concatenation and f is a specification of the 1-way permutation. Clearly, anyone can easily compute m from a replica by computing f in the forward direction and calling T^{-1}. It turns out that this construction is secure if the adversary computes the state to store for later in a very restricted way, namely he forgets all information about at least one replica, say the i'th one. Namely, the adversary forgets both the encoding $(f, f^{-1}(T(m||i)))$ and the intermediate value $T(m||i)$.

---

[3] It is hard to compare our analysis with that of Hourglass since in [VDJO+12] only an informal security argument of incompressibility is given.

[4] One can think of the random permutation T as a random oracle which can be invoked in both directions.

We can now argue that if the adversary is nevertheless able to produce the i'th replica, he will have to invert the one-way permutation: from the output of the adversary $(f, f^{-1}(T(m||i)))$ we can (as the encoding can be decoded efficiently), extract $T(m||i)$. But, we assumed that the state did not contain any information about this value (except for a negligible amount following from the fact that it must be different from other outputs). Hence he must call the oracle to get $T(m||i)$. Therefore, in a security reduction, we can take a challenge value y and reprogram T such that $T(m||i) = y$. Now, the i'th replica (that we assumed the adversary could produce) is exactly the preimage of y under f.

Of course, we cannot reasonably assume that the adversary behaves in this simple-minded way. As mentioned, we only want to assume that the state stored is smaller than the combined size of the replicas, say by a constant factor. To overcome this problem, we iterate the above construction several times, so that T is called several times while preparing a replica. Now there are many more outputs from T than the adversary can remember, and we show that by the setting the parameters right, at least one of these is almost uniform in the view of the adversary. Now we can place a challenge value for the one-way permutation in this position by an argument similar to the above.

2   Preliminaries

Notation. We denote the concatenation of two bit strings x and y by $x||y$. Throughout, we use κ to denote the security parameter. We denote a probabilistic polynomial time algorithm by PPT. A function is negligible if for all large enough values of the input, it is smaller than the inverse of any polynomial. We use negl to denote a negligible function. We use $[1, n]$ to represent the set of numbers $\{1, 2, \ldots, n\}$. For a randomized algorithm Alg, we use $y \leftarrow \mathsf{Alg}(x)$ to denote that y is the output of Alg on x. We write $y \xleftarrow{R} \mathcal{Y}$ to mean sampling a value y uniformly from the set $\mathcal{Y}$.

2.1   Trapdoor Permutations

A collection of trapdoor permutations is a family $\mathcal{F} = \{f_{pk} : \mathcal{D}_{pk} \to \mathcal{D}_{pk}\}$ such that:

- There exists a PPT algorithm KeyGen such that $(pk, sk) \leftarrow \mathsf{KeyGen}(1^\kappa)$, f_{pk} is a permutation.
- There exists a PPT algorithm that given pk samples uniformly from $\mathcal{D}_{pk}$.
- There exists a PPT algorithm that on input pk and $x \in \mathcal{D}_{pk}$, computes $f_{pk}(x)$.
- There exists a PPT algorithm that on input sk and $f_{pk}(x)$, computes x, that is, $f_{sk}^{-1}(f_{pk}(x)) = x$.

Definition 1. *A trapdoor permutation family* $\mathcal{F} = \{f_{pk} : \mathcal{D}_{pk} \to \mathcal{D}_{pk}\}$ *is said to be hard to invert if the following holds: for all PPT algorithms A, there exists a negligible function* negl *such that*

$$\Pr[f_{pk}(z) = y : (pk, sk) \leftarrow \mathsf{KeyGen}(1^\kappa), x \leftarrow \mathcal{D}_{pk}, y \leftarrow f_{pk}(x),$$
$$z \leftarrow A(pk, y)] \leq \mathsf{negl}(\kappa)$$

When the domain and range is clear from context, we omit the subscript pk and only write $\mathcal{D}$.

Definition 2. *We call a trapdoor permutation family a B-leakage trapdoor permutation if the following holds: For all PPT algorithms (A_1, A_2), there exists a negligible function* negl *such that*

$$\Pr[f_{pk}(z) = y : (pk, sk) \leftarrow \mathsf{KeyGen}(1^\kappa), x \leftarrow \mathcal{D}_{pk},$$
$$L \leftarrow A_1(x, pk), y \leftarrow f_{pk}(x), z \leftarrow A_2(y, L(x))] \leq \mathsf{negl}(\kappa)$$

where the output length of L is bounded by B bits.

Note that every trapdoor function family is also a B-leakage trapdoor permutation family for $B = \log \kappa$.

RSA trapdoor permutation. The RSA trapdoor permutation is given by:

- $\mathsf{KeyGen}(1^\kappa)$: Choose κ-bit primes p, q, let $N = pq$. Choose e such that $\gcd(e, (p-1)(q-1)) = 1$, let d be such that $ed = 1 \bmod (p-1)(q-1)$. Return $(pk = (e, N), sk = d)$.
- For $x \in \mathbb{Z}_N^*$, given $pk = (e, N)$, compute $f_{pk}(x) = y = x^e \bmod N$.
- For $y \in \mathbb{Z}_N^*$, and $sk = d$, compute $f_{sk}^{-1}(y) = y^d \bmod N$

The RSA inversion problem is assumed to be hard for any $\mathcal{A}$ running in time polynomial in κ.

Invertible Random Oracle. We assume the algorithms of the construction and the adversary have access to an invertible random oracle (IRO): that is oracle access to $\Pi : \mathcal{D} \to \mathcal{D}$ and $\Pi^{-1} : \mathcal{D} \to \mathcal{D}$.

We discuss here how to plausibly implement such an oracle: The indifferentiability framework, first proposed by Maurer et al. [MRH04], informally says that given ideal primitives G and F, a construction C^G is indifferentiable from F, if there exists a simulator S with oracle access to F such that (C^G, G) is indistinguishable from (F, S^F). Coron et al. [CHK+16] showed that a 14-round Feistel network where the round functions are independent random oracles is indifferentiable from a random permutation. A series of subsequent works [DKT16, DS16] show that 8 rounds is sufficient. Thus, using a Feistel network appears like a plausible way of instantiating the oracle we need.

Unfortunately, the indifferentiability composition theorem is not known to apply to security notions that are captured by games that have multiple stages [RSS11]. Our security notion of proof of replication is captured using a multi-stage game, and therefore the result of [RSS11] applies.

Therefore, the construction described below should only be seen as a plausible instantiation of an invertible random oracle.

A plausible oracle instantiation. In our constructions, we make use of an invertible random oracle H that acts on strings of arbitrary length, and an invertible random oracle T that has the same domain as a trapdoor permutation. H is instantiated using a regular Feistel network. In the following we discuss an heuristic instantiation of T on pairs of outputs of RSA and obtain trapdoor permutation f and IRO T with the same domain.

We define a trapdoor permutation $f : (\mathbb{Z}_N)^2 \to (\mathbb{Z}_N)^2$ as follows: $f(x_1, x_2) = (f'(x_1), f'(x_2))$ where f' is the RSA permutation $f' : \mathbb{Z}_N \to \mathbb{Z}_N$. Note that N is part of the public key of the RSA permutation. The input and output of T are elements in $(\mathbb{Z}_N)^2$. We note that we can instantiate the Feistel construction in this domain as well by replacing XOR with multiplication modulo N i.e., given a random oracle G that maps inputs in $\mathbb{Z}_N^*$ to strings that are twice the length, we can define $\mathcal{F} : (\mathbb{Z}_N)^2 \to (\mathbb{Z}_N)^2$ on pairs of values modulo N as follows:

$$\mathcal{F}^H(L\|R) = s\|t, \text{ where } s = L \cdot G(R) \bmod N, t = R \cdot G(s) \bmod N$$

where $\cdot$ is product modulo N. Note that $G(x) \bmod N$ is close to uniform in $\mathbb{Z}_N^*$, therefore, $\mathcal{F}$ is invertible except with negligible probability i.e., if $\mathcal{F}$ is not invertible then a non-trivial factor of N is found.

2.2 Proof of Retrievability

Proofs of retrievability, introduced by Juels and Kaliski [JK07] allow a client to store data on a server that is untrusted, and admit an *audit* protocol in which the server proves to the client that it is still storing all of the data. A scheme without random oracle was given in [DVW09], whereas [SW08] allows public verifiability. A proof of retrievability (PoR) scheme consists of three algorithms, $\mathsf{Gen}, \mathcal{P}, \mathcal{V}$. We recall the definition from [SW08, DVW09] below.

- The generation algorithm takes as input a file $F \in \{0,1\}^*$ and outputs a file to be stored on the server and a tag (verification information) for the client.

$$(F^*, \tau) \leftarrow \mathsf{Gen}(F)$$

- The $\mathcal{P}, \mathcal{V}$ algorithms define an audit protocol to prove retrievability of the file. The $\mathcal{P}$ algorithm takes as input the processed file F^* and the $\mathcal{V}$ algorithm takes the tag τ. At the end of the audit protocol, the verifier outputs a bit indicating whether the proof succeeds or not.

$$\{0,1\} \leftarrow \langle \mathcal{P}(F^*), \mathcal{V}(\tau) \rangle$$

A PoR scheme needs to satisfy correctness and soundness. Correctness requires that for all file $F \in \{0,1\}^*$, and for all (F^*, τ) output by $\mathsf{Gen}(F)$, an honest prover will make the verifier accept in the audit protocol.

$$\langle \mathcal{P}(F^*), \mathcal{V}(\tau) \rangle = 1$$

Informally, a PoR scheme is sound if for any prover that convinces the verifier that it is storing the file, there exists an algorithm called the extractor that interacts with the prover and extracts the file. We give the formal definition below.

Experiment $\mathsf{Expt}_{\mathcal{A}}^{PoR\text{-}sound}(\kappa)$

- The adversary $\mathcal{A}$ picks a file $F \in \{0,1\}^n$.
- The challenger creates $(F^*, \tau) \leftarrow \mathsf{Gen}(F)$ and returns F^* to $\mathcal{A}$.
- $\mathcal{A}$ can interact with $\mathcal{V}(\tau)$ by running many proofs and seeing whether $\mathcal{V}$ outputs 0 or 1.
- $\mathcal{A}$ outputs a prover algorithm (ITM) $\mathcal{P}^*$ and returns this to the challenger.
- The challenger runs $b \leftarrow \langle \mathcal{P}^*, \mathcal{V}(\tau) \rangle$, and runs the extractor, $\tilde{F} = \mathsf{ext}^{\mathcal{P}^*}(\tau, n, \kappa)$
- Output 1 if $b = 1 \wedge \tilde{F} \neq F$, or 0 otherwise.

Fig. 1. Soundness for Proofs of Retrievability.

Definition 3 (Soundness for Proof of Retrievability). *A proof of retrievability (PoR)* $\mathsf{Gen}, \mathcal{P}, \mathcal{V}$ *satisfies* soundness *if for any PPT adversary* $\mathcal{A}$*, there exists an extractor* ext *such that the advantage of* $\mathcal{A}$

$$\mathsf{Adv}_{\mathcal{A}}^{PoR\text{-}Sound}(\kappa) = \Pr[\mathsf{Expt}_{\mathcal{A}}^{PoR\text{-}Sound}(\kappa) = 1]$$

in the experiment described in Fig. 1 is negligible in κ.

The definition in [DVW09] discusses the notion of knowledge soundness versus information soundness. If the definition holds for the class of efficient extractors, the scheme satisfies knowledge soundness. A somewhat weaker notion is that of information soundness where the running time of the extractor is not restricted.

2.3 Min Entropy

Recall that the predictability of a random variable X is $\max_x \Pr[X = x]$ and its min-entropy $\mathsf{H}_\infty(X)$ is $-\log(\max_x \Pr[X = x])$. The average case min-entropy is defined as follows. Let X and Y be random variables.

$$\tilde{\mathsf{H}}_\infty(X|Y) = -\log\left(\mathbb{E}_{y \leftarrow Y}\left(2^{-\mathsf{H}_\infty(X|Y=y)}\right)\right)$$

We make use of the following lemma which states that the average min-entropy of a variable (from the point of view of an adversary) does not go down by more than the number of bits (correlated with the variable) observed by the adversary. We recall the entropy weak chain rule for average case min entropy below in Lemma 1.

Lemma 1. *([DORS08]) Let X and Y be random variables. If Y has at most 2^λ values, then*

$$\tilde{H}_\infty(X|Y) \geq H_\infty(X) - H_0(Y) = H_\infty(X) - \lambda$$

where $H_0(Y) = \log |\mathsf{support}(Y)|$.

3 Defining Proof of Replication

While several candidates of proof of replication have already been proposed, they all use timing assumptions, and we are not aware of any formal definition of the security properties that such a proof should satisfy without timing assumption. It is indeed non-trivial to come up with the "right" definition, due to the fact that we ask the adversary to store many copies *of the same file.* Thus simply requiring the existence of an extractor algorithm (as in proof of knowledge or proof of storage) is not sufficient: it is not enough that the adversary knows the file, the adversary should know multiple replicas of the same file. But what does it mean for an extractor to extract replicas of the same file? Before providing our definition, we introduce some notions of encodings which will be used to build up our solution.

3.1 Replica Encodings

We now define ReplicaEncoding as a tuple of algorithms $(\mathsf{rEnc}, \mathsf{rDec})$ where rEnc takes a message $m \in \{0,1\}^*$ and outputs a replica encoding of $m \in \{0,1\}^*$,

$$y \leftarrow \mathsf{rEnc}(\kappa, m)$$

The rDec algorithm takes a replica encoding and returns a message i.e., $m \leftarrow \mathsf{rDec}(y)$.

Definition 4 (Replica encoding). *A pair $(\mathsf{rEnc}, \mathsf{rDec})$ is a secure replica encoding if the following holds:*

- *Completeness: The probability of incorrect decoding is negligible i.e.,*

$$\Pr[\mathsf{rDec}(\mathsf{rEnc}(\kappa, m)) \neq m] < \mathsf{negl}(\kappa)$$

- *Soundness: Consider the game $\mathsf{sound}_{\mathcal{A}_1, \mathcal{A}_2}$ between an adversary and a challenger defined in Fig. 2. A replica encoding scheme is c-sound (for a constant $c, 0 < c < 1$) if for any $(\mathcal{A}_1, \mathcal{A}_2)$, there exists a negligible function negl such that the following holds.*

$$\Pr\left[|\mathsf{state}| < cv\beta|v \leftarrow \mathsf{sound}_{\mathcal{A}_1, \mathcal{A}_2}\right] \leq \mathsf{negl}(\kappa)$$

where β is the bit-length of an encoding y.
- *Efficiency: $|y| = |m| + O(\kappa)$.*

Experiment sound$_{\mathcal{A}_1,\mathcal{A}_2}$

- The adversary $\mathcal{A}_1$ chooses a file $m \in \{0,1\}^k$
- The challenger outputs n encodings of m

$$y^{(i)} \leftarrow \mathsf{rEnc}(\kappa, m)$$

for $i \in [1,n]$ and returns $(y^{(1)}, \ldots, y^{(n)})$ to $\mathcal{A}_1$.
- $\mathcal{A}_1$ outputs a state $\mathsf{state} \leftarrow \mathcal{A}_1(y^{(1)}, \ldots, y^{(n)})$
- The challenger runs $\mathcal{A}_2$ on state.

$$(\tilde{y}^{(1)}, \ldots, \tilde{y}^{(n)}) \leftarrow \mathcal{A}_2(\kappa, \mathsf{state})$$

- Let $v_i = 1$ if $\tilde{y}^{(i)} = y^{(i)}$, and 0 otherwise. Output $v = \sum_{i=1}^{n} v_i$.

Fig. 2. Soundness of a Replica Encoding scheme

Discussion. The main measure of efficiency for a replica encoding is its expansion factor, in other words the ratio $|y|/|m|$. Clearly, the smaller the expansion factor the more interesting the scheme is. Looking ahead, all our constructions will have $|y| = |m| + O(\kappa)$.

We motivate here some of the choices in our definition. First note that the completeness requirement allows the file to be reconstructed from a single replica encoding. This captures the functional requirement in the honest usage of proofs of replication, where a client would store different encodings of the file on different servers and should be able to recover the file as long as one server is storing their encoding.

When defining soundness, we consider a monolithic adversary $\mathcal{A}$ which controls all colluding servers. To be able to meaningfully talk about the *space* that the adversary uses for storing the file, we split the adversary $\mathcal{A}$ into two parts $\mathcal{A}_1$ and $\mathcal{A}_2$, where $\mathcal{A}_1$ receives the replica encoding from the challenger (representing the honest client) and $\mathcal{A}_2$ is the part of the adversary returning (some of) the encodings to the client at a later stage, using the state that $\mathcal{A}_1$ transferred to $\mathcal{A}_2$. We do not require that $\mathcal{A}_2$ outputs all of the received encoding, instead, we use the variable v to count how many of the replica encodings $\mathcal{A}_2$ is able to return. The definition of soundness then intuitively states that the adversary can at most return the number of replicas that "fit" into the state (where we allow for a constant "slack" c, to avoid trivial attacks where the adversary forgets few bits and then "guesses" them right before returning the encodings – in practice one should think of c as any constant close to 1).

As a sanity check of our definition, let's consider a construction of replica encoding that is "too trivial": define $y^{(i)} = (m, r_i)$ i.e., every replica is simply the message concatenated with some random string r_i. Due to incompressibility of random data the adversary needs to store all the r_i's, but clearly only needs to store one copy of m and can still recompute all encodings. This is of course not desirable, so our definition had better not accept this construction. Indeed it does not: the adversary can break the soundness property because he can choose to return $v \geq 2$ encodings using storage only $|m| + v|r| < cv|y|$ - which is trivially true for any interesting case (remember in efficient encodings $|y| \approx |m|$ and c is close to 1).

3.2 Proof of Replication

We now use the notion of encodings to meaningfully capture the replication property. A proof of replication scheme consists of a tuple of algorithms create, retrieve and an audit protocol defined by two algorithms, $\mathcal{P}, \mathcal{V}$ for the prover and verifier respectively. create is a randomized algorithm that takes as input a file $m \in \{0,1\}^*$, that is to be replicated and stored, a replication factor n; and produces n replicas $y^{(1)}, \ldots, y^{(n)}$ together with verification information ver. Each replica $y^{(i)}$ is sent the server i to be stored, and ver with the client to be used for verification in the audit protocol. retrieve is a deterministic algorithm run by anyone that takes as input a replica $y^{(i)}$ and outputs a file m^*.

In the audit protocol, each server (prover) has a replica $y^{(i)}$, and the client (verifier) has ver. At the end of the audit, the verifier outputs a bit b indicating whether the audit was successful or not. We denote the protocol executing the prover and verifier algorithms by $\langle \mathcal{P}_i(\tilde{y}^{(i)}), \mathcal{V}(\text{ver}, i) \rangle$.

We require the scheme to satisfy completeness and soundness properties as defined below. Note that when considering the honest usage of the our protocol (e.g., completeness), each server is able to prove to the client that they are storing the file independently[5]. On the other hand, when considering adversarial behaviour (e.g., soundness), we assume that all servers are under the control of a monolithic adversary.

All our algorithms below are parametrized by a security parameter, even when omitted as in the description below.

Definition 5 (Proof of Replication). *A scheme* PoRep $= ($create, retrieve, $\mathcal{P}, \mathcal{V})$ *where,*

$$(y^{(1)}, \ldots, y^{(n)}, \text{ver}) \leftarrow \text{create}(m, n), \text{ for } m \in \{0,1\}^*, n \in \mathbb{Z}$$

$$m_i^* = \text{retrieve}(y^{(i)}), i \in [1, n]$$

$$\{0,1\} \leftarrow \langle \mathcal{P}_i(\tilde{y}^{(i)}), \mathcal{V}(\text{ver}, i) \rangle$$

is a proof of replication scheme if the following properties are satisfied.

---

[5] For instance, an honest server does not need to communicate with the other servers, nor know that they exist.

– *Completeness. For an honest client and honest server,*
  - *for* $(y^{(1)}, \ldots, y^{(n)}, \mathsf{ver}) \leftarrow \mathsf{create}(m, n), m_i^* = \mathsf{retrieve}(y^{(i)}), m_i^* = m \ \forall i \in [1, n]$
  - *The audit protocol interaction between honest client and honest server succeeds, that is, the client accepts and outputs* $b = 1$.

$$\langle \mathcal{P}_i(\tilde{y}^{(i)}), \mathcal{V}(\mathsf{ver}, i) \rangle = 1$$

– *Soundness. We define the soundness game* $\mathsf{sound}_{\mathcal{A}_1, \mathcal{A}_2}^{\mathcal{E}}$ *between an adversary and a challenger in Fig. 3. The scheme* PoRep *is c-sound (for a constant* $c, 0 < c < 1$) *if for any* $(\mathcal{A}_1, \mathcal{A}_2)$, *there exists an extractor* $\mathcal{E}$ *and a negligible function* negl *such that the following holds.*

$$\Pr\left[u < v \lor |\mathsf{state}| < cv\beta | (u, v) \leftarrow \mathsf{sound}_{\mathcal{A}_1, \mathcal{A}_2}^{\mathcal{E}}\right] \leq \mathsf{negl}(\kappa)$$

where β *is the bitlength of an encoding* y.

Experiment $\mathsf{sound}_{\mathcal{A}_1, \mathcal{A}_2}^{\mathcal{E}}$

- The adversary $\mathcal{A}_1$ chooses a file $m \in \{0,1\}^k$
- The challenger runs $(y^{(1)}, \ldots, y^{(n)}, \mathsf{ver}) \leftarrow \mathsf{create}(m, n)$ and returns $(y^{(1)}, \ldots, y^{(n)})$ to $\mathcal{A}_1$.
- $\mathcal{A}_1$ outputs a state $\mathsf{state} \leftarrow \mathcal{A}_1(y^{(1)}, \ldots, y^{(n)})$
- The challenger runs $\langle \mathcal{A}_2(\mathsf{state}), \mathcal{V}(\mathsf{ver}, i) \rangle$, let v_i be the output of $\mathcal{V}$ for all $i \in [1, n]$ and $v = \sum_{i=1}^{n} v_i$.
- The challenger runs the extractor.

$$(\tilde{y}^{(1)}, \ldots, \tilde{y}^{(n)}) = \mathcal{E}^{A_2}(\kappa, \mathsf{ver}, k)$$

- For all $i \in [1, n]$, define $u_i = 1$ if $\tilde{y}^{(i)} = y^{(i)}$, and $u = \sum_{i=1}^{n} u_i$
  The output of the game $\mathsf{sound}_{\mathcal{A}_1, \mathcal{A}_2}^{\mathcal{E}}$ is (u, v).

Fig. 3. Soundness of a proof of replication scheme

The definition above guarantees that the malicious servers, even colluding, cannot make the verifier accept more proofs than the storage they have used.

4   Constructing Proof of Replication

We begin by giving a high-level overview of our construction. Following the idea behind our definition, we create many independent encodings, and use a proof of retrievability on the encodings. Even though each encoding can independently be decoded to the same file without any secret information, the proof of retrievability on the encodings enforces that the server stores each encoding and therefore dedicates space for *each* replica. Recall that in Sect. 1.2 we have already described a simple solution which works in a restricted model in which the adversary is restricted to either store or delete entire replicas. Of course this is not a realistic threat model and a malicious server could choose to forget arbitrary parts of each encoding (say, a constant fraction). Now, to pass the audit, the server would have to compute a preimage of the underlying trapdoor permutation, but *given* a constant fraction of bits of the preimage. Unfortunately, the definition of security for trapdoor permutation does not allow us to say that this is not possible; in other words, we cannot construct a reduction for this kind of adversaries.

To address this problem, we use the following approach: we start by applying an (invertible) random oracle (IRO) on the message concatenated with a short seed (which is different for each replica), and then we use the trapdoor permutation on the result. We then iterate the IRO and the trapdoor permutation as a round function sufficiently many times. Intuitively the trapdoor permutation of the round function ensures that the adversary has to do something "hard" in every round, while the IRO of the round function is used to make sure that the "hard tasks" are all independent.

Again, in any given round, we cannot rule out that the adversary might have stored some (small) information that allows to easily invert the trapdoor permutation. However, since we repeat this for many rounds and the adversary must store some pre-image information at every round to potentially break the trapdoor permutation, eventually the total information that the adversary would have to store will exceed the bound necessary for replicated storage.

When dealing with large files (e.g., larger than the size of the input/output of T), we split the file in blocks. To make sure that all blocks depend on the entire file (for instance, to prevent the server from "de-duplicating" individual blocks which might appear in multiple files), we first apply a "large" IRO on the entire file. Then, in the round function, we apply a "small" IRO on each individual block. Thanks to this, the number of rounds in the encoding only needs to be proportional to the block size, instead of the entire file size (as it was the case in an earlier version of this paper).

Note that our combination of the RSA trapdoor permutation with a random oracle is reminiscent of full domain hash-signatures and, to a greater extent, CCA secure encryption via RSA and OAEP. Note however that, in our construction, we apply the oracle and the trapdoor permutation for multiple rounds, and the domain of the random oracle is a pair of blocks for the RSA permutation. The idea of iterating a combination of RSA with a random oracle was used before in [VDJO+12], however (apart from their work having a less in-depth treatment) there are two major differences, namely that they did not consider replication as an application, and that they use a strictly weaker notion of security, namely "near-incompressibility".

Efficiency of decoding. We note that, when instantiating the construction with the RSA trapdoor permutation, it is possible to use a small exponent (i.e., $e = 3$). Now decoding would be much faster then encoding, which is a desirable property in applications where a single user uploads a file which is then retrieved by a large number of users.

4.1 Replica Encodings

We now proceed to describe our construction in detail, and first construct a replica encoding scheme ReplicaEncoding = (rEnc, rDec) in Figs. 4 and 5.

Let $m \in \{0,1\}^{k'}$ be a message to be encoded.

- Choose a string γ uniformly at random from $\{0,1\}^\kappa$, and let $y_0 = H(m||\gamma)$, where $H : \{0,1\}^\lambda \to \{0,1\}^\lambda$ is a invertible random oracle (IRO), and $\lambda = k' + \kappa$.
- Let $(\mathsf{KeyGen}, f^{-1}, f)$ be trapdoor permutation over domain $\mathcal{D}$. $(sk, pk) \leftarrow \mathsf{KeyGen}(1^\kappa)$. Divide y_0 into s blocks such that each block is in $\mathcal{D}$. That is, $y_0 = Y_{10}||\cdots||Y_{s0}$. Let $T : \mathcal{D} \to \mathcal{D}$ be an IRO over $\mathcal{D}$. We then iterate the following round function: For each round j from 1 to r, and for each block $t \in [1, s]$ define
  - Apply the IRO T,
  $$Z_{tj} = T(Y_{tj-1})$$
  - Invert the trapdoor permutation block-wise,
  $$Y_{tj} = f_{sk}^{-1}(Z_{tj})$$

  Let $y_j = Y_{1j}||\cdots||Y_{sj}$
- Let $R = (y_r, pk)$
- Return R

Fig. 4. The Replica Encoding Algorithm rEnc(κ, m)

Soundness of the scheme. Before formally proving the soundness of the scheme, we give an overview of the proof idea. If the state state that is passed from $\mathcal{A}_1$ to $\mathcal{A}_2$ is small, then the adversary $\mathcal{A}_2$ cannot "remember" all the answers to the queries that $\mathcal{A}_1$ made in the first part of the game since the outputs of a random oracle are incompressible. However, we can extract the outputs of the random oracle used during the encoding from the adversary since the replica encodings can be efficiently decoded. This implies that the adversary must make some queries to the random oracle in phase 2 of the game. Now, for each of the queries the adversary makes, there are two options: either the response to the query has full entropy in the view of the adversary, or it doesn't. If it has full entropy, i.e., if the state contained no (or very little) information about what the

For a replica $R = (y_r, pk)$, Parse y_r as $Y_{1r}|| \cdots ||Y_{sr}$. For each round j from r down to 1, and each block $t \in [1, s]$, compute

- Round j:
  - Apply the trapdoor permutation block-wise,

  $$Z_{tj} = f_{pk}(Y_{tj})$$

  - Invert the IRO,

  $$Y_{tj-1} = T^{-1}(Z_{tj})$$

- Let $y_0 = Y_{10}|| \cdots ||Y_{s0}$. Compute $H^{-1}(y_0)$ and parse the output as $m||\gamma$ where m is the first k' bits. Return m.

Fig. 5. The replica decoding algorithm $\mathsf{rDec}(R)$

oracle would answer, then we are done, as we will elaborate next. But first let us consider if not; that is, the response to the query made did not have full entropy in $\mathcal{A}_2$'s view. This means that the state must have contained some information about the answer to the query. Now, since the encoding uses the random oracle in each round, and since the state that the adversary is allowed to remember is small, by carefully accounting for the entropy budget for each query made, we argue that after a certain round, the entropy in the state is exhausted and therefore there is at least one query that the adversary had to make to the oracle whose response has full entropy in order to win the game. Finally, once we have found such a query for which we know that the output of the oracle has full entropy that $\mathcal{A}_2$ *had to make* to win the game, we can reprogram the random oracle with a challenge for the trapdoor permutation. Thus since $\mathcal{A}_2$ is nevertheless able to produce the replicas, we use it to break the assumption and reach a contradiction.

Theorem 1. *Assuming T, H are invertible random oracles, the construction* $\mathsf{ReplicaEncoding} = (\mathsf{rEnc}, \mathsf{rDec})$ *using trapdoor permutation f is a secure replica encoding scheme, replication parameter n as per Definition 4. For number of rounds $r > \frac{(cn+1)k}{B}$, it is complete and c-sound with soundness error*

$$\epsilon \le \left(\epsilon' + 2^{-k(1-c)} + qs^2 2^{-k}\right) nrs$$

where $k = \log |\mathcal{D}|$, $\mathcal{D}$ is the domain of f and T, s is the number of blocks, q the number of queries to the RO and the advantage of any adversary in B-leakage inversion of the permutation f is at most ϵ'.

Proof. We use the notation $R^{(i)}$ to identify the encoding stored on server i.

Completeness. For n encodings that are created honestly, $R^{(i)} \leftarrow \mathsf{rEnc}(m, \kappa)$, $m^* = \mathsf{rDec}(R^{(i)})$. Then, due to the invertibility of T, H and the trapdoor permutation f, $m^* = m$, $\forall i$.

Soundness. Assume there exists an adversary $(\mathcal{A}_1, \mathcal{A}_2)$ such that

$$\Pr\left[\,|\mathsf{state}| < cv\beta |v \leftarrow \mathsf{sound}_{\mathcal{A}_1,\mathcal{A}_2}\right] > \epsilon.$$

Therefore, the adversary $\mathcal{A}_2^T$ outputs $R^{(i_1)}, \cdots, R^{(i_v)}$, where each $i_j \in [1, n]$. Let $I \subset [1, n], |I| = v$ be the set of indices indicating the replicas that $\mathcal{A}_2$ outputs correctly. We argue that if the state is too small, then the adversary does not have enough entropy to store information about $R^{(i)}, \forall i \in I$ and therefore one of the $R^{(i)}$ must have been recomputed, (by making relevant queries to T), which we use to invert the B-leakage trapdoor permutation. The proof idea is that since the state is small, in round r, $\mathcal{A}_2$ must have learned some of the Z values of round r from responses of T. If the response of T to these queries do not have full entropy in $\mathcal{A}_2$'s view given the state, then this deficit must be accounted for in the size of the state. We continue this argument for every round going backwards from the last round, by reasoning about the set of relevant queries made in each round, and accounting for every query made that did not have entropy in $\mathcal{A}_2$'s view with B bits in the state. We then hit a round where the response of T for one of $\mathcal{A}_2$'s queries must have high enough entropy from $\mathcal{A}_2$'s point of view. Such a query is guaranteed to exist since the state size is used up after enough queries of the former kind. We use the response to this query to embed a challenge and invert the trapdoor permutation. We now proceed to give the reduction.

Let $\mathcal{B}$ be an adversary whose task is to invert the trapdoor permutation. $\mathcal{B}$ receives a challenge $(\hat{pk}, \hat{x})$, and wins if it outputs $\hat{y}$ such that $f_{\hat{pk}}(\hat{y}) = \hat{x}$. $\mathcal{B}$ interacts with $(\mathcal{A}_1, \mathcal{A}_2)$ in the soundness game. $\mathcal{B}$ receives a file $m \in \{0, 1\}^{k'}$ from $\mathcal{A}_1$. $\mathcal{B}$ creates encoded replicas honestly, except for one of the replicas chosen at random (call its index $i^* \in [1, n]$), in which the challenge will be embedded. For now we only use the public key $\hat{pk}$. Since $\mathcal{B}$ does not know the corresponding secret key, $\mathcal{B}$ cannot compute this encoding honestly. Thus, $\mathcal{B}$ defines the encoding $R^{(i^*)}$ as $(\hat{pk}, y_r)$ for a uniformly random y_r. Then it "decodes" y_r down to y_0 (by following the decoding procedure) and finally programs the random oracle H such that $H^{-1}(y_0) = (m||\gamma^{(i^*)})$ for some random string $\gamma^{(i^*)}$. More in detail:

- Choose random $y_r^{(i^*)} \in \{0, 1\}^\lambda$.
- For each round j from r down to 1, parse $y_j^{(i^*)} = Y_{1j}||\cdots||Y_{sj}$ and, for each block $t \in [1, s]$, compute:
  - Apply the trapdoor permutation block-wise,

  $$Z_{tj} = f_{\hat{pk}}(Y_{tj})$$

  - Invert the IRO,

  $$Y_{tj-1} = T^{-1}(Z_{tj})$$

- Let $y_0 = Y_{10}||\cdots||Y_{s0}$.
- Pick a random value $\gamma \in \{0, 1\}^\kappa$ and program the IRO H to output y_0 on input (m, γ).
- Return $R^{(i^*)} = (y^{(i^*)}, \hat{pk})$.

$\mathcal{B}$ responds to any other oracle queries of $\mathcal{A}_1$ honestly, and finally gives $(R^{(1)}, \cdots, R^{(n)})$ to $\mathcal{A}_1$, where $R^{(i)}$ for $i \neq i^*$ is created honestly. $\mathcal{A}_1$ outputs a state state. Now, $\mathcal{B}$ interacts with $\mathcal{A}_2$. It runs $\mathcal{A}_2$ on state, and receives and responds to $\mathcal{A}_2$'s oracle queries in the following way. $\mathcal{B}$ chooses a random round $j^* \in [1, r]$, and a random block $t^* \in [1, s]$ to embed the challenge $\hat{x}$ in. If $\mathcal{A}_2$ queries T on $Y^{(i^*)}_{t^* j^* - 1}$, $\mathcal{B}$ sets the response to embed its challenge $\hat{x}$ in the following way. Set $Z_{t^* j^*} = \hat{x}$ and,

$$T(Y^{(i^*)}_{t^* j^* - 1}) = Z_{t^* j^*}$$

The rest of the queries are answered honestly. If $\mathcal{A}_2$ makes a query $Y^{(i^*)}_{t^* j^*} = \hat{y}$ such that, $f_{\hat{pk}}(\hat{y}) = \hat{x}$, $\mathcal{B}$ outputs $\hat{y}$. If there is no such query, $\mathcal{B}$ outputs $\perp$. We now compute the probability that $\mathcal{B}$ wins in the trapdoor permutation inversion game. Consider the case when $(m||\gamma)$ fits into $\mathcal{D}$, and therefore there is only one block in the encoding. We later show how the argument extends to multiple blocks. Let k be the block length, that is, the bit length of elements in $\mathcal{D}$. We therefore have $|\text{state}| < cvk, c < 1$. Consider the min-entropy of the random variable state, which is at most the bit length, $\mathsf{H}_\infty(\text{state}) \leq cvk$. $\mathcal{A}_2$ on state returns,

$$\{R^{(i)}\}_{i \in I} \leftarrow \mathcal{A}_2(\text{state})$$

for $R^{(i)} = (y^{(i)}_r, pk_i)$. Since there is only one block in the encoding, $y^{(i)}_r \in \mathcal{D}$ and can be decoded to obtain $z^{(i)}_r = f_{pk_i}(y^{(i)}_r)$.

Let $\mathcal{Y}_r = y^{(i_1)}_r || \cdots || y^{(i_v)}_r$ and $\mathcal{Z}_r = z^{(i_1)}_r || \cdots || z^{(i_v)}_r, i_j \in I$.

Since each replica is computed by using independent randomness γ_i, the queries to the oracle are different for each replica, and therefore each $z^{(i)}_r$ is unpredictable. We have,

$$\mathsf{H}_\infty(z^{(i)}_r | z^{(1)}_r, \cdots, z^{(i-1)}_r, z^{(i+1)}_r, \cdots, z^{(n)}_r) = k$$

and therefore, $\mathsf{H}_\infty(\mathcal{Z}_r) = vk$. Since $\mathcal{Z}_r$ can be extracted from $\mathcal{A}_2^T(\text{state})$ by decoding, either the state contains information about each $z^{(i)}$ in $z^{(1)}|| \cdots ||z^{(v)}$, or $\mathcal{A}_2$ must make relevant RO queries, that is, query the RO on the inputs corresponding to $z^{(i)}$. By the conditional rule for average case min-entropy (Lemma 1),

$$\tilde{\mathsf{H}}_\infty(\mathcal{Z}_r | \text{state}) \geq \mathsf{H}_\infty(\mathcal{Z}_r) - \mathsf{H}_0(\text{state})$$

$$\tilde{\mathsf{H}}_\infty(\mathcal{Z}_r | \text{state}) \geq \mathsf{H}_\infty(\mathcal{Z}_r) - cvk = vk - cvk$$

$\mathcal{Z}_r$ is extracted by making no RO queries only with probability less than $2^{-vk(1-c)} < 2^{-k(1-c)}$ which is negligible for constant c (even in the worse case where the adversary replies with a single replica). Therefore, there is at least one RO query. Let $\mathcal{Q}_r$ be the indices in I that indicates the queries which are y-values of round r. That is, $\forall u \in \mathcal{Q}_r$, $\mathcal{A}_2$ queried T on $y^{(u)}_{r-1}$, and $T(y^{(u)}_{r-1}) = z^{(u)}_r$. Let $q_r = |\mathcal{Q}|$ denote the number of "relevant" r-round queries. For each query, either the state contains information about the response or not; we consider the two cases where the state stores $< B$ bits of information or $\geq B$ of information of a query response. If the state contains $< B$ bits of information about responses in round r, then $\mathcal{B}$ wins if the challenge is embedded in that response and we are done. Otherwise, the state contains information about each $z_r^{(u)}$ which means the state stores at least B bits of information for each query.

$$\mathsf{H}_\infty(\mathsf{state}) \geq q_r B$$

Now, let us consider the set of queries made with indices in $\mathcal{Q}_r$. For each $y_{r-1}^{(u)}, u \in \mathcal{Q}_r$, we can extract $z_{r-1}^{(u)}$ by computing the decoding. That is, $z_{r-1}^{(u)} = f_{pk_u}(y_{r-1}^{(u)})$, for $y_{r-1}^{(u)} \in \mathcal{D}$. These q_r elements are outputs of RO on different inputs, and therefore have full entropy. Let $\mathcal{Z}_{r-1} = z_{r-1}^{(u_1)} || \cdots || z_{r-1}^{(u_{q_r})}$ where each $u_i \in \mathcal{Q}_r$. We have $\mathsf{H}_\infty(\mathcal{Z}_{r-1}) = q_r k$. If $\mathcal{Z}_{r-1}$ can be extracted from $\mathcal{A}_2^T(\mathsf{state})$, either the state contains information about $z_{r-1}^{(i)}, \forall i \in \mathcal{Q}_r$, or $\mathcal{A}_2$ must make more RO queries. If there are no more queries, then $\mathsf{H}_\infty(\mathsf{state}) \geq vk$. Therefore, there must be more queries on inputs corresponding to the indices in $\mathcal{Q}_r$.

Let q_{r-1} be the number of relevant round $(r-1)$ queries. Define a set of query indices $\mathcal{Q}_{r-1}$, from which we can extract $\mathcal{Z}_{r-2} = z_{r-2}^{(u_1)} || \cdots || z_{r-2}^{(u_{q_{r-1}})}$, for $u_i \in \mathcal{Q}_{r-1}$. Again, for each query, either the state dedicates $< B$ bits of information, in which case $\mathcal{B}$ wins if the challenge is embedded in that response and we are done. Otherwise, the state stores at least B bits of information about each $y_{r-1}^{(u)}$, and therefore we have,

$$\mathsf{H}_\infty(\mathsf{state}) \geq q_r B + q_{r-1} B$$

Making a similar argument as before, there must be more RO queries corresponding to the indices in set $\mathcal{Q}_{r-1}$. Thus, we have, after r rounds, $\mathcal{Z}_r, \ldots, \mathcal{Z}_1$ are extracted from $\mathcal{A}_2(\mathsf{state})$, and we have

$$\mathsf{H}_\infty(\mathsf{state}) \geq \sum_{i=1}^{r} q_i B$$

Let $\mathcal{A}_2$ make RO queries in each round j for the replicas given by the indices in $\mathcal{Q}_j$ such that the reduction could not successfully embed a challenge in any of the responses. Then after r rounds, setting,

$$\sum_{i=1}^{r} q_i B - cvk = k$$

We get $\tilde{\mathsf{H}}_\infty(\mathcal{Z}_1 | \mathsf{state}) \geq k$, when $r > k(cv+1)/B$.

Therefore, at some round $\ell \leq r$, the entropy of the response is full when making an RO query at round ℓ. That is, $\exists \ell \in [1, r], w \in [1, n]$ such that,

$$\tilde{\mathsf{H}}_\infty(z_\ell^{(w)} | \mathsf{state}) = k$$

When there are multiple blocks, we have $|\mathsf{state}| < cv\beta$. Since the permutation H is applied to the entire file concatenated with a random string γ, before r rounds of T and f, the adversary can find files such that the output of H results in the same blocks only with probability $((qs)^2 + 1)/2^k$ where q is the number of queries and s the number of blocks. Then the above argument holds for each block independently.

The probability that the challenge is programmed into the RO response of one of the blocks of $z_\ell^{(w)}$ is the probability that $i^* = w, j^* = \ell$ which is $1/vrs > 1/nrs$ (in the worse case where $n = v$). Thus the probability that $\mathcal{B}$ wins is at least $\frac{\epsilon}{nrs} - 2^{-k(1-c)} - qs^2 2^{-k}$.   □

As any trapdoor function is also trivially B-leakage secure for $B = \log(k)$, we obtain the following corollary.

Corollary 1. *Assuming T, H are invertible random oracles, the construction* $\mathsf{ReplicaEncoding} = (\mathsf{rEnc}, \mathsf{rDec})$ *using trapdoor permutation f is a secure replica encoding scheme for replication parameter n as per Definition 4. For number of rounds $r > \frac{(cn+1)k}{\log k}$, it is complete and c-sound with soundness error*

$$\epsilon \leq \left(\epsilon' + 2^{-k(1-c)} + qs^2 2^{-k}\right) nrs$$

where $k = \log|\mathcal{D}|$, $\mathcal{D}$ is the domain of f and T, s is the number of blocks, q the number of queries to the RO and the advantage of any adversary in inverting the permutation f is at most ϵ'.

Of course, for specific trapdoor permutations, it might be possible to assume B-leakage security for larger values of B thus achieving better round complexity.

4.2   From Replica Encodings to Proofs of Replication

We now construct a proof of replication scheme $\mathsf{create}, \mathsf{retrieve}, \mathcal{P}, \mathcal{V}$. The idea is very simple: to construct a proof of replication we use the replica encoding scheme from the previous section to create replicas, and then apply a proof of retrievability on the encoded replicas. The proof of security is also simple, as an adversary that breaks soundness for the proof of replication can be used to break the soundness property of the proof of retrievability scheme or the soundness of the replica encoding scheme.

The create procedure is formally described in Fig. 6. The prover, and verifier algorithms $\mathcal{P}, \mathcal{V}$ are the same as the prover and verifier in the proof of retrievability. Finally, the $\mathsf{retrieve}$ algorithm simply runs the replica decoding algorithm rDec if the proof of retrievability accepts.

Theorem 2. $\mathsf{PoRep} = (\mathsf{create}, \mathsf{retrieve}, \mathcal{P}, \mathcal{V})$ *is a proof of replication scheme for replication parameter n secure as per Definition 5. It is complete and c-sound with soundness error $\gamma \leq \delta + \epsilon$ where the underlying PoR scheme has soundness error δ, and the replica encoding scheme has soundness error ϵ.*

Let PoR = $(\mathsf{Gen}, \mathcal{P}, \mathcal{V})$ be a proof of retrievability scheme. Given a file $m \in \{0,1\}^{k'}$, and a replication factor n:

- For each $i \in [1, n]$
  - Run $R^{(i)} \leftarrow \mathsf{rEnc}(m, \kappa)$
  - $(\{\tilde{R}^{(i)}\}_i, \tau_i) = \mathsf{PoR.Gen}(R^{(i)})$
- Set $\mathsf{ver} = \{\tau_i\}_i$
- $\tilde{R}^{(i)}$ is sent to the server i for storage and ver is returned to the client.

Fig. 6. $\mathsf{create}(m, n)$: Create replicated storage

Proof. We first argue completeness: Given $R^{(i)}$ and pk, for encodings that are created honestly, an honest server can recover $m^* = \mathsf{retrieve}(R^{(i)})$. By completeness of the replica encoding scheme rEnc, we have $\mathsf{rDec}(R^{(i)}) = \mathsf{rDec}(y^{(i)}, pk^{(i)}) = m, \forall i$.

We now argue the soundness of the construction. Let $(\mathcal{A}_1, \mathcal{A}_2)$ be an adversary, that wins the soundness game $\mathsf{sound}^{\mathcal{E}}_{\mathcal{A}_1, \mathcal{A}_2}$ with advantage γ. Let $(u, v) \leftarrow \mathsf{sound}^{\mathcal{E}}_{\mathcal{A}_1, \mathcal{A}_2}$. We consider the two cases:

Case 1. $u < v$. Let ext be the extractor of the PoR scheme, and let the file output by ext be $\{\tilde{R}^{(i)}\}_{i=1}^n$. By assumption that $u < v$ there must be an index $i \in [1, n]$ such that the adversary $\mathcal{A}_2$ succeeds in the audit protocol (i.e., $v_i = 1$), but $\tilde{R}^{(i)} \neq R^{(i)}$ (i.e., $u_i = 0$). By the soundness of the proof of retrievability scheme PoR, this happens only with probability δ.

Case 2. $|\mathsf{state}| \leq cv\beta$. In this case the adversary $\mathcal{A}_2^T$ succeeds in v audit protocols, and since $u \geq v$, the extractor $\mathcal{E}$ outputs $\tilde{R}^{(i)} = R^{(i)}$ for $i \in I \subset [1, n], |I| = v$. Let $(\mathcal{B}_1, \mathcal{B}_2)$ be an adversary whose task is to break the soundness of the replica encoding scheme rEnc. $\mathcal{B}_1$ interacts with $(\mathcal{A}_1, \mathcal{A}_2)$ in the soundness game. $\mathcal{B}_1$ receives a file $m \in \{0,1\}^{k'}$ from $\mathcal{A}_1$, and outputs m to its challenger. $\mathcal{B}_1$ receives n replica encodings $(R^{(1)}, \cdots, R^{(n)})$ from the challenger, where the bit length of each encoding is β. $\mathcal{B}_1$ runs the PoR on the replicas. $(\{\tilde{R}^{(i)}\}_i, \mathsf{ver}) \leftarrow \mathsf{PoR.Gen}\{R^{(i)}\}_i$ and returns $\{\tilde{R}^{(i)}\}_i$ to $\mathcal{A}_1$. $\mathcal{B}_1$ outputs as state whatever $\mathcal{A}_1$ outputs with $|\mathsf{state}| \leq cv\beta$. For every successful audit proof given by $\mathcal{A}_2$, $\mathcal{B}_2$ runs the extractor $\mathcal{E}(\mathsf{ver}, n, \kappa)$ of the scheme. Thus $\mathcal{B}_2$ outputs $\tilde{R}^{(i)} = R^{(i)}$ for each $i \in I$ with probability at least γ.

5   Dealing with Malicious Clients

We discuss here some limitations and possible extensions of our approach.

Our definition and construction so far has concentrated on the case where the client is honest. This is not a problem for our base use-case where a user wants to make sure they will be able to retrieve their files in the future, but it is a problem in the Filecoin use case where servers are rewarded for the files they store.

In this case, we need to prevent against the so called *generation attack* and it is therefore important to have some security guarantees when the client is corrupt and might work with a set of corrupt servers to convince honest users that they store many replicas whereas in fact the replicas are generated "on-the-fly" for each proof.

Our solution from the previous section does not work in this case, as a corrupt user could share the trapdoor function secret key with the servers and now they can indeed encode a replica on the fly. If the client who owns the file is corrupt and is the only user involved in the encoding process, then the adversary knows everything about the encoding process, and a different solution is needed. One way to go is to involve several users in the encoding process and work under the assumption that at least one of them is honest.

In a Filecoin-like scenario one could implement such a solution by rewarding users for helping others to encode. We now describe two different approaches to such multi-user encoding.

Parallel Encoding. Given one-way trapdoor functions $f_1, ..., f_n$ that act on k-bit strings, we define a new function F on kn bit strings by $F(x_1, ..., x_n) = (f_1(x_1), ..., f_n(x_n))$, where each x_i is a k-bit string. It is clear that F is a one-way trapdoor function even with respect to an adversary who knows all but one of the trapdoors for $f_1, ..., f_n$. Namely, if the j'th trapdoor is unknown, we can take a challenge y_j, choose $y_i = f_i(x_i)$ for $i \neq j$ and random x_i and give $(y_1, ..., y_n)$ to the adversary. If he computes a preimage, then the j'th component is the answer to challenge y_j.

Note that our main result gives a construction that is secure based on any one-way trapdoor function and so it also works for F.

Now, in the practical use-case, we will assume that n users are involved, such that user i has f_i as part of his public key and knows the corresponding trapdoor. A public-key infrastructure is one of several ways to realize this. Then the n users can collaborate to encode: whenever we need to compute F, we can assume the input to the current round is known (initially it will be the file to encode), so each user i can apply the permutation oracle and compute and broadcast f_i^{-1} on his part of the result.

It follows immediately from the above that if at least one user is honest, then this construction results in a secure replica encoding. Note also that the contributions of each user can be verified by computing his function in the forward direction. Moreover, the overhead in encoding size and the cost per bit of encoding and decoding is the same as for the single honest user case. On the other hand, we need a number of rounds for the encoding protocol that equals the number of rounds in the encoding process.

Sequential Encoding. An obvious alternative is to do the encoding sequentially. Namely, the first user does an encoding of the input file using his (set of) trapdoor functions and broadcasts the result. The second user encodes the output of the first, etc. In the end, we have an encoding that is essentially done just like our original construction, only with more rounds. Note that one can decode the output of each user and check the result is correct.

The intuition behind the security of this approach is the following: under the assumption that at least one user is honest, we have the same security as in the original construction assuming that at least one of the users is honest. This is simply because the adversary does not know the trapdoors for the honest member, and his encoding process involves the same number of random oracle responses that we considered in the original proof. This approach increases the size of the encodings but not significantly (the complexity would grow from $O(|m| + \kappa)$ to $O(|m| + n \cdot \kappa)$ with n users). The cost of encoding and decoding in this solution is a factor n larger than for the single honest user case. On the other hand, the number of rounds in the encoding protocol is n, which may be better than parallel encoding, depending on the concrete scenario.

6 Conclusions and Future Work

We gave two possible solutions to multi-user encoding above. However, there is also a solution of a different nature that comes to mind: namely we can share a trapdoor (say, an RSA key) between a set of users and have them collaborate to compute the encoding using that trapdoor function securely. This has the advantage that an encoding looks just like what an honest client would produce, we are not forced to have larger block size when many users are involved. Also, decoding is as fast as in the honest client case, and one can set up the protocol such that just one participating client needs to be honest in order for the secret key to not leak. On the other hand, encoding requires more work. For the encoding protocol, one can take advantage of the huge body of literature on distributed RSA key generation and distributed signing. Finding the optimal solution for this approach is left for future work.

We also leave as an open question the problem of finding a secure replica encoding where the number of rounds in the encoding process does not depend on the number of replicas.

References

[AAC+17] Abusalah, H., Alwen, J., Cohen, B., Khilko, D., Pietrzak, K., Reyzin, L.: Beyond Hellman's time-memory trade-offs with applications to proofs of space. In: Takagi, T., Peyrin, T. (eds.) ASIACRYPT 2017, Part II. LNCS, vol. 10625, pp. 357–379. Springer, Cham (2017). https://doi.org/10.1007/978-3-319-70697-9_13

[ABBK16] Armknecht, F., Barman, L., Bohli, J.-M., Karame, G.O.: Mirror: enabling proofs of data replication and retrievability in the cloud. In: USENIX Security Symposium, pp. 1051–1068 (2016)

[BBBF18] Boneh, D., Bonneau, J., Bünz, B., Fisch, B.: Verifiable delay functions. In: Shacham, H., Boldyreva, A. (eds.) CRYPTO 2018, Part I. LNCS, vol. 10991, pp. 757–788. Springer, Cham (2018). https://doi.org/10.1007/978-3-319-96884-1_25

[BH11] Barsoum, A.F., Anwar Hasan, M.: On verifying dynamic multiple data copies over cloud servers. IACR Cryptology ePrint Archive 2011, p. 447 (2011)

[CFMJ18]   Cecchetti, E., Fisch, B., Miers, I., Juels, A.: PIEs: public incompressible
            encodings for decentralized storage. Cryptology ePrint Archive, Report
            2018/684 (2018). https://eprint.iacr.org/2018/684
[chi17]   Chia network (2017). https://chia.network/
[CHK+16]   Coron, J.-S., Holenstein, T., Künzler, R., Patarin, J., Seurin, Y., Tes-
            saro, S.: How to build an ideal cipher: the indifferentiability of the Feistel
            construction. J. Cryptol. **29**(1), 61–114 (2016)
[CKBA08]   Curtmola, R., Khan, O., Burns, R., Ateniese, G.: MR-PDP: multiple-
            replica provable data possession. In: The 28th International Conference on
            Distributed Computing Systems, ICDCS 2008, pp. 411–420. IEEE (2008)
[DFKP15]   Dziembowski, S., Faust, S., Kolmogorov, V., Pietrzak, K.: Proofs of space.
            In: Gennaro, R., Robshaw, M. (eds.) CRYPTO 2015, Part II. LNCS, vol.
            9216, pp. 585–605. Springer, Heidelberg (2015). https://doi.org/10.1007/
            978-3-662-48000-7_29
[DKT16]   Dachman-Soled, D., Katz, J., Thiruvengadam, A.: 10-round Feistel is
            indifferentiable from an ideal cipher. In: Fischlin, M., Coron, J.-S. (eds.)
            EUROCRYPT 2016, Part II. LNCS, vol. 9666, pp. 649–678. Springer,
            Heidelberg (2016). https://doi.org/10.1007/978-3-662-49896-5_23
[DORS08]   Dodis, Y., Ostrovsky, R., Reyzin, L., Smith, A.: Fuzzy extractors: how
            to generate strong keys from biometrics and other noisy data. SIAM J.
            Comput. **38**(1), 97–139 (2008)
[DS16]   Dai, Y., Steinberger, J.: Indifferentiability of 8-round Feistel networks. In:
            Robshaw, M., Katz, J. (eds.) CRYPTO 2016, Part 1. LNCS, vol. 9814,
            pp. 95–120. Springer, Heidelberg (2016). https://doi.org/10.1007/978-3-
            662-53018-4_4
[DVW09]   Dodis, Y., Vadhan, S., Wichs, D.: Proofs of retrievability via hardness
            amplification. In: Reingold, O. (ed.) TCC 2009. LNCS, vol. 5444, pp.
            109–127. Springer, Heidelberg (2009). https://doi.org/10.1007/978-3-642-
            00457-5_8
[EK13]   Etemad, M., Küpçü, A.: Transparent, distributed, and replicated dynamic
            provable data possession. In: Jacobson, M., Locasto, M., Mohassel, P.,
            Safavi-Naini, R. (eds.) ACNS 2013. LNCS, vol. 7954, pp. 1–18. Springer,
            Heidelberg (2013). https://doi.org/10.1007/978-3-642-38980-1_1
[FBBG18]   Fisch, B., Bonneau, J., Benet, J., Greco, N.: Proofs of replication using
            depth robust graphs (2018). https://cyber.stanford.edu/bpase18
[Fis18]   Fisch, B.: Tight proofs of space and replication. Cryptology ePrint
            Archive, Report 2018/702 (2018). https://eprint.iacr.org/2018/702
[HY10]   Hao, Z., Yu, N.: A multiple-replica remote data possession checking pro-
            tocol with public verifiability. In: 2010 Second International Symposium
            on Data, Privacy and E-Commerce (ISDPE), pp. 84–89. IEEE (2010)
[JK07]   Juels, A., Kaliski Jr., B.S.: PORs: proofs of retrievability for large files.
            In: Ning, P., di Vimercati, S.D.C., Syverson, P.F. (eds.) ACM CCS 2007,
            pp. 584–597. ACM Press, October 2007
[Lab17a]   Protocol Labs. Filecoin: a decentralized storage network (2017). https://
            filecoin.io/filecoin.pdf
[Lab17b]   Protocol Labs. Proof of replication (2017). https://filecoin.io/proof-of-
            replication.pdf
[MRH04]   Maurer, U., Renner, R., Holenstein, C.: Indifferentiability, impossibility
            results on reductions, and applications to the Random Oracle methodol-
            ogy. In: Naor, M. (ed.) TCC 2004. LNCS, vol. 2951, pp. 21–39. Springer,
            Heidelberg (2004). https://doi.org/10.1007/978-3-540-24638-1_2

[Pie18]   Pietrzak, K.: Proofs of catalytic space. Cryptology ePrint Archive, Report 2018/194 (2018). https://eprint.iacr.org/2018/194

[PPK+15] Park, S., Pietrzak, K., Kwon, A., Alwen, J., Fuchsbauer, G., Gaži, P.: SpaceMint: a cryptocurrency based on proofs of space. Cryptology ePrint Archive, Report 2015/528 (2015). http://eprint.iacr.org/2015/528

[RD16]   Ren, L., Devadas, S.: Proof of space from stacked expanders. In: Hirt, M., Smith, A. (eds.) TCC 2016, Part I. LNCS, vol. 9985, pp. 262–285. Springer, Heidelberg (2016). https://doi.org/10.1007/978-3-662-53641-4_11

[RSS11]   Ristenpart, T., Shacham, H., Shrimpton, T.: Careful with composition: limitations of the indifferentiability framework. In: Paterson, K.G. (ed.) EUROCRYPT 2011. LNCS, vol. 6632, pp. 487–506. Springer, Heidelberg (2011). https://doi.org/10.1007/978-3-642-20465-4_27

[SW08]   Shacham, H., Waters, B.: Compact proofs of retrievability. In: Pieprzyk, J. (ed.) ASIACRYPT 2008. LNCS, vol. 5350, pp. 90–107. Springer, Heidelberg (2008). https://doi.org/10.1007/978-3-540-89255-7_7

[VDJO+12] Dijk, M.V., Juels, A., Oprea, A., Rivest, R.L., Stefanov, E., Triandopoulos, N.: Hourglass schemes: how to prove that cloud files are encrypted. In: Proceedings of the 2012 ACM Conference on Computer and Communications Security, pp. 265–280. ACM (2012)

Simple Proofs of Space-Time and Rational Proofs of Storage

Tal Moran[1]([⊠]) and Ilan Orlov[2]

[1] IDC Herzliya, Herzliya, Israel
talm@idc.ac.il
[2] Outbrain, New York, USA

Abstract. We introduce a new cryptographic primitive: Proofs of Space-Time (PoSTs) and construct an extremely simple, practical protocol for implementing these proofs. A PoST allows a prover to convince a verifier that she spent a "space-time" resource (storing data—space—over a period of time). Formally, we define the PoST resource as a tradeoff between CPU work and space-time (under reasonable cost assumptions, a rational user will prefer to use the lower-cost space-time resource over CPU work).

Compared to a proof-of-work, a PoST requires less energy use, as the "difficulty" can be increased by extending the time period over which data is stored without increasing computation costs. Our definition is very similar to "Proofs of Space" [ePrint 2013/796, 2013/805] but, unlike the previous definitions, takes into account amortization attacks and storage duration. Moreover, our protocol uses a very different (and much simpler) technique, making use of the fact that we explicitly allow a space-time tradeoff, and doesn't require any non-standard assumptions (beyond random oracles). Unlike previous constructions, our protocol allows incremental difficulty adjustment, which can gracefully handle increases in the price of storage compared to CPU work. In addition, we show how, in a crypto-currency context, the parameters of the scheme can be adjusted using a market-based mechanism, similar in spirit to the difficulty adjustment for PoW protocols.

1 Introduction

A major problem in designing secure decentralized protocols for the internet is a lack of identity verification. It is often easy for an attacker to create many "fake" identities that cannot be distinguished from the real thing. Several strategies have been suggested for defending against such attacks (often referred to as "sybil attacks"); one of the most popular is to force users of the system to spend resources in order to participate. Creating multiple identities would require an attacker to spend a correspondingly larger amount of resources, making this attack much more expensive.

T. Moran—Supported by ISF grant no. 1790/13 and the Bar-Ilan Cyber-center.

A. Boldyreva and D. Micciancio (Eds.): CRYPTO 2019, LNCS 11692, pp. 381–409, 2019.
https://doi.org/10.1007/978-3-030-26948-7_14

Any bounded resource can be used as the "payment"; one of the more common is computing resources, since they do not require any additional infrastructure beyond that already needed to access the Internet. In order to ensure that users actually do spend the appropriate resource payment, the users must employ a "proof of work".

Proofs of work have been used for reducing spam [9], for defending against denial-of-service attacks [23] and fairly recently, as the underlying mechanism for implementing a decentralized bulletin-board—this is the technical heart of the Bitcoin protocol [17].

While effective, proofs-of-work have a significant drawback; they require energy in direct proportion to the resource used (i.e., the amount of electricity required to run the CPU during the proof of work generally depends linearly on the amount of work being performed). This is especially problematic in the context of the Bitcoin protocol, since the security of the system relies on all honest parties *constantly* performing proofs of work. In addition to having an environmental impact, this also sets a lower bound on transaction fees (since rational parties would only participate in the protocol if their reward exceeds their energy cost). Motivated in large part by the need to replace proofs-of-work as a basis for crypto-currencies, two (very similar) proposals for *Proofs of Space* (PoS) have been published [5,10]. Park et al. also designed an alternative crypto-currency that is based on Proofs of Space [18], and several new crypto-currency companies are also basing their protocols on similar ideas [1,2,15].

A PoS is a two-phase protocol[1]: it consists of an initialization phase and (sometime later) an execution phase. In an (N_0, N_1, T)-PoS the prover shows that she either (1) had access to at least N_0 storage between the initialization and execution phases and at least N_1 space during the execution phase, or (2) used more than T time during the execution phase.

At first glance, this definition might seem sufficient as a replacement for proof-of-work. However, in contrast to work, space can be reused. Using the PoS definition as a "resource payment" scheme thus violates two properties we would like any such scheme to satisfy:

1. **Amortization-Resistance**: A prover with access to max (N_0, N_1) space can, without violating the formal PoS security guarantee, generate an arbitrary number of different (N_0, N_1, T)-PoS proofs while using the same amount of resources as an honest prover generating a single proof; thus, the *amortized* cost per proof can be arbitrarily low.
2. **Rationally Stored Proofs**: Loosely speaking, in a *rationally stored proof* a verifier is convinced that a rational prover has expended a space resource over a period of time. There may exist a successful adversarial strategy that does not require the adversary to expend space over time, but this strategy will be more costly than the honest one. If we are interested in designing a crypto-currency that replaces CPU work with a space-based resource, our proof of resource consumption must be a rationally stored proof, otherwise rational

---

[1] For the purposes of this paper, we use the formal definitions of [10].

parties will prefer to use the adversarial strategy, and we can no longer claim that the crypto-currency is energy-efficient.

The *cost* of storage is proportional to the product of the storage space and the time it is used (e.g., in most cloud storage services, it costs the same to store 10 TB for two months or 20 TB for one month[2]). Under the PoS definition, a prover can pay an arbitrarily small amount by discarding almost all stored data after the initialization phase and rerunning the initialization in the execution phase (the prover only needs to store the communication from the verifier in the initialization phase). More generally, a *rational* prover will prefer to use computation over storage whenever the cost of storing the data between the phases is greater than the cost of rerunning the initialization; when this occurs the PoS basically devolves into a standard proof-of-work in terms of energy usage.

Even if we ignore energy use, this is a problem if the PoS is used in a protocol where the prover must generate many proofs, but only some will be verified: the dishonest prover will not have to expend resources on the unverified proofs in this case.

We note that though the definition of a PoS is insufficient to guarantee rational storage, the existing PoS *constructions* actually do achieve this under some parameters. However, this is more than just a definitional problem. Almost all previous PoS constructions [5,10,12,21,22] are based on the memory-hardness of labeling a specially-constructed directed graph, such that the label of each vertex is a hash (random-oracle) of its predecessors in the graph. The constructions use graph-pebbling games to show that correctly answering the verifier's challengers forces the prover to have either used the required amount of space or a much larger amount of oracle queries.

In all of these constructions, the *work* performed by the honest prover in the initialization phase is proportional to the work required to access the graph (i.e., $O(N_0)$). It's not clear how to increase the initialization costs without increasing either the memory size or verification cost linearly. This strongly bounds the time that can be allowed between the initialization and execution phases if we want rational provers to use space resources rather than CPU work. In the Spacemint protocol, for example, the authors suggest running the proofs every minute or so [18]. If one wanted to run a proof only once a month, a rational miner might prefer to rerun the initialization phase each time.

1.1 Our Contributions

"Fixed" Definition. In this paper, we define a new proof-of-resource-payment scheme: a "Proof of Spacetime" (PoST), that we believe is better suited as a

---

[2] Of course, this is also true for a local disk; during the interval in which we are using the disk to store data A, we can't use it to store anything else, so our "cost" is the utility we could have gained over the same period (e.g., by renting out the disk to a cloud-storage company).

scalable energy-efficient replacement for proof-of-work. Our definition is similar to a Proof of Space, but addresses both amortization and rationality of storage.

In a PoST, we consider two different "spendable" resources: one is CPU work (i.e., as in previous proofs-of-work), and the second is "spacetime": filling a specified amount of storage for a specified period of time (during which it cannot be used for anything else); we believe spacetime is the "correct" space-based analog to work (which is a measure of CPU power over time). Like work, spacetime is directly convertible to cost.

Rational Storage vs. Space. Rather than require the prover to show exactly which resource was spent in the execution phase, we allow the prover to choose arbitrarily the division between the two, as long as the total amount of resources spent is enough.

That is, the prover convinces a verifier that she *either* spent a certain amount of CPU work, *or* reserved a certain amount of storage space for some specified period of time or spent some linear combination of the two. However, by setting parameters correctly, we can ensure that *rational* provers will prefer to use space-time over work; when this is the case we say that a PoST is *Rationally Stored* (we give a formal definition in Sect. 2.2). In situations where it is reasonable to assume rational adversaries (such as in crypto-currencies), our definition opens the door to new constructions that might not satisfy the PoS requirements. For example, the PoS definition essentially requires a memory-hard function, while our construction is rationally stored but is *not* memory-hard!

Simple, Novel Construction. We construct a PoST based on *incompressible* proofs-of-work (IPoW); a variant of proofs-of-work for which we can lower-bound the storage required for the proof itself. We give two simple candidate constructions based on the standard "hash preimage" PoW and on storing part of a single hash output. Our protocols and proofs use a very different technique than existing proofs of space, and are much simpler to implement. (We note that although the constructions are extremely simple, proving their security is non-trivial.)

Incremental Difficulty Adjustment. Since the relative price of CPU and storage may change over time, use of a PoST (or PoS) protocol in a crypto-currency setting could require adjusting the parameters (in particular, if the relative price of storage increases, it may no longer be rational to use storage as the preferred resource). In existing PoS constructions, this appears to require rerunning the entire initialization protocol. In contrast, our PoST construction supports simple *incremental* difficulty adjustment—that is, users only have to pay the marginal work cost between difficulty levels.

Market-Based Parameter Adjustment. A related issue when designing a crypto-currency based on PoST (or PoS) is deciding when and how to adjust the initialization difficulty. We show how to do this automatically via a *market-based* mechanism (similar in spirit to the difficulty adjustment in PoW-based crypto-currencies). The idea is to incentivize users to honestly report whether they are recomputing or storing data (see Sect. 7 for details), allowing us to build protocols that automatically increase the difficulty when the price of storage rises sufficiently (in which case we'd expect to see more users choosing computation over storage). The detection technique is general, and may be of independent interest—it can be applied to existing PoS constructions as well.

Different Parameter Regimes. In comparison with existing PoS constructions, we think of the time between the initialization and proof phases as *weeks* rather than minutes (this could enable, for example, a crypto-currency in which the "miners" could be completely powered off for weeks at a time). One can think of our constructions as complementary to the existing PoS constructions for different parameter regimes—On the one hand, the proof phase of our PoST protocol is less efficient (it requires access to the entire storage, so a proof might take minutes rather than seconds, as is the case for the pebbling-based constructions. This means it is not as well suited to very short periods between proofs). On the other hand—unlike the existing PoS constructions—the computational difficulty of our initialization phase is tunable *independently* of the amount of space, so it is possible to use it to prove reasonable storage size over long periods (e.g., weeks or months). In this parameter regime, a proof that takes several minutes would be reasonable.

Compared to pebbling-based constructions, the big loss of efficiency is on the *prover*'s side. In our construction, the prover must read the entire table in order to generate a valid response to a challenge. This is indeed much worse asymptotically. Of course this is a drawback of our construction, and improving this is certainly a worthwhile goal. In practical terms, however, our efficiency doesn't preclude the use-cases we describe (e.g., even on a mid-range consumer HDD, sequential throughput is about 150 MB/s; this means reading through a 100 GB table in about 10 min, which is reasonable even if challenges occur every few hours, much less every few weeks).

Improvements to Spacemint. Finally, we propose a modification to the Spacemint crypto-currency protocol that removes some restrictions on the types of PoS protocols it can use—allowing it to use PoSTs rather than the specific PoS constructions it is currently based on (for reasons of space, this description is omitted here, but can be found in the eprint version).

1.2 Related Work

Random-Function-Inversion PoS. A recent work by Abusalah et al. [3] shows how to construct a PoS protocol based on inverting a random function. This construction is significantly simpler than the pebbling-based constructions (although still more complex than our construction). However, the initialization difficulty is also fixed, and it does not seem trivial to increase initialization difficulty without at the same time increasing verification difficulty linearly, and it does not appear to support incremental difficulty adjustment. Hence it does not appear suitable for long intervals between proofs.

Proofs of Storage/Retrievability. In a proof-of-storage/retrievability a prover convinces a verifier that she is correctly storing a file previously provided by the verifier [6,7,13,14,20]. The main motivation behind these protocols is verifiable cloud storage; they are not suitable for use in a PoST protocol due to high communication requirements (the verifier must send the entire file to the server in the first phase), and because they are not publicly verifiable. That is, if the prover colludes with the owner of the file, she could use a very small amount of storage space and still be able to prove that she can retrieve a large amount of pseudorandom data.

Proofs of Replication. In a Proof of Replication [11], a party would like to prove that they are storing multiple redundant copies of a file. The PoRep definitions combine a PoS and a Proof of Retrievability. Similarly to the PoST definition, PoReps don't (and can't) guarantee that the prover actually stores redundant copies of the data, but instead make it an ε-Nash equilibrium (so a rational prover does not lose much by doing so). The existing constructions of PoReps depend on depth-robust graphs for the PoS and on sequential timing assumptions (the prover must respond to a challenge quickly, and the timing assumptions ensure that the prover cannot recompute its data in that time).

Memory-Hard Functions. Loosely speaking, a memory-hard function is a function that requires a large amount of memory to evaluate [4,19]. One of the main motivations for constructing such functions is to construct proofs-of-work that are "ASIC-resistant" (based on the assumption that the large memory requirement would make such chips prohibitively expensive). Note that the proposed memory-hard functions are still proofs-of-*work*; the prover must constantly utilize her CPU in order to produce additional proofs. PoSTs, on the other hand, allow the prover to "rest" (e.g., by turning off her computer) while still expending space-time (since expending this resource only requires that storage be filled with data for a period of time).

Filecoin. Filecoin [15] is a crypto-currency protocol based on Proofs of Replication, whose underlying idea is to base the consensus algorithm resource on "useful" space. The Filecoin whitepaper also defines a "Proof of Spacetime",[3] however in their definitions the proof must include a proof of the elapsed time (requiring assumptions such sequential work timing assumptions). Moreover, their constructions make use of very heavy cryptographic machinery (such as zkSNARKS).

Permacoin. Miller, Juels, Shi, Parno and Katz proposed the Permacoin protocol, a cryptocurrency that includes, in addition to the standard PoWs, a special, distributed, proof of retrievability that allows the cryptocurrency to serve as a distributed backup for *useful* data [16]. In strict contrast to PoSTs, the Permacoin construction is amortizable *by design*—an adversary who stores the entire dataset can reuse it for as many clients as it wishes. Thus, Permacoin still requires regular PoWs, and cannot be used to replace them entirely with a

---

[3] We note that the our PoST definitions precede theirs.

storage-based resource. Also by design, clients require a large amount of communication to retrieve the data they must store, in contrast to PoSs and PoSTs in which clients trade computation for communication.

2   Proofs of Spacetime

A PoST deals in two types of resources: one is processing power and the other is storage. All our constructions are in the random oracle model—we model processing power by counting the number of queries to the random oracle.

Modeling storage is a bit trickier. Our purpose is to allow an *energy-efficient* proof-of-resource-consumption for rational parties, where we assume that the prover is rewarded for each successful proof (this is, roughly speaking, the case in Bitcoin). Thus, simply proving that you used a lot of space in a computation is insufficient; otherwise it would be rational to perform computations without pause (reusing the same space). Instead, we measure spacetime—a unit of space "reserved" for a unit of time (and unusable for anything else during that time). To model this, we separate the computation into two phases; we think of the first phase as occurring at time $t = 0$ and the second at time $t = 1$ (after a unit of time has passed). After executing the first phase, the prover outputs a state $\sigma \in \{0,1\}^*$ to be transferred to the second phase; this is the only information that can be passed between phases. The size of the state $|\sigma|$ (in bits) measures the space used by the prover over the time period between phases.

Informally, the soundness guarantee of a PoST is that the *total* number of resource units used by the adversary is lower bounded by some specified value—the adversary can decide how to divide them between processing units and spacetime units.

We give the formal definition of a PoST in Sect. 2.2, in Sect. 3 we present a simple construction of a PoST, and in Sect. 3.1 we prove its security.

2.1   Units and Notation

Our basic units of measurement are CPU throughput, Space and Time. These can correspond to arbitrary real-world units (e.g., 2^{30} hash computations per minute, one Gigabyte and one minute, respectively). We define the rest of our units in terms of the basics:

- Work: CPU × time; A unit of CPU effort expended (e.g., 2^{30} hash computations).
- Spacetime: space × time; A space unit that is "reserved" for a unit of time (and unusable for anything else during that time).

In our definitions, and in particular when talking about the behavior of *rational* adversaries, we would like to measure the total cost incurred by the prover, regardless of the type of resource expended. To do this, we need to specify the conversion ratio between work and spacetime:

Real-world Cost. We define γ to be the work-per-spacetime cost ratio in terms of real-world prices. That is, in the real-world one spacetime unit costs as much as γ work units (the value of γ may change over time, and depends on the relative real-world costs of storage space and processing power).

We define the corresponding cost function, the *real-world cost* of a PoST to be a normalized cost in work units: a PoST that uses $|\sigma|$ spacetime units and x work units has real-world cost $c = \gamma|\sigma| + x$.

2.2   Defining a PoST Scheme

A PoST scheme consists of two phases, each of which is an interactive protocol between a prover $P = (P_{\text{init}}, P_{\text{exec}})$ and a verifier $V = (V_{\text{init}}, V_{\text{exec}})$.[4] (for brevity, we drop the *init* and *exec* subscripts when they are clear from the context.) Both parties have access to a random oracle $H^{(\text{work})}$.

Initialization Phase Both parties receive as input an id string $id \in \{0,1\}^*$. At the conclusion of this phase, both the prover and the verifier output state strings ($\sigma_P \in \{0,1\}^*$ and $\sigma_V \in \{0,1\}^*$, respectively):

$$(\sigma_P, \sigma_V) \leftarrow \left\langle P_{\text{init}}^{H^{(\text{work})}}(id), V_{\text{init}}^{H^{(\text{work})}}(id) \right\rangle .$$

Execution Phase Both parties receive the id and their corresponding state from the initialization phase. At the end of this phase, the verifier either accepts or rejects ($out_V \in \{0,1\}$, where 1 is interpreted as "accept"). The prover has no output:

$$(\cdot, out_V) \leftarrow \left\langle P_{\text{exec}}^{H^{(\text{work})}}(id, \sigma_P), V_{\text{exec}}^{H^{(\text{work})}}(id, \sigma_V) \right\rangle .$$

The execution phase can be repeated multiple times without rerunning the initialization phase. This is critical, since the initialization phase requires work, while the execution phase is energy-efficient. Thus, although a single execution of the PoST does not give any advantage over proof-of-work, the amortized work per execution can be made arbitrary low.

PoST Parameters. A PoST has three parameters: w, the *Honest Initialization Work*, m, the *Honest Storage Space*, and f, the *Soundness Bound*.

Honest Initialization Work (w). This is the expected work performed by the *honest* prover in the initialization phase. This should be "tunable" to ensure that storing the output remains the rational choice rather than recomputing the initialization as the space-time to work cost ratio changes.

If the cost of the initialization phase is too low, the adversary can generate a proof more cheaply than an honest prover by deleting all data after initialization,

---

[4] Although the definition allows general interaction, in our construction the first phase is non-interactive (the prover sends a single message) and the second consists of a single round.

then rerunning the initialization just before the proof phase. In this case, the adversary does not store any data between phases, so does not pay *any* space-time cost. We formalize this in Definition 8 as a *rationality* attack. **Note that this is a general attack that also applies to PoS schemes**—hence they must also have a lower bound on the work required for initialization.

Honest Storage Space (m). This is the amount of storage the honest prover must expend during the period between the initialization and execution phases (and between successive execution phases).

Definition 1 (PoST). *A protocol* (P, V) *as defined above is a* (w, m, ε, f)*-PoST if it satisfies the properties of completeness and* f*-soundness defined below.*

Completeness

Definition 2 (PoST η-Completeness). *We say that a PoST is* η*-complete if for every* $id \in \{0,1\}^{poly(k)}$ *and every oracle* $H^{(work)}$,

$$\Pr\left[out_V = 1 : (\sigma_P, \sigma_V) \leftarrow \left\langle P_{init}^{H^{(work)}}(id), V_{init}^{H^{(work)}}(id) \right\rangle, \right.$$
$$\left. (\cdot, out_V) \leftarrow \left\langle P_{exec}^{H^{(work)}}(id, \sigma_P), V_{exec}^{H^{(work)}}(id, \sigma_V) \right\rangle \right] \geq \eta .$$

When $\eta = 1$ completeness is perfect (in this case we sometimes omit the η).

Soundness. We define a security game with two phases; each phase has a corresponding adversary. We denote the adversary $\mathcal{A} = (\mathcal{A}_1, \mathcal{A}_2)$, where $\mathcal{A}_1$ and $\mathcal{A}_2$ correspond to the first and the second phases of the game. $\mathcal{A}_1$ and $\mathcal{A}_2$ can coordinate arbitrarily before the beginning of the game, but cannot communicate during the game itself (or between phases).

Definition 3 (PoST (n, s, T_1, T_2)-Security Game). *Each phase of the security game corresponds to a PoST phase:*

1. *Initialization.* $\mathcal{A}_1$ *chooses a set of ids* $\{id_1, \ldots, id_n\}$ *where* $id_i \in \{0,1\}^*$. *It then interacts in parallel with* n *independent (honest) verifiers executing the initialization phase of the PoST protocol, where verifier* i *is given* id_i *as input. Let* $\sigma_{\mathcal{A}}$ *be the output of* $\mathcal{A}_1$ *after this interaction and* $(\sigma_{V_1}, \ldots, \sigma_{V_n})$ *be the outputs of the verifiers.*
2. *Execution. The adversary* $\mathcal{A}_2(id_1, \ldots, id_n, \sigma_{\mathcal{A}})$ *interacts with* n *independent verifiers executing the execution phase of the PoST protocol, where verifier* i *is given* (id_i, σ_{V_i}) *as input.*[5]

We say the adversary has succeeded if $|\sigma_{\mathcal{A}}| \leq s$, $\mathcal{A}_1$ *makes at most* T_1 *queries to the oracle* $H^{(work)}$, $\mathcal{A}_2$ *makes at most* T_2 *queries to the oracle and all of the verifiers output 1 (we denote this event* $\mathbf{Succ}_{n,s,T_1,T_2}$)

---

[5] Each of the verifiers runs a copy of the honest verifier code with independent random coins; $\mathcal{A}_2$, however, can correlate its sessions with the verifiers.

Definition 4 (PoST f-Soundness). *We say a PoST protocol is ε, f-sound if for all $T_1, T_2, s, \geq 0$ and all $n \geq 1$, every adversary $\mathcal{A} = (\mathcal{A}_1, \mathcal{A}_2)$ must satisfy the following conditions in the PoST security game:*

1. *Rational Storage: If $\mathcal{A}_1$ made less than $\varepsilon \cdot w$ queries to the work oracle, then the probability of success is negligible (in the security parameter).*
2. *Space-Time Trade-Off: $\Pr\left[\mathbf{Succ}_{n,s,T_1,T_2}\right] \leq f(n, s, T_1, T_2)$.*

The first condition checks that the adversary spends at least an ε fraction of the honest work in the initialization phase. This prevents the adversary from launching a "rationality attack": if the initialization phase requires very little computational effort, the prover can "throw out" the stored data from the initialization phase and rerun the phase to regenerate any needed data during the execution phase. This would make its total space-time cost negligible (since the "time" component vanishes).

The second condition bounds the trade-off between space-time and work. Intuitively, a PoST satisfying this definition forces an adversary to trade space for queries. The use of n ids rather than just one prevents an amortization attack, wherein the adversary reuses the same space for different proofs. Naïvely, to generate n proofs the prover would require n times the queries, splitting the storage equally between them. Ideally using anything less we'd like the adversary to fail with overwhelming probability. However, this is impossible to achieve, even if it might be true for an individual PoST. This is because the adversary can always "forget" the entire data for a subset of the n instances, and rerun the initialization phase for those instances in the proof phase.

Rationally Stored Proofs of Work. Our high-level goal in this paper is to construct *energy-efficient* proofs, by forcing provers to use storage rather than work. Unfortunately, our definitions (and constructions) don't allow a prover to *prove* they used storage (this is actually impossible if the adversary can simulate the initialization phase without a lot of storage—which is always the case unless communication in the initialization phase is proportional to storage or we use non-standard assumptions). However, we can still give conditions under which a *rational* prover (whose goal is to minimize expected total cost) would prefer to use storage. As long as these conditions are met, it seems reasonable to assume that real-world users would choose storage over work (especially in a crypto-currency setting, where profit is the main motive for participating).

Definition 5 ((γ, ε')-Rationally-Stored PoST). *We say a PoST is (γ, ε')-rationally stored if, when the real-world cost of a space unit is less than γ, then for any given resource budget C, the optimal execution strategy (maximizing the expected number of successful PoST proofs for that budget) requires that at least an ε'-fraction of the budget be used for storage).*

We don't count the initialization cost in Definition 5. This is because it is only incurred once, while the cost of the execution phase is incurred repeatedly.

We can identify a sufficient condition for a PoST to be rationally stored:

Lemma 1. *If a (w, m, ε, f)-PoST is η-complete, and for all $C > 0$, $s < \varepsilon' \cdot C/\gamma$ it holds that*

$$\sum_{i=1}^{\infty} f(i, s, C - \gamma \cdot s) < \eta \cdot C/(\gamma \cdot m)$$

then it is (γ, ε')-Rationally-Stored.

(Note that we assume $f(i, s, T) \leq 1$ for all values i, s and T—otherwise we use instead $f^*(i, s, T) = \min\{1, f(i, s, T)\}$.)

Proof. Denote $\#G$ the random variable for the number of successful PoST proofs produced by the adversary. Then

$$\mathbb{E}[\#G] = \sum_{i=1}^{\infty} i \cdot \Pr[\#G = i] = \sum_{i=1}^{\infty} i \cdot \left(\Pr[\#G \geq i] - \Pr[\#G \geq i + 1] \right)$$
$$= \sum_{i=1}^{\infty} \Pr[\#G \geq i] .$$

By the definition of f-soundness, for an adversary using s space and $C - \gamma \cdot s$ oracle queries, the expectation is thus bounded by

$$\mathbb{E}[\#G] \leq \sum_{i=1}^{\infty} f(i, s, C - \gamma \cdot s)$$

On the other hand, using the honest proof strategy, and allocating the entire C budget to space will give $C/(\gamma \cdot m)$ proofs, each successful with probability at least η, hence the expected number of successful proofs for the honest space-only strategy is $\eta \cdot C/(\gamma \cdot m)$.

Thus, the honest proof strategy generates, in expectation, more successful proofs (i.e., higher reward) than any adversarial strategy that spends less than an ε' fraction of its budget on storage space. □

Note that the adversary can always rerun the initialization phase instead of storing data, so for any η-complete, (w, m, ε, f)-PoST we must have $f(i, 0, i \cdot w) \geq \eta$, hence if $\gamma \cdot m > w$ the condition of Lemma 1 cannot be satisfied.

Comparison with the PoS definition. As we remarked in the introduction, an (N_0, N_1, T)-PoS does not give any formal security guarantees with respect to the PoST definition (even if we ignore amortization), since it does not address rationality attacks at all. In the other direction, even an optimally-sound (w, m, f)-PoST can't guarantee a (x, x, w)-PoS, for any $x \in (0, w)$, since we don't place any lower bound on the space required to generate a proof—the adversary can always trade space for polynomial work. Thus, the parameters are not truly comparable.

Note that even if we did add a space lower bound, similar to the PoS definition, in order to make use of it in practice one would have to add additional non-standard assumptions (such as timing assumptions); this is because the adversary can perform the space-time tradeoff at the level of entire PoS instances (e.g., generate n instances, but use space for only a single instance at a time).

Thus, one can think of the two definitions as being targeted at different "regimes": a PoS forces the prover to use a lot of space, but is not well suited to high storage costs and requires frequent proof phases (to prevent a space/time tradeoff), while the PoST definition does allow long periods of elapsed time between proofs (with a suitably hard initialization step), but relies on the rationality of the adversary to enforce use of storage rather than work.

Non-Interactive Proofs of SpaceTime (NIPSTs)

Sigma-PoST. A *Sigma-PoST* is a PoST scheme that has the form of a Sigma-protocol: $P_{\mathrm{init}}(id)$ sends a single commitment message to the verifier; V_{init} responds with a random challenge string, after which P_{init} sends a single response message. For the execution phase, the commitment message is the same as the initialization commitment (hence does not need to be resent); V_{exec} sends a random challenge string, and P_{exec} responds in turn with a single message.

We note that our PoST construction is a Sigma-PoST.

Making Sigma-PoSTs Non-Interactive. The initialization phase of a Sigma-PoST can be made non-interactive in the random oracle model by using the Fiat-Shamir heuristic (replacing the verifier's response with a hash of the commitment message). However, interaction cannot be removed entirely—the execution phase requires a challenge that cannot be predicted by the prover at initialization time—hence, under standard assumptions it cannot be solely a function of the prover's inputs.

Using Proofs of Sequential Work. By introducing a sequential timing assumption, we *can* make the proof entirely non-interactive; the idea is to use the output of the initialization phase (or the previous execution phase if we're running multiple times) as the input to a publicly-verifiable *proof of sequential work* (PoSW). We can then use (a hash of) the output of the PoSW as the challenge to the execution phase. If we assume a lower bound on the elapsed time for an adversary to perform a given amount of sequential work, this construction ensures that the adversary must have used sufficient spacetime resources between the initialization and execution phases.

This NIPST construction appears to violate our main goal—it requires continuous CPU work even for an honest user. The trick is that a *single* PoSW instance can be shared between an arbitrary number of provers, so the *amortized* CPU cost vanishes as the number of users grows. Instead of using the previous proof directly as the input to the PoSW, we create a Merkle tree whose leaves are the inputs from each prover, and use the root of the tree as the input to the single, shared PoSW.

The full NIPST consists of (1) the initialization phase output, (2) a Merkle path from the output to the root of the tree, (3) a PoSW whose input is the Merkle root and (4) the execution phase proof, with the PoSW as the challenge.

We note that some PoSW constructions (such as that of Cohen and Pietrzak [8]) don't have *unique* proofs; an adversary can generate multiple different proofs for the same input that will all be accepted by a verifier. When used in a NIPST, this means the PoST execution-phase challenges come from a distribution that can be biased by the adversary. However, our PoST construction can handle this as long as the distribution has enough min-entropy (which must be the case, since otherwise an adversary could solve the PoSW by trying to guess the result and running the verifier to check—this can be done in parallel, so would violate the sequential work security of the PoSW).

2.3   Constructing a PoST: High-Level Overview

Our proof of spacetime has each prover generate the data they must store on their own. To ensure that this data is cheaper to store than to generate (and to allow public verifiability), we require the stored data to be a proof-of-work. We construct our protocol using the abstract notion of an incompressible-proof-of-work (IPoW); this is a proof-of-work (PoW) that is non-compressible in the sense that storing n different IPoWs requires n times the space compared to storing one IPoW (we define them more formally below; see Sect. 2.4).

As long as the cost of storing an IPoW proof is less than the cost of recomputing it, the prover will prefer to store it. However, this solution is very inefficient: it requires the prover to send its entire storage to the verifier. In order to verify the proof with low communication, instead of one large proof of work, we generate a table containing τ entries; each entry in the table is a proof of work that can be independently verified.

Why the Naïve Construction Fails. At first glance, it would seem that there is an easy solution for verifying that the prover stored a large fraction of the table:

1. In the initialization phase: the prover commits to the table contents (using a Merkle tree whose leaves are the table entries)
2. In the execution phase: the verifier sends a random set of indices to the prover, who must then respond with the corresponding table entries and commitment openings (merkle paths to the root of the tree).

Unfortunately, this doesn't work: the prover can discard the entire table and reconstruct only those entries requested by the verifier during the execution phase.

A Simple Solution. Our construction overcomes this problem by forcing the prover to commit to the entire table *at the time of the challenge*, and only then learn the random entries to be sent back (this is made non-interactive using the Fiat-Shamir heuristic). Intuitively, the prover is forced to either reconstruct a large fraction of the table (in which case it must either store many IPoWs, or recompute them), or spend a lot of computational work trying to find a commitment that will produce a "good" challenge. By setting the parameters correctly, we can ensure that in the second case the amount of work the prover must do is more than the initialization cost (see Sect. 3 for details).

2.4   Incompressible Proofs of Work

The standard definitions of PoWs do not rule out an adversary that can store a small amount of data and can use it to regenerate an entire table of proofs with very low computational overhead. Thus, to ensure the adversary must indeed store the entire table we need a more restrictive definition:

An *Incompressible Proof of Work* (IPoW) can be described as a protocol between a verifier V and a prover P:

1. The prover P is given a challenge ch as input, and outputs a "proof" π:
2. The verifier receives (ch, π) and outputs 1 (accept) or 0 (reject).

For simplicity, we denote IPoW (ch) the output of the honest prover on challenge ch (this is a random variable that depends on the random oracle and the prover's coins).

Defining an IPoW. Let $q_P^\#$ denote the number of oracle calls made by P in the protocol (this is a random variable that depends on ch and the random coins of P).

Definition 6 ((w', m, f)-IPoW). *A protocol is a (w', m, f)-IPoW if:*

1. $\mathbb{E}\left[q_P^\#\right] \leq w'$ *(the honest prover's expected work is bounded by w'),*
2. $|\pi| \leq m$ *(the honest prover's storage is bounded by m) and*
3. *The IPoW is complete (c.f. Definition 7) and f-sound (c.f. Definition 8).*

Definition 7 (IPoW Completeness). *An IPoW protocol is complete if, for every challenge ch, the probability that the verifier rejects is negligible in the security parameter (the probability is over the coins of the prover and the random oracle).*

Definition 8 (IPoW $f(n, s, T)$-Soundness). *We say $\mathcal{A} = (\mathcal{A}_1, \mathcal{A}_2)$ is an $[n, s, T]$-adversary if $\mathcal{A}_1$ outputs a string σ with length $|\sigma| \leq s$, while $\mathcal{A}_2$ gets σ as input, makes at most T queries to the random oracle and outputs n pairs $(ch_1, \pi_1, \ldots, ch_n, \pi_n)$.*

*Denote **Succ** the event (over the randomness of $\mathcal{A}$ and the random oracle) that all the challenges are distinct and $\forall i \in [n] : V(ch_i, \pi_i) = 1$. An IPoW protocol is f-sound if for every adversary and all $n \geq 1$, $s \geq 0$ and $T \geq 0$*

$$\Pr\left[\mathbf{Succ}\right] < f(n, s, T)$$

Note that we don't restrict the number of queries $\mathcal{A}_1$ makes to the oracle.

As in the PoST definition, this condition bounds the trade-off between space-time and work for the IPoW adversary. Ideally, we'd like f to be negligible when $s < n \cdot m$ and $T < n \cdot w'$ (this implies that the adversary must either store the same amount as the honest prover, or do enough work to reconstruct the proof from scratch). Unfortunately, we can't hope to achieve this; for example, for any $i \in (0, n)$. if an adversary stores only i IPoWs, and reconstructs the remaining $n - i$, it will have overwhelming probability of success while storing $i \cdot m$ bits and doing $(n - i) \cdot w'$ work. Moreover, the adversary can always "forget" j bits of storage and guess them correctly with 2^{-j} probability. Thus, in any f-sound IPoW, we must have, for all $j \geq 0$ and $i \in (0, n)$ that $f(n, i \cdot m - j, (n-i) \cdot w', T) \geq 2^{-j} - \varepsilon$ for some negligible ε (that depends on the completeness of the protocol).

3   Our Simple PoST Construction: The Details

Formally, we describe the protocol in the presence of two types of random oracles, a "work" oracle $H^{(\mathrm{work})}$ and "Merkle" oracles H_i (for $i \neq j$, H_i and H_j are independent random oracles).[6] We assume the work oracle has a much higher cost than the calls to the Merkle oracles (in implementation, we can think of the Merkle oracles as a single iteration of a fast hash function, while the work oracle can be implemented by a slower hash function or multiple sequential iterations). In the analysis, we track the number of calls separately, using T to denote the number of calls to $H^{(\mathrm{work})}$ and T^* the number of calls to the Merkle oracles.

The formal PoST protocol description appears as Protocol 1. To construct it, we use a (w', m, f)-IPoW. (We construct two oracle-based IPoW schemes in Sect. 4.)

The soundness of our Simple PoST protocol is summarized in the following theorem. (For our construction we allow $\mathcal{A}_1$ unbounded access to the work oracle, so we don't include a T_1 parameter.)

Theorem 1 (PoST Soundness). *Let k_{ch} be the min-entropy of the distribution from which PoST challenges are sampled. The Simple PoST protocol, instantiated with an f'-sound IPoW, is f-sound for*

$$f(n, s, T_1^*, (T, T^*)) = \min\{$$
$$\min_{\varepsilon \in (0,1)} \left\{ f'(\varepsilon \cdot n \cdot \tau, s + n \cdot (k_H + \log T^* + \tau), T) + T^* \cdot \varepsilon^k \right\} + (T^*)^2 \cdot 2^{-k_H} + T_1^* \cdot 2^{-k_{ch}} ,$$
$$2^{-k_H \cdot (n - \max\{T_1^*, T^*\})}\} .$$

(Note that the second term in the outer min is relevant only when $n > \max\{T_1^*, T^*\}$.)

---

[6] This is just for convenience of notation, we can implement them all using a single oracle by assigning a unique prefix to the oracle queries (e.g., $\mathrm{H}_i(x) = \mathrm{H}(i||x)$.).

Protocol 1. SIMPLE-POST

Public Parameters: k_H: hash output size, k: security parameter, τ: table size and IPoW (ch) is a (w', m, f)-IPoW.

Storing Phase: (Performed by the prover P)

Inputs: $id \in \{0, 1\}^*$.

1. Generate an array G of size τ as follows:

   For each $0 \leq i < \tau$, set $G[i] \stackrel{\text{def}}{=} \text{IPoW} (id||i)$ (where the IPoW is given access to $H^{(\text{work})}$ as its underlying work oracle).

2. Run the proof phase with fixed challenge 0.

3. Publish the string id and the initial proof.

Proof Phase: (Performed by the prover P)

Upon receiving a challenge ch from the verifier V:

1: Construct a Merkle tree whose leaves are labeled with the entries of G, and each internal node's label is the output of the random oracle H_{ch} on the concatenation of its children's labels. Let com be the root label.

2: Parse $H_{ch} (com)$ as a set of k indices $(i_1, \ldots, i_k) \in \{0, \tau - 1\}^k$.

3: Let π_j be the Merkle path from the table entry $G[i_j]$ to the root com. // The first element of π_j is the table entry itself.

4: Output $com, \pi_1, \ldots, \pi_k$. // This can be made more communication efficient by eliminating common labels.

The honest prover does not need any calls to $H^{(\text{work})}$, but needs up to 2τ calls to the Merkle oracle (or temporary space to store the Merkle tree).

Proof Phase: (Performed by the verifier V)

Generate a random challenge ch and send it to the prover. Wait to receive the list $com, \pi_1 \ldots, \pi_k$

1: Parse $H_{ch} (com)$ as a set of k indices $(i_1, \ldots, i_k) \in \{0, \tau - 1\}^k$.

2: **for all** $j \in \{1, \ldots, k\}$ **do**

3:     Verify that $G[i_j]$ (the first element of π_j) is a valid IPoW for the challenge $id||i_j$ (using the oracle $H^{(\text{work})}$).

4:     Verify that π_j is a valid Merkle path from the leaf i_j to the root com (using the oracle H_{ch}).

5: **end for**

Corollary 1. *When instantiated with the m-Partial-Hash IPoW, the Simple PoST is f-sound for*

$$f(n, s, T_1^*, (T, T^*)) = \min_{\varepsilon \in (0,1)} \left\{ 2^{-(\varepsilon \cdot n \cdot \tau \cdot m - (T \cdot m + s + n \cdot (k_H + \log T^* + \tau)))} + T^* \cdot \varepsilon^k \right\} +$$

$$(T^*)^2 \cdot 2^{-k_H} + T_1^* \cdot 2^{-k_{ch}} .$$

3.1   Security Proof

Proof (of Theorem 1). Let $\mathcal{A} = (\mathcal{A}_1, \mathcal{A}_2)$ be an adversary that wins the $(n, s, T_1^*, (T, T^*))$-PoST security game with probability p. For every $\varepsilon < 1$, we can use $\mathcal{A}$ to construct an IPoW adversary $\mathcal{A}^{(IPoW)} = (\mathcal{A}_1^{(IPoW)}, \mathcal{A}_2^{(IPoW)})$ as follows:

Let $ch_1, \ldots, ch_n$ be random challenges independently selected from a distribution with min-entropy k_{ch}.[7]

IPoW Adversary Initialization $(\mathcal{A}_1^{(IPoW)})$:

1. Execute $\mathcal{A}_1$, recording the n ids $id_1, \ldots, id_n$ and storing its output σ.
2. Execute $\mathcal{A}_2$, with inputs $id_1, \ldots, id_n, \sigma$ and challenges $ch_1, \ldots, ch_n$. While executing, keep track of all calls to H_{ch_i}. Denote $com_1, \ldots, com_n$ the first elements of each $\mathcal{A}_2$ proof (which, for an honest prover, would each correspond to the root of a merkle tree).
3. For all $i \in [n]$:
   (a) Denote Q_i the set of queries to H_{ch_i}.
   (b) For every $q \in Q_i$, attempt to reconstruct a merkle tree with root $H_{ch_i}(q)$. Obviously, this may not be possible for every query q, and even when possible may not result in a full tree. We will say a leaf (i, j) *exists* for q if some subset of Q_i comprises a valid Merkle path from the leaf j to the root $H_{ch_i}(q)$. (Note that the reconstruction doesn't make any *additional* calls to the Merkle oracle, it just uses the stored results.)
   (c) For all q, and every existing leaf (i, j) for q, run the IPoW verifier with challenge $id_i\|j$ to check if the leaf is a valid IPoW proof. In this case, we say the leaf (i, j) is *valid* for q.
   (d) We say a query q is ε-*good* if there exist $\varepsilon \cdot \tau$ different leaves that are valid for q.
   (e) If there does not exist an ε-good query in Q_i, output $\perp$ and abort. Otherwise, denote g_i the index of the first ε-good query in Q_i, and let v_i be a bit-vector indicating the valid leaves ($v_{i,j} = 1$ iff (i, j) is a valid leaf for q_{g_i}).
4. Output $(\sigma, id_1, \ldots, id_n, g_1, \ldots, g_n, v_1, \ldots, v_n)$.

Note that the output length for $\mathcal{A}_1^{(IPoW)}$ is $s + n \cdot k_H + n \cdot \log T^* + n \cdot \tau = s + n \cdot (k_H + \log T^* + \tau)$ bits (since for all i, $|Q_i| < T^*$, and assuming, w.l.o.g, that the id size is k_H—we can always use a hash of the id if its larger).

IPoW Adversary Prover $(\mathcal{A}_2^{(IPoW)})$:

1. Run Steps 2 and 3 from the execution of $\mathcal{A}_1^{(IPoW)}$.
2. For each $i \in [n]$, reconstruct the Merkle tree rooted at $H_{ch_i}(q_{g_i})$ and for every valid leaf (i, j), as indicated by v_i, output $id_i\|j$ as an IPoW challenge and leaf (i, j) as the corresponding proof.

Note that $\mathcal{A}_2^{(IPoW)}$ makes at most T calls to the work oracle and T^* calls to the Merkle oracle, since it executes $\mathcal{A}_2$ exactly once.

---

[7] These can be chosen by hardwiring a seed in the code of both $\mathcal{A}_1^{(IPoW)}$ and $\mathcal{A}_2^{(IPoW)}$, and computing ch_i using the Merkle oracle, which is not counted against the query budget of $\mathcal{A}_2^{(IPoW)}$.

When $\mathcal{A}_2^{(IPoW)}$ succeeds, we're guaranteed that for each of the n challenges it can extract an ε-fraction of valid leaves, hence it outputs at least $\varepsilon \cdot n \cdot \tau$ valid IPoW proofs.

The storage space it requires is at most $s + n \cdot (k_H + \log T^* + \tau)$ bits. Thus, $\mathcal{A}^{(IPoW)}$ is an $(\varepsilon \cdot n \cdot \tau, s + n \cdot (k_H + \log T^* + \tau), T)$-IPoW adversary.

IPoW Adversary Success Probability: To bound the probability of success, we first rule out two "catastrophic" events:

- $\mathcal{A}_1$ makes a query to H_{ch_i}. Since $\mathcal{A}_1$ makes at most T_1^* queries in total to the Merkle oracles, and ch_i is chosen from a distribution with min-entropy k_{ch}, the probability of this occurring for challenge ch_i is at most $T_1^* \cdot 2^{-k_{ch}}$.
- $\mathcal{A}_2$ finds a collision in H_{ch_i} for some i. Since the Merkle oracle has output length k_H, and $\mathcal{A}_2$ makes at most T^* queries to H_{ch_i}, by the Birthday Bound the probability of finding any collision is less than $(T^*)^2 \cdot 2^{-k_H}$.

Now, consider instance i of the PoST proofs generated by $\mathcal{A}_2$. We claim that unless $p < 2^{-k_H}$, com_i must be the result of a query $\mathcal{A}_2$ makes to H_{ch_i}. To see this, recall that we assume $\mathcal{A}_1$ did not query H_{ch_i} on any input. Thus, if $\mathcal{A}_2$ did not receive com_i as the result of an oracle query, the probability that it can generate a valid Merkle path that terminates at com_i is at most 2^{-k_H}.

Since $\mathcal{A}_2$ can make at most T^* Merkle queries, each execution of $\mathcal{A}_2$ can have at most T^* potential Merkle roots for instance i.

Denote $\mathbf{Bad}_i$ the event that there are no ε-good queries in Q_i. Denote $\mathbf{Succ}$ the event that $\mathcal{A}_2$ is successful (for all n instances). We claim that for all i, $T_1^*, \ldots, T_n^*$ such that $\Pr\left[\mathbf{Bad}_i \bigwedge_{j=1}^{n} |Q_j| = T_j^*\right] > 0$, it holds that

$$\Pr\left[\mathbf{Succ} \,\middle|\, \mathbf{Bad}_i \bigwedge_{j=1}^{n} |Q_j| = T_j^*\right] < T_i^* \cdot \varepsilon^k .$$

To see this, consider an execution of $\mathcal{A}_2$. In order for $\mathcal{A}_2$ to be successful, it must output a good PoST proof for instance id_i. This means it must output a Merkle root com_i and the k merkle paths from valid leaves that are selected by $H_{ch_i}(com_i)$.

For every new query q_i made by $\mathcal{A}_2$, conditioned on $\mathbf{Bad}_i$ the probability that $H_{ch_i}(q_i)$ selects k valid leaves in *any* Merkle tree in $\mathcal{A}_2$'s view is at most ε^k; this is because, conditioning on $\mathbf{Bad}_i$, no Merkle tree in $\mathcal{A}_2$'s view has more than an ε-fraction of valid leaves. Since q_i has not been previously queried, $H_{ch_i}(q_i)$ is independent of the view up to that point, hence the probability that k random indices are all valid is at most ε^k. Since there are exactly T_i^* queries to H_{ch_i}, the claim follows by the union bound.

Denote $\mathbf{Bad} = \mathbf{Bad}_1 \vee \cdots \vee \mathbf{Bad}_n$ the event that for some i there did not exist an ε-good query. Since $\mathcal{A}$ is bounded by T^* queries to the Merkle oracles, it must hold that $\sum_{i=1}^{n} |Q_i| \leq T^*$. Thus,

$$\Pr[\mathbf{Succ} \wedge \mathbf{Bad}]$$

$$= \Pr\left[\mathbf{Succ} \wedge \mathbf{Bad} \wedge \sum_{i=1}^{n} |Q_i| \leq T^*\right]$$

$$= \Pr\left[\mathbf{Succ} \wedge (\mathbf{Bad}_1 \vee \cdots \vee \mathbf{Bad}_n) \wedge \sum_{i=1}^{n} |Q_i| \leq T^*\right]$$

$$= \sum_{T_1^*,\ldots,T_n^*} \Pr\left[\bigwedge_{i=1}^{n} |Q_i| = T_i^*\right] \cdot$$

$$\Pr\left[\mathbf{Succ} \wedge (\mathbf{Bad}_1 \vee \cdots \vee \mathbf{Bad}_n) \wedge \sum_{i=1}^{n} |Q_i| \leq T^* \,\middle|\, \bigwedge_{i=1}^{n} |Q_i| = T_i^*\right]$$

$$= \sum_{\substack{T_1^*,\ldots,T_n^* \mid \\ \sum_{i=1}^{n} T_i^* \leq T^*}} \Pr\left[\bigwedge_{i=1}^{n} |Q_i| = T_i^*\right] \Pr\left[\mathbf{Succ} \wedge (\mathbf{Bad}_1 \vee \cdots \vee \mathbf{Bad}_n) \,\middle|\, \bigwedge_{i=1}^{n} |Q_i| = T_i^*\right]$$

By the union bound,

$$\leq \sum_{\substack{T_1^*,\ldots,T_n^* \mid \\ \sum_{i=1}^{n} T_i^* \leq T^*}} \Pr\left[\bigwedge_{i=1}^{n} |Q_i| = T_i^*\right] \sum_{i=1}^{n} \Pr\left[\mathbf{Succ} \wedge \mathbf{Bad}_i \,\middle|\, \bigwedge_{j=1}^{n} |Q_j| = T_j^*\right]$$

By the definition of conditional probability,

$$= \sum_{\substack{T_1^*,\ldots,T_n^* \mid \\ \sum_{i=1}^{n} T_i^* \leq T^*}} \Pr\left[\bigwedge_{i=1}^{n} |Q_i| = T_i^*\right] \cdot$$

$$\sum_{i=1}^{n}\left(\Pr\left[\mathbf{Bad}_i \,\middle|\, \bigwedge_{j=1}^{n} |Q_j| = T_j^*\right] \Pr\left[\mathbf{Succ} \,\middle|\, \mathbf{Bad}_i \, \bigwedge_{j=1}^{n} |Q_j| = T_j^*\right]\right)$$

Since $\Pr[\mathbf{Bad}_i] \leq 1$,

$$\leq \sum_{\substack{T_1^*,\ldots,T_n^* \mid \\ \sum_{i=1}^{n} T_i^* \leq T^*}} \Pr\left[\bigwedge_{i=1}^{n} |Q_i| = T_i^*\right] \sum_{i=1}^{n} \Pr\left[\mathbf{Succ} \,\middle|\, \mathbf{Bad}_i \, \bigwedge_{j=1}^{n} |Q_j| = T_j^*\right]$$

By our bound on $\Pr[\mathbf{Succ}|\mathbf{Bad}_i]$ above,

$$\leq \sum_{\substack{T_1^*,\dots,T_n^* | \\ \sum_{i=1}^n T_i^* \leq T^*}} \Pr\left[\bigwedge_{i=1}^n |Q_i| = T_i^*\right] \sum_{i=1}^n (T_i^* \cdot \varepsilon^k)$$

$$= \varepsilon^k \sum_{\substack{T_1^*,\dots,T_n^* | \\ \sum_{i=1}^n T_i^* \leq T^*}} \Pr\left[\bigwedge_{i=1}^n |Q_i| = T_i^*\right] \sum_{i=1}^n T_i^*$$

$$\leq \varepsilon^k \sum_{\substack{T_1^*,\dots,T_n^* | \\ \sum_{i=1}^n T_i^* \leq T^*}} \Pr\left[\bigwedge_{i=1}^n |Q_i| = T_i^*\right] T^*$$

$$\leq T^* \cdot \varepsilon^k \ .$$

Therefore

$$\Pr[\neg\mathbf{Bad}] \geq \Pr[\mathbf{Succ} \wedge \neg\mathbf{Bad}] = \Pr[\mathbf{Succ}] - \Pr[\mathbf{Succ} \wedge \mathbf{Bad}] \geq p - T^* \cdot \varepsilon^k \ .$$

Note that if the event **Bad** did not occur, and neither catastrophic event occurred, then $\mathcal{A}_1^{(IPoW)}$ does not abort and $\mathcal{A}_2^{(IPoW)}$ is guaranteed to be successful.

Since $\mathcal{A}^{(IPoW)}$ is a $(\varepsilon \cdot n \cdot \tau, s + n \cdot (k_H + \log T^* + \tau), T)$-IPoW adversary that succeeds with probability $p - T^* \cdot \varepsilon^k$, by the f'-soundness of the IPoW it follows that $p < f'(\varepsilon \cdot n \cdot \tau, s + n \cdot (k_H + \log T^* + \tau), T) + T^* \cdot \varepsilon^k + (T^*)^2 \cdot 2^{-k_H} + T_1^* \cdot 2^{-k_{ch}}$.

Finally, note that if $n > \max\{T_1^*, T^*\}$, then there are at least $n - \max\{T_1^*, T^*\}$ challenges which the adversary did not query at all; in this case its success probability is bounded by $2^{-k_H \cdot (n - \max\{T_1^*, T^*\})}$. □

4   Hash-Preimage IPoW

One of the most popular proofs of work is the hash-preimage PoW: given a challenge $ch \in \{0,1\}_H^k$, interpret the random oracle's output as a binary fraction in $[0,1]$ and find $x \in \{0,1\}_H^k$ s.t.

$$H^{(\text{work})}(ch||x) < p \tag{1}$$

p is a parameter that sets the difficulty of the proof. For any adversary, the expected number of oracle calls to generate a proof-of-work of this form is at least $1/p$.

At first glance, this might seem to be an incompressible PoW already—after all, the random oracle entries are uniformly distributed and independent, so compressing the output of a random oracle is information-theoretically impossible. Unfortunately, this intuition is misleading. The reason is that we need the proof to be incompressible *even with access to the random oracle*. However, given access to the oracle, it's enough to compress the *input* to the oracle. Indeed, the hash-preimage PoW is vulnerable to a very simple compression attack: Increment a counter x until the first valid solution is found, but don't store the zero prefix of the counter. Since the expected number of oracle calls until finding a valid x is only $1/p$, on average that means only $\log \frac{1}{p}$ bits need to be stored (rather than the full length of an oracle entry).

We show that this is actually an optimal compression scheme. Therefore, to make this an *incompressible* PoW, we instruct the honest user to use this strategy, and store exactly the $\left\lceil \log \frac{1}{p} \right\rceil$ least significant bits of the counter. We note that $\frac{1}{p}$ is the *expected* number of attempts—in the worst case the prover may require more; thus, we allow the prover to search up to $\frac{k}{p}$ entries; the verifier will check k possible prefixes for the $\log \frac{1}{p}$ bits sent by the prover (with overwhelming probability, there will be a valid solution in this range). Thus, the verifier may have to make k oracle queries in the worst case in order to check a proof (however, in expectation it will be only slightly more than one).[8]

Formally,

Definition 9 (w'-Hash-Preimage IPoW). *The honest prover and verifier are defined as follows: Set $p = 1/w'$.*

Prover *Given a challenge y, calls $H^{(work)}$ on the inputs $\{y||x\}_{x \in \{0,1\}^{\log \frac{k}{p}}}$ in lexicographic order, returning as the proof π the least significant $\log \frac{1}{p}$ bits of the first x for which $H^{(work)}(y||x) < p$.*

Verifier *Given challenge y and proof π, verifies that $|\pi| \leq \log \frac{1}{p}$ and that there exists a prefix z of length $\log k$ such that $H^{(work)}(y||z||\pi) < p$ (where π is zero-padded to the maximum length).*

The security of the Hash-Preimage IPoW is summarized in the following theorem:

Theorem 2. *The w'-hash-preimage protocol is a $(w', \log w', f)$-IPoW for $f(n, s, T) = 2^{-(n \log w' - s - n(2 + \log \lceil T/n \rceil))}$.*

(The proof appears in Sect. 6.1.)

5   Partial Hash IPoW

Our choice of parameters for the IPoW is constrained by several real-world variables:

- The maximal time period between proofs that we would like to support
- The amount of storage we would like to fill
- The cost of storage per time period

---

[8] We note that this computation can be performed by the prover instead, but it will simplify our analysis to assume the verifier performs the checks.

- The cost of a hash invocation
- The maximum cost we can tolerate for PoST initialization.

For the Hash Preimage IPoW, given a maximum initialization cost and the cost of a hash invocation, we can upper bound the amount of storage we can fill: each hash invocation can "contribute" at most a single bit to the total storage (this is because the amount of space needed to store a single Hash-Preimage IPoW is logarithmic in the expected number of hash invocations needed to generate the proof; hence the largest space is taken when each proof requires on average only a single invocation).

If we would like to fill more space without increasing our initialization cost, we need to use a different IPoW.

The Partial Hash IPoW is a simple solution that can fill up to k bits per hash invocation (but *at least* one bit per invocation). In this case, the amount of work per IPoW is always a single hash invocation, as is the verification cost. We parameterize with the amount of space required to store an IPoW.

Formally,

Definition 10 (m-Partial-Hash IPoW). *The honest prover and verifier are defined as follows (where m is the space required to store an IPoW for the honest user):*

Prover *Given a challenge y, calls $H^{(work)}(y)$ and returns as the proof the m least-significant bits of $H^{(work)}(y)$.*

Verifier *Given challenge y and proof π, verifies that π consists of the m least-significant bits of $H^{(work)}(y)$.*

The security of the Partial-Hash IPoW is summarized in the following theorem:

Theorem 3. *The m-partial-hash IPoW protocol is a $(1, m, f(n, s, T) = 2^{-(n \cdot m - (T \cdot m + s))})$-IPoW.*

(For reasons of space, the proof is omitted here, but can be found in the eprint version.)

6   IPoW Security Analysis

In the proofs of security for both of our IPoW schemes, we use the following simple claim bounding the probability to compress a random string.

Let $(Compress, Decompress)$ be an arbitrary pair of probabilistic algorithms (possibly computationally unbounded), such that $Compress : \{0,1\}^k \mapsto \left\{\{0,1\}^{k-m}, bot\right\}$ and $Decompress : \{0,1\}^{k-m} \mapsto \{0,1\}^k$, and for all $(x, y) \in \{0,1\}^k \times \{0,1\}^{k-m}$, if $y \in \Im(Compress(x))$ then $Decompress(y) = x$. (That is, if $Compress$ "succeeds" then decompression is perfect).

Claim 1. Let U_k be a uniformly selected from $\{0,1\}^k$. Then $\Pr[Compress(U_k) \neq \perp] \leq 2^{-m}$.

Proof. Denote $Y = \Im(Compress) \setminus \{\perp\}$. Then $|Y| \leq 2^{k-m}$. Note that since decompression is perfect, for any $y \in Y$ there can be only a single pre-image (if we have $x_1 \neq x_2$ such that $Compress(x_1) = y = Compress(x_2)$, then for at least one of them $Decompress(y)$ will fail with non-zero probability). Let $X = \{x | Compress(x) \in Y\}$. Then $|X| \leq 2^{k-m}$. By the definitions of p and X, $p = \Pr[Compress(U_k) \neq \perp] = \Pr[U_k \in X]$, but since $|X| \leq 2^{k-m}$ and U_k is uniform, we have $p \leq 2^{-m}$. □

6.1   Proof of Theorem 2

Proof. The honest prover uses w' expected queries, by the setting of $p = 1/w'$ and stores $\log \frac{1}{p} = \log w'$ bits. Given an (n,s,T)-adversary $\mathcal{A} = (\mathcal{A}_1, \mathcal{A}_2)$ that succeeds with probability p, we can construct a compression algorithm as described in Protocols 2 and 3.

Protocol 2. Hash-IPoW Decompression algorithm

1: **function** DECOMPRESS(Z)
2:   Parse Z as $(\sigma, \Delta_1, \ldots, \Delta_{|X'|}, \Delta_{|X'|+1}, H(q_1), \ldots, H(q_{T \cdot n}), H|_{X \setminus Q}, H|_{\neg(X \cup Q)})$
3:   Reconstruct $\hat{X} = \{i | q_i \in X'\}$ from $\Delta_1, \ldots, \Delta_{|X'|}$: $\hat{X}_i = \sum_j = 1^i \Delta_i$. (note: we know when we've reached $\Delta_{|X'|+1}$ when the sum is exactly $T \cdot n$)
4:   Execute $\mathcal{A}_2$ with σ as input
  – For the ith query made by $\mathcal{A}_2(\sigma)$:
    • If $i \in \hat{X}$ then reconstruct $H(q_i)$ by reading the $k-m$ next bits and treating them as a k-bit value with m zero MSBs
    • If $i \notin \hat{X}$ then reconstruct $H(q_i)$ by reading the k next bits
  The execution will give Q and X as output.
5:   Reconstruct $H|X \setminus Q$ by reading the next $(n - |X'|)(k - m)$ bits and treating them as $(n - |X'|)$ values
6:   Reconstruct $H|_{\neg(X \cup Q)}$ by reading the next $(2^\ell - (n + T \cdot n - |X'|))k$ bits.
7: **end function**

This algorithm can, with probability p, compress a string of length $2^\ell \cdot k_H$ into a string of length $2^\ell k_H - (n \log w' - s - n(2 + \log \lceil T/n \rceil))$ (the analysis of the encoding length appears in the algorithm description). Thus, by Claim 1, we must have $p \leq 2^{-(n \log w' - s - n(2 + \log \lceil T/n \rceil))}$. □

7   Market-Based Mechanisms for Difficulty Adjustment

One of the very nice properties of PoW-based cryptocurrency schemes is that the tunable parameter of PoWs—their difficulty—can be set dynamically using a market-based solution: by counting the number of published PoW solutions,

---

Protocol 3. Hash-IPoW Compression algorithm

1: **function** COMPRESS(H) // Treat $H \in \{0,1\}^{2^\ell \cdot k}$ as the truth table of a function: $H : \{0,1\}^\ell \mapsto \{0,1\}^k$
2:   Run $\mathcal{A}_1$ to get σ. // Assume w.l.o.g that $|\sigma| = s$
3:   Run $\mathcal{A}_2$ with σ and H as input.
4:   Let $X = (ch_1\|x_1, \ldots, ch_n\|x_n)$ be the outputs of $\mathcal{A}_2$, sorted lexicographically.
5:   Let $Q = (q_1, \ldots, q_T)$ be the set of oracle queries made by $\mathcal{A}_2$, sorted lexicographically. (We can assume w.l.o.g. that $|Q| = T$.)
6:   **if** $\forall i$, the $\log w'$ MSBs of $H(ch_i\|x_i)$ are all 0s **then** // the output of $\mathcal{A}_2$ verifies; occurs w.p. p
7:     Let $X' = X \cap Q = (x'_1, \ldots, x'_{|X'|})$, the subset of outputs that were also queried.
8:     **for all** $j \in \{1, \ldots, |X'|\}$ **do**
9:       Denote $\mathbf{idx}(j)$ the index of x'_j in Q (i.e., $q_{\mathbf{idx}(j)} = x'_j$).
10:      Let $\Delta_j = \mathbf{idx}(j) - \mathbf{idx}(j-1)$ // we define $\mathbf{idx}(0) = 1$
11:     **end for**
12:     Let $\Delta_{|X'|+1} = T - \sum_{j=1}^{|X'|-1} \Delta_j$ // $\sum_{j=1}^{|X'|} \Delta_j = T$
13:     **return** $(\sigma, \Delta_1, \ldots, \Delta_{|X'|}, \Delta_{|X'|+1}, H(q_1), \ldots, H(q_T), H|_{X\backslash Q}, H|_{\neg(X\cup Q)})$
         – We will represent Δ_j in the following way:
           • $\left\lfloor \frac{\Delta_j}{\lceil T/n\rceil} \right\rfloor$ represented in unary (between 0 and $\lceil T/n\rceil$ one bits)
           • a zero bit.
           • $\Delta_j \bmod (\lceil T/n\rceil)$ represented in binary ($\log\lceil T/n\rceil$ bits)
         Since $\sum_j \Delta_j \leq T$, the total number of bits in the unary representations is at most n. Thus, in total we use at most $n + |X'|(1 + \log\lceil T/n\rceil)$ bits.
         – We represent $H(q_i)$ as follows:
           • If $q_i \in X'$, we store the $k - \log w'$ LSBs of $H(q_i)$
           • Otherwise, we store the full k bits.
         In total, this uses $|X'|(k - \log w') + (|Q| - |X'|)k$ bits.
         – We represent $H|_{X\backslash Q}$ by storing the $k - \log w'$ LSBs of each entry. The entries are stored consecutively without padding. This uses $(n - |X'|)(k - \log w')$ bits.
         – We will represent $H|_{\neg(X\cup Q)}$ by storing the full entries. The entries are stored consecutively without padding. This uses $(2^\ell - n - |Q| + |X'|)k$ bits.
       All together, since $|X'| \leq n$, the length of the encoding is at most

$$Z = s + n + |X'|(1 + \log\lceil T/n\rceil) + |X'|(k - \log w') +$$
$$(|Q| - |X'|)k + (n - |X'|)(k - \log w') + (2^\ell - n - |Q| + |X'|)k$$
$$\leq 2^\ell k - (n \log w' - s - n(2 + \log\lceil T/n\rceil)) \, .$$

14:   **else**
15:      **return** $\perp$
16:   **end if**
17: **end function**

---

we can estimate the total computational power expended on producing PoWs, and thus update the difficulty accordingly.

A PoST scheme has two main tunable parameters—the amount of space it requires (m), and the computational cost of initialization, or difficulty parameter (w). The first parameter determines the cost of generating a good proof (since amortized over multiple proofs, the initialization cost becomes irrelevant). This parameter can be set dynamically in a similar fashion to the PoW-based schemes, by counting the total amount of space invested over a specified time period.

The difficulty parameter, on the other hand, determines the rationality of storage: the higher the cost of storage, the higher the difficulty parameter must be set in order to ensure that rational provers will prefer storage over recomputing the PoST. Unfortunately, the price of storage (relative to computation cost) can't readily be estimated simply by observing the PoST proofs (in particular, the proofs generated by recomputing the initialization are identical to "honest" proofs).

However, by choosing an appropriate incentive scheme, it turns out that we *can* dynamically set the difficulty. The main idea is to give a prover two *identifiable* options for generating proofs: the standard, storage-based PoST, and an alternative that is computation-based. By giving a small "bonus" reward for solutions that use the computation-based proofs, we incentivize users to identify themselves as "computational solvers" when the price of storage is high enough to make computation a more attractive option. When we observe that the fraction of computational solvers changes, we can adjust the difficulty parameter to compensate.

The challenge in instantiating such a scheme is that we must ensure that (1) the difficulty of the alternative proof is equivalent to the difficulty of recomputing the PoST proof and (2) that the work expended in the alternative proof is tied to a specific instance of the PoST proof phase (i.e., that it can't be amortized across multiple instances).

To solve both of these problems, we use the PoST initialization itself as the basis for the alternative proof. However, instead of allowing an arbitrary *id* string, we require the id for the proof to be a function of the original id and the challenge from the PoST proof phase.

7.1   PoSTs with Computation Bonus

More formally, we define a PoST with Computational Bonus to be a PoST scheme with an additional "computational" prover P_{bonus} and corresponding verifier V_{bonus}.

Definition 11 (PoST with Computational Bonus). $P = (P_{init}, P_{exec}, P_{bonus})$, $V = (V_{init}, V_{exec}, V_{bonus})$ *is a* (w, m, ε, f)-*PoST with a computational bonus if* $P' = (P_{init}, P_{exec})$ *and* $V' = (V_{init}, V_{exec})$ *comprise an* (w, m, ε, f)-*PoST and the prover* P_{bonus} *and verifier* V_{bonus} *comprise a* w'-*PoW such that* $w' \leq w$.

Computational Solvers Will Self-Identify. To receive the computational bonus, we will require the prover to send the proof for P_{bonus}. The expected cost to compute this proof is w', while the expected cost to recompute the PoST initialization is $w \geq w'$. Thus, the strategy of using P_{bonus} dominates the strategy of recomputing the PoST, meaning that rational computational solvers will self-identify.

Rational Storage is Still Preferred. The adversary's expected cost for using the computational proof is w'. Thus, the expected number of successful proofs for a given budget C using the bonus proof method is C/w'. Denote β the bonus multiplier (i.e., a successful "standard" proof gets reward 1, while a computational bonus proof gets reward β).

Lemma 2. *If a PoST is (γ, ε')-rationally stored and $\beta < \frac{\eta \cdot w'}{\gamma \cdot m}$ then the PoST with a β computational bonus is (γ, ε')-rationally stored.*

Proof. Suppose the adversary uses $\alpha \cdot C$ of its budget for the standard PoST proofs (using an optimal adversarial strategy) and $(1 - \alpha) \cdot C$ for computational bonus proofs.

For every choice of α, if the adversary allocates less than $\varepsilon' \cdot \alpha \cdot C$ of the budget to storage, then the expected reward for the adversary is bounded by

$$\mathbb{E}\left[\#G\right] \leq \beta \cdot (1 - \alpha) \cdot C/w' + \max_{s \in [0, \varepsilon' \cdot \alpha \cdot C/\gamma]} \left\{ \sum_{i=1}^{\infty} f(i, s, \alpha \cdot C - \gamma s) \right\}$$

using the (γ, ε')-rational storage property:

$$< \beta \cdot (1 - \alpha) \cdot C/w' + \eta \cdot \alpha \cdot C/(\gamma \cdot m)$$

By our assumption about β

$$:\leq \frac{\eta \cdot w'}{\gamma \cdot m} \cdot (1 - \alpha) \cdot C/w' + \eta \cdot \alpha \cdot C/(\gamma \cdot m)$$
$$= \eta \cdot (1 - \alpha) \cdot C/(\gamma \cdot m) + \eta \cdot \alpha \cdot C/(\gamma \cdot m) = \eta \cdot C/(\gamma \cdot m) \ .$$

In particular, this holds for $\alpha = 1$, which gives the desired result.   □

7.2   Constructing PoSTs with Computational Bonus (Sketch)

Given any (w, m, ε, f)-PoST with a non-interactive initialization phase (e.g., as can be construction from a Sigma-PoST), we can extend it to a PoST with computational bonus by defining the following computational prover and verifier:

Let id be the id used in the PoST initialization phase. The computational prover/verifier are defined to be

$$P_{\text{bonus}}(id, ch) := P_{\text{init}}(id \| ch) \text{ and } V_{\text{bonus}}(id, ch) := V_{\text{init}}(id \| ch)$$

The security of this construction (with $w = w'$)) follows immediately from the rational storage condition of PoST soundness: this implies that PoST initialization is a proof of work. Moreover, since we use the same parameters as the underlying PoST (just with a different id), the cost is identical to initializing the PoST.

7.3   Incremental Difficulty Adjustment

Although in our analysis we treat the initialization phase as a one-time operation (and hence can amortize away its complexity), if we increase the difficulty, the data generated by a previous init phase will no longer be valid (since the IPoWs in our PoST table will not satisfy the new difficulty level).

However, a nice property of the hash-based Simple-PoSTs is that we can incrementally increase the difficulty. For the Hash-Preimage IPoW, if we increase difficulty from p to $p' < p$, then on average p/p' of the entries will already satisfy the new difficulty level. Moreover, for those that do not, since we stored the last index we reached in the search for a good solution, we can simply "continue" running the Hash-IPoW solver where it left off. Thus, the total work we expend (including the first initialization phase) will be only $1/p'$. For the Partial-Hash IPoW, increasing the difficulty means reducing the number of bits stored per IPoW; this requires the prover to delete some data, and generate additional IPoWs (increasing the number of table entries) in order to maintain the same amount of space.

8   Discussion and Open Questions

Improving Proving Complexity. Compared to PoS, our prover complexity (at least asymptotically) is much worse: the PoST prover has read the entire table in order to generate a proof. It might be possible to combine the PoS pebbling-based protocols with our IPoW construction to get both fast proving time and finely-tunable difficulty—by having each pebble be an IPoW (whose challenge is given by the hash of its predecessor pebbles).[9] Proving the security of this construction appears to be non-trivial, however.

Best-of-Both-Worlds? All the existing PoS constructions that don't require the prover to read its entire data don't support incremental difficulty adjustment. An interesting open question is whether it is possible to get a "best of both worlds" construction, combining low prover complexity with incremental difficulty adjustment.

Constructing additional IPoW constructions using different techniques is also an interesting open question.

Acknowledgements. The authors would like to thank Siyao Guo for some very helpful discussions on compression arguments.

---

[9] Thanks to the anonymous reviewer who suggested this idea!

References

1. The chia network. https://chia.net/
2. Spacemesh. https://spacemesh.io/
3. Abusalah, H., Alwen, J., Cohen, B., Khilko, D., Pietrzak, K., Reyzin, L.: Beyond Hellman's time-memory trade-offs with applications to proofs of space. In: Takagi, T., Peyrin, T. (eds.) ASIACRYPT 2017, Part II. LNCS, vol. 10625, pp. 357–379. Springer, Cham (2017). https://doi.org/10.1007/978-3-319-70697-9_13
4. Alwen, J., Serbinenko, V.: High parallel complexity graphs and memory-hard functions. In: Servedio, R.A., Rubinfeld, R. (eds.) Proceedings of the Forty-Seventh Annual ACM on Symposium on Theory of Computing, STOC 2015, Portland, OR, USA, 14–17 June 2015, pp. 595–603. ACM (2015). https://doi.org/10.1145/2746539.2746622. http://doi.acm.org/10.1145/2746539.2746622
5. Ateniese, G., Bonacina, I., Faonio, A., Galesi, N.: Proofs of space: when space is of the essence. In: Abdalla, M., De Prisco, R. (eds.) SCN 2014. LNCS, vol. 8642, pp. 538–557. Springer, Cham (2014). https://doi.org/10.1007/978-3-319-10879-7_31
6. Ateniese, G., et al.: Provable data possession at untrusted stores. IACR Cryptology ePrint Archive 2007:202 (2007)
7. Bowers, K.D., Juels, A., Oprea, A.: Proofs of retrievability: theory and implementation. In: Sion, R., Song, D. (eds.) CCSW, pp. 43–54. ACM (2009)
8. Cohen, B., Pietrzak, K.: Simple proofs of sequential work. In: Nielsen, J.B., Rijmen, V. (eds.) EUROCRYPT 2018, Part II. LNCS, vol. 10821, pp. 451–467. Springer, Cham (2018). https://doi.org/10.1007/978-3-319-78375-8_15
9. Dwork, C., Naor, M.: Pricing via processing or combatting junk mail. In: Brickell, E.F. (ed.) CRYPTO 1992. LNCS, vol. 740, pp. 139–147. Springer, Heidelberg (1993). https://doi.org/10.1007/3-540-48071-4_10
10. Dziembowski, S., Faust, S., Kolmogorov, V., Pietrzak, K.: Proofs of space. In: Gennaro, R., Robshaw, M. (eds.) CRYPTO 2015. LNCS, vol. 9216, pp. 585–605. Springer, Heidelberg (2015). https://doi.org/10.1007/978-3-662-48000-7_29
11. Fisch, B.: PoReps: proofs of space on useful data. IACR Cryptology ePrint Archive, 2018:678 (2018). https://eprint.iacr.org/2018/678
12. Fisch, B.: Tight proofs of space and replication. Cryptology ePrint Archive, Report 2018/702 (2018). https://eprint.iacr.org/2018/702
13. Golle, P., Jarecki, S., Mironov, I.: Cryptographic primitives enforcing communication and storage complexity. In: Blaze, M. (ed.) FC 2002. LNCS, vol. 2357, pp. 120–135. Springer, Heidelberg (2003). https://doi.org/10.1007/3-540-36504-4_9
14. Juels, A., Kaliski Jr., B.S.: Pors: proofs of retrievability for large files. In: Ning, P., di Vimercati, S.D.C., Syverson, P.F. (eds.) ACM Conference on Computer and Communications Security, pp. 584–597. ACM (2007)
15. Protocol Labs: Filecoin: a decentralized storage network (2017). https://filecoin.io/filecoin.pdf
16. Miller, A., Juels, A., Shi, E., Parno, B., Katz, J.: Permacoin: repurposing bitcoin work for data preservation. In: 2014 IEEE Symposium on Security and Privacy, SP 2014, Berkeley, CA, USA, 18–21 May 2014, pp. 475–490. IEEE Computer Society (2014). https://doi.org/10.1109/SP.2014.37
17. Nakamoto, S.: Bitcoin: a peer-to-peer electronic cash system (2008). https://bitcoin.org/bitcoin.pdf
18. Park, S., Kwon, A., Fuchsbauer, G., Gazi, P., Alwen, J., Pietrzak, K.: SpaceMint: a cryptocurrency based on proofs of space. In: Proceedings of the 22nd International Conference on Financial Cryptography and Data Security (FC). Springer, Heidelberg (2018). http://fc18.ifca.ai/preproceedings/78.pdf

19. Percival, C.: Stronger key derivation via sequential memory-hard functions. In: BSDCan 2009 (2009)
20. Pietro, R.D., Mancini, L.V., Law, Y.W., Etalle, S., Havinga, P.J.M.: LKHW: a directed diffusion-based secure multicast scheme for wireless sensor networks. In: ICPP Workshops, p. 397. IEEE Computer Society (2003)
21. Pietrzak, K.: Proofs of catalytic space. In: Blum, A. (ed.) 10th Innovations in Theoretical Computer Science Conference, ITCS 2019. LIPIcs, San Diego, California, USA, 10–12 January 2019, vol. 124, pp. 59:1–59:25. Schloss Dagstuhl - Leibniz-Zentrum fuer Informatik (2019). https://doi.org/10.4230/LIPIcs.ITCS.2019.59
22. Ren, L., Devadas, S.: Proof of space from stacked expanders. In: Hirt, M., Smith, A. (eds.) TCC 2016-B, Part I. LNCS, vol. 9985, pp. 262–285. Springer, Heidelberg (2016). https://doi.org/10.1007/978-3-662-53641-4_11
23. Waters, B., Juels, A., Halderman, J.A., Felten, E.W.: New client puzzle outsourcing techniques for dos resistance. In: Atluri, V., Pfitzmann, B., McDaniel, P.D. (eds.) ACM Conference on Computer and Communications Security, pp. 246–256. ACM (2004)

Non-Malleable Codes

Non-malleable Codes for Decision Trees

Marshall Ball[1]($\boxtimes$), Siyao Guo[2]($\boxtimes$), and Daniel Wichs[3]

[1] Columbia University, New York, USA
marshall@cs.columbia.edu
[2] New York University Shanghai, Shanghai, China
siyao.guo@nyu.edu
[3] Northeastern University, Boston, USA
wichs@ccs.neu.edu

Abstract. We construct efficient, unconditional non-malleable codes that are secure against tampering functions computed by decision trees of depth $d = n^{1/4-o(1)}$. In particular, each bit of the tampered codeword is set arbitrarily after adaptively reading up to d arbitrary locations within the original codeword. Prior to this work, no efficient unconditional non-malleable codes were known for decision trees beyond depth $O(\log^2 n)$.

Our result also yields efficient, unconditional non-malleable codes that are $\exp(-n^{\Omega(1)})$-secure against constant-depth circuits of $\exp(n^{\Omega(1)})$-size. Prior work of Chattopadhyay and Li (STOC 2017) and Ball et al. (FOCS 2018) only provide protection against $\exp(O(\log^2 n))$-size circuits with $\exp(-O(\log^2 n))$-security.

We achieve our result through simple non-malleable reductions of decision tree tampering to split-state tampering. As an intermediary, we give a simple and generic reduction of leakage-resilient split-state tampering to split-state tampering with improved parameters. Prior work of Aggarwal et al. (TCC 2015) only provides a reduction to split-state non-malleable codes with decoders that exhibit particular properties.

1 Introduction

Motivated by applications in tamper-resilience, non-malleable codes were first introduced by Dziembowski, Pietrzak, and Wichs [DPW10] as an extension of error-correcting codes that give meaningful guarantees even when every bit of a codeword may be altered. To define the non-malleability of an encoding scheme (Enc, Dec) for a class of tampering functions $\mathcal{F}$, consider the following experiment for any $f \in \mathcal{F}$: (1) encode a message x via Enc, (2) tamper the resulting codeword with f, and (3) decode the tampered codeword with Dec. Roughly, (Enc, Dec) is non-malleable if $\tilde{x} = \text{Dec}(f(\text{Enc}(x)))$ is either completely unrelated to the original message x or identical to x, for any x. In particular, the outcome of the experiment should be simulatable without any knowledge of x, up to allowing the simulator to output a special symbol "same" to indicate that the message is unchanged.

The initial work of Dziembowski et al. [DPW10] observed that achieving non-malleability against arbitrary tampering is strictly impossible. The goal, as

© International Association for Cryptologic Research 2019
A. Boldyreva and D. Micciancio (Eds.): CRYPTO 2019, LNCS 11692, pp. 413–434, 2019.
https://doi.org/10.1007/978-3-030-26948-7_15

in many coding tasks, is to construct a code against as large a class of tampering functions (channels) as possible with best information rate and strongest security guarantees. And, since 2010 a flurry of work has done just that, studying this object in a variety of models. Of particular interest, both at large and in this work, is explicit constructions of statistically secure non-malleable codes for specific families of tampering functions and the efficiency of these constructions (in both information rate and computational complexity).

Much of the work on explicit constructions has focused on split-state tampering, where the codeword is broken into blocks according to some (fixed a priori) partition and each block may be tampered with independently of all other blocks [DKO13, CG14, CZ14, ADL14, Agg15, CGL16, AB16, KOS17, Li17, Li18]. However, a recent strand of work has focused on tampering functions that aren't restricted to fixed partitions. Since initial work on tampering via permutations and bit-flipping [AGM+15] many of these works have looked at tampering functions that are restricted under some measure of computational complexity.

In 2016, Ball et al. [BDKM16] constructed non-malleable codes for ℓ-local tampering functions (functions where each output only depends on ℓ inputs) for $\ell = o(n/\log n)$ with rate proportional to ℓ restriction and negligible error. This class contains NC^0, functions computed by circuits composed from a constant depth of constant fan-in gates. In 2017, Chattopadhyay and Li [CL17] constructed non-malleable codes for AC^0 (polynomial size circuits of constant depth, unbounded fan-in AND and OR gates, as well as NOT gates). Their construction achieved a negligible error, but had exponentially larger codewords of length $n = 2^{\sqrt{k}}$ for messages of length k.[1] In 2018, Ball et al. [BDG+18] constructed non-malleable codes for AC^0 with negligible error and codewords of almost linear length ($n = k^{1+o(1)}$).[2]

However, none of the known constructions for small-depth circuits can support tampering via *large size* small-depth circuits nor can they provide security guarantees beyond $\exp(-\omega(\log^2 n))$ even for AC^0 itself. This leads to the following problem which we address in this work:

Construct non-malleable codes for AC^0 with error bounds $\exp(-\omega(\log^2 n))$.

In fact, the techniques of [BDG+18] immediately suggest a path to improving non-malleable codes for small-depth circuits, by resolving another open question which is interesting, independent of the above motivation:

Construct non-malleable codes for decision trees of depth $d = \omega(\log^2 n)$, or ideally $d = n^{\Omega(1)}$.

---

[1] [CL17] also gave a construction for local functions with polynomial length codewords and sub-exponential error.

[2] Actually, the construction of [BDG+18] can handle a slightly wider range of parameters including polynomial size circuits of depth $o(\log n/\log\log n)$ and constant depth circuits of size $n^{O(\log n)}$. Note that depth d decision trees are also a strict subclass of 2^d-local functions. Accordingly, Ball et al.'s codes for $n^{1-\varepsilon}$-local tampering handle decision tree tampering of depth up to $(1 - \varepsilon)\log n$.

Decision trees of depth d capture tampering where each output bit is set arbitrarily after adaptively reading d locations of the input, where the choice of which input location to read next at any point in time can depend on the values of all the previous locations read. While tampering via decision trees has been studied in the Common Reference String (CRS) model under cryptographic assumptions [BDKM18], prior to the present work no efficient or explicit information-theoretic codes were known for decision trees of $\omega(\log^2 n)$ depth.[3]

1.1   Our Results

Theorem 1 (Informal). *There exists an explicit, efficient, information theoretic non-malleable code for decision trees of depth $n^{1/4-o(1)}$.*

Given the above, the following theorem is a straightforward corollary to a lemma of [BDG+18] that reduces small-depth circuit tampering to tampering functions that may adaptively leak limited information from the codeword before selecting local functions to modify the codeword with. It is easy to observe that this class is subsumed by decision tree tampering of sufficient depth (See Lemma 8 in Sect. 5 for more details).

Theorem 2 (Informal). *For $d \leq c_1 \log n / \log \log n$, there exists an explicit, efficient, information theoretic non-malleable code for d-depth circuits (of unbounded fan-in) of size $\exp(n^{c_2/d})$ with error $\exp(-n^{\Omega(1/d)})$ and encoding length $n = k^{1+c}$, where $c, c_1, c_2 \in (0,1)$ are constants.*

In particular, for constant-depth circuits, our result yields efficient, unconditional non-malleable codes that are $\exp(-n^{\Omega(1)})$-secure against $\exp(n^{\Omega(1)})$-size circuits. Prior work [BDG+18, CL17] only provides protection against circuits of size $\exp(O(\log^2 n))$ with $\exp(-O(\log^2 n))$ security.[4]

It is easy to observe that a non-malleable code (Enc, Dec) with error ε for most classes $\mathcal{C}$ implies a strong average-case lower bound on the power of that class – in particular, Dec is ε-hard to compute on average via $\mathcal{C}$ with respect to the distribution $Enc(b)$ where b is uniformly chosen.[5] For this reason, explicit constructions of non-malleable codes (with good error) for even a slightly larger class $AC^0[2]$ (AC^0 with the addition of mod 2 gates) would necessitate a better structural understanding of this class than is currently known.

Along the way, we also construct new leakage-resistant split-state codes. Our construction allows up to a $1/4$-fraction of the codeword to be leaked which, to our knowledge, is the best known.[6]

---

[3]   Note that any decision tree of depth d can also be represented by a 2^d-local function or as a DNF with 2^d clauses of width d.

[4]   Note that if security $2^{-\lambda}$ is required, these codes will no longer be efficient. In particular, the codeword lengths in both cases will be super-polynomial in λ.

[5]   For tampering functions such that each output bit is in the class $\mathcal{C}$, the implications follows so long as $\mathcal{C}$ contains the constant functions and is closed under negation.

[6]   [CL18] does not give an explicit bound on leakage and [ADKO15b] allows $1/12$-fraction leakage (or $1/6$ in a more restricted model where the leakage amount from each side has to be the same).

Theorem 3 (Informal). *There is an explicit split-state non-malleable code supporting leakage of up to a $1/4$-fraction of the bits with rate $\Omega(\log\log n/\log n)$ and error $\exp(-\Omega(n\log\log n/\log n))$.*

In particular, our construction allows one to reduce leakage-resilient split-state tampering to *any* split-state tampering with just a constant factor increase in codeword size. Previously, such reductions were only known with worse parameters and if the underlying split-state code had decoder with certain properties [ADKO15b]. On the other hand, [CL18] show that certain split-state seedless non-malleable extractors *are*, in fact, leakage-resilient, yielding codes with rate comparable to that of the present work (but the leakage bound is left unspecified). Unlike either of these previous construction, our reduction would yield improved leakage-resilient split-state non-malleable codes from *any* future improvement in the rate of explicit split-state non-malleable codes. Finally, our analysis is much simpler than that of [ADKO15b].

1.2 Our Techniques

We construct our codes for decision trees by constructing a *non-malleable reduction* from decision tree tampering to split-state tampering. A non-malleable reduction, first defined in [ADKO15a], from $\mathcal{F}$ to $\mathcal{G}$ is simply an encoding scheme, (Enc, Dec) such that for any $f \in \mathcal{F}$ and any message x, the value $\text{Dec}(f(\text{Enc}(x)))$ is statistically close to $g(x)$ for g chose from some distribution over functions in $\mathcal{G}$. In particular a non-malleable code for $\mathcal{F}$ is a non-malleable reduction from $\mathcal{F}$ to the family $\mathcal{G}$ consisting of the identity function and constant functions.

Both the reduction and its analysis are surprisingly simple. We also note that our reduction can be seen as distillation of the core ideas behind the construction for local tampering from [BDKM16, BDG+18]. One can view the reductions in these papers as, in fact, performing two reductions: local tampering to leaky split-state tampering, and leaky split-state tampering to split-state tampering. Viewed this way, these works implicitly construct a very weak form a leakage-resilient split-state code. It is weak in that it can only handle the leakage of a few bits chosen in advance, in particular it is not robust enough to handle even adaptive choices of the bits. While leakage-resilient split-state codes are already known [ADKO15b, CL18], this alone is not enough. In particular, the implicit reduction from local tampering to leaky split-state tampering in [BDKM16, BDG+18] does not seem to hold for decision trees. However, this modular perspective simplifies the analysis tremendously, even for this original case of local tampering.

We will outline our new reduction for decision tree tampering. The key idea here, as in [BDKM16, BDG+18], is to exploit size differences. Our encoder and decoder will work independently on the left and right pieces of the message, so we will in turn think of having left and right encoders, decoders, codewords, and tampering functions (corresponding to the respective outputs).

First, let us suppose that the right piece of the message (corresponding to the right split-state codeword) is much longer than that of the left. Then, suppose both the right and left encoders and decoders are simply the identity function. Then, all the left tampering functions together will make a number of queries to the right codeword that is below our leakage threshold.

However, because the right is much longer than the left, the above analysis won't help in simulating tampering on the right with low leakage from the left. Instead, we modify the left encoder/decoder to make it much longer than the right, but while retaining the property that the left can be decoded from just a few decision trees. To do so, we sample a random small set, whose size is that of the message, in a much larger array. We plant the message in these locations and zero everything else out. Then, we bit-wise secret share a description of the small set (i.e., its seed) such that the secrecy threshold is relatively large. To decode, we can simply extract the seed and output what is in the corresponding locations of the array.

Now, note that decoding the left still only requires at most relatively few queries to the right: decision tree depth times both encoded seed length plus message length. But we can't make the encoded seed too long or we will be dead again. Instead, we critically use the fact that tampering is by a *forest* of decision trees. In particular, for any small set of tampering functions on the right, the seed remains uniformly chosen regardless of what queries the set makes, so we expect only a small fraction of any queries made to the array to actually hit the message locations. Strong concentrations bounds guarantee that this is more or less what actually happens. Finally we simply union bound over all such subsets to guarantee that collectively the right tampering function makes few queries to the left with overwhelming probability.

Finally, we apply the same style of encoding used on the left to the right side to fix the syntactic mismatch and reduce to the case where the right and left messages are the same size.

As mentioned above, non-malleable codes for leakage-resilient split-state are known from prior work [ADKO15b, CL18]. However, we give a new reduction from leakage-resilient split-state tampering to split-state tampering that, when combined with the state-of-the-art split-state non-malleable codes [Li18], improves on the (explicit) parameters of what was known before.

Our leakage-resilient reduction is quite intuitive. We show that given a statistically-secure leakage-resilient encryption scheme (where an adversary can receive bounded leakage from both ciphertext *and* the key used to encrypt it) it suffices to simply encrypt the left and right split-state codewords independently (with their own keys) and place the keys in the opposite state. By the strong security property of the encryption scheme, the ciphertext hides each underlying split-state codeword piece, whatever (bounded amount) is leaked from the key in the opposite state.

To complete the reduction, we construct such a statistically-secure leakage-resilient encryption scheme from extractors. Our notion of leakage-resilience essentially combines the notions of "forward-secure storage" [Dzi06] and "leakage-resilient storage" [DDV10] to get the best of both worlds, and our construction essentially combines the ideas behind the constructions of the above two objects.

Related Work in Other Models. The aforementioned work of [BDKM18] constructs a generic framework for converting correlation bounds into non-malleable codes. They instantiate their framework to construct non-malleable codes both for decision trees and large small-depth circuits. However, this work (a) requires a Common Reference String, and (b) is secure in a game-based model against efficient adversaries, assuming unproven cryptographic assumptions. In fact, one of the assumptions, public key encryption with decryption in AC^0, necessarily limits their error term to be at most $\exp(-\log^{O(1)}(n))$.

A very recent follow-up work, [BDSK+18], improves upon [BDKM18] showing how to remove the Common Reference String, but still does not achieve unconditional or statistical guarantees.

2   Preliminaries

For a positive integer n, we use $[n]$ to denote $\{1, \ldots, n\}$. For $x = (x_1, \ldots, x_n) \in \{0,1\}^n$ and $i \leq j \in [n]$, we define $x_{i:j} := (x_i, \ldots, x_j)$. For a set $S \subseteq [n]$ or a string $S \in \{0,1\}^n$, x_S denotes the projection of x to S. For $x, y \in \{0,1\}^n$, if they disagree on at least $\varepsilon \cdot n$ indices, we say they are ε-far, otherwise, they are ε-close to each other.

For a set Σ, we use Σ^Σ to denote the set of all functions from Σ to Σ. Given a distribution $\mathcal{D}$, $z \leftarrow \mathcal{D}$ denotes sample z according to $\mathcal{D}$. For two distributions $\mathcal{D}_1$, $\mathcal{D}_2$ over Σ, their statistical distance is defined as $\Delta(\mathcal{D}_1, \mathcal{D}_2) := \frac{1}{2} \sum_{z \in \Sigma} |\mathcal{D}_1(z) - \mathcal{D}_2(z)|$.

2.1   Non-malleable Reductions and Codes

Non-malleable codes were first defined in [DPW10]. Here we use a simpler, but equivalent, definition based on the following notion of non-malleable reduction by Aggarwal et al. [ADKO15a].

Definition 1 (Non-Malleable Reduction [ADKO15a]). *Let $\mathcal{F} \subset A^A$ and $\mathcal{G} \subset B^B$ be some classes of functions. We say $\mathcal{F}$ reduces to $\mathcal{G}$, $(\mathcal{F} \Rightarrow \mathcal{G}, \varepsilon)$, if there exists an efficient (randomized) encoding function $\mathrm{Enc} : B \rightarrow A$, and an efficient decoding function $\mathrm{Dec} : A \rightarrow B$, such that*

(a) $\forall x \in B, \Pr[\mathrm{Dec}(\mathrm{Enc}(x)) = x] = 1$ (over the randomness of E).
(b) $\forall f \in \mathcal{F}, \exists G$ s.t. $\forall x \in B$, $\Delta(\mathrm{Dec}(f(\mathrm{Enc}(x))); G(x)) \leq \varepsilon$, where G is a distribution over $\mathcal{G}$ and $G(x)$ denotes the distribution $g(x)$, where $g \leftarrow G$.

If the above holds, then $(\mathrm{Enc}, \mathrm{Dec})$ is an $(\mathcal{F}, \mathcal{G}, \varepsilon)$-non-malleable reduction.

Definition 2 (Non-Malleable Code [ADKO15a]). *Let NM_k denote the set of trivial manipulation functions on k-bit strings, consisting of the identity function $id(x) = x$ and all constant functions $f_c(x) = c$, where $c \in \{0,1\}^k$. $(\mathrm{Enc}, \mathrm{Dec})$ defines an $(\mathcal{F}_{n(k)}, k, \varepsilon)$-non-malleable code, if it defines an $(\mathcal{F}_{n(k)}, \mathrm{NM}_k, \varepsilon)$-non-malleable reduction. Moreover, the rate of such a code is taken to be $k/n(k)$.*

The following useful theorem allows us to compose non-malleable reductions.

Theorem 4 (Composition [ADKO15a]). *If $(\mathcal{F} \Rightarrow \mathcal{G}, \varepsilon_1)$ and $(\mathcal{G} \Rightarrow \mathcal{H}, \varepsilon_2)$, then $(\mathcal{F} \Rightarrow \mathcal{H}, \varepsilon_1 + \varepsilon_2)$.*

2.2 Tampering Function Classes

Definition 3 (Split-State Model [DPW10]). *The split-state model, SS_k, denotes the set of all functions:*

$$\{f = (f_1, f_2) : f(x) = (f_1(x_{1:k}) \in \{0,1\}^k, f_2(x_{k+1:2k}) \in \{0,1\}^k), x \in \{0,1\}^{2k}\}.$$

One natural extension of split-state model is leaky/bounded-communication split-state functions considered by Aggarwal et al. [ADKO15b] and Chattopadhyay et al. [CL18].

Definition 4 (Leaky/Bounded-Communication Split-State Model). *Let $\alpha \in [0,1]$ be a parameter. We say $f \in \{0,1\}^{2k} \to \{0,1\}^{2k}$ is in α-leaky split-state model, $\alpha - SS_k$ if there exists a communication protocol between Alice and Bob such that for $x = (x_{1:k}, x_{k+1:2k}) \in \{0,1\}^{2k}$, $f(x)$ can be computed by a communication protocol with parameter α between Alice and Bob where Alice has access to $x_{1:k}$, Bob has access to $x_{k+1:2k}$. Alice and Bob send information back and forth depending on their own inputs and the current transcript of the communication so far. Overall the total communication is at most αk bits and finally Alice outputs $f(x)_{1:k}$ and Bob outputs $f(x)_{k+1:2k}$.*

Definition 5 (Decision Trees). *A decision tree with n input bits is a binary tree whose internal nodes have labels from $x_1, \ldots, x_n$ and whose leaves have labels from $\{0,1\}$. If a node has label x_i then the test performed at that node is to examine the i-th bit of the input. If the result is 0, one descends into the left subtree, whereas if the result is 1, one descends into the right subtree. The label of the leaf so reached is the output value on that particular input. The depth of a decision tree is the number of edges in a longest path from the root to a leaf. Let $DT(t)$ denote decision trees with depth at most t.*

Definition 6 (Small Depth Circuits). *A Boolean circuit with n input bits is a directed acyclic graph in which every node (also called gate) is either an input node of in-degree 0 labeled by one of the n input bits, an AND gate, an OR gate, or a NOT gate. One of these gates is designated as the output gate. The size of a circuit is its number of gates and the depth of a circuit is the length of its longest path from an input gate to the output gate. Let $AC_d(S)$ denote depth d circuits of size at most S with unbounded fan-in.*

For a set of boolean circuits $\mathcal{C}$ (respectively decision trees), we say that a boolean function f is in $\mathcal{C}$, if there exists a $C \in \mathcal{C}$ which agrees with f on every input. We say that **a multiple output function $f = (f_1, \ldots, f_m)$ is in $\mathcal{C}$** if $f_i \in \mathcal{C}$ for any $i \in [m]$.

2.3   Pseudorandom Objects

Extractors

Definition 7 (Weak Random Sources). *The min-entropy of a distribution* X *over* $\{0,1\}^n$ *is* $H_\infty(X) := -\log(\max_{x \in \{0,1\}^n} \Pr[X = x])$. *A distribution* X *over* $\{0,1\}^n$ *is called an* (n,k) *source if* $H_\infty(X) \geq k$.

Definition 8 (Strong Extractors [NZ96]). *A function* Ext : $\{0,1\}^{n+d} \rightarrow \{0,1\}^m$ *is a* (k,ε) *extractor if for every* (n,k) *source* X, Y, Ext(X, Y) *is* ε-*close to* Y, U_m *where* Y *is uniformly distributed over* $\{0,1\}^d$ *and* U_m *is uniformly distributed over* $\{0,1\}^m$. *An extractor is explicit if it is computable in polynomial time.*

Theorem 5 (Explicit Strong Extractors [GUV09]). *For every constant* $\alpha > 0$, *and all positive integers* n, k *and all* $\varepsilon > 0$, *there is an explicit construction of a* (k,ε) *extractor* Ext : $\{0,1\}^n \times \{0,1\}^d \rightarrow \{0,1\}^m$ *with* $d = O(\log n + \log(1/\varepsilon))$ *and* $m \geq (1 - \alpha)k$.

Definition 9 (Two Source Extractors [CG88]). *A function* 2Ext : $\{0,1\}^n \times \{0,1\}^n \rightarrow \{0,1\}^m$ *is a* (k,ε) *two source extractor if for independent source* X *and sources* Y *such that* $H_\infty(X) + H_\infty(Y) \geq k$, (Y, 2Ext(X, Y)) *is* ε-*close to* (Y, U_m) *and* (X, 2Ext(X, Y)) *is* ε-*close to* (X, U_m) *where* U_m *is uniformly distributed over* $\{0,1\}^m$. *An extractor is explicit if it is computable in polynomial time.*

Theorem 6 (Explicit Two Source Extractors [CG88]). *For all positive integers* m, n *such that* n *is a multiple of* m *and for all* $\varepsilon \geq 0$, *there exists an efficient* $(n + m + 2\log 1/\varepsilon, \varepsilon)$ *2-source extractor with* n-*bit sources and* m-*bit output.*[7]

Binary Ramp Secret Sharing Encoding Schemes

Definition 10 (Binary Ramp Secret Sharing Encoding Schemes). *We say* (Enc, Dec) *is a* binary ramp secret sharing encoding scheme *with parameters* (k, n, c_{sec}), *where* $k, n \in \mathbb{N}$, $0 \leq c_{sec} < 1$, *if it satisfies the following properties:*

1. **Reconstruction.** *Enc*: $\{0,1\}^k \rightarrow \{0,1\}^n$ *is an efficient probabilistic procedure, which maps a message* $x \in \{0,1\}^k$ *to a distribution over* $\{0,1\}^n$, *and* *Dec*: $\{0,1\}^n \rightarrow \{0,1\}^k$ *is an efficient procedure. For any* $x \in \{0,1\}^k$, *it holds that* $\Pr[\text{Dec}(\text{Enc}(x)) = x] = 1$.
2. **Secrecy of partial views.** *For any* $x \in \{0,1\}^k$ *and any non-empty set* $S \subset [n]$ *of size* $\leq \lfloor c_{sec} \cdot n \rfloor$, *Enc*$(x)_S$ *is identically distributed to the uniform distribution over* $\{0,1\}^{|S|}$.

As observed by Ball et al. [BDG+18] (cf. Lemma 2), such a coding scheme can be constructed efficiently from any linear error correcting code. We reproduce their construction here for convenience and refer the reader to [BDG+18] for further discussion.

---

[7] [CG88] implies this theorem and the parameters have been taken from [ADKO15b].

Lemma 1 ([BDG+18]). *Suppose there exists a binary linear error correcting code with parameters (k, n, d), then there is a binary ramp secret sharing scheme with parameters $(k, n, (d-1)/n)$.*

Proof. For a linear error correcting code with (k, n, d), let A denote its encoding matrix, H denote its parity check matrix. Let B be a matrix so that $BA = I$ where I is the $k \times k$ identity matrix (such B exists because A has rank k and can be found efficiently). By property of parity check matrix, $HA = \mathbf{0}$ and $Hs \neq 0$ for any $0 < \|s\|_0 < d$ where $\mathbf{0}$ is the $(n-k) \times k$ all 0 matrix.

We define (Enc, Dec) as follows: for $x \in \{0, 1\}^k$ and randomness $r \in \{0, 1\}^{n-k}$, $\text{Enc}(x; r) := B^T x + H^T r$, for $c \in \{0, 1\}^n$; $\text{Dec}(c) := A^T c$.

(Enc, Dec) is an encoding scheme because $\text{Dec} \circ \text{Enc} = A^T B^T = I^T = I$. For secrecy property, note that for any non-empty $S \subseteq [n]$ of size at most $d - 1$, $(Hr)_S$ is distributed uniformly over $\{0, 1\}^{|S|}$, because for any $a \in \{0, 1\}^{|S|}$,

$$\Pr_r[(H^T r)_S = a] = \mathrm{E}[\Pi_{i \in S} \frac{1 + (-1)^{(H^T r)_i + a_i}}{2}]$$
$$= 2^{-|S|} \sum_{S' \subseteq S} \mathrm{E}[\Pi_{i \in S'}(-1)^{(H^T r)_i + a_i}] = 2^{-|S|},$$

where the last equality is because the only surviving term is $S' = \emptyset$ and for other S', $\sum_{i \in S'} H_i^T \neq 0$ so $\mathrm{E}[\Pi_{i \in S'}(-1)^{(H^T r)_i}] = 0$. It implies $\text{Enc}(x)_S$ is also distributed uniformly over $\{0, 1\}^S$. Hence (Enc, Dec) is a binary ramp secret sharing encoding scheme with parameters $(k, n, (d-1)/n)$.

The following lemma is an immediate consequence of the former and any construction of a good code, such as a Justesen code.

Lemma 2. *For any $k \in \mathbb{N}$, there exist constants $0 < c_{rate}, c_{sec} < 1$ such that there is a binary RSS scheme with parameters $(k, c_{rate}k, c_{sec})$.*

To achieve longer encoding lengths n, with the same c_{sec} parameter, one can simply pad the message to an appropriate length.

2.4   Concentration Inequalities

Theorem 7 (Generalized Chernoff Bound [PS97]). *Let $X_1, \ldots, X_n$ be boolean random variables such that, for some $0 \leq \delta \leq 1$, we have that, for every subset $S \subseteq [n]$, $\mathrm{E}[\Pi_{i \in S} X_i] \leq \delta^{|S|}$. Then $\Pr[\sum_{i=1}^n X_i \geq 2\delta n] \leq \exp(-n\delta/3)$.*

3   Decision Trees to Leaky Split-State Model

In this section, we give a non-malleable reduction from decision tree tampering to leaky split-state tampering.

Lemma 3. *For any constant $\alpha \in (0, 1)$ and $t = O(n^{1/4}/\log^{3/2} n)$, there is a $(\text{DT}(t) \Rightarrow \alpha - \text{SS}_k, \varepsilon)$-non-malleable reduction with rate $\Omega(1/t^2 \log^3 n)$ where $\varepsilon \leq \exp(-\Omega(n/t^4 \log^5 n))$.*

A single decision tree from $\{0,1\}^n$ to $\{0,1\}$ of depth t can be viewed as an adversary (or computation) that first adaptively queries at most t input coordinates, and then outputs a bit. Given a tampering function f from $\{0,1\}^n$ to $\{0,1\}^n$ such that each output bit is computed by a decision tree of depth t (i.e., each output is the result of adaptively querying at most t coordinates from the input, here a codeword), we will non-malleably reduce f to a special subclass of leaky split-state functions.

Recall that an α-leaky split-state function $g = (g_L, g_R)$ from $\{0,1\}^{2k}$ to $\{0,1\}^{2k}$ can be computed by a communication protocol with parameter α between Alice and Bob where Alice has access to $x_L := x_{1:k}$ and Bob has access to $x_R := x_{k+1:2k}$. Alice and Bob send information back and forth depending on their own inputs and the current transcript of the communication so far. And finally, Alice outputs $g_L(x_L, x_R)$ and Bob outputs $g_R(x_L, x_R)$. We consider a special subclass of α-leaky split-state function where Alice and Bob simply make a bounded number of adaptive queries to each other's input. In particular, when Alice (resp. Bob) makes a query to x_R (resp. x_L), Alice (resp. Bob) sends location $i \in [k]$ and ask Bob (resp. Alice) to send back the ith coordinate of x_R (resp. x_L).

Note that the communication cost for each query (and answer) is $\lceil \log k \rceil + 1$ bits. (For the remainder of this section, we will assume that both k and n are powers of 2.) So if both Alice and Bob make at most $\alpha k / (2(\log k + 1))$ queries to each other's input, the total communication is at most αk and g is an α-leaky split-state function. We will show that our reduction reduces decision tree tampering functions (of appropriate depth) to this subclass of leaky split-state functions.

Our reduction relies on a ramp secret sharing scheme over binary alphabet. For parameter m, let $(\text{Enc}_{RSS}, \text{Dec}_{RSS})$ be an efficient coding scheme such that Enc_{RSS} maps an m-bit to a (random) $4m$-bit string so that for any $\zeta \in \{0,1\}^m$ and subset $S \neq \emptyset$ of size at most m, $\text{Enc}_{RSS}(\zeta)_S$ distributes uniformly and randomly over $\{0,1\}^{|S|}$. As observed by Ball et al. [BDG+18] (see Lemma 2), such a coding scheme can be constructed efficiently from any linear error correcting code from m bits to $4m$ bits with minimal distance $m + 1$. We choose constant 4 to simplify the presentation.

Based on $(\text{Enc}_{RSS}, \text{Dec}_{RSS})$, we define a coding scheme that hides a message in random locations. Let $G_{k,n}$ be the function that given a short "seed," ζ, of k distinct indices in $[n]$ expands it to the corresponding n-bit string with hamming weight k (where the ones are in locations indexed by ζ). Let $D_{k,n}$ be a distribution such that $G_{k,n}(D_{k,n})$ is uniform over n-bit strings with hamming weight k. Note that $G_{k,n}$ can be computed efficiently and $D_{k,n}$ can be sampled efficiently by simply sampling k locations from $[n]$ without replacement. For k, n and $m \geq k \log n$, we define an encoding $\text{Enc}^*_{n,k,m} : \{0,1\}^k \to \{0,1\}^{4m} \times \{0,1\}^n$, as follows: on a k-bit string x, sample a random seed $\zeta \leftarrow D_{k,n}$ for $G_{k,n}$, and output $(\text{Enc}_{RSS}(\zeta), c)$ so that c is 0 everywhere except $c_{G(\zeta)} = x$. $\text{Dec}^*_{n,k,m}$ is defined in the straightforward way (it first decodes ζ using Dec_{RSS}, then outputs $c_{G(\zeta)}$).

Given $f = (f_L, f_R) \in DT(t)$, we sample an α-split state g from the distribution G_f as follows: sample and hardwire the randomness required for $\mathrm{Enc}_L, \mathrm{Enc}_R$. Let ζ_L and ζ_R be the respective seeds used for G in Enc_L and Enc_R. Then, $g = (g_L, g_R)$ is defined as follows: on input $x = (x_L, x_R)$

- $g_L(x)$ simulates $\mathrm{Dec}_L(f_L(\mathrm{Enc}_L(x_L), \mathrm{Enc}_R(x_R)))$ with at most $\alpha k/2(\log k + 1)$ queries to x_R (*)
    1. Decode the tampered seed $\widetilde{\zeta_L}$ by computing the first $4m_L$ outputs of $f_L(\mathrm{Enc}_L(x_L), \mathrm{Enc}_R(x_R))$ then applying Dec_{RSS}.
    (To evaluate the necessary portion f_L the simulator evaluates the corresponding decision trees. When a bit is queried in $\mathrm{Enc}_R(x_R)$ we have three cases (recall that these encodings consist of two parts, $\mathrm{Enc}_{RSS}(\zeta_R)$ and c_R): (a) if the index corresponds to a location in $\mathrm{Enc}_{RSS}(\zeta_R)$, it is hardwired already in g_L; (b) if the index corresponds to c_R and a location specified by ζ_R, query/request the relevant bit from x_R; (c) if the index corresponds to c_R and a location *not* specified by ζ_R, simply use 0.)
    2. Compute the output bits of $f_L(\mathrm{Enc}_L(x_L), \mathrm{Enc}_R(x_R))$ indexed by set $G(\widetilde{\zeta_L})$.
    (The decision trees corresponding to indices specified by $\widetilde{\zeta_L}$ are evaluated identically to the preceeding step.)
    (*) whenever $g_L(x)$ makes more than $\alpha k/(2(\log k + 1))$ queries to x_R, abort and output 0^k.
- $g_R(x)$ simulates $\mathrm{Dec}_R(f_R(\mathrm{Enc}_L(x_L), \mathrm{Enc}_R(x_R)))$ with at most $\alpha k/2(\log k + 1)$ queries to x_L (*)
    1. Compute $\widetilde{y_R} = f_R(\mathrm{Enc}_L(x_L), \mathrm{Enc}_R(x_R))$.
    (The corresponding decision trees in f_R are evaluated in a symmetric manner to those needed for g_L.)
    2. Compute $\mathrm{Dec}_R(\widetilde{y_R})$.
    (*) whenever $g_R(x)$ makes more than $\alpha k/(2(\log k + 1))$ queries to x_L, abort and output 0^k.

Fig. 1. Simulator for $(\mathrm{Enc}, \mathrm{Dec})$

The high level idea of our reduction is to use two copies of Enc^* to hide inputs x_L and x_R independently inside two long messages (with different length). Let n_L, m_L, n_R, m_R be parameters to be determined later. We define Enc as $\mathrm{Enc}(x_L, x_R) = (\mathrm{Enc}_L(x_L), \mathrm{Enc}_R(x_R))$ where $\mathrm{Enc}_L = \mathrm{Enc}^*_{n_L, k, m_L}$ and $\mathrm{Enc}_R = \mathrm{Enc}^*_{n_R, k, m_R}$. And we define Dec as $\mathrm{Dec}(y_L, y_R) = (\mathrm{Dec}_L(y_L), \mathrm{Dec}_R(y_R))$ where $\mathrm{Dec}_L = \mathrm{Dec}^*_{n_L, k, m_L}$ and $\mathrm{Dec}_R = \mathrm{Dec}^*_{n_R, k, m_R}$.

Now we show $(\mathrm{Enc}, \mathrm{Dec})$ non-malleably reduces $DT(t)$ to α-SS_k and prove Lemma 3. First observe that $\mathrm{Dec} \circ \mathrm{Enc}$ is the identity function due to the correctness of $(\mathrm{Enc}_L, \mathrm{Dec}_L)$ and $(\mathrm{Enc}_R, \mathrm{Dec}_R)$. It remains to show that for any $f: \{0,1\}^n \to \{0,1\}^n \in DT(t)$, $\mathrm{Dec} \circ f \circ \mathrm{Enc}$ becomes α-split state functions. In fact, in Fig. 1, we reduce decision trees to a simpler subclass of α-SS_k where Alice and Bob, in parallel, make at most $\alpha k/(2(\log k + 1))$-bounded number of adaptive queries to locations of the other party's inputs, then output tampered values.

By the special condition (∗) in g_L, g_R, $g = (g_L, g_R)$ is indeed α-split state function because Alice and Bob communicates at most $\log k + 1$ bits per query (including the answer). Moreover, for any x, $G_f(x)$ distributes identically to Deco $f \circ \mathrm{Enc}(x)$ conditioning on that (∗) doesn't happen. Therefore ε, the difference between the simulation and the real experiment, is at most the probability that (∗) happens. To bound the event that (∗) happens, we begin by proving the following more general proposition.

Proposition 1. *For integers $n, k, m \geq k \log n$. Let A be an arbitrary algorithm that makes at most m adaptive queries to $(\mathrm{Enc}_{RSS}(\zeta), G(\zeta))$. Let Y denote the number of distinct 1's in $G(\zeta)$ which are queried by A. It holds that over the randomness of ζ and Enc_{RSS},*

$$\Pr[Y \geq 2mk/n] \leq \exp(-mk/3n).$$

Proof. Note that, for any fixed ζ, any A that makes at most m adaptive queries cannot distinguish $(\mathrm{Enc}_{RSS}(\zeta), G(\zeta))$ and $(U, G(\zeta))$ where U is uniformly distributed over $\{0, 1\}^{4m}$. That's because $(U, G(\zeta))$ generates any possible transcript $(i_1, b_1, \ldots, i_m, b_m)$, $(\mathrm{Enc}_{RSS}(\zeta), G(\zeta))$ with exactly the same probability due to the secrecy property of Enc_{RSS}. Because U and ζ are independent, it suffices to bound the probability that $A^{U, G(\zeta)}$ queries more than $2mk/n$ number of 1's for an arbitrary fixed choice of U and a random ζ.

Without loss of generality, we assume A queries m distinct locations of $G(\zeta)$ because any algorithm can be made into one which sees more ones from $G(\zeta)$ by querying distinct locations. Let $Y_1, \ldots, Y_m$ be indicators that $G(\zeta)$ returns 1 for these m queries made by A. Note that $Y = Y_1 + \cdots + Y_m$ and $\mathrm{E}[Y] \leq mk/n$. In addition, observe that for any $b_1, \ldots, b_m \in \{0, 1\}$, $\Pr[\forall i \in [m], Y_i = b_i] = \binom{n-m}{k-|b|_0}/\binom{n}{k}$. It follows that for any set $S \subseteq [m]$, $\mathrm{E}[\Pi_{i \in S} Y_i] = \binom{n-|S|}{k-|S|}/\binom{n}{k} \leq (k/n)^{|S|}$. By the generalized Chernoff bound by Theorem 7 with $\delta = k/n$, we obtain the desired conclusion.

We then apply Proposition 1 in following two claims to bound (∗), the probability that the number of bits required from the opposite side exceeds some threshold for either half of the simulated tampering function. We will handle each side separately. In particular, these claims will bound the number of queries or probes made to bits on the opposite side that depend on the input (if we fix the randomness of encoding). Because in the simulated tampering, both Alice and Bob jointly know the randomness of encoding, if a bit on the opposite side is not dependent on the input, then both Alice and Bob know this and do not need to request its value. So, in order to complete the proof we only need to bound queries the simulator makes to the opposite side that additionally correspond to locations specified by the respective ζ (in the respective Enc^*).

Claim. Suppose $m_R \geq (4m_L + k)t$, then for any $x \in \{0, 1\}^{2k}$, the event that g_L makes more than $2(4m_L + k)tk/n_R$ queries to x_R happens with probability at most $\exp(-(4m_L + k)tk/3n_R)$.

Proof. Fix any x_L, x_R and the randomness for $\mathrm{Enc}_L(x_L)$. Note that Dec_L reads at most $4m_L + k$ coordinates from its input, $4m_L$ to reconstruct the tampered "seed" $\tilde{\zeta}$ and then the at most k locations specified by $G(\tilde{\zeta})$. Each decision tree tampering one of these bits makes at most t queries $\mathrm{Enc}_R(x_R)$ (it makes at most t queries total). Therefore g_L, in order to simulate the tampering of the bits Dec_L requires, makes at most $(4m_L+k)t$ queries to $\mathrm{Enc}_R(x_R) = (\mathrm{Enc}_{RSS}(\zeta_R), G(\zeta_R))$. By Proposition 1, g_L queries more than $2(4m_L+k)tk/n_R$ locations happens with probability at most $\exp(-(4m_L + k)tk/3n_R)$.

Claim. Suppose $m_L \geq t$, then for any $x \in \{0,1\}^{2k}$, the event that g_R makes more than $2(4m_R + n_R)tk/n_L$ queries to x_L happens with probability at most $(n_R + 4m_R)t/m_L \cdot \exp(-m_L k/3n_L)$.

Proof. Fix any x_L, x_R and the randomness for $\mathrm{Enc}_R(x_R)$. Note that any subset of m_L/t outputs of f_R makes at most m_L queries to $\mathrm{Enc}_L(x_L)$. By Proposition 1, the probability that $2m_L k/n_L$ ones in $G(\zeta_L)$ are queried is at most $\exp(-m_L k/3n_L)$. We partition the output bits of f_R into $(n_R + 4m_R)t/m_L$ disjoint subsets of size m_L/t. By a union bound over these subsets, the even that f_R makes more than $2(4m_R + n_R)tk/n_L$ queries to x_L happens with probability at most $(n_R + 4m_R)t/m_L \cdot \exp(-m_L k/3n_L)$. The number of queries made by g_R to x_L is at most the queries made by f_R and the desired conclusion follows.

Then for fixed α, there exists constants c_1, c_2, c_3 (only dependent on α) such that if we set $m_L = c_1 k \log n, n_R = m_R = c_2 tk \log n \log k$ and $n_L = c_3 t^2 k \log n \log^2 k$, then (*) (the event that the number of queries to either opposing side exceeds $\alpha k/(2(\log k + 1))$ happens with probability at most $(t^2 \log k) \cdot \exp(-\Omega(k/t^2 \log^2 k))$. Note that it follows that the rate is $k/n = \Omega(1/t^2 \log^3 n)$ and for $t = O(n^{1/4}/\log^{3/2} n)$, the error can be simplified to $\exp(-\Omega(n/t^4 \log^5 n))$ because $\Omega(n/t^4 \log^5 n) = \Omega(\log n)$ and $t^2 \log k = \exp(O(\log n))$.

4   Leaky Split-State to Split-State Model

In this section, we show how to reduce leaky split-state to split-state non-malleability. In other words, we show how to add leakage-resilience generically to any split-state non-malleable code. Our construction handles up to $\frac{1}{4}$ fraction leakage. Concretely, we prove the following lemma, where the tampering classes SS_k (split-state) and $\alpha\text{-}\mathrm{SS}_n$ (leaky split-state) are defined in Definitions 3 and 4 respectively.

Lemma 4. *For any constant $\alpha \in [0, 1/4)$, $\alpha\text{-}\mathrm{SS}_n$ non-malleably reduces to SS_k with loss $\exp(-\Omega(n)))$ and constant rate.*

Our main tool is new notion of (information-theoretic, one-time) leakage-resilient encryption defined below.

Definition 11 (Leakage-Resilient Encryption). *We consider a (randomized) encryption scheme* (Encrypt, Decrypt) *which encrypts message x of length $|x| = k$ using a key of size $|\mathsf{key}| = m$. For some message $x \in \{0,1\}^k$ we consider the following randomized experiment* $\mathsf{Game}^{\mathsf{LRENC}}(x)$:

- *Choose* key $\leftarrow \{0,1\}^m$, ct $\leftarrow$ Encrypt(key, x).
- *Alice gets* ct *and Bob gets* key. *They can run an arbitrary protocol with each other subject to the total communication being at most ℓ_1 bits. Let* trans $\in \{0,1\}^{\ell_1}$ *be the transcript.*
- *At the end of the protocol, Alice also outputs an additional value* aux $\in \{0,1\}^{\ell_2}$.
- *The output of the game is* key, trans, aux.

We say that an encryption scheme is $(\ell_1, \ell_2, \varepsilon)$-leakage-resilient if for any adversarial strategy of Alice and Bob and for any x_0, x_1 the outputs of Game$^{\mathsf{LRENC}}(x_0)$ *and* Game$^{\mathsf{LRENC}}(x_1)$ *have statistical distance at most ε.*

The above definition is similar to the "forward-secure storage" of Dziembowski [Dzi06], which corresponds to our notion with $\ell_1 = 0$ (there is only leakage on the ciphertext; it is completely independent of the key but can be much larger than the key). It is also similar to the notion of "leakage-resilient storage" of Davi, Dziembowski and Venturi [DDV10], which corresponds to our notion with $\ell_2 = 0$ (there is back-and-forth leakage on the ciphertext and the key but the total leakage is smaller than either the ciphertext or the key). Our definition combines the two notions. We will crucially rely on a setting of parameters where, if the key size is m and the message size is k then we need $\ell_1 < m \le \ell_2 < k$. In other words, we allow ℓ_1 bits of back-and-forth leakage between the ciphertext and the key where ℓ_1 is smaller than either component, but then allow and additional ℓ_2 bits of leakage on the ciphertext where ℓ_2 is larger than the key.

Reduction via Leakage-Resilient Encryption. We first show how to use leakage-resilient encryption as defined above to construct a reduction from leaky split-state to split-state tampering. We do so by encrypting the two states x_L, x_R using leakage-resilient encryption and storing the key with the other state (i.e., the key used to encrypt the left state is stored on the right sides and vice versa). Intuitively, the leakage-resilient encryption ensures that the leakage is independent of the actual states x_L, x_R. However, we face the challenge that, by tampering the key on the right side we can influence how the left side is decrypted and vice versa. We get around this by thinking of the tampered keys as additional leakage (aux).

Let $\mathcal{E} = (\mathsf{Encrypt}, \mathsf{Decrypt})$ be a leakage-resilient encryption with message size k and key length m. We define our reduction (Enc, Dec) below:

- Enc(x_L, x_R): Sample key$_L \leftarrow \{0,1\}^m$, ct$_L \leftarrow$ Encrypt(x_L), key$_R \leftarrow \{0,1\}^m$, ct$_R \leftarrow$ Encrypt(x_R). Output (y_L, y_R) where $y_L = ($ct$_L,$ key$_R), y_R = ($ct$_R,$ key$_L)$.
- Dec(y_L, y_R): Parse $y_L = ($ct$_L,$ key$_R), y_R = ($ct$_R,$ key$_L)$ and output $x_L =$ Decrypt(key$_L$, ct$_L$) and $x_R =$ Decrypt(key$_R$, ct$_R$).

Lemma 5. *Assume $\mathcal{E}$ is an $(\ell_1, \ell_2, \varepsilon)$-leakage-resilient encryption with message length k, key length $m \le \ell_2$ and ciphertext length c. Then* (Enc, Dec) *defined above is a 2ε-non-malleable reduction from $(\ell_1/(c+m))$-leaky split-state to split-state. For a messages (x_L, x_R) of length $2k$, the resulting codeword* Enc(x_L, x_R) *has length $2(c+m)$.*

Proof. Consider the following game: $\mathsf{Game}^{\mathsf{NM}}(x_L, x_R)$:

1. Compute $(y_L = (\mathsf{ct}_L, \mathsf{key}_R), y_R = (\mathsf{ct}_R, \mathsf{key}_L)) \leftarrow \mathsf{Enc}(x_L, y_L)$
2. Give Alice y_L and Bob y_R. They can run an arbitrary protocol with each other subject to the total communication being at most ℓ_1 bits. Let $\mathsf{trans} \in \{0,1\}^{\ell_1}$ be the transcript.
3. At the end of the protocol Alice outputs $y'_L = (\mathsf{ct}'_L, \mathsf{key}'_R)$ and Bob outputs $y'_R = (\mathsf{ct}'_R, \mathsf{key}'_L)$.
4. The output of the game $(x'_L, x'_R) = \mathsf{Dec}(y'_L, y'_R)$, so that $x'_L = \mathsf{Decrypt}(\mathsf{key}'_L, \mathsf{ct}'_L)$ and $x'_R = \mathsf{Decrypt}(\mathsf{key}'_R, \mathsf{ct}'_R)$.

To prove the Lemma, we fix an arbitrary strategy of Alice and Bob and need to show that there exist some distribution G over functions (g_L, g_R) such that for every x_L, x_R the output of $\mathsf{Game}^{\mathsf{NM}}(x_L, x_R)$ is 2ε-statistically close to $g_L(x_L), g_R(x_R)$ where $(g_L, g_R) \leftarrow G$.

Let us define the distribution $z \leftarrow D(x_L, x_R)$ to be the distribution of the values

$$z = (\mathsf{key}_L, \mathsf{key}_R, \mathsf{trans}, \mathsf{key}'_L, \mathsf{key}'_R)$$

in the context of $\mathsf{Game}^{\mathsf{NM}}(x_L, x_R)$. We make two observations, which we then combine to prove our lemma.

Observation 1. In $\mathsf{Game}^{\mathsf{NM}}(x_L, x_R)$, if we condition on some particular choice of $z \leftarrow D(x_L, x_R)$, then the distribution of x'_L a is completely independent of (x_R, x'_R) and similarly x'_R is independent of (x_L, x'_L). In particular, we can define the randomized process g_L^z which has z hard-coded and samples $x'_L \leftarrow g_L^z(x_L)$ by first sampling Alice's view in the game conditioned on z and x_L, computing her output ct'_L and setting $x'_L = \mathsf{Decrypt}(\mathsf{key}'_L, \mathsf{ct}'_L)$. We can define the randomized process $x'_R \leftarrow g_R^z(x_R)$ analogously. It is easy to see that the distribution of $\mathsf{Game}^{\mathsf{NM}}(x_L, x_R)$ is then identical to sampling $z \leftarrow D(x_L, x_R)$ and outputting $x'_L \leftarrow g_L^z(x_L), x'_R \leftarrow g_R^z(x_R)$.

Observation 2. For any x_L, x_R the distribution of $D(x_L, x_R)$ is 2ε-statistically close to $D(0^k, 0^k)$. We argue that this holds via two steps. We first argue that $D(x_L, x_R)$ is ε-close to $D(0^k, x_R)$ and then argue that $D(0^k, x_R)$ is ε-close to $D(0^k, 0^k)$. For the first step, we can fix any worst case choice of $\mathsf{key}_R, \mathsf{ct}_R$ and use the security of leakage-resilient encryption to argue that the joint distribution of $\mathsf{key}_L, \mathsf{trans}, \mathsf{key}'_R$ is ε-close between $D(x_L, x_R)$ and $D(0^k, x_R)$; we set $\mathsf{aux} = \mathsf{key}'_R$ in this argument and use the fact that $|\mathsf{key}'_R| = m \le \ell_2$. We then note that key'_L is just a function of $\mathsf{ct}_R, \mathsf{key}_L$ and trans and therefore the total distribution of $(\mathsf{key}_L, \mathsf{key}_R, \mathsf{trans}, \mathsf{key}'_L, \mathsf{key}'_R)$ is ε close between $D(x_L, x_R)$ and $D(0^k, x_R)$. The argument that $D(0^k, x_R)$ is ε-close to $D(0^k, 0^k)$ is identical.

By combining observations 1 and 2, we see the distribution of $\mathsf{Game}^{\mathsf{NM}}(x_L, x_R)$ is 2ε statistically close to sampling $z \leftarrow D(0^k, 0^k)$ and outputting $x'_L \leftarrow g_L^z(x_L), x'_R \leftarrow g_R^z(x_R)$. This concludes our reduction as desired; we define the distribution G over functions (g_L, g_R) by sampling $z \leftarrow D(0^k, 0^k)$ and setting $g_L = g_L^z$ and $g_R = g_R^z$. The output of $\mathsf{Game}^{\mathsf{NM}}(x_L, x_R)$ is 2ε-statistically close to $g_L(x_L), g_R(x_R)$ where $(g_L, g_R) \leftarrow G$.

Construction of Leakage-Resilient Encryption. Let Ext be a seeded strong extractor with r-bit source, d-bit seed and output size k which is $(r - \ell_1 - \ell_2, \varepsilon_1)$-secure. Let 2Ext be a strong two-source extractor with m-bit sources and d-bit output which is $(2m - \ell_1, \varepsilon_2)$-secure.

Define the scheme (Encrypt, Decrypt) as follows:

- Encrypt(key, x):
  Choose $u \leftarrow \{0,1\}^r$, $y \leftarrow \{0,1\}^m$, $s = 2\mathsf{Ext}(\mathsf{key}, y)$, $z = \mathsf{Ext}(u; s) \oplus x$.
  Output ct $= (u, y, z)$.
- Decrypt(key, ct $= (u, y, z)$):
  Compute $s = 2\mathsf{Ext}(\mathsf{key}, y)$ and output $z \oplus \mathsf{Ext}(u; s)$.

Claim. Consider a variant of the leakage-resilient encryption game, which we denote "weak leakage resilience", where Alice does not get the z part of the ciphertext during the game but the output of the game is key, trans, aux, z. If the scheme is $(\ell_1, \ell_2, \varepsilon)$-"weak leakage resilient" then it also satisfies $(\ell_1, \ell_2, \varepsilon \cdot 2^k)$-leakage resilience.

Proof. Assume there exists some (Alice, Bob, Distinguisher) strategy in the original game such that the Distinguisher has an $\varepsilon 2^k$ advantage in distinguishing the game with x_0 and x_1. We convert this into an (Alice', Bob, Distinguisher') strategy for the weak game by guessing a random value $v \leftarrow \{0,1\}^k$ at the beginning of the game and having Alice' run Alice with v in place of z. Then Distinguisher' gets z and if $v = z$ it runs the original Distinguisher else outputs 0. It's easy to see that the advantage of Distinguisher' is the same as that of Distinguisher when $v = z$, which happens with probability 2^{-k}, and 0 otherwise. Therefore, Distinguisher' has advantage 2^{-k} smaller than Distinguisher which proves the claim.

Lemma 6. (Encrypt, Decrypt) *is* $(\ell_1, \ell_2, (\varepsilon_1 + \varepsilon_2)2^{k+1})$-*leakage-resilient.*

Proof. It suffices to show that the scheme is $(\ell_1, \ell_2, 2(\varepsilon_1 + \varepsilon_2))$ weak leakage resilient and the rest follows by the preceding claim. We use a statistical hybrid argument.

Hybrid 1: This is the weak leakage resilient game with message x_0. Recall that in the game Alice gets (u, y) and Bob gets key. They run a protocol with ℓ_1 bits of communication resulting in transcript trans. At the termination of the protocol, Bob also outputs an additional ℓ_2-bit value aux. The output of the protocol is key, trans, aux, z where $z = \mathsf{Ext}(u; s) \oplus x_0$ and $s = 2\mathsf{Ext}(\mathsf{key}, y)$.

Hybrid 2: Note that, in Hybrid 1, conditioned on the random variable $V_1 = (s, y, \mathsf{trans})$ the random variables $V_2 = (u, \mathsf{aux}, z)$ and $V_3 = \mathsf{key}$ are independent. Therefore, we can define Hybrid 2 to run the same game as Hybrid 1, which defines (V_1, V_2, V_3), but then, instead of key, output a freshly resampled key' from the correct distribution of V_3 conditioned on V_1. This is distributed identically to Hybrid 1.

Hybrid 3: In this hybrid, we choose s uniformly at random instead of $s = 2\mathsf{Ext}(\mathsf{key}, y)$ and set $z = \mathsf{Ext}(r; s) \oplus x_0$. We still sample key' from the same distribution of V_3 conditioned on V_1 at the end of the game, just like in Hybrid 2. The statistical distance between Hybrid 2 and Hybrid 3 is ε_2. We rely on the fact that $2\mathsf{Ext}$ is a strong extractor and that trans amounts to ℓ_1 bits of entropy loss from key to argue that, even given (u, y, trans) the value s is ε_2-close to uniform.

Hybrid 4: In this hybrid, we set z to uniform instead of $z = \mathsf{Ext}(u; s) \oplus x_0$. The statistical distance between Hybrid 3 and Hybrid 4 is ε_1. This follows from the strong-extractor property of Ext and the fact that $\mathsf{trans}, \mathsf{aux}$ gives $\ell_2 + \ell_1$ bits of leakage on u.

Hybrid 5, 6, 7: Are the same as 3, 2, 1 with x_0 replaced by x_1. In particular Hybrid 7 is the weak leakage resilience game with message x_1.

Hybrids 4,5 are ε_1 close (same argument as Hybrids 3, 4), Hybrids 5, 6 are ε_2 close (same argument as Hybrids 2, 3) and Hybrids 6, 7 are identical (same argument as 1, 2).

Combining the above we get a total distance of $2(\varepsilon_1 + \varepsilon_2)$ between Hybrids 1 and 7 as we wanted to show.

We can now plug in parameters using the inner-product two-source extractor [CG88], and the strong extractor [GUV09] to prove the main Lemma of this section:

Proof (Proof of Lemma 4). For $\varepsilon \in (0,1)$, let $\varepsilon_1 = \varepsilon_2 = \varepsilon/2^{k+3}$ and $\ell_2 = m$. By Theorem 5, there exists some constant $c_1, c_2 \geq 1$ and explicit Ext such that for $r - \ell_1 - \ell_2 \geq c_1 \cdot k$, Ext can extract k bits from $(r, r - \ell_1 - \ell_2)$ source with $d = c_2 \log(r/\varepsilon_1)$-bit seed and error ε_1. By Theorem 6, for $2m - \ell_1 \geq m + d + 2\log(1/\varepsilon_2)$, there exists explicit $2\mathsf{Ext}$ that extracts d bits with error ε_2 from m-bit sources with entropy $2m - \ell_1$. Plugging in Ext and $2\mathsf{Ext}$, by Lemma 6 and Lemma 5, we obtain $(\ell_1, \ell_2, (\varepsilon_1 + \varepsilon_2)2^{k+1})$ leakage-resilient encryption and a $(\varepsilon_1 + \varepsilon_2)2^{k+2}$-non-malleable reduction from (ℓ_1/n)-split state to split state with $n = r + 2m + k$. By setting $r = \ell_1 + m + c_2 k$, $m = \ell_1 + d + 2\log(1/\varepsilon_2)$ and $d = c_2(\log(r/\varepsilon_1))$, we obtain that $n \leq 4\ell_1 + c_3(k + \log 1/\varepsilon)$ for some constant $c_3 \geq 1$. Therefore for any $\alpha < 1/4$ and $\ell_1 = \alpha n$, we can set $n = \Theta(\frac{k + \log(1/\varepsilon)}{1/4 - \alpha})$. The desired conclusion follows from setting $\varepsilon = \exp(-\Omega(k))$ and $n = \Theta(k)$.

5 Putting Things Together

Combining Lemmas 3 and 4, we obtain a non-malleable reduction from decision trees to split-state model.

Lemma 7. *For $t = O(n^{1/4}/\log^{3/2} n)$, there is a $(\mathrm{DT}(t) \Rightarrow \mathsf{SS}_k, \varepsilon)$ non-malleable reduction with rate $\Omega(1/t^2 \log^3 n)$ where $\varepsilon \leq \exp(-\Omega(n/t^4 \log^5 n))$.*

Plugging in the construction of non-malleable codes for split state model [Li18] with rate $\Omega(\log \log n/ \log n)$ and error $\exp(-\Omega(n \log \log n/ \log n))$, we obtain our main theorem.

Theorem 8. *For any* $t = O(n^{1/4}/ \log^{3/2} n)$, *there is an explicit and efficient non-malleable code that is unconditionally secure against depth-t decision trees with codeword length* $n = O(kt^2 \log^4 n/ \log \log n)$ *and error* $\exp(-\Omega(n/t^4 \log^5 n))$ *for a k-bit message.*

Ball et al. [BDG+18] gave a non-malleable reduction from small-depth circuits to a leaky variant of decision trees, $LL^{d,m,n}[DT(t)]$ (See Definition 12).

Lemma 8. *[BDG+18] For* $S,d,n,t \in \mathbb{N}, p, \delta \in (0,1)$, *there exist*

$$\sigma = \text{poly}(t, \log(2^t S), \log(1/\delta), \log(1/p))^8$$

and $m = O(\sigma \log n)$ *such that, for any* $2m \leq k \leq n(p/4)^d$,

$$(AC_d(S) \implies LL^{d,m,n}[DT(t)], d\varepsilon)$$

where

$$\varepsilon = nS \left(2^{2t+1}(5pt)^t + \delta\right) + \exp(-\tfrac{\sigma}{2\log(1/p)}).$$

Ball et al. [BDG+18] used the fact that for $t < \log n$, leaky depth-t decision trees is a subclass of leaky 2^t-local functions and gave a non-malleable code for leaky local functions based on a construction of Ball et al. [BDKM16]. Their approach only works for $t < \log n$. This limits the error of the composed code to be $n^{-O(\log n)}$ which, in turns, requires $S = n^{O(\log n)}$. (The same restrictions also appear in [CL17], but for other reasons.)

We note that the "leakage" is simply a restricted form of dm adaptive queries to depth-t decision trees. Thus, $LL^{d,m,n}[DT(t)] \subseteq DT(dmt)$. Therefore a non-malleable code for large depth decision trees immediately yields a new non-malleable code for small depth circuits (with improved error). In particular, $LL^{d,m,n}[DT(t)]$ gives decision trees that are identical excepting (up to) the last t queries before output (and that the last t-queries must be consistent with one of n depth-t decision trees). Combining Lemma 8 and our new non-malleable reduction from decision trees to split-state functions, we obtain an improved non-malleable reduction from small-depth circuits to split-state functions.

Lemma 9. *For* $S,d,n,t \in \mathbb{N}, p, \delta \in (0,1)$, *there exist*

$$\sigma = \text{poly}(t, \log(2^t S), \log(1/\delta), \log(1/p))$$

and $m = O(\sigma \log n)$ *such that, for* $t' = dmt = O(n^{1/4}/ \log^{3/2} n)$, $k \geq O(\sigma \log n)$ *and* $k = \Omega(n(p/4)^d/(t')^2 \log^3 n)$,

$$(AC_d(S) \implies SS_k, d\varepsilon + \exp(-\Omega(n/(t')^4 \log^5 n)))$$

---

[8] The exponent of this polynomial is a fixed absolute constant independent of all other parameters.

where

$$\varepsilon = nS\left(2^{2t'+1}(5pt')^{t'} + \delta\right) + \exp(-\frac{\sigma}{2\log(1/p)}).$$

For constant-depth polynomial-size circuits (i.e., AC^0), by setting $p = n^{-O(1/d)}$ (such as $n^{-1/100d}$), $t' = 1/40p$ and $\delta = \exp(n^{-\Omega(1/d)})$, we improve the error of the non-malleable reduction from AC^0 to split-state from $n^{-\log n}$ to $\exp(-n^{\Omega(1)})$.

Corollary 1. $\left(\mathsf{AC}^0 \implies \mathsf{SS}_k, \exp(-n^{\Omega(1)})\right)$ *for* $n = k^{1+c}$ *for a constant* $0 < c < 1$.

The same setting of parameters lead to non-malleable reduction for circuits of depth as large as $\Theta(\log(n)/\log\log(n))$ and size $S = \exp(n^{O(1/d)})$ with error $\exp(-n^{\Omega(1/d)})$. Combining the non-malleable code for split state from [Li18] with rate $\Omega(\log\log n/\log n)$ and error $\exp(-\Omega(n\log\log n/\log n))$, we obtain our main theorem.

Theorem 9. *For any constant* $c \in (0,1)$, *there exist constants* $c_1, c_2 \in (0,1)$ *such that for any* $d \leq c_1 \log n/\log\log n$ *and* $S = \exp(n^{c_2/d})$ *there is an explicit, efficient, information theoretic non-malleable code for depth* d *size* S *circuits with error* $\exp(-n^{\Omega(1/d)})$ *and encoding length* $n = k^{1+c}$.

Acknowledgements. We would like to thank Dana Dachman-Soled, Tal Malkin, and Li Yang Tan for many insightful conversations and helping to pose the initial question and its connections to small depth circuits. We would like to additionally thank Justin Holmgren and Ron Rothblum for stimulating discussions. The first author is supported by an IBM Research PhD Fellowship, NSF grant CCF1423306, and the Leona M. & Harry B. Helmsley Charitable Trust. Part of this work was completed while the author was visiting IDC Herzilya. The second author is supported by NSF grants CNS1314722 and CNS-1413964. The third author is supported by NSF grants CNS-1314722, CNS-1413964, CNS-1750795 and the Alfred P. Sloan Research Fellowship.

A   Leaky Function Classes

Ball et al. [BDG+18] considered a leaky variant of a given tampering class $\mathcal{C}$.

Definition 12 (Leaky Function Families). *[BDG+18] Let* $\mathsf{LL}^{i,m,N}[\mathcal{C}]$ *denote tampering functions generated via the following game:*

1. *The adversary first commits to* N *functions from a class* $\mathcal{C}$, $F_1, \ldots, F_N = \mathbf{F}$. *(Note:* $F_j : \{0,1\}^N \to \{0,1\}$ *for all* $j \in [N]$.)*
2. *The adversary then has* i-*adaptive rounds of leakage. In each round* $j \in [i]$,
   - *the adversary selects* s *indices from* $[N]$, *denoted* S_j,
   - *the adversary receives* $\mathbf{F}(x)_{S_j}$.
   Formally, we take $h_j : \{0,1\}^{m(j-1)} \to [N]^m$ *to be the selection function such that*
   $$h_j(F(X)_{S_1}, \ldots, F(X)_{S_{j-1}}) = S_j.$$
   Let h_1 *be the constant function that outputs* S_1.

3. *Finally, selects a sequence of n functions* $(F_{t_1}, \ldots, F_{t_n})$ $(T = \{t_1, \ldots, t_n\} \subseteq [N]$ *such that* $t_1 < t_2 < \cdots < t_n)$ *to tamper with.*

Formally, we take $h : \{0,1\}^{mi} \to [N]^n$ *such that* $h(F(X)_{S_1}, \ldots, F(X)_{S_i}) = T$.

Thus, any $\tau \in \mathrm{LL}^{i,m,N}[\mathcal{C}]$ *can be described as* $(\boldsymbol{F}, h_1, \cdots, h_i, h)$ *and denote the tampering function described above via* $\tau = \mathrm{Eval}(\boldsymbol{F}, h_1, \cdots, h_i, h)$.

References

[AB16]   Aggarwal, D., Briët, J.: Revisiting the Sanders-Bogolyubov-Ruzsa theorem in fp^n and its application to non-malleable codes. In: IEEE International Symposium on Information Theory, ISIT 2016, Barcelona, Spain, 10–15 July 2016, pp. 1322–1326 (2016)

[ADKO15a]   Aggarwal, D., Dodis, Y., Kazana, T., Obremski, M.: Non-malleable reductions and applications. In: Servedio, R.A., Rubinfeld, R. (eds.) Proceedings of the Forty-Seventh Annual ACM on Symposium on Theory of Computing, STOC 2015, Portland, OR, USA, 14–17 June 2015, pp. 459–468. ACM (2015)

[ADKO15b]   Aggarwal, D., Dziembowski, S., Kazana, T., Obremski, M.: Leakage-resilient non-malleable codes. In: Dodis, Y., Nielsen, J.B. (eds.) TCC 2015, Part I. LNCS, vol. 9014, pp. 398–426. Springer, Heidelberg (2015). https://doi.org/10.1007/978-3-662-46494-6_17

[ADL14]   Aggarwal, D., Dodis, Y., Lovett, S.: Non-malleable codes from additive combinatorics. In: Shmoys, D.B. (ed.) Symposium on Theory of Computing, STOC 2014, New York, NY, USA, 31 May–03 June 2014, pp. 774–783. ACM (2014)

[Agg15]   Aggarwal, D.: Affine-evasive sets modulo a prime. Inf. Process. Lett. **115**(2), 382–385 (2015)

[AGM+15]   Agrawal, S., Gupta, D., Maji, H.K., Pandey, O., Prabhakaran, M.: Explicit non-malleable codes against bit-wise tampering and permutations. In: Gennaro, R., Robshaw, M. (eds.) CRYPTO 2015, Part I. LNCS, vol. 9215, pp. 538–557. Springer, Heidelberg (2015). https://doi.org/10.1007/978-3-662-47989-6_26

[BDG+18]   Ball, M., Dachman-Soled, D., Guo, S., Malkin, T., Tan, L.-Y.: Non-malleable codes for small-depth circuits. IACR Cryptology ePrint Archive 2018, p. 207 (2018)

[BDKM16]   Ball, M., Dachman-Soled, D., Kulkarni, M., Malkin, T.: Non-malleable codes for bounded depth, bounded fan-in circuits. In: Fischlin, M., Coron, J.-S. (eds.) EUROCRYPT 2016, Part II. LNCS, vol. 9666, pp. 881–908. Springer, Heidelberg (2016). https://doi.org/10.1007/978-3-662-49896-5_31

[BDKM18]   Ball, M., Dachman-Soled, D., Kulkarni, M., Malkin, T.: Non-malleable codes from average-case hardness: AC^0, decision trees, and streaming space-bounded tampering. In: Nielsen, J.B., Rijmen, V. (eds.) EUROCRYPT 2018, Part III. LNCS, vol. 10822, pp. 618–650. Springer, Cham (2018). https://doi.org/10.1007/978-3-319-78372-7_20

[BDSK+18] Ball, M., Dachman-Soled, D., Kulkarni, M., Lin, H., Malkin, T.: Non-malleable codes against bounded polynomial time tampering. Cryptology ePrint Archive, Report 2018/1015 (2018). https://eprint.iacr.org/2018/1015

[CG88] Chor, B., Goldreich, O.: Unbiased bits from sources of weak randomness and probabilistic communication complexity. SIAM J. Comput. **17**(2), 230–261 (1988)

[CG14] Cheraghchi, M., Guruswami, V.: Non-malleable coding against bit-wise and split-state tampering. In: Lindell, Y. (ed.) TCC 2014. LNCS, vol. 8349, pp. 440–464. Springer, Heidelberg (2014). https://doi.org/10.1007/978-3-642-54242-8_19

[CGL16] Chattopadhyay, E., Goyal, V., Li, X.: Non-malleable extractors and codes, with their many tampered extensions. In: Proceedings of the 48th Annual ACM SIGACT Symposium on Theory of Computing, STOC 2016, Cambridge, MA, USA, 18–21 June 2016, pp. 285–298 (2016)

[CL17] Chattopadhyay, E., Li, X.: Non-malleable codes and extractors for small-depth circuits, and affine functions. In: Proceedings of the 49th Annual ACM SIGACT Symposium on Theory of Computing, STOC 2017, Montreal, QC, Canada, 19–23 June 2017, pp. 1171–1184 (2017)

[CL18] Chattopadhyay, E., Li, X.: Non-malleable extractors and codes in the interleaved split-state model and more. CoRR, abs/1804.05228 (2018)

[CZ14] Chattopadhyay, E., Zuckerman, D.: Non-malleable codes against constant split-state tampering. In: 55th IEEE Annual Symposium on Foundations of Computer Science, FOCS 2014, Philadelphia, PA, USA, 18–21 October 2014, pp. 306–315. IEEE Computer Society (2014)

[DDV10] Daví, F., Dziembowski, S., Venturi, D.: Leakage-resilient storage. In: Garay, J.A., De Prisco, R. (eds.) SCN 2010. LNCS, vol. 6280, pp. 121–137. Springer, Heidelberg (2010). https://doi.org/10.1007/978-3-642-15317-4_9

[DKO13] Dziembowski, S., Kazana, T., Obremski, M.: Non-malleable codes from two-source extractors. In: Canetti, R., Garay, J.A. (eds.) CRYPTO 2013, Part II. LNCS, vol. 8043, pp. 239–257. Springer, Heidelberg (2013). https://doi.org/10.1007/978-3-642-40084-1_14

[DPW10] Dziembowski, S., Pietrzak, K., Wichs, D.: Non-malleable codes. In: Yao, A.C.-C. (ed.) Innovations in Computer Science - ICS 2010, Tsinghua University, Beijing, China, 5–7 January 2010, Proceedings, pp. 434–452. Tsinghua University Press (2010)

[Dzi06] Dziembowski, S.: On forward-secure storage. In: Dwork, C. (ed.) CRYPTO 2006. LNCS, vol. 4117, pp. 251–270. Springer, Heidelberg (2006). https://doi.org/10.1007/11818175_15

[GUV09] Guruswami, V., Umans, C., Vadhan, S.P.: Unbalanced expanders and randomness extractors from parvaresh-vardy codes. J. ACM **56**(4), 20:1–20:34 (2009)

[KOS17] Kanukurthi, B., Obbattu, S.L.B., Sekar, S.: Four-state non-malleable codes with explicit constant rate. In: Kalai, Y., Reyzin, L. (eds.) TCC 2017, Part II. LNCS, vol. 10678, pp. 344–375. Springer, Cham (2017). https://doi.org/10.1007/978-3-319-70503-3_11

[Li17] Li, X.: Improved non-malleable extractors, non-malleable codes and independent source extractors. In: Hatami, H., McKenzie, P., King, V. (eds.) Proceedings of the 49th Annual ACM SIGACT Symposium on Theory of Computing, STOC 2017, Montreal, QC, Canada, 19–23 June 2017, pp. 1144–1156. ACM (2017)

[Li18] Li, X.: Pseudorandom correlation breakers, independence preserving mergers and their applications. In: Electronic Colloquium on Computational Complexity (ECCC), vol. 25, p. 28 (2018)

[NZ96] Nisan, N., Zuckerman, D.: Randomness is linear in space. J. Comput. Syst. Sci. **52**(1), 43–52 (1996)

[PS97] Panconesi, A., Srinivasan, A.: Randomized distributed edge coloring via an extension of the Chernoff-Hoeffding bounds. SIAM J. Comput. **26**(2), 350–368 (1997)

Explicit Rate-1 Non-malleable Codes
for Local Tampering

Divya Gupta[1], Hemanta K. Maji[2], and Mingyuan Wang[2(✉)]

[1] Microsoft Research, Bangalore, India
divya.gupta@microsoft.com
[2] Department of Computer Science, Purdue University, West Lafayette, USA
{hmaji,wang1929}@purdue.edu

Abstract. This paper constructs high-rate non-malleable codes in the information-theoretic plain model against tampering functions with bounded locality. We consider δ-local tampering functions; namely, each output bit of the tampering function is a function of (at most) δ input bits. This work presents the first explicit and efficient rate-1 non-malleable code for δ-local tampering functions, where $\delta = \xi \lg n$ and $\xi < 1$ is any positive constant. As a corollary, we construct the first explicit rate-1 non-malleable code against NC^0 tampering functions.

Before our work, no explicit construction for a constant-rate non-malleable code was known even for the simplest 1-local tampering functions. Ball et al. (EUROCRYPT–2016), and Chattopadhyay and Li (STOC–2017) provided the first explicit non-malleable codes against δ-local tampering functions. However, these constructions are rate-0 even when the tampering functions have 1-locality. In the CRS model, Faust et al. (EUROCRYPT–2014) constructed efficient rate-1 non-malleable codes for $\delta = O(\log n)$ local tampering functions.

Our main result is a general compiler that bootstraps a rate-0 non-malleable code against leaky input and output local tampering functions to construct a rate-1 non-malleable code against $\xi \lg n$-local tampering functions, for any positive constant $\xi < 1$. Our explicit construction instantiates this compiler using an appropriate encoding by Ball et al. (EUROCRYPT–2016).

1 Introduction

Dziembowski, Pietrzak, and Wichs [18] introduced the notion of non-malleable codes as an extension of the standard objective of error-correction. Non-malleable codes provide message-integrity assurances even when error-detection, let alone error-correction, is impossible. Suppose a sender encodes a message $m \in \{0,1\}^\ell$ and transmits the codeword over a channel. If the channel adds an error that

H. K. Maji—The research effort is supported in part by an NSF CRII Award CNS–1566499, an NSF SMALL Award CNS–1618822, and an REU CNS–1724673.
H. K. Maji and M. Wang—The research effort is supported in part by a Purdue Research Foundation grant.

A. Boldyreva and D. Micciancio (Eds.): CRYPTO 2019, LNCS 11692, pp. 435–466, 2019.
https://doi.org/10.1007/978-3-030-26948-7_16

has a small Hamming weight, then the sender can encode the message using an error-correcting code and the receiver can error-correct and retrieve the original message. Algebraic Manipulation Detection codes [16] help the receiver detect if the transmitted codeword is tampered using algebraic operations. For more sophisticated classes of tampering function $\mathcal{F}$, demanding manipulation detection or error-correction might be far-fetched. For example, suppose the channel replaces the original codeword with a fixed valid codeword. In this case, error-correction or error-detection is impossible. Non-malleable codes provide a meaningful message integrity assurance against sophisticated tampering families.

Let us fix an encoding and a decoding scheme (Enc, Dec), and a tampering function family $\mathcal{F}$. Non-malleable codes ensure that for any message $m \in \{0, 1\}^{\ell}$ and tampering function $f \in \mathcal{F}$, the tampered message $\mathsf{Dec}(f(\mathsf{Enc}(m)))$ is either identical to the original message m or a simulator Sim_f can simulate this distribution (that is, it is independent of the original message). Even such a weak message integrity assurance turns out to be cryptographically useful, for example, in storing secret-keys for cryptographic primitives [18,28] and non-malleable messaging [22,23]. Naturally, we measure the quality of non-malleable codes using the following two parameters.

1. **Rate.** The ratio of the length of the message to the length of its encoding.
2. **Sophistication of the tampering family.** The complexity of the tampering attacks captured by the tampering functions in this family.

Constructing explicit non-malleable codes with high rate against sophisticated tampering function families is the guiding principle for the research in non-malleable codes. However, both these objectives, even independently, have been significantly non-trivial to achieve. Only recently, using elegant probabilistic arguments, [13,20] constructed rate-1 non-malleable codes in the *CRS model* for tampering families of bounded size.[1]

In this paper, for any positive constant $\xi < 1$, we present the first *rate-1* explicit non-malleable codes against any tampering function that has $\xi \lg n$ *output locality*, i.e., at most $\xi \lg n$ input-bits influence any output bit of the tampering function. Note that there is no bound on the input locality, i.e., the number of output positions one input bit can influence during tampering. Here lg represents the logarithm with base 2, and n represents the length of the codeword. Notably, our construction is in the information-theoretic plain model. We emphasize that our construction does not rely on any computational hardness assumption or a CRS.

1.1   Prior Relevant Works

Note that it is impossible to construct a non-malleable code (NMC) that is secure for all tampering functions. Consider a tampering function that obtains an advantage in predicting the first bit m_1 of the message m. Then, the tampering function f overwrites the codeword with a *fixed* encoding of m_1^{ℓ}, which we

---

[1] Tampering functions can access the CRS; however, they cannot tamper the CRS.

hardwire into it. This result indicates that, given the codeword c, no tampering function $f \in \mathcal{F}$ should have an advantage in predicting any bit of the message $m \in \{0,1\}^{\ell}$. Consequently, we fix the class of tampering function family $\mathcal{F}$, and construct a non-malleable encoding scheme (Enc, Dec) for that tampering family.

Monte-Carlo Constructions. Dziembowski et al. [18], introduced the notion of non-malleable codes and showed the existence of rate-1 NMC against bit-wise tampering (each output bit is a function of the corresponding input bit). Next, Faust et al. [20] showed the existence of rate-1 non-malleable codes against any tampering family of size $2^{\mathrm{poly}(n)}$.[2] Cheraghchi and Guruswami [13] proved that there exists (possibly inefficient) $(1 - \alpha)$-rate NMC against any tampering function family of size $2^{2^{\alpha n}}$. These results are probabilistic in nature and it is unknown whether we can derandomize them to obtain explicit constructions in the plain model. Note that there are (roughly) $\left(\binom{n}{\delta} 2^{2^{\delta}} \right)^{n} \approx 2^{n 2^{\delta}}$ distinct δ-local tampering functions. If $\delta = O(\log n)$ then [20] indicates the existence of an efficient rate-1 non-malleable code. Further, for $\delta = o(n)$, [13] implies the existence of a (possibly inefficient) rate-1 non-malleable code.

Explicit Constructions. A famous line of research explores designing NMCs against k-split-state tampering functions where k different locations store the k shares of the encoding. The tampering of each share is performed arbitrarily, albeit independently. The maximum achievable rate in this setting is $R \leqslant 1 - 1/k$ [13]. Dziembowski et al. [17] constructed NMC for one-bit messages in the 2-split-state model. A sequence of highly influential works have constructed near-optimal constant-rate NMCs using only $k = 3$ shares of the encoding [2,3,10, 12,24,27,28]. Currently, Li's construction [29,30] achieves the highest rate $R = O(\log \log \log n / \log \log n)$ for 2-split-state tampering.

Another research direction allows the tampering function to tamper the entire codeword but constrains its computational power. For example, local tampering functions have an a priori upper bound of how many input bits influence each output bit. [7,11] construct explicit NMC for local tampering functions. The rate of [7] is at most the product of inverse of locality and rate of the 2-split-state NMC. Hence, their construction has rate-0 even for constant locality. Recently, [6] consider constant depth circuits and construct the first explicit NMC against AC^0 tampering. Both [11] and [6] have inverse-polynomial rate.

Explicit Rate-1 Constructions. Explicit rate-1 NMC constructions are even more scarce. Cheraghchi and Guruswami [14,18] construct a rate-1 NMC for bit-wise tampering. Agrawal et al. [4,5] provide an explicit rate-1 NMC against tampering functions that perform bit-wise tampering after permuting the input bits. Both these constructions amplify the rate of a base NMC (possibly, with additional properties) that has sub-optimal rate into a rate-1 NMC using a compiler. We emphasize that these two particular tampering families are not only 1-local but also have the constraint that each input bit influences at most

---

[2] This construction is also an efficient rate-1 construction in the CRS model.

one output bit (that is, 1-input local). Note that the focus of this work is δ-local tampering functions with $\delta > 1$ and no bound on input locality.

In the computationally bounded setting, [1] construct a rate-1 NMC against 2-split-state tampering based on the existence of one-way functions. Furthermore, there are constructions of NMC that rely on a CRS [8,20,31].

Non-malleable codes have also been considered in the continual tampering model, for example, [19,26,33]; covering which is beyond the scope of this work.

1.2 Our Contribution

Our work focuses on constructing non-malleable codes, in the information-theoretic plain model, against tampering functions that are δ-local, i.e., at most δ input bits influence any output bit. We emphasize that δ can be a function of n, the size of the codeword. Our work, for any positive constant $\xi < 1$, constructs explicit rate-1 NMC against δ-local tampering functions, where $\delta = \xi \lg n$, which has a tampering family of size $2^{n^{1+o(1)}}$. In our case, the locality $\delta = \omega(1)$ and, hence, the set of all δ-local tampering functions subsumes the family of NC^0 tampering functions.

We present a general black-box compiler that takes three ingredients as input and constructs a non-malleable code for local functions. At an intuitive level, we prove the following result.

Informal Theorem 1. *For any positive constant $\xi < 1$, there exists an explicit and efficient rate-1 NMC against $\xi \lg n$-local tampering functions using the following primitives in a black-box manner (refer to Fig. 2).*

1. *Rate-1 linear error-correcting code[3] with (near) linear distance and dual-distance (see Definition 7),*
2. *Rate-$1/\eta^{o(1)}$ NMC against leaky input and output local tampering for message length η (referred to as the base NMC) (see Definition 6), and*
3. *A pseudorandom generator for finite state machines with super-polynomial stretch (see Definition 9).*

The compiler (refer to Fig. 1 for an outline) encodes the message m using the error-correcting code. Then, it samples a few entries of the codeword (at a suitable rate) and adds errors at half of them. The compiler tabulates all the sampled entries (both the erroneous and unaltered ones) along with their respective locations. The erroneous codeword forms the primary payload of the message m. The list of tabulated entries is appropriately encoded using a combination of the base NMC and the PRG and is juxtaposed (at the end) for consistency checks during decoding. If the rate of subsampling is sufficiently low, then the overall construction is rate-1. The security argument proceeds by demonstrating that if the subsampling rate is sufficiently high, then any local function cannot change

---

[3] Error-correcting codes can be converted into error-correcting secret sharing schemes using standard share-packing techniques [9,21,34].

the payload without being inconsistent with the tabulated entries themselves. Section 1.3 provides an intuitive overview of our compiler's construction.

Finally, we instantiate the respective primitives using (1) Reed-Solomon Codes over characteristic 2 fields, (2) An appropriate encoding introduced by Ball et al. [7], and (3) Nisan's PRG [32]. As a consequence, we construct explicit efficient rate-1 NMC against $\xi \lg n$-local tampering functions, for any positive constant $\xi < 1$, with negligible simulation error (refer Theorem 2).

Remark. We note that the resulting decoding function for our construction is randomized. However, the randomization stems solely from the randomized decoding function of the base NMC construction of [7]. Given an appropriate NMC against leaky input and output local tampering with deterministic decoding, our construction will have deterministic decoding.

Remark. If the base NMC is only rate-1/ poly n, then our compiler with suitably modified parameters, constructs an explicit rate-1 NMC against $o(\log n)$-local tampering functions. We defer this modification to the full version.

1.3   Technical Overview

As a starting point, it is instructive to understand the construction of Agrawal et al. [5] for a rate-1 NMC against tampering functions with input and output locality 1. The conceptual hurdles in generalizing this approach to δ-local functions, we believe, motivates the components used in our construction.

Construction of Agrawal et al. [5]. The construction of Agrawal et al. [5] encodes the message m with an error correcting secret sharing (ECSS) scheme to obtain a. Then, it samples a small number of bits from a indexed by E, which are represented by a_E, and replaces a_E with a (uniformly random) error e. This creates an erroneous codeword c. Observe that half of the bits of e match the original entries in a_E and the remaining do not. Next, an NMC of rate-1/ poly encodes the consistency checks (E, e) as c_{err}, and the final encoding is (c, c_{err}). The decoding algorithm error-corrects c to obtain a (and hence, m) and checks the *consistency* between a, c, c_{err}. For an appropriately chosen size of the set E, the encoding (c, c_{err}) is non-malleable and has rate-1.

We represent the tampered codeword and error, respectively, by $\widetilde{c}$ and $\widetilde{c_{\mathrm{err}}}$. The security argument proceeds, roughly, as follows.

(1) The tampering on c_{err} is independent of the message m. This argument crucially relies on the output-locality of the tampering function. The independence[4] of the ECSS is sufficiently high to permit the simulation of the tampering on c_{err} independent of the message m.

(2) The non-malleability of the encoding c_{err} ensures that $\widetilde{c_{\mathrm{err}}}$ encodes either (a) the original (E, e), or (b) an entirely unrelated (E^*, e^*). The case of the tampering function creating an invalid encoding is not particularly insightful.

---

[4] An ECSS of independence t has the property that any t shares are uniformly and independently random.

(3.a.) Consider the case where the tampering function preserves error; namely, the same* case. In this case, they argue that the only way to get a valid tampered codeword is by keeping $\widetilde{c}$ identical to c and that the probability of encoding being valid independent of the original message m. For this argument, they perform a case analysis based on the number of bits that the tampering function *does not* directly copy from the codeword (a.k.a., the *not-copied-bits*). The tampering function, by definition, directly *copies* the remaining bits from the codeword into the tampered codeword.

If the number of not-copied-bits in the tampering function is small, then the simulation proceeds as follows. Since the tampering function has a small number of not-copied-bits, most bits in $\widetilde{c}$ are identical to their corresponding bits in c. These copied bits define a unique codeword (using the high distance property of ECSS[5]). Decoding succeeds if every not-copied-bit of $\widetilde{c}$ matches the corresponding bit in c. Moreover, decoding fails if any not-copied bit of $\widetilde{c}$ does not match the corresponding input bit in c. Since, the number of the not-copied-bits is small and they have output locality 1, we can simulate this check independent of the original message m by leveraging the (sufficiently large) independence of the ECSS.

On the other hand, if the number of not-copied-bits is large, then they argue that the tampered codeword is invalid (w.h.p.). The following intuition underlies their argument. Due to the input-locality 1 of the tampering functions, the error c_{err} can influence only a few bits in $\widetilde{c}$. Consequently, there still remains a large number of bits in $\widetilde{c}$ that are not-copied-bits and are not influenced by c_{err}. Therefore, the subset of these bits that is sampled in E is also large (over the random choice of E). Among these indices, leveraging the high independence of the ECSS and input locality 1 of the tampering function, there is a large subset where each indexed bit in the tampered codeword independently disagrees with the tabulated (E, e) with probability (at least)[6] $1/2$. So, with high probability, the tampered codeword fails the consistence check.

(3.b.) Consider the case where the tampering function replaces the error with an unrelated (E^*, e^*). In this case, they argue that the only way to get valid tampered codeword is by replacing c by an unrelated c^* that is consistent with (E^*, e^*). For this argument, they perform a case analysis based on the number of output-bits of the tampering function that are non-constant (a.k.a., the *non-constant-bits*). If the number of non-constant-bits is small, then the tampered message is simulatable independent of the message due to the high independence of the ECSS and output locality 1 of tampering function. On the other hand, if the number of non-constant-bits is large, then the decoding fails with high probability. In this case, each bit in $\widetilde{c}$ that is influenced by a bit in c risks creating an independent inconsistency with (E^*, e^*) with probability $1/2$. Hence, if there is a large number of these bits where each of them is inconsistent

---

[5] An ECSS with distance d ensures that, for two different secrets, at least d secret shares are different.

[6] If the tampering function flips the input bit then the probability of disagreement is 1; otherwise, the probability of disagreement is $1/2$.

with (E^*, e^*) independently with probability $1/2$, then the overall codeword will be invalid with high probability. Similar to case 3.a., this argument relies on leveraging the high independence of the ECSS, input locality 1 of the tampering function, and the fact that E is randomly chosen.

To summarize, two key properties are crucial to our arguments.

(A) Being non-committal to the errors. We rely on randomness of errors to argue inconsistency with tabulated errors in c_{err}.
(B) Independence of failure. Our objective is to identify output bits that cause decoding failure independently.

Consequently, we have the following objective.

> "Find a *large subset* of bits in $\widetilde{c}$ that *independently* fail the consistency check" while, simultaneously, "remaining *noncommittal* to (most of) the error (E, e)"

In the sequel, we elaborate the unique challenges to achieve this objective against δ-local functions, with $\delta > 1$, and no a priori bound on the input-locality.

Intuition underlying Our Construction. For a tampering function with output locality δ (referred to as a δ-local function), intuitively, every bit in the tampered codeword is influenced by some bits in c and some bits in c_{err}. The 2-local tampering functions suffice to capture these two influences and we use these to illustrate some primary challenges and key components of our construction.

Using the output locality of the tampering function, we can argue that tampering on c_{err} would be independent of the message m. Next, we use non-malleablity of encoding c_{err} to simulate whether $\widetilde{c_{\mathrm{err}}}$ encodes (a) the original errrors, (2) an unrelated (E^*, e^*), or (3) $\bot$. Let us consider the case when the tampering function preserves the original errors. In this case, we perform a case analysis on the number of *not-copied-bits*. So the first (somewhat minor) hurdle is how to define not-copied-bits for δ-local functions. Since a bit in $\widetilde{c}$ can be influenced by δ bits, it is a not-copied-bit if it is not a copy for (at least) 1 out of the 2^δ possible inputs. Hence, in the final argument, this bit shall fail the consistency check with probability $1/2^\delta$. Thus, as δ increases, we need to find *exponentially more* bits that *independently* fail to be consistent.

The second hurdle is that, unlike Agrawal et al. [5], our tampering functions are *not* input-local. So, for instance, one bit in the (c, c_{err}) can influence every bit of the tampered codeword. Therefore, even though there might be many not-copied-bits, their probability of being inconsistent is possibly correlated. To resolve this challenge, Viola [35] proposed a technique to fix the values of the *highly influential* input bits (sampled from an appropriate distribution) of the tampering function. This technique, intuitively, transforms an output local tampering function into a convex combination of tampering function that are both input and output local. We use this technique to fix the highly influential bits in c to be uniform random bits (relying on output locality of tampering function and independence of ECSS). However, as we discuss below, many challenges remain related to the bits in c_{err} that are highly influential for $\widetilde{c}$.

Consider the following representative 2-local tampering function. Each bit is $\tilde{c}$ is influenced by corresponding bit in c and a bit in c_{err} while ensuring that all bits in c_{err} have an identical number of output neighbors.

(1) If the threshold to identify "highly influential" input bits is set too low, then the procedure mentioned above might fix the entire c_{err}, because the size of c_{err} is very small. Consequently, the error (E, e) gets fixed. Thereafter, it is unclear how to proceed and catch any non-trivial tampering of c. So, the threshold to identify "highly influential" *cannot* be too low. Therefore, in this case, it is possible that no bit in c_{err} is fixed and c_{err} cumulatively influences a lot of bits in $\tilde{c}$.

(2) Ideally, we would like that the bits we pick from $\tilde{c}$ to argue failure do not depend on c_{err}. However, in this case, all the bits in $\tilde{c}$ depend on c_{err}.

(3) Furthermore, there is another subtle issue. Conditioning on the fact that the tampered $\widetilde{c_{\text{err}}}$ encodes the same error or a fixed (E^*, e^*) distorts the distribution of c_{err}, which, in turn, influences the distribution of the tampered $\tilde{c}$. To summarize, the distributions $\tilde{c}$ and (E, e) are correlated when conditioned on whether the $\widetilde{c_{\text{err}}}$ encodes the same c_{err} or a fixed c_{err}.

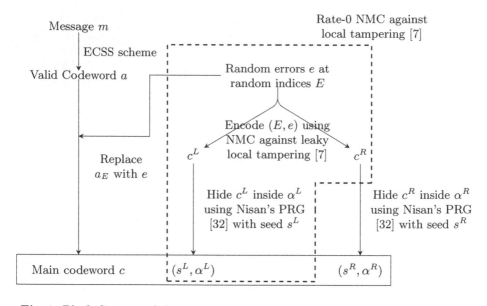

Fig. 1. Block diagram of the compiler to construct NMC against local tampering.

To resolve these concerns simultaneously, the high level idea is to hide the informative bits about (E, e), i.e., c_{err}, in a polynomially larger string, say α (refer to Fig. 1 for a block diagram of our compiler). We use a PRG with a super-polynomial stretch to determine the positions with informative bits inside α and store the PRG seed s along with α as the new payload. So our final codeword is (c, s, α).[7] We argue that for any tampering function, the number of bits from c_{err} that are highly influential for $\tilde{c}$ is small. To simulate these bits, we perform a small leakage on c_{err}. Since our base NMC from [8] is resilient to small leakage, we stay non-committal to (E, e) even conditioned on this leakage. Note that the rest of the bits in c_{err} have a bounded input locality onto $\tilde{c}$ and hence, c_{err} influences only a small subset of bits in $\tilde{c}$.

Now, if we had a large number of not-copied-bits in $\tilde{c}$, we have a large number of not-copied-bits in $\tilde{c}$ that are not influenced by c_{err}. But these bits might share input neighbors in c and have correlated probability of failing consistency checks. Recall that we have already fixed the highly influential bits in c. Finally, we can use the bounded input and output locality to identify independent bits in $\tilde{c}$ (using the greedy neighbor-of-neighbor argument of Viola [35]).

This section presents only the intuitive rationale underlying the cryptographic primitives needed for our construction. There are further subtleties involved in the security arguments. Section 5.1 presents the full proof of our compiler using a hybrid argument.

Remark: Limit of Our Approach. We present a simple rationale for why our construction works for δ-local functions, where $\delta = \xi \lg n$ and $\xi < 1$ is a positive constant. Note that in steps 3.a. and 3.b., the probability of inconsistency with the tabulated error was at least $1/2$ in a 1-local tampering function. However, the probability of inconsistency in a δ-local tampering function can be as low as $2^{-\delta}$. The probability of u independent consistency checks to simultaneously pass is $(1 - 2^{-\delta})^u$. We need $u = \omega(2^{\delta} \log n)$ for this quantity to be negligible. On the other hand, we have $u \leqslant n$. Consequently, we must have $2^{\delta} \ll n / \log n$, or, in particular, $\delta \ll \lg n$.

2   Preliminaries

We use $[n]$ to denote the set $\{1, 2, \ldots, n\}$. For $x = (x_1, x_2, \ldots, x_n)$ and $S \subseteq [n]$, we use x_S to denote $(x_{s_1}, x_{s_2}, \ldots, x_{s_k})$, where $S = \{s_1, s_2, \ldots, s_k\}$ and $s_1 < s_2 < \cdots < s_k$. For brevity, we write x_{-i} for $x_{[n] \setminus \{i\}}$. We use U_S to represent the uniform distribution over the set S. If $\mathcal{D}$ is a distribution, we write $x \sim \mathcal{D}$ to denote that x is sampled according to distribution $\mathcal{D}$. The support of a distribution $\mathcal{D}$, represented by $\mathsf{Supp}(\mathcal{D})$, is the set $\{x \colon \Pr[\mathcal{D} = x] > 0\}$. For any binary strings $x, y \in \{0, 1\}^n$, we use $\mathsf{HD}(x, y)$ to denote their Hamming distance defined by $\mathsf{HD}(x, y) := |\{i \colon x_i \neq y_i \text{ and } 1 \leqslant i \leqslant n\}|$.

2.1   Local Functions

Let $f \colon \{0, 1\}^n \to \{0, 1\}^n$ be a deterministic function. We write f as $(f_1, f_2, \ldots, f_n)$ such that $f(x) = (f_1(x), f_2(x), \ldots, f_n(x))$, where each

---

[7] Similar to [6], hash function families with sufficiently high independence also suffice in this context.

$f_i \colon \{0,1\}^n \to \{0,1\}$ and $1 \leqslant i \leqslant n$. We say that the *i-th bit (of the input) has influence on the j-th bit (of the output)* if there exists an x^*_{-i} such that

$$f_j(x^*_1, \ldots, x^*_{i-1}, 0, x^*_{i+1}, \ldots, x^*_n) \neq f_j(x^*_1, \ldots, x^*_{i-1}, 1, x^*_{i+1}, \ldots, x^*_n)$$

For every output position $1 \leqslant j \leqslant n$, we define the input neighbors $\mathrm{Inp}_f(j)$ to be $\{i | 1 \leqslant i \leqslant n, i \text{ has influence on } j\}$. Similarly, for an input position $1 \leqslant i \leqslant n$, we define its output neighbors $\mathrm{Out}_f(i)$ to be $\{j | 1 \leqslant j \leqslant n, i \text{ has influence on } j\}$. We extend this notion naturally to a set of indices. We write $\mathrm{Inp}_f(S) = \cup_{s \in S} \mathrm{Inp}_f(s)$ and $\mathrm{Out}_f(S) = \cup_{s \in S} \mathrm{Out}_f(s)$.

A function f has *input locality* δ, if, for all $1 \leqslant i \leqslant n$, we have $|\mathrm{Out}_f(i)| \leqslant \delta$. Similarly, a function f has *output locality* δ, if for all $1 \leqslant j \leqslant n$, we have $|\mathrm{Inp}_f(j)| \leqslant \delta$.

Definition 1 (Local Functions). *A function $f : \{0,1\}^n \longrightarrow \{0,1\}^n$ is called a δ-local function if it has output locality δ.*

We use Local^δ to represent the set of all such functions because n shall be implicit from our context.

Recall that NC^0 is the set of all functions f such that for all i, f_i can be computed by a circuit of fan-in 2 and constant depth. Trivially, $\mathsf{NC}^0 \subseteq \mathsf{Local}^{O(1)}$.

We follow the convention in the literature and define the restriction of boolean functions as follows.

Definition 2 (Restriction). *Let $g : \{0,1\}^n \to \{0,1\}$ be a boolean function and $(I, \bar{I})$ be a partition of $[n]$. Let $x \in \{0,1\}^I$. Then, we write $g_{I|x} \colon \{0,1\}^n \to \{0,1\}$ for function g with input of indices in I being restricted to x. For function $f : \{0,1\}^n \to \{0,1\}^n$ such that $f = (f_1, f_2, \ldots, f_n)$ we write $f_{I|x}$ to denote $((f_1)_{I|x}, (f_2)_{I|x}, \ldots, (f_n)_{I|x})$. We say that $i \in \bar{I}$ has influence on j if there exists a x^*_{-i} such that $x^*_I = x$ and*

$$(f_{I|x})_j(x^*_1, \ldots, x^*_{i-1}, 0, x^*_{i+1}, \ldots, x^*_n) \neq (f_{I|x})_j(x^*_1, \ldots, x^*_{i-1}, 1, x^*_{i+1}, \ldots, x^*_n)$$

Note that for all $j \in [n]$, $\mathrm{Inp}_{f_{I|x}}(j) = \{i | 1 \leqslant i \leqslant n, i \text{ has influence on } j\} \subseteq \bar{I}$.

2.2 Non-malleable Codes

We define non-malleable codes below similar to previous works.

Definition 3 (Coding Schemes). *Let* $\mathrm{Enc} \colon \{0,1\}^\ell \to \{0,1\}^n$ *and* $\mathrm{Dec} \colon \{0,1\}^n \to \{0,1\}^\ell \cup \{\bot\}$ *be randomized functions (that is, they has access to private randomness). The pair $(\mathrm{Enc}, \mathrm{Dec})$ defines an encoding scheme with block length n and message length ℓ if it satisfies perfect (resp., statistical) correctness. That is, for all $m \in \{0,1\}^\ell$, over the randomness of Enc and Dec, $\Pr[\mathrm{Dec}(\mathrm{Enc}(m)) = m] = 1$ (resp., $\Pr[\mathrm{Dec}(\mathrm{Enc}(m)) = m] = 1 - \mathsf{negl}(\ell)$). The rate R of this encoding scheme is defined as $R = \ell/n$.*

Let $\mathcal{F}_n$ denote the set of all functions $f \colon \{0,1\}^n \to \{0,1\}^n$. Non-malleable codes are defined w.r.t. a family of tampering functions, say $\mathcal{F} \subseteq \mathcal{F}_n$, as follows.

Definition 4 ((n, ℓ, ε)-Non-malleable Codes). *A coding scheme $(\mathrm{Enc}, \mathrm{Dec})$ with block length n and message length ℓ is said to be non-malleable against tampering family $\mathcal{F} \subseteq \mathcal{F}_n$ with (simulation) error ε, if for all functions $f \in \mathcal{F}$, there exists a distribution $\mathrm{Sim}(f)$ over $\{0,1\}^\ell \cup \{\bot\} \cup \{\text{same}^*\}$ such that for all messages $m \in \{0,1\}^\ell$,*

$$\mathrm{Tamper}_f^m \approx_\varepsilon \mathrm{copy}\,(\mathrm{Sim}(f), m)$$

where Tamper_f^m stands for the following distribution of the tampered message

$$\mathrm{Tamper}_f^m := \left\{ \begin{array}{c} c \sim \mathrm{Enc}(m),\ \widetilde{c} = f(c),\ \widetilde{m} = \mathrm{Dec}(\widetilde{c}) \\ \textit{Output: } \widetilde{m}. \end{array} \right\}$$

and

$$\mathrm{copy}(x, y) = \begin{cases} y, & \textit{if } x = \text{same}^*; \\ x, & \textit{otherwise.} \end{cases}$$

2.3   Hypergeometric Distribution

Consider a universe of size N with K success samples. An (N, K, n)-hypergeometric distribution is the probability distribution of number of success samples picked when n random samples are picked from the universe without replacement. Specifically, we define the distribution as follows.

Definition 5. *A distribution $\mathcal{D}$ over the sample space $[n]$ is an (N, K, n)-hypergeometric distribution if, for any $k \in [n]$, we have*

$$\mathrm{Pr}[\mathcal{D} = k] = \binom{K}{k}\binom{N-K}{n-k}\binom{N}{n}^{-1}$$

Using standard coupling arguments, it is known that the hypergeometric distribution is more concentrated than the corresponding Bernoulli distribution. Consequently, we have the following tail bound.

Lemma 1. *([15, 25]) Let X be a random variable sampled from a (N, K, n)-hypergeometric distribution. Then for any $\varepsilon \in (0, \frac{K}{N})$,*

$$\mathrm{Pr}\left[X \leqslant (K/N - \varepsilon) \cdot n\right] \leqslant \exp\left(-2\varepsilon^2 n\right)$$

The following corollary suffices for our proof.

Corollary 1. *Let $A \subseteq [n]$ be an arbitrary subset of size a. Let $B \subseteq [n]$ be a random subset of size b. Then*

$$\mathrm{Pr}\left[|A \cap B| \leqslant ab/2n\right] \leqslant \exp\left(-a^2 b/2n^2\right)$$

Note that $|A \cap B|$ is an (n, a, b)-hypergeometric distribution. The corollary follows from the previous lemma with $\varepsilon = a/2n$.

3 Building Blocks

In this section we describe the building blocks of our compiler.

3.1 Non-malleable Codes Against Leaky Input and Output Local Tampering

Our construction relies on an encoding scheme that satisfies non-malleability against leaky input and output local tampering that we define below.

Definition 6. *Let* $(\mathrm{Enc}, \mathrm{Dec})$ *be a coding scheme such that* $\mathrm{Enc} : \{0,1\}^k \to \{0,1\}^{n_L} \times \{0,1\}^{n_R}$ *and* $\mathrm{Dec} : \{0,1\}^{n_L} \times \{0,1\}^{n_R} \to \{0,1\}^k$. *We call* $(\mathrm{Enc}, \mathrm{Dec})$ *a* $(\lambda, \mu, \ell_i, \ell_o)$-*non-malleable code against leaky input and output local tampering with simulation error* ε *if it satisfies the following conditions.*

Let $\mathcal{L}^L \subseteq [n_L]$ *and* $\mathcal{L}^R \subseteq [n_R]$ *be arbitrary subsets of size at most* λn_L *and* λn_R, *respectively. Consider any function* F *with domain* $\{0,1\}^{|\mathcal{L}^L|} \times \{0,1\}^{|\mathcal{L}^R|}$ *that outputs a tampering function* $g : \{0,1\}^{n_L} \times \{0,1\}^{n_R} \to \{0,1\}^{n_L} \times \{0,1\}^{n_R}$ *such that for any* $x \in \{0,1\}^{|\mathcal{L}^L|}$, $y \in \{0,1\}^{|\mathcal{L}^R|}$, *and* $g = F(x,y)$

1. *The output locality of the tampering function* g *is at most* ℓ_o, *and*
2. *All but (at most)* μn_L *input-bits of the first* n_L *input-bits of* g *have input locality (at most)* ℓ_i.

Then, there exists a distribution $\mathrm{Sim}(\mathcal{L}^L, \mathcal{L}^R, F)$ *over* $\left(\{0,1\}^k \cup \{\bot, \mathrm{same}^*\}\right) \times \{0,1\}^{|\mathcal{L}^L|} \times \{0,1\}^{|\mathcal{L}^R|}$ *such that for any message* $m \in \{0,1\}^k$,

$$\mathrm{Tamper}^m_{\mathcal{L}^L, \mathcal{L}^R, F} \approx_\varepsilon \mathrm{copy}(\mathrm{Sim}(\mathcal{L}^L, \mathcal{L}^R, F), m), \quad \text{where}$$

$$\mathrm{Tamper}^m_{\mathcal{L}^L, \mathcal{L}^R, F} := \left\{ \begin{array}{c} (c^L, c^R) \sim \mathrm{Enc}(m), x := c^L_{\mathcal{L}^L}, y := c^R_{\mathcal{L}^R} \\ g := F(x, y) \\ (\widetilde{c^L}, \widetilde{c^R}) = g(c^L, c^R), \widetilde{m} = \mathrm{Dec}(\widetilde{c^L}, \widetilde{c^R}) \\ \mathrm{Output}\ (\widetilde{m}, x, y) \end{array} \right\}$$

Intuitively, leaky input and output local tampering allows the adversary to first pick a subset of indices and peek into the codeword at those places, then use this leakage as an advice to select a output-local, (almost) input-local tampering function. Then, non-malleability against leaky input and output local tampering guarantees that the tampered message and the leakage are simulatable independent of the original message only given the position of leaked indices and the map F from leakage to the tampering function. Ball et al. [7] construct this non-malleable code as an intermediate step toward their final rate-0 non-malleable codes against local tampering. As a corollary of their results, we have the following lemma, which suffices for our construction.

Lemma 2 ([7]). *There exist constants* λ, μ *such that, for any* $\ell_i, \ell_o = O(\log k)$, *there exists an explicit and efficient* $(\lambda, \mu, \ell_i, \ell_o)$*-non-malleable code against leaky input and output local tampering with simulation error* $\varepsilon = \mathsf{negl}(k)$ *and rate* $1/k^{o(1)}$, *where* k *is the length of the message.*

Remark 1. Note that [7] reduces the problem of constructing non-malleable codes against leaky input and output local tampering to the problem of constructing non-malleable codes against 2-split-state tampering family. The rate of their final construction will be the product of the rate of the reduction, which is inverse of the locality (i.e., $1/\max(\ell_i, \ell_o)$) and the rate of the given 2-split-state non-malleable code. Instantiated with the state-of-the-art 2-split-state construction by Li [29,30], which has rate $\Omega(\log \log \log k/\log \log k)$, the final rate of [7]'s construction can be as high as $1/\operatorname{polylog}(k)$, which is $1/k^{o(1)}$ and satisfies this lemma.

3.2 Error-Correcting Secret-Sharing Schemes

Definition 7. *An encoding scheme* $(\mathsf{Enc}, \mathsf{Dec})$ *with block length* n *and message length* ℓ *is said to be an* (n, ℓ, d, t)*-error-correcting secret sharing scheme (ECSS scheme) if it satisfies the following conditions.*

1. **Distance** d. *For any two codewords* c, c', $\mathsf{HD}(c, c') > d$.
2. **Independence** t. *For any message* $m \in \{0, 1\}^\ell$ *and a subset* $S \subseteq [n]$ *such that* $|S| \leqslant t$, *the distribution of* $\mathsf{Enc}(m)_S$ *is identical to the uniform distribution* $U_{\{0,1\}^{|S|}}$.
3. **Error Correction** $d/2$. *There exists an error-correcting function* ECorr *such that for any* $c \in \{0, 1\}^n$, $\mathsf{ECorr}(c)$ *outputs a codeword* c^* *such that* $\mathsf{HD}(c, c^*) \leqslant d/2$. *If no such codeword exists, then it outputs* $\perp$.

Lemma 3. *For every* $\zeta \in (0, 1)$, *there exists an explicit* (n, ℓ, d, t)*-ECSS scheme with* $n = (1 + o(1))\ell$ *and* $d, t \geqslant n^{1-\zeta}$.

Standard Reed-Solomon codes over characteristic 2 fields achieve the properties required by Lemma 3. We defer such a construction to the full version.

3.3 Pseudorandom Generator for Finite State Machines

Definition 8 (Finite State Machine). *A finite state machine (FSM) Q with space w over the alphabet Σ satisfies the following properties.*

1. *There exists a state-transition function* $q: \{0, 1\}^w \times \Sigma \to \{0, 1\}^w$ *that takes as input the current state* $s \in \{0, 1\}^w$ *and an alphabet* $x \in \Sigma$, *and outputs the new state* $q(s, x)$.
2. *There exists a subset* $S \subseteq \{0, 1\}^w$ *such that if the final state* $s \in S$ *then the FSM accepts the input and outputs 1. Otherwise, it outputs 0.*

Definition 9. *A function* $G \colon \{0,1\}^p \to \Sigma^u$ *is a* pseudorandom generator for FSMs *with space* w *and alphabet* Σ *with error* ε *if for any distinguisher FSM* Q *with space* w *and alphabet* Σ *we have*

$$\left| \Pr\left[Q\left(U_{\Sigma^u} \right) = 1 \right] - \Pr\left[Q\left(G(U_{\{0,1\}^p}) \right) \right) = 1 \right] \right| \leqslant \varepsilon$$

Lemma 4 ([32]). *There exists a constant* $\kappa > 0$ *such that for all integers* $d > 0$ *and* $u \leqslant \kappa d$, *there is an explicit pseudorandom generator* $G \colon \Sigma^{3u} \to \Sigma^{2^u}$ *for FSMs with alphabet* $\Sigma = \{0,1\}^d$ *and space* κd *with error* $2^{-\kappa d}$.

4 Our Compiler

In this section, we will present our compiler. That is, for all constants $\xi < 1$, given a rate-1 ECSS scheme, a rate $1/\eta^{o(1)}$ non-malleable code against leaky input and output local tampering (for η length messages) and a PRG secure against finite state machines with appropriate parameters, we construct a rate-1 non-malleable coding scheme against all δ-local tampering family Local^δ for $\delta = \xi \cdot \lg n$. Here n is the length of the codeword. We begin by giving some notation, specifying the building blocks used followed by our construction overview.

Notation: Throughout our construction and proof, we use the notation that after the tampering is done, any variable of original codeword, for example, a, will have a tilde on it, i.e., $\widetilde{a}$. For example, c is the original main codeword and $\widetilde{c}$ would be the tampered version of the main codeword. Thus, when we talk about bits from c, it refers to the input-bits of the tampering function and on the other hand, bits from $\widetilde{c}$ are output-bits of the tampering function.

Building blocks used. We use the following three building blocks. Let $\delta = \xi \cdot \lg n$ for $\xi < 1$ be the locality of the tampering function.

1. An (n, ℓ, d, t)-ECSS scheme with $d, t \geqslant n^{1-\varsigma}$ and $n = (1 + o(1))\ell$ for an appropriate constant ς to be fixed later. This is provided by Lemma 3.
2. For any constant λ, μ and $\eta = n^{\Theta(1)}$, a $(\lambda, \mu, \ell_i, \ell_o)$-NMC against leaky input and output local tampering for messages in $\{0,1\}^\eta$, rate $1/\eta^{o(1)}$, $\ell_o = \delta = O(\log \eta)$, $\ell_i = 4\delta/\mu = O(\log \eta)$, simulation error negligible in η. This is provided by Lemma 2. We denote the corresponding simulator by Sim_0.
3. A PRG $G : (\{0,1\}^{\log^2 n})^{3\Lambda \log n} \longrightarrow (\{0,1\}^{\log^2 n})^{n^\Lambda}$ that is secure against all FSMs with alphabet $\Sigma = \{0,1\}^{\log^2 n}$ and space $\kappa \log^2 n$ with error $2^{-\kappa \log^2 n}$ for an appropriate constant Λ to be fixed later. Here, κ is a constant provided by Lemma 4 for $u = \Lambda \log n$ and $d = \log^2 n$.

Building blocks:
- $\circ$ (ECSS. Enc, ECSS. Dec) is an (n, ℓ, d, t) ECSS scheme.
- $\circ$ $(\mathrm{NMEnc}_0, \mathrm{NMDec}_0)$ is a $(\lambda, \mu, \ell_i, \ell_o)$-non-malleable code against leaky input and output local tampering.
- $\circ$ $G : (\{0,1\}^{\log^2 n})^{3\Lambda \log n} \longrightarrow (\{0,1\}^{\log^2 n})^{n^\Lambda}$ is a PRG that fools all FSMs with space $\kappa \log^2 n$. We set Λ below.

$\mathrm{NMEnc}_1(m)$:

1. Sample a random $E \subseteq [n]$ of size $n^{1-\varepsilon_1}$, where ε_1 is a small constant.
2. For all $i \in E$, sample $e_i \sim U_{\{0,1\}}$.
3. Sample $a \sim \mathrm{ECSS.\,Enc}(m)$.
4. Define c as $c_i = \begin{cases} a_i, & i \notin E \\ e_i, & i \in E \end{cases}$
5. Let $(c^L, c^R) \sim \mathrm{NMEnc}_0(E, e)$
6. Pick seeds $s^L, s^R \xleftarrow{\$} \{0,1\}^{3\Lambda \cdot \log^3 n}$.
7. Let $\mathrm{Embed}^L, \mathrm{Embed}^R$ be as below.
   - $\circ$ $\alpha^L = \mathrm{Embed}^L(s^L, c^L)$
   - $\circ$ $\alpha^R = \mathrm{Embed}^R(s^R, c^R)$
8. Output $(c, s^L, \alpha^L, s^R, \alpha^R)$

$\mathrm{NMDec}_1(\widetilde{c}, \widetilde{s^L}, \widetilde{\alpha^L}, \widetilde{s^R}, \widetilde{\alpha^R})$:

1. Let $\mathrm{Recover}^L, \mathrm{Recover}^R$ be as below.
   - $\circ$ $\widetilde{c^L} = \mathrm{Recover}^L(\widetilde{s^L}, \widetilde{\alpha^L})$
   - $\circ$ $\widetilde{c^R} = \mathrm{Recover}^R(\widetilde{s^R}, \widetilde{\alpha^R})$
2. If $\mathrm{NMDec}_0(\widetilde{c^L}, \widetilde{c^R}) = \bot$, output $\bot$
3. (Else) $(\widetilde{E}, \widetilde{e}) = \mathrm{NMDec}_0(\widetilde{c^L}, \widetilde{c^R})$
4. If $\mathrm{ECSS.\,ECorr}(\widetilde{c}) = \bot$, output $\bot$
5. (Else) $\widetilde{a} = \mathrm{ECSS.\,ECorr}(\widetilde{c})$
6. Define c' as $c'_i = \begin{cases} \widetilde{a}_i, & i \notin \widetilde{E} \\ \widetilde{e}_i, & i \in \widetilde{E} \end{cases}$
7. if $c' \neq \widetilde{c}$, output $\bot$
8. (Else) $\widetilde{m} = \mathrm{ECSS.\,Dec}(\widetilde{a})$
9. Output $\widetilde{m}$

Let lengths of c^L and c^R be n^{β_1} and n^{β_2}, respectively. First, pick[a] a constant γ s.t. $\max(\beta_1, \beta_2) < \gamma < 1$. Next, let $\tau > 0$ be a constant s.t. $\Lambda = \gamma + 2\tau < 1$.

$\mathrm{Embed}^L, \mathrm{Recover}^L$: Let $\rho^L : \{0,1\}^{\log^2 n} \longrightarrow \{0,1\}$ be any function with bias[b] $2n^{-(\Lambda - \beta_1)}$. First, compute $G(s^L) = (y_1, y_2, \ldots, y_{n^\Lambda})$ s.t. each $y_i \in \{0,1\}^{\log^2 n}$ and $\mathrm{Adv}^L = (\rho^L(y_1), \rho^L(y_2), \ldots, \rho^L(y_{n^\Lambda}))$. Then, $\alpha^L = \mathrm{Embed}^L(s^L, c^L)$ is defined as:

$$\alpha^L_i := \begin{cases} c^L_j & \text{If } \mathrm{Adv}^L_i \text{ is the } j^{th} \text{ 1 in } \mathrm{Adv}^L \\ 0 & \text{Otherwise.} \end{cases}$$

To recover during decoding, compute $G(\widetilde{s^L}) = (\widetilde{y_1}, \widetilde{y_2}, \ldots, \widetilde{y_{n^\Lambda}})$ and $\widetilde{\mathrm{Adv}}^L = (\rho^L(\widetilde{y_1}), \ldots, \rho^L(\widetilde{y_{n^\Lambda}}))$. Then, if $\widetilde{\mathrm{Adv}}^L$ does not contain $\geqslant n^{\beta_1}$ many 1's, quit decoding by outputing $\bot$. Otherwise, $\widetilde{c^L} = \mathrm{Recover}^L(\widetilde{s^L}, \widetilde{\alpha^L})$ is defined as:

$$\widetilde{c^L_j} := \widetilde{\alpha^L_i} \quad \text{where } \widetilde{\mathrm{Adv}}^L_i \text{ is the } j^{th} \text{ 1 in } \widetilde{\mathrm{Adv}}^L$$

$\mathrm{Embed}^R, \mathrm{Recover}^R$: Let $\rho^R : \{0,1\}^{\log^2 n} \longrightarrow \{0,1\}$ be any function with bias $2n^{-(\Lambda - \beta_2)}$. Now $\mathrm{Embed}^R, \mathrm{Recover}^R$ are defined analogously to above using ρ^R.

---

[a] This is possible because (E, e) has length $\eta = n^{1-\varepsilon_1}(\log n + 1)$ and $(\mathrm{NMEnc}_0, \mathrm{NMDec}_0)$ is a $1/\eta^{o(1)}$ rate coding scheme.

[b] Bias of a function is the probability that output is 1 for a uniformly sampled input.

Fig. 2. Our rate-1 non-malleable codes against δ-local functions

Construction Overview. Our construction starts with encoding the message $m \in \{0,1\}^{\ell}$ using ECSS scheme $a \sim \text{ECSS.Enc}(m)$ such that $a \in \{0,1\}^{n}$. Next, we sample a random subset $E \subseteq [n]$ of size $n^{1-\varepsilon_1}$ for a small constant ε_1 specified later. Next, for each index $i \in E$, we sample a random bit e_i. These will be our planted errors. Then, all bits at E in codeword a are replaced by these random bits e_i to produce c. We refer to this an erroneous codeword c as the main codeword. We note that a bit at index in E has probability $1/2$ of being an error.

Next, for the second part of our codeword, we record the error indices E as well as planted errors $e = (e_1, e_2, \ldots, e_{|E|})$ using (poor-rate) non-malleable codes against leaky input and output local tampering. We sample $(c^L, c^R) \sim \text{NMEnc}_0(E, e)$. Finally, we hide the codeword (c^L, c^R) inside a larger code (α^L, α^R) at pseudorandom locations as follows: We will sample two seeds s^L, s^R of appropriate length (See Fig. 2). And invoke our pseudorandom generator G on s^L (resp., s^R) and use appropriate bias function ρ^L (resp., ρ^R) to generate advice string Adv^L (resp., Adv^R). At a high level, positions having a 1 in the advice string will store an actual bit of the code, and positions with 0 will store a redundant 0. Intuitively, this step ensures that when bits from α^L or α^R are used for tampering, most of these bits would be redundant 0's. Our final codeword is $(c, s^L, \alpha^L, s^R, \alpha^R)$.

Conversely, to decode, we use seeds $\widetilde{s^L}, \widetilde{s^R}$ to determine the indices of $\widetilde{c^L}, \widetilde{c^R}$ in $\widetilde{\alpha^L}, \widetilde{\alpha^R}$. Then, we decode $(\widetilde{c^L}, \widetilde{c^R})$ to get the error index set $\widetilde{E}$ and error bits $\widetilde{e}$. Next, we compare $\widetilde{c}$ with planted errors $(\widetilde{E}, \widetilde{e})$ to check (1) whether all the bits from $\widetilde{c}$ with index in $\widetilde{E}$ and $\widetilde{e}$ are equal; (2) we error correct $\widetilde{c}$ to obtain correct codeword $\widetilde{a}$ and check whether all the errors in $\widetilde{c}$ were recorded in $\widetilde{E}$. If both conditions are satisfied, we will consider the codeword valid and output the decoding of $\widetilde{a}$ as the decoded message.

Setting the parameters. Next, we will set the various constants used in our construction (as well as proof of non-malleability).

○ λ, μ: We pick constants λ, μ arbitrarily.
○ Λ, γ, τ: Let $|c^L| = n^{\beta_1}$ and $|c^R| = n^{\beta_2}$. Since $\eta = |(E, e)| = n^{1-\varepsilon_1}(\log n)$ and rate of NMEnc_0 is $1/\eta^{o(1)}$, we have that $\max(\beta_1, \beta_2) < 1$. We pick positive constants γ, τ such that $\max(\beta_1, \beta_2) < \gamma < 1$ and $\gamma + 2\tau < 1$. Set $\Lambda = \gamma + 2\tau$.
○ $\varepsilon_1, \varepsilon_2$: The number of erroneous indices $|E| = n^{1-\varepsilon_1}$. In our security hybrids, we have another small constant ε_2 and we require $\varepsilon_1 + 2\varepsilon_2 < 1 - \xi$, where ξ is defined by the tampering family. Hence, given ξ, we pick two positive constants satisfying the condition.
○ ζ: In our construction, we use an (n, ℓ, d, t)-ECSS scheme with $d, t \geqslant n^{1-\zeta}$. In our security proof, we require $\zeta < \min(\varepsilon_1, \varepsilon_2, \tau, 1 - \Lambda)$ and hence, ζ can be picked as a sufficiently small positive constant satisfying the constraint.

Theorem 1. *Let $\{0,1\}^{\ell}$ be the message space and $\delta = \xi \cdot \lg n$, for some constant $\xi < 1$. There exists an explicit and efficient rate-1 NMC against Local$^{\delta}$ with simulation error that is negligible in n and uses the following primitives in a black-box manner.*

1. For appropriate $\zeta > 0$, an (n, ℓ, d, t)-ECSS scheme with $d, t \geqslant n^{1-\zeta}$ and $n = (1 + o(1))\ell$.
2. For some constant λ, μ and $\eta = n^{\Theta(1)}$, a $(\lambda, \mu, \ell_i, \ell_o)$-NMC against leaky input and output local tampering for messages in $\{0, 1\}^\eta$, rate $1/\eta^{o(1)}$, $\ell_o = O(\log \eta)$, $\ell_i = O(\log \eta)$, simulation error negligible in η.
3. For some constant $\Lambda > 0$, a PRG $G : (\{0, 1\}^{\log^2 n})^{3\Lambda \log n} \longrightarrow (\{0, 1\}^{\log^2 n})^{n^\Lambda}$ that is secure against FSM with alphabet size $\log^2 n$ and space $\Theta(\log^2 n)$ with error that is negligible in n.

The above theorem when instantiated with Lemmas 3, 2 and 4 gives following theorem.

Theorem 2. *For all constants $\xi < 1$, there exists an explicit rate-1 non-malleable code against* $Local^{\xi \cdot \lg n}$ *with negligible in n simulation error, where n is the length of the codeword.*

In particular, this implies an explicit rate-1 non-malleable code against NC^0 tampering.

4.1 Proof of Theorem 1

Here, we will prove that the our construction has rate-1 and perfect correctness. We provide proof of non-malleability in the next section.

Rate of our construction. Our codeword is $(c, s^L, \alpha^L, s^R, \alpha^R)$. Note that our main codeword c has length $n = \ell + o(\ell)$. Next, $|s^L| = |s^R| = 3\Lambda \log^3 n$. And, $-\alpha^L| = |\alpha^R| = n^\Lambda$. Since, $\Lambda = \gamma + 2\tau < 1$ (see parameter setting above), the overall codeword has length $\ell + o(\ell)$.

Correctness. We first argue that our scheme has statistical correctness, and then show how the scheme in Fig. 2 can be tweaked slightly to give perfect correctness. It is easy to see that the correctness of our scheme in Fig. 2 is broken only when Adv^L does not have enough number of 1's to store all of c^L in α^L or similarly, when Adv^R does not have enough number of 1's to store all of c^R in α^R. If this happens, the decoding algorithm would output $\perp$. Note that whether this event happens or not depends on the choice of seeds s^L and s^R only. We prove the following lemma that states that probability of this event happening is negligible.

Lemma 5. *With probability at least $1 - 2^{-\Omega(\log^2 n)}$ over the random choice of s_L and s_R, α^L and α^R will contain all the bits from c^L and c^R.*

Proof. We will prove the lemma for (s^L, α^L) and same argument holds for (s^R, α^R). We first show that the lemma holds when G is a random function. Next, we argue that if lemma does not hold for a PRG G, then there exists a distinguisher FSM Q with space $\kappa \log^2 n$ that breaks PRG security with non-negligible probability in n.

Firstly, when $G(s^L)$ outputs uniform random string, the expected number of 1's in Adv^L is $n^\Lambda \cdot 2n^{-(\Lambda-\beta_1)} = 2n^{\beta_1}$. Next, using Chernoff bound, with probability at least $1 - \exp(-\Theta(n^{\beta_1}))$, there are at least n^{β_1} many 1's in Adv^L and hence, α^L will contain all the bits from c^L.

Now suppose that the lemma does not hold when we use PRG G that fools FSMs with space $\kappa \log^2 n$. Consider the following FSM Q that takes $(y_1, y_2, \ldots, y_{n^\Lambda})$ as input and a state in Q stores ctr, which denotes number of indices i for which $\rho^{I'}(y_i)$ output 1. The final output of Q is 1 when $\text{ctr} \geqslant n^{\beta_1}$. Clearly, by our argument above, on a true uniform string, Q will output 1 with probability at least $1 - \exp(-\Theta(n^{\beta_1}))$. If this lemma is incorrect for a PRG G, Q will output 1 with probability at most $1 - 2^{-\Omega(\log^2 n)}$ and hence Q will break the underlying PRG with success probability greater than $2^{-\Omega(\log^2 n)}$. Finally, note that Q only needs $\Lambda \log n < \kappa \log^2 n$ space to record Λ. This completes the proof.   □

Getting perfect correctness. We can tweak our scheme slightly to give perfect correctness as follows: If s^L or s^R is bad, i.e., (α^L, α^R) will not contain all bits in (c^L, c^R), then we ignore $\text{Adv}^L, \text{Adv}^R$ and store the codeword in default location. More precisely, we store c^L in first $|c^L|$ locations in α^L and similarly for c^R. It is easy to see that this gives perfect correctness. In the proof of non-malleability, our simulator can simply give up when this case happens. (Since s^L, s^R are uniform seeds independent of the message, it is easy to check for this case.) This would increase the simulation error by the probability of this event occurring. But, above Lemma 5 proves that this happens with negligible probability. Hence, this only increases the simulation error by $\text{negl}(n)$.

5   Proof of Non-malleability of Our Compiler

Non-malleability. Recall that to prove non-malleability of the resulting scheme against δ-local tampering family Local^δ, we need to show that for any $f \in \text{Local}^\delta$, there exists a simulator $\text{Sim}_1(f)$ such that, for all message $m \in \{0,1\}^\ell$, we have the following

$$\left\{ \begin{array}{c} (c, s^L, \alpha^L, s^R, \alpha^R) \sim \text{NMEnc}_1(m) \\ (\widetilde{c}, \widetilde{s^L}, \widetilde{\alpha^L}, \widetilde{s^R}, \widetilde{\alpha^R}) = f(c, s^L, \alpha^L, s^R, \alpha^R) \\ \widetilde{m} = \text{NMDec}_1(\widetilde{c}, \widetilde{s^L}, \widetilde{\alpha^L}, \widetilde{s^R}, \widetilde{\alpha^R}) \\ \text{Output} \widetilde{m} \end{array} \right\} = \text{Tamper}_f^m \approx_\varepsilon \text{copy}(\text{Sim}_1(f), m)$$

Our simulator is formally defined in Fig. 3. In the simulator and the hybrids, $n_e = |(s^L, \alpha^L, s^R, \alpha^R)|$. A detailed proof using a sequence of indistinguishable hybrids is presented in the next section. We shall use the following lemma in our hybrid argument. We defer the proof of this lemma to the full version.

1. Let $P = \{i | i \in [n], |\text{Out}_f(i) \cap [n]| \geq n^{\varepsilon_2}\}$
2. Let $Q = \{i | i \in [n], \text{Out}_f(i) \backslash [n] \neq \emptyset\}$
3. Let $X = P \cup Q$. Sample $a_X \sim U_{\{0,1\}^{|X|}}$
4. Sample a random $E_1 \subseteq X$ s.t. $|E_1| \sim (n, |X|, n^{1-\varepsilon_1})$-hypergeometric distribution.
5. For all $i \in E_1$, sample $e_i \sim U_{\{0,1\}}$.
6. For all $i \in E_1$, replace a_i with e_i, we get c_X.
7. Sample seeds s^L, s^R uniformly from $\{0,1\}^{3\Lambda \log^3 n}$.
8. Given s^L (resp., s^R), indices of c^L (resp., c^R) in α^L (resp., α^R) are determined.
   Let $\text{Bad}^L = \{$Indices of c^L with more than $n^{1-\gamma-\tau}$ output neighbors in $\widetilde{c}\}$,
   $\text{Leak}^L = \{$Indices of c^L with output neighbors in either $\widetilde{s^L}$ or $\widetilde{s^R}\}$,
   $\text{Bad}^R = \{$Indices in c^R with more than $n^{1-\gamma-\tau}$ output neighbors in $\widetilde{c}\}$, and
   $\text{Leak}^R = \{$Indices in c^R with output neighbors in either $\widetilde{s^L}$ or $\widetilde{s^R}\}$
9. Let $\mathcal{L}^L = \text{Bad}^L \cup \text{Leak}^L$ and $\mathcal{L}^R = \text{Bad}^R \cup \text{Leak}^R$.
10. Let f_0 be the following mapping from leakage at $(\mathcal{L}^L, \mathcal{L}^R)$ to tampering function
    g for NMEnc_0: First, use (s^L, s^R), leakage at $(\text{Leak}^L, \text{Leak}^R)$ and c_Q to compute
    $\widetilde{s^L}$ and $\widetilde{s^R}$. These determine indices of $\widetilde{c^L}$ and $\widetilde{c^R}$ in α^L and α^R. Then, define g to
    be the tampering function from indices of (c^L, c^R) to indices of $(\widetilde{c^L}, \widetilde{c^R})$.
11. If $(|\mathcal{L}^L| \geq \lambda n^{\beta_1})$ or $(|\mathcal{L}^R| \geq \lambda n^{\beta_2})$ or (f_0 does not satisfy Definition 6), output $\perp$
12. (Else) $(\text{ans}, x, y) = \text{Sim}_0(\mathcal{L}^L, \mathcal{L}^R, f_0)$.
13. Let S^L, S^R denote indices of s^L, s^R. Define function h as a restriction of f_1:

$$h := (f_1)_{(X, S^L, S^R, \mathcal{L}^L, \mathcal{L}^R) | (c_X, s^L, s^R, x, y)} \qquad \text{(See Definition 2)}$$

14. $V := \{i | i \in [n], \text{Inp}_h(i) \neq \emptyset\}$
15. $W := \{i | i \in [n], \text{Inp}_h(i) \backslash [n] \neq \emptyset\}$
16. $Z := \{i \in [n] | \exists z \in \{0,1\}^{n+n_e}, z_{(X, S^L, S^R, \mathcal{L}^L, \mathcal{L}^R)} = (c_X, s^L, s^R, x, y), h_i(z) \neq z_i\}$
17. Sample $a \sim \text{ECSS.Enc}(0^\ell) | (\text{ECSS.Enc}(0^\ell))_X = a_X$
18. Sample a random $E_2 \subseteq [n] \backslash X$ of size $n^{1-\varepsilon_1} - |E_1|$, let $E = E_1 \cup E_2$
19. For all $i \in E_2$, sample $e_i \sim U_{\{0,1\}}$
20. Define c as $c_i = \begin{cases} a_i, & i \notin E \\ e_i, & i \in E \end{cases}$
21. $(\widetilde{E}, \widetilde{e}) = \text{copy}(\text{Sim}_0(\mathcal{L}^L, \mathcal{L}^R, f_0), (E, e))$
22. $(c^L, c^R) \sim \text{NMEnc}_0(E, e)$ s.t. $\text{NMDec}_0(g(c^L, c^R)) = (\widetilde{E}, \widetilde{e})$ and $c^L_{\mathcal{L}^L} = x, c^R_{\mathcal{L}^R} = y$
23. $\alpha^L = \text{Embed}^L(s^L, c^L)$, $\alpha^R = \text{Embed}^R(s^R, c^R)$
24. $\widetilde{c} = f_1(c, s^L, \alpha^L, s^R, \alpha^R)$
25. If ans =
    - $\perp$: Output $\perp$
    - same*: If $|Z \backslash (W \cup X)| \geq n^{1-\varepsilon_2}$, output $\perp$
      (Else) If $\widetilde{c}_Z = c_Z$, output same*; (Else) Output $\perp$.
    - (E^*, e^*): If $|V \backslash W| \geq n^{1-\varepsilon_2}$, output $\perp$
      (Else) If $\text{ECSS.ECorr}(\widetilde{c}) \perp$, output $\perp$;
      (Else) $\widetilde{a} = \text{ECSS.ECorr}(\widetilde{c})$
      Define c' as $c'_i = \begin{cases} \widetilde{a}_i, & i \notin \widetilde{E} \\ \widetilde{e}_i, & i \in \widetilde{E} \end{cases}$
      If $c' \neq \widetilde{c}$, output $\perp$; (Else) Output $\widetilde{m} = \text{ECSS.Dec}(\widetilde{a})$

Fig. 3. Simulator $\text{Sim}_1(f)$

Lemma 6. *For any δ-local tampering function, with probability at least $1 - 2^{-\Omega(\log^2 n)}$ over the random choice of s_L and s_R, the following conditions hold.*
(1) At most μn^{β_1} bits from c^L will have input locality higher than $4\delta/\mu$ onto $\widetilde{\alpha^R}$;
(2) Number of bits in c^L and c^R that have greater than $n^{1-\gamma-\tau}$ input locality onto $\widetilde{c}$ are bounded by $4\delta n^{\beta_1-\tau}$ and $4\delta n^{\beta_2-\tau}$, respectively.
And as a consequence, we have
(3) Number of bits in $\widetilde{c}$ that are influenced by low input locality bits from c^L and c^R are bounded by $n^{\beta_1} \cdot n^{1-\gamma-\tau} = o(n^{1-\tau})$ and $n^{\beta_2} \cdot n^{1-\gamma-\tau} = o(n^{1-\tau})$, respectively.

5.1 Detailed Hybrid Argument

In this section, we are going to use a series of statistically close hybrids to prove that Tamper_f^m and $\text{copy}\left(\text{Sim}_1(f), m\right)$ are indistinguishable. Throughout this subsection, we use the following color/highlight notation. In a current hybrid, the text in red denotes the changes from the previous hybrid. The text in shaded part represents the steps that will be replaced by red part of the next hybrid. We call c (resp., $\widetilde{c}$) the main codeword and $(s^L, \alpha^L, s^R, \alpha^R)$ (resp., $(\widetilde{s^L}, \widetilde{\alpha^L}, \widetilde{s^R}, \widetilde{\alpha^R})$) the error codeword.

$H_1(f, m)$: Our first hybrid is the real world Tamper_f^m, we simply open up the definition of NMEnc_1 and NMDec_1 and write tampering function f as (f_1, f_2). Both functions are given as input the entire codeword and f_1 is doing the tampering on the main codeword, i.e., outputs $\widetilde{c}$, while f_2 is doing the tampering on the error codeword, i.e., outputs $(\widetilde{s^L}, \widetilde{\alpha^L}, \widetilde{s^R}, \widetilde{\alpha^R})$. This way of writing f would be useful in later hybrids.

$H_2(f, m)$: In the next hybrid H_2, we change the way we sample ECSS codeword of m. We define two subsets of indices P and Q. Intuitively, P is the *popular* input bits of the main codeword, i.e., bits in c that influence more than n^{ε_2} bits of $\widetilde{c}$. And Q is the set of bits in main codeword c that influence the error codeword $(\widetilde{s^L}, \widetilde{\alpha^L}, \widetilde{s^R}, \widetilde{\alpha^R})$. Now, let $X = P \cup Q$. We first sample a uniform string a_X of length $|X|$ and then sample $a \sim \text{ECSS.Enc}(m)$ condition on that $\text{ECSS.Enc}(m)_X = a_X$. We argue that this does not change the distribution of a and hence it is identical to the previous hybrid.

To argue this we use the independence property of our ECSS scheme. In particular, since $t \geqslant n^{1-\varsigma}$, the distribution of a_X is indeed uniform as long as $|X| = o(n^{1-\varsigma})$. Now, $|P|$ can be bound as follows: The total number of input neighbors of $\widetilde{c}$ is δn and at most $\delta n^{1-\varepsilon_2}$ many bits in c can influence more than n^{ε_2} bits from $\widetilde{c}$. Hence $|P| = o(n^{1-\varsigma})$ as long as we pick $\boxed{\varsigma < \varepsilon_2}$. Next, the length of the error codeword is $|s^L| + |\alpha^L| + |s^R| + |\alpha^R| = O(n^\Lambda)$ and hence, by output locality δ, the size of Q is at most $\delta \cdot O(n^\Lambda) = o(n^{1-\varsigma})$ as long as $\boxed{\varsigma < 1 - \Lambda}$.

$H_1(f, m)$:

1. Sample a random $E \subseteq [n]$ of size $n^{1-\varepsilon_1}$
2. For all $i \in E$, sample $e_i \sim U_{\{0,1\}}$
3. Sample $a \sim \mathrm{ECSS.Enc}(m)$
4. Define c as $c_i = \begin{cases} a_i, & i \notin E \\ e_i, & i \in E \end{cases}$
5. Let $(c^L, c^R) \sim \mathrm{NMEnc}_0(E, e)$
6. Sample seeds s^L, s^R uniformly from $\{0,1\}^{3\Lambda \log^3 n}$
7. $\alpha^L = \mathrm{Embed}^L(s^L, c^L)$ and $\alpha^R = \mathrm{Embed}^R(s^R, c^R)$
8. $\widetilde{c} = f_1(c, s^L, \alpha^L, s^R, \alpha^R)$
9. $(\widetilde{s^L}, \widetilde{\alpha^L}, \widetilde{s^R}, \widetilde{\alpha^R}) = f_2(c, s^L, \alpha^L, s^R, \alpha^R)$
10. $\widetilde{c^L} = \mathrm{Recover}^L(\widetilde{s^L}, \widetilde{\alpha^L})$ and $\widetilde{c^R} = \mathrm{Recover}^R(\widetilde{s^R}, \widetilde{\alpha^R})$
11. If $\mathrm{NMDec}_0(\widetilde{c^L}, \widetilde{c^R}) = \bot$, output $\bot$; (Else) $(\widetilde{E}, \widetilde{e}) = \mathrm{NMDec}_0(\widetilde{c^L}, \widetilde{c^R})$
12. If $\mathrm{ECSS.ECorr}(\widetilde{c}) = \bot$, output $\bot$; (Else) $\widetilde{a} = \mathrm{ECSS.ECorr}(\widetilde{c})$
13. Define c' as $c'_i = \begin{cases} \widetilde{a}_i, & i \notin \widetilde{E} \\ \widetilde{e}_i, & i \in \widetilde{E} \end{cases}$
14. If $c' \neq \widetilde{c}$, output $\bot$; (Else) $\widetilde{m} = \mathrm{ECSS.Dec}(\widetilde{a})$
15. Output $\widetilde{m}$

$H_2(f, m)$:

1. Let $P = \{i | i \in [n], |\mathrm{Out}_f(i) \cap [n]| \geqslant n^{\varepsilon_2}\}$
2. Let $Q = \{i | i \in [n], \mathrm{Out}_f(i) \backslash [n] \neq \emptyset\}$
3. Let $X = P \cup Q$. Sample $a_X \sim U_{\{0,1\}^{|X|}}$
4. Sample $a \sim \mathrm{ECSS.Enc}(m)|(\mathrm{ECSS.Enc}(m))_X = a_X$
5. Sample a random $E \subseteq [n]$ of size $n^{1-\varepsilon_1}$
6. For all $i \in E$, sample $e_i \sim U_{\{0,1\}}$
7. Define c as $c_i = \begin{cases} a_i, & i \notin E \\ e_i, & i \in E \end{cases}$
8. Let $(c^L, c^R) \sim \mathrm{NMEnc}_0(E, e)$
9. Sample seeds s^L, s^R uniformly from $\{0,1\}^{3\Lambda \log^3 n}$
10. $\alpha^L = \mathrm{Embed}^L(s^L, c^L)$ and $\alpha^R = \mathrm{Embed}^R(s^R, c^R)$
11. $\widetilde{c} = f_1(c, s^L, \alpha^L, s^R, \alpha^R)$
12. $(\widetilde{s^L}, \widetilde{\alpha^L}, \widetilde{s^R}, \widetilde{\alpha^R}) = f_2(c, s^L, \alpha^L, s^R, \alpha^R)$
13. $\widetilde{c^L} = \mathrm{Recover}^L(\widetilde{s^L}, \widetilde{\alpha^L})$ and $\widetilde{c^R} = \mathrm{Recover}^R(\widetilde{s^R}, \widetilde{\alpha^R})$
14. If $\mathrm{NMDec}_0(\widetilde{c^L}, \widetilde{c^R}) = \bot$, output $\bot$; (Else) $(\widetilde{E}, \widetilde{e}) = \mathrm{NMDec}_0(\widetilde{c^L}, \widetilde{c^R})$
15. If $\mathrm{ECSS.ECorr}(\widetilde{c}) = \bot$, output $\bot$; (Else) $\widetilde{a} = \mathrm{ECSS.ECorr}(\widetilde{c})$
16. Define c' as $c'_i = \begin{cases} \widetilde{a}_i, & i \notin \widetilde{E} \\ \widetilde{e}_i, & i \in \widetilde{E} \end{cases}$
17. If $c' \neq \widetilde{c}$, output $\bot$; (Else) $\widetilde{m} = \mathrm{ECSS.Dec}(\widetilde{a})$
18. Output $\widetilde{m}$

$H_3(f, m)$:

1. Let $P = \{i | i \in [n], |\mathrm{Out}_f(i) \cap [n]| \geqslant n^{\varepsilon_2}\}$
2. Let $Q = \{i | i \in [n], \mathrm{Out}_f(i) \backslash [n] \neq \emptyset\}$
3. Let $X = P \cup Q$. Sample $a_X \sim U_{\{0,1\}^{|X|}}$
4. Sample $a \sim \mathrm{ECSS.\,Enc}(m) | (\mathrm{ECSS.\,Enc}(m))_X = a_X$
5. Sample a random $E \subseteq [n]$ of size $n^{1-\varepsilon_1}$
6. For all $i \in E$, sample $e_i \sim U_{\{0,1\}}$
7. Define c as $c_i = \begin{cases} a_i, & i \notin E \\ e_i, & i \in E \end{cases}$
8. Sample seeds s^L, s^R uniformly from $\{0,1\}^{3\Lambda \log^3 n}$
9. Given s^L (resp., s^R), indices of c^L (resp., c^R) in α^L (resp., α^R) are determined. Let $\mathrm{Bad}^L = \{$Indices of c^L with more than $n^{1-\gamma-\tau}$ output neighbors in $\widetilde{c}\}$, $\mathrm{Leak}^L = \{$Indices of c^L with output neighbors in either $\widetilde{s^L}$ or $\widetilde{s^R}\}$, $\mathrm{Bad}^R = \{$Indices in c^R with more than $n^{1-\gamma-\tau}$ output neighbors in $\widetilde{c}\}$, and $\mathrm{Leak}^R = \{$Indices in c^R with output neighbors in either $\widetilde{s^L}$ or $\widetilde{s^R}\}$
10. Let $\mathcal{L}^L = \mathrm{Bad}^L \cup \mathrm{Leak}^L$ and $\mathcal{L}^R = \mathrm{Bad}^R \cup \mathrm{Leak}^R$.
11. Let f_0 be the following mapping from leakage at $(\mathcal{L}^L, \mathcal{L}^R)$ to tampering function g for NMEnc_0: First, use (s^L, s^R), leakage at $(\mathrm{Leak}^L, \mathrm{Leak}^R)$ and c_Q to compute $\widetilde{s^L}$ and $\widetilde{s^R}$. These determine indices of $\widetilde{c^L}$ and $\widetilde{c^R}$ in $\widetilde{\alpha^L}$ and $\widetilde{\alpha^R}$. Then, define g to be the tampering function from indices of (c^L, c^R) to indices of $(\widetilde{c^L}, \widetilde{c^R})$.
12. If $(|\mathcal{L}^L| \geqslant \lambda n^{\beta_1})$ or $(|\mathcal{L}^R| \geqslant \lambda n^{\beta_2})$ or (f_0 does not satisfy Definition 6), output $\perp$
13. (Else) $(\widetilde{E}, \widetilde{e}, x, y) = \mathrm{Tamper}_{\mathcal{L}^L, \mathcal{L}^R, f_0}^{(E,e)}$
14. If $(\widetilde{E}, \widetilde{e}) = \perp$, output $\perp$
15. $(c^L, c^R) \sim \mathrm{NMEnc}_0(E, e)$ s.t. $\mathrm{NMDec}_0(g(c^L, c^R)) = (\widetilde{E}, \widetilde{e})$ and $c_{\mathcal{L}^L}^L = x$, $c_{\mathcal{L}^R}^R = y$
16. $\alpha^L = \mathrm{Embed}^L(s^L, c^L)$, $\alpha^R = \mathrm{Embed}^R(s^R, c^R)$
17. $\widetilde{c} = f_1(c, s^L, \alpha^L, s^R, \alpha^R)$
18. If $\mathrm{ECSS.\,ECorr}(\widetilde{c}) = \perp$, output $\perp$; (Else) $\widetilde{a} = \mathrm{ECSS.\,ECorr}(\widetilde{c})$
19. Define c' as $c_i' = \begin{cases} \widetilde{a}_i, & i \notin \widetilde{E} \\ \widetilde{e}_i, & i \in \widetilde{E} \end{cases}$
20. If $c' \neq \widetilde{c}$, output $\perp$; (Else) $\widetilde{m} = \mathrm{ECSS.\,Dec}(\widetilde{a})$
21. Output $\widetilde{m}$

$H_3(f, m)$: In the next hybrid H_3, we rewrite the way how $(\widetilde{E}, \widetilde{e})$ is generated from (E, e) given seeds s^L and s^R. Here, we would generate $(\widetilde{E}, \widetilde{e})$ as output of a tampering experiment on (E, e) with an appropriate tampering function from the leaky input and output local tampering family. Note that (E, e) is first encoded to (c^L, c^R) and then is hidden among (α^L, α^R) using seeds s^L, s^R. We note that if we are given the seed s^L and s^R, the places where c^L are c^R are stored among α^L and α^R is known. Similarly, if we know $\widetilde{s^L}$ and $\widetilde{s^R}$, the places where $\widetilde{c^L}$ and $\widetilde{c^R}$ are stored among $\widetilde{\alpha^L}$ and $\widetilde{\alpha^R}$ are also known. Therefore, we define Leak^L and Leak^R as the input neighbors of both $\widetilde{s^L}$ and $\widetilde{s^R}$ from c^L and c^R respectively. Now let f_0 be the mapping that given the leakage Leak^L and Leak^R, first computes[8] $\widetilde{s^L}$ and $\widetilde{s^R}$, and then outputs the tampering function g. Now that we know indices of (c^L, c^R) and $(\widetilde{c^L}, \widetilde{c^R})$, function g maps (c^L, c^R) to $(\widetilde{c^L}, \widetilde{c^R})$.[9] We note that leaking bits at Bad^L and Bad^R from c^L and c^R would be used in later hybrids. So the total leakage from c^L and c^R are $\mathcal{L}^L = \text{Leak}^L \cup \text{Bad}^L$ and $\mathcal{L}^R = \text{Leak}^R \cup \text{Bad}^R$. Now we need to argue that the tampering f_0 and leakage $\mathcal{L}^L, \mathcal{L}^R$ forms a valid tampering experiment onto our base NMC against leaky input and output local tampering. It is easy to see that if it is valid, then the two hybrids are identical. When they are not valid we output $\bot$ in this hybrid and we need to argue that probability of output $\bot$ due this is negligible.

$H_4(f, m)$:

1. Let $P = \{i | i \in [n], |\text{Out}_f(i) \cap [n]| \geqslant n^{\varepsilon_2}\}$
2. Let $Q = \{i | i \in [n], \text{Out}_f(i) \backslash [n] \neq \emptyset\}$
3. Let $X = P \cup Q$. Sample $a_X \sim U_{\{0,1\}^{|X|}}$
4. Sample $a \sim \text{ECSS.Enc}(m) | (\text{ECSS.Enc}(m))_X = a_X$
5. Sample a random $E \subseteq [n]$ of size $n^{1-\varepsilon_1}$
6. For all $i \in E$, sample $e_i \sim U_{\{0,1\}}$
7. Define c as $c_i = \begin{cases} a_i, & i \notin E \\ e_i, & i \in E \end{cases}$
8. Sample seeds s^L, s^R uniformly from $\{0,1\}^{3\Lambda \log^3 n}$
9. Given s^L, define: $\text{Bad}^L, \text{Leak}^L$ as in $H_3(f, m)$
   Given s^R, define: $\text{Bad}^R, \text{Leak}^R$ as in $H_3(f, m)$
10. Let $\mathcal{L}^L = \text{Bad}^L \cup \text{Leak}^L$ and $\mathcal{L}^R = \text{Bad}^R \cup \text{Leak}^R$.
11. Define mapping f_0 and its output g as in $H_3(f, m)$
12. If $(|\mathcal{L}^L| \geqslant \lambda n^{\beta_1})$ or $(|\mathcal{L}^R| \geqslant \lambda n^{\beta_2})$ or (f_0 does not satisfy Definition 6), output $\bot$
13. (Else) $(\text{ans}, x, y) = \text{Sim}_0(\mathcal{L}^L, \mathcal{L}^R, f_0)$
14. If $\text{ans} = \bot$, output $\bot$; (Else) $(\widetilde{E}, \widetilde{e}) = \text{copy}(\text{ans}, (E, e))$
15. $(c^L, c^R) \sim \text{NMEnc}_0(E, e)$ s.t. $\text{NMDec}_0(g(c^L, c^R)) = (\widetilde{E}, \widetilde{e})$ and $c^L_{\mathcal{L}^L} = x$, $c^R_{\mathcal{L}^R} = y$
16. $\alpha^L = \text{Embed}^L(s^L, c^L)$, $\alpha^R = \text{Embed}^R(s^R, c^R)$
17. $\widetilde{c} = f_1(c, s^L, \alpha^L, s^R, \alpha^R)$
18. If $\text{ECSS.ECorr}(\widetilde{c}) = \bot$, output $\bot$; (Else) $\widetilde{a} = \text{ECSS.ECorr}(\widetilde{c})$
19. Define c' as $c'_i = \begin{cases} \widetilde{a}_i, & i \notin \widetilde{E} \\ \widetilde{e}_i, & i \in \widetilde{E} \end{cases}$
20. If $c' \neq \widetilde{c}$, output $\bot$; (Else) $\widetilde{m} = \text{ECSS.Dec}(\widetilde{a})$
21. Output $\widetilde{m}$

Firstly, f_0 might not satisfy Definition 6 if one of the following happens: (i) Not all the bits from c^L, c^R are contained in α^L and α^R, respectively and thus, f_0 cannot produce function g; (ii) g has output locality higher than $\ell_o = \delta$; (iii) under g, more than μn^{β_1} many bits from c^L have input locality higher than

---

[8] Note that at this point, the original seed s^L and s^R and their input neighbors c_Q from main codeword c is already fixed.

[9] If $\widetilde{c^L}$ or $\widetilde{c^R}$ are not contained in $\widetilde{\alpha^L}$ or $\widetilde{\alpha^R}$, f_0 will simply set g to be a $\bot$ function.

$\ell_i = 4\delta/\mu$ to $\widetilde{c^R}$. Note that our tampering function f is δ-local and therefore, the output function g will also be δ-local, thus (ii) will never happen. And the probability of (i) or (iii) happening is negligible as guaranteed by Lemma 5 and (1) from Lemma 6, respectively.

We bound the size of the leakage $|\mathcal{L}^L| = |\text{Leak}^L \cup \text{Bad}^L|$ by $o(n^{\beta_1})$. First, we observe that our seeds s^L and s^R are of length $O(\log^3 n)$ and hence $|\text{Leak}^L|$ is at most $O(\delta \log^3 n) = o(n^{\beta_1})$. And the size of Bad^L is $o(n^{\beta_1})$ is guaranteed by (2) of Lemma 6. The argument for $\mathcal{L}^R$ is analogous to $\mathcal{L}^L$. This proves that this hybrid and the previous one are $2^{-\Omega(\log^2 n)}$-close.

Note that we still need the error codeword $(s^L, \alpha^L, s^R, \alpha^R)$ to do the tampering f_1 onto $\widetilde{c}$. Hence, we sample c^L and c^R under the condition that the tampering experiment outputs $(\widetilde{E}, \widetilde{e}, x, y)$ and construct the error codeword as defined by our compiler.

$H_5(f, m)$:

1. Let $P = \{i | i \in [n], |\text{Out}_f(i) \cap [n]| \geqslant n^{\varepsilon_2}\}$
2. Let $Q = \{i | i \in [n], \text{Out}_f(i) \backslash [n] \neq \emptyset\}$
3. Let $X = P \cup Q$. Sample $a_X \sim U_{\{0,1\}^{|X|}}$
4. Sample a random $E_1 \subseteq X$ s.t. $|E_1| \sim (n, |X|, n^{1-\varepsilon_1})$-hypergeometric distribution
5. For all $i \in E_1$, sample $e_i \sim U_{\{0,1\}}$
6. For all $i \in E_1$, replace a_i with e_i, we get c_X
7. Sample seeds s^L, s^R uniformly from $\{0,1\}^{3\Lambda \log^3 n}$
8. Given s^L, define: $\text{Bad}^L, \text{Leak}^L$ as in $H_3(f, m)$
   Given s^R, define: $\text{Bad}^R, \text{Leak}^R$ as in $H_3(f, m)$
9. Let $\mathcal{L}^L = \text{Bad}^L \cup \text{Leak}^L$ and $\mathcal{L}^R = \text{Bad}^R \cup \text{Leak}^R$.
10. Define mapping f_0 and its output g as in $H_3(f, m)$
11. If $(|\mathcal{L}^L| \geqslant \lambda n^{\beta_1})$ or $(|\mathcal{L}^R| \geqslant \lambda n^{\beta_2})$ or $(f_0$ does not satisfy Definition 6), output $\perp$
12. (Else) $(\text{ans}, x, y) = \text{Sim}_0(\mathcal{L}^L, \mathcal{L}^R, f_0)$.
13. If $\text{ans} = \perp$, output $\perp$
14. Sample $a \sim \text{ECSS.Enc}(m)|(\text{ECSS.Enc}(m))_X = a_X$
15. Sample a random $E_2 \subseteq [n] \backslash X$ of size $n^{1-\varepsilon_1} - |E_1|$, Let $E = E_1 \cup E_2$
16. For all $i \in E_2$, sample $e_i \sim U_{\{0,1\}}$
17. Define c as $c_i = \begin{cases} a_i, & i \notin E \\ e_i, & i \in E \end{cases}$
18. $(\widetilde{E}, \widetilde{e}) = \text{copy}(\text{ans}, (E, e))$
19. $(c^L, c^R) \sim \text{NMEnc}_0(E, e)$ s.t. $\text{NMDec}_0(g(c^L, c^R)) = (\widetilde{E}, \widetilde{e})$ and $c^L_{\mathcal{L}^L} = x$, $c^R_{\mathcal{L}^R} = y$
10. $\alpha^L = \text{Embed}^L(s^L, c^L)$, $\alpha^R = \text{Embed}^R(s^R, c^R)$
21. $\widetilde{c} = f_1(c, s^L, \alpha^L, s^R, \alpha^R)$
22. If $\text{ECSS.ECorr}(\widetilde{c}) = \perp$, output $\perp$; (Else) $\widetilde{a} = \text{ECSS.ECorr}(\widetilde{c})$
23. Define c' as $c'_i = \begin{cases} \widetilde{a}_i, & i \notin \widetilde{E} \\ \widetilde{e}_i, & i \in \widetilde{E} \end{cases}$
24. If $c' \neq \widetilde{c}$, output $\perp$; (Else) $\widetilde{m} = \text{ECSS.Dec}(\widetilde{a})$
25. Output $\widetilde{m}$

$H_4(f, m)$: In the next hybrid H_4, we simply replace the tampering experiment onto our base non-malleable codes with its corresponding simulator Sim_0 and incur a negligible error by Lemma 2.

$H_5(f, m)$: In this hybrid, we break the error indices E into two parts: $E_1 = E \cap X$ and $E_2 = E \backslash E_1$. Next, we note that c_Q is needed to define the tampering on the error codeword. Hence, we sample E_1 and the error bits from E_1 early before defining tampering on error codeword. However, rest of errors, i.e., E_2 is not used before we invoke simulator Sim_0. Based on these observations, we re-arrange parts of the hybrids and this hybrid is identical to the previous one. Note that the size of E_1 and E_2 are distributed according to $(n, |X|, n^{1-\varepsilon_1})$-hypergemetric distribution and $(n, n - |X|, n^{1-\varepsilon_1})$-hyper geometric distribution, respectively. By Corollary 1, it is easy to see that with probability $1 - \exp(-\Theta(n^{1-\varepsilon_1}))$, the size of E_2 is at least $n^{1-\varepsilon_1}/2$.

$H_6(f, m)$: In this hybrid, we only introduce some new notation to be used in later hybrids and hence, this hybrid is identical to the previous one.

We focus on the tampering of the main codeword using function f_1. Note that so far in the previous hybrid, we have already fixed certain bits in the input main codeword c (that is, c_X), picked PRG seeds s^L, s^R and also leaked certain parts of c^L, c^R, i.e., $\mathcal{L}^L, \mathcal{L}^R$.[10] Using this information, we define a restriction h of function f_1 that fixes all the above bits in the input.

We next define three subsets of $[n]$ corresponding to h, namely, V, W and Z as follows. V is the subset of bits i such that $\tilde{c}_i$ is not fixed given the fixing of bits done so far. And W is the subset of bits that are influenced by some bits in the error codeword (that have not been leaked and fixed so far). And Z is the subset of bits i, such that the output of h_i is not always the i-th input bit (In the definition of Z, recall that $n_e = |(s^L, \alpha^L, s^R, \alpha^R)|$).

Intuitively, Z is the set of bits that are not-copied-bits under the tampering function h, V is the set of non-constant-bits and W is the set of bits that are influenced by the error codeword. As we explained in technical overview Sect. 1.3, if ans = same* and the size of $Z \backslash W$ is large or if ans = (E^*, e^*) and the size of $V \backslash W$ is large, then the tampered codeword will be invalid with probability $1 - \mathsf{negl}(n)$. This intuition is formally proved in the next hybrid.

$H_7(f, m)$: In the next hybrid H_7, we add a sanity check right after we define V, W, Z. (a) When ans = $\bot$, we will output $\bot$ immediately. This is the same as the previous hybrid. (b) When ans = same*, we check the size of $Z \backslash (W \cup X)$. If it is larger than $n^{1-\varepsilon_2}$, we directly output $\bot$ without any further computation. On the other hand, if it is less than $n^{1-\varepsilon_2}$, we only compare c and $\tilde{c}$ at locations Z. If they are the same, we output same*, otherwise, we output $\bot$. (c) When ans = (E^*, e^*), we check the size of $V \backslash W$. If $|V \backslash W| \geqslant n^{1-\varepsilon_2}$, we directly output $\bot$ without further computation. Below, we prove that the previous hybrid $H_6(f, m)$ and copy($H_7(f, m), m$) are statistically close. We break the proof into two parts: ans = same* case and ans = (E^*, e^*) case.

---

[10] Note that those places in α^L, α^R that are not used to store c^L and c^R are also fixed (to be 0 by the compiler).

$H_6(f, m)$:

1. Let $P = \{i | i \in [n], |\text{Out}_f(i) \cap [n]| \geq n^{\varepsilon_2}\}$
2. Let $Q = \{i | i \in [n], \text{Out}_f(i) \backslash [n] \neq \emptyset\}$
3. Let $X = P \cup Q$. Sample $a_X \sim U_{\{0,1\}^{|X|}}$
4. Sample a random $E_1 \subseteq X$ s.t. $|E_1| \sim (n, |X|, n^{1-\varepsilon_1})$-hypergeometric distribution.
5. For all $i \in E_1$, sample $e_i \sim U_{\{0,1\}}$
6. For all $i \in E_1$, replace a_i with e_i, we get c_X
7. Sample seeds s^L, s^R uniformly from $\{0,1\}^{3\Lambda \log^3 n}$
8. Given s^L, define: $\text{Bad}^L, \text{Leak}^L$ as in $H_3(f, m)$
   Given s^R, define: $\text{Bad}^R, \text{Leak}^R$ as in $H_3(f, m)$
9. Let $\mathcal{L}^L = \text{Bad}^L \cup \text{Leak}^L$ and $\mathcal{L}^R = \text{Bad}^R \cup \text{Leak}^R$.
10. Define mapping f_0 and its output g as in $H_3(f, m)$
11. If $(|\mathcal{L}^L| \geq \lambda n^{\beta_1})$ or $(|\mathcal{L}^R| \geq \lambda n^{\beta_2})$ or (f_0 does not satisfy Definition 6), output $\bot$
12. (Else) $(\text{ans}, x, y) = \text{Sim}_0(\mathcal{L}^L, \mathcal{L}^R, f_0)$.
13. Let S^L, S^R denote indices of s^L, s^R. Define function h as a restriction of f_1 (Definition 2): $h := (f_1)_{(X, S^L, S^R, \mathcal{L}^L, \mathcal{L}^R)|(c_X, s^L, s^R, x, y)}$
14. $V := \{i \in [n] | \text{Inp}_h(i) \neq \emptyset\}$.
15. $W := \{i \in [n] | \text{Inp}_h(i) \backslash [n] \neq \emptyset\}$.
16. $Z := \{i \in [n] | \exists z \in \{0,1\}^{n+n_c}, z_{(X, S^L, S^R, \mathcal{L}^L, \mathcal{L}^R)} = (c_X, s^L, s^R, x, y), h_i(z) \neq z_i\}$.
17. If $\text{ans} = \bot$, output $\bot$
18. Sample $a \sim \text{ECSS}.\text{Enc}(m)|(\text{ECSS}.\text{Enc}(m))_X = c_X$
19. Sample a random $E_2 \subseteq [n] \backslash X$ of size $n^{1-\varepsilon_1} - |E_1|$, let $E = E_1 \cup E_2$
20. For all $i \in E_2$, sample $e_i \sim U_{\{0,1\}}$
21. Define c as $c_i = \begin{cases} a_i, & i \notin E \\ e_i, & i \in E \end{cases}$
22. $(\widetilde{E}, \widetilde{e}) = \text{copy}(\text{Sim}_0(\mathcal{L}^L, \mathcal{L}^R, f_0), (E, e))$
23. $(c^L, c^R) \sim \text{NMEnc}_0(E, e)$ s.t. $\text{NMDec}_0(g(c^L, c^R)) = (\widetilde{E}, \widetilde{e})$ and $c^L_{\mathcal{L}^L} = x, c^R_{\mathcal{L}^R} = y$
24. $\alpha^L = \text{Embed}^L(s^L, c^L), \alpha^R = \text{Embed}^R(s^R, c^R)$
25. $\widetilde{c} = f_1(c, s^L, \alpha^L, s^R, \alpha^R)$
26. If $\text{ECSS}.\text{ECorr}(\widetilde{c}) = \bot$, output $\bot$; (Else) $\widetilde{a} = \text{ECSS}.\text{ECorr}(\widetilde{c})$
27. Define c' as $c'_i = \begin{cases} \widetilde{a}_i, & i \notin \widetilde{E} \\ \widetilde{e}_i, & i \in \widetilde{E} \end{cases}$
28. If $c' \neq \widetilde{c}$, output $\bot$; (Else) $\widetilde{m} = \text{ECSS}.\text{Dec}(\widetilde{a})$
29. Output $\widetilde{m}$

Case ans = same*: Let us first look at that the case when $|Z \backslash (W \cup X)| < n^{1-\varepsilon_2}$. Note that by the definition of Z, all the bits of $\widetilde{c}$ in $[n] \backslash Z$ are identical to those in c. Recall c is obtained by planting $|E| = n^{1-\varepsilon_1}$ errors into a valid ECSS codeword a. We have $\text{HD}(\widetilde{c}, a) \leq \text{HD}(\widetilde{c}, c) + \text{HD}(c, a) = |Z| + |E| \leq (|Z \backslash (W \cup X)| + |W| + |X|) + |E|$. Using $|W| = o(n^{1-\tau})$ from (3) of Lemma 6, $|X| = o(n^{1-\varsigma})$ from hybrid 2, and $|E| = n^{1-\varepsilon_1}$, we get $\text{HD}(\widetilde{c}, a) \leq n^{1-\varepsilon_2} + o(n^{1-\tau}) + o(n^{1-\varsigma}) + n^{1-\varepsilon_1} = o(n^{1-\varsigma})$ by setting $\boxed{\varsigma < \varepsilon_2}$, $\boxed{\varsigma < \tau}$ and $\boxed{\varsigma < \varepsilon_1}$. Hence, using the fact that the distance of the ECSS scheme, $d \geq n^{1-\varsigma}$, we get

ECSS. $\mathrm{ECorr}(\widetilde{c}) = a$. Consequently, if we error-correct $\widetilde{c}$ and plant in the original errors (E, e), we get c. Hence, experiment would output $\bot$ iff $\widetilde{c} \neq c$. This happens only when $\widetilde{c}_Z \neq c_Z$.

Now consider the case when $|Z \backslash (W \cup X)| \geqslant n^{1-\varepsilon_2}$. We begin by computing a lower bound on number of error indices in $Z \backslash (W \cup X)$, i.e., size of set $A = (Z \backslash (W \cup X)) \cap E_2$. First, note that E_2 is a random subset of $[n] \backslash X$ of size at least $n^{1-\varepsilon_1}/2$ with probability $1 - \exp(-\Omega(n^{1-\varepsilon_1}))$ by Corollary 1. Next, we observe that sets Z, W, X are defined independent of E_2 and hence, by Corollary 1, $|A| \geqslant \frac{1}{4} \cdot n^{1-\varepsilon_1-\varepsilon_2}$ with probability at least $1 - \exp(-\Omega(n^{1-\varepsilon_1-2\varepsilon_2}))$.

Next, we pick a subset $A' \subseteq A$ such that bits in A' have disjoint input neighbors. That is, $\forall i, j \in A', \mathrm{Inp}_h(i) \cap \mathrm{Inp}_h(j) = \emptyset$. We use following two properties to ensure that we can pick A' of sufficiently large size. First, for every bit $i \in A$, $\mathrm{Inp}_h(i) \subseteq [n]$ (because $A \cap W = \emptyset$). Second, all the bits in $[n]$ with more than n^{ε_2} output neighbors in $[n]$ belong to subset P and have already been fixed. This implies that for any bit $i \in A$, all bits in $\mathrm{Inp}_h(i)$ have at most n^{ε_2} output neighbours in $[n]$. Therefore, it is guaranteed that we can pick a set $A' \subseteq A$ s.t. $|A'| \geqslant \frac{|A|}{\delta n^{\varepsilon_2}} = \frac{n^{1-\varepsilon_1-2\varepsilon_2}}{4\delta}$. (This can be done greedily by picking an arbitrary index $i \in A$ and discarding all the bits in A that are influenced by $\mathrm{Inp}_h(i)$. Since h has at output locality δ and each bit in $\mathrm{Inp}_h(i)$ influences at most n^{ε_2}-many bits in A, we discard at most δn^{ε_2} indices from A for picking one index in A'. Now, we recurse on the remaining indices in A.)

For the rest of the proof, we consider such a set A' of size exactly $\frac{n^{1-\varepsilon_1-2\varepsilon_2}}{4\delta}$. We note that for all indices $i \in A'$ following conditions are satisfied (1) c_i is a planted error $(A' \subseteq E_2)$; (2) h_i does not always output e_i $(A' \subseteq Z)$; (3) the input neighbors of i are all in $[n]$ $(A' \cap W = \emptyset)$. For the tampered main codeword to be consistent with recorded errors, we need that for all $i \in A'$, The i-th bit after tampering, i.e. $\widetilde{c}_i$ needs to be equal to e_i. We show that this happens with probability at most $(1 - 1/2^\delta)^{n^{1-\varepsilon_1-2\varepsilon_2}8\delta}$, which is negligible for $\delta = \xi \cdot \lg n$ when $\boxed{\varepsilon_1 + 2\varepsilon_2 < 1 - \xi}$. Hence, it suffices to output $\bot$ always.

We first argue that all of A' input neighbors are independent uniform bits. We use the fact that A' is of size $\frac{n^{1-\varepsilon_1-2\varepsilon_2}}{4\delta}$ and its (at most $\delta \cdot \frac{n^{1-\varepsilon_1-2\varepsilon_2}}{4\delta}$-many) input neighbors are all from our ECSS codeword with planted errors. Since we have only fixed X of size $o(t)$ from c so far and our ECSS has independence $t \geqslant n^{1-\varsigma}$ and $n^{1-\varepsilon_1-2\varepsilon_2} = o(t)$, all the input neighbors of A' are indeed independent uniform bits. Given the uniformly random input, we examine the bits from A' one by one. For any $i \in A'$, there are following two possibilities

○ If c_i (i.e., e_i) is the input neighbor of $\widetilde{c}_i$, then since h_i does not always output c_i, there exists a setting of the other (at most) $\delta - 1$ neighbors, such that $\widetilde{c}_i$ is either fixed 0, fixed 1, or flipped e_i. Because of uniformity of value at input neighbors, this setting happens with probability at least $\frac{1}{2^{\delta-1}}$ and when it happens, with probability at least $1/2$, $\widetilde{c}_i \neq e_i$. Hence, $\widetilde{c}_i = e_i$ with probability at most $1 - \frac{1}{2^\delta}$. We remove i from A' and recurse on remaining bits.

○ If c_i (i.e., e_i) is not the input neighbor of $\widetilde{c}_i$, then since all of the input neighbors are independent of uniform bit e_i, the probability $\widetilde{c}_i = e_i$ is at most $1/2$.

However, we need to address a small subtlety here. Since e_i is not the input neighbor of itself, it can be in the input neighbor of another bit in A'. To keep failure probabilities independent, if such a bit j exists (s.t. e_i is an input neighbor of $\widetilde{c}_j$), we only include i in our witness set of failed indices but we remove both indices i and j before recursing to remaining bits in A'.

H_7:

1. Let $P = \{i | i \in [n], |\mathrm{Out}_f(i) \cap [n]| \geqslant n^{\varepsilon_2}\}$
2. Let $Q = \{i | i \in [n], \mathrm{Out}_f(i) \backslash [n] \neq \emptyset\}$
3. Let $X = P \cup Q$. Sample $a_X \sim U_{\{0,1\}^{|X|}}$
4. Sample a random $E_1 \subseteq X$ s.t. $|E_1| \sim (n, |X|, n^{1-\varepsilon_1})$-hypergeometric distribution
5. For all $i \in E_1$, sample $e_i \sim U_{\{0,1\}}$
6. For all $i \in E_1$, replace a_i with e_i, we get c_X
7. Sample seeds s^L, s^R uniformly from $\{0,1\}^{3\Lambda \log^3 n}$
8. Given s^L, define: $\mathrm{Bad}^L, \mathrm{Leak}^L$ as in $H_3(f, m)$
   Given s^R, define: $\mathrm{Bad}^R, \mathrm{Leak}^R$ as in $H_3(f, m)$
9. Let $\mathcal{L}^L = \mathrm{Bad}^L \cup \mathrm{Leak}^L$ and $\mathcal{L}^R = \mathrm{Bad}^R \cup \mathrm{Leak}^R$.
10. Define mapping f_0 and its output g as in $H_3(f, m)$
11. If $(|\mathcal{L}^L| \geqslant \lambda n^{\beta_1})$ or $(|\mathcal{L}^R| \geqslant \lambda n^{\beta_2})$ or (f_0 does not satisfy Definition 6), output $\perp$
12. (Else) $(\mathrm{ans}, x, y) = \mathrm{Sim}_0(\mathcal{L}^L, \mathcal{L}^R, f_0)$.
13. Let S^L, S^R denote indices of s^L, s^R. Then, $h := (f_1)_{(X, S^L, S^R, \mathcal{L}^L, \mathcal{L}^R)|(c_X, s^L, s^R, x, y)}$
14. $V := \{i | i \in [n], \mathrm{Inp}_h(i) \neq \emptyset\}$
15. $W := \{i | i \in [n], \mathrm{Inp}_h(i) \backslash [n] \neq \emptyset\}$
16. $Z := \{i \in [n] | \exists z \in \{0,1\}^{n+n_e}, z_{(X, S^L, S^R, \mathcal{L}^L, \mathcal{L}^R)} = (c_X, s^L, s^R, x, y), h_i(z) \neq z_i\}$
17. If $\mathrm{ans} = \perp$, output $\perp$
    If $\mathrm{ans} = \mathrm{same}^*$ and $|Z \backslash (W \cup X)| \geqslant n^{1-\varepsilon_2}$, output $\perp$
    If $\mathrm{ans} = (E^*, e^*)$ and $|V \backslash W| \geqslant n^{1-\varepsilon_2}$, output $\perp$
18. Sample $a \sim$ ECSS.Enc(m) $|(\mathrm{ECSS.Enc}(m))_X = c_X$
19. Sample a random $E_2 \subseteq [n] \backslash X$ of size $n^{1-\varepsilon_1} - |E_1|$, let $E = E_1 \cup E_2$
20. For all $i \in E_2$, sample $e_i \sim U_{\{0,1\}}$
21. Define c as $c_i = \begin{cases} a_i, & i \notin E \\ e_i, & i \in E \end{cases}$
22. $(\widetilde{E}, \widetilde{e}) = \mathrm{copy}(\mathrm{Sim}_0(\mathcal{L}^L, \mathcal{L}^R, f_0), (E, e))$
23. $(c^L, c^R) \sim \mathrm{NMEnc}_0(E, e)$ s.t. $\mathrm{NMDec}_0(g(c^L, c^R)) = (\widetilde{E}, \widetilde{e})$ and $c^L_{\mathcal{L}^L} = x, c^R_{\mathcal{L}^R} = y$
24. $\alpha^L = \mathrm{Embed}^L(s^L, c^L), \alpha^R = \mathrm{Embed}^R(s^R, c^R)$
25. $\widetilde{c} = f_1(c, s^L, \alpha^L, s^R, \alpha^R)$
26. If $\mathrm{ans} =$
    ○ same^*: If $\widetilde{c}_Z = c_Z$, output same^*
        (Else) Output $\perp$.
    ○ (E^*, e^*): If $\mathrm{ECSS.ECorr}(\widetilde{c}) = \perp$, output $\perp$; (Else) $\widetilde{a} = \mathrm{ECSS.ECorr}(\widetilde{c})$
        Define c' as $c'_i = \begin{cases} \widetilde{a}_i, & i \notin \widetilde{E} \\ \widetilde{e}_i, & i \in \widetilde{E} \end{cases}$
        If $c' \neq \widetilde{c}$, output $\perp$; (Else) $\widetilde{m} = \mathrm{ECSS.Dec}(\widetilde{a})$
        Output $\widetilde{m}$

Now, we have shown that either a bit has probability at most $1 - \frac{1}{2^\delta}$ to be consistent or two bits have probability at most $1/2$ to be consistent at the same time. And all of those events are independent, hence, the probability that all the bits are consistent with errors (E, e) is at most $(1 - \frac{1}{2^\delta})^{|A'|/2}$.

Case ans $= (E^*, e^*)$: For the case when ans $= (E^*, e^*)$, this hybrid is only different from previous one when $|V \backslash W| \geqslant n^{1-\varepsilon_2}$. We show that if this happens, the output of previous hybrid is not $\perp$ with only negligible probability.

We first pick a $B \subseteq (V \backslash W)$ such that $\forall i, j \in B, \mathrm{Inp}_h(i) \cap \mathrm{Inp}_h(j) = \emptyset$. Similar to above, all the input neighbors of $V \backslash W$ are contained in $[n]$ and have output locality at most n^{ε_2} in $[n]$. Hence, it is guaranteed that we could pick B such that $|B| = \frac{n^{1-2\varepsilon_2}}{\delta}$. (Similar to same* case, this can be done greedily by picking an arbitrary index from $V \backslash W$ into B and removing all the bits its input neighbors have influence on. We only discard at most δn^{ε_2} bits for picking one bit.)

Note that $B \subseteq V$ implies that for all $i \in B$, $\mathrm{Inp}_h(i) \neq \emptyset$ and since all the bits in B has disjoint input neighbors, we have $|\mathrm{Inp}_h(B)| \geqslant |B|$. Now, consider a subset $B' \subseteq B$ such that each bit in B' has an input neighbour in errors E_2. That is,

$$B' = \left\{ i \middle| i \in B, \mathrm{Inp}_h(i) \cap E_2 \neq \emptyset \right\}$$

Again E_2 is a random subset of size at least $n^{1-\varepsilon_1}/2$ with probability $1 - \exp(-\Omega(n^{1-\varepsilon_1}))$ and is independent of B. Thus, by Corollary 1, with probability at least $1 - \exp(-\Omega(n^{1-\varepsilon_1-4\varepsilon_2}))$, $|\mathrm{Inp}_h(B) \cap E_2| \geqslant \frac{1}{4\delta} n^{1-\varepsilon_1-2\varepsilon_2}$. Hence, $|B'| \geqslant \frac{n^{1-\varepsilon_1-2\varepsilon_2}}{4\delta^2}$ (Because of δ-locality).

For the rest of proof, we consider such a set B' of size exactly $\frac{n^{1-\varepsilon_1-2\varepsilon_2}}{4\delta^2}$. Next, we argue that input neighbors of B' (at most $\delta \cdot n^{1-\varepsilon_1-2\varepsilon_2}/(4\delta^2)$ in number) are independently uniformly distributed. This is because they are all from our ECSS codeword with planted errors. Since we have only fixed X of size $o(t)$ from c so far and our ECSS has independence $t = n^{1-\zeta}$ with $\boxed{\zeta < \varepsilon_1 + 2\varepsilon_2}$, all the input neighbors of B' are indeed independent uniform bits. So, bits in B' satisfy the following conditions: its input neighbors (1) are disjoint; (2) contain at least one bit from E_2; (3) are contained in $[n]$; (4) are independently uniform bits.

Next, we define $M = \mathrm{Out}_h(\mathrm{Inp}_h(B'))$. This is the set of all indices that is being influenced by the input neighbor of B'. Obviously $B' \subseteq M$. And the size of M is bounded by $n^{\varepsilon_2} \cdot \delta \cdot n^{1-\varepsilon_1-2\varepsilon_2}/(4\delta^2) = n^{1-\varepsilon_1-\varepsilon_2}/(4\delta)$. We first observe that fix any $c^*_{[n]\backslash M}$, there is at most one c_M that is consistent with $c^*_{[n]\backslash M}$ and the fixed errors E^*, e^*. This is because if there exist two $c^{(1)}, c^{(2)}$ s.t. $c^{(1)}_{[n]\backslash M} = c^{(2)}_{[n]\backslash M}$, their distance is bounded by $n^{1-\varepsilon_1-\varepsilon_2}/(4\delta)$ which is smaller than the distance $d \geqslant n^{1-\zeta}$ as long as $\boxed{\zeta < \varepsilon_1 + \varepsilon_2}$. Therefore, those two codewords will be error-corrected to the same correct codeword and after being reconstructed from errors (E^*, e^*), they will be the same. Therefore, for every fixing $c^*_{[n]\backslash M}$, there is at most one codeword c^* (equivalently, one c_M^*), which is consistent with (E^*, e^*). Since $B' \subseteq M$, there is at most one choice for $c_{B'}^*$ as well.

Finally, we prove that the probability that $c_{B'}^*$ takes the fixed value needed to be consistent is negligible. Now, for any $i \in B'$, we know some bit E_j is the input neighbors of i. Therefore, at least one out of at most $2^{\delta-1}$ possible settings of all the other input neighbors $\text{Inp}_h(i)\backslash[j]$, flipping the value of e_j will flip the output of h_i. Note that by definition of M, E_j cannot be the input neighbors of any bits in $[n]\backslash M$, hence c_j is independent of $c_{[n]\backslash M}^*$. And thus, whenever this setting happens, with probability $1/2$, the output at i will not be consistent with (E^*, e^*). Therefore, since the input neighbors of i are uniformly distributed, the probability that $\tilde{c}_i$ is not consistent with fixed errors (E^*, e^*) is at least $\frac{1}{2^\delta}$. Since all the input neighbors of B' are all independent uniform bits, the probability that all the bits from B' are consistent is at most $(1 - \frac{1}{2^\delta})^{n^{1-\varepsilon_1-2\varepsilon_2}/(4\delta^2)}$, which is negligible when $\delta = \xi \cdot \lg n$ with $\boxed{\varepsilon_1 + 2\varepsilon_2 < 1 - \xi}$.

$H_8(f, m)$: Our final hybrid is identical to our simulator Fig. 3. In this final hybrid, we simply switch message m with 0^ℓ.

Note that the only bits from ECSS.$\text{Enc}(m)$ that affect the output of the hybrid is (1) the neighbors of Z and also c_Z when ans = same* and $|Z\backslash(W \cup X)| < n^{1-\varepsilon_2}$; (2) the neighbors of V, when ans $\notin$ {same*, $\bot$} and $|V\backslash W| < n^{1-\varepsilon_2}$.[11] For (1), as shown in hybrid 7, the size of Z is $o(t)$ when $|Z\backslash(W \cup X)| < n^{1-\varepsilon_2}$ and hence the neighbor of $|Z|$ is of size at most $\delta \cdot |Z| = o(t)$. For (2), $|V| \leqslant |V\backslash W| + |W|$. Both are $o(t)$ as require in hybrid 7 and therefore so is $|V|$ and the size of the neighbors of V. Hence the number of bits in c that influence the hybrid output is at most $o(t)$. Any $o(t)$ bits from ECSS.$\text{Enc}(m)$ condition on c_X is uniformly distributed. Hence, we can switch the encoding of m with encoding of 0^ℓ.

This completes our hybrid argument.

References

1. Aggarwal, D., Agrawal, S., Gupta, D., Maji, H.K., Pandey, O., Prabhakaran, M.: Optimal computational split-state non-malleable codes. In: Kushilevitz, E., Malkin, T. (eds.) TCC 2016. LNCS, vol. 9563, pp. 393–417. Springer, Heidelberg (2016). https://doi.org/10.1007/978-3-662-49099-0_15
2. Aggarwal, D., Dodis, Y., Kazana, T., Obremski, M.: Non-malleable reductions and applications. In: STOC (2015)
3. Aggarwal, D., Dodis, Y., Lovett, S.: Non-malleable codes from additive combinatorics. In: STOC (2014)
4. Agrawal, S., Gupta, D., Maji, H.K., Pandey, O., Prabhakaran, M.: Explicit non-malleable codes against bit-wise tampering and permutations. In: Gennaro, R., Robshaw, M. (eds.) CRYPTO 2015. LNCS, vol. 9215, pp. 538–557. Springer, Heidelberg (2015). https://doi.org/10.1007/978-3-662-47989-6_26

---

[11] Note that, by the definition of V, all the output bits from $[n]\backslash V$ are fixed to some values with no input neighbors. Hence, it suffices to have the neighbor of V to finish the hybrid completely.

5. Agrawal, S., Gupta, D., Maji, H.K., Pandey, O., Prabhakaran, M.: A rate-optimizing compiler for non-malleable codes against bit-wise tampering and permutations. In: Dodis, Y., Nielsen, J.B. (eds.) TCC 2015. LNCS, vol. 9014, pp. 375–397. Springer, Heidelberg (2015). https://doi.org/10.1007/978-3-662-46494-6_16

6. Ball, M., Dachman-Soled, D., Guo, S., Malkin, T., Tan, L.-Y.: Non-malleable codes for small-depth circuits. In: FOCS (2018)

7. Ball, M., Dachman-Soled, D., Kulkarni, M., Malkin, T.: Non-malleable codes for bounded depth, bounded fan-in circuits. In: Fischlin, M., Coron, J.-S. (eds.) EUROCRYPT 2016. LNCS, vol. 9666, pp. 881–908. Springer, Heidelberg (2016). https://doi.org/10.1007/978-3-662-49896-5_31

8. Ball, M., Dachman-Soled, D., Kulkarni, M., Malkin, T.: Non-malleable codes from average-case hardness: AC^0, decision trees, and streaming space-bounded tampering. In: Nielsen, J.B., Rijmen, V. (eds.) EUROCRYPT 2018. LNCS, vol. 10822, pp. 618–650. Springer, Cham (2018). https://doi.org/10.1007/978-3-319-78372-7_20

9. Blakley, G.R., Meadows, C.: Security of ramp schemes. In: Blakley, G.R., Chaum, D. (eds.) CRYPTO 1984. LNCS, vol. 196, pp. 242–268. Springer, Heidelberg (1985). https://doi.org/10.1007/3-540-39568-7_20

10. Chattopadhyay, E., Goyal, V., Li, X.: Non-malleable extractors and codes, with their many tampered extensions. In: STOC (2016)

11. Chattopadhyay, E., Li, X.: Non-malleable codes and extractors for small-depth circuits, and affine functions. In: STOC (2017)

12. Chattopadhyay, E., Zuckerman, D.: Non-malleable codes against constant split-state tampering. In: FOCS (2014)

13. Cheraghchi, M., Guruswami, V.: Capacity of non-malleable codes. In: ITCS (2014)

14. Cheraghchi, M., Guruswami, V.: Non-malleable coding against bit-wise and split-state tampering. In: Lindell, Y. (ed.) TCC 2014. LNCS, vol. 8349, pp. 440–464. Springer, Heidelberg (2014). https://doi.org/10.1007/978-3-642-54242-8_19

15. Chvátal, V.: The tail of the hypergeometric distribution. Discret. Math. **25**(3), 285–287 (1979)

16. Cramer, R., Dodis, Y., Fehr, S., Padró, C., Wichs, D.: Detection of algebraic manipulation with applications to robust secret sharing and fuzzy extractors. In: Smart, N. (ed.) EUROCRYPT 2008. LNCS, vol. 4965, pp. 471–488. Springer, Heidelberg (2008). https://doi.org/10.1007/978-3-540-78967-3_27

17. Dziembowski, S., Kazana, T., Obremski, M.: Non-malleable codes from two-source extractors. In: Canetti, R., Garay, J.A. (eds.) CRYPTO 2013. LNCS, vol. 8043, pp. 239–257. Springer, Heidelberg (2013). https://doi.org/10.1007/978-3-642-40084-1_14

18. Dziembowski, S., Pietrzak, K., Wichs, D.: Non-malleable codes. In: ICS (2010)

19. Faust, S., Mukherjee, P., Nielsen, J.B., Venturi, D.: Continuous non-malleable codes. In: Lindell, Y. (ed.) TCC 2014. LNCS, vol. 8349, pp. 465–488. Springer, Heidelberg (2014). https://doi.org/10.1007/978-3-642-54242-8_20

20. Faust, S., Mukherjee, P., Venturi, D., Wichs, D.: Efficient non-malleable codes and key-derivation for poly-size tampering circuits. In: Nguyen, P.Q., Oswald, E. (eds.) EUROCRYPT 2014. LNCS, vol. 8441, pp. 111–128. Springer, Heidelberg (2014). https://doi.org/10.1007/978-3-642-55220-5_7

21. Franklin, M.K., Yung, M.: Communication complexity of secure computation (extended abstract). In: STOC (1992)

22. Goyal, V., Kumar, A.: Non-malleable secret sharing. In: STOC (2018)

23. Goyal, V., Kumar, A.: Non-malleable secret sharing for general access structures. In: Shacham, H., Boldyreva, A. (eds.) CRYPTO 2018. LNCS, vol. 10991, pp. 501–530. Springer, Cham (2018). https://doi.org/10.1007/978-3-319-96884-1_17

24. Gupta, D., Maji, H.K., Wang, M.: Non-malleable codes against lookahead tampering. In: Chakraborty, D., Iwata, T. (eds.) INDOCRYPT 2018. LNCS, vol. 11356, pp. 307–328. Springer, Cham (2018). https://doi.org/10.1007/978-3-030-05378-9_17

25. Hoeffding, W.: Probability inequalities for sums of bounded random variables. J. Am. Stat. Assoc. **58**(301), 13–30 (1963)

26. Jafargholi, Z., Wichs, D.: Tamper detection and continuous non-malleable codes. In: Dodis, Y., Nielsen, J.B. (eds.) TCC 2015. LNCS, vol. 9014, pp. 451–480. Springer, Heidelberg (2015). https://doi.org/10.1007/978-3-662-46494-6_19

27. Kanukurthi, B., Obbattu, S.L.B., Sekar, S.: Four-State non-malleable codes with explicit constant rate. In: Kalai, Y., Reyzin, L. (eds.) TCC 2017. LNCS, vol. 10678, pp. 344–375. Springer, Cham (2017). https://doi.org/10.1007/978-3-319-70503-3_11

28. Kanukurthi, B., Obbattu, S.L.B., Sekar, S.: Non-malleable randomness encoders and their applications. In: Nielsen, J.B., Rijmen, V. (eds.) EUROCRYPT 2018. LNCS, vol. 10822, pp. 589–617. Springer, Cham (2018). https://doi.org/10.1007/978-3-319-78372-7_19

29. Li, X.: Improved non-malleable extractors, non-malleable codes and independent source extractors. In: STOC (2017)

30. Li, X.: Pseudorandom correlation breakers, independence preserving mergers and their applications. In: ECCC 25 (2018)

31. Liu, F.-H., Lysyanskaya, A.: Tamper and leakage resilience in the split-state model. In: Safavi-Naini, R., Canetti, R. (eds.) CRYPTO 2012. LNCS, vol. 7417, pp. 517–532. Springer, Heidelberg (2012). https://doi.org/10.1007/978-3-642-32009-5_30

32. Nisan, N.: Pseudorandom generators for space-bounded computation. In: STOC (1990)

33. Ostrovsky, R., Persiano, G., Venturi, D., Visconti, I.: Continuously non-malleable codes in the split-state model from minimal assumptions. In: Shacham, H., Boldyreva, A. (eds.) CRYPTO 2018. LNCS, vol. 10993, pp. 608–639. Springer, Cham (2018). https://doi.org/10.1007/978-3-319-96878-0_21

34. Shamir, A.: How to share a secret. Commun. ACM **22**(11), 612–613 (1979)

35. Viola, E.: Extractors for circuit sources. In: FOCS (2011)

Continuous Space-Bounded Non-malleable Codes from Stronger Proofs-of-Space

Binyi Chen[1(✉)], Yilei Chen[2(✉)], Kristina Hostáková[3], and Pratyay Mukherjee[2]

[1] University of California, Santa Barbara, USA
binyichen@cs.ucsb.edu
[2] VISA Research, Palo Alto, USA
{yilchen,pratmukh}@visa.com
[3] Technische Universität Darmstadt, Darmstadt, Germany
kristina.hostakova@cs.tu-darmstadt.de

Abstract. Non-malleable codes are encoding schemes that provide protections against various classes of tampering attacks. Recently Faust et al. (CRYPTO 2017) initiated the study of *space-bounded* non-malleable codes that provide such protections against tampering within small-space devices. They put forward a construction based on any *non-interactive proof-of-space (NIPoS)*. However, the scheme only protects against an a priori bounded number of tampering attacks.

We construct non-malleable codes that are resilient to an unbounded polynomial number of space-bounded tamperings. Towards that we introduce a stronger variant of NIPoS called *proof-extractable* NIPoS (PExt-NIPoS), and propose two approaches of constructing such a primitive. Using a new proof strategy we show that the generic encoding scheme of Faust et al. achieves unbounded tamper-resilience when instantiated with a PExt-NIPoS. We show two methods to construct PExt-NIPoS:

1. The first method uses a special family of "memory-hard" graphs, called *challenge-hard graphs* (CHG), a notion we introduce here. We instantiate such family of graphs based on an *extension of* stack of localized expanders (first used by Ren and Devadas in the context of proof-of-space). In addition, we show that the graph construction used as a building block for the proof-of-space by Dziembowski et al. (CRYPTO 2015) satisfies challenge-hardness as well. These two CHG-instantiations lead to continuous space-bounded NMC with different features in the random oracle model.
2. Our second instantiation relies on a new measurable property, called *uniqueness* of NIPoS. We show that standard extractability can be upgraded to proof-extractability if the NIPoS also has uniqueness. We propose a simple heuristic construction of NIPoS, that achieves (partial) uniqueness, based on a candidate memory-hard function in the standard model and a publicly verifiable computation with small-space verification. Instantiating the encoding scheme of Faust et al. with this NIPoS, we obtain a continuous space-bounded NMC

Work done at VISA Research.

A. Boldyreva and D. Micciancio (Eds.): CRYPTO 2019, LNCS 11692, pp. 467–495, 2019.
https://doi.org/10.1007/978-3-030-26948-7_17

that supports the "most practical" parameters, complementing the provably secure but "relatively impractical" CHG-based constructions. Additionally, we revisit the construction of Faust et al. and observe that due to the lack of uniqueness of their NIPoS, the resulting encoding schemes yield "highly impractical" parameters in the continuous setting.

We conclude the paper with a comparative study of all our non-malleable code constructions with an estimation of concrete parameters.

1   Introduction

Non-malleable codes and tamper-resilience. The notion of non-malleable codes (NMC) was put forward by Dziembowski, Pietrzak and Wichs [20] as an abstract tool for protecting cryptographic devices against tampering attacks (e.g. [12]). Intuitively, an encoding scheme (Encode, Decode) is called non-malleable with respect to a class of tampering adversaries (modeled as functions or algorithms) $\mathcal{A}$ if for any adversary A $\in$ $\mathcal{A}$ and any message x, the output Decode ∘ A ∘ Encode(x) is independent of x, unless it is equal to x. It is straightforward to see that $\mathcal{A}$ can not contain all efficiently computable functions because in that case it is always possible to just decode a codeword c to x, modify (for example add 1) and re-encode $x + 1$; hence one must consider a restricted class $\mathcal{A}$ which excludes functions able to encode or decode. Therefore, the NMC literature (for example [1,2,15,16,24,25,29,32]) focuses on constructing encoding schemes that are non-malleable against a meaningful, broad class of tampering functions; notice that non-malleability against a broader $\mathcal{A}$ translates to protection against stronger tampering attacks.

Leaky NMC for space-bounded tampering. One such interesting tampering class is space-bounded tampering, in that the only restriction on $\mathcal{A}$ is that any (efficient) tampering algorithm in this class can only use a limited amount of memory. Space-bounded tampering captures the essence of mauling attacks performed by malware that infect small-space devices like mobile phones. However, as noticed by Faust et al. [22] (henceforth FHMV), for such tampering class it is unreasonable to assume that a tampering algorithm can not decode. For example, if decoding requires more space than what is available for the attacker, then the encoded secret becomes unusable inside the device. The encoding algorithm, on the other hand, can be reasonably space-intense and performed outside the device. Therefore, it is possible to assume the space-bounded adversary cannot perform encoding, therefore avoiding the aforementioned impossibility.

Moreover, even if $\mathcal{A}$ includes only Decode, "full-fledged" non-malleability is still not achievable. To see this, consider an attacker that decodes c, learns the message x and based on the first bit of x overwrites the memory of the device with a precomputed encoding—leaking the first bit (this can be easily extended to an attack that leaks any $\log(|x|)$ bits by tampering once). However, Faust et al. [22] observed that all hope may not be lost if it is possible to guarantee that the leakage is "not too much". Formally FHMV defines a weaker notion called *leaky non-malleability*, which guarantees that an encoding scheme satisfying the notion would leak only a limited amount of information about x. FHMV also showed that this is sufficient for many applications. For example, they showed how one can use such leaky NMC by trading-off tampering with leakage when x comes from a high-entropy distribution (see Section 7 of [23] for more details).

Continuous space-bounded tampering. Traditional NMC (as defined in [20]) guarantees non-malleability when the attacker tampers only once. To use such NMC for tamper-resilience (see [20] for more details), one needs to refresh the encoding after each tampering. To combat this issue, in 2014, Faust et al. [24] proposes the notion of *continuous non-malleable codes* that tolerates an unbounded number of tampering attempts, which consequently removes the necessity of re-encoding in the tampering application. Though FHMV's definition of (leaky) non-malleability allows continuous tampering, their construction (see Theorem 3 of [23]) only allows an a priori bounded number of tampering attempts (say θ) because their parameters are related in a way that the leakage (say, ℓ) is directly proportional to θ. Hence, after a few tampering attempts, the leakage becomes as large as $|x|$. Coming up with a construction that tolerates an unbounded (polynomially large) θ was left open in FHMV (see Remark 2 of [23]).

1.1   Our Work

Leaky NMC for continuous space-bounded tampering. In this work we address the open problem by proposing various constructions of non-malleable codes, in all of which the leakage ℓ is proportional to the logarithm of the number of tamperings, i.e. $\log(\theta)$.[1] No prior bound is required for θ in this case. However, we do not claim that our solutions are strictly stronger than that provided in FHMV, because we assume a "self-destruct" mechanism similar to the prior works on continuous non-malleability (e.g. [24]). Roughly speaking, the "self-destruct" mechanism requires the small-space device to erase its entire state (or make it non-functional) once a tampering is detected. As already shown by FHMV, this is a *necessary* requirement for achieving unbounded continuous space-bounded tampering.

Our approach: Stronger non-interactive proof-of-space. FHMV's encoding scheme relies on any extractable non-interactive proof of space (simply called NIPoS) In contrast, we introduce a *new* and *stronger* property of NIPoS called *proof-extractability* and prove that when FHMV's encoding scheme is instantiated with a proof-extractable NIPoS (PExt-NIPoS), then we obtain a continuous space-bounded NMC (CSNMC). We take two different approaches to construct PExt-NIPoS — in the following few paragraphs we choose to outline them through the natural flow of our attempts, instead of dividing strictly into two distinct approaches.

---

[1] In the rest of the paper whenever we say that an encoding scheme satisfies continuous space-bounded non-malleability or is a CSNMC, we mean that the encoding scheme is a leaky NMC for space-bounded tampering with $\ell \propto \log(\theta)$.

Proof-extractability from any NIPoS with uniqueness. Our starting point is the construction of FHMV [22] which is based on any NIPoS. We show that any NIPoS can be upgraded to a PExt-NIPoS if it has a special property called *uniqueness*, which we define as a quantitative measure of a NIPoS. We notice that the parameters of the resulting PExt-NIPoS (and consequently the CSNMC scheme yielded via FHMV's generic construction) is directly related to the uniqueness parameter of the starting NIPoS. For example, if a NIPoS has "maximal uniqueness", then the resulting CSNMC incurs "minimal leakage", which is equal to $p - |c|$ bits, where $|c|$ is the codeword length and p is the available (persistent) space. Unfortunately, we do not know of a provably secure NIPoS construction with maximal, or even a "reasonably good measure" of uniqueness (later we propose a construction that satisfies partial uniqueness based on heuristic assumptions). In fact, we show that the NIPoS used in FHMV (which is in turn based on the PoS proposed by Ren and Devadas in [38]) has poor uniqueness parameters and thus, when adapted to our proof-extractability technique, yields a CSNMC which suffers from a leakage that is as large as $\approx p - |x|$.

Modeling space-bounded adversary with bounded description. The lack of a NIPoS with "good uniqueness" drives us to revisit the adversarial model of FHMV, in particular, how they formalize the notion of space. In FHMV, which in turn follows the notion introduced by Dziembowski et al. [19], the adversary is separated into two parts: a "big adversary" which is a PPT adversary with no space-bound, and a "small adversary" that is a space-bounded poly-time adversary. In a security game, the big adversary starts interacting with the challenger, and then outputs small adversaries which will then have access to the target codeword (or the proof, in case of NIPoS) and execute tampering in a space-bounded manner.

We notice that FHMV assumes that the small adversary can have arbitrary amount of auxiliary information hardcoded in its description (see Page-5 of [23]). In reality this seems to be an overkill, because if the small adversary (e.g. malware) has a huge description, it might not even fit into a small-space device (e.g. a mobile device), let alone executing tampering. So, it is reasonable to assume that such adversary has a bounded size description. In particular, we define a class of space-bounded adversaries as $\mathcal{A}_{\mathsf{space}}^{s,f}$ containing all poly-time adversaries that have a description of size at most f-bit and which require at most s-bit to execute.

PExt-NIPoS from Challenge-hard Graphs (CHG). We define a new family of "memory-hard graphs" called *challenge-hard-graphs* and construct PExt-NIPoS for the class of space-bounded adversaries $\mathcal{A}_{\mathsf{space}}^{s,f}$ from that. We provide two instantiations of CHG: (i) The first one extends the stack of local expanders (SoLEG), used by Ren and Devadas [38] in the context of proof-of-space. We uses a novel technique to connect a gadget with a standard SoLEG in order to amplify crucial challenge-hardness parameters. This technique may be of independent interest. (ii) The second one uses the graph designed by Paul et al. [37] and used by Dziembowski et al. [17], who use the notion of challenge-hardness *implicitly* to construct proof-of-space. Both of the constructions use standard graph-pebbling techniques to ensure memory-hardness (and challenge-hardness) and work in the random oracle model. Plugging-in these PExt-NIPoS constructions into FHMV's encoding scheme, we obtain CSNMC schemes with "almost minimal leakage" $\ell \approx p - |c|$.

A NIPoS with partial uniqueness based on heuristics. The constructions mentioned above all come with rigorous security proofs (in the random oracle model). However, it turns out that in order to achieve reasonable security, the concrete parameters of these constructions are fairly impractical. For example, for a message of size 1 MB, the size of a codeword is almost 800 MB for the CHG-based NMC constructions. To complement this, we take a step back on our initial idea of constructing NIPoS with "good uniqueness", and propose a simple and practical instantiation of NIPoS based on heuristic assumptions. The construction uses a concrete instantiation of a *memory-hard-function* (MHF), and applies a (non-interactive) publicly verifiable computation where the verification requires small space. When the MHF is instantiated with the SoLEG-based construction of Ren and Devadas [38], the resulting NIPoS has extractability and a "good measure of uniqueness". This yields a PExt-NIPoS with very good parameters and, consequently, plugging-in that to FHMV's encoding scheme we obtain a CSNMC with very small proof size (in kilobytes), that also allows a leakage, as small as $p - 0.99|c|$, in certain settings.

While the above scheme is practical, it is not provably secure, since we can not assume that the hash-functions within the MHF are random oracles, as the prover needs to access the circuit of the MHF to produce a proof of computation. Note that any MHF, while used in practice with concrete hash functions (for example SHA3) for important practical applications [39], provides provable guarantees only in the random oracle model (see, e.g. [6]). Instead, we rely on heuristic assumptions that intuitively state that the MHF remains memory-hard when the random oracle is instantiated with a standard hash function like SHA3.

Roadmap. We summarize our contributions below in Sect. 1.2. In Sect. 1.3 we provide an elaborative technical overview. Then, after providing preliminaries in Sect. 3 and basic definitions of Continuous Space-bounded Tampering in Sect. 4, we define the new NIPoS properties (uniqueness and proof-extractability) in Sect. 5 where we also discuss their relations. In Sect. 6, we show that the FHMV's encoding scheme satisfies continuous space-bounded non-malleability when instantiated with PExt-NIPoS. Section 7 introduces the notion of challenge-hard-graphs and shows how to use them to construct PExt-NIPoS. We provide a heuristic construction of NIPoS with (partial) uniqueness relying on memory-hard functions in Sect. 8 and finally in Sect. 9, we conclude with a instantiations and comparison of the important concrete parameters of different encoding schemes we constructed.

1.2   Summary of Our Contributions

Our overall contributions can be summarized as follows:

– We propose the first constructions of continuous space-bounded (leaky) non-malleable codes (with a necessary "self-destruct" mechanism) and thus resolve an open problem posed by FHMV [22]. Overall we propose *four* different constructions of different merits; we provide a comparison in Table 1:

Table 1. Among the above constructions, the MHF-based one is the most practical one whereas the SoLEG-based one has the best concrete parameters among the provably-secure constructions. For a detail comparison of the concrete parameters please see Table 2 in Sect. 9.

Approach	PExt-NIPoS type	Assumptions	Leakage	Size of A
CHG	SoLEG-based	RO	$\approx p - |c|$	Bounded
	PTC-based	RO	$\approx p - |c|$	Bounded
Uniqueness	FHMV-based	RO	$\approx p - |x|$	Unbounded poly
	MHF-based	Heuristic	$\approx p - 0.99|c|$	Unbounded poly

– We introduce various abstract notions of NIPoS, like *proof-extractability* and *uniqueness*, and show relations among them. The abstractions are targeted towards constructing CSNMC as the main end goal, but may be of independent interests. We prove that the FHMV encoding scheme is a CSNMC when instantiated with any PExt-NIPoS.
– We propose different techniques to construct a PExt-NIPoS. We introduce the notion of *challenge-hard graphs* and show how to build PExt-NIPoS from that. We propose a novel technique to bootstrap the important *challenge-hardness parameters* of a CHG by carefully connecting a gadget to a special type of memory-hard graphs (SoLEG). Furthermore, we provide a simple construction of *partially unique* NIPoS that yields "reasonably practical" parameters for the resulting PExt-NIPoS and CSNMC. It is based on heuristic assumptions on memory-hard functions and complements the provably secure but "relatively impractical" CHG-based constructions.
– Finally we provide a comparative study of the most important parameters of all our CSNMC constructions with respect to concrete instantiations. This helps us to understand the practical impacts of different techniques and constructions proposed in this work.

1.3   Technical Overview

Revisiting FHMV's construction. We start by briefly revisiting the construction of FHMV [22]. Recall that FHMV's generic encoding scheme is based on any extractable (non-interactive) proof-of-space (NIPoS).

First let us briefly recall the notion of proof-of-space introduced in [7,17]. In an interactive proof-of-space (PoS) protocol, a prover P interactively proves that she has "sufficient amount of space/memory" to a space-bounded verifier V. One can use Fiat-Shamir transformation [27] to make it non-interactive, in that the entire proof can be represented as one single string, say π_{id}, with respect to an identity id. The verifier is able to verify the pair (id, π_{id}) within bounded space. Extractability of NIPoS guarantees that: given an honestly generated pair (id, π_{id}), if a space-bounded "small adversary" A is able to compute another valid (i.e. correctly verified) pair $(id', \pi_{id'})$ such that $id \neq id'$, then id' can be *efficiently* extracted from the RO queries made by the "big adversary" B (that has no space-restriction and may be represented by a PPT algorithm) given a "small hint"[2].

Given a NIPoS, FHMV's encoding scheme works as follows. On input a message x, the space-intense encoding algorithm runs the prover of NIPoS on an identity x to generate a proof π_x. The codeword c is simply the pair (x, π_x). The space-bounded decoding algorithm, on receiving $c = (x, \pi_x)$, runs the (space-bounded) verifier. If the verification passes, it returns x, otherwise it returns $\perp$ denoting the invalidity of c. Intuitively, non-malleability follows from the guarantee provided by NIPoS; namely, whenever the small adversary tampers to a valid codeword $(x', \pi_{x'})$, the new message x' must be independent of the input message x.

To be slightly more formal, to show that this encoding scheme is non-malleable against space-bounded attacker, one needs to simulate the tampering experiment with "a small leakage" on x. Given the extractability, the simulator can be constructed as follows: the leakage is obtained using the "small hint". As guaranteed by the extractability of NIPoS, since the "small hint" (of length η, say) is sufficient to extract id', each tampering can be simulated by first obtaining the hint as a leakage and then running the NIPoS-extractor to obtain id'. Clearly, this strategy runs into problem for unbounded continuous tampering as the overall leakage ℓ becomes proportional to $\theta \cdot \eta$ (where θ denotes the number of tampering queries).

Proof-extractability to the recovery. The above discussion shows that we possibly need a stronger guarantee from the underlying NIPoS to make FHMV's encoding scheme a CSNMC. Towards that, we introduce a stronger property of a NIPoS called *proof-extractability* (PExt-NIPoS). It guarantees that, given a "small hint" (of length η', say), it is possible to construct a stronger extractor that extracts not only the changed identity, but also the changed proof: $(id', \pi_{id'})$. Intuitively, this means that if a small adversary computes a valid pair $(id', \pi_{id'})$, then the "big adversary" must have computed the *entire* proof $\pi_{id'}$ (as opposed to a part of the proof as for NIPoS) outside the small-space device; hence, enabling extracting the entire proof from the RO queries made by B only.

---

[2] Note that we made some syntactical change to FHMV's definition of extractability by introducing an explicit hint-producing function. We introduce the length of the hint as a new extractability parameter which must be small for making the definition meaningful. For example, if the leakage function leaks the entire pair (id', π'_{id}), then the definition would be trivially satisfied. Looking ahead, in the proof of CSNMC this hint will be used by the NMC simulator as a leakage to simulate the tampering experiment. For more details we refer to Sect. 5.

Given the proof-extractor, the new NMC simulator works as follows: it uses the hint to get a "small leakage" and then runs the proof-extractor to obtain $(id', \pi_{id'})$. Furthermore, the simulator also needs an extra leakage, which consists of the "extra persistent space" (of size $p - |c|$)—now the simulator reconstructs the entire persistent tampered state and can continue the rest of the tampering experiment without having to make any further leakage query. However, to avoid any leakage before the first tampering takes place (for example, if the first 100 tampering functions are identities), the simulator needs to know the index when the target codeword changes for the first time in the sequence of tampering and for that the leakage becomes proportional to $\log(\theta)$. Overall, the simulator only needs to make a constant number of leakage queries (two, to be precise) to simulate any (polynomial) number of tampering, as opposed to making one leakage query for each tampering. The overall leakage becomes $\ell \propto \log(\theta) + \eta' + (p - |c|)$ thereby achieving CSNMC. Therefore, the main question that remains is how to construct PExt-NIPoS, which will be described in the next few paragraphs.

Uniqueness and Proof-extractability. We observe that, if a NIPoS has a special property, called *uniqueness*, then it satisfies *proof-extractability*. Intuitively, uniqueness means for a fixed identity id, there exists exactly one string π_{id} such that π_{id} verifies correctly with respect to id. Unfortunately, we do not know how to construct a NIPoS with such property (even under heuristic assumptions). Therefore, to have a more relaxed and fine-grained notion, we define uniqueness as a *quantitative measure*: a NIPoS has u_{pos}-uniqueness means that, for any identity id, the first u_{pos} bits of any valid π_{id} are fixed and can be computed efficiently with overwhelming probability.

We then show (in Lemma 1) that any u_{pos}-unique NIPoS satisfies proof-extractability, where the size η' of the hint required for PExt-NIPoS depends on u_{pos} as: $\eta' = \eta + n_{\text{pos}} - u_{\text{pos}}$, where η denotes the size of the hint of the starting NIPoS and n_{pos} denotes the size of the proof. This follows naturally from the construction of the hint-producing function of PExt-NIPoS, as the hint for the proof extractor needs to contain enough information to extract both id' and $\pi_{id'}$. Now id' can be extracted from the hint produced via the starting NIPoS (by standard extractability); given id' the proof-extractor can compute the first u_{pos} bits of $\pi_{id'}$; but the remaining part, which has length $n_{\text{pos}} - u_{\text{pos}}$, must be separately output by the hint-producing function of PExt-NIPoS. Notice that, maximal uniqueness means $u_{\text{pos}} = n_{\text{pos}}$ which in turn implies $\eta' = \eta$. Hence, if FHMV's encoding scheme is instantiated with a maximally unique NIPoS, part of the leakage of the resulting CSNMC would be determined by only η and hence would be minimal. We leave the task of constructing a maximally unique NIPoS as an interesting open problem. On the other hand, we observe that the NIPoS considered by FHMV has $u_{\text{pos}} \approx 0$ and hence the leakage is largely dominated by $\eta + n_{\text{pos}}$, resulting in much worse parameters.

Partially unique-NIPoS from memory-hard functions. We are able to construct an NIPoS with reasonably large u_{pos} from heuristic assumptions on memory-hard functions. The construction is very simple: let M be a concrete instantiation of a memory-hard function, which guarantees that any space-bounded adversary can not compute the function on a randomly chosen input in polynomial time. Let us assume a verifiable computation scheme (VC) where the verification can be done in small-space. Then the NIPoS prover works as follows: given an identity id, first compute a hash (that is assumed to be a random oracle) to generate a random value $x := \mathcal{H}(id)$, then compute $y := M(x)$ and finally run the VC prover to produce a proof π_{vc} to prove that y is indeed obtained by computing $M(x)$. The proof-of-space is then defined to be the pair $(M(x), \pi_{vc})$. The NIPoS verifier works naturally by first computing $x = \mathcal{H}(id)$ and then verifying the proof π_{vc} in small-space.

To see that the construction above yields a NIPoS with good uniqueness, first note that the extractability follows from the fact that the function M is memory-hard and can not be computed on a random input by a space-bounded "small adversary"; hence, the "big adversary" must have queried on id' beforehand enabling extraction of id' from B's RO queries. Note that here we also need to rely on the soundness of VC as otherwise the small adversary could just compute a different "memory-easy" function and "fake" the proof of computation to fool the verifier. Moreover, note that, the first part of the NIPoS proof is indeed uniquely determined (with overwhelming probability any other string would fail to verify as guaranteed by the soundness of the VC scheme), whereas the second part, i.e. the proof π_{vc}, is not. So, overall we have a NIPoS with $u_{pos} = |y|$. Since the VC produces a short proof to enable small-space verification (we use Pinocchio [36] to instantiate), we are able to have a NIPoS with fairly large u_{pos}, which in turn leads to a CSNMC with very good parameters.

PExt-NIPoS from Challenge-hard graphs (CHG). In addition to the heuristic construction above, we also construct a provably secure PExt-NIPoS in the random oracle model, albeit with an additional restriction on the class of space-bounded adversaries, namely assuming that the description size of a small-space adversary is also bounded (as discussed in Sect. 1.1).

To do so, we define a new notion of memory-hard graphs, called challenge-hard graphs (CHG). Recall that, special types of DAGs are used for memory-hardness and for constructing proof-of-space via graph-labeling games. Usually, labels are the output of the hash functions modeled as random oracles (therefore are not "compressible"). In a graph-based proof of space constructions (e.g. [38]), an honest prover computes the labeling of the entire graph ensuring the usage of significant amount of space. Small-space verification is done by checking the labels of a few randomly selected nodes (or challenge nodes) of the graph—this guarantees that the "small adversary" cannot put too many fake labelings (a.k.a. faults) without storing them and thereby ending up using less memory.

However, such verification leaves room for computing a small part of the proof inside the small-space device—for example, consider a multi-layered DAG (e.g. a stack of bipartite graphs), for which a "big adversary" computes the labeling of the entire graph except for *a single* node in the last layer, and the "small adversary" easily computes the label of the node inside the small-space device.

As a result the entire proof can not be extracted only from B's RO queries, making proof-extractability impossible.

To remedy this issue, we replace the traditional memory hard graphs with CHG, which contains another carefully chosen set of challenges and guarantees that, even if a "big adversary" computes the labeling of the entire graph except for a few nodes and send a bounded hint to the "small adversary", it is still infeasible to compute the labels of the new challenge nodes with a small-space device. Let us remark that such a guarantee is only possible when the small adversary has a small description size (i.e., the hint from the "big adversary" is small), as otherwise the small adversary, for example, can hard-code the entire labeling for whole graph including all possible challenges, making challenge hardness impossible. As discussed in Sect. 1.1, we propose two instantiations of CHGs with different merits with respect to their parameters.

2   Related Works

Our work can be categorized among the work on non-malleable codes against global tampering, where the entire codeword is subject to tampering, as opposed to granular tampering, where the codeword is split into independently tamperable parts. In the NMC literature, majority of work, e.g. [1,2,13,15,28,30–32] falls into the the later category; among them [13] considers, a weaker notion (non-malleability with replacement) of NMC like us (leaky-NMC). A few other works, e.g. [5,9,10,26] consider global tampering. Moreover, most of these work consider one-time tampering. Continuous tampering, first proposed in [24], is addressed also in [3,4,21,25,35]. Except FHMV [22], the recent work by Ball et al. [10] also considers space-bounded NMC, albeit in a streaming model. Our modeling of space-bounded adversary, which is also adapted in FHMV is used in earlier woks like [18,19] for constructing different schemes. For more detail on different NMC-based compilers for tamper-resilience we refer to [34].

3   Preliminaries

3.1   Notation

For a string x, we denote its length by $|x|$; a truncated string from i-th bit to j-th bit is denoted by $x[i\ldots j]$; for a $a \in \mathbb{N}$, bit$(a) \in \{0,1\}^*$ is its boolean representation and bit^{-1} is the corresponding inverse function; if $\mathcal{X}$ is a set, $|\mathcal{X}|$ represents the number of elements in $\mathcal{X}$. When x is chosen randomly in $\mathcal{X}$, we write $x \leftarrow_\$ \mathcal{X}$. When A is an algorithm, we write $y \leftarrow \mathsf{A}(x)$ to denote a run of A on input x and output y; if A is probabilistic, then y is a random variable and $\mathsf{A}(x;r)$ denotes a run of A on input x and randomness r. An algorithm A is *probabilistic polynomial-time* (PPT) if A is probabilistic and for any input x and a randomly chosen $r \in \{0,1\}^*$ the computation of $\mathsf{A}(x;r)$ terminates in at most a polynomial (in the input size) number of steps. We often consider *oracle-aided* algorithms $\mathsf{A}^{\mathcal{O}(\cdot)}$, with access to an oracle $\mathcal{O}(\cdot)$.

For any string x, and any hash function $\mathcal{H}$, we use the notation $\mathcal{H}_x$ to denote the specialized hash function that accepts only inputs with prefix equal to x. Often the hash function is modeled as a random oracle.

We consider Turing Machine as our model of computation where any algorithm A is formally represented as a binary string. Any string w hardwired into A is denoted in the subscript as A_w and also becomes part of its description. An algorithm A has a state $st_A \in \{0,1\}^*$ that does not include the description of A. st_A is typically initialized with the input x and (optionally) some other auxiliary information. At each time step st_A is updated. At termination A returns an output y also denoted as $A(x)$. If A is a stateful algorithm then it also outputs the state st_A.

We denote with $\lambda \in \mathbb{N}$ the security parameter. In the rest of the paper λ will always be an implicit security parameter and any other parameter will be a function of λ. A function $\nu : \mathbb{N} \to [0,1]$ is negligible in the security parameter (or simply negligible), denoted $\nu(\lambda) \in \text{negl}(\lambda)$, if it vanishes faster than the inverse of any polynomial in λ, i.e. $\nu(\lambda) = \lambda^{-\omega(1)}$. A function $\mu : \mathbb{N} \to \mathbb{R}$ is a polynomial in the security parameter, written $\mu(\lambda) \in \text{poly}(\lambda)$, if, for some constant $c \geq 1$, we have $\mu(\lambda) \in O(\lambda^c)$.

We defer a few basic definitions to the full version [14].

3.2   Bounded Algorithms

In this paper we will be dealing with algorithms that are restricted in terms of different resources. In particular we consider two main types of resource: time and space. Importantly, in contrast with [22] we split the space-usage into two parts: (i) the space required to store the algorithm and (ii) additional space used by it. Faust et al. [22] only assumes concrete measure of the latter one and the former one was implicitly assumed to be an unbounded polynomial in the security parameter. We formalize the notion of bounded algorithms below.

Definition 1 (Bounded algorithms). *Let* A *be an algorithm such that (i) f-bits arc sufficient to describe the code of* A, *(ii) at any time during its execution, the state of* A *can be described by at most s bits and (iii) on any input,* A *runs for at most t time-steps. Then we say that* A *is a (s, f, t)-bounded algorithm. For such algorithms we have $f_A \leq f, s_A \leq s$ and $t_A \leq t$ (with the obvious meaning). Sometimes, for simplicity, we will call an $(s, \text{poly}(\lambda), \text{poly}(\lambda))$-bounded algorithm just s-space-bounded, an $(s, \text{poly}(\lambda), t)$-bounded algorithm (s, t)-space-time bounded and an $(s, f, \text{poly}(\lambda))$-bounded algorithm (s, f)-total-space-bounded.*

Note that the bound f the size of A is also an upper bound on the hardwired auxiliary information. We stress that, similarly to previous works [18,19], in case A is modeled as a Turing machine, we count the length of the input tape and the position of all the tape heads within the space bound s. Given an input $x \in \{0,1\}^n$, and an initial configuration $\sigma \in \{0,1\}^{s-n}$, we write $(y, \tilde{\sigma}) := A(x; \sigma)$ for the output y of A including its final configuration $\tilde{\sigma} \in \{0,1\}^{s-n}$.

Intuitively, a coding scheme can be decoded in bounded space if the decoding algorithm is space bounded. A formal definition is deferred to full version [14].

4 Continuous Space-Bounded Tampering

Space-bounded Tampering algorithms. We assume that tampering algorithms are deterministic[3], sequential and (s, f)-total-space-bounded, where $s, f \in \mathbb{N}$ are tunable parameters and are usually functions of the security parameter λ. Let us denote the class of all such algorithms by $\mathcal{A}_{\text{space}}^{s,f}$. When the context is clear, we might just refer to $\mathcal{A}_{\text{space}}^{s,f}$ by $\mathcal{A}_{\text{space}}$ for simplicity. Generally any $A \in \mathcal{A}_{\text{space}}^{s,f}$ will be often referred to as a *space-bounded tampering algorithm*.

Oracles. Next we define *space-bounded tampering oracle with self-destruct*. In contrast with [22] (Definition 5) our tampering oracle has the "self-destruct" mechanism.

Definition 2 (Space-bounded Tampering Oracle with Self-destruct). *A space-bounded tampering oracle with self-destruct* $\mathcal{O}_{\text{real-sd}}^{\Pi, x, \text{pp}, s, f, p}$ *is parametrized by a* (k, n)-*code* $\Pi = (\text{Init}^{\mathcal{H}}, \text{Encode}^{\mathcal{H}}, \text{Decode}^{\mathcal{H}})$, *a string* $x \in \{0, 1\}^k$, *public parameters* $\text{pp} \in \{0, 1\}^*$ *and integers* $s, p \in \mathbb{N}$ *(with* $s \geq p \geq n$*). Initially, the oracle assigns a flag* $\text{sd} := 0$, *and sets a state* $\text{st} := (c, \sigma)$, *where* $c := \text{Encode}^{\mathcal{H}}(\text{pp}, x)$, *and* $\sigma := \sigma_0 \| \sigma_1 := 0^{p-n} \| 0^{s-p}$. *Given input a space-bounded tampering algorithm* $A \in \mathcal{A}_{\text{space}}^{s,f}$, *the oracle works as follows:*

Oracle $\mathcal{O}_{\text{real-sd}}^{\Pi, x, \text{pp}, s, f, p}(A)$:

Parse $\text{st} = (c, \sigma_0, \sigma_1)$
$(\tilde{c}, \tilde{\sigma}_0, \tilde{\sigma}_1) := A^{\mathcal{H}}(c; \sigma_0 \| \sigma_1)$
Update $\text{st} := (\tilde{c}, \tilde{\sigma}_0, 0^{s-p})$
$\tilde{x} := \text{Decode}^{\mathcal{H}}(\text{pp}, \tilde{c})$; *If* $\tilde{x} = \bot$ *then* $\text{sd} := 1$
If $\text{sd} = 1$ *return* $\bot$
Return $\tilde{x}$.

We recall from [22] the definitions of the leakage $\mathcal{O}_{\text{leak}}^{\ell, x}$ that can be queried in order to retrieve up-to ℓ bits of information about x and the simulation oracle which would use the leakage oracle to simulate the output of the tampering experiment.

Definition 3 (Leakage oracle). *A leakage oracle* $\mathcal{O}_{\text{leak}}^{\ell, x}$ *is a stateful oracle that maintains a counter* ctr *that is initially set to* 0. *The oracle is parametrized by a string* $x \in \{0, 1\}^k$ *and a value* $\ell \in \mathbb{N}$. *When* $\mathcal{O}_{\text{leak}}^{\ell, x}$ *is invoked on a polynomial-time computable leakage function* L, *the value* $L(x)$ *is computed, its length is added to* ctr, *and if* $\text{ctr} \leq \ell$, *then* $L(x)$ *is returned; otherwise,* $\bot$ *is returned.*

Definition 4 (Simulation oracle). *A simulation oracle* $\mathcal{O}_{\text{sim}}^{S_2, \ell, x, s, f, \text{pp}}$ *is an oracle parametrized by a stateful PPT algorithm* S_2, *values* $\ell, s \in \mathbb{N}$, *some string* $x \in \{0, 1\}^k$, *and public parameters* $\text{pp} \in \{0, 1\}^*$. *Upon input a space-bounded tampering algorithm* $A \in \mathcal{A}_{\text{space}}^{s,f}$, *the output of the oracle is defined as follows.*

---
[3] This is without loss of generality, as in the tampering setting A is chosen by PPT distinguisher D ("big adversary" in our case) who can just hardwires its truly random coin to A.

$Oracle\ \mathcal{O}_{\text{sim}}^{S_2,\ell,x,s,f,\text{pp}}(\mathsf{A}):$

Let $\tilde{x} \leftarrow \mathsf{S}_2^{\mathcal{O}_{\text{leak}}^{\ell,x}(\cdot)}(1^\lambda, \text{pp}, \mathsf{A})$

If $\tilde{x} = \mathsf{same}^\star$ set $\tilde{x} := x.$

Return $\tilde{x}.$

Space-bounded Continuous Non-malleability. Our definition is broadly the same as in [22] with slight modifications: here the real tampering oracle $\mathcal{O}_{\text{real-sd}}$ has self-destruct in it and we consider a concrete non-malleability error-bound ε_{nm}.

Definition 5 (Space-bounded continuous non-malleability with self-destruct). *For parameters $k, n, \ell, s, f, p, \theta, d, n_\mathcal{H} \in \mathbb{N}$ (with $s \geq p \geq n$) and $\varepsilon_{\text{nm}} \in [0,1)$ let $\mathcal{H} : \{0,1\}^* \to \{0,1\}^{n_\mathcal{H}}$ be a random oracle, then we say a (k,n)-code $\Pi = (\mathsf{Init}^\mathcal{H}, \mathsf{Encode}^\mathcal{H}, \mathsf{Decode}^\mathcal{H})$ is an ℓ-leaky (s,f,p)-space-bounded[4] $(\theta, \varepsilon_{\text{nm}})$-continuously non-malleable code with self-destruct with d-space-bounded decoding (or $(\ell, s, f, p, \theta, d, \varepsilon_{\text{nm}})$-SP-NMC-SD) in the ROM if Π satisfies the following conditions:*

- **Space-bounded decoding:** *$\mathsf{Decode}^\mathcal{H}$ is d-space-bounded.*
- $(\ell, \theta, \varepsilon_{\text{nm}})$**-continuous non-malleability:** *For any PPT distinguisher D that makes at most θ queries to the tampering oracle $\mathcal{O}_{\text{real-sd}}$, there exists a pair of PPT algorithms (also called the simulator) $\mathsf{S} = (\mathsf{S}_1, \mathsf{S}_2)$, such that for all $x \in \{0,1\}^k$ and $\lambda \in \mathbb{N}$,*

$$\left| \Pr\left[\mathsf{D}^{\mathcal{H}(\cdot), \mathcal{O}_{\text{real-sd}}^{\Pi,x,\text{pp},s,f,p}(\cdot)}(\text{pp}) = 1 : \text{pp} \leftarrow \mathsf{Init}^\mathcal{H}(1^\lambda) \right] \right.$$

$$\left. - \Pr\left[\mathsf{D}^{\mathsf{S}_1(\cdot), \mathcal{O}_{\text{sim}}^{S_2,\ell,x,s,f,\text{pp}}(\cdot)}(\text{pp}) = 1 : \text{pp} \leftarrow \mathsf{Init}^{S_1}(1^\lambda) \right] \right| \leq \varepsilon_{\text{nm}},$$

the randomness coming from $\mathcal{H}$, Init, D, $\mathsf{S} = (\mathsf{S}_1, \mathsf{S}_2)$ and encoding of $\mathcal{O}_{\text{real-sd}}$.

We are interested in constructing an encoding scheme which satisfies Definition 5 with any choice of $\theta = \text{poly}(\lambda)$. Recall from Section 3.2 of [22] that, in this case, self-destruct is necessary in order to achieve a meaningful notion of non-malleability as otherwise whenever $\theta \geq n$ it is impossible to achieve space-bounded non-malleability for any non-trivial[5] leakage ℓ.

5 Non-Interactive Proof of Space (NIPoS)

As in [22], the main building block of our NMC construction is Non-Interactive Proof of Space (for short NIPoS). Intuitively, a NIPoS allows a prover to convince a verifier that she has a lot of space/memory. Importantly, the verification done on the verifier's side is space efficient.

---

[4] Note that the terminology "space-bounded" is slightly overloaded as we use it both for an encoding scheme as well as for an algorithm (cf. Definition 1).

[5] Recall that for any non-trivial leakage we must have $\ell \leq k - \omega(\log k)$ as otherwise the tampering adversary learns (almost) all information about the input rendering the notion useless.

We start by recalling the definition of NIPoS from [22] adjusted to (s, f, t)-bounded algorithms. We split the definitions completeness and extractability here. Then we define property called *proof-extractability*. We made some syntactical changes to the definition of extractability to align it with the proof-extractability definition. Finally we define a new quantitative measure of NIPoS called *uniqueness* and show that uniqueness, when combined with extractability gives proof-extractability.

Definition 6 (Non-interactive proof of space (NIPoS)). *For parameters* $s_P, s_V, k_{pos}, n_{pos} \in \mathbb{N}$ *with* $s_V \leq s < s_P$ *an* $(k_{pos}, n_{pos}, s_P, s_V)$-*non-interactive proof of space scheme (NIPoS for short) in the ROM consists of a tuple of PPT algorithms* $(\mathsf{Setup}^{\mathcal{H}}, \mathsf{P}^{\mathcal{H}}, \mathsf{V}^{\mathcal{H}})$ *with the following syntax.*

- $\mathsf{Setup}^{\mathcal{H}}(1^\lambda)$: *This is a randomized polynomial-time (in λ) algorithm with no space restriction. It takes as input the security parameter and outputs public parameters* $\mathsf{pp}_{pos} \in \{0,1\}^*$.
- $\mathsf{P}^{\mathcal{H}}_{\mathsf{pp}_{pos}}(id)$: *This is a probabilistic polynomial-time (in λ) algorithm that is s_P-space-bounded. It takes as input an identity* $id \in \{0,1\}^{k_{pos}}$ *and hard-wired public parameters* pp_{pos}, *and it returns a proof of space* $\pi \in \{0,1\}^{n_{pos}}$.
- $\mathsf{V}^{\mathcal{H}}_{\mathsf{pp}_{pos}}(id, \pi)$: *This algorithm is s_V-space-bounded and deterministic. It takes as input an identity id, hard-wired public parameters* pp_{pos}, *and a candidate proof of space π, and it returns a decision bit.*

We require completeness to hold:

Completeness: *For all $id \in \{0,1\}^{k_{pos}}$, we have that*

$$\Pr\left[\mathsf{V}^{\mathcal{H}}_{\mathsf{pp}_{pos}}(id, \pi) = 1 : \mathsf{pp}_{pos} \leftarrow \mathsf{Setup}^{\mathcal{H}}(1^\lambda); \pi \leftarrow \mathsf{P}^{\mathcal{H}}_{\mathsf{pp}_{pos}}(id)\right] = 1,$$

where the probability is taken over the internal random coins of the algorithms Setup *and* P, *and over the choice of the random oracle.*

We define the extractability of a NIPoS separately as follows.

Definition 7 (Extractability of NIPoS). *Let* $\mathsf{NIPoS} = (\mathsf{Setup}^{\mathcal{H}}, \mathsf{P}^{\mathcal{H}}, \mathsf{V}^{\mathcal{H}})$ *be an* $(k_{pos}, n_{pos}, s_P, s_V)$-*non-interactive proof of space scheme. Let* $s, f, t, \eta \in \mathbb{N}$ *and* $\varepsilon_{pos} \in [0,1)$ *be parameters with* $s_V \leq s < s_P$. *Then we say that* NIPoS *is* $(s, f, t, \eta, \varepsilon_{pos})$-*extractable (Ext-NIPoS) if there exists a polynomial-time deterministic algorithm* K *(the knowledge extractor) and a deterministic efficiently computable function* $F_{hint} : \{0,1\}^* \to \{0,1\}^\eta$ *such that for any probabilistic polynomial-time algorithm* B, *we have*

$$\Pr[\mathbf{G}^{ext}_{\mathsf{B},id}(\lambda) = 1] \leq \varepsilon_{pos},$$

for the game $\mathbf{G}^{ext}_{\mathsf{B},id}(\lambda)$ *defined as follows:*

Game $\mathbf{G}^{ext}_{\mathsf{B},id}(\lambda)$:

1. *Sample* $\mathsf{pp}_{pos} \leftarrow \mathsf{Setup}^{\mathcal{H}}(1^\lambda)$ *and* $\pi \leftarrow \mathsf{P}^{\mathcal{H}}_{\mathsf{pp}_{pos}}(id)$.

2. Let $\mathsf{A} \leftarrow \mathsf{B}^{\mathcal{H}}_{\mathsf{pp}_{\mathsf{pos}}}(id, \pi)$ such that $\mathsf{A} \in \mathcal{A}^{s,f}_{\mathsf{space}}$ (if this condition fails, then output 0 and stop).
3. Let $(\tilde{id}, \tilde{\pi}) := \mathsf{A}^{\mathcal{H}}(id, \pi)$.
4. Let $z := F_{\mathsf{hint}}(\mathsf{pp}_{\mathsf{pos}}, \mathcal{Q}_{\mathcal{H}}(\mathsf{B}), \tilde{id})$.
5. Let $\alpha := \mathsf{K}(\mathsf{pp}_{\mathsf{pos}}, \mathcal{Q}_{\mathcal{H}}(\mathsf{B}), z)$.
6. Output 1 if and only if: (i) $\mathsf{V}^{\mathcal{H}}_{\mathsf{pp}_{\mathsf{pos}}}(\tilde{id}, \tilde{\pi}) = 1$; (ii) $\tilde{id} \neq id$ and (iii) $\tilde{id} \neq \alpha$; otherwise output 0,

where the set $\mathcal{Q}_{\mathcal{H}}(\mathsf{B})$ contains the sequence of queries of B to $\mathcal{H}$ and the corresponding answers, and where the probability is taken over the coin tosses of $\mathsf{Setup}, \mathsf{B}, \mathsf{P}$ and over the choice of the random oracle.

Extractability guarantees that if the space bounded adversary A successfully tampers to a new pair $(\tilde{id}, \tilde{\pi})$, the identity $\tilde{id}$ can be extracted from the query table of the algorithm B, i.e., the pair $(\tilde{id}, \tilde{\pi})$ was (partially) precomputed by B. Let us stress that knowledge of $\tilde{id}$ does not generally imply knowledge of the entire pair $(\tilde{id}, \tilde{\pi})$. This is because there might be many different $\tilde{\pi}$ for which $\mathsf{V}^{\mathcal{H}}_{\mathsf{pp}_{\mathsf{pos}}}(\tilde{id}, \tilde{\pi}) = 1$, unless, of course, there is a unique such $\tilde{\pi}$. In order guarantee extraction of the entire pair $(\tilde{id}, \tilde{\pi})$, we need NIPoS to satisfy a stronger extractability property, which we call Proof-Extractability and define next.

Definition 8 (Proof-Extractability of NIPoS). Let $\mathsf{NIPoS} := (\mathsf{Setup}^{\mathcal{H}}, \mathsf{P}^{\mathcal{H}}, \mathsf{V}^{\mathcal{H}})$ be a $(k_{\mathsf{pos}}, n_{\mathsf{pos}}, s_{\mathsf{P}}, s_{\mathsf{V}})$-non-interactive proof of space scheme. Let $s, f, t, \eta \in \mathbb{N}$ and $\varepsilon_{\mathsf{p\text{-}ext}} \in [0, 1)$ be parameters such that $s_{\mathsf{V}} \leq s < s_{\mathsf{P}}$. Then NIPoS is called $(s, f, t, \eta, \varepsilon_{\mathsf{p\text{-}ext}})$-proof extractable (PExt-NIPoS) if there exists a polynomial time deterministic algorithm K (the proof-extractor) and an efficiently computable deterministic function $F_{\mathsf{hint}} : \{0, 1\}^* \rightarrow \{0, 1\}^\eta$ such that for any PPT algorithm B and any identity $id \in \{0, 1\}^{k_{\mathsf{pos}}}$, it holds that

$$\Pr[\mathbf{G}^{\mathsf{pext}}_{\mathsf{B}, id}(\lambda) = 1] \leq \varepsilon_{\mathsf{p\text{-}ext}},$$

for the game $\mathbf{G}^{\mathsf{pext}}_{\mathsf{B}, id}(\lambda)$ defined as follows:

Game $\mathbf{G}^{\mathsf{pext}}_{\mathsf{B}, id}(\lambda)$:

1. Sample $\mathsf{pp}_{\mathsf{pos}} \leftarrow \mathsf{Setup}^{\mathcal{H}}(1^\lambda)$ and $\pi \leftarrow \mathsf{P}^{\mathcal{H}}_{\mathsf{pp}_{\mathsf{pos}}}(id)$.
2. Let $\mathsf{A} \leftarrow \mathsf{B}^{\mathcal{H}}_{\mathsf{pp}_{\mathsf{pos}}}(id, \pi)$ such that $\mathsf{A} \in \mathcal{A}^{s,f}_{\mathsf{space}}$ (if this condition fails, then output 0 and stop).
3. Let $(\tilde{id}, \tilde{\pi}) := \mathsf{A}^{\mathcal{H}}(id, \pi)$.
4. Let $z := F_{\mathsf{hint}}(\mathsf{pp}_{\mathsf{pos}}, \mathcal{Q}_{\mathcal{H}}(\mathsf{B}), (\tilde{id}, \tilde{\pi}))$
5. Let $\alpha := \mathsf{K}(\mathsf{pp}_{\mathsf{pos}}, \mathcal{Q}_{\mathcal{H}}(\mathsf{B}), z)$
6. Output 1 if and only if: (i) $\mathsf{V}^{\mathcal{H}}_{\mathsf{pp}_{\mathsf{pos}}}(\tilde{id}, \tilde{\pi}) = 1$; (ii) $\tilde{id} \neq id$ and (iii) $(\tilde{id}, \tilde{\pi}) \neq \alpha$; otherwise output 0,

where the set $\mathcal{Q}_{\mathcal{H}}(\mathsf{B})$ is the random oracle query table of B.[6] The probability is over the choice of the random oracle, and the coin tosses of $\mathsf{Setup}, \mathsf{B}$.

---

[6] Note that B does not make RO queries after outputting the small adversary A.

Remark 1. Note that, in the above definition the hint-producing function takes the pair $(\tilde{id}, \tilde{\pi})$ as opposed to only $\tilde{id}$ as in Definition 7. Intuitively this means that, given some small hint, the extractor does not only return the changed identity, but the identity-proof pair. Clearly this makes the latter definition stronger.

As mentioned above, when there is a unique valid proof corresponding to each identity, then proof-extractability reduces to simply extractability. Nevertheless, it may also be possible that only a part of the proof is uniquely determined. We formalize this by the following definition.

Definition 9 (Uniqueness of NIPoS). *Let* NIPoS $:= (\text{Setup}^{\mathcal{H}}, \text{P}^{\mathcal{H}}, \text{V}^{\mathcal{H}})$ *be a* $(k_{\text{pos}}, n_{\text{pos}}, s_{\text{P}}, s_{\text{V}})$-*NIPoS. Then* NIPoS *is called* $(u_{\text{pos}}, \varepsilon_{\text{unique}})$-*unique (where* $u_{\text{pos}} \leq n_{\text{pos}}$, $u_{\text{pos}} \in \mathbb{N}$ *and* $\varepsilon_{\text{unique}} \in \text{negl}(\lambda))$ *if for any* $\lambda \in \mathbb{N}$, *there is a deterministic function* $J : \{0,1\}^* \times \{0,1\}^{k_{\text{pos}}} \to \{0,1\}^{u_{\text{pos}}}$ *such that for* $\text{pp}_{\text{pos}} \leftarrow \text{Setup}^{\mathcal{H}}(\lambda)$, *any identity* $id \in \{0,1\}^{k_{\text{pos}}}$ *and any* $\pi \in \{0,1\}^{n_{\text{pos}}}$, *if* $\text{V}_{\text{pp}}^{\mathcal{H}}(id, \pi) = 1$, *then* $J(\text{pp}_{\text{pos}}, id) = \pi[1 \ldots u_{\text{pos}}]$ *with probability at least* $1 - \varepsilon_{\text{unique}}$ *(where the probability is over the randomnesses of* $\text{Setup}^{\mathcal{H}}$ *and* $\text{P}^{\mathcal{H}}$).

Remark 2. Intuitively, the definition says that for a valid proof π, a part of π (first u_{pos} bits in this case) can be *uniquely* and *efficiently* determined given the id and the public parameters pp with overwhelming probability.

In the following lemma, we formally show that uniqueness and extractability together imply proof-extractability. To see this, observe that, e.g., maximal uniqueness implies that given $\tilde{id}$, the corresponding $\pi_{\tilde{id}}$ is fixed and hence it suffices to provide the PExt-NIPoS hint-producer only with $\tilde{id}$.

Lemma 1. *Let* NIPoS $:= (\text{Setup}^{\mathcal{H}}, \text{P}^{\mathcal{H}}, \text{V}^{\mathcal{H}})$ *be a* $(k_{\text{pos}}, n_{\text{pos}}, s_{\text{P}}, s_{\text{V}})$-*NIPoS that is* $(u_{\text{pos}}, \varepsilon_{\text{unique}})$-*unique and* $(s, f, t, \eta, \varepsilon_{\text{pos}})$-*extractable. Then* NIPoS *is* $(s, f, t, \eta',$ $\varepsilon_{\text{p-ext}})$-*proof-extractable where*

$$\eta' = \eta + n_{\text{pos}} - u_{\text{pos}} \qquad \varepsilon_{\text{p-ext}} \leq \varepsilon_{\text{pos}} + \varepsilon_{\text{unique}}$$

The proof is deferred to the full version [14].

6   Space-Bounded NMC from Proof-Extractable NIPoS

The following theorem, which is proven in the full version [14], states that the above construction is a continuous non-malleable code for any $\theta \in \text{poly}(\lambda)$.

Theorem 1. *Let* λ *be a security parameter and* $\mathcal{H}$: $\{0,1\}^* \to \{0,1\}^{n_{\mathcal{H}}}$ *be a hash function modeled as a random oracle. Let* $\{\text{PRF}_\chi : \{0,1\}^* \to \{0,1\}^{n_{\mathcal{H}}}\}_{\chi \in \{0,1\}^{n_{\text{key}}}}$ *be any* $(*, n_{\mathcal{H}}, n_{\text{key}}, \varepsilon_{\text{pr}})$-*PRF, (defined formally in full version [14]) where* $n_{\text{key}} \in \text{poly}(\lambda)$. *Let* $(\text{Setup}^{\mathcal{H}}, \text{P}^{\mathcal{H}}, \text{V}^{\mathcal{H}})$ *be any* $(k_{\text{pos}}, n_{\text{pos}}, s_{\text{P}}, s_{\text{V}})$-*NIPoS that is* $(s, f, \text{poly}(\lambda), \eta, \varepsilon_{\text{p-ext}})$-*proof-extractable. Then for any* $\theta \in \text{poly}(\lambda)$, the (k,n)-code $\Pi = (\mathsf{Init}^{\mathcal{H}}, \mathsf{Encode}^{\mathcal{H}}, \mathsf{Decode}^{\mathcal{H}})$ defined above is an $(\ell, s, f, p, \theta, s_{\mathsf{V}}, \varepsilon_{\mathsf{nm}})$-SP-NMC-SD in the ROM, where

$$k = k_{\mathsf{pos}} \qquad n = k_{\mathsf{pos}} + n_{\mathsf{pos}} \qquad k_{\mathsf{pos}} + n_{\mathsf{pos}} \le p < n + k - O(\log(\lambda))$$
$$\ell = p - n + \lceil \log \theta \rceil + \eta + 2 \qquad \varepsilon_{\mathsf{nm}} = \varepsilon_{\mathsf{pr}} + \varepsilon_{\mathsf{p\text{-}ext}}$$

The above theorem together with Lemma 1 imply that the encoding scheme of Faust et al. satisfies Definition 5 also when instantiated with any Ext-NIPoS with (partial) uniqueness. This is formalized in the following corollary:

Corollary 1. *Let λ be a security parameter and $\mathcal{H} : \{0,1\}^* \to \{0,1\}^{n_{\mathcal{H}}}$ be a hash function modeled as a random oracle. Let $\{\mathsf{PRF}_{\chi} : \{0,1\}^* \to \{0,1\}^{n_{\mathcal{H}}}\}_{\chi \in \{0,1\}^{n_{\mathsf{key}}}}$ be any $(*, n_{\mathcal{H}}, n_{\mathsf{key}}, \varepsilon_{\mathsf{pr}})$-PRF where $n_{\mathsf{key}} \in \mathrm{poly}(\lambda)$. Let $(\mathsf{Setup}^{\mathcal{H}}, \mathsf{P}^{\mathcal{H}}, \mathsf{V}^{\mathcal{H}})$ be any $(k_{\mathsf{pos}}, n_{\mathsf{pos}}, s_{\mathsf{P}}, s_{\mathsf{V}})$-NIPoS that is $(s, \mathrm{poly}(\lambda), \mathrm{poly}(\lambda), \eta, \varepsilon_{\mathsf{pos}})$-extractable and $(u_{\mathsf{pos}}, \varepsilon_{\mathsf{unique}})$-unique. Then for any $\theta \in \mathrm{poly}(\lambda)$, the (k,n)-code $\Pi = (\mathsf{Init}^{\mathcal{H}}, \mathsf{Encode}^{\mathcal{H}}, \mathsf{Decode}^{\mathcal{H}})$ of FHMV is an $(\ell, s, \mathrm{poly}(\lambda), p, \theta, s_{\mathsf{V}}, \varepsilon_{\mathsf{nm}})$-SP-NMC-SD in the ROM, where*

$$k = k_{\mathsf{pos}} \qquad n = k_{\mathsf{pos}} + n_{\mathsf{pos}} \qquad k_{\mathsf{pos}} + n_{\mathsf{pos}} \le p < n + k - O(\log(\lambda))$$
$$\ell = p - k - u_{\mathsf{pos}} + \lceil \log \theta \rceil + \eta + 2 \qquad \varepsilon_{\mathsf{nm}} = \varepsilon_{\mathsf{pr}} + \varepsilon_{\mathsf{pos}} + \varepsilon_{\mathsf{unique}}.$$

7 Constructing Proof-Extractable NIPoS from CHG

7.1 Challenge-Hard Graphs (CHG)

In this section we introduce the concept of *challenge-hard graphs* (CHG for short) which we use it to construct proof-extractable NIPoS. We remark that the notion of challenge hardness has similarities with a notion introduced in [17]. In particular, in Section 4 of [17], the authors informally described a pebbling game which is similar to the game in our notion (Definition 10).

Challenge hard graphs are parameterized by the following variables: $N_c, \beta, N, \tau_c, t, \varepsilon$, where N is the size of the graph; τ_c is the number of challenge nodes, where all the challenges are in a pre-defined target set V_c; N_c is the size of the target set V_c; $\beta \cdot N_c = \Omega(N_c)$ is the budget on the number of pebbles available; t is an upper bound on the running time of pebbling strategies; and ε is an upper bound on the winning probability of the pebbling challenge game.

Definition 10 (Challenge Hard Graphs (CHG)). *A family of directed acyclic graphs $\{G_\lambda\}_{\lambda \in \mathbb{N}}$ (with constant in-degree)[7] is $(\beta, N_c, N, \tau_c, t, \varepsilon)$-challenge-hard (where $\beta \in (0,1)$ is a constant, and other parameters are functions of λ),*

---

[7] We require the in-degree of the graph to be a constant, because for graph-labeling in the ROM this captures the essence of the standard model. To see this assume that $\mathcal{H}$ is implemented by an iteration-based scheme (e.g., Merkle-Damgård extension), and thereby to compute the hash output, it is sufficient to store only a few labels at each iteration step. However, while in the ROM computing a label $\mathsf{label}(v) := \mathcal{H}(v, \mathsf{label}(\mathsf{pred}(v)))$ is only possible if the entire labeling $\mathsf{label}(\mathsf{pred}(v))$ is stored. If the in-degree is high (e.g. super-constant) this distinction would affect the parameters. We refer to Appendix B.3 in [11] for more discussions.

if for every $\lambda \in \mathbb{N}$ *and graph* $G = G_\lambda = (V, E)$ *(with* $N = N(\lambda)$ *vertices), there exist* τ_c *target sets (possibly with overlapping)* $V_c^{(1)}, \ldots, V_c^{(\tau_c)} \subseteq V$ *such that the union of the target sets*

$$V_c := V_c^{(1)} \cup \cdots \cup V_c^{(\tau_c)} \subseteq V$$

has N_c *vertices, and the following property is satisfied:*

For any pebbling strategy $\mathsf{B} = (\mathsf{B}_1, \mathsf{B}_2)$ *it holds that*

$$\mathsf{Adv}^{\mathsf{peb}}_{\mathsf{B},\beta,t,\tau_c,G}(\lambda) := \Pr\left[\mathbf{G}^{\mathsf{peb}}_{\mathsf{B},\beta,t,\tau_c,G}(\lambda) = 1\right] \leq \varepsilon,$$

where the pebbling game $\mathbf{G}^{\mathsf{peb}}_{\mathsf{B},\beta,t,\tau_c,G}(\lambda)$ *is defined as follows.*

Game $\mathbf{G}^{\mathsf{peb}}_{\mathsf{B},\beta,t,\tau_c,G}(\lambda)$:

1. *Let* $P_0 \leftarrow \mathsf{B}_1$ *be a pebbling configuration, where* $|P_0| \leq \beta \cdot N_c$.
2. *Let* $\mathsf{chal} \leftarrow \mathcal{D}^{\tau_c}$ *be* τ_c *random challenge vertices (possibly with overlapping), where* $\mathcal{D}^{\tau_c}$ *is the uniform distribution over* $V_c^1 \times \cdots \times V_c^{(\tau_c)}$.
3. *Let* $\mathbf{P} = (P_0, \ldots, P_{t(\mathbf{P})}) \leftarrow \mathsf{B}_2(P_0, \mathsf{chal})$ *be a pebbling strategy.*
4. *Output 1 iff*
   - $\mathbf{P}$ *follows the rule of a sequential pebbling strategy.*
   - *For every* $i \in \{0, \ldots, t(\mathbf{P})\}$, *it holds that* $|P_i| \leq \beta \cdot N_c$.
   - $\mathsf{chal} \subseteq P_0 \cup \cdots \cup P_{t(\mathbf{P})}$.
   - $t(\mathbf{P}) \leq t$.

We define N_c/τ_c *and* N/N_c *as the* **challenge sparseness** *and* **graph compactness** *of* G.

Intuitively, challenge sparseness defines what fraction of the target nodes will be challenged. Graph compactness determines what fraction of all node in the graph are in the target set. Looking ahead, these two metrics of CHG will play crucial roles in determining the parameters of the NIPoS and the encoding schemes.

7.2   Construction of PExt-NIPoS from CHG

Now we present our main PExt-NIPoS construction based on challenge-hard graphs and show that it satisfies proof-extractability. The construction is quite similar to the one presented in [22] with only a few minor modifications.

The scheme consists of three algorithms $(\mathsf{Setup}^\mathcal{H}, \mathsf{P}^\mathcal{H}, \mathsf{V}^\mathcal{H})$ that use the following ingredients:

- a DAG $G = (V, E)$ with $N = |V|$ vertices and maximal in-degree $\deg \in O(1)$, which has τ_c target sets $V_c^{(1)}, \ldots, V_c^{(\tau_c)} \subseteq V$ such that

$$V_c := V_c^{(1)} \cup \cdots \cup V_c^{(\tau_c)} \subseteq V$$

and V_c has N_c vertices.

– a set of random oracles $\{\mathcal{H}_{id}\}_{id \in \{0,1\}^{k_{pos}}} \cup \{\mathcal{H}_{com}\} \cup \{\mathcal{H}_{chal}\}$ defined as follows: $\mathcal{H}_{id} : \{0,1\}^{\leq \log N + \deg \cdot n_{\mathcal{H}}} \rightarrow \{0,1\}^{n_{\mathcal{H}}}$ for every $id \in \{0,1\}^{k_{pos}}$; $\mathcal{H}_{com}$: $\{0,1\}^{2n_{\mathcal{H}}} \rightarrow \{0,1\}^{n_{\mathcal{H}}}$; $\mathcal{H}_{chal}$ takes as input a $\{0,1\}^{k_{pos}+n_{\mathcal{H}}}$-bit string and outputs a random challenge set check plus τ_c challenge nodes:

$$(\text{check}, \text{chal} := (\text{chal}_1, \ldots, \text{chal}_{\tau_c})) \in V^\tau \times V_c^{(1)} \times \cdots \times V_c^{(\tau_c)} \,.$$

For simplicity of explanation, we assume that the output length of $\mathcal{H}_{chal}$ is exactly $n_{\mathcal{H}}$ (where $n_{\mathcal{H}} \geq \tau \cdot \log |V| + \tau_c \cdot \log |V_c|$), and we define the corresponding challenge sets (check, chal) as the first $\tau \cdot \log |V| + \tau_c \cdot \log |V_c|$ bits of the RO output.[8] Note that by a typical domain separation technique (e.g., used in [7] and [33]), we can instantiate the three random oracles using a unified random oracle $\mathcal{H} : \{0,1\}^* \rightarrow \{0,1\}^{n_{\mathcal{H}}}$.

The construction is presented in detail in Fig. 1. We provide a high-level overview here. The prover first computes the labeling of a graph $G = (V, E)$, and then commits the labeling using a Merkle tree. From the merkle root value $\tilde{\phi}_\ell$, the prover computes the Fiat-Shamir challenge $\mathcal{H}(\tilde{\phi}_\ell)$, which consists of two sets (check, chal). The set check contains τ random nodes in V, and the set chal has τ_c random nodes in a target set $V_c \subseteq V$. The proof is the Merkle tree opening paths for nodes in check $\cup$ pred(check) $\cup$ chal, where pred(check) are the parents of nodes in check.

Memory usage of the prover and the verifier. In our PExt-NIPoS construction, the honest prover has to store the complete labeling of the graph G plus the entire Merkle tree, thus the size of the prover's space is

$$s_{\mathsf{P}} := N \cdot n_{\mathcal{H}} + (N - 1) \cdot n_{\mathcal{H}} \,,$$

where $n_{\mathcal{H}}$ is the random oracle output length. On the other hand, the verifier only needs to store a single proof-of-space, which consists of a Merkle root value, two challenge sets, and $\tau \cdot (\deg + 1) + \tau_c$ tree paths. Since each tree path is of length $\log N$, the size of the verifier's space is given by:

$$s_{\mathsf{V}} := n_{\mathcal{H}} + \tau \cdot \log N + \tau_c \cdot \log N_c + (\tau \cdot (\deg + 1) + \tau_c) \cdot \log N \cdot n_{\mathcal{H}} \,.$$

It is not hard to see that our PExt-NIPoS scheme satisfies *completeness*.

Theorem 2. *Let λ be a security parameter. Suppose $G := G_{\text{HARD}}$ is a $(\beta, N_c, N, \tau_c, t, \epsilon_{\text{peb}})$-challenge hard graph with indegree $\deg = O(1)$, let $\gamma_{\text{sp}} = N_c/\tau_c$ and $\gamma_{\text{cp}} = N/N_c$ denote the challenge sparseness and graph compactness of G. $\mathcal{H} : \{0,1\}^* \rightarrow \{0,1\}^{n_{\mathcal{H}}}$ is a hash function modeled as a random oracle; and Π_G is a (τ_c, τ, ν)-Merkle-tree-based PExt-NIPoS scheme (defined in Fig. 1) built upon G, where*

$$\nu := (\tau \cdot (\deg + 1) + \tau_c) \cdot \log N + 1 \approx N_c \log N / \gamma_{\text{sp}} \,.$$

---

[8] For ease of explanation, we assume that $|V|$ and $|V_c|$ are powers of 2.

PExt-NIPoS Construction

$\mathsf{Setup}^{\mathcal{H}}(1^\lambda)$: On input the security parameter 1^λ output a set of public parameters $\mathsf{pp_{pos}} \in \{0,1\}^*$, which consist of values $\tau, \tau_c, N_c, N \in \mathbb{N}$, the DAG G as described above.

$\mathsf{P}^{\mathcal{H}}_{\mathsf{pp_{pos}}}(id)$: Given public parameters $\mathsf{pp_{pos}} \in \{0,1\}^*$ and identity $id \in \{0,1\}^{k_{\mathsf{pos}}}$, do as follows:

1. For every node $v \in V$, compute a $\mathcal{H}_{id}$-labeling of v as $\mathsf{label}(v) := \mathcal{H}_{id}(v, \mathsf{label}(\mathsf{pred}(v)))$, where $\mathsf{label}(\mathsf{pred}(v))$ are the $\mathcal{H}_{id}$-labelings of v's parents in G. Let $\ell := (\mathsf{label}(v))_{v \in V} \in \{0,1\}^{N \cdot n_{\mathcal{H}}}$ be the $\mathcal{H}_{id}$-labeling of the graph G.

2. Given labeling ℓ compute the Merkle commitment $\phi_\ell := \mathsf{MCom}^{\mathcal{H}_{\mathsf{com}}}(\ell)$, where $\phi_\ell \in \{0,1\}^{n_{\mathcal{H}}}$ is the Merkle root.

3. Determine the set of challenges $(\mathsf{check}, \mathsf{chal}) := \mathcal{H}_{\mathsf{chal}}(id, \phi_\ell)$.

4. Output the proof-of-space π which consists of two parts:
   - The Merkle-root value and the two challenge sets

$$(\phi_\ell, \mathsf{check}, \mathsf{chal}) \in \{0,1\}^{n_{\mathcal{H}}} \times V^\tau \times V_c^{(1)} \times \cdots \times V_c^{(\tau_c)}.$$

   - Let $\mathsf{pred}(\mathsf{check})$ be the set of predecessors for nodes in check. For every node $v \in \mathsf{check} \cup \mathsf{pred}(\mathsf{check}) \cup \mathsf{chal}$, output the Merkle-tree opening path from the v-th leaf (with label $\mathsf{label}(v)$) to the Merkle-root (with value ϕ_ℓ): $\mathsf{MOpen}^{\mathcal{H}_{\mathsf{com}}}(\ell, v)$.

$\mathsf{V}^{\mathcal{H}}_{\mathsf{pp_{pos}}}(id, \pi)$: Given public parameters $\mathsf{pp_{pos}}$, identity $id \in \{0,1\}^{k_{\mathsf{pos}}}$ and a *candidate* proof-of-space $\pi \in \{0,1\}^{n_{\mathsf{pos}}}$, check the correctness of π with respec to id as follows:

1. Parse
$$\left[(\phi_\ell, \mathsf{check}, \mathsf{chal}), \left\{\left(z_v; (y_v^{(1)}, \ldots, y_v^{(\log N)})\right)\right\}_{v \in \mathsf{check} \cup \mathsf{pred}(\mathsf{check}) \cup \mathsf{chal}}\right] := \pi$$

2. Check $(\mathsf{check}, \mathsf{chal}) = \mathcal{H}_{\mathsf{chal}}(id, \phi_\ell)$.

3. For every node $v \in \mathsf{check}$, denote by z_v the opening for v, and $z_{\mathsf{pred}(v)}$ the openings for v's parents in graph G. The check: $z_v = \mathcal{H}_{id}(v, z_{\mathsf{pred}(v)})$

4. For every node $v \in \mathsf{check} \cup \mathsf{pred}(\mathsf{check}) \cup \mathsf{chal}$, denote by $(z_v, (y_v^{(1)}, \ldots, y_v^{(\log N)}))$ the opening path for v, V checks that
$$\mathsf{MVer}^{\mathcal{H}_{\mathsf{com}}}(v, \phi_\ell, z_v, (y_v^{(1)}, \ldots, y_v^{(\log N)})) = 1.$$

5. Output 1 if and only if all of the above check passes; otherwise output 0.

Fig. 1. Our PExt-NIPoS construction: Denoting by ν the number of RO input-output pairs in the proof we call this construction a (τ_c, τ, ν)-**Merkle-tree-based PExt-NIPoS** scheme built upon the DAG G.

For any $s, f \in \mathbb{N}$ such that there exists a constant $\delta^* \in (0,1)$ where

$$s + f \leq (\beta - \delta^* - 0.01) \cdot N_c \cdot n_{\mathcal{H}},$$

it holds that Π_G is a $(k_{pos}, n_{pos}, s_P, s_V)$-NIPoS that is $(s, f, t, \eta, \varepsilon_{p\text{-}ext})$-proof-extractable, as long as[9]

$$s_P \geq k_{pos} + (2N - 1) \cdot n_{\mathcal{H}} \qquad s \geq s_V \geq k_{pos} + \nu \cdot n_{\mathcal{H}} \qquad \eta = O(\nu \log \lambda)$$

$$n_{pos} = \nu \cdot n_{\mathcal{H}} \qquad \varepsilon_{p\text{-}ext} \leq \mathrm{poly}(\lambda) \cdot \left(2^{-n_{\mathcal{H}}} + \exp(-\kappa) + \epsilon_{peb}\right),$$

where $\kappa = \tau \cdot \delta^* \cdot N_c / N = \tau \cdot \delta^* / \gamma_{cp}$.

Remark 3. To guarantee that the verifier space $s_V \approx \nu \cdot n_{\mathcal{H}}$ is smaller than the tampering space $s \approx N_c \cdot n_{\mathcal{H}}$, we need the underlying CHG to be **at least** $\Omega(\log N)$-challenge sparse (defined as N_c / τ_c).

7.3   Instantiating CHG

We propose two instantiations (details deferred to full version [14]). First, we provide a new construction of CHG from Stack of Localized Expander Graphs (SoLEG) (see the full version [14] for details on SoLEGs) used by Ren and Devadas [38] in the context of proof-of-space. We use a novel technique to construct an **extension of SoLEG** by connecting a gadget in order to "boot-strap" challenge sparseness. Second, as observed by [17] (in Section 6.1 of [17]), the graph introduced by Paul, Tarjan and Celoni [37] (in short, **PTC's graph**) does satisfy challenge hardness.

7.4   Instantiations of PExt-NIPoS from CHGs

We obtain two PExt-NIPoS constructions by plugging-in the parameters from two CHG constructions, namely the SoLEG-extension and the PTC's graph respectively into Theorem 2. The details of the concrete instantiations and the comparison of the two PExt-NIPoS constructions are deferred to full version [14].

8   PExt-NIPoS from Memory-Hard Functions

In this section we propose a simple construction of NIPoS with extractability. Our construction is based on memory-hard functions (MHF for short) and verifiable computations.

8.1   Memory-Hard Functions

Here we formalize memory-hard functions. The definition of our second building block, publicly verifiable computation, can be found in full version [14].

Definition 11 (Memory-hard Functions (MHF)). *Let $\mathcal{H} : \{0,1\}^* \rightarrow \{0,1\}^k$ be a random oracle. For parameters $k, n, s_{mhf}, t_{mhf}, s, f, t \in \mathbb{N}$ and $\varepsilon_{mhf} \in [0,1)$, where $s_{mhf} \geq s$, a function $M : \{0,1\}^k \rightarrow \{0,1\}^n$ is called a $(k, n, s_{mhf}, t_{mhf}, s, f, t, \varepsilon_{mhf})$-memory-hard function (or MHF for short) in the ROM if:*

---

[9] The polynomial factor in $\varepsilon_{p\text{-}ext}$ depends on the number of RO queries made by the adversary. We refer to full version [14] for the exact probability upper bound.

- M is computable by a $(s_{\mathsf{mhf}}, t_{\mathsf{mhf}})$-space-time-bounded algorithm.
- for any (s, f, t)-bounded deterministic algorithm $\mathsf{A}^{\mathcal{H}}$, any $x \in \{0,1\}^*$ we have that:

$$\Pr_{\mathcal{H}}[M(\mathcal{H}(x)) = \mathsf{A}^{\mathcal{H}}(x)] \leq \varepsilon_{\mathsf{mhf}}$$

Remark 4. It is worth noting that, though our definition is in the ROM, the function M itself does not have access to random oracles, but in the security game the adversary A has access to the random oracle.

8.2 Partially-Unique Ext-NIPoS from MHF and VC

In this section, we construct a partially-unique NIPoS with extractability based on a MHF and a VC with space-bounded verification. At a high level, the NIPoS scheme is designed as follows. Let M be a memory-hard function and (Gen, Prove, Ver) a publicly verifiable scheme. The NIPoS prover on input id first queries the random oracle to obtain $x := \mathcal{H}(id)$ and then runs the algorithm Prove on input x and outputs whatever the algorithm outputs, i.e. the value $y := M(x)$ and the proof of correct computation π_{vc}. The NIPoS verifier on input id and the proof of space (y, π_{vc}) first queries the random oracle to obtain $x := \mathcal{H}(id)$ and the runs the algorithm Ver on input x, y, π_{vc} and outputs whatever the algorithm outputs.

Our Construction. Let M be a $(k, n, s_{\mathsf{mhf}}, t_{\mathsf{mhf}}, s, f, t, \varepsilon_{\mathsf{mhf}})$-MHF, (Gen, Prove, Ver) be a $(s_{\mathsf{mhf}}, t_{\mathsf{mhf}}, s_{\mathsf{P}}^{vc}, t_{\mathsf{P}}^{vc}, s_{\mathsf{V}}^{vc}, t_{\mathsf{V}}^{vc}, k, n, n_{\mathsf{vc}}, \varepsilon_{\mathsf{vc}})$-VC scheme for M and $\mathcal{H}$: $\{0,1\}^* \rightarrow \{0,1\}^k$ be a hash-function modeled as random oracle such that $t_{\mathsf{mhf}}, t_{\mathsf{P}}^{vc}, t_{\mathsf{V}}^{vc} \in \mathrm{poly}(\lambda)$ and $s_{\mathsf{V}}^{vc} \leq s < s_{\mathsf{P}}^{vc}$. Then define the following algorithms:

Setup(1^λ): On input the security parameter, run $(vk_M, ek_M) \leftarrow \mathsf{Gen}_M(1^\lambda)$ and set $\mathsf{pp}_{\mathsf{pos}} := (vk_M, ek_M)$.

$\mathsf{P}^{\mathcal{H}}_{\mathsf{pp}_{\mathsf{pos}}}(id)$: Given public parameters $\mathsf{pp}_{\mathsf{pos}} := (vk_M, ek_M)$ and an identity $id \in \{0,1\}^{k_{\mathsf{pos}}}$, compute the proof-of-space as follows:
  1. Obtain $x := \mathcal{H}(id)$ by querying $\mathcal{H}$.
  2. Compute $(y, \pi_{\mathsf{vc}}) := \mathsf{Prove}_{ek_M}(x)$.
  3. Return $\pi := (y, \pi_{\mathsf{vc}})$.

$\mathsf{V}^{\mathcal{H}}_{\mathsf{pp}_{\mathsf{pos}}}(id, \pi)$: Given public parameters $\mathsf{pp}_{\mathsf{pos}} := (vk_M, ek_M)$ an identity $id \in \{0,1\}^{k_{\mathsf{pos}}}$ and a candidate proof $\pi \in \{0,1\}^{n_{\mathsf{pos}}}$, check the correctness of π with respect to id as follows:
  1. Obtain $x := \mathcal{H}(id)$ by querying $\mathcal{H}$.
  2. Parse $(y, \pi_{\mathsf{vc}}) := \pi$.
  3. Return $\mathsf{Ver}_{vk_M}(x, y, \pi_{\mathsf{vc}})$.

Lemma 2. *The above construction is $(k_{\mathsf{pos}}, n_{\mathsf{pos}}, s_{\mathsf{P}}, s_{\mathsf{V}})$-NIPoS with $(u_{\mathsf{pos}}, \varepsilon_{\mathsf{unique}})$-uniqueness and $(s, f, t, \eta, \varepsilon_{\mathsf{pos}})$-extractability as long as:*

$$k_{\mathsf{pos}} \in \mathrm{poly}(\lambda) \qquad n_{\mathsf{pos}} = n + n_{\mathsf{vc}} \qquad s_{\mathsf{P}} \geq \max(s_{\mathsf{P}}^{vc}, k_{\mathsf{pos}})$$

$$s_{\mathsf{V}} \leq s_{\mathsf{V}}^{vc} + k + n + k_{\mathsf{pos}} + n_{\mathsf{vc}} \qquad \eta = \log|\mathcal{Q}_{\mathcal{H}}(\mathsf{B})|$$

$$u_{\mathsf{pos}} = n \qquad \varepsilon_{\mathsf{unique}} \leq \varepsilon_{\mathsf{vc}} \qquad \varepsilon_{\mathsf{pos}} \leq \varepsilon_{\mathsf{vc}} + \varepsilon_{\mathsf{mhf}} + \frac{1}{2^k - |\mathcal{Q}_{\mathcal{H}}(\mathsf{B})|}$$

where $|Q_{\mathcal{H}}(\mathsf{B})|$ is the total number of random-oracle query made by B.

8.3   Instantiating MHF

Our MHF instantiation is a slight variant of a graph-based proof of space construction;[10] in particular, we choose the one provided in [38] (also used in [22]). However, similar formal arguments of space-hardness does not work in our case. Instead, we rely on a heuristic assumption (and also Assumption 1) that our construction, provided below, satisfies our definition of MHF (cf. Definition 11) for useful parameters.

Our construction $M_{G,\mathsf{Hash}}$: On input $x \in \{0,1\}^k$, define the MHF $M_{G,\mathsf{Hash}}$ as follows: consider the SoLEG $G_{N_c,k_G,\gamma_1,\gamma_2}$; recall that the number of nodes of $G_{N_c,k_G,\gamma_1,\gamma_2}$ is given by $N = N_c(k_G + 1)$ and the in-degree is deg $\in O(1)$. Let $\mathsf{Hash} : \{0,1\}^* \to \{0,1\}^{n_{hs}}$ be a standard hash function (for example SHA3) with collision-probability ε_{hs}. On input $x \in \{0,1\}^k$, first compute a Hash_x-labeling of $G_{N_c,k_G,\gamma_1,\gamma_2}$. Denote the labeling by $\mathbf{z} = (z_1,\dots,z_N) \in \{0,1\}^{n_{hs}N}$, where each $z_i \in \{0,1\}^{n_{hs}}$. Output y where $y := \mathcal{H}_x(\mathbf{z}) \in \{0,1\}^{n_{hs}}$.

For a standard instantiation of $\mathcal{H}$, we assume the following facts about labeling a SoLEG. (For basic definitions and facts about graph labeling we refer to full version [14].)

Assumption 1 (Efficient labeling with Hash). *Let* $G_{N_c,k_G,\gamma_1,\gamma_2}$ *be a SoLEG and* $\mathcal{H}: \{0,1\}^* \to \{0,1\}^{n_{\mathcal{H}}}$ *be a "standard hash function" like SHA3. There exists a polynomial time algorithm* A *that computes the $\mathcal{H}$-labeling of the graph* $G_{N_c,k_G,\gamma_1,\gamma_2}$ *in at most $N_c n_{\mathcal{H}}$-space.*

Assumption 2 (Memory-hardness of Graph-labeling with Hash). *Suppose that Assumption 1 is true for the hash function* $\mathsf{Hash} : \{0,1\}^* \to \{0,1\}^{n_{hs}}$ *(with collision-probability ε_{hs}). Then for any $k, s_{mhf}, t_{mhf}, s, f, t \in \mathrm{poly}(\lambda)$ such that $t < 2^{k_G}\gamma_1 N_c$ and $s \le \delta N_c n_{hs}$ for some $\delta \in [0, \gamma_2 - 2\gamma_1)$, the above construction is $(k, n, s_{mhf}, t_{mhf}, s, f, t, \varepsilon_{mhf})$-MHF where:*

$$n = n_{hs} \qquad s_{mhf} \ge k + n_{hs}(N_c + \log(N) + 1) + n$$

$$\varepsilon_{mhf} \le \exp\left(\frac{-n_{hs}N_c(\beta - \delta)}{N\log(N)}\right) + (s+f)\varepsilon_{hs} + 2^{-\gamma_{hs}n_{hs}} + 2^{-k}$$

for $\beta = \gamma_2 - 2\gamma_1$ and a constant $\gamma_{hs} \in (0, \frac{1}{2}]$.

We defer some important notes on the above assumptions to full version [14].

From Assumption 2 we get the following corollary about our MHF-candidate:[11]

Corollary 2. *Suppose that Assumption 1 holds for the hash function* $\mathsf{Hash} :$ $\{0,1\}^* \to \{0,1\}^{n_{hs}}$ *and based on that Assumption 2 holds for our construction*

---

[10] Since popular memory-hard functions like SCrypt [39] are not conjectured to provide exponential space-time trade-off, we are unable to use them here.

[11] We remark that this corollary is very similar to Corollary 1 of [23] as one may expect. However the parameters here are much better in terms of efficiency.

based on a SoLEG $G_{N_c, k_G, \gamma_1, \gamma_2}$ with $N = N_c(k_G + 1)$ nodes and $\deg = O(1)$ in-degree such that:

$$n_{\mathsf{hs}} = \lambda^2 \qquad \beta = \gamma_2 - 2\gamma_1 \in (0,1) \qquad k_G = \lambda - 1$$
$$N_c = \lambda^3 \qquad \varepsilon_{\mathsf{hs}} \in \mathrm{negl}(\lambda).$$

Then, for any $\delta \in (0, \beta)$, any $\varepsilon > 0$ and any $\gamma_{\mathsf{hs}} \in (0, \frac{1}{2}]$ our construction is a $(k, n, s_{\mathsf{mhf}}, t_{\mathsf{mhf}}, s, f, t, \varepsilon_{\mathsf{mhf}})$-MHF for $t, f, t_{\mathsf{mhf}} \in \mathrm{poly}(\lambda)$ and:

$$k = O(\lambda^\varepsilon) \qquad n = \lambda^2 \qquad s_{\mathsf{mhf}} = O(\lambda^5)$$

$$s \leq \delta \cdot \lambda^5 \qquad \varepsilon_{\mathsf{mhf}} \leq \exp\left(\frac{-(\beta - \delta)\lambda}{\log(\lambda)}\right) + \mathrm{negl}(\lambda) \in \mathrm{negl}(\lambda)$$

Furthermore, for making $\varepsilon_{\mathsf{mhf}} \approx 2^{-80}$, we need to have $\lambda \approx 2300$. Choosing standard values for other parameters, $\delta = 0.1, \beta = 0.9, \gamma_{\mathsf{hs}} = 0.001$ we get concrete parameters for our MHF-construction as:

$$k \geq 80 \qquad n \approx 670 \text{ KB} \qquad s_{\mathsf{mhf}} \approx 8000 \text{ TB} \qquad s \leq 800 \text{ TB} \qquad \varepsilon_{\mathsf{mhf}} \approx 2^{-80}$$

8.4   Instantiating VC

Our NIPoS construction can be instantiated with any VC for which the verification can be done in small space (compared to computing the function itself). In this work we concretely consider such a scheme, known as Pinocchio [36].

Space requirements of Pinocchio Verifier. Without giving formal arguments on the space-bound, we rely on the following assumption on the Pinocchio verification algorithm. Note that these bounds are independent of the space-bound of the function (in this case that is $M_{G,\mathsf{Hash}}$) to be verified. We briefly provide some justifications of that afterwards. We refer the reader for more details about the algorithm and the time complexity to the original paper [36].

Assumption 3 (Space-bounded Verification). *Let $\mathbb{G}$ be a (as considered in [36]) cyclic subgroup of points in $E(\mathbb{F}_p)$; $E(\mathbb{F}_p)$ denotes an elliptic curve over $\mathbb{F}_p$ where $p \in \exp(\lambda)$ is a prime.[12] Then for a function $F : \{0,1\}^k \to \{0,1\}^n$, the Pinocchio verification algorithm (see Protocol 2 of [36]) requires $k + n + O(\lambda)$-bit space asymptotically and $\approx k + n + 300 \cdot \lceil \log p \rceil$ bits concretely.*

We defer some important notes on the above assumptions to full version [14].

Assumption 4 (Lower-bound on Prover's space). *Let $\mathbb{G}$ be a (as considered in [36]) cyclic subgroup of points in $E(\mathbb{F}_p)$, where $E(\mathbb{F}_p)$ denotes an elliptic curve over a $\mathbb{F}_p$ where $p \in \exp(\lambda)$ is a prime. Consider a function F that is computable by a (s_F, t_F)-bounded algorithm for $s_F, t_F \in \mathrm{poly}(\lambda)$ and also assume that $s_F \gg \lceil 16 \log(p) \rceil$. Then the Pinocchio prove algorithm (see Protocol 2 of [36]) requires at least s_F-bit space.*

---

[12] To achieve 128-bits of security, as suggested by [8], we will set $\lceil \log(p) \rceil \approx 1536$.

Combining Assumptions 3 and 4 we conclude:

Corollary 3. *Let $\lambda \in \mathbb{N}$ be the security parameter and let $F : \{0,1\}^k \to \{0,1\}^n$ be a deterministic function that is computable by an $(s_F, \mathrm{poly}(\lambda))$-space-time bounded algorithm. Then there exists an explicit $(s_F, \mathrm{poly}(\lambda), s_V^{vc}, \mathrm{poly}(\lambda), s_P^{vc}, \mathrm{poly}(\lambda), k, n, n_{vc}, \mathrm{negl}(\lambda))$-non-interactive publicly verifiable computation construction, where:*

$$s_V^{vc} = k + n + O(\lambda) \qquad s_P^{vc} \geq s_F \qquad n_{vc} = O(\lambda)$$

Furthermore, in concrete terms, to get $\varepsilon_{vc} \approx 2^{-128}$, choosing $\lceil \log p \rceil \approx 1536$ (following [8]) we can have estimations of the verifier's space $s_V^{vc} \approx 58$ KB$+k+n$ and the proof-size $n_{vc} \approx 3$ KB.

8.5 Instantiating Partially Unique NIPoS and PExt-NIPoS

Putting together the instantiations of MHF and VC, we can get a (partially) unique extractable NIPoS based on four heuristic assumptions (Assumptions 1–4). Plugging in the parameters from Corollaries 2 and 3 into Lemma 2, we obtain the following corollary:

Corollary 4 (MHF-based NIPoS with uniqueness). *For any $\varepsilon > 0$ and a $\delta \in (0,1)$ there is an explicit construction of $(k_{\mathsf{pos}}, n_{\mathsf{pos}}, s_P, s_V)$-NIPoS which has $(u_{\mathsf{pos}}, \varepsilon_{\mathsf{unique}})$-uniqueness and $(s, f, t, \eta, \varepsilon_{\mathsf{pos}})$-extractability for any $f, t \in \mathrm{poly}(\lambda)$ as long as:*

$$k_{\mathsf{pos}} \in \mathrm{poly}(\lambda^{\varepsilon}) \qquad n_{\mathsf{pos}} = O(\lambda^2) \qquad s_P = \Omega(\lambda^5) \qquad s \leq \delta\lambda^5$$
$$s_V = O(\lambda^2) \qquad u_{\mathsf{pos}} = \lambda^2 \qquad \varepsilon_{\mathsf{unique}} \in \mathrm{negl}(\lambda) \qquad \eta = O(\log(\lambda)) \qquad \varepsilon_{\mathsf{pos}} \in \mathrm{negl}(\lambda).$$

9 Instantiating and Comparing Our NMC Constructions

9.1 Instantiations from Different PExt-NIPoS

We obtain four constructions in total, two of them through CHG and other two (including FHMV one) through the uniqueness. For more details we refer to the full version [14].

9.2 Comparing Concrete Parameters

We propose four constructions of space-bounded (leaky) non-malleable codes that support unbounded tampering. All of them are based on NIPoS. Two of them (described in Sect. 7) require proof-extractability whereas other two can be based on standard extractability (described in Sects. 6 and 8). Our constructions have different merits. While the asymptotic bounds for the parameters have already been provided, we believe that a comparison with respect to the concrete values is important.

Our setting. Since our constructions are obtained from different techniques and achieve different bounds, it is important to fix a common measure with respect to which a comparison makes sense. We choose to fix a standard security measure. In particular, we set $\varepsilon_{nm} = 2^{-80}$ in the Definition 5—that is how we can estimate the values of the other parameters (namely, k, n, ℓ, s, f, p, d) to get 80-bit security. We also choose a reasonable values for the number of tampering queries: $\theta = 2^{16}$.[13] Whenever there is a term that depends on the number of RO queries made by a poly-time adversary, (for example $|\mathcal{Q}_{\mathcal{H}}(\Lambda)|$) we set that to 2^{64}. We assume that a poly-time adversary runs for 2^{80} time steps. Since in our setting ℓ is always as big as $p - n$ we compare the parameters considering $p \approx n$ to have *minimal leakage*. We choose small values for k (close to ℓ) within the supported range, although for most of our constructions much higher k is supported. Using concrete instantiations of PExt-NIPoS (see the full version [14] for detail) and plugging-in them to Theorem 1 we get the concrete parameters for the resulting CSNMCs: we provide a comparative study in Table 2.

Table 2. This table shows approximate concrete parameters for the setting when $p \approx n$. Note that for PExt-NIPoS-based constructions the last column has bound on $s + f$, whereas for Ext-NIPoS-based constructions the bound is only on s as f can be set to arbitrary large value.

Technique	NIPoS-type	k	$n, (\approx p)$	ℓ	d	$s(+f)$
CHG	SoLEG-based	1 MB	801 MB	0.8 MB	801 MB	1.1 GB$(+f)$
	PTC-based	257 MB	256 GB	256 MB	256 GB	256 GB$(+f)$
Ext	FHMV-based	226 TB	415 TB	225 TB	452 TB	800 TB
	MHF-based	4 KB	677 KB	3 KB	740 KB	800 TB

Assumptions. The first three constructions are based on "memory-hard graphs". The hardness can be proven in the random oracle model via standard pebbling games. The main proof relies on combinatorial arguments. In contrast Construction-4 relies on heuristic arguments for space bounds. The main assumptions are (Assumption 2 and 1) that memory-hard graphs retain their space-hardness when instantiated with concrete hash functions. This is needed because the standard pebbling arguments fall short when the hash function is not modeled as a random oracle. We also rely on a few other assumptions (namely Assumption 3 and 4) regarding the underlying verfiable computation. For all of the above constructions we need a PRF with standard security as the proofs depend on the pseudorandomness guarantee of the PRF.

---

[13] We stress that this value can be set much higher without affecting the main parameters significantly.

References

1. Aggarwal, D., Agrawal, S., Gupta, D., Maji, H.K., Pandey, O., Prabhakaran, M.: Optimal computational split-state non-malleable codes. In: Kushilevitz, E., Malkin, T. (eds.) TCC 2016, Part II. LNCS, vol. 9563, pp. 393–417. Springer, Heidelberg (2016). https://doi.org/10.1007/978-3-662-49099-0_15

2. Aggarwal, D., Dodis, Y., Lovett, S.: Non-malleable codes from additive combinatorics. In: Shmoys, D.B. (ed.) 46th Annual ACM Symposium on Theory of Computing, pp. 774–783, 31 May–3 June 2014. ACM Press, New York (2014)

3. Aggarwal, D., Dottling, N., Nielsen, J.B., Obremski, M., Purwanto, E.: Continuous non-malleable codes in the 8-split-state model. Cryptology ePrint Archive, Report 2017/357 (2017). https://eprint.iacr.org/2017/357

4. Aggarwal, D., Kazana, T., Obremski, M.: Inception makes non-malleable codes stronger. In: Kalai, Y., Reyzin, L. (eds.) TCC 2017, Part II. LNCS, vol. 10678, pp. 319–343. Springer, Cham (2017). https://doi.org/10.1007/978-3-319-70503-3_10

5. Agrawal, S., Gupta, D., Maji, H.K., Pandey, O., Prabhakaran, M.: Explicit non-malleable codes against bit-wise tampering and permutations. In: Gennaro, R., Robshaw, M. (eds.) CRYPTO 2015, Part I. LNCS, vol. 9215, pp. 538–557. Springer, Heidelberg (2015). https://doi.org/10.1007/978-3-662-47989-6_26

6. Alwen, J., Chen, B., Pietrzak, K., Reyzin, L., Tessaro, S.: Scrypt is maximally memory-hard. In: Coron, J.-S., Nielsen, J.B. (eds.) EUROCRYPT 2017, Part III. LNCS, vol. 10212, pp. 33–62. Springer, Cham (2017). https://doi.org/10.1007/978-3-319-56617-7_2

7. Ateniese, G., Bonacina, I., Faonio, A., Galesi, N.: Proofs of space: when space is of the essence. In: Abdalla, M., De Prisco, R. (eds.) SCN 2014. LNCS, vol. 8642, pp. 538–557. Springer, Cham (2014). https://doi.org/10.1007/978-3-319-10879-7_31

8. Guillevic, A., Morain, F.: Discrete logarithms. Book Chapter 9. https://hal.inria.fr/hal-01420485v1/document

9. Ball, M., Dachman-Soled, D., Kulkarni, M., Malkin, T.: Non-malleable codes for bounded depth, bounded fan-in circuits. In: Fischlin, M., Coron, J.-S. (eds.) EUROCRYPT 2016, Part II. LNCS, vol. 9666, pp. 881–908. Springer, Heidelberg (2016). https://doi.org/10.1007/978-3-662-49896-5_31

10. Ball, M., Dachman-Soled, D., Kulkarni, M., Malkin, T.: Non-malleable codes from average-case hardness: AC^0, decision trees, and streaming space-bounded tampering. In: Nielsen, J.B., Rijmen, V. (eds.) EUROCRYPT 2018, Part III. LNCS, vol. 10822, pp. 618–650. Springer, Cham (2018). https://doi.org/10.1007/978-3-319-78372-7_20

11. Boneh, D., Corrigan-Gibbs, H., Schechter, S.: Balloon hashing: a memory-hard function providing provable protection against sequential attacks. Cryptology ePrint Archive, Report 2016/027 (2016). http://eprint.iacr.org/2016/027

12. Boneh, D., DeMillo, R.A., Lipton, R.J.: On the importance of eliminating errors in cryptographic computations. J. Cryptology 14(2), 101–119 (2001)

13. Chandran, N., Goyal, V., Mukherjee, P., Pandey, O., Upadhyay, J.: Block-wise non-malleable codes. In: Chatzigiannakis, I., Mitzenmacher, M., Rabani, Y., Sangiorgi, D. (eds.) ICALP 2016. 43rd International Colloquium on Automata, Languages and Programming, LIPIcs, Rome, Italy, 11–15 July 2016, vol. 55, pp. 31:1–31:14. Schloss Dagstuhl - Leibniz-Zentrum fuer Informatik (2016)

14. Chen, B., Chen, Y., Hostáková, K., Mukherjee, P.: Continuous space-bounded non-malleable codes from stronger proofs-of-space. Cryptology ePrint Archive, Report 2019/552 (2019). https://eprint.iacr.org/2019/552

15. Cheraghchi, M., Guruswami, V.: Non-malleable coding against bit-wise and split-state tampering. In: Lindell, Y. (ed.) TCC 2014. LNCS, vol. 8349, pp. 440–464. Springer, Heidelberg (2014). https://doi.org/10.1007/978-3-642-54242-8_19
16. Dachman-Soled, D., Liu, F.-H., Shi, E., Zhou, H.-S.: Locally decodable and updatable non-malleable codes and their applications. In: Dodis, Y., Nielsen, J.B. (eds.) TCC 2015, Part I. LNCS, vol. 9014, pp. 427–450. Springer, Heidelberg (2015). https://doi.org/10.1007/978-3-662-46494-6_18
17. Dziembowski, S., Faust, S., Kolmogorov, V., Pietrzak, K.: Proofs of space. In: Gennaro, R., Robshaw, M. (eds.) CRYPTO 2015, Part II. LNCS, vol. 9216, pp. 585–605. Springer, Heidelberg (2015). https://doi.org/10.1007/978-3-662-48000-7_29
18. Dziembowski, S., Kazana, T., Wichs, D.: Key-evolution schemes resilient to space-bounded leakage. In: Rogaway, P. (ed.) CRYPTO 2011. LNCS, vol. 6841, pp. 335–353. Springer, Heidelberg (2011). https://doi.org/10.1007/978-3-642-22792-9_19
19. Dziembowski, S., Kazana, T., Wichs, D.: One-time computable self-erasing functions. In: Ishai, Y. (ed.) TCC 2011. LNCS, vol. 6597, pp. 125–143. Springer, Heidelberg (2011). https://doi.org/10.1007/978-3-642-19571-6_9
20. Dziembowski, S., Pietrzak, K., Wichs, D.: Non-malleable codes. In: Yao, A.C.-C. (ed.) ICS 2010: 1st Innovations in Computer Science, pp. 434–452. Tsinghua University, Beijing, China, 5–7 January 2010. Tsinghua University Press (2010)
21. Faonio, A., Nielsen, J.B., Simkin, M., Venturi, D.: Continuously non-malleable codes with split-state refresh. In: Preneel, B., Vercauteren, F. (eds.) ACNS 2018. LNCS, vol. 10892, pp. 121–139. Springer, Cham (2018). https://doi.org/10.1007/978-3-319-93387-0_7
22. Faust, S., Hostáková, K., Mukherjee, P., Venturi, D.: Non-malleable codes for space-bounded tampering. In: Katz, J., Shacham, H. (eds.) CRYPTO 2017, Part II. LNCS, vol. 10402, pp. 95–126. Springer, Cham (2017). https://doi.org/10.1007/978-3-319-63715-0_4
23. Faust, S., Hostakova, K., Mukherjee, P., Venturi, D.: Non-malleable codes for space-bounded tampering. Cryptology ePrint Archive, Report 2017/530 (2017). http://eprint.iacr.org/2017/530
24. Faust, S., Mukherjee, P., Nielsen, J.B., Venturi, D.: Continuous non-malleable codes. In: Lindell, Y. (ed.) TCC 2014. LNCS, vol. 8349, pp. 465–488. Springer, Heidelberg (2014). https://doi.org/10.1007/978-3-642-54242-8_20
25. Faust, S., Mukherjee, P., Nielsen, J.B., Venturi, D.: A tamper and leakage resilient von Neumann architecture. In: Katz, J. (ed.) PKC 2015. LNCS, vol. 9020, pp. 579–603. Springer, Heidelberg (2015). https://doi.org/10.1007/978-3-662-46447-2_26
26. Faust, S., Mukherjee, P., Venturi, D., Wichs, D.: Efficient non-malleable codes and key-derivation for poly-size tampering circuits. In: Nguyen, P.Q., Oswald, E. (eds.) EUROCRYPT 2014. LNCS, vol. 8441, pp. 111–128. Springer, Heidelberg (2014). https://doi.org/10.1007/978-3-642-55220-5_7
27. Fiat, A., Shamir, A.: How to prove yourself: practical solutions to identification and signature problems. In: Odlyzko, A.M. (ed.) CRYPTO 1986. LNCS, vol. 263, pp. 186–194. Springer, Heidelberg (1987). https://doi.org/10.1007/3-540-47721-7_12
28. Goyal, V., Pandey, O., Richelson, S.: Textbook non-malleable commitments. In: Wichs, D., Mansour, Y. (eds.) 48th Annual ACM Symposium on Theory of Computing, Cambridge, MA, USA, 18–21 June 2016, pp. 1128–1141. ACM Press (2016)
29. Jafargholi, Z., Wichs, D.: Tamper detection and continuous non-malleable codes. In: Dodis, Y., Nielsen, J.B. (eds.) TCC 2015, Part I. LNCS, vol. 9014, pp. 451–480. Springer, Heidelberg (2015). https://doi.org/10.1007/978-3-662-46494-6_19

30. Kanukurthi, B., Obbattu, S.L.B., Sekar, S.: Four-state non-malleable codes with explicit constant rate. In: Kalai, Y., Reyzin, L. (eds.) TCC 2017, Part II. LNCS, vol. 10678, pp. 344–375. Springer, Cham (2017). https://doi.org/10.1007/978-3-319-70503-3_11

31. Kanukurthi, B., Obbattu, S.L.B., Sekar, S.: Non-malleable Randomness encoders and their applications. In: Nielsen, J.B., Rijmen, V. (eds.) EUROCRYPT 2018, Part III. LNCS, vol. 10822, pp. 589–617. Springer, Cham (2018). https://doi.org/10.1007/978-3-319-78372-7_19

32. Liu, F.-H., Lysyanskaya, A.: Tamper and leakage resilience in the split-state model. In: Safavi-Naini, R., Canetti, R. (eds.) CRYPTO 2012. LNCS, vol. 7417, pp. 517–532. Springer, Heidelberg (2012). https://doi.org/10.1007/978-3-642-32009-5_30

33. Mahmoody, M., Moran, T., Vadhan, S.P.: Publicly verifiable proofs of sequential work. In: Kleinberg, R.D. (ed.) ITCS 2013: 4th Innovations in Theoretical Computer Science, Berkeley, CA, USA, 9–12 January 2013, pp. 373–388. Association for Computing Machinery (2013)

34. Mukherjee, P.: Protecting cryptographic memory against tampering attack. Ph.D thesis (2015)

35. Ostrovsky, R., Persiano, G., Venturi, D., Visconti, I.: Continuously non-malleable codes in the split-state model from minimal assumptions. In: Shacham, H., Boldyreva, A. (eds.) CRYPTO 2018. LNCS, vol. 10993, pp. 608–639. Springer, Cham (2018). https://doi.org/10.1007/978-3-319-96878-0_21

36. Parno, B., Howell, J., Gentry, C., Raykova, M.: Pinocchio: nearly practical verifiable computation. In: 2013 IEEE Symposium on Security and Privacy, Berkeley, CA, USA, 19–22 May 2013, pp. 238–252. IEEE Computer Society Press (2013)

37. Paul, W.J., Tarjan, R.E., Celoni, J.R.: Space bounds for a game on graphs. Math. Syst. Theory 10(1), 239–251 (1976)

38. Ren, L., Devadas, S.: Proof of space from stacked expanders. In: Hirt, M., Smith, A. (eds.) TCC 2016, Part I. LNCS, vol. 9985, pp. 262–285. Springer, Heidelberg (2016). https://doi.org/10.1007/978-3-662-53641-4_11

39. Tarsnap. The scrypt key derivation function. https://eprint.iacr.org/2017/1125

SNARKs and Blockchains

Synchronous, with a Chance
of Partition Tolerance

Yue Guo[1,2], Rafael Pass[1,2], and Elaine Shi[1,2(✉)]

[1] Thunder Research, Sunnyvale, USA
[2] Cornell University, Ithaca, USA
{yue.guo,rafael,elaine}@thundercore.com

Abstract. Murphy, Murky, Mopey, Moody, and Morose decide to write
a paper together over the Internet and submit it to the prestigious
CRYPTO'19 conference that has the most amazing PC. They encounter
a few problems. First, not everyone is online every day: some are lazy
and go skiing on Mondays; others cannot use git correctly and they are
completely unaware that they are losing messages. Second, a small subset
of the co-authors may be secretly plotting to disrupt the project (e.g.,
because they are writing a competing paper in stealth).

Suppose that each day, sufficiently many honest co-authors are online
(and use git correctly); moreover, suppose that messages checked into git
on Monday can be correctly received by honest and online co-authors on
Tuesday or any future day. Can the honest co-authors successfully finish
the paper in a small number of days such that they make the CRYPTO
deadline; and perhaps importantly, can all the honest co-authors, including even those who are lazy and those who sometimes use git incorrectly,
agree on the final theorem?

1 Introduction

The "synchronous" model is one of the most commonly studied models in the
past 30 years of distributed computing and cryptography literature. In the synchronous model, it is assumed that whenever an honest node sends a message,
an honest recipient is guaranteed to have received it within a bounded delay Δ,
and the protocol is aware of the maximum delay Δ.

We love the synchronous model because it allows us to achieve robustness
properties that would otherwise be impossible. For example, assuming synchrony,
we can achieve distributed consensus even when arbitrarily many nodes may
be malicious [8]. In comparison, it is well-known that if message delays can
be arbitrarily long [9], consensus is impossible in the presence of $\frac{1}{3}$ fraction of
corrupt nodes. On the other hand, the synchrony assumption has been criticized
for being too strong [3,19]: if an honest node ever experiences even a short outage
(e.g., due to network jitter) during which it is not able to receive honest messages
within Δ delay, this node is now considered as corrupt. From this point on, a
consensus protocol proven secure under a synchronous model is not obliged to
provide consistency and liveness to that node any more, even if the node may
wake up shortly afterwards and wish to continue participating in the protocol.

A. Boldyreva and D. Micciancio (Eds.): CRYPTO 2019, LNCS 11692, pp. 499–529, 2019.
https://doi.org/10.1007/978-3-030-26948-7_18

Similarly, as soon as P has even a short-term outage, a multi-party computation (MPC) protocol proven secure under a synchronous model is not obliged to provide privacy for party P's inputs—for example, some protocols that aim to achieve fairness and guaranteed output would now have the remaining online parties reconstruct P's secret-shared input and thus P loses its privacy entirely.

We stress that this is not just a theoretical concern. Our work is in fact directly motivated by conversations with real-world blockchain engineers who were building and deploying a fast cryptocurrency and pointed out what seems to be a fatal flaw in a blockchain protocol [20] that was proven secure in the classical synchronous model: even when all nodes are benign and only a few crash in a specific timing pattern, transactions that were "confirmed" can be "undone" from the perspective of an honest node who just experienced short-term jitter possibly unknowingly (see the online full version [14] for a detailed description of this real-world example).

Not only so, in fact to the best of our knowledge, all known classical-style, *synchronous* consensus protocols [2,15,18] are *underspecified* and *unimplementable* in practice: if a node ever experiences even a short-term outage and receives messages out of sync, these protocols [2,15,18] provide no explicit instructions for such nodes to join back and continue to enjoy consistency and liveness!

Of course, one known solution to this problem is to simply adopt a partially synchronous [9] or asynchronous [6] model. In a partially synchronous or asynchronous model, a short-term outage would be treated in the same way as a long network delay, and a node that is transiently offline will not be penalized. For this reason, partially synchronous (or asynchronous) protocols are known to be arbitrarily *partition tolerant*; while synchronous protocols are *not*. Unfortunately, as mentioned, partially synchronous or asynchronous protocols can tolerate only $1/3$ fraction of corruptions!

Can we achieve the best of both worlds, i.e., design distributed computing protocols that resist more than $1/3$ corruption and meanwhile achieve a practical notion of partition tolerance?

1.1   Definitional Contribution: A "Weak Synchronous" Network

At a very high level, we show that synchrony and partition tolerance are not binary attributes, and that we can guarantee a notion called "best-possible partition tolerance" under a quantifiable measure of synchrony. To this end, we propose a new model called a χ-*weakly-synchronous* network.

A natural but overly restrictive notion. One natural way to quantify the degree of synchrony is to count the fraction of nodes that always respect the synchrony assumption. For example, we may want a distributed computing protocol to satisfy desired security properties (e.g., consistency, liveness, privacy), as long as more than χ fraction of nodes are not only honest but also always have good connectivity (i.e., bounded Δ delay) among themselves. This model, however, is overly restrictive especially in long-running distributed computing tasks such as a blockchain: after all, no node can guarantee 100% up-time [1], and over a few years duration, it could be that every node was at some point, offline.

χ-*weak-synchrony.* We thus consider a more general model that allows us to capture network churn. We now require only the following:

> [χ-weakly-synchronous assumption:] In every round, more than χ fraction nodes are not only honest but also *online*; however, the set of honest and online nodes in adjacent rounds need not be the same.

Throughout the paper we use the notation $\mathcal{O}_r$ to denote a set of at least $\lfloor \chi n \rfloor + 1$ honest nodes who are online in round r—henceforth $\mathcal{O}_r$ is also called the "honest and online set of round r". Note that the remaining set $[n] \backslash \mathcal{O}_r$ may contain a combination of honest or corrupt nodes and an honest node in $[n] \backslash \mathcal{O}_r$ is said to be offline in round r.

We assume that the network delivery respects the following property where multicast means "send to everyone":

> [network assumption:] when a node in $\mathcal{O}_r$ multicasts a message in round r, every node in $\mathcal{O}_t$ where $t \geq r + \Delta$ must have received the message in round t.

We allow the adversary to choose the honest and online set of each round (even after observing the messages that honest nodes want to send in the present round), and delay or erase honest messages, as long as the above χ-weak-synchrony and network delivery constraints are respected. For example, the adversary may choose to delay an honest but offline node's messages (even to online nodes) for as long as the node remains offline. The adversary can also selectively reveal an arbitrary subset of honest messages to an honest and offline node.

Therefore, our weak synchrony notion can be viewed as a generalization of the classical synchronous notion (henceforth also called strong synchrony). In a strongly synchronous network, it is required that the honest and online set of every round must contain all honest nodes.

We ask whether we can achieve secure distributed computing tasks under such a χ-weakly-synchronous network. With the exception of liveness (or guaranteed output) which we shall discuss shortly, we would like to guarantee all security properties, including consistency and privacy, for *all* honest nodes, regardless of whether or when they are online/offline. Defining liveness (or guaranteed output) in the χ-weakly-synchronous model, however, is more subtle. Clearly we cannot hope to guarantee liveness for an honest but offline node for as long as it remains offline. Therefore, we aim to achieve a "best-effort" notion of liveness: a protocol has T-liveness iff for any honest node that becomes online in some round $r \geq T$, it must have produced output by the end of round r.

The challenges. We are faced with a few apparent challenges when designing distributed protocols secure under χ-weak-synchrony. First, the online nodes may change rapidly in adjacent rounds. For example, if $\chi = 0.5$ and everyone is honest, the honest and online sets belonging to adjacent rounds can be almost disjoint. Second, we stress that *offline nodes may not be aware they are offline,* e.g., a DoS attack against a victim's egress router clearly will not announce itself in advance. Further, the adversary can selectively reveal a subset of messages to offline nodes such that they cannot detect they are offline from the protocol messages they receive either. Because of these facts, designing protocols in our χ-weakly-synchronous model is significantly more challenging than the classical synchronous model (or even the above restrictive model where we may assume a sufficiently large set of honest and persistently online nodes).

1.2   Results: Consensus in a Weakly Synchronous Network

We consider the feasibility and infeasibility of achieving Byzantine Agreement (BA) in a χ-weakly-synchronous network. In a BA protocol, a designated sender has an input bit that it wants to convey to all other nodes. We would like to achieve the following guarantees for all but a negligible fraction of executions: (1) *consistency*, i.e., all honest nodes must output the same bit; (2) *validity*, i.e., if the designated sender is honest and online in the starting round (i.e., round 0) of the protocol, every honest node's output (if any) must agree with the sender's input bit; and (3) T-*liveness*, i.e., every node in $\mathcal{O}_r$ where $r \geq T$ must have produced an output by the end of round r. Note that if the designated sender is honest but offline initially, the protocol cannot make up for the time lost when the sender is offline—thus validity requires that the sender not only be honest but also online in the starting round.

As mentioned, we are primarily interested in protocols that tolerate more than $1/3$ corruptions since otherwise one could adopt a partially synchronous or asynchronous model and achieve arbitrary partition tolerance. To avoid a well-known lower bound by Lamport et al. [17], throughout the paper we will assume the existence of a public-key infrastructure (PKI).

Impossibility when minority are honest and online. Unfortunately, we show that it is impossible to have a χ-weakly-synchronous consensus protocol for $\chi < 0.5 - 1/n$, i.e., if the honest and online set of each round contains only minority number of nodes (and this lower bound holds even assuming any reasonable setup assumption such as PKI, random oracle, common reference string (CRS), or the ability of honest nodes to erase secrets from memory). The intuition for the lower bound is simple: there can be two honest well-connected components that are partitioned from each other, i.e., the minority honest nodes inside each component can deliver messages to each other within a single round; however messages in between incur very long delay. In this case, by liveness of the consensus protocol, each honest well-connected component will reach agreement independently of each other. We formalize this intuition later in Sect. 4.

Best-possible partition tolerance. Due to the above impossibility, a consensus protocol that achieves consistency, validity, and liveness under 0.5-weak-synchrony is said to be *best-possible partition tolerant*.

A refinement of synchronous consensus. First, it is not hard to see that any best-possible partition tolerant Byzantine Agreement (BA) protocol (i.e., secure under 0.5-weak-synchrony) must also be secure under honest majority in the classical, strong synchronous model. On the other hand, the converse is not true. Interestingly, we examined several classical, honest-majority BA protocols [2,15,18,20] and found none of them to satisfy best-possible partition tolerance. In this sense, our notion of best-possible partition tolerance can also be viewed as a refinement of classical honest-majority BA, i.e., we can tease out a proper subset of honest-majority BA protocols that satisfy good-enough partition tolerance in practice—and we strongly recommend this robust subset for practical applications.

Round-efficient, best-possible partition tolerant BA. Of course, to show that our notion is useful, we must show existence of a best-possible partition tolerant BA that is efficient; and this turns out to be non-trivial.

Theorem 1 (Informal). *Assume the existence of a PKI and enhanced trapdoor permutations. Then, there exists an expected constant-round* BA *protocol secure under 0.5-weak-synchrony.*

Note that here, expected constant-round means that there is a random variable T whose expectation is constant, such that if an honest node becomes online in round $r \geq T$, it must have produced an output in round r.

We additionally show how to extend the above result and construct a best-possible partition tolerant BA protocol that is optimistically responsive [20]: specifically, under the following optimistic conditions, the honest and online nodes in $\mathcal{O}$ will produce an output in $O(\delta)$ amount of time where δ is the actual maximum network delay (rather than the a-priori upper bound Δ):

O := "there exists a set $\mathcal{O}$ containing at least $3n/4$ honest and persistently online nodes, and moreover, the designated sender is not only honest but also online in the starting round"

Corollary 1 (Informal). *Assume the existence of a PKI and enhanced trapdoor permutations. Then, there exists an expected constant-round* BA *protocol secure under χ-weak-synchrony; moreover, if the optimistic conditions* **O** *specified above also holds, then the honest and online nodes in $\mathcal{O}$ would produce output in $O(\delta)$ time where δ is the actual maximum network delay.*

Classical, corrupt-majority BA *protocols inherently sacrifice partition tolerance.* As is well-known, in the classical, strongly synchronous model, we can achieve BA even when arbitrarily many nodes can be corrupt. We show, however, the set of corrupt-majority protocols are disjoint from the set of best-possible partition tolerant protocols. Not only so, we can show that the more corruptions one hopes to tolerate, the less partition tolerant the protocol becomes. Intuitively, the lower bound is simple because in a corrupt majority protocol, a minority honest well-connected component must independently reach agreement among themselves in a bounded amount of time; and obviously there can be two such components that are disconnected from each other and thus consistency among the two components is violated (with constant probability).

This simple observation, however, raises another philosophical point: if we adopted the classical synchronous model, it would be tempting to draw the conclusion that corrupt-majority BA is strictly more robust than honest-majority BA. However, we show that one must fundamentally sacrifice partition tolerance to trade for the ability to resist majority corruption and this tradeoff is, unfortunately, inherent.

1.3   Results: MPC in a Weakly Synchronous Network

We next consider the feasibility of realizing multi-party computation in a χ-weakly-synchronous network. Imagine that n parties would like to jointly evaluate the function $f(x_1, \ldots, x_n)$ over their respectively inputs $x_1, x_2, \ldots, x_n$ such that only the outcome is revealed and nothing else. Again, a couple of subtleties arise in formulating the definition. First, one cannot hope to incorporate the inputs of offline nodes if one would like online nodes to obtain outputs quickly. Thus, we require that at least $\lfloor \chi n \rfloor + 1$ number of honest nodes' inputs be included and moreover, every honest node who has always been online throughout the protocol should get their inputs incorporated. Concretely, we require that the ideal-world adversary submit a subset $\mathfrak{I} \subseteq [n]$ to the ideal functionality, such that $\mathfrak{I} \cap \mathsf{Honest} \geq \lfloor \chi n \rfloor + 1$ where Honest denotes the set of honest nodes, and moreover $\mathfrak{I}$ must include every honest node who has been online throughout the protocol. Henceforth, the subset $\mathfrak{I}$ is referred to as the "effective input set":

- for every $i \in \mathfrak{I}$ that is honest, the computation should use node i's true inputs;
- for every $i \in \mathfrak{I}$ that is corrupt, we allow the ideal-world adversary to replace the input to any value of its choice; and
- for every $i \notin \mathfrak{I}$, the computation simply uses a canonical input $\perp$ as its input.

Second, the notion of guaranteed output must be treated in the same manner as liveness for BA since we cannot hope that honest but offline nodes can obtain output for as long as they remain offline. We say that an execution of the multi-party protocol completes in T rounds, iff for any honest node in $\mathcal{O}_t$ where $t \geq T$, it must have produced an output by the end of round t.

Under the above definition, we prove the following theorem (informally stated):

Theorem 2 (Informal). *Assume the existence of a PKI, enhanced trapdoor permutations, and that the Learning with Errors (LWE) assumption holds. Then, there is an expected constant-round protocol that allows multiple parties to securely evaluate any function f under 0.5-weak-synchrony.*

We further extend our results in a non-trivial manner and achieve optimistically responsive MPC in the online full version [14].

Additional related work. We provide comparison with additional related work in our online full version [14].

2   Technical Roadmap

The most technically non-trivial part of our result is how to realize Byzantine Agreement (BA) under 0.5-weak-synchrony. Existing synchronous, honest-majority protocols [15,18] completely fail in our model. Since the honest and online set can change rapidly in every round, it could be that by the end of the protocol, very few or even no honest nodes have been persistently online, and everyone honest was offline at some point. In other words, it could be that from the view of every honest node, message delivery was asynchronous at some point in the protocol. Indeed, interestingly many of our core techniques are in fact reminiscent of asynchronous consensus rather than synchronous approaches.

Although at a very high level, we follow a well-known recipe that constructs BA from a series of building blocks:

$$\text{Reliable Broadcast (RBC)} \Rightarrow \text{Verifiable Secret Sharing (VSS)}$$
$$\Rightarrow \text{Leader Election (LE)} \Rightarrow \text{Byzantine Agreement (BA)}$$

as it turns out, for all these building blocks, even how to define them was non-trivial: the definitional subtleties arise partly due to the new χ-weakly-synchronous model, and partly due to compositional issues.

2.1   Reliable Broadcast (RBC)

Definition. Reliable broadcast (RBC) allows a designated sender to convey a message to other nodes. The primitive can be viewed as a relaxed version of BA: assuming 0.5-weak-synchrony, RBC always guarantees the following for all but a negligible fraction of executions:

1. *Consistency:* if two honest nodes output x and x' respectively, it must be that $x = x'$. For technical reasons that will become clear later, we actually need a strengthening of the standard consistency notion, requiring that an efficient extractor can extract the value that honest nodes can possibly output, given honest nodes' transcript in the initial T rounds of the protocol.
2. *Validity:* if the sender is honest, then honest nodes' output must be equal to the honest sender's input;
3. *T-liveness (under an honest and initially online sender):* if the sender is not only honest but also online in the starting round, then every node in $\mathcal{O}_t$ where $t \geq T$ must have produced an output by the end of round t;
4. *Close termination:* if any honest node (even if offline) produces and output in round r, then anyone in $\mathcal{O}_t$ where $t \geq r + 2\Delta$ must have produced an output by the end of round t too.

Interestingly, note that the T-liveness property is reminiscent of classical synchronous definitions whereas the close termination property is reminiscent of asynchronous definitions.

Construction. At a very high level, our RBC construction combines techniques from classical synchronous "gradecast" [10,15] and asynchronous "reliable broadcast" [5,6]. We defer the concrete construction to Sect. 5; the construction is constant round, i.e., achieves T-liveness where $T = O(1)$.

2.2   Verifiable Secret Sharing (VSS)

Definition. Verifiable secret sharing (VSS) allows a dealer to share a secret among all nodes and later reconstruct it. We propose a new notion of (a computationally secure) VSS that is composable and suitable for a 0.5-weakly-synchronous network. Somewhat imprecisely, we require the following properties:

– *Binding (formally referred to as Validity in Sect. 6.2).* Standard notions of VSS [6] require that the honest transcript of the sharing phase binds to the honestly reconstructed secret. For technical reasons needed later in the proof of the Leader Election (LE), we require a stronger notion: an efficient extractor $\mathcal{E}$, knowing honest nodes' public and secret keys, must be able to extract this secret from the honest transcript during the sharing phase, and the honestly reconstructed secret must agree with the extractor's output.
– *Secrecy and non-malleability.* If the dealer is honest, then the shared value must remain secret from the adversary before reconstruction starts. Not only so, we also need a non-malleability: an adversary, after interacting in VSS instances each with an honest dealer, cannot act as a dealer in another VSS instance and share a secret that is related to the honest secrets.
– *Liveness.* For liveness, we require that if the dealer is honest and online in the initial round of the sharing phase, for $t \geq T$, everyone in $\mathcal{O}_t$ must have output "sharing-succeeded". Even when the dealer is corrupt or initially offline, if any honest node (even if offline) ever outputs "sharing-succeeded" in some round r, then everyone in $\mathcal{O}_t$ where $t \geq r + 2\Delta$ must have output "sharing-succeeded" by the end of round t. If some honest node has output "sharing-succeeded", then reconstruction must be successful and will terminate in T rounds for honest and online nodes.

Just like the RBC definition, our VSS definition also has both synchronous and asynchronous characteristics.

Construction. Informally our construction works as follows:

– Share. In the starting round of the sharing phase, the dealer secret splits its input s into n shares denoted $s_1, s_2, \ldots, s_n$ using a $(\lfloor n/2 \rfloor + 1)$-out-of-$n$ secret-sharing scheme. It then encrypts the share s_j to node i's public key pk_j using a public-key encryption scheme—let CT_j be the resulting ciphertext. Now, the node proves in zero-knowledge, non-interactively, that the ciphertexts $\mathsf{CT}_1, \ldots, \mathsf{CT}_n$ are correct encryptions of an internally consistent sharing of some secret—let π denote the resulting proof. Assuming PKI and honest majority, we can realize a Non-interactive Zero-Knowledge Proof (NIZK) system (without CRS) using a technique called multi-string honest majority NIZK proposed by Groth and Ostrovsky [13] (see online full version [14]). Finally, the dealer invokes an RBC instance (henceforth denoted RBC_0) to reliably broadcast the tuple $(sid, \{\mathsf{CT}_j\}_{j \in [n]}, \pi)$ to everyone—here sid denotes the current instance's unique identifier and this term is needed here and also included in the NIZK statement for compositional reasons.

Suppose that the RBC scheme employed satisfies T_{rbc}-liveness. Now in round T_{rbc} (assuming that the starting round is renamed to round 0), if a tuple has been output from the RBC_0 instance with a valid NIZK proof, then reliably broadcast the message "ok"; otherwise reliably broadcast the message $\perp$—note that here n instances of RBC are spawned and each node i will act as the designated sender in the i-th instance. Finally, output "sharing-succeeded" iff not only RBC_0 has output a tuple with a valid NIZK proof but also at least $\lfloor n/2 \rfloor + 1$ RBC instances have output "ok"—note that at this moment, the node (denoted i) can decrypt its own share s'_i from the corresponding ciphertext component contained in the output of RBC_0.

- Reconstruct: If the sharing phase has output "sharing-succeeded" and moreover the reconstruction phase has been invoked, then node i multicasts the decrypted share s'_i as well as a NIZK proof that the decryption was done correctly (in a way that is consistent with its public key). Finally, as soon as $\lfloor n/2 \rfloor + 1$ decryption shares with valid NIZK proofs are received, one can reconstruct the secret.

2.3   Leader Election (LE)

Definition. Leader Election (LE) is an inputless protocol that allow nodes to elect a leader denoted $L \in [n]$ among the n nodes. For the outcome of LE to be considered "good", we want that not only every honest node must agree on the leader, but also that this leader belongs to $\mathcal{O}_r$ for some a-priori known round r—jumping ahead, later in our BA protocol, everyone would attempt to propose a value during this round r and the proposal of the elected leader will be chosen.

Intuitively, we would like that the LE achieves a good outcome with $O(1)$ probability. Our actual definition turns out to be tricky due to compositional issues that arise due to multiple LE instances sharing the same PKI. We would like that even when multiple LE instances share the same PKI, roughly speaking, almost surely there is still *independent* constant probability that each individual instance's outcome is good. In formal definition (see Sect. 7), we will precisely specify which subset of honest coins that are freshly chosen in each LE instance allow us to capture this desired independence. Note that this independence property is desired because later in our BA protocol, we need to argue that after a bounded number of trials, an honest leader must be elected except with negligible probability.

Construction. Our LE protocol is in fact inspired by the *asynchronous* leader election protocol by Canetti and Rabin [6]. Since our LE construction is rather technical, we explain a high-level intuition here while deferring the full protocol to Sect. 7. The idea is for everyone i to choose n coins denoted $c_{i,1}, \ldots, c_{i,n} \in \mathbb{F}$, one for each person. All these coins will be committed to using a VSS protocol such that corrupt nodes cannot choose their coins after seeing honest coins. Each person j's *charisma* is the product of the coins chosen for him by at least $\lfloor n/2 \rfloor + 1$ others, i.e., $\prod_{i \in D_j} c_{i,j}$ where $D_j \subseteq [n]$ and $|D_j| \geq \lfloor n/2 \rfloor + 1$—in this way, at least one in D_j is honest and has chosen a random coin. In our protocol, every person j will announce this set D_j itself through an RBC protocol. Ideally we would like nodes to agree on a set of candidates that contain many nodes in

$\mathcal{O}_r$ for some r, and elect the candidate with the maximum charisma (lexicographically) from this set—unfortunately at this moment we do not have Byzantine Agreement yet. Thus we must accomplish this task without reaching agreement. Our idea is for each node to *independently calculate a sufficiently large set of candidates; and although honest nodes may not agree on this candidate set, honest nodes' candidate sets must all contain every node in* $\mathcal{O}_r$. We stress that the challenge is that honest offline nodes' candidate sets must also satisfy this property even though they are receiving only an arbitrary subset of messages chosen by the adversary—note that these nodes basically have "asynchronous" networks. Perhaps more challengingly, it could be that every honest node may be offline in some round, and thus everyone's network may be asynchronous at some point.

Towards this end, we adapt Canetti and Rabin's leader election idea [6] to our weakly synchronous setting: specifically, everyone first reliably broadcasts a *tentative* candidate set S, but they keep maintaining and growing a local candidate set denoted $S^* \supseteq S$. They would keep adding nodes that they newly deem eligible to their local set S^*, until at some point, they decide that their local set S^* is sufficiently inclusive based on sufficiently many tentative candidate sets that have been reliably broadcast. At this moment, the node stops growing its local candidate set and outputs the candidate with maximum charisma from its current local set. We refer the reader to Sect. 7 for a detailed description.

2.4   Byzantine Agreement (BA)

The next question is how to construct BA given weakly synchronous LE. This step turns out to be non-trivial too. In particular, we stress that existing synchronous BA protocols [2,15,18] are broken under 0.5-weak-synchrony, not only because they lack a good leader election (or common coin) algorithm—in fact even if we replaced the leader election in existing schemes with an ideal version (e.g., our own leader election scheme in Sect. 7), the resulting BA schemes would still be broken under 0.5-weak-synchrony. All existing synchronous BA schemes make use of synchrony in a *strong* manner: they rely on the fact that if an honest node i sees some message m in round t, then i is surely able to propagate the message to *every* honest node by the end of round $t + \Delta$. This assumption is not true in our model since our model does not provide any message delivery guarantees for offline honest nodes. Instead, our protocol makes use of only weak synchrony and specifically the following observation (and variants of it): if $\lfloor n/2 \rfloor + 1$ number of nodes declare they have observed a message m by the end of round t, then at least one of them must be in $\mathcal{O}_t$ and if all of these nodes try to propagate the message m to others in round t, then everyone in $\mathcal{O}_{t^*}$ where $t^* \geq t + \Delta$ must have observed m by the end of round t^*.

At a very high level, our protocol proceeds in epochs. We make the following simplifying assumptions for the time being: (1) $\Delta = 1$, and (2) every node keeps echoing every message they have seen in every round (in our later technical sections we will remove the need for infinite echoing):

- *Propose:* For the first epoch, the designated sender's signature on a bit is considered a valid proposal. For all other epochs, at epoch start a leader election protocol is invoked to elect a leader. Recall that with constant probability, the leader election algorithm guarantees the following "good" event G: (1) the LE protocol guarantees that the elected leader is in $\mathcal{O}_r$ for some pre-determined round r; and (2) no two honest nodes output inconsistent leaders. Now imagine that in precisely round r of this epoch, everyone tentatively proposes a random bit b—and if the node indeed gets elected as a leader the proposed bit will be recognized as a valid proposal[1].

- *Vote (formally called "Prepare" later):* Let T_{le} be the liveness parameter of the LE scheme. In round T_{le} of the epoch e, a node votes on the elected leader's proposal if in epoch $e - 1$ majority nodes complained of not having received majority votes for either bit—in this case no honest node can have made a decision yet. Otherwise if the node has observed majority votes for some bit b' from the previous epoch $e - 1$, it votes for b'—in this case some honest node might have made a decision on b' and thus we might need to carry on the decision. Henceforth the set of majority votes for b' from epoch $e - 1$ is said to be an epoch-e pseudo-proposal for b'.
- *Commit:* In round $T_{le} + 1$ of the epoch e, a node sends an epoch-e commit message for a bit b, iff it has observed majority epoch-e votes on b, and no epoch-e proposal or pseudo-proposal for $1 - b$ has been seen.
- *Complain:* In round $T_{le} + 2$ of the epoch e, send a complaint if neither bit gained majority votes in this epoch.

At any time, if $\lfloor n/2 \rfloor + 1$ number of commits from the same epoch and for the same bit b have been observed, output b and continue participating in the protocol (we describe a termination technique in the online full version [14]).

Remark 1. We point out that although our BA protocol might somewhat resemble the recent work by Abraham et al. [2], their protocol is in fact broken under 0.5-weak-synchrony (even if they adopted an ideal leader election protocol) for a couple of reasons. In their protocol, in essence a node makes a decision if the node itself has seen majority votes and no conflicting proposal. To ensure consistency under weak synchrony, our protocol makes a decision when majority votes have been collected and moreover, *majority nodes have declared that they have not seen a conflicting proposal (or pseudo-proposal).* Finally, we introduce a "complain" round, and technically this (and together with the whole package) allows us to achieve liveness under 0.5-weak-synchrony—in comparison, Abraham et al.'s protocol [2] appears to lack liveness under weak synchrony.

2.5   Multi-party Computation

We now consider multi-party computation in a weakly synchronous network. Specifically, we will consider the task of secure function evaluation (SFE). Imagine that n nodes each has an input where node i's input is denoted x_i.

---

[1] This is necessary because if a single proposer made a proposal *after* being elected, the adversary could make the proposer offline in that precise round.

The nodes would like to jointly compute a function $f(x_1, \ldots, x_n)$ over their respective inputs. The privacy requirement is that besides learning the outcome, each node must learn nothing else (possibly in a computational sense). Recall that earlier in our Byzantine Agreement (BA) protocols, there is no privacy requirement, and therefore our goal was to ensure that honest nodes who drop offline do not risk inconsistency with the rest of the network. With SFE, we would like to protect not only the consistency but also the *input-privacy* of those who are benign but drop offline or have unstable network connection.

Of course, in a weakly synchronous environment, if we would like online nodes to obtain outputs in a bounded amount of time, we cannot wait forever for offline honest nodes to come online. Thus, in our definition, we require that (1) *at least $n/2$ honest nodes' inputs be included in the computation*; and (2) every honest node that remains online during the protocol must get their inputs incorporated. Note that the second requirement ensures that our notion is strictly stronger (i.e., more robust) than classical synchronous MPC under honest majority.

Construction. Our goal is to construct an expected constant-round SFE protocol secure under 0.5-weak-synchrony. The naïve approach of taking *any* existing MPC and replacing the "broadcast" with our weakly synchronous BA (see earlier subsections of this section) may not solve the problem. Specifically, we need to additionally address the following challenges:

1. Classical synchronous MPC protocols are not required to provide secrecy for honest nodes who even temporarily drop offline. Once offline, an honest node's input may be reconstructed and exposed by honest nodes who still remain online.
2. Many standard MPC protocols [4,11] require many pairs of nodes to have finished several rounds of pairwise interactions to make progress. Even if such protocols required only constant number of rounds in the classical synchronous model, they may suffer from bad round complexity in our model— recall that in a weakly synchronous network, nodes do not have persistent online presence; thus it can take (super-)linear number of rounds for sufficiently many pairs of nodes to have had an opportunity to rendezvous.

To tackle these challenges we rely on a Threshold Multi-Key Fully Homomorphic Encryption (TMFHE) scheme [3,12]. In a TMFHE scheme [3],

1. Each node i can independently generate a public key denoted pk_i and register it with a PKI.
2. Now, each node i can encrypt its input x_i resulting in a ciphertext CT_i.
3. After collecting a set of ciphertexts $\{\mathsf{CT}_i\}_{i \in S}$ corresponding to the nodes $S \subseteq [n]$, any node can independently perform homomorphic evaluation (for the function f) on the ciphertext-set $\{\mathsf{CT}_i\}_{i \in S}$ and obtain an encryption (denoted $\widetilde{\mathsf{CT}}$) of $f(\{x_i\}_{i \in S})$.
4. Now, each node i can evaluate a partial decryption share of $\widetilde{\mathsf{CT}}$ such that if sufficiently many partial decryption shares are combined, one can reconstruct the plaintext evaluation outcome $f(\{x_i\}_{i \in S})$.

In our protocol, in round 0, every node i will compute an TMFHE ciphertext (denoted CT_i) that encrypts its own input and compute a NIZK proof (denoted π_i) attesting to well-formedness of the ciphertext. The pair (CT_i, π_i) will be broadcast by invoking an instance of our BA protocol described in Sect. 8. Let T_{ba} be the liveness parameter of BA. Now, every honest node in $\mathcal{O}_{T_{ba}}$ will have obtained outputs from all BA instances at the beginning of round T_{ba}. From the outputs of these BA instances, nodes in $\mathcal{O}_{T_{ba}}$ can determine the effective-input set $\mathfrak{I}$—specifically if any BA instance that has produced a well-formed output with a valid NIZK proof, the corresponding sender will be included in the effective-input set. Observe that everyone in $\mathcal{O}_0$ will be included in $\mathfrak{I}$. Now, in round T_{ba}, any node who has produced outputs from all n BA instances will perform homomorphic evaluation independently over the collection of ciphertexts $\{CT_i\}_{i \in \mathfrak{I}}$. They will then compute and multicast a partial decryption share and a NIZK proof vouching for the correctness of the partial decryption share. Now, everyone in $\mathcal{O}_t$ for $t \geq T_{ba}$ will have received sufficiently many decryption shares in round t to reconstruct the evaluation outcome.

Comparison with "lazy MPC". Interestingly, the recent work by Badrinarayanan et al. [3] propose a related notion called "lazy MPC"; and their goal is also to safeguard the inputs of those who are benign but drop out in the middle of the protocol. Their model, however, is overly restrictive:

1. first, Badrinarayanan et al. [3] require that a set of majority number of honest nodes to be online *forever*;
2. not only so, they also make the strong assumption that nodes who drop offline never come back (and thus we need not guarantee liveness for nodes who ever drop offline).

As mentioned, in long-running distributed computation environments (e.g., decentralized blockchains where a secure computation task may be repeated many times over the course of years), most likely no single node can guarantee 100% up-time (let alone majority). From a technical perspective, the existence of a majority "honest and persistent online" set also makes the problem significantly easier. For example, for BA, there is in fact a simple compiler that compiles any existing honest-majority, strongly synchronous BA to a setting in which the existence of majority "honest and persistent online" set is guaranteed: basically, simply run an honest-majority, strongly synchronous BA protocol denoted BA_0. If BA_0 outputs a value v, multicast a signed tuple $(\texttt{finalize}, v)$. Output v iff $\lfloor n/2 \rfloor + 1$ number of $(\texttt{finalize}, v)$ messages have been received with valid signatures from distinct nodes. In fact, this simple protocol also ensures liveness for drop-outs who come back online.

Under our definition of weak synchrony, realizing BA is highly non-trivial (see earlier subsections of this section). Once we realize BA, our approach for realizing MPC is reminiscent of Badrinarayanan et al. [3]. There is, in fact, a notable difference in a low-level subtlety: in Badrinarayanan et al. [3]'s lazy MPC model, they can afford to have sufficiently many pairs of nodes engage in several rounds of pairwise interaction, whereas in our model, it can take (super-)linear number of rounds for sufficiently many pairs of nodes to have had an opportunity to rendezvous. For this reason, we need to use a strengthened notion of Threshold Multi-Key Fully Homomorphic Encryption (TMFHE) in comparison with Badrinarayanan et al. [3]. More detailed discussion of these technicalities are included in the online full version [14].

3   Defining a Weakly Synchronous Execution Model

A protocol execution is formally modeled as a set of Interactive Turing Machines (ITMs). The execution proceeds in *rounds*, and is directed by a non-uniform probabilistic polynomial-time (p.p.t.) environment denoted $\mathcal{Z}(1^\kappa)$ parametrized by a security parameter $\kappa \in \mathbb{N}$. Henceforth we refer to ITMs participating in the protocol as *nodes* and we number the nodes from 1 to $n(\kappa)$ where n is chosen by $\mathcal{Z}$ and may be a polynomial function in κ.

3.1   Modeling Corruption and Network Communication

We assume that there is a non-uniform p.p.t. adversary $\mathcal{A}(1^\kappa)$ that may communicate with $\mathcal{Z}$ freely at any time during the execution. $\mathcal{A}$ controls a subset of nodes that are said to be *corrupt*. All corrupt nodes are fully within the control of $\mathcal{A}$: $\mathcal{A}$ observes a node's internal state the moment it becomes corrupt and henceforth all messages received by the corrupt node are forwarded to $\mathcal{A}$; further, $\mathcal{A}$ decides what messages corrupt nodes send in each round. In this paper, we assume that corruption is *static*, i.e., the adversary $\mathcal{A}$ decides which nodes to corrupt prior to the start of the protocol execution.

Nodes that are not corrupt are said to be *honest*, and honest nodes faithfully follow the prescribed protocol for as long as they remain honest. In each round, an honest node can either be *online* or *offline*.

Definition 1 (Honest and online nodes). *Throughout the paper, we shall use the notation $\mathcal{O}_r$ to denote the set of honest nodes that are online in round r. The set $\mathcal{O}_r$ is also called the "honest and online set" of round r. For $i \in \mathcal{O}_r$, we often say that i is honest and online in round r.*

We make the following assumption about network communication—note that our protocol is in the *multicast* model, i.e., every protocol message is sent to the set of all nodes:

Assumption 1 (Message delivery assumption). *We assume that if someone in $\mathcal{O}_r$ multicasts a message m in round r, then everyone in $\mathcal{O}_t$ where $t \geq r + \Delta$ will have received m at the beginning of round t.*

In other words, an honest and online node is guaranteed to be able to deliver messages to the honest and online set of nodes Δ or more rounds later. The adversary $\mathcal{A}$ may delay or erase honest messages arbitrarily as long as Assumption 1 is respected.

Remark 2 (Offline nodes' network communication). Note that the above message delivery assumption implies that messages sent by honest but offline nodes can be arbitrarily delayed or even completely erased by the adversary. Further, the adversary can control which subset of honest messages each offline node receives in every round; it can omit an arbitrary subset of messages or even all of them from the view of honest offline nodes for as long as they remain offline.

Remark 3. We stress that *a node is not aware whether it is online or offline.* This makes protocol design in this model more challenging since the adversary can carefully choose a subset of messages for an offline (honest) node to receive, such that the offline node's view can appear perfectly "normal" such that it is unable to infer that it is offline. Jumping ahead, a consensus protocol secure in our model should guarantee that should an offline node make a decision while it is offline, such decisions would nonetheless be safe and would not risk inconsistency with the rest of the network.

Our protocol needs to be aware of the parameters Δ and n. Throughout we shall assume that Δ and n are polynomial functions in κ. Formally, we can imagine that $\mathcal{Z}$ inputs Δ and n to all honest nodes at the start of the execution. Throughout the paper, we assume that $(\mathcal{A}, \mathcal{Z})$ respects the following constraints:

$\mathcal{Z}$ always provides the parameters n and Δ to honest nodes at the start of the execution such that n is the total number of nodes spawned in the execution, and moreover, the adversary $\mathcal{A}$ respects Assumption 1.

Schedule within a round. More precisely, in each round r, the following happens:

1. First, each honest node receives inputs from $\mathcal{Z}$ and receives incoming messages from the network; note that at this moment, $\mathcal{A}$'s decision on which set of incoming messages an honest node receives will have bearings on whether this honest node can be included in $\mathcal{O}_r$;
2. Each honest node then performs polynomially bounded computation and decides what messages to send to other nodes—these messages are immediately revealed to $\mathcal{A}$. Further, after the computation each honest node may optionally send outputs to $\mathcal{Z}$.
3. At this moment, $\mathcal{A}$ decides which nodes will belong to $\mathcal{O}_r$ where r denotes the current round. Note that $\mathcal{A}$ can decide the honest and online set $\mathcal{O}_r$ of the present round after seeing what messages honest nodes intend to send in this round.
4. $\mathcal{A}$ now decides what messages each corrupt node will send to each honest node. Note also that $\mathcal{A}$ is *rushing* since it can see all the honest messages before deciding the corrupt nodes' messages.
5. Honest nodes send messages over the network to other nodes (which may be delayed or erased by $\mathcal{A}$ as long as Assumption 1 is satisfied).

Definition 2 (χ-weak-synchrony). *We say that $(\mathcal{A}, \mathcal{Z})$ respects χ-weak-synchrony (or that $\mathcal{A}$ respects χ-weak-synchrony), iff in every round r, $|\mathcal{O}_r| \geq \lfloor \chi \cdot n \rfloor + 1$.*

To aid understanding, we make a couple of remarks regarding this definition. First, observe that the set of honest and online nodes need not be the same in every round. This allows us to model churns in the network: nodes go offline and come online; and we wish to achieve consistency for *all* honest nodes, regardless of whether they are online or offline, as long as sufficiently many nodes are online in each round. Second, the requirement of χ-weak-synchrony also imposes a corruption budget. As an example, consider the special case when $\chi = 0.5$ and n is an even integer: if $(\mathcal{A}, \mathcal{Z})$ respects 0.5-weak-synchrony, it means that the adversary controls at most $n/2 - 1$ nodes. It could be that the adversary in fact controls fewer, say, $n/3$ number of nodes. In this case, up to $n/2 - 1 - n/3$ honest nodes may be offline in each round, and jumping ahead, in a consensus protocol we will require that consistency hold for these honest but offline nodes as well.

Finally, note also that our weakly-synchronous model is a generalization of the classical synchronous model: in the classical synchronous model, it is additionally required that for every r, $\mathcal{O}_r$ must be equal to the set of all nodes that remain honest till the end of round r (or later).

3.2   Modeling Setup Assumptions

In the plain model without any setup assumptions, Lamport et al. [17] showed that no consensus protocol could tolerate 1/3 or more corruptions; however for $< 1/3$ corruptions, one can construct protocols that tolerate arbitrary network partitions by adopting the partially synchronous model [7,9,16]. It is also known that assuming a public-key infrastructure (PKI) and computationally bounded adversaries, one can construct consensus protocols that tolerate arbitrarily many corruptions in the classical fully synchronous model. Thus the interesting open question is whether, assuming the existence of a PKI and computationally bounded adversaries, we can construct protocols that tolerate more than 1/3 corruptions and yet provide some quantifiable degree of partition tolerance. Therefore, throughout this paper we shall assume the existence of a PKI and computationally bounded adversaries. We assume that the adversary chooses which nodes to corrupt before the PKI is established.

3.3   Weakly Synchronous Byzantine Agreement

We now define Byzantine Agreement (BA) in a weakly synchronous network. The consistency definition is standard except that now we require consistency for honest nodes regardless of whether they are online or offline. For validity, if the sender is honest but offline initially, we cannot hope that the protocol will somehow make up for the time lost waiting for the sender to come online, such that honest and online nodes would output by the same deadline. Thus we require validity to hold only if the sender is not only honest but also online in the starting round. For liveness, we cannot hope that honest but offline nodes obtain outputs quickly without the risk of being inconsistent with the rest of the network. Thus, we require that as soon as an honest node is online at time T or greater (where T is also called the liveness parameter), it must produce an output if it has not done so already.

Syntax. A Byzantine Agreement (BA) protocol must satisfy the following syntax. Without loss of generality, we assume that node 1 is the designated sender. Before protocol start, the sender receives an input bit b from $\mathcal{Z}$; and all other nodes receive no input. The nodes then run a protocol, and during the protocol every node may output a bit.

Security. Let $T(\kappa, n, \Delta)$ be a polynomial function in the stated parameters. For $P \in \{\text{consistency, validity, } T\text{-liveness}\}$, a BA protocol is said to satisfy property P w.r.t. some non-uniform p.p.t. $(\mathcal{A}, \mathcal{Z})$ that is allowed to spawn multiple possibly concurrent BA instances sharing the same PKI, iff there exists a negligible function $\mathsf{negl}(\cdot)$ such that for every $\kappa \in \mathbb{N}$, except with $\mathsf{negl}(\kappa)$ probability over the choice of protocol execution, the corresponding property as explained below is respected in all BA instances spawned—henceforth we rename the starting round of each BA instance to be round 0 and count rounds within the same instance accordingly afterwards:

– *Consistency.* If honest node i outputs b_i and honest node j outputs b_j, it must be that $b_i = b_j$.
– *Validity.* If the sender is in $\mathcal{O}_0$, any honest node's output must be equal to the sender's input.
– *T-liveness.* Any node in $\mathcal{O}_r$ for $r \geq T$ must have output a bit by the end of round r.

We say that a BA protocol satisfies property $P \in \{\text{consistency, validity, and } T\text{-liveness}\}$ under χ-weak-synchrony if it satisfies the property P w.r.t. any non-uniform p.p.t. $(\mathcal{A}, \mathcal{Z})$ that respects χ-weak-synchrony and is allowed to spawn multiple possibly concurrent BA instances sharing the same PKI. Henceforth, if a BA protocol satisfies consistency, validity, and T-liveness under χ-weak-synchrony, we also say that the protocol is a "χ-weakly-synchronous BA protocol".

Remark 4 (Worst-case vs expected notions of liveness). We note that T-liveness defines a worst-case notion of liveness. In the remainder of the paper, we sometimes use an expected round complexity notion. We say that our BA protocol is expected constant round, iff there is a random variable R whose expectation is constant such that everyone in $\mathcal{O}_r$ where $r \geq R$ should have produced an output by the end of round r.

Multi-valued agreement. The above definition can be extended to multi-valued agreement where nodes agree on a value from the domain $\{0,1\}^{\ell(\kappa)}$ rather than a single bit. Multi-valued agreement can be obtained by parallel composition of ℓ instances of BA. In this paper, we will refer to the multi-valued version as Byzantine Agreement (BA) too.

4   Lower Bounds

4.1   Impossibility of Weakly-Synchronous Consensus for $\chi \leq 0.5$

First, we show that for any $\chi \leq 0.5 - \frac{1}{n}$, it is impossible to achieve BA under χ-weak-synchrony. The intuition for this lower bound is simple: if a BA protocol allows a minority set of online nodes to reach agreement without hearing from the offline nodes, then two minority camps could independently reach agreement thus risking consistency. We formalize this intuition in the following theorem.

Theorem 3. *For any $\chi \leq 0.5 - \frac{1}{n}$, for any polynomial function T, no BA protocol Π can simultaneously achieve consistency, validity, and T-liveness under χ-weak-synchrony.*

Proof. Please refer to the online full version [14].

We point out that the above the lower bound holds even if $\mathcal{A}$ is restricted to scheduling the same honest and online set throughout, i.e., $\mathcal{O}_0 = \mathcal{O}_1 = \ldots$, has to decide the message delivery schedule in advance, and even when no node is corrupt. Moreover, the lower bound holds even for randomized protocols, allowing computational assumptions, and allowing additional setup assumptions (e.g., PKI, random oracle, or the erasure model).

Best-possible partition tolerance. In light of Theorem 3, a BA protocol secure under 0.5-weak-synchrony is also said to be best-possible partition tolerant.

4.2   Corrupt-Majority Protocols Sacrifice Partition Tolerance

It is well-known that there exist Byzantine Agreement protocols that tolerate arbitrarily many byzantine faults [8] under the classical synchronous model henceforth referred to as *strong* synchrony. If we adopted the classical strong synchrony model we might be misled to think that protocols that tolerate corrupt majority are strictly more robust than those that tolerate only corrupt minority. In this section, however, we show that corrupt-majority protocols (under strong synchrony) in fact sacrifice partition tolerance in exchange for tolerating corrupt majority, and this is inherent. As explained earlier, in real-world scenarios such as decentralized cryptocurrencies, partition tolerance seems to be a more important robustness property.

It is not too difficult to see that any corrupt-majority, strongly-synchronous protocol cannot be secure under 0.5-weak-synchrony. Specifically, with a corrupt-majority strongly-synchronous protocol, if the network partitions into multiple minority connected components, each component will end up reaching its own independent decision. We can generalize this intuition and prove an even stronger statement: any strongly-synchronous protocol that tolerates more than $\nu \geq 0.5$ fraction of corruptions cannot be secure under ν-weak-synchrony, i.e., such a protocol cannot guarantee consistency for all honest nodes (including offline ones) even if we make the strong assumption that at least ν fraction of honest nodes are online. In other words, *the more corruptions the protocol tolerates under strong synchrony, the less partition tolerant it becomes.* To state our theorem precisely, we introduce the following notation:

- We say that $(\mathcal{A}, \mathcal{Z})$ respects μ-strongly-synchronous iff at least $\lfloor \mu n \rfloor + 1$ nodes are honest and moreover all honest nodes are forever online. We say that a BA protocol satisfies property $P \in \{$consistency, validity, and T–liveness$\}$ under μ-strong-synchrony iff it satisfies property P w.r.t. any non-uniform p.p.t. $(\mathcal{A}, \mathcal{Z})$ that respects μ-strong-synchrony.
- Let $\mathcal{BA}\{\mu\}$ be the family that contains every protocol Π satisfying the following: $\exists$ a polynomial function $T(\cdot, \cdot, \cdot)$ s.t. Π that satisfy consistency, validity, and $T(\kappa, n, \Delta)$-liveness under μ-strong-synchrony.
- Let $\mathcal{BA}^+\{\chi\}$ be the family that contains every protocol Π satisfying the following: $\exists$ a polynomial function $T(\cdot, \cdot, \cdot)$ s.t. Π that satisfy consistency, validity, and T-liveness under χ-weak-synchrony.

Theorem 4. $\forall 0 < \mu < 0.5, \chi \leq 1 - \mu - 2/n, \ \mathcal{BA}\{\mu\} \cap \mathcal{BA}^+\{\chi\} = \emptyset.$

Proof. Please refer to the online full version [14].

5   Reliable Broadcast (RBC)

In our upper bound sections (Sects. 5, 6.2, 7, 8, and the MPC upper bound in the online full version [14]) for convenience, we will make a slightly stronger assumption on the underlying network—but in fact this stronger assumption can be realized from Assumption 1 described earlier.

Assumption 2 (Strong message delivery assumption). *If $i \in \mathcal{O}_r$ and i has multicast or received a message* m *before the end of round r, then everyone in $\mathcal{O}_t$ where $t \geq r + \Delta$ will have received* m *at the beginning of round t.*

In the online full version [14], we describe how to realize Assumption 2 through a simple echo mechanism: roughly speaking, nodes echo and retry sending messages they have seen until they believe that the message has become part of the honest and online nodes' view.

5.1   Definition

We define a primitive called reliable broadcast (RBC) that allows a designated sender to broadcast a message, guaranteeing consistency regardless of whether the sender is honest or online, and additionally guaranteeing liveness when the sender is not only honest but also online in the starting round. We also require a "close termination" property: even when the designated sender is corrupt, we require that if some honest node outputs in round r, then everyone in $\mathcal{O}_t$ where $t \geq r + 2\Delta$ must have output by the end of round t too. The liveness notion is defined in a similar fashion as in Sect. 3.3: since under weak synchrony we cannot guarantee progress for offline nodes, we require that any honest node who comes back online in some time T or greater will have received output (assuming an honest and initially online sender). For technical reasons that will be useful later in the proof of our Leader Election (LE) protocol, we need a stronger version of the standard consistency property: not only must honest nodes' outputs agree, there must be an efficient extractor that outputs either a bit $b \in \{0, 1\}$ or $\bot$ when given the PKI and the honest nodes' transcript in the initial T rounds as input. If any honest node indeed makes an output, the output must be consistent with the extractor's output b.

Syntax. An RBC protocol consists of the following algorithms/protocols:

- **PKI setup:** at the very beginning every node i registers a public key pk_i with the PKI;
- **RBC protocol:** all instances of RBC share the same PKI. In each RBC instance, a designated sender (whose identifier is pre-determined and publicly-known) receives a value x from the environment $\mathcal{Z}$ whereas all other nodes receive nothing. Whenever a node terminates, it outputs a value y. Henceforth we shall assume that an admissible $\mathcal{Z}$ must instruct all nodes to start protocol execution in the same round[2];
- **Extractor $\mathcal{E}$:** a polynomial-time deterministic extractor $\mathcal{E}$ that is needed only in our security definitions and proofs, not in the real-world protocol.

Security. Let $T(n, \Delta, \kappa)$ be a polynomial function in the stated parameters. For $P \in \{T\text{-consistency, validity, } T\text{-liveness, close termination}\}$, we say that an RBC protocol Π satisfies property P under χ-weak-synchrony iff for any non-uniform p.p.t. $(\mathcal{A}, \mathcal{Z})$ that respects χ-weak-synchrony and can spawn multiple instances of RBC sharing the same PKI, there exists a negligible function $\mathsf{negl}(\cdot)$ such that for every $\kappa \in \mathbb{N}$, except for $\mathsf{negl}(\kappa)$ fraction of the executions in the experiment $\mathsf{EXEC}^{\Pi}(\mathcal{A}, \mathcal{Z}, \kappa)$, the following properties hold for every RBC instance:

- *T-consistency.* Let $y := \mathcal{E}(\{\mathsf{pk}_i\}_{i \in [n]}, \mathsf{Tr})$ where Tr denotes the transcript of all honest nodes in the initial T rounds of the RBC instance. Then, if any honest node ever outputs y', it must be that $y' = y$.
- *Validity.* If the sender is honest and its input is x, then if any honest node outputs x', it must be that $x' = x$.
- *T-liveness (under an honest and initially online sender).* If the sender is not only honest and but also online in the starting round of this RBC instance (henceforth the starting round is renamed to be round 0 for convenience), then every node that is honest and online in round $r \geq T$ will have produced an output by the end of round r.
- *Close termination.* If an honest node outputs in some round r, then every node that is honest and online in round $r' \geq r + 2\Delta$ will have output by the end of round r'.

---

[2] Later in our VSS and LE protocols that invoke RBC, the fact that the RBC's environment $\mathcal{Z}$ is admissible is guaranteed by construction.

Remark 5. Although in general, consistency and liveness can be parametrized by different delay functions, without loss of generality we may assume that two parameters are the same T (since we can always take the maximum of the two).

5.2 Construction

During the PKI setup phase (shared across all subsequent RBC instances), every node calls $(\mathsf{vk}, \mathsf{ssk}) \leftarrow \varSigma.\mathsf{K}(1^\kappa)$ and registers the vk with the PKI. The portion ssk is kept secret and henceforth the node will use ssk to sign protocol messages in all future RBC instances. Henceforth, although not explicitly noted, we assume that every message is by default tagged with the current session's identifier denoted sid. Every signature computation and verification will include the sid. We also assume that each message is tagged with the purported sender such that a recipient knows under which public key to verify the signature.

1. **Propose (round 0):** In round 0, the sender multicasts $(\mathtt{propose}, x)$ where x is its input, attached with a signature on the tuple.
2. **ACK (round Δ):** At the beginning of round Δ, if a tuple $(\mathtt{propose}, y)$ with a valid signature has been received from the sender, multicast $(\mathtt{ack}, y)$ along with a signature on the tuple.
3. **Commit (round 2Δ):** At the beginning of round 2Δ, if the node has observed $\lfloor n/2 \rfloor + 1$ number of $(\mathtt{ack}, y)$ messages for the same y and with valid signatures from distinct nodes, and moreover, it has not received any conflicting $(\mathtt{propose}, y')$ message (with a valid signature from the sender) for $y' \neq y$, then multicast $(\mathtt{commit}, y)$ along with a signature on the tuple.
4. **Finalize (any time):** At any time, if the node has received $\lfloor n/2 \rfloor + 1$ valid $(\mathtt{commit}, y)$ messages for the same y and from distinct nodes, multicast $(\mathtt{finalize}, y)$ along with a signature on the tuple. At any time, if a collection of $\lfloor n/2 \rfloor + 1$ $(\mathtt{finalize}, y)$ messages with valid signatures from distinct nodes have been observed, output y.

We defer the constructor of the extractor $\mathcal{E}$ to the proofs since it is needed only in the security definitions and proofs and not in the real-world protocol.

Theorem 5. *Suppose that the signature scheme employed is secure, then the above* RBC *protocol satisfies 2Δ-consistency, validity, 4Δ-liveness, and close termination under 0.5-weak-synchrony.*

Proof. Please refer to the online full version [14].

6 Verifiable Secret Sharing (VSS)

6.1 Definitions

A Verifiable Secret Sharing (VSS) allows a dealer to share a secret among all nodes and later reconstruct the secret. Standard notions of VSS [6] require that the honest transcript of the sharing phase binds to the honestly reconstructed secret. For technical reasons needed later in the proof of the Leader Election (LE), we require a stronger notion, i.e., an efficient extractor $\mathcal{E}$, knowing honest nodes' public and secret keys, must be able to extract this secret from the honest transcript during the sharing phase (and later the honestly reconstructed secret must agree with the extractor's output). We need a composable notion of secrecy which we call non-malleability—note that composition was a non-issue in previous works that achieve security against unbounded adversaries [6]. Finally, for liveness, we require that if the dealer is honest and online in the initial round, for $t \geq T$, everyone in $\mathcal{O}_t$ must have output "sharing succeeded". Even when the dealer is corrupt or offline, if any honest node ever outputs "sharing succeeded" in some round r, then everyone in $\mathcal{O}_t$ where $t \geq r + 2\Delta$ must have output "sharing succeeded" by the end of round t. If some honest node has output "sharing succeeded", then reconstruction must be successful and will terminate in T rounds for honest and online nodes.

Syntax. A Verifiable Secret Sharing (VSS) scheme for a finite field $\mathbb{F}$ consists of a setup algorithm K that is run once upfront and henceforth shared among all protocol instances where each protocol instance contains two sub-protocols called Share and Reconstruct:

1. $(\mathsf{pk}_i, \mathsf{sk}_i) \leftarrow \mathsf{K}(1^\kappa)$: every node i calls this algorithm to generate a public and secret key pair denoted pk_i and sk_i; and pk_i is registered with the PKI.
2. Share: A designated node called the dealer receives an input $s \in \mathbb{F}$ from $\mathcal{Z}$ and all other nodes receive no input. Now all nodes execute the Share sub-protocol for the dealer to secret-share its input. We assume that for the same VSS instance, an admissible $\mathcal{Z}$ always instructs all honest nodes to start executing Share in the same round. Should execution of Share successfully terminate, a node would output a canonical output "sharing succeeded".
3. Reconstruct: All nodes execute the Reconstruct sub-protocol to reconstruct a secret that is shared earlier in the Share sub-protocol. We assume that an admissible $\mathcal{Z}$ always instructs all honest nodes to start executing Reconstruct in the same round. Should execution of Reconstruct successfully terminate, a node would output a reconstructed secret $s' \in \mathbb{F}$.

Besides these real-world algorithms, a VSS scheme additionally has a polynomial-time extractor algorithm $\mathcal{E}$ that is needed later in the security definitions (including the definitions of validity and non-malleability). We shall explain the extractor $\mathcal{E}$ later when we define security.

T-Liveness. Consider a pair $(\mathcal{A}, \mathcal{Z})$ that may spawn multiple (concurrent or sequential) VSS instances all of which share the same n, PKI setup, and the same Δ. Let $T(n, \Delta, \kappa)$ be a polynomial function in n, Δ, κ. We say that a VSS protocol satisfies T-liveness under χ-weak-synchrony iff for any non-uniform p.p.t. $(\mathcal{A}, \mathcal{Z})$

that respects χ-weak-synchrony (and may spawn multiple instances sharing the same PKI), there exists $\mathsf{negl}(\cdot)$ such that for any $\kappa \in \mathbb{N}$, such that except with $\mathsf{negl}(\kappa)$ probability, the following holds for every VSS instance spawned:

1. *Termination of* Share *under honest and initially online dealer:* suppose that the Share sub-protocol is spawned in round r_0, and moreover the dealer is in $\mathcal{O}_{r_0}$, then any node in $\mathcal{O}_r$ for $r \geq r_0 + T$ must have output "sharing succeeded" by the end of round r;
2. *Close termination of* Share*:* if an honest node i has terminated the Share sub-protocol outputting "sharing succeeded" in round r, then for every $r' \geq r + 2\Delta$, every node in $\mathcal{O}_{r'}$ must have terminated the Share sub-protocol outputting "sharing succeeded" by the end of round r';
3. *Termination of* Reconstruct*:* if by the end of some round r, some honest node has terminated the Share sub-protocol outputting "sharing succeeded", and moreover honest nodes have been instructed to start Reconstruct, then, anyone in $\mathcal{O}_t$ for $t \geq r + T$ must have terminated the Reconstruct sub-protocol outputting some reconstructed value in $\mathbb{F}$ by the end of round t.

T-Validity. As before, we consider an $(\mathcal{A}, \mathcal{Z})$ pair that is allowed to spawn multiple (concurrent or sequential) VSS instances, all of which share the same n, PKI setup, and Δ. Let $T(n, \Delta, \kappa)$ be a polynomial function in its parameters. Henceforth let Honest $\subseteq [n]$ denote the set of honest nodes. We say that a VSS protocol satisfies T-validity under χ-weak-synchrony, iff for every non-uniform p.p.t. $(\mathcal{A}, \mathcal{Z})$ that respects χ-weak-synchrony (and may spawn multiple VSS instances sharing the same PKI where each instance has a unique sid), there exists a negligible function $\mathsf{negl}(\cdot)$ such that except with $\mathsf{negl}(\kappa)$ probability, the following holds for every VSS instance spawned: let $s' := \mathcal{E}(\{\mathsf{pk}_i\}_{i \in [n]}, \{\mathsf{sk}_i\}_{i \in \mathsf{Honest}}, \mathsf{Tr})$ where Tr denotes the transcript observed by all honest nodes in the initial T rounds of the Share sub-protocol; it must be that

(a) if an honest node ever outputs a reconstructed secret, the value must agree with s';
(b) if $\mathcal{E}$ outputs $\perp$, then no honest node ever outputs "sharing succeeded"[3];
(c) if the dealer is honest and online in the round in which the Share sub-protocol was invoked, and moreover it received the input s from $\mathcal{Z}$, then $s' = s$.

Non-malleability. Consider the following experiment $\mathsf{Expt}^{\mathcal{A}}(1^\kappa, s)$ involving an adversary $\mathcal{A}$ and a challenger $\mathcal{C}$, as well as a challenge input $s \in \mathbb{F}$. We assume that throughout the experiment, *if an honest node outputs a string in any* VSS *instance, the adversary $\mathcal{A}$ is notified of the node's identifier, the identifier of the* VSS *instance, as well as the corresponding output.*

1. **Setup.** First, $\mathcal{A}$ chooses which set of nodes to corrupt. Henceforth the challenger $\mathcal{C}$ acts on behalf of all honest nodes and interact with $\mathcal{A}$. The honest nodes run the honest key generation algorithm such that each picks a public/secret-key pair. The public keys are given to $\mathcal{A}$. $\mathcal{A}$ now chooses corrupt nodes' public keys arbitrarily and sends them to $\mathcal{C}$.

---

[3] Note that (a) implies that if $\mathcal{E}$ outputs $\perp$, then no honest node will ever output a reconstructed secret.

2. **Queries.** The adversary $\mathcal{A}$ is now allowed to (adaptively) instruct $\mathcal{C}$ to spawn as many VSS instances as it wishes. The queries can be issued at any time, including before, during, or after the challenge phase (see the **Challenge** paragraph later).

   – Whenever $\mathcal{A}$ sends $\mathcal{C}$ a tuple $(sid, \mathsf{Share}, u, x)$ where $sid \in \{0,1\}^*$ and $u \in [n]$, $\mathcal{C}$ spawns instance sid with node u as the dealer. If u is honest, $\mathcal{A}$ must additionally specify the honest dealer u's input x in this instance (otherwise the field x is ignored). Now, $\mathcal{C}$ invokes the instance's Share sub-protocol (if this has not been done already);

   – Whenever $\mathcal{A}$ sends $\mathcal{C}$ a tuple $(sid, \mathsf{Reconstruct})$ where $sid \in \{0,1\}^*$, $\mathcal{C}$ does the following: if the instance sid has been spawned, then invoke the Reconstruct sub-protocol for that instance (if this has not been done).

   – Whenever $\mathcal{A}$ sends $\mathcal{C}$ a tuple $(sid, \mathsf{Extract})$ and instance sid has executed for at least T rounds, then $\mathcal{C}$ computes $\mathcal{E}(\{\mathsf{pk}_i\}_{i \in [n]}, \{\mathsf{sk}_i\}_{i \in \mathsf{Honest}}, \mathsf{Tr})$ where Tr is the transcript of honest nodes in the initial T rounds of the Share sub-protocol; $\mathcal{C}$ returns the result to $\mathcal{A}$.

3. **Challenge.** At any time, $\mathcal{A}$ may send the tuple $(\mathtt{challenge}, sid, u)$ to $\mathcal{C}$ where u must be an honest node and the challenge sid must not be specified in any Extract or Reconstruct query throughout the experiment (in the past or future). $\mathcal{C}$ then spawns a challenge VSS instance identified by sid where u is the designated dealer and receives the input s; further $\mathcal{C}$ invokes the challenge instance's Share sub-protocol.

4. **Output.** Whenever the adversary $\mathcal{A}$ outputs a bit $b \in \{0,1\}$, this bit is defined as the experiment's output.

We assume that an admissible $\mathcal{A}$ never attempts to create two VSS instances with the same sid, i.e., $\mathcal{A}$ chooses distinct session identifiers for all instances. Further, throughout the experiment, $\mathcal{A}$ is allowed to decide which honest nodes are online/offline in each round (after seeing the messages honest nodes want to send in that round). $\mathcal{A}$ also controls the message delivery schedule[4].

Definition 3 (Non-malleability for VSS). *We say that a VSS scheme satisfies non-malleability under χ-weak-synchrony iff for any non-uniform p.p.t. $\mathcal{A}$ that respects χ-weak-synchrony, there exists a negligible function $\mathsf{negl}(\cdot)$ such that for any $s, s' \in \mathbb{F}$, $\left| \Pr[\mathsf{Expt}^{\mathcal{A}}(1^\kappa, s) = 1] - \Pr[\mathsf{Expt}^{\mathcal{A}}(1^\kappa, s') = 1] \right| \le \mathsf{negl}(\kappa)$.*

6.2   A 0.5-Weakly-Synchronous VSS Scheme

We show how to construct a 0.5-weakly synchronous VSS scheme. We will rely on the following cryptographic primitives:

1. let $\mathsf{NIZK} := (\mathsf{K}, \widetilde{\mathsf{K}}, \mathsf{P}, \mathsf{V})$ denote multi-CRS NIZK scheme that satisfies completeness, zero-knowledge, and simulation soundness (see the online full version [14]);

---

[4] Specifically, when honest nodes running inside $\mathcal{C}$ want to send messages, the messages are forwarded to $\mathcal{A}$, and $\mathcal{A}$ tells $\mathcal{C}$ when each honest node receives what message.

2. let $\mathsf{PKE} := (\mathsf{K}, \mathsf{Enc}, \mathsf{Dec})$ denote a perfectly correct public-key encryption scheme that preserves IND-CCA security; and

3. let RBC denote a reliable broadcast scheme that satisfies T_{rbc}-consistency, T_{rbc}-liveness, validity, and close termination under 0.5-weak-synchrony for some polynomial function T_{rbc}.

PKI setup (shared across all VSS instances): During the PKI setup phase, every node i performs the following:

- let $(\mathsf{epk}_i, \mathsf{esk}_i) \leftarrow \mathsf{PKE}.\mathsf{K}(1^\kappa)$; $(\mathsf{vk}_i, \mathsf{ssk}_i) := \Sigma.\mathsf{K}(1^\kappa)$; $\mathsf{crs}_i \leftarrow \mathsf{NIZK}.\mathsf{K}(1^\kappa)$; and let $(\mathsf{rpk}_i, \mathsf{rsk}_i) \leftarrow \mathsf{RBC}.\mathsf{K}(1^\kappa)$;
- node i registers its public key $\mathsf{pk}_i := (\mathsf{epk}_i, \mathsf{crs}_i, \mathsf{vk}_i, \mathsf{rpk}_i)$ with the PKI; and it retains its secret key comprised of $\mathsf{sk}_i := (\mathsf{esk}_i, \mathsf{ssk}_i, \mathsf{rsk}_i)$.

Share (executed by the dealer): Let s be the input received from the environment, the dealer does the following:

- it splits s into n shares using a $(\lfloor n/2 \rfloor + 1)$-out-of-$n$ Shamir Secret Sharing scheme, where the i-th share is henceforth denoted s_i;
- for $i \in [n]$, it computes $\mathsf{CT}_i := \mathsf{PKE}.\mathsf{Enc}_{\mathsf{epk}_i}(sid, s_i)$ where sid is the identifier of the current instance;
- it calls $\mathsf{NIZK}.\mathsf{P}(\{\mathsf{crs}_i\}_{i \in [n]}, x, w)$ to compute a proof π where x and w are defined as below: $x := (sid, \{\mathsf{pk}_i, \mathsf{CT}_i\}_{i \in [n]})$ is the statement declaring that there is a witness $w := (s, \{s_i\}_{i \in [n]})$ such that for each $i \in [n]$, CT_i is a valid encryption[5] of (sid, s_i) under epk_i (which is part of pk_i); and moreover, the set of shares $\{s_i\}_{i \in [n]}$ is a valid sharing of the secret s.
- finally, the dealer relies on RBC to reliably broadcast the tuple $(sid, \{\mathsf{CT}_i\}_{i \in [n]}, \pi)$—henceforth this RBC instance is denoted RBC_0.

Share (executed by everyone): Every node i does the following (where the starting round of Share is renamed round 0):

- **Any time:** whenever the RBC_0 instance outputs a tuple of the form $(sid, \{\mathsf{CT}_j\}_{j \in [n]}, \pi)$, call $\mathsf{NIZK}.\mathsf{V}$ to verify the proof π w.r.t. the statement $(sid, \{\mathsf{pk}_i, \mathsf{CT}_i\}_{i \in [n]})$; and if the check succeeds, set $\mathsf{flag} := 1$ (we assume that flag was initially 0).
- **Round T_{rbc}:** if $\mathsf{flag} = 1$, reliably broadcast the message "ok"; else reliably broadcast the message "$\perp$";
- **Any time:** whenever more than $\lfloor n/2 \rfloor + 1$ RBC instances have output "ok" and RBC_0 has output a tuple; decrypt CT_i contained in the tuple output by RBC_0 using secret key esk_i; let $(\_, s_i)$ be the decrypted outcome; now record the share s_i and output "sharing-succeeded".

Reconstruct (executed by everyone): when the Reconstruct sub-protocol has been invoked, every node i waits till the instance's Share sub-protocol has output "sharing-succeeded" and then performs the following where the set $\mathbb{S}$ is initially empty:

- let s_i be the share recorded at the end of the Share sub-protocol;

---

[5] For simplicity, we omit writing the randomness consumed by $\mathsf{PKE}.\mathsf{Enc}$ which is also part of the witness.

- call NIZK.P($\{crs_i\}_{i\in[n]}, x, w$) to compute a proof (henceforth denoted π_i) for the following statement $x := (sid, i, s_i, CT_i)$ declaring that there is random string that causes PKE.K to output the tuple (epk_i, esk_i) where $epk_i \in pk_i$; and moreover, (sid, s_i) is a correct decryption of CT_i using esk_i—the witness w includes the randomness used in PKE.K, esk_i, and the randomness of PKE.Dec.
- multicast the tuple (sid, i, s_i, π_i);
- upon receiving a tuple (sid, j, s_j, π_j) such that π_j verifies w.r.t. the statement (sid, j, s_j, CT_j) where CT_j was the output of RBC_0 during the Share sub-protocol, add s_j to the set $\mathbb{S}$.
- whenever the set $\mathbb{S}$'s size is at least $\lfloor n/2 \rfloor + 1$, call the reconstruction algorithm of Shamir Secret Sharing to reconstruct a secret s, and if reconstruction is successful, output the result.

Since the extractor algorithm $\mathcal{E}$ is only needed in the proofs, we defer its presentation to the online full version [14].

Theorem 6. *Without loss of generality, assume that $T_{rbc} \geq 3\Delta$ (if not, we can simply define $T_{rbc} := 3\Delta$); and moreover assume that the RBC scheme employed satisfies T_{rbc}-liveness, validity, T_{rbc}-consistency, and close termination under 0.5-weak-synchrony; the NIZK scheme employed satisfies zero-knowledge and simulation soundness; and the PKE scheme satisfies IND-CCA security and is perfectly correct. Then, the above VSS protocol satisfies $2T_{rbc}$-liveness, T_{rbc}-validity, and non-malleability under 0.5-weak-synchrony.*

Proof. Please refer to the online full version [14].

7   Leader Election (LE)

7.1   Definition

A leader election (LE) protocol is an inputless protocol such that when a node terminates, it outputs an elected leader $L \in [n]$. For the outcome of LE to be considered good, we want that not only every honest node must agree on the leader, but also that this leader belongs to $\mathcal{O}_r$ for some a-priori known round r. We would like that the LE achieves a good outcome with $O(1)$ probability. Our actual definition below is somewhat tricky due to compositional issues that arise due to multiple LE instances sharing the same PKI. We would like that even when multiple LE instances share the same PKI, roughly speaking, almost surely there is still *independent* constant probability that each individual instance's outcome is good. In our formal definition below, we will precisely specify which subset of honest coins that are freshly chosen in each LE instance allow us to capture this desired independence. Note that this independence property is desired because later in our BA protocol, we need to argue that after super-logarithmically many trials, an honest leader must be elected except with negligible probability. We formalize the definitions below.

T-liveness. Consider an $(\mathcal{A}, \mathcal{Z})$ pair that is allowed to spawn multiple concurrent or sequential LE instances all of which share the same n, PKI setup, and Δ.

Let $T(n, \Delta, \kappa)$ be a polynomial function in its parameters. We say that an LE protocol denoted Π satisfies T-liveness under χ-weak-synchrony if for every non-uniform p.p.t. $(\mathcal{A}, \mathcal{Z})$ that respects χ-weak-synchrony and may spawn multiple LE instances sharing the same PKI, there exists a negligible function $\mathsf{negl}(\cdot)$ such that for every $\kappa \in \mathbb{N}$, except with $\mathsf{negl}(\kappa)$ probability, the following holds for every LE instance spawned (for the LE instance of interest, we rename its starting round to round 0):

> every node in $\mathcal{O}_r$ for $r \geq T$ must have output by the end of round r.

(T^*, q)-*quality.* We consider an $(\mathcal{A}, \mathcal{Z})$ pair who can spawn $m(\kappa)$ LE instances possibly running concurrently. Henceforth let ρ_ℓ^* denote the collection of the following randomness:

> for each node honest and online in the starting round (i.e., round 0) of the ℓ-th instance: the first $d(\kappa, n)$ bits of randomness consumed by this node in this round,

where $d(\kappa, n)$ is an appropriate polynomial function that depends on the construction. Let ρ be all randomness consumed by the entire experiment (including by $(\mathcal{A}, \mathcal{Z})$ and by honest nodes and the randomness of the PKI), and let $\rho \backslash \rho_\ell^*$ denote all other randomness besides ρ_ℓ^*.

We say that a leader election (LE) protocol satisfies (T^*, q)-quality under χ-weak-synchrony, iff for any polynomial function $m(\kappa)$, for any non-uniform p.p.t. $(\mathcal{A}, \mathcal{Z})$ that respects χ-weak-synchrony and spawns $m(\kappa)$ LE instances possibly executing concurrently, there exists a negligible function $\mathsf{negl}(\cdot)$ such that for all $\kappa \in \mathbb{N}$, for every $1 \leq \ell \leq m(\kappa)$, except for a $\mathsf{negl}(\kappa)$ fraction of choices for $\rho \backslash \rho_\ell^*$, there exist at least q fraction of choices for ρ_ℓ^*, such that the experiment (determined by the joint randomness choice above) would guarantee the following good events for the ℓ-th instance:

1. *Consistency:* if an honest node outputs L and another honest node outputs L', it holds that $L = L'$; and
2. *Fairness:* let L be the leader output by an honest node, we have that $L \in \mathcal{O}_{T^*}$ (assuming that the start round of the ℓ-th instance is renamed round 0).

7.2   Construction

The construction is a bit involved and thus we refer the reader to Sect. 2.3 for an intuitive explanation of our protocol. Below we focus on a formal description.

Let VSS denote a verifiable secret sharing scheme for inputs over the finite field $\mathbb{F}$. (see Sect. 6.2) and let T_{vss} be its liveness parameter. We now show how to construct leader election from verifiable secret sharing. In our protocol below, there are n^2 instances of VSS. Henceforth we use $\mathsf{VSS}[i, j]$ to denote the j-th instance where node i is the designated dealer. Additionally, let RBC denote a reliable broadcast protocol (see Sect. 5) whose liveness parameter is denoted T_{rbc}. Let $\Sigma := (\mathsf{K}, \mathsf{Sign}, \mathsf{Ver})$ denote a digital signature scheme.

The following protocol is executed by every node, below we describe the actions taken by node $i \in [n]$—for simplicity we implicitly assume that every message is tagged with its purported sender:

- **PKI setup** (shared across all LE instances): each node i calls $(\mathsf{rpk}_i, \mathsf{rsk}_i) \leftarrow$ RBC.K(1^κ); $(\mathsf{vpk}_i, \mathsf{vsk}_i) \leftarrow$ VSS.K(1^κ); and $(\mathsf{vk}_i, \mathsf{ssk}_i) \leftarrow \Sigma$.K$(1^\kappa)$. Now its public key is $(\mathsf{rpk}_i, \mathsf{vpk}_i, \mathsf{vk}_i)$ and its secret key is $(\mathsf{rsk}_i, \mathsf{vsk}_i, \mathsf{ssk}_i)$.
  In the following, we describe the leader election (LE) protocol. We assume that all LE protocols share the same PKI. Moreover, whenever a node i uses ssk_i to sign messages, the message to be signed is always tagged with the session identifier sid of the current instance and signature verification also verifies the signature to the same sid.
- **Round 0:** Node i chooses n random coins $c_{i,1}, \ldots, c_{i,n} \in \mathbb{F}$. For instances VSS$[i,1]$, $\ldots$, VSS$[i,n]$ where node i is the dealer, node i provides the inputs $c_{i,1}, \ldots, c_{i,n}$ respectively to each instance. Then, node i invokes the Share sub-protocol of all n^2 instances of VSS.
- **Any round:** At any time during the protocol, if in node i's view, all n VSS instances where node j is the dealer has terminated outputting "sharing succeeded", we say that node i now considers j as a *qualified dealer*.
- **Round T_{vss}:** If in round T_{vss}, at least $\lfloor n/2 \rfloor + 1$ qualified dealers have been identified so far: let D be the current set of all qualified dealers; reliably broadcast the message (qualified-set, D) using RBC. Henceforth, we use RBC$[j]$ to denote the RBC instance where j is the sender. If not enough qualified dealers have been identified, reliably broadcast the message $\perp$.
- **Any round:** In any round during the protocol, if RBC$[j]$ has output (qualified-set, D_j) such that D_j is a subset of $[n]$ containing at least $\lfloor n/2 \rfloor + 1$ nodes, and moreover every node in D_j has become qualified w.r.t. node i's view so far, then node i considers j as a *candidate*, and node i records the tuple (j, D_j).
- **Round $T_{\mathrm{vss}} + T_{\mathrm{rbc}}$:** In round $T_{\mathrm{vss}} + T_{\mathrm{rbc}}$, do the following:
  • invoke the Reconstruct sub-protocol of all VSS instances;
  • if at least $\lfloor n/2 \rfloor + 1$ nodes are now considered candidates: let S be the set of all candidates so far; now multicast (candidate-set, S) along with a signature on the message.
- **Any round:** At any time, if a node i has observed a (candidate-set, S_j) message with a valid signature from the purported sender j where $S_j \subseteq [n]$ is at least $\lfloor n/2 \rfloor + 1$ in size, and moreover, every node in S_j is now considered a candidate by node i too, we say that node i becomes *happy* with j.
- **As soon as** node i becomes happy with at least $\lfloor n/2 \rfloor + 1$ nodes, let S_i^* be the current set of nodes that are considered candidates;
- **As soon as** the relevant VSS instances (needed in the following computation) have terminated the reconstruction phase outputting a reconstructed secret—henceforth let $c'_{u,v}$ be the secret reconstructed from instance VSS$[u,v]$:

- For every $u \in S_i^*$: let (u, D_u) be a previously recorded tuple when u first became a candidate; compute node u's *charisma* as $C_u := \prod_{v \in D_u} c'_{v,u}$.
- Output the node $u^* \in S_i^*$ with maximum charisma (where ordering between elements in $\mathbb{F}$ is determined using lexicographical comparisons).

Theorem 7. *Suppose that the* VSS *scheme satisfies* T_{vss}*-liveness,* T_{vss}*-validity, and non-malleability under 0.5-weak-synchrony; the* RBC *scheme satisfies* T_{rbc}*-consistency,* T_{rbc}*-liveness, validity, and close termination under 0.5-weak-synchrony, and the signature scheme satisfies existential unforgeability under chosen-message attack. Then, the above* LE *scheme satisfies* $(2T_{\text{vss}} + T_{\text{rbc}})$*-liveness and* $(T_{\text{vss}}, 1/2)$*-quality under 0.5-weak-synchrony.*

Proof. Please refer to the online full version [14].

8   Byzantine Agreement

Let LE be a leader election scheme that satisfies T_{le}-liveness and $(T'_{\text{le}}, 1/2)$-quality under 0.5-weak-synchrony where $T_{\text{le}} > T'_{\text{le}}$.

PKI setup. Upfront, every node performs PKI setup as follows: every node calls $(\mathsf{LE.pk}, \mathsf{LE.sk}) \leftarrow \mathsf{LE.K}(1^\kappa)$; further, it calls $(\mathsf{vk}, \mathsf{ssk}) \leftarrow \Sigma.\mathsf{K}(1^\kappa)$. The tuple $(\mathsf{LE.pk}, \mathsf{vk})$ is the node's public key and registered with the PKI, and the tuple $(\mathsf{LE.sk}, \mathsf{ssk})$ is the node's secret key.

As before we assume that all messages, excluding the ones within the LE instance[6], are signed (using each node's ssk) and tagged with the purported sender, and honest recipients verify the signature (using the purported sender's vk) upon receiving any message. To allow multiple BA instances to share the same PKI, we assume that a message is always tagged with the current instance's session identifier *sid* before it is signed and the verification algorithm checks the *sid* accordingly. Messages with invalid signatures are discarded immediately.

Protocol. In the following, an epoch-e commit evidence for $b \in \{0, 1\}$ is a set of signatures from $\lfloor n/2 \rfloor + 1$ number of distinct nodes on the message $(\texttt{prepare}, e, b)$. Our protocol works as follows. For each epoch $e = 1, 2, \ldots$, do the following (henceforth the initial round of each epoch is renamed round 0 of this epoch):

- **Propose.** For the initial T_{le} rounds in each epoch, do the following:
  1. If the current epoch is $e = 1$, then in round 0 of epoch 1, the sender multicasts a signed tuple $(\texttt{propose}, b)$ where b is its input bit.
  2. Round 0 of every epoch: invoke an instance of the LE protocol.
  3. Round T'_{le} of every epoch: every node $i \in [n]$ flips a random coin $b_i \leftarrow_\$ \{0, 1\}$, and multicasts a signed tuple $(\texttt{propose}, b_i)$

---

[6] Recall that the LE instance deals with its own message signing internally.

- **Prepare (round $T_{le} + \Delta$ of each epoch).** If $e = 1$ and a node has heard an epoch-1 proposal for b from the sender, then it multicasts the signed tuple $(\texttt{prepare}, e, b)$. Else if $e > 1$, every node performs the following:
  1. if an epoch-e proposal of the form $(\texttt{propose}, e, b)$ has been heard from an eligible epoch-e proposer which is defined by the output of LE and moreover, either an epoch-$(e - 1)$ commit evidence vouching for b or $\lfloor n/2 \rfloor + 1$ epoch-$(e - 1)$ complaints from distinct nodes have been observed, multicast the signed tuple $(\texttt{prepare}, e, b)$.
  If LE has not produced an output in the range $[n]$ at the beginning of this round, act as if no valid proposal has been received.
  2. else multicast the signed tuple $(\texttt{prepare}, e, b)$ if the node has seen an epoch-$(e - 1)$ commit evidence vouching for the bit b (if both bits satisfy this then send a prepare message for each bit).
- **Commit (round $T_{le} + 2\Delta$ of each epoch).** If by the beginning of the commit round of the current epoch e, a node
  1. has heard an epoch-e commit evidence for the bit b;
  2. has not observed a valid epoch-e proposal for $1 - b$ (from an eligible proposer); and
  3. has not observed any epoch-$(e - 1)$ commit evidence for $1 - b$;
  then multicast the signed tuple $(\texttt{commit}, e, b)$.
- **Complain (round $T_{le} + 3\Delta$ of each epoch).** If no epoch-e commit evidence has been seen, multicast the signed tuple $(\texttt{complain}, e)$.
- End of this epoch and beginning of next epoch (round $T_{le} + 4\Delta$).

Finalization. At any time during the protocol, if a node has collected $\lfloor n/2 \rfloor + 1$ commit messages (from distinct nodes) for the same epoch and vouching for the same bit b, then output b if no bit has been output yet and continue participating in the protocol (we devise a termination technique in the online full version [14]).

Theorem 8. *Suppose that the* LE *scheme satisfies T_{le}-liveness and $(T_{le}', 1/2)$-quality under 0.5-weak-synchrony, the digital signature scheme employed is secure, and let λ be any super-logarithmic function in the security parameter κ. Then, the* BA *scheme above satisfies consistency, validity, and $\lambda \cdot (T_{le} + 4\Delta)$-liveness under 0.5-weak-synchrony.*

Proof. Please refer to the online full version [14].

References

1. Gmail and Google Drive are experiencing issues, and naturally people are complaining about it on Twitter. https://www.huffingtonpost.com/entry/gmail-issue_n_3099988
2. Abraham, I., Devadas, S., Dolev, D., Nayak, K., Ren, L.: Efficient synchronous Byzantine consensus. In: Financial Crypto (2019)
3. Badrinarayanan, S., Jain, A., Manohar, N., Sahai, A.: Secure MPC: laziness leads to GOD. Cryptology ePrint Archive, Report 2018/580 (2018)

4. Ben-Or, M., Goldwasser, S., Wigderson, A.: Completeness theorems for non-cryptographic fault-tolerant distributed computation. In: STOC, pp. 1–10 (1988)
5. Cachin, C., Kursawe, K., Petzold, F., Shoup, V.: Secure and efficient asynchronous broadcast protocols. In: Kilian, J. (ed.) CRYPTO 2001. LNCS, vol. 2139, pp. 524–541. Springer, Heidelberg (2001). https://doi.org/10.1007/3-540-44647-8_31
6. Canetti, R., Rabin, T.: Fast asynchronous Byzantine agreement with optimal resilience. In: STOC, pp. 42–51 (1993)
7. Castro, M., Liskov, B.: Practical Byzantine fault tolerance. In: OSDI (1999)
8. Dolev, D., Strong, H.R.: Authenticated algorithms for Byzantine agreement. SIAM J. Comput. SIAMCOMP 12(4), 656–666 (1983)
9. Dwork, C., Lynch, N., Stockmeyer, L.: Consensus in the presence of partial synchrony. J. ACM 35, 288–323 (1988)
10. Feldman, P., Micali, S.: An optimal probabilistic protocol for synchronous Byzantine agreement. SIAM J. Comput. 26, 873–933 (1997)
11. Goldreich, O., Micali, S., Wigderson, A.: How to play ANY mental game. In: ACM Symposium on Theory of Computing (STOC) (1987)
12. Dov Gordon, S., Liu, F.-H., Shi, E.: Constant-round MPC with fairness and guarantee of output delivery. In: Gennaro, R., Robshaw, M. (eds.) CRYPTO 2015. LNCS, vol. 9216, pp. 63–82. Springer, Heidelberg (2015). https://doi.org/10.1007/978-3-662-48000-7_4
13. Groth, J., Ostrovsky, R.: Cryptography in the multi-string model. In: Menezes, A. (ed.) CRYPTO 2007. LNCS, vol. 4622, pp. 323–341. Springer, Heidelberg (2007). https://doi.org/10.1007/978-3-540-74143-5_18
14. Guo, Y., Pass, R., Shi, E.: Synchronous, with a chance of partition tolerance. https://eprint.iacr.org/2019/179.pdf
15. Katz, J., Koo, C.-Y.: On expected constant-round protocols for Byzantine agreement. J. Comput. Syst. Sci. 75(2), 91–112 (2009)
16. Lamport, L.: The part-time parliament. ACM Trans. Comput. Syst. 16, 133–169 (1998)
17. Lamport, L., Shostak, R., Pease, M.: The Byzantine generals problem. ACM Trans. Program. Lang. Syst. 4, 382–401 (1982)
18. Micali, S., Vaikuntanathan, V.: Optimal and player-replaceable consensus with an honest majority. MIT CSAIL Technical report, 2017-004 (2017)
19. Pass, R., Shi, E.: The sleepy model of consensus. In: Takagi, T., Peyrin, T. (eds.) ASIACRYPT 2017. LNCS, vol. 10625, pp. 380–409. Springer, Cham (2017). https://doi.org/10.1007/978-3-319-70697-9_14
20. Pass, R., Shi, E.: Thunderella: blockchains with optimistic instant confirmation. In: Nielsen, J.B., Rijmen, V. (eds.) EUROCRYPT 2018. LNCS, vol. 10821, pp. 3–33. Springer, Cham (2018). https://doi.org/10.1007/978-3-319-78375-8_1

Subvector Commitments with Application to Succinct Arguments

Russell W. F. Lai[1]($\boxtimes$) and Giulio Malavolta[2]($\boxtimes$)

[1] Friedrich-Alexander-Universität Erlangen-Nürnberg, Erlangen, Germany
giulio.malavolta@hotmail.it
[2] Carnegie Mellon University, Pittsburgh, USA
russell.lai@cs.fau.de

Abstract. We put forward the notion of subvector commitments (SVC): An SVC allows one to open a committed vector at a set of positions, where the opening size is independent of length of the committed vector and the number of positions to be opened. We propose two constructions under variants of the root assumption and the CDH assumption, respectively. We further generalize SVC to a notion called linear map commitments (LMC), which allows one to open a committed vector to its images under linear maps with a single short message, and propose a construction over pairing groups.

Equipped with these newly developed tools, we revisit the "CS proofs" paradigm [Micali, FOCS 1994] which turns any arguments with public-coin verifiers into non-interactive arguments using the Fiat-Shamir transform in the random oracle model. We propose a compiler that turns any (linear, resp.) PCP into a non-interactive argument, using exclusively SVCs (LMCs, resp.). For an approximate 80 bits of soundness, we highlight the following new implications:

1. There exists a succinct non-interactive argument of knowledge (SNARK) with public-coin setup with proofs of size 5360 bits, under the adaptive root assumption over class groups of imaginary quadratic orders against adversaries with runtime 2^{128}. At the time of writing, this is the shortest SNARK with public-coin setup.
2. There exists a non-interactive argument with private-coin setup, where proofs consist of 2 group elements and 3 field elements, in the generic bilinear group model.

1 Introduction

Commitment schemes are one of the fundamental building blocks and one of the most well-studied primitives in cryptography. Due to their pivotal importance in the design of cryptographic protocols, even small efficiency improvements have magnified repercussions in the field. In a recent work, Catalano and Fiore [27] put forth the notion of Vector Commitments (VC): A VC allows a prover to commit to a vector x of ℓ messages, such that it can later open the commitment at any position $i \in [\ell]$ of the vector, *i.e.*, reveal a message and show that it equals to the i-th committed message. The distinguishing

G. Malavolta—Part of the work done while at Friedrich-Alexander-Universität Erlangen-Nürnberg.

A. Boldyreva and D. Micciancio (Eds.): CRYPTO 2019, LNCS 11692, pp. 530–560, 2019.
https://doi.org/10.1007/978-3-030-26948-7_19

feature of VCs is that the size of the commitments and openings is independent of ℓ. A VC scheme is required to be position binding, meaning that no efficient algorithm can open a commitment at some position i to two distinct messages $x_i \neq x_i'$. Catalano and Fiore [27] constructed two VC schemes based on the CDH assumption over pairing groups and the RSA assumption, respectively. In both schemes, a commitment and an opening both consist of a single group element (in the respective groups). Furthermore, the scheme based on the RSA assumption has public parameters whose size is independent of the length of the vectors to be committed.

This concept was later generalized by Libert et al. [48], who formalized the notion of functional commitment (FC). Intuitively, an FC allows the prover to commit to a vector x, and to open the commitment to function-value tuples (f, y) such that $y = f(x)$. Libert et al. [48] proposed a construction for *linear forms*[1] based on the Diffie-Hellman exponent assumption over pairing groups, where a commitment and an opening both consist of a single group element. VCs and FCs for linear forms are very versatile tools and turned out to be useful for a variety of applications, such a zero-knowledge sets [54], polynomial commitments [44], accumulators, and credentials, to mention a few.

While a short commitment is certainly an appealing feature, there are contexts where there is still a lot to be desired. For example, in case the prover wants to reveal multiple locations of the committed vector (resp. multiple function outputs) the best known solution is to repeat the above protocol in parallel. This means that the size of the openings grows linearly with the amount of revealed locations (resp. function outputs).

1.1   Commitments with Even Shorter Openings

We introduce the notion of *subvector commitments* (SVCs). An SVC allows one to commit to a vector x of length ℓ and later open to a *subvector* of an arbitrary length $\leq \ell$. Given an *ordered* index set $I \subseteq [\ell]$, we define the I-subvector of x as the vector formed by collecting the i-th component of x for all $i \in I$. While a VC is required to be succinct, namely the commitment size and the size of the proof of the opening are independent of the length of the committed vector, an SVC has a stronger compactness[2] property which additionally requires that these sizes do not depend on the length of the subvector to be opened. This difference is going to be critical for our applications (explained later). Improving upon the VC constructions of Catalano and Fiore [27], we propose two constructions of SVCs based on the CDH assumption over pairing groups and the RSA assumption, respectively. We further generalize the RSA-based scheme to work over modules over Euclidean rings [51], where variants of the root assumption are conjectured to hold. Loosely speaking, the root assumption states that it is hard to find the e-th root of a random ring element, for any non-trivial e. In these settings we obtain public-coin-setup instantiations of SVCs using class groups of imaginary quadratic orders.

---

[1] A linear form is a linear map from a vector space to its field of scalars. Libert et al. [48] used the more general term linear functions to refer to linear forms.

[2] The term "compactness" is borrowed from the literature of randomized encodings (RE) and functional encryption, and not to be confused with the compactness notion of homomorphic encryption. For example, a compact RE of a computation with n outputs should have size independent of n [49].

We then generalize the notion of SVCs to allow the prover to reveal arbitrary *linear maps* $f : \mathbb{F}^\ell \to \mathbb{F}^q$ computed over the committed vector. We call such class of schemes *linear map commitments* (LMC). As in SVC, it is important to require an LMC to be compact, meaning that both the commitment and the proofs are of size independent of ℓ and q, whereas succinctness only requires their size to be independent of ℓ. Note that an SVC can be viewed as an LMC restricted to the class of linear maps whose matrix representation has exactly one 1 in each row and 0 everywhere else.

Table 1. Comparison of subvector and linear map commitments for messages of length ℓ, with binding against adversaries of runtime 2^λ. All constants are omitted. pp: public parameters, C: commitment, Λ: proof, Pub: public-coin, Pri: private-coin, CRH: collision-resistant hash, Root: strong or adaptive root, SD: subgroup decision, GGM: generic bilinear group model.

Scheme	$|pp|$	$|C|$	$|\Lambda|$	time(Com)	time(Open)	time(Verify)	Setup	Assumption
Merkle Tree [52]	1	λ	$\lambda q \log \ell$	$\lambda \ell$	$\lambda q \log \ell$	$\lambda q \log \ell$	Pub	CRH
VC (RSA) [27]	$\lambda^3 \ell$	λ^3	$\lambda^3 q$	$\lambda^3 \ell$	$\lambda^3 q \ell^2$	$\lambda^3 q$	Pri	RSA
VC (CDH) [27]	$\lambda \ell^2$	λ	λq	$\lambda \ell$	$\lambda q \ell$	λq	Pri	CDH
SVC (Class Group)	$\lambda^2 \ell$	λ^2	λ^2	$\lambda^2 \ell$	$\lambda^2 (\ell - q^2)$	$\lambda^2 q$	Pub	Root
SVC (CDH)	$\lambda \ell^2$	λ	λ	$\lambda \ell$	$\lambda q \ell$	λq	Pri	CDH
FC (linear form) [48]	$\lambda^3 \ell$	λ^3	$\lambda^3 q$	$\lambda^3 \ell$	$\lambda^3 q \ell$	$\lambda^3 q \ell$	Pri	SD
LMC	$\lambda q \ell$	λ	λ	$\lambda \ell$	$\lambda q \ell^2$	$\lambda q \ell$	Pri	GGM

Naively, one may attempt to generalize position binding for LMC by requiring that the prover cannot open a commitment to (f, y) and (f, y') with $y \neq y'$, where f is a linear map and $y, y' \in \mathbb{F}^k$ are now vectors. This turns out to be insufficient for our applications: This is because the prover may be able to open to (f, y) and (f', y') where $f \neq f'$ and $y \neq y'$ such that they form an inconsistent system of linear equations, yet the attack is not captured by the definition. We tackle this issue by defining a more general *function binding* notion which requires that no efficient algorithm can produce openings for Q function-value tuples $\{(f_k, y_k)\}_{k \in [Q]}$ for any $Q \in \mathrm{poly}(\lambda)$, such that there does not exist x with $f_k(x) = y_k$ for all $k \in [Q]$.

We then modify the construction of Libert *et al.* [48] to support batch openings to linear forms or, equivalently opening to a linear map. Since the verification equation of their construction is linear, a natural way to support batch openings is to define the new verification equation as a random linear combination of previous ones. With this observation, we embed a secret linear combination in the public parameters, and show that the resulting construction is function binding in the generic bilinear group model. In Table 1 we compare our SVC and LMC constructions with existing schemes.

1.2 The Quest of Constructing Ever Shorter Arguments

In addition to enabling batching in the original applications of VCs and FCs for linear forms mentioned above, the compactness of SVCs and LMCs opens the new possibilities of application in constructing succinct argument systems.

Background. An argument system for an NP language $\mathcal{L}$ allows a prover, with a witness w, to convince a verifier that a certain statement x is in $\mathcal{L}$. In contrast with proof systems, argument systems are only required to be computationally sound. Due to this relaxation, it is possible that the interaction between the prover and the verifier is succinct, *i.e.*, the communication complexity is bounded by some polynomial $\mathrm{poly}(\lambda)$ in the security parameter and is independent of the size of w. Other desirable properties of an argument system are:

- "of knowledge": a successful prover implies an extractor that can recover the witness;
- non-interactive: the protocol consists of a single message from the prover;
- (verifier) public-coin: messages from the verifier are sampled from public domains.

Recently, much progress has been made both in theory and practice to construct succinct non-interactive arguments of knowledge (SNARK) for general NP languages. We distinguish between SNARKs in the public-coin-setup model and the pre-processing model. In the public-coin-setup model, the prover and the verifier do not share any input other than the statement x to be proven. In the pre-processing model, they share a common reference string, generated by a trusted third party, which may depend on the language $\mathcal{L}$ and the statement x. In general, existing SNARKs in the pre-processing model are more efficient, in terms of both communication and computation, than those in the public-coin-setup model. This reflects the intuition that pushing the majority of the verifier's workload to the offline pre-processing phase reduces its workload in the online phase. On the other hand, in some applications, such as cryptocurrencies, it is crucial to have a public-coin setup, which can be publicly initialized via, *e.g.*, a random oracle [8].

Public-Coin-Setup SNARKs. While it is known that public-coin-setup non-interactive arguments for NP do not exists in the standard model [15], one can circumvent this impossibility by working in the random oracle model [8]. A common way to obtain public-coin-setup SNARKs is through the "CS proofs" paradigm [45,53] based on probabilistically checkable proofs (PCP) [3]. To recall, a q-query $2^{-\sigma}$-soundness PCP scheme allows the prover to efficiently compute a PCP string which encodes the witness of the statement to be proven. The verifier can then decide whether the statement is true with probability close to $1 - 2^{-\sigma}$ by inspecting q entries of the PCP string. Given a PCP, a SNARK under the CS proofs paradigm are constructed in two steps. First, the PCP is turned into an interactive argument system: The prover first commits to the PCP string, typically using a Merkle-tree commitment. The verifier then sends the indices of the entries to be inspected. Next, the prover opens the commitment at these entries. Finally, by inspecting the revealed entries, the verifier can decide whether the statement is valid. Typically, an argument system constructed this way has a public-coin verifier and can be made non-interactive using the Fiat-Shamir transform [35].

Under the CS proofs paradigm, a proof (*e.g.*, in the scheme by Micali [53]) consists of a λ-bit Merkle-tree commitment of a ℓ-bit PCP string, q bits of the PCP string, and q openings of the commitment, each of size $\lambda \log \ell$ bits. For concreteness, assuming a 3-query PCP and $\ell = 2^{30}$, for 2^{-80}-soundness against a 2^{128}-time adversary, the proof size is around 113 KB. Despite having linear verification time (hence not being a SNARK) Bulletproof [21,26] is arguably the most practically efficient non-interactive argument to date. A proof in [26] consists of $2 \log n + 13$ (group and field) elements, where n is the number of multiplication gates in the arithmetic circuit representation of the verification algorithm of $\mathcal{L}$. In their instantiation over the curve secp256k1, each of the group elements and integers can be represented by ~ 256 bits, thus a proof consists of roughly $512 \log n + 3328$ bits.

Pre-Processing SNARKs. In the pre-processing model, there exist plenty of SNARK constructions originated by [37] based on pairings and linear interactive proofs (LIP), where the latter can be constructed from linear PCPs. To recall, linear PCPs [42] generalizes traditional PCPs in the sense that the PCP string now encodes a linear form. In a q-query linear PCP, the verifier, who is given oracle access to the linear form, can decide the veracity of the statement with overwhelming probability by making only q queries. SNARK constructions in this category typically have a computationally expensive statement-dependent pre-processing phase, meaning that one set of public parameters has to be generated per statement to be proven.

In this setting, the scheme with the shortest proofs (4 group elements) in the standard model is due to Danezis *et al.* [32]. In the generic bilinear group model, Groth [40] proposed a scheme [60] with only 3 group elements, and showed that proofs constructed from LIP must consist of at least 2 group elements. These schemes can be instantiated over pairing-friendly elliptic curves. A popular choice is the 256-bit Barreto-Naehrig curve [7], in which a group element can be represented using 256 bits.

Our Approach. Equipped with our newly developed tools, we revisit the CS proofs paradigm. In previous schemes following this paradigm, the proof size is dominated by the factor $q \log \ell$ due to the q Merkle-tree commitment openings. Moreover, due to the lack of structure of a Merkle-tree commitment, prior schemes do not work with linear PCPs. The main idea is thus to replace the Merkle-tree commitment with an SVC/LMC, so that the q openings can be compressed into a single one which has size independent of ℓ and q. By doing so, we obtain a compiler which compiles any (resp. linear) PCP into an interactive argument using an SVC (resp. LMC).

We highlight two interesting instantiations of our construction. The first instantiation is with classical PCPs and our public-coin-setup SVC based on $Cl(\Delta)$, the class group of imaginary quadratic order with discriminant Δ.

Instantiation 1. *If the adaptive root assumption holds in $Cl(\Delta)$, then there exist public-coin-setup SNARKs for NP with soundness error $2^{-\sigma}$ in which a proof consists of 2 $Cl(\Delta)$ elements and q bits in the random oracle model, using any q-query $2^{-\sigma}$-soundness PCP.*

If one aims for an extremely short proof and is willing to accept expensive prover computation, then a 3-query 2^{-1}-soundness PCP can be amplified into a 3σ-query $2^{-\sigma}$-soundness PCP and gives the shortest SNARK. Based on the best known attacks on the root problem in class groups [41], for a soundness error of 2^{-80} against a 2^{128}-time adversary, we obtain a proof size of 5360 bits, which is shorter than that of Bulletproof [26] for $n > 16$, *i.e.*, the verification circuit has more than 16 multiplication gates. We view this instantiation as a feasibility for extremely succinct proofs and a step forward towards optimal ($O(\lambda)$-sized) public-coin-setup SNARKs. Next we turn our attention to the instantiation with linear PCPs and our pairing-based LMCs.

Table 2. Comparison of SNARKs with $2^{-\lambda}$-soundness against adversaries of runtime 2^{128}. All constants are omitted. pp: public parameters, π: proof, n: size of circuit, ℓ_{PCP}: length of PCP proof, ℓ_{LPCP}: length of linear PCP proof, Pub: public-coin, Pri: private-coin, Pre-Proc: pre-processing, Root: strong or adaptive root assumption, GGM: generic group model.

Scheme	|pp|	|π|	Setup	Assumption
CS Proof (Merkle Tree Compiler) [45,53]	1	$\lambda^2 \log n$	Pub	ROM
Bulletproof [21,26]	λn	$\lambda \log n$	Pub	DLog, ROM
Aurora [12]	1	$\lambda \log^2 n$	Pub	ROM
SVC Compiler (Class Group)	$\lambda^2 \ell_{\text{PCP}}$	λ^2	Pub	Root, ROM
Groth [40]	λn	λ	Pre-Proc	GGM
SVC Compiler (CDH)	$\lambda \ell_{\text{LPCP}}^2$	λ	Pri	CDH, ROM
LMC Compiler	$\lambda \ell_{\text{LPCP}}$	λ	Pri	GGM, ROM

Instantiation 2. *In the generic bilinear group and random oracle model, there exist pre-processing non-interactive arguments for NP in which a proof consists of 2 $\mathbb{G}$ elements and q field elements, using any q-query linear PCP.*

Using a 3-query linear PCP (*e.g.* [17]) and instantiating the pairing group over the 256-bit Barreto-Naehrig curve yields a proof consisting of 5 elements or 1280 bits. Compared to other pairing-based compilers from linear PCPs to preprocessing SNARKs (*e.g.*, [40]), our compiler has the advantages that it supports *any* linear PCPs, but not only those where the verifier is restricted to only evaluate quadratic polynomials. Moreover the setup phase is independent of the statements to be proven, and thus the same public parameters can be reused for proving many statements.

A comparison with the shortest succinct arguments from the literature is given in Table 2. To summarize, our approach yields extremely short proofs in exchange for a higher prover complexity and the usage of public-key cryptography. We also stress that our compiler is compatible with a broader class of PCPs, when compared with schemes under the CS proofs paradigm and pairing-based schemes. Being a very active area of research, we expect significant advancements in the design of more efficient PCPs, which are going to benefit from the generality of our approach.

Other Applications. Catalano and Fiore [27] suggested a number of applications of VC, including verifiable databases with efficient updates, updatable zero-knowledge elementary databases, and universal dynamic accumulators. In all of these applications, one can gain efficiency by replacing the VC scheme with an SVC scheme which allows for batch opening and updating. When instantiated with our first construction of SVC, one can further avoid the private-coin setup, which is especially beneficial to database applications as trusted third parties are no longer required.

The notion of SVC has already attracted the attention of the community. A follow up work by Boneh *et al.* [20] shows how SVCs can be used as a drop-in replacement for Merkle-trees in SNARKs based on interactive oracle proofs (IOPs) which generalizes PCPs. They leverage the structure of class group-based SVCs to reduce the proof size to $(r + 1)$ group elements and r integers, where r is the number of iterations of the underlying IOP. They also propose a technique to improve the efficiency of the verification algorithm and they estimate a decrease in verification time of $\sim 80\%$. Finally, they discuss how to use SVCs to improve the current design of blockchain-based transaction ledger in such a way that no user has to store the entire state of the ledger in memory.

1.3   Related Work

Succinct arguments were introduced by Kilian [45,46] and later improved, in terms of round complexity, by Lipmaa and Di Crescenzo [34]. Succinct non-interactive arguments, or computationally sound proofs, were first proposed by Micali [53]. These early approaches rely on PCP and have been recently extended [9] to handle interactive oracle proofs [13] (also known as probabilistic checkable interactive proofs [57]), largely improving the efficiency of the prover. A recent manuscript by Ben-Sasson *et al.* [10] improves the concrete efficiency of interactive oracle proofs. The first usage of knowledge assumptions to construct SNARKs appeared in the work of Mie [55]. Later, Groth [39] and Lipmaa [50] upgraded this approach to non-interactive proofs.

Ishai, Kushilevitz, and Ostrovsky [42] observed that linear PCPs can be combined with a linearly homomorphic encryption to construct more efficient arguments, with pre-processing. The also introduced a new (interactive) commitment scheme with private-coin verifier for linear functions. However, in contrast with LMC, their binding definition does not ensure that the committed function is actually linear. Gennaro *et al.* [37] presented a very elegant linear PCP that gave rise to a large body of work to improve the practical efficiency of non-interactive arguments [5,11,14,28,29,33]. All of these constructions assume a highly structured and honestly generated common reference string (of size proportional to the circuit to be evaluated) and rely on some variant of the knowledge of exponent assumption. Recently, Ames *et al.* [2] proposed an argument based on the MPC-in-the-head [43] paradigm to prove satisfiability of a circuit C with proofs of size $O(\lambda\sqrt{|C|})$. Zhang *et al.* [64] show how to combine interactive proofs and verifiable polynomial delegation schemes to construct succinct interactive arguments. The scheme requires a private-coin pre-processing and the communication complexity is $O(\lambda \log |w|)$. A recent result by Whaby *et al.* [62] introduces a prover-efficient construction with proofs of size $O(\lambda\sqrt{|w|})$. Recent works [1,36] investigate on the resilience of SNARKs against a subverted setup. Libert, Ramanna, and Yung [48] constructed an accumulator for subset queries. Although similar in spirit to SVC, the critical difference is that accumulators are not position binding, which is crucial for the soundness of our argument system.

2   Preliminaries

Throughout this work we denote by $\lambda \in \mathbb{N}$ the security parameter, and by $\mathsf{poly}(\lambda)$ and $\mathsf{negl}(\lambda)$ the sets of polynomials and negligible functions in λ, respectively. We say that a Turing machine is probabilistic polynomial time (PPT) if its running time is bounded by some polynomial function $\mathrm{poly}(\lambda)$. An interactive protocol Π between two machines A and B is referred to as $(A, B)_\Pi$. Given a set S, we denote sampling a random element from S as $s \leftarrow_\$ S$ and the output of an algorithm A on input x is written as $z \leftarrow A(x)$. Let $\ell \in \mathbb{N}$, the set $[\ell]$ is defined as $[\ell] := \{1, \ldots, \ell\}$. Vectors are written vertically.

2.1 Subvectors

We define the notion of subvectors. Roughly speaking, a subvector $(x_{i_1}, \ldots, x_{i_{|I|}})^T$ is an ordered subset (indexed by I) of the entries of a given vector $(x_1, \ldots, x_\ell)^T$.

Definition 1 (Subvectors). *Let $\ell \in \mathbb{N}$, $\mathcal{X}$ be a set, and $(x_1, \ldots, x_\ell)^T \in \mathcal{X}^\ell$ be a vector. Let $I = (i_1, \ldots, i_{|I|}) \subseteq [q]$ be an ordered index set. The I-subvector of x is defined as $x_I := (x_{i_1}, \ldots, x_{i_{|I|}})^T$.*

2.2 Arguments of Knowledge

Let $\mathcal{R} : \{0,1\}^* \times \{0,1\}^* \to \{0,1\}$ be an NP-relation with corresponding NP-language $\mathcal{L} := \{x : \exists w \text{ s.t. } \mathcal{R}(x, w) = 1\}$. We define arguments of knowledge [22] for interactive Turing machines [38]. To be as general as possible, we define an additional setup algorithm $\mathcal{S}$, which is executed once and for all by a possibly trusted party. If the argument is secure without a setup, then such an algorithm can be omitted.

Definition 2 (Arguments of knowledge). *A tuple $(\mathcal{S}, (\mathcal{P}, \mathcal{V})_\Pi)$ is a $2^{-\sigma}$-sound (succinct) argument of knowledge for $\mathcal{R}$ if the following conditions hold.*

(Completeness). If $\mathcal{R}(x, w) = 1$ then $\Pr_{y \leftarrow \mathcal{S}(1^\lambda)} [(\mathcal{P}(x, w, y), \mathcal{V}(x, y))_\Pi = 1] = 1$.

(Soundness). For any PPT adversary $\mathcal{A}$, all $x \notin \mathcal{L}$, and all $z \in \{0,1\}^*$, $\Pr_{y \leftarrow \mathcal{S}(1^\lambda)} [(\mathcal{A}(x, z, y), \mathcal{V}(x, y))_\Pi = 1] < 2^{-\sigma}$.

(Argument of Knowledge). For any PPT adversary $\mathcal{A}$, there exists a PPT extractor $\mathcal{E}$, such that for all $x, z \in \{0,1\}^*$, $\Pr_{y \leftarrow \mathcal{S}(1^\lambda)} [(\mathcal{A}(x, z, y), \mathcal{V}(x, y))_\Pi = 1] > \mathsf{negl}(\lambda)$, then $\Pr[\mathcal{R}(x, w) = 1 | w \leftarrow \mathcal{E}^\mathcal{A}(x)] > \mathsf{negl}(\lambda)$.

(Succinctness). The communication between $\mathcal{P}$ and $\mathcal{V}$ is at most $\mathrm{poly}(\lambda, \log |x|)$.

2.3 Probabilistically Checkable Proofs

One of the principal tools in the construction of argument systems is probabilistic checkable proofs (PCP) [3]. It is known that any witness w for an NP-statement can be encoded into a PCP of length $\mathrm{poly}(|w|)$ bits such that it is sufficient to probabilistically test $O(1)$ bits of the encoded witness.

Definition 3 (Probabilistically Checkable Proofs). *A pair of machines $(\mathcal{P}_{PCP}, \mathcal{V}_{PCP})$ is a ℓ-long q-query $2^{-\sigma}$-sound PCP for an NP-relation $\mathcal{R}$ if the following hold.*

(Completeness). If $\mathcal{R}(x, w) = 1$, then $\Pr\left[\mathcal{V}_{PCP}^{\pi}(x) = 1 | \pi \leftarrow \mathcal{P}_{PCP}(x, w)\right] = 1$.
(Soundness). For all $x \notin \mathcal{L}$, $\Pr\left[\mathcal{V}_{PCP}^{\pi}(x) = 1 | \pi \leftarrow \mathcal{P}_{PCP}(x, w)\right] < 2^{-\sigma}$.
(Proof Length). If $\mathcal{R}(x, w) = 1$, then for all $\pi \in \mathcal{P}_{PCP}(x, w)$, $|\pi| \leq \ell$.
(Query Complexity). For all $x, \pi \in \{0, 1\}^{*}$, $\mathcal{V}_{PCP}^{\pi}(x)$ queries at most q locations of π.

The notation $\mathcal{V}_{PCP}^{\pi}(x)$ means that $\mathcal{V}_{PCP}$ does not read the entire string π directly, but is given oracle access to the string. On input a position $i \in [\|\pi\|]$, the oracle returns the value π_i. It is well known that one can diminish the soundness error to a negligible function by repetition. We additionally require that the witness can be efficiently recovered from the encoding of the witness π [61].

Definition 4 (Proof of Knowledge). *A PCP is of knowledge if there exists a PPT algorithm $\mathcal{E}_{PCP}$ such that, given any strings x and π with $\Pr\left[\mathcal{V}_{PCP}^{\pi}(x) = 1\right] > \mathsf{negl}(\lambda)$, $\mathcal{E}_{PCP}^{\pi}(x)$ extracts an NP witness w for x.*

Linear PCPs. Ishai et al. [42] considered the notion of *linear* PCP, where the string π is instead a vector in $\mathbb{F}^{\ell}$ for some finite field $\mathbb{F}$ (or in general a ring) and positive integer ℓ. The oracle given to the verifier is modified, such that on input $f \in \mathbb{F}^{\ell}$, it returns the inner product $\langle f, \pi \rangle$. Note that this generalizes the classical notion of PCP as one can recover the original definition by restricting the queries f to be unit vectors. In this paper we are interested in the notion of linear PCP where soundness is only guaranteed to hold against linear functions (same as considered in [17]).

3   Mathematical Background and Assumptions

To capture the minimal mathematical structure required for one of our constructions, we follow the module-based cryptography framework of Lipmaa [51].

Background. A (left) R-module R_D over the ring R (with identity) consists of an Abelian group $(D, +)$ and an operation $\circ : R \times D \rightarrow D$, denoted $r \circ A$ for $r \in R$ and $A \in D$, such that for all $r, s \in R$ and $A, B \in D$, we have

- $r \circ (A + B) = r \circ A + r \circ B$,
- $(r + s) \circ A = r \circ A + s \circ A$,
- $(r \cdot s) \circ A = r \circ (s \circ A)$, and
- $1_R \circ r = r$, where 1_R is the multiplicative identity of R.

Let $S = (s_1, \ldots, s_\ell) \subseteq \mathbb{N}$ be an ordered set, and $r = (r_{s_1}, \ldots, r_{s_\ell})^T \in R^\ell$ and $A = (A_{s_1}, \ldots, A_{s_\ell})^T \in D^\ell$ be vectors of ring and group elements respectively. For notational convenience, we denote $\sum_{i \in S} r_i \circ A_i$ by $\langle r, A \rangle$.

A commutative ring R with identity is called an *integral domain* if for all $r, s \in R$, $rs = 0_R$ implies $r = 0_R$ or $s = 0_R$, where 0_R is the additive identity of R. A ring R is *Euclidean* if it is an integral domain and there exists a function $\deg : R \rightarrow \mathbb{Z}^+$, called the Euclidean degree, such that (i) if $r, s \in R$, then there exist $q, k \in R$ such that $r = qs + k$ with either $k = 0_R$, $k \neq 0_R$ and $\deg(k) < \deg(q)$, and (ii) if

$r, s \in R$ with $rs \neq 0_R$ and $r \neq 0_R$, then $\deg(r) < \deg(rs)$. The set of units $U(R) := \{u \in R : \exists v \text{ s.t. } uv = vu = 1_R\}$ contains all invertible elements in R. An element $r \in R \setminus (\{0_R\} \cup U(R))$ is said to be *irreducible* if there are no elements $s, t \in R \setminus \{1_R\}$ such that $r = st$. The set of all irreducible elements of R is denoted by $\mathrm{IRR}(R)$. An element $r \in R \setminus (\{0_R\} \cup U(R))$ is said to be *prime* if for all $s, t \in R$, whenever r divides st, then r divides s or r divides t. If R is Euclidean, then an element is irreducible if and only if it is prime.

Adaptive Root. The adaptive root assumption (over unknown order groups, and in particular over class groups of imaginary quadratic orders) was introduced by Wesolowski [63] and re-formulated by Boneh *et al.* [19] to establish the security of the verifiable delay function scheme of Wesolowski [63]. Here we state the same assumption over modules in two variants – with private and public coins. Note that Wesolowski [63] and Boneh et al. [19] implicitly considered the *public-coin-setup* variant.

Definition 5 ((Public-Coin) Adaptive Root). *Let I be some ordered set. Let $\mathcal{R}_D = ((R_i)_{D_i})_{i \in I}$ be a family of modules. Let $\mathsf{MGen}(1^\lambda; \omega)$ be a deterministic algorithm which picks some $i \in I$ (hence some $R_D = (R_i)_{D_i} \in \mathcal{R}_D$) and some element $A \in D$. For a ring R, let $\mathrm{IRR}_\lambda(R) \subseteq \mathrm{IRR}(R)$ be some set of prime elements in R of size 2^λ. The adaptive root assumption is said to hold over the family of modules $\mathcal{R}_D$ with respect to IRR_λ, if for any PPT adversary $\mathcal{A} = (\mathcal{A}_1, \mathcal{A}_2)$ there exists $\epsilon(\lambda) \in \mathsf{negl}(\lambda)$ such that*

$$\Pr\left[e \circ Y = X \,\middle|\, \begin{array}{c} \omega \leftarrow_\$ \{0,1\}^\lambda; (R_D, A) := \mathsf{MGen}(1^\lambda; \omega) \\ X \leftarrow \mathcal{A}_1(R_D, A, \boxed{\omega}); e \leftarrow_\$ \mathrm{IRR}_\lambda(R); Y \leftarrow \mathcal{A}_2(e) \end{array} \right] \leq \epsilon(\lambda),$$

where $\mathcal{A}$ is not given ω (highlighted by the dashed box). If the inequality holds even if $\mathcal{A}$ is given ω, then we say that the assumption is public-coin.

Strong Distinct-Prime-Product Root. We define the following variant of the "strong root assumption" [30] over modules over Euclidean rings, which is a generalization of the strong RSA assumption. Let R_D be a module over some Euclidean ring R, and A be an element of D. The strong distinct-prime-product root problem with respect to A asks to find a set of distinct prime elements $\{e_i\}_{i \in S}$ in R and an element Y in D such that $(\prod_{i \in S} e_i) \circ Y = A$. We define the assumption in two variants depending on whether R_D and A are sampled with public coins.

Definition 6 ((Public-Coin) Strong Distinct-Prime-Product Root). *Let I be an ordered set, $\mathcal{R}_D = ((R_i)_{D_i})_{i \in I}$ be a family of modules, and $\mathsf{MGen}(1^\lambda; \omega)$ be a deterministic algorithm which picks some $i \in I$ (hence some $R_D = (R_i)_{D_i} \in \mathcal{R}_D$) and some element $A \in D$. The strong distinct-prime-product root assumption is said to hold over the family $\mathcal{R}_D$, if for any PPT adversary $\mathcal{A}$ there exists $\epsilon(\lambda) \in \mathsf{negl}(\lambda)$ such that*

$$\Pr\left[\begin{array}{c} (\prod_{i \in S} e_i) \circ Y = A \\ \forall i \in S, e_i \in \mathrm{IRR}(R) \\ \forall i \neq j \in S, e_i \neq e_j \end{array} \,\middle|\, \begin{array}{c} \omega \leftarrow_\$ \{0,1\}^\lambda \\ (R_D, A) := \mathsf{MGen}(1^\lambda; \omega) \\ (\{e_i\}_{i \in S}, Y) \leftarrow \mathcal{A}(R_D, A, \boxed{\omega}) \end{array} \right] \leq \epsilon(\lambda),$$

where $\mathcal{A}$ is not given ω (highlighted by the dashed box). If the inequality holds even if $\mathcal{A}$ is given ω, then we say that the assumption is public-coin.

Lipmaa [51] defined several variants of the (strong) root assumption with respect to a random element in D sampled with *private coin*, given the description of the module R_D sampled with *public coin*. Note that the (resp. public-coin) strong distinct-prime-product root assumption is weaker than the (resp. public-coin) strong root assumption, where the latter requires the adversary to simply output (e, Y) such that $e \neq 1_R$ and $e \circ Y = A$. It is apparent that the strong distinct-prime-product root assumption over RSA groups is implied by the strong RSA assumption.

4   Subvector Commitments

In the following we define the main object of interest for our work. Subvector commitments are a generalization of vector commitments [27], where the opening is performed with respect to subvectors.

Definition 7 (Subvector Commitments (SVC)). *A subvector commitment scheme* SVC *over $\mathcal{X}$ consists of the following* PPT *algorithms* (Setup, Com, Open, Verify):

Setup($1^\lambda, 1^\ell; \omega$): *The* deterministic *setup algorithm inputs the security parameter 1^λ, the vector size 1^ℓ, and a random tape ω. It outputs a public parameter* pp. *We assume that all other algorithms input* pp *which we omit.*

Com($\boldsymbol{x}$): *The committing algorithm inputs a vector $\boldsymbol{x} \in \mathcal{X}^\ell$. It outputs a commitment string C and some auxiliary information* aux.

Open($I, \boldsymbol{x}'_I, \text{aux}$): *The opening algorithm inputs an index set I, an I-subvector $\boldsymbol{x}'_I$, and some auxiliary information* aux. *It outputs a proof Λ_I that $\boldsymbol{x}'_I$ is the I-subvector of the committed vector.*

Verify($C, I, \boldsymbol{x}'_I, \Lambda_I$): *The verification algorithm inputs a commitment string C, an index set I, an I-subvector $\boldsymbol{x}'_I$, and a proof Λ_I. It accepts (i.e., it outputs 1) if and only if C is a commitment to $\boldsymbol{x}$ and $\boldsymbol{x}'_I$ is the I-subvector of $\boldsymbol{x}$.*

The definition of correctness is given as follows.

Definition 8 (Correctness). *A subvector commitment* SVC *over $\mathcal{X}$ is said to be* correct *if, for any security parameter $\lambda, \ell \in \mathbb{N}$, random tape $\omega \in \{0, 1\}^\lambda$, public parameters* pp $\in$ Setup($1^\lambda, 1^\ell; \omega$), $\boldsymbol{x} \in \mathcal{X}^\ell$, *index set $I \in [\ell]$, $(C, \text{aux}) \in$ Com($\boldsymbol{x}$), $\Lambda_I \in$ Open($I, \boldsymbol{x}_I, \text{aux}$), there exists $\epsilon(\lambda) \in$ negl(λ) such that*

$$\Pr\left[\text{Verify}(C, I, \boldsymbol{x}_I, \Lambda_I) = 1\right] \geq 1 - \epsilon(\lambda).$$

The distinguishing property for SVCs is compactness. Loosely speaking it says that the size of the commitment strings C and the proofs Λ_I are not only independent of the length of the committed vector $\boldsymbol{x}$, but also that of $\boldsymbol{x}_I$.

Definition 9 (Compactness). *A subvector commitment* SVC *over* $\mathcal{X}$ *is compact if there exists a universal polynomial* $p \in \text{poly}(\lambda)$ *such that for any* $\ell \in \text{poly}(\lambda)$, *random tape* $\omega \in \{0,1\}^{\lambda}$, *public parameters* pp $\in$ Setup$(1^{\lambda}, 1^{\ell}; \omega)$, *vector* $\boldsymbol{x} \in \mathcal{X}^{\ell}$, *index set* $I \in [\ell]$, $(C, \text{aux}) \in \text{Com}(\boldsymbol{x})$, $\Lambda_I \in \text{Open}(I, \boldsymbol{x}_I, \text{aux})$, *it holds that* $|C| \leq p(\lambda)$ *and* $|\Lambda_I| \leq p(\lambda)$.

We consider the notion of position binding for subvector commitments with public-coin setup. Recall that position binding for vector commitments requires that it is infeasible to open a commitment with respect to some position i to two distinct messages $\boldsymbol{x}_i$ and $\boldsymbol{x}'_i$. We extend this notion to subvector commitments, by requiring that it is infeasible to open a commitment with respect to some index sets I and J to subvectors $\boldsymbol{x}_I$ and $\boldsymbol{x}'_J$, respectively, such that there exists an index $i \in I \cap J$ where $x_i \neq x'_i$. Furthermore, we require this property to hold even if the setup algorithm is public coin.

Definition 10 ((Public-Coin) Position Binding). *A subvector commitment* SVC *over* $\mathcal{X}$ *is position binding if for any* PPT *adversary* $\mathcal{A}$, *there exists a negligible function* $\epsilon(\lambda) \in \text{negl}(\lambda)$ *such that*

$$\text{Pr}\left[\begin{array}{c}\text{Verify}(C, I, \boldsymbol{x}_I, \Lambda_I) = 1 \\ \text{Verify}(C, J, \boldsymbol{x}'_J, \Lambda'_J) = 1 \\ \exists i \in I \cap J \text{ s.t. } x_i \neq x'_i\end{array} \middle| \begin{array}{c}\omega \leftarrow_{\$} \{0,1\}^{\lambda} \\ \text{pp} \leftarrow \text{Setup}(1^{\lambda}, 1^{\ell}; \omega) \\ (C, I, J, \boldsymbol{x}_I, \boldsymbol{x}'_J, \Lambda_I, \Lambda'_J) \leftarrow \mathcal{A}(\text{pp}^{\bar{\lceil}, \bar{\omega}\bar{\rceil}})\end{array}\right] \leq \epsilon(\lambda)$$

where $\mathcal{A}$ *is not given* ω *(highlighted by the dashed box). If the inequality holds even if* $\mathcal{A}$ *is given* ω, *then we say that* SVC *is function binding with* public coins.

We do not define hiding as it is not needed for our purpose. However, as discussed in [27], one can construct a hiding VC generically by committing to (normal) commitments using VC. This naturally extends to SVC as well.

4.1 Linear Map Commitments

Functional commitments for linear functions, specifically for linear forms $f : \mathbb{F}^{\ell} \to \mathbb{F}$ for some field $\mathbb{F}$, were introduced by Libert, Ramanna and Yung [48] and is a generalization of vector commitments (VC) introduced by Catalano and Fiore [27]. Here we refine the notion to capture a more general class of function families, which allows the prover to open a commitment to the output of *multiple* linear forms or, equivalently, to the output of a *linear map* $f : \mathbb{F}^{\ell} \to \mathbb{F}^{q}$. Note that any linear map from $\mathbb{F}^{\ell}$ to $\mathbb{F}^{q}$ can be represented by a matrix $F \in \mathbb{F}^{q \times \ell}$.

Definition 11 (Linear Map Commitments (LMC)). *A linear map commitment scheme* LMC *over* $\mathbb{F}$ *consists of the following* PPT *algorithms* (Setup, Com, Open, Verify):

Setup$(1^{\lambda}, \mathcal{F}; \omega)$: *Let* $\ell, q \in \text{poly}(\lambda)$ *be positive integers, and* $\mathcal{F} \subseteq \{f : \mathbb{F}^{\ell} \to \mathbb{F}^{q}\}$ *be a family of linear maps. The* deterministic *setup algorithm inputs the security parameter* 1^{λ}, *the description of the family* $\mathcal{F}$, *and a random tape* ω. *It outputs a public parameter* pp. *We assume that all other algorithms input* pp *which we omit.*

$\underline{\mathsf{Com}(x)}$: *The committing algorithm inputs a vector $x \in \mathbb{F}^\ell$. It outputs a commitment string C and some auxiliary information* aux.

$\underline{\mathsf{Open}(f, y, \mathsf{aux})}$: *The opening algorithm inputs an $f \in \mathcal{F}$, an image $y \in \mathbb{F}^q$, and some auxiliary information* aux. *It outputs a proof Λ that $y = f(x)$.*

$\underline{\mathsf{Verify}(C, f, y, \Lambda)}$: *The verification algorithm inputs a commitment string C, an $f \in \mathcal{F}$, an image y, and a proof Λ. It accepts (i.e., it outputs 1) if and only if C is a commitment to x and $y = f(x)$.*

In the following we define correctness and compactness for LMCs.

Definition 12 (Correctness). *A linear map commitment scheme* LMC *over $\mathbb{F}$ is said to be correct if, for any security parameter and length $\lambda, \ell, q \in \mathbb{N}$, random tape $\omega \in \{0,1\}^\lambda$, linear map family $\mathcal{F} \subseteq \{f : \mathbb{F}^\ell \to \mathbb{F}^q\}$, public parameters $\mathsf{pp} \in \mathsf{Setup}(1^\lambda, \mathcal{F}; \omega)$, $x \in \mathbb{F}^\ell$, linear map $f \in \mathcal{F}$, $(C, \mathsf{aux}) \in \mathsf{Com}(x)$, $\Lambda \in \mathsf{Open}(f, f(x), \mathsf{aux})$, there exists $\epsilon(\lambda) \in \mathsf{negl}(\lambda)$ such that*

$$\Pr\left[\mathsf{Verify}(C, f, f(x), \Lambda) = 1\right] \geq 1 - \epsilon(\lambda).$$

Definition 13 (Compactness). *A linear map commitment scheme* LMC *over $\mathbb{F}$ is compact if there exists a universal polynomial $p \in \mathsf{poly}(\lambda)$, such that for any $\ell, q \in \mathsf{poly}(\lambda)$, family of linear maps $\mathcal{F} \subseteq \{f : \mathbb{F}^\ell \to \mathbb{F}^q\}$, random tape $\omega \in \{0,1\}^\lambda$, public parameters $\mathsf{pp} \in \mathsf{Setup}(1^\lambda, \mathcal{F}; \omega)$, vector $x \in \mathbb{F}^\ell$, linear map $f \in \mathcal{F}$, $(C, \mathsf{aux}) \in \mathsf{Com}(x)$, $\Lambda \in \mathsf{Open}(f, f(x), \mathsf{aux})$, it holds that $|C| \leq p(\lambda)$ and $|\Lambda| \leq p(\lambda)$.*

We next generalize the notion of function binding for linear maps. The original definition, as considered by Libert, Ramanna and Yung [48], requires that it is hard to open a commitment to (f, y) and (f, y') where $y \neq y'$. When considering broader classes of functions, such as linear maps where the target space is multidimensional, each opening defines a system of equations. Note that in this case one might be able to generate an inconsistent system with just a single opening, or generate openings to (f, y) and (f', y') with $f \neq f'$ but the systems defined by the tuples are inconsistent. Therefore, our definition explicitly forbids the adversary to generate inconsistent equations.

Definition 14 ((Public-Coin) Function Binding). *A linear map commitment* LMC *over $\mathbb{F}$ is function binding if for any* PPT *adversary $\mathcal{A}$, positive integers $Q, \ell, q \in \mathsf{poly}(\lambda)$, and family of linear maps $\mathcal{F} \subseteq \{f : \mathbb{F}^\ell \to \mathbb{F}^q\}$, there exists a negligible function $\epsilon(\lambda) \in \mathsf{negl}(\lambda)$ such that*

$$\Pr\left[\begin{array}{l} \forall k \in [Q], \quad f_k \in \mathcal{F} \wedge y_k \in \mathbb{F}^q \wedge \\ \quad\quad \mathsf{Verify}(C, f_k, y_k, \Lambda_k) = 1 \\ \nexists x \in \mathcal{X}^\ell \text{ s.t. } \forall k \in [Q], \ f_k(x) = y_k \end{array} \middle| \begin{array}{l} \omega \leftarrow_\$ \{0,1\}^\lambda \\ \mathsf{pp} \leftarrow \mathsf{Setup}(1^\lambda, \mathcal{F}; \omega) \\ (C, \{(f_k, y_k, \Lambda_k)\}_{k\in[Q]}) \leftarrow \mathcal{A}(\mathsf{pp}, \omega) \end{array}\right] \leq \epsilon(\lambda)$$

where $\mathcal{A}$ is not *given ω (highlighted by the dashed box). If the inequality holds even if $\mathcal{A}$ is given ω, then we say that* LMC *is function binding with* public coins.

As for SVC, we omit the hiding definition as it is not needed for our purpose.

5 Constructions for SVCs

We propose two direct constructions of SVC, one from modules over Euclidean rings where certain variants of the root assumption hold, and one from pairing groups where the CDH assumption holds. Both schemes allow one to commit to binary strings (i.e., we consider the field $\mathcal{X} = \mathbb{F}_2$). Our constructions are inspired by the work of Catalano and Fiore [27] and extend the opening algorithms of their vector commitment schemes to simultaneously handle multiple positions. These modifications introduce several complications in the security proofs that require a careful manipulation of the exponents.

5.1 SVC from Modules over Euclidean Rings

Our first SVC scheme relies on modules over Euclidean rings where some variants of the root problem (the natural generalization of the RSA problem) is hard. Let $\ell \in \text{poly}(\lambda)$ be a positive integer. Let MGen be an efficient module sampling algorithm as defined in Sect. 3 and let R be an Euclidean ring sampled by MGen. Let $\text{IRR}_\lambda(R)$ be a set of prime elements in R of size 2^λ. Let $H : \{0,1\}^* \to \text{IRR}_\lambda(R)^\ell$ be a prime-valued function which maps finite bit strings to tuples of ℓ distinct elements in $\text{IRR}_\lambda(R)$. That is, for all string $s \in \{0,1\}^*$, if $(e_1, \ldots, e_\ell) = H(s)$, then $e_i \neq e_j$ for all $i, j \in [q]$ where $i \neq j$. Let $\mathcal{X} := \{0_R, 1_R\}^3$ where 0_R and 1_R are the additive and multiplicative identity elements of R respectively. We construct our first subvector commitment scheme in Fig. 1. Note that in the opening algorithm, it is required to compute

$$\Lambda_I := \left(\prod_{i \in I} e_i \right)^{-1} \circ \langle \boldsymbol{x}_{[\ell] \setminus I}, \boldsymbol{S}_{[\ell] \setminus I} \rangle.$$

Setup($1^\lambda, 1^\ell; \omega$)	Open($I, \boldsymbol{x}'_I, \text{aux}$)
$(R_D, X) \leftarrow_{\$} \text{MGen}(1^\lambda, \omega)$	**parse** aux as $\boldsymbol{x}$
$(e_1, \ldots, e_\ell) \leftarrow H(R_D, X)$	$\Lambda_I := \left(\prod_{i \in I} e_i \right)^{-1} \circ \langle \boldsymbol{x}_{[\ell] \setminus I}, \boldsymbol{S}_{[\ell] \setminus I} \rangle$
$\forall i \in [\ell], S_i := \left(\prod_{j \in [\ell] \setminus \{i\}} e_j \right) \circ X$	**return** Λ_I
$\boldsymbol{S} := (S_1, \ldots, S_\ell)^T$, $\boldsymbol{e} := (e_1, \ldots, e_\ell)^T$	
return pp $:= (R_D, X, \boldsymbol{S}, \boldsymbol{e})$	Verify($C, I, \boldsymbol{x}'_I, \Lambda_I$)
	$b_0 := (\boldsymbol{x}'_I \in \mathcal{M}^{|I|})$
Com($\boldsymbol{x}$)	$b_1 := (C = \langle \boldsymbol{x}'_I, \boldsymbol{S}_I \rangle + \left(\prod_{i \in I} e_i \right) \circ \Lambda_I)$
return $(C, \text{aux}) := (\langle \boldsymbol{x}, \boldsymbol{S} \rangle, \boldsymbol{x})$	**return** $b_0 \cap b_1$

Fig. 1. SVC from the root assumption.

---

[3] In general, $\mathcal{X}$ can be set such that for all $x, x' \in \mathcal{X}$, $\gcd(x - x', e_i) = 1$ for all $i \in [q]$.

Although multiplicative inverses of ring elements do not exist in general, and if so, they may be hard to compute, the above are efficiently computable because, for all $i \in [\ell] \setminus I$ and hence for all $i \in J \setminus I$, we have

$$S_i := \left(\prod_{j \in [\ell] \setminus \{i\}} e_j \right) \circ X = \left(\prod_{j \in I} e_j \prod_{j \in [\ell] \setminus (I \cup \{i\})} e_j \right) \circ X.$$

The correctness of the construction follows straightforwardly by inspection. Depending on the instantiation of H, we can prove our scheme secure against different assumptions:

- H is a (non-cryptographic) hash: Our construction is secure if the strong distinct-prime-product root assumption (introduced in Sect. 3) holds over the module family $\mathcal{R}_\mathcal{D}$. This is shown in Theorem 1.
- H is a random oracle: Our construction is secure if the adaptive root problem (introduced in [19]) is hard over the module family. This is shown in Theorem 2.

Theorem 1. *If the (resp. public-coin) strong distinct-prime-product root assumption holds over the module family $\mathcal{R}_\mathcal{D}$, then the scheme in Fig. 1 is (resp. public-coin) position binding.*

Proof. Suppose not, let $\mathcal{A}$ be a PPT adversary such that

$$\Pr \left[\begin{matrix} \mathsf{Verify}(C, I, \boldsymbol{x}_I, \Lambda_I) = 1 \\ \mathsf{Verify}(C, J, \boldsymbol{x}'_J, \Lambda'_J) = 1 \\ \exists i \in I \cap J \ s.t. \ x_i \neq x'_i \end{matrix} \middle| \begin{matrix} \omega \leftarrow_\$ \{0,1\}^\lambda \\ \mathsf{pp} \leftarrow \mathsf{Setup}(1^\lambda, 1^\ell; \omega) \\ (C, I, J, \boldsymbol{x}_I, \boldsymbol{x}'_J, \Lambda_I, \Lambda'_J) \leftarrow \mathcal{A}(1^\lambda, \mathsf{pp}, \overline{\omega}) \end{matrix} \right] > \frac{1}{f(\lambda)}$$

for some polynomial $f(\lambda) \in \mathsf{poly}(\lambda)$, where $\mathcal{A}$ gets ω as input (highlighted by the dashed box) only in the public-coin variant. We construct an algorithm $\mathcal{C}$ as follows, whose existence contracts the fact that $\mathcal{R}_\mathcal{D}$ is a (public-coin) strong distinct-prime-product root modules family.

In the private-coin setting, $\mathcal{C}$ receives as input (R_D, A) generated by $\mathsf{MGen}(1^\lambda; \omega)$ for some $\omega \leftarrow_\$ \{0,1\}^\lambda$. It sets $X := A$, and computes $(e_1, \ldots, e_\ell) \leftarrow H(R_D, X)$. It then sets $S_i := \left(\prod_{j \in [\ell] \setminus \{i\}} e_j \right) \circ X$ for all $i \in [\ell]$, $\boldsymbol{S} := (S_1, \ldots, S_q)^T$, and $\boldsymbol{e} := (e_1, \ldots, e_\ell)$. It sets $\mathsf{pp} := (R_D, X, \boldsymbol{S}, \boldsymbol{e})$ and runs $\mathcal{A}$ on input $(1^\lambda, \mathsf{pp})$. In the public-coin setting, $\mathcal{C}$ receives additionally ω and runs $\mathcal{A}$ on $(1^\lambda, \mathsf{pp}, \omega)$ instead. In any case, it is clear that pp and ω obtained above distribute identically as

$$\{(\mathsf{pp}, \omega) : \omega \leftarrow_\$ \{0,1\}^\lambda; \mathsf{pp} \leftarrow \mathsf{Setup}(1^\lambda, 1^\ell; \omega)\}_\lambda.$$

Hence, with probability at least $1/f(\lambda)$, $\mathcal{C}$ obtains $(C, I, J, \boldsymbol{x}_I, \boldsymbol{x}'_J, \Lambda_I, \Lambda'_J)$ such that

$$\langle \boldsymbol{x}_I, \boldsymbol{S}_I \rangle + \left(\prod_{i \in I} e_i \right) \circ \Lambda_I = \langle \boldsymbol{x}'_J, \boldsymbol{S}_J \rangle + \left(\prod_{i \in J} e_i \right) \circ \Lambda'_J$$

which implies

$$\langle \boldsymbol{x}_{I \setminus J}, \boldsymbol{S}_{I \setminus J} \rangle - \langle \boldsymbol{x}'_{J \setminus I}, \boldsymbol{S}_{J \setminus I} \rangle + \langle \boldsymbol{x}_{I \cap J} - \boldsymbol{x}'_{I \cap J}, \boldsymbol{S}_{I \cap J} \rangle$$

$$= \left(\prod_{i \in I \cap J} e_i \right) \left(\left(\prod_{i \in J \setminus I} e_i \right) \circ \Lambda'_J - \left(\prod_{i \in I \setminus J} e_i \right) \circ \Lambda_I \right).$$

Recall that $S_i = \left(\prod_{j \in [\ell] \setminus \{i\}} e_j \right) \circ A$. Define $\delta_i := \begin{cases} x_i & i \in I \setminus J \\ -x'_i & i \in J \setminus I \\ x_i - x'_i & i \in I \cap J \end{cases}$ and

$\Lambda := \left(\left(\prod_{i \in J \setminus I} e_i \right) \circ \Lambda'_J - \left(\prod_{i \in I \setminus J} e_i \right) \circ \Lambda_I \right)$. $\mathcal{C}$ obtains

$$\left(\sum_{i \in I \cup J} \delta_i \prod_{j \in [\ell] \setminus \{i\}} e_j \right) \circ A = \left(\prod_{i \in I \cap J} e_i \right) \circ \Lambda.$$

Let $K_0 := \{i \in I \cap J : \delta_i = 0_R\}$ and $K_1 := \{i \in I \cup J : \delta_i \neq 0_R\}$. Next, we show that $d := \gcd \left(\sum_{i \in I \cup J} \delta_i \prod_{j \in [\ell] \setminus \{i\}} e_j, \prod_{i \in I \cap J} e_i \right) = \prod_{j \in K_0} e_j$. Furthermore, suppose that this is the case, we have $(I \cap J) \setminus K_0 \neq \emptyset$ since there exists $i \in I \cap J$ such that $\delta_i = x_i - x'_i \neq 0_R$. To prove the above, we first note that

$$\sum_{i \in I \cup J} \delta_i \prod_{j \in [\ell] \setminus \{i\}} e_j = \sum_{i \in K_1} \delta_i \prod_{j \in [\ell] \setminus \{i\}} e_j = \prod_{j \in [\ell] \setminus (I \cup J)} e_j \left(\sum_{i \in K_1} \delta_i \prod_{j \in (I \cup J) \setminus \{i\}} e_j \right).$$

Hence

$$d = \gcd \left(\sum_{i \in K_1} \delta_i \prod_{j \in (I \cup J) \setminus \{i\}} e_j, \prod_{i \in I \cap J} e_i \right)$$

$$= \prod_{j \in K_0} e_j \cdot \gcd \left(\sum_{i \in K_1} \delta_i \prod_{j \in (I \cup J) \setminus (K_0 \cup \{i\})} e_j, \prod_{i \in (I \cap J) \setminus K_0} e_i \right).$$

It remains to show that $d' := \gcd \left(\sum_{i \in K_1} \delta_i \prod_{j \in (I \cup J) \setminus (K_0 \cup \{i\})} e_j, \prod_{i \in (I \cap J) \setminus K_0} e_i \right) = 1_R$. Suppose not, let $d' = \prod_{i \in L} e_i$ for some $L \subseteq (I \cap J) \setminus K_0$. Suppose $\ell \in L \neq \emptyset$. This means $\delta_\ell \neq 0_R$ and hence $\ell \in K_1$. Then there exists $r \in R$ such that

$$e_\ell \cdot r = \sum_{i \in K_1} \delta_i \prod_{j \in (I \cup J) \setminus (K_0 \cup \{i\})} e_j$$

$$= \delta_\ell \prod_{j \in (I \cup J) \setminus (K_0 \cup \{\ell\})} e_j + e_\ell \sum_{i \in K_1 \setminus \{\ell\}} \delta_i \prod_{j \in (I \cup J) \setminus (K_0 \cup \{i\})} e_j.$$

Let $r' := r - \sum_{i \in K_1 \setminus \{\ell\}} \delta_i \prod_{j \in (I \cup J) \setminus (K_0 \cup \{i\})} e_j$. We have

$$e_\ell \cdot r' = \delta_\ell \prod_{j \in (I \cup J) \setminus (K_0 \cup \{\ell\})} e_j.$$

Since $\delta_\ell \neq 0_R$, i.c., $\delta_\ell \in \{-1_R, 1_R\}$, the above contradicts the fact that e_ℓ is a prime element. Thus we must have $L = \emptyset$ and hence $d' = 1_R$.

Now that we have concluded $d = \gcd\left(\sum_{i \in I \cup J} \delta_i \prod_{j \in [\ell] \setminus \{i\}} e_j, \prod_{i \in I \cap J} e_i\right) = \prod_{j \in K_0} e_j$, $\mathcal{C}$ can use the extended Euclidean algorithm to find $a, b \in R$ such that

$$a \sum_{i \in I \cup J} \delta_i \prod_{j \in [\ell] \setminus \{i\}} e_j + b \prod_{i \in I \cap J} e_i = \prod_{j \in K_0} e_j.$$

Multiplying this to A, it gets

$$\left(\prod_{j \in K_0} e_j\right) \circ A = \left(a \sum_{i \in I \cup J} \delta_i \prod_{j \in [\ell] \setminus \{i\}} e_j + b \prod_{i \in I \cap J} e_i = \prod_{j \in K_0} e_j\right) \circ A$$

$$= \left(a \prod_{i \in I \cap J} e_i\right) \circ \Lambda + \left(b \prod_{i \in I \cap J} e_i\right) \circ A$$

$$= \left(\prod_{i \in I \cap J} e_i\right) (a \circ \Lambda + b \circ A).$$

Since $(I \cap J) \setminus K_0 \neq \emptyset$, $\mathcal{C}$ can set $S := (I \cap J) \setminus K_0$ and $Y := (a \circ \Lambda + b \circ A)$, and output $(\{e_i\}_{i \in S}, Y)$ as a solution to the strong distinct-prime-product root problem. □

Theorem 2. *If the (resp. public-coin) adaptive root assumption holds over the module family $\mathcal{R}_\mathcal{D}$ with respect to IRR_λ, then the scheme in Fig. 1 is (resp. public-coin) position binding in the random oracle model.*

Due to space constraints, we refer to [47] for a full proof.

Efficiency and Optimizations. Our construction admits two complementary instantiations, discussed in the following.

- Efficient Verifier (assuming random access to public parameters): The vectors S and e are explicitly included in the public parameters (as it is currently described). In this case, and suppose the verifier has random access to each e_i and S_i, the computational effort of the verifier is only proportional to $|I|$, the size of the subvector. The shortcoming of this scheme is that the size of the public parameters is linear in ℓ, which can be very large depending on the application.
- Short Public Parameters: One can reduce the size of the public parameters to a constant by including only the module description $(R_\mathcal{D}, X)$ and letting each algorithm

recompute the terms of S needed for the computations. This however increases the computational complexity of the verifier, since the computation needed for each element of S is linear in the vector length ℓ. This can be partially amortized by observing that the values $(S_1, \ldots, S_\ell)$ do not depend on the committed vector and can be precomputed by both parties.

Another possible tradeoff is given by the assumption that one is willing to rely on: Note that the main workload for the verifier (in the verifier-optimized variant) is to compute the term $\left(\prod_{i \in I} e_i\right) \circ \Lambda_I$. Assuming $R = \mathbb{Z}$ and the term is computed by repeated squaring, the complexity of the computation depends on the bit-length of the primes e_i. In the adaptive root assumption, the primes $(e_1, \ldots, e_\ell)$ are sampled randomly from a set of primes of size 2^λ, therefore representing each prime requires at least λ bits. On the other hand, under the strong distinct-prime-product root assumption we can set $(e_1, \ldots, e_\ell)$ to be the smallest ℓ primes. Since $\ell \in \mathrm{poly}(\lambda)$, each prime can be represented by $O(\log \lambda)$ bits. This greatly reduces the computational effort of the verifier.

5.2 SVC from the Computational Diffie-Hellman Assumption

Next we present our SVC construction from pairing groups. In favor of a simpler presentation and a more general result we describe our scheme assuming symmetric pairings. However, we stress that the scheme can be easily adapted to work over the more efficient asymmetric (type III) bilinear groups without affecting computational efficiency nor opening size by, e.g., replicating all public parameters in both source groups.

The public parameters consist of a set of random elements $\{G_i = G^{z_i}\}_{i \in [q]}$ and their pairwise "Diffie-Hellman products" $H_{i,i'} = G^{z_i z_{i'}}$ with $i \neq i'$. To commit to a vector $\boldsymbol{x}$ one computes $C := \prod_i G_i^{x_i}$. The opening of a subvector $\boldsymbol{x}_I$ is then $\prod_{i \in I} \prod_{i' \notin I} H_{i,i'}^{x_{i'}}$. Note that since $i \in I$ and $i' \notin I$, it is always true that $i \neq i'$.

$\mathsf{Setup}(1^\lambda, 1^\ell; \omega)$	$\mathsf{Open}(I, \boldsymbol{x}'_I, \mathsf{aux})$

$(p, \mathbb{G}, \mathbb{G}_T, G, e) \leftarrow \mathsf{GGen}(1^\lambda; \omega)$

$\forall i \in [\ell], \ z_i \leftarrow_\$ \mathbb{Z}_p$

$\forall i, i' \in [\ell], \ G_i := G^{z_i}, \ H_{i,i'} := G^{z_i z_{i'}}$

$\mathsf{pp} := \begin{pmatrix} p, \mathbb{G}, \mathbb{G}_T, G, \{G_i\}_{i \in [\ell]}, \\ \{H_{i,i'}\}_{i,i' \in [\ell], i \neq i'}, e \end{pmatrix}$

return pp

$\mathsf{Com}(\boldsymbol{x})$

return $(C, \mathsf{aux}) := \left(\prod_{i \in [\ell]} G_i^{x_i}, \boldsymbol{x} \right)$

parse aux as $\boldsymbol{x}$

return $\Lambda_I := \prod_{i \in I} \prod_{i' \notin I} H_{i,i'}^{x_{i'}}$

$\mathsf{Verify}(C, I, \boldsymbol{x}'_I, \Lambda_I)$

$b_0 := (\boldsymbol{x}'_I \in \mathcal{X}^{|I|})$

$b_1 := \left(e\left(\dfrac{C}{\prod_{i \in I} G_i^{x_i}}, \prod_{i \in I} G_i \right) = e(\Lambda_I, G) \right)$

return $b_0 \cap b_1$

Fig. 2. SVC from CDH.

Therefore the product is efficiently computable for an honest prover. Assuming that the verifier has random access to each G_i in the public parameters, it can check the relation by accessing $|I|$ entries in the public parameters, and computing $2 \cdot |I|$ group operations and 2 pairings (which are independent of ℓ). Since the public parameters are highly structured, this scheme does not admit an instantiation with short public parameters, which grow quadratically with the vector size ℓ.

Let GGen be an efficient bilinear group sampling algorithm. Let $(p, \mathbb{G}, \mathbb{G}_T, G, e)$ be a group description output by GGen. Let $\mathcal{X} := \mathbb{Z}_p$. Our second subvector commitment scheme is shown in Fig. 2. In the following we show that our SVC scheme is position binding with a private-coin setup.

Theorem 3. *If the computational Diffie-Hellman (CDH) assumption holds with respect to* GGen, *then the scheme in Fig. 2 is position binding.*

Proof. Suppose not, let $\mathcal{A}$ be a PPT adversary such that

$$
\Pr\left[
\begin{array}{c}
\mathsf{Verify}(C, I, \boldsymbol{x}_I, \Lambda_I) = 1 \\
\mathsf{Verify}(C, J, \boldsymbol{x}'_J, \Lambda'_J) = 1 \\
\exists i \in I \cap J \text{ s.t. } x_i \neq x'_i
\end{array}
\middle|
\begin{array}{c}
\omega \leftarrow_{\$} \{0,1\}^{\lambda} \\
\mathsf{pp} \leftarrow \mathsf{Setup}(1^{\lambda}, 1^{\ell}; \omega) \\
(C, I, J, \boldsymbol{x}_I, \boldsymbol{x}'_J, \Lambda_I, \Lambda'_J) \leftarrow \mathcal{A}(1^{\lambda}, \mathsf{pp})
\end{array}
\right] > \frac{1}{f(\lambda)}
$$

for some $f(\lambda) \in \mathrm{poly}(\lambda)$. We construct a square-DH solver $\mathcal{C}$, which implies a CDH solver [6], as follows.

$\mathcal{C}$ receives as input $(p, \mathbb{G}, \mathbb{G}_T, G, H, e)$, where $(p, \mathbb{G}, \mathbb{G}_T, G, e) \leftarrow \mathsf{GGen}(1^{\lambda})$ and $H = G^z$ for some random $z \leftarrow_{\$} \mathbb{Z}_p$, and must output G^{z^2}. It picks an index $i^* \leftarrow_{\$} [\ell]$ and set $G_{i^*} := H$. Symbolically, let $z_{i^*} := z$, which is not known by $\mathcal{C}$. For the other indices $i, i' \in [\ell] \setminus \{i^*\}$, it samples $z_i \leftarrow_{\$} \mathbb{Z}_p$ and sets $G_i := G^{z_i}$ and $H_{i,i'} := G^{z_i z_{i'}}$. It also sets $H_{i^*,i} = H_{i,i^*} = G^{z z_i}$ for each $i \in [\ell] \setminus \{i^*\}$. It then sets $\mathsf{pp} = (p, \mathbb{G}, \mathbb{G}_T, G, \{G_i\}_{i \in [\ell]}, \{H_{i,i'}\}_{i,i' \in [\ell], i \neq i'}, e)$, which is identically distributed as pp output by Setup. $\mathcal{C}$ runs $\mathcal{A}$ on input $(1^{\lambda}, \mathsf{pp})$. With probability at least $1/f(\lambda)$, it obtains $(C, I, J, \boldsymbol{x}_I, \boldsymbol{x}'_J, \Lambda_I, \Lambda'_J)$ such that $\mathsf{Verify}(C, I, \boldsymbol{x}_I, \Lambda_I) = 1$, $\mathsf{Verify}(C, J, \boldsymbol{x}'_J, \Lambda'_J) = 1$, and $\exists i \in I \cap J$ s.t. $x_i \neq x'_i$. Conditioning on the above, with probability $1/\ell$, it holds that $i^* \in I \cap J$ and $x_{i^*} \neq x'_{i^*}$. By examining the verification equations, we have

$$
e\left(\prod_{i \in I} G_i^{x_i}, \prod_{i \in I} G_i\right) \cdot e(\Lambda_I, G) = e\left(\prod_{i \in J} G_i^{x'_i}, \prod_{i \in J} G_i\right) \cdot e(\Lambda_J, G)
$$

$$
e\left(\prod_{i \in J} G_i^{x'_i}, \prod_{i \in J} G_i\right) \cdot e\left(\prod_{i \in I} G_i^{-m_i}, \prod_{i \in I} G_i\right) = e(\Lambda, G), \text{ where } \Lambda := \Lambda_I / \Lambda_J
$$

$$
\left(\sum_{i \in J} z_i x'_i\right)\left(\sum_{i \in J} z_i\right) - \left(\sum_{i \in I} z_i x_i\right)\left(\sum_{i \in I} z_i\right) = \log_G \Lambda
$$

$$
\alpha z_{i^*}^2 + \beta z_{i^*} + \gamma = \log_G \Lambda
$$

where

$$\alpha := (x'_{i*} - x_{i*}) \qquad \beta := \sum_{i \in J \setminus \{i*\}} z_i(x'_i + x'_{i*}) - \sum_{i \in I \setminus \{i*\}} z_i(x_i + x_{i*})$$

$$\gamma := \left(\sum_{i \in J \setminus \{i*\}} z_i x'_i \right) \left(\sum_{i \in J \setminus \{i*\}} z_i \right) - \left(\sum_{i \in I \setminus \{i*\}} z_i x_i \right) \left(\sum_{i \in I \setminus \{i*\}} z_i \right)$$

are computable by $\mathcal{C}$ since they do not depend on $z = z_{i*}$. $\mathcal{C}$ then outputs $G^{z^2} = \left(\frac{\Lambda}{H^\beta G^\gamma} \right)^{1/\alpha}$ which is the solution to the square-DH instance. $\qquad \square$

6 Construction for LMC

Our LMC construction is inspired by the scheme presented in [48] and it is based upon the following observations. First, when the vectors $\boldsymbol{x}, \boldsymbol{f} \in \mathbb{F}^\ell$ for some field $\mathbb{F}$ are encoded as the polynomials $p_f(\alpha) := \sum_{j \in [\ell]} f_j \alpha^{\ell+1-j}$ and $p_x(\alpha) := \sum_{j \in [\ell]} x_j \alpha^j$ with variable α respectively, their inner product is the coefficient of the monomial $\alpha^{\ell+1}$ in the polynomial product $p_f(\alpha) p_x(\alpha)$. Second, due to linearity of polynomial multiplication, if a matrix $F \in \mathbb{F}^{q \times \ell}$ is encoded in the polynomial $p_F(\alpha) := \sum_{i \in [q], j \in [\ell]} f_{i,j} z_i \alpha^{\ell+1-j}$ with variables $(\alpha, z_1, \ldots, z_q)$, then the matrix-vector product $F\boldsymbol{x}$ is given in the coefficients of the monomials $z_i \alpha^{\ell+1}$ for $i \in [q]$ in the polynomial $p_F(\alpha) p_x(\alpha)$.

With the above observations, we give an overview of our construction. We let the commitment C to $\boldsymbol{x}$ be $G^{p_x(\alpha)}$, which is computable by combining elements of the form

Setup$(1^\lambda, \mathcal{F}; \omega)$	Open$(F, \boldsymbol{y}, \text{aux})$
$(p, \mathbb{G}, \mathbb{G}_T, G, e) \leftarrow \mathsf{GGen}(1^\lambda; \omega)$	**parse aux as $\boldsymbol{x}$**
$\alpha, z_1, \ldots, z_q \leftarrow_{\$} \mathbb{Z}_p$	$\Lambda := \prod_{i \in [q]} \prod_{j \in [\ell]} \prod_{j' \in [\ell] \setminus \{j\}} H_{i, \ell+1+j-j'}^{f_{i,j} x_{j'}}$
$\forall j \in [\ell],\ G_j := G^{\alpha^j}$	
$\forall i \in [q], j \in [2\ell],\ H_{i,j} := G^{z_i \alpha^j}$	**return** Λ
$\mathsf{pp} := \left(\begin{array}{l} p, \mathbb{G}, \mathbb{G}_T, G, \{G_j\}_{j \in [\ell]}, \\ \{H_{i,j}\}_{i \in [q], j \in [2\ell] \setminus \{\ell+1\}}, e \end{array} \right)$	Verify$(C, F, \boldsymbol{y}, \Lambda)$
return pp	$b_0 := (\boldsymbol{y} \in \mathbb{Z}_p^q)$
Com$(\boldsymbol{x})$	$b_1 := \left(\dfrac{e \left(C, \prod_{i \in [q]} \prod_{j \in [\ell]} H_{i, \ell+1-j}^{f_{i,j}} \right) =}{e(G_1, \prod_{i \in [q]} H_{i,\ell}^{y_i}) \cdot e(\Lambda, G)} \right)$
return $(C, \text{aux}) := \left(\prod_{j \in [\ell]} G_j^{x_j}, \boldsymbol{x} \right)$	**return** $b_0 \cap b_1$

Fig. 3. LMC from bilinear pairings.

G^{α^j} given in the public parameters. Given (F, y), to verify that $Fx = y$, the verifier computes via pairing $e(G^{p_F(\alpha, z_1, \ldots, z_q)}, G^{p_x(\alpha)})$, where the left-input is computable by combining elements of the form $G^{z_i \alpha^j}$ given in the public parameters. If the relation $Fx = y$ indeed holds, then the coefficients of y must be encoded as the coefficients of the (lifted) monomials $G^{z_i \alpha^{\ell+1}}$. To convince the verifier that this is the case, it suffices for the prover to provide the remaining terms of the product polynomial.

Let GGen be an efficient bilinear group sampling algorithm. Let $(p, \mathbb{G}, \mathbb{G}_T, G, e)$ be a group description output by GGen. Let $\mathbb{F} = \mathbb{Z}_p$, $\ell, q \in \mathbb{N}$, and $\mathcal{F}$ be the set of all linear maps from $\mathbb{Z}_p^\ell$ to $\mathbb{Z}_p^q$. Our LMC for $\mathbb{Z}_p$ is given in Fig. 3. For full generality we present the construction over symmetric pairings, however one can easily convert it to the more efficient asymmetric pairing groups via standard techniques, without affecting the size of the openings. Although we do not aim to achieve the hiding property, our construction can be easily modified to be hiding, by introducing randomness similar to that in Pedersen commitment [56]. Indeed this is how the FC of [48] achieves hiding. We show that our construction is function binding (in the generic bilinear group model) in the following.

Theorem 4. *Let $\ell, q \in \mathsf{poly}(\lambda)$ and $1/p \in \mathsf{negl}(\lambda)$. The scheme in Fig. 3 is function binding in the generic bilinear group model.*

Proof. The proof uses the generic group model abstraction of Shoup [59] and we refer the reader to [18] for a comprehensive introduction to the bilinear group model. Here we state the central lemma useful for proving facts about generic attackers.

Lemma 1 (Schwartz-Zippel). *Let $F(X_1, \ldots, X_m)$ be a non-zero polynomial of degree $d \geq 0$ over a field $\mathbb{F}$. Then the probability that $F(x_1, \ldots, x_m) = 0$ for randomly chosen values $(x_1, \ldots, x_m)$ in $\mathbb{F}^n$ is bounded from above by $\frac{d}{|\mathbb{F}|}$.*

Fix $Q \in \mathbb{N}$. Suppose there exists an adversary $\mathcal{A}$, who only performs generic bilinear group operations, such that there exists a polynomial $f \in \mathsf{poly}(\lambda)$ with

$$\Pr\left[\begin{array}{l} \forall k \in [Q], \begin{array}{l} F_k \in \mathbb{Z}_p^{q \times \ell} \wedge y_k \in \mathbb{Z}_p^q \wedge \\ \mathsf{Verify}(C, f_k, y_k, \Lambda_k) = 1 \end{array} \\ \nexists x \in \mathbb{Z}_p^\ell \ s.t. \ \forall k \in [Q], \ F_k(x) = y_k \end{array} \middle| \begin{array}{l} \mathsf{pp} \leftarrow \mathsf{Setup}(1^\lambda, \mathcal{F}) \\ (C, \{(F_k, y_k, \Lambda_k)\}_{k \in [Q]}) \leftarrow \mathcal{A}(1^\lambda, \mathsf{pp}) \end{array} \right] > \frac{1}{f(\lambda)}.$$

Since $\mathcal{A}$ is generic, and C and each of Λ_k are $\mathbb{G}$ elements, we can write $\log_G C$ and each $\log_G \Lambda_k$ in the following form:

$$\log_G C = \gamma_0 + \sum_{j \in [\ell]} \gamma_j \alpha^j + \sum_{\substack{i \in [q] \\ j \in [2\ell] \setminus \{\ell+1\}}} \gamma_{i,j} z_i \alpha^j$$

$$\log_G \Lambda_k = \lambda_{k,0} + \sum_{j \in [\ell]} \lambda_{k,j} \alpha^j + \sum_{\substack{i \in [q] \\ j \in [2\ell] \setminus \{\ell+1\}}} \lambda_{k,i,j} z_i \alpha^j$$

for some integer coefficients γ_j, $\gamma_{i,j}$, $\lambda_{k,j}$, and $\lambda_{k,i,j}$ for i, j, and k in the appropriate ranges. Since for each $k \in [Q]$, $\mathsf{Verify}(C, F_k, \boldsymbol{y}_k, \Lambda_k) = 1$, the following relations hold:

$$(\log_G C) \left(\sum_{i \in [q]} \sum_{j \in [\ell]} f_{k,i,j} z_i \alpha^{\ell+1-j} \right) = \sum_{i \in [q]} y_{k,i} z_i \alpha^{\ell+1} + \log_G \Lambda_k.$$

Note that the above defines a $(n+1)$-variate polynomial of degree $3\ell+2$ which evaluates to zero at a random point $(\alpha, z_1, \ldots, z_q)$. Suppose that the polynomial is non-zero. By the Schwartz-Zippel lemma, the probability that the above happens is bounded by $\frac{3\ell+2}{p}$ which is negligible as $\ell \in \mathsf{poly}(\lambda)$ and $1/p \in \mathsf{negl}(\lambda)$. We can therefore assume that the polynomial is always zero. In particular, the coefficients of the monomials $z_i \alpha^{\ell+1}$ are zero for all $i \in [q]$. Thus, we have the following relations for all $k \in [Q]$ and $i \in [q]$:

$$\sum_{j \in [\ell]} f_{k,i,j} \gamma_j = y_{k,i}.$$

In other words, there exists $\boldsymbol{x} := (\gamma_1, \ldots, \gamma_q)^T \mod p \in \mathbb{Z}_p^q$ such that $F_k(\boldsymbol{x}) = \boldsymbol{y}_k$, for all $k \in [Q]$, which contradicts the assumption about $\mathcal{A}$. We thus conclude that such adversaries exist only with negligible probability. Since the above holds for any $Q \in \mathbb{N}$, we conclude that the construction is function binding. $\qquad\square$

7 Succinct Arguments of Knowledge from SVC/LMC

We present our compiler for constructing interactive arguments of knowledge either from traditional PCPs and subvector commitments (Sect. 5), or from linear PCPs [42] and linear map commitments (Sect. 6). The constructions for both cases are in fact identical and we present only the latter since it is strictly more general (an traditional PCP can be seen as a linear PCP where queries are restricted to unit vectors).

Let $(\mathcal{P}_{\mathsf{PCP}}, \mathcal{V}_{\mathsf{PCP}})$ be an ℓ-long q-query (linear) PCP over some field $\mathbb{F}$ for NP with r being the length of the random coins of the possibly adaptive verifier. Let $\mathsf{PRG} : \{0,1\}^\lambda \rightarrow \{0,1\}^r$ be a pseudo-random generator and let $\mathsf{LMC} := (\mathsf{Setup}, \mathsf{Com}, \mathsf{Open}, \mathsf{Verify})$ be a linear map commitment for the set of all linear maps $\mathcal{F}$ from $\mathbb{F}^\ell$ to $\mathbb{F}^q$, possibly with public-coin setup. We present a 4-move interactive argument of knowledge in Fig. 4.

7.1 Protocol Description

We first describe some subroutines to be used in the protocol. We construct polynomial time algorithms Record, Reconstruct, and Decide which perform the following:

- Record: On input a statement x, a proof π, a randomness ρ, it runs $\mathcal{V}_{\mathsf{PCP}}^\pi(x; \rho)$ and records the queries $\boldsymbol{f}_1, \ldots, \boldsymbol{f}_q \in \mathbb{F}^q$ made by $\mathcal{V}_{\mathsf{PCP}}$. It outputs a query matrix $F := [\boldsymbol{f}_1 | \ldots | \boldsymbol{f}_q]^T \in \mathbb{F}^{q \times \ell}$.
- Reconstruct: On input a statement x, a response vector $\boldsymbol{y} \in \mathbb{F}^q$, and a randomness ρ, it runs $\mathcal{V}_{\mathsf{PCP}}^\pi(x; \rho)$ by simulating the oracle π using the response vector $\boldsymbol{y}$. That is, when $\mathcal{V}_{\mathsf{PCP}}$ makes the i-th query $\boldsymbol{f}_i$ for $i \in [q]$, it responds by returning the value y_i. It outputs a query matrix $F := [\boldsymbol{f}_1 | \ldots | \boldsymbol{f}_q]^T \in \mathbb{F}^{q \times \ell}$.

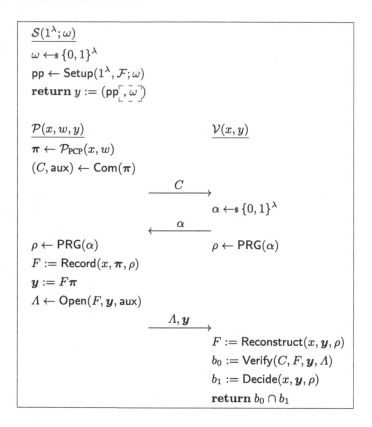

Fig. 4. Succinct argument of knowledge for NP from SVC/LMC

- Decide: On input a statement x, a response vector $\boldsymbol{y} \in \mathbb{F}^q$, it runs $\mathcal{V}^\pi_{\mathrm{PCP}}(x; \rho)$ by simulating the oracle π as in Reconstruct, and outputs whatever $\mathcal{V}^\pi_{\mathrm{PCP}}(x; \rho)$ outputs.

It is clear that for any strings x and π and randomness ρ, if $\boldsymbol{y}$ is formed in such a way that y_i is the response to the i-th query made by $\mathcal{V}^\pi_{\mathrm{PCP}}(x; \rho)$, then $\mathsf{Record}(x, \boldsymbol{\pi}, \rho) = \mathsf{Reconstruct}(x, \boldsymbol{y}, \rho)$, and $\mathsf{Decide}(x, \boldsymbol{y}, \rho) = \mathcal{V}^\pi_{\mathrm{PCP}}(x; \rho)$.

We now describe the protocol. The setup algorithm $\mathcal{S}$ samples a random string ω and computes the public parameters pp of LMC using ω. It outputs pp if an LMC with private-coin setup is used, which results in an argument system with private-coin setup. Alternatively, if an LMC with public-coin setup is used, it outputs additionally ω (as highlighted in the dashed box). This results in a public-coin setup.

In the rest of the protocol, the verifier is entirely public-coin. On input the public parameter pp, the statement x and the witness w, the prover $\mathcal{P}$ produces π as the PCP encoding of the witness w, then it commits to π and sends its commitment C to the verifier $\mathcal{V}$. Upon receiving the commitment C, $\mathcal{V}$ responds with a random string α. The prover $\mathcal{P}$ stretches α with a PRG into ρ and executes $\mathcal{V}_{\mathrm{PCP}}$ on ρ. Here the PRG is used to compress the (possibly large) randomness of the verifier, which is strictly needed only for linear PCPs (standard PCPs typically have low randomness complexity and therefore the random coins can be sent in plain).

The prover $\mathcal{P}$ then records the sets of queries $F = \mathsf{Record}(x, \boldsymbol{\pi}, \rho)$ of $\mathcal{V}_{\mathrm{PCP}}$ using randomness ρ to $\boldsymbol{\pi}$, and computes the responses $\boldsymbol{y} = F\boldsymbol{\pi}$. Next, it computes the opening Λ of the commitment C to the tuple $(F, \boldsymbol{y})$. The opening Λ along with the response $\boldsymbol{y}$ are sent to the verifier $\mathcal{V}$. The verifier $\mathcal{V}$ runs $\mathsf{Reconstruct}(x, \boldsymbol{y}, \rho)$ to reconstruct the query matrix F. It then checks if Λ is a valid opening of C to $(F, \boldsymbol{y})$. Finally, it checks if $\mathsf{Decide}(x, \boldsymbol{y}, \rho)$ returns 1. If all checks are passed, it outputs 1. Otherwise, it outputs 0.

7.2 Analysis

Clearly, if $(\mathcal{P}_{\mathrm{PCP}}, \mathcal{V}_{\mathrm{PCP}})$ is a complete linear PCP, and LMC is a correct LMC, then the argument system is complete. Alternatively, if $(\mathcal{P}_{\mathrm{PCP}}, \mathcal{V}_{\mathrm{PCP}})$ is a complete (traditional) PCP, and LMC is a correct SVC, then the system is also complete. The succinctness of the system follows directly from the compactness of LMC. Next, we show that the argument system is of knowledge by the following theorem. Due to space constraints, we refer to [47] for a full proof.

Theorem 5. *Let* $(\mathcal{P}_{\mathrm{PCP}}, \mathcal{V}_{\mathrm{PCP}})$ *be a* $2^{-\sigma}$*-sound linear PCP of knowledge for NP, PRG be a pseudo-random generator, and* LMC $:=$ (Setup, Com, Open, Verify) *be (resp. public-coin) function binding. Then the protocol in Fig. 4 is a* $2^{-\sigma}$*-sound (resp. public-coin) argument of knowledge.*

7.3 Instantiations and Efficiency

Since our argument system has a public-coin verifier, we can apply the Fiat-Shamir transformation to turn it into a non-interactive argument and sometimes a SNARK.[4] We highlight some interesting instantiations of our compiler: Regardless of the specific root assumption used, we can instantiate our first SVC construction over $Cl(\Delta)$, the class group of an imaginary quadratic order with discriminant Δ. Considering the current best attacks, we can assume that root problems for a $O(\lambda^2)$-bit Δ are hard for a 2^{λ}-time adversary. Concretely, with a 2560-bit Δ, which roughly offers security against a 2^{128}-time adversary, each element in $Cl(\Delta)$ can be represented by at most 2560 bits (see Sect. 8 for more details). Using a 240-query 2^{-80}-sound PCP, the resulting proof size is $2 \cdot 2560 + 240 = 5360$ bits. When using the verifier-optimized SVC (see Sect. 5.1) the workload of the verifier is dominated by 240 exponentiations, regardless of the witness size. However the public parameters grow linearly with the length of the PCP encoding. One can reduce the size of the public parameters to constant at the cost of having an inefficient verifier. We stress that class groups of imaginary quadratic orders have a public-coin setup and so does the resulting SNARK.

Alternatively, we can use our second SVC construction over the pairing-friendly 256-bit Barreto-Naehrig curve [7], which roughly offers security against 2^{128}-time

---

[4] In the original definition of Bitansky *et al.* [16], a SNARK verifier is a Turing machine with runtime logarithmic in that of the corresponding NP verifier. We consider a relaxed definition where the SNARK verifier is a random access machine.

adversaries. In such a curve, each group element can be represented by 256 bits. Therefore the resulting proof size is $2 \cdot 256 + 240 = 752$ bits. This marginally improves over the shortest proofs known [40]. A shortcoming of this approach is that the public parameters of the resulting SNARK grow quadratically in the length of the PCP proof.

An unsatisfactory aspect of the instantiations above is that PCPs with such short queries have typically a very high prover complexity and are therefore very expensive to compute, which means that our arguments described above have a high prover complexity. One approach to address this issue is to leverage the large body of work on linear PCPs [17,42], which significantly improve the complexity of the prover. Any of these schemes can be used in combination with an LMC (such as the construction of Sect. 6) to obtain a non-interactive argument with slightly larger proofs (by a constant factor) but with a more efficient prover. We stress that our compiler supports *any* linear PCP, whereas existing compilers only support those with a verifier who only evaluates quadratic polynomials. Moreover, although our pairing-based instantiations inherit the private-coin setup from underlying SVC/LMC, the setup is statement-independent. In contrast, the setup in existing pairing-based schemes such as [40] depends on the statement to be proven. We shall mention however that our LMC has a linear verifier complexity and therefore it yields an argument with verifier computation linear in the length of the PCP.

For the efficiency of the verifier, there are several techniques to reduce its computational overhead: As an example, one could compose our scheme with a verifier-optimized SNARK to prove the validity of the verification equation, instead of having the verifier computing it. Very recently, Boneh et al. [20] presented a special-purpose proof of knowledge of co-prime roots (PoKCR) that drastically reduces the running time of the verifier in class group-based SVCs (see Sect. 5) by trading group operations for modular multiplications and additions, which are orders of magnitude more efficient. We refer the reader to [20] for a detailed analysis of the concrete costs.

8   Candidate Module Families

In the following we suggest some candidate instantiations for modules (specifically groups) where the strong distinct-prime-root assumption and/or the adaptive root assumption are believed to hold.

8.1   Class Groups of Imaginary Quadratic Orders

The use of class groups in cryptography was first proposed by Buchmann and Williams [25]. We refer to, *e.g.*, [23,24], for more detailed discussions. We recall the basic properties of class groups necessary for our purpose. Let Δ be a negative integer such that $\Delta \equiv 0$ or $1 \pmod 4$. The ring $\mathcal{O}_\Delta := \mathbb{Z} + \frac{\Delta + \sqrt{\Delta}}{2}\mathbb{Z}$ is called an *imaginary quadratic order of discriminant Δ*. Its field of fractions is $\mathbb{Q}(\sqrt{\Delta})$. The discriminant is *fundamental* if $\Delta/4$ (resp. Δ) is square-free in the case of $\Delta \equiv 0 \pmod 4$ (resp. $\Delta \equiv 1 \pmod 4$). If Δ is fundamental, then $\mathcal{O}_\Delta$ is a *maximal* order. The *fractional ideals* of $\mathcal{O}_\Delta$ are of the form $q\left(a\mathbb{Z} + \frac{b + \sqrt{\Delta}}{2}\mathbb{Z}\right)$ with $q \in \mathbb{Q}$, $a \in \mathbb{Z}^+$, and $b \in \mathbb{Z}$, subject to the constraint that there exists $c \in \mathbb{Z}^+$ such that $\Delta = b^2 - 4ac$ and $\gcd(a, b, c) = 1$. A fractional ideal can therefore be represented by a tuple (q, a, b). If $q = 1$, then the ideal is called *integral* and can be represented by a tuple (a, b). An integral ideal (a, b) is *reduced* if it satisfies $-a < b \leq a \leq c$ and $b > 0$ if $a = c$. It is known that if an ideal (a, b) is reduced, then $a \leq \sqrt{|\Delta|/3}$. Two ideals $\mathfrak{a}, \mathfrak{b} \subseteq \mathcal{O}_\Delta$ are *equivalent* if there exists $0 \neq \alpha \in \mathbb{Q}(\sqrt{\Delta})$ such that $\mathfrak{b} = \alpha \mathfrak{a}$. It is known that, for each equivalence class of ideals, there exists exactly one reduced ideal which serves as the representative of the equivalence class. The set of equivalence classes of ideals equipped with ideal multiplication forms an Abelian group $Cl(\Delta)$ known as a *class group*.

Properties Useful in Cryptography. Since for all reduced ideals, $|b| \leq a \leq \sqrt{|\Delta|/3}$, $Cl(\Delta)$ is finite. For sufficiently large $|\Delta|$, no efficient algorithm is known for finding the cardinality of $Cl(\Delta)$, also known as the class number. Group operations can be performed efficiently, as there exist efficient algorithms for ideal multiplication and computing reduced ideals [23]. Assuming the extended Riemann hypothesis, $Cl(\Delta)$ is generated by the classes of all invertible prime ideals of norm smaller than $12(\log |\Delta|)^2$ [4], where the norm of a fractional ideal (q, a, b) is defined as $q^2 a$ ($= a$ for integral ideals). Since these ideals have norms logarithmic in $|\Delta|$, they can be found in polynomial time through exhaustive search. A random element can then be sampled by computing a power product of the elements in the generating set, with exponents randomly chosen from $[|\Delta|]$.

(Strong) Root Problem and its Variants in $Cl(\Delta)$. To recall, the strong root problem in $Cl(\Delta)$ is to find a prime $e \in \mathbb{Z}$ and a group element $Y \in Cl(\Delta)$ such that $Y^e = X$, for some given element $X \in Cl(\Delta)$. It is widely believed that root problems in $Cl(\Delta)$ for a large enough Δ are hard if the problem instances are sampled randomly with private coin [25]. Although the strong root problem in $Cl(\Delta)$ is not as well studied, it is shown to be hard for generic group algorithms [31]. The best attacks currently known are the ones for the root problem which runs in time proportional to $L_{|\Delta|}(\frac{1}{2}, 1)$ [41], where $L_x(d, c) := \exp(c(\log x)^d (\log \log x)^{1-d})$. As discussed in [41], using a 2560-bit Δ offers approximately 128 bits of computational security.

The (resp. public-coin setup) position binding property of our first construction of SVC can be proven under either the (resp. public-coin setup) strong distinct-prime-product root assumption or the (resp. public-coin setup) adaptive root assumption. Note that these two assumptions are somewhat "dual" to each other, in the sense that the former allows the adversary to choose which root it is going to compute, while the latter allows the adversary to choose the element whose root is to be found.

In the private-coin setup setting, it is clear that the strong distinct-prime-product root assumption is implied by the standard strong root assumption. In the public-coin setup setting, it is conjectured [19, 63] that the adaptive root assumption holds in $Cl(\Delta)$. In the following, we first propose a simple candidate sampling algorithm MGen for sampling $Cl(\Delta)$ and random elements in $Cl(\Delta)$ with public coin, and then elaborate more about the strong distinct-prime-product root assumption with respect to MGen.

The sampling algorithm MGen first samples random integers of the appropriate length until it finds a fundamental discriminant Δ. Let $\{G_1, \ldots, G_k\}$ be a generating set of $Cl(\Delta)$. Our sampling algorithm samples random primes $c_1, \ldots, c_k \in [|\Delta|]$ subject to the constraint that the c_i's are pairwise coprime[5]. That is $\gcd(c_i, c_j) = 1$ for all $i, j \in [k]$ with $i \neq j$. The algorithm then outputs Δ along with $A = \prod_{i \in [k]} G_i^{c_i}$.

With the above restriction in place, it seems that the best strategy of finding an e-th root of A is to find an e-th root of G_i for all $i \in [k]$ simultaneously. On the other hand, the additional constraint seems necessary for the strong distinct-prime-product root problem with respect to A to be hard. Suppose that (1) there exists a subset $I = \{c_{i_1}, \ldots, c_{i_\ell}\} \subseteq [k]$ such that $\gcd(c_{i_1}, \ldots, c_{i_\ell}) = d \neq 1$; (2) d can be efficiently factorized into $\{e_i\}_{i \in S}$ such that $d = \prod_{i \in S} e_i$ for distinct primes $e_i \neq 1$; and (3) for all $j \in [k] \setminus I$, G_j can be efficiently represented as a product $G_j = \prod_{i \in I} G_i^{a_{i,j}}$ for some $a_{i,j}$. Then one can efficiently find a d-th root of A, say Y, and output $(\{e_i\}_{i \in S}, Y)$ as a solution to the strong distinct-prime-product root problem. Since it seems unreasonable to assume that d cannot be efficiently factorized into a product of distinct primes (see also the discussion of RSA-UFO below), nor is it sound to assume that none of the G_j can be represented with a power product of the G_i's where $i \neq j$, we impose the more reasonable restriction that the c_i's are pairwise coprime.

8.2 RSA Groups

RSA-based cryptosystems operate over $\mathbb{Z}_N^*$, the group of positive integers smaller and coprime with N, equipped with modular multiplication, where N is an integer with at least two distinct large prime factors. The security of these systems relies on the hardness of the (strong) root problem over $\mathbb{Z}_N^*$, known as the (strong) RSA assumption. Typically, N is chosen as a product of two secret distinct large primes p, q. However, the (strong) root problem over $\mathbb{Z}_N^*$ is easy if p and q are known. In other words, for N generated this way, the (strong) root assumption with *public-coin setup* does not hold over $\mathbb{Z}_N^*$.

RSA-UFOs. The problem of constructing RSA-based accumulators without trapdoors was considered by Sander [58], who proposed a way to generate (k, ϵ)-"generalized RSA moduli of unknown complete factionization (RSA-UFOs)" N which has at least two distinct k-bit prime factors with probability $1 - \epsilon$, summarized as follows. Let $N_1, \ldots, N_r$ be random $3k$-bit integers with $r = O(\log 1/\epsilon)$. It is known that with constant probability N_i has at least two distinct k-bit prime factors [58]. It then follows that $N := \prod_{i \in [r]} N_i$ has at least two distinct k-bit prime factors. An important observation is that N can be generated with public coin, e.g., using a random oracle. However, since N is a $3kr$-bit integer, any cryptosystem based on $\mathbb{Z}_N^*$ seems impractical. Nevertheless, one can show that strong RSA over RSA-UFO groups is implied by the standard strong RSA assumption in the presence of a random oracle. This result is implicitly shown by Sander [58] and a proof sketch is given in [47].

Acknoweldgements. We thank Yuval Ishai and Eran Tromer for insighful discussions and comments on an earlier draft of this work. Research supported in part by a gift from DoS Networks.

---

[5] This is assuming $k > 1$, else just set $c_1 = 1$.

References

1. Abdolmaleki, B., Baghery, K., Lipmaa, H., Zając, M.: A subversion-resistant SNARK. In: Takagi, T., Peyrin, T. (eds.) ASIACRYPT 2017. LNCS, vol. 10626, pp. 3–33. Springer, Cham (2017). https://doi.org/10.1007/978-3-319-70700-6_1
2. Ames, S., Hazay, C., Ishai, Y., Venkitasubramaniam, M.: Ligero: lightweight sublinear arguments without a trusted setup. In: Proceedings of the 2017 ACM SIGSAC Conference on Computer and Communications Security, pp. 2087–2104. ACM (2017)
3. Arora, S., Safra, S.: Probabilistic checking of proofs: a new characterization of NP. J. ACM (JACM) **45**(1), 70–122 (1998)
4. Bach, E.: Explicit bounds for primality testing and related problems. Math. Comput. **55**(191), 355–380 (1990)
5. Backes, M., Barbosa, M., Fiore, D., Reischuk, R.M.: ADSNARK: nearly practical and privacy-preserving proofs on authenticated data. In: 2015 IEEE Symposium on Security and Privacy, pp. 271–286. IEEE Computer Society Press, May 2015
6. Bao, F., Deng, R.H., Zhu, H.F.: Variations of Diffie-Hellman problem. In: Qing, S., Gollmann, D., Zhou, J. (eds.) ICICS 2003. LNCS, vol. 2836, pp. 301–312. Springer, Heidelberg (2003). https://doi.org/10.1007/978-3-540-39927-8_28
7. Barreto, P.S.L.M., Naehrig, M.: Pairing-friendly elliptic curves of prime order. In: Preneel, B., Tavares, S. (eds.) SAC 2005. LNCS, vol. 3897, pp. 319–331. Springer, Heidelberg (2006). https://doi.org/10.1007/11693383_22
8. Bellare, M., Rogaway, P.: Random oracles are practical: a paradigm for designing efficient protocols. In: Denning, D.E., Pyle, R., Ganesan, R., Sandhu, R.S., Ashby, V. (eds.) ACM CCS 1993, pp. 62–73. ACM Press, November 1993
9. Ben-Sasson, E., et al.: Computational integrity with a public random string from quasi-linear PCPs. In: Coron, J.-S., Nielsen, J.B. (eds.) EUROCRYPT 2017, Part III. LNCS, vol. 10212, pp. 551–579. Springer, Cham (2017). https://doi.org/10.1007/978-3-319-56617-7_19
10. Ben-Sasson, E., Bentov, I., Horesh, Y., Riabzev, M.: Fast Reed-Solomon interactive oracle proofs of proximity. In: Electronic Colloquium on Computational Complexity (ECCC), vol. 24, p. 134 (2017)
11. Ben-Sasson, E., Chiesa, A., Genkin, D., Tromer, E., Virza, M.: SNARKs for C: verifying program executions succinctly and in zero knowledge. In: Canetti, R., Garay, J.A. (eds.) CRYPTO 2013, Part II. LNCS, vol. 8043, pp. 90–108. Springer, Heidelberg (2013). https://doi.org/10.1007/978-3-642-40084-1_6
12. Ben-Sasson, E., Chiesa, A., Riabzev, M., Spooner, N., Virza, M., Ward, N.P.: Aurora: transparent succinct arguments for R1CS. In: Ishai, Y., Rijmen, V. (eds.) EUROCRYPT 2019, Part I. LNCS, vol. 11476, pp. 103–128. Springer, Cham (2019). https://doi.org/10.1007/978-3-030-17653-2_4
13. Ben-Sasson, E., Chiesa, A., Spooner, N.: Interactive oracle proofs. In: Hirt, M., Smith, A. (eds.) TCC 2016-B, Part II. LNCS, vol. 9986, pp. 31–60. Springer, Heidelberg (2016). https://doi.org/10.1007/978-3-662-53644-5_2
14. Ben-Sasson, E., Chiesa, A., Tromer, E., Virza, M.: Scalable zero knowledge via cycles of elliptic curves. In: Garay, J.A., Gennaro, R. (eds.) CRYPTO 2014, Part II. LNCS, vol. 8617, pp. 276–294. Springer, Heidelberg (2014). https://doi.org/10.1007/978-3-662-44381-1_16
15. Bitansky, N., et al.: The hunting of the SNARK. J. Cryptol. **30**(4), 989–1066 (2017)
16. Bitansky, N., Canetti, R., Chiesa, A., Tromer, E.: From extractable collision resistance to succinct non-interactive arguments of knowledge, and back again. In: Goldwasser, S. (ed.) ITCS 2012, pp. 326–349. ACM, January 2012
17. Bitansky, N., Chiesa, A., Ishai, Y., Paneth, O., Ostrovsky, R.: Succinct non-interactive arguments via linear interactive proofs. In: Sahai, A. (ed.) TCC 2013. LNCS, vol. 7785, pp. 315–333. Springer, Heidelberg (2013). https://doi.org/10.1007/978-3-642-36594-2_18

18. Boneh, D., Boyen, X.: Efficient selective-ID secure identity-based encryption without random oracles. In: Cachin, C., Camenisch, J.L. (eds.) EUROCRYPT 2004. LNCS, vol. 3027, pp. 223–238. Springer, Heidelberg (2004). https://doi.org/10.1007/978-3-540-24676-3_14

19. Boneh, D., Bünz, B., Fisch, B.: A survey of two verifiable delay functions. Technical report, Cryptology ePrint Archive, Report 2018/712 (2018). https://eprint.iacr.org/2018/712

20. Boneh, D., Bünz, B., Fisch, B.: Batching techniques for accumulators with applications to IOPs and stateless blockchains. Cryptology ePrint Archive, Report 2018/1188 (2018). https://eprint.iacr.org/2018/1188

21. Bootle, J., Cerulli, A., Chaidos, P., Groth, J., Petit, C.: Efficient zero-knowledge arguments for arithmetic circuits in the discrete log setting. In: Fischlin, M., Coron, J.-S. (eds.) EUROCRYPT 2016, Part II. LNCS, vol. 9666, pp. 327–357. Springer, Heidelberg (2016). https://doi.org/10.1007/978-3-662-49896-5_12

22. Brassard, G., Chaum, D., Crépeau, C.: Minimum disclosure proofs of knowledge. J. Comput. Syst. Sci. 37(2), 156–189 (1988)

23. Buchmann, J., Hamdy, S.: A survey on IQ-cryptography. Technical report TI-4/01, Technische Universitäat Darmstadt, Fachbereich Informatik (2000)

24. Buchmann, J., Takagi, T., Vollmer, U.: Number field cryptography. In: High Primes and Misdemeanours: Lectures in Honour of the 60th Birthday of Hugh Cowie Williams, vol. 41, pp. 111–125 (2004)

25. Buchmann, J., Williams, H.C.: A key-exchange system based on imaginary quadratic fields. J. Cryptol. 1(2), 107–118 (1988)

26. Bünz, B., Bootle, J., Boneh, D., Poelstra, A., Wuille, P., Maxwell, G.: Bulletproofs: short proofs for confidential transactions and more. In: 2018 IEEE Symposium on Security and Privacy, pp. 315–334. IEEE Computer Society Press, May 2018

27. Catalano, D., Fiore, D.: Vector commitments and their applications. In: Kurosawa, K., Hanaoka, G. (eds.) PKC 2013. LNCS, vol. 7778, pp. 55–72. Springer, Heidelberg (2013). https://doi.org/10.1007/978-3-642-36362-7_5

28. Chiesa, A., Tromer, E., Virza, M.: Cluster computing in zero knowledge. In: Oswald, E., Fischlin, M. (eds.) EUROCRYPT 2015, Part II. LNCS, vol. 9057, pp. 371–403. Springer, Heidelberg (2015). https://doi.org/10.1007/978-3-662-46803-6_13

29. Costello, C.: Geppetto: versatile verifiable computation. In: 2015 IEEE Symposium on Security and Privacy, pp. 253–270. IEEE Computer Society Press, May 2015

30. Damgård, I., Fujisaki, E.: A statistically-hiding integer commitment scheme based on groups with hidden order. In: Zheng, Y. (ed.) ASIACRYPT 2002. LNCS, vol. 2501, pp. 125–142. Springer, Heidelberg (2002). https://doi.org/10.1007/3-540-36178-2_8

31. Damgård, I., Koprowski, M.: Generic lower bounds for root extraction and signature schemes in general groups. In: Knudsen, L.R. (ed.) EUROCRYPT 2002. LNCS, vol. 2332, pp. 256–271. Springer, Heidelberg (2002). https://doi.org/10.1007/3-540-46035-7_17

32. Danezis, G., Fournet, C., Groth, J., Kohlweiss, M.: Square span programs with applications to succinct NIZK arguments. In: Sarkar, P., Iwata, T. (eds.) ASIACRYPT 2014, Part I. LNCS, vol. 8873, pp. 532–550. Springer, Heidelberg (2014). https://doi.org/10.1007/978-3-662-45611-8_28

33. Danezis, G., Fournet, C., Groth, J., Kohlweiss, M.: Square span programs with applications to succinct NIZK arguments. In: Sarkar, P., Iwata, T. (eds.) ASIACRYPT 2014, Part I. LNCS, vol. 8873, pp. 532–550. Springer, Heidelberg (2014). https://doi.org/10.1007/978-3-662-45611-8_28

34. Di Crescenzo, G., Lipmaa, H.: Succinct NP proofs from an extractability assumption. In: Beckmann, A., Dimitracopoulos, C., Löwe, B. (eds.) CiE 2008. LNCS, vol. 5028, pp. 175–185. Springer, Heidelberg (2008). https://doi.org/10.1007/978-3-540-69407-6_21

35. Fiat, A., Shamir, A.: How to prove yourself: practical solutions to identification and signature problems. In: Odlyzko, A.M. (ed.) CRYPTO 1986. LNCS, vol. 263, pp. 186–194. Springer, Heidelberg (1987). https://doi.org/10.1007/3-540-47721-7_12

36. Fiat, A., Shamir, A.: How to prove yourself: practical solutions to identification and signature problems. In: Odlyzko, A.M. (ed.) CRYPTO 1986. LNCS, vol. 263, pp. 186–194. Springer, Heidelberg (1987). https://doi.org/10.1007/3-540-47721-7_12

37. Gennaro, R., Gentry, C., Parno, B., Raykova, M.: Quadratic span programs and succinct NIZKs without PCPs. In: Johansson, T., Nguyen, P.Q. (eds.) EUROCRYPT 2013. LNCS, vol. 7881, pp. 626–645. Springer, Heidelberg (2013). https://doi.org/10.1007/978-3-642-38348-9_37

38. Goldwasser, S., Micali, S., Rackoff, C.: The knowledge complexity of interactive proof systems. SIAM J. Comput. 18(1), 186–208 (1989)

39. Groth, J.: Short pairing-based non-interactive zero-knowledge arguments. In: Abe, M. (ed.) ASIACRYPT 2010. LNCS, vol. 6477, pp. 321–340. Springer, Heidelberg (2010). https://doi.org/10.1007/978-3-642-17373-8_19

40. Groth, J.: On the size of pairing-based non-interactive arguments. In: Fischlin, M., Coron, J.-S. (eds.) EUROCRYPT 2016, Part II. LNCS, vol. 9666, pp. 305–326. Springer, Heidelberg (2016). https://doi.org/10.1007/978-3-662-49896-5_11

41. Hamdy, S., Möller, B.: Security of cryptosystems based on class groups of imaginary quadratic orders. In: Okamoto, T. (ed.) ASIACRYPT 2000. LNCS, vol. 1976, pp. 234–247. Springer, Heidelberg (2000). https://doi.org/10.1007/3-540-44448-3_18

42. Ishai, Y., Kushilevitz, E., Ostrovsky, R.: Efficient arguments without short PCPs. In: Twenty-Second Annual IEEE Conference on 2007 Computational Complexity, CCC 2007, pp. 278–291. IEEE (2007)

43. Ishai, Y., Kushilevitz, E., Ostrovsky, R., Sahai, A.: Zero-knowledge from secure multiparty computation. In: Johnson, D.S., Feige, U. (eds.) 39th ACM STOC, pp. 21–30. ACM Press, June 2007

44. Kate, A., Zaverucha, G.M., Goldberg, I.: Constant-size commitments to polynomials and their applications. In: Abe, M. (ed.) ASIACRYPT 2010. LNCS, vol. 6477, pp. 177–194. Springer, Heidelberg (2010). https://doi.org/10.1007/978-3-642-17373-8_11

45. Kilian, J.: A note on efficient zero-knowledge proofs and arguments (extended abstract). In: 24th ACM STOC, pp. 723–732. ACM Press, May 1992

46. Kilian, J.: Improved efficient arguments (preliminary version). In: Coppersmith, D. (ed.) CRYPTO 1995. LNCS, vol. 963, pp. 311–324. Springer, Heidelberg (1995). https://doi.org/10.1007/3-540-44750-4_25

47. Lai, R.W.F., Malavolta, G.: Subvector commitments with applications to succinct arguments. Cryptology ePrint Archive, Report 2018/705 (2018). https://eprint.iacr.org/2018/705

48. Libert, B., Ramanna, S., Yung, M.: Functional commitment schemes: from polynomial commitments to pairing-based accumulators from simple assumptions. In: Chatzigiannakis, I., Mitzenmacher, M., Rabani, Y., Sangiorgi, D. (eds.) ICALP 2016, LIPIcs, vol. 55, pp. 30:1–30:14. Schloss Dagstuhl, July 2016

49. Lin, H., Pass, R., Seth, K., Telang, S.: Output-compressing randomized encodings and applications. In: Kushilevitz, E., Malkin, T. (eds.) TCC 2016, Part I. LNCS, vol. 9562, pp. 96–124. Springer, Heidelberg (2016). https://doi.org/10.1007/978-3-662-49096-9_5

50. Lipmaa, H.: Progression-free sets and sublinear pairing-based non-interactive zero-knowledge arguments. In: Cramer, R. (ed.) TCC 2012. LNCS, vol. 7194, pp. 169–189. Springer, Heidelberg (2012). https://doi.org/10.1007/978-3-642-28914-9_10

51. Lipmaa, H.: Secure accumulators from Euclidean rings without trusted setup. In: Bao, F., Samarati, P., Zhou, J. (eds.) ACNS 2012. LNCS, vol. 7341, pp. 224–240. Springer, Heidelberg (2012). https://doi.org/10.1007/978-3-642-31284-7_14

52. Merkle, R.C.: A digital signature based on a conventional encryption function. In: Pomerance, C. (ed.) CRYPTO 1987. LNCS, vol. 293, pp. 369–378. Springer, Heidelberg (1988). https://doi.org/10.1007/3-540-48184-2_32

53. Micali, S.: CS proofs (extended abstracts). In: 35th FOCS, pp. 436–453. IEEE Computer Society Press, November 1994

54. Micali, S., Rabin, M., Kilian, J.: Zero-knowledge sets. In: 44th FOCS, pp. 80–91. IEEE Computer Society Press, October 2003

55. Mie, T.: Polylogarithmic two-round argument systems. J. Math. Cryptol. **2**(4), 343–363 (2008)

56. Pedersen, T.P.: Non-interactive and information-theoretic secure verifiable secret sharing. In: Feigenbaum, J. (ed.) CRYPTO 1991. LNCS, vol. 576, pp. 129–140. Springer, Heidelberg (1992). https://doi.org/10.1007/3-540-46766-1_9

57. Reingold, O., Rothblum, G.N., Rothblum, R.D. Constant-round interactive proofs for delegating computation. In: Wichs, D., Mansour, Y. (eds.) 48th ACM STOC, pp. 49–62. ACM Press, June 2016

58. Sander, T.: Efficient accumulators without trapdoor extended abstract. In: Varadharajan, V., Mu, Y. (eds.) ICICS 1999. LNCS, vol. 1726, pp. 252–262. Springer, Heidelberg (1999). https://doi.org/10.1007/978-3-540-47942-0_21

59. Shoup, V.: Lower bounds for discrete logarithms and related problems. In: Fumy, W. (ed.) EUROCRYPT 1997. LNCS, vol. 1233, pp. 256–266. Springer, Heidelberg (1997). https://doi.org/10.1007/3-540-69053-0_18

60. Shoup, V.: OAEP reconsidered. In: Kilian, J. (ed.) CRYPTO 2001. LNCS, vol. 2139, pp. 239–259. Springer, Heidelberg (2001). https://doi.org/10.1007/3-540-44647-8_15

61. Valiant, P.: Incrementally verifiable computation or proofs of knowledge imply time/space efficiency. In: Canetti, R. (ed.) TCC 2008. LNCS, vol. 4948, pp. 1–18. Springer, Heidelberg (2008). https://doi.org/10.1007/978-3-540-78524-8_1

62. Wahby, R.S., Tzialla, I., Shelat, A., Thaler, J., Walfish, M.: Doubly-efficient zkSNARKs without trusted setup (2018)

63. Wesolowski, B.: Efficient verifiable delay functions. IACR Cryptology ePrint Archive 2018/623 (2018)

64. Zhang, Y., Genkin, D., Katz, J., Papadopoulos, D., Papamanthou, C.: vSQL: verifying arbitrary SQL queries over dynamic outsourced databases. In: 2017 IEEE Symposium on Security and Privacy, pp. 863–880. IEEE Computer Society Press, May 2017

Batching Techniques for Accumulators with Applications to IOPs and Stateless Blockchains

Dan Boneh, Benedikt Bünz$^{(\boxtimes)}$, and Ben Fisch$^{(\boxtimes)}$

Stanford University, Stanford, USA
benedikt@cs.stanford.edu, benafisch@gmail.com

Abstract. We present batching techniques for cryptographic accumulators and vector commitments in groups of unknown order. Our techniques are tailored for distributed settings where no trusted accumulator manager exists and updates to the accumulator are processed in batches. We develop techniques for non-interactively aggregating membership proofs that can be verified with a constant number of group operations. We also provide a constant sized batch non-membership proof for a large number of elements. These proofs can be used to build the first positional vector commitment (VC) with constant sized openings and constant sized public parameters. As a core building block for our batching techniques we develop several succinct proof systems in groups of unknown order. These extend a recent construction of a succinct proof of correct exponentiation, and include a succinct proof of knowledge of an integer discrete logarithm between two group elements. We circumvent an impossibility result for Sigma-protocols in these groups by using a short trapdoor-free CRS. We use these new accumulator and vector commitment constructions to design a stateless blockchain, where nodes only need a constant amount of storage in order to participate in consensus. Further, we show how to use these techniques to reduce the size of IOP instantiations, such as STARKs. The full version of the paper is available online [BBF18b].

1 Introduction

A cryptographic accumulator [Bd94] is a primitive that produces a short binding commitment to a set of elements together with short membership and/or non-membership proofs for any element in the set. These proofs can be publicly verified against the commitment. The simplest accumulator is the Merkle tree [Mer88], but several other accumulators are known, as discussed below. An accumulator is said to be *dynamic* if the commitment and membership proofs can be updated efficiently as elements are added or removed from the set, at unit cost independent of the number of accumulated elements. Otherwise we say that the accumulator is *static*. A *universal* accumulator is dynamic and supports both membership and non-membership proofs.

© International Association for Cryptologic Research 2019
A. Boldyreva and D. Micciancio (Eds.): CRYPTO 2019, LNCS 11692, pp. 561–586, 2019.
https://doi.org/10.1007/978-3-030-26948-7_20

A *vector commitment* (VC) is a closely related primitive [CF13]. It provides the same functionality as an accumulator, but for an ordered list of elements. A VC is a *position binding* commitment and can be opened at any position to a unique value with a short proof (sublinear in the length of the vector). The Merkle tree is a VC with logarithmic size openings. Subvector commitments [LM18] are VCs where a subset of the vector positions can be opened in a single short proof (sublinear in the size of the subset).

The typical way in which an accumulator or VC is used is as a communication-efficient authenticated data structure (ADS) for a remotely stored database where users can retrieve individual items along with their membership proofs in the data structure. Accumulators have been used for many applications within this realm, including accountable certificate management [BLL00, NN98], timestamping [Bd94], group signatures and anonymous credentials [CL02], computations on authenticated data [ABC+12], anonymous e-cash [STS99b, MGGR13], privacy-preserving data outsourcing [Sla12], updatable signatures [PS14, CJ10], and decentralized bulletin boards [FVY14, GGM14].

Our present work is motivated by two particular applications of accumulators and vector commitments: stateless transaction validation in blockchains, or "stateless blockchains" and short interactive oracle proofs (IOPs) [BCS16].

"Stateless" blockchains. A *blockchain* has become the popular term for a ledger-based payment system, in which peer-to-peer payment transactions are asynchronously broadcasted and recorded in an ordered ledger that is replicated across nodes in the network. Bitcoin and Ethereum are two famous examples. Verifying the validity of a transaction requires querying the ledger *state*. The state can be computed uniquely from the ordered log of transactions, but provides a more compact index to the information required for transaction validation.

For example, in Ethereum the state is a key/value store of account balances where account keys are the public key addresses of users. In Bitcoin, the state is the set of *unspent transaction outputs* (UTXOs). In Bitcoin, every transaction completely transfers all the funds associated with a set of source addresses to a set of target addresses. It is only valid if every source address is the output of a previous transaction that has not yet been consumed (i.e. "spent"). It is important that all nodes agree on the ledger state.

Currently, in Bitcoin, every node in the system stores the entire UTXO set in order to verify incoming transactions. This has become cumbersome as the size of UTXO set has grown to gigabytes. An accumulator commitment to the UTXO set would alleviate this need. Transactions would include membership proofs for all its inputs. A node would only need to store the current state of the accumulator and verify transactions by checking membership proofs against the UTXO accumulator state. In fact, with dynamic accumulators, no single node in the network would be required to maintain the entire UTXO set. Only the individual nodes who are interested in a set of UTXOs (e.g. the users who can spend these outputs) would need to store them along with their membership proofs.

Every node can efficiently update the UTXO set commitment and membership proofs for individual UTXOs with every new batch of transactions. The same idea can be applied to the Ethereum key-value store using a VC instead of an accumulator.

This design concept is referred to as a "stateless blockchain" [Tod16] because nodes may participate in transaction validation without storing the entire state of the ledger, but rather only a short commitment to the state. The idea of committing to a ledgers state was introduced long before Bitcoin by Sanders and Ta-Shma for E-Cash [STS99a]. While the stateless blockchain design reduces the storage burden of node performing transaction validation, it increases the network communication due to the addition of membership proofs to each transaction payload. A design goal is to minimize the communication impact. Therefore, stateless blockchains would benefit from an accumulator with smaller membership proofs, or the ability to aggregate many membership proofs for a batch of transactions into a single constant-size proof.

Interactive oracle proofs (IOPs). Micali [Mic94] showed how *probabilistically checkable proofs* (PCPs) can be used to construct succinct non-interactive arguments. In this construction the prover commits to a long PCP using a Merkle tree and then uses a random oracle to generate a few random query positions. The prover then verifiably opens the proof at the queried positions by providing Merkle inclusion paths.

This technique has been generalized to the broader class of *interactive oracle proofs* (IOPs) [BCS16]. In an IOP the prover sends multiple proof oracles to a verifier. The verifier uses these oracles to query a small subsets of the proof, and afterwards accepts or rejects the proof. If the proof oracle is instantiated with a Merkle tree commitment and the verifier is public coin, then an IOP can be compiled into a non-interactive proof secure in the random oracle model [BCS16]. In particular, this compiler is used to build short non-interactive (zero-knowledge) proof of knowledge with a quasilinear prover and polylogarithmic verifier. Recent practical instantiations of proof systems from IOPs include Ligero [AHIV17], STARKs [BBHR18], and Aurora [BSCR+18].

IOPs use Merkle trees as a vector commitment. Merkle trees have two significant drawbacks for this application: first, position openings are not constant size, and second, the openings of several positions cannot be compressed into a single constant size proof (i.e. it is not a subvector commitment). A vector commitment with these properties would have dramatic benefits for reducing the communication of an IOP (or size of the non-interactive proof compiled from an IOP).

1.1   Summary of Contributions

Our technical contributions consist of a set of batching and aggregation techniques for accumulators. The results of these techniques have a wide range of implications, from concrete practical improvements in the proof-size of IOP-based succinct arguments (e.g. STARKS) and minimizing the network communication blowup of stateless blockchains to theoretical achievements in VCs and IOPs.

To summarize the theoretical achievements first, we show that it is possible to construct a VC with constant size subvector openings and constant size public parameters. Previously, it was only known how to construct a VC with constant size subvector openings and public parameters *linear* in the length of the vector. This has immediate implications for IOP compilers. The Merkle-tree IOP compiler outputs a non-interactive proof that is $O(\lambda q \log n)$ larger (additive blowup) than the original IOP communication, where q is the number of oracle queries, n is the maximum length[1] of the IOP proof oracles, and λ is the Merkle tree security parameter. When replacing the Merkle-tree in the IOP compiler with our new VC, we achieve only $O(r\lambda)$ blowup in proof size, independent of q and n, but dependent on the number of IOP rounds r. In the special case of a PCP there is a single round (i.e. $r = 1$). A similar result was recently demonstrated [LM18] using the vector commitments of Catalano and Fiore (CF) [CF13], but the construction requires the verifier to access public parameters linear in n. It was not previously known how to achieve this with constant size public parameters.

Lai and Malavolta apply the CF vector commitments to "CS-proofs", a special case of a compiled IOP where the IOP is a single round PCP. Instantiated with theoretical PCPs [Kil92, Mic94], this results in the shortest known setup-free non-interactive arguments (for NP) with random oracles consisting of just 2 elements in a hidden order group and 240 additional bits of the PCP proof for 80-bit statistical security. Instantiating the group with class groups and targeting 100-bit security yields a proof of ≈540 bytes. However, the verifier must either use linear storage or perform linear work for each proof verification to generate the public proof parameters. In similar vein, we can use our new VCs to build the same non-interactive argument system, but with sublinear size parameters (in fact constant size). Under the same parameters our proofs are slightly larger, consisting of 5 group elements, a 128-bit integer, and the 240 bits of the PCP proof (≈1.3 KB).

Our VCs also make concrete improvements to practical IOPs. Targeting 100-bit security with class groups, replacing Merkle trees with our VCs would incur only 1 KB per round of the IOP. In Aurora [BSCR+18], it was reported that Merkle proofs take up 154 KB of the 222 KB proof for a circuit of size 2^{20}. Our VCs would reduce the size of the proof to less than 100 KB, a 54% reduction. For STARKs, a recent benchmark indicates that the Merkle paths make up over 400 KB of the 600 KB proof for a circuit of 2^{52} gates [BBHR18]. With our VCs, under the same parameters the membership proofs would take up roughly 22 KB, reducing the overall proof size to approximately 222 KB, nearly a 63% reduction.

Furthermore, replacing Merkle trees with our new VCs maintains good performance for proof verification. Roughly, each Merkle path verification of a k-bit block is substituted with k modular multiplications of λ-bit integers. The performance comparison is thus $\log n$ hashes vs k multiplications, which is even an improvement for $k < \log n$. In the benchmarked STARK example, Merkle path verification comprises roughly 80% of the verification time.

---

[1] In each round of an IOP, the prover prepares a message and sends the verifier a "proof oracle", which gives the verifier random read access to the prover's message. The "length" of the proof oracle is the length of this message.

1.2 Overview of Techniques

Batching and aggregation. We use the term *batching* to describe a single action applied to n items instead of one action per item. For example a verifier can batch verify n proofs faster than n times verifying a single membership proof. *Aggregation* is a batching technique that is used when non-interactively combining n items to a single item. For example, a prover can aggregate n membership proofs to a single constant size proof.

Succinct proofs for hidden order groups. Wesolowski [Wes18] recently introduced a constant sized and efficient to verify proof that a triple (u, w, t) satisfies $w = u^{2^t}$, where u and w are elements in a group $\mathbb{G}$ of unknown order. The proof extends to exponents that are not a power of two and still provides significant efficiency gains over direct verification by computation.

We expand on this technique to provide a new proof of knowledge of an exponent, which we call a *PoKE* proof. It is a proof that a computationally bounded prover knows the discrete logarithm between two elements in a group of unknown order. The proof is succinct in that the proof size and verification time is independent of the size of the discrete-log and has good soundness. We also generalize the technique to pre-images of homomorphisms from $\mathbb{Z}^q$ to $\mathbb{G}$ of unknown order. We prove security in the generic group model, where an adversarial prover operates over a generic group. Nevertheless, our extractor is classical and does not get to see the adversary's queries to the generic group oracles. We also rely on a short unstructured common reference string (CRS). Using the generic group model for extraction and relying on a CRS is necessary to bypass certain impossibility results for proofs of knowledge in groups of unknown order [BCK10, TW12].

We also extend the protocol to obtain a (honest verifier zero-knowledge) Σ-Protocol of DLOG in $\mathbb{G}$. This protocol is the first succinct Σ-protocol of this kind.

Distributed accumulator with batching. Next, we extend current RSA-based accumulators [CL02, LLX07] to create a universal accumulator for a distributed/decentralized setting where no single trusted accumulator manager exists and where updates are processed in batches. Despite this we show how membership and non-membership proofs can be efficiently aggregated. Moreover, items can efficiently be removed from the accumulator without a trapdoor or even knowledge of the accumulated set. Since the trapdoor is not required for our construction we can extend Lipmaa's [Lip12] work on accumulators in groups of unknown order without a trusted setup by adding dynamic additions and deletions to the accumulator's functionality. Class groups of imaginary quadratic order are a candidate group of unknown order without a trusted setup [BH01].

Batching non-membership proofs. We next show how our techniques can be amplified to create a succinct and efficiently verifiable batch membership and batch non-membership proofs. We then use these batch proofs to create the first vector commitment construction with constant sized batch openings (recently called subvector commitments [LM18]) and $O(1)$ setup. This improves on previous work [CF13,LRY16] which required superlinear setup time and linear public parameter size. It also improves on Merkle tree constructions which have logarithmic sized non-batchable openings. The efficient setup also allows us to create sparse vector commitments which can be used as a key-value map commitment.

Soundness lower bounds in hidden order groups. Certain families of sigma protocols for a relation in a generic group of unknown order can achieve at most soundness $1/2$ per challenge [BCK10,TW12]. Yet, our work gives sigma protocols in a generic group of unknown order that have negligible soundness error. This does not contradict the known impossibility result because our protocols involve a CRS, whereas the family of sigma protocols to which the $1/2$ soundness lower bound applies do not have a CRS. Our results are significant as we show that it suffices to have a CRS containing two fresh random generic group generators to circumvent the soundness lower bound.

Note that we only prove how to extract a witness from a successful prover that is restricted to the generic group model. Proving extraction from an arbitrary prover under a falsifiable assumption is preferable and remains an open problem.

2 Preliminaries

Notation

- $a \parallel b$ is the concatenation of two lists a, b
- $\boldsymbol{a}$ is a vector of elements and a_i is the ith component
- $[\ell]$ denotes the set of integers $\{0, 1, \ldots, \ell - 1\}$.
- $\mathsf{negl}(\lambda)$ is a negligible function of the security parameter λ
- $\mathsf{Primes}(\lambda)$ is the set of integer primes less than 2^λ
- $x \xleftarrow{\$} S$ denotes sampling a uniformly random element $x \in S$.
  $x \xleftarrow{\$} \mathcal{A}(\cdot)$ denotes the random variable that is the output of a randomized algorithm $\mathcal{A}$.
- $GGen(\lambda)$ is a randomized algorithm that generates a group of unknown order in a range $[a, b]$ such that a, b, and $a - b$ are all integers exponential in λ.

2.1 Assumptions

The adaptive root assumption, introduced in [Wes18], is as follows.

Definition 1. *We say that the **adaptive root assumption** holds for GGen if there is no efficient adversary $(\mathcal{A}_0, \mathcal{A}_1)$ that succeeds in the following task. First, $\mathcal{A}_0$ outputs an element $w \in \mathbb{G}$ and some state. Then, a random prime ℓ in $\mathsf{Primes}(\lambda)$ is chosen and $\mathcal{A}_1(\ell, \mathsf{state})$ outputs $w^{1/\ell} \in \mathbb{G}$. More precisely, for all efficient $(\mathcal{A}_0, \mathcal{A}_1)$:*

$$\mathsf{Adv}^{\mathrm{AR}}_{(\mathcal{A}_0, \mathcal{A}_1)}(\lambda) := \Pr \left[u^\ell = w \neq 1 \; : \; \begin{array}{c} \mathbb{G} \xleftarrow{\$} GGen(\lambda) \\ (w, \mathsf{state}) \xleftarrow{\$} \mathcal{A}_0(\mathbb{G}) \\ \ell \xleftarrow{\$} \mathsf{Primes}(\lambda) \\ u \xleftarrow{\$} \mathcal{A}_1(\ell, \mathsf{state}) \end{array} \right] \leq \mathsf{negl}(\lambda).$$

The adaptive root assumption implies that the adversary can't compute the order of any non trivial element. For any element with known order the adversary can compute arbitrary roots that are co-prime to the order. This immediately allows the adversary to win the adaptive root game. For the group Z_N this means that we need to exclude $\{-1, 1\}$.

We will also need the strong RSA assumption for general groups of unknown order. The adaptive root and strong RSA assumptions are incomparable. The former states that it is hard to take a random root of a chosen group element, while the latter says that it is hard to take a chosen root of a random group element. In groups of unknown order that do not require a trusted setup the adversary A additionally gets access to $GGen$'s random coins.

Definition 2 (Strong RSA assumption). *GGen satisfies the strong RSA assumption if for all efficient $\mathcal{A}$:*

$$\Pr\left[u^\ell = g \text{ and } \ell \text{ is an odd prime} : \begin{array}{c} \mathbb{G} \xleftarrow{\$} GGen(\lambda), \ g \xleftarrow{\$} \mathbb{G}, \\ (u, \ell) \in \mathbb{G} \times \mathbb{Z} \xleftarrow{\$} \mathcal{A}(\mathbb{G}, g) \end{array}\right] \leq \mathsf{negl}(\lambda).$$

2.2 Generic Group Model for Groups of Unknown Order

We will use the generic group model for groups of unknown order as defined by Damgard and Koprowski [DK02]. The group is parameterized by two integer public parameters A, B. The order of the group is sampled uniformly from $[A, B]$. The group $\mathbb{G}$ is defined by a random injective function $\sigma : \mathbb{Z}_{|\mathbb{G}|} \to \{0, 1\}^\ell$, for some ℓ where $2^\ell \gg |\mathbb{G}|$. The group elements are $\sigma(0), \sigma(1), \ldots, \sigma(|\mathbb{G}| - 1)$. A *generic group algorithm $\mathcal{A}$* is a probabilistic algorithm. Let $\mathcal{L}$ be a list that is initialized with the encodings given to $\mathcal{A}$ as input. The algorithm can query two generic group oracles:

- $\mathcal{O}_1$ samples a random $r \in \mathbb{Z}_{|\mathbb{G}|}$ and returns $\sigma(r)$, which is appended to the list of encodings $\mathcal{L}$.
- When $\mathcal{L}$ has size q, the second oracle $\mathcal{O}_2(i, j, \pm)$ takes two indices $i, j \in \{1, \ldots, q\}$ and a sign bit, and returns $\sigma(x_i \pm x_j)$, which is appended to $\mathcal{L}$.

Note that unlike Shoup's generic group model [Sho97], the algorithm is not given $|\mathbb{G}|$, the order of the group $\mathbb{G}$.

2.3 Argument Systems

An argument system for a relation $\mathcal{R} \subset \mathcal{X} \times \mathcal{W}$ is a triple of randomized polynomial time algorithms $(\mathsf{Pgen}, \mathsf{P}, \mathsf{V})$, where Pgen takes an (implicit) security parameter λ and outputs a common reference string (crs) pp. If the setup algorithm uses only public randomness we say that the setup is transparent and that the crs is unstructured. The prover P takes as input a statement $x \in \mathcal{X}$, a witness $w \in \mathcal{W}$, and the crs pp. The verifier V takes as input pp and x and after interaction with P outputs 0 or 1. We denote the transcript between the prover and verifier by $\langle V(pp, x), P(pp, x, w) \rangle$ and write $\langle V(pp, x), P(pp, x, w) \rangle = 1$ to indicate that the verifier accepted the transcript. If V uses only public randomness we say that the protocol is *public coin*.

Definition 3 (Completeness). *We say that an argument system* (Pgen, P, V) *for a relation $\mathcal{R}$ is **complete** if for all $(x, w) \in \mathcal{R}$:*

$$\Pr\left[\langle V(pp, x), P(pp, x, w) \rangle = 1 : pp \overset{\$}{\leftarrow} \text{Pgen}(\lambda) \right] = 1.$$

We now define soundness and knowledge extraction for our protocols. The adversary is modeled as two algorithms $\mathcal{A}_0$ and $\mathcal{A}_1$, where $\mathcal{A}_0$ outputs the instance $x \in \mathcal{X}$ *after* Pgen is run, and $\mathcal{A}_1$ runs the interactive protocol with the verifier using a state output by $\mathcal{A}_0$. In our soundness definition the adversary $\mathcal{A}_1$ succeeds if he can make the verifier accept when no witness for x exists. For the stronger *argument of knowledge* definition we require that an extractor with access to $\mathcal{A}_1$'s internal state can extract a valid witness whenever $\mathcal{A}_1$ is convincing. We model this by enabling the extractor to rewind $\mathcal{A}_1$ and reinitialize the verifier's randomness.

Definition 4 (Arguments (of Knowledge)). *We say that an argument system* (Pgen, P, V) *is sound if for all poly-time adversaries $\mathcal{A} = (\mathcal{A}_0, \mathcal{A}_1)$:*

$$\Pr\left[\begin{array}{l} \langle V(pp, x), \mathcal{A}_1(pp, x, state) \rangle = 1 \\ \text{and } \not\exists w \ (x, w) \in \mathcal{R} : \end{array} \quad \begin{array}{l} pp \overset{\$}{\leftarrow} \text{Pgen}(1^\lambda) \\ (x, state) \leftarrow \mathcal{A}_0(pp) \end{array} \right] = \text{negl}(\lambda).$$

Additionally, the argument system is an argument of knowledge if for all poly-time adversaries $\mathcal{A}_1$ there exists a poly-time extractor Ext *such that for all poly-time adversaries $\mathcal{A}_0$:*

$$\Pr\left[\begin{array}{l} \langle V(pp, x), \mathcal{A}_1(pp, x, state) \rangle = 1 \\ \text{and } (x, w') \notin \mathcal{R} : \end{array} \quad \begin{array}{l} pp \overset{\$}{\leftarrow} \text{Pgen}(1^\lambda) \\ (x, state) \leftarrow \mathcal{A}_0(pp) \\ w' \overset{\$}{\leftarrow} \text{Ext}(pp, x, state) \end{array} \right] = \text{negl}(\lambda).$$

Any argument of knowledge is also sound. In some cases we may further restrict $\mathcal{A}$ in the security analysis, in which case we would say the system is an argument of knowledge for a restricted class of adversaries. For example, in this work we construct argument systems for relations that depend on a group $\mathbb{G}$ of unknown order. In the analysis we replace $\mathbb{G}$ with a generic group and restrict $\mathcal{A}$ to a generic group algorithm that interacts with the oracles for this group. For simplicity, although slightly imprecise, we say the protocol is an *argument of knowledge in the generic group model*.

Definition 5 (Non interactive arguments). *A **non-interactive argument system** is an argument system where the interaction between P and V consists of only a single round. We then write the prover P as $\pi \overset{\$}{\leftarrow} \text{Prove}(pp, x, w)$ and the verifier as $\{0, 1\} \leftarrow \text{Vf}(pp, x, \pi)$.*

The Fiat-Shamir heuristic [FS87] and its generalization to multi-round protocols [BCS16] can be used to transform public coin argument systems to noninteractive systems.

3 Succinct Proofs for Hidden Order Groups

In this section we present several new succinct proofs in groups of unknown order. The proofs build on a proof of exponentiation recently proposed by Wesolowski [Wes18] in the context of verifiable delay functions [BBBF18]. We show that the Wesolowski proof is a *succinct* proof of knowledge of a discrete-log in a group of unknown order. We then derive a *succinct* zero-knowledge argument of knowledge for a discrete-log relation, and more generally for knowledge of the inverse of a homomorphism $h : \mathbb{Z}^n \to \mathbb{G}$, where $\mathbb{G}$ is a group of unknown order. Using the Fiat-Shamir heuristic, the non-interactive version of this protocol is a special purpose SNARK for the pre-image of a homomorphism.

3.1 A Succinct Proof of Exponentiation

Let $\mathbb{G}$ be a group of unknown order. Let $[\ell] := \{0, 1, \ldots, \ell - 1\}$ and let $\mathsf{Primes}(\lambda)$ denote the set of odd prime numbers in $[0, 2^\lambda]$. We begin by reviewing Wesolowski's (non-ZK) proof of exponentiation [Wes18] in the group $\mathbb{G}$. Here both the prover and verifier are given (u, w, x) and the prover wants to convince the verifier that $w = u^x$ holds in $\mathbb{G}$. That is, the protocol is an argument system for the relation

$$\mathcal{R}_{\mathsf{PoE}} = \left\{ \left((u, w \in \mathbb{G}, x \in \mathbb{Z}); \perp \right) \; : \; w = u^x \in \mathbb{G} \right\}.$$

The verifier's work should be much less than computing u^x by itself. Note that $x \in \mathbb{Z}$ can be much larger than $|\mathbb{G}|$, which is where the protocol is most useful. The protocol works as follows:

Protocol PoE (Proof of exponentiation) for $\mathcal{R}_{\mathsf{PoE}}$ [Wes18]

Params: $\mathbb{G} \xleftarrow{\$} GGen(\lambda)$; Inputs: $u, w \in \mathbb{G}$, $x \in \mathbb{Z}$; Claim: $u^x = w$

1. Verifier sends $\ell \xleftarrow{\$} \mathsf{Primes}(\lambda)$ to prover.
2. Prover computes the quotient $q = \lfloor x/\ell \rfloor \in \mathbb{Z}$ and residue $r \in [\ell]$ such that $x = q\ell + r$.
   Prover sends $Q \leftarrow u^q \in \mathbb{G}$ to the Verifier.
3. Verifier computes $r \leftarrow (x \bmod \ell) \in [\ell]$ and accepts if $Q^\ell u^r = w$ holds in $\mathbb{G}$.

The protocol above is a minor generalization of the protocol from [Wes18] in that we allow an arbitrary exponent $x \in \mathbb{Z}$, where as in [Wes18] the exponent was restricted to be a power of two. This does not change the soundness property captured in the following theorem, whose proof is given in [Wes18, Prop. 2] (see also [BBF18a, Thm. 2]) and relies on the adaptive root assumption for $GGen$.

Theorem 1 (Soundness PoE [Wes18]). *Protocol PoE is an argument system for Relation $\mathcal{R}_{PoE}$ with negligible soundness error, assuming the adaptive root assumption holds for GGen.*

For the protocol to be useful the verifier must be able to compute $r = x \bmod \ell$ faster than computing $u^x \in \mathbb{G}$. The original protocol presented by Wesolowski assumed that $x = 2^T$ is a power of two, so that computing $x \bmod \ell$ requires only $\log(T)$ multiplications in $\mathbb{Z}_\ell$ whereas computing u^x requires T group operations.

For a general exponent $x \in \mathbb{Z}$, computing $x \bmod \ell$ takes $O((\log x)/\lambda)$ multiplications in $\mathbb{Z}_\ell$. In contrast, computing $u^x \in \mathbb{G}$ takes $O(\log x)$ group operations in $\mathbb{G}$. Hence, for the current groups of unknown order, computing u^x takes λ^3 times as long as computing $x \bmod \ell$. Concretely, when ℓ is a 128 bit integer, a multiplication in $\mathbb{Z}_\ell$ is approximately 5000 time faster than a group operation in a 2048-bit RSA group. Hence, the verifier's work is much less than computing $w = u^x$ in $\mathbb{G}$ on its own.

The PoE protocol can be generalized to a relation involving any homomorphism $\phi : \mathbb{Z}^n \to \mathbb{G}$ for which the adaptive root assumption holds in $\mathbb{G}$. The details of this generalization are discussed in the full version.

3.2   A Succinct Proof of Knowledge of a Discrete-Log

We next show how the protocol PoE can be adapted to provide an argument of knowledge of discrete-log, namely an argument of knowledge for the relation:

$$\mathcal{R}_{PoKE} = \big\{ \big((u, w \in \mathbb{G}); \ x \in \mathbb{Z}\big) \ : \ w = u^x \in \mathbb{G}\big\}.$$

The goal is to construct a protocol that has communication complexity that is much lower than simply sending x to the verifier. As a stepping stone we first provide an argument of knowledge for a modified PoKE relation, where the base $u \in \mathbb{G}$ is fixed and encoded in a CRS. Concretely let CRS consist of the unknown-order group $\mathbb{G}$ and the generator g. We construct an argument of knowledge for the following relation:

$$\mathcal{R}_{PoKE^*} = \big\{\big(w \in \mathbb{G}; \ x \in \mathbb{Z}\big) \ : \ w = g^x \in \mathbb{G}\big\}.$$

The argument modifies the PoE Protocol in that x is not given to the verifier, and the remainder $r \in [\ell]$ is sent from the prover to the verifier:

Protocol PoKE* (Proof of knowledge of exponent) for Relation $\mathcal{R}_{PoKE^*}$

Params: $\mathbb{G} \xleftarrow{\$} GGen(\lambda)$, $g \in \mathbb{G}$; Inputs: $w \in \mathbb{G}$; Witness: $x \in \mathbb{Z}$;
Claim: $g^x = w$

1. Verifier sends $\ell \xleftarrow{\$} \text{Primes}(\lambda)$.
2. Prover computes the quotient $q \in \mathbb{Z}$ and residue $r \in [\ell]$ such that $x = q\ell + r$. Prover sends the pair $(Q \leftarrow g^q, \ r)$ to the Verifier.
3. Verifier accepts if $r \in [\ell]$ and $Q^\ell g^r = w$ holds in $\mathbb{G}$.

Here the verifier does not have the witness x, but the prover additionally sends $r := (x \bmod \ell)$ along with Q in its response to the verifier's challenge. Note that the verifier no longer computes r on its own, but instead relies on the value from the prover. We will demonstrate an extractor that extracts the witness $x \in \mathbb{Z}$ from a successful prover, and prove that this extractor succeeds with overwhelming probability against a generic group prover. In fact, in the full version of the paper [BBF18b] we present a generalization of Protocol PoKE* to group representations in terms of bases $\{g_i\}_{i=1}^n$ included in the CRS, i.e. a proof of knowledge of an integer vector $\mathbf{x} \in \mathbb{Z}^n$ such that $\prod_i g_i^{x_i} = w$. We will prove that this protocol is an argument of knowledge against a generic group adversary. The security of Protocol PoKE* above follows as a special case. Hence, the following theorem is a special case of Theorem 7 in the full version.

Theorem 2. Protocol PoKE* *is an argument of knowledge for relation* $\mathcal{R}_{\mathsf{PoKE}^*}$ *in the generic group model.*

An attack. Protocol PoKE* requires the discrete logarithm base g to be encoded in the CRS. When this protocol is applied to a base freely chosen by the adversary it becomes insecure. In other words, Protocol PoKE* is not a secure protocol for the relation $\mathcal{R}_{\mathsf{PoKE}}$.

To describe the attack, let g be a generator of $\mathbb{G}$ and let $u = g^x$ and $w = g^y$ where $y \neq 1$ and x does not divide y. Suppose that the adversary knows both x and y but not the discrete log of w base u. Computing an integer discrete logarithm of w base u is still difficult in a generic group, however an efficient adversary can nonetheless succeed in fooling the verifier as follows. Since the challenge ℓ is co-prime with x with overwhelming probability, the adversary can compute $q, r \in \mathbb{Z}$ such that $q\ell + rx = y$. The adversary sends $(Q = g^q, r)$ to the verifier, and the verifier checks that indeed $Q^\ell u^r = w$. Hence, the verifier accepts despite the adversary not knowing the discrete log of w base u.

This does not qualify as an "attack" when $x = 1$, or more generally when x divides y, since then the adversary does know the discrete logarithm y/x such that $u^{y/x} = w$.

Extending PoKE for general bases. To obtain a protocol for the relation $\mathcal{R}_{\mathsf{PoKE}}$ we start by modifying protocol PoKE* so that the prover first sends $z = g^x$, for a fixed base g, and then executes two PoKE* style protocols, one base g and one base u, in parallel, showing that the discrete logarithm of w base u equals the one of z base g. We show that the resulting protocol is a secure argument of knowledge (in the generic group model) for the relation $\mathcal{R}_{\mathsf{PoKE}}$. The transcript of this modified protocol now consists of two group elements instead of one.

Protocol PoKE (Proof of knowledge of exponent)

Params: $\mathbb{G} \xleftarrow{\$} GGen(\lambda)$, $g \in \mathbb{G}$; Inputs: $u, w \in \mathbb{G}$; Witness: $x \in \mathbb{Z}$;
Claim: $u^x = w$

1. Prover sends $z = g^x \in \mathbb{G}$ to the verifier.
2. Verifier sends $\ell \xleftarrow{\$} \mathsf{Primes}(\lambda)$.
3. Prover finds the quotient $q \in \mathbb{Z}$ and residue $r \in [\ell]$ such that $x = q\ell + r$.
   Prover sends $Q = u^q$ and $Q' = g^q$ and r to the Verifier.
4. Verifier accepts if $r \in [\ell]$, $Q^\ell u^r = w$, and $Q'^\ell g^r = z$.

The intuition for the security proof is as follows. The extractor first uses the same extractor for Protocol PoKE* to extract the discrete logarithm x of z base g. It then suffices to argue that this extracted discrete logarithm x is a *correct* discrete logarithm of w base u. We use the adaptive root assumption to argue that the extracted x is a correct discrete logarithm of w base u.

We can optimize the protocol to bring down the proof size back to a single group element. We do so in the protocol PoKE2 below by adding one round of interaction. The additional round has no effect on proof size after making the protocol non-interactive using Fiat-Shamir. The protocol is presented in the full version [BBF18b].

Theorem 3 (PoKE Argument of Knowledge). *Protocol PoKE and Protocol PoKE2 are arguments of knowledge for relation* $\mathcal{R}_{\mathsf{PoKE}}$ *in the generic group model.*

The PoKE argument of knowledge can be extended to an argument of knowledge for the pre-image of a homomorphism $\phi : \mathbb{Z}^n \to \mathbb{G}$. This is included in the full version.

We can also construct a (honest-verifier) zero-knowledge version of the PoKE argument of knowledge protocol using a method similar to the classic Schnorr Σ-protocol for hidden order groups. This is covered in the full version [BBF18b].

3.3 Aggregating Knowledge of Co-prime Roots

Unlike exponents, providing a root of an element in a hidden order group is already succinct (it is simply a group element). There is a simple aggregation technique for providing a succinct proof of knowledge for multiple *co-prime* roots $x_1, ..., x_n$ simultaneously. This is useful for aggregating PoKE proofs.

In the full version of the proof we describe the PoKCR. It is a proof for the relation:

$$\mathcal{R}_{\mathsf{PoKCR}} = \left\{ (\alpha \in \mathbb{G}^n;\ \mathbf{x} \in \mathbb{Z}^n)\ :\ w = \phi(\mathbf{x}) \in \mathbb{G} \right\}.$$

4 Trapdoorless Universal Accumulator

In this section we describe a number of new techniques for manipulating accumulators built from the strong RSA assumption in a group of unknown order.

We show how to efficiently remove elements from the accumulator, how to use the proof techniques from Sect. 3 to give short membership proofs for multiple elements, and how to non-interactively aggregate inclusion and exclusion proofs. All our techniques are geared towards the setting where there is no trusted setup. We begin by defining what an accumulator is and what it means for an accumulator to be secure.

Our presentation of a trapdoorless universal accumulator mostly follows the definitions and naming conventions of [BCD+17]. Figure 1 summarizes the accumulator syntax and list of associated operations. One notable difference in our syntax is the presence of a common reference string pp generated by the **Setup** algorithm in place of private/public keys.

The security definition we follow [Lip12] formulates an *undeniability* property for accumulators. For background on how this definition relates to others that have been proposed see [BCD+17], which gives generic transformations between different accumulators with different properties and at different security levels.

The following definition states that an accumulator is secure if an adversary cannot construct an accumulator, an element x and a valid membership witness w_x^t and a non-membership witness u_x^t where w_x^t shows that x is in the accumulator and u_x^t shows that it is not. Lipmaa [Lip12] also defines undeniability without a trusted setup. In that definition the adversary has access to the random coins used by **Setup**.

λ: Security Parameter
t: A discrete time counter
A_t: Accumulator value at time t
S_t: The set of elements currently accumulated
w_x^t, u_x^t: Membership and non-membership proofs
pp: Public parameters implicitly available to all methods
upmsg: Information used to update proofs
Setup$(\lambda, z) \to$ pp, A_0 Generate the public parameters
Add$(A_t, x) \to \{A_{t+1}, \mathbf{upmsg}\}$ Update the accumulator
Del$(A_t, x) \to \{A_{t+1}, \mathbf{upmsg}\}$ Delete a value from the accumulator
MemWitCreate$(A_t, S, x) \to w_x^t$ Create an membership proof
NonMemWitCreate$(A_t, S, x) \to u_x^t$ Create a non-membership proof
MemWitUp$(A_t, w_x^t, x, \mathbf{upmsg}) \to w_x^{t+1}$ Update an membership proof
NonMemWitUp$(A_t, w_x^t, x, \mathbf{upmsg}) \to u_x^{t+1}$ Update a non-membership proof
VerMem$(A_t, x, w_x^t) \to \{0, 1\}$ Verify membership proof
VerNonMem$(A_t, x, u_x^t) \to \{0, 1\}$ Verify non-membership proof

---

Fig. 1. A trapdoorless universal accumulator.

Definition 6 (Accumulator Security (Undeniability)).

$$
\Pr \left[\begin{array}{l} pp, A_0 \in \mathbb{G} \xleftarrow{\$} \textbf{Setup}(\lambda) \\ (A, x, w_x, u_x) \xleftarrow{\$} \mathcal{A}(pp, A_0) \\ \textbf{VerMem}(A, x, w_x^t) \wedge \textbf{VerNonMem}(A, x, u_x^t) \end{array} \right] = \mathsf{negl}(\lambda)
$$

4.1   Accumulator Construction

Several sub-procedures that are used heavily in the construction are summarized below. **Bezout**(x,y) refers to a sub-procedure that outputs Bezout coefficients $a, b \in \mathbb{Z}$ for a pair of co-prime integers x, y (i.e. satisfying the relation $ax + by = 1$). **ShamirTrick** uses Bezout coefficient's to compute an (xy)-th root of a group element g from an x-th root of g and a yth root of g. **RootFactor** is a procedure that given an element $y = g^x$ and the factorization of the exponent $x = x_1 \cdots x_n$ computes an x_i-th root of y for all $i = 1, \ldots, n$ in total time $O(n \log(n))$. Naively this procedure would take time $O(n^2)$. It is related to the **MultiExp** algorithm described earlier and was originally described by [STSY01].

ShamirTrick(w_1, w_2, x, y): [Sha83]
1. **if** $w_1^x \neq w_2^y$ **return** $\perp$
2. $a, b \leftarrow$ **Bezout**(x, y)
3. **return** $w_1^b w_2^a$

$H_{\text{prime}}(x)$:
1. $y \leftarrow H(x)$
2. **while** y is not odd prime:
3. $y \leftarrow H(y)$
4. **return** y

RootFactor$(g, x_1, \ldots, x_n)$:
1. **if** $n = 1$ **return** g
2. $n' \leftarrow \lfloor \frac{n}{2} \rfloor$
3. $g_L \leftarrow g^{\Pi_{j=1}^{n'} x_j}$
4. $g_R \leftarrow g^{\Pi_{j=n'+1}^{n} x_j}$
5. $L \leftarrow$ **RootFactor**$(g_R, x_1, \ldots, x_{n'})$
6. $R \leftarrow$ **RootFactor**$(g_L, x_{n'+1}, \ldots, x_n)$
7. **return** $L \parallel R$

Groups of unknown order. The accumulator requires a procedure $GGen(\lambda)$ which samples a group of unknown order in which the strong root assumption (Definition 2) holds. One can use the quotient group $(\mathbb{Z}/N)^*/\{-1, 1\}$, where N is an RSA modulus, which may require a trusted setup to generate the modulus N. Alternatively, one can use a class group which eliminates the trusted setup. Note that the adaptive root assumption requires that these groups have no known elements of low order, and hence the group $(\mathbb{Z}/N)^*$ is not suitable because $(-1) \in (\mathbb{Z}/N)^*$ has order two [BBF18a]. Given an element of order two it is possible to convince a PoE-verifier that $g^x = -y$ when in fact $g^x = y$.

The basic RSA accumulator. We review he classic RSA accumulator [CL02, Lip12] below, omitting all the procedures that require trapdoor information. All accumulated values are odd primes. If the strong RSA assumption (Definition 2) holds in $\mathbb{G}$, then the accumulator satisfies the undeniability definition [Lip12].

The core procedures for the basic dynamic accumulator are the following:

- **Setup** generates a group of unknown order and initializes the group with a generator of that group.
- **Add** takes the current accumulator A_t, an element from the odd primes domain, and computes $A_{t+1} = A_t$.
- **Del** does not have such a trapdoor and therefore needs to reconstruct the set from scratch. The **RootFactor** algorithm can be used for pre-computation. Storing 2^k elements and doing $n \cdot k$ work, the online removal will only take $(1 - \frac{1}{2}^k) \cdot n$ steps.

- A membership witness is simply the accumulator without the aggregated item.
- A membership non-witness, proposed by [LLX07], uses the fact that for any $x \notin S$, $\gcd(x, \prod_{s \in S} s) = 1$. The Bezout coefficients $(a, b) \leftarrow$ **Bezout**$(x, \prod_{s \in S} s)$ are therefore a valid membership witness. The actual witness is the pair (a, g^b) which is short because $|a| \approx |x|$.
- Membership and non-membership witnesses can be efficiently updated as in [LLX07]

Setup(λ):

1. $\mathbb{G} \xleftarrow{\$} GGen(\lambda)$
2. $g \xleftarrow{\$} \mathbb{G}$
3. **return** $\mathbb{G}, g$

Add(A_t, S, x):

1. **if** $x \in S$: **return** A_t
2. **else** :
3. $S \leftarrow S \cup \{x\}$
4.   **upmsg** $\leftarrow x$
5.   **return** A_t^x, **upmsg**

Del(A_t, S, x):

1. **if** : $x \notin S$: **return** A_t
2. **else** :
3. $S \leftarrow S \setminus \{x\}$
4. $A_{t+1} \leftarrow g^{\prod_{s \in S} s}$
5.   **upmsg** $\leftarrow \{x, A_t, A_{t+1}\}$
6.   **return** A_{t+1}, **upmsg**

MemWitCreate(A, S, x) :

1. $w_x^t \leftarrow g^{\prod_{s \in S, s \neq x} s}$
2. **return** w_x^t

NonMemWitCreate(A, S, x) :

1. $s^* \leftarrow \prod_{s \in S} s$
2. $a, b \leftarrow$ **Bezout**(s^*, x)
3. $B \leftarrow g^b$
4. **return** $u_x^t \leftarrow \{a, B\}$

VerMem(A, w_x, x) :

1. **return** 1 **if** $(w_x)^x = A$

VerNonMem(A, u_x, x) :

1. $\{a, B\} \leftarrow u_x$
2. **return** 1 **if** $A^a B^x = g$

Theorem 4 (Security accumulator [Lip12]). *Assume that the strong RSA assumption (Definition 2) holds in $\mathbb{G}$. Then the accumulator satisfies undeniability (Definition 6) and is therefore secure.*

Proof. We construct an $\mathcal{A}_{RSA}$ that given an $\mathcal{A}_{Acc}$ for the accumulator breaks the strong RSA assumption. $\mathcal{A}_{RSA}$ receives a group $\mathbb{G} \leftarrow GGen(\lambda)$ and a challenge $g \xleftarrow{\$} \mathbb{G}$. We now run $\mathcal{A}_{Acc}$ on input $\mathbb{G}$ and $A_0 = g$. $\mathcal{A}_{Acc}$ returns a tuple (A, x, w_x, u_x) such that **VerMem**$(A, x, w_x) = 1$ and **VerNonMem**$(A, x, u_x) = 1$. $\mathcal{A}_{RSA}$ parses $(a, B) = u_x$ and computes $B \cdot (w_x)^a$ as the xth root of g. x is an odd prime by definition and $(B \cdot w_x^a)^x = B^x \cdot A^b = g$. This contradicts the strong RSA assumption and thus shows that the accumulator construction satisfies undeniability.

4.2   Batching and Aggregation of Accumulator Witnesses

Aggregating membership witnesses. Aggregating membership witnesses for many elements into a single membership witness for the set is straightforward using **ShamirTrick**. However, verification of this membership witness is linear in the number of group operations. Note that the individual membership witnesses can still be extracted from the aggregated witness as $w_x = w_{xy}^y$. Security, therefore, still holds for an accumulator construction with aggregated membership witnesses. The succinct proof of exponentiation (NI-PoE) enables us to produce a single membership witness that can be verified in constant time. The verification **VerAggMemWit** simply checks the proof of exponentiation.

Aggregating existing membership witnesses for elements in several distinct accumulators (that use the same setup parameters) can be done as well. The algorithm **MemWitX** simply multiplies together the witnesses w_x for an element $x \in A_1$ and w_y for $y \in A_2$ to create an inclusion proof w_{xy} for x and y. The verification checks $w_{xy}^{x \cdot y} = A_1^y A_2^x$. If x and y are co-prime then we can directly recover w_x and w_y from the proof w_{xy}. In particular $w_x = \textbf{ShamirTrick}(A_1^y, A_1, w_{xy}^y A_2^{-1}, y, x)$ and $w_y = \textbf{ShamirTrick}(A_2^x, A_2, w_{xy}^x A_1^{-1}, x, y)$.

AggMemWit(A, w_x, w_y, x, y) :
1. $w_{x \cdot y} \leftarrow \textbf{ShamirTrick}(A, w_x, w_y, x, y)$
2. **return** $w_{x \cdot y}$, NI-PoE$(w_{x \cdot y}, x \cdot y, A)$

MemWitCreate*$(A, \{x_1, \ldots, x_n\})$:
1. $x^* = \prod_{i=1}^n x_i$
2. $w_{x^*} \leftarrow \textbf{MemWitCreate}(A, x^*)$
3. **return** w_{x^*}, NI-PoE(x, w_{x^*}, A)

VerMem*$(A, \{x_1, \ldots, x_n\}, w = \{w_x, \pi\})$:
1. **return** NI-PoE.verify$(\prod_{i=1}^n x_i, w, A, \pi)$

MemWitX$(A_1, A_2, w_x, w_y, x, y)$:
1. **return** $w_{xy} \leftarrow w_x \cdot w_y$

VerMemWitX(A_1, A_2, w_{xy}, x, y) :
1. **if** $gcd(x, y) \neq 1$
2.   **return** $\perp$
3. **else**
4.   **return** $w_{xy}^{x \cdot y} \leftarrow A_1^y A_2^x$

Distributed accumulator updates. In the decentralized/distributed setting, the accumulator is managed by a distributed network of participants who only store the accumulator state and a subset of the accumulator elements along with their membership witnesses. These participants broadcast their own updates and listen for updates from other participants, updating their local state and membership witnesses appropriately when needed[2].

---

[2] The condition that $gcd(x, y) = 1$ is minor as we can simply use a different set of primes as the domains for each accumulator. Equivalently we can utilize different collision resistant hash functions with prime domain for each accumulator. The concrete security assumption would be that it is difficult to find two values a, b such that both hash functions map to the same prime. We utilize this aggregation technique in our IOP application (Sect. 6.2).

We observe that the basic accumulator functions do not require a trapdoor or knowledge of the entire state, summarized in Fig. 2. In particular, deleting an item requires knowledge of the item's current membership witness (the accumulator state after deletion is this witness). Moreover, operations can be performed in batches as follows:

The techniques are summarized as follows:

- **BatchAdd** An NI-PoE proof can be used to improve the amortized verification efficiency of a batch of updates that add elements $x_1, ..., x_m$ at once and update the accumulator to $A_{t+1} \leftarrow A_t^{x^*}$. A network participant would check that $x^* = \prod_i x_i$ and verify the proof rather than compute the m exponentiations.
- **BatchDel** Deleting elements in a batch uses the **AggMemWit** function to a compute the aggregate membership witness from the individual membership witnesses of each element. This is the new state of the accumulator. A NI-PoE proof improves the verification efficiency of this batch update.
- **CreateAllMemWit** It is possible for users to update membership and non-membership witnesses [LLX07]. The updates do not require knowledge of the accumulated set S but do require that every accumulator update is processed. Since this is cumbersome some users may rely on service providers for maintaining the witness. The service provider may store the entire state or just the users witnesses. Creating all users witnesses naively requires $O(n^2)$ operations. Using the **RootFactor** algorithm this time can be reduced to $O(n \log(n))$ operations or amortized $O(\log(n))$ operations per witness.
- **CreateManyNonMemWit** Similarly to **CreateAllMemWit** it is possible to create m non-membership witness using $O(\max(n, m) + m \log(m))$ operations. This stands in contrast to the naive algorithm that would take $O(m \cdot n)$ operations. The algorithm is in Fig. 3.

Add(A_t, x):
1. **return** A_t^x

BatchAdd$(A_t, \{x_1, \ldots, x_m\})$:
1. $x^* \leftarrow \prod_{i=1}^m x_i$
2. $A_{t+1} \leftarrow A_t^{x^*}$
3. **return** $A_{t+1}, \text{NI-PoE}(x^*, A_t, A_{t+1})$

DelWMem(A_t, w_x^t, x):
1. **if** **VerMem**$(A_t, w_x^t, x) = 1$
2. **return** w_x^t

BatchDel$(A_t, (x_1, w_{x_1}^t) \ldots, (x_m, w_{x_m}^t))$:
1. $A_{t+1} \leftarrow w_{x_1}^t$
2. $x^* \leftarrow x_1$
3. **for** $i \leftarrow 2, i \leq m$
4. $\quad A_{t+1} \leftarrow \textbf{ShamirTrick}(A_{t+1}, w_{x_i}^t, x, x_i)$
5. $\quad x^* \leftarrow x^* \cdot x_i$
6. **return** $A_{t+1}, \text{NI-PoE}(x^*, A_{t+1}, A_t)$

CreateAllMemWit(S) :
1. **return** **RootFactor**(g, S)

Fig. 2. Distributed and stateless accumulator functions.

CreateManyNonMemWit$(A, S, \{x_1, \ldots, x_m\})$:
1. $x^* = \prod_{i=1}^{m} x_i$
2. $\{a, B\} = $ **NonMemWitCreate**(A, S, x^*)
3. **return BreakUpNonMemWit**$(A, \{a, B\}, \{x_1, \ldots, x_m\})$

BreakUpNonMemWit$(A, \{a, B\}, \{x_1, \ldots, x_m\})$:
1. **if** $m = 1$ **return** $\{a, B\}$
2. $x_L = \prod_{i=1}^{m/2} x_i$
3. $x_R = \prod_{i=\lfloor m/2 \rfloor + 1}^{m} x_i$
4. $B_L = B^{x_R} A^{\lfloor \frac{a}{x_L} \rfloor}, a_L = a \bmod x_L$
5. $B_R = B^{x_L} A^{\lfloor \frac{a}{x_R} \rfloor}, a_R = a \bmod x_R$
6. $u_L = $ **BreakUpNonMemWit**$(A, \{a_L, B_L\}, \{x_1, \ldots, x_{\lfloor m/2 \rfloor}\})$
7. $u_R = $ **BreakUpNonMemWit**$(A, \{a_R, B_R\}, \{x_{\lfloor m/2 \rfloor + 1}, \ldots, x_m\})$
8. **return** $u_L \| u_R$

Fig. 3. Algorithm for creating multiple non membership witnesses

Batching non-membership witnesses. A non-membership witness u_x for x in an accumulator with state A for a set S is $u_x = \{a, g^b\}$ such that $as^* + bx = 1$ for $s^* \leftarrow \prod_{s \in S} s$. The verification checks $A^a g^{bx} = g$. Since $gcd(s^*, x) = 1$ and $gcd(s^*, y) = 1$ if and only if $gcd(s^*, xy) = 1$, to batch non-membership witnesses we could simply construct a non-membership witness for $x \cdot y$. A prover computes $a', b' \leftarrow$ **Bezout**(s^*, xy) and sets $u_{xy} \leftarrow a', g^{b'}$. This is still secure as a non-membership witness for both x and y because we can easily extract a non-membership witness for x as well as for y from the combined witness (a', B') by setting $u_x = (a', (B')^y)$ and $u_y = (a', (B')^x)$.

Unfortunately, $|a'| \approx |xy|$ so the size of this batched non-membership witness is linear in the number of elements included in the batch. A natural idea is to set $u_{xy} = (V, B) \leftarrow (A^{a'}, g^{b'}) \in \mathbb{G}^2$ instead of $(a', B) \in \mathbb{Z} \times \mathbb{G}$ as the former has constant size. The verification would check that $VB^{xy} = g$. This idea doesn't quite work as an adversary can simply set $V = gB^{-xy}$ without knowing a discrete logarithm between A and V. Our solution is to use the NI-PoKE2 protocol to ensure that V was created honestly. Intuitively, soundness is achieved because the knowledge extractor for the NI-PoKE2 can extract a' such that (a', B) is a standard non-membership witness for xy.

The new membership witness is $V, B, \pi \leftarrow$ NI-PoKE(A,v;b). The size of this witness is independent of the size of the statement. We can further improve the verification by adding a proof of exponentiation that the verification equation holds: NI-PoE$(x \cdot y, B, g \cdot V^{-1})$. Lastly, recall from Sect. 3 that the two independent NI-PoKE2 and NI-PoE proofs can be aggregated into a single group element.

We present the non-membership protocol bellow as **NonMemWitCreate***. The verification algorithm **VerNonMem*** simply verifies the NI-PoKE2 and NI-PoE.

NonMemWitCreate*(A, s^*, x^*) : //
$A = g^{s^*}$, $s^* = \prod_{s \in S} s$, $x = \prod x_i, x_i \in \mathsf{Primes}(\lambda)$
 1. $a, b \leftarrow \mathbf{Bezout}(s^*, x^*)$
 2. $V \leftarrow A^a, B \leftarrow g^b$
 3. $\pi_V \leftarrow \mathsf{NI\text{-}PoKE2}(A, V; a)$ // $V = A^a$
 4. $\pi_g \leftarrow \mathsf{NI\text{-}PoE}(x^*, B, g \cdot V^{-1})$// $B^x = g \cdot V^{-1}$
 5. **return** $\{V, B, \pi_V, \pi_g\}$
VerNonMem*$(A, u = \{V, B, \pi_V, \pi_g\}, \{x_1, \ldots, x_n\})$:
 1. **return** $\mathsf{NI\text{-}PoKE2.verify}(A, V, \pi_V) \wedge \mathsf{NI\text{-}PoE.verify}(\prod_{i=1}^n x_i, B, g \cdot V^{-1}, \pi_g)$

Batch accumulator security. We now formally define security for an accumulator with batch membership and non-membership witnesses. The definition naturally generalizes Definition 6. We omit a correctness definition as it follows directly from the definition of the batch witnesses. We assume that correctness holds perfectly.

Definition 7 (Batch Accumulator Security (Undeniability)).

$$
\Pr \left[
\begin{array}{l}
pp, A_0 \in \mathbb{G} \overset{\$}{\leftarrow} \textbf{\textit{Setup}}(\lambda) \\
(A, I, E, w_I, u_E) \overset{\$}{\leftarrow} \mathcal{A}(pp, A_0) : \\
\textbf{\textit{VerMem}}^*(A, I, w_I) \wedge \textbf{\textit{VerNonMem}}^*(A, S, u_S) \wedge I \cap S \neq \emptyset
\end{array}
\right] = \mathsf{negl}(\lambda)
$$

From the batch witnesses w_I and u_S we can extract individual accumulator witnesses for each element in I and S. Since the intersection of the two sets is not empty we have an element x and extracted witnesses w_x and u_x for that element. As in the proof of Theorem 4 this lets us compute and xth root of g which directly contradicts the strong RSA assumption. Our security proof will be in the generic group model as it implies the strong RSA assumption, the adaptive root assumption and can be used to formulate extraction for the PoKE2 protocol. Our security proof uses the interactive versions of PoKE2 and PoE protocols but extraction/soundness holds for their non-interactive variants as well.

Theorem 5. *The batch accumulator construction presented in Sect. 4.2 is secure (Definition 7) in the generic group model.*

For the security proof see the full version [BBF18b].

Aggregating non-membership witnesses. In the full version of the paper [BBF18b] we show how non-membership witnesses can be aggregated non-interactively. Multiple independently created non-membership witnesses can be aggregated into a single witness. We can use similar batching techniques as discussed above to make this witness constant sized.

5 Batchable Vector Commitments with Small Parameters

5.1 VC Definitions

We review briefly the formal definition of a vector commitment. We only consider static commitments that do not allow updates, but our scheme can naturally be modified to be dynamic.

Vector commitment syntax. A VC is a tuple of four algorithms: VC.Setup, VC.Com, VC.Open, VC.Verify.

1. VC.Setup($\lambda, n, \mathcal{M}$) → pp Given security parameter λ, length n of the vector, and message space of vector components $\mathcal{M}$, output public parameters pp, which are implicit inputs to all the following algorithms.
2. VC.Com($\boldsymbol{m}$) → τ, com Given an input $\boldsymbol{m} = (m_1, ..., m_n)$ output a commitment com and advice τ.
3. VC.Update(com, m, i, τ) → τ, com Given an input message m and position i output a commitment com and advice τ.
4. VC.Open(com, m, i, τ) → π On input $m \in \mathcal{M}$ and $i \in [1, n]$, the commitment com, and advice τ output an opening π that proves m is the ith committed element of com.
5. VC.Verify(com, m, i, π) → 0/1 On input commitment com, an index $i \in [n]$, and an opening proof π output 1 (accept) or 0 (reject).

If the vector commitment does not have an VC.Update functionality we call it a *static* vector commitment.

Definition 8 (Static Correctness). *A static vector commitment scheme VC is correct if for all $\boldsymbol{m} \in \mathcal{M}^n$ and $i \in [1, n]$:*

$$\Pr \left[VC.\text{Verify}(com, m_i, i, \pi) = 1 : \begin{array}{l} pp \leftarrow VC.\text{Setup}(\lambda, n, \mathcal{M}) \\ \tau, com \leftarrow VC.\text{Com}(\boldsymbol{m}) \\ \pi \leftarrow VC.Open(com, m_i, i, \tau) \end{array} \right] = 1$$

The correctness definition for dynamic vector commitments also incorporates updates. Concretely whenever VC.Update is invoked the underlying committed vector $\boldsymbol{m}$ is updated correctly.

Binding commitments. The main security property of vector commitments (of interest in the present work) is position binding. The security game augments the standard binding commitment game.

Definition 9 (Binding). *A vector commitment scheme VC is position binding if for all $O(\text{poly}(\lambda))$-time adversaries $\mathcal{A}$ the probability over pp $\leftarrow$ VC.Setup($\lambda, n, \mathcal{M}$) and $(com, i, m, m', \pi, \pi') \leftarrow \mathcal{A}(pp)$ the probability that VC.Verify(com, m, i, π) = VC.Verify(com, m', i, π') = 1 and $m \neq m'$ is negligible in λ.*

5.2   VC Construction

We first present a VC construction for bit vectors, i.e. using the message space $\mathcal{M} = \{0, 1\}$. We then explain how this can be easily adapted for a message space of arbitrary bit length.

Our VC construction associates a unique prime[3] integer p_i with each ith index of the bitvector m and uses an accumulator to commit to the set of all primes corresponding to indices where $m_i = 1$. The opening of the ith index to $m_i = 1$ is an inclusion proof of p_i and the opening to $m_i = 0$ is an exclusion proof of p_i. By using our accumulator from Sect. 4, the opening of each index is constant-size. Moreover, the opening of several indices can be batched into a constant-size proof by aggregating all the membership witnesses for primes on the indices opened to 1 and batching all the non-membership witnesses for primes on the indices opened to 0.

The VC for vectors on a message space of arbitrary bit length is exactly the same, interpreting the input vector as a bit vector. Opening a λ-bit component is then just a special case of batch opening several indices of a VC to a bit vector. The full details are in Figure 4 of the full version [BBF18b].

Both the accumulator's CRS as well as PrimeGen can be represented in constant space independent of n. This means that the public parameters for the vector commitment are also constant-size and independent of n, unlike all previous vector commitments with $O(1)$ size openings [CF13, LRY16, LM18]. The batch opening of several (mixed value) indices consists of 2 elements in $\mathbb{G}$ for the aggregate membership-witness and an additional 5 elements in $\mathbb{G}$ for the batch non-membership witness, plus one λ-bit integer.

Aggregating Openings, Key-Value commitment and Optimizations. In the full version [BBF18b] we describe how vector commitment openings can be non-interactively aggregated. We also discuss how a vector commitment with constant sized setup can be used as a commitment to a key value map as well as several optimizations.

5.3   Key-Value Map Commitment

Our vector-commitment can be used to build a commitment to a key-value map. A key-value map can be built from a sparse vector. The key-space is represented by positions in the vector and the associated value is the data at the keys position. The vector length is exponential in the key length and most positions are zero (null). Our VC commitment naturally supports sparse vectors because the complexity of the commitment is proportional to the number of bit indices that are set to 1, and otherwise independent of the vector length.

---

[3] Examples include $\mathsf{H}_{\mathsf{prime}}$ (described earlier), or alternatively the function that maps i to the next prime after $f(i) = 2(i+2) \cdot \log_2(i+2)^2$, which maps the integers $[0, N)$ to smaller primes than $\mathsf{H}_{\mathsf{prime}}$ (in expectation).

6   Applications

6.1   Stateless Blockchains

UTXO commitment. We first consider a simplified blockchain design which closely corresponds to Bitcoin's UTXO design where users own coins and issue transaction by spending old coins and creating new coins. We call the set of unspent coins the UTXO set. Updates to the blockchain can be viewed as asynchronous updates to the UTXO set. In most current blockchain designs (with some exceptions [MGGR13, BCG+14]) nodes participating in transaction validation store the whole UTXO set and use it to verify whether a coin was unspent. Instead, we consider a blockchain design where the network maintains the UTXO set in a dynamic accumulator [STS99a, TMA13, Tod16, Dra]. We instantiate this accumulator with our new construction from Sect. 4.1, taking advantage of our distributed batch updates and aggregate membership proofs.

Each transaction block will contain an accumulator state, which is a commitment to the current UTXO set. To spend a coin, a user provides a membership witness for the coin (UTXO) that is being spent inside a transaction. Any validator (aka miner) may verify the transactions against the latest accumulator state and also uses **BatchDel** to delete all spent coins from the accumulator, derive its new state, and output a proof of correctness for the deletions. The proof is propagated to other validators in the network. For the newly minted coins, the validator uses **BatchAdd** to add them to the accumulator and produce a second proof of correctness to propagate. Other validators are able to verify that the accumulator was updated correctly using only a constant number of group operations and highly efficient arithmetic over λ-bit integers.

In this design, users store the membership witnesses for their own coins and are required to update their witnesses with every block of transactions. It is plausible that users use third-party services to help with this maintenance. These services are not trusted for integrity, but only for availability. Note that a may produce many (e.g. n) membership witnesses at once in $O(n \log(n))$ time using the **CreateAllMemWit** algorithm.

Accounts commitment. Some currencies such as Ethereum [Woo14] use an account-based system where the state is a key-value map. A transaction updates the balances of the sending and the receiving accounts. To enable stateless validation in this setting, a user can provide proofs of the balances of the sending and receiving accounts in the current ledger state. Instead of using an accumulator to commit to this state, we use the new key-value map commitment from Sect. 5.3. This commitment supports batch distributed updates, similar to our new accumulator. Using the aggregation of vector commitment openings a miner or validator can perform the aggregation and batching operations without storing the state providing efficient proofs that the openings are correct. Other nodes can verify these opening proofs efficiently requiring only a constant number of group operations.

6.2   Short IOPs

Merkle tree paths contribute significant overhead to both the proof size of a compiled IOP proof and its verification time. Vector commitments with smaller openings than Merkle trees, or batchable openings (i.e. subvector commitments), can help reduce this overhead [LM18]. Using our new VCs, the opening proof for each round of the compiled IOP is just 4 group elements in $\mathbb{G}$ and a λ-bit integer (plus one additional element for the VC commitment itself). Instantiating $\mathbb{G}$ with a class group of quadratic imaginary order and tuning security to 128-bits requires elements of size approximately 2048-bits [HM00]. Thus, the VC openings contribute 8320 bits to the proof size per IOP round. When applied to the "CS-proof" SNARK considered by Lai and Malavolta, which is based on a theoretical PCP that checks 3 bits per query and has 80 queries, the proof size is $5 \cdot 2048 + 128 + 3 \cdot 80 = 10608$ bits, or 1.3 KB. This is the shortest (theoretical) setup-free SNARK with sublinear public parameters to date.

Our VCs also achieve concrete improvements to practical IOPs. Targeting 100-bit security in the VC component and otherwise apples-to-apples comparisons with benchmarks for Aurora [BSCR+18] and STARKS [BBHR18], we can conservatively use 2048-bit class group elements. With these parameters, our VCs reduce the size of the Aurora proofs on a 2^{20} size circuit from 222 KB to less than 100 KB, a 54% reduction, and the size of STARK proofs for a circuit of 2^{52} gates from 600 KB to approximately 222 KB, a 63% reduction. This rough estimate is based on the Merkle path length 42 and round number 21 extrapolated from the most recent STARK benchmarks for this size circuit [BBHR18].

Replacing Merkle trees with our VCs does not significantly impact the verification cost, and in some cases it may even improve verification time. Recall that verifying a batch VC proof costs approximately one *lamdba*-bit integer multiplication and a primality check per bit. Furthermore, using the optimization described in the full version eliminates the primality checks for the verifier (at a slight cost to the prover). Computing a SHA256 hash function (whether SHA256 or AES with Davies-Meyer) is comparable to the cost of a λ-bit integer multiplication. Thus, as a loose estimate, replacing each Merkle path per query with a single λ-bit multiplication would achieve a factor $\log n = 36$ reduction. In STARKS, Merkle paths are constructed over 256-bit blocks of the proof rather than bits, thus the comparison is 36 hashes vs 256 modular multiplications. The Merkle path validation accounts for 80% of the verification time.

While using our vector commitment has many benefits for IOPs, there are several sever downsides. Our vector commitment is not quantum secure as a quantum computer can find the order of the group and break the Strong-RSA assumption. Merkle trees are more plausibly quantum secure. Additionally, the prover for an IOP instantiated with our vector commitment would be significantly slower than one with a Merkle tree.

Acknowledgments. This work was partially supported by NSF, ONR, the Simons Foundation and the ZCash foundation.

References

[ABC+12] Ahn, J.H., Boneh, D., Camenisch, J., Hohenberger, S., shelat, A., Waters, B.: Computing on authenticated data. In: Cramer, R. (ed.) TCC 2012. LNCS, vol. 7194, pp. 1–20. Springer, Heidelberg (2012). https://doi.org/10.1007/978-3-642-28914-9_1

[AHIV17] Ames, S., Hazay, C., Ishai, Y., Venkitasubramaniam, M.: Ligero: lightweight sublinear arguments without a trusted setup. In: Thuraisingham, B.M., Evans, D., Malkin, T., Xu, D. (eds.) ACM CCS 2017, pp. 2087–2104. ACM Press, October–November 2017

[BBBF18] Boneh, D., Bonneau, J., Bünz, B., Fisch, B.: Verifiable delay functions. In: Shacham, H., Boldyreva, A. (eds.) CRYPTO 2018, Part I. LNCS, vol. 10991, pp. 757–788. Springer, Cham (2018). https://doi.org/10.1007/978-3-319-96884-1_25

[BBF18a] Boneh, D., Bünz, B., Fisch, B.: A survey of two verifiable delay functions. Cryptology ePrint Archive, Report 2018/712 (2018). https://eprint.iacr.org/2018/712

[BBF18b] Boneh, D., Bünz, B., Fisch, B.: Batching techniques for accumulators with applications to IOPs and stateless blockchains. Cryptology ePrint Archive, Report 2018/1188 (2018). https://eprint.iacr.org/2018/1188

[BBHR18] Ben-Sasson, E., Bentov, I., Horesh, Y., Riabzev, M.: Scalable, transparent, and post-quantum secure computational integrity. Cryptology ePrint Archive, Report 2018/046 (2018). https://eprint.iacr.org/2018/046

[BCD+17] Baldimtsi, F., et al.: Accumulators with applications to anonymity-preserving revocation. Cryptology ePrint Archive, Report 2017/043 (2017). http://eprint.iacr.org/2017/043

[BCG+14] Ben-Sasson, E., et al.: Zerocash: decentralized anonymous payments from bitcoin. In: 2014 IEEE Symposium on Security and Privacy, pp. 459–474. IEEE Computer Society Press, May 2014

[BCK10] Bangerter, E., Camenisch, J., Krenn, S.: Efficiency limitations for Σ-protocols for group homomorphisms. In: Micciancio, D. (ed.) TCC 2010. LNCS, vol. 5978, pp. 553–571. Springer, Heidelberg (2010). https://doi.org/10.1007/978-3-642-11799-2_33

[BCS16] Ben-Sasson, E., Chiesa, A., Spooner, N.: Interactive oracle proofs. In: Hirt, M., Smith, A. (eds.) TCC 2016, Part II. LNCS, vol. 9986, pp. 31–60. Springer, Heidelberg (2016). https://doi.org/10.1007/978-3-662-53644-5_2

[Bd94] Benaloh, J., de Mare, M.: One-way accumulators: a decentralized alternative to digital signatures. In: Helleseth, T. (ed.) EUROCRYPT 1993. LNCS, vol. 765, pp. 274–285. Springer, Heidelberg (1994). https://doi.org/10.1007/3-540-48285-7_24

[BH01] Buchmann, J., Hamdy, S.: A survey on IQ cryptography. In: Public-Key Cryptography and Computational Number Theory, pp. 1–15 (2001)

[BLL00] Buldas, A., Laud, P., Lipmaa, H.: Accountable certificate management using undeniable attestations. In: Jajodia, S., Samarati, P. (eds) ACM CCS 2000, pp. 9–17. ACM Press, November 2000

[BSCR+18] Ben-Sasson, E., Chiesa, A., Riabzev, M., Spooner, N., Virza, M., Ward, N.P.: Aurora: Transparent succinct arguments for r1cs. Cryptology ePrint Archive, Report 2018/828 (2018). https://eprint.iacr.org/2018/828

[CF13] Catalano, D., Fiore, D.: Vector commitments and their applications. In: Kurosawa, K., Hanaoka, G. (eds.) PKC 2013. LNCS, vol. 7778, pp. 55–72. Springer, Heidelberg (2013). https://doi.org/10.1007/978-3-642-36362-7_5

[CJ10] Canard, S., Jambert, A.: On extended sanitizable signature schemes. In: Pieprzyk, J. (ed.) CT-RSA 2010. LNCS, vol. 5985, pp. 179–194. Springer, Heidelberg (2010). https://doi.org/10.1007/978-3-642-11925-5_13

[CL02] Camenisch, J., Lysyanskaya, A.: Dynamic accumulators and application to efficient revocation of anonymous credentials. In: Yung, M. (ed.) CRYPTO 2002. LNCS, vol. 2442, pp. 61–76. Springer, Heidelberg (2002). https://doi.org/10.1007/3-540-45708-9_5

[DK02] Damgård, I., Koprowski, M.: Generic lower bounds for root extraction and signature schemes in general groups. In: Knudsen, L.R. (ed.) EURO-CRYPT 2002. LNCS, vol. 2332, pp. 256–271. Springer, Heidelberg (2002). https://doi.org/10.1007/3-540-46035-7_17

[Dra] Drake, J.: Accumulators, scalability of utxo blockchains, and data availability. https://ethresear.ch/t/accumulators-scalability-of-utxo-blockchains-and-data-availability/176

[FS87] Fiat, A., Shamir, A.: How to prove yourself: practical solutions to identification and signature problems. In: Odlyzko, A.M. (ed.) CRYPTO 1986. LNCS, vol. 263, pp. 186–194. Springer, Heidelberg (1987). https://doi.org/10.1007/3-540-47721-7_12

[FVY14] Fromknecht, C., Velicanu, D., Yakoubov, S.: A decentralized public key infrastructure with identity retention. Cryptology ePrint Archive, Report 2014/803 (2014). http://eprint.iacr.org/2014/803

[GGM14] Garman, C., Green, M., Miers, I.: Decentralized anonymous credentials. In: NDSS 2014. The Internet Society, February 2014

[HM00] Hamdy, S., Möller, B.: Security of cryptosystems based on class groups of imaginary quadratic orders. In: Okamoto, T. (ed.) ASIACRYPT 2000. LNCS, vol. 1976, pp. 234–247. Springer, Heidelberg (2000). https://doi.org/10.1007/3-540-44448-3_18

[Kil92] Kilian, J.: A note on efficient zero-knowledge proofs and arguments (extended abstract). In: 24th ACM STOC, pp. 723–732. ACM Press, May 1992

[Lip12] Lipmaa, H.: Secure accumulators from euclidean rings without trusted setup. In: Bao, F., Samarati, P., Zhou, J. (eds.) ACNS 2012. LNCS, vol. 7341, pp. 224–240. Springer, Heidelberg (2012). https://doi.org/10.1007/978-3-642-31284-7_14

[LLX07] Li, J., Li, N., Xue, R.: Universal accumulators with efficient nonmembership proofs. In: Katz, J., Yung, M. (eds.) ACNS 2007. LNCS, vol. 4521, pp. 253–269. Springer, Heidelberg (2007). https://doi.org/10.1007/978-3-540-72738-5_17

[LM18] Lai, R.W.F., Malavolta, G.: Optimal succinct arguments via hidden order groups. Cryptology ePrint Archive, Report 2018/705 (2018). https://eprint.iacr.org/2018/705

[LRY16] Libert, B., Ramanna, S.C., Yung, M.: Functional commitment schemes: from polynomial commitments to pairing-based accumulators from simple assumptions. In: Chatzigiannakis, I., Mitzenmacher, M., Rabani, Y., Sangiorgi, D. (eds) ICALP 2016, volume 55 of LIPIcs, pp. 30:1–30:14. Schloss Dagstuhl, July 2016

[Mer88]   Merkle, R.C.: A digital signature based on a conventional encryption function. In: Pomerance, C. (ed.) CRYPTO 1987. LNCS, vol. 293, pp. 369–378. Springer, Heidelberg (1988). https://doi.org/10.1007/3-540-48184-2_32

[MGGR13] Miers, I., Garman, C., Green, M., Rubin, A.D.: Zerocoin: anonymous distributed E-cash from bitcoin. In: 2013 IEEE Symposium on Security and Privacy, pp. 397–411. IEEE Computer Society Press, May 2013

[Mic94]   Micali, S.: CS proofs (extended abstracts). In: 35th FOCS, pp. 436–453. IEEE Computer Society Press, November 1994

[NN98]   Nissim, K., Naor, M.: Certificate revocation and certificate update. In: Usenix (1998)

[PS14]   Pöhls, H.C., Samelin, K.: On updatable redactable signatures. In: Boureanu, I., Owesarski, P., Vaudenay, S. (eds.) ACNS 2014. LNCS, vol. 8479, pp. 457–475. Springer, Cham (2014). https://doi.org/10.1007/978-3-319-07536-5_27

[Sha83]   Shamir, A.: On the generation of cryptographically strong pseudorandom sequences. ACM Trans. Comput. Syst. (TOCS) 1(1), 38–44 (1983)

[Sho97]   Shoup, V.: Lower bounds for discrete logarithms and related problems. In: Fumy, W. (ed.) EUROCRYPT 1997. LNCS, vol. 1233, pp. 256–266. Springer, Heidelberg (1997). https://doi.org/10.1007/3-540-69053-0_18

[Sla12]   Slamanig, D.: Dynamic accumulator based discretionary access control for outsourced storage with unlinkable access. In: Keromytis, A.D. (ed.) FC 2012. LNCS, vol. 7397, pp. 215–222. Springer, Heidelberg (2012). https://doi.org/10.1007/978-3-642-32946-3_16

[STS99a] Sander, T., Ta-Shma, A.: Auditable, anonymous electronic cash. In: Wiener, M. (ed.) CRYPTO 1999. LNCS, vol. 1666, pp. 555–572. Springer, Heidelberg (1999). https://doi.org/10.1007/3-540-48405-1_35

[STS99b] Sander, T., Ta-Shma, A.: Flow control: a new approach for anonymity control in electronic cash systems. In: Franklin, M. (ed.) FC 1999. LNCS, vol. 1648, pp. 46–61. Springer, Heidelberg (1999). https://doi.org/10.1007/3-540-48390-X_4

[STSY01] Sander, T., Ta-Shma, A., Yung, M.: Blind, auditable membership proofs. In: Frankel, Y. (ed.) FC 2000. LNCS, vol. 1962, pp. 53–71. Springer, Heidelberg (2001). https://doi.org/10.1007/3-540-45472-1_5

[TMA13]   Todd, P., Maxwell, G., Andreev, O.: Reducing UTXO: users send parent transactions with their merkle branches, October 2013. https://bitcointalk.org

[Tod16]   Todd, P.: Making UTXO Set Growth Irrelevant With Low-Latency Delayed TXO Commitments, May 2016. https://petertodd.org/2016/delayed-txo-commitments

[TW12]   Terelius, B., Wikström, D.: Efficiency limitations of $\sum$-protocols for group homomorphisms revisited. In: Visconti, I., De Prisco, R. (eds.) SCN 2012. LNCS, vol. 7485, pp. 461–476. Springer, Heidelberg (2012). https://doi.org/10.1007/978-3-642-32928-9_26

[Wes18]   Wesolowski, B.: Efficient verifiable delay functions. Cryptology ePrint Archive, Report 2018/623 (2018). https://eprint.iacr.org/2018/623

[Woo14]   Wood, G.: Ethereum: A secure decentralized transaction ledger (2014). http://gavwood.com/paper.pdf

Homomorphic Cryptography

On the Plausibility of Fully Homomorphic Encryption for RAMs

Ariel Hamlin[1]($\boxtimes$), Justin Holmgren[2]($\boxtimes$), Mor Weiss[3], and Daniel Wichs[1]

[1] Khoury College of Computer Sciences, Northeastern University,
Boston, MA, USA
{ahamlin,wichs}@ccs.neu.edu
[2] Department of Computer Science, Princeton University,
Princeton, NJ, USA
justin.holmgren@princeton.edu
[3] Department of Computer Science, IDC Herzliya, Herzliya, Israel
mor.weiss01@post.idc.ac.il

Abstract. We initiate the study of fully homomorphic encryption for RAMs (RAM-FHE). This is a public-key encryption scheme where, given an encryption of a large database D, anybody can efficiently compute an encryption of $P(D)$ for an arbitrary RAM program P. The running time over the encrypted data should be as close as possible to the worst case running time of P, which may be sub-linear in the data size.

A central difficulty in constructing a RAM-FHE scheme is hiding the sequence of memory addresses accessed by P. This is particularly problematic because an adversary may homomorphically evaluate many programs over the same ciphertext, therefore effectively "rewinding" any mechanism for making memory accesses oblivious.

We identify a necessary prerequisite towards constructing RAM-FHE that we call *rewindable oblivious RAM* (rewindable ORAM), which provides security even in this strong adversarial setting. We show how to construct rewindable ORAM using *symmetric-key doubly efficient PIR (SK-DEPIR)* (Canetti-Holmgren-Richelson, Boyle-Ishai-Pass-Wootters: TCC '17). We then show how to use rewindable ORAM, along with virtual black-box (VBB) obfuscation for specific circuits, to construct RAM-FHE. The latter primitive can be heuristically instantiated using existing indistinguishability obfuscation candidates. Overall, we obtain a RAM-FHE scheme where the multiplicative overhead in running time is polylogarithmic in the database size N. Our basic scheme is single-hop, but we also extend it to obtain multi-hop RAM-FHE with overhead N^ϵ for arbitrarily small $\epsilon > 0$.

We view our work as the first evidence that RAM-FHE is likely to exist.

Justin Holmgren is supported in part by the Simons Collaboration on Algorithms and Geometry and by NSF grant CCF-1714779. This research was done in part while affiliated with MIT, supported in part by the NSF MACS project CNS-1413920. Mor Weiss is supported in part by ISF grants 1861/16 and 1399/17, and AFOSR Award FA9550-17-1-0069. Daniel Wichs and Ariel Hamlin are supported by NSF grants CNS-1314722, CNS-1413964, CNS-1750795 and the Alfred P. Sloan Research Fellowship.

© International Association for Cryptologic Research 2019
A. Boldyreva and D. Micciancio (Eds.): CRYPTO 2019, LNCS 11692, pp. 589–619, 2019.
https://doi.org/10.1007/978-3-030-26948-7_21

1   Introduction

Fully Homomorphic Encryption. Fully Homomorphic Encryption (FHE), proposed by Rivest, Adleman, and Dertouzos [RAD78], is an extension of standard semantically secure encryption that supports computations "underneath" encryption. That is, given an encryption of some data D, anybody can compute an encryption of $P(D)$ for arbitrary programs P, while D remains computationally hidden. We currently have constructions of FHE schemes based on the Learning With Errors (LWE) assumption (either satisfying a relaxation called "leveled" FHE, or additionally requiring a circular security assumption) [Gen09, BV11].

FHE has proven to be an indispensable tool in the foundational study of cryptography, with wide-ranging applications including functional encryption [GKP+b], program obfuscation [GGH+], verifiable computation [GGP10, KRR14], cryptographic hash functions [CCH+19], and more.

The most immediate use-case of FHE is to outsource private computation. A client Alice stores her sensitive database D on an untrusted server, and the server non-interactively executes computations on Alice's behalf (by computing encryptions of $P(D)$ for arbitrary programs P), but learns nothing about D. In known FHE schemes, Alice's work is asymptotically optimal: encrypting her database takes $|D| \cdot \mathsf{poly}(\lambda)$ work, and decrypting the server's ciphertexts takes $|P(D)| \cdot \mathsf{poly}(\lambda)$ work. The server's work is also optimal; however, the program P *must be represented as a circuit* C, and the server's work is then $|C| \cdot \mathsf{poly}(\lambda)$.

There has been much work towards making FHE more practical by minimizing the $\mathsf{poly}(\lambda)$ factors [BGH13, GHS12, BGV12, GSW, GHPS13], but the necessity of representing P as a circuit can lead to a much larger asymptotic loss in efficiency. Indeed, we typically think of programs and their efficiency in the *Random-Access Memory (RAM)* model of computation. Although any RAM program can be converted into a circuit, this may result in a large efficiency loss: in general, a RAM program that runs in time T over a database of size N can be converted into a circuit of size $\widetilde{O}(N + T^2)$ [CR72, PF79]. As a result, for RAM computations running in time $T \ll N$ (e.g., binary search, whose RAM running time is $O(\log N)$), the circuit conversion can incur an exponential efficiency loss. Even for RAM computations with longer running times $T > N$, circuit conversion incurs a quadratic overhead, which asymptotically will be more significant than any $\mathsf{poly}(\lambda)$ multiplicative factor. Therefore, it is crucial to ask the question: Can an FHE scheme "natively" support RAM computations?

1.1   Our Results

RAM-FHE. We define and construct two notions of RAM-FHE. In both notions, given an encryption $\widehat{D}$ of an N-bit database D, a RAM program P, and a bound T on the running time of P, anyone can obtain an encryption $\widehat{y}$ of $P(D)$ in time roughly T. We note that the bound T on evaluation runtime is necessary for semantic security: if homomorphic evaluation preserved the input-specific running time of P, then one could completely learn D by measuring the time to homomorphically evaluate several carefully chosen programs.

Our basic notion is *single-hop*, in which the output ciphertext $\widehat{y}$ and any changes made to D by P, cannot be meaningfully used by future homomorphic computations. We also consider a *multi-hop* variant, in which one can homomorphically evaluate a sequence of RAM programs, which may read *and* write to D, with the changes made by each program execution visible to the next.

We give the first evidence that these notions are possible by constructing (single- and multi-hop) RAM-FHE schemes using extremely strong but plausible assumptions. Specifically, we rely on a recent primitive called *Secret Key Doubly-Efficient Private Information Retrieval (SK-DEPIR)*, as well as *Virtual Black-Box (VBB) obfuscation* for specific circuits. We have candidate SK-DEPIR constructions based on non-standard assumptions related to permuted and noisy Reed-Muller codes [BIPW17, CHR17]. While VBB obfuscation for general circuits is impossible [BGI+01], it appears reasonable to assume that it can be done for most specific circuits and, indeed, any of the candidate constructions of indistinguishability obfuscation (iO) [GMM+16, BMSZ16, MZ18, CVW18, BGMZ18, Agr, LM18, AJS18] can be used to heuristically instantiate it. We view such use of VBB obfuscation as analogous to the random-oracle heuristic: although it is known to be unsound in general, all examples where it fails tend to be contrived, and natural uses of it appear to be sound.[1]

Our constructions have the following efficiency guarantees:

- In the single-hop setting, encryptions of an N-bit database have size $\mathsf{poly}(\lambda, N)$, and the cost of homomorphically evaluating a program P with description size $|P|$ and run-time T is $(T + |P|) \cdot \mathsf{poly}(\lambda, \log N)$.
- In the multi-hop setting, for any constant $\epsilon > 0$, ciphertext sizes are $N^{1+\epsilon} \cdot \mathsf{poly}(\lambda)$ and homomorphic evaluation takes time $(T + |P|) \cdot N^\epsilon \cdot \mathsf{poly}(\lambda)$.

Rewindable Oblivious RAM. As explained in Sect. 1.2 below, the main difficulty in constructing RAM-FHE is hiding the memory access pattern when the evaluator *repeatedly runs different programs on the same initial ciphertext*. We abstract this as a strengthening of Oblivious RAM (ORAM) [Gol87, Ost90, GO96] that we call *rewindable* ORAM, which we believe may be of interest beyond its applications to RAM-FHE. Recall that a standard ORAM scheme allows a client with a small local state k to privately access his own database whose encoding $\widetilde{D}$ is stored on a remote untrusted server. Informally, rewindable ORAM extends this notion to guarantee privacy even when the server can reset the client's state to a previous value.

We construct rewindable ORAM schemes based on any SK-DEPIR scheme. We do not assume the existence of any type of obfuscator and obtain different tradeoffs between efficiency and the types of rewinding attacks, specifically:

---

[1] Furthermore, it is possible to replace VBB obfuscation by a small stateless hardware token, resulting in a RAM-FHE scheme where ciphertexts contain such tokens, which appears to still be non-trivial. We note that VBB was similarly used to construct a public-key DEPIR scheme [BIPW17].

- If the server is only allowed to rewind the client to his initial state, then following a poly (λ, N)-time setup, accessing the database costs poly $(\lambda, \log N)$.
- If the server is allowed to rewind the client to *any* previous state, then following an $N^{1+\epsilon} \cdot$ poly (λ)-time setup, accessing the database costs $N^{\epsilon} \cdot$ poly (λ), for any $\epsilon > 0$.

1.2   Our Techniques

As alluded to above, the main difficulty in constructing RAM-FHE arises from the fact that the *memory access pattern* induced by evaluating P on D may be highly dependent on the database D, whereas the access pattern of the *homomorphic* evaluation of P must hide everything about D. One natural approach towards hiding the access pattern is to force the evaluator to emulate P via an ORAM. However, the RAM-FHE evaluator should be able to evaluate arbitrarily many different programs on *the same* ciphertext $\widehat{D}$, and is *not* required to update his state between executions. This raises the concern that (even a semi-honest) evaluator evaluating two different programs P_1, P_2 on $\widehat{D}$ may potentially deduce non-trivial information about the database D from the *correlations* between the two memory access patterns during these evaluations. This strategy corresponds to a "rewinding" attack on the underlying ORAM, and is not just a theoretical concern - all known ORAM constructions are *indeed insecure* in this case. (For example, if an ORAM client accesses an address a_0, fails to update his state, and then accesses a_1, the server's view will reveal whether or not $a_0 = a_1$.)

Main Component: Rewindable ORAM. We consider (Sect. 3.1) two flavors of *rewindable ORAM*, which provide security against this type of attack. The weaker flavor, called *Initial-State Rewindable ORAM* (ISR-ORAM) allows the adversary to observe the ORAM access patterns of various programs $P_1, P_2, \ldots$ executed on D, where between executions the client/server states are reset to their initial values $k, \widetilde{D}$. The adversary should learn nothing about the underlying access patterns of the programs.

We also define a stronger flavor called *Any-State Rewindable ORAM* (ASR-ORAM) where the adversary can rewind the client/server states to *any point in time*.[2] The ORAM access patterns that the adversary observes should reveal nothing about the underlying access patterns of the programs.

Rewindable ORAM Constructions. Constructing rewindable (even ISR-) ORAM appears to be difficult, and none of the standard ORAM constructions suffice. Indeed, all standard ORAM constructions follow the "balls and bins" model in which each data block is represented as a "ball" and stored on the server in some "bin". Such structures cannot guarantee even ISR-ORAM security since, as noted above, if the client state is reset between accesses then the server can distinguish

---

[2] For example, the adversary can observe the sequential ORAM execution of programs P_1, P_2, P_3, then rewind the client/server state to the point immediately after P_1's execution and observe the execution of a different program P_2', etc.

whether the client is accessing the same data block or not (when accessing the same block, the client will access the same "ball" on the server). Thus, we need fundamentally different techniques than prior ORAM constructions.

Our new approach to rewindable ORAM leverages a powerful recent tool called SK-DEPIR [BIPW17, CHR17], which can be viewed as a *stateless read-only* ORAM. Informally, following a setup phase in which the client receives a secret key k and the server receives an encoding $\widetilde{D}$ of the database D, the client can privately read arbitrary locations i of D by reading a few positions in $\widetilde{D}$, without having to update the client/server state during the process. The server should learn nothing about the underlying locations i being read. In particular, we can think of SK-DEPIR as a very restricted form of ISR-ORAM for the class of RAM program $P_i(D)$ that read and output the i'th location of D.

The works of [BIPW17, CHR17] constructed SK-DEPIR schemes under non-standard assumptions relating to permuted and noisy Reed-Muller codes. Note that such SK-DEPIR cannot exist in the "balls and bins" model, and must encode the data in some complex way that intertwines many data locations together. Indeed, repeatedly accessing the same data location i in a SK-DEPIR should be indistinguishable from accessing completely random and unrelated data locations, so there must be many different, and seemingly unrelated, tuples of locations in $\widetilde{D}$ that contain information about data location i. We use SK-DEPIR to construct both ISR- and ASR-ORAM schemes.

ISR-ORAM from SK-DEPIR and standard ORAM. The ISR-ORAM scheme is simple. Recall that SK-DEPIR is read-only, while ISR-ORAM supports arbitrary RAM programs that can both read and write to the database. In both cases, we can rewind the state to its initial value after an execution while maintaining privacy of the underlying access pattern. The high-level idea is to use the SK-DEPIR to support reads, and use a *standard* ORAM scheme to support writes.

Specifically, the initial states in our ISR-ORAM are the client and server states $k, \widetilde{D}$ of the SK-DEPIR. To execute a RAM program P, the client initializes a fresh copy of a standard, non-rewindable ORAM O, which is initially empty. (We provide an explicit construction of an ORAM scheme for initially empty databases in the full version [HHWW].) Writes are executed using the ORAM scheme O. To read some location i, the client reads i from both the ORAM O and the SK-DEPIR. If location i was found in O, the client uses that value, otherwise he uses the SK-DEPIR value. Thus, the client always gets the freshest copy of the value in any location. Note that rewinding the ISR-ORAM client/server to their initial states erases all information about O (which was initialized only in the first access), so we do not require rewindable security from O: the next access will instantiate a completely fresh ORAM scheme O for the execution. The scheme is described in the full version [HHWW].

ASR-ORAM from SK-DEPIR via a hierarchical structure. The ASR-ORAM construction is more complex. ASR-ORAM should support repeated sequential execution of different programs, and remain secure when the adversary can rewind to any intermediate state from which it starts a new sequence of program executions. Unfortunately, this precludes our previous solution of storing intermediate values written during the execution in a standard, non-rewindable ORAM: rewinding to an intermediate point will rewind the ORAM.

We solve this problem by combining SK-DEPIR with techniques from hierarchical ORAM [Ost90, GO96]. In particular, our ASR-ORAM consists of a hierarchy of SK-DEPIR schemes of exponentially increasing size, where the top-most scheme has size 1 and the bottom-most scheme has size N. Initially, the data is entirely contained in the bottom-most scheme. To read a location i we try to read it using the SK-DEPIR schemes at all levels, and use the value found in the top-most scheme that contains i. To write a location i, we write it to the top level (which requires re-generating its SK-DEPIR scheme). As in Hierarchical ORAM this requires "reshuffles": every pre-determined number of writes, we need to merge sufficiently many of the top levels to ensure that their combined size is large enough to hold the database. Since levels are implemented using SK-DEPIR, this requires reading and re-writing the levels in their entirety. However, as levels get larger, they are "reshuffled" with decreasing frequency so the overall amortized[3] complexity is low. Notice that reshuffles reveal no information, even under arbitrary rewinding, because they occur at pre-determined times (independent of the access history), and reads are secure by the security of the (stateless) SK-DEPIR even under arbitrary rewinding.

We note that the actual construction (Sect. 3.2) is somewhat more involved. One issue arises because SK-DEPIR schemes are designed for array structures (i.e., reading a data block requires knowing its location in D), whereas the hierarchical construction imposes a map structure at each level because it contains a subset of (not necessarily consecutive) data blocks. To resolve this we use the standard data-structures trick of pseudorandomly mapping data blocks into buckets, thus guaranteeing that the block's location in each level in which it appears is independent of the history of accesses.

RAM-FHE from Rewindable ORAM. We construct RAM-FHE from rewindable ORAM using VBB obfuscation. At a high level, to encrypt some database D, we first construct the rewindable ORAM client/server states $k, \widetilde{D}$ for D. We then obfuscate the ORAM client program, with k hard-wired into it, and output the ciphertext consisting of $\widetilde{D}$ and the obfuscated program. The evaluator can then use the obfuscated ORAM client to execute an arbitrary RAM program over the encrypted database $\widetilde{D}$ and derive an encrypted output. During the execution, the evaluator emulates the ORAM server using $\widetilde{D}$ (performing read/write operations as instructed by the client).

Formalizing the above approach is challenging, and requires some adaptations. The final construction is obtained through the following steps.

Step (1): emulating statefulness. We cannot directly use a circuit obfuscator to obfuscate the rewindable ORAM client, because the client is *stateful*, and

---

[3] We note that as in [OS97], reshuffles can be "spread-out" over many operations to achieve low *worst-case* complexity.

state is needed even for correctness. Instead, we obfuscate the circuit emulating a *single* client step in the ORAM scheme. This circuit takes the client state as input, and returns the updated client state as part of its output. We note that representing the client as a circuit in this way is fundamentally different (and significantly more efficient) than representing an entire RAM program as a circuit. Indeed, the circuit performs *a single execution step*, thus the overhead is independent of the database size or the worst-case runtime of the program.

For simplicity of the exposition, we assume for now that the program's description is short (of size $p(\lambda)$ for some a-priori fixed polynomial p), and can therefore be given in its entirety to the obfuscated circuit in the first execution step. We explain below how to remove this restriction.

Step (2): hiding client state. (Standard/rewindable) ORAM security assumes the adversary does not see the client state, but in our construction the evaluator sees the client's internal states throughout the execution (since the obfuscated circuit outputs them). To hide the client states, we have the obfuscated circuit encrypt the state, using a hard-wired (symmetric) encryption key.

Step (3): forcing honest behavior. The rewindable ORAM is secure only as long as the ORAM client behaves honestly, and the ORAM server behaves semi-honestly. However, RAM-FHE should guarantee semantic security of the encrypted database against arbitrary (possibly malicious) evaluators. A malicious evaluator may deviate from a semi-honest emulation of the rewindable ORAM scheme in two ways.

First, the evaluator may emulate a malicious server whose answers to `read` requests are inconsistent with the database, and who fails to perform requested `write` operations. Such attacks can be prevented using the standard approach of maintaining a Merkle Hash Tree (MHT) of the server state. More specifically, we hard-code the initial MHT root into the obfuscated circuit. Answers to `read` requests include also the MHT path proving consistency of the answer (which is verified by the obfuscated circuit using the MHT root). Answers to `write` requests outputted by the obfuscated circuit additionally include an updated MHT path proving that the root was updated correctly.

Second, the evaluator may emulate a malicious client, by providing incorrect/inconsistent client states to the obfuscated circuit. We prevent such attacks by hard-wiring a Message-Authentication Code (MAC) key into the obfuscated circuit, and having it verify the input state and MAC the output state.

Step (4): hiding the output. Recall from Step (2) that the internal ORAM client state is encrypted using a "temporary" symmetric encryption key that is chosen at encryption time. Consequently, this key cannot be used to encrypt the computation output (which should be encrypted using a persistent public key that is chosen during key generation). We encrypt the output using a standard PKE scheme, where the public key is hard-wired into the obfuscated circuit.

Step (5): generating randomness for the execution. Even if the emulated RAM program is deterministic, the obfuscated circuit described above needs random coins for encryption, and to emulate the ORAM client. We use a PRF (applied to the MHT root, and the entire execution history) to derive the needed randomness, where the PRF key is hard-wired into the circuit.

An additional point that needs to be handled is the fact that a RAM program P has a volatile tape (a "scratch tape") which is used only during P's execution, after which it is erased. We use a *standard ORAM* to instantiate the scratch tape at the onset of the execution. Notice that standard ORAM security suffices here, since each execution instantiates a fresh ORAM for the scratch tape.[4]

The construction described above gives a single-hop RAM-FHE scheme when the underlying ORAM is an ISR-ORAM (see Sect. 6). The multi-hop RAM-FHE scheme is obtained by instantiating the ORAM with an ASR-ORAM, with some modifications to allow the evaluator to perform sequential computations on the database. (For example, this requires MAC-ing the initial state of the ASR-ORAM client together with the MHT root of the updated database, see the full version [HHWW] for more details.)

Generalizing to programs of any length. The construction described above assumed the entire program description was given as input to the obfuscated circuit (this requires an a-priori fixed bound on the description size). To support longer programs, we first copy the program description into the scratch tape at the onset of the computation. More specifically, the evaluator provides a MHT root for the program description as input to the obfuscated circuit, and the circuit then copies the program bit-by-bit into the scratch-tape, verifying consistency with the MHT root in each step. See the full version for details.

On the necessity of rewindable ORAM and DEPIR. As a final note, we informally argue that rewindable ORAM is inherent to the construction of RAM-FHE, by explaining how to construct ISR/ASR-ORAM from single-hop/multi-hop RAM-FHE. To initialize the ORAM with a database D, the client generates a random encryption-decryption key pair, encrypts D using the encryption key, and stores the ciphertext $\widehat{D}$ on the server. To execute a RAM program P on D, the client homomorphically evaluates P on $\widehat{D}$ by accessing all relevant bits of $\widehat{D}$ remotely on the server. Finally, the client decrypts the computation output using the decryption key. These ORAM access patterns reveal nothing about the database because the RAM-FHE scheme is semantically secure.[5] If we use multi-hop RAM-FHE then we can sequentially execute many programs and rewind to any intermediate state; semantic security still ensures that the access patterns

---

[4] We note that if an a-priori bound on the scratch tape size is known during encryption, then in the single-hop setting the scratch tape can be included as part of the encrypted database, since any updates to the database during execution are anyway lost when the execution ends.

[5] More formally, there is a discrepancy since the access pattern of homomorphic evaluation, though revealing nothing about D, may reveal something about P. To prevent this, we can append an encryption secret key sk to the database D, and execute a program $\widetilde{P}$ in which P's code is encrypted under sk, where $\widetilde{P}$ first decrypts P and then executes it over D. This way, the access pattern of the FHE evaluation cannot reveal anything about neither P nor D.

reveal nothing about the underlying database, so we obtain ASR-ORAM. If we use a single-hop RAM-FHE, the ORAM only allows for the execution of a single program before rewinding to the initial state, so we only get ISR-ORAM. As discussed above, SK-DEPIR can be thought of as a read-only ISR-ORAM, so RAM-FHE also implies SK-DEPIR.

1.3 Related Work

Supporting RAM computations directly, without first representing the RAM program as a circuit, has been considered for several cryptographic primitives.

Similar to RAM-FHE, Garbled RAM [LO13, GHL+14] (also known as private RAM delegation) allows a user to garble a database D, following which an evaluator can run RAM computations on the garbled D. (There are also works on non-private RAM delegation, e.g., [KP16].) However, in garbled RAM the evaluator can only compute specific RAM programs P which the garbler generated. Similar to RAM-FHE, the size of the garbled program, and the garbling and evaluation times, are proportional to P's running time. There has been a large body of works on garbled RAM, improving its efficiency, underlying assumptions, properties, and applications [GLOS, CHJV15, CH16, CCHR16, ACC+16, BCP, CCC+, Mia16, GGMP16, HY16, LO17, GOS18]. Succinct garbled RAMs together with iO for circuits also imply indistinguishability Obfuscation (iO) for RAMs [CHJV15, BCG+18].

Functional Encryption (FE) for RAMs, namely an FE scheme in which the master secret key can be used to generate function keys for *RAM programs*, was studied in [AIT16, GHRW, BCG+18]. These constructions are not function-private, and [AIT16] additionally do not hide the access pattern of the RAM program (which, as discussed in Sect. 1.2, seems to be a central difficulty in constructing RAM-FHE).

The notion of FHE for Turing machines was considered in [GKP+a], who construct FHE schemes with *input-specific* running time during evaluation. However, the runtime is still at least linear in the database size, whereas RAM-FHE evaluation time may be sublinear in the database size (if the original RAM program runs in sublinear time). Moreover, their model is somewhat restricted in that the Turing machine and its input are encrypted together (so one cannot execute arbitrary Turing machines on the input).

2   Preliminaries

Throughout this paper, λ denotes a security parameter. We use $\mathsf{poly}\,(\lambda)$ and $\mathsf{negl}\,(\lambda)$ to denote unspecified functions that are polynomial and negligible in λ, respectively. We use standard cryptographic definitions of one-way functions (OWFs), pseudorandom functions (PRFs), collision-resistant hash functions (CRHFs), and message authentication codes (MACs) (see, e.g., [Gol01, Gol04]). For a randomized algorithm A with n inputs, we use $A\,(x_1, \ldots, x_n; r)$ to denote the output of A on inputs $x_1, \ldots, x_n$ when it uses randomness r. We use $\approx$ to denote computational indistinguishability.

We use PPT to refer to probabilistic polynomial-time algorithms, and non-uniform PPT to refer to (ensembles of) polynomial-sized probabilistic circuits. We use the notion of Virtual Black Box (VBB) obfuscation with auxiliary input (see the full version [HHWW]).

2.1 Doubly-Efficient Private Information Retreival (DEPIR)

Definition 1 (Secret-Key Doubly-Efficient PIR (SK-DEPIR) [CHR17, BIPW17]). *A secret-key doubly-efficient PIR (SK-DEPIR) scheme consists of procedures* (KeyGen, Process, Query, Decode) *where* KeyGen, Process, Query *are randomized and* Decode *is deterministic, with the following syntax:*

- KeyGen (1^λ) *takes as input a security parameter λ, and outputs a client secret-key* sk.
- Process $(\mathsf{sk}, \mathsf{DB})$ *takes as input a client secret-key* sk *and a database* $\mathsf{DB} \in \{0,1\}^N$, *and outputs a processed database* $\widetilde{\mathsf{DB}} \in \{0,1\}^{\tilde{N}}$.
- Query $(\mathsf{sk}, \mathsf{addr})$ *takes as input a client secret-key* sk *and an address* $\mathsf{addr} \in [N]$, *and outputs a set* $\mathcal{Q} \subseteq \left[\tilde{N} \right]$ *of queries, and a temporary state* st.
- Decode $\left(\mathsf{sk}, \mathsf{st}, \left\{ \widetilde{\mathsf{DB}}_i \ : \ i \in \mathcal{Q} \right\} \right)$ *takes as input a secret key* sk, *a temporary state* st, *and a set of values from the processed database* $\left\{ \widetilde{\mathsf{DB}}_i \ : \ i \in \mathcal{Q} \right\}$, *and outputs a value* val.

We require that the scheme satisfies the following properties:

- **Correctness:** *for every* $N \in \mathbb{N}$, *every* $\mathsf{DB} \in \{0,1\}^N$, *and every* $\mathsf{addr} \in [N]$, *it holds that:*

$$\Pr\left[\mathsf{Decode}\left(\mathsf{sk}, \mathsf{st}, \left\{ \widetilde{\mathsf{DB}}_i \ : \ i \in \mathcal{Q} \right\} \right) = \mathsf{DB}_i \ : \ \begin{array}{l} \mathsf{sk} \leftarrow \mathsf{KeyGen}\left(1^\lambda \right) \\ \widetilde{\mathsf{DB}} \leftarrow \mathsf{Process}\left(\mathsf{sk}, \mathsf{DB} \right) \\ (\mathcal{Q}, \mathsf{st}) \leftarrow \mathsf{Query}\left(\mathsf{sk}, \mathsf{addr} \right) \end{array} \right] = 1$$

- **Security:** *Any non-uniform PPT adversary $\mathcal{A}$ has only* $\mathsf{negl}\left(\lambda \right)$ *advantage in the following security game with a challenger $\mathcal{C}$:*
  1. *$\mathcal{A}$ sends to $\mathcal{C}$ a database* $\mathsf{DB} \in \{0,1\}^N$.
  2. *$\mathcal{C}$ picks a random bit $b \leftarrow \{0,1\}$, and runs* $\mathsf{sk} \leftarrow \mathsf{KeyGen}\left(1^\lambda \right)$ *to obtain a client secret-key* sk, *and then runs* $\widetilde{\mathsf{DB}} \leftarrow \mathsf{Process}\left(\mathsf{sk}, \mathsf{DB} \right)$ *to obtain a processed database* $\widetilde{\mathsf{DB}}$, *which it sends to $\mathcal{A}$.*
  3. *$\mathcal{A}$ selects two addresses* $\mathsf{addr}^0, \mathsf{addr}^1 \in [N]$, *and sends* $(\mathsf{addr}^0, \mathsf{addr}^1)$ *to $\mathcal{C}$.*
  4. *$\mathcal{C}$ samples* $(Q, \mathsf{st}) \leftarrow \mathsf{Query}(\mathsf{sk}, \mathsf{addr}^b)$, *and sends Q to $\mathcal{A}$.*
  5. *Steps 3 and 4 are repeated an arbitrary (polynomial) number of times.*
  6. *$\mathcal{A}$ outputs a bit b', and his advantage in the game is defined to be* $\Pr[b = b'] - \frac{1}{2}$.

- **Efficiency.** *The runtime of* KeyGen *is* poly (λ), *the runtime of* Process *is* poly (N, λ), *and the runtime of* Query, Decode *is* $o(N) \cdot$ poly (λ), *where N is the database size.*

We will need a SK-DEPIR scheme with the additional guarantee that preprocessing is oblivious of the database contents. We note that both the SK-DEPIR constructions of [CHR17, BIPW17] satisfy this guarantee.

Definition 2 (Security with oblivious preprocessing). *We say that a SK-DEPIR scheme is* secure with oblivious preprocessing *if the security property of Definition 1 holds even when in Step 2 above, the adversary is given the sequence of memory accesses (including which address was accessed, whether it was read or written, and what value was written) performed during the execution of* Process (sk, DB).

Remark on existence of SK-DEPIR schemes with specific parameters and oblivious preprocessing. The works [BIPW17, CHR17] prove that under a new assumption on noisy Reed-Muller codes, there exist SK-DEPIR schemes with either of the following parameters for databases of size N and security parameter λ:

- **Sublinear SK-DEPIR:** For any $\epsilon > 0$, the running time of Process can be $N^{1+\epsilon} \cdot$ poly (λ), and the running time of Query and Decode can be $N^{\epsilon} \cdot$ poly (λ).
- **Polylog SK-DEPIR:** The running time of Process can be poly (λ, N), and the running time of Query and Decode can be poly $(\lambda, \log N)$.

We note that both of these schemes have oblivious preprocessing. Indeed, in these constructions Process randomly permutes a (noisy) Reed-Muller encoding of an encryption of the database. The encoding is data-oblivious since it is applied to ciphertexts, and using oblivious sorting algorithms the permuting operation can also be done obliviously.

3   Rewindable Oblivious RAM

We define two ORAM variants which guarantee security against rewinding attacks. The two notions differ in the type of attacks they can handle. We first recall the notion of an access pattern, and the standard ORAM definition [Gol87, Ost90, GO96].

Notation 1 (Access pattern). A length-q *access pattern* Q consists of a list $(\mathsf{op}_l, \mathsf{val}_l, \mathsf{addr}_l)_{1 \leq l \leq q}$ of instructions, where instruction $(\mathsf{op}_l, \mathsf{val}_l, \mathsf{addr}_l)$ denotes that the client performs operation $\mathsf{op}_l \in \{\mathtt{read}, \mathtt{write}\}$ at address addr_l with value val_l (which, if $\mathsf{op}_l = \mathtt{read}$, is $\bot$).

Informally, an ORAM scheme allows a client to store his database, or "logical memory", remotely on a server, or "physical memory". Following a Setup procedure which generates client and server states, reads and writes to logical memory are performed through an interactive protocol Access between the client and server, where in each round the client generates a read request and an update request for the server. The access pattern to physical memory during the Access protocol completely hides from the server the database contents and access pattern to logical memory (see the full version for the formal definition).

3.1 Rewindable ORAM Security

We now describe a game that formalizes the security of our ORAM variants. The adversarial server in the game chooses a pair of initial databases, and (as in standard ORAM) two sequences of access patterns, with the goal of distinguishing between the executions of these sequences on the two databases. Unlike standard ORAM, the adversarial server in our security game can also *rewind* the execution to a previous state, and continue the execution from that state.

Definition 3 (Rewindable ORAM security game). *The ORAM security game is run between an adversary $\mathcal{A}$, and a challenger $\mathcal{C}$.*

1. *$\mathcal{A}$ sends to $\mathcal{C}$ two databases $\mathsf{DB}^0, \mathsf{DB}^1 \in \{0,1\}^N$.*
2. *$\mathcal{C}$ picks a random bit $b \leftarrow \{0,1\}$, and runs $\mathsf{Setup}\left(1^\lambda, \mathsf{DB}^b\right)$ to obtain client and server states ck, st. $\mathcal{C}$ sends st to $\mathcal{A}$.*
3. *Let $\mathsf{st}_0 = \mathsf{st}$ and $\mathsf{ck}_0 = \mathsf{ck}$. Repeat the following $\mathrm{poly}(\lambda)$ times, where in the i'th iteration:*
   (a) *$\mathcal{A}$ sends to $\mathcal{C}$ an index $j_i \in \{0, 1, \ldots, i-1\}$, as well as two sequences of instructions $Q_i^0 = \left(\mathsf{op}_{i,l}, \mathsf{addr}_{i,l}^0, \mathsf{val}_{i,l}^0\right)_{l \in [q_i]}$, and $Q_i^1 = \left(\mathsf{op}_{i,l}, \mathsf{addr}_{i,l}^1, \mathsf{val}_{i,l}^1\right)_{l \in [q_i]}$, where $q_i \leq \mathrm{poly}(\lambda)$, $\mathsf{op}_{i,l} \in \{\texttt{read}, \texttt{write}\}$, $\mathsf{addr}_{i,l}^0, \mathsf{addr}_{i,l}^1 \in [N]$, and $\mathsf{val}_{i,l}^0, \mathsf{val}_{i,l}^1 \in \{0,1\}$.*
   (b) *Starting from server state st_{j_i} and client state ck_{j_i}, $\mathcal{C}$ executes $\mathsf{Access}\left(\mathsf{op}_{i,l}, \mathsf{addr}_{i,l}^b, \mathsf{val}_{i,l}^b\right)$ for $1 \leq l \leq q_i$. Let $\mathsf{ck}_i, \mathsf{st}_i$ denote the updated client and server states (respectively) at the end of this sequence of executions. Let $\mathcal{ACC}_i$ denote the access pattern to physical memory during this sequence of Access executions.*
   (c) *$\mathcal{C}$ sends $\mathcal{ACC}_i$ to $\mathcal{A}$.*
4. *$\mathcal{A}$ outputs a bit b', and his advantage in the game is defined as $\Pr[b = b'] - \frac{1}{2}$.*

Discussion. The rewindable ORAM security game of Definition 3 captures several security variants, depending on the permissible choice of j_i. First, notice that the security game with $\mathrm{poly}(\lambda)$ iterations in the security game, when the adversary is restricted to choose $j_i = i - 1$ in each iteration, and $\mathsf{DB}^0 = \mathsf{DB}^1$, yields the standard ORAM security definition without rewinds. Second, restricting the adversary to choose $j_i = \{0, i - 1\}$ in every iteration i means the adversary can only rewind the execution to the initial state, but can adaptively decide to "extend" a previous execution. Restricting the adversary to choose $j_i = 0$ in every iteration corresponds to an adversary that can only rewind the execution to the initial state, where any rewind "finalizes" the current branch of the execution, and the adversary cannot later extend it. In the most general form, when j_i can take any value in $\{0, 1, \ldots, i-1\}$, we can assume without loss of generality that the adversary chooses a length-1 sequence in each iteration of the security game. This corresponds to an adversary that can rewind the ORAM to any intermediate state. The security game of Definition 3 can be used to capture various other security variants; we choose to focus on the latter two notions. Formally,

Definition 4 (Any-State Rewindable ORAM (ASR-ORAM)). *We say that an ORAM scheme is* Any-State Rewindable (ASR) *if any PPT adversary $\mathcal{A}$ has a* negl(λ) *advantage in the rewindable ORAM security game of Definition 3.*

Definition 5 (Initial-State Rewindable ORAM (ISR-ORAM)). *We say that an adversary $\mathcal{A}$ is* initial-state restricted *if in every iteration i of the rewindable ORAM security game of Definition 3, it chooses $j_i = 0$. We say that an ORAM scheme is* Initial-State Rewindable (ISR) *if any initial-state restricted PPT adversary $\mathcal{A}$ has a* negl(λ) *advantage in the rewindable ORAM security game of Definition 3.*

3.2 Rewindable ORAM Constructions

In this section we construct ISR- and ASR-ORAM schemes from SK-DEPIR and standard ORAM schemes. Our ISR-ORAM scheme, despite having a weaker security guarantee than ASR-ORAM, has the advantage of being simpler and more efficient. In the full version [HHWW], we construct an ISR-ORAM scheme from a SK-DEPIR scheme along with an ORAM scheme for initially-empty databases, proving the following:

Theorem 2 (ISR-ORAM). *Assume there exist OWFs and SK-DEPIR. Then there exists an ISR-ORAM scheme.*

Moreover, if the Query *and* Decode *algorithms of the SK-DEPIR scheme have* poly(λ) *complexity for databases of size N and security parameter λ, and the client (resp., server) state has size* poly(λ) *(resp.,* poly(λ, N)), *then the* Access *complexity of the ISR-ORAM is* poly(λ), *and the client (resp., server) state has size* poly(λ) *(*poly(λ, N)*).*

We now construct an ASR-ORAM scheme from SK-DEPIR and PRFs, proving the following (the proof appears in the full version):

Theorem 3 (ASR-ORAM). *Assume the existence of OWFs and SK-DEPIR, then there exists an ASR-ORAM scheme. Moreover, if for $\epsilon > 0$ the* Query *and* Decode *algorithms of the SK-DEPIR scheme have $N^\epsilon \cdot$ poly(λ) complexity, and* Process *has $N^{1+\epsilon} \cdot$ poly(λ) complexity for databases of size N and security parameter λ, then:*

- *The complexity of* Access *is $N^\epsilon \cdot$ poly(λ).*
- *The client state has size* poly(λ), *and the server state has size $N^{1+\epsilon} \cdot$ poly(λ).*

The construction. Recall from Sect. 1.2 that we use a hierarchical structure whose levels contain SK-DEPIR schemes. Since a SK-DEPIR scheme is designed for array structures, we use PRFs to map the data blocks of the level into buckets, thus guaranteeing that a block's location in each level (if it appears in the level) is independent of the access history. To allow for more efficient reshuffles, each level i also contains the (encrypted, unprocessed) database stored in the SK-DEPIR of the level. We note that whenever a level is initialized as part of a reshuffle, we pick new PRF and SK-DEPIR keys for the level. This guarantees security even under rewinds. Indeed, though a SK-DEPIR is rewind-secure, by rewinding the ORAM the adversary may rewind a reshuffle. However, this will result in a completely fresh SK-DEPIR scheme, and therefore doesn't violate security. In the following, we use $\mathsf{B} = \lambda$ to denote the bucket size.

Construction 1 (ASR-ORAM from SK-DEPIR and PRFs). The scheme uses:

- A PRF F.
- A SK-DEPIR scheme (DEPIR.KeyGen, Process, Query, Decode) with oblivious preprocessing (Definition 2).
- A CPA-secure symmetric encryption scheme (SE.KeyGen, Encrypt, Decrypt).

The scheme consists of the following procedures.

Setup(1^λ, DB): Recall that λ denotes the security parameter, and DB $\in \{0,1\}^N$. Let DB′ be the database obtained from DB by concatenating the address to each bit, i.e., entries of DB′ have the form $(\mathsf{addr}, \mathsf{DB_{addr}})$. (This will be needed when blocks are mapped to buckets.) Let $\ell = \log N$, and proceed as follows.

- <u>Counter initialization:</u> initialize a counter count_W to 0. (count_W counts the total number of writes performed so far.)
- <u>Encryption initialization:</u> run $\mathsf{sk} \leftarrow \mathsf{SE.KeyGen}\left(1^\lambda\right)$ to generate a secret-key sk for the encryption scheme.
- <u>PRF and SK-DEPIR key initialization for all levels:</u> for every level $1 \le i \le \ell$, set $\widetilde{K}^i = \widetilde{\mathsf{sk}}^i =\bot$. (Later, $\widetilde{K}^i, \widetilde{\mathsf{sk}}^i$ will contain encryptions of level-specific PRF and SK-DEPIR keys, respectively.)
- <u>Initializing level ℓ:</u> encrypt the database by running DB″ $\leftarrow$ Encrypt $(\mathsf{sk}, \mathsf{DB}')$. Run $\left(\mathsf{DB}'', \widetilde{\mathsf{DB}}, \widetilde{K}^{\ell'}, \widetilde{\mathsf{sk}}^{\ell'}\right) \leftarrow$ InitLevel (ℓ, DB'') (Fig. 1 on page 604) to obtain the processed SK-DEPIR database $\widetilde{\mathsf{DB}}$, and the PRF and SK-DEPIR keys for level ℓ. Initialize level ℓ to be $\mathsf{L}^\ell = \left(\mathsf{DB}'', \widetilde{\mathsf{DB}}\right)$, and all other levels L^i to be empty. Replace $\widetilde{K}^\ell, \widetilde{\mathsf{sk}}^\ell$ with $\widetilde{K}^{\ell'}, \widetilde{\mathsf{sk}}^{\ell'}$, respectively.
- <u>Output:</u> the client state $\mathsf{ck} = \mathsf{sk}$ consists of the encryption key. The server state $\mathsf{st} = \left(\mathsf{count}_W, \left(\mathsf{L}^i, \widetilde{K}^i, \widetilde{\mathsf{sk}}^i\right)_{i \in [\ell]}\right)$ consist of the counter, the contents of all levels, and the (encrypted) PRF and SK-DEPIR keys for all levels (which are currently empty, except for the keys of level ℓ).

The Access protocol. To perform the operation op on location addr $\in [N]$ in the database with value val, the client C with state $\mathsf{ck} = \mathsf{sk}$, and the server with state $\mathsf{st} = \left(\mathsf{count}_W, \left(\mathsf{L}^i, \widetilde{K}^i, \widetilde{\mathsf{sk}}^i \right)_{i \in [\ell]} \right)$ operate as follows.

- **If op $=$ read:**
  - Initialize an output value val' to $\bot$.
  - For every non-empty level i from 1 to ℓ, do:
    * Computing bucket index: read $\widetilde{K}^i, \widetilde{\mathsf{sk}}^i$ from the server, and decrypt $K^i = \mathsf{Decrypt}\left(\mathsf{sk}, \widetilde{K}^i \right), \mathsf{sk}^i = \mathsf{Decrypt}\left(\mathsf{sk}, \widetilde{\mathsf{sk}}^i \right)$. Compute $l = F\left(K^i, \mathsf{addr} \right)$. (If addr appears in level i, it will be in the l'th bucket.)
    * Looking for data block addr in level i: look for block addr in the l'th bucket by running the procedure $\mathsf{ReadBucket}\left(l, i, \mathsf{sk}^i, \mathsf{addr} \right)$ of Fig. 2 to obtain a value val^i. If $\mathsf{val}' \neq \bot$ then set $\mathsf{val}' := \mathsf{val}^i$.
  - Output: output val' to the client.

If op $=$ write:

- Encrypt the data block as $c \leftarrow \mathsf{Encrypt}\left(\mathsf{sk}, (\mathsf{addr}, \mathsf{val}) \right)$, and generate a "dummy" level 0 database which contains a single (encrypted) data block c.
- Update the server state as follows:
  - $\mathsf{count}_W := \mathsf{count}_W + 1$.
  - For $i = 0, 1, \ldots, \ell$ such that 2^i divides count_W, reshuffle level i into level $i + 1$ using the $\mathsf{ReShuffle}$ procedure of Fig. 3, namely executes $\mathsf{ReShuffle}\left(i, \mathsf{L}^i, \mathsf{L}^{i+1} \right)$.[6]

4   Definition of RAM-FHE

We first informally describe the RAM model we work with, which is a simple model of RAM computation that captures their essential efficiency advantage over Turing machines. Specifically, we define RAM machines via a transition circuit δ, with the following functionality. The circuit δ is designed to be evaluated repeatedly in a prescribed way, such that the main output of the i'th evaluation is an operation on one of the RAM machine's tapes, which is either the "persistent" tape containing the database, a volatile work tape which we call the "scratch tape", or the input and output tapes. The main input to δ is the result of the previously outputted operation. Additionally, the circuit δ simulates statefulness by taking as input and producing as output an internal state. We now define single-hop RAM-FHE. (See full version [HHWW] for the formal definition of RAM model and the multi-hop version.)

---

[6] Using a technique of Ostrovsky and Shoup [OS97], these operations can be spread-out over multiple **write** operations. We analyze the scheme below assuming the reshuffle operations are indeed spread-out across all **write** operations.

Definition 6 (Single-hop RAM FHE). *A* public-key (single-hop) RAM FHE *scheme is a tuple of PPT^7 algorithms (*KeyGen, Enc, Dec, Eval*) such that:*

- *Syntax.*
    - KeyGen (1^λ) *takes as input a security parameter λ, and outputs public and secret keys* pk, sk.

The InitLevel procedure

<u>Constant:</u> the encryption key sk, and the security parameter λ.

<u>Inputs:</u>

i: the index of the level to initialize.

DB^i: a size-2^i database DB^i encrypted using Encrypt (sk, $\cdot$).

<u>Operation:</u>

1. Pick a (fresh) random PRF key $K^{i\prime}$ for level i, generate a (fresh) SK-DEPIR key $sk^{i\prime} \leftarrow$ DEPIR.KeyGen (1^λ) for level i, and encrypt the keys by running $\widetilde{K}^{i\prime} \leftarrow$ Encrypt $(sk, K^{i\prime})$, $\widetilde{sk}^{i\prime} \leftarrow$ Encrypt $(sk, sk^{i\prime})$.

2. Generate 2^i buckets, each with B "empty" blocks,[a] and encrypt the bucket contents using Encrypt.

3. Randomly and obliviously permute DB^i using the Fisher-Yates shuffle, to obtain a permuted database $\widehat{DB}^i$. In each step of the shuffle, the blocks touched during that step are re-encrypted. (That is, if a step of the shuffle touches blocks i, j then these blocks are downloaded from the server, decrypted, encrypted with fresh randomness, and then uploaded to the server again, in the correct order as determined by the shuffle.)

4. Insert $\widehat{DB}^i$ into the buckets as follows. For every $1 \le j \le 2^i$, compute the index l of the bucket into which block j is mapped, as follows:
    - If block j is "empty", then pick l at random from 2^i.
    - Otherwise, let addr be the logical address of block j (recall that each block contains its logical address). Set $l = F\left(K^{i\prime}, \text{addr}\right)$.

    Insert block j into bucket l by downloading the entire bucket l from the server, decrypting all blocks in the bucket, replacing the first "empty" block with block j, encrypting each block in the bucket, and reloading the bucket to the server.[b]

5. Run Process $(sk^{i\prime}, L)$ to obtain a processed database $\widetilde{DB}^i$, and output $\left(DB^i, \widehat{DB}^i, \widetilde{K}^{i\prime}, \widetilde{sk}^{i\prime}\right)$.

---

[a] See remark on physical memory block contents in full version for a discussion of empty blocks.

[b] To obtain perfect correctness, if a bucket overflows then the contents of the level are stored "in the clear" (i.e., the block encryptions are stored in an array). As we show in the full version, this happens with negligible probability.

Fig. 1. The InitLevel procedure used in Construction 1

---

[7] In fact, in our construction Eval and Dec are deterministic.

The ReadBucket procedure

Input:

l: the index of the bucket to read.
i: the index of the level in which the bucket resides.
sk^i: the secret key of the SK-DEPIR of level i.
addr: the address of the block to read.

Operation: recall that B denotes the bucket size.

- Initialize an output value val to $\bot$.
- For every $(l-1) \cdot \mathsf{B} + 1 \leq m \leq l \cdot \mathsf{B}$:
  - Run $\mathsf{Query}\left(\mathsf{sk}^i, m\right)$ to obtain queries Q and a short-term client state st_C, send Q to S, and obtains answers $\{a_j\}_{j \in Q}$.
  - Run $\mathsf{Decode}\left(\mathsf{sk}^i, \mathsf{st}_C, \{a_j\}_{j \in Q}\right)$ to obtain value $(\mathsf{addr}^m, \mathsf{val}^m)$.
  - If $\mathsf{addr}^m = \mathsf{addr}$ then set $\mathsf{val} := \mathsf{val}^m$.
- Output val.

Fig. 2. The ReadBucket procedure used in Construction 1

- $\mathsf{Enc}\left(\mathsf{pk}, D, 1^B\right)$ *takes as input a pubic key* pk, *a database* D, *and a bound* B *on the description size of RAM machines. It outputs a database-ciphertext* $\hat{D}$. *For improved efficiency, it may also take as input a bound* s *(in unary) on the space usage of the RAM machines for which homomorphic evaluation will be supported.*
- $\mathsf{Eval}\left(M, x, 1^T\right)$ *takes as input a description* M *of a RAM machine, an input* x, *and a running time bound* T, *and is given read/write random-access to a database-ciphertext* $\hat{D}$. Eval *outputs an output-ciphertext* $\hat{y}$, *and may also change the contents of* $\hat{D}$ *to some new value* $\hat{D}'$. *We write* $(\hat{y}, \hat{D}') = \mathsf{Eval}^{\hat{D}}(M, x, 1^T)$.
- $\mathsf{Dec}\left(\mathsf{sk}, \hat{y}\right)$ *takes as input a secret key* sk *and an output-ciphertext* $\hat{y}$, *and outputs a plaintext message* y.
- **Correctness.** *For any security parameter* λ, *any size bound* B, *any RAM machine* M *satisfying* $|M| \leq B$, *any database* $D \in \{0,1\}^*$, *any input* x, *and any* $T \in \mathbb{Z}^+$ *with* $\mathsf{Time}(M, x, D) \leq T$, *in the probability space defined by sampling*

$$
\begin{aligned}
&(\mathsf{pk}, \mathsf{sk}) \leftarrow \mathsf{KeyGen}(1^\lambda) \\
&\hat{D} \leftarrow \mathsf{Enc}(\mathsf{pk}, D, 1^B) \\
&\left(\hat{y}, \hat{D}'\right) := \mathsf{Eval}^{\hat{D}}(M, x, 1^T) \\
&(y, D') := M^D(x) \\
&y' := \mathsf{Dec}(\mathsf{sk}, \hat{y}),
\end{aligned}
\tag{1}
$$

it holds that $y = y'$ *except with* $\mathsf{negl}\,(\lambda)$ *probability.*

The ReShuffle procedure

<u>Constant:</u> the encryption key sk.

<u>Inputs:</u>

i: the index of a level to reshuffle.

$\left(\mathsf{DB}^j, \widetilde{\mathsf{DB}}^j\right), j \in \{i, i+1\}$: the databases DB^j (encrypted with $\mathsf{Encrypt}\,(\mathsf{sk}, \cdot)$), and the processed databases $\widetilde{\mathsf{DB}}^j$, of levels $i, i+1$.

<u>Operation:</u>

1. For $j \in \{i, i+1\}$, if DB^j is empty (because it was not initialized yet, or following a previous reshuffle), instantiate DB^j with 2^j "empty" blocks, encrypted with $\mathsf{Encrypt}\,(\mathsf{sk}, \cdot)$. (See full version for a discussion of empty blocks.)
2. For $j \in \{i, i+1\}$, perform a linear scan of DB^j, concatenating encryptions of the label "$j - i$" to all blocks. (That is, level-i blocks are given label 0, and blocks from level $i + 1$ are given label 1.)
3. Let A be the array of size $\left(2^i + 2^{i+1}\right)$ obtained by concatenating $\mathsf{DB}^i, \mathsf{DB}^{i+1}$.
4. Obliviously sort A according to block addresses, breaking ties using the labels created in Step 2. Each touched block is re-encrypted before being uploaded to the server. (After this step, duplicate block copies appear consecutively, and the copy from level i appears first.)
5. Perform a linear scan over A, replacing all duplicate blocks with "empty" blocks, and updating the labels (created in Step 2) of all non-duplicate blocks to 0. This is done as follows: the client locally stores the address of the previous block in A (initialized to 0). When traversing the current block, if its address is the same as the previous block, then replace the block with an "empty" block with label 1, otherwise update the block label to 0. Each block is re-encrypted before being uploaded to the server.
6. Obliviously sort A according to the labels, breaking ties according to block addresses. Each touched block is re-encrypted before being uploaded to the server. (After this step, real blocks appear before "empty" blocks.)
7. Perform a linear scan over A, removing the labels. Truncate A to size 2^{i+1}. (Notice that the truncated A still contains the freshest version of all blocks from $\mathsf{DB}^i, \mathsf{DB}^{i+1}$.)
8. Run the procedure $\left(\mathsf{DB}^{i+1\prime}, \widetilde{\mathsf{DB}}^{i+1\prime}, \widetilde{K}^{i+1\prime}\widetilde{\mathsf{sk}}^{i+1\prime}\right) \leftarrow \mathsf{InitLevel}\,(i+1, A)$ of Figure 1 to obtain the processed database $\widetilde{\mathsf{DB}}^{i+1\prime}$ of level $i + 1$, and fresh (encrypted) PRF and SK-DEPIR keys $\widetilde{K}^{i+1\prime}, \widetilde{\mathsf{sk}}^{i+1\prime}$ (respectively). Replace $\widetilde{K}^{i+1}, \widetilde{\mathsf{sk}}^{i+1}$ with $\widetilde{K}^{i+1\prime}, \widetilde{\mathsf{sk}}^{i+1\prime}$ (respectively). Update level i to be empty $\mathsf{L}^i = \perp$, and level $i + 1$ to $\mathsf{L}_{i+1} = \left(\mathsf{DB}^{i+1\prime}, \widetilde{\mathsf{DB}}^{i+1\prime}\right)$.

Fig. 3. The ReShuffle protocol used in Construction 1

- **IND-CPA Security.** *For all non-uniform PPT* $\mathcal{A}_0$ *and* $\mathcal{A}_1$, *there is a negligible function* negl *such that for every security parameter* λ,

$$\Pr\left[b' = b \ : \ \begin{array}{r} (\mathsf{pk}, \mathsf{sk}) \leftarrow \mathsf{KeyGen}(1^\lambda) \\ (\mathsf{st}, D_0, D_1, 1^B) := \mathcal{A}_0(\mathsf{pk}) \\ b \leftarrow \{0,1\} \\ \hat{D} \leftarrow \mathsf{Enc}(\mathsf{pk}, D_b, B) \\ b' := \mathcal{A}_1(\mathsf{st}, \hat{D}) \end{array} \right] \leq \frac{1}{2} + \mathsf{negl}(\lambda).$$

- $\eta\,(|D|)$**-Efficiency.** *With probability* 1, *the running time of* Eval *in the experiment described in Eq.* (1) *is at most* $T \cdot \eta\,(|D|) \cdot \mathsf{poly}\,(B, \lambda)$.
- **Compactness.** *In the experiment described in Eq.* (1), $|\hat{y}| \leq \mathsf{poly}(\log |\mathcal{Y}|, \lambda)$.

Remark 1. We note that when Enc is executed with the additional space-bound parameter s, then correctness holds for every RAM machine M whose volatile tape throughout the execution has size at most s, and the adversary in the security game is also allowed to choose s.

5 Road Map Towards Constructing RAM-FHE

As described in Sect. 1.2, the encryption of a database D consists of the server state in a rewindable ORAM for D, together with a VBB obfuscation of the circuit that emulates a single execution step of the rewindable ORAM client. Formalizing this idea requires two steps. First, we need to emulate a *consistent* client state throughout the execution (because the ORAM client is stateful, while the obfuscated circuit is not), as well as guarantee semi-honest emulation of the ORAM server. This covers steps (1) and (3) from Sect. 1.2. Second, we need to hide the ORAM client state from the evaluator, using pseudorandom bits for encryption, which was described as steps (2) and (5) in Sect. 1.2. We obtain both of these using a new abstraction which we call a **database-dependent RAM-VBB obfuscator** (Sect. 5.1) in which, informally, the obfuscator takes as input not only a database D, but also a *specific* RAM machine M, and the evaluator can run M on different inputs x with RAM access to (the mutable) D. We provide two constructions (Sect. 5.2) to handle each of the issues described above. We obtain the RAM-FHE by applying the RAM-VBB obfuscator to the universal RAM machine (which takes as input a description M of a RAM machine, and an input x for it, and outputs $M^D(x)$, where D is the database), that additionally encrypts its output using a PKE scheme (step (4) in Sect. 1.2).

5.1 Database-Dependent RAM-VBB Obfuscation

We define two notions of RAM-VBB obfuscation, in which the RAM machine is obfuscated with relation to a specific database. These notions, which we call *database-dependent* RAM-VBB, provide weaker security than RAM-FHE, and incomparable correctness. We note that though such obfuscation is unlikely to exist in general, similar to circuit-VBB obfuscation it might exist for restricted ensembles of RAM machines, and in particular might exist for the *specific* ensemble we consider in this work.

Informally, the obfuscator $\mathcal{O}$ is parameterized by an ensemble $\mathcal{M} = \{\mathcal{M}_N\}_N$ of classes of RAM programs. It takes as input not only a database $D_0 \in \{0,1\}^N$, but also a RAM machine $M \in \mathcal{M}_N$. The evaluator is able to compute $M^D(x)$ for any input x and any database D that is either D_0 or was obtained by a previous execution of M. Formally,

Definition 7 (Database-dependent RAM-VBB obfuscator). *Let $n \in \mathbb{N}$ be an input length, $N \leq 2^\lambda$ be a database size, and $\mathcal{M} = \{\mathcal{M}_N\}_N$ be an ensemble of classes of RAM programs. A* database-dependent RAM-VBB obfuscator *for $\mathcal{M}$ is an algorithm $\mathcal{O}$ that takes as input a security parameter 1^λ, a database $D_0 \in \{0,1\}^N$, and a RAM machine $M \in \mathcal{M}_N$. It outputs a database $\widetilde{D}_0$, a RAM machine $\widetilde{M}$, and some auxiliary input $\mathcal{I}_0$ for $\widetilde{M}$. We require that $\mathcal{O}$ satisfies the following requirements:*

- **Correctness.** *For every $n, k, N \in \mathbb{N}$, every $M \in \mathcal{M}_N$, every database $D_0 \in \{0,1\}^N$, and every inputs $x_1, \dots, x_m \in \{0,1\}^n$, the following two experiments yield the same values of $(y_1, \dots, y_m) \in \left(\{0,1\}^k\right)^m$ except with $\mathsf{negl}\,(\lambda)$ probability.*

$$(\widetilde{D}_0, \widetilde{M}, \mathcal{I}_0) \leftarrow \mathcal{O}(1^\lambda, D_0, M)$$
$$(y_1, \widetilde{D}_1, \mathcal{I}_1) \leftarrow \widetilde{M}^{\widetilde{D}_0}(x_1, \mathcal{I}_0)$$
$$\dots$$
$$(y_m, \widetilde{D}_m, \mathcal{I}_m) \leftarrow \widetilde{M}^{\widetilde{D}_{m-1}}(x_m, \mathcal{I}_{m-1})$$

and

$$(y_1, D_1) \leftarrow M^{D_0}(x_1)$$
$$\dots \tag{2}$$
$$(y_m, D_m) \leftarrow M^{D_{m-1}}(x_m)$$

- **Efficiency.** *In the above experiments, it holds that*

$$\mathsf{Time}(\widetilde{M}, (x_i, \mathcal{I}_{i-1}), \widetilde{D}_{i-1}) \leq \mathsf{Time}(M, x_i, D_{i-1}) \cdot \mathsf{poly}(|M|, \lambda)$$

where $|M|$ denotes the combined length of the internal state and the description of M.

We define two security notions for database-dependent RAM-VBB obfuscation. The first, which we call transcript-simulatable, is roughly that any adversary (with single-bit output) given an obfuscation of (D_0, M) is simulatable given only the execution trace (see full version [HHWW] for definition), namely given oracle access to the function that takes a sequence of inputs $x_1, \dots, x_d$, and returns the operations performed by M when sequentially executed (i.e., with a mutable database D that is initially D_0 but persists across executions) on the inputs $x_1, \dots, x_d$. The second security property, which we call address simulatable, is stronger since it gives the simulator less information. Specifically, the simulator no longer sees the entire computation transcripts but instead sees only the *addresses* of the physical memory which are operated on, the *type* (read or write) of memory operation, and the outcome of the computation. The simulator does *not* see the *values* read from/written to memory, or the contents D_0 of the initial database, but instead sees only its size $|D_0|$. These definitions appear in the full version [HHWW]. We abbreviate transcript/address-simulatable database-dependent RAM-VBB as transcript/address-simulatable RAM-VBB.

5.2 Database-Dependent RAM-VBB Obfuscation: Constructions

In this section we construct (single-hop) transcript-simulatable and address-simulatable RAM-VBB obfuscators. These will be used in Sect. 6 to construct a RAM-FHE scheme.

In the single hop setting, we can assume without loss of generality that the database is read-only, since database updates can be emulated in the scratch tape, causing a multiplicative factor-2 increase in the scratch tape size, and the number of **read** accesses. Therefore, we can (by performing dummy accesses if needed) assume without impact that every execution step performs a single **read** from the database and scratch tape, and a single **write** to the scratch tape.

We now construct a single-hop transcript-simulatable RAM-VBB obfuscator (see full version for a multi-hop variant). The high level idea is to use MACs and Merkle hash trees to enforce consistent execution, and to obfuscate the transition circuit (computing the transition function δ of the RAM machine) which has the MAC key hard-wired into it. This intuition is formalized in the next construction. In the full version [HHWW], we prove the following construction is a transcript Simulatable RAM-VBB obfuscator.

Construction 2 (Transcript-simulatable RAM-VBB obfuscation). The transcript-simulatable RAM-VBB obfuscator $\mathcal{O}_{\text{trans}}$ uses:

- A family $\mathcal{H}$ of hash functions.
- A MAC scheme (KeyGen, Tag, Verify), in which Tag, Verify are deterministic (this assumption is without loss of generality).
- A circuit obfuscator $\mathcal{O}$.

Given a security parameter λ, a database D_0, and a RAM machine M, $\mathcal{O}_{\text{trans}}$:

- Generates a random MAC key $K_{\text{MAC}} \leftarrow \text{KeyGen}\left(1^\lambda\right)$, and picks a description of a hash function $h \leftarrow \mathcal{H}$.
- Generate a MHT MT for D_0, and let Rt denote its root.
- Let st_M denote the initial state of the RAM machine M, set $\text{st} = (\text{true}, \text{st}_M, \text{Rt})$, and pad st with zeros to have the same size as st in Fig. 4. (The boolean value true in st indicates that the execution hasn't started yet.) $\mathcal{O}_{\text{trans}}$ generates a tag $\sigma = \text{Tag}\left(K_{\text{MAC}}, (\text{false}, \text{st})\right)$. (The signature is on the state st, as well as a boolean variable b_{fin} indicating whether the execution has already terminated.)
- Runs the obfuscator $\widetilde{C} \leftarrow \mathcal{O}\left(1^\lambda, C_{\text{Exec}}\right)$ to obfuscate the circuit C_{Exec} described in Fig. 5, with the constants described in Fig. 4 hard-wired into it.

- Outputs $\left(\mathsf{MT}, M_{\mathsf{wrap}}, \mathcal{I} = \left(\mathsf{st}, \sigma, \widetilde{C}\right)\right)$, where M_{wrap} is the RAM machine described in Fig. 6.

The constants and inputs used in the circuit C_{Exec} of Figure 5

Constants: a description h of a CRHF, and a key K_{MAC} for a MAC scheme.

Inputs:

$x \in \{0,1\}^n$: an input for the RAM machine M.

b_{fin}: a boolean variable indicating whether the computation has already terminated.

$\mathsf{st} = (b_{\mathsf{first}}, \mathsf{st}_M, \mathsf{Rt}, \mathsf{Rt}_{\mathsf{hist}}, \mathcal{P}_{\mathsf{hist}}, \mathsf{addr}_{\mathsf{DB}}, \mathsf{addr}_{\mathsf{stape}}, \mathsf{addr}_w, \mathsf{val}_w, x')$: an internal state st, consisting of: a boolean variable b_{first} indicating whether this is the first operation, the internal state st_M of a RAM machine, the root Rt for a MHT MT for a database, the root $\mathsf{Rt}_{\mathsf{hist}}$ of a MHT $\mathsf{MT}_{\mathsf{hist}}$ of the history of accesses performed so far, and the path $\mathcal{P}_{\mathsf{hist}}$ to the right-most (i.e., last) node in $\mathsf{MT}_{\mathsf{hist}}$, addresses $\mathsf{addr}_{\mathsf{DB}}, \mathsf{addr}_{\mathsf{stape}}$ read from the database and scratch tape (respectively) in the previous execution step, the value val_w written in the last execution step to address addr_w of the scratch tape, and an input x' for M.

σ: a MAC tag for $(b_{\mathsf{fin}}, \mathsf{st})$.

$\mathsf{val}_{\mathsf{DB}}, \mathsf{val}_{\mathsf{stape}}$: the values at locations $\mathsf{addr}_{\mathsf{DB}}, \mathsf{addr}_{\mathsf{stape}}$ (respectively) in the database and scratch tape, respectively.

$\mathcal{P}_{\mathsf{DB}}, \mathcal{P}_{\mathsf{stape}}, \mathcal{P}_w$: the paths of nodes $\mathsf{addr}_{\mathsf{DB}}, \mathsf{addr}_{\mathsf{stape}}, \mathsf{addr}_w$ (respectively) in MT.

Fig. 4. Description of the constants and inputs of C_{Exec}

In full version [HHWW], we construct an address-simulatable RAM-VBB obfuscator from a transcript-simulatable RAM-VBB obfuscator. The high level idea is to apply the transcript-simulatable VBB obfuscator to a RAM program M that has a hard-wired encryption key, which the transition circuit uses to encrypt the internal state. One issue that arises is how to generate randomness for encryption, when M cannot toss coins. This is done by applying a PRF to the current execution state. We also include a counter in the internal state to guarantee that the states are unique throughout the execution.

6 A RAM-FHE Scheme

In this section we describe our single-hop RAM-FHE scheme, which uses an address-simulatable RAM-VBB as a building block. We assume that (polynomial) a-priori bounds on the input, output, and description lengths of the RAM machine are known. In the full version [HHWW], we discuss extensions to the general setting (in which no such bounds are a-priori known) and how we upgrade the scheme to a multi-hop scheme. Concretely, we prove (in the full version) the following theorem:

The execution circuit C_{Exec}

<u>Constants and inputs:</u> as described in Figure 4.

1. **Verify input consistency:** verify that $\mathsf{Verify}\,(K_{\mathsf{MAC}}, (b_{\mathsf{fin}}, \mathsf{st}), \sigma) = 1$. If $b_{\mathsf{first}} = \mathsf{false}$ then verify additionally that:
   (a) $\mathcal{P}_{\mathsf{DB}}, \mathcal{P}_{\mathsf{stape}}, \mathcal{P}_w$ are paths to the nodes $\mathsf{addr}_{\mathsf{DB}}, \mathsf{addr}_{\mathsf{stape}}, \mathsf{addr}_w$ in the MHT whose root is Rt, and the values at $\mathsf{addr}_{\mathsf{DB}}, \mathsf{addr}_{\mathsf{stape}}$ are $\mathsf{val}_{\mathsf{DB}}, \mathsf{val}_{\mathsf{stape}}$ (respectively).
   (b) $\mathcal{P}_{\mathsf{hist}}$ is the path to the right-most node in the MHT whose root is $\mathsf{Rt}_{\mathsf{hist}}$.
   (c) $x' = x$. (Verifying the same input is used throughout the execution.)
   If any of these checks fail, output **abort**.
2. **Updating database MHT:** if $b_{\mathsf{first}} = \mathsf{false}$, use $\mathcal{P}_w$ to compute the root Rt' of the MHT obtained from MT by replacing the value of the node addr_w with val_w.
3. **Emulating next transition step:**
   (a) Execute the next command of M, as described in st_M (which indicates which command is next), by applying the transition function δ using $\mathsf{val}_{\mathsf{DB}}, \mathsf{val}_{\mathsf{stape}}$ as the values obtained from the last command executed. (If $b_{\mathsf{first}} = \mathsf{true}$ then $\mathsf{val}_{\mathsf{DB}}, \mathsf{val}_{\mathsf{stape}}$ are not needed and are therefore ignored.) The execution results in an updated internal state st'_M of M (i.e., the state outputted by the transition circuit).
   (b) If M terminated in the current step with output y, then set $b_{\mathsf{fin}} = \mathsf{true}$ and $\mathsf{out} = (b_{\mathsf{fin}}, y)$, and go to Step 5.
   (c) Otherwise, the execution step results in accesses $\mathsf{addr}'_{\mathsf{DB}}, \mathsf{addr}'_{\mathsf{stape}}, (\mathsf{addr}'_w, \mathsf{val}'_w)$ reading addresses $\mathsf{addr}'_{\mathsf{DB}}, \mathsf{addr}'_{\mathsf{stape}}$ from the database and scratch tape (respectively), and writing value val'_w to address addr'_w in the scratch tape. Set $b_{\mathsf{fin}} = \mathsf{false}$.
4. **Updating history and state:** set $\mathsf{leaves} = (\mathsf{val}_{\mathsf{DB}}, \mathsf{val}_{\mathsf{stape}}, \mathsf{addr}'_{\mathsf{DB}}, \mathsf{addr}'_{\mathsf{stape}}, \mathsf{addr}'_w, \mathsf{val}'_w)$. If $b_{\mathsf{first}} = \mathsf{false}$, use $\mathcal{P}_{\mathsf{hist}}$ to compute the root $\mathsf{Rt}'_{\mathsf{hist}}$ of the MHT $\mathsf{MT}'_{\mathsf{hist}}$ obtained from $\mathsf{MT}_{\mathsf{hist}}$ by adding the leaves leaves. If $b_{\mathsf{first}} = \mathsf{true}$, set $b_{\mathsf{first}} = \mathsf{false}$ and generate a (new) MHT $\mathsf{MT}'_{\mathsf{hist}}$ for leaves (see remark on page 28). In either case, let $\mathcal{P}'_{\mathsf{hist}}$ be the path to the right-most node in $\mathsf{MT}'_{\mathsf{hist}}$, and set $\mathsf{st}' = (b_{\mathsf{first}}, \mathsf{st}'_M, \mathsf{Rt}', \mathsf{Rt}'_{\mathsf{hist}}, \mathcal{P}'_{\mathsf{hist}}, \mathsf{addr}'_{\mathsf{DB}}, \mathsf{addr}'_{\mathsf{stape}}, \mathsf{addr}'_w, \mathsf{val}'_w, x)$, compute $\sigma' = \mathsf{Tag}\,(K_{\mathsf{MAC}}, (b_{\mathsf{fin}}, \mathsf{st}'))$, and set $\mathsf{out} = (b_{\mathsf{fin}}, \mathsf{st}', \sigma')$.
5. **Output:** return out.

Fig. 5. Description of the circuit used to emulate a single transition of the RAM machine

Theorem 4 (Single-hop RAM-FHE). *Assume the existence of OWFs, CRHFs, PKE schemes, and SK-DEPIR which for size-N databases has* $\mathsf{poly}(\lambda, \log N)$ *Query and Decode complexity, where λ denotes the security parameter. Then for every $d = \mathsf{poly}\,(\lambda)$ there exists a $\mathsf{poly}\log N$-efficient single-hop RAM-FHE scheme in the circuit-VBB hybrid model for RAM machines with input length, output length, description size, and space usage at most d.*

The wrapper program M_{wrap}

RAM access to: a MHT MT for a database D (which contains an initial database, concatenated with a scratch tape).

Inputs:

$x \in \{0,1\}^n$: an input for a RAM machine M.
st: the internal state used in the execution of C_{Exec}.
σ: a MAC tag for st.
$\widetilde{C}$: an obfuscation of the circuit C_{Exec} of Figure 5.

Operation:

1. **Initialization:** Set $\mathcal{P}_{\text{hist}}$ to be empty (this is a "place holder" for the right-most path in a MHT MT_{hist} of the access history so far), and $z = (x, \text{false}, \text{st}, \sigma)$, padded with zeros to have the size of inputs to $\widetilde{C}$.

2. Repeat:
   - **Emulate an execution step:** execute $(b_{\text{fin}}, y) = \widetilde{C}(z)$ to obtain a bit b_{fin} indicating whether the execution has terminated, and an additional output y.
   - **Generate output when the execution ends:** if $b_{\text{fin}} = \text{true}$ then output y and halt.
   - **Emulate database and scratch tape accesses:**
     - Interpret y as (st', σ'), where σ' is a MAC tag for $(b_{\text{fin}}, \text{st}')$, and st' is the current internal execution state, consists of: a bit b, the current internal state st_M of M (as outputted by the transition circuit), the root Rt of an updated MHT for D, a root Rt_{hist} for a MHT MT_{hist}, the path $\mathcal{P}_{\text{hist}}$ to the right-most node in MT_{hist}, addresses addr_{DB}, $\text{addr}_{\text{stape}}$ to read from D, a value val_w to write to address addr_w of D, and an input x' for M.
     - Read the path $\mathcal{P}_{\text{DB}}$ to the node addr_{DB} in MT, and let val_{DB} be the value of the node.
     - Read the path $\mathcal{P}_{\text{stape}}$ to the node $\text{addr}_{\text{stape}}$ in MT, and let $\text{val}_{\text{stape}}$ be the value of the node.
     - Read the path $\mathcal{P}_w$ to the node addr_w in MT. Replace the value in addr_w with val_w, and update its path in MT.
   - **Compute input for next execution step:** Set $z = (x, b_{\text{fin}}, \text{st}', \sigma', \text{val}_{\text{DB}}, \text{val}_{\text{stape}}, \mathcal{P}_{\text{DB}}, \mathcal{P}_{\text{stape}}, \mathcal{P}_w)$.

Fig. 6. Description of the wrapper RAM machine

The Construction. The high level idea is to combine the address-simulatable RAM-VBB for the universal RAM machine, with an ISR-ORAM (which is replaced with an ASR-ORAM in the multi-hop setting). The address-simulatable RAM-VBB guarantees that the RAM machine emulation only reveals the sequence of physical memory addresses it accesses, which by ISR-ORAM security reveals no information about the access pattern to logical memory. One technical issue is that the universal machine should encrypt its output (using a persistent encryption key that is generated during KeyGen, independent of the database and any RAM machine that will be run on it) which requires generating randomness. We use a PRF to generate this randomness.

Construction 3 (Single-hop RAM-FHE). The RAM-FHE scheme uses:

- An address-simulatable RAM-VBB obfuscator $\mathcal{O}$.
- An ISR-ORAM scheme (ISR $-$ ORAM.Setup, ISR $-$ ORAM.Access) with a deterministic client during ISR $-$ ORAM.Access.
- A PKE scheme (PKE.KeyGen, PKE.Encrypt, PKE.Decrypt).
- An unbounded-input PRF F.

It consists of the following algorithms:

- KeyGen (1^λ) generates a public-secret key pair $(\mathsf{pk}', \mathsf{sk}') \leftarrow$ PKE.KeyGen (1^λ), and outputs $(\mathsf{pk} = (1^\lambda, \mathsf{pk}'), \mathsf{sk} = \mathsf{sk}')$.
- Encrypt $(\mathsf{pk} = (1^\lambda, \mathsf{pk}'), \mathsf{DB}, 1^d, 1^s)$ takes as input a public key pk, a database DB, and bounds d, s on the description size and space usage of RAM machines (respectively). It operates as follows:
  - Set DB$'$ to be the database of size $|\mathsf{DB}| + s$ obtained by concatenating s empty blocks to DB. (Intuitively, these blocks are "place holders" for the contents of the scratch tape of a RAM machine; see remark on physical memory block contents in the full version for a discussion of empty blocks.)
  - Initialize an ISR-ORAM with DB$'$, by running ISR $-$ ORAM.Setup $(1^\lambda, \mathsf{DB}')$, to obtain a client state $\mathsf{ck}_{\mathsf{ISR}}$ and a server state $\mathsf{st}_{\mathsf{ISR}}$.
  - Pick a random PRF key $K \leftarrow \{0,1\}^\lambda$.
  - Run $(\widetilde{\mathsf{DB}}, \widetilde{M_\mathcal{U}}, \mathcal{I}) \leftarrow \mathcal{O}(1^\lambda, \mathsf{st}_{\mathsf{ISR}}, M_\mathcal{U})$, where $M_\mathcal{U}$ is the RAM machine described in Fig. 7, with hard-wired values $|\mathsf{DB}|, \mathsf{pk}', K$, and internal variable $\mathsf{ck}_{\mathsf{ISR}}$.
  - Output the ciphertext $c_{\mathsf{DB}} = (\widetilde{\mathsf{DB}}, \widetilde{M_\mathcal{U}}, \mathcal{I})$.
- Eval$^{c_{\mathsf{DB}}}(M, x, 1^T)$ takes as input a description M of size at most d of a RAM machine, an input x for M, and a bound T on the runtime of M. It also has RAM access to a database-ciphertext $c_{\mathsf{DB}} = (\widetilde{\mathsf{DB}}, \widetilde{M_\mathcal{U}}, \mathcal{I})$. It runs $\widetilde{M_\mathcal{U}}^{\widetilde{\mathsf{DB}}}(M, 1^T, x, \mathcal{I})$, and outputs whatever it outputs.
- Decrypt (sk, c) takes as input a secret key sk, and an output-ciphertext c. It outputs PKE.Decrypt (sk, c).

Remark on growing Merkel Hash Trees. Our construction (in particular, the circuit C_{Exec} of Fig. 5 on page 611) generate and grow MHTs. The hash trees use an underlying hash function $H : \{0,1\}^{2n} \rightarrow \{0,1\}^n$ for some $n \in \mathbb{N}$. Generating a MHT T for a string s is done in the standard way by hashing adjacent pairs of nodes repeatedly, and we say that the resultant tree T *represents* s. Growing an existing MHT T which represents a string s is done as follows. Assume T has

---

The RAM machine $M_{\mathcal{U}}$ with RAM access to $\widetilde{DB}$

Hard-wired value: a database size N, a public key pk for a PKE scheme, and a PRF key K.

Internal variables:

ck: a client state in an ISR-ORAM.

y: the output of a RAM machine (initialized to 0).

fin: a boolean variable indicating whether the execution has terminated or not (initialized to false).

count: a counter of the number of operations performed so far (initialized to 0).

Inputs:

M: a description (of length at most d) of a RAM machine.

T: a bound on the runtime of M.

$x \in \{0,1\}^*$: the input for the RAM machine M.

Operation:

1. **Initialize the run:** set val$_{DB}$, val$_{stape}$ to be empty. (This is the first operation, no values were previously read from the database and scratch tape.)
2. **Execute M for T steps:** for $i = 1, \ldots, T$, do:
   - **Emulate a transition step:** execute the procedure from Figure 8 with val$_{DB}$, val$_{stape}$ as the values read from the database and the scratch tape, respectively.
   - **Access DB and scratch tape:** if count $\leq T$ then for $j = 1, 2, 3$: execute the procedure from Figure 9.
3. **Output:** set $r = F(K, (M, T, x))$, encrypt $c = \mathsf{PKE.Encrypt}(pk, y; r)$ and output c.

Fig. 7. RAM machine used in Construction 3

height h growing from the leaves to the root, and let $v_1, \ldots, v_h$ be the right-most nodes in each level of T, i.e., v_1 is a suffix of s, and v_h is the root. To generate a MHT representing the string $s \circ s'$ for some $s' \in \{0,1\}^n$, concatenate s' to level 1 of the tree as the new right-most node, and let $v_1' := s'$. Compute a new right-most path in the tree by generating, for every $1 < i \leq h$ the node $v_i' = H(v_{i-1}, v_{i-1}')$ and concatenating v_i' to the right of node v_i in level i. Finally, generate a new root at level $h + 1$ by computing $H(v_h, v_h')$. To grow T be a string of length $> n$, partition the string into length-n substrings, and apply this procedure sequentially on each of the substrings.

Emulating a single transition of M in $M_{\mathcal{U}}$

Hard-wired values, internal variables, M: as in Figure 7.

1. **If fin = true, perform a dummy step:** perform a no-op operation,[a] and set $\mathsf{addr}_{\mathsf{DB}} = 0$, $\mathsf{addr}_{\mathsf{stape}} = \mathsf{addr}_w = N$, and $\mathsf{val}_w = 0$ (these are dummy accesses which read address 0 from the database and scratch tape, and write 0 to address 0 of the scratch tape).
2. **If fin = false, perform the next transition step:**
   (a) Execute the next command of M using $\mathsf{val}_{\mathsf{DB}}, \mathsf{val}_{\mathsf{stape}}$ as the values read from the database and the scratch tapes, respectively.
   (b) If M terminated in the current step with output out, then set $y = \mathsf{out}$ and fin = true.
   (c) Otherwise, if count $< T$ then this step results in accesses $\mathsf{addr}_{\mathsf{DB}}, \mathsf{addr}_{\mathsf{stape}}$, $(\mathsf{addr}_w, \mathsf{val}_w)$ reading addresses $\mathsf{addr}_{\mathsf{DB}}, \mathsf{addr}_{\mathsf{stape}}$ (respectively) from the database and scratch tape, and writing value val_w to address addr_w of the scratch tape. Set $\mathsf{addr}_{\mathsf{stape}} := \mathsf{addr}_{\mathsf{stape}} + N$, $\mathsf{addr}_w := \mathsf{addr}_w + N$. (This "translates" the addresses in the scratch tape to addresses in $\widetilde{\mathsf{DB}}$, since M's scratch tape appears in $\widetilde{\mathsf{DB}}$ after the size-N database.)
3. **Update the counter:** set count = count + 1.

---

[a] This is needed to hide whether a command of M was executed or not, which would reveal information about the actual runtime of M.

Fig. 8. Emulating a single transition of M

Emulating a database or scratch tape access of M in $M_{\mathcal{U}}$

Hard-wired value, internal variables, j: as in Figure 7.

Memory accesses $\mathsf{addr}_{\mathsf{DB}}, \mathsf{addr}_{\mathsf{stape}}, (\mathsf{addr}_w, \mathsf{val}_w)$: as in Figure 8.

1. **Determine ORAM client input:** if $j = 1$ (i.e., **read** from database) set $v = (\mathsf{addr}_{\mathsf{DB}}, \perp)$. If $j = 2$ (i.e., **read** from scratch tape) set $v = (\mathsf{addr}_{\mathsf{stape}}, \perp)$. If $j = 3$ (i.e., **write** to scratch tape), set $v = (\mathsf{addr}_w, \mathsf{val}_w)$.
2. **Initiate ORAM access:** run the ISR-ORAM client from state ck with input v, to obtain a query q to the physical memory, and an update instruction update to the physical memory. (This results also in an updated client state which is updated in $M_{\mathcal{U}}$'s internal state).
3. **Emulate ORAM access:** until the ORAM client halts, do:
   − Read the value val written in block q of $\widetilde{\mathsf{DB}}$, and perform update on $\widetilde{\mathsf{DB}}$.
   − Run the ORAM client from state ck, given val as the server's answer to the last query q. The client outputs either the next query q and an update instruction update to the physical memory, or an output value $\mathsf{val}_{\mathsf{out}}$ (in this case, the ORAM client halts; in either case, this also results in an updated ORAM client state).
4. **Output:** if $j = 1$ (i.e., a value was read from the database), set $\mathsf{val}_{\mathsf{DB}} = \mathsf{val}_{\mathsf{out}}$, and if $j = 2$ (i.e., a value was read from the scratch tape), set $\mathsf{val}_{\mathsf{stape}} = \mathsf{val}_{\mathsf{out}}$.

Fig. 9. Emulating a database or scratch tape access in M

References

[ACC+16] Ananth, P., Chen, Y.-C., Chung, K.-M., Lin, H., Lin, W.-K.: Delegating RAM computations with adaptive soundness and privacy. In: Hirt, M., Smith, A. (eds.) TCC 2016-B, Part II. LNCS, vol. 9986, pp. 3–30. Springer, Heidelberg (2016). https://doi.org/10.1007/978-3-662-53644-5_1

[Agr] Agrawal, S.: New methods for indistinguishability obfuscation: bootstrapping and instantiation. IACR Cryptology ePrint Archive 2018:633 (2018)

[AIT16] Arriaga, A., Iovino, V., Tang, Q.: Updatable functional encryption. IACR Cryptology ePrint Archive 2016:1179 (2016)

[AJS18] Ananth, P., Jain, A., Sahai, A.: Indistinguishability obfuscation without multilinear maps: iO from LWE, bilinear maps, and weak pseudorandomness. IACR Cryptology ePrint Archive 2018:615 (2018)

[BCG+18] Bitansky, N., et al.: Indistinguishability obfuscation for RAM programs and succinct randomized encodings. SIAM J. Comput. 47(3), 1123–1210 (2018)

[BCP] Boyle, E., Chung, K.-M., Pass, R.: Oblivious parallel RAM and applications. In: Kushilevitz, E., Malkin, T. (eds.) TCC 2016-A, Part II. LNCS, vol. 9563, pp. 175–204. Springer, Heidelberg (2016). https://doi.org/10.1007/978-3-662-49099-0_7

[BGH13] Brakerski, Z., Gentry, C., Halevi, S.: Packed ciphertexts in LWE-based homomorphic encryption. In: Kurosawa, K., Hanaoka, G. (eds.) PKC 2013. LNCS, vol. 7778, pp. 1–13. Springer, Heidelberg (2013). https://doi.org/10.1007/978-3-642-36362-7_1

[BGI+01] Barak, B., et al.: On the (im)possibility of obfuscating programs. In: Kilian, J. (ed.) CRYPTO 2001. LNCS, vol. 2139, pp. 1–18. Springer, Heidelberg (2001). https://doi.org/10.1007/3-540-44647-8_1

[BGMZ18] Bartusek, J., Guan, J., Ma, F., Zhandry, M.: Return of GGH15: provable security against zeroizing attacks. In: Beimel, A., Dziembowski, S. (eds.) TCC 2018, Part II. LNCS, vol. 11240, pp. 544–574. Springer, Cham (2018). https://doi.org/10.1007/978-3-030-03810-6_20

[BGV12] Brakerski, Z., Gentry, C., Vaikuntanathan, V.: (Leveled) fully homomorphic encryption without bootstrapping. In: Proceedings of ITCS 2012, pp. 309–325. ACM (2012)

[BIPW17] Boyle, E., Ishai, Y., Pass, R., Wootters, M.: Can we access a database both locally and privately? In: Kalai, Y., Reyzin, L. (eds.) TCC 2017, Part II. LNCS, vol. 10678, pp. 662–693. Springer, Cham (2017). https://doi.org/10.1007/978-3-319-70503-3_22

[BMSZ16] Badrinarayanan, S., Miles, E., Sahai, A., Zhandry, M.: Post-zeroizing obfuscation: new mathematical tools, and the case of evasive circuits. In: Fischlin, M., Coron, J.-S. (eds.) EUROCRYPT 2016, Part II. LNCS, vol. 9666, pp. 764–791. Springer, Heidelberg (2016). https://doi.org/10.1007/978-3-662-49896-5_27

[BV11] Brakerski, Z., Vaikuntanathan, V.: Efficient fully homomorphic encryption from (standard) LWE. In: ECCC 2011, vol. 18, p. 109 (2011)

[CCC+] Chen, Y.-C., Chow, S.S.M., Chung, K.-M., Lai, R.W.F., Lin, W.-K., Zhou, H.-S.: Cryptography for parallel RAM from indistinguishability obfuscation. In: Proceedings of ITCS 2016, pp. 179–190 (2016)

[CCH+19]   Canetti, R., et al.: Fiat-Shamir: from practice to theory (2019)
[CCHR16]   Canetti, R., Chen, Y., Holmgren, J., Raykova, M.: Adaptive succinct garbled RAM or: how to delegate your database. In: Hirt, M., Smith, A. (eds.) TCC 2016-B, Part II. LNCS, vol. 9986, pp. 61–90. Springer, Heidelberg (2016). https://doi.org/10.1007/978-3-662-53644-5_3
[CH16]   Canetti, R., Holmgren, J.: Fully succinct garbled RAM. In: Proceedings of ITCS 2016, pp. 169–178 (2016)
[CHJV15]   Canetti, R., Holmgren, J., Jain, A., Vaikuntanathan, V.: Succinct garbling and indistinguishability obfuscation for RAM programs. In: Proceedings of STOC 2015, pp. 429–437 (2015)
[CHR17]   Canetti, R., Holmgren, J., Richelson, S.: Towards doubly efficient private information retrieval. In: Kalai, Y., Reyzin, L. (eds.) TCC 2017, Part II. LNCS, vol. 10678, pp. 694–726. Springer, Cham (2017). https://doi.org/10.1007/978-3-319-70503-3_23
[CR72]   Cook, S.A., Reckhow, R.A.: Time-bounded random access machines. In: Proceedings of STOC 1972, pp. 73–80 (1972)
[CVW18]   Chen, Y., Vaikuntanathan, V., Wee, H.: GGH15 beyond permutation branching programs: proofs, attacks, and candidates. In: Shacham, H., Boldyreva, A. (eds.) CRYPTO 2018, Part II. LNCS, vol. 10992, pp. 577–607. Springer, Cham (2018). https://doi.org/10.1007/978-3-319-96881-0_20
[Gen09]   Gentry, C.: Fully homomorphic encryption using ideal lattices. In: Proceedings of STOC 2009, pp. 169–178. ACM (2009)
[GGH+]   Garg, S., Gentry, C., Halevi, S., Raykova, M., Sahai, A., Waters, B.: Candidate indistinguishability obfuscation and functional encryption for all circuits. In: Proceedings of STOC 2013, pp. 40–49 (2013)
[GGMP16]   Garg, S., Gupta, D., Miao, P., Pandey, O.: Secure multiparty RAM computation in constant rounds. In: Hirt, M., Smith, A. (eds.) TCC 2016-B, Part I. LNCS, vol. 9985, pp. 491–520. Springer, Heidelberg (2016). https://doi.org/10.1007/978-3-662-53641-4_19
[GGP10]   Gennaro, R., Gentry, C., Parno, B.: Non-interactive verifiable computing: outsourcing computation to untrusted workers. In: Rabin, T. (ed.) CRYPTO 2010. LNCS, vol. 6223, pp. 465–482. Springer, Heidelberg (2010). https://doi.org/10.1007/978-3-642-14623-7_25
[GHL+14]   Gentry, C., Halevi, S., Lu, S., Ostrovsky, R., Raykova, M., Wichs, D.: Garbled RAM revisited. In: Nguyen, P.Q., Oswald, E. (eds.) EUROCRYPT 2014. LNCS, vol. 8441, pp. 405–422. Springer, Heidelberg (2014). https://doi.org/10.1007/978-3-642-55220-5_23
[GHPS13]   Gentry, C., Halevi, S., Peikert, C., Smart, N.P.: Field switching in BGV-style homomorphic encryption. J. Comput. Secur. 21(5), 663–684 (2013)
[GHRW]   Gentry, C., Halevi, S., Raykova, M., Wichs, D.: Outsourcing private RAM computation. In: Proceedings of FOCS 2014, pp. 404–413 (2014)
[GHS12]   Gentry, C., Halevi, S., Smart, N.P.: Fully homomorphic encryption with polylog overhead. In: Pointcheval, D., Johansson, T. (eds.) EUROCRYPT 2012. LNCS, vol. 7237, pp. 465–482. Springer, Heidelberg (2012). https://doi.org/10.1007/978-3-642-29011-4_28
[GKP+a]   Goldwasser, S., Kalai, Y.T., Popa, R.A., Vaikuntanathan, V., Zeldovich, N.: How to run turing machines on encrypted data. In: Canetti, R., Garay, J.A. (eds.) CRYPTO 2013, Part II. LNCS, vol. 8043, pp. 536–553. Springer, Heidelberg (2013). https://doi.org/10.1007/978-3-642-40084-1_30

[GKP+b] Goldwasser, S., Kalai, Y.T., Popa, R.A., Vaikuntanathan, V., Zeldovich, N.: Reusable garbled circuits and succinct functional encryption. In: Proceedings of STOC 2013, pp. 555–564. ACM (2013)

[GLOS]   Garg, S., Lu, S., Ostrovsky, R., Scafuro, A.: Garbled RAM from one-way functions. In: Proceedings of STOC 2015, pp. 449–458 (2015)

[GMM+16] Garg, S., Miles, E., Mukherjee, P., Sahai, A., Srinivasan, A., Zhandry, M.: Secure obfuscation in a weak multilinear map model. In: Hirt, M., Smith, A. (eds.) TCC 2016-B, Part II. LNCS, vol. 9986, pp. 241–268. Springer, Heidelberg (2016). https://doi.org/10.1007/978-3-662-53644-5_10

[GO96]   Goldreich, O., Ostrovsky, R.: Software protection and simulation on oblivious RAMs. J. ACM 43(3), 431–473 (1996)

[Gol87] Goldreich, O.: Towards a theory of software protection and simulation by oblivious RAMs. In: Proceedings of STOC 1987, pp. 182–194 (1987)

[Gol01] Goldreich, O.: The Foundations of Cryptography - Volume 1, Basic Techniques. Cambridge University Press, Cambridge (2001)

[Gol04] Goldreich, O.: The Foundations of Cryptography - Volume 2, Basic Applications. Cambridge University Press, Cambridge (2004)

[GOS18] Garg, S., Ostrovsky, R., Srinivasan, A.: Adaptive garbled RAM from laconic oblivious transfer. In: Shacham, H., Boldyreva, A. (eds.) CRYPTO 2018, Part III. LNCS, vol. 10993, pp. 515–544. Springer, Cham (2018). https://doi.org/10.1007/978-3-319-96878-0_18

[GSW]   Gentry, C., Sahai, A., Waters, B.: Homomorphic encryption from learning with errors: conceptually-simpler, asymptotically-faster, attribute-based. In: Canetti, R., Garay, J.A. (eds.) CRYPTO 2013, Part I. LNCS, vol. 8042, pp. 75–92. Springer, Heidelberg (2013). https://doi.org/10.1007/978-3-642-40041-4_5

[HHWW]   Hamlin, A., Holmgren, J., Weiss, M., Wichs, D.: On the plausibility of fully homomorphic encryption for RAMs. IACR Cryptology ePrint Archive 2019:632 (2019)

[HY16]   Hazay, C., Yanai, A.: Constant-round maliciously secure two-party computation in the RAM model. In: Hirt, M., Smith, A. (eds.) TCC 2016-B, Part I. LNCS, vol. 9985, pp. 521–553. Springer, Heidelberg (2016). https://doi.org/10.1007/978-3-662-53641-4_20

[KP16]   Kalai, Y.T., Paneth, O.: Delegating RAM computations. In: Hirt, M., Smith, A. (eds.) TCC 2016-B, Part II. LNCS, vol. 9986, pp. 91–118. Springer, Heidelberg (2016). https://doi.org/10.1007/978-3-662-53644-5_4

[KRR14] Kalai, Y.T., Raz, R., Rothblum, R.D.: How to delegate computations: the power of no-signaling proofs. In: Proceedings of STOC 2014, pp. 485–494. ACM (2014)

[LM18]   Lin, H., Matt, C.: Pseudo flawed-smudging generators and their application to indistinguishability obfuscation. IACR Cryptology ePrint Archive 2018:646 (2018)

[LO13]   Lu, S., Ostrovsky, R.: How to garble RAM programs? In: Johansson, T., Nguyen, P.Q. (eds.) EUROCRYPT 2013. LNCS, vol. 7881, pp. 719–734. Springer, Heidelberg (2013). https://doi.org/10.1007/978-3-642-38348-9_42

[LO17] Lu, S., Ostrovsky, R.: Black-box parallel garbled RAM. In: Katz, J., Shacham, H. (eds.) CRYPTO 2017, Part II. LNCS, vol. 10402, pp. 66–92. Springer, Cham (2017). https://doi.org/10.1007/978-3-319-63715-0_3

[Mia16] Miao, P.: Cut-and-choose for garbled RAM. IACR Cryptology ePrint Archive 2016:907 (2016)

[MZ18] Ma, F., Zhandry, M.: The MMap strikes back: obfuscation and new multilinear maps immune to CLT13 zeroizing attacks. In: Beimel, A., Dziembowski, S. (eds.) TCC 2018, Part II. LNCS, vol. 11240, pp. 513–543. Springer, Cham (2018). https://doi.org/10.1007/978-3-030-03810-6_19

[OS97] Ostrovsky, R., Shoup, V.: Private information storage (extended abstract). In: Proceedings of STOC 1997, pp. 294–303 (1997)

[Ost90] Ostrovsky, R.: Efficient computation on oblivious RAMs. In: Proceedings of STOC 1990, pp. 514–523 (1990)

[PF79] Pippenger, N., Fischer, M.J.: Relations among complexity measures. J. ACM 26(2), 361–381 (1979)

[RAD78] Rivest, R.L., Adleman, L., Dertouzos, M.L.: On data banks and privacy homomorphisms. In: DeMillo, R.A., Lipton, R.J., Dobkin, D.P., Jones, A.K. (eds.) Foundations of Secure Computation, pp. 169–179. Academia Press, New York (1978)

Homomorphic Time-Lock Puzzles
and Applications

Giulio Malavolta$^{1(\boxtimes)}$ and Sri Aravinda Krishnan Thyagarajan$^{2(\boxtimes)}$

^{1} Carnegie Mellon University, Pittsburgh, USA
giulio.malavolta@hotmail.it
^{2} Friedrich-Alexander-Universität Erlangen-Nürnberg, Erlangen, Germany
sri.aravinda.krishnan.thyagarajan@cs.fau.de

Abstract. Time-lock puzzles allow one to encrypt messages for the future, by efficiently generating a puzzle with a solution s that remains hidden until time $\mathcal{T}$ has elapsed. The solution is required to be concealed from the eyes of any algorithm running in (parallel) time less than $\mathcal{T}$. We put forth the concept of *homomorphic time-lock puzzles*, where one can evaluate functions over puzzles without solving them, i.e., one can manipulate a set of puzzles with solutions $(s_1, \ldots, s_n)$ to obtain a puzzle that solves to $f(s_1, \ldots, s_n)$, for any function f. We propose candidate constructions under concrete cryptographic assumptions for different classes of functions. Then we show how homomorphic time-lock puzzles overcome the limitations of classical time-lock puzzles by proposing new protocols for applications of interest, such as e-voting, multi-party coin flipping, and fair contract signing.

1 Introduction

Time-lock puzzles [30] allow one to encapsulate messages for a precise amount of time or, equivalently, to encrypt messages for the future. On input a secret s and a hardness parameter $\mathcal{T}$, the puzzle generation algorithm allows one to compute a Z such that s can be recovered only after time $\mathcal{T}$. Time-lock puzzles are characterized by the following properties.

- *Fast puzzle generation:* The time needed to generate a puzzle is much shorter than $\mathcal{T}$. This is crucial when secrets are hidden for a long time, e.g., 10 years.
- *Security against parallel algorithms:* The secret s is hidden for circuits of depth less than $\mathcal{T}$, regardless of their size.

The latter can be seen as a more fine-grained notion of the classical semantic security [19], where simply lowering the security parameter may enable faster algorithms that exploit massive parallelization to solve the puzzle. Note that ignoring either of the above properties makes the problem trivial since it can be either solved with standard probabilistic encryption or any inherently sequential computation (such as repeated hashing). Applications of time-lock puzzles

---

G. Malavolta—Part of the work done while at Friedrich-Alexander-Universität Erlangen-Nürnberg.

A. Boldyreva and D. Micciancio (Eds.): CRYPTO 2019, LNCS 11692, pp. 620–649, 2019.
https://doi.org/10.1007/978-3-030-26948-7_22

include sealed-bid auctions [30], fair contract signing [6], zero-knowledge arguments [12], and non-malleable commitments [23], to mention a few.

To compensate for the absence of a trusted party, time-lock puzzles force the decrypter to perform a long computation before being able to recover the secret. When time-lock puzzles are deployed within large scale protocols, this slight drawback is magnified and parties may incur in a significant computational burden. While performing *some* computation is clearly unavoidable, this effort should not become the bottleneck of the protocol. To the best of our knowledge, there is currently no solution to mitigate this problem.

1.1 Limitations of Time-Lock Puzzles

To illustrate the aforementioned limitations of time-lock puzzles, we consider the scenario of e-voting in the absence of a trusted authority, one of the motivating examples for the usage of the primitive. Throughout the following discussion we assume that the voters have access to a public and append-only bulletin board, e.g., a blockchain, and we will not consider the privacy of the votes nor their authenticity. Both problems are well studied and can be dealt with using standard techniques, e.g., unlinkable transactions and anonymous credentials. Instead, we are going to focus on constructing a system that allows a large set of voters to cast their preference without any bias.

If one were to assume a trusted administrator, then the voters could simply encrypt their preference and let the administrator count and announce the result. However, the absence of trusted authorities makes the problem non-trivial. The standard approach to avoid voters being biased by the current majority is to divide the protocol in two phases: In the *voting phase* the voters commit to their vote and post the commitment on the bulletin board. In the *counting phase*, new commitments are ignored, and voters are asked to reveal their openings, which makes it possible to compute and announce the result of the election.

This however leaves open the question of how to handle users who send valid commitments in the first phase but fail to reveal their openings in the second. One could either (i) repeat the voting phase or (ii) ignore such "unopened" votes. Repeating the voting process could empower an attacker to successfully mount a denial-of-service attack at essentially no cost. On the other hand, the latter solution might be exploited to manipulate the final outcome: An attacker controlling the network traffic might block those openings corresponding to an unwanted candidate, thereby generating a bias towards a the preferred side.

Time-lock puzzles elegantly resolve this by replacing commitments as the hiding mechanism for the votes. The votes of those users who fail to publish their coins (i.e., reveal their vote) can be simply determined by solving their time-lock puzzles. Setting the hardness parameter T to be a safe amount longer than the voting phase makes sure that the votes are kept secret until such a phase is over, thereby avoiding any bias. Unfortunately, this solution does not come without additional costs: Consider what happens when a large amount of voters, say 100.000, fail to open their puzzles. Then the computation of the election winner tally requires brute-forcing those puzzles, which means that a massive amount of (parallel) computation is needed in order to complete the election within reasonable time. Taking into account the typical number of voters for an election which is usually in the range of millions, it is safe to say that the problem is of practical relevance.

We stress that, even though e-voting exemplifies well the scalability issues of time-lock puzzles, it is certainly not the only scenario where they emerge. Essentially any other application that involves a large number of users (e.g., sealed bid auctions or multi-party coin flipping), encounters similar problems. We conjecture that such constraints constitute one of the main obstacles that so far prevented the large scale adoption of time-lock puzzles.

1.2   Our Solution

Put in different words, the main shortcoming of time-lock puzzle-based solutions is that one needs to solve (brute-force) many puzzles before computing some function over the embedded secrets. What if we could (homomorphically) evaluate the function first and then solve a *single puzzle* containing the function output? This would dramatically reduce the computational burden of time-lock puzzle-based protocols. Consider the e-voting example as described above: To compute the election winner one could homomorphically evaluate the corresponding circuit over the puzzles and then solve *a single puzzle*, regardless of the number of offline voters.

Motivated by this question, we propose the notion of *Homomorphic Time-Lock Puzzles* (HTLP): Loosely speaking, an HTLP is an augmented time-lock puzzle that allows anyone to evaluate a circuit C over sets of puzzles $(Z_1, \ldots, Z_n)$ homomorphically, without necessarily knowing the secret messages $(s_1, \ldots, s_n)$ encapsulated within these puzzles. The resulting output (which is also a puzzle) contains the circuit output $C(s_1, \ldots, s_n)$ and the timing hardness of this puzzle does not depend on the size of the circuit C that was evaluated (compactness). We stress that the compactness of the evaluation algorithm is a crucial requirement for HTLP (as it is the case for fully-homomorphic encryption [16]): If we were to ignore it, then the trivial solution of solving the puzzles $(Z_1, \ldots, Z_n)$ and then evaluating C over the secrets would suffice.

In this work we put forward the concept of HTLPs and we formally characterize their security guarantees. We then propose several schemes that support the homomorphic evaluation of different classes of circuits and we demonstrate their usefulness by presenting several concrete applications.

1.3   Technical Overview

Towards instantiating HTLPs, our starting point is the classical construction of Rivest, Shamir, and Wagner [30], whose hardness is rooted in the (conjectured) inherent sequentiality of squaring in finite fields. Let $N = p \cdot q$ be an RSA integer, a time-lock puzzle for a secret s and for a time $\mathcal{T}$ consists of the tuple

$$(N, \mathcal{T}, x, x^{2^{\mathcal{T}}} \cdot k, \mathsf{Enc}(k, s))$$

where (x, k) are uniformly sampled elements from $\mathbb{Z}_N^*$, and $\mathsf{Enc}(k, s)$ is a symmetric encryption of the secret s. Note that knowing the group order $\varphi(N)$ allows one to efficiently compute the term x^{2^T} by reducing 2^T modulo $\varphi(N)$ first. On the other hand the decrypter has to perform $\mathcal{T}$-many squarings before recovering the key k. Here the hybrid encryption approach breaks the structure of the group, and therefore the scheme has no homomorphic properties.

Linearly Homomorphic. Our first observation is that the term x^{2^T} acts essentially as a one-time pad and we can choose a more structured embedding that admits an efficiently computable homomorphism. We follow the blueprint of Paillier [28], i.e., we exploit the fact that the group $\mathbb{Z}_{N^2}^*$ can be written as the product of the group generated by $(1 + N)$, which has order N, and the group of N-th residues $\{x^N : x \in \mathbb{Z}_N^*\}$, which has order $\varphi(N)$. Consider the following (flawed) attempt to construct HTLPs for linear functions:

$$(N, \mathcal{T}, x, x^{N \cdot 2^T} \cdot (1 + N)^s),$$

for a random $x \in \mathbb{Z}_N^*$. Assume for the moment that N is fixed across all puzzles, then the scheme is clearly linearly homomorphic as shown below:

$$(N, \mathcal{T}, x \cdot y, x^{N \cdot 2^T} \cdot y^{N \cdot 2^T} \cdot (1+N)^s \cdot (1+N)^{s'}) = (N, \mathcal{T}, (x \cdot y), (x \cdot y)^{N \cdot 2^T} \cdot (1+N)^{s+s'}).$$

Observe that the time needed to homomorphically add secrets is independent of $\mathcal{T}$. Further recall that the group generated by $(1 + N)$ admits a polynomial-time algorithm to compute discrete logarithms, so recovering the output is easy once $x^{N \cdot 2^T}$ is computed. Unfortunately there are two major issues with the current scheme: (i) If N is shared across all users who also generated them, then everybody potentially knows the factorization of N (and therefore $\varphi(N)$), which is a problem for security, and (ii) the blinding factor $x^{N \cdot 2^T}$ is trivially distinguishable from a uniform element in $\mathbb{Z}_N^*$ as the Jacobi symbol of $x^{N \cdot 2^T}$ is always $+1$. The latter issue can be easily countered by restricting the random choice to those elements in $\mathbb{Z}_N^*$ whose Jacobi symbol is equal to $+1$. Our idea to sidestep the former limitation is to use the random self-reducibility of the problem: In our augmented scheme, the tuple (N, x, x^{2^T}), where x is a random element of $\mathbb{Z}_N^*$ with Jacobi symbol $+1$, is fixed in a setup phase. A freshly-looking HTLP can now be computed as

$$(N, \mathcal{T}, x^r, (x^{N \cdot 2^T})^r \cdot (1 + N)^s) = (N, \mathcal{T}, y, y^{N \cdot 2^T} \cdot (1 + N)^s),$$

where r is uniformly sampled from $\{1, \ldots, N^2\}$, whose distribution (modulo $\varphi(N)$) is statistically close to sampling from $\{1, \ldots, \varphi(N)\}$. Note that the newly generated puzzle is correctly distributed and the knowledge of $\varphi(N)$ is not needed to compute it. It can be shown that the scheme is an HTLP for linear functions, assuming the inherent sequentiality of squaring modulo N and other standard intractability assumptions over hidden-order groups.

Multiplicatively Homomorphic. Armed with the tools discussed above, we can easily switch the message encoding to obtain HTLPs that supports the evaluation of multiplication gates. This is done by adapting the scheme of above to a Diffie-Hellman structure in a natural way: Given that the tuple (N, x, x^{2^T})

is fixed in a setup phase, a puzzle to encapsulate a secret $s \in \mathbb{J}_N$ (where $\mathbb{J}_N$ is the subgroup of $\mathbb{Z}_N^*$ whose elements have Jacobi symbol $+1$) is generated as

$$(N, \mathcal{T}, x^r, (x^{2^{\mathcal{T}}})^r \cdot s)$$

for some uniformly chosen r. The procedure to recover the puzzle is essentially unchanged, except that now all the operations are performed in the subgroup $\mathbb{J}_N$. Clearly, there is no need to compute any discrete logarithm since s is already in its plain form. In [10] it was shown that the decisional Diffie-Hellman (DDH) assumption over $\mathbb{J}_N$ is implied by the DDH assumption over $\mathbb{Z}_p^*$ and $\mathbb{Z}_q^*$ and the quadratic residuosity assumption over $\mathbb{Z}_N^*$. Thus the security of our scheme follows from the same set of hard problems (in addition to assuming the sequential nature of squaring modulo N).

Fully Homomorphic. The schemes constructed above support the homomorphic evaluation of some restricted classes of functions over the secrets. The next natural question is whether there exists an HTLP for *any* polynomially-computable function. It seems like the techniques developed so far are not very helpful in this context since constructing homomorphic encryption from RSA groups (and related assumptions) has been an elusive task so far. For this reason we turn our attention to constructions based on indistinguishability obfuscation [14]. The scheme that we obtain shall be interpreted as a feasibility result. We leave constructing HTLPs for any function without the aid of obfuscation as a fascinating open problem. Our candidate solution follows the blueprint of the fully-homomorphic encryption (FHE) scheme from [9]. Omitting most of the technicalities, their FHE is constructed from standard public-key encryption by obfuscating a program that decrypts two input ciphertexts, computes a NAND gate over the messages, and re-encrypts the output. This approach allows one to construct FHE without relying on circular assumptions, since the obfuscated program can evaluate circuits of any depth without growing in size.

At a first glance, this strategy does not seem to translate directly to the time-lock puzzle settings, since puzzles do not necessarily have a trapdoor that allows one to efficiently recover the secret (see, e.g., the construction from [2]). Instead of replacing the public key encryption, our scheme *augments it* by additionally time-locking the message: The puzzle consists of a tuple (c, Z), where the ciphertext c and any (non-homomorphic) time-lock puzzle Z encode the same message. To open it, one simply ignores c and solves Z. To support homomorphic computations, we obfuscate a program that takes as input two puzzles (c_0, Z_0) and (c_1, Z_1), decrypts c_0 and c_1, computes the NAND of the messages and produces a fresh pair (c', Z') encoding the output bit. Note that, although the program discards Z_0 and Z_1, the output puzzle is still well-formed. Such a program is obfuscated in the setup phase and it is made available to all parties.

Extensions. The constructions presented above constitute the backbone of our results, but there are still a few shortcomings that need to be addressed in order to enjoy all advantages of HTLPs. For example, all of the schemes (as described above) require a trusted setup that needs to be re-initialized once time $\mathcal{T}$ has passed. We show that this is in fact not necessary for our RSA-based schemes and that the common reference string (N, x, x^{2^T}) can be fixed once and for all in a *one-time setup*, assuming a mildly stronger version of the sequential squaring problem. We also show how to compute homomorphic operations over puzzles generated under different hardness parameters and we explore the feasibility of a non-trusted (public-coin) setup. Finally, we present a semi-compact HTLP for branching programs (a superclass of NC1), where the size of the evaluated puzzle grows with the length of the program but not with its size.

1.4 Applications

We substantiate our claims with concrete examples of scenarios where HTLPs are useful. Due to the different nature of our constructions, we focus on how to exploit our efficient (RSA-based) schemes to build applications of interest.

E-Voting and Sealed Bid Auctions over Blockchains. We consider the settings where n voters choose one among m candidates and we assume that $n \gg m$. In our protocol, each voter generates a vector of m *linearly-homomorphic* puzzles $(Z_1, \ldots, Z_m)$ encapsulating 0, except for the j-th puzzle Z_j that encodes 1, where j is the index of the preferred candidate.[1] The vector of each voter is made available to all parties (by, e.g., posting it on a blockchain) during the voting phase. Afterwards, the outcome of the election can be determined by simply summing up all vectors and opening the resulting m puzzles. The resulting vector will contain the amount of votes per candidate and the winner can then be easily determined. Note that this is a public operation and therefore there is no need for a trusted tallying authority. Furthermore, the computational effort needed to determine the result of the election is that of solving m puzzles, regardless on the amount of voters. The typical values for m are in the order of tens, which corresponds to a manageable amount of computation for essentially any machine. This is a significant improvement with respect to the original solution that required the opening of potentially hundreds of thousands puzzles.

Similar techniques can be used to design a sealed bid auction protocol: Each bidder time-locks its bid and the index corresponding to the highest bidder is homomorphically computed over the puzzles. The winner of the auction can be determined by solving a single puzzle. Unfortunately the resulting protocol is not yet practical since the circuit being evaluated exceeds the capability of linear functions and requires *fully-homomorphic* time-lock puzzles.

Multi-Party Coin Flipping. Coin flipping protocols are one of the classical problems in cryptography [3] and have recently found applications in real-life cryptocurrencies [22]. The security required by an n-party coin flipping protocol is that $n-1$ colluding parties should not be able to bias the final outcome. Boneh and Naor [6] proposed a solution for coin flipping among two parties based on time-lock puzzles. However, naively extending their protocol to the multi-party setting suffers from predictable drawbacks: The computational effort of the participants is proportional to the amount of parties that do not reveal their random

---

[1] We implicitly assume that all puzzles are honestly generated, which can be enforced with standard cryptographic tools.

coins. This becomes very significant when coin flipping protocols are executed on a large scale (e.g., thousands of participants). Using *linearly-homomorphic* time-lock puzzles we obtain a very simple solution to this problem. Each participant encapsulates a random bit for a safe amount of time and broadcasts it to all parties. Then each party homomorphically add all puzzles, without the need for further interactions. Solving the resulting output puzzle and isolating the least significant bit of the solution gives us an unbiased coin.

Multi-party Contract Signing. Consider the scenario where n mutually distrusting parties want to exchange signatures on a document. Boneh and Naor [6] proposed a protocol for fair exchange of signatures based on time-lock puzzles. The protocol proceeds in rounds where each party generates a time-lock puzzle of their signature and broadcasts it. When all signatures are published, the protocol repeats except that the hardness parameter of the time-lock puzzle is halved. The protocol is strongly fair in the sense that the work required to recover the signatures by all parties differs at most by a factor of (roughly) 2.

Observe that if at any round *any* party fails to broadcast its puzzle, then all other parties need to solve *all* the puzzles ($(n - 1)$-many) from the previous round to learn the signatures necessary for the validity of the contract. Our *multiplicatively-homomorphic* time-lock puzzles can be plugged in this protocol to solve exactly this issue. More specifically, we can leverage a recent result on RSA-aggregate signatures [20], where Hohenberger and Waters proposed a scheme where signatures live in $\mathbb{QR}_N$, where N is fixed in the setup, and can be aggregated by simply multiplying them modulo N. Recall that $\mathbb{QR}_N$ is a subgroup of $\mathbb{J}_N$ and therefore signatures encapsulated in our HTLP can be aggregated homomorphically.

Equipped with this tool, we can simply replace the time-lock puzzle of Boneh and Naor with our multiplicatively homomorphic construction and combine it with the signature scheme of Hohenberger and Waters. Then, in the case that any party goes offline ahead of time, each other party can homomorphically aggregate the signatures from the previous round and then solve a *single* time-lock puzzle, regardless of the number of participants.

1.5   Related Work

Time-lock puzzles were envisioned in the seminal work by Rivest, Shamir, and Wagner [30]. Their scheme builds on the (conjectured) inherent sequentiality of repeated squaring in RSA groups. Recently, Bitanski et al. [2] proposed a different approached to construct time-lock puzzles, assuming the existence of succinct randomized encodings [1] and non-parallelizable languages. We also mention a new construction paradigm from Liu et al. [24] that combines witness encryption [15] with a reference clock, such as a blockchain.

A related but different notion is that of verifiable delay functions [4], which allow a prover to convince a verifier that a certain amount of sequential computation has been performed. The two notions are incomparable since verifiable delay functions (in general) do not allow one to encapsulate secrets and time-lock puzzles are (in general) not efficiently verifiable. Proofs of sequential work [26] can be seen as a non-unique verifiable delay functions. Interestingly, Mahmoody et al. [25] showed a blackbox separation between time-lock puzzles and proofs of sequential work.

2   Preliminaries

We denote by $\lambda \in \mathbb{N}$ the security parameter. We say that a function μ is negligible if it vanishes faster than any polynomial. Given two ensembles D_0 and D_1, we write $D_0 \approx_\mu D_1$ if all probabilistic polynomial-time distinguishers succeed with probability μ-close to $1/2$. Given a set U, we denote by $u \leftarrow_s U$ the uniform sampling from U. Recall the definition of statistical distance.

Definition 1 (Statistical Distance). *Let X and Y be two random variables over a finite set U. The statistical distance between X and Y is defined as*

$$\mathbb{SD}\,[X, Y] = \sum_{u \in U} |\Pr[X = u] - \Pr[Y = u]|\,.$$

We say that an ensemble D is ε-uniform in U if the statistical distance between D and uniformly sampling from U is at most ε. We recall the following useful lemma from [7].

Lemma 1. *Let $(n, \tilde{n}) \in \mathbb{N}^2$ and let $x \leftarrow_s \{1, \ldots, \tilde{n}\}$, then $x \ (mod \ n)$ is $(n/\tilde{n})$-uniform in $\mathbb{Z}_n$.*

Proof. Let $d = \tilde{n} \ (\mathrm{mod} \ n)$, then conditioned on the event that $x \in \{1, \ldots, \tilde{n}-d\}$, it holds that $x \ (\mathrm{mod} \ n)$ is uniformly distributed in $\mathbb{Z}_n$. Therefore $x \ (\mathrm{mod} \ n)$ is $(d/\tilde{n}) \le (n/\tilde{n})$-uniform.

2.1   Number Theory and Assumptions

Let $N = p \cdot q$, where p and q are random primes of equal length, we define $\mathbb{Z}_N^* := \{x \in \mathbb{Z}_N : \gcd(x, N) = 1\}$ and $\mathbb{J}_N$ as the group of elements of $\mathbb{Z}_N^*$ with Jacobi symbol $+1$ and we denote by g a generator of $\mathbb{J}_N$. Euler totient function is denoted by $\varphi(\cdot)$. We say that N is a strong RSA integer if $p = 2p' + 1$ and $q = 2q' + 1$, where p' and q' are also primes. Note that if N is a strong RSA integer then $\mathbb{J}_N$ is cyclic and has order $\varphi(N)/2$. Also note that a generator g for $\mathbb{J}_N$ can be found by sampling $\tilde{g} \leftarrow_s \mathbb{Z}_N^*$ and setting $g := -\tilde{g}^2$ since the order of $\tilde{g}$ is either $\varphi(N)/2$ or $\varphi(N)/4$ with all but negligible probability.

We state and prove the following simple lemma, which is going to be useful in the analysis of our schemes.

Lemma 2. *For every $x \in \mathbb{N}$ and every $N \in \mathbb{N}$ it holds that*

$$x^N \ (mod \ N^2) = (x \ (mod \ N))^N \ (mod \ N^2).$$

Proof. Let us rewrite $x = \tilde{x} + kN$, for some k and some $\tilde{x} < N$. Then we have

$$
\begin{aligned}
x^N \ (\mathrm{mod}\ N^2) &= (\tilde{x} + kN)^N \ (\mathrm{mod}\ N^2) \\
&= \tilde{x}^N + \left(\tilde{x}^{N-1}kN\right)N + \dots \ (\mathrm{mod}\ N^2) \\
&= \tilde{x}^N \ (\mathrm{mod}\ N^2) \\
&= (x \ (\mathrm{mod}\ N))^N \ (\mathrm{mod}\ N^2).
\end{aligned}
$$

Sequential Squaring. In the following we recall the intractability assumption (implicitly) introduced by Rivest, Shamir, and Wagner [30].

Assumption 1 (Sequential Squaring). *Let N be a uniform strong RSA integer, g be a generator of $\mathbb{J}_N$, and $\mathcal{T}(\cdot)$ be a polynomial. Then there exists some $0 < \varepsilon < 1$ such that for every polynomial-size adversary $\mathcal{A} = \{\mathcal{A}_\lambda\}_{\lambda \in \mathbb{N}}$ who's depth is bounded from above by $\mathcal{T}^\varepsilon(\lambda)$, there exists a negligible function $\mu(\cdot)$ such that*

$$
\Pr\left[b \leftarrow \mathcal{A}(N, g, \mathcal{T}(\lambda), x, y) : \begin{array}{l} x \leftarrow_\$ \mathbb{J}_N; b \leftarrow_\$ \{0,1\} \\ \text{if } b = 0 \text{ then } y \leftarrow_\$ \mathbb{J}_N \\ \text{if } b = 1 \text{ then } y := x^{2^{\mathcal{T}(\lambda)}} \end{array} \right] \leq \frac{1}{2} + \mu(\lambda).
$$

Note that we restrict the domain of x and y to $\mathbb{J}_N$ to avoid trivial attacks where the distinguisher computes the Jacobi symbol of the group element.

Decisional Composite Residuosity. Here we recall the decisional composite residuosity (DCR) assumption as of [28].

Assumption 2 (Decisional Composite Residuosity). *Let N be a uniform strong RSA integer. Then for every polynomial-size adversary $\mathcal{A} = \{\mathcal{A}_\lambda\}_{\lambda \in \mathbb{N}}$ there exists a negligible function $\mu(\cdot)$ such that*

$$
\Pr\left[b \leftarrow \mathcal{A}(N, y) : \begin{array}{l} x \leftarrow_\$ \mathbb{Z}_N^*; b \leftarrow_\$ \{0,1\} \\ \text{if } b = 0 \text{ then } y \leftarrow_\$ \mathbb{Z}_{N^2}^* \\ \text{if } b = 1 \text{ then } y := x^N \end{array} \right] \leq \frac{1}{2} + \mu(\lambda).
$$

Decisional Diffie-Hellman. Here we recall the decisional composite Diffie-Hellman (DDH) assumption over $\mathbb{J}_N$ as stated in [10]. In the same work, it was shown that such a conjecture is implied by the DDH assumption over $\mathbb{Z}_p^*$ and $\mathbb{Z}_q^*$ and by the quadratic residuosity assumption over $\mathbb{Z}_N^*$.

Assumption 3 (Decisional Diffie-Hellman). *Let N be a uniform strong RSA integer and g be a generator of $\mathbb{J}_N$. Then for every polynomial-size adversary $\mathcal{A} = \{\mathcal{A}_\lambda\}_{\lambda \in \mathbb{N}}$ there exists a negligible function $\mu(\cdot)$ such that*

$$
\Pr\left[b \leftarrow \mathcal{A}(N, g, g^x, g^y, g^z) : \begin{array}{l} (x, y) \leftarrow_\$ \{1, \dots, \varphi(N)/2\}; b \leftarrow_\$ \{0,1\} \\ \text{if } b = 0 \text{ then } z \leftarrow_\$ \{1, \dots, \varphi(N)/2\} \\ \text{if } b = 1 \text{ then } z := x \cdot y \ (mod \ \varphi(N)/2) \end{array} \right] \leq \frac{1}{2} + \mu(\lambda).
$$

2.2 Cryptographic Building Blocks

In the following we introduce the cryptographic primitives used in our work.

Puncturable PseudoRandom Functions. A puncturable pseudorandom function (PRF) is an augmented PRF that has an additional puncturing algorithm. Such an algorithm produces a punctured version of the key that can evaluate the PRF at all points except for the punctured one. It is required that the PRF value at that specific point is pseudorandom even given the punctured key. A puncturable PRF can be constructed from any one-way function [18].

Definition 2 (Puncturable PRFs). *A puncturable family of PRFs is a tuple of polynomial-time algorithms* (Key, Puncture, PRF) *defined as follows.*

- $K \leftarrow \mathsf{Key}(1^\lambda)$ *a probabilistic algorithm that takes as input the security parameter and outputs a key* K.
- $K_{-i} \leftarrow \mathsf{Puncture}(K, i)$ *a deterministic algorithm that takes as input a key* K *and a position* $i \in \{0,1\}^n$ *and returns a punctured key* K_{-i}.
- $y \leftarrow \mathsf{PRF}(K, i)$ *a deterministic algorithm that takes as input a key* K *and an index* $i \in \{0,1\}^n$ *and returns a string* $y \in \{0,1\}^m$.

Definition 3 (Correctness). *For all* $\lambda \in \mathbb{N}$, *for all outputs* $K \leftarrow \mathsf{Key}(1^\lambda)$, *for all points* $i \in \{0,1\}^n$ *and* $x \in \{0,1\}^n \setminus i$, *and for all* $K_{-i} \leftarrow \mathsf{Puncture}(K, i)$, *we have that* $\mathsf{PRF}(K_{-i}, x) = \mathsf{PRF}(K, x)$.

Definition 4 (Pseudorandomness). *For all* $\lambda \in \mathbb{N}$ *and for every polynomial-time adversaries* $(\mathcal{A}_1, \mathcal{A}_2)$ *there is a negligible function* $\mu(\cdot)$, *such that*

$$\Pr\left[b \leftarrow \mathcal{A}_2(\tau, K_{-i}, i, y) : \begin{array}{l} (i, \tau) \leftarrow \mathcal{A}_1(1^\lambda) \\ K \leftarrow \mathsf{Key}(1^\lambda) \\ K_{-i} \leftarrow \mathsf{Puncture}(K, i) \\ b \leftarrow_{\$} \{0, 1\} \\ \textit{if } b = 0 \textit{ then } y \leftarrow_{\$} \{0,1\}^m \\ \textit{if } b = 1 \textit{ then } y \leftarrow \mathsf{PRF}(K, i) \end{array} \right] \leq \frac{1}{2} + \mu(\lambda).$$

Time-Lock Puzzles. We recall the definition of standard time-lock puzzles [2]. For conceptual simplicity we consider only schemes with binary solutions.

Definition 5 (Time-Lock Puzzles). *A time-lock puzzle is a tuple of two algorithms* (PGen, PSolve) *defined as follows.*

- $Z \leftarrow \mathsf{PGen}(\mathcal{T}, s)$ *a probabilistic algorithm that takes as input a hardness-parameter* $\mathcal{T}$ *and a solution* $s \in \{0,1\}$, *and outputs a puzzle* Z.
- $s \leftarrow \mathsf{PSolve}(Z)$ *a deterministic algorithm that takes as input a puzzle* Z *and outputs a solution* s.

Definition 6 (Correctness). *For all* $\lambda \in \mathbb{N}$, *for all polynomials* $\mathcal{T}$ *in* λ, *and for all* $s \in \{0,1\}$, *it holds that* $s = \mathsf{PSolve}(\mathsf{PGen}(\mathcal{T}, s))$.

Definition 7 (Security). *A scheme* (PGen, PSolve) *is secure with gap* $\varepsilon < 1$ *if there exists a polynomial* $\tilde{T}(\cdot)$ *such that for all polynomials* $T(\cdot) \geq \tilde{T}(\cdot)$ *and every polynomial-size adversary* $\mathcal{A} = \{\mathcal{A}_\lambda\}_{\lambda \in \mathbb{N}}$ *of depth* $\leq T^\varepsilon(\lambda)$, *there exists a negligible function* $\mu(\cdot)$, *such that for all* $\lambda \in \mathbb{N}$ *it holds that*

$$\Pr\left[b \leftarrow \mathcal{A}(Z) : Z \leftarrow \mathsf{PGen}(T(\lambda), b)\right] \leq \frac{1}{2} + \mu(\lambda).$$

Trapdoor Encryption. A trapdoor encryption scheme is a public key encryption scheme that allows one to generate a trapdoor version of the public key. Such trapdoor key is indistinguishable from a normal public key, however encrypting under the trapdoor key hides the message in an information-theoretic sense. Canetti et al. [9] showed that any public-key encryption with perfect re-randomization (such as ElGamal or Paillier encryption) can be used generically to construct such a primitive.

Definition 8 (Trapdoor Encryption). *A trapdoor encryption scheme is a tuple of polynomial-time algorithms* (KeyGen, Enc, Dec, tKeyGen) *defined as follows.*

- $(pk, sk) \leftarrow \mathsf{KeyGen}(1^\lambda)$ *a probabilistic algorithm that takes as input the security parameter and outputs a key pair* (pk, sk).
- $pk \leftarrow \mathsf{tKeyGen}(1^\lambda)$ *a probabilistic algorithm that takes as input the security parameter and outputs a trapdoor key* pk.
- $c \leftarrow \mathsf{Enc}(pk, m)$ *a probabilistic algorithm that takes as input a message* $m \in \{0, 1\}$ *and a key* pk *and returns a ciphertext* c.
- $m \leftarrow \mathsf{Dec}(sk, c)$ *a deterministic algorithm that takes as input a secret key* sk *and a ciphertext* c *and returns a message* m.

Definition 9 (Correctness). *For all* $\lambda \in \mathbb{N}$, *for all* $m \in \{0, 1\}$ *it holds that* $m = \mathsf{Dec}(sk, \mathsf{Enc}(pk, m))$, *where* $(pk, sk) \leftarrow \mathsf{KeyGen}(1^\lambda)$.

Definition 10 (Trapdoor Public Keys). *For all* $\lambda \in \mathbb{N}$ *and for all probabilistic polynomial-time adversaries* $\mathcal{A}$ *there exists a negligible function* $\mu(\cdot)$ *such that*

$$\Pr\left[b \leftarrow \mathcal{A}(pk) : \begin{array}{c} b \leftarrow_\$ \{0, 1\} \\ \textit{if } b = 0 \textit{ then } pk \leftarrow \mathsf{tKeyGen}(1^\lambda) \\ \textit{if } b = 1 \textit{ then } (pk, sk) \leftarrow \mathsf{KeyGen}(1^\lambda) \end{array}\right] \leq \frac{1}{2} + \mu(\lambda).$$

Definition 11 (μ-Hiding). *For all* $\lambda \in \mathbb{N}$ *and for all unbounded adversaries* $\mathcal{A}$ *there exists a negligible function* $\mu(\cdot)$ *such that*

$$\Pr\left[b \leftarrow \mathcal{A}(pk, \mathsf{Enc}(pk, b)) : \begin{array}{c} b \leftarrow_\$ \{0, 1\} \\ pk \leftarrow \mathsf{tKeyGen}(1^\lambda) \end{array}\right] \leq \frac{1}{2} + \mu(\lambda).$$

Probabilistic Obfuscation. A probabilistic obfuscator $pi\mathcal{O}$ is an algorithm that obfuscates probabilistic circuits and it can be constructed assuming sub-exponentially secure indistinguishability obfuscation [14] and sub-exponentially secure one-way functions [9].

Definition 12 (*piO* for a class of samplers S). *A uniform polynomial-size machine piO is an* indistinguishable obfuscator *for a class of samplers* **S** *over the (possibly randomized) circuit family* $\mathcal{C} = \{C_\lambda\}_{\lambda \in \mathbb{N}}$ *if, on input a (possibly probabilistic) circuit* $C \in \mathcal{C}_\lambda$ *and the security parameter* 1^λ, *outputs a deterministic circuit* Λ *of size* $p(|C|, \lambda)$, *for some fixed polynomial* $p(\cdot)$.

Definition 13 (Correctness). *For every non-uniform polynomial-size distinguisher* $\mathcal{D}$, *every (possibly probabilistic) circuit* $C \in \mathcal{C}_\lambda$ *and string* y, *we define the following experiments*

- $\mathsf{EXP}_0^{\mathcal{D}}(1^\lambda, C, y)$: $\mathcal{D}$ *on input* $1^\lambda, C, y$, *participates in as many number of iterations as he wants. In iteration* i, *it chooses an input* x_i; *if* $x_i = x_j$ *for* $j < i$, *then abort; else,* $\mathcal{D}$ *gets back* $(C(x_i, r_i))$ *where* r_i *are fresh randomness (* $r_i = null$, *if* C *is deterministic). At the end of the final iteration,* $\mathcal{D}$ *outputs a bit* b. *(Note that* $\mathcal{D}$ *is stateful.)*
- $\mathsf{EXP}_1^{\mathcal{D}}(1^\lambda, C, y)$: *Obfuscate circuit* C *to obtain* $\Lambda \leftarrow piO(1^\lambda, C; r)$ *using fresh randomness* r. *Run* $\mathcal{D}$ *as described in the above experiment, except that in each iteration give* $\Lambda(x_i)$ *to* $\mathcal{D}$ *instead.*

We require that for every non-uniform polynomial-size distinguisher $\mathcal{D}$, *there is a negligible function* $\mu(\cdot)$, *such that, for every* $\lambda \in \mathbb{N}$, *every* $C \in \mathcal{C}_\lambda$, *and every polynomial-size auxiliary input* y *it holds that*

$$\Pr[b \leftarrow \mathsf{EXP}_b^{\mathcal{D}}(1^\lambda, C, y)] \le \frac{1}{2} + \mu(\lambda).$$

Definition 14 (Security with respect to S). *For every sampler* $D = \{D_\lambda\}_{\lambda \in \mathbb{N}} \in \mathbf{S}$, *and for every non-uniform polynomial-size machine* $\mathcal{A}$, *there exists a negligible function* $\mu(\cdot)$ *such that*

$$\Pr[b \leftarrow \mathcal{A}(C_0, C_1, piO(1^\lambda, C_b), y) : b \leftarrow_{\!*} \{0, 1\}; (C_0, C_1, y) \leftarrow D_\lambda)]. \tag{1}$$

Indistinguishability Obfuscation. We can cast the definition of indistinguishability obfuscation (iO) for circuits as a special case of worst-case input piO for the class $\mathcal{C}' = \{\mathcal{C}'_\lambda\}_{\lambda \in \mathbb{N}}$ of deterministic circuits as done in [9].

Definition 15 (iO for Circuits [14]). *A uniform PPT machine iO is an* indistinguishable obfuscator *for circuits, if it is a piO for the class of worst-case input Indistinguishability samplers* $\mathbf{S}^{\mathsf{w-Ind}}$ *over* $\mathcal{C}'$ *that includes all deterministic circuits of size at most* λ.

What is left to be defined is the class of worst-case input samplers.

Definition 16 (Worst-case input Indistinguishable Samplers). *The class* $\mathbf{S}^{\mathsf{w-Ind}}$ *of worst-case input indistinguishable samplers for a circuit family* $\mathcal{C}$ *contains all circuit samplers* $D = \{D_\lambda\}_{\lambda \in \mathbb{N}}$ *for* $\mathcal{C}$ *with the following property: For all adversary* $\mathcal{A} = \{(\mathcal{A}_1, \mathcal{A}_2)_\lambda\}_{\lambda \in \mathbb{N}}$ *where* $\mathcal{A}_1$ *is an unbounded non-uniform machine and* $\mathcal{A}_2$ *is PPT, there is a negligible function* $\mu(\cdot)$, *such that*

$$\Pr\left[b \leftarrow \mathcal{A}_2(st, C_0, C_1, z, x, y) : \begin{array}{l} (C_0, C_1, z) \leftarrow D_\lambda \\ (x, st) \leftarrow \mathcal{A}_1(C_0, C_1, z) \\ b \leftarrow_{\$} \{0, 1\} \\ y \leftarrow C_b(x) \end{array}\right] \leq \frac{1}{2} + \mu(\lambda).$$

3   Homomorphic Time-Lock Puzzles

In the following we give a definition for the main object of interest of this work, homomorphic time-lock puzzles (HTLP). The syntax follows the standard notation for time-lock puzzles except that we consider an additional setup phase that depends on the hardness parameter but not on the secret. Furthermore, HTLPs are augmented with an evaluation algorithm that allows one to manipulate puzzles in a meaningful way.

Definition 17 (Homomorphic Time-Lock Puzzles). *Let $\mathcal{C} = \{\mathcal{C}_\lambda\}_{\lambda \in \mathbb{N}}$ be a class of circuits and let $\mathcal{S}$ be a finite domain. A homomorphic time-lock puzzle (HTLP) with respect to $\mathcal{C}$ and with solution space $\mathcal{S}$ is tuple of four algorithms* (HP.PSetup, HP.PGen, HP.PSolve, HP.PEval) *defined as follows.*

- *$pp \leftarrow$ HP.PSetup$(1^\lambda, \mathcal{T})$ a probabilistic algorithm that takes as input a security parameter 1^λ and a time hardness parameter $\mathcal{T}$, and outputs public parameters pp.*
- *$Z \leftarrow$ HP.PGen(pp, s) a probabilistic algorithm that takes as input public parameters pp, and a solution $s \in \mathcal{S}$, and outputs a puzzle Z.*
- *$s \leftarrow$ HP.PSolve(pp, Z) a deterministic algorithm that takes as input public parameters pp and a puzzle Z and outputs a solution s.*
- *$Z' \leftarrow$ HP.PEval$(C, pp, Z_1, \ldots, Z_n)$ a probabilistic algorithm that takes as input a circuit $C \in \mathcal{C}_\lambda$, public parameters pp and a set of n puzzles $(Z_1, \ldots, Z_n)$ and outputs a puzzle Z'.*

Security requires that the solution of the puzzles is hidden for all adversaries that run in (parallel) time less than $\mathcal{T}$. Here we consider a basic version where the time is counted from the moment the public parameters are published. We also consider a stronger version, i.e., where the time is taken from the moment each puzzle is generated, in Sect. 5.2.

Definition 18 (Security of HTLP). *An HTLP scheme* (HP.PSetup, HP.PGen, HP.PSolve, HP.PEval) *is secure with gap $\varepsilon < 1$ if there exists a polynomial $\tilde{\mathcal{T}}(\cdot)$ such that for all polynomials $\mathcal{T}(\cdot) \geq \tilde{\mathcal{T}}(\cdot)$ and every polynomial-size adversary $(\mathcal{A}_1, \mathcal{A}_2) = \{(\mathcal{A}_1, \mathcal{A}_2)_\lambda\}_{\lambda \in \mathbb{N}}$ where the depth of $\mathcal{A}_2$ is bounded from above by $\mathcal{T}^\varepsilon(\lambda)$, there exists a negligible function $\mu(\cdot)$, such that for all $\lambda \in \mathbb{N}$ it holds that*

$$\Pr\left[b \leftarrow \mathcal{A}_2(pp, Z, \tau) : \begin{array}{l} (\tau, s_0, s_1) \leftarrow \mathcal{A}_1(1^\lambda) \\ pp \leftarrow \text{HP.PSetup}(1^\lambda, \mathcal{T}(\lambda)) \\ b \leftarrow_{\$} \{0, 1\} \\ Z \leftarrow \text{HP.PGen}(pp, s_b) \end{array}\right] \leq \frac{1}{2} + \mu(\lambda)$$

and $(s_0, s_1) \in \mathcal{S}^2$.

We consider the basic notion of correctness, that concerns with a single application of the evaluation algorithm. The definition can be easily extended to the multi-hop settings (in the same spirit as [17]) in a natural way.

Definition 19 (Correctness). *Let* $C = \{C_\lambda\}_{\lambda \in \mathbb{N}}$ *be a class of circuits (together with their respective representations). An HTLP scheme* (HP.PSetup, HP.PGen, HP.PSolve, HP.PEval) *is correct (for the class* C*) if for all* $\lambda \in \mathbb{N}$*, all polynomials* T *in* λ*, all circuits* $C \in C_\lambda$ *and respective inputs* $(s_1, \ldots, s_n) \in S^n$*, all pp in the support of* HP.PSetup($1^\lambda, T$)*, and all* Z_i *in the support of* HP.PGen(pp, s_i)*, the following two conditions are satisfied:*

- *There exists a negligible function* $\mu(\cdot)$ *such that*

$$\Pr\left[\mathsf{HP.PSolve}(pp, \mathsf{HP.PEval}(C, pp, Z_1, \ldots, Z_n)) \neq C(s_1, \ldots, s_n) \right] \leq \mu(\lambda).$$

- *There exists a fixed polynomial* $p(\cdot)$ *such that the runtime of* HP.PSolve(pp, Z) *is bounded by* $p(\lambda, T)$*, where* $Z \leftarrow$ HP.PEval($C, pp, Z_1, \ldots, Z_n$)*.*

The central property for HTLPs is compactness, which requires that the size of evaluated ciphertexts is independent of the size of the circuit and that the running time of the evaluation algorithm is independent of the hardness parameter.

Definition 20 (Compactness). *Let* $C = \{C_\lambda\}_{\lambda \in \mathbb{N}}$ *be a class of circuits (together with their respective representations). An HTLP scheme* (HP.PSetup, HP.PGen, HP.PSolve, HP.PEval) *is compact (for the class* C*) if for all* $\lambda \in \mathbb{N}$*, all polynomials* T *in* λ*, all circuits* $C \in C_\lambda$ *and respective inputs* $(s_1, \ldots, s_n) \in S^n$*, all pp in the support of* HP.PSetup($1^\lambda, T$)*, and all* Z_i *in the support of* HP.PGen(pp, s_i)*, the following two conditions are satisfied:*

- *There exists a fixed polynomial* $p(\cdot)$ *such that* $|Z| = p(\lambda, |C(s_1, \ldots, s_n)|)$*, where* $Z \leftarrow$ HP.PEval($C, pp, Z_1, \ldots, Z_n$)*.*
- *There exists a fixed polynomial* $\tilde{p}(\cdot)$ *such that the runtime of* HP.PEval ($C, pp, Z_1, \ldots, Z_n$) *is bounded by* $\tilde{p}(\lambda, |C|)$*.*

Finally we observe that one can define circuit privacy for HTLPs analogously to the FHE notion. Since it is not of significance for our applications we refrain from giving a formal definition and we refer the reader to [27].

4   Constructions

In this section we describe our HTLP schemes for different classes of functions.

4.1   Linearly Homomorphic

We describe a scheme (LHTLP) homomorphic over the ring $(\mathbb{Z}_N, +)$ below.

LHP.PSetup($1^\lambda, \mathcal{T}$) :

- Sample a pair of primes (p, q) such that $p = 2p' + 1$ and $q = 2q' + 1$, where p' and q' are also primes, and set $N := p \cdot q$.
- Sample a uniform $\tilde{g} \leftarrow_\$ \mathbb{Z}_N^*$ and set $g := -\tilde{g}^2 \pmod{N}$.
  Compute $h := g^{2^{\mathcal{T}}}$, which can be optimized by reducing $2^{\mathcal{T}}$ modulo $\varphi(N)/2$ first.
- Output $pp := (\mathcal{T}, N, g, h)$.

LHP.PGen(pp, s) :

- Parse $pp := (\mathcal{T}, N, g, h)$.
- Sample a uniform $r \leftarrow_\$ \{1, \ldots, N^2\}$.
- Generate the elements $u := g^r \pmod{N}$ and $v := h^{r \cdot N} \cdot (1 + N)^s \pmod{N^2}$.
- Output $Z := (u, v)$ as the puzzle.

LHP.PSolve(pp, Z) :

- Parse $pp := (\mathcal{T}, N, g, h)$.
- Parse the puzzle $Z := (u, v)$.
- Compute $w := u^{2^{\mathcal{T}}} \pmod{N}$ by repeated squaring.
- Output $s := \dfrac{v/(w)^N \pmod{N^2} - 1}{N}$ as the solution.

LHP.PEval($\oplus, pp, Z_1, \ldots, Z_n$) :

- Parse $pp := (\mathcal{T}, N, g, h)$.
- Parse every $Z_i := (u_i, v_i) \in \mathbb{J}_N \times \mathbb{Z}_{N^2}^*$.
- Compute $\tilde{u} := \prod_{i=1}^n u_i \pmod{N}$ and $\tilde{v} := \prod_{i=1}^n v_i \pmod{N^2}$.
- Output the puzzle $(\tilde{u}, \tilde{v})$.

To see why the scheme is correct, observe that

$$
\tilde{s} = \frac{\tilde{v}/(\tilde{w})^N \pmod{N^2} - 1}{N}
$$

$$
= \frac{\prod_{i=1}^n v_i / \left(\prod_{i=1}^n u_i^{2^{\mathcal{T}}} \pmod{N} \right)^N \pmod{N^2} - 1}{N}
$$

$$
= \frac{\prod_{i=1}^n h^{r_i \cdot N} \cdot (1 + N)^{s_i} / \left(\prod_{i=1}^n h^{r_i} \pmod{N} \right)^N \pmod{N^2} - 1}{N}
$$

$$
= \frac{\prod_{i=1}^n h^{r_i \cdot N} \cdot (1 + N)^{s_i} / \prod_{i=1}^n h^{r_i \cdot N} \pmod{N^2} - 1}{N}
$$

$$
= \frac{(1 + N)^{\sum_{i=1}^n s_i} \pmod{N^2} - 1}{N}
$$

by Lemma 2. Furthermore,

$$
\tilde{s} = \frac{(1 + N)^{\sum_{i=1}^n s_i} \pmod{N^2} - 1}{N} = \frac{1 + N \cdot \sum_{i=1}^n s_i - 1}{N} = \sum_{i=1}^n s_i
$$

by binomial expansion. The security of our construction is shown in the following.

Theorem 1. *Let N be a strong RSA integer. If the sequential squaring assumption and the DDH assumptions hold over $\mathbb{J}_N$ and the DCR assumption hold over $Z_{N^2}^*$, then the scheme* LHTLP *is a secure homomorphic time-lock puzzle.*

Proof. Consider the following sequence of hybrids.

Hybrid $\mathcal{H}_0$: Is defined as the original scheme.

Hybrid $\mathcal{H}_1$: In this hybrid h is sampled uniformly from $\mathbb{J}_N$, instead of being computed as $h := g^{2^T}$. Let $(\mathcal{A}_1, \mathcal{A}_2)$ be an efficient distinguisher where the depth of $\mathcal{A}_2$ is less than T. We construct the following reduction against the sequential squaring assumption: The reduction runs the adversary $\mathcal{A}_1$ on input the security parameter 1^λ and receives two secrets (s_0, s_1) and some advice τ. Then receives as input the tuple (N, g, T, x, y), sets $pp := (T, N, x, y)$ and computes Z exactly as specified by the scheme using s_b as the solution, for a random $b \leftarrow_\$ \{0, 1\}$. Then it invokes the adversary $\mathcal{A}_2$ on input (pp, Z, τ) and outputs whatever $\mathcal{A}_2$ returns. Observe that the depth of the reduction is only a constant fraction larger than that of $\mathcal{A}_2$. We the analyze the two cases separately.

1. (N, g, x, y) is a uniform tuple: Then $x = g$ and $y = h$ are uniform in $\mathbb{J}_N$. Thus

$$(T, N, x, y) = (T, N, g, h)$$

   is distributed as in $\mathcal{H}_1$.
2. (N, g, x, y, z) is a squared tuple: In this case we have that $(N, g, x, y) = (N, g, x, x^{2^T})$. Which means that the tuple

$$(T, N, x, y) = (T, N, g, g^{2^T})$$

   is distributed according to $\mathcal{H}_0$.

Thus the existence of an efficient distinguisher (with depth smaller than T) between the two hybrids contradicts the sequential squaring assumption.

Hybrid $\mathcal{H}_2$: In this hybrid r is sampled from the set $\{1, \ldots, \varphi(N)/2\}$, rather than $\{1, \ldots, N^2\}$. The two hybrids are statistically indistinguishable by Lemma 1. We stress that the encrypter does not know $\varphi(N)/2$, however the argument is purely statistical and therefore there is no need for a polynomial-time simulation.

Hybrid $\mathcal{H}_3$: In this hybrid u is sampled uniformly at random from $\mathbb{J}_N$. We show indistinguishability with a reduction against the DDH assumption over $\mathbb{J}_N$. The reduction runs the adversary on input the security parameter to receive (τ, s_0, s_1). On input (N, g, g^x, g^y, g^z), the reduction sets the public parameters of the scheme to (T, N, g, g^x) and the puzzle to $(g^y, (g^z)^N \cdot (1 + N)^{s_b})$, then feeds $\mathcal{A}_2$ with those inputs and it returns whatever the adversary returns. Clearly the reduction is efficient, so what is left to be shown is that the inputs are distributed correctly, according to the two hybrids.

1. (N, g, g^x, g^y, g^z) is a uniform tuple: Then $g^x = h$ is uniform in $\mathbb{J}_N$, $g^y = u$ is uniform in $\mathbb{J}_N$, and g^z is uniform in $\mathbb{J}_N$, so we rewrite it as $g^z = h^r$ (for some random $r \in \{1, \ldots, \varphi(N)/2\}$). Thus

$$(\mathcal{T}, N, g, g^x), (g^y, (g^z)^N \cdot (1 + N)^{s_b}) = (\mathcal{T}, N, g, h), (u, h^{r \cdot N} \cdot (1 + N)^{s_b})$$

   are distributed identically to $\mathcal{H}_3$.
2. (N, g, g^x, g^y, g^z) is a DDH tuple: For the sake of clarity we rewrite the input tuple as (N, g, g^x, g^y, g^{xy}). Fix $g^x = h$ and observe that the tuples

$$(\mathcal{T}, N, g, g^x), (g^y, (g^{xy})^N \cdot (1 + N)^{s_b}) = (\mathcal{T}, N, g, h), (g^y, h^{y \cdot N} \cdot (1 + N)^{s_b})$$

   are distributed according to $\mathcal{H}_2$.

It follows that any non negligible advantage in distinguishing the two hybrids directly implies an attack against DDH.

Hybrid $\mathcal{H}_4$: In this hybrid v is computed as $w \cdot (1 + N)^{s_b} \pmod{N^2}$, where w is uniformly sampled from $\mathbb{Z}_{N^2}^*$ (constrained on having Jacobi symbol $+1$). Consider the following reduction against the DCR assumption: Prior to the challenge, the reduction runs $\mathcal{A}_1$ on input 1^λ and receives (τ, s_0, s_1). On input (N, y), the reduction sets N as the modulus and samples g and h uniformly from $\mathbb{J}_N$ (as specified in the $\mathcal{H}_3$). Then it computes the Jacobi symbol of y and samples some $\tilde{y}$ with the same Jacobi symbol as y. Then it samples some $u \leftarrow_s \mathbb{J}_N$ and sets $v := y \cdot \tilde{y}^N \cdot (1 + N)^{s_b} \pmod{N^2}$, for a uniform $b \leftarrow_s \{0, 1\}$. Finally it runs $\mathcal{A}_2$ on input $((\mathcal{T}, N, g, h), (u, v))$ and returns whatever $\mathcal{A}_2$ returns. Note that the reduction is efficient since the Jacobi symbol is efficiently computable without the factorization of N. If y is uniform in $\mathbb{Z}_{N^2}^*$, then so is $y \cdot \tilde{y}^N \pmod{N^2}$, and therefore the reduction perfectly simulates $\mathcal{H}_4$. On the other hand if y is an N-th residue, then $y \cdot \tilde{y}^N = x^N \cdot \tilde{y}^N = (x\tilde{y})^N \pmod{N^2}$ is also an N-th residue. Note that the Jacobi symbol of $x\tilde{y}$ is $+1$, since the Jacobi symbol is multiplicatively homomorphic. It follows that in this case the inputs of the reduction are identical to that of $\mathcal{H}_3$. We can therefore bound from above the distance between these two hybrids by a negligible amount.

Observe that in the last hybrid every bit of information about the message is lost. This concludes our proof.

4.2 Multiplicatively Homomorphic

In the following we describe our scheme (MHTLP) which is multiplicatively homomorphic over the ring $(\mathbb{J}_N, \cdot)$. The algorithms are described below.

MHP.PSetup($1^\lambda, \mathcal{T}$) :

- Sample a pair of primes (p, q) such that $p = 2p' + 1$ and $q = 2q' + 1$, where p' and q' are also primes, and set $N := p \cdot q$.
- Sample a uniform $\tilde{g} \leftarrow_s \mathbb{Z}_N^*$ and set $g := -\tilde{g}^2 \pmod{N}$.
- Compute $h := g^{2^\mathcal{T}}$, which can be optimized by reducing $2^\mathcal{T}$ modulo $\varphi(N)/2$ first.
- Output $pp := (\mathcal{T}, N, g, h)$.

MHP.PGen(pp, s) :

- Parse $pp := (\mathcal{T}, N, g, h)$.
- Sample a uniform $r \leftarrow_\$ \{1, \ldots, N^2\}$.
- Generate the elements $u := g^r \pmod{N}$ and $v := h^r \cdot s \pmod{N}$.
- Output $Z := (u, v)$ as the puzzle.

MHP.PSolve(pp, Z) :

- Parse $pp := (\mathcal{T}, N, g, h)$.
- Parse the puzzle $Z := (u, v)$.
- Compute $w := u^{2^\mathcal{T}} \pmod{N}$ by repeated squaring.
- Output $s := v/w$ as the solution.

MHP.PEval$(\otimes, pp, Z_1, \ldots, Z_n)$:

- Parse $pp := (\mathcal{T}, N, g, h)$.
- Parse every $Z_i := (u_i, v_i) \in \mathbb{J}_N^2$.
- Compute $\tilde{u} := \prod_{i=1}^n u_i \pmod{N}$ and $\tilde{v} := \prod_{i=1}^n v_i \pmod{N}$.
- Output the puzzle $(\tilde{u}, \tilde{v})$.

For correctness it suffices to observe that

$$\tilde{s} = \frac{\tilde{v}}{\tilde{w}} = \frac{\tilde{v}}{\tilde{u}^{2^\mathcal{T}}} = \frac{\prod_{i=1}^n v_i}{\prod_{i=1}^n u_i^{2^\mathcal{T}}} = \frac{\prod_{i=1}^n h^{r_i} \cdot s_i}{\prod_{i=1}^n g^{r_i \cdot 2^\mathcal{T}}} = \frac{\prod_{i=1}^n h^{r_i} \cdot s_i}{\prod_{i=1}^n h^{r_i}} = \prod_{i=1}^n s_i.$$

For security we prove the following theorem.

Theorem 2. *Let N be a strong RSA integer. If the sequential squaring and the DDH assumptions hold over $\mathbb{J}_N$, then the scheme* MHTLP *is a secure homomorphic time-lock puzzle.*

Proof. Consider the following sequence of hybrids.

Hybrid $\mathcal{H}_0$: Is defined as the original scheme.

Hybrid $\mathcal{H}_1$: Same as Theorem 1.

Hybrid $\mathcal{H}_2$: Same as Theorem 1.

Hybrid $\mathcal{H}_3$: In this hybrid v is computed as $w \cdot s$, for a uniform $w \leftarrow_\$ \mathbb{J}_N$. Indistinguishability follows from an invocation of the DDH assumption over $\mathbb{J}_N$: The reduction runs the adversary on input the security parameter and receives (τ, s_0, s_1). On input (N, g, g^x, g^y, g^z), the reduction sets the public parameters of the scheme to $(\mathcal{T}, N, g, g^x)$ and computes the puzzle Z as $(g^y, g^z \cdot s_b)$, for a randomly sampled $b \leftarrow_\$ \{0, 1\}$. The adversary is fed with (pp, Z, τ) and the reduction returns whatever the adversary returns. The reduction is clearly polynomial-time. We consider the two distributions in the following.

1. (N, g, g^x, g^y, g^z) is a uniform tuple: Then the tuples

$$(\mathcal{T}, N, g, g^x), (g^y, g^z \cdot s_b) = (\mathcal{T}, N, g, h), (g^y, w \cdot s_b)$$

are distributed identically to $\mathcal{H}_3$.

2. (N, g, g^x, g^y, g^z) is a DDH tuple: For the sake of clarity we rewrite the input tuple as (N, g, g^x, g^y, g^{xy}). Fix $g^x = h$ and observe that the tuples

$$(\mathcal{T}, N, g, g^x), (g^y, g^{xy} \cdot s_b) = (\mathcal{T}, N, g, h), (g^y, h^y \cdot s_b)$$

are distributed according to $\mathcal{H}_2$.

It follows that any non negligible advantage in distinguishing the two hybrids directly implies an attack against DDH.

The proof is concluded by observing that in $\mathcal{H}_3$ the secret s_b is information-theoretically hidden by w.

XOR-Homomorphism. If we set N to be a Blum integer and encode the secret $s \in \{0,1\}$ as $(-1)^s$, then the same construction gives us an XOR homomorphic scheme. This is because if N is a Blum integer, then $(\pm 1, \cdot)$ is a subgroup of $\mathbb{J}_N$.

4.3   Fully Homomorphic

In the following we describe our construction for a fully-homomorphic time-lock puzzle (FHTLP). Without loss of generality we consider binary secrets and circuits that are composed exclusively by NAND gates. Let $(\mathsf{KeyGen}, \mathsf{Enc}, \mathsf{Dec}, \mathsf{tKeyGen})$ be a trapdoor encryption scheme, $(\mathsf{Key}, \mathsf{Puncture}, \mathsf{PRF})$ be a puncturable PRF, $(\mathsf{PGen}, \mathsf{PSolve})$ be any (non-homomorphic) time-lock puzzle, $pi\mathcal{O}$ be an obfuscator for probabilistic circuits, and $i\mathcal{O}$ be an obfuscator for deterministic circuits. Define the circuit $\mathsf{Prog}^{(sk,pk)}(\alpha, \beta)$ and $\mathsf{MProg}^{(sk_0,k,k')}(i)$ as

$\mathsf{Prog}^{(sk,pk)}(\alpha, \beta):$	$\mathsf{MProg}^{(sk_0,k,k')}(i):$
parse $\alpha := (z_\alpha, c_\alpha)$	$r_{i-1} \leftarrow \mathsf{PRF}(k, i-1)$
parse $\beta := (z_\beta, c_\beta)$	$r_i \leftarrow \mathsf{PRF}(k, i), r_i' \leftarrow \mathsf{PRF}(k', i)$
$s_\alpha \leftarrow \mathsf{Dec}(sk, c_\alpha), s_\beta \leftarrow \mathsf{Dec}(sk, c_\beta)$	$(pk_{i-1}, sk_{i-1}) \leftarrow \mathsf{KeyGen}(1^\lambda; r_{i-1})$
$s := s_\alpha \text{ NAND } s_\beta$	$(pk_i, sk_i) \leftarrow \mathsf{KeyGen}(1^\lambda, r_i)$
$z \leftarrow \mathsf{PGen}(\mathcal{T}, s)$	$P_i \leftarrow \mathsf{Prog}^{(sk_{i-1}, pk_i)}$
$c \leftarrow \mathsf{Enc}(pk, s)$	$\Lambda_i \leftarrow pi\mathcal{O}(1^p, P_i; r_i')$
return (z, c)	**return** (Λ_i)

Let $\mathcal{L}$ be a super-polynomial function $\mathcal{L}(\lambda) := 2^{\omega(\log(\lambda))}$. The four algorithms of the scheme are described below.

$\mathsf{FHP.PSetup}(1^\lambda, \mathcal{T}):$

- Sample a pair of keys $(pk_0, sk_0) \leftarrow \mathsf{KeyGen}(1^\lambda)$
- Sample two PRF keys $k, k' \leftarrow \mathsf{Key}(1^\lambda)$
- Obfuscate using $i\mathcal{O}$ the circuit $\mathsf{MProg}^{(sk_0,k,k')}$, that is, sample $MEvk \leftarrow i\mathcal{O}(1^p, \mathsf{MProg}^{(sk_0,k,k')})$ where the security parameter $p = p(\lambda)$ for obfuscation is an upper-bound on the size of $\mathsf{MProg}^{(sk_0,k,k')}$.
- Output $pp := (\mathcal{T}, pk_0, MEvk)$.

FHP.PGen(pp, s) :

- Parse $pp := (\mathcal{T}, pk_0, MEvk)$.
- Generate a ciphertext $c \leftarrow \mathsf{Enc}(pk_0, s)$.
- Generate a puzzle $z \leftarrow \mathsf{PGen}(\mathcal{T}, s)$.
- Output $Z := (z, c)$ as the puzzle.

FHP.PSolve(pp, Z) :

- Parse the puzzle $Z := (z, c)$.
- Compute $s \leftarrow \mathsf{PSolve}(z)$ and output s as the solution.

FHP.PEval$(C, pp, Z_1, \ldots, Z_n)$:

- Evaluate C (of depth $\ell \leq \mathcal{L}(\lambda)$) layer by layer. For iteration $i \in \{0, \ldots, \ell\}$, generate the evaluation key for the layer as $\Lambda_i \leftarrow MEvk(i)$.
- For each NAND gate g in this layer i, let $\alpha(g), \beta(g)$ be the puzzles of the values of its input wires
- Evaluate g homomorphically by computing $\gamma(g) = \Lambda_i(\alpha(g), \beta(g))$ as the puzzle of the value of g's output wire.
- Output the puzzle generated in the last iteration ℓ.

Correctness easily follows from the correctness of the underlying primitives. Towards arguing about security, we define a useful subroutine $\mathsf{tProg}^{(tpk)}(\alpha, \beta)$ as follows

$\underline{\mathsf{tProg}^{(tpk)}(\alpha, \beta)}$:

$z \leftarrow \mathsf{PGen}(\mathcal{T}, 0)$

$c \leftarrow \mathsf{Enc}(tpk, 0)$

return (z, c)

which is instrumental for probabilistic obfuscator $pi\mathcal{O}$. Let $SK = \{sk_\lambda\}$ be the set of all strings of length $n = n(\lambda)$. Define the distribution D^{SK} as follows: Sample a trapdoor key $tpk \leftarrow \mathsf{tKeyGen}(1^\lambda)$ and some $sk \leftarrow_\$ SK$ and return $(C_0 = \mathsf{Prog}^{(sk, tpk)}, C_1 = \mathsf{tProg}^{(tpk)}, tpk)$. Then **S** is the class of samplers that include the distribution ensembles D^{SK} for all strings SK of length n. Security is established by the following theorem and the proof is given in the full version.

Theorem 3. *Let* $(\mathsf{PGen}, \mathsf{PSolve})$ *be a secure time-lock puzzle. Define* $\mu(\lambda) := \tilde{\mu}(\lambda) \cdot \mathcal{L}^{-1}$, *where* $\tilde{\mu}(\cdot)$ *is some negligible function. Assume the following primitives with distinguishing gaps bounded by* $\mu(\lambda)$ *against a polynomial-size adversary who's depth is bounded by* $\mathcal{T}^\varepsilon(\lambda)$, *for some constant* $\varepsilon < 1$:

- $(\mathsf{KeyGen}, \mathsf{Enc}, \mathsf{Dec}, \mathsf{tKeyGen})$ *is a secure* μ-*hiding trapdoor encryption scheme*,
- $pi\mathcal{O}$ *is a secure indistinguishable obfuscator for the class of samplers* **S**,
- $i\mathcal{O}$ *is a secure indistinguishable obfuscator for circuits, and*
- $(\mathsf{Key}, \mathsf{Puncture}, \mathsf{PRF})$ *is a secure puncturable PRF.*

Then, the scheme FHTLP *is a secure homomorphic time-lock puzzle.*

5   Extensions

In the following we explore and discuss several extensions of our constructions.

5.1   Semi-compact Scheme for Branching Programs

The linearly homomorphic scheme described in Sect. 4.1 can be easily generalized to higher powers of N, along the lines of the work of Damgård and Jurik [11], where the message domain is $\mathbb{Z}_{N^{y-1}}$ and the ciphertexts live in $\mathbb{Z}_{N^y}$, for an arbitrary $y \in \mathbb{N}$. The public parameters are identical to the ones generated by LHP.PSetup, whereas the puzzle is generated as

$$u := g^r \pmod{N} \text{ and } v := h^{r \cdot N^{y-1}} \cdot (1+N)^s \pmod{N^y}.$$

The solving algorithm factors $h^{r \cdot N^{y-1}} \pmod{N^y}$ out of v, via a series of sequential squarings, and recovers s from $(1+N)^s \pmod{N^y}$ using the polynomial-time discrete-logarithm algorithm described in [11]. Security follows from a natural generalization of the DCR assumption, also introduced in [11].

Note that the asymptotic message-ciphertext rate approaches 1 as y grows. This is desirable from a practical perspective but also it allows us to instantiate the compiler of Ishai and Paskin [21] with our extended scheme: As a corollary we obtain a (semi-compact) HTLP for branching programs (a superclass of NC1) where the ciphertext size grows linearly in the length of the branching program but does not depend on its width.

5.2   Reusing the Setup

A shortcoming of our primitive is that security is guaranteed to hold against a depth-constrained adversary that takes as input both the public parameters pp and the puzzle Z. This is equivalent to saying that the secrets are hidden until time $\mathcal{T}$ since the generation of the setup rather than the generation of the puzzle. From a practical perspective, this cripples the applicability of our primitive since the public parameters need to be re-initialized after time $\mathcal{T}$.

Ideally, we would like to set the public parameters once and for all and compute polynomially many puzzles at arbitrary time intervals. Each puzzle should then hide the secret until time $\mathcal{T}$, starting from the generation of the puzzle itself. Thus we consider a two stage adversary $(\mathcal{A}_1, \mathcal{A}_2)$, where $\mathcal{A}_1$ is polynomial-size (unbounded depth) and is allowed to craft the polynomial-size advice τ *after* being given the public parameters pp. Then the depth-bounded $\mathcal{A}_2$ is asked to guess the bit b on input the puzzle Z and the advice τ. This is formalized in the following.

Definition 21 (Reusable Security of HTLP). *An HTLP scheme* (HP.PSetup, HP.PGen, HP.PSolve, HP.PEval) *is reusable secure with gap* $\varepsilon < 1$ *if there exists a polynomial* $\tilde{\mathcal{T}}(\cdot)$ *such that for all polynomials* $\mathcal{T}(\cdot) \geq \tilde{\mathcal{T}}(\cdot)$ *and every polynomial-size adversary* $(\mathcal{A}_1, \mathcal{A}_2) = \{(\mathcal{A}_1, \mathcal{A}_2)_\lambda\}_{\lambda \in \mathbb{N}}$ *where the depth of*

$\mathcal{A}_2$ is bounded from above by $\mathcal{T}^{\varepsilon}(\lambda)$, there exists a negligible function $\mu(\cdot)$, such that for all $\lambda \in \mathbb{N}$ it holds that

$$\Pr \left[b \leftarrow \mathcal{A}_2(Z, \tau) : \begin{array}{l} pp \leftarrow \mathsf{HP.PSetup}(1^{\lambda}, \mathcal{T}(\lambda)) \\ (\tau, s_0, s_1) \leftarrow \mathcal{A}_1(pp) \\ b \leftarrow_{\$} \{0, 1\} \\ Z \leftarrow \mathsf{HP.PGen}(pp, s_b) \end{array} \right] \leq \frac{1}{2} + \mu(\lambda)$$

and $(s_0, s_1) \in \mathcal{S}^2$.

Arguing about the security of the constructions described in Sects. 4.1 and 4.2 in these settings requires a slightly modified version of the standard sequential squaring assumption (Assumption 1) that we describe below.

Assumption 4 (Strong Sequential Squaring). *Let N be a uniformly sampled strong RSA integer, g be a generator of $\mathbb{J}_N$, and $\mathcal{T}(\cdot)$ be a polynomial. Then there exists some $0 < \varepsilon < 1$ such that for every polynomial-size adversary $(\mathcal{A}_1, \mathcal{A}_2) = \{(\mathcal{A}_1, \mathcal{A}_2)_{\lambda}\}_{\lambda \in \mathbb{N}}$, where the depth of $\mathcal{A}_2$ is bounded from above by $\mathcal{T}^{\varepsilon}(\lambda)$, there exists a negligible function $\mu(\cdot)$ such that*

$$\Pr \left[b \leftarrow \mathcal{A}_2(x, y, \tau) : \begin{array}{l} \tau \leftarrow \mathcal{A}_1(N, g, \mathcal{T}(\lambda)) \\ x \leftarrow_{\$} \mathbb{J}_N; b \leftarrow_{\$} \{0, 1\} \\ \text{if } b = 0 \text{ then } y \leftarrow_{\$} \mathbb{J}_N \\ \text{if } b = 1 \text{ then } y := x^{2^{\mathcal{T}(\lambda)}} \end{array} \right] \leq \frac{1}{2} + \mu(\lambda).$$

This essentially corresponds to stating that the prior knowledge of the group structure does not help one breaking the sequentiality of the squaring operation, which seems to be a mild strengthening of the original conjecture. We remark that similar assumptions have already appeared in the context of verifiable delay functions [5,29,31]. We are now ready to state the following theorems.

Theorem 4. *Let N be a strong RSA integer. If the strong sequential squaring assumption and the DCR assumption hold over $\mathbb{J}_N$ and $Z^*_{N^2}$, respectively, then the scheme LHTLP is a reusable secure homomorphic time-lock puzzle.*

Proof. Consider the following sequence of hybrids.

Hybrid $\mathcal{H}_0$: This is the original experiment.

Hybrid $\mathcal{H}_1$: In this hybrid r is randomly sampled from $\{1, \ldots, \varphi(N)/2\}$. By Lemma 1, $\mathcal{H}_0$ and $\mathcal{H}_1$ are statistically close.

Hybrid $\mathcal{H}_2$: In this hybrid v is computed as $z^N \cdot (1 + N)^{s_b} \pmod{N^2}$, for a uniform $z \leftarrow_{\$} \mathbb{J}_N$. Let $(\mathcal{A}_1, \mathcal{A}_2)$ be an efficient distinguisher where the depth of $\mathcal{A}_2$ is less than $\mathcal{T}$. We construct the following reduction $(\mathcal{R}_1, \mathcal{R}_2)$ against the strong sequential squaring assumption: $\mathcal{R}_1$ takes as input the tuple $(N, g, \mathcal{T})$ and computes $h := g^{2^{\mathcal{T}}}$, then it sets $pp := (\mathcal{T}, N, g, h)$ and runs $\mathcal{A}_1(pp)$, who outputs some (τ, s_0, s_1), which is also the output of $\mathcal{R}_1$. The challenger sends to $\mathcal{R}_2$ the triple $(x, y, (\tau, s_0, s_1))$, who sets $u := x$ and $v := y^N \cdot (1 + N)^{s_b} \pmod{N^2}$, for a random $b \leftarrow_\$ \{0, 1\}$, and runs $\mathcal{A}_2((u, v), \tau)$ outputting whatever the adversary outputs. Observe that $\mathcal{R}_1$ is efficient, since $\mathcal{T}$ is a polynomial, and that the depth of $\mathcal{R}_2$ is identical (up to a constant factor) to that of $\mathcal{A}_2$. We distinguish two cases.

1. $y = x^{2^\mathcal{T}}$: Let $x = g^r$, for some $r \in \{1, \ldots, \varphi(N)/2\}$. Then the puzzle

$$(u, v) = (x, x^{2^\mathcal{T} \cdot N} \cdot (1 + N)^{s_b} \pmod{N^2}) = (g^r, h^{r \cdot N} \cdot (1 + N)^{s_b} \pmod{N^2})$$

   is distributed according to $\mathcal{H}_1$.
2. $y \leftarrow_\$ \mathbb{J}_N$: In this case the puzzle

$$(u, v) = (x, y^N \cdot (1 + N)^{s_b} \pmod{N^2})$$

   is distributed according to $\mathcal{H}_2$.

Thus the existence of $(\mathcal{R}_1, \mathcal{R}_2)$ contradicts the sequential squaring assumption.

Hybrid $\mathcal{H}_3$: In this hybrid v is computed as $w \cdot (1 + N)^{s_b} \pmod{N^2}$, where w is uniformly sampled from $\mathbb{Z}_{N^2}^*$ (constrained to have Jacobi symbol $+1$). The indistinguishability follows from an invocation of the DCR assumption and the argument is identical to the last hybrid of Theorem 1.

The proof concludes by observing that the message in the last hybrid is hidden in an information-theoretic sense.

Theorem 5. *Let N be a strong RSA integer. If the strong sequential squaring assumption holds over $\mathbb{J}_N$, then the scheme MHTLP is a secure reusable homomorphic time-lock puzzle.*

Proof. Consider the following sequence of hybrids.

Hybrid $\mathcal{H}_0$: This is the original experiment.

Hybrid $\mathcal{H}_1$: Same as Theorem 4.

Hybrid $\mathcal{H}_2$: In this hybrid we compute v as $w \cdot s$, for a uniform $w \leftarrow_\$ \mathbb{J}_N$. The two hybrids are indistinguishable by the sequential squaring assumption over $\mathbb{J}_N$. Consider the following two-stage reduction: $\mathcal{R}_1$ takes as input the tuple $(N, g, \mathcal{T})$ and computes $h := g^{2^\mathcal{T}}$, then it sets $pp := (\mathcal{T}, N, g, h)$ and runs $\mathcal{A}_1(pp)$, who outputs some message (τ, s_0, s_1). The output of $\mathcal{R}_1$ is the string (τ, s_0, s_1). The challenger provides $\mathcal{R}_2$ with the triple $(x, y, (\tau, s_0, s_1))$, who sets $u := x$ and $v := y \cdot s_b$ and runs $\mathcal{A}_2((u, v), \tau)$ and outputs whatever the adversary outputs. Observe that $\mathcal{R}_1$ is efficient, since $\mathcal{T}$ is a polynomial, and that the depth of $\mathcal{R}_2$ is close to that of $\mathcal{A}$. It is not hard to see that whenever $y = x^{2^\mathcal{T}}$ then reduction reproduces the distribution of $\mathcal{H}_1$, whereas if y is uniformly sampled in $\mathbb{J}_N$, then the simulation is identical to $\mathcal{H}_2$. Thus the success probability of $\mathcal{R}$ is identical to that of $\mathcal{A}$. This contradicts the sequential squaring assumption and bounds the difference between the two hybrids to a negligible factor.

Observe that in $\mathcal{H}_2$ the puzzle consists of two uniform elements of $\mathbb{J}_N$.

5.3   Public-Coin Setup

All of our schemes require a trusted setup where the random coins have to be kept private. If revealed, they would give one an unfair advantage in solving any puzzle. This does not seem to be an inherent limitation of the primitive and we could envision a dream-version of HTLPs where the setup can be run with public random coins. Towards this objective, one can generalize the techniques presented in Sects. 4.1 and 4.2 to hidden-order groups with public-coin setups [8], however this would hinder the efficiency of the schemes as the tuple $(g, h = g^{2^T})$ is no longer efficiently computable (by assumption). Depending on T, this may require a significant initial investment in terms of computation.

Nevertheless, for certain applications (e.g., e-voting or sealed bid auctions) it might be perfectly acceptable to run T sequential squarings ahead of time to generate the tuple (g, h). Note that, in the variants described above, the puzzle is guaranteed to hide the payload for time proportional to T, starting from the moment the puzzle is published. Therefore arbitrarily many puzzles can be efficiently spawned once (g, h) is fixed. Constructing an HTLP with an efficient public-coin setup is a fascinating open question.

5.4   Combining Puzzles of Different Hardness

Another limitation of our schemes is that the time parameter T is fixed once and for all in the setup. An easy solution to make our construction more flexible is to augment the setup with multiple $(T_1, \dots, T_n)$. For the constructions in Sects. 4.1 and 4.2 is sufficient to set the public parameters as

$$pp := \left(g, h_1 := g^{2^{T_1}}, \dots, h_n := g^{2^{T_n}} \right)$$

which can be efficiently computed using the factors of N. Our scheme in Sect. 4.3 can also be extended by producing different obfuscated circuits $(MEvk^{(1)}, \dots, MEvk^{(n)})$, with the appropriate T_i hardwired. Here it is important that the obfuscated circuits are sampled with fresh coins, so also the corresponding keys $(pk_0^{(1)}, \dots, pk_0^{(n)})$ must be included in the setup.

It turns out that one can even combine puzzles generated with different parameters T_1 and T_2 in a natural way: Assume without loss of generality that $T_1 > T_2$, then clearly $2^{T_2} \cdot \tilde{t} = 2^{T_1}$, for some integer $\tilde{t} = 2^t$. Then the homomorphic evaluation over two puzzles (u_1, v_1) and (u_2, v_2) is done as follows

$$\tilde{u} := u_1^{2^t} \cdot u_2 \ (\mathrm{mod}\ N) \text{ and } \tilde{v} := v_1 \cdot v_2 \ (\mathrm{mod}\ N^2)\ /\ (\mathrm{mod}\ N),$$

where the second modulus depends on whether we are considering linearly or multiplicatively homomorphic puzzles. Note that the hardness of the resulting puzzles $(\tilde{u}, \tilde{v})$ corresponds to the time proportional to solving it (T_2) + homomorphic evaluation $(t) = T_1$. This is aligned with the expectation that the evaluation algorithm does not decrease the difficulty of a puzzle. For the fully-homomorphic construction the argument is a bit more delicate since the obfuscated circuits contain a trapdoor to efficiently solve the puzzles. Therefore, one has to ensure that the puzzles are re-encoded with the correct hardness parameter. This can be done via standard techniques, e.g., signing the puzzles and verifying the signatures inside the obfuscated circuits.

6   Applications

In this section we present some of the most interesting applications of HTLPs. We stress that our purpose is to demonstrate the usefulness of our primitive in broader contexts and not to construct systems that are ready to be deployed in practice. The precise implementation and the complete characterization of the security of such systems is beyond the scope of this work. In favor of a simpler presentation, we implicitly assume that all HTLPs are well-formed and all secrets are sampled from the correct domains. This can be always enforced by augmenting our schemes with non-interactive zero-knowledge proofs [13].

6.1   E-Voting

We construct an *e-voting* protocol with n voters and m candidates. An e-voting protocol consists of a *voting* phase and a *counting* phase and proceeds as follows: During the voting phase, each voter casts a vote for one of the candidates and the votes are counted during the subsequent counting phase. Finally the candidate with the largest amount of votes is announced as the winner of the election. The votes must be kept hidden for the duration of the first phase to avoid any bias.

Let $\mathcal{T}$ be the time bound of the *voting phase*. We propose an e-voting protocol based on our linearly homomorphic time-lock puzzle from Sect. 4.1. Here, the i-th vote, denoted by vote_i, consists of a tuple of m time-lock puzzles where the secret encoded is always 0 except at position j, where the secret is 1. This encodes the preference for the j-th candidate C_j. After receiving votes from all the voters, the puzzles are combined homomorphically to sum up the number of preferences for each candidate. We eventually obtain a final vote consisting of m puzzles, which are then solved to obtain the final vote tallies for each candidate.

Election Setup: Generate the public parameters $pp \leftarrow \mathsf{LHP.PSetup}(1^\lambda, \mathcal{T})$ and publish them so that they are accessible to all the voters.

Voting Phase: Each voter V_i, on deciding to vote the j-th candidate C_j (where $j \in \{1, \dots, m\}$) does the following.

- For all $j' \in \{1, \dots, m\}/j$, generate $Z_{j'} \leftarrow \mathsf{LHP.PGen}(pp, 0)$.
- Generate $Z_j \leftarrow \mathsf{LHP.PGen}(pp, 1)$.
- Compute $\mathsf{vote}_i = (Z_1, \dots, Z_m)$ and output vote_i as the vote.

Counting Phase: Collect votes from all voters denoted by $(\mathsf{vote}_1, \dots, \mathsf{vote}_n)$ and do the following.

- Parse each vote as $\mathsf{vote}_i = (Z_1^{(i)}, \dots, Z_m^{(i)})$.

- For all $j \in \{1, \ldots, m\}$:
  - Compute the puzzle $\tilde{Z}_j \leftarrow \mathsf{LHP.PEval}(\oplus, pp, Z_j^{(1)}, \ldots, Z_j^{(n)})$.
  - Count the votes received by j-candidate by $v_j \leftarrow \mathsf{LHP.PSolve}(pp, \tilde{Z}_j)$.
- Output j^*-th candidate as the winner of the election, where $v_{j^*} = \max(v_1, \ldots, v_m)$.

By the security of LHTLP, the votes remain hidden for the whole duration of the voting phase. Furthermore, observe that we eventually need to only solve m puzzles, one puzzle per candidate. This is regardless on how many users go offline before the counting phase.

6.2   Multi-party Coin Flipping

We consider the settings where n parties want to flip a coin in such a way that (i) the value of the coin is unbiased even if $n - 1$ parties collude and (ii) all parties agree on the same value for the coin. Consider the protocol where parties commit to a bit and the result is the XOR of all the bits. The problem with this simple solution is that one party that controls the network traffic might learn all of the other bits and go offline if he does not agree with the outcome, thus biasing the result.

We propose the use of our linearly homomorphic time-lock puzzles to solve this problem. Let $\mathcal{T}$ be a bound on the runtime of the protocol. In our protocol, $\mathsf{LHP.PSetup}(1^\lambda, \mathcal{T})$ is run first to generate the public parameters pp. Then, every party P_i randomly chooses a bit $b_i \leftarrow_\$ \{0, 1\}$ and generates a time-lock puzzle as $Z_i \leftarrow \mathsf{LHP.PGen}(pp, b_i)$ before publishing it. Once P_i receives the puzzles from all other parties, it runs $Z \leftarrow \mathsf{LHP.PEval}(\oplus, pp, Z_1, \ldots, Z_n)$ to obtain the puzzle Z encoding the sum of all secrets. Each party P_i can solve Z to recover the corresponding s and output its least significant bit as the result of the coin flipping. Observe that only one puzzle needs to be solved regardless of the number of participants, even if everyone goes offline after the first phase. Since the time-lock puzzle is correct, then so is our protocol, furthermore the coins is unbiased by the security of LHTLP (in the timing model).

Setup: Generate the public parameters $pp \leftarrow \mathsf{LHP.PSetup}(1^\lambda, \mathcal{T})$ and publish them so that they are accessible to all the parties.

Coin Flipping: Each party P_i does the following.

- Choose $b_i \leftarrow_\$ \{0, 1\}$,
- Generate $Z_i \leftarrow \mathsf{LHP.PGen}(pp, b_i)$.
- Broadcast Z_i to all other parties.

Announcement of the Result: Each party P_i collects all the puzzles $Z_1, \ldots, Z_n$ from other parties and does the following.

- Compute the final puzzle $Z \leftarrow \mathsf{LHP.PEval}(\oplus, pp, Z_1, \ldots, Z_n)$.
- Solve the final puzzle as $s \leftarrow \mathsf{LHP.PSolve}(pp, Z)$
- Output $b \leftarrow \mathsf{LSB}(s)$ as the final result of the coin flipping.

6.3   Sealed Bid Auctions

Consider the settings where an auction is conducted with a set of n bidders $(B_1, \ldots, B_n)$. The bids are sealed throughout the bidding phase and disclosed during the opening phase. Once all of the bids are revealed, the highest bidder (or some other bidder depending on the allocation rule of the auction) is awarded as the winner. Sealed-bid auctions are one of the motivating examples for the usage of time-lock puzzles [6]. However, current solutions do not scale well with the amount of users going offline after the first phase.

To counter this issue we propose a protocol very similar to the coin-flipping one, where the setup generates the public parameters of the time-lock puzzles pp. In the bidding phase, each bidder generates a puzzle Z_i on input a bound T and his bid. The winner of the auction is the recovered by homomorphically evaluating the circuit Γ over all bids, where Γ computes the highest bid from a given list of bids and outputs the index of the corresponding bidder. Also in this case, only one puzzle has to be solved in the announcement phase. However, the function that needs to be homomorphically evaluated is no longer linear and therefore one needs to resort to fully-homomorphic time-lock puzzles (such as the scheme described in Sect. 4.3).

6.4   Multi-party Contract Signing

Consider the settings where n mutually distrusting parties want to jointly sign a contract. The contract is enforceable only if signed by all parties. In a naive approach, a party P_i collects the signatures that were broadcast by all other parties and add its own to seal the contract. However, if P_i fails to broadcast its own signature, other parties are left empty-handed.

We propose a solution based on the combination of multiplicatively homomorphic time-lock puzzles (as described in Sect. 4.2) and RSA-aggregate signatures [20]. Loosely speaking, an aggregate signature scheme allows one to publicly combine signatures over different messages and under different keys in such a way that the digest is still efficiently verifiable. The crucial property of the construction of Hohenberger and Waters [20] is that signatures σ are elements of $\mathbb{QR}_N$, for some fixed RSA integer N, and the aggregation of $((pk_1, m_1, \sigma_1), \ldots, (pk_n, m_n, \sigma_n))$ is computed as

$$\sigma_{agg} = \prod_{j=1}^{n} \sigma_j \pmod{N}.$$

Since $\mathbb{QR}_N$ is a subgroup of $\mathbb{J}_N$, we can seamlessly compute the aggregation function homomorphically. Let M be the contract to be signed. Our contract-signing protocol proceeds as follows: In the setup phase, the public parameters of the Hohenberger-Waters signature scheme (Setup, KeyGen, Sign) and of MHTLP (with reusable setup) are generated. Note that we implicitly assume that both setup algorithms sample the same strong RSA integer N. Then we fix $T_1 := T$ for some fixed T (which is suggested to be in the order of $2^{30} - 2^{50}$ in [6]) and each $\mathcal{T}_i$ is defined as $\frac{\mathcal{T}_{i-1}}{2}$, until $\mathcal{T}_\ell := 2$. Each user generates a key pair (pk_i, sk_i) and enters in the following loop. In the k-th iteration, each party P_i generates a signature $\sigma_i^{(k)}$ on the contract M via the signing algorithm Sign[2]. Then it time-locks $\sigma_i^{(k)}$ with a timing hardness $\mathcal{T}_k$ via $Z_i^{(k)} \leftarrow \mathsf{MHP.PGen}(pp_2, \sigma_i^{(k)}, \mathcal{T}_k)$ and broadcasts $Z_i^{(k)}$. If every user successfully broadcasts $Z_i^{(k)}$, then the protocol proceeds to the next iteration. Otherwise each party collects the puzzles $(Z_1^{(k-1)}, \ldots, Z_n^{(k-1)})$ from the previous iteration and generates the final puzzle as $Z^{(k-1)} \leftarrow \mathsf{MHP.PEval}(\otimes, pp_2, Z_1^{(k-1)}, \ldots, Z_n^{(k-1)})$. Solving this final puzzle reveals the aggregated signature σ_{agg} on M.

Setup Phase: Generate the public parameters of the aggregate signature scheme as $pp_1 \leftarrow \mathsf{Setup}(1^\lambda, 1^T)$ and the public parameters of the time-lock puzzle MHTLP (with reusable setup and multiple hardness parameters) as $pp_2 \leftarrow \mathsf{MHP.PSetup}(1^\lambda, \mathcal{T}_1, \mathcal{T}_2, \ldots, \mathcal{T}_\ell)$ and broadcast it to all parties.

Key Generation Phase: Before the start of the first iteration, each party P_i executes the key generation algorithm $(pk_i, sk_i) \leftarrow \mathsf{KeyGen}(pp_1)$ to generate a public and private key pair (pk_i, sk_i).

Signing Phase: At the beginning of the k-th iteration, each party P_i does the following.

- Generate a signature on M as $\sigma_i^{(k)} \leftarrow \mathsf{Sign}(pp_1, sk_i, M)$.
- Time-lock the signature via $Z_i^{(k)} \leftarrow \mathsf{MHP.PGen}(pp_2, \sigma_i^{(k)}, \mathcal{T}_k)$ with timing hardness $\mathcal{T}_k$ and broadcast the puzzle.

Aggregation phase: If all parties had broadcast their puzzles, proceed to $(k+1)$-th iteration. If not (or if $k = \ell$), each party P_i does the following.

- Collect the puzzles $(Z_1^{(k-1)}, \ldots, Z_n^{(k-1)})$ from the $(k-1)$-th iteration.
- Generate the final puzzle as
  $Z^{(k-1)} \leftarrow \mathsf{MHP.PEval}(\otimes, pp_2, Z_1^{(k-1)}, \ldots, Z_n^{(k-1)})$.
- Solve the puzzle to obtain the aggregated signature
  $\sigma_{agg} \leftarrow \mathsf{MHP.PSolve}(pp_2, Z^{(k-1)})$ on M.
- Output (M, σ_{agg}).

Acknowledgements. Research supported in part by a gift from Ripple, a gift from DoS Networks, a grant from Northrop Grumman, a Cylab seed funding award, and a JP Morgan Faculty Fellowship.

References

1. Bitansky, N., Garg, S., Lin, H., Pass, R., Telang, S.: Succinct randomized encodings and their applications. In: Servedio, R.A., Rubinfeld, R. (eds.) 47th ACM STOC, pp. 439–448. ACM Press, June 2015

---

[2] In [20] the signing algorithm requires an additional timing parameter, which we fix to be the round number and omit for the sake of clarity.

2. Bitansky, N., Goldwasser, S., Jain, A., Paneth, O., Vaikuntanathan, V., Waters, B.: Time-lock puzzles from randomized encodings. In: Sudan, M. (ed.) ITCS 2016, pp. 345–356. ACM, Cambridge (2016)

3. Blum, M., Micali, S.: How to generate cryptographically strong sequences of pseudo random bits. In: 23rd FOCS, pp. 112–117. IEEE Computer Society Press, November 1982

4. Boneh, D., Bonneau, J., Bünz, B., Fisch, B.: Verifiable delay functions. In: Shacham, H., Boldyreva, A. (eds.) CRYPTO 2018. LNCS, vol. 10991, pp. 757–788. Springer, Cham (2018). https://doi.org/10.1007/978-3-319-96884-1_25

5. Boneh, D., Bünz, B., Fisch, B.: A survey of two verifiable delay functions. Cryptology ePrint Archive, Report 2018/712 (2018). https://eprint.iacr.org/2018/712

6. Boneh, D., Naor, M.: Timed commitments. In: Bellare, M. (ed.) CRYPTO 2000. LNCS, vol. 1880, pp. 236–254. Springer, Heidelberg (2000). https://doi.org/10.1007/3-540-44598-6_15

7. Brakerski, Z., Goldwasser, S.: Circular and leakage resilient public-key encryption under subgroup indistinguishability. In: Rabin, T. (ed.) CRYPTO 2010. LNCS, vol. 6223, pp. 1–20. Springer, Heidelberg (2010). https://doi.org/10.1007/978-3-642-14623-7_1

8. Buchmann, J., Williams, H.C.: A key-exchange system based on imaginary quadratic fields. J. Cryptol. 1(2), 107–118 (1988)

9. Canetti, R., Lin, H., Tessaro, S., Vaikuntanathan, V.: Obfuscation of probabilistic circuits and applications. In: Dodis, Y., Nielsen, J.B. (eds.) TCC 2015. LNCS, vol. 9015, pp. 468–497. Springer, Heidelberg (2015). https://doi.org/10.1007/978-3-662-46497-7_19

10. Couteau, G., Peters, T., Pointcheval, D.: Encryption switching protocols. In: Robshaw, M., Katz, J. (eds.) CRYPTO 2016. LNCS, vol. 9814, pp. 308–338. Springer, Heidelberg (2016). https://doi.org/10.1007/978-3-662-53018-4_12

11. Damgård, I., Jurik, M.: A generalisation, a simplification and some applications of Paillier's probabilistic public-key system. In: Kim, K. (ed.) PKC 2001. LNCS, vol. 1992, pp. 119–136. Springer, Heidelberg (2001). https://doi.org/10.1007/3-540-44586-2_9

12. Dwork, C., Naor, M.: Zaps and their applications. In: 41st FOCS, pp. 283–293. IEEE Computer Society Press, November 2000

13. Feige, U., Lapidot, D., Shamir, A.: Multiple non-interactive zero knowledge proofs based on a single random string (extended abstract). In: 31st FOCS, pp. 308–317. IEEE Computer Society Press, October 1990

14. Garg, S., Gentry, C., Halevi, S., Raykova, M., Sahai, A., Waters, B.: Candidate indistinguishability obfuscation and functional encryption for all circuits. In: 54th FOCS, pp. 40–49. IEEE Computer Society Press, October 2013

15. Garg, S., Gentry, C., Sahai, A., Waters, B.: Witness encryption and its applications. In: Boneh, D., Roughgarden, T., Feigenbaum, J. (eds.) 45th ACM STOC, pp. 467–476. ACM Press, June 2013

16. Gentry, C.: Fully homomorphic encryption using ideal lattices. In: Mitzenmacher, M. (ed.) 41st ACM STOC, pp. 169–178. ACM Press, May/June 2009

17. Gentry, C., Halevi, S., Vaikuntanathan, V.: i-Hop homomorphic encryption and rerandomizable yao circuits. In: Rabin, T. (ed.) CRYPTO 2010. LNCS, vol. 6223, pp. 155–172. Springer, Heidelberg (2010). https://doi.org/10.1007/978-3-642-14623-7_9

18. Goldreich, O., Goldwasser, S., Micali, S.: How to construct random functions (extended abstract). In: 25th FOCS, pp. 464–479. IEEE Computer Society Press, October 1984

19. Goldwasser, S., Micali, S.: Probabilistic encryption and how to play mental poker keeping secret all partial information. In: 14th ACM STOC, pp. 365–377. ACM Press, May 1982
20. Hohenberger, S., Waters, B.: Synchronized aggregate signatures from the RSA assumption. In: Nielsen, J.B., Rijmen, V. (eds.) EUROCRYPT 2018. LNCS, vol. 10821, pp. 197–229. Springer, Cham (2018). https://doi.org/10.1007/978-3-319-78375-8_7
21. Ishai, Y., Paskin, A.: Evaluating branching programs on encrypted data. In: Vadhan, S.P. (ed.) TCC 2007. LNCS, vol. 4392, pp. 575–594. Springer, Heidelberg (2007). https://doi.org/10.1007/978-3-540-70936-7_31
22. Kiayias, A., Russell, A., David, B., Oliynykov, R.: Ouroboros: a provably secure proof-of-stake blockchain protocol. In: Katz, J., Shacham, H. (eds.) CRYPTO 2017. LNCS, vol. 10401, pp. 357–388. Springer, Cham (2017). https://doi.org/10.1007/978-3-319-63688-7_12
23. Lin, H., Pass, R., Soni, P.: Two-round and non-interactive concurrent non-malleable commitments from time-lock puzzles. In: 58th FOCS, pp. 576–587. IEEE Computer Society Press (2017)
24. Liu, J., Jager, T., Kakvi, S.A., Warinschi, B.: How to build time-lock encryption. Des. Codes Crypt. **86**, 2549–2586 (2018)
25. Mahmoody, M., Moran, T., Vadhan, S.: Time-lock puzzles in the random Oracle model. In: Rogaway, P. (ed.) CRYPTO 2011. LNCS, vol. 6841, pp. 39–50. Springer, Heidelberg (2011). https://doi.org/10.1007/978-3-642-22792-9_3
26. Mahmoody, M., Moran, T., Vadhan, S.P.: Publicly verifiable proofs of sequential work. In: Kleinberg, R.D. (ed.) ITCS 2013, pp. 373–388. ACM, January 2013
27. Ostrovsky, R., Paskin-Cherniavsky, A., Paskin-Cherniavsky, B.: Maliciously circuit-private FHE. In: Garay, J.A., Gennaro, R. (eds.) CRYPTO 2014. LNCS, vol. 8616, pp. 536–553. Springer, Heidelberg (2014). https://doi.org/10.1007/978-3-662-44371-2_30
28. Paillier, P.: Public-key cryptosystems based on composite degree residuosity classes. In: Stern, J. (ed.) EUROCRYPT 1999. LNCS, vol. 1592, pp. 223–238. Springer, Heidelberg (1999). https://doi.org/10.1007/3-540-48910-X_16
29. Pietrzak, K.: Simple verifiable delay functions. Cryptology ePrint Archive, Report 2018/627 (2018). https://eprint.iacr.org/2018/627
30. Rivest, R.L., Shamir, A., Wagner, D.A.: Time-lock puzzles and timed-release crypto. Technical report, Cambridge, MA, USA (1996)
31. Wesolowski, B.: Efficient verifiable delay functions. Cryptology ePrint Archive, Report 2018/623 (2018). https://eprint.iacr.org/2018/623

Symmetric Primitives
with Structured Secrets

Navid Alamati[1]([✉]), Hart Montgomery[2]([✉]), and Sikhar Patranabis[2,3]

[1] University of Michigan, Ann Arbor, USA
alamati@umich.edu
[2] Fujitsu Laboratories of America, Sunnyvale, USA
hmontgomery@us.fujitsu.com, sikharpatranabis@gmail.com
[3] IIT Kharagpur, Kharagpur, India

Abstract. Securely managing encrypted data on an untrusted party is a challenging problem that has motivated the study of a wide variety of cryptographic primitives. A special class of such primitives allows an untrusted party to transform a ciphertext encrypted under one key to a ciphertext under another key, using some auxiliary information that does not leak the underlying data. Prominent examples of such primitives in the symmetric setting are key-homomorphic (weak) PRFs, updatable encryption, and proxy re-encryption. Although these primitives differ significantly in terms of their constructions and security requirements, they share two important properties: (a) they have *secrets with structure or extra functionality*, and (b) all known constructions of these primitives satisfying reasonably strong definitions of security are based on *concrete* public-key assumptions, e.g., DDH and LWE.

This raises the question of whether these objects inherently belong to the world of public-key primitives, or they can potentially be built from simple symmetric-key objects such as pseudorandom functions. In this work, we show that the latter possibility is unlikely. More specifically, we show that:

- Any (bounded) key-homomorphic *weak* PRF with an abelian output group implies a (bounded) *input-homomorphic* weak PRF, which has recently been shown to imply not only public-key encryption but also a variety of primitives such as PIR, lossy TDFs, and even IBE.
- Any ciphertext-independent updatable encryption scheme that is forward and post-compromise secure implies PKE. Moreover, any symmetric-key proxy re-encryption scheme with reasonably strong security guarantees implies a forward and post-compromise secure ciphertext-independent updatable encryption, and hence PKE.

In addition, we show that unbounded (or exact) key-homomorphic weak PRFs over abelian groups are *impossible* in the quantum world. In other words, over abelian groups, bounded key-homomorphism is the best that we can hope for in terms of post-quantum security. Our attack also works over other structured primitives with abelian groups and exact homomorphisms, including homomorphic one-way functions and input-homomorphic weak PRFs.

© International Association for Cryptologic Research 2019
A. Boldyreva and D. Micciancio (Eds.): CRYPTO 2019, LNCS 11692, pp. 650–679, 2019.
https://doi.org/10.1007/978-3-030-26948-7_23

1   Introduction

Examining the practicality and security of cryptographic primitives has always been one of the most important aspects of cryptographic research. When a new cryptographic protocol is developed, it is often somewhat inefficient and relies on a relatively strong assumption. We might ask a question that captures the essence of "lower bounds" for cryptographic algorithms: is it possible to improve this cryptosystem, or is the proposed scheme close to optimal?

A plausible approach for understanding the gap between known constructions and "reasonable" lower bounds is to determine the power of a cryptographic primitive, i.e., what other cryptographic objects can be built from it in a generic way. For instance, if a certain primitive is known to imply public-key encryption (PKE), then it does not seem likely that this primitive can be built in a generic manner from one-way functions (OWFs) [IR89, GHMM18]. However, for certain classes of primitives, this gap might be substantial.

One such class of primitives that has been studied considerably is what we will term *symmetric primitives with structured secrets*. Perhaps the most iconic member of this (informal) class, and one we will use to illustrate our points here, is the *key-homomorphic PRF*. Recall that, informally, a key-homomorphic PRF is a function $F : \mathcal{K} \times \mathcal{X} \to \mathcal{Y}$ with key space $\mathcal{K}$ and output space $\mathcal{Y}$ endowed with group operations $\oplus$ and $\otimes$, respectively, that meets all of the requirements of a pseudorandom function with the following extra property:[1]

$$F(k_1, x) \otimes F(k_2, x) = F(k_1 \oplus k_2, x).$$

Key-homomorphic PRFs (KHPRFs) were first implicitly shown in [NPR99] in the random oracle model and then formally defined and constructed in the standard model in [BLMR13]. There are a number of interesting applications of KHPRFs, including primitives like distributed PRFs [NPR99, BLMR13, LST18], updatable encryption [EPRS17, LT18], and PRFs that are secure against related key attacks [LMR14].

Since [BLMR13], there have been a number of works constructing improved variants of KHPRFs [BP14, BV15, BFP+15]. However, despite this quantity of research, the known constructions of KHPRFs still require powerful assumptions. For instance, we only know how to build exact key-homomorphic PRFs in the standard model from multilinear maps or related assumptions [BLMR13]. If we relax these requirements to almost KHPRFs in the standard model, all known constructions still require an LWE assumption with superpolynomial modulus. Even constructions in the random oracle model require public-key assumptions like DDH [NPR99].

All of these assumptions and constructions are seemingly very heavyweight for an ostensibly symmetric-key primitive that is typically targeted for applications in the symmetric-key setting. This leads us to a natural question: can we

---

[1] We note that this equality can be relaxed to achieve *approximate* key-homomorphic PRFs, and these (approximate) key-homomorphic PRFs can be built from lattice-based assumptions, like LWE.

construct more efficient key-homomorphic PRFs, or is there some fundamental lower bound limiting their efficiency? Boneh et. al state, optimistically, "Another interesting area of research is to construct key-homomorphic PRFs whose performance is comparable to real-world block ciphers such as AES," [BLMR13] but so far there are no known realizations of such a construction.

However, key-homomorphic PRFs are far from the only symmetric primitive with structured secrets for which the gap between known constructions and lower bounds appears to be relatively large. There are a number of other seemingly symmetric-key primitives that are only known to be implementable from concrete public-key assumptions.

Updatable Encryption. Suppose that Alice wants to perform key rotation on encrypted data in the cloud, but does not trust the cloud with her secret key. *Updatable encryption*, first defined in [BLMR13] as an application of key-homomorphic PRFs, allows third parties to periodically rotate encryption keys by moving ciphertexts from an old key to a new one, without actually learning the contents of the ciphertexts.

Boneh *et al.* [BLMR13] proposed the first formal definitions and concrete realizations of updatable encryption, which were subsequently refined by Everspaugh *et al.* in [EPRS17]. In a more recent work, Lehmann and Tackmann [LT18] introduced stronger security notions for updatable encryption that are desirable for real-world applications, and also pointed out that none of the existing constructions satisfy these notions. They addressed this issue by presenting a new, non-KHPRF updatable encryption protocol called RISE that achieves these stronger security requirements.

However, all of the constructions from the stronger security assumptions in [LT18] are either built from key-homomorphic PRFs or from concrete public-key assumptions. Yet again, the question remains: can we build similar schemes using simple symmetric-key primitives? Lehmann and Tackmann [LT18] are pessimistic, "secure updatable encryption schemes seem to inherently require techniques from the public-key world" but no formal bounds were given.

Proxy Re-Encryption. A *proxy re-encryption* scheme is a cryptosystem where, given a special update token, a third party can transform a ciphertext encrypted under Alice's public key to a ciphertext encrypted under Bob's public key, while learning nothing about the underlying message. Proxy re-encryption was initially developed in [BBS98] and then formalized in [AFGH05, AFGH06]. A number of subsequent works proposed improved schemes, including CCA-secure proxy re-encryption [CH07], identity-based proxy re-encryption [GA07], and CCA-secure unidirectional proxy re-encryption [LV08].

Proxy re-encryption has also been studied extensively in the symmetric-key setting [SNS11]. In particular, many of the proposed definitions and security notions associated with proxy re-encryption [nBL17, DKL+18, FKKP19] can be adopted to the symmetric-key setting. Interestingly, while some of the simpler definitions of security may be realized from known symmetric primitives, the stronger definitions only have known realizations from public-key assumptions like DDH and LWE [ABPW13, CCL+14]. This leads to the following question: are these stronger definitions of symmetric-key proxy re-encryption achievable from symmetric-key encryption?

Downside of Structure. A common property underlying each of the cryptographic primitives discussed so far is that they have structured secrets. While the presence of structure potentially allows building rich cryptosystems from simple primitives, it may also make these primitives vulnerable to potential attacks [Bar17]. This motivates us to pose the following question: can the structure inherent in KHwPRFs (and related primitives) lead to attacks?

1.1 Our Contributions

We show that the answer to many of these questions is negative. Our results can be summarized as follows:

Key-Homomorphic Weak PRFs. We show that any key-homomorphic *weak* PRF (KHwPRF) $F : \mathcal{K} \times \mathcal{X} \to \mathcal{Y}$ with an abelian output group $\mathcal{Y}$ implies PKE. In fact, we show that KHwPRFs with abelian output groups imply a much stronger primitive called *input-homomorphic weak PRF* (IHwPRF) which, by the recent work of [AMPR19], implies a large number of public-key primitives, including identity-based encryption [Sha84], private information retrieval [KO97], and lossy trapdoor functions [PW08]. In essence, our results indicate that it is seemingly unlikely that KHwPRFs, and hence KHPRFs, with abelian output groups are implied by symmetric-key primitives [IR89, GHMM18]. Our results also hold for *bounded* KHwPRFs with abelian output groups (encompassing nearly all applications of *almost* KHPRFs from lattice-based assumptions). To our knowledge, all existing constructions of KHwPRFs (and almost KHwPRFs) have abelian output groups.

Interestingly, our constructions of PKE and IHwPRF *only* use the output group $\mathcal{Y}$ of the KHwPRF. We use the security of the KHwPRF to argue security of our constructions. It may be possible that this seemingly novel construction technique has other applications.

These results on KHwPRFs lend evidence to support the idea that many "symmetric-key" cryptosystems that are currently only known from KHPRFs, do, in fact, belong to the world of public-key primitives. We note that some primitives (such as distributed PRFs) have KHPRF-based constructions that require abelian key and output groups, further strengthening the argument that these constructions are unlikely to be built from symmetric-key primitives.

Finally, we show how to construct a Naor-Reingold style PRF [NR97] from any key-homomorphic weak PRF. As we explain in Sect. 3.4, this allows us to construct highly parallel and potentially efficient PRFs from any KHwPRF. To the best of our knowledge, prior to this work, it was not known how to construct a Naor-Reingold style PRF from a *generic* primitive.

Updatable Encryption. We show that any ciphertext-independent updatable encryption scheme that satisfies the adaptive notions of forward and post-compromise security proposed in [LT18] implies PKE. As pointed out in [LT18], forward and post-compromise security are desirable for real-world applications, since they guarantee that message confidentiality is preserved even in the presence of temporary key compromise. Our result confirms the pessimism expressed in [LT18] that updatable encryption schemes with desirable security properties inherently belong to the class of asymmetric primitives.

Proxy Re-Encryption. We show that any symmetric-key proxy re-encryption scheme that satisfies the adaptive notion of indistinguishability-based security formalized in [FKKP19] implies updatable encryption with forward and post-compromise security, and hence PKE. We remark that the definition presented in [FKKP19] captures the desirable properties of proxy re-encryption, namely unidirectionality and adaptive security, and unifies the security notions achieved by a large number of existing constructions [AFGH05, AFGH06, ABH09, CCL+14].

Quantum Attacks on Primitives with Structure. We show that any exact (not bounded) homomorphic one-way function (HOWF) with abelian input and output groups can be broken in polynomial time using a quantum computer. This immediately rules out the existence of abelian, exact KHwPRFs (and hence KHPRFs) in the quantum setting. In other words, over abelian groups, KHw-PRFs (and KHPRFs) with bounded homomorphism are the best that we can hope for in the quantum world.

We can also extend this attack to essentially all exact input-homomorphic weak unpredictable functions (IHwUFs) and IHwPRFs over abelian groups using the results from [AMPR19], which in turn yields quantum attacks on essentially all exact (group-)homomorphic encryption schemes over abelian groups. We note that a similar result with respect to homomorphic encryption was achieved in [AGKP14], albeit using different techniques.

1.2   Related Works

We have already discussed a number of papers related to key-homomorphic PRFs, updatable encryption, and proxy re-encryption. However, we want to note the construction [DKPW12] of Dodis et al. which showed how to build efficient MACs from key-homomorphic weak PRFs, even predating [BLMR13].

Previous works have studied the relationship between cryptographic primitives and structure. Recently, [AMPR19] examined simple primitives with structured inputs. In a work on a similar topic, Pietrzak and Sjödin [PS08] showed that weak PRFs with a certain input property imply PKE. In a different line of works that show PKE from other primitives, Berman et al. showed that laconic zero-knowledge protocols imply PKE [BDRV18], Fischlin and Harasser [FH18] showed that PKE is implied by invisible sanitizable signatures, and Rothblum [Rot11] demonstrated (homomorphic) PKE from a secret-key encryption scheme with some form of weak homomorphism. For a comprehensive treatment of PRFs and related primitives, see [BR17].

1.3   Technical Overview

In this section, we explain at a high level the techniques behind our constructions and proofs.

Key-Homomorphic Weak PRFs. Informally, a key-homomorphic weak PRF is a function $F : \mathcal{K} \times \mathcal{X} \to \mathcal{Y}$ with keyspace $\mathcal{K}$ and output space $\mathcal{Y}$ endowed with group operations $\oplus$ and $\otimes$, respectively, that meets the definition of a weak pseudorandom function[2] with the following extra property:

$$F(k_1, x) \otimes F(k_2, x) = F(k_1 \oplus k_2, x).$$

As a warm-up, we first show that a KHwPRF with an abelian output group $\mathcal{Y}$ implies PKE. To illustrate how this works, we will show how our construction works with a simple DDH-based KHwPRF from [NPR99][3] in parallel with a generic construction. First, we use the following notation for two weak PRFs:

Generic KHwPRF	DDH Instantiation
$F(k \in \mathcal{K}, x \in \mathcal{X}) \in \mathcal{Y}$	$F_{DDH}(g \in \mathbb{G}, k \in \mathbb{Z}_q) \in \mathbb{G}$
$F(k, x) = y$	$F_{DDH}(g, k) = g^k$

Now consider many instances of the same KHwPRF in parallel, with different keys. By a hybrid argument, we know that such a set of KHwPRF outputs is still indistinguishable from random. One can visualize this as follows:

Generic KHwPRF	DDH Instantiation

$$
\begin{matrix}
F(k_1, x_1) & F(k_2, x_1) & \dots & F(k_\ell, x_1) \\
F(k_1, x_2) & F(k_2, x_2) & \dots & F(k_\ell, x_2) \\
\vdots & \vdots & \ddots & \vdots \\
F(k_1, x_m) & F(k_2, x_m) & \dots & F(k_\ell, x_m)
\end{matrix}
\qquad
\begin{matrix}
g_1^{k_1} & g_1^{k_2} & \dots & g_1^{k_\ell} \\
g_2^{k_1} & g_2^{k_2} & \dots & g_2^{k_\ell} \\
\vdots & \vdots & \ddots & \vdots \\
g_m^{k_1} & g_m^{k_2} & \dots & g_m^{k_\ell}
\end{matrix}
$$

Now suppose we take a random "subset sum"[4] of the columns of these many instances of KHwPRFs in parallel. If $\mathbf{s} = (s_1, \dots, s_\ell) \in \{0, 1\}^\ell$ is a random vector denoting our subset sum choice, we get new "columns" as follows:

---

[2] A weak PRF is a PRF for which the pseudorandomness guarantee holds when the inputs are sampled uniformly at random.

[3] This was originally envisioned by the authors of [NPR99] as a PRF in the random oracle model, but we note that it is equivalent to a weak PRF in the standard model.

[4] We use the term "subset sum" loosely to essentially indicate subset group-operation over the output space of the KHwPRF. Depending on whether the group is additive or multiplicative, we perform either subset sums or subset products.

Generic KHwPRF	DDH Instantiation
$\bigotimes_{j=1}^{\ell} s_j \cdot F(k_j, x_1) = F(k^*, x_1)$	$\prod_{j=1}^{\ell} g_1^{s_j \cdot k_j} = g_1^{k^*}$
$\bigotimes_{j=1}^{\ell} s_j \cdot F(k_j, x_2) = F(k^*, x_2)$	$\prod_{j=1}^{\ell} g_2^{s_j \cdot k_j} = g_2^{k^*}$
$\vdots$	$\vdots$
$\bigotimes_{j=1}^{\ell} s_j \cdot F(k_j, x_m) = F(k^*, x_m)$	$\prod_{j=1}^{\ell} g_m^{s_j \cdot k_j} = g_m^{k^*}$

If $\ell > 3 \log |\mathcal{K}|$, then the distribution of $k^* = \oplus_{j=1}^{\ell} s_j k_j$ will be statistically close to uniform over $\mathcal{K}$. This can be shown by a relatively simple application of the leftover hash lemma [IZ89]. It now follows by the pseudorandomness of the KHwPRFs F and F_{DDH} that these new columns are computationally indistinguishable from random, even given the outputs of the other columns.

We now present the critical step of our argument: if such subset sums of KHwPRF outputs are indistinguishable from random even if the randomness for the subset sum is reused, then, by a series of hybrid arguments, it follows that similar subset sums of randomly chosen elements of the output group $\mathcal{Y}$ are indistinguishable from random: otherwise, we would have a distinguisher for the original KHwPRF. In other words, the following must hold:

Generic KHwPRF	DDH Instantiation
$\mathbf{Y} \leftarrow \mathcal{Y}^{m \times \ell}, \mathbf{s} \leftarrow \{0,1\}^{\ell}$	$\mathbf{G} \leftarrow \mathbb{G}^{m \times \ell}, \mathbf{s} \leftarrow \{0,1\}^{\ell}$
$(\mathbf{Y}, \mathbf{Y}\mathbf{s}) \overset{c}{\approx} (\mathbf{Y}, \mathbf{u})$	$(\mathbf{G}, \mathbf{G}\mathbf{s}) \overset{c}{\approx} (\mathbf{G}, \mathbf{h})$
where $\mathbf{u} \leftarrow \mathcal{Y}^m$.	where $\mathbf{h} \leftarrow \mathbf{G}^m$.

Note that for a matrix of group elements $\mathbf{Y} \in \mathcal{Y}^{m \times \ell}$ and a vector $\mathbf{s} \in \{0,1\}^{\ell}$, we denote by $\mathbf{Y}\mathbf{s} \in \mathcal{Y}^m$ the vector of group elements

$$\left(\bigotimes_{j=1}^{\ell} s_j \cdot y_{1,j}, \ldots, \bigotimes_{j=1}^{\ell} s_j \cdot y_{m,j} \right).$$

Given this hard problem, which is based on the weak pseudorandomness of F, it is simple to construct a two-party noninteractive key exchange protocol (which is sufficient for PKE), as visualized in the following figure (note that the public parameter pp consists of an $m \times m$ matrix of uniformly chosen group elements for a fixed $m > 3 \log |\mathcal{K}|$).

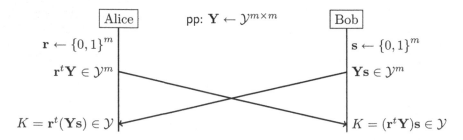

It turns out that the technique described above is actually versatile enough to construct a number of stronger cryptographic primitives. More specifically, we show how to build an input-homomorphic weak PRF (IHwPRF), which by [AMPR19] implies a variety of public-key primitives.

Informally, an IHwPRF is a function $F' : \mathcal{K} \times \mathcal{X} \to \mathcal{Y}$ with input space $\mathcal{X}$ and output space $\mathcal{Y}$ endowed with group operations $\oplus$ and $\otimes$, respectively, that also meets the definition of a weak pseudorandom function. However, the homomorphism is over the input space rather than the key space:

$$F'(k, x_1) \otimes F'(k, x_2) = F'(k, x_1 \oplus x_2).$$

First, note that the DDH-based KHwPRF is already input homomorphic. But the DDH assumption is very special in this regard, and we cannot guarantee that other constructions of KHwPRFs are also implicitly IHwPRFs. In general, for a KHwPRF $F : \mathcal{K} \times \mathcal{X} \to \mathcal{Y}$, the input space $\mathcal{X}$ might not even be a group.

We now illustrate the construction of an IHwPRF $F' : \{0,1\}^\ell \times \mathcal{Y}^\ell \to \mathcal{Y}$ from any KHwPRF with an abelian output group $\mathcal{Y}$ (where $\ell > 3 \log |\mathcal{K}|$):

Generic KHwPRF	DDH Instantiation
$F' : \{0,1\}^\ell \times \mathcal{Y}^\ell \to \mathcal{Y}$	$F'_{\text{DDH}} : \{0,1\}^\ell \times \mathbb{G}^\ell \to \mathbb{G}$
$F'(\mathbf{s}, (y_1, ..., y_\ell)) = \bigotimes_{j=1}^\ell s_j \cdot y_j$	$F'_{\text{DDH}}(\mathbf{s}, (g_1, ..., g_\ell)) = \prod_{j=1}^\ell g_j^{s_j}$

First, note that the input homomorphism of F' and F'_{DDH} follows from that fact that the underlying groups $\mathcal{Y}$ and $\mathbb{G}$ are abelian, respectively. If $\mathcal{Y}$ is not abelian, then F' would still be pseudorandom, but not input homomorphic. It is an interesting open problem to remove this restriction on $\mathcal{Y}$ while retaining input-homomorphism.

Notice that in the actual *constructions* of PKE and IHwPRF, we do not explicitly use the key space or the input space of the underlying KHwPRF; we essentially use the pseudorandomness of the KHwPRF to argue their security. In Sect. 3, we present the detailed constructions and proofs, and extend our techniques to work for *almost* KHwPRFs.

On the negative side, we rule out the existence of *exact* KHwPRFs with output groups over which a system of linear equations (with binary variables) can be solved efficiently, because such an algorithm can be used to break the hard problem instance described above, and hence to break the pseudorandomness of the underlying exact KHwPRF.[5]

Updatable Encryption. We show that any ciphertext-independent updatable encryption (UE) scheme that meets the notion of "adaptive indistinguishability of updates" formalized by Lehmann and Tackmann in [LT18] implies a PKE

---

[5] We remark that known algorithms to solve systems of linear equations over abelian groups need an *explicit representation* of the group, see [GR02] for more details. For example, such an explicit representation is not known to an adversary against a DDH-hard group $\mathbb{G}$.

scheme. Recall that a UE scheme allows publishing an update token $\Delta_{0,1}$ that can be used by a third party to transform a ciphertext encrypted under a key sk_0 to a ciphertext encrypted under another key sk_1, without knowing the underlying message.

In our PKE construction from UE, the public key consists of a pair of UE ciphertexts encrypting 0 and 1 respectively under a key sk_0, and an update token $\Delta_{0,1}$. Depending on the plaintext bit b, the encryption algorithm updates one of the two ciphertexts, and the decryption algorithm in turn decrypts using the updated key sk_1. To prove CPA security, we show a reduction in which the challenge ciphertext for the UE game is transformed into the public key for the PKE game, which then allows us to switch between knowledge of secrets and knowledge of update tokens. The detailed construction and proof of security are presented in Sect. 4.1.

As a side note, our construction of PKE assumes that the update algorithm of the underlying UE scheme is *randomized*. We point out that all existing UE schemes satisfying the notion of update indistinguishability (notably, the RISE scheme in [LT18]) have randomized update algorithms.

Proxy Re-Encryption. We show that any symmetric-key proxy re-encryption scheme that satisfies the indistinguishability-based security notions formalized in [FKKP19] implies a ciphertext-independent UE scheme with indistinguishability of updates. By the result mentioned above, it thus implies a PKE scheme.

Our construction of UE from a symmetric-key PRE essentially maps PRE secret keys associated with different identifiers to UE secret keys associated with different epochs. To prove security, we show a reduction where any *valid* oracle query from the adversary in the UE game can be mapped into a corresponding *valid* oracle query to the challenger in the PRE game.

We remark that while existing PRE schemes typically support *multi-hop updates* [AFGH05, FKKP19], UE schemes as formalized in [LT18] support a more sequential flavor of updates. It is unlikely that such UE schemes would imply PRE schemes with desirable security properties, unless the definitions for UE are further strengthened to encompass functionalities similar to multi-hop-updates.

Quantum Attacks on Generic Primitives. In the body of the paper, we show that there exist quantum attacks on a number of generic exact primitives over abelian groups. However, since all of these attacks essentially follow from our attack on an exact homomorphic one-way function (HOWF) over an abelian group, we will focus our attention here on this attack. Informally, an HOWF is a function $f : \mathcal{X} \rightarrow \mathcal{Y}$ with input group $(\mathcal{X}, \oplus)$ and output group $(\mathcal{Y}, \otimes)$ (where both group operations are efficiently computable), that meets the definition of a one-way function with the following extra property:

$$f(x_1) \otimes f(x_2) = f(x_1 \oplus x_2).$$

Our attack relies on the fact that there exists a quantum algorithm such that given black-box access to an abelian group $\mathcal{G}$ with certain properties, it outputs an *explicit representation* of the group; in other words, it outputs an isomorphism $\psi : \mathcal{G} \to \mathbb{Z}_{q_1} \oplus \cdots \oplus \mathbb{Z}_{q_m}$ such that both ψ and ψ^{-1} are efficiently computable (see [CM01] and Section 6.2 of [Chi17] for more details).

At a high level, our attack works as follows: given an exact HOWF $f : \mathcal{X} \to \mathcal{Y}$ such that $\mathcal{X}$ and $\mathcal{Y}$ are both abelian groups, we use their explicit representations to construct *linear systems of modular equations*, and efficiently solve them to find a preimage for any given HOWF output. The detailed description of the attack is presented in Sect. 5.

2 Preliminaries

2.1 Notation

For any positive integer n, we use $[n]$ to denote the set $\{1, \ldots, n\}$. We use λ for the security parameter. We use the symbols $\oplus$ and $\otimes$ as group operations defined in the context. For a finite set S, we use $s \leftarrow S$ to sample uniformly from the set S.

Let $(\mathcal{Y}, \otimes)$ be an efficiently samplable group, such that the group operation is efficiently computable. Let $\mathbf{Y} \in \mathcal{Y}^{m \times \ell}$ be an $m \times \ell$ matrix of group elements sampled from $\mathcal{Y}$. Also, let $\mathbf{s} = (s_1, \ldots, s_\ell) \in \{0,1\}^\ell$ be an arbitrary binary vector. We denote by $\mathbf{Y}\mathbf{s} \in \mathcal{Y}^m$ the vector of group elements

$$\left(\bigotimes_{j:s_j=1} y_{1,j}, \ldots, \bigotimes_{j:s_j=1} y_{m,j} \right).$$

Similarly, let $\mathbf{S} = [s_{j,j'}] \in \{0,1\}^{\ell \times \ell'}$ be an arbitrary binary matrix. We denote by $\mathbf{Y}\mathbf{S} \in \mathcal{Y}^{m \times \ell'}$ the matrix of group elements

$$\begin{bmatrix} \bigotimes_{j:s_{j,1}=1} y_{1,j} & \cdots & \bigotimes_{j:s_{j,\ell'}=1} y_{1,j} \\ \vdots & \ddots & \vdots \\ \bigotimes_{j:s_{j,1}=1} y_{m,j} & \cdots & \bigotimes_{j:s_{j,\ell'}=1} y_{m,j} \end{bmatrix}.$$

2.2 Cryptographic Primitives

Pseudorandom Functions. Informally, an efficiently computable function is called pseudorandom if there exists no PPT adversary that can distinguish it from a truly random function. More formally, a PRF family is an efficiently computable function family $\{F(k, \cdot) : \mathcal{X} \to \mathcal{Y}\}_{k \in \mathcal{K}}$ (where K, $\mathcal{X}$ and $\mathcal{Y}$ are indexed by the security parameter λ) such that for all PPT adversaries $\mathcal{A}$ we have

$$\left| \Pr[\mathcal{A}^{F(k,\cdot)}(1^\lambda) = 1] - \Pr[\mathcal{A}^{f(\cdot)}(1^\lambda) = 1] \right| \leq \mathrm{negl}(\lambda),$$

where $k \leftarrow \mathcal{K}$ and $f : \mathcal{X} \to \mathcal{Y}$ is a (truly) random function.

Weak Pseudorandom Functions. Let $F^\$(k, \cdot)$ be a *randomized* oracle that responds to queries by sampling $x \leftarrow \mathcal{X}$ and outputting $(x, F(k, x))$. A weak pseudorandom function (wPRF) family is an efficiently computable function family $\{F(k, \cdot) : \mathcal{X} \to \mathcal{Y}\}_{k \in \mathcal{K}}$ (where K, $\mathcal{X}$ and $\mathcal{Y}$ are indexed by the security parameter λ) such that for all PPT adversaries $\mathcal{A}$ we have

$$\left| \Pr[\mathcal{A}^{F^\$(k, \cdot)}(1^\lambda) = 1] - \Pr[\mathcal{A}^{f^\$(\cdot)}(1^\lambda) = 1] \right| \le \mathrm{negl}(\lambda),$$

where $k \leftarrow \mathcal{K}$ and $f : \mathcal{X} \to \mathcal{Y}$ is a (truly) random function.

Definition 1. (Homomorphic One-Way Function.) *A homomorphic one-way function (HOWF) is a function $f : \mathcal{X} \to \mathcal{Y}$ with input group $(\mathcal{X}, \oplus)$ and output group $(\mathcal{Y}, \otimes)$ (where both group operations are efficiently computable), that meets the definition of a one-way function with the following extra property:*

$$f(x_1) \otimes f(x_2) = f(x_1 \oplus x_2).$$

Definition 2. (Key-Homomorphic Functions.) *A function family $\{F(k, \cdot) : \mathcal{X} \to \mathcal{Y}\}_{k \in \mathcal{K}}$ is key-homomorphic if the following conditions hold:*

- *$(\mathcal{K}, \oplus)$ and $(\mathcal{Y}, \otimes)$ are efficiently samplable groups, and the group operations and the inverse operation in each group are efficiently computable.*
- *For any pair of keys $k_1, k_2 \in \mathcal{K}$ and any input $x \in \mathcal{X}$, we have*

$$F(k_1, x) \otimes F(k_2, x) = F(k_1 \oplus k_2, x).$$

A key-homomorphic weak PRF (KHwPRF) family is a weak PRF family that is also key homomorphic. Similarly, a key-homomorphic PRF (KHPRF) family is a PRF family that is also key homomorphic.

Definition 3. (Input-Homomorphic Weak PRF.) *A weak pseudorandom function family $\{F'(k, \cdot) : \mathcal{X} \to \mathcal{Y}\}_{k \in \mathcal{K}}$ is an IHwPRF family if the following conditions are satisfied:*

- *$(\mathcal{X}, \oplus)$ and $(\mathcal{Y}, \otimes)$ are efficiently samplable groups, and the group operations and the inverse operation in each group are efficiently computable.*
- *For any pair of inputs $x_1, x_2 \in \mathcal{X}$ and any key $k \in \mathcal{K}$, we have*

$$F'(k, x_1) \otimes F'(k, x_2) = F'(k, x_1 \oplus x_2).$$

Definition 4. (γ-Bounded IHwPRF.) *A weak pseudorandom function family $\{F(k, \cdot) : \mathcal{X} \to \mathcal{Y}\}_{k \in \mathcal{K}}$ is a γ-bounded IHwPRF family if there is an (efficiently computable) universal mapping $\mathcal{R} : \mathcal{Y} \to \mathcal{Z}$ such that*

- *$(\mathcal{K}, \oplus)$ and $(\mathcal{Y}, \otimes)$ are efficiently samplable groups, and the group operations and the inverse operation in each group are efficiently computable.*
- *For a randomly chosen input vector $(x_1, \ldots, x_L) \leftarrow \mathcal{X}^L$ such that $L \le \gamma$, and a randomly chosen key $k \leftarrow \mathcal{K}$, the following holds with overwhelming probability:*

$$\mathcal{R}\left(F\left(k, \bigoplus_{j \in [L]} x_j\right)\right) = \mathcal{R}\left(\bigotimes_{j \in [L]} F(k, x_j)\right).$$

3   Key-Homomorphic Weak PRFs and Implications

In this section we show how to construct PKE and input-homomorphic weak PRF (IHwPRF) from a key-homomorphic weak PRF (KHwPRF). First, we introduce a hardness assumption over the *output group* of a KHwPRF. This hardness assumption has the advantage that it does not directly involve the input set $\mathcal{X}$ of the KHwPRF, which may be algebraically unstructured. Here (and in the following two subsections), we assume that the KHwPRF has unbounded (or exact) homomorphism. Later in this section, we show how to extend our results to "almost" KHwPRFs. Finally, we provide a construction of Naor-Reingold style PRF from KHwPRFs.

Theorem 1. *Let $F : \mathcal{K} \times \mathcal{X} \to \mathcal{Y}$ be a KHwPRF, and let $m = \mathrm{poly}(\lambda)$ be an (arbitrary) positive integer. Assume that $d = \mathrm{poly}(\lambda)$ be a positive integer such that $d > 3 \log|\mathcal{K}|$. Let $\mathbf{Y} \in \mathcal{Y}^{m \times d}$ be a matrix of group elements such that each entry $y_{i,j}$ (for $i \in [m], j \in [d]$) is drawn uniformly and independently from $\mathcal{Y}$. If $\mathbf{s} \leftarrow \{0,1\}^d$, then for any PPT adversary we have*

$$(\mathbf{Y}, \mathbf{Ys}) \overset{c}{\approx} (\mathbf{Y}, \mathbf{u}),$$

where $\mathbf{u} \leftarrow \mathcal{Y}^m$ is a a vector of m uniformly chosen elements from $\mathcal{Y}$.

Proof. Let $\mathbf{F} \in \mathcal{Y}^{m \times d}$ be a matrix formed in the following way: first sample m uniform elements from $\mathcal{X}$ as $\{x_i \leftarrow \mathcal{X}\}_{i \in [m]}$, and generate d uniform elements from $\mathcal{K}$ as $\{k_j \leftarrow \mathcal{K}\}_{j \in [d]}$. Now we set $\mathbf{F}_{i,j} = F(k_j, x_i)$, i.e., each row (respectively, column) has the same input (respectively, key).

In the first part we prove that $\mathbf{F} \overset{c}{\approx} \mathbf{Y}$. We define the hybrids $\mathcal{H}_j$ over the columns as follows: let $\mathcal{H}_j$ be the hybrid that the first j columns are generated using the weak PRF and the remaining columns are generated using uniform and independent values. By construction, we have $\mathcal{H}_0 \equiv \mathbf{Y}$ and $\mathcal{H}_d \equiv \mathbf{F}$. It is enough to show that $\mathcal{H}_{j-1} \overset{c}{\approx} \mathcal{H}_j$ for each $j \in [d]$. Given access to an oracle $\mathcal{O}$ which is either F or a truly random function, the reduction invokes its oracle m times and receives $\{x_{i'}, \mathcal{O}(x_{i'})\}_{i' \in [m]}$. It then samples $j - 1$ keys as $\{k_{j'} \leftarrow \mathcal{K}\}_{j' \in [j-1]}$ and forms the matrix $\mathbf{M} \in \mathcal{Y}^{m \times d}$ as follows:

- If $j' < j$, set $\mathbf{M}_{i',j'} = F(k_{j'}, x_{i'})$.
- If $j' = j$, set $\mathbf{M}_{i',j'} = \mathcal{O}(x_{i'})$.
- If $j' > j$, for each $i' \in [m]$ and $j' \in \{j+1, \ldots, d\}$ sample a fresh $y \leftarrow \mathcal{Y}$ and set $\mathbf{M}_{i',j'} = y$.

Observe that $\mathbf{M} \equiv \mathcal{H}_{j-1}$ if $\mathcal{O}$ corresponds to a truly random function, and $\mathbf{M} \equiv \mathcal{H}_j$ if $\mathcal{O}$ corresponds to the pseudorandom function F. It follows that $\mathcal{H}_{j-1} \overset{c}{\approx} \mathcal{H}_j$.

In the second part of the proof, we show that $(\mathbf{F}, \mathbf{Fs}) \overset{c}{\approx} (\mathbf{F}, \mathbf{u})$. Given an attacker $\mathcal{A}$ that distinguishes $(\mathbf{F}, \mathbf{Fs})$ from $(\mathbf{F}, \mathbf{u})$, we describe an attacker $\mathcal{B}$ against the weak pseudorandomness of F. Given access to an oracle $\mathcal{O}$ which is either F or a truly random function, $\mathcal{B}$ invokes its oracle m times and receives $\{x_i, \mathcal{O}(x_i)\}_{i \in [m]}$. The reduction then samples d keys as $\{k_j \leftarrow \mathcal{K}\}_{j \in [d]}$ and forms the matrix $\mathbf{F}$ as $\mathbf{F}_{i,j} = F(k_j, x_i)$. Define the vectors $\mathbf{y}^* \in \mathcal{Y}^m$ and $\mathbf{k} \in \mathcal{K}^d$ as

$$\mathbf{k} = (k_1, \ldots, k_d), \qquad \mathbf{y}^* := (\mathcal{O}(x_1), \ldots, \mathcal{O}(x_m)).$$

Finally, $\mathcal{B}$ runs $\mathcal{A}$ on the input $(\mathbf{F}, \mathbf{y}^*)$ and $\mathcal{B}$ outputs whatever $\mathcal{A}$ outputs. It is easy to see that if $\mathcal{O}$ is a truly random function we have $(\mathbf{F}, \mathbf{y}^*) \equiv (\mathbf{F}, \mathbf{u})$. Observe that by the leftover hash lemma, we have $(\mathbf{k}, \bigoplus_{\mathbf{s}} \mathbf{k}) \overset{s}{\approx} (\mathbf{k}, k^*)$ where k^* is uniform over $\mathcal{K}$. If $\mathbf{y}^*$ corresponds to the weak PRF outputs ($\mathcal{O}$ is the weak PRF), by key homomorphism of F we have

$$\mathbf{Fs} = \begin{pmatrix} F\left(\bigoplus_{\mathbf{s}} \mathbf{k}, x_1\right) \\ F\left(\bigoplus_{\mathbf{s}} \mathbf{k}, x_2\right) \\ \vdots \\ F\left(\bigoplus_{\mathbf{s}} \mathbf{k}, x_m\right) \end{pmatrix} \overset{s}{\approx} \begin{pmatrix} F\left(k^*, x_1\right) \\ F\left(k^*, x_2\right) \\ \vdots \\ F\left(k^*, x_m\right) \end{pmatrix} \equiv \mathbf{y}^*.$$

Therefore, the advantage of $\mathcal{B}$ (in the weak PRF game) is negligibly different from the advantage of $\mathcal{A}$. It follows that $(\mathbf{F}, \mathbf{Fs}) \overset{c}{\approx} (\mathbf{F}, \mathbf{u})$, as required.

Using the first part of the proof by a straightforward reduction we have $(\mathbf{Y}, \mathbf{Ys}) \overset{c}{\approx} (\mathbf{F}, \mathbf{Fs})$ and $(\mathbf{F}, \mathbf{u}) \overset{c}{\approx} (\mathbf{Y}, \mathbf{u})$. Using the second part, it follows that

$$(\mathbf{Y}, \mathbf{Ys}) \overset{c}{\approx} (\mathbf{F}, \mathbf{Fs}) \overset{c}{\approx} (\mathbf{F}, \mathbf{u}) \overset{c}{\approx} (\mathbf{Y}, \mathbf{u}),$$

and hence we get $(\mathbf{Y}, \mathbf{Ys}) \overset{c}{\approx} (\mathbf{Y}, \mathbf{u})$.

3.1   Public-Key Encryption

Now we describe a non-interactive key exchange protocol (which is sufficient to realize PKE) based on any KHwPRF. Later, we explain construction of an IHwPRF from any KHwPRF, which in turn implies a variety of cryptographic primitives. We first start with an inefficient protocol, and then we show how to improve its efficiency.

Given a KHwPRF $F : \mathcal{K} \times \mathcal{X} \to \mathcal{Y}$ such that $\mathcal{Y}$ is an abelian group, fix some integer $m > 3 \log|\mathcal{K}|$ and let $\mathbf{Y} \in \mathcal{Y}^{m \times m}$ be a matrix of uniformly chosen group elements from $\mathcal{Y}$. Alice (respectively, Bob) chooses binary vector $\mathbf{r} \leftarrow \{0,1\}^m$ (respectively, $\mathbf{s} \leftarrow \{0,1\}^m$), and sends $\mathbf{r}^t \mathbf{Y}$ (respectively, $\mathbf{Ys}$) to Bob (respectively, Alice). The final secret will be $\mathbf{r}^t(\mathbf{Ys}) = (\mathbf{r}^t\mathbf{Y})\mathbf{s} \in \mathcal{Y}$. The following figure is a simple visualization of the key exchange protocol.

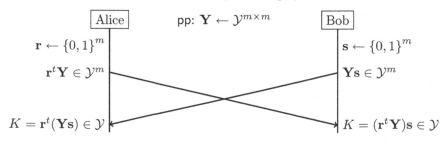

We sketch the security proof for the mentioned protocol. It is enough to show

$$(\mathbf{Y}, \mathbf{r}^t \mathbf{Y}, \mathbf{Ys}, \mathbf{r}^t \mathbf{Ys}) \stackrel{c}{\approx} (\mathbf{Y}, \mathbf{y}_1, \mathbf{y}_2, y),$$

where $\mathbf{Y} \leftarrow \mathcal{Y}^{m \times m}, \mathbf{r} \leftarrow \{0,1\}^m, \mathbf{s} \leftarrow \{0,1\}^m, \mathbf{y}_1 \leftarrow \mathcal{Y}^m, \mathbf{y}_2 \leftarrow \mathcal{Y}^m, y \leftarrow \mathcal{Y}$.

Observe that by Theorem 1 and a simple hybrid argument we can replace $\mathbf{r}^t \mathbf{Y}$ with a random vector $\mathbf{u} \leftarrow \mathcal{Y}^m$ and so

$$(\mathbf{Y}, \mathbf{u}, \mathbf{Ys}, \mathbf{us}) \stackrel{c}{\approx} (\mathbf{Y}, \mathbf{y}_1, \mathbf{y}_2, y).$$

Now let $\hat{\mathbf{Y}} \in \mathcal{Y}^{(m+1) \times m}$ be the matrix that has $\mathbf{Y}$ as its top submatrix and $\mathbf{u}$ as its last row. By applying Theorem 1 again, it follows that

$$(\hat{\mathbf{Y}}, \hat{\mathbf{Y}}\mathbf{s}) \stackrel{c}{\approx} (\hat{\mathbf{Y}}, y),$$

as required.

The reader may notice that the aforementioned key exchange protocol is too expensive in terms of communication complexity, i.e, to agree on some group element the parties need to exchange $2m^2$ group elements. Using the following lemma, we immediately get a key exchange protocol for which the whole cost of communication is twice the size of the final secret (like DDH).

Lemma 1. *Let $F : \mathcal{K} \times \mathcal{X} \rightarrow \mathcal{Y}$ be a KHwPRF, and let $m > 3\log|\mathcal{K}|$ be a positive integer. For any PPT adversary we have*

$$(\mathbf{Y}, \mathbf{RY}, \mathbf{YS}, \mathbf{RYS}) \stackrel{c}{\approx} (\mathbf{Y}, \mathbf{Y}', \mathbf{Y}'', \mathbf{Y}'''),$$

where $\mathbf{Y}, \mathbf{Y}', \mathbf{Y}'', \mathbf{Y}'''$ are matrices of uniform group elements in $\mathcal{Y}^{m \times m}$, and $\mathbf{S}, \mathbf{R}$ are uniform binary matrices, i.e., $\mathbf{R} \leftarrow \{0,1\}^{m \times m}$ and $\mathbf{S} \leftarrow \{0,1\}^{m \times m}$.[6]

Proof. The lemma follows from Theorem 1, and a standard hybrid argument.

3.2 Input-Homomorphic Weak PRF

Here we show a simple construction of an IHwPRF from any KHwPRF. We remark that although an IHwPRF implies a variety of cryptographic primitives, the constructions will not be necessarily efficient. More efficient constructions can be obtained by directly building the primitive using the assumption in Lemma 1.

Lemma 2. *Let $F : \mathcal{K} \times \mathcal{X} \rightarrow \mathcal{Y}$ be a KHwPRF. If $d > 3\log|\mathcal{K}|$ be a positive integer and $\mathcal{Y}$ is an abelian group, the function $\tilde{F} : \{0,1\}^d \times \mathcal{Y}^d \rightarrow \mathcal{Y}$ defined as*

$$\tilde{F}(\mathbf{s} = (s_1, \ldots, s_d), \mathbf{y} = (y_1, \ldots, y_d)) = \bigotimes_{\mathbf{s}} \mathbf{y} = \bigotimes_{j : s_j = 1} y_j$$

is an IHwPRF.

---

[6] Notice that for the correctness of key exchange, we require the group $\mathcal{Y}$ to be abelian.

Proof. First, observe that $\tilde{F}$ is input homomorphic since for any $\mathbf{y}, \mathbf{y}' \in \mathcal{Y}^d$ and $\mathbf{s} \in \{0,1\}^d$ we have

$$
\begin{aligned}
\tilde{F}(\mathbf{s}, \mathbf{y}) \otimes \tilde{F}(\mathbf{s}, \mathbf{y}') &= \left(\bigotimes_{\mathbf{s}} \mathbf{y} \right) \otimes \left(\bigotimes_{\mathbf{s}} \mathbf{y}' \right) \\
&= \left(\bigotimes_{j:s_j=1} y_j \right) \otimes \left(\bigotimes_{j:s_j=1} y'_j \right) \\
&= \bigotimes_{j:s_j=1} (y_j \otimes y'_j) \\
&= \bigotimes_{\mathbf{s}} (\mathbf{y} \otimes \mathbf{y}') = \tilde{F}(\mathbf{s}, \mathbf{y} \otimes \mathbf{y}').
\end{aligned}
$$

Given m (where $m = \mathrm{poly}(\lambda)$) samples of the form $(\mathbf{y}_i, \mathcal{O}(\mathbf{y}_i))$, form the matrix $\mathbf{Y} \in \mathcal{Y}^{m \times d}$ such that the i'th row of $\mathbf{Y}$ is $\mathbf{y}_i$. In addition, define $\mathbf{y}^*$ as $\mathbf{y}^* := (\mathcal{O}(\mathbf{y}_1), \ldots, \mathcal{O}(\mathbf{y}_m))$. Observe that if $\mathcal{O}$ is a truly random function then $\mathbf{y}^*$ is uniformly distributed in $\mathcal{Y}^m$. On the other hand, if $\mathcal{O}$ is the weak PRF, we have $\mathbf{y}^* = \mathbf{Y}\mathbf{s}$ for some uniform $\mathbf{s} \in \{0,1\}^d$. By applying Theorem 1 and observing the fact that $m = \mathrm{poly}(\lambda)$, it follows that F is a weak PRF.

Implications. By plugging in the results of [AMPR19], and using the Lemma 2 it follows that KHwPRFs imply noninteractive key exchange, private information retrieval [KO97], lossy trapdoor functions [PW08], identity-based encryption (in a non-blackbox manner) [DG17b, DG17a, BLSV18], and hinting PRGs [KW19].

We remark that KHwPRFs trivially imply homomorphic one-way functions (HOWFs) and hence using the results of [AMPR19], KHwPRFs imply collision-resistant hash functions, Schnorr signatures, and chameleon hash functions.

3.3   Asymmetric Primitives from Bounded KHwPRFs

In this part, we show that the "approximate" (some papers called it "almost") version of key-homomorphic weak PRFs with certain properties imply a variety of asymmetric primitives, such as public-key encryption (PKE). Approximate KHwPRFs have the property that $F_{k \oplus k'}(x)$ is *close* to $F_k(x) \otimes F_{k'}(x)$ where closeness is measured with respect to some distance function.

An Algebraic Definition. Formalizing a general definition for "approximate" homomorphism requires a somewhat involved *geometric* definition that needs a distance function, which also does not nicely fit into the recent (algebraic) framework of [AMPR19]. In this work, we provide a natural *algebraic* definition for *bounded* Key-Homomorphic weak PRFs, which is similar to the definition of bounded IHwPRFs of [AMPR19].

We remark that all existing constructions of approximate KHwPRFs with an appropriate choice of parameters can be viewed as bounded KHwPRFs.

Definition 5. *A weak pseudorandom function family* $\{F(k,\cdot) : \mathcal{X} \to \mathcal{Y}\}_{k \in \mathcal{K}}$ *is a γ-bounded KHwPRF family if there exists (efficiently computable) universal mappings* $\mathcal{R}_{\mathsf{in}} : \mathcal{Y} \to \mathcal{Z}_{\mathsf{in}}$ *and* $\mathcal{R}_{\mathsf{out}} : \mathcal{Z}_{\mathsf{in}} \to \mathcal{Z}_{\mathsf{out}}$ *such that*

- $(\mathcal{K}, \oplus)$, $(\mathcal{Y}, \otimes)$, *and* $(\mathcal{Z}_{\mathsf{in}}, \odot)$ *are efficiently samplable groups, and the group operations and the inverse operation in each group are efficiently computable.*
- *For a randomly chosen key vector* $(k_1, \ldots, k_L) \leftarrow \mathcal{K}^L$ *such that* $L \leq \gamma$, *and a randomly chosen input* $x \leftarrow \mathcal{X}$, *the following holds with overwhelming probability:*

$$\mathcal{R}_{\mathsf{in}}\Big(F\Big(\bigoplus_{j \in [L]} k_j, x\Big)\Big) = \mathcal{R}_{\mathsf{in}}\Big(\bigotimes_{j \in [L]} F(k_j, x)\Big),$$

$$\mathcal{R}_{\mathsf{out}}\Big(\bigodot_{j \in [L]} \mathcal{R}_{\mathsf{in}}\big(F(k_j, x)\big)\Big) = \mathcal{R}_{\mathsf{out}}\Big(\mathcal{R}_{\mathsf{in}}\Big(\bigotimes_{j \in [L]} F(k_j, x)\Big)\Big).$$

Bounded KHwPRFs and LWR. All of the currently known instantiations of "approximate" key-homomorphic (weak) PRFs use Learning With Rounding (LWR) [BPR12] as their underlying assumption. It is easy to see that if the *output* group of some LWR-based KHwPRF is $\mathbb{Z}_p^n$ for some *superpolynomial* modulus p and some dimension n, we can define the mapping $\mathcal{R}_{\mathsf{in}}$ (respectively, $\mathcal{R}_{\mathsf{out}}$) to be rounding with respect to some modulus p_{in} (respectively, p_{out}) such that p/p_{in} and $p_{\mathsf{in}}/p_{\mathsf{out}}$ are both superpolynomial.

This immediately yields bounded KHwPRFs from approximate KHwPRFs that have the mentioned property. We remark that this property seems to be necessary for most of the applications of KH-PRFs in [BLMR13] (and in some cases to get an efficient construction). The reader may note that the resulting construction of bounded KHwPRFs from LWR has a triple rounding, one that is embedded in the (weak) PRF F and one for each mapping $\mathcal{R}_{\mathsf{out}}$ and $\mathcal{R}_{\mathsf{in}}$ defined above. Although this property is inherent for the LWR-based construction, in general there may not be any similarity between F and $\mathcal{R}_{\mathsf{in}}$ or $\mathcal{R}_{\mathsf{out}}$ for a bounded KHwPRF.

PKE Construction from Bounded KHwPRF. Using the definition above, we now construct a public-key encryption scheme from a *bounded* KHwPRF. The construction is almost identical to the case of unbounded KHwPRFs, with the difference being applying the mappings $\mathcal{R}_{\mathsf{in}}$ and $\mathcal{R}_{\mathsf{out}}$ of the bounded KHwPRF. The argument for the security is also very similar to the exact/unbounded case, and we omit the details.

Given a γ-bounded KHwPRF $F : \mathcal{K} \times \mathcal{X} \to \mathcal{Y}$ (with mappings $\mathcal{R}_{\mathsf{in}}$ and $\mathcal{R}_{\mathsf{out}}$ defined as above) such that $\mathcal{Y}$ and $\mathcal{Z}_{\mathsf{in}}$ are abelian groups and $\gamma > 3\log|\mathcal{K}|$, fix some integer $m > 3\log|\mathcal{K}|$ and let $\mathbf{Y} \in \mathcal{Y}^{m \times m}$ be a matrix of uniformly chosen group elements from $\mathcal{Y}$. Alice (respectively, Bob) chooses binary vector $\mathbf{r} \leftarrow \{0,1\}^m$ (respectively, $\mathbf{s} \leftarrow \{0,1\}^m$), and sends $\mathcal{R}_{\mathsf{in}}(\mathbf{r}^t \mathbf{Y})$ (respectively, $\mathcal{R}_{\mathsf{in}}(\mathbf{Y}\mathbf{s})$) to Bob (respectively, Alice). The final secret will be

$$\mathcal{R}_{\mathsf{out}}\big(\mathbf{r}^t \mathcal{R}_{\mathsf{in}}(\mathbf{Y}\mathbf{s})\big) = \mathcal{R}_{\mathsf{out}}\big(\mathcal{R}_{\mathsf{in}}(\mathbf{r}^t\mathbf{Y})\mathbf{s}\big) \in \mathcal{Z}_{\mathsf{out}}.$$

Bounded IHwPRF from Bounded KHwPRF. Using the definition above, we now construct a bounded IHwPRF from a *bounded* KHwPRF. The construction is almost identical to the case of unbounded KHwPRFs, with the difference being applying the mappings $\mathcal{R}_{in}$ and $\mathcal{R}_{out}$ of the bounded KHwPRF.

Given a γ-bounded KHwPRF $F : \mathcal{K} \times \mathcal{X} \to \mathcal{Y}$ (with mappings $\mathcal{R}_{in}$ and $\mathcal{R}_{out}$ defined as above) such that $\mathcal{Y}$ and $\mathcal{Z}_{in}$ are abelian groups and $\gamma > 3 \log|\mathcal{K}|$, fix some integer d such that $3 \log|\mathcal{K}| < d \le \gamma$ we define a bounded IHwPRF $\tilde{F} : \{0,1\}^d \times \mathcal{Y}^d \to \mathcal{Z}_{in}$ with its associated mapping $\tilde{\mathcal{R}} : \mathcal{Z}_{in} \to \mathcal{Z}_{out}$ as

$$\tilde{F}\big(\mathbf{s} = (s_1, \dots, s_d), \mathbf{y} = (y_1, \dots, y_d)\big) = \mathcal{R}_{in}\Big(\bigotimes_{\mathbf{s}} \mathbf{y}\Big) = \mathcal{R}_{in}\Big(\bigotimes_{j : s_j = 1} y_j\Big),$$

where $\tilde{\mathcal{R}}$ (the associated mapping with $\tilde{F}$) is identical to $\mathcal{R}_{out}$. The security proof is very similar to the exact/unbounded case, and hence we omit the details.

3.4   Naor-Reingold PRF

Here we show a construction of Naor-Reingold style PRF from any KHwPRF. Before we do so, however, we will provide some background on the Naor-Reingold PRF and explain why PRFs in this style are important. We start by recalling the original Naor-Reingold PRF [NR97]:

Let $\mathbb{G}$ be a group of order p, and let $F_{NR} : (\mathbb{Z}_p^{(\ell+1)} \times \mathbb{G}) \times \{0,1\}^\ell \to \mathbb{G}$ be the function defined by

$$F_{NR}\left(\{\alpha_j\}_{j \in [0,\ell]} \in \mathbb{Z}_p^{(\ell+1)}, g \in \mathbb{G}, \mathbf{x} \in \{0,1\}^\ell\right) = g^{\alpha_0 \prod_{i=1}^{\ell} \alpha_i^{x_i}},$$

where the values $\alpha_0, \alpha_1, \dots, \alpha_\ell$ form the key and $\mathbf{x}$ is the input. Informally, a Naor-Reingold style PRF requires a constant number of computations (for instance, the exponentiation in F_{NR}) on which the assumption related to its hardness depends, while all of the operations that scale with the length of the input (for instance, the integer multiplications in the exponent of F_{NR}) are less expensive. This feature allows Naor-Reingold style PRFs to be potentially efficient. In particular, assuming that the underlying operations have reasonably low circuit depth, such PRFs typically have polylogarithmic evaluation circuits.

We now show a simple construction of Naor-Reingold style PRF from any exact KHwPRF with abelian output group. Our construction involves a subset product of binary matrices and one "multiplication" of a group matrix and an integer matrix. The depth of the PRF evaluation circuit is polylogarithmic provided that the group operation can be done efficiently.

Theorem 2. *Let $\tilde{F} : \mathcal{K} \times \mathcal{X} \to \mathcal{Y}$ be a KHwPRF, and fix some $m > 3 \log|\mathcal{K}|$. Let $\mathbf{Y} \in \mathcal{Y}^{m \times m}$ be a (public) matrix of group elements such that each entry $y_{i,j}$ (for $i \in [m], j \in [m]$) is drawn uniformly and independently from $\mathcal{Y}$. The function $F : \mathcal{Y}^{(\ell+1) \times m^2} \times \{0,1\}^\ell \to \mathcal{Y}^{m \times m}$ defined as*

$$F\left((\mathbf{S}_0, \mathbf{S}_1, \dots, \mathbf{S}_\ell), \mathbf{x} = (x_1, \dots, x_\ell)\right) = \mathbf{Y}\mathbf{S}_0 \prod_{i=1}^{\ell} \mathbf{S}_i^{x_i}$$

is a pseudorandom function where $\mathbf{S}_i \leftarrow \{0,1\}^{m \times m}$ for $i \in \{0, \dots, \ell\}$.

Proof. To prove this theorem, we use the following lemma.

Lemma 3. *Let* $\mathbf{Y}_1, \ldots, \mathbf{Y}_Q \in \mathcal{Y}^{m \times m}$ *be matrices with uniformly and independently sampled entries from* $\mathcal{Y}$ *for some* $Q = \text{poly}(\lambda)$, *and let* $\mathbf{S} \leftarrow \{0,1\}^{m \times m}$ *be a uniformly sampled binary matrix. Then for any PPT adversary we have*

$$\{(\mathbf{Y}_q, \mathbf{Y}_q \mathbf{S})\}_{q \in [Q]} \overset{c}{\approx} \{(\mathbf{Y}_q, \mathbf{U}_q)\}_{q \in [Q]}.$$

where for each $q \in [Q]$, $\mathbf{U}_q \leftarrow \mathcal{Y}^{m \times m}$ *is a matrix of uniformly chosen elements from* $\mathcal{Y}$.

This lemma follows directly from Theorem 1, and a standard hybrid argument over the columns of $\mathbf{S}$. The proof of pseudorandomness now proceeds via a series of $(\ell + 1)$ hybrid games, where for each $j \in [0, \ell]$, the jth game is as described below.

1. The challenger samples $(\ell - j)$ uniform binary matrices as $\mathbf{S}_i \leftarrow \{0,1\}^{m \times m}$ for $i \in [j + 1, \ell]$. It also maintains a list $\mathcal{L}$ of $m \times m$ matrices over the group $\mathcal{Y}$. Initially, this list is empty. The challenger also creates and stores an $m \times m$ matrix $\mathbf{Y}_0$ consisting of uniformly and independently sampled entries from $\mathcal{Y}$.
2. The adversary adaptively issues a maximum of $Q = \text{poly}(\lambda)$ PRF queries of the form $\mathbf{x}_1, \ldots, \mathbf{x}_Q$, where for each $q \in [Q]$, we have $\mathbf{x}_q = (x_{1,q}, \ldots, x_{\ell,q})$. For ease of representation, we divide each query string as $\mathbf{x}_q = (\mathbf{x}_q^{(0)}, \mathbf{x}_q^{(1)})$, where

$$\mathbf{x}_q^{(0)} = (x_{1,q}, \ldots, x_{j,q}), \quad \mathbf{x}_q^{(1)} = (x_{j+1,q}, \ldots, x_{\ell,q}).$$

3. Upon receipt of the qth query, the challenger proceeds as follows:
   (a) If $j = 0$, it sets $\mathbf{Y}_q = \mathbf{Y}_0$.
   (b) Otherwise, it checks if there exists a $q' < q$ such that $\mathbf{x}_q^{(0)} = \mathbf{x}_{q'}^{(0)}$.
       i. If yes, it sets $\mathbf{Y}_q = \mathbf{Y}_{q'}$.
       ii. Otherwise, it sets $\mathbf{Y}_q$ to be an $m \times m$ matrix with uniformly and independently sampled entries from $\mathcal{Y}$.
   (c) It updates the list $\mathcal{L}$ as $\mathcal{L} = \mathcal{L} \cup \{\mathbf{Y}_q\}$ and responds to the qth query as

$$f_{j,q} = \mathbf{Y}_q \prod_{i=j+1}^{\ell} \mathbf{S}_i^{x_{i,q}}.$$

Note that in the zeroth hybrid, we replaced the component $\mathbf{YS}_0$ in the original PRF construction by an $m \times m$ matrix $\mathbf{Y}_0$ consisting of uniformly and independently sampled entries from $\mathcal{Y}$. It follows from Theorem 1 that this hybrid is indistinguishable from the real PRF experiment.

Now, for each $j \in [0, \ell]$, let $\mathcal{F}_j = \{f_{j,q}\}_{q \in [Q]}$ be the set of responses generated by the challenger in the jth game. The proof of Theorem 2 now follows immediately from the following claim:

Claim. For each $j \in [0, \ell - 1]$ and for any PPT adversary we have

$$\mathcal{F}_j \stackrel{c}{\approx} \mathcal{F}_{j+1}.$$

Let $\mathcal{A}$ be a PPT adversary such that for some $j \in [\ell]$, $\mathcal{A}$ efficiently distinguishes between $\mathcal{F}_j$ and $\mathcal{F}_{j+1}$. We construct an attacker $\mathcal{B}$ against the assumption in Lemma 3. $\mathcal{B}$ receives as input a tuple of the form $\{(\mathbf{Y}_q, \mathbf{Z}_q)\}_{q \in [Q']}$ for some $Q' > Q$, where either each $\mathbf{Z}_q$ is of the form $\mathbf{Y}_q \mathbf{S}_j$ for some uniformly random $m \times m$ binary matrix $\mathbf{S}_j$, or each $\mathbf{Z}_q$ is a uniformly random matrix over $\mathcal{Y}^{m \times m}$. It proceeds as follows:

1. $\mathcal{B}$ samples $(\ell - j - 1)$ uniform binary matrices as $\mathbf{S}_i \leftarrow \{0, 1\}^{m \times m}$ for $i \in [j + 2, \ell]$. It also maintains a counter variable cnt. Initially, cnt $= 1$.
2. $\mathcal{A}$ adaptively issues a maximum of $Q = \text{poly}(\lambda)$ PRF queries of the form $\mathbf{x}_1, \ldots, \mathbf{x}_Q$, where for each $q \in [Q]$, we have $\mathbf{x}_q = (x_{1,q}, \ldots, x_{\ell,q})$. Again, for ease of representation, we divide each query string as $\mathbf{x}_q = (\mathbf{x}_q^{(0)}, \mathbf{x}_q^{(1)})$, where

$$\mathbf{x}_q^{(0)} = (x_{1,q}, \ldots, x_{j,q}), \quad \mathbf{x}_q^{(1)} = (x_{j+1,q}, \ldots, x_{\ell,q}).$$

3. Upon receipt of the qth query, $\mathcal{B}$ checks if there exists a $q' < q$ such that $\mathbf{x}_q^{(0)} = \mathbf{x}_{q'}^{(0)}$.
   (a) If yes, it sets $\widetilde{\mathbf{Y}}_q = \widetilde{\mathbf{Y}}_{q'}$ and $\widetilde{\mathbf{Z}}_q = \widetilde{\mathbf{Z}}_{q'}$.
   (b) Otherwise, it sets $\widetilde{\mathbf{Y}}_q = \mathbf{Y}_{\text{cnt}}$ and $\widetilde{\mathbf{Z}}_q = \mathbf{Z}_{\text{cnt}}$, and updates cnt $= \text{cnt} + 1$.
4. $\mathcal{B}$ now responds to the qth query as

$$\tilde{f}_{j,q} = \begin{cases} \widetilde{\mathbf{Y}}_q \prod_{i=j+2}^{\ell} \mathbf{S}_i^{x_{i,q}} & \text{if } x_{j+1,q} = 0 \\ \widetilde{\mathbf{Z}}_q \prod_{i=j+2}^{\ell} \mathbf{S}_i^{x_{i,q}} & \text{if } x_{j+1,q} = 1. \end{cases}$$

5. Eventually, the adversary $\mathcal{A}$ outputs a bit b. $\mathcal{B}$ outputs the same bit b.

Let $\widetilde{\mathcal{F}} = \{\tilde{f}_{j,q}\}_{q \in [Q]}$ be the set of responses generated by $\mathcal{B}$. It is easy to see the following:

- If each $\mathbf{Z}_q$ is of the form $\mathbf{Y}_q \mathbf{S}_j$ for some uniformly random $m \times m$ binary matrix $\mathbf{S}_j$, then the distribution of $\widetilde{\mathcal{F}}$ is identical to that of $\mathcal{F}_j$.
- On the other hand, if each $\mathbf{Z}_q$ is a uniformly random matrix over $\mathcal{Y}^{m \times m}$, then the distribution of $\widetilde{\mathcal{F}}$ is identical to that of $\mathcal{F}_{j+1}$.

It now follows that the advantage of $\mathcal{B}$ is identical to that of $\mathcal{A}$. This completes the proof of Claim 3.4. The proof of Theorem 2 follows immediately.

NR-style PRFs from Bounded KHwPRFs. Our definition of bounded KHwPRFs does not allow a direct construction of NR-style PRFs. However, there are known constructions of NR-style PRFs from lattice-based assumptions. A notable example is the lattice-based KHPRF from [BLMR13], which proves security by progressively rounding further at each hybrid argument to ensure that "exactness" holds at each step. However, while actually computing the PRF, this is simulated by rounding once to a specially chosen modulus. In practical scenarios, this construction seems substantially less efficient than related pseudorandom synthesizer constructions [NR95, Mon18].

Our algebraic definition of bounded KHwPRFs does not encompass multiple levels of "rounding" (or any other compressing operation), since it seemingly makes bounded KHwPRFs inherently inefficient for constructing NR-style PRFs. Thus, we omit constructing NR-style PRFs from bounded KHwPRFs.

4 Updatable Encryption and Symmetric PRE

In this section, we show that any ciphertext-independent updatable encryption scheme that satisfies the adaptive notions of forward and post-compromise security proposed in [LT18] implies PKE. We also show that any symmetric-key proxy re-encryption scheme that satisfies the adaptive notion of indistinguishability-based security formalized in [FKKP19] implies updatable encryption with forward and post-compromise security, and hence PKE.

4.1 PKE from Updatable Encryption

An updatable encryption scheme is, informally speaking, a symmetric key encryption scheme with the following extra property: a user with a secret key k_1 can provide an update token $\sigma_{1,2}$ that maps ciphertexts encrypted under key k_1 to new ciphertexts encrypted under some other key k_2. The main application of updatable encryption is handling key rotation of data in the cloud where a data owner does not trust the cloud owner enough to provide them with a secret key in the clear.

Updatable encryption was first defined in [BLMR13] as an application of KHPRFs. The definitions proposed in [BLMR13] were subsequently refined by Everspaugh et al. in [EPRS17]. In a more recent work, Lehmann and Tackmann [LT18] introduced more rigorous security notions for updatable encryption that are desirable for real-world applications, and also pointed out that none of the existing constructions satisfy these notions. In this section, we show that updatable encryption with adaptive update indistinguishability (IND-UPD) as defined by Lehmann and Tackmann [LT18] implies public-key encryption. We start by defining the general functionality of any UE scheme. Note that all of the definitions we use here are from [LT18].

Definition 6. (Updatable Encryption). *An updatable encryption scheme* UE *for a message space* $\mathcal{M}$ *is a tuple of five PPT algorithms* (Setup, Next, Enc, Dec, Update) *defined as follows:*

- Setup(1^λ): *Given the security parameter* λ, *it generates a secret key* sk_0.
- Next(sk_e): *On input a secret key* sk_e *for epoch* e, *it generates a new secret key* sk_{e+1} *and a new update token* $\Delta_{e,e+1}$ *for epoch* $(e+1)$.
- Enc(sk_e, m): *On input a secret key* sk_e *for epoch* e *and a message* m $\in \mathcal{M}$, *it generates a ciphertext* ct_e.

- Dec(sk_e, ct_e): *On input a secret key* sk_e *and a ciphertext* ct_e *for some epoch e, it either outputs a message* $\mathsf{m}' \in \mathcal{M}$ *or* $\perp$.
- Update($\Delta_{e,e+1}$, ct_e): *On input an update token* $\Delta_{e,e+1}$ *and a ciphertext* ct_e *for some epoch e, it outputs an updated ciphertext* ct_{e+1} *for epoch* $(e+1)$.

Correctness. For any message $\mathsf{m} \in \mathcal{M}$, for any $\mathsf{sk}_0 \leftarrow \mathsf{Setup}(1^\lambda)$, and for any sequence of key/update token pairs $(\mathsf{sk}_1, \Delta_{0,1}), \dots, (\mathsf{sk}_e, \Delta_{c-1,e})$ obtained recursively as $(\mathsf{sk}_j, \Delta_{j-1,j}) \leftarrow \mathsf{Next}(\mathsf{sk}_{j-1})$ for each $j \in [e]$, we have

$$\mathsf{Dec}(\mathsf{sk}_j, \mathsf{ct}_j) = \mathsf{m},$$

for any $j \in [e]$, where the sequence of ciphertexts $\mathsf{ct}_0, \mathsf{ct}_1, \dots, \mathsf{ct}_e$ is obtained as $\mathsf{ct}_0 = \mathsf{Enc}(\mathsf{sk}_0, \mathsf{m})$ and $\mathsf{ct}_j \leftarrow \mathsf{Update}(\Delta_{j-1,j}, \mathsf{ct}_{j-1})$ for each $j \in [e]$.

Security Notions for UE. In their paper [LT18], Lehmann and Tackmann define several notions of security for updatable encryption. Previous works had somewhat non-accurate notions of security, so we consider the definitions from [LT18] to be the only suitable ones currently known for UE. In this section, we focus on their IND-UPD security definition, which we explain below. In our opinion, this definition reflects the security needs of a user storing data and updating ciphertexts in an untrusted cloud. However, debating the definitions of UE is out of scope of this paper, and we refer to the sections 3 and 4 of [LT18] for a discussion of notions of UE security.

Forward and Post-Compromise Security. We adopt the definition of post-compromise security for UE schemes proposed and formalized by Lehmann and Tackmann in a recent work [LT18]. More specifically, we focus on the notion of *adaptive update indistinguishability*, or IND-UPD in short (also referred to as *unlinkability*), which ensures that an updated ciphertext obtained via the Update algorithm does not reveal any information about the previous ciphertext to a PPT adversary $\mathcal{A}$, even when $\mathcal{A}$ adaptively compromises polynomially many keys and tokens before and after the challenge epoch.

Adaptive Update Indistinguishability. We recall the formal definitions for adaptive update indistinguishability from [LT18]. We assume that the adversary has access to the following oracles (e is an epoch counter initialized to 0 and $\mathcal{L}$ is a list initialized to empty):

1. $\mathcal{O}_{\mathsf{Enc}}$: On input a message m, this oracle outputs $\mathsf{ct}_e \leftarrow \mathsf{Enc}(\mathsf{sk}_e, \mathsf{m})$, where sk_e is the secret key corresponding to the current epoch e, and adds the tuple (ct_e, e) to the list $\mathcal{L}$.
2. $\mathcal{O}_{\mathsf{Next}}$: When queried, this oracle generates a new key/update token pair as $(\mathsf{sk}_{e+1}, \Delta_{e,e+1}) \leftarrow \mathsf{Next}(\mathsf{sk}_e)$, updates the epoch counter to $(e+1)$ and adds $(e+1, \mathsf{sk}_{e+1}, \Delta_{e,e+1})$ to the global state of the challenger. If issued post challenge-query phase, it also updates the challenge ciphertext to the new epoch as $\mathsf{ct}_e^* \leftarrow \mathsf{Update}(\Delta_{e-1,e}, \mathsf{ct}_{e-1}^*)$, and adds (ct_e^*, e) to the list $\mathcal{L}$.
3. $\mathcal{O}_{\mathsf{Update}}$: On input a ciphertext ct_{e-1} such that $(\mathsf{ct}_{e-1}, e-1) \in \mathcal{L}$ (i.e., the input ciphertext is honestly generated during the previous epoch), this oracle outputs $\mathsf{ct}_e \leftarrow \mathsf{Update}(\Delta_{e-1,e}, \mathsf{ct}_{e-1})$, and adds (ct_e, e) to the list $\mathcal{L}$.

4. $\mathcal{O}_{\text{corrupt}}$: This oracle takes as input an epoch $e' \leq e$ (where e is the current epoch) and either key or token. On input (e', key), it outputs the key $\text{sk}_{e'}$. On input (e', token), it outputs the token $\Delta_{e'-1,e'}$.
5. $\mathcal{O}_{\text{challenge}}$: This oracle returns the current challenge ciphertext ct_e^* from the list $\mathcal{L}$.

For each bit $b \in \{0, 1\}$, define the following experiment $\text{Expt}_b^{\text{ind-upd}}$ between a challenger and an adversary $\mathcal{A}$:

Experiment $\text{Expt}_b^{\text{ind-upd}}$:

1. The challenger generates $\text{sk}_0 \leftarrow \text{Setup}(1^\lambda)$.
2. The challenger maintains an epoch counter e, a challenge epoch counter e^* and a list $\mathcal{L}$. Initially, $e = 0$, $e^* = \perp$ and $\mathcal{L} = \phi$.
3. The adversary $\mathcal{A}$ adaptively issues any number of queries to the $\mathcal{O}_{\text{Enc}}$, $\mathcal{O}_{\text{Next}}$, $\mathcal{O}_{\text{Update}}$ and $\mathcal{O}_{\text{corrupt}}$ oracles. These oracles update the epoch counter e and the list $\mathcal{L}$ as described above.
4. The adversary $\mathcal{A}$ eventually outputs a pair of ciphertexts $(\text{ct}_0, \text{ct}_1)$, subject to the restriction that $(\text{ct}_0, e-1), (\text{ct}_1, e-1) \in \mathcal{L}$ and $|\text{ct}_0| = |\text{ct}_1|$.
5. The challenger queries the $\mathcal{O}_{\text{Next}}$ oracle to obtain the key/update token pair $(\text{sk}_e, \Delta_{e-1,e})$.
6. The challenger sets $\text{ct}_e^* \leftarrow \text{Update}(\Delta_{e-1,e}, \text{ct}_b)$ and adds the tuple (ct_e^*, e) to the list $\mathcal{L}$. It also sets $e^* = e$.
7. The adversary $\mathcal{A}$ continues to adaptively issue any number of queries to the $\mathcal{O}_{\text{Enc}}$, $\mathcal{O}_{\text{Next}}$, $\mathcal{O}_{\text{Update}}$, $\mathcal{O}_{\text{corrupt}}$ and $\mathcal{O}_{\text{challenge}}$ oracles, albeit subject to the following restrictions:
   (a) $\mathcal{A}$ has not made an *update-query* to the $\mathcal{O}_{\text{corrupt}}$ oracle during the challenge epoch e^*, that is, it does not know the update token Δ_{e^*-1,e^*}.
   (b) If $\mathcal{E}_0^*$ is the set of all epochs during which $\mathcal{A}$ has queried the $\mathcal{O}_{\text{challenge}}$ oracle and $\mathcal{E}_1^*$ is the set of all epochs during which $\mathcal{A}$ has made *key-queries* to the $\mathcal{O}_{\text{corrupt}}$ oracle, then $\mathcal{E}_0^* \cap \mathcal{E}_1^* = \{\}$.

Definition 7. (IND-UPD secure Updatable Encryption). *An updatable encryption scheme* (Setup, Next, Enc, Dec, Update) *is said to be* IND-UPD*-secure if for all PPT adversaries $\mathcal{A}$, the views of $\mathcal{A}$ in the experiments $\text{Expt}_0^{ind-upd}$ and $\text{Expt}_1^{ind-upd}$ are computationally indistinguishable. (Note that in the aforementioned definition, we implicitly assumed that the update algorithm of the underlying UE scheme is randomized.)*

We now show that any updatable encryption scheme that satisfies adaptive update indistinguishability implies a PKE scheme. More formally, let UE = (Setup, Next, Enc, Dec, Update) be an IND-UPD secure scheme. We construct a PKE scheme as follows.

- Key Generation: The key generation algorithm receives as input the security parameter λ. It first generates a secret key for the UE scheme as $\mathsf{sk}_0 \leftarrow \mathsf{Setup}(1^\lambda)$. It then recursively updates this secret key $(e+1)$ times for some arbitrarily chosen epoch e, as

$$(\mathsf{sk}_j, \Delta_{j-1,j}) \leftarrow \mathsf{Next}(\mathsf{sk}_{j-1}) \text{ for each } j \in [e+1].$$

Finally, it chooses two messages $\mathsf{m}_0, \mathsf{m}_1 \in \mathcal{M}$ such that $\mathsf{m}_0 \neq \mathsf{m}_1$, sets

$$\mathsf{ct}_0^* = \mathsf{Enc}(\mathsf{sk}_e, \mathsf{m}_0), \quad \mathsf{ct}_1^* = \mathsf{Enc}(\mathsf{sk}_e, \mathsf{m}_1),$$

and outputs the secret key/public key pair $(\mathsf{sk}_{\mathrm{PKE}}, \mathsf{pk}_{\mathrm{PKE}})$ as

$$\mathsf{sk}_{\mathrm{PKE}} = \mathsf{sk}_{e+1}, \quad \mathsf{pk}_{\mathrm{PKE}} = ((\mathsf{m}_0, \mathsf{ct}_0^*), (\mathsf{m}_1, \mathsf{ct}_1^*), \Delta_{e,e+1}).$$

- Encryption: To encrypt a bit $b \in \{0,1\}$, the encryption algorithm outputs a randomized update of ct_b^* to the epoch $e+1$ using the publicly available update token $\Delta_{e,e+1}$. More formally, on input a bit $b \in \{0,1\}$, the encryption algorithm outputs

$$\mathsf{ct}_{\mathrm{PKE}} \leftarrow \mathsf{Update}(\Delta_{e,e+1}, \mathsf{ct}_b^*).$$

- Decryption: On input a ciphertext $\mathsf{ct}_{\mathrm{PKE}}$, the decryption algorithm computes

$$\mathsf{m}' = \mathsf{Dec}(\mathsf{sk}_{\mathrm{PKE}}, \mathsf{ct}_{\mathrm{PKE}}).$$

If $\mathsf{m}' = \mathsf{m}_b$ for some $b \in \{0,1\}$, it outputs b. Otherwise, it outputs $\perp$.

Correctness is straightforward to verify. We now formally prove the following theorem.

Theorem 3. *If* UE *is* IND-UPD *secure, then the aforementioned* PKE *scheme is* IND-CPA *secure.*

Proof. Let $\mathcal{A}$ be an adversary that breaks the IND-CPA security of the PKE scheme with non-negligible advantage ε. We construct an algorithm $\mathcal{B}$ that breaks the IND-UPD security of UE with advantage $\varepsilon' = \varepsilon/2$. $\mathcal{B}$ proceeds as follows:

1. $\mathcal{B}$ plays the IND-UPD security game with the challenger for UE till some epoch $e-1$ for some arbitrarily chosen challenge epoch e. At this point, $\mathcal{B}$ chooses a pair of arbitrary messages $\mathsf{m}_0, \mathsf{m}_1 \in \mathcal{M}$ such that $\mathsf{m}_0 \neq \mathsf{m}_1$, and queries the $\mathcal{O}_{\mathsf{Enc}}$ oracle to obtain $(\mathsf{ct}_0, \mathsf{ct}_1)$, where

$$\mathsf{ct}_0 = \mathsf{Enc}(\mathsf{sk}_{e-1}, \mathsf{m}_0), \quad \mathsf{ct}_1 = \mathsf{Enc}(\mathsf{sk}_{e-1}, \mathsf{m}_1).$$

2. $\mathcal{B}$ outputs $(\mathsf{ct}_0, \mathsf{ct}_1)$ as the pair of challenge ciphertexts, and receives the challenge ciphertext ct_e^*, which is a randomized update of ct_b to the epoch e for $b \leftarrow \{0,1\}$.

3. Next, $\mathcal{B}$ issues the following additional queries:

   (a) It queries the $\mathcal{O}_{\mathsf{Update}}$ oracle to receive $\widetilde{\mathsf{ct}}_e^*$, which is a randomized update of ct_1 to the epoch e.

   (b) It issues a query to the $\mathcal{O}_{\mathsf{Next}}$ oracle, followed by a *token-query* to the $\mathcal{O}_{\mathsf{corrupt}}$ oracle, to obtain an update token $\Delta_{e,e+1}$.

   Note that none of the aforementioned queries violate any of the constraints described in the IND-UPD security experiment.

4. $\mathcal{B}$ now provides the adversary $\mathcal{A}$ with the public key $\mathsf{pk}_{\mathrm{PKE}}$, where

$$\mathsf{pk}_{\mathrm{PKE}} = \left((\mathsf{m}_0, \mathsf{ct}_e^*), (\mathsf{m}_1, \widetilde{\mathsf{ct}}_e^*), \Delta_{e,e+1} \right).$$

5. $\mathcal{B}$ uniformly samples $b' \leftarrow \{0,1\}$ and outputs the challenge ciphertext $\mathsf{ct}_{\mathrm{PKE}}^*$, where

$$\mathsf{ct}_{\mathrm{PKE}}^* = \begin{cases} \mathsf{Update}(\Delta_{e,e+1}, \mathsf{ct}_e^*) & \text{if } b' = 0, \\ \mathsf{Update}(\Delta_{e,e+1}, \widetilde{\mathsf{ct}}_e^*) & \text{if } b' = 1. \end{cases}$$

6. $\mathcal{B}$ outputs whatever $\mathcal{A}$ outputs.

Observe that when $b = 0$, the distribution of the public key $\mathsf{pk}_{\mathrm{PKE}}$ in the view of $\mathcal{A}$ is exactly as in the real IND-CPA experiment. On the other hand, if $b = 1$, then ct_e^* and $\widetilde{\mathsf{ct}}_e^*$ are sampled from the same distribution. It follows that the advantage of $\mathcal{B}$ in the IND-UPD experiment is $\varepsilon' = \varepsilon/2$. This completes the proof of Theorem 3.

5   Negative Results in Quantum Setting

In this section we show that any homomorphic one-way function (HOWF) with exact/unbounded homomorphism over abelian groups can be broken using a quantum algorithm. Since exact (or unbounded) KHwPRFs (and hence KHPRFs) over abelian groups trivially imply unbounded HOWFs, it follows that there is no secure construction of an unbounded KHPRF/KHwPRF in quantum world. As a result, a secure KHwPRF either needs to have an approximate homomorphism, or the homomorphism should hold over a non-abelian group.

At a high level, given any abelian group with certain conditions there are known quantum algorithms to determine the structure of the group. That is, given an abelian group $\mathcal{G}$, there is an efficient quantum algorithm to find (an efficiently computable) isomorphism $\psi : \mathcal{G} \to \mathbb{Z}_{q_1} \oplus \cdots \oplus \mathbb{Z}_{q_m}$. We apply this to both the input and output group of a candidate HOWF f. Then we show a simple classic algorithm that given these isomorphisms over the input and output group of f, one can simply break one-wayness of f.

Theorem 4. *Let $f : \mathcal{X} \to \mathcal{Y}$ be a (classic) HOWF such that $\mathcal{X}$ and $\mathcal{Y}$ are abelian groups, and there exists an efficient algorithm to find a generating set* *for $\mathcal{Y}$. There exists a polynomial quantum algorithm that breaks the one-wayness of f with non-negligible advantage.*[7]

First we recall the following fact from algebra. A proof can be found in any standard textbook.

Theorem 5. *Any finite abelian group is isomorphic to a direct sum of cyclic groups, and each cyclic group has a prime power order.*

We also rely on the following quantum algorithm (see [CM01] and Section 6.2 of [Chi17] for more details).

Theorem 6. *Let $\mathcal{G}$ be a finite abelian group such that (1) each element of $\mathcal{G}$ has a unique decoding, (2) there is an efficient algorithm to do group operations on the elements of $\mathcal{G}$, and (3) there is an efficient algorithm to find a generating set for $\mathcal{G}$. There is a polynomial time quantum algorithm such that decomposes the group $\mathcal{G}$ as*

$$\mathcal{G} = \langle g_1 \rangle \oplus \cdots \oplus \langle g_M \rangle,$$

in terms of the generators $g_1, \ldots, g_M$, and for every $m, m' \in [M]$ such that $m \neq m'$ we have $\langle g_m \rangle \cap \langle g_{m'} \rangle = \{e\}$, where e is the identity element of $\mathcal{G}$. Moreover, the isomorphism

$$\psi : \mathcal{G} \to \mathbb{Z}_{|\langle g_1 \rangle|} \oplus \cdots \oplus \mathbb{Z}_{|\langle g_M \rangle|},$$

(in both ways) can be computed efficiently.

Now we are ready to proceed to the proof of Theorem 4. Let $f : \mathcal{X} \to \mathcal{Y}$ be an unbounded HOWF such that $\mathcal{X}$ and $\mathcal{Y}$ are abelian groups. Given a challenge $y^* \in \mathcal{Y}$ such that $y^* := f(x^*)$ for some uniform $x^* \leftarrow \mathcal{X}$, we want to find a preimage x such that $f(x) = y^*$. Let

$$\tilde{\mathcal{X}} := \mathbb{Z}_{p_1} \oplus \cdots \oplus \mathbb{Z}_{p_M} \quad , \quad \tilde{\mathcal{Y}} := \mathbb{Z}_{q_1} \oplus \cdots \oplus \mathbb{Z}_{q_N}$$

be the decomposition of groups $\mathcal{X}$ and $\mathcal{Y}$, respectively, where p_i (respectively, q_j) is a prime power for $m \in [M]$ (respectively, $n \in [N]$). We fix some arbitrary order for the cyclic groups, and we call $\tilde{\mathcal{X}}$ an *explicit representation* of $\mathcal{X}$. Using Theorem 6, we can efficiently compute the isomorphisms $\psi_{\mathcal{X}}, \psi_{\mathcal{Y}}$ (and their inverses) for any element in the domain of the isomorphism where

$$\psi_{\mathcal{X}} : \mathcal{X} \to \tilde{\mathcal{X}} \quad , \quad \psi_{\mathcal{Y}} : \mathcal{Y} \to \tilde{\mathcal{Y}}.$$

We define $\tilde{f} : \tilde{\mathcal{X}} \to \tilde{\mathcal{Y}}$ as the analog of f over the explicit representations of $\mathcal{X}$ and $\mathcal{Y}$, i.e., define

$$\tilde{f}(\tilde{x}) = \psi_{\mathcal{Y}}(f(\psi_{\mathcal{X}}^{-1}(\tilde{x}))).$$

---

[7] Notice that it is almost always the case that $\mathcal{Y}$ is an efficiently samplable group. By Theorem 5 of [AGKP14], a set of uniform elements with size $3\log|\mathcal{Y}|$ forms a generating set for $\mathcal{Y}$ with an overwhelming probability.

It is not hard to see that $f(x) = y$ is equivalent to $\tilde{f}(\psi_{\mathcal{X}}(x)) = \psi_{\mathcal{Y}}(y)$. Because the isomorphisms $\psi_{\mathcal{X}}, \psi_{\mathcal{Y}}$ and their inverses are efficiently computable, it is enough to show an attack against one-wayness of $\tilde{f}$.

For each $n \in [N]$, we define $\mathbf{e}_n \in \mathbb{Z}_{p_1} \oplus \cdots \oplus \mathbb{Z}_{p_N}$ to be the (unit) vector whose nth component is 1, and all other components are 0.[8] For an element $\tilde{y} \in \tilde{\mathcal{Y}}$, let $[\tilde{y}]_m \in \mathbb{Z}_{q_m}$ be the mth component of $\tilde{y}$. We compute the index set I_m for each $m \in M$ as

$$I_m = \{n \in [N] \mid [\tilde{f}(\mathbf{e}_n)]_m \neq 0\}.$$

All index sets $\{I_m\}_{m \in [M]}$ can be computed efficiently since both N and M are polynomially bounded. Define a vector of variables $\mathbf{z} = (z_1, \dots, z_N) \in \mathbb{Z}^N$, and for each $m \in [M]$, consider the following system of modular equations where $\{z_i\}_{i \in I_m}$ are the (unknown) variables:

$$S_m : \quad \sum_{i \in I_m} z_i [\tilde{f}(\mathbf{e}_i)]_m \equiv [\tilde{y}]_m \pmod{q_m}$$

Consider the following observations:

- Without loss of generality we can assume that for two distinct $m, m' \in [M]$, we have $\gcd(q_m, q'_m) = 1$. If $q_m = q'_m$, we can simply merge S_m and $S_{m'}$. If $q_m < q_{m'}$ and $\gcd(q_m, q'_m) > 1$, we can "lift" the equation in $S_{m'}$ simply by multiplying the both sides by $q^{m'}/q^m$ and adding the resulting equation to $S_{m'}$. We refer to this part as "merging step".
- Observe that for any two integers $p > 1, q > 1$, if there is a non-trivial homomorphism from $\mathbb{Z}_p$ to $\mathbb{Z}_q$ then either $p \mid q$ or $q \mid p$. Therefore, if z_n appears in S_m (or equivalently $n \in I_m$), we either have $p_n \mid q_m$ or $q_m \mid p_n$.

Let $\overline{M} \subseteq M$ be the set of indices after the "merging step". Using the previous observations, it follows that

- For any two distinct $\overline{m}_1, \overline{m}_2 \in \overline{M}$, we have $\gcd(q_{\overline{m}_1}, q_{\overline{m}_2}) = 1$.
- For any $n \in N$, there is at most one $\overline{m} \in \overline{M}$ such that the variable z_n appears in $S_{\overline{m}}$.

Each system of equation(s) $S_{\overline{m}}$ can be seen as a system of linear equation(s) over the group $\mathbb{Z}_{q_{\overline{m}}}$, and it can solved using the known algorithms for solving linear equations over finite abelian groups, e.g., [GR02]. One can equivalently interpret each $S_{\overline{m}}$ as a system of equations over the finite *ring* $\mathbb{Z}_{q_{\overline{m}}}$ (since $q_{\overline{m}}$ is not necessarily prime).

By solving each system $S_{\overline{m}}$, we can determine the vector $\mathbf{z} \in \mathbb{Z}^N$. Finally, we output $\tilde{x}$ as the preimage of $\tilde{y}$ the attacker where

$$\tilde{x} = (z_1 \bmod p_1, \dots, z_N \bmod p_n).$$

By construction, we know that the vector $\mathbf{z}$ satisfies all system of equation(s) $\{S_m\}_{m \in M}$. It follows that $\tilde{f}(\tilde{x}) = \tilde{y}$, as required.

---

[8] Notice that each component may live in a different cyclic group.

Building Quantum-Secure Primitives from Abelian Groups. Our results here may have some implications for the construction of quantum-secure primitives over abelian groups. For instance, in [AMPR19], the authors showed that many public-key cryptosystems can be built from generic primitives with exact homomorphism. Our results here give evidence that such constructions are not going to be quantum-secure when instantiated with new assumptions that rely on abelian groups. Lattice-based primitives do not support exact homomorphisms, which makes them immune to a wide class of quantum attacks. However, there do exist other assumptions relying on abelian groups, such as isogeny-based assumptions [JD11], for which similar notions of homomorphism are yet to be explored [dOPS18].

References

[ABH09]   Ateniese, G., Benson, K., Hohenberger, S.: Key-private proxy re-encryption. In: Fischlin, M. (ed.) CT-RSA 2009. LNCS, vol. 5473, pp. 279–294. Springer, Heidelberg (2009). https://doi.org/10.1007/978-3-642-00862-7_19

[ABPW13] Aono, Y., Boyen, X., Phong, L.T., Wang, L.: Key-private proxy re-encryption under LWE. In: Paul, G., Vaudenay, S. (eds.) INDOCRYPT 2013. LNCS, vol. 8250, pp. 1–18. Springer, Cham (2013). https://doi.org/10.1007/978-3-319-03515-4_1

[AFGH05] Ateniese, G., Fu, K., Green, M., Hohenberger, S.: Improved proxy re-encryption schemes with applications to secure distributed storage. In: NDSS 2005. The Internet Society, February 2005

[AFGH06] Ateniese, G., Fu, K., Green, M., Hohenberger, S.: Improved proxy re-encryption schemes with applications to secure distributed storage. ACM Trans. Inf. Syst. Secur. (TISSEC) 9(1), 1–30 (2006)

[AGKP14] Armknecht, F., Gagliardoni, T., Katzenbeisser, S., Peter, A.: General impossibility of group homomorphic encryption in the quantum world. In: Krawczyk, H. (ed.) PKC 2014. LNCS, vol. 8383, pp. 556–573. Springer, Heidelberg (2014). https://doi.org/10.1007/978-3-642-54631-0_32

[AMPR19] Alamati, N., Montgomery, H., Patranabis, S., Roy, A.: Minicrypt primitives with algebraic structure and applications. In: Ishai, Y., Rijmen, V. (eds.) EUROCRYPT 2019, Part II. LNCS, vol. 11477, pp. 55–82. Springer, Cham (2019). https://doi.org/10.1007/978-3-030-17656-3_3

[Bar17]   Barak, B.: The complexity of public-key cryptography. In: Lindell, Y. (ed.) Tutorials on the Foundations of Cryptography. ISC, pp. 45–77. Springer, Cham (2017). https://doi.org/10.1007/978-3-319-57048-8_2

[BBS98]   Blaze, M., Bleumer, G., Strauss, M.: Divertible protocols and atomic proxy cryptography. In: Nyberg, K. (ed.) EUROCRYPT 1998. LNCS, vol. 1403, pp. 127–144. Springer, Heidelberg (1998). https://doi.org/10.1007/BFb0054122

[BDRV18] Berman, I., Degwekar, A., Rothblum, R.D., Vasudevan, P.N.: From laconic zero-knowledge to public-key cryptography. In: Shacham, H., Boldyreva, A. (eds.) CRYPTO 2018, Part III. LNCS, vol. 10993, pp. 674–697. Springer, Cham (2018). https://doi.org/10.1007/978-3-319-96878-0_23

[BFP+15] Banerjee, A., Fuchsbauer, G., Peikert, C., Pietrzak, K., Stevens, S.: Key-homomorphic constrained pseudorandom functions. In: Dodis, Y., Nielsen, J.B. (eds.) TCC 2015, Part II. LNCS, vol. 9015, pp. 31–60. Springer, Heidelberg (2015). https://doi.org/10.1007/978-3-662-46497-7_2

[BLMR13] Boneh, D., Lewi, K., Montgomery, H., Raghunathan, A.: Key homomorphic PRFs and their applications. In: Canetti, R., Garay, J.A. (eds.) CRYPTO 2013, Part I. LNCS, vol. 8042, pp. 410–428. Springer, Heidelberg (2013). https://doi.org/10.1007/978-3-642-40041-4_23

[BLSV18] Brakerski, Z., Lombardi, A., Segev, G., Vaikuntanathan, V.: Anonymous IBE, leakage resilience and circular security from new assumptions. In: Nielsen, J.B., Rijmen, V. (eds.) EUROCRYPT 2018, Part I. LNCS, vol. 10820, pp. 535–564. Springer, Cham (2018). https://doi.org/10.1007/978-3-319-78381-9_20

[BP14] Banerjee, A., Peikert, C.: New and improved key-homomorphic pseudorandom functions. In: Garay, J.A., Gennaro, R. (eds.) CRYPTO 2014, Part I. LNCS, vol. 8616, pp. 353–370. Springer, Heidelberg (2014). https://doi.org/10.1007/978-3-662-44371-2_20

[BPR12] Banerjee, A., Peikert, C., Rosen, A.: Pseudorandom functions and lattices. In: Pointcheval, D., Johansson, T. (eds.) EUROCRYPT 2012. LNCS, vol. 7237, pp. 719–737. Springer, Heidelberg (2012). https://doi.org/10.1007/978-3-642-29011-4_42

[BR17] Bogdanov, A., Rosen, A.: Pseudorandom functions: three decades later. In: Lindell, Y. (ed.) Tutorials on the Foundations of Cryptography. ISC, pp. 79–158. Springer, Cham (2017). https://doi.org/10.1007/978-3-319-57048-8_3

[BV15] Brakerski, Z., Vaikuntanathan, V.: Constrained key-homomorphic PRFs from standard lattice assumptions. In: Dodis, Y., Nielsen, J.B. (eds.) TCC 2015, Part II. LNCS, vol. 9015, pp. 1–30. Springer, Heidelberg (2015). https://doi.org/10.1007/978-3-662-46497-7_1

[CCL+14] Chandran, N., Chase, M., Liu, F.-H., Nishimaki, R., Xagawa, K.: Re-encryption, functional re-encryption, and multi-hop re-encryption: a framework for achieving obfuscation-based security and instantiations from lattices. In: Krawczyk, H. (ed.) PKC 2014. LNCS, vol. 8383, pp. 95–112. Springer, Heidelberg (2014). https://doi.org/10.1007/978-3-642-54631-0_6

[CH07] Canetti, R., Hohenberger, S.: Chosen-ciphertext secure proxy re-encryption. In: Ning, P., De Capitani di Vimercati, S., Syverson, P.F. (eds.) ACM CCS 2007, pp. 185–194. ACM Press, October 2007

[Chi17] Childs, A.M.: Lecture notes on quantum algorithms (2017). https://www.cs.umd.edu/~amchilds/qa/qa.pdf

[CM01] Cheung, K.K.H., Mosca, M.: Decomposing finite abelian groups. Quantum Inf. Comput. **1**(3), 26–32 (2001)

[DG17a] Döttling, N., Garg, S.: From selective IBE to Full IBE and selective HIBE. In: Kalai, Y., Reyzin, L. (eds.) TCC 2017, Part I. LNCS, vol. 10677, pp. 372–408. Springer, Cham (2017). https://doi.org/10.1007/978-3-319-70500-2_13

[DG17b] Döttling, N., Garg, S.: Identity-based encryption from the Diffie-Hellman assumption. In: Katz, J., Shacham, H. (eds.) CRYPTO 2017, Part I. LNCS, vol. 10401, pp. 537–569. Springer, Cham (2017). https://doi.org/10.1007/978-3-319-63688-7_18

[DKL+18]   Derler, D., Krenn, S., Lorünser, T., Ramacher, S., Slamanig, D., Striecks, C.: Revisiting proxy re-encryption: forward secrecy, improved security, and applications. In: Abdalla, M., Dahab, R. (eds.) PKC 2018, Part I. LNCS, vol. 10769, pp. 219–250. Springer, Cham (2018). https://doi.org/10.1007/978-3-319-76578-5_8

[DKPW12]   Dodis, Y., Kiltz, E., Pietrzak, K., Wichs, D.: Message authentication, revisited. In: Pointcheval, D., Johansson, T. (eds.) EUROCRYPT 2012. LNCS, vol. 7237, pp. 355–374. Springer, Heidelberg (2012). https://doi.org/10.1007/978-3-642-29011-4_22

[dOPS18]   de Saint Guilhem, C., Orsini, E., Petit, C., Smart, N.P.: Secure oblivious transfer from semi-commutative masking. Cryptology ePrint Archive, Report 2018/648 (2018). https://eprint.iacr.org/2018/648

[EPRS17]   Everspaugh, A., Paterson, K., Ristenpart, T., Scott, S.: Key rotation for authenticated encryption. In: Katz, J., Shacham, H. (eds.) CRYPTO 2017, Part III. LNCS, vol. 10403, pp. 98–129. Springer, Cham (2017). https://doi.org/10.1007/978-3-319-63697-9_4

[FH18]   Fischlin, M., Harasser, P.: Invisible sanitizable signatures and public-key encryption are equivalent. In: Preneel, B., Vercauteren, F. (eds.) ACNS 2018. LNCS, vol. 10892, pp. 202–220. Springer, Cham (2018). https://doi.org/10.1007/978-3-319-93387-0_11

[FKKP19]   Fuchsbauer, G., Kamath, C., Klein, K., Pietrzak, K.: Adaptively secure proxy re-encryption. In: Lin, D., Sako, K. (eds.) PKC 2019, Part II. LNCS, vol. 11443, pp. 317–346. Springer, Cham (2019). https://doi.org/10.1007/978-3-030-17259-6_11

[GA07]   Green, M., Ateniese, G.: Identity-based proxy re-encryption. In: Katz, J., Yung, M. (eds.) ACNS 2007. LNCS, vol. 4521, pp. 288–306. Springer, Heidelberg (2007). https://doi.org/10.1007/978-3-540-72738-5_19

[GHMM18]   Garg, S., Hajiabadi, M., Mahmoody, M., Mohammed, A.: Limits on the power of garbling techniques for public-key encryption. In: Shacham, H., Boldyreva, A. (eds.) CRYPTO 2018, Part III. LNCS, vol. 10993, pp. 335–364. Springer, Cham (2018). https://doi.org/10.1007/978-3-319-96878-0_12

[GR02]   Goldmann, M., Russell, A.: The complexity of solving equations over finite groups. Inf. Comput. **178**(1), 253–262 (2002)

[IR89]   Impagliazzo, R., Rudich, S.: Limits on the provable consequences of one-way permutations. In: 21st ACM STOC, pp. 44–61. ACM Press, May 1989

[IZ89]   Impagliazzo, R., Zuckerman, D.: How to recycle random bits. In: 30th FOCS, pp. 248–253. IEEE Computer Society Press, October/November 1989

[JD11]   Jao, D., De Feo, L.: Towards quantum-resistant cryptosystems from supersingular elliptic curve isogenies. In: Yang, B.-Y. (ed.) PQCrypto 2011. LNCS, vol. 7071, pp. 19–34. Springer, Heidelberg (2011). https://doi.org/10.1007/978-3-642-25405-5_2

[KO97]   Kushilevitz, E., Ostrovsky, R.: Replication is NOT needed: SINGLE database, computationally-private information retrieval. In: 38th FOCS, pp. 364–373. IEEE Computer Society Press, October 1997

[KW19]   Koppula, V., Waters, B.: Realizing chosen ciphertext security generically in attribute-based encryption and predicate encryption. In: Boldyreva, A., Micciancio, D. (eds.) CRYPTO 2019. LNCS, vol. 11693, pp. 671–700 (2019)

[LMR14] Lewi, K., Montgomery, H., Raghunathan, A.: Improved constructions of PRFs secure against related-key attacks. In: Boureanu, I., Owesarski, P., Vaudenay, S. (eds.) ACNS 2014. LNCS, vol. 8479, pp. 44–61. Springer, Cham (2014). https://doi.org/10.1007/978-3-319-07536-5_4

[LST18] Libert, B., Stehlé, D., Titiu, R.: Adaptively secure distributed PRFs from LWE. In: Beimel, A., Dziembowski, S. (eds.) TCC 2018, Part II. LNCS, vol. 11240, pp. 391–421. Springer, Cham (2018). https://doi.org/10.1007/978-3-030-03810-6_15

[LT18] Lehmann, A., Tackmann, B.: Updatable encryption with post-compromise security. In: Nielsen, J.B., Rijmen, V. (eds.) EUROCRYPT 2018, Part III. LNCS, vol. 10822, pp. 685–716. Springer, Cham (2018). https://doi.org/10.1007/978-3-319-78372-7_22

[LV08] Libert, B., Vergnaud, D.: Unidirectional chosen-ciphertext secure proxy re-encryption. In: Cramer, R. (ed.) PKC 2008. LNCS, vol. 4939, pp. 360–379. Springer, Heidelberg (2008). https://doi.org/10.1007/978-3-540-78440-1_21

[Mon18] Montgomery, H.: More efficient lattice PRFs from keyed pseudorandom synthesizers. In: Chakraborty, D., Iwata, T. (eds.) INDOCRYPT 2018. LNCS, vol. 11356, pp. 190–211. Springer, Cham (2018). https://doi.org/10.1007/978-3-030-05378-9_11

[nBL17] (née Berners-Lee), E.L.: Improved security notions for proxy re-encryption to enforce access control. Cryptology ePrint Archive, Report 2017/824 (2017). https://eprint.iacr.org/2017/824

[NPR99] Naor, M., Pinkas, B., Reingold, O.: Distributed pseudo-random functions and KDCs. In: Stern, J. (ed.) EUROCRYPT 1999. LNCS, vol. 1592, pp. 327–346. Springer, Heidelberg (1999). https://doi.org/10.1007/3-540-48910-X_23

[NR95] Naor, M., Reingold, O.: Synthesizers and their application to the parallel construction of pseudo-random functions. In: 36th FOCS, pp. 170–181. IEEE Computer Society Press, October 1995

[NR97] Naor, M., Reingold, M.: Number-theoretic constructions of efficient pseudo-random functions. In: 38th FOCS, pp. 458–467. IEEE Computer Society Press, October 1997

[PS08] Pietrzak, K., Sjödin, J.: Weak pseudorandom functions in Minicrypt. In: Aceto, L., Damgård, I., Goldberg, L.A., Halldórsson, M.M., Ingólfsdóttir, A., Walukiewicz, I. (eds.) ICALP 2008, Part II. LNCS, vol. 5126, pp. 423–436. Springer, Heidelberg (2008). https://doi.org/10.1007/978-3-540-70583-3_35

[PW08] Peikert, C., Waters, B.: Lossy trapdoor functions and their applications. In: Ladner, R.E., Dwork, C. (eds.) 40th ACM STOC, pp. 187–196. ACM Press, May 2008

[Rot11] Rothblum, R.: Homomorphic encryption: from private-key to public-key. In: Ishai, Y. (ed.) TCC 2011. LNCS, vol. 6597, pp. 219–234. Springer, Heidelberg (2011). https://doi.org/10.1007/978-3-642-19571-6_14

[Sha84] Shamir, A.: Identity-based cryptosystems and signature schemes. In: Blakley, G.R., Chaum, D. (eds.) CRYPTO 1984. LNCS, vol. 196, pp. 47–53. Springer, Heidelberg (1985). https://doi.org/10.1007/3-540-39568-7_5

[SNS11] Syalim, A., Nishide, T., Sakurai, K.: Realizing proxy re-encryption in the symmetric world. In: Abd Manaf, A., Zeki, A., Zamani, M., Chuprat, S., El-Qawasmeh, E. (eds.) ICIEIS 2011. CCIS, vol. 251, pp. 259–274. Springer, Heidelberg (2011). https://doi.org/10.1007/978-3-642-25327-0_23

Leakage Models and Key Reuse

Unifying Leakage Models on a Rényi Day

Thomas Prest[1]([envelope]), Dahmun Goudarzi[1], Ange Martinelli[2],
and Alain Passelègue[3,4]

[1] PQShield, Oxford, UK
{thomas.prest,dahmun.goudarzi}@pqshield.com
[2] Thales, Gennevilliers, France
ange.martinelli@thalesgoup.com
[3] Inria, Paris, France
alain.passelegue@inria.fr
[4] ENS Lyon, Lyon, France

Abstract. In the last decade, several works have focused on finding the best way to model the leakage in order to obtain provably secure implementations. One of the most realistic models is the noisy leakage model, introduced in [PR13,DDF14] together with secure constructions. These works suffer from various limitations, in particular the use of ideal leak-free gates in [PR13] and an important loss (in the size of the field) in the reduction in [DDF14].

In this work, we provide new strategies to prove the security of masked implementations and start by unifying the different noisiness metrics used in prior works by relating all of them to a standard notion in information theory: the pointwise mutual information. Based on this new interpretation, we define two new natural metrics and analyze the security of known compilers with respect to these metrics. In particular, we prove (1) a tighter bound for reducing the noisy leakage models to the probing model using our first new metric, (2) better bounds for amplification-based security proofs using the second metric.

To support that the improvements we obtain are not only a consequence of the use of alternative metrics, we show that for concrete representation of leakage (*e.g.,* "Hamming weight + Gaussian noise"), our approach significantly improves the parameters compared to prior works. Finally, using the Rényi divergence, we quantify concretely the advantage of an adversary in attacking a block cipher depending on the number of leakage acquisitions available to it.

1 Introduction

In modern cryptography, it is common to prove the security of a construction by relying on the security of its underlying building blocks or on the hardness

---

T. Prest—Part of this work was done when the author was an engineer at Thales.
D. Goudarzi—Part of this work was done when the author was a PhD student at CryptoExperts and École Normale Supérieure.

A. Boldyreva and D. Micciancio (Eds.): CRYPTO 2019, LNCS 11692, pp. 683–712, 2019.
https://doi.org/10.1007/978-3-030-26948-7_24

of standard computational problems. This approach has allowed the community to propose a wide variety of cryptographic primitives based on only a limited number of different assumptions (e.g., factoring, learning parity with noise, existence of one-way functions, security of AES or SHA-3, etc). Unfortunately, there is still a significant gap between the *ideal security models* that are used in provable security, and the *actual environments* in which these cryptosystems are deployed. Notably, standard security models usually assume that attackers have only a black-box access to the cryptosystem: attackers do not have any information beyond the input/output behavior.

Yet, it is well known that this is generally *not true in practice*. These cryptosystems are run by physical devices, hence an adversary might be able to learn partial information such as the running-time, the power consumption, the electromagnetic emanation, or several other physical measures of the device. As revealed by Kocher et al. in [Koc96, KJJ99], these additional information, referred to as the *leakage of the computation*, are valuable and can be used to mount *side-channel attacks* against cryptographic *implementations*. Hence, a cryptosystem that is proven secure in an ideal security model can become completely vulnerable when deployed in the real-world.

Due to the fundamental importance of secure implementations of cryptographic primitives, constructing leakage-resilient cryptography has become a major area of research. Many empirical countermeasures have been proposed over the last decades and an important line of works has aimed at formalizing the notion of leakage towards obtaining provably secure implementations.

The presence of leakage in the real-world has been formalized by introducing new security models in which the attacker can obtain additional information about the computation. In a seminal work from 2003 by Ishai, Sahai, and Wagner [ISW03], the authors introduced the d-probing (or d-threshold probing) model, in which an attacker can learn a *bounded number d of intermediate results* (i.e. wire values, also called *probes*) of a computation C. A circuit is then secure in this model if any subset of at most d probes does not reveal any information about the inputs of the computation. That is, the distribution of values obtained by probing should be independent of the inputs of the computation. While this model is ideal and does not fully catch the behavior of a device in the real-world (*e.g.*, physical leakages reveal information about the whole computation), it is simple enough to get efficient compilers that transform any circuit into a secure one in the d-probing model, as shown in [ISW03]. They built secure addition and multiplication in the d-probing model based on secret-sharing techniques[1] and immunize any arithmetic circuit by replacing every gate by its secure variant. This transformation blows up the size of the circuit by a factor $O(d^2)$. A different and more realistic model was proposed by Micali and Reyzin in 2004 [MR04]. They defined a model of cryptography in presence of arbitrary forms of leakage about the whole computation. The above two works

---

[1] Basically, their secure variants take as input additive shares of the input and produce additive shares of the output. Their secure multiplication that operates on additive shares is often referred to as the ISW-multiplication.

are cornerstones of leakage-resilient cryptography. In particular, the assumption that *only computation leaks information* (thus a program can still hide some secrets) originated in these works. Following the path of [MR04], Dziembowski and Pietrzak proposed in 2008 a simplified model for *leakage-resilient cryptography* in [DP08]. In this model, any elementary operation on some input x leaks a partial information about x, modeled as the evaluation $f(x)$ of a *leakage function* whose range is bounded, so an adversary is given access to the leakage $f(x)$ for every intermediate result x of the evaluation of C. Unfortunately, this model has a drawback: the range of the leakage function is bounded and fairly small (e.g., 128-bit strings) compared to the actual amount of information that can be obtained from a device (e.g., a power trace on an AES computation can contain several megabytes of information).

To circumvent this limitation, Prouff and Rivain proposed in [PR13] a more realistic leakage model, called the *noisy leakage model*. The authors modified the above definition of leakage by making an *additional but realistic assumption*: the information $f(x)$ leaked by an elementary operation on some input x is *noisy*. Specifically, the authors assumed that f is a randomized function such that the leakage $f(x)$ only implies a bounded bias in the distribution of x, which is formally defined as distributions X and $X|f(X)$ being close (up to some fixed bound δ), where X denotes the distribution of x. The authors measured *closeness* with the Euclidean Norm (denoted EN) between the distributions (over finite sets) and propose solutions to immunize symmetric primitives in this model. Their model is inspired by the seminal work of Chari et al. [CJRR99] that considered the leakage as inherently noisy and proved that using additive secret-sharing (or masking) on a variable X decreases the information revealed by the leakage by an exponential factor in the number of shares (or masking order). This kind of proof is referred to as amplification-based, and Prouff and Rivain extended it to a whole block cipher evaluation.

A drawback of this model is the difficulty to design proofs. In addition, the constructions in [PR13] rely on a fairly strong assumption: the existence of *leak-free refresh gates* (i.e. gates that do not leak any information and refresh additive shares of x)[2]. Both limitations were solved by Duc, Dziembowski, and Faust in [DDF14]. In the latter work, using the statistical distance (denoted SD) instead of the Euclidean norm as measure of closeness, the authors showed that constructions proven secure in the ideal d-probing model of Ishai et al. are also secure in the δ-noisy leakage model, provided d is large enough (function of δ). As a consequence, the simple compilers for building d-probing secure circuits can serve for achieving security in the noisy leakage model, proving a conjecture broadly admitted for several years based on empirical observations.

The present work extends the two above results and proposes general solutions to immunize cryptographic primitives in the noisy leakage model. We start by giving a more formal overview of these two works.

---

[2] In practice, refresh gates are often implemented via an ISW-multiplication with additive shares of 1 (*e.g.,* shares $(1, 0, \ldots, 0)$).

1.1   Previous Works

As explained above, two distinct approaches for immunizing cryptosystems in the noisy leakage model have been considered: (1) a direct approach, used in [PR13], that proves the security of a construction directly in the model via noise amplification, and (2) an indirect approach, used in [DDF14], that consists in reducing security in the noisy leakage model to security in ideal models (*e.g.*, the probing model) and then applying compilers for the latter models.

A direct approach. In [PR13], the authors propose a way to immunize block ciphers of a particular form (succession of linear functions and substitution boxes, a.k.a. s-boxes, *e.g.*, AES). Their approach consists in replacing elementary operations of such block ciphers by subprotocols that operate on masked inputs and produce a masked output. They bound the leakage on each subprotocol and as a consequence are able to bound the leakage of a single evaluation of the *masked block cipher* (i.e. the block cipher obtained by replacing every elementary operation by the corresponding subprotocol and applying leak-free refresh gates between each subprotocol). They conclude by proving an upper bound on the information (in an information-theoretic sense) revealed by the leakage about the input (plaintext/key) from evaluations of the masked block cipher, in particular proving that it decreases exponentially in the masking order.

While this paper makes great progress towards constructing provably-secure leakage-resilient block ciphers, it suffers from a few limitations. First, as already mentioned, the security proof relies on leak-free refresh gates. Second, the fact that the final analysis relies on the mutual information implies a rather paradoxal situation: from an information theory perspective, a single pair of plaintext-ciphertext can reveal the key. To get around this problem, the authors assume that both the plaintext and the ciphertext are secret, which is fairly unrealistic compared to standard security models for block ciphers. Finally, to offer strong security guarantees, the mutual information should be upper bounded by $2^{-O(\lambda)}$, with λ being the security parameter. Hence, the masking order for reaching this bound only depends on λ, which is independent of the number of queries (and therefore the amount of leakage) the adversary makes.

An indirect approach. In [DDF14], the authors propose an elegant approach that applies to any form of computation. Their main result proves that any information obtained in the δ-noisy leakage model (so information of the form $f(x)$ for any intermediate result x of the computation) can be simulated from a sufficiently large number d of probes. As such a set of probes does not carry any information about the inputs if the circuit is secure in the $(d+1)$-probing model, this guarantees that the information obtained in the δ-noisy leakage model does not carry any useful information either. Hence, using standard compilers to secure a cryptosystem in the $(d+1)$-probing model makes it secure when deployed in the real-world, assuming the leakage is δ-noisy. Unfortunately, this reduction incurs an important blow-up in the parameters ($\delta \rightarrow d$). Notably d has to be at least

N times larger than δ to guarantee security, where N is the size of the field on which the circuit operates. This loss appears in an intermediate step of their reduction when first reducing the noisy leakage model to the random probing model[3]. Typically, for AES, we have $N = 256$, so the required order d of security is very large (and so is the size of the masked circuit since applying the ISW compiler increases the size by a factor d^2).

This loss is seemingly an artifact of the reduction and has not been observed in empirical measures [DFS15a]. A first attempt to circumvent this issue was made in [DFS15b] by introducing a new model, called the average random probing model, which is a tweak of the random probing model. The authors prove a tight equivalence between the noisy leakage and the average random probing models and show that the ISW compiler is secure in their model.

Yet, there are two caveats. First, their proof of security of the ISW compiler introduce leak-free gates, whereas [DDF14] does not. Second, [DFS15b] does not establish a reduction from the average random probing to the threshold probing model, hence leaving open the question of improving the reductions provided in [DDF14]. In this paper, we overcome these two issues and provide a tight reduction from a[4] noisy leakage model to the threshold probing model without leak-free gates nor a loss in the size of the field.

1.2   Our Contributions

We extend the previous studies of leakage-resilient cryptography in several directions. Our approach starts by relating the noisiness of a leakage to a standard notion in information theory: the pointwise mutual information (PMI).

From pointwise mutual information to noisiness metrics. Our first observation is that the two metrics used in prior works to measure the distance between X and $X|f(X)$, namely the Euclidean norm (EN) and the statistical distance (SD), can be easily expressed as different averages of the pointwise mutual information of the same distributions. Given this interpretation, it is easy to see that these two measures are *average-case* metrics of noisiness.

We investigate the benefits of considering the problem of building leakage-resilient cryptography based on two other *worst-case* metrics that naturally follow from the pointwise mutual information: the Average Relative Error (ARE) and the Relative Error (RE). Using these two metrics, we propose tighter proofs for immunizing cryptosystems in the noisy leakage model. We emphasize that

---

[3] In the ϵ-random probing model, the adversary learns each exact wire value with probability ϵ (and nothing about it with probability $1 - \epsilon$).

[4] Noisy-leakage models are inherently associated to the metric used to measure noisiness. [PR13] is based on the Euclidean norm, [DDF14] on the statistical distance. We introduce new metrics, therefore new models. Yet, the overall result remain comparable as only the noisiness of the leakage is impacted by the metric, but not the leakage itself, so the metric is just a tool to argue the security (security against the leakage being independent of the metric).

even though we introduce new metrics (and therefore new noisy leakage models), our goal remains to prove that we can simulate *perfectly* the leakage (which depends on the intermediate values but *does not depend* on the metric) from a certain amount of probes. The metric only plays a role in determining the amount of probes that is needed for simulating the leakage, i.e. the sufficient masking order to immunize the computation, but does not play any role in measuring the quality of the simulation (which remains perfect). We are able (in general) to prove better bounds for the amount of probes needed for the simulation. In particular, combining our results with known compilers is particularly interesting for typical forms of concrete leakage such as the "Hamming weight + Gaussian noise" model.

A tighter reduction from noisy leakage to random probing. We propose a reduction from the noisy leakage model to the random probing model, when the noise is measured with the ARE metric. Our reduction is analogous to the reduction proposed from [DDF14]. Once reduced to the random probing model, it is easy to go to the threshold probing model by a simple probabilistic argument (observed in [DDF14]). Using the ARE metric, we are able to reduce the δ-noisy leakage model (where the noise is measured with the ARE metric) to the δ-random probing model (instead of the $\delta \cdot N$-random probing model for prior work using the SD metric). Again, we emphasize that, despite using different metrics, these reductions allows to simulate the exact distribution of the leakage, which is completely independent of the underlying metric.

This tighter reduction has immediate, tangible consequences when considering compilers which are proven secure in the threshold probing model [ISW03] or in the random probing model [ADF16, GJR17, AIS18]: for a specific form of noisy leakage, as long as the ARE-noisiness is smaller than N times than the SD-noisiness, our reduction guarantees security using a smaller masking order than the reduction based on the SD metric. In particular, we show for the concrete "Hamming weight + Gaussian noise" model of leakage that our result reduces the required masking order by a factor $O(N/\sqrt{\log N})$ compared to [DDF14].

Actually, even though we do not start from the same metrics (and then from the exact same noisy leakage model), we prove that the ARE-noisiness of any function is upper bounded (up to a factor $2 \cdot N$) by its SD-noisiness. Then, even in the worst case, our reduction (which is tighter by a factor N) gives as good results (up to a factor 2) as the reduction in [DDF14]. Reversely the SD-noisiness is upper bounded by the ARE-noisiness (up to a factor 2), so the loss of a factor N in the reduction is not compensated, which explains the large improvement we gain from our approach in certain cases such as the aforementioned one.

As a side contribution, and perhaps surprisingly, we are also able to prove a converse reduction: we show that the random probing model reduces to the ARE-noisy leakage model (though it incurs a loss of a factor $N - 1$). This follows from observing that the random probing model is a special instance of the ARE-noisy leakage model. This implies that the SD-noisy leakage, ARE-noisy leakage and (average) random probing models are all equivalent. We believe that this result is of independent interest and could find applications in future works.

While we focus on using a compiler introduced in [ISW03], which has also been studied in [PR13, DDF14, DFS15b], other compilers also benefit from our work in obvious ways (e.g., the compilers described in [ADF16, GJR17, AIS18] are secure in the random probing model, hence benefit from our reduction to the noisy leakage model).

Our reductions and previously known reductions are summarized in Fig. 1. This diagram represents the interactions between various leakage models (from very concrete ones, like "Hamming weight with Gaussian noise", to theoretical models such as the threshold probing model) and circuit compilers. The physical noise model is displayed on the first line, noisy leakage models on the second line, probing models on the third line, and circuit compilers are displayed on the fourth line. Arrows from a model M to a compiler C means that C is proven secure in the model M. An arrow from a model M_1 to a model M_2 means that an adversary in M_1 can be simulated in M_2 with the overhead indicated next to the arrow. Our contributions (models and reductions) are displayed in bold. For the sake of clarity, constant factors are omitted. N denotes the size of the underlying finite field, and λ denotes the security parameter of the scheme to protect.

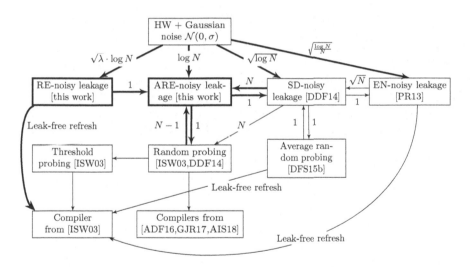

Fig. 1. From concrete leakages to secure circuit compilers: an overview of reduction-based proofs and our contributions.

An amplification-based proof with the Rényi divergence. Our second main contribution is a new amplification-based proof which improves over existing ones in some aspects. Once again, we put our result in perspective with concrete noisy leakage models where the noise follows a Gaussian distribution $\mathcal{N}(0, \sigma)$ with standard deviation σ, *e.g.,* the "Hamming weight + Gaussian noise" model. In the context of leakage-resilient cryptography, known amplification-based proofs show that if σ is large enough, then the leakage of a masked circuit decreases exponentially in the masking order; equivalently (and we will use this perspective for convenience), it shows that the required amount of Gaussian noise decreases when the masking order increases.

The most notable amplification-based proofs of masked circuits are due to [PR13], which uses the EN-noisy leakage model, and [DFS15b], which uses the average random probing model (or equivalently, the SD-noisy leakage model). Both works yield a condition on σ, precisely they impose $\sigma = \Omega(d \times f \times g^{1/(d+1)})$, where the functions f and g are constant in the masking order d. Here, f acts like a factor of σ which is *fixed* (it does not depend of d), whereas g acts like a *compressible* part whose impact on σ can be decreased by increasing the masking order. Both terms are important, because f cannot be compressed, but g can be very large in practice. Our new amplification-based proof relies on the RE-noisiness, and can be seen as revisiting the proof of [PR13]. Compared to the previous works, it provides several qualitative and quantitative gains:

- Whereas in the previous works, σ was exponential in the security level λ (more precisely, larger than $2^{\lambda/(d+1)}$), in our case it is only proportional to $\sqrt{\lambda}$; This is thanks to our use of the Rényi divergence, which allows to replace $2^{\lambda/(d+1)}$ by $q^{1/(d+1)}$, where q denotes the number of traces (i.e. the number of evaluations with known leakage) obtained by the attacker. This is a far lighter constraint, since in cryptography it is typical to take $\lambda = 256$, whereas it is extremely rare to have more than 2^{32} traces available.
- Our Rényi divergence-based proof shows that the view of a black-box adversary is not significantly different from the view of an adversary which has access to leakage, and we relate the distance between these two views to the masking order and the number of traces available to the adversary (in particular upper bounded by the number of queries).
- Compared to [DFS15b], our fixed part f is larger, but our compressible part g is much smaller: for the above values of q and λ, g will be 2^{32} in our case, whereas it would be larger than 2^{1024} in the case of [DFS15b]. In addition, [DFS15b, Lemma 14 and Theorem 1] implicitly impose d to be linear in $\lambda + \log N$, which gives an extremely high masking order. Our proof imposes no such bound.

In Fig. 1, amplification proofs correspond to *Leak-Free Refresh* arrows.

Finally, in Table 1, we compare our results with the state-of-the-art approaches in the case of Hamming weight + Gaussian noise for both reduction-based proofs and amplification-based proofs. Our bound for the noisiness are taken from Proposition 3. The conditions on the Gaussian noise level σ are given,

Table 1. Comparison with prior works (combined with Proposition 3).

Work	Condition on σ	Other condition	LFR	Model	Tool
[DDF14, Thm 1]	$\Omega\left(dN\sqrt{\ln N}\right)$	$d = \Omega(\lambda + \ln|\Gamma|)$	No	CPA	Δ_{SD}
This work (Sect. 5)	$\Omega\left(d\ln N\right)$	$d = \Omega(\lambda + \ln|\Gamma|)$	No	CPA	Δ_{SD}
[PR13, Cor 2, Thm 4]	$\Omega\left(dN\sqrt{\ln N} \times (N^3 2^\lambda|\Gamma|)^{1/(d+1)}\right)$	$d = \Omega(dN^{3/2}\sqrt{\ln N})$	Yes	RPA	MI
[DFS15b, Cor 4]	$\Omega\left(d\sqrt{\ln N} \times [(Nd2^\lambda)^4|\Gamma|]^{1/d}\right)$	$d = \Omega(\lambda + \ln(N|\Gamma|))$	Yes	CPA	Δ_{SD}
This work (Sect. 6)	$\Omega\left(d\sqrt{\lambda}\ln N \times (q|\Gamma|)^{1/(d+1)}\right)$	-	Yes	CPA	R_∞

as well as additional conditions when they exist. *LFR* indicates whether leak-free refresh gates are required in the security proof. *Model* states the model of attacker (random-plaintext or chosen-plaintext). The model of attack is actually not considered in [DFS15b], but [DFS16, Lemma 2] shows that in the case of [DFS15b], random plaintext attacks reduce to chosen plaintext attacks and that it is therefore sufficient to consider only the former. *Tool* indicates the main notion the security proof relies on (statistical distance, mutual information or Rényi divergence of order infinity). λ denotes the security parameter of the scheme, d the masking order, N the size of the underlying field, and q the number of traces available to an attacker.

Organization of the paper. The remainder of the paper is organized as follows. Section 2 presents some theoretical background and notation. Section 3 provides a unifying background for the metrics used in prior works as well as those we introduce. Section 4 builds the bridge from a standard, concrete model of leakage (Hamming weight with Gaussian noise) to noisy leakage models. In Sect. 5, we detail our tight reduction from the noisy leakage model to the probing model. Our amplification-based proofs are described Sect. 6.

2   Preliminaries

In this section we recall basic notation and notions used throughout the paper.

2.1   Notation

For any $\ell \geq 1$, we denote by $[\ell]$ the set $\{1, \ldots, \ell\}$. We denote by $\mathcal{X}$ a finite set, by x an element of $\mathcal{X}$, by X a random variable over $\mathcal{X}$, and by $\mathcal{P}_X$ the corresponding probability mass function (i.e. the function $\mathcal{P}_X : x \mapsto \mathbb{P}[X = x]$). We often abuse notation and denote by P the distribution defined by a probability mass function $\mathcal{P}$. For a distribution P over $\mathcal{X}$, we denote by $x \leftarrow P$ the action of sampling x from the distribution P.

For any distribution P and any function f over $\mathcal{X}$, we denote by $f(P)$ the distribution of $f(x)$ induced by sampling $x \leftarrow P$. We denote by $\mathrm{Supp}(X) := \{x \in \mathcal{X} \mid \mathcal{P}_X(x) > 0\}$ the support of a random variable X over $\mathcal{X}$ (and we define similarly the support of a distribution).

For any random variable X over $\mathcal{X}$ and a function $f : \mathcal{X} \to \mathcal{Y}$, we use the following notation:

$$\mathbb{E}_X[f(X)] = \sum_x f(x) \cdot \mathbb{P}[X = x] \ .$$

For two random variables X, Y over $\mathcal{X}$, the *statistical distance* between X and Y is defined as:

$$\varDelta_{\mathrm{SD}}(X;Y) := \frac{1}{2} \sum_{x \in \mathcal{X}} |\mathbb{P}[X = x] - \mathbb{P}[Y = x]| \ .$$

Similarly, the Euclidean norm between X and Y is defined as:

$$\varDelta_{\mathrm{EN}}(X;Y) = \sqrt{\sum_{x \in \mathcal{X}} (\mathbb{P}[X = x] - \mathbb{P}[Y = x])^2} \ .$$

Finally, if X, Y have the same support, their relative error is:

$$\varDelta_{\mathrm{RE}}(X;Y) := \max_{x \in \mathrm{Supp}(X)} \left| \frac{\mathbb{P}[X = x]}{\mathbb{P}[Y = x]} - 1 \right| \ .$$

We now recall these two definitions from [DDF14] and [PR13]:[5]

$$\mathrm{SD}(X|Y;X) = \sum_y \mathbb{P}[Y = y] \cdot \varDelta_{\mathrm{SD}}(X|Y = y; X)$$

$$\mathrm{EN}(X|Y;X) = \sum_y \mathbb{P}[Y = y] \cdot \varDelta_{\mathrm{EN}}(X|Y = y; X)$$

2.2   The Rényi Divergence

The Rényi divergence [Ré61] is a measure of divergence between distributions. In the recent years, it has found several applications in lattice-based cryptography [BLL+15, Pre17]. When used in security proofs, its peculiar properties allow designers of cryptographic schemes to set some parameters according to the number of queries allowed to an attacker, rather than to the security level, and this has often resulted in improved parameters. We first recall its definition as well as some standard properties.

---

[5] Instead of SD and EN, [DDF14] and [PR13] used the notations $\varDelta$ and β; we prefer our notation as it avoids any confusion with greek letters denoting scalars.

Definition 1 (Rényi divergence). *Let P, Q be two distributions over X such that* $\text{Supp}(P) \subseteq \text{Supp}(Q)$. *For $a \in (1, +\infty)$, their Rényi divergence of order a is:*

$$R_a(P\|Q) = \left(\sum_{x \in \text{Supp}(P)} \frac{P(x)^a}{Q(x)^{a-1}} \right)^{\frac{1}{a-1}} .$$

In addition, the Rényi divergence of order $+\infty$ is

$$R_\infty(P\|Q) = \max_{x \in \text{Supp}(P)} \frac{P(x)}{Q(x)} .$$

This definition is common in the lattice-based cryptography literature, whereas the information theory literature favors its logarithm as the definition. Classical properties of the Rényi divergence may be found in [FHT03], and cryptographic properties may be found in [BLL+15, Pre17]. In this paper, we use the following composition properties from [BLL+15].

Lemma 1. *For two distributions P, Q and two families of distributions $(P_i)_i, (Q_i)_i$, the Rényi divergence verifies the following properties:*

- **Data processing inequality:** *For any function f, $R_a(f(P)\|f(Q)) \leq R_a(P\|Q)$.*
- **Multiplicativity:** $R_a(\prod_i P_i \| \prod_i Q_i) = \prod_i R_a(P_i\|Q_i)$.
- **Probability preservation:** *For any event $E \subseteq \text{Supp}(Q)$ and $a \in (1, +\infty)$,*

$$Q(E) \geq P(E)^{\frac{a}{a-1}}/R_a(P\|Q) ,$$
$$Q(E) \geq P(E)/R_\infty(P\|Q) .$$

2.3   Pointwise Mutual Information

The pointwise mutual information is a common tool in computational linguistics [CH89], where it serves as a measure of co-occurence between words. For example, the pmi of "Sean" and "Penn" is high because Sean Penn is a well-known person, whereas the pmi of "bankruptcy" and "success" is low because the two words are rarely used in the same sentence.

Formally, the pointwise mutual information is defined as follows.

Definition 2 (Pointwise mutual information). *Let X, Y be random variables over $\mathcal{X}$. Then, for any $(x, y) \in \text{Supp}(X) \times \text{Supp}(Y)$, we have:*

$$\text{pmi}_{X,Y}(x, y) = \log \left(\frac{\mathbb{P}[X = x, Y = y]}{\mathbb{P}[X = x]\mathbb{P}[Y = y]} \right) .$$

We also define its exponential form as:

$$\text{PMI}_{X,Y}(x, y) = e^{\text{pmi}_{X,Y}(x,y)} - 1 = \frac{\mathbb{P}[X = x, Y = y]}{\mathbb{P}[X = x]\mathbb{P}[Y = y]} - 1 .$$

We note that when they are close to 0, $\text{pmi}_{X,Y}(x, y) \sim \text{PMI}_{X,Y}(x, y)$. The mutual information between X and Y can be simply expressed from the pointwise mutual information, since we have:

$$\text{MI}(X; Y) = \mathbb{E}_{(X,Y)} \left[\text{pmi}_{X,Y} \right] ,$$

where (X, Y) denotes the joint distribution of X and Y. When X and Y are clear from context, we may omit the subscripts and simply note pmi and PMI.

Interestingly, as we show in the next section, several metrics in leakage-resilient cryptography can be defined simply using the pointwise mutual information.

3   Unifying Leakage Models via the Pointwise Mutual Information

As already explained, in the noisy leakage model (defined below), an adversary learns noisy information $f(x)$ about every intermediate result x of a computation. The hope is that this leakage does not reveal much information about the actual value x, which is translated by the fact that the distribution X is *close* to the distribution $X|f(X)$. Two main notions of *closeness* (corresponding to two noisiness metrics) have been proposed, namely EN and SD.

3.1   Noisiness Metrics from Pointwise Mutual Information

It appears that the above noisiness metrics can easily be related to the pointwise mutual information, as we state in the following immediate proposition. Other natural metrics can also be derived from the pointwise mutual information, and we define two additional metrics in the subsequent definition.

Let us define the following four metrics with respect to the PMI.

Definition 3 (Noisiness metrics). *Let X, Y be random variables over sets $\mathcal{X}, \mathcal{Y}$ respectively. We define the following metrics based on the pointwise mutual information:*

- $\text{SD}(X|Y) := \frac{1}{2} \cdot \mathbb{E}_X \mathbb{E}_Y \left[|\text{PMI}| \right];$
- $\text{EN}(X|Y) := \mathbb{E}_Y \sqrt{\mathbb{E}_X \left[\mathbb{P}[X]\text{PMI}^2 \right]};$
- $\text{RE}(X|Y) := \max_{x,y} |\text{PMI}|;$
- $\text{ARE}(X|Y) := \mathbb{E}_Y \left[\max_x |\text{PMI}| \right].$

The four notions of noisiness defined here compute different norms of the $(\text{PMI})_{x,y}$: SD compute the average value of $|\text{PMI}|$, RE computes its max, and ARE computes something in between.

Note that this difference in their definition (average-case vs worst-case) is mirrored in the random probing models (average random probing vs random probing), so it is perhaps unsurprising that reductions between worst-case models (ARE-noisy leakage to random probing in Sect. 5) incur no loss, as well as those between average-case models (SD-noisy leakage and average random probing in [DFS15b]), but that the worst-case-average-case reduction of [DDF14] incurs a loss by a factor $|\mathcal{X}|$.

We note that these definitions of SD and EN match the ones given in Sect. 2.1: $SD(X|Y) = SD(X|Y;X)$ and $EN(X|Y) = EN(X|Y;X)$. This is done on purpose as we aim at introducing new noisiness metrics without discarding previously defined ones. We do so by expressing them all with a single common notion: the pointwise mutual information. The acronyms RE and ARE stand for Relative Error and Average Relative Error. We note that $RE(X|Y) = \max_y \Delta_{RE}(X|Y = y; X)$ and $ARE(X|Y) = \mathbb{E}_Y \Delta_{RE}(X|Y; X)$.

We now define a generic notion of noisy functions, parameterized by any of the above metrics.

Definition 4 (Noisy functions). *Let $D \in \{SD, EN, RE, ARE\}$ be one of the metrics defined in Definition 3, X be a random variable over a set $\mathcal{X}$ and $\delta \geq 0$. We say that a function $f : \mathcal{X} \to \mathcal{Y}$ is δ-noisy for the metric D and the random variable X (or for short, δ-D-noisy for X) if:*

$$D(X|f(X)) \leq \delta .$$

If X follows the uniform distribution, we simply say that f is δ-D-noisy.

This definition highlights an important caveat of the noisy leakage model: the notion of noisy function is implicitly parameterized by an underlying distribution X. However, we will later show in Lemma 2 than for RE- and ARE-noisy functions, we can abstract ourselves from the underlying distribution at the cost of essentially a factor 2 in the noise parameter δ.

3.2 Basic Properties

Before moving to the core results of the paper, we detail a few properties relating the above noisiness metrics to each other.

Proposition 1. *Let X, Y denote random variables over finite sets. Then we have:*

1. $SD(X|Y) = SD(Y|X)$;
2. $RE(X|Y) = RE(Y|X)$;
3. $2 \cdot SD(X|Y) \leq ARE(X|Y) \leq RE(X|Y)$.

Moreover, if X follows the uniform distribution over a set $\mathcal{X}$ of size N, then:

$$ARE(X|Y) \leq 2N \cdot SD(X|Y) . \tag{1}$$

The above properties are immediate from Definition 3. We however provide a proof for the last one. Note that, as mentioned in the introduction, our reduction from the ARE-noisy leakage model to the random probing model described in Sect. 5 is tighter by a factor N compared to reduction from the SD-noisy leakage model to the random probing model from [DDF14]. Hence (1) implies that even in the worst case, our results give at least as good bounds (up to a factor 2) as prior reductions.

Proof. Since X is uniform, $\mathbb{P}[X = x] = \frac{1}{N}$ for any $x \in \mathcal{X}$. Hence for any fixed y:

$$\max_{x} |\text{PMI}| \leq \sum_{x \in \mathcal{X}} |\text{PMI}| = N \cdot \mathbb{E}_X |\text{PMI}| \ .$$

Then (1) follows from the definitions of SD and ARE.

Remark 1. Note that the item 3 is tight. Indeed, considering the "checkerboard distribution" $Z = (X, Y)$ defined over $[\![0, m-1]\!] \times [\![0, n-1]\!]$ via:

$$\mathbb{P}[X = x, Y = y] = \frac{1}{mn} \left(1 + (-1)^{x+y} \delta\right) \ ,$$

One can easily check that $2\text{SD}(X|Y) = \text{ARE}(X|Y) = \text{RE}(X|Y) = \delta$.

We can also relate the SD-noisiness and the RE-noisiness to the mutual information via the following inequalities, whose proofs are detailed in the full version [GMPP19]:

Proposition 2. *Let X, Y denote random variables over finite sets. Then, we have:*

$$2\text{SD}(X|Y)^2 \leq \text{MI}(X; Y) \leq 2\text{RE}(X|Y)\text{SD}(X|Y) \ .$$

The left inequality was already proven in [DFS15a, Theorem 1]. However, our proof relies on a completely different interpretation of the mutual information, and is arguably much simpler.[6] On the other hand, the right inequality improves a previous bound given in [DDF14] by a factor $\frac{N}{\ln(2)\text{RE}(X|Y)}$. Overall, it allows to bound $\text{MI}(X; Y)$ up to a factor $\frac{\text{SD}(X|Y)}{\text{RE}(X|Y)}$.

Finally, we provide a self-reducibility lemma for RE-noisy and ARE-noisy functions. We show that the underlying distribution is not too important, as a function f which is δ-noisy for a distribution X is also $\Theta(\delta)$-noisy for any other distribution X'.

Lemma 2 (Self-reducibility). *Let X, X' be two arbitrary distributions of support $\mathcal{X}$ and $f : \mathcal{X} \to \mathcal{Y}$ be a randomized function. Suppose that f is δ_{RE}-RE-noisy (resp. δ_{ARE}-ARE-noisy) for X. Then:*

1. *f is $\left(\frac{2 \cdot \delta_{\text{RE}}}{1 - \delta_{\text{RE}}}\right)$-RE-noisy for X';*
2. *f is $\left(\frac{2 \cdot \delta_{\text{ARE}}}{(1 - \delta_{\text{ARE}})(1 - \delta_{\text{RE}})}\right)$-ARE-noisy for X'.*

Lemma 2 is similar to [DFS16, Lemma 2], which shows that if f is δ-SD-noisy for X the uniform distribution, then it is $(3N\delta)$-SD-noisy for any distribution X'. Our proposition is more powerful than [DFS16, Lemma 2]: X can be any distribution, and the tightness loss is $O(1)$ as long as $\delta_{\text{RE}} \leq 1 - c$ for a constant c. The proof of Lemma 2 is given in the full version [GMPP19].

---

[6] In addition, this interpretation of MI in terms of the Kullback-Leibler divergence gives us for free several bounds which are tighter for non-negligible values of SD: for example $\text{MI} \geq \log\left(\frac{1+\text{SD}}{1-\text{SD}}\right) - \frac{2\text{SD}}{1+\text{SD}}$ [Vaj70] or $\text{MI} \geq 2\text{SD}^2 + \frac{4}{9}\text{SD}^4 + O(\text{SD}^6)$ [FHT03].

3.3   Noisy Leakage Adversary

We finally define the noisy leakage model. We consider an arbitrary sequence $(x_1, \ldots, x_\ell) \in \mathcal{X}^\ell$, with $\mathcal{X}$ being some finite set and ℓ being some parameter (typically the number of intermediate results in a computation). We denote by $\mathcal{A}$ a (possibly unbounded) adversary.

Definition 5 (Noisy Leakage Adversary). *Let $D \in \{\text{SD}, \text{EN}, \text{RE}, \text{ARE}\}$. For $0 \le \delta \le 1$, a δ-D-noisy adversary on $\mathcal{X}^\ell$ is a machine $\mathcal{A}$ that plays the following game against an oracle that knows $(x_1, \ldots, x_\ell) \in \mathcal{X}^\ell$:*

1. *$\mathcal{A}$ picks δ-D-noisy functions $(f_i)_{i \in [\ell]}$ with range $\mathcal{Y}$;*
2. *$\mathcal{A}$ receives $(f_i(x_i))_{i \in [\ell]} \in \mathcal{Y}^\ell$ and outputs $\mathsf{out}_{\mathcal{A}}(x_1, \ldots, x_\ell)$.*

4   From Concrete Leakage to Noisy Leakage Models

In order to have a full-fledged security proof of a circuit compiler with a leakage model, the first step consists in linking the concrete representation of the leakage to a noisy leakage model. This allows to ground firmly our metrics and models in the reality, and guarantee that the gains observed in subsequent sections are not artifacts of definitions.

4.1   A Concrete Modelization of the Leakage

A common representation of the leakage $f(X)$ corresponding to the manipulation of an intermediate variable X is a function $l(X)$ tempered by the addition of a Gaussian noise $\mathcal{N}(0, \sigma)$. The function l is then defined by the consumption model. The most widely used consumption model is the Hamming weight model initially used by Brier, Clavier, and Olivier in [BCO04], namely:

$$f(x) = \mathsf{HW}(x) + \mathcal{N}(0, \sigma) \ ,$$

Our goal is now to determine how (RE/ARE/SD/EN)-noisy the function f is. We consider that x is distributed according to a uniformly random variable X over the set $[\![0, N-1]\!]$, where $N = 2^n$ is a power of two. This assumption is realistic since in a cryptographic algorithm, the diffusion of the random private key throughout the computation makes any intermediate variable looks like a random variable. As an illustration, we give in Fig. 2 a toy example for the distributions of $f(X)$ and $f(X)|(\mathsf{HW}(X) = k)$.

4.2   A Visual Interpretation of the Noisiness Metrics

We give an intuition on how the different noisiness metrics are connected to the Hamming weight consumption model with the help of Fig. 2. Let $Y = f(X)$ and $Y_k = f(X)|(\mathsf{HW}(X) = k)$. By Definition 3, we can link the four metrics to the pointwise mutual information. The pointwise mutual information can be depicted as the ratio between one of the Y_k curves and the Y curve, minus 1: $\text{PMI}(x, y) = \frac{Y_{\mathsf{HW}(x)}(y)}{Y(y)} - 1$. With this in mind, we can provide a visual interpretation of the four metrics as follows:

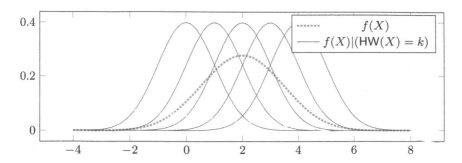

Fig. 2. Distribution of the noisy function $f(X) = \mathsf{HW}(X) + \mathcal{N}(0,1)$ when X is uniformly distributed over $[\![0, 2^4 - 1]\!]$. The conditional distributions $f(X)|(\mathsf{HW}(X) = k)$ (for $k = 0, \ldots, 4$) are also represented.

- **SD.** The metric SD simply computes a ponderated mean of $|\mathrm{PMI}|$.
- **RE.** Since RE is the max of $|\mathrm{PMI}|$, it is essentially the maximum, minus 1, of the ratio Y_0/Y: this maximum is reached at the far right of Fig. 2, and imposes a tailcut for the reasons detailed in Remark 2;
- **ARE.** Since ARE computes the mean (over Y) of the max (over X) of $|\mathrm{PMI}|$, it can be visually interpreted as the mean on the right side of the Fig. 2 of "the ratio Y_0/Y, minus 1".
- **EN.** The visual interpretation of EN is a little more complex. Since here X is uniform, we have $\mathrm{EN}(X|Y) = \frac{1}{\sqrt{N}}\mathbb{E}_Y\sqrt{\mathbb{E}_X\left[\mathrm{PMI}^2\right]}$, so EN is essentially the scaled expected value (over Y) of Euclidean norm (over X) of the PMI.

Remark 2. We note that $\mathrm{RE}(X|f(X))$ is not formally defined as the value $|\mathrm{PMI}(x,y)|$ can be arbitrarily large. We overcome this issue by observing, see the full version [GMPP19], that with overwhelming probability $f(X)$ lies in the interval $[-\tau\sigma, \tau\sigma + \log N]$, where $\tau = \sqrt{-2\log(2^{-\lambda}\sqrt{2\pi})} = \Theta(\sqrt{\lambda})$. We can then define $\mathrm{RE}(X|f(X))$ with a tailcut argument.

4.3 Estimating the Noisiness Metrics in Practice

In order to estimate the noisiness of f (with respect to RE, ARE, SD, and EN), we derive asymptotic bounds as shown in Proposition 3. To back up our theoretical results, we used a Sage implementation (which source code is given in the full version [GMPP19]) and obtained numerical values which match exactly our results.

Proposition 3. *Let X be a uniformly random variable over the set $\mathcal{X} = [\![0, N - 1]\!]$, where $N = 2^n$ is a power-of-two. Let $\mathcal{Y} = \mathbb{R}$, and $f : \mathcal{X} \to \mathcal{Y}$ be defined with the Hamming weight model, namely:*

$$f(x) = \mathsf{HW}(x) + \mathcal{N}(0, \sigma) \ .$$

Let $\tau \in [1; \sigma]$ be a tailcut rate such that $|\mathcal{N}(0, \sigma)| \leq \tau \cdot \sigma$ with overwhelming probability. Then, for sufficiently large values of σ and N it holds that:

$$\mathrm{RE}(X|f(X)) \quad \sim C_1 \cdot \tfrac{1}{\sigma} \cdot \tau \cdot \log N \quad , \ with\ C_1 = \tfrac{1}{2}$$

$$\mathrm{ARE}(X|f(X)) \sim C_2 \cdot \tfrac{1}{\sigma} \cdot \log N \qquad , \ with\ C_2 = \tfrac{1}{\sqrt{2\pi}}$$

$$\mathrm{SD}(X|f(X)) \quad \sim C_3 \cdot \tfrac{1}{\sigma} \cdot \sqrt{\log N} \quad , \ with\ C_3 = \tfrac{1}{2\pi}$$

$$\mathrm{EN}(X|f(X)) \quad \sim C_2 \cdot \tfrac{1}{\sigma} \cdot \sqrt{\tfrac{\log N}{N}} \quad .$$

The proof of Proposition 3 can be found in the full version [GMPP19]. We note that a different model of the concrete leakage (say, x added to binomial noise) could lead to completely different equations.

RE vs ARE. The noisiness metric RE incurs an overhead of $O(\tau)$ compared to ARE. All other parts being equal, it is therefore more desirable to use the latter than the former. This observation is the ground motivation behind the use of ARE to show the reduction between the noisy leakage model and the probing model in Sect. 5.

ARE vs SD. Since ARE incurs an overhead of $O(\sqrt{\log N})$ compared to SD, one could be tempted to say that the latter leads to tighter bounds. However, we show in Sect. 5 that when reducing to the random probing model, SD incurs an overhead of $O(N)$ compared to ARE. When linking the random probing model to a concrete model of leakage, ARE therefore allows a total gain of $O(N/\sqrt{\log N})$ compared to SD.

EN vs others. Unlike the other noisiness metrics, EN is $\tilde{O}(1/\sqrt{N})$. This suggest that this metric should lead to the most efficient discrimination of the four, but we see in Sect. 6 that in amplification-based proofs, the EN currently incurs a total overhead which is polynomial in N (compared to RE).

On the definition of EN. The presence in practice of a factor $\tilde{O}(1/\sqrt{N})$ in EN (as highlighted in item 4.3) suggests that the definition of EN is perhaps not the right one, along with other circumstantial evidence:

- In Proposition 3, the definition of EN in terms of the pointwise mutual information is not as clean as for the other metrics;
- Several noise amplification theorems in [PR13] have an overhead $O(N^{O(d)})$. One could think this overhead is an artifact of the proof, but in some cases (such as [PR13, Theorem 1]), it is in fact an artifact of the definition.

5   From ARE-Noisy Leakage Model to Threshold-Probing Model

While noisy-leakage models defined in Sect. 3.3 capture well what leaks from an actual computation on physical devices, it is fairly hard to build cryptosystems that achieve security in these complex models. Therefore, simpler and more idealistic models are often considered for constructing leakage-resilient cryptography. The most common model is the threshold-probing model, introduced by Ishai, Sahai, and Wagner in [ISW03]. In this model, an adversary can learn a bounded number of *exact* intermediate results of the computation (instead of noisy information about every intermediate results). This probing model being much simpler, it is easy to immunize any computation against such adversaries, and the hope is that secure constructions in this model offer some guarantees against more realistic forms of leakage.

Fortunately, it was recently proven in [DDF14] that this intuition is correct: Duc et al. proved that a construction secure in the threshold probing model is also secure in the SD-noisy leakage model. However, the reduction comes with an overhead in the size of the field. In [DFS15a], the authors showed with empirical methods that this overhead can be significantly reduced. In this section, we aim to demonstrate an improvement of [DFS15a] by using the ARE-noisy leakage model[7] instead of the SD-noisy-leakage model. Our proof follows a similar strategy as the original proof in [DDF14]. As an outcome, the reduction between the two leakage models produces a tighter bound compared to the previous results in the state-of-the-art, thus providing stronger security guarantees for probing-secure constructions in the real world.

5.1   Probing Models

We first recall standard models of adversaries relevant in our context, as defined in [DDF14].

Random-Probing Model. For $0 \le \epsilon \le 1$, we denote by $\mathsf{id}_\epsilon : \mathcal{X} \to \mathcal{X} \cup \{\bot\}$ the function that on input $x \in \mathcal{X}$ outputs x with probability ϵ and $\bot$ otherwise. For $0 \le \epsilon \le 1$, an ϵ-random-probing adversary on $\mathcal{X}^\ell$ is a machine $\mathcal{A}$ that plays the following game against an oracle that knows $(x_1, \ldots, x_\ell) \in \mathcal{X}^\ell$:

1. $\mathcal{A}$ picks a $(\epsilon_1, \ldots, \epsilon_\ell) \in [0; \epsilon]^\ell$;
2. $\mathcal{A}$ receives $(\mathsf{id}_{\epsilon_i}(x_i))_{i \in [\ell]} \in (\mathcal{X} \cup \{\bot\})^\ell$ and outputs $\mathsf{out}_{\mathcal{A}}(x_1, \ldots, x_\ell)$.

Threshold-Probing Model. For $0 \le d \le \ell$, a d-threshold-probing adversary on $\mathcal{X}^\ell$ is a machine $\mathcal{A}$ that plays the following game against an oracle that knows $(x_1, \ldots, x_\ell) \in \mathcal{X}^\ell$:

---

[7] Note that the reduction can also work with the RE-noisy leakage model. However, as shown in previous section using the ARE metric always induces tighter reduction than the RE metric.

1. $\mathcal{A}$ picks a set $\mathcal{I} \subseteq [\ell]$ with $|\mathcal{I}| \leq d$;
2. $\mathcal{A}$ receives $(x_i)_{i \in \mathcal{I}} \in \mathcal{X}^{|\mathcal{I}|}$ and outputs $\mathsf{out}_{\mathcal{A}}(x_1, \ldots, x_\ell)$.

Following the methodology of [DDF14], our proof proceeds in two steps:

1. reduction from the ARE-noisy leakage model to the random-probing model (Sect. 5.2);
2. reduction from the random-probing model to the threshold probing model (Sect. 5.3).

5.2   From ARE-Noisy Leakage Model to Random-Probing Model

The first step consists in reducing the ARE-noisy leakage model to the random-probing model. The main technicality consists in proving the following lemma, which is the ARE-noisy version of [DDF14, Lemma 2] that was given in the SD-noisy setting. The proof of this lemma is analogous to its SD-noisy counterpart and is detailed in the full version of the paper. We denote the equality between two distributions P and Q by $P \overset{d}{=} Q$.

Lemma 3. *Let $f\colon \mathcal{X} \to \mathcal{Y}$ denote a δ-ARE-noisy function for some distribution X. Then, there exists a (randomized) function $f^{\perp}\colon \mathcal{X} \cup \{\perp\} \to \mathcal{Y}$ such that for all $x \in \mathcal{X}$:*

$$f(x) \overset{d}{=} f^{\perp}(\mathsf{id}_\delta(x)) \ .$$

Moreover, if f is poly-time-noisy[8], then $f^{\perp}$ is efficiently computable.

We then obtain the following corollary:

Corollary 1. *Let $\mathcal{A}$ be a δ-ARE-noisy adversary on $\mathcal{X}^\ell$. Then there exists a δ-random-probing adversary $\mathcal{S}$ on $\mathcal{X}^\ell$ such that for all $(x_1, \ldots, x_\ell) \in \mathcal{X}^\ell$:*

$$\mathsf{out}_{\mathcal{S}}(x_1, \ldots, x_\ell) \overset{d}{=} \mathsf{out}_{\mathcal{A}}(x_1, \ldots, x_\ell) \ .$$

Moreover, if $\mathcal{A}$ is poly-time-noisy[9], then $\mathcal{S}$ runs in polynomial time.

Proof. It immediately follows from Lemma 3. $\mathcal{S}$ simply runs $\mathcal{A}$ which it provides with $(f_i^{\perp}(\mathsf{id}_\delta(x)))_{i \in [\ell]} \overset{d}{=} (f_i(x))_{i \in [\ell]}$ as inputs. When $\mathcal{A}$ halts, so does $\mathcal{S}$ with the same output. ☐

Interestingly we have an opposite reduction from random probing model to ARE-noisy leakage model. However this reduction comes with a loss in tightness by a factor $N - 1$.

Lemma 4. *If $\mathcal{A}$ is a δ-random probing adversary on $\mathcal{X}^\ell$, then it is also a $(|\mathcal{X}| - 1) \cdot \delta$-ARE-noisy leakage adversary on $\mathcal{X}^\ell$.*

Proof. From the definitions, it is immediate that the δ-identity id_δ is also a $(|\mathcal{X}| - 1) \cdot \delta$-ARE-noisy function for any distribution.

---

[8] By poly-time-noisy, we mean that f is poly-time computable, produces outputs in a finite set $\mathcal{Y}$, and $\mathbb{P}[f_i(x) = y]$ is poly-time computable for all x, y, i.

[9] By poly-time-noisy, we mean that $\mathcal{A}$ queries only poly-time-noisy functions $(f_i)_i$.

5.3   From Random-Probing Model to Threshold-Probing Model

The second step consists in reducing the random-probing model to the threshold-probing model. This step follows immediately from the results in [DDF14] and is independent of the metric.

Lemma 5 (Lemma 4 of [DDF14]). *Let $\mathcal{A}$ be a δ-random-probing adversary on $\mathcal{X}^\ell$. Then, there exists a $(2\delta\ell - 1)$-threshold-probing adversary $\mathcal{S}$ on $\mathcal{X}^\ell$ with similar running-time such that $\forall(x_1,\ldots,x_\ell) \in \mathcal{X}^\ell$:*

$$\mathsf{out}_{\mathcal{A}}(x_1,\ldots,x_\ell) \overset{d}{=} \mathsf{out}_{\mathcal{S}}(x_1,\ldots,x_\ell) \ ,$$

as long as $\mathsf{out}_{\mathcal{S}}(x_1,\ldots,x_\ell) \neq \perp$. Moreover, the latter happens with probability:

$$\mathbb{P}[\mathsf{out}_{\mathcal{S}}(x_1,\ldots,x_\ell) \neq \perp] \geq 1 - \exp\left(-\frac{\delta\ell}{3}\right) \ .$$

The proof immediately follows from the fact that with probability at least $1 - \exp\left(-\frac{\delta\ell}{3}\right)$ (thanks to the Chernoff bound), a δ-random-probing adversary on $\mathcal{X}^\ell$ obtain at most $2\delta\ell - 1$ of the x_i's.

5.4   Putting Everything Together

Combining Corollary 1 and Lemma 5, we then obtain the following theorem:

Theorem 1. *Let $\mathcal{A}$ be a δ-ARE-noisy adversary on $\mathcal{X}^\ell$. Then, there exists a $(2\delta\ell - 1)$-threshold-probing adversary $\mathcal{S}$ on $\mathcal{X}^\ell$ such that:*

$$\mathsf{out}_{\mathcal{A}}(x_1,\ldots,x_\ell) \overset{d}{=} \mathsf{out}_{\mathcal{S}}(x_1,\ldots,x_\ell) \ ,$$

as long as $\mathsf{out}_{\mathcal{S}}(x_1,\ldots,x_\ell) \neq \perp$, which happens with probability:

$$\mathbb{P}[\mathsf{out}_{\mathcal{S}}(x_1,\ldots,x_\ell) \neq \perp] \geq 1 - \exp\left(-\frac{\delta\ell}{3}\right) \ .$$

Moreover, if $\mathcal{A}$ is poly-time-noisy, then $\mathcal{S}$ runs in polynomial time.

For comparison, the main theorem from [DDF14] states that a δ-SD-noisy adversary can be simulated by a $(2\delta\ell \cdot |\mathcal{X}| - 1)$-threshold probing adversary, with success probability at least $1 - \exp\left(-\delta\ell/(3|\mathcal{X}|)\right)$. Hence, we gain a multiplicative factor $\mathcal{X}$ in the number of probes and reduce the failure probability by an exponential factor in $\mathcal{X}$.

5.5   Circuit Leakage Resilience

Let us define a circuit compiler as in [DDF14]. Let us consider an adversary able to probe at most $\lfloor (d-1)/2 \rfloor$ wires from each gadget (i.e. masked operations) of the implementation. We define a (δ, ζ)-noise resilient implementation as follows:

Definition 6 (*D*-noise resilient implementation). *Let Γ be an stateful arithmetic circuit over $\mathcal{X}$ and Γ' denote the resulting masked circuit obtained via applying the compiler. Let Enc denote a randomized encoding function (i.e. that transform an input into a masked input). Let $D \in \{\mathrm{SD, EN, RE, ARE}\}$ be a noisiness metric. We say that Γ' is a (δ, ζ)-D-noise resilient implementation of Γ with respect to Enc if the following properties hold for every input k:*

1. *the input-output behavior of $\Gamma(k)$ and $\Gamma'(Enc(k))$ is identical, i.e. for every sequence of inputs $a_1, \ldots, a_m$ and outputs $b_1, \ldots, b_m$ we have*

$$\mathbb{P}[\Gamma(k, a_1, \ldots, a_m) = (b_1, \ldots, b_m)] = \mathbb{P}[\Gamma'(Enc(k), a_1, \ldots, a_m) = (b_1, \ldots, b_m)]$$

2. *for every δ-D-noisy adversary $\mathcal{A}$ there exists a black-box circuit adversary $\mathcal{S}$ such that*

$$\Delta_{\mathrm{SD}} \left(\mathsf{out} \left(\mathcal{A} \overset{noisy}{\hookrightarrow} \Gamma'(Enc(k)) \right) ; \mathsf{out} \left(\mathcal{S} \overset{bb}{\hookrightarrow} \Gamma(k) \right) \right) \leq \zeta$$

Then we have the following theorem.

Theorem 2. *Let Γ be an arbitrary stateful arithmetic circuit over $\mathcal{X}$. Let Γ' be the masked circuit. Then Γ' is a $(\delta, |\Gamma| exp(-d/12))$-RE-noise-resilient implementation of Γ with efficient simulation where*

$$\delta = \frac{1}{28d + 16} = O(1/d)$$

The proof is the exact same as the one given in [DDF14] with a numerical gain of a factor $|\mathcal{X}|$ in δ due to the use of ARE in Theorem 1.

6   A New Amplification-Based Proof for Block Ciphers

In this section, we revisit the approach initiated in [PR13] by Prouff and Rivain. Recall that in the latter work, the authors propose a solution to immunize block-ciphers in the noisy-leakage model (with the Euclidian norm EN measuring noisiness). They propose a secret-sharing based immunization for block-ciphers, basically by replacing every operations (linear functions and s-box evaluations) by one that operates on additive shares of the inputs and produce additive shares of the output. They analyze the security by decomposing the resulting proto-col into 4 types of basic subsequences of operations: two types corresponding to simple subsequences and two types corresponding to more complex subse-quences. The overall protocol is then proven secure by composition, assuming leak-free refresh gates can be used between each subsequence to refresh the addi-tive shares. We refer the reader to Section 4 of [PR13] for the details about how to construct the secure subprotocols. The 4 types of subsequences needed for the analysis are recalled below. We propose a different security analysis in the noisy-leakage model using the RE metric instead of the Euclidian norm. Doing so, we are able to prove much tighter bounds for the security.

The 4 types of subsequences to consider are:

T1. $(z_i \leftarrow g(x_i))_{0 \leq i \leq d}$, with g being a linear function (of the block-cipher);
T2. $(z_i \leftarrow g(x_i))_{0 \leq i \leq d}$, with g being an affine function (of an s-box evaluation);
T3. $(v_{i,j} \leftarrow a_i \times b_j)_{0 \leq i,j \leq d}$ (first step of secure non-linear multiplication);
T4. $(t_{i,j} \leftarrow t_{i,j-1} \oplus v_{i,j})_{0 \leq i,j \leq d}$ (fourth step of secure non-linear multiplication).

While type 1 is obviously a particular case of type 2, we treat them separately as we are able to prove a better bound for linear functions than for affine functions.

In the rest of this section, we first provide several basic properties on the RE metric (Sect. 6.1). Then, in Sect. 6.2 we analyze the leakage of each type of subsequences. Next, we argue about the security of a complete evaluation of the block-cipher in Sect. 6.3. Finally, in Sect. 6.4 we apply the Rényi divergence to get a tight amplification-based proof and overcome the limitations in [PR13].

6.1   Basic Properties and Amplification for the Relative Error

First, we give several basic properties of RE-noisy functions and of the RE-noisiness metric that are used in our proofs. We essentially show that the relative error is preserved under function, application, projection and lifting on X. We also prove an amplification result (Lemma 6) that is central throughout our security analysis.

Proposition 4. *Let X, Y, W denote random variables over finite sets $\mathcal{X}, \mathcal{Y}$ and $\mathcal{W}$ respectively. Then we have the following:*

1. **Data processing.** *Let $f : \mathcal{X} \to \mathcal{Y}$ be a δ-RE-noisy function for X, and $g : \mathcal{X} \to \mathcal{X}$ be a (non necessarily deterministic) function. It holds that:*

$$\mathrm{RE}(X|f \circ g(X)) \leq \frac{2\delta}{1 - \delta} \underset{\delta \to 0}{\sim} 2\delta \ .$$

In addition, if g is deterministic and bijective, then $\mathrm{RE}(X|f \circ g(X)) = \delta$.
2. **Conservation under projection and lifting.**

$$\mathrm{RE}(X|Y) \leq \mathrm{RE}((X,W)|Y) \ . \tag{2}$$

In addition, if X and W are independent and $f : \mathcal{W} \to \mathcal{Y}$ is a RE-noisy function for W, then:

$$\mathrm{RE}((X,W)|f(W)) = \mathrm{RE}(W|f(W)) \ . \tag{3}$$

The proof of Proposition 4 is detailed in the full version of the paper.

Remark 3. Note that Inequality 1 is tight: Indeed, if we consider the checkerboard distribution of Remark 1, take $f(X) = Y$, $g(0) = 0$ and for any $x > 0$, $g(x) = 1$, then:

$$\mathrm{RE}(X|f(X)) = \delta \text{ and } \mathrm{RE}(X|f \circ g(X)) = \frac{2(1 - 1/m)\delta}{1 - (1 - 2/m)\delta} \underset{m \to \infty}{\sim} \frac{2\delta}{1 - \delta} \ .$$

Note that Inequality 2 is also tight via (3).

We also prove the following amplification lemma for the relative error. It is the relative error counterpart (though the proof is completely different) of an amplification lemma by Maurer, Pietrzak and Renner [MPR07, Lemma 1]. In the context of leakage-resilient cryptography, the latter result was used and improved by [DFS15b, DFS16].

Lemma 6. *Let $\mathbb{F}$ be a finite field. Let $Z = U(\mathbb{F})$ be the uniform distribution over $\mathbb{F}$, and $Z_1, \ldots, Z_d$ be d independent random variables over $\mathbb{F}$. It holds that:*

$$\Delta_{\mathrm{RE}}\left(\left(\sum_{i=1}^{d} Z_i\right); Z\right) \leq \prod_{i=1}^{d} \Delta_{\mathrm{RE}}(Z_i; Z) .$$

6.2   Security Analysis of Subsequences

We now detail our security analysis for the 4 different types of subsequences to be considered.

Type 1 and type 2 subsequences. We first deal with the simple case of subsequences where all the shares of a secret value are processed separately, i.e. for linear and affine functions. From a security perspective, these are the simplest subsequences as each share only leaks partial information once.

Type 1 subsequences. We first prove the following theorem for type 1 subsequences, which follows almost immediately from Lemma 6. For the sake of completeness, we provide a proof in the full version [GMPP19].

Theorem 3. *Let X be a uniform random variable over a finite field $\mathcal{X}$ and $(X_i)_{i \in \{0,\ldots,d\}}$ be a $(d+1)$-additive sharing of X[10]. Let $\delta \in [0,1)$ and $f_0, f_1, \ldots, f_d$ be δ-RE-noisy-leakage functions over $\mathcal{X}$. Then, we have:*

$$\mathrm{RE}(X|f_0(X_0), \ldots, f_d(X_d)) \leq \delta^{d+1} .$$

Unlike [PR13, Theorem 1], we do not get a overhead of $N^{d/2}$ in our amplification theorem. One could think that this overhead is an artifact of their proof, but circumstantial evidence such as the presence in practice of a factor $1/\sqrt{N}$ in $\mathrm{EN}(X_i|f_i(X_i))$ let us think that it is inherent to the use of the Euclidean norm.

Type 2 subsequences. We can now easily analyze the security of type 2 subsequences, i.e. affine functions of s-box evaluations. Such evaluations are handled via Lagrange interpolation in [PR13], so each elementary calculation processes a share G_i of an encoding of $g(X)$, where X is a uniform s-box input, and g is a polynomial function. This case is covered by Corollary 2, whose proof immediately follows from Theorem 3 and Proposition 4, and is detailed in the full version [GMPP19].

---

[10] Precisely, $\sum_{i=0}^{d} X_i = X$ and the distribution of any strict subset of the X_i's is uniform.

Corollary 2. *Let X be a uniform random variable over a finite field $\mathcal{X}$, $g :$ $\mathcal{X} \to \mathcal{X}$ be a deterministic function, d be a positive integer and $(G_i)_{i \in \{0,\dots,d\}}$ be a $(d+1)$-additive sharing of $g(X)$. Let $\delta \in [0,1)$ and let $f_0, f_1, \dots, f_d$ be δ-RE-noisy leakage functions over $\mathcal{X}$. Then, we have:*

$$\mathrm{RE}(X|f_0(G_0),\dots,f_d(G_d)) \leq \frac{2\delta^{d+1}}{1 - \delta^{d+1}} \underset{\delta \to 0}{\sim} 2\delta^{d+1} \ .$$

Type 3 and type 4 subsequences. We now consider more complex subsequences, where a share is processed several times, and therefore may leak several times in the same subsequence. We first give a generic theorem regarding the bias induced by multiple leakages. We then use this theorem (whose proof is given in the full version [GMPP19]) to bound the leakage of subsequences of type 3 and type 4.

Theorem 4. *Let X be a uniform random variable over a finite field $\mathcal{X}$ and t be a strictly positive integer. Let $\delta \in [0,1)$ and $L_1, \dots, L_t$ be t random variables such that $\mathrm{RE}(X|L_i) \leq \delta$ for every i. We further assume that the random variables $(L_i|X = x)$ are mutually independent for every $x \in \mathcal{X}$. Then, we have:*

$$\mathrm{RE}(X|L_1,\dots,L_t) \leq \left(\frac{1+\delta}{1-\delta}\right)^t - 1 \underset{t\delta \to 0}{=} 2 \cdot t\delta + O((t\delta)^2) \ .$$

In addition, if $\delta \leq 1/t$, then:

$$\mathrm{RE}(X|L_1,\dots,L_t) \leq \frac{t\delta}{1-(t-1)\delta} \underset{t\delta \to 0}{=} t\delta + O((t\delta)^2) \ .$$

Depending on the situation, we use one bound or the other in what follows.

Type 4 subsequences. We start by analyzing subsequences of type 4. Each elementary computation of these subsequences computes $T_{i,j} \leftarrow T_{i,j-1} \oplus V_{i,j}$, with $0 \leq i, j \leq d$ and $T_{i,0} = V_{i,0}$. At the end, the shares $(Z_i)_i = (T_{i,d})_i$ form an additive sharing of $g(X)$, where X is a uniform s-box input and g is a polynomial function over $\mathcal{X}$. Our goal here is to bound the bias of X given the leakages of all these elementary computations. We give a first theorem (whose proof is given in the full version [GMPP19]) which bounds the bias of the shares $(Z_i)_i = (T_{i,d})_i$.[11]

Theorem 5. *Let $T_0, T_1, \dots, T_d$ be $d+1$ independent uniformly random variables over a finite set $\mathcal{X}$. Let $\delta \in \mathbb{R}$ such that $\delta \leq \frac{1}{2d+1}$ and $f_1, f_2, \dots, f_d$ be a family of δ-RE-noisy functions defined over $\mathcal{X} \times \mathcal{X}$. We have:*

$$\mathrm{RE}(T_d|f_1(T_0,T_1),\dots,f_1(T_{d-1},T_d)) \leq \frac{d\delta}{1-(d-1)\delta} \ .$$

---

[11] For concision, Theorem 5 omits the subscript i and writes $(T_j)_j$ instead of $(T_j)_{i,j}$.

This implies the following corollary for the security of a subsequence of type 4:

Corollary 3. *The leakage of type 4 subsequences is upper bounded by:*

$$\mathrm{RE}(X|(f_{i,j}(T_{i,j-1},V_{i,j})_{0\leq i,j\leq d}) \leq \frac{2\delta'^{d+1}}{1-\delta'^{d+1}}, \ \ with \ \delta' = \frac{d\delta}{1-(d-1)\delta} \ .$$

Type 3 subsequences. Only the case of type 3 subsequences remains, which is the most delicate one. As a preliminary result, we provide an upper bound on the bias for a uniform pair (A, B) given the leakage $(f_{i,j}(A_i, B_j))_{i,j}$.

Theorem 6. *Let A, B be two uniform random variables over a finite field $\mathcal{X}$, d a positive integer, and $(A_i)_i, (B_i)_i$ be $d+1$-additive-sharings of A and B respectively. Let $\delta \in \mathbb{R}$ such that $\delta \leq \frac{1}{2d+1}$, and $(f_{i,j})_{i,j}$ be a family of randomized and mutually independent functions such that each $f_{i,j} : \mathcal{X} \times \mathcal{X} \to \mathcal{Y}$ is δ-RE-noisy. We have:*

$$\mathrm{RE}((A, B)|(f_{i,j}(A_i, B_j))_{i,j}) \leq 3\left(\frac{(d+1)\delta}{1-d\delta}\right)^{d+1} \ .$$

The proof of Theorem 6 essentially combines Theorems 3 and 4, and is detailed in the full version [GMPP19].

We now give the leakage of type 3 subsequences. The difference with Theorem 6 is that A and B are not uniformly random, but rather $A = g(X)$ and $B = h(X)$ for some polynomial functions g, h. We then have the following corollary:

Corollary 4. *Let X be a uniform random variable over a finite field $\mathcal{X}$, let g, h be two deterministic functions from $\mathcal{X}$ to $\mathcal{X}$, d be a positive integer, and $(G_i)_i, (H_i)_i$ be $d+1$-additive-sharings of $g(X)$ and $h(X)$ respectively. Let $\delta \in \mathbb{R}$ such that $\delta \leq \frac{1}{2d+1}$, and $(f_{i,j})_{i,j}$ be δ-RE-noisy functions over $\mathcal{X} \times \mathcal{X}$. We have:*

$$\mathrm{RE}(X|(f_{i,j}(G_i, H_j))_{i,j}) \leq \frac{2\delta'}{1-\delta'}, \ \ with \ \delta' = 3\left(\frac{(d+1)\delta}{1-d\delta}\right)^{d+1} \ .$$

Corollary 4 results from combining Theorem 6 with Proposition 4. It is detailed in the full version [GMPP19].

6.3 From Subsequences to a Complete Computation

Now that we have bounded the leakages of the individual subsequences, the next step is to bound the leakage of a single complete execution of a block cipher.

Modeling a block cipher. We use the same notations as in [PR13] and consider the resulting block cipher (after applying their compiler to the original block cipher), hereafter referred to as the *masked block cipher.* An evaluation of the masked block cipher gives $\mathcal{I} = (C_i, f_i)_i$, where the C_i's denote elementary computations (or gates) of the masked block cipher, each C_i being associated to an RE-noisy function f_i. We assume that the (original) cipher involves t_{lin} linear transformations (corresponding to as many type 1 subsequences), t_{aff} affine functions (type 2 subsequences), and t_{nlm} nonlinear multiplications (types 3, 4).

Uniformity of the key and of the subsequence inputs. The block cipher is parameterized by a secret key k which is sampled from the uniform distribution K over $\mathcal{K} = \mathcal{X}^m$. Each subsequence subseq_j operates on an additive-sharing of a random variable X_j. We can write $X_j = g_j(K, \mathsf{msg})$, where msg denotes the message being processed by the block cipher, and g_j is a publicly-known function such that $g_j(\cdot, \mathsf{msg})$ maps the uniform distribution over $\mathcal{K}$ to the uniform distribution over $\mathcal{X}$, which is the case for block ciphers in practice. Therefore the inputs X_j's of each subsequence are uniformly random variables. Alternatively, one could rely on Lemma 2.

Leakage of a block cipher evaluation. For a given subseq_j, let L_j denote its leakage. Since each $g_j(\cdot, \mathsf{msg})$ maps the uniform distribution to the uniform distribution, we have $\mathrm{RE}(K|L_j) = \mathrm{RE}(X_j|L_j)$ from Proposition 4. Since the $t = t_{\mathsf{lin}} + t_{\mathsf{aff}} + 2t_{\mathsf{nlm}}$ subsequences composing the circuit are interleaved with leak-free refresh gates (by assumption), each of them operates on fresh random shares, therefore the leakages $(L_j|K = k)$ are mutually independent.

We suppose that there exists a $\delta_{\mathsf{subseq}} \geq 0$ such that $\forall j, \mathrm{RE}(X_j|L_j) \leq \delta_{\mathsf{subseq}}$. Theorems 3 and 5 as well as Corollaries 2 and 4 give us explicit conditions to fulfill this bound for each subsequence. Via Theorem 4, the leakage δ_{circ} of the whole secure evaluation is bounded by:

$$\delta_{\mathsf{circ}} \leq \frac{t\delta_{\mathsf{subseq}}}{1 - (t-1)\delta_{\mathsf{subseq}}} \approx t\delta_{\mathsf{subseq}}$$

which is non-vacuous as long as $\delta_{\mathsf{subseq}} \leq 1/(t-1)$.

6.4   Overall Security Proof with the Rényi Divergence

Now that we have bounded the overall leakage of one evaluation of the block cipher, we want to analyze the impact of this leakage on the concrete security of the block cipher. This last section corresponds somehow to the end of [PR13], where the leakage of an evaluation is translated into a bound on the mutual information provided by the leakage. Yet, this incurs the following limitations.

Limitations of the Prouff-Rivain approach. The use of the mutual information is somewhat problematic in the sense that it provokes paradoxical situations like the fact that a single pair of plaintext-ciphertext can information-theoretically reveal the key. The authors circumvent this by considering a random-plaintext attack where plaintexts and ciphertexts are both unknown. This does not cover many situations encountered in cryptography and is highly unusual compared to most works, which consider at least a chosen-plaintext attack. Finally, while not stated explicitly, for concrete security we need the mutual information to be upper bounded by $2^{-O(\lambda)}$, where λ is the targeted security parameter of the block cipher, hence the masking order depends only on λ and in particular does not depend on the amount of leakage the adversary can observe.

A proof based on the Rényi divergence. In this section, we provide an alternative security proof based on the Rényi divergence instead of the mutual information. This provides two main benefits compared to the previous work: (1) We can consider classical chosen-plaintext attacks, and (2) the requirement on the noise is much lower because it does not depend on the security level anymore but *on the number of leakages*, denoted q in what follows.

Description of the games. We consider two games. The first game models a black-box interaction of an attacker with an encryption oracle and corresponds to the standard security model such as the IND-CPA security game model. The second game models a grey-box interaction where the attacker has, in addition, access to leakage. This grey-box interaction captures the behavior of a block cipher in the real-world. We also introduce a third artificial (but easier) game which we use to connect the latter two games. These three games are summarized in Figs. 3, 4, and 5 and are precisely described below.

Let $\mathcal{A}$ be an adversary interacting with an (encryption and decryption) oracle $\mathcal{O}$ in the following fashion:

1. $\mathcal{O}$ draws a secret key $k \leftarrow K$, where K denotes the uniform distribution over a finite set $\mathcal{K}$;
2. $\mathcal{A}$ makes a finite number q of queries to $\mathcal{O}$. This is the part where the three games differ:
   - Game 1 (*black-box*): $\mathcal{A}$ sends q plaintexts $\mathsf{msg}_1, \ldots, \mathsf{msg}_q$ to $\mathcal{O}$, who sends back the q corresponding ciphertexts $\mathsf{ctxt}_1 = E_k(\mathsf{msg}_1), \ldots, \mathsf{ctxt}_q = E_k(\mathsf{msg}_q)$;
   - Game 2 (*grey-box*): $\mathcal{A}$ sends q plaintexts $\mathsf{msg}_1, \ldots, \mathsf{msg}_q$ to $\mathcal{O}$. For each plaintext msg_i, $\mathcal{O}$ sends back the corresponding ciphertexts ctxt_i but also some value L_i which modelizes the physical leakage occurring during the computation $\mathsf{ctxt}_i \leftarrow E_k(\mathsf{msg}_i)$, and gets recorded by $\mathcal{A}$;
   - Game 3 (*hybrid*): This is a 2-stage game:
     (a) first, $\mathcal{A}$ sends q plaintexts $\mathsf{msg}'_1, \ldots, \mathsf{msg}'_q$, and $\mathcal{O}$ sends back the corresponding leakages L_i but *not* the ciphertexts $E_k(\mathsf{msg}'_i)$.
     (b) second, $\mathcal{A}$ sends q plaintexts $\mathsf{msg}_1, \ldots, \mathsf{msg}_q$, and $\mathcal{O}$ sends back the ciphertexts $E_k(\mathsf{msg}'_i)$ *but not* the corresponding leakages L_i.
3. After the query-reply phase, $\mathcal{A}$ outputs a value k'. $\mathcal{A}$ wins the game if $k = k'$.

Relationships between the games. It is clear that any attacker $\mathcal{A}$ that succeeds in Game 1 also does in Game 2, since $\mathcal{A}$ can choose to discard the additional leakage $L_1, \ldots, L_q$, in which case Game 2 becomes identical to Game 1. Similarly, any attacker that succeeds in Game 2 also does in Game 3 by simply querying $\mathsf{msg}'_i = \mathsf{msg}_i, \forall i$. Hence, it is sufficient to prove that the success probability of an adversary in Game 3 is close (in a precisely quantifiable way) to its success probability in the ideal Game 1 to argue that security holds in the real-world (Game 2). This is what we do in the rest of this section.

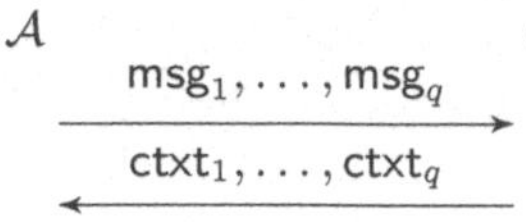

$$\mathcal{A} \xrightarrow{\quad \mathsf{msg}_1,\ldots,\mathsf{msg}_q \quad} \mathcal{O}$$

Fig. 3. Game 1: Black-box 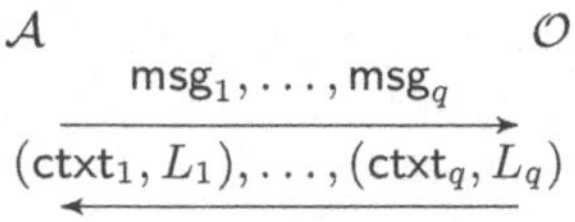   **Fig. 4.** Game 2: Grey-box 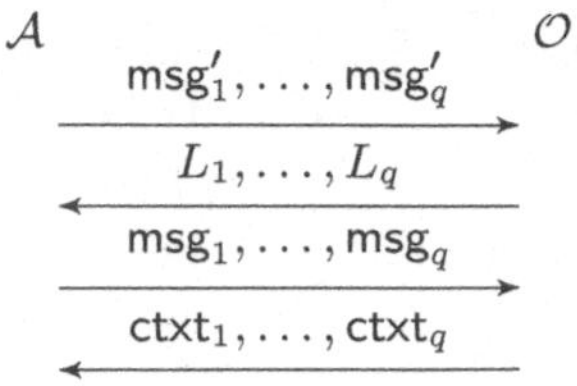   **Fig. 5.** Game 3: Hybrid

Applying the Rényi divergence. At the end of the first step of Game 3, $\mathcal{A}$ has learnt leakages $L_1, \ldots, L_q$. These leakages imply a bias in the distribution of possible secret keys K (which was originally the uniformly random distribution). We denote by K' the distribution $(K|L_1, \ldots, L_q)$. Hence, after the first step of Game 3, the vision of $\mathcal{A}$ is the same as playing Game 1 with the secret key being taken from distribution K' (instead of uniformly at random).

Suppose that $\forall i, \mathrm{RE}(K|L_i) \leq \delta_{\mathsf{circ}}$ for some $\delta_{\mathsf{circ}} \in [0,1)$. Assuming leak-free refresh gates, it follows from Theorem 4 that:

$$\Delta_{\mathrm{RE}}(K'; K) = \mathrm{RE}(K|L_1, \ldots, L_q) \leq \left(\frac{1 + \delta_{\mathsf{circ}}}{1 - \delta_{\mathsf{circ}}}\right)^n - 1 \ . \tag{4}$$

Let $E \subseteq \mathrm{Supp}(K)$ be an arbitrary event. We recall that $K(E)$ denotes the probability of E occurring under the distribution K. First, from the probability preservation property of the Rényi divergence (Lemma 1):

$$K'(E) \leq K(E) \cdot R_\infty(K' \| K). \tag{5}$$

On the other hand, from the definition of the Rényi divergence:

$$R_\infty(K' \| K) \leq 1 + \Delta_{\mathrm{RE}}(K'; K) \tag{6}$$

Combining (4), (5) and (6) yields

$$K'(E) \leq K(E) \cdot \left(\frac{1 + \delta_{\mathsf{circ}}}{1 - \delta_{\mathsf{circ}}}\right)^q$$

Practical implications. The consequence of this security proof is that as long as the number of leakage queries q is in $O(1/\delta_{\mathsf{circ}})$, an adversary does not have significantly larger chances to break a leaking block cipher implementation than it does for the black-box implementation.

For example, let E be the event that $\mathcal{A}$ solves a search problem (finding a secret key, forging a signature, decrypting a message, etc). If we take $q \leq 1/\delta_{\mathsf{circ}}$, then $K'(E) \leq e^2 K(E)$, which means that the leakages do no improve the probability of $\mathcal{A}$ solving the search problem by more than a factor e^2; this means that less than 3 bits of security have been lost between the black-box (Game 1) and leaking (Game 2) implementations. In contrast, an analysis based on the statistical distance or the mutual information would require $\delta_{\text{circ}} = 2^{-O(\lambda)}$.

We note that this Rényi-divergence based analysis is only valid for search problems: achieving the same efficiency for decision problems is still an open question [BLL+15, Pre17].

References

[ADF16] Andrychowicz, M., Dziembowski, S., Faust, S.: Circuit compilers with $O(1/\log(n))$ leakage rate. In: Fischlin, M., Coron, J.-S. (eds.) EURO-CRYPT 2016. LNCS, vol. 9666, pp. 586–615. Springer, Heidelberg (2016). https://doi.org/10.1007/978-3-662-49896-5_21

[AIS18] Ananth, P., Ishai, Y., Sahai, A.: Private circuits: a modular approach. Cryptology ePrint Archive, Report 2018/566 (2018). https://eprint.iacr.org/2018/566

[BCO04] Brier, E., Clavier, C., Olivier, F.: Correlation power analysis with a leakage model. In: Joye, M., Quisquater, J.-J. (eds.) CHES 2004. LNCS, vol. 3156, pp. 16–29. Springer, Heidelberg (2004). https://doi.org/10.1007/978-3-540-28632-5_2

[BLL+15] Bai, S., Langlois, A., Lepoint, T., Stehlé, D., Steinfeld, R.: Improved security proofs in lattice-based cryptography: using the Rényi divergence rather than the statistical distance. In: Iwata, T., Cheon, J.H. (eds.) ASIACRYPT 2015. LNCS, vol. 9452, pp. 3–24. Springer, Heidelberg (2015). https://doi.org/10.1007/978-3-662-48797-6_1

[CH89] Church, K.W., Hanks, P.: Word association norms, mutual information and lexicography. In: ACL, pp. 76–83. ACL (1989)

[CJRR99] Chari, S., Jutla, C.S., Rao, J.R., Rohatgi, P.: Towards sound approaches to counteract power-analysis attacks. In: Wiener, M. (ed.) CRYPTO 1999. LNCS, vol. 1666, pp. 398–412. Springer, Heidelberg (1999). https://doi.org/10.1007/3-540-48405-1_26

[DDF14] Duc, A., Dziembowski, S., Faust, S.: Unifying leakage models: from probing attacks to noisy leakage. In: Nguyen, P.Q., Oswald, E. (eds.) EUROCRYPT 2014. LNCS, vol. 8441, pp. 423–440. Springer, Heidelberg (2014). https://doi.org/10.1007/978-3-642-55220-5_24

[DFS15a] Duc, A., Faust, S., Standaert, F.-X.: Making masking security proofs concrete. In: Oswald, E., Fischlin, M. (eds.) EUROCRYPT 2015. LNCS, vol. 9056, pp. 401–429. Springer, Heidelberg (2015). https://doi.org/10.1007/978-3-662-46800-5_16

[DFS15b] Dziembowski, S., Faust, S., Skorski, M.: Noisy leakage revisited. In: Oswald, E., Fischlin, M. (eds.) EUROCRYPT 2015. LNCS, vol. 9057, pp. 159–188. Springer, Heidelberg (2015). https://doi.org/10.1007/978-3-662-46803-6_6

[DFS16] Dziembowski, S., Faust, S., Skórski, M.: Optimal amplification of noisy leakages. In: Kushilevitz, E., Malkin, T. (eds.) TCC 2016. LNCS, vol. 9563, pp. 291–318. Springer, Heidelberg (2016). https://doi.org/10.1007/978-3-662-49099-0_11

[DP08] Dziembowski, S., Pietrzak, K.: Leakage-resilient cryptography. In: FOCS, pp. 293–302. IEEE Computer Society (2008)

[FHT03] Fedotov, A.A., Harremoes, P., Topsoe, F.: Refinements of Pinsker's inequality. IEEE Trans. Inf. Theory **49**(6), 1491–1498 (2003)

[GJR17] Goudarzi, D., Joux, A., Rivain, M.: How to securely compute with noisy leakage in quasilinear complexity. Cryptology ePrint Archive, Report 2017/929 (2017). https://eprint.iacr.org/2017/929

[GMPP19] Goudarzi, D., Martinelli, A., Passelègue, A., Prest, T.: Unifying leakage models on a Rényi day. IACR Cryptology ePrint Archive 2019, p. 138 (2019)

[ISW03] Ishai, Y., Sahai, A., Wagner, D.: Private circuits: securing hardware against probing attacks. In: Boneh, D. (ed.) CRYPTO 2003. LNCS, vol. 2729, pp. 463–481. Springer, Heidelberg (2003). https://doi.org/10.1007/978-3-540-45146-4_27

[KJJ99] Kocher, P., Jaffe, J., Jun, B.: Differential power analysis. In: Wiener, M. (ed.) CRYPTO 1999. LNCS, vol. 1666, pp. 388–397. Springer, Heidelberg (1999). https://doi.org/10.1007/3-540-48405-1_25

[Koc96] Kocher, P.C.: Timing attacks on implementations of Diffie-Hellman, RSA, DSS, and other systems. In: Koblitz, N. (ed.) CRYPTO 1996. LNCS, vol. 1109, pp. 104–113. Springer, Heidelberg (1996). https://doi.org/10.1007/3-540-68697-5_9

[MPR07] Maurer, U., Pietrzak, K., Renner, R.: Indistinguishability amplification. In: Menezes, A. (ed.) CRYPTO 2007. LNCS, vol. 4622, pp. 130–149. Springer, Heidelberg (2007). https://doi.org/10.1007/978-3-540-74143-5_8

[MR04]   Micali, S., Reyzin, L.: Physically observable cryptography. In: Naor, M. (ed.) TCC 2004. LNCS, vol. 2951, pp. 278–296. Springer, Heidelberg (2004). https://doi.org/10.1007/978-3-540-24638-1_16

[PR13]   Prouff, E., Rivain, M.: Masking against side-channel attacks: a formal security proof. In: Johansson, T., Nguyen, P.Q. (eds.) EUROCRYPT 2013. LNCS, vol. 7881, pp. 142–159. Springer, Heidelberg (2013). https://doi.org/10.1007/978-3-642-38348-9_9

[Pre17] Prest, T.: Sharper bounds in lattice-based cryptography using the Rényi divergence. In: Takagi, T., Peyrin, T. (eds.) ASIACRYPT 2017. LNCS, vol. 10624, pp. 347–374. Springer, Cham (2017). https://doi.org/10.1007/978-3-319-70694-8_13

[Ré61]   Rényi, A.: On measures of entropy and information. In: Proceedings of the Fourth Berkeley Symposium on Mathematical Statistics and Probability, Volume 1: Contributions to the Theory of Statistics, pp. 547–561. University of California Press, Berkeley (1961)

[Vaj70] Vajda, I.: Note on discrimination information and variation (corresp.). IEEE Trans. Inf. Theory **16**(6), 771–773 (1970)

Leakage Certification Revisited: Bounding Model Errors in Side-Channel Security Evaluations

Olivier Bronchain[1], Julien M. Hendrickx[1], Clément Massart[1], Alex Olshevsky[2], and François-Xavier Standaert[1($\boxtimes$)]

[1] ICTEAM Institute, Université catholique de Louvain, Louvain-la-Neuve, Belgium
fstandae@uclouvain.be
[2] Department of Electrical and Computer Engineering,
Boston University, Boston, MA, USA

Abstract. Leakage certification aims at guaranteeing that the statistical models used in side-channel security evaluations are close to the true statistical distribution of the leakages, hence can be used to approximate a worst-case security level. Previous works in this direction were only qualitative: for a given amount of measurements available to an evaluation laboratory, they rated a model as "good enough" if the model assumption errors (i.e., the errors due to an incorrect choice of model family) were small with respect to the model estimation errors. We revisit this problem by providing the first quantitative tools for leakage certification. For this purpose, we provide bounds for the (unknown) *Mutual Information* metric that corresponds to the true statistical distribution of the leakages based on two easy-to-compute information theoretic quantities: the *Perceived Information*, which is the amount of information that can be extracted from a leaking device thanks to an estimated statistical model, possibly biased due to estimation and assumption errors, and the *Hypothetical Information*, which is the amount of information that would be extracted from an hypothetical device exactly following the model distribution. This positive outcome derives from the observation that while the estimation of the Mutual Information is in general a hard problem (i.e., estimators are biased and their convergence is distribution-dependent), it is significantly simplified in the case of statistical inference attacks where a target random variable (e.g., a key in a cryptographic setting) has a constant (e.g., uniform) probability. Our results therefore provide a general and principled path to bound the worst-case security level of an implementation. They also significantly speed up the evaluation of any profiled side-channel attack, since they imply that the estimation of the Perceived Information, which embeds an expensive cross-validation step, can be bounded by the computation of a cheaper Hypothetical Information, for any estimated statistical model.

1 Introduction

State-of-the-art. Side-Channel Attacks (SCAs) are among the most important threats against the security of modern embedded devices [20]. They leverage

© International Association for Cryptologic Research 2019
A. Boldyreva and D. Micciancio (Eds.): CRYPTO 2019, LNCS 11692, pp. 713–737, 2019.
https://doi.org/10.1007/978-3-030-26948-7_25

physical leakages such as the power consumption or electromagnetic radiation of an implementation in order to recover sensitive data. Concretely, SCAs consist in two main steps: information extraction and information exploitation. In the first step, the adversary collects partial information about some intermediate computations of the leaking implementation. For this purpose, he generally compares key-dependent leakage models with actual measurements thanks to a distinguisher such as the popular Correlation Power Analysis (CPA) [2] or Template Attacks (TAs) [5]. In the second step, the adversary combines this partial information in order to recover the sensitive data in full (e.g., by performing a key recovery). For this purpose, the most frequent solution is to exploit a divide-and-conquer strategy (e.g., to recover each key byte independently), and to perform key enumeration if needed [22,27,34].[1]

Based on this description, the (worst-case) security evaluation of actual implementations and side-channel countermeasures requires estimating the amount of information leaked by a target device [33]. Fair evaluations ideally require exploiting a perfect leakage model (i.e., a model that perfectly corresponds to the leakage distribution) with a Bayesian distinguisher. Yet, such a perfect leakage model is in general unknown. Therefore, side-channel security evaluators (and adversaries) have to approximate the statistical distribution of the leakages using density estimation techniques. It raises the problem that security evaluations can become inaccurate due to estimation and assumption errors in the leakage model. Estimation errors are due to an insufficient number of measurements for the model parameters to converge. Assumption errors are due to incorrect choices of density estimation tools (e.g., assuming Gaussian leakages for non-Gaussian leakages).

The problem of ensuring that a leakage model is "good enough" so that it does not lead to over-estimating the security of an implementation has been formalized by Durvaux et al. as *leakage certification* [13]. In the first leakage certification test introduced at Eurocrypt 2014, a leakage model is defined as good enough if its assumption errors are small with respect to its estimation errors. Intuitively, it guarantees that given the amount of measurements used by the evaluator/adversary to estimate a model, any improvement of his (possibly incorrect) assumptions will not lead to noticeable degradations of the security level (since the impact of improved assumptions will be hidden by estimation errors). In a heuristic simplification proposed at CHES 2016, a model is considered as good enough if the statistical moments of the model do not noticeably deviate from the statistical moments of the actual leakage distribution [12]. In both cases, the certification tests are based on challenging the model against fresh samples in a cross-validation step. In both cases, the certification tests are qualitative and conditional to the number of measurements available to build the model. By increasing the number of measurements (and if the model is imperfect), one can make estimation errors arbitrarily small, which inevitably leads to

---

[1] More advanced strategies, such as Algebraic Side-Channel Attacks (ASCA) [29] or Soft Analytical Side-Channel Attacks (SASCA) [35] can also be considered. Our following tools apply identically to these attacks.

the possible detection of assumption errors. As a result, a fundamental challenge in side-channel security evaluations (which we tackle in this paper) is to *bound the information loss due to model errors quantitatively.*

We note that from an information theoretic viewpoint, the risk of under-estimating the leakages due to model errors in side-channel security evaluations can be captured with the notion of Perceived Information (PI) initially introduced in [30] to analyze model variability in nanoscale devices. Informally, the PI corresponds to the amount of information that can be extracted from some data thanks to a statistical model possibly affected by estimation or assumption errors. If the model is perfect, the PI is identical to Shannon's standard definition of Mutual Information (MI). Otherwise, the difference between the MI and the PI provides a quantitative view of the information loss. (Yet, at this stage not a usable one since the MI is unknown, just as the perfect model).

Contribution. The main contributions of the paper are to provide simple and efficient information theoretic tools in order to bound the model errors in side-channel security evaluations, and to validate these tools empirically based on simulated leakages and actual measurements.

Our starting point for this purpose is a third information theoretic quantity that was introduced as part as a negative result on the way towards the CHES 2016 heuristic leakage certification test. Namely, the Hypothetical Information (HI), which is the amount of information that would be extractable from the samples if the true distribution was the statistical model. As discussed in [12], as such the HI seems useless since in case of incorrect model, it can be completely disconnected from the true leakage distribution (i.e., models with positive HI may not lead to successful attacks). Yet, we show next how it can be used in combination with the PI in order to enable quantitative leakage certification. In particular, our main results in this direction are twofold:

First, we show that – *under the assumption that the target random variable (e.g., the secret key) has constant (e.g., uniform) probability* – the empirical HI (eHI), which corresponds to the HI estimated directly based on the empirical leakage distribution, is in expected value an upper bound for the MI and that it converges monotonically towards the true MI as the number of measurements used in order to estimate the leakage model increases. Second, we show that (under the same assumptions) the PI is a lower bound for the MI.

Our experiments then show that these tools can be concretely exploited in the analysis of actual leakage models and speed up side-channel security evaluations. They also sometimes illustrate the difficulty to obtain tight worst-case bounds in practice, and the interest of exploiting some additional (e.g., Gaussian) leakage assumptions in order to more efficiently obtain "close to worst-case" evaluations. In this case as well, we show that bounding the PI with the HI can lead to efficiency gains, especially for distributions with larger number of dimensions.

Related works. The fact that we may bound the MI is surprising since it is actually known to be impossible in general. As for example discussed by Paninski [26], there are no unbiased estimators for the MI (and the rate at which the error decreases depends on the data structure, for any estimator).

This had led some works aiming at leakage detection to exploit more positive results for the distribution of the zero MI (i.e., the case with no information leakage) [6,7,24]. We follow a different path by observing that in the context of side-channel security evaluations, every key (or target intermediate variable) has a uniform distribution a priori, and it is easy for the evaluator to enforce that the number of leakages collected for every key (or target intermediate variable) is identical. In this case, where the probability of the key (or target intermediate variable) does not need to be estimated, we fall back on a situation where the maximum likelihood estimation of the MI is biased upwards everywhere. Combined with the good properties of the empirical distribution (which converges towards the true distribution) it leads to our first result. The result for the PI is even more direct, holds for any model, and is obtained by solving an optimization problem.

Besides, the problem of leakage certification shares strong similarities with the application of the bias-variance decomposition [9], introduced as a diagnosis tool for the evaluation of side-channel leakage models by Lerman et al. [18]. Note that we here mean the bias (and variance) of the leakage model, not the bias of the MI estimator as when previously referring to Paninski. Conceptually, evaluating the bias and variance of a leakage model can be viewed as similar to evaluating its estimation and assumption errors. Yet, the problem of this decomposition is again that it requires the knowledge of the perfect leakage model. Lerman et al. alleviate this difficulty by assuming that the perfect leakage model directly provides the key (in one trace). However, this leads their estimation of the bias and variance to gradually become inaccurate as the target implementations become protected, so that this idealizing assumption becomes more and more incorrect.

2   Notations and Background

In this section, we provide the background and definitions needed to describe our results, with a particular focus on the different metrics we suggest for side-channel security evaluations.

True distributions. Given a (discrete) secret key variable K and a (discrete or continuous) leakage variable L, we denote the true conditional Probability Mass Function (PMF) – which corresponds to discrete leakages – as $\Pr(L = l|K = k)$ and the true conditional Probability Density Function (PDF) – which corresponds to continuous leakages – as $f(L = l|K = k)$.

Mutual Information (MI). For discrete leakages, it is defined as [8]:

$$\text{MI}(K; L) = \text{H}(K) + \sum_{l \in \mathcal{L}} \Pr(L = l) \cdot \sum_{k \in \mathcal{K}} \Pr(K = k|L = l) \cdot \log_2 \Pr(K = k|L = l), \quad (1)$$

$$= \text{H}(K) + \sum_{k \in \mathcal{K}} \Pr(K = k) \cdot \sum_{l \in \mathcal{L}} \Pr(L = l|K = k) \cdot \log_2 \Pr(K = k|L = l). \quad (2)$$

Using the simplified notation $\Pr(X = x) := \mathsf{p}(x)$, it leads to:

$$\mathrm{MI}(K; L) = \mathrm{H}(K) + \sum_{k \in \mathcal{K}} \mathsf{p}(k) \cdot \sum_{l \in \mathcal{L}} \mathsf{p}(l|k) \cdot \log_2 \mathsf{p}(k|l). \tag{3}$$

Assuming uniformly distributed keys, $\mathsf{p}(k|l)$ is computed as $\frac{\mathsf{p}(l|k)}{\sum_{k^* \in \mathcal{K}} \mathsf{p}(l|k^*)}$ and $\mathrm{H}(K) = \log_2(|\mathcal{K}|)$. Similarly, in the case of continuous leakages, we can define the MI as follows:

$$\mathrm{MI}(K; L) = \mathrm{H}(K) + \sum_{k \in \mathcal{K}} \Pr(k) \cdot \int_{l \in \mathcal{L}} \mathsf{f}(l|k) \cdot \log_2 \mathsf{p}(k|l) \, dl. \tag{4}$$

MI and statistical inference attacks. We are interested in the MI in the context of side-channel analysis because it is a good predictor of the success probability of a continuous "statistical inference attack", where an adversary uses his leakages in order to recover a secret key.[2] Precisely, it is shown in [11] that a higher MI generally implies a more efficient maximum likelihood attack where the adversary selects the most likely key $\tilde{k}$ among all the candidates k^* as:

$$\tilde{k} = \underset{k^* \in \mathcal{K}}{\mathrm{argmax}} \prod_{l \in \mathcal{L}} \mathsf{p}(k^*|l). \tag{5}$$

Note that this implication only holds independently for each key k manipulated by the leaking device. That is, a higher "MI per key" $\mathrm{MI}(k; L)$ implies a higher probability of success $\Pr(\tilde{k} = k)$.

Intuitively, the link between such an attack and $\mathrm{MI}(k; L)$ comes from the similarity between the product of probabilities in the attack and the sum of log probabilities in the metric.

Sampling process. The true distributions are generally unknown, but we can sample them in order to produce data sets for estimating leakage models and testing these models. We denote these sampling processes as $\mathcal{M} \overset{n}{\leftarrow} \mathsf{p}(l|k)$ and $\mathcal{T} \overset{n_t}{\leftarrow} \mathsf{p}(l|k)$ in the discrete case, with n and n_t (resp., $n(k)$ and $n_t(k)$) the number of i.i.d. samples measured and stored (resp., per key) in the multisets of samples $\mathcal{M}$ and $\mathcal{T}$ (which have repetitions). We replace p by f for the continuous case.

Computing the MI by sampling. The MI metric can be computed directly thanks to Eqs. 3 or 4. It can also be computed "by sampling" (for discrete and continuous leakages) as:

$$\widehat{\mathrm{MI}}(K; L) = \mathrm{H}(K) + \sum_{k \in \mathcal{K}} \mathsf{p}(k) \cdot \sum_{i=1}^{n_t(k)} \frac{1}{n_t(k)} \cdot \log_2 \mathsf{p}(k|l_k(i)), \tag{6}$$

where $l_k(i) \in \mathcal{T}$ is the ith leakage sample observed for the key k. In the discrete case, it is easy to see that the blue part of the equation corresponds to the

---

[2] We consider so-called noisy leakages, where the adversary can observe a noisy function of secret variables [28].

empirical distribution. So Eq. 6 essentially replaces the true distribution $p(l|k)$ by the empirical one, and the hat sign is used to reflect that the MI is computed by sampling. Since the empirical distribution converges towards the real one as $n_t \to \infty$, $\widehat{\text{MI}}(K; L)$ also tends towards $\text{MI}(K; L)$. In the continuous case, the convergence requires more elaboration (details are given in the full version of the paper [3]). For simplicity, we next refer to the blue part of Eq. 6 as the empirical in both the discrete and continuous cases.

Note that the PMF after the log in Eq. 6 is fixed (i.e., it is not an estimate). So this equation does not describe an estimation of the MI in the usual sense, where the joint probability of two random variables has to be estimated: it only provides an alternative way to compute the MI of some known distribution. Hence it does not suffer from the bias issues discussed in [26].

Model estimation. Given a set of n modeling samples $\mathcal{M}$, we denote the process of estimating the conditional leakage distribution as $\tilde{\mathsf{m}}_n(l|k) \leftarrow \mathcal{M}$, where we use the red color to highlight the model and the tilde sign to reflect that it is the result of a statistical estimation.

We will consider two types of models: *exhaustive models* where we directly estimate the empirical distribution (e.g., in the discrete case they correspond to histograms on the full support of the observations); *simplified models* which may for example correspond to histograms with reduced numbers of bins in the discrete case, or to parametric (e.g., Gaussian) PDF estimation in the continuous case. Simplified models are aimed to converge faster (i.e., to require lower n values before becoming informative), possibly at the cost of some information loss when $n \to \infty$. In other words, exhaustive models (sometimes slowly) converge towards the real distribution as $n \to \infty$, while simplified models may be affected by assumption errors appearing for large n's (i.e., bad choices of parametric estimation such as assuming Gaussian noise for non-Gaussian leakages).

Finally, we use the term *model* for the (parametric or non-parametric) estimation of a distribution from a given number of profiling leakages n, and the term *model family* for the set of all the models that can be produced with a defined set of parameters. For example, the (univariate) Gaussian model family denotes all the models that can be produced by estimating a sample mean and a sample variance, and a Gaussian model corresponds to one estimation given n leakages.

Hypothetical and Perceived information. Given that the true distributions $p(l|k)$ or $f(l|k)$ are unknown, we cannot directly compute the MI. One option to get around this impossibility is to estimate it, which is known to be a hard problem (i.e., there are no unbiased and distribution-independent estimators [26]). We next study an alternative approach which is to analyze the information that is revealed by estimated models thanks to two previously introduced and easy-to-compute quantities. First the *Perceived Information* (PI), which is the amount of information that can be extracted from some data thanks to an estimated model, possibly affected by estimation or assumption errors [13]. Second the

Hypothetical Information (HI), which is the amount of information that would be revealed by (hypothetical) data following the model distribution [12].

Informally, the PI predicts the concrete success probability of a maximum likelihood attack exploiting an estimated model just as the (unknown) MI predicts the theoretical success probability of a worst-case maximum likelihood attack exploiting the true leakage distribution [15]. It can be negative if the estimated model is too different from the true distribution, and therefore can underestimate the information available in the leakages. By contrast, the HI is a purely hypothetical value that is always non-negative and can therefore overestimate the information available in the leakages. We next aim to formalize their properties, and in particular to show that they can be used to (lower and upper) bound the worst-case security level captured by the unknown MI.

The HI is defined as follows in the discrete case:

$$\text{HI}_n(K; L) = \text{H}(K) + \sum_{k \in \mathcal{K}} \mathsf{p}(k) \cdot \sum_{l \in \mathcal{L}} \tilde{\mathsf{m}}_n(l|k) \cdot \log_2 \tilde{\mathsf{m}}_n(k|l). \tag{7}$$

(Replace $\sum$ by $\int$ in the continuous case) For an estimated model $\tilde{\mathsf{m}}_n(l|k)$, the HI can be computed based on Eq. 7, or by sampling (just as for the MI). In the latter case, we use the notation $\widehat{\text{HI}}_n(K; L)$:

$$\widehat{\text{HI}}_n(K; L) = \text{H}(K) + \sum_{k \in \mathcal{K}} \mathsf{p}(k) \cdot \sum_{i=1}^{n_t(k)} \frac{1}{n_t(k)} \cdot \log_2 \tilde{\mathsf{m}}_n(k|l_k(i)), \tag{8}$$

with as main difference from the MI case that the test samples come from a set $\mathcal{T}_\text{m}$ which has been picked up from the model distribution rather than the true distribution. We denote this process as $\mathcal{T}_\text{m} \overset{n_t}{\leftarrow} \tilde{\mathsf{m}}_n(l|k)$, and use the green color to denote the empirical distribution of the model.

Note that, as in Eq. 6, the model after the log in Eq. 8 is fixed. Similarly to the MI estimation process, the value of the estimation $\widehat{\text{HI}}(K; L)$ when $n_t \to \infty$ equals $\text{HI}(K; L)$. *In most practical cases, the HI will be estimated directly via Eq. 7 (which is simpler and faster).*

Next, the PI is theoretically defined as follows in the discrete case:

$$\text{PI}_n(K; L) = \text{H}(K) + \sum_{k \in \mathcal{K}} \mathsf{p}(k) \cdot \sum_{l \in \mathcal{L}} \mathsf{p}(l|k) \cdot \log_2 \tilde{\mathsf{m}}_n(k|l), \tag{9}$$

and as follows in the continuous case:

$$\text{PI}_n(K; L) = \text{H}(K) + \sum_{k \in \mathcal{K}} \mathsf{p}(k) \cdot \int_{l \in \mathcal{L}} \mathsf{f}(l|k) \cdot \log_2 \tilde{\mathsf{m}}_n(k|l) \, dl. \tag{10}$$

In contrast with the HI, these equations cannot be computed directly since they require the knowledge of the true distributions $\mathsf{p}(l|k)$ and $\mathsf{f}(l|k)$ which are unknown. *So concretely, the PI will always be computed thanks to the following sampling process* (where we keep the red color code for the model and the blue color code for the true empirical distribution):

$$\widehat{\mathrm{PI}}_n(K; L) = \mathrm{H}(K) + \sum_{k \in \mathcal{K}} \mathsf{p}(k) \cdot \sum_{i=1}^{n_t(k)} \frac{1}{n_t(k)} \cdot \log_2 \tilde{\mathsf{m}}(k | l_k(i)). \qquad (11)$$

This is feasible in practice since, even though the analytical form of the true distributions is unknown to the evaluator, he can sample these distributions, by measuring his target implementation.

Note again that, as in Eq. 6, the model after the log in Eq. 11 is fixed. So the PI captures the amount of information that can be extracted from some fixed model (usually obtained by estimation in an earlier phase). In other words, the PI computation is a two-step process: first a model is estimated, second the amount of information it provides is estimated. This is captured in our equations with the tilde and hat notations: the first one is for the estimation of the model, the second one for the computation of the information theoretic metrics by sampling.

Other useful facts. We next list a few additional former results.

- *A sufficient condition for successful (maximum likelihood) attacks.* As previously mentioned, the PI can be negative, indicating an estimated model that is too different from the true distribution. Also, the link between information theoretic metrics and the success rate of maximum likelihood attacks only holds per key. A sufficient condition for successful maximum likelihood attacks, first stated in [33], can therefore be given based on the "PI per key". For this purpose, and again assuming uniformly distributed keys, we first define a PI matrix (PIM) as follows:

$$\widehat{\mathrm{PIM}}_n(k, k^*) = \mathrm{H}(K) + \sum_{i=1}^{n_t(k)} \frac{1}{n_t(k)} \cdot \log_2 \tilde{\mathsf{m}}_n(k^* | l). \qquad (12)$$

It captures the correlation between a key generating leakages k and a key candidate in a maximum likelihood attack k^*. The sufficient condition of successful attack against this key k is:

$$k = \operatorname*{argmax}_{k^* \in \mathcal{K}} \widehat{\mathrm{PIM}}_n(k, k^*). \qquad (13)$$

The PI is connected to the PIM: $\widehat{\mathrm{PI}}_n(K; L) = \underset{k \in \mathcal{K}}{\mathsf{E}} \left(\widehat{\mathrm{PIM}}_n(k, k) \right)$.

- *Key equivalence in the standard DPA setting.* In the usual (divide-and-conquer) side-channel analysis context, formalized in [21] as the standard DPA setting that we consider next, the adversary can continuously accumulate information about the key thanks to multiple input plaintexts x. Information theoretic metrics such as the MI, HI and PI therefore have to include another sum over these inputs to be reflective of this setting. For example in the discrete MI case, it yields:

$$\text{MI}(K; L, X) = \text{H}(K) + \sum_{k \in \mathcal{K}} \mathsf{p}(k) \cdot \sum_{x \in \mathcal{X}} \mathsf{p}(x) \cdot \sum_{l \in \mathcal{L}} \mathsf{p}(l|k, x) \cdot \log_2 \mathsf{p}(k|l, x). \quad (14)$$

Concretely, the adversary exploits the leakages after a first group operation between uniformly distributed plaintexts x and a key k took place. For example, he can target an intermediate operation $y = x \oplus k$ or $y = \mathsf{S}(x \oplus k)$ with S a block cipher S-box.[3] As a result, one can leverage the "key equivalence property" also proven in [21], which states that $\text{MI}(K; L, X) = \text{MI}(k; L, X) = \text{MI}(Y; L)$ (i.e., there are no weak keys with respect to standard DPA and all the information exploited depends on the target intermediate computation Y).[4] Again, we use the $\text{MI}(k; L, X)$ notation for a "MI per key" (i.e., Eq. 14 for a fixed value of K, which is the same for all k's). The same type of result holds with the HI and PI. In the following, and in order to keep notations concise, we will therefore state our results for $\text{MI}(Y; L)$, $\text{HI}_n(Y; L)$ and $\text{PI}_n(Y; L)$:

$$\text{MI}(Y; L) = \text{H}(Y) + \sum_{y \in \mathcal{Y}} \mathsf{p}(y) \cdot \sum_{l \in \mathcal{L}} \mathsf{p}(l|y) \cdot \log_2 \mathsf{p}(y|l), \quad (15)$$

$$\text{HI}_n(Y; L) = \text{H}(Y) + \sum_{y \in \mathcal{Y}} \mathsf{p}(y) \cdot \sum_{l \in \mathcal{L}} \tilde{\mathsf{m}}_n(l|y) \cdot \log_2 \tilde{\mathsf{m}}_n(y|l), \quad (16)$$

$$\text{PI}_n(Y; L) = \text{H}(Y) + \sum_{y \in \mathcal{Y}} \mathsf{p}(y) \cdot \sum_{l \in \mathcal{L}} \mathsf{p}(l|y) \cdot \log_2 \tilde{\mathsf{m}}_n(y|l), \quad (17)$$

where the n subscript is the amount of leakages used to estimate the model.
- *Cross-validation.* When computing a metric by sampling, one generally uses cross-validation in order to better take advantage of the collected data. As detailed in [13], it allows all the measured leakages to be used both as profiling and as test samples (but not both at the same time).
- *Metrics convergence and confidence intervals.* When estimating a metric by sampling, one is generally interested in knowing whether the computed value is close enough to the asymptotic one. In the context of side-channel analysis considered here, the amount of collected data is generally sufficient to build a "convergence plot" (see the experimental section) enabling to gain simple (visual) confidence that the metric is well estimated. If needed (e.g., in case of limited amount of data available), the bootstrap confidence intervals proposed in [17] can be used.

---

[3] It is shown in [36] that their adaptive selection only marginally improves the attacks, and in [10,11] how this average metric can be used to state a sufficient condition for secure masked implementations.

[4] The second equality is turned into an inequality in case of non-bijective S-boxes.

- *Outliers.* We finally note that outliers may prevent the PI metric computed from real data to converge (e.g., in case a probability zero is assigned to the correct y, leading to a $\log(0)$ in the PI equation). The treatment of these outliers will be discussed in the next section.

3   Theoretical Bounds for the MI Metric

Given the motivation that the MI metric is a good predictor of the success probability of a worst-case side-channel attack using the true leakage model, and the impossibility to compute it directly for unknown distributions, we now provide our main theoretical results and show how the HI and PI metrics can be used to bound the MI. We first state our results for discrete leakages and discuss the continuous case in Sect. 3.4. We will consider three quantities for this purpose:

- The previously defined MI with $\mathsf{p}(y|l)$ computed thanks to Bayes assuming uniform y's (uniform y's are typically encountered in the aforementioned standard DPA setting):

$$\mathrm{MI}(Y;L) = \mathrm{H}(Y) + \sum_{y \in \mathcal{Y}} \mathsf{p}(y) \cdot \sum_{l \in \mathcal{L}} \mathsf{p}(l|y) \cdot \log_2 \mathsf{p}(y|l), \qquad (18)$$

$$= \mathrm{H}(Y) + \sum_{y \in \mathcal{Y}} \mathsf{p}(y) \cdot \sum_{l \in \mathcal{L}} \mathsf{p}(l|y) \cdot \log_2 \frac{\mathsf{p}(l|y)}{\sum_{y^* \in \mathcal{Y}} \mathsf{p}(l|y^*)}.$$

- The PI (i.e., Eq. 17) under a similar uniformity assumption.
- The empirical HI (eHI), which is Eq. 16 taking as model $\tilde{\mathsf{m}}_n(l|y)$ the empirical distribution, that we denote by $\tilde{\mathsf{e}}_n(l|y)$, under a similar uniformity assumption:

$$\mathrm{eHI}_n(Y;L) = \mathrm{H}(Y) + \sum_{y \in \mathcal{Y}} \mathsf{p}(y) \cdot \sum_{l \in \mathcal{L}} \tilde{\mathsf{e}}_n(l|y) \cdot \log_2 \tilde{\mathsf{e}}_n(y|l). \qquad (19)$$

Note that the eHI is exactly the biased maximum likelihood estimator of the MI that is used in the leakage detection test of Chatzikokolaki et al. [6], applied in the SCA setting by Mather et al. [24]. As detailed next, under our uniformity assumption this estimator of the MI is biased upwards everywhere, which explains why the eHI provides an upper bound of the unknown MI.

3.1   Technical Lemmas

We start with a few technical lemmas that we need to prove our two main theorems. Note that some of them are variations of well-known results given in textbooks such as [8]. We provide the proofs for the sake of completeness and for readers not familiar with information theory. Considering a discrete random variable taking values $1, 2, \ldots, t$, we next denote the actual probability of a value v as $\mathsf{p}(v)$, and the t-dimensional vector containing these probabilities as p.

Lemma 1. *Denoting by $\tilde{e}_n$ the empirical distribution estimated from n i.i.d. leakage samples indexed $1, 2, \ldots, n$, and by $\tilde{e}_n^j$ the empirical distribution estimated from the same samples excluding the sample j, the following equality holds:*

$$\tilde{e}_n = \sum_{j=1:n} \frac{1}{n} \, \tilde{e}_n^j,$$

and each empirical distribution $\tilde{e}_n^j$ follows the same distribution as $\tilde{e}_{n-1}$.

Proof. Let $x \in \{1, 2, \ldots, t\}^n$ be the random i.i.d. samples. For any subset $\mathcal{S}$ of $\{1, \ldots, n\}$, we denote by $\tilde{e}_{\mathcal{S}}$ the empirical distribution of the sample whose indices are in $\mathcal{S}$. Observe that:

$$\tilde{e}_{\mathcal{S}} = \frac{1}{|\mathcal{S}|} \sum_{i \in \mathcal{S}} I_{x_i},$$

with I_{x_i} the indicator function taking the value 1 for the entry x_i and 0 otherwise. We then have:

$$\sum_{j=1:n} \frac{1}{n} \, \tilde{e}_n^j = \frac{1}{n} \sum_{j=1}^{n} \left(\sum_{i \in \{1:n\} \backslash \{j\}} \frac{1}{n-1} I_{x_i} \right),$$

$$= \frac{1}{n(n-1)} \sum_{j=1}^{n} \left(\left(\sum_{i=1}^{n} I_{x_i} \right) - I_{x_j} \right),$$

$$= \frac{1}{n(n-1)} \left(n \left(\sum_{i=1}^{n} I_{x_i} \right) - \sum_{j=1}^{n} I_{x_j} \right),$$

$$= \frac{1}{n(n-1)} (n-1) \left(\sum_{i=1}^{n} I_{x_i} \right),$$

$$= \frac{1}{n} \sum_{i=1}^{n} I_{x_i} = \tilde{e}_n,$$

which proves the equality in the lemma. Moreover, since the samples are i.i.d., all $\tilde{e}_n^j$ follow the same distribution, and in particular the same distribution as $\tilde{e}_n^n = \tilde{e}_{n-1}$. □

Lemma 2. *Let $\gamma : [0,1]^t \to \mathbb{R}$ be a convex function. Then for any $n > 1$, we have:*

$$\gamma(\mathsf{p}) \leq \mathsf{E}\Big(\gamma(\tilde{e}_n) \Big) \leq \mathsf{E}\Big(\gamma(\tilde{e}_{n-1}) \Big).$$

Moreover, if γ is continuous at p and bounded from above on $[0,1]^t$, then:

$$\mathsf{E}\Big(\gamma(\tilde{e}_n) \Big) \to \gamma(\mathsf{p}),$$

monotonically with n. Similarly, if γ is concave and under the assumption that it is continuous and bounded from below, the same result holds with reverse inequalities.

Proof. We focus on the convex case and begin with the first inequality. Observe that:

$$p = E(\tilde{e}_n). \tag{20}$$

Indeed, by linearity of the expected value, we have $E(\tilde{e}_n) = \frac{1}{n}\sum_{i=1}^{n} E(I_{x_i})$, with I_{x_i} the indicator function, whose t-dimensional value is 1 for the entry x_i and 0 otherwise. Therefore, for any i and entry $v \in \{1, \ldots, t\}$:

$$E(I_{x_i})_v = 1 \cdot \Pr(x_i = v) + 0 \cdot \Pr(x_i \neq v) = p(v),$$

from which (20) follows. Hence, due to the convexity of γ, we have:

$$\gamma(p) = \gamma\Big(E(\tilde{e}_n)\Big) \leq E\Big(\gamma(\tilde{e}_n)\Big).$$

For the second inequality, it follows from Lemma 1 that:

$$\tilde{e}_n = \sum_{j=1:n} \frac{1}{n} \, \tilde{e}_n^j.$$

Hence we have:

$$\gamma(\tilde{e}_n) = \gamma\left(\sum_{j=1:n} \frac{1}{n} \, \tilde{e}_n^j\right) \leq \sum_{j=1:n} \frac{1}{n} \gamma\left(\tilde{e}_n^j\right).$$

Moreover, each $\tilde{e}_n^j$ has the same distribution as $\tilde{e}_{n-1}$. Hence:

$$E\Big(\gamma(\tilde{e}_n)\Big) \leq E\left(\sum_{j=1:n} \frac{1}{n}\, \gamma\left(\tilde{e}_n^j\right)\right),$$

$$= \sum_{j=1:n} \frac{1}{n}\, E\Big(\gamma(\tilde{e}_n^j)\Big),$$

$$= \sum_{j=1:n} \frac{1}{n}\, E\Big(\gamma(\tilde{e}_{n-1})\Big) = E\gamma(\tilde{e}_{n-1}).$$

Let us now show the convergence under the assumption that γ is continuous at p and uniformly bounded by some M. By continuity of γ at p, for every ϵ there is a δ such that $\|\tilde{e}_n - p\| \leq \delta$ implies $|\gamma(\tilde{e}_n) - \gamma(p)| \leq \epsilon$. Moreover, $\tilde{e}_n$ converges in probability to p, meaning that for every (δ, ϵ') there is a n' such that $\Pr(\|\tilde{e}_n - p\| > \delta) < \epsilon'$ for any $n > n'$. As a consequence, for $n > n'$, we have:

$$\Pr(|\gamma(\tilde{e}_n) - \gamma(p)| > \epsilon) < \epsilon'.$$

Remembering that $\gamma(.) < M$, we then have that for every $n > n'$:

$$E\Big(\gamma(f^n)\Big) - \gamma(p) = E\Big(\gamma(\tilde{e}_n) - \gamma(p)\Big),$$

$$\leq \epsilon \Pr\Big(|\gamma(\tilde{e}_n) - \gamma(p)| \leq \epsilon\Big) + \Big(M - \gamma(p)\Big)\Pr\Big(|\gamma(\tilde{e}_n) - \gamma(p)| > \epsilon\Big),$$

$$\leq \epsilon(1 - \epsilon') + \epsilon'\Big(M - \gamma(p)\Big),$$

for every $n > n'$. Combining this with $\gamma(\mathsf{p}) \leq \mathsf{E}\Big(\gamma(\tilde{\mathsf{e}}_n)\Big)$ yields the desired convergence result. □

Lemma 3. *Let* $y \in \mathbb{R}_+^m$ *be a vector of positive entries. Then for any positive* $x \in \mathbb{R}_+^m$, *we have:*

$$\sum_i y_i \log_2 \frac{x_i}{\sum_j x_j} \leq \sum_i y_i \log_2 \frac{y_i}{\sum_j y_j},$$

with equality if and only if $x_i = ky_i$ *for some* $k > 0$.

Proof. Let $x' = x/(\sum_j x_j)$ and $y' = y/(\sum_j y_j)$. These vectors can be viewed as probability distributions since they are non-negative and sum to 1. Hence we can compute the following KL-divergence, which is always non-negative, and zero if and only if $x' = y'$:

$$0 \leq D_{KL}(y'||x') = \sum_i \left(y_i' \log \left(\frac{y_i'}{x_i'} \right) \right).$$

Using $\log(y_i'/x_i') = \log y_i' - \log x_i'$, we obtain:

$$\sum_i (y_i' \log x_i') \leq \sum_i (y_i' \log y_i'),$$

from which the result follows by replacing x_i', y_i' and multiplying by $\sum_j y_j$. Equality holds if and only if $x' = y'$, that is, if $x = ky$ for some $k > 0$. □

3.2 Bound from the HI

We first recall the following standard result from Cover and Thomas:

Theorem 1 (Cover & Thomas, 2.7.4 [8]). *The mutual information* $\mathrm{MI}(Y; L)$ *is a concave function of* $\mathsf{p}(y)$ *for fixed* $\mathsf{p}(l|y)$ *and a convex function of* $\mathsf{p}(l|y)$ *for fixed* $\mathsf{p}(y)$.

Combined with the technical Lemma 2, it leads to our main result:

Theorem 2. *On average over the profiling sets* $\mathcal{M}$ *used to estimate the eHI and assuming that the target random variable* Y *has (constant) uniform probability, we have:*

$$\underset{\mathcal{M} \overset{n}{\leftarrow} \mathsf{p}(l|y)}{\mathsf{E}} \Big(\mathrm{eHI}_n(Y; L)\Big) \geq \underset{\mathcal{M} \overset{n-1}{\leftarrow} \mathsf{p}(l|y)}{\mathsf{E}} \Big(\mathrm{eHI}_{n-1}(Y; L)\Big) \geq \mathrm{MI}(Y; L).$$

Moreover, $\lim_{n \to \infty} \mathrm{eHI}_n(Y; L) = \mathrm{MI}(Y; L)$ *(i.e., the eHI monotonically converges towards the MI).*

Proof. Observe that $\mathrm{eHI}_n(Y; L)$ is the mutual information between Y and the empirical distribution of the leakages. Hence (thanks to Theorem 1), it is convex in $\tilde{\mathsf{e}}_n(l|y)$ for a fixed distribution of y (which we have by assumption). The result then follows from Lemma 2. □

3.3 Bound from the PI

Theorem 3. *Assuming that the target random variable Y has (constant) uniform probability and given any model $\tilde{\mathsf{m}}_n(l|y)$ for the conditional probabilities $\mathsf{p}(l|y)$, we have:*

$$\mathrm{PI}_n(Y;L) := \mathrm{II}(Y) + \sum_y \mathsf{p}(y) \sum_l \mathsf{p}(l|y) \log_2 \frac{\tilde{\mathsf{m}}_n(l|y)}{\sum_{y^*} \tilde{\mathsf{m}}_n(l|y^*)} \le \mathrm{MI}(Y;L).$$

Proof. Since $\mathsf{p}(y)$ is a constant c, we have:

$$\mathrm{PI}_n(Y;L) = \mathrm{H}(Y) + c \sum_l \left(\sum_y \mathsf{p}(l|y) \log_2 \frac{\tilde{\mathsf{m}}_n(l|y)}{\sum_{y^*} \tilde{\mathsf{m}}_n(l|y^*)} \right). \tag{21}$$

Now for any l, it follows from Lemma 3 that:

$$\sum_y \mathsf{p}(l|y) \log_2 \frac{\tilde{\mathsf{m}}_n(l|y)}{\sum_{y^*} \tilde{\mathsf{m}}_n(l|y^*)} \le \sum_y \mathsf{p}(l|y) \log_2 \frac{\mathsf{p}(l|y)}{\sum_{y^*} \mathsf{p}(l|y^*)}. \tag{22}$$

Re-introducing this in Eq. 21 leads to:

$$\mathrm{PI}_n(Y;L) \le \mathrm{H}(Y) + c \sum_l \left(\sum_y \mathsf{p}(l|y) \log_2 \frac{\mathsf{p}(l|y)}{\sum_{y^*} \mathsf{p}(l|y^*)} \right), \tag{23}$$

$$= \mathrm{H}(Y) + \sum_y \mathsf{p}(y) \sum_l \mathsf{p}(l|y) \log_2 \frac{\mathsf{p}(l|y)}{\sum_{y^*} \mathsf{p}(l|y^*)},$$

$$= \mathrm{MI}(Y;L).$$

$\square$

Additional observation. It would be nice to know that $\mathrm{PI}_n(Y;L) = \mathrm{MI}(Y;L)$ if and only if $\tilde{\mathsf{m}}_n(l|y) = \mathsf{p}(l|y)$. However, this is not true in general. Suppose for example that l and y only take two values l_1, l_2 and y_1, y_2, and that $\mathsf{p}(l_i|y_j) = 1/2$ for all four cases. Then consider the model defined by $\tilde{\mathsf{m}}_n(l_1|y_j) = \alpha$ and $\tilde{\mathsf{m}}_n(l_2|y_j) = 1 - \alpha$ for both y_j and some $\alpha \in [0,1]$. Again assuming a constant $\mathsf{p}(y) = 1/2$, the perceived information of any such model would be:

$$\mathrm{PI}_n(Y;L) = \mathrm{H}(Y) + \frac{1}{2} \sum_l \sum_y \frac{1}{2} \log_2 \frac{\tilde{\mathsf{m}}_n(l|y)}{\sum_{y^*} \tilde{\mathsf{m}}_n(l|y^*)},$$

$$= \mathrm{H}(Y) + \frac{1}{4} \left(\log_2 \frac{\tilde{\mathsf{m}}_n(l_1|y_1)}{\tilde{\mathsf{m}}_n(l_1|y_1) + \tilde{\mathsf{m}}_n(l_1|y_2)} + \log_2 \frac{\tilde{\mathsf{m}}_n(l_1|y_2)}{\tilde{\mathsf{m}}_n(l_1|y_1) + \tilde{\mathsf{m}}_n(l_1|y_2)} \right.$$

$$\left. + \log_2 \frac{\tilde{\mathsf{m}}_n(l_2|y_1)}{\tilde{\mathsf{m}}_n(l_2|y_1) + \tilde{\mathsf{m}}_n(l_2|y_2)} + \log_2 \frac{\tilde{\mathsf{m}}_n(l_2|y_2)}{\tilde{\mathsf{m}}_n(l_2|y_1) + \tilde{\mathsf{m}}_n(l_2|y_2)} \right),$$

$$= \mathrm{H}(Y) + \frac{1}{4} \left(\log_2 \frac{\alpha}{\alpha + \alpha} + \log_2 \frac{\alpha}{\alpha + \alpha} + \log_2 \frac{1-\alpha}{1-\alpha+1-\alpha} + \log_2 \frac{1-\alpha}{1-\alpha+1-\alpha} \right),$$

$$= \mathrm{H}(Y) + \log_2 \frac{1}{2},$$

irrespectively of α. The value obtained for any α is the same as for $\alpha = 1/2$ (i.e., the only value for which $\tilde{\mathsf{m}}_n(l|y) = \mathsf{p}(l|y)$). We therefore conclude that $\mathrm{PI}_n(Y;L) = \mathrm{MI}(Y;L)$ does not imply that the model accurately describes the distribution of leakage.

As a complement of this observation, we next characterize the conditions under which $\tilde{\mathsf{m}}_n(l|y) = \mathsf{p}(l|y)$ is the only maximum.

Proposition 1. *Let $\mathbf{P}$ be the matrix defined by $\mathbf{P}_{l,y} = \mathsf{p}(l|y)$. If $\mathbf{P}$ is full row rank, then $\mathrm{PI}_n(Y;L) = \mathrm{MI}(Y;L)$ if and only if $\tilde{\mathsf{m}}_n(l|y) = \mathsf{p}(l|y)$. If $\mathbf{P}$ is not full row rank then one can build alternative models leading to $\mathrm{PI}_n(Y;L) = \mathrm{MI}(Y;L)$.*

Proof. Let $\tilde{\mathsf{m}}_n(l|y)$ be a conditional probability distribution. Keeping the notations of Theorem 3, $\mathrm{PI}_n(Y;L) = \mathrm{MI}(Y;L)$ holds if and only if equality holds in Eq. 23, and therefore if and only if it holds in Eq. 22 for every l. By Lemma 3, this is equivalent to the existence of a positive vector k such that $\tilde{\mathsf{m}}_n(l|y) = k_l \cdot \mathsf{p}(l|y)$ holds for every y, l. Clearly, $\tilde{\mathsf{m}}_n(l|y) = \mathsf{p}(l|y)$ for all y, l if and only if all k_l's are equal to 1 (i.e., $\mathbf{k} = \mathbf{1}$). Now, for an arbitrary positive vector $\mathbf{k}$, the quantities $\tilde{\mathsf{m}}_n(l|y) = k_l \, \mathsf{p}(l|y)$ define valid conditional probabilities if and only if (i) they all belong to $[0, 1]$, and (ii) $\sum_l \tilde{\mathsf{m}}_n(l|y) = 1$ for every y. We show next that these conditions imply $\mathbf{k} = \mathbf{1}$ if and only if $\mathbf{P}$ is full row-rank, which will imply our result. Define the matrix $\mathbf{M}$ as $\mathbf{M}_{l,y} = \tilde{\mathsf{m}}_n(l|y)$ and the diagonal matrix $\mathbf{K}$ as $\mathbf{K}_{ll} = k_l$ (so that $\mathbf{k} = \mathbf{K}\mathbf{1}$). Condition (ii) can be rewritten as $\mathbf{1}^T \mathbf{M} = \mathbf{1}^T = \mathbf{1}^T \mathbf{P}$, and $\tilde{\mathsf{m}}_n(l|y) = k_l \, \mathsf{p}(l|y)$ can be re-expressed as $\mathbf{M} = \mathbf{K}\mathbf{P}$. Therefore:

$$(k - 1)^T \mathbf{P} = (\mathbf{1}^T \mathbf{K} - \mathbf{1}^T)\mathbf{P} = \mathbf{1}^T \mathbf{K}\mathbf{P} - \mathbf{1}^T \mathbf{P} = \mathbf{1}^T \mathbf{M} - \mathbf{1}^T \mathbf{P} = \mathbf{1}^T - \mathbf{1}^T = 0.$$

That is, the vector $(k - 1)^T$ is in the left-kernel of $\mathbf{P}$. Hence, if $\mathbf{P}$ has full-row rank, the only vector $\mathbf{k}$ for which (ii) is satisfied is $\mathbf{k} = \mathbf{1}$. Otherwise, any vector of the form $\mathbf{k} = \mathbf{1} + \alpha v$ for $\alpha \neq 0$ and $v \neq 0$ in the left-kernel of $\mathbf{P}$ would lead $\tilde{\mathsf{m}}_n(l|y)$ to satisfy condition (ii). To finish the proof, we show that we can also have condition (i) satisfied. By taking a sufficiently small α, we can ensure that $\mathbf{k}$ is positive, and therefore that the $\tilde{\mathsf{m}}_n(l|y)$'s are non-negative. Because $\sum_l \tilde{\mathsf{m}}_n(l|y) = 1$ by condition (ii), this implies that $\tilde{\mathsf{m}}_n(l|y) \leq 1$ for every l, y and that condition (i) is satisfied. $\qquad\square$

Note that this full row rank condition may not be achieved in so-called Simple Power Analysis (SPA) attacks with "compressive" leakage functions. For example, imagine an implementation leaking the noise-free Hamming weight of an n-bit key. Then, the number of leakages (i.e., $n + 1$) is lower then the number of keys (i.e., 2^n) and $\mathbf{P}$ cannot have full row rank. By contrast, in the DPA setting, the amount of leakages that the adversary can observe is multiplied by the number of plaintexts (i.e., 2^n) and the matrix $\mathbf{P}_{(l,x),k} = \mathsf{p}(l, x|k)$ is expected to be of full row rank.

3.4   Discussion and Application of the Results

The previous theorems can be quite directly applied in a side-channel evaluation context. Yet the following clarifications are worth being pointed out before moving to experiments.

First and as previously mentioned, one technical difficulty that may arise is the presence of outliers (or simply rare events) leading to zero probabilities for the good key candidate, and therefore to a log(0) in the PI equation (for the HI equation, we assume $0 \cdot \log(0) = 0$). A simple heuristic to deal with these cases is to lower-bound such probabilities to $\frac{1}{n_t(k)}$ and to report the fraction of corrected probabilities (which vanishes as n increases) with the experimental results.

Second, the HI bound of Sect. 3.2 is stated for the empirical distribution that is straightforward to estimate in a discrete case with finite support thanks to histograms. In this respect, we observe that actual leakages are measured thanks to sampling devices (hence are inherently discrete and finite). We also refer to the fast leakage assessment methodology in [31] for a motivation why this may lead to performance gains for the evaluator. Yet, there is actually nothing specific to discrete distributions in the way we obtain this bound (up to the slightly different convergences discussed in the full version of the paper [3]). So it is applicable to continuous distributions and estimators. For example, we could replace the estimation of the discrete MI based on histograms that we use to compute the eHI by a Kernel-based one such as used in [7,24]). In the next section, we also consider a simplified (Gaussian) model family and show how the HI bound can be useful in this context.

4   Empirical Confirmation

4.1   Simulated Experiments

In order to demonstrate the relevance of the previous tools, we start by investigating a standard simulation setting where the evaluator/adversary exploits the leakages corresponding to several executions of the AES S-box. Our first scenario corresponds to a univariate attack against an unprotected implementation of this S-box, where the leakage samples are of the form:

$$l_i^1 = \mathsf{HW}\Big(\mathsf{S}(x \oplus k)\Big) + r_i,$$

with HW the Hamming weight function, and r_i a Gaussian distributed noise sample with variance σ^2. The noise level is a parameter of our simulations. For convenience (and simpler interpretation) we report it as a Signal-to-Noise Ratio (SNR) which is defined as in [19] as the variance of the signal (which is worth 2 in the case of a random 8-bit Hamming weight value) divided by σ^2.

Our second simulated scenario corresponds to a bivariate attack against the same unprotected implementation of the AES S-box, where the leakage vectors are of the form:

$$l_i^2 = \Big[\mathsf{HW}(x \oplus k) + r_i; \; \mathsf{HW}\Big(\mathsf{S}(x \oplus k)\Big) + r_i'\Big].$$

Finally, our third scenario corresponds to a univariate attack against a masked (i.e., secret shared [4]) implementation of this S-box, where the leakage samples are of the form:

$$l_i^3 = \left[\mathsf{HW}\Big(\mathsf{S}(x \oplus k) \oplus q\Big) + \mathsf{HW}(q) + r_i \right],$$

with q a secret mask picked up uniformly at random by the leaking device.

The results of our first scenario for high and medium SNRs are in Fig. 1, where we plot the MI (that is known since we are in a simulated setting), the eHI, the ePI (considered in our bounds) and the Gaussian PI (gPI) which is the PI corresponding to a Gaussian leakage model. The IT metrics are plot in function of the number of traces in the profiling set n.[5] As expected, the eHI provides an average upper bound that converges monotonically towards the MI, and the ePI provides a lower bound. Besides, the gPI converges rapidly towards the true MI since in our simulations, the leakages are generated based on a Gaussian distribution. So making this additional assumption in such an ideal setting allows faster model convergence without information loss.

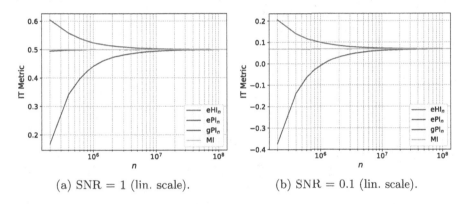

(a) SNR = 1 (lin. scale).   (b) SNR = 0.1 (lin. scale).

Fig. 1. Simulations, unprotected S-box, high & medium SNRs, univariate.

These results are confirmed with the similar plots given in Fig. 2 for a lower SNR of 0.01. For readability, the right plot switches to a logarithmic scale for the Y axis. It illustrates a context where it is possible to formally bound the mutual information to values lower than 10^{-2}.

Figures 1 and 2 correspond to simple (unprotected, univariate) cases where the estimation of the empirical distribution (despite significantly more expensive than the one of a Gaussian distribution) leads to reasonably tight bounds for the MI. We complement this observation with experiments corresponding to

---

[5] We use $n_t = n$, which leads to good estimations since the number of measurements needed to estimate a model is usually larger than the number of leakages needed to recover the key with a well-estimated model [32].

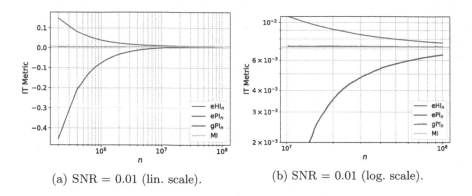

(a) SNR = 0.01 (lin. scale).   (b) SNR = 0.01 (log. scale).

Fig. 2. Simulations, unprotected S-box, low SNR, univariate.

our second (unprotected, bivariate) context. As illustrated in Fig. 3 for medium and low SNRs, this more challenging context leads to considerably less tight bounds, which can be explained by the (much) slower convergence of multivariate histograms. Note that we could not reach a positive ePI with $n = 10^7$ in this case (and the gPI still does it rapidly).

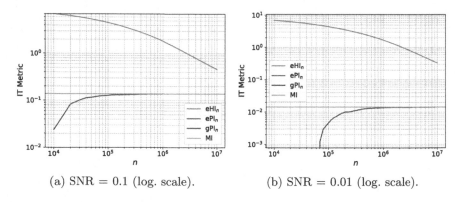

(a) SNR = 0.1 (log. scale).   (b) SNR = 0.01 (log. scale).

Fig. 3. Simulations, unprotected S-box, medium & low SNR, bivariate.

We finally report the results of the simulated masked implementation in Fig. 4 for very high and high SNRs. The very high SNR case is intended to illustrate a context where the Gaussian assumption is not satisfied (since the masked leakage distribution is actually a Gaussian mixture), so that the gPI is considerably lower than the ePI. By contrast, and as observed (for example) in [14], Fig. 1 (right), this Gaussian approximation becomes correct and the gPI gets close to the ePI as the noise increases, which we also see on the right part of Fig. 4.
An open source code allowing to reproduce these results is given in [1].

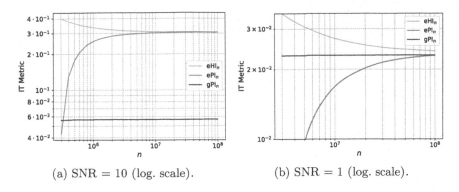

(a) SNR = 10 (log. scale).   (b) SNR = 1 (log. scale).

Fig. 4. Simulations, masked S-box, very high & high SNR, univariate.

4.2   Real Measurements

We complement the previous simulated experiments with analyzes performed on actual measurements obtained from an FPGA implementation of the AES S-box. In order to instantiate a noise parameter as in our simulations, we consider different architectures for this purpose: the target S-box is computed in parallel with $\pi \in \{0, 3, 7, 11)$ other S-boxes whose computations (for random inputs) generate "algorithmic noise". We implemented our design on a SAKURA-X board embedding a Xilinx Kintex-7 FPGA. The target device was running at 4 MHz and sampled at 500 ms/s (i.e., 125 leakage points per cycle). We split our experiments in two parts. In a first part, we consider a univariate evaluation (similar to the first setting of our simulated setup) allowing reasonably tight worst-case bounds. In a second part, we consider a highly multivariate evaluation (i.e., an adversary exploiting all the 125 points of each clock cycle) and discuss how to connect this context with nearly worst-case security arguments for (e.g., masked) cryptographic implementations.

Univariate analyses & theoretical worst-case bounds. The eHI/ePI bounds computed for the most informative leakage points of our measurements for $\pi = 0$ and 7 are in Fig. 5. The $\pi = 3$ and 11 cases are given in the full version of the paper [3]. We again observe that it is possible to obtain reasonably tight bounds (e.g., to bound the MI below 10^{-1} which is a sufficient noise for the masking countermeasure to be effective). Yet, as π increases and the MI decreases, we also see that tightening the bounds becomes increasingly data-intensive.

In view of the important amount of samples n needed to bound the MI, and of the popularity of the Gaussian assumption in SCAs [5], we additionally considered the Gaussian HI (gHI) which is the HI corresponding to a Gaussian model, and evaluated it based on the formula:

$$\text{approx-gHI}_n(Y, L) = -\frac{1}{2} \cdot \log_2 \left(1 - \rho(M, L)^2 \right), \tag{24}$$

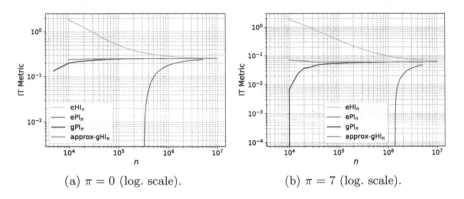

(a) $\pi = 0$ (log. scale).   (b) $\pi = 7$ (log. scale).

Fig. 5. Actual measurements, unprotected S-box, univariate.

where ρ is Pearson's correlation coefficient, L the leakage random variable (as previously) and M the model random variable. As discussed in [19], $\rho(Y, M)$ can be related to the leakages' SNR, which (in the case of Gaussian leakages) can be linked to the MI metric [11]. As observed in [21], the formula holds well for noisy Hamming weight leakages in case of "reasonably small" correlations values (i.e., typically $\rho < 0.1$). The latter is confirmed in our experiments of Figs. 5. Namely, these figures first illustrate that the gHI is also an upper bound for the gPI and converges monotonically (as expected from the results in Sect. 3). They additionally show that the gHI and gPI are very close to the worst-case MI in our experimental setting. The latter is particularly interesting since the gHI converges very fast compared to the other metrics.

Multivariate analyzes and efficient evaluations. Ultimately, an evaluator would be interested in efficiently and tightly bounding the total amount of information provided by his leakage points. As clear from the Sect. 4.1 (and the bivariate analysis of Fig. 3), obtaining tight MI bounds with two dimensions is already data-intensive. Hence, applying such a straightforward approach to our measurements where each clock cycle has 125 points is unlikely to provide any tight result. So here as well, we considered the multivariate gHI as a useful alternative (yet, this time without possibility to compare it to the eHI). For this purpose, we use the formula for the differential entropy of a multivariate Gaussian distribution:

$$\text{gH}(\boldsymbol{Z}) = \frac{\frac{1}{2} \log \left(\det(2\pi e \boldsymbol{\Sigma}) \right)}{\log(2)}, \tag{25}$$

where $\boldsymbol{\Sigma}$ is the covariance matrix of the Gaussian-distributed random variable $\boldsymbol{Z}$, $\det(.)$ denotes the matrix determinant and the $\log(2)$ of the denominator is to obtain a value in bits. We then used this standard formula to approximate the multivariate gHI as:

$$\text{MV approx-gHI}_n(Y, \boldsymbol{L}) = \text{gH}(\boldsymbol{M}) + \text{gH}(\boldsymbol{L}) - \text{gH}(\boldsymbol{M}; \boldsymbol{L}), \tag{26}$$

which is the multivariate generalization of Eq. 24. Note that as in Eq. 24, this approximation is based on the (multivariate) model random variable, which captures the possibility that different leakage points can have different leakage behaviors despite depending on the same Y.

Note also that as the number of dimensions increases, using such an approximation is increasingly useful from the time complexity viewpoint. Indeed, while the univariate gHI can be computed directly by integration, computing the multivariate gHI in our experimental case study (where we exploit the measurements of two clock cycles corresponding to 250 leakage points) would require integrating a 250-dimension distribution. By contrast, evaluating Eq. 26 only requires estimating the covariances matrices of the model, leakages and their joint distribution.

The approximations of the multivariate gHI for the cases $\pi = 3$ and 11 are in Fig. 6. The $\pi = 0$ and 7 cases are given in the full version of the paper [3]. For completeness, the plots first report the univariate gHI for each time sample (in red). The multivariate Gaussian approximations of Eq. 26 are then reported in purple in a cumulative manner: the value for time sample x corresponds to the x-variate estimation for dimensions 1 to x. Eventually, we added a conservative bound in blue, based on the assumption that each leakage point provides independent information and is summed. Those results are practically-relevant for two main reasons:

- First, they allow estimating the information of a very powerful yet realistic, close to worst-case adversary (since the univariate gHI is close to the eHI) in a more accurate (and less conservative) manner than bounds obtained based on an independence assumption. For example, the most informative point of Fig. 6(b) has a (univariate) gHI of $4 \cdot 10^{-2}$ while our approximation of the multivariate gHI is worth $2 \cdot 10^{-1}$ (i.e., a factor 5 more) and the bound would suggest a gHI larger than one (i.e., no security). So it illustrates a case where our approximation provides a useful intermediate between a too optimistic univariate analysis and a too conservative bound based on an independence assumption. We note that as for the univariate case, the approximation of Eq. 26 only holds for small HI values (i.e., typically below 0.1). For example, the approximation for the $\pi = 0$ case (given in the full version of the paper [3]) overestimates the information leakages. Yet, the quantitative analysis of those cases is anyway not very interesting (since they correspond to a too weak security).

- Second, these close to worst-case evaluations of the information leakages are obtained very efficiently (from the data complexity viewpoint). Taking again the $\pi = 11$ case for illustration, the Gaussian approximation of the 250-variate gHI already reaches a good convergence after approximately $n = 10^6$ samples (while the gPI is still negative with this amount of measurements). For completeness, we report the convergence plots of the multivariate gPI and gHI in the full version of the paper [3], where we can observe this faster convergence for lower number of dimensions (for which the gPI is positive).

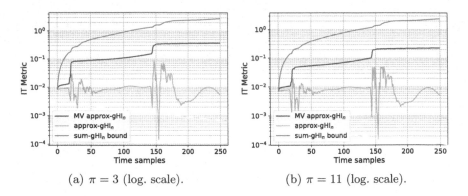

(a) $\pi = 3$ (log. scale).   (b) $\pi = 11$ (log. scale).

Fig. 6. Actual measurements, unprotected S-box, multivariate.

5 Conclusions

This paper provides first quantitative tools to bound the information leakages exploited in SCAs, taking into account the risk of a "false sense of security" due to incorrect assumptions about the leakage distributions. In case of low-dimensional leakages, we are able to formally bound the amount of information obtained on a target random variable. In case of high-dimensional leakages (which typically happen in case of strong adversaries trying to exploit all the information in power or electromagnetic measurements), tightening these bounds usually requires an unrealistic amount of data. Yet, even in these cases, our tools can be used to approximate the information provided by more specialized (close to worst-case) adversaries, by exploiting simplifying (e.g., Gaussian) assumptions. As a result, a natural approach to leakage certification is to mix (*i*) a low-dimension analysis estimating both the empirical and (for example) the Gaussian HI and PI metrics, in order to gauge the quality of the simplifying (e.g., Gaussian) assumption and (*ii*) a high-dimension analysis based on the simplifying assumption(s) only. Such an approach can considerably speed up security evaluations. First, estimating an HI bound is significantly less expensive than estimating the PI, both in terms of data complexity (as clear from the convergence plots of the previous section) and in terms of time complexity. For example, the multivariate gHI estimations of Sect. 4.2 are obtained within minutes of computations on a desktop computer whereas the gPI estimations take several hours (due to their expensive cross-validation step). Next, such information theoretic metrics can be used to bound the success rate of actual side-channel attacks much faster than by directly mounting attacks. These bounds can be used both in the context of standard divide-and-conquer adversaries as usually considered in current security evaluations (e.g., using the formulas in [11]), and for analyzing more advanced adversaries trying to combine the information leakages beyond the operations that can be easily guessed by a divide-and-conquer adversary (e.g., using the Local Random Probing Model in [16]). We believe these tools are important ingredients to strengthen the understanding of side-channel security evaluations and the design of countermeasures with strong security guarantees. We also believe they are of general interest and could find applications in other contexts such as timing attacks or privacy-related applications [23].

Acknowledgments. The authors thank Philippe Delsarte for stimulating discussions and Carolyn Whitnall for useful feedback on the HI/PI definitions and comments on early versions of this manuscript. Julien Hendrickx holds a WBI.World excellence fellowship. François-Xavier Standaert is a Senior Research Associate of the Belgian Fund for Scientific Research (FNRS-F.R.S.). This work has been funded in parts by the EU through the ERC project SWORD (Consolidator Grant 724725) and the H2020 project REASSURE, and by a Concerted Research Action of the "Communauté Française de Belgique".

References

1. https://github.com/obronchain/Leakage_Certification_Revisited
2. Brier, E., Clavier, C., Olivier, F.: Correlation power analysis with a leakage model. In: Joye, M., Quisquater, J.-J. (eds.) CHES 2004. LNCS, vol. 3156, pp. 16–29. Springer, Heidelberg (2004). https://doi.org/10.1007/978-3-540-28632-5_2
3. Bronchain, O., Hendrickx, J.M., Massart, C., Olshevsky, A., Standaert, F.: Leakage certification revisited: bounding model errors in side-channel security evaluations. IACR Cryptology ePrint Archive 2019, p. 132 (2019)
4. Chari, S., Jutla, C.S., Rao, J.R., Rohatgi, P.: Towards sound approaches to counteract power-analysis attacks. In: Wiener, M. (ed.) CRYPTO 1999. LNCS, vol. 1666, pp. 398–412. Springer, Heidelberg (1999). https://doi.org/10.1007/3-540-48405-1_26
5. Chari, S., Rao, J.R., Rohatgi, P.: Template attacks. In: Kaliski, B.S., Koç, K., Paar, C. (eds.) CHES 2002. LNCS, vol. 2523, pp. 13–28. Springer, Heidelberg (2003). https://doi.org/10.1007/3-540-36400-5_3
6. Chatzikokolakis, K., Chothia, T., Guha, A.: Statistical measurement of information leakage. In: Esparza, J., Majumdar, R. (eds.) TACAS 2010. LNCS, vol. 6015, pp. 390–404. Springer, Heidelberg (2010). https://doi.org/10.1007/978-3-642-12002-2_33
7. Chothia, T., Guha, A.: A statistical test for information leaks using continuous mutual information. In: Proceedings of the 24th IEEE Computer Security Foundations Symposium, CSF 2011, Cernay-la-Ville, France, 27–29 June 2011, pp. 177–190. IEEE Computer Society (2011)
8. Cover, T.M., Thomas, J.A.: Elements of Information Theory, 2nd edn. Wiley, New York (2006)
9. Domingos, P.M.: A unified bias-variance decomposition and its applications. In: Langley, P. (ed) Proceedings of the Seventeenth International Conference on Machine Learning (ICML 2000), Stanford University, Stanford, CA, USA, 29 June–2 July 2000, pp. 231–238. Morgan Kaufmann (2000)
10. Duc, A., Dziembowski, S., Faust, S.: Unifying leakage models: from probing attacks to noisy leakage. In: Nguyen and Oswald [25], pp. 423–440
11. Duc, A., Faust, S., Standaert, F.-X.: Making masking security proofs concrete. In: Oswald, E., Fischlin, M. (eds.) EUROCRYPT 2015. LNCS, vol. 9056, pp. 401–429. Springer, Heidelberg (2015). https://doi.org/10.1007/978-3-662-46800-5_16
12. Durvaux, F., Standaert, F., Pozo, S.M.D.: Towards easy leakage certification: extended version. J. Cryptographic Eng. **7**, 129–147 (2017)

13. Durvaux, F., Standaert, F., Veyrat-Charvillon, N.: How to certify the leakage of a chip? In: Nguyen and Oswald [25], pp. 459–476
14. Grosso, V., Standaert, F.-X., Prouff, E.: Low entropy masking schemes, revisited. In: Francillon, A., Rohatgi, P. (eds.) CARDIS 2013. LNCS, vol. 8419, pp. 33–43. Springer, Cham (2014). https://doi.org/10.1007/978-3-319-08302-5_3
15. Guilley, S., Heuser, A., Rioul, O., Standaert, F.: Template attacks, optimal distinguishers and the perceived information metric, Cryptarchi (2015). https://perso.uclouvain.be/fstandae/PUBLIS/162.pdf
16. Guo, Q., Grosso, V., Standaert, F.: Modeling soft analytical side-channel attacks from a coding theory viewpoint. IACR Cryptology ePrint Archive 2018, p. 498 (2018)
17. Lange, J., Massart, C., Mouraux, A., Standaert, F.: Side-channel attacks against the human brain: the PIN code case study (extended version). Brain Inform. **5**, 12 (2018)
18. Lerman, L., Veshchikov, N., Markowitch, O., Standaert, F.: Start simple and then refine: bias-variance decomposition as a diagnosis tool for leakage profiling. IEEE Trans. Comput. **67**, 268–283 (2018)
19. Mangard, S.: Hardware countermeasures against DPA – a statistical analysis of their effectiveness. In: Okamoto, T. (ed.) CT-RSA 2004. LNCS, vol. 2964, pp. 222–235. Springer, Heidelberg (2004). https://doi.org/10.1007/978-3-540-24660-2_18
20. Mangard, S., Oswald, E., Popp, T.: Power Analysis Attacks - Revealing the Secrets of Smart Cards, 1st edn. Springer, Heidelberg (2007). https://doi.org/10.1007/978-0-387-38162-6
21. Mangard, S., Oswald, E., Standaert, F.: One for all - all for one: unifying standard differential power analysis attacks. IET Inf. Secur. **5**, 100–110 (2011)
22. Martin, D.P., O'Connell, J.F., Oswald, E., Stam, M.: Counting keys in parallel after a side channel attack. In: Iwata, T., Cheon, J.H. (eds.) ASIACRYPT 2015. LNCS, vol. 9453, pp. 313–337. Springer, Heidelberg (2015). https://doi.org/10.1007/978-3-662-48800-3_13
23. Massart, C., Standaert, F.: Revisiting location privacy from aside-channel analysis viewpoint (extended version). IACR Cryptology ePrint Archive 2019, p. 467 (2019)
24. Mather, L., Oswald, E., Bandenburg, J., Wójcik, M.: Does my device leak information? an *a priori* statistical power analysis of leakage detection tests. In: Sako, K., Sarkar, P. (eds.) ASIACRYPT 2013. LNCS, vol. 8269, pp. 486–505. Springer, Heidelberg (2013). https://doi.org/10.1007/978-3-642-42033-7_25
25. Nguyen, P.Q., Oswald, E. (eds.): EUROCRYPT 2014. LNCS, vol. 8441. Springer, Heidelberg (2014). https://doi.org/10.1007/978-3-642-55220-5
26. Paninski, L.: Estimation of entropy and mutual information. Neural Comput. **15**, 1191–1253 (2003)
27. Poussier, R., Standaert, F.-X., Grosso, V.: Simple key enumeration (and rank estimation) using histograms: an integrated approach. In: Gierlichs, B., Poschmann, A.Y. (eds.) CHES 2016. LNCS, vol. 9813, pp. 61–81. Springer, Heidelberg (2016). https://doi.org/10.1007/978-3-662-53140-2_4
28. Prouff, E., Rivain, M.: Masking against side-channel attacks: a formal security proof. In: Johansson, T., Nguyen, P.Q. (eds.) EUROCRYPT 2013. LNCS, vol. 7881, pp. 142–159. Springer, Heidelberg (2013). https://doi.org/10.1007/978-3-642-38348-9_9

29. Renauld, M., Standaert, F.-X., Veyrat-Charvillon, N.: Algebraic side-channel attacks on the AES: why time also matters in DPA. In: Clavier, C., Gaj, K. (eds.) CHES 2009. LNCS, vol. 5747, pp. 97–111. Springer, Heidelberg (2009). https:// doi.org/10.1007/978-3-642-04138-9_8
30. Renauld, M., Standaert, F.-X., Veyrat-Charvillon, N., Kamel, D., Flandre, D.: A formal study of power variability issues and side-channel attacks for nanoscale devices. In: Paterson, K.G. (ed.) EUROCRYPT 2011. LNCS, vol. 6632, pp. 109–128. Springer, Heidelberg (2011). https://doi.org/10.1007/978-3-642-20465-4_8
31. Reparaz, O., Gierlichs, B., Verbauwhede, I.: Fast leakage assessment. In: Fischer, W., Homma, N. (eds.) CHES 2017. LNCS, vol. 10529, pp. 387–399. Springer, Cham (2017). https://doi.org/10.1007/978-3-319-66787-4_19
32. Standaert, F.-X., Koeune, F., Schindler, W.: How to compare profiled side-channel attacks? In: Abdalla, M., Pointcheval, D., Fouque, P.-A., Vergnaud, D. (eds.) ACNS 2009. LNCS, vol. 5536, pp. 485–498. Springer, Heidelberg (2009). https://doi.org/ 10.1007/978-3-642-01957-9_30
33. Standaert, F.-X., Malkin, T.G., Yung, M.: A unified framework for the analysis of side-channel key recovery attacks. In: Joux, A. (ed.) EUROCRYPT 2009. LNCS, vol. 5479, pp. 443–461. Springer, Heidelberg (2009). https://doi.org/10.1007/978-3-642-01001-9_26
34. Veyrat-Charvillon, N., Gérard, B., Renauld, M., Standaert, F.-X.: An optimal key enumeration algorithm and its application to side-channel attacks. In: Knudsen, L.R., Wu, H. (eds.) SAC 2012. LNCS, vol. 7707, pp. 390–406. Springer, Heidelberg (2013). https://doi.org/10.1007/978-3-642-35999-6_25
35. Veyrat-Charvillon, N., Gérard, B., Standaert, F.-X.: Soft analytical side-channel attacks. In: Sarkar, P., Iwata, T. (eds.) ASIACRYPT 2014. LNCS, vol. 8873, pp. 282–296. Springer, Heidelberg (2014). https://doi.org/10.1007/978-3-662-45611-8_15
36. Veyrat-Charvillon, N., Standaert, F.-X.: Adaptive chosen-message side-channel attacks. In: Zhou, J., Yung, M. (eds.) ACNS 2010. LNCS, vol. 6123, pp. 186–199. Springer, Heidelberg (2010). https://doi.org/10.1007/978-3-642-13708-2_12

Security in the Presence of Key Reuse: Context-Separable Interfaces and Their Applications

Christopher Patton[✉] and Thomas Shrimpton[✉]

Computer and Information Science and Engineering, Florida Institute for Cybersecurity Research, University of Florida, Gainesville, USA
{cjpatton,teshrim}@ufl.edu

Abstract. Key separation is often difficult to enforce in practice. While key reuse can be catastrophic for security, we know of a number of cryptographic schemes for which it is provably safe. But existing formal models, such as the notions of joint security (Haber-Pinkas, CCS '01) and agility (Acar et al., EUROCRYPT '10), do not address the full range of key-reuse attacks—in particular, those that break the abstraction of the scheme, or exploit protocol interactions at a higher level of abstraction. This work attends to these vectors by focusing on two key elements: the *game* that codifies the scheme under attack, as well as its intended adversarial model; and the underlying *interface* that exposes secret key operations for use by the game. Our main security experiment considers the implications of using an interface (in practice, the API of a software library or a hardware platform such as TPM) to realize the scheme specified by the game when the interface is shared with other unspecified, insecure, or even malicious applications. After building up a definitional framework, we apply it to the analysis of two real-world schemes: the EdDSA signature algorithm and the Noise protocol framework. Both provide some degree of *context separability*, a design pattern for interfaces and their applications that aids in the deployment of secure protocols.

Keywords: Key reuse · APIs · Diffie-Hellman · EdDSA · Noise

1 Introduction

The principle of *key separation*, or ensuring that distinct cryptographic functionalities use distinct keys, is a widely accepted tenet of applied cryptography. It appears to be difficult to follow, however, as there are many instances of *key reuse* in deployed cryptosystems, some having significant impact on the security of applications. There are a number of practical matters that lead to key resuse. First, operational requirements of the system often demand some degree of it. For example, it is common to use a signing key deployed for TLS [32] in other protocols, as this is permitted by certificate authorities and avoids the cost of certifying a distinct key for each protocol. But doing so has side effects that

© International Association for Cryptologic Research 2019
A. Boldyreva and D. Micciancio (Eds.): CRYPTO 2019, LNCS 11692, pp. 738–768, 2019.
https://doi.org/10.1007/978-3-030-26948-7_26

must be addressed in the design of these protocols, as well as the interface that exposes the key to applications [9]. Second, it is often not clear what constitutes a "distinct functionality". Intel's Trusted Platform Module (TPM) standard [36] supports a variety of protocols for remote attestation that use an Intel-certified key stored on chip. The TPM exposes a core set of operations involving this key via its application-programming interface (API), which applications make calls to in order to implement attestation schemes. But the requirement to support so many protocols has lead to a flexibile API with subtle vulnerabilities [2,12].

Prior work sheds light on when key reuse is safe among specific primitives. Haber and Pinkas [16] introduce the notion of *joint* security, which captures the security of a target cryptosystem (say, a digital signature scheme) in the presence of an oracle that exposes a related secret-key operation (say, the decryption operation of a public-key encryption scheme). Many widely used primitives are jointly secure, including RSA-PSS/OAEP [16] and Schnorr signatures/hybrid encryption [13]. Acar et al. [1] address the related problem of *agility*, where the goal is to identify multiple instantiations of a particular primitive (e.g., sets of AEAD schemes, PRFs, or signature schemes) that can securely use the same key material. But the range of potential key-reuse attacks goes well beyond what these works cover; attack vectors sometimes break the intended abstraction boundary of the scheme by exposing lower level operations [2,11], or involve unforeseen protocol interactions at a higher level of abstraction [9,18]. We believe that a comprehensive treatment of key reuse can and should account for these attack vectors as well.

To this end, we propose to surface the API as a first class security object. For our purposes, the API (or just "interface") is the component of a system that exposes to applications a fixed set of operations involving one or more secret keys. APIs are often the root-of-trust of applications: TPM, Intel's Software Guard Extensions (SGX), hardware security modules (HSMs), and even chip-and-pin credit cards all provide cryptographic APIs that aim to be trustworthy-by-design. But pressure to meet operational requirements, while exporting interfaces that are suitable for a variety of applications, often leads to vulnerabilities [2,10,13,21]. An analogous situation arises in the development of software that uses a cryptographic library; software engineers tend to trust that any use case *permitted* by an API is secure, without fully grasping its side-effects [27]. This phenomenon tends to lead to vulnerable code [3,28].

In light of these issues, this work seeks to develop security-oriented design principles for interfaces and their applications. We devise a definitional framework for reasoning about the security of an application when the interface it consumes is used in other, perhaps unintended or even insecure ways. We model these "other applications" very conservatively, as follows: to assist it in its attack against the target application, we assume the adversary has *direct* access to the underlying interface, allowing it to mount *exposed interface attacks* on a target application. We apply this framework to the design and analysis of two real-world cryptosystems: the EdDSA signature algorithm [17] and the Noise protocol framework [30]. In doing so, we elicit a property of interfaces and their applications we call *context separability*, which we will show to be an invaluable tool for secure protocol design.

The Full Version [29]. This is an extended abstract; the full version of this paper includes all deferred proofs, as well as additional results, remarks, and discussion.

The Framework. We begin by motivating our definitional viewpoint, which draws abstraction boundaries a bit differently than usual. Game-based notions of security [6] typically specify (in pseudocode) a game $\mathcal{G}$ that makes calls to a cryptographic scheme Π (a primitive or protocol, also specified in pseudocode). The game captures an attack model—that is, the capabilities and goal of the adversary—and establishes boundaries on the permitted uses of Π. Model-specific adversarial capabilities are captured as oracle procedures specified by $\mathcal{G}$, which the adversary may query during its attack. Its goal is formalized by an explicit winning condition that depends on its queries and the random choices of the game. The security of the scheme, when used as specified by $\mathcal{G}$, is measured by executing an adversary with $\mathcal{G}$.

Suppose that Π is specified in terms of calls to an underlying interface $\mathcal{I}$, which defines the set of operations that can be performed on the secret key. Our goal is to measure the security of Π in the sense of $\mathcal{G}$ when the adversary playing the game is also provided direct access to $\mathcal{I}$, i.e., when the adversary is able to mount exposed interface attacks on the security of Π that $\mathcal{G}$ codifies.

We formalize our syntax for interfaces and games in Sect. 3. Rather than refer explicitly to Π, we allow the game $\mathcal{G}$ to realize Π as pseudocode that makes calls to $\mathcal{I}$. Interfaces may expose conventional primitive operations like signing or decryption, or they may expose lower level operations that are composed into higher level ones by the game. (This is precisely what TPM does; more on this in Sect. 5.1.) Our syntax for interfaces admits operations on symmetric and asymmetric keys. In the latter case, all secret-key operations are handled by the interface, and all public-key operations are specified by the game.

Security Under Exposed Interface Attack. The objects of our study are an interface and a target application; we formalize the latter as a game that defines the scheme, how it is used, and what is its goal. With some details suppressed, Fig. 1 visualizes the execution flow of our main security experiment SEC/I, which acts as an analysis harness for an interface $\mathcal{I}$, game $\mathcal{G}$, and adversary $\mathcal{A}$. The experiment first generates the public and secret keys (pk, sk) as specified by $\mathcal{I}$, then runs $\mathcal{A}$ on input of pk and with access to oracles **Init**, **Call**, and **Final** used to "play" the game $\mathcal{G}$. The game is comprised of three algorithms: the first, $\mathcal{G}$.Init, takes pk as input and outputs the game's initial state; the second, $\mathcal{G}$.Call, specifies the capabilities of $\mathcal{A}$ in the game and advances the state in response to its queries; and the last, $\mathcal{G}$.Final, computes the game's winning condition and outputs a bit win. Both $\mathcal{G}$.Call and $\mathcal{G}$.Final are given access to $\mathcal{I}$ for performing secret key operations, and the adversary is given direct access to $\mathcal{I}$ via a fourth oracle **Op**. As usual [6], the adversary must call **Init** first and **Final** last; the outcome of the experiment is the value of win.

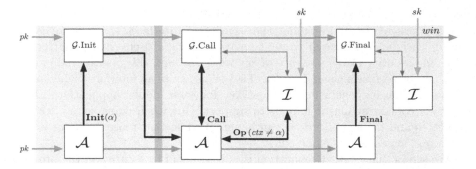

Fig. 1. Illustration of the SEC/I experiment, which has three "phases": first, the adversary $\mathcal{A}$ chooses the game context α and initializes the game $\mathcal{G}$; second, $\mathcal{A}$ plays $\mathcal{G}$ and interacts with $\mathcal{I}$; and third, $\mathcal{A}$ finalizes $\mathcal{G}$ and the experiment outputs the outcome *win*.

The central goal of our work is to measure the security "gap" between this and the "usual setting" in which the underlying interface is only used for the target application. This setting is formalized by the SEC experiment, which is defined just like SEC/I, except the adversary is denied access to **Op**. We will formalize both experiments in Sect. 4.

Context Separability. Security in our setting often requires a property we call context separability. Loosely, a context-separable interface is one whose operations can be bound to the context in which they are used. When *context separation* is enforced, this binding prevents context-separable *games* from interacting in unintended ways. Let us consider an illustrative example. TLS is designed to prevent signatures produced in the context of the protocol from being used in other applications, and vice versa. To accomplish this, whenever a message is to be signed, it is signed together with a short *context string* that uniquely identifies the protocol version and the signer (i.e., the client or server, see [32, Sect. 4.4.3]). This makes it unlikely that another protocol would *inadvertently* produce a signature that could be used in TLS, but nothing about the protocol or the signature scheme ensures this; depending on how signing operations are exposed and whether key separation is enforced, this could lead to practical cross-protocol attacks [9].

As reflected in both our syntax and security notions, our framework sheds formal light on the affect of these design challenges on security. In addition to the secret key and operand, an interface is formalized to take as input a context string *ctx*, which is meant to uniquely identify the application making the API call; correspondingly, a game is initialized with context that is meant to uniquely identify it. In the SEC/I experiment, the game $\mathcal{G}$ is initialized with an adversarially chosen *game context* string α, which the adversary may not use for its interface queries. (See Fig. 1.) This is akin to enforcing non-repeating nonces in the security experiment for symmetric encryption; in practice, it is an operational requirement that the environment must enforce.

On the Role of Context Separation. The high-level goal of our work is to provide a framework for reasoning about the security of interfaces that expose secrets to applications. We uncover context separability as a useful design pattern for achieving security in the presence of key reuse. In fact, this operational requirement can be seen as a generalization of key separation; an interface could enforce key separation by generating a unique key for each unique application (identified by a context string) it intends to support. But when doing so is infeasible, interfaces and their applications can be designed so that reuse is secure as long as context separation is enforced.

We stress that context separation is not essential to security in the presence of key reuse. We could have formalized other operational requirements; it may suffice to ensure that no single operation is used in multiple applications, or that distinct applications provide distinct inputs, etc. However, our choice to enforce context separation in the SEC/I experiment was not arbitrary. First and foremost, it reflects a design pattern often explicit (but sometimes implicit) in real standards, two of which we analyze in this paper (EdDSA and Noise). Second, it is our hope that clarifying this simple requirement will reduce some of the complexity inherent to protocol design.

A Composition Theorem. To measure the "gap" between SEC and SEC/I— that is, to measure the security impact of exposing the underlying interface—in Sect. 4.2 we formulate and prove sufficiency of a condition under which security in the former sense implies security in the latter. The GAP1 experiment is associated to an interface $\mathcal{I}$, a game $\mathcal{G}$, a simulator $\mathcal{S}$, and a distinguisher $\mathcal{D}$. The experiment allows $\mathcal{D}$ to play the game via **Init**, **Call**, and **Final** as above; likewise, the adversary can query the interface via **Op**. In the "real" world, **Op** exposes $\mathcal{I}$, but in the "simulated" world, the distinguisher's queries are evaluated by $\mathcal{S}$, which is given the public key but *no* access to $\mathcal{I}$. The adversary's goal is to distinguish between these two worlds. We show that for any $\mathcal{I}$ and $\mathcal{G}$, if $\mathcal{I}$ is both SEC and GAP1 secure for $\mathcal{G}$, then $\mathcal{I}$ is also SEC/I secure for $\mathcal{G}$ (Theorem 1(i)). Thus, proving GAP1 security of $\mathcal{I}$ for $\mathcal{G}$ will be our primary goal, as it succinctly characterizes conditions under which it is safe to compose applications that share the same interface.

We also consider the security impact of changing an interface, by, for example, exposing additional operations on the key. The GAP2 experiment is similar to GAP1, except it involves a *pair* of interfaces $(\mathcal{I}^1, \mathcal{I}^0)$. In the "real" world, both the game and distinguisher are given oracle access to $\mathcal{I}^1$; in the "simulated" world, the game is given an oracle for $\mathcal{I}^0$ and the distinguisher's **Op** queries are answered by the simulator, which is also given an oracle for $\mathcal{I}^0$. We prove that if $(\mathcal{I}^1, \mathcal{I}^0)$ is GAP2 secure for $\mathcal{G}$ and $\mathcal{I}^0$ is SEC/I secure for $\mathcal{G}$, then so is $\mathcal{I}^1$ (Theorem 1(ii)). We also formulate a *necessary* condition, wGAP2, that allows us to characterize key operations that are not generally safe to expose in an interface.

Application to Discrete Log Interfaces. We apply our framework to various *discrete log (DL) interfaces*, whose key pairs are $(p = g^s, s)$ where g is the generator of a finite, cyclic group. They are so named because the security of their applications is predicated on the hardness of computing discrete logarithms (in particular, $s = \log_g p$) in the given group. They are particularly interesting in our setting because they admit a wide variety of primitives and protocols.

Diffie-Hellman and EdDSA. A well-known design challenge for DL interfaces is avoiding accidental exposure of a static Diffie-Hellman (DH) oracle [2,12]: given p and an oracle that on input of q returns q^s, there is an algorithm [11] for computing s that is much faster than generic DL [31]. As a first exercise of our framework, we rule out the security of (inadvertently) exposing static DH in *any* DL interface by proving wGAP2 insecurity of their composition (Sect. 5.1). We then consider the security of the EdDSA signature scheme [8] in our setting (Sect. 5.2). The standardized version of this algorithm [17] admits variants that are context separable, allowing us to prove in the random oracle model (ROM) [5] that the signing operation is GAP1 secure for any game in which all signing and verification operations use the game context. We also show (in the ROM) that exposing the signing operation of *any* EdDSA variant in a DL interface that meets certain requirements is GAP2 secure in general.

Noise. Having addressed the security of these relatively simple operations, in Sect. 6 we turn to analyzing Noise [30], a framework for designing two-party secure-channel protocols. Participants in these protocols negotiate and execute *handshake patterns*, which define the sequence of messages sent between them and thereby the security of the communication channel they establish. We specify as an interface the set of *processing rules* that determine how each party consumes and produces messages, and how their state is updated as a side-effect. This allows handshake patterns to be executed by making calls to this interface.

Our results for Noise are largely positive. With a simple tweak of the processing rules, we are able to prove GAP1 security of our interface while making only minimal (and natural) assumptions about the target application. This implies, in particular, that all handshake patterns that can be executed by our interface are jointly secure (up to context separation). We cannot support all patterns, however, because some give rise to GAP1 distinguishing attacks in any interface that could be used to implement them. As a result of these limitations, our analysis leaves the security of key-reuse in Noise *as it is* an open question. Nevertheless, our work shows that Noise's approach to protocol design makes it possible to reason about protocol interactions in a very general way.

Finally, in the full version of this paper [29], we will directly address the composition of the security of using a key deployed for EdDSA in Noise (and vice versa).

Limitations of the Framework. Our syntax for games is such that a wide variety of security goals can be expressed with them. However, the execution semantics of games in the SEC/I experiment excludes some important settings, including the multi-user setting [7] and those captured by multi-stage adversaries [33]. In the full version of this paper [29] we will briefly discuss how to formalize these settings as extensions to the SEC/I experiment. In addition, our interfaces are all *stateless*, which we found necessary for composition in general. (This is in line with prior works that address related problems [33].)

Related Work. Here we highlight the works that inspired or are technically related to our framework and leave a broader overview of this area to the full version [29]. Our framework generalizes the setting of Shrimpton, Stam, and Warinschi [35], who study HSMs implementing the PKCS#11 standard for cryptographic APIs [15]. Their formulation of a "primitive" is closely related to our formulation of interfaces, and their framework allows for expressing arbitrary security goals for primitives, as ours does for interfaces.

Our security goals are reminiscent of joint security, and many of the proof techniques we use are borrowed from that area [13,16]. However, our notions are ultimately incompatible with theirs. To adapt our framework to the consideration of joint security, one would partition the set of operations exposed by the interface into those available to the target system (i.e., the game) and those available to the adversary.

The GAP2 notion can be viewed as a restricted form of indifferentiability [24]. In particular, the GAP2 experiment for $(\mathcal{I}^1, \mathcal{I}^0)$, $\mathcal{G}$, adversary $\mathcal{A}$, and simulator $\mathcal{S}$ is equivalent to the indifferentiability of $(\mathcal{I}^1, \mathcal{I}^0)$ with respect to the *specific* distinguisher $\mathcal{D}$ that is the composition of $\mathcal{G}$ and $\mathcal{A}$ prescribed by the GAP2 experiment. To be clear, this does *not* allow us to directly use the indifferentiability composition theorem. Our own result is about composing game $\mathcal{G}$ with interfaces $\mathcal{I}^1$ and, separately, $\mathcal{I}^0$; and although our composition theorem looks quite similar to [33, Theorem 1], the things being composed are not the same.

2 Pseudocode and Conventions

This section enumerates our conventions for pseudocode, algorithms, adversaries, and experiments. The reader may wish to skip this section and refer to it later as needed.

Pseudocode. Our pseudocode is based on Rogaway and Stegers [34]. Variables are statically typed. Available types are **set** (a set), **tup** (a tuple), **bool** (an element of $\{0,1\}$), **int** (an element of $\mathbb{Z}$), and **str** (an element of $\{0,1\}^*$). In general, if $X \in \mathcal{X}$, then we say that X has type $\mathbf{elem}_\mathcal{X}$. Variables are declared with the keyword **dec**, e.g., **dec int** x; **str** A. Variables need not be explicitly declared, in which case their type must be inferable from their initialization (i.e., the first use of the variable in an assignment statement). There are two *compound* types. The first is associative arrays, denoted by "[]", which map tuples (that is, a finite sequence of quantities of any type) to values of a specific type. For example, **dec str** $\pi[]$ declares an associative array π whose values are strings. We let $\pi[k]$ and π_k denote the value in π associated with k. The second is **struct**, which is used to recursively define new types; see Fig. 7 for an example. We will also refer to the type of a procedure (i.e., an algorithm) by its interface. For instance, the type $\mathcal{A}(\mathbf{str}\ X, Y) \mapsto (\mathbf{int}\ i, \mathbf{str}\ A)$ indicates that $\mathcal{A}$ takes as input a pair of strings (X, Y) and outputs an integer i and a string A.

Nil and Bottom. Uninitialized variables implicitly have the value $\diamond$, read "nil". If a variable of one type is set to a value of another type, then the variable takes the value $\diamond$. The symbol $\diamond$ is interpreted as $\emptyset$ in an expression involving sets, as the 0-length tuple in an expression involving tuples, as 0 (i.e., false) in a boolean expression, as 0 in an expression involving integers, and as ε in an expression involving strings. A non-**bool** variable X is interpreted as "$(X \neq \diamond)$" (i.e., "X is defined") in a boolean expression. If X is an associative array, then $X \leftarrow \diamond$ "resets" the array so that $X_k = \diamond$ for all k. Likewise, if X is a **struct**, then $X \leftarrow \diamond$ sets each field of X to $\diamond$. The symbol $\perp$, read "bottom", can be assigned to any variable regardless of type. Unlike $\diamond$, its interpretation in an expression is always undefined, except that $X = \perp$ and $\perp = X$ should evaluate to true just in case the previous assignment to X was $\perp$. (We remark that $\perp$ has the usual semantics in cryptographic pseudocode.)

Represented Groups. We say that a group $\mathbb{G}$ is *represented* if $\diamond \notin \mathbb{G}$. We define an additional type, **elem**$_\mathbb{G}$, parameterized by a represented group $\mathbb{G}$. We emphasize that, unlike **set**, **tup**, **bool**, **int**, or **str**, using the symbol $\diamond$ in an expression involving values of this type is not well-defined, since $\diamond$ has no interpretation as an element of $\mathbb{G}$.

Refined Types. Variable declarations may be written as set-membership assertions. For example, **dec int** s; **elem**$_\mathbb{G} P$ may be written like **dec** $s \in \mathbb{Z}$; $P \in \mathbb{G}$. Where appropriate, these types may also be refined, e.g. **dec** $s \in \mathbb{N}$.

String and Tuple Operations. Let $|X|$ denote the length of a string (or tuple) X. We denote the i-th element of X by X_i or $X[i]$. We define $X \| Y$ to be the concatenation of X with string (or tuple) Y. Let $X[i{:}j]$ denote the sub-string (or sub-tuple) $X_i \| \cdots \| X_j$ of X. If $i \notin [1..j]$ or $j \notin [i..|X|]$, then define $X[i{:}j] = \diamond$. Let $X[i{:}] = X[i{:}|X|]$ and $X[{:}j] = X[1{:}j]$.

Encoding of Types. A value of any type can be encoded as a string. We will not define this encoding explicitly, but assume it possesses the following properties. Let $\underline{x_1, \ldots, x_m}$ denote the encoding of a tuple $(x_1, \ldots, x_m)$ as a string. Decoding is written as $\underline{x_1, \ldots, x_m} \leftarrow X$ and works like this (slightly deviating from [34, Sect. 2]): if there exist $y_1, \ldots y_n$ such that $X = \underline{y_1, \ldots, y_n}$, $m = n$, and each y_i has the same type as x_i, then set $x_i \leftarrow y_i$ for each $1 \leq i \leq m$. Otherwise, set $x_i \leftarrow \diamond$ for each $1 \leq i \leq m$. Let $\underline{x}_n$ denote the encoding of an integer $x \geq 0$ as an n-bit string. We write $\underline{x}_n \leftarrow X$ to denote decoding X as an n-bit, non-negative integer and assigning it to x. Finally, we say that a group $\mathbb{G}$ is v-*encoded* if it is represented and for all $X \in \mathbb{G}$ it holds that $|\underline{X}| = v$.

Passing Variables by Reference. It is customary in cryptographic pseudocode to pass all variables by *value*; we also permit variables to be passed by *reference*. (This idea is due to Rogaway and Stegers [34], but our semantics deviates from theirs.) Specifically, variables passed to procedures may be embellished with the symbol "&". If the variable appears on the left hand side of an assignment statement, then this immediately changes the value of the variable; when used in an expression, the variable is treated as its value. A procedure's interface makes explicit each input that is passed by reference. For example, in a procedure $\mathcal{A}(\&\textbf{int } x, \textbf{int } y) \mapsto \textbf{int } z$, variable y is passed by value, while x is passed by reference. For example, after executing $x, y \leftarrow 0$; $z \leftarrow \mathcal{A}(\&x, y)$, the value of x may be non-0, but y is necessarily equal to 0.

Algorithms, Experiments, and Adversaries. Algorithms are randomized unless stated otherwise. An algorithm is t-time if for every choice of random coins, the algorithm halts in at most t time steps.[1] When an algorithm $\mathcal{A}$ is deterministic we write $y \leftarrow \mathcal{A}(x)$ to denote executing $\mathcal{A}$ on input of x and assigning its output to y; if $\mathcal{A}$ is randomized, then we write $y \twoheadleftarrow \mathcal{A}(x)$. Let $[\mathcal{A}(x)]$ denote the set of possible outputs of $\mathcal{A}$ when run on input x. Algorithms may have access to one or more oracles, written as superscripts, e.g., $y \twoheadleftarrow \mathcal{A}^{\mathcal{O}, \cdots}(x)$. When this notation becomes cumbersome we may write $y \twoheadleftarrow \langle \mathcal{A} : \mathcal{O}, \ldots \rangle(x)$ instead. When we specify a procedure, if the procedure halts without an explicit **ret**-statement (i.e., a "return" statement), then it returns $\bot$.

We regard security experiments as algorithms whose output is always a bit. If "XXX" is an experiment associated with an adversary $\mathcal{A}$, we write $\mathbf{Exp}^{xxx}(\mathcal{A})$ to denote the event that the experiment is run with $\mathcal{A}$ and the output is 1, i.e., $\Pr\left[\mathbf{Exp}^{xxx}(\mathcal{A})\right]$ denotes the probability that XXX run with $\mathcal{A}$ outputs 1, where the probability is over the coins of XXX and $\mathcal{A}$. An adversary is an algorithm associated to a security experiment in which it is executed exactly once. (Thus, in this paper we restrict ourselves to the single-stage adversary setting [33].) Our convention will be that an adversary is t-time if its experiment is t-time. That is, an XXX-adversary $\mathcal{A}$ is t-time if $\mathbf{Exp}^{xxx}(\mathcal{A})$ is t-time.

Miscellaneous. Logarithms are base-2 unless the base is given explicitly. If $\mathcal{X}$ is a set, then we write $x \twoheadleftarrow \mathcal{X}$ to denote sampling x randomly from $\mathcal{X}$ according to some distribution associated to $\mathcal{X}$; if $\mathcal{X}$ is finite and the distribution is unspecified, then it is uniform.

3   Interfaces and Games

In this section we define the syntax for *interfaces* and *games*, the fundamental components of our framework. A game captures an attack model (the capabilities and goals of an adversary) as well as an intended use of cryptographic operations that are provided (via black-box calls) by an interface. Typically, this use will be to realize some cryptographic scheme (i.e., primitive or protocol) that is under attack.

Definition 1 (Interfaces). An *interface* is a pair of algorithms $\mathcal{I} = (\mathrm{Gen}, \mathrm{Op})$ defined as follows:

- $\mathrm{Gen}(\,) \mapsto \mathbf{str}\ pk, sk$. The *key generator* outputs pair of key strings.
- $\mathrm{Op}(\mathbf{str}\ sk, ctx, op, in) \mapsto \mathbf{str}\ out$. The *key operator* exposes operations involving the key sk. It takes as input the context ctx, the operation identifier op, and the operand in, and it outputs the result out.

For compactness, we may denote $\mathcal{I}.\mathrm{Op}(sk, ctx, op, in)$ by $\mathcal{I}_{sk}(ctx, op, in)$ in the remainder.   ◆

---

[1] What constitutes a "time step" depends on the model of computation, which we leave implicit.

In our security experiments, the "public key" pk will be made available to all parties, but the "secret key" sk will be kept private by the interface. We note that $pk = \varepsilon$ is allowed, so that symmetric-key operations are within scope.

Definition 2 (Games). A *game* is a triple of algorithms $\mathcal{G} = (\text{Init}, \text{Call}, \text{Final})$ defined as follows:

- $\text{Init}(\mathbf{str}\ pk, \alpha) \mapsto \mathbf{str}\ st, out$. This is the game *initiator*. It takes as input the public key pk and game context α and outputs the initial state st and a string out.
- $\text{Call}^{\mathcal{O}}(\&\mathbf{str}\ st, \mathbf{str}\ in) \mapsto \mathbf{str}\ out$. The *caller* is used to advance the state of an already initialized game. It abstracts all oracle queries except initialization and finalization. The first input is a reference to the game state, which may be updated as a side-effect of invoking the caller; the interpretation of the second input is up to the game. The caller expects access to an oracle $\mathcal{O}$, which we will call the *interface oracle*. It takes as input three strings and returns one.
- $\text{Final}^{\mathcal{O}}(\mathbf{str}\ st, in) \mapsto \mathbf{bool}\ r$. The *finalizer* is used to decide if a game is in a winning state. Its inputs are the game state st and a string in, which is used to compute the winning condition. Oracle $\mathcal{O}$ is as defined for the caller.

For compactness, we occasionally denote $\mathcal{G}.\text{Call}^{\mathcal{O}}(\&st, in)$ by $\mathcal{G}_{st}^{\mathcal{O}}(in)$. We say that $\mathcal{G}$ is *c-bound* if the caller and finalizer each make at most c calls to $\mathcal{O}$ during any one execution of the algorithm. ♦

4   Security Under Exposed Interface Attack

The goal of this work is to understand the security of cryptographic schemes when they are realized by an interface that may also be exposed to other, possibly insecure or (or even malicious) applications. The following experiment (SEC/I) captures this formally, allowing us prove or disprove security of a scheme (both codified by a game $\mathcal{G}$) when a given interface $\mathcal{I}$ is callable by both the game $\mathcal{G}$ and the adversary $\mathcal{A}$. An adversary in this experiment is said to be mounting an *exposed interface attack* on $\mathcal{G}$. We define another experiment (SEC) that captures the usual setting in which the adversary does not have this access.

Definition 3 (SEC/I and SEC security). Figure 2 defines two security experiments: SEC/I includes the boxed statement (but not the shaded one), and SEC includes the shaded statement (but not the boxed one). Both experiments begin by running the key generator $\mathcal{I}.\text{Gen}$ and executing the adversary $\mathcal{A}$ on input of the public key and with access to four oracle procedures:

- **Init** initializes $\mathcal{G}$ by calling the initiator $\mathcal{G}.\text{Init}$ on the public key and the game context chosen by $\mathcal{A}$ and returns the output out of the initiator.
- **Call** advances the game by invoking the caller $\mathcal{G}.\text{Call}$ on input in provided by $\mathcal{A}$ and with oracle access to the interface $\mathcal{I}.\text{Op}(sk, \cdot, \cdot, \cdot)$. It returns the output out of the caller.

$$\boxed{\mathbf{Exp}_{\mathcal{I},\mathcal{G}}^{\text{sec/i}}(\mathcal{A})} \ / \ \mathbf{Exp}_{\mathcal{I},\mathcal{G}}^{\text{sec}}(\mathcal{A})$$

1 **dec str** sk, st, α; **bool** win
2 $(pk, sk) \twoheadleftarrow \mathcal{I}.\text{Gen}(\,)$
3 $\boxed{\langle \mathcal{A}: \mathbf{Init}, \mathbf{Final}, \mathbf{Call}, \mathbf{Op} \rangle (pk)}$
4 $\langle \mathcal{A}: \mathbf{Init}, \mathbf{Final}, \mathbf{Call} \rangle (pk)$
5 **ret** win

Init(ctx)

6 $(st, out) \twoheadleftarrow \mathcal{G}.\text{Init}(pk, ctx)$
7 $\alpha \leftarrow ctx$; **ret** out

Final(in)

8 $win \twoheadleftarrow \mathcal{G}.\text{Final}^{\mathcal{I}.\text{Op}(sk,\cdot,\cdot,\cdot)}(st, in)$
9 **ret** win

Call(in)

10 **ret** $\mathcal{G}.\text{Call}^{\mathcal{I}.\text{Op}(sk,\cdot,\cdot,\cdot)}(\&st, in)$

Op(ctx, op, in)

11 **if** $ctx = \alpha$ **then ret** $\bot$
12 **ret** $\mathcal{I}.\text{Op}(sk, ctx, op, in)$

Fig. 2. The SEC/I and SEC experiments for interface $\mathcal{I}$, game $\mathcal{G}$, and adversary $\mathcal{A}$.

- **Op** exposes $\mathcal{I}.\text{Op}(sk, \cdot, \cdot, \cdot)$ to $\mathcal{A}$ directly with the restriction that each query use a context string ctx that is different from the game context used to initialize the game.
- **Final** finalizes $\mathcal{G}$ by running the finalizer $\mathcal{G}.\text{Final}$ on input in provided by $\mathcal{A}$ and setting win to the output and returning the value of win to $\mathcal{A}$.

The outcome of the experiment is the value of win when $\mathcal{A}$ halts. A valid SEC/I adversary makes a single query to **Init**, this being its first; it may then make any number of queries to **Call** and **Op**.[2] It completes its execution by making a single query to **Final**. We define the advantage of a (valid) SEC/I-adversary $\mathcal{A}$ in attacking $\mathcal{I}$ with respect to $\mathcal{G}$ as

$$\mathbf{Adv}_{\mathcal{I},\mathcal{G}}^{\text{sec/i}}(\mathcal{A}) = \Pr\left[\,\mathbf{Exp}_{\mathcal{I},\mathcal{G}}^{\text{sec/i}}(\mathcal{A})\,\right].$$

We call a SEC/I adversary (t, q_G, q_I)-resource if it is t-time and makes at most q_G and q_I queries to **Call** and **Op** respectively. We define the maximum advantage of any r-resource SEC/I-adversary as $\mathbf{Adv}_{\mathcal{I},\mathcal{G}}^{\text{sec/i}}(r)$. SEC security of $\mathcal{I}$ with respect to $\mathcal{G}$ is defined in kind, except that **Op** is not given to $\mathcal{A}$. We denote the advantage of SEC-adverseary $\mathcal{A}$ in attacking $\mathcal{I}$ with respect to $\mathcal{G}$ by $\mathbf{Adv}_{\mathcal{I},\mathcal{G}}^{\text{sec}}(\mathcal{A}) = \Pr\left[\,\mathbf{Exp}_{\mathcal{I},\mathcal{G}}^{\text{sec}}(\mathcal{A})\,\right]$, and we define $\mathbf{Adv}_{\mathcal{I},\mathcal{G}}^{\text{sec}}(r)$ as above. Informally, we say that $\mathcal{I}$ is SEC/I (resp. SEC) secure for $\mathcal{G}$ if every efficient SEC/I (resp. SEC) adversary has small advantage.

Finally, if each of $\mathcal{G}.\text{Call}$'s and $\mathcal{G}.\text{Final}$'s interface queries is a triple (α, op, in) such that α is the context with which the game was initialized, then we say $\mathcal{G}$ is *regular* for SEC/I (resp. SEC). ♦

Regular Games and Context Separation. We remark that a game being regular is a property of the execution semantics of the game in the experiment,

---

[2] Disallowing **Op** queries prior to **Init** is necessary for enforcing context separation. This restriction could be lifted by, say, allowing pre-**Init** access to **Op**, but demanding that none of these queries uses the (adversarially chosen) game context α.

$\mathbf{Exp}_{\mathcal{I},\mathcal{G}}^{\text{gap1}}(\mathcal{S},\mathcal{D})$	$\mathbf{Exp}_{\mathcal{I}^1,\mathcal{I}^0,\mathcal{G}}^{\text{gap2}}(\mathcal{S},\mathcal{D})$
1 **dec str** sk, st, σ, α; $b \twoheadleftarrow \{0,1\}$	12 **dec str** sk, st, σ, α; $b \twoheadleftarrow \{0,1\}$
2 $(pk, sk) \twoheadleftarrow \mathcal{I}.\text{Gen}(\,)$; $\sigma \twoheadleftarrow \mathcal{S}.\text{Init}(pk)$	13 $(pk, sk) \twoheadleftarrow \mathcal{I}^b.\text{Gen}(\,)$; $\sigma \twoheadleftarrow \mathcal{S}.\text{Init}(pk)$
3 $d \twoheadleftarrow \langle \mathcal{D}: \mathbf{Init}, \mathbf{Final}, \mathbf{Call}, \mathbf{Op}\rangle(pk)$	14 $d \twoheadleftarrow \langle \mathcal{D}: \mathbf{Init}, \mathbf{Final}, \mathbf{Call}, \mathbf{Op}\rangle(pk)$
4 **ret** $(d = b)$	15 **ret** $(d = b)$
Init(ctx)	**Init**(ctx)
5 $(st, out) \twoheadleftarrow \mathcal{G}.\text{Init}(pk, ctx)$	16 $(st, out) \twoheadleftarrow \mathcal{G}.\text{Init}(pk, ctx)$
6 $\alpha \leftarrow ctx$; **ret** out	17 $\alpha \leftarrow ctx$; **ret** out
Final(in)	**Final**(in)
7 **ret** $\mathcal{G}.\text{Final}^{\mathcal{I}_{sk}}(st, in)$	18 **ret** $\mathcal{G}.\text{Final}^{\mathcal{I}_{sk}^b}(st, in)$
Call(in)	**Call**(in)
8 **ret** $\mathcal{G}.\text{Call}^{\mathcal{I}_{sk}}(\&st, in)$	19 **ret** $\mathcal{G}.\text{Call}^{\mathcal{I}_{sk}^b}(\&st, in)$
Op(ctx, op, in)	**Op**(ctx, op, in)
9 **if** $ctx = \alpha$ **then ret** $\bot$	20 **if** $ctx = \alpha$ **then ret** $\bot$
10 **if** $b = 1$ **then ret** $\mathcal{I}_{sk}(ctx, op, in)$	21 **if** $b = 1$ **then ret** $\mathcal{I}_{sk}^1(ctx, op, in)$
11 **ret** $\mathcal{S}.\text{Op}^{\bot}(\&\sigma, ctx, op, in)$	22 **ret** $\mathcal{S}.\text{Op}^{\mathcal{I}_{sk}^0}(\&\sigma, ctx, op, in)$

Fig. 3. Top-left: the GAP1 experiment for interface $\mathcal{I}$, game $\mathcal{G}$, simulator $\mathcal{S}$, and adversary $\mathcal{D}$. Top-right: the GAP2 experiment for interfaces $\mathcal{I}^1$ and $\mathcal{I}^0$, $\mathcal{G}$, $\mathcal{S}$, and $\mathcal{D}$.

and not a syntactic property of the game itself. This is because an experiment might execute the game differently; for example, instead of invoking the initiator before the caller, the experiment could invoke the caller with state $st = \varepsilon$ each time. This may sound silly, but we have not given a syntactic condition on games that excludes this execution semantics. Because all experiments will run the game in the same way, we silently extend this definition of regularity to all experiments in the remainder of the paper. In our analyses in Sects. 5 and 6, we will prove SEC/I security with respect to regular games. This condition is sufficient for ensuring context sepparability between operations performed by the adversary via direct access to the interface and those performed by the game.

Indistinguishability Variants. We note that our definitions of SEC/I and SEC advantage are not appropriate for every game. For example, $\mathcal{G}$ might be a bit-*guessing* game (e.g., IND-CCA) in which the initiator flips a coin and the finalizer interprets its input as the adversary's guess. In order to normalize the adversary's advantage in such games, we define the IND-SEC/I advantage of SEC/I-adversary $\mathcal{A}$ as $\mathbf{Adv}_{\mathcal{I},\mathcal{G}}^{\text{ind-sec/i}}(\mathcal{A}) = 2\mathbf{Adv}_{\mathcal{I},\mathcal{G}}^{\text{sec/i}}(\mathcal{A}) - 1$. (Similarly for IND-SEC.)

4.1 Simulatability of an Interface

Intuitively, the "gap" between the SEC/I and SEC security of an interface $\mathcal{I}$ with respect to game $\mathcal{G}$ is driven by any extra leverage the attacker gains by interacting with $\mathcal{I}$ directly. In this section, we formalize an experiment that aims to measure the size of this gap for a given $\mathcal{I}$ and $\mathcal{G}$. We also define a related experiment that measures the relative security "gap" between a pair of interfaces $(\mathcal{I}_1, \mathcal{I}_0)$ with respect to a given game. This is particularly useful when the operations permitted by $\mathcal{I}_1$ are a superset of those permitted by $\mathcal{I}_0$. For example, in Sect. 5, we will use this notion to analyze the change in security when operations are added to an existing interface. Both of these experiments will make use of simulators, so let us first define these.

Definition 4 (Simulators). A simulator $\mathcal{S}$ is a tuple of algorithms (Init, Op) defined as follows:

- Init(**str** pk) $\mapsto$ **str** σ. The *initiator* takes as input a public key and outputs the simulator's initial state σ.
- Op$^{\mathcal{O}}$($\&$**str** σ, **str** ctx, op, in) $\mapsto$ **str** out. The *operator* takes as input a reference to the simulator state (which it may update as a side-effect) and a triple of strings (ctx, op, in) and outputs a string out. Oracle $\mathcal{O}$ is an interface oracle defined just as for games.

In the remainder, we may denote $\mathcal{S}.\mathrm{Op}^{\mathcal{O}}(\&\sigma, ctx, op, in)$ by $\mathcal{S}_\sigma^{\mathcal{O}}(ctx, op, in)$. We say that $\mathcal{S}$ is (t, q_I)-resource if each algorithm is t-time and the caller makes at most q_I queries to its oracle.   ◆

Definition 5 (GAP1/2 security). Figure 3 defines two experiments: GAP1 and GAP2. Each involves a simulator $\mathcal{S}$, an adversary $\mathcal{D}$, and a game $\mathcal{G}$; GAP1 involves a single interface $\mathcal{I}$, while GAP2 involves a pair interfaces $(\mathcal{I}_1, \mathcal{I}_0)$. Both begin by choosing a challenge bit b at random, executing the key generator ($\mathcal{I}.\mathrm{Gen}$ in GAP1 and $\mathcal{I}^b.\mathrm{Gen}$ in GAP2), and initializing the simulator via $\mathcal{S}.\mathrm{Init}$ on input of the public key. The adversary is then executed on input of the public key and with four oracles:

- **Init**, **Final**, and **Call** execute the game just like in the SEC/I experiment; interface queries are answered by $\mathcal{I}.\mathrm{Op}$ in GAP1 and $\mathcal{I}^b.\mathrm{Op}$ in GAP2.
- **Op** processes (ctx, op, in) as follows. If ctx is equal to the game context, then it returns $\bot$ (just as in SEC/I). If $b = 1$, then it returns $\mathcal{I}.\mathrm{Op}(sk, ctx, op, in)$ in GAP1 and $\mathcal{I}^1.\mathrm{Op}(sk, ctx, op, in)$ in GAP2; if $b = 0$, theni the oracle returns $\mathcal{S}.\mathrm{Op}^\bot(\&\sigma, ctx, op, in)$ in GAP1 and $\mathcal{S}.\mathrm{Op}^{\mathcal{I}^0_{sk}}(\&\sigma, ctx, op, in)$ in GAP2. (The "$\bot$" oracle given to $\mathcal{S}$ denotes the interface oracle that just returns $\bot$ on any query.)

The outcome of the experiment is the bit d output by $\mathcal{D}$ when it halts. A valid GAP1 (resp. GAP2) adversary makes a single query to **Init**, this being its first query; it may then make any number of queries to **Call** and **Op**. It completes its execution by making a single query to **Final**. We define the advantage of a (valid) GAP1-adversary $\mathcal{D}$ in attacking $\mathcal{I}$ with respect to $\mathcal{G}$ as

$$\mathbf{Adv}_{\mathcal{I},\mathcal{G}}^{\mathrm{gap1}}(\mathcal{S}, \mathcal{D}) = 2\Pr\left[\mathbf{Exp}_{\mathcal{I},\mathcal{G}}^{\mathrm{gap1}}(\mathcal{S}, \mathcal{D})\right] - 1.$$

We call an GAP1 adversary (t, q_G, q_I)-resource if it is t-time and makes at most q_G and q_I queries to **Call** and **Op** respectively. We define the maximum advantage of any r-resource GAP1 adversary (for a given $\mathcal{I}, \mathcal{G}, \mathcal{S}$) as $\mathbf{Adv}_{\mathcal{I},\mathcal{G}}^{\mathrm{gap1}}(\mathcal{S}, r)$.

Define $\mathbf{Adv}^{\mathrm{gap2}}_{\mathcal{I}^1,\mathcal{I}^0,\mathcal{G}}(\mathcal{S},\mathcal{D})$ and $\mathbf{Adv}^{\mathrm{gap2}}_{\mathcal{I}^1,\mathcal{I}^0,\mathcal{G}}(\mathcal{S},r)$ in kind. Informally, we say that $\mathcal{I}$ (resp. $(\mathcal{I}^1,\mathcal{I}^0)$) is GAP1 (resp. GAP2) secure for $\mathcal{G}$ if for every efficient GAP1 (resp. GAP2) adversary $\mathcal{D}$ there exists an efficient $\mathcal{S}$ such that $\mathcal{D}$ has small advantage.

Finally, we say that a simulator is *regular* for GAP1 (resp. GAP2) if each time it is called with input context ctx, each of its interface queries have the form (ctx, op, in) for some $op, in \in \{0,1\}^*$. ♦

4.2   The Composition Theorem

An interface $\mathcal{I}$ being GAP1 secure for $\mathcal{G}$ means that whatever information an SEC/I adversary learns in its attack against $\mathcal{G}$ it can (efficiently) compute on its own without interacting with the **Op** oracle. Thus, if $\mathcal{I}$ is both SEC and GAP1 secure for $\mathcal{G}$, then it should be that $\mathcal{I}$ is also SEC/I secure for $\mathcal{G}$. Relatedly, for any pair of interfaces $(\mathcal{I}^1,\mathcal{I}^0)$ and game $\mathcal{G}$, if $(\mathcal{I}^1,\mathcal{I}^0)$ is GAP2 secure for $\mathcal{G}$ and $\mathcal{I}^0$ is SEC/I secure for $\mathcal{G}$, then $\mathcal{I}^1$ is SEC/I-secure for $\mathcal{G}$, too. Theorem 1 makes these claims precise. To support upcoming results in Sects. 5 and 6, we state and prove our composition theorem in the ROM. So, let us first formalize the ROM in our setting.

The ROM. When modeling a function $H : \mathcal{X} \to \mathcal{Y}$ as a random oracle (RO) in an experiment, we declare an associative array $\mathbf{elem}_{\mathcal{Y}}\pi[]$ and a set $\mathcal{Q}$ (initially empty) and define three oracles: **P**, **Q**, and **R**. The last of these is the usual RO: on input of $X \in \mathcal{X}$, oracle **R** checks to see if π_X is defined (i.e., $\pi_X \neq \diamond$); if not, then it samples π_X from $\mathcal{Y}$ according to the distribution induced on $\mathcal{Y}$ by H. (Usually $\mathcal{Y}$ will be finite and the distribution will be uniform.) Finally, it returns π_X. We call an algorithm q_R-*ro-bound* if it makes at most q_R queries to **R** during any execution; a game, interface, or simulator is q_R-ro-bound if each of its constituent algorithms is q_R-ro-bound. Experiments are lifted to the ROM by providing each named algorithm oracle access to **R**. In addition, each query X to **R** made by the adversary is added to the set $\mathcal{Q}$.

Just as we measure an adversary's runtime using the experiment in which it is executed, our convention will be that an adversary's RO-query budget accounts for all queries to **R** made by it or any other algorithm (including the simulator) during the course of the experiment. That is, XXX-adversary $\mathcal{A}$ is q_R-ro-bound if $\mathbf{Exp}^{\mathrm{xxx}}(\mathcal{A})$ is q_R-ro-bound. We say an algorithm is $(r \,\|\, q_R)$-resource if it is r-resource and q_R-ro-bound. (Note that $r \,\|\, q_R$ is a tuple, since r is a tuple and q_R is a singleton.) Let $\psi : \{0,1\}^* \times \mathcal{X} \to \{0,1\}$ be a function. We say that a game $\mathcal{G}$ is ψ-*ro-regular* (for the associated experiment) if each of its RO queries $X \in \mathcal{X}$ satisfies $\psi(\alpha, X)$, where α is the game context used to initialize it in the experiment. Similarly, we say that an interface $\mathcal{I}$ is ψ-ro-regular if each of $\mathcal{I}.$Op's RO queries $X \in \mathcal{X}$ satisfies $\psi(ctx, X)$, where ctx is the provided context string.

The other two oracles (**P** and **Q**) are used to specify additional powers made available to simulators in security proofs. Oracle **P** takes as input a pair $(X,Y) \in \mathcal{X} \times \mathcal{Y}$ and sets $\pi[X] \leftarrow Y$, allowing the simulator to "program" the RO.

Oracle $\mathbf{Q}$ simply returns the set $\mathcal{Q}$ of RO queries made by the adversary so far, allowing the simulator to "observe" the adversary's RO queries as it makes them. We emphasize that $\mathbf{P}$ and $\mathbf{Q}$ formalize powers of the simulator that are usually left implicit, but are essential to certain proof techniques [13,16]. We introduce *oracle-relative* simulators as a means of formalizing the requirements of the simulator for composition.

Definition 6 (Oracle-relative simulators). Let $\mathcal{O}$ be an oracle in an experiment. An $\mathcal{O}$-*relative* simulator $\mathcal{S}$ is one for which both the initiator and operator expect oracle access to $\mathcal{O}$; we say that $\mathcal{S}$ is c-$\mathcal{O}$-*bound* if each algorithm makes at most c such queries on any execution. Let $\mathcal{X}$ and $\mathcal{Y}$ be sets and let $\mu_1, \mu_2 \geq 0$ be real numbers. In the ROM we say that a $\mathbf{P}$-relative simulator is (μ_1, μ_2)-*min-entropy* if for all $(X', Y') \in \mathcal{X} \times \mathcal{Y}$ and each query (X, Y) to $\mathbf{P}$, it holds that $\Pr\left[X = X'\right] \leq 2^{-\mu_1}$ and $\Pr\left[Y = Y'\right] \leq 2^{-\mu_2}$. ◆

Theorem 1. *Let $\mathcal{I}^1$ and $\mathcal{I}^0$ be interfaces, let $\mathcal{G}$ be a game, and let $H : \{0,1\}^* \to \{0,1\}^h$ be a function modeled as a random oracle. Let $q_G, q_I, q_R, t, c_I, c_R, c_P, s \geq 0$ be integers such that $s = O(t/(q_I+1))$, and let $\mu_1, \mu_2 \geq 0$ be real numbers such that $\mu_2 \leq h$. Let $\boldsymbol{r} = (t, q_G, q_I, q_R)$. Then, for every regular, $\mathbf{P}$- and $\mathbf{Q}$-relative simulator $\mathcal{S}$ that is (s, c_I, c_R)-resource, c_P-$\mathbf{P}$-bound, and (μ_1, μ_2)-min-entropy, it holds that*

(i) $\mathbf{Adv}^{\text{sec/i}}_{\mathcal{I}^1, \mathcal{G}}(\boldsymbol{r}) \leq \epsilon + \mathbf{Adv}^{\text{sec}}_{\mathcal{I}^1, \mathcal{G}}(O(t), q_G, \hat{r}_R) + \mathbf{Adv}^{\text{gap1}}_{\mathcal{I}^1, \mathcal{G}}(\mathcal{S}, \hat{\boldsymbol{r}})$ *and*

(ii) $\mathbf{Adv}^{\text{sec/i}}_{\mathcal{I}^1, \mathcal{G}}(\boldsymbol{r}) \leq \epsilon + \mathbf{Adv}^{\text{sec/i}}_{\mathcal{I}^0, \mathcal{G}}(O(t), q_G, c_I q_I, \hat{r}_R) + \mathbf{Adv}^{\text{gap2}}_{\mathcal{I}^1, \mathcal{I}^0, \mathcal{G}}(\mathcal{S}, \hat{\boldsymbol{r}})$,

where $\epsilon = (c_P q_I)(q_R/2^{\mu_1-1} + 2^{h-\mu_2} - 1)$, $\hat{r}_R = q_R + (c_R + c_P)(q_I + 1)$, and $\hat{\boldsymbol{r}} = (O(t), q_G, q_I, \hat{r}_R)$.

We must defer the proof to the full version [29]. Except for accounting for the simulator's powers in the ROM, the proof is closely related to [33, Theorem 1]. A few observations about this result are in order. First, we note that the ϵ term in the bound is only non-zero for simulators that program the RO. Second, it is sufficient for the domain points programmed by the simulator to be high min-entropy, but the bound is vacuous unless the corresponding range points are essentially uniform (because of the $2^{h-\mu_2}$ term in the expression for ϵ). When the programmed domain points are high min-entropy, neither the game nor the GAP2 distinguisher is likely to call the RO on the domain points programmed by the simulator. This fact, and the uniformity of programmed range points, allows us to compose the GAP1/2 distinguisher and the simulator $\mathcal{S}$ into a new SEC/I adversary, despite the fact that $\mathcal{S}$ may program the RO, but the SEC/I adversary may not. Likewise, the simulator "observing" the distinguisher's RO queries is not an issue for this composition.

A Necessary Condition for Theorem 1(ii). Condition (ii) of the composition theorem characterizes a sufficient property of $(\mathcal{I}^1, \mathcal{I}^0)$ and $\mathcal{G}$ such that it is safe to replace $\mathcal{I}^0$ with $\mathcal{I}^1$ (GAP2). This tells us, in particular, what sorts of operations are safe to expose in an API without breaking applications. We would also like a characterization of what sorts of operations are *not* safe, i.e., a necessary condition for Theorem 1(ii). We find that if wGAP2 security (defined below) does not hold for $(\mathcal{I}^1, \mathcal{I}^0)$, then there are games $\mathcal{G}$ for which $\mathcal{I}^1$ is not SEC/I secure, even if $\mathcal{I}^0$ is SEC/I secure for $\mathcal{G}$ (Theorem 2). We will use this result to rule out certain API-design choices in the remainder of the paper.

Definition 7 (wGAP2 security). The wGAP2 experiment is defined much like GAP2, except it does not involve a game. (Pseudocode for this definition is provided in the full version [29].) A wGAP2 adversary takes as input a string and outputs a bit and expects access to an interface oracle. Let $\mathcal{I}^1$ and $\mathcal{I}^0$ be interfaces, $\mathcal{S}$ be a simulator, and $\mathcal{D}$ be a wGAP2 adversary. The wGAP2 experiment for $(\mathcal{I}^1, \mathcal{I}^0)$, $\mathcal{S}$, and $\mathcal{D}$, denoted $\mathbf{Exp}_{\mathcal{I}^1,\mathcal{I}^0}^{\mathrm{wgap2}}(\mathcal{S},\mathcal{D})$, is defined just like the GAP2 experiment in Fig. 3, except that $\mathcal{D}$ is only executed with access to oracle **Op**, and since there is no game context, we remove line 3:20. Define the advantage of $\mathcal{D}$ in distinguishing $\mathcal{I}^1$ from $\mathcal{I}^0$ with respect to simulator $\mathcal{S}$ as $\mathbf{Adv}_{\mathcal{I}^1,\mathcal{I}^0}^{\mathrm{wgap2}}(\mathcal{S},\mathcal{D}) = 2\Pr\left[\mathbf{Exp}_{\mathcal{I}^1,\mathcal{I}^0}^{\mathrm{wgap2}}(\mathcal{S},\mathcal{D})\right] - 1$. Informally, we say that $(\mathcal{I}^1, \mathcal{I}^0)$ is wGAP2 secure if for every efficient adversary $\mathcal{D}$, there is an efficient simulator $\mathcal{S}$ such that $\mathcal{D}$'s advantage is small. We say $\mathcal{D}$ is (t, q_I)-resource if it is t-time and makes at most q_I queries to **Op**. ♦

Theorem 2 (wGAP2 is necessary for Theorem 1(ii)). *Let $\mathcal{I}^1$ and $\mathcal{I}^0$ be interfaces, let $\mathcal{B}$ be an SEC/I adversary, and let $\mathcal{D}$ be a wGAP2 adversary. There exist a game $\mathcal{G}$, SEC/I-adversary $\mathcal{A}$, and simulator $\mathcal{S}$ such that*

$$\mathbf{Adv}_{\mathcal{I}^1,\mathcal{I}^0}^{\mathrm{wgap2}}(\mathcal{S},\mathcal{D}) + \mathbf{Adv}_{\mathcal{I}^0,\mathcal{G}}^{\mathrm{sec/i}}(\mathcal{B}) \le \mathbf{Adv}_{\mathcal{I}^1,\mathcal{G}}^{\mathrm{sec/i}}(\mathcal{A}).$$

Moreover, if $\mathcal{D}$ is (s,r)-resource, $\mathcal{B}$ is (t, q_G, q_I)-resource, and $t = O(s)$, then $\mathcal{A}$ is $(O(t), q_G, q_I + r)$-resource and $\mathcal{S}$ is $(t, 1)$-resource.

Note that this result is easily lifted to the ROM. The proof (provided in the full version [29]) is in the same spirit as that of [24, Theorem 2], but there are some subtleties. The crux of the argument, which was adapted from Maurer, Renner, and Holenstein [24], is that the game $\mathcal{G}$ is defined using the adversary $\mathcal{D}$ so that the winning condition depends on $\mathcal{D}$ doing something "bad" (in particular, outputting 1). This allows us to relate $\mathcal{B}$'s advantage to $\mathcal{D}$'s. (We remark on the necessity of GAP1 itself for composition in the full version [29].)

5   Discrete Log Interfaces

In this section we bring our framework to bear on a few common operations for discrete log (DL) interfaces. We first recall some standard definitions from the cryptographic literature and formally define *DL* interfaces and *signing* interfaces.

Preliminaries. Refer to the CDH and GDH experiments in Fig. 4. Define the advantage of an adversary $\mathcal{A}$ in solving an instance of the *computational DH (CDH)* problem for $\mathbb{G}$ as $\mathbf{Adv}_{\mathbb{G}}^{\mathrm{cdh}}(\mathcal{A}) = \Pr[\mathbf{Exp}_{\mathbb{G}}^{\mathrm{cdh}}(\mathcal{A})]$ and let $\mathbf{Adv}_{\mathbb{G}}^{\mathrm{cdh}}(t)$ denote the maximum advantage of any t-time CDH-adversary. Define the advantage of an adversary $\mathcal{A}$ in solving an instance of the *gap DH (GDH)* problem [26] for $\mathbb{G}$

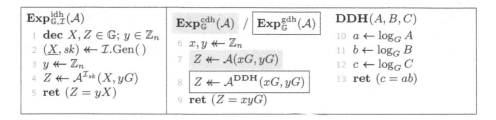

Fig. 4. Let $\mathbb{G} = \langle G \rangle$ be a represented, additive group of order n and let $\mathcal{I}$ be a DL interface for $\mathbb{G}$. Left: IDH problem for $(\mathbb{G}, \mathcal{I})$. Right: CDH and GDH problems for $\mathbb{G}$.

as $\mathbf{Adv}_{\mathbb{G}}^{\mathrm{gdh}}(\mathcal{A}) = \Pr[\mathbf{Exp}_{\mathbb{G}}^{\mathrm{gdh}}(\mathcal{A})]$. Depending on the group $\mathbb{G}$ and the model of computation, it may not be possible to evaluate $\mathcal{A}$'s **DDH** queries efficiently; for the purpose of accounting for $\mathcal{A}$'s resources, we will regard the discrete log computations on lines 4:7–8 as constant time operations. Let $\mathbf{Adv}_{\mathbb{G}}^{\mathrm{gdh}}(t, q)$ denote the maximum advantage of any t-time GDH-adversary that makes at most q queries to its **DDH** oracle. Informally, we say CDH (resp. CDH) is hard for $\mathbb{G}$ if the CDH (resp. GDH) advantage of any efficient adversary is small.

Define the CR advantage of an adversary $\mathcal{C}() \mapsto \mathbf{elem}_{\mathcal{X} \times \mathcal{X}}$ in finding collisions for function $H : \mathcal{X} \to \mathcal{Y}$ as $\mathbf{Adv}_H^{\mathrm{cr}}(\mathcal{C}) = \Pr[X \neq Y \wedge H(X) = H(Y) : (X, Y) \twoheadleftarrow \mathcal{C}()]$.

Definition 8 (DL and signing interfaces). Let $\mathbb{G} = \langle G \rangle$ be a represented, additive group of order n. A DL interface for $\mathbb{G}$ is an interface $\mathcal{I}$ with an associated *scalar computer*, a deterministic algorithm $\mathrm{Scal}(\mathbf{str}\ sk) \mapsto \mathbf{int}\ s$ such that for every $(pk, sk) \in [\mathcal{I}.\mathrm{Gen}()]$ it holds that $pk = \underline{sG}$, where $s = \mathcal{I}.\mathrm{Scal}(sk)$. We say that $\mathcal{I}$ is *simple* if $\mathcal{I}.\mathrm{Scal}(sk) = s$ just in case $sk = \underline{s}$.

A *signing interface* is an interface $\mathcal{DS}$ with an associated deterministic algorithm $\mathcal{DS}.\mathrm{Verify}(\mathbf{str}\ pk, ctx, M, T) \mapsto \mathbf{bool}\ v$, called the *verifier*, for which $T \in [\mathcal{DS}(sk, ctx, \mathrm{sig}, M)]$ iff $\mathcal{DS}.\mathrm{Verify}(pk, ctx, M, T) = 1$ for all $ctx, M, T \in \{0,1\}^*$ and $(pk, sk) \in [\mathcal{DS}.\mathrm{Gen}()]$. (This is analogous to the correctness condition for standard signature schemes.) We may denote $\mathcal{DS}.\mathrm{Op}(sk, ctx, \mathrm{sig}, M)$ by $\mathcal{DS}.\mathrm{Sign}(sk, ctx, M)$ and refer to $\mathcal{DS}.\mathrm{Sign}$ as the *signer*. We say that a game is *$\mathcal{DS}$-regular* (for the associated experiment) if each time it invokes $\mathcal{DS}.\mathrm{Verify}$, it does so on input of (pk, α, M, T), where α is the game context used to initialize it and $pk, M, T \in \{0,1\}^*$. ♦

5.1 Diffie-Hellman

Let $\mathbb{G} = \langle G \rangle$ be an additive, represented group of order n. Let $\mathcal{I}$ be a DL interface for $\mathbb{G}$ and define $\mathcal{I}_{+\mathrm{dh}}$ as the pair of algorithms $(\mathcal{I}.\mathrm{Gen}, \mathrm{Op})$, where Op is defined as follows. On input of (sk, ctx, op, in), if $op = \mathrm{dh}$ and $Q \in \mathbb{G}$, where Q is the element of $\mathbb{G} \cup \{\diamond\}$ encoded by in, then return $\underline{sQ}$, where $s = \mathcal{I}.\mathrm{Scal}(sk)$; otherwise return $\mathcal{I}(sk, ctx, op, in)$. We refer to dh as the *DH operator*. (Note that point validation [22] for this operation is implicitly enforced by our conventions for represented groups; see Sect. 2.)

It is well known that exposing such a "static DH oracle" is not generally secure [11], but its practical impact on security can be subtle, and its presence in an interface is often hard to recognize [2,12]. In order to rule out the security of exposing the DH operation (inadvertently or not), we formalize a property of $\mathcal{I}$ that, if it holds, implies that $(\mathcal{I}_{+\mathrm{dh}}, \mathcal{I})$ is wGAP2 *insecure*; by Theorem 2, this implies that $\mathcal{I}_{+\mathrm{dh}}$ is not SEC/I secure in general. We then build on this result by considering whether it is safe to expose some function of the output (e.g., a hash or key-derivation function); when we model the function as a random oracle, we find that this is not wGAP2 secure.

Insecurity of exposing DH easily follows from the hardness of a variant of the CDH problem for $\mathbb{G}$ associated with $\mathcal{I}$. The *interface-relative DH (IDH)* problem for $(\mathbb{G}, \mathcal{I})$ is as follows.

Definition 9 (The IDH problem). Refer to the IDH experiment for $\mathbb{G}$ and $\mathcal{I}$ in Fig. 4. The experiment first runs $\mathcal{I}$.Gen to get the public key X and secret key sk. It then chooses a random $y \in \mathbb{Z}_n$ and runs the adversary $\mathcal{A}$ on input of (X, yG) and with oracle access to $\mathcal{I}_{sk}$; the adversary wins if it outputs yX. Define the advantage of IDH-adversary $\mathcal{A}$ as $\mathbf{Adv}_{\mathbb{G},\mathcal{I}}^{\mathrm{idh}}(\mathcal{A}) = \Pr\left[\mathbf{Exp}_{\mathbb{G},\mathcal{I}}^{\mathrm{idh}}(\mathcal{A})\right]$. An IDH adversary is (t, q)-resource if it is t-time and makes at most q queries to its interface oracle; as usual, we denote the maximum advantage of any r-resource IDH adversary by $\mathbf{Adv}_{\mathbb{G},\mathcal{I}}^{\mathrm{idh}}(r)$. Informally, we say the IDH problem is hard for $(\mathbb{G}, \mathcal{I})$ if $\mathbf{Adv}_{\mathbb{G},\mathcal{I}}^{\mathrm{idh}}(\mathcal{A})$ is small for every efficient $\mathcal{A}$. ◆

We will use this problem as a sort of litmus test to rule out insecure API designs. In Sect. 5.2 we show (via Theorem 1(i)) that CDH and IDH are equivalent relative to EdDSA, and in Sect. 6 we show that GDH and IDH are equivalent relative to Noise. To prove that hardness of the IDH problem for $(\mathbb{G}, \mathcal{I})$ implies the wGAP2 insecurity of $(\mathcal{I}_{+\mathrm{dh}}, \mathcal{I})$, we exhibit a wGAP2 adversary $\mathcal{D}$ such that in order for any simulator $\mathcal{S}$ to thwart $\mathcal{D}$, it must solve an instance of IDH for $(\mathbb{G}, \mathcal{I})$.

Theorem 3. *Suppose that n is prime and let $t, q_I \geq 0$ be integers. There is a $(O(t), 1)$-resource wGAP2-adversary $\mathcal{D}$ such that for all (t, q_I)-resource $\mathcal{S}$, there is a $(O(t), q_I)$-resource IDH-adversary $\mathcal{A}$ such that $\mathbf{Adv}_{\mathcal{I}_{+\mathrm{dh}},\mathcal{I}}^{\mathrm{wgap2}}(\mathcal{S}, \mathcal{D}) = 1 - \mathbf{Adv}_{\mathbb{G},\mathcal{I}}^{\mathrm{idh}}(\mathcal{A})$.*

Proof. Define adversary $\mathcal{D}^{\mathbf{Op}}(\underline{P})$ as follows. First run $r \twoheadleftarrow \mathbb{Z}_n^*$, then ask $\underline{Z} \twoheadleftarrow \mathbf{Op}(\varepsilon, \mathrm{dh}, \underline{rG})$. If $r^{-1}Z = P$, then return 1; otherwise return 0. Let d_{b1} denote the probability that $\mathcal{D}$ outputs 1 conditioned on the event that its challenge bit is b. First, if $b = 1$, then the response to $\mathcal{D}$'s query will be $Z = srG$, where $P = sG$. Since n is prime, r has a unique inverse $1/r \pmod{n}$, and so $r^{-1}Z = r^{-1}srG = sG = P$. It follows that $d_{11} = 1$. Now consider the probability that $r^{-1}Z = P$ given that $b = 0$ and define adversary $\mathcal{A}^{\mathcal{O}}(P, Q)$ as follows. It first executes $\sigma \twoheadleftarrow \mathcal{S}.\mathrm{Init}(\underline{P})$, then $\underline{Z} \twoheadleftarrow \mathcal{S}^{\mathcal{O}}(\&\sigma, \varepsilon, \mathrm{dh}, \underline{Q})$. Finally, it returns Z. Then the probability that $\mathcal{A}$ wins is precisely the probability that, in $\mathcal{D}$'s game, simulator $\mathcal{S}$ outputs $\underline{Z}$ such that $r^{-1}Z = P \iff rP = Z$, and so $d_{01} = \Pr\left[\mathbf{Exp}_{\mathbb{G},\mathcal{I}}^{\mathrm{idh}}(\mathcal{A})\right]$. □

Functional DH. Many applications do not make direct use of static DH, but some function of its output. In particular, it is common to apply a hash or key-derivation function to the shared secret, perhaps binding it to some context, e.g., the transcript hash in TLS or, as we will see, the CipherState in Noise. Therefore, it is worth considering whether exposing this intermediate functionality is secure.

Let $\mathcal{F} : \mathbb{G} \times \{0,1\}^* \to \{0,1\}^h$ be a function. Define the interface $\mathcal{I}_{+\mathrm{fdh}}$ as the pair of algorithms $(\mathcal{I}.\mathrm{Gen}, \mathrm{Op})$, where Op is defined as follows. On input of (sk, ctx, op, in), if $op = \mathrm{fdh}$ and $Q \in \mathbb{G}$, where Q is the element of $\mathbb{G} \cup \{\diamond\}$ encoded by in, then return $\mathcal{F}(sQ, ctx)$; otherwise return $\mathcal{I}.\mathrm{Op}(sk, ctx, op, in)$. We call $op = \mathrm{fdh}$ the *functional DH operator*.

Exposing functional DH is also wGAP2 insecure. The proof is more involved, but follows similar lines as Theorem 3. We cannot directly exploit the algebraic structure of the DH operator as we did above, since rather than getting sQ in response to its query, adversary $\mathcal{D}$ gets $\mathcal{F}(sQ, ctx)$. Instead, we model $\mathcal{F}$ as a random oracle and hope that the simulator manages to query the oracle with the correct point. We prove the following in the full version [29]:

Theorem 4. *Suppose that n is prime and let $t, q_I, q_R \geq 0$ be integers. When $\mathcal{F}$ is modeled as a random oracle, there is a $(O(t), 1, 1)$-resource wGAP2-adversary $\mathcal{D}$ such that for all (t, q_I, q)-resource, **P**- and **Q**-relative, and p-**P**-bound $\mathcal{S}$, there is a $(O(t + q), q_I)$-resource IDH-adversary $\mathcal{A}$ such that*

$$\mathbf{Adv}^{\mathrm{wgap2}}_{\mathcal{I}_{+\mathrm{fdh}}, \mathcal{I}}(\mathcal{S}, \mathcal{D}) + \epsilon \geq 1 - \mathbf{Adv}^{\mathrm{idh}}_{\mathbb{G}, \mathcal{I}}(\mathcal{A}),$$

where $\mathcal{I}$ is 0-ro-bound, $\epsilon = \hat{q}/n + \hat{q}^2/2^{h-1}$, and $\hat{q} = 2(q + p)$.

Discussion. The existence of a static DH oracle in an interface can be difficult to recognize, and its impact on security is often quite subtle. Acar, Ngyuen, and Zavarucha [2] discovered that an early version of the TPM standard exposed such an oracle via flexible API calls designed to support a wide variety of protocols. Indeed, a rigorous analysis of the standard in our attack model would have unearthed this subtlety. It would be worthwhile to study the proposal of Camenish et al. [12], which aims to remove the TPM oracle while still supporting a large variety of useful applications. More generally, we suggest that the approach developed in this paper could be used to vet API standards before they are implemented to help uncover such flaws. Though the problem with TPM was obvious in hindsight, it is possible that more flaws lurk in this and other API designs.

5.2   EdDSA

Unlike signature schemes like RSA-PSS or ECDSA, the standardized version of EdDSA (RFC 8032 [17]) admits variants that are context separable, allowing us to prove it GAP1 secure (in the ROM) for any game in which all signing and verifying operations are regular (Definition 8). We also show that any variant can be securely composed with any simple DL interface. After presenting our results, we will make the case for designing and deploying context-separable signatures in practice.

```
Gen( )                                        Scal(K)
  1  K ←$ {0,1}^b; s ← Scal(K)                  8  ret cl(H(K)[:b])
  2  ret (sG, K)
                                              Sign(K, ctx, M)
Verify(pk, ctx, M, T)                           9  dec r, t ∈ ℕ
  3  dec P, R ∈ 𝔾; x, t ∈ ℕ                    10  s ← Scal(K); X ← H(K)[b + 1:]
  4  P ← pk; R, x ← T                          11  r_2b ← H(vr(ctx) ‖ X ‖ ph(M))
  5  if ¬R ∨ ¬x then ret 0                     12  t_2b ← H(vr(ctx) ‖ rG ‖ sG ‖ ph(M))
  6  t_2b ← H(vr(ctx) ‖ R ‖ P ‖ ph(M))         13  x ← r + st (mod n)
  7  ret (x2^c G = 2^c R + t2^c P)             14  ret rG, x
```

Fig. 5. Signing/DL interface $\mathcal{ED}$ for EdDSA. Let $b, c \in \mathbb{N}$ and let $\mathbb{G} = \langle G \rangle$ be a represented, additive group of order n. Let $\mathcal{H} : \{0,1\}^* \to \{0,1\}^{2b}$, $cl : \{0,1\}^b \to \mathbb{Z}_n \setminus \{0\}$, and $vr, ph : \{0,1\}^* \to \{0,1\}^*$ be functions.

The standard specifies two concrete instantiations of EdDSA: Ed22519 and Ed448, whose names indicate the underlying group. The signing interface $\mathcal{ED}$ defined in Fig. 5 specifies generic EdDSA; a concrete scheme is instantiated by selecting the group $\mathbb{G}$, integers b and c, and functions $\mathcal{H}$, cl, vr, and ph. The group is determined by a prime number $p > 2$, parameters for a (twisted) Edwards curve E (see [8, Sect. 2]), and a generator G of a prime order subgroup of $E(\mathbb{F}_p)$, where $E(\mathbb{F}_p)$ denotes the group of points $(x, y) \in \mathbb{F}_p \times \mathbb{F}_p$ that lie on the curve E, and $\mathbb{F}_p$ denotes the finite field of order p. Define b so that $2^{b-1} > p$ and define c so that $\#E(\mathbb{F}_p) = n2^c$ (i.e., 2^c is the cofactor of $\mathbb{G}$). This choice of b makes it possible to encode signatures with $2b$ bits, and this choice of c is intended to mitigate small subgroup attacks [22]. The "clamping" function cl is similarly tailored to the underlying group: for Ed25519 and its variants, this function clears the first 3 bits, sets the second to last bit, and clears the last bit. (This ensures that $s = 2^{254} + 8x$ for a uniform random $x \in \mathbb{Z}_{2^{251}}$.) Finally, the algorithm variant is determined by the functions vr and ph. For example, the most common Ed25519 variant is obtained by setting $vr(X) = \varepsilon$ and $ph(X) = X$ for all X, but the standard also specifies variants that permit context (Ed25519ctx) and pre-hashing of the message (Ed25519ph). To provide context separability, the function vr must be collision resistant.

We begin our analysis by proving that the context-separable variants of EdDSA are GAP1 secure in the ROM for games in which the signing and verifying operations are regular (Theorem 5). The upcoming Corollary 1, which follows from Theorems 1(1) and 5, combined with the straightforward result that IDH implies CDH, gives a qualitative equivalence between CDH and IDH in terms of the security of (any variant of) EdDSA. We will then show that exposing any variant of EdDSA in any *simple* DL interface is GAP2 secure in general (Theorem 6). Fix EdDSA parameters $(\mathbb{G}, \mathcal{H}, cl, vr, ph, b, c)$ and let $\mathcal{ED}$ be the signing interface instantiated with these parameters as specified in Fig. 5. Let $n = |\mathbb{G}|$.

Theorem 5. *Let $\mathcal{G}$ be an ($\mathcal{ED}$-)regular game and suppose that $n \leq 2^{b-1}$. When $\mathcal{H}$ is modeled as a random oracle, there exists a regular, $\mathbf{P}$-relative simulator $\mathcal{S}$ such that for all $t, q_G, q_I, q_R, c \geq 0$ there exists a $O(t + q_R q_I)$-time CR-adversary $\mathcal{C}$ such that $\mathbf{Adv}_{\mathcal{ED},\mathcal{G}}^{\mathrm{gap1}}(\mathcal{S}, r) \leq 2c q_I \mathbf{Adv}_{vr}^{\mathrm{cr}}(\mathcal{C}) + 6 q_R q_I / n$, where $\mathcal{G}$ is c-bound, $\mathcal{S}$ is $(\log n/2, 2b)$-min-entropy, $(O(t/(q_I + 1)), 1, 0)$-resource, and 1-$\mathbf{P}$-bound, and $r = (t, q_G, q_I, q_R)$.*

We only give the high level idea of the a argument here; refer to the full version for the proof [29]. The simulator programs the random oracle with valid EdDSA signatures in the usual way (cf. [13, Section 4.4]). We must ensure, however, that signatures programmed by the simulator cannot be used by the adversary in an attack against the game $\mathcal{G}$. To do so, we use the collision resistance of vr to bound the probability that any interface query made via **Call** coincides with an interface query made via **Op**. For this argument to work, we must require that $\mathcal{G}$ is ($\mathcal{ED}$-)regular.

If the game in Theorem 5 makes no interface queries (i.e., is 0-bound), then CR security of vr is not required. This allows us to prove equivalence of IDH and CDH regardless of how vr is realized. The following corollary follows almost immediately from Theorems 1(i) and 5.

Corollary 1. *Let $r = |Rng\ cl|$ and suppose that $r \mid 2^b$ and $n \leq 2^{b-1}$. Then for all $t, q_I, q_R \geq 0$ it holds that $\mathbf{Adv}_{\mathbb{G},\mathcal{ED}}^{\mathrm{idh}}(t, q_I, q_R) \leq n/r \mathbf{Adv}_{\mathbb{G}}^{\mathrm{cdh}}(O(t+\hat{q})) + 7 q_R q_I / n$, where $\mathcal{H}$ is modeled as a random oracle and $\hat{q} = q_R + q_I + 1$.*

The IDH experiment is equivalent to the SEC/I experiment with $\mathcal{ED}$ and a game $\mathcal{G}^{\mathrm{cdh}}$ that specifies the CDH problem with one of the inputs being the public key provided to the game as input. We reduce the SEC security of $\mathcal{G}^{\mathrm{cdh}}$ to SEC/I via Theorem 1(i) with help of the simulator exhibited in Theorem 5. Note that $\mathcal{G}^{\mathrm{cdh}}$ is 0-ro-bound, and so CR security of vr does not arise in the bound. The result is obtained by observing that the SEC experiment for $\mathcal{ED}$ and $\mathcal{G}^{\mathrm{cdh}}$ is essentially the CDH experiment for $\mathbb{G}$ modulo the distribution on the first input induced by $\mathcal{ED}$.Gen, which accounts for the n/r term. We refer the reader to the full version for the complete proof [29].

Finally, we show that EdDSA can be composed with any *simple* DL interface $\mathcal{I}$ without affecting the security of $\mathcal{I}$'s intended application. Let $\mathcal{I}$ be a simple DL interface for $\mathbb{G}$. We define a new interface $\mathcal{ED}_{+\mathcal{I}} = (\mathcal{ED}.\mathrm{Gen}, \mathrm{Op})$, where on input of (sk, ctx, op, in), algorithm Op returns $\mathcal{ED}.\mathrm{Sign}(sk, ctx, in)$ if $op = \mathrm{sig}$ and returns $\mathcal{I}.\mathrm{Op}(\underline{s}, ctx, op, in)$ otherwise, where $s = \mathcal{ED}.\mathrm{Scal}(sk)$.

Theorem 6. *Let $\mathcal{G}$ be a game and suppose that $n \leq 2^{b-1}$. When $\mathcal{H}$ is modeled as a random oracle, there exists a regular, $\mathbf{P}$-relative simulator $\mathcal{S}$ such that for all $t, q_G, q_I, q_R \geq 0$ it holds that $\mathbf{Adv}_{\mathcal{ED}_{+\mathcal{I}},\mathcal{I},\mathcal{G}}^{\mathrm{gap2}}(\mathcal{S}, r) \leq 7 q_R q_I / n$, where $\mathcal{S}$ is $(\log n/2, 2b)$-min-entropy, $(O(t/(q_I+1)), 1, 0)$-resource, and 1-$\mathbf{P}$-bound, and $r = (t, q_G, q_I, q_R)$.*

The restriction to simple interfaces is so that we can achieve context separation in the proof without using collision resistance of vr. The argument leverages the fact that $\mathcal{I}$ does not make use of the string X computed by the signer. Otherwise the proof is closely related to Theorem 5; we defer the details to the full version of this paper [29].

Discussion. The restrictions imposed on the game in Theorem 5 and the interface in Theorem 6 are very mild, but are required for context separability. If the game encodes the UF-CMA security of $\mathcal{ED}$, then this ensures that a signature generated via the interface cannot be used as a forgery in the game. But this "attack" is rather uninteresting and is only an artifact of our model. On the other hand, the game might specify the use of a signature scheme in a complex protocol like TLS in which digital signatures have a variety of uses, including client and server authentication and delegation of credentials for terminating TLS on a party's behalf [4]. In each of these cases the protocol binds the signature to a unique context string identifying its use (e.g., [32, Sect. 4.4.3]). Our abstraction boundary makes the requirements for such applications explicit. Because Ed25519ctx and Ed448ctx are context separable, Theorem 5 makes clear the conditions under which these algorithms are secure for their intended application, no matter how else they are used: the implementer must ensure that (1) the interface enforces context separation, and (2) signing/verification operations in the application always use the context that identify the application. We believe that exploiting this property of context-separable signatures would reduce the inherent complexity of designing and deploying protocols. (Indeed, it is also not difficult to design signature schemes to have this property.)

6   Noise

In this section we consider the GAP1 security of Noise [30], a framework for designing DL-based, two-party protocols. Noise provides a set of rules for processing *handshake patterns*, which define the sequence of interactions between an *initiator* and *responder* in a protocol. The processing rules involve three primitives: Diffie-Hellman (DH), an AEAD scheme, and a hash function. Each message sent or received by a host updates the host's state, which consists of the host's *ephemeral* (i.e., short-lived) and *static* (long-lived) secret keys, the peer's ephemeral and static public keys, shared state used to derive the symmetric key and associated data, the current symmetric key, and the current nonce. The symmetric key, nonce, and associated data are used to encrypt *payloads* accompanying each message, providing implicit authentication of a peer via confirmation of knowledge of their static secret.

Noise admits a wide variety of protocols. The processing rules are designed to make it easy to verify properties of handshake patterns, and considerable effort has gone into their formal analysis [14, 19, 23]. But the study of handshake patterns in isolation does not fully address the complexity of using Noise to build and deploy protocols. In practice, it is often necessary for the communicants to negotiate the details of the handshake, including the pattern, primitives, and cryptographic artifacts such as static keys and their certificates. All of this is out of scope of the core Noise specification, which aims to be as rigid as possible. As a result, there is an apparent gap between our understanding of the security that Noise provides and how it might be used in practice. One question that arises, which we will address here, is whether it is safe to reuse a single static key in many patterns.

We cast the Noise framework as an interface that exposes a host's static key for use in Noise protocols. The interface specifies how the host consumes (resp. produces) messages sent by (resp. to send to) the peer, and how its handshake state is updated as a side-effect. In other words, it implements the processing rules such that Noise patterns can be executed by making calls to the interface. Our goal is to prove GAP1 security with respect to the largest possible set of games, which would provide two benefits in practice. First and foremeost, it would imply joint security (up to context separation) of all patterns the interface implements; second it would provide a degree of robustness to cross protocol attacks by ensuring that, as long as context separation is enforced, vulnerabilities in one application cannot creep into another.

Our analysis sheds light on two limitations of Noise with respect to our security notions. The first is that *some* handshake patterns, if implemented by our interface, would allow for GAP1 attacks. We provide a formal characterization of the actions that give rise to these attacks, and we prove GAP1 security of our interface when they are excluded. The second issue is more subtle. To prove GAP1 security with respect to games in which the adversary may compromise the handshake state—for example, when modeling forward secrecy—it is necessary to tweak the Noise spec slightly. The processing rules explicitly bind the protocol context (i.e., a string that uniquely defines the handshake pattern and parameters) to the initial state of the protocol. While this provides a certain degree of context separability, the lack of binding to each state update precludes a proof of security relative to such games. We propose a simple and efficient modification of the processing rules that ensures context separability under these conditions, allowing us to prove security under minimal (and natural) assumptions about the game.

Of course, a consequence of these restrictions is that our analysis leaves open the security of key reuse in Noise *as it is*. In the full version of this paper [29], we will discuss what our results mean for Noise in practice and suggest directions for future work.

Preliminaries. Our analysis will use the standard notion of ciphertext integrity of AEAD schemes. A scheme for *authenticated encryption with associated data (AEAD)* is a pair of deterministic algorithms $\mathcal{AE} = (\text{Enc}, \text{Dec})$. The first, $\text{Enc}(\textbf{str } K, N, A, M) \mapsto \textbf{str } C$, maps a key K, nonce N, associated data A, and plaintext M to a ciphertext C. The second, $\text{Dec}(\textbf{str } K, N, A, C) \mapsto \textbf{str } M$, maps K, N, A, and C to M. We respectively define the key, nonce, associated-data (AD), and message space as the sets $\mathcal{K}, \mathcal{N}, \mathcal{A}, \mathcal{M} \subseteq \{0,1\}^*$ for which $\text{Enc}(K, N, A, M) \neq \perp$ if and only if $(K, N, A, M) \in \mathcal{K} \times \mathcal{N} \times \mathcal{A} \times \mathcal{M}$;

NN:	NK:	NX:	IKpsk2:
→ e,	← s	→ e	← s
← e, ee	...	← e, ee, s, es	...
	→ e, es		→ e, es, s, ss
	← e, ee		← e, ee, se, psk

Fig. 6. Examples of Noise handshake patterns.

correctness requires that $\mathrm{Dec}(K, K, N, A, \mathrm{Enc}(K, N, A, M)) = M$ for every such (K, N, A, M). (This condition implies that $\mathcal{AE}$ is both *correct* and *tidy* in the sense of Namprempre, Rogaway, and Shrimpton [25].) We say that $\mathcal{AE}$ has key-length k if $\mathcal{K} = \{0,1\}^k$ and nonce-length n if $\mathcal{N} = \{0,1\}^n$. We will use the standard notion of ciphertext integrity (INT-CTXT) for AEAD schemes in the presence of nonce-respecting adversaries; refer to the full version [29] for its precise definition. Define the advantage of an adversary $\mathcal{A}$ in breaking the ciphertext integrity of $\mathcal{AE}$ as $\mathbf{Adv}_{\mathcal{AE}}^{\text{int-ctxt}}(\mathcal{A}) = \Pr\left[\mathbf{Exp}_{\mathcal{AE}}^{\text{int-ctxt}}(\mathcal{A})\right]$. Let $\mathbf{Adv}_{\mathcal{AE}}^{\text{int-ctxt}}(t, q_E, q_D)$ denote the maximum advantage of any t-time adversary making at most q_E (resp. q_D) queries to **Enc** (resp. **Dec**).

6.1   Handshake and Message Patterns

By way of eliciting the formal tools we will need in our analysis, we begin this section with a brief overview of how handshake patterns are specified. Figure 6 recalls four patterns from the standard [30]. The first, referred to as the "NN" pattern, encodes an unauthenticated DH key exchange as a sequence of *handshake messages*, which in turn encode sequences of *tokens*. In the first message (→ e) the initiator generates an ephemeral DH key pair and sends the public key to the responder. In the next handshake message (← e, ee), the responder generates an ephemeral key pair (e), computes the DH shared secret and derives a symmetric key (ee), then sends the ephemeral public key in its response. Every message includes a possibly AEAD-encrypted *payload*. Encryption is opportunistic. Once a shared secret is established, everything that can be encrypted will be encrypted; if the caller does not provide a payload, then the payload is the empty string.

The NK pattern is a variant of NN that provides authentication of the responder. The main difference is an additional message preceding the ellipses (← s) indicating that the responder's static public key is known to the initiator before the protocol begins. In its first action, the initiator computes the shared secret between this and its ephemeral secret (es) and uses it to encrypt the message payload. This has two effects: first, the initiator proves knowledge of the shared secret to the responder; and second, the responder authenticates itself by proving knowledge of the shared secret to the initiator. These properties are due to the sequence of actions induced by the pattern; if decryption fails, then this indicates that the sender does not know the correct shared secret. This works because each key derivation depends on all shared secrets computed in the protocol so far.

The NX pattern is similar except that the public key is *transmitted* to the initiator during the handshake, rather than out-of-band. For our purposes, the significant difference between NK and NX is that, in the former pattern, the initiator confirms knowledge of the shared secret *before* the responder consumes the message and produces its response. On the other hand, in the NX pattern the initiator can send an arbitrary element of the DH group as its ephemeral key and observe a valid response without demonstrating knowledge of its discrete logarithm. This leads to information leakage beyond what is learned by honest initiators (that is, for computationally bounded attackers). It is akin to providing the adversary with a functional DH oracle, which enables an attack against the GAP1 security of the interface; as we did in Theorem 4, one can exhibit a distinguisher that gets high advantage if the IDH problem is hard for the underlying group. (More on this attack in the full version [29].) To reason about this attack in our analysis, we require an abstraction for handshake patterns and the actions they induce.

Definition 10 (Patterns, actions, and tokenizers). A handshake pattern is a sequence of *message patterns* that specify the sequence of *tokens* processed when producing or consuming a message. A message pattern is a string that can be parsed by a *tokenizer*, which determines the set of valid *actions*. A tokenizer is a deterministic algorithm $T(\text{bool } f, r, \text{str } pat) \mapsto \text{tup } t, \text{str } err$. String pat is the message pattern, f indicates whether or not the host is producing a message, and r indicates whether the host is the initiator. The outputs are a tuple t comprised of the sequence of tokens to be processed and a string err indicating whether an error occurred. A valid action for T is a triple (f, r, pat) for which $err = \diamond$, where $(t, err) = T_f(r, pat)$. We say that T has *action count* ℓ if $|t| \leq \ell$ for every valid action (f, r, pat).

A *token action* is a triple $(f, r, t) \in \{0,1\} \times \{0,1\} \times \{0,1\}^*$. We say that a tokenizer T *includes* a set of token actions $\mathcal{X}$ if for each $(f, r, t) \in \mathcal{X}$ the following is true: there exists a valid pattern pat for T such that $t = t_i$ for some $1 \leq i \leq |t|$ and $(t, err) = T_f(r, t)$. If this condition holds for no such token action, then T *excludes* $\mathcal{X}$.   ♦

6.2   The Interface

The interface is specified as the composition of a tokenizer and the DH, AEAD, and hash primitives. Let $\mathbb{G} = \langle G \rangle$ be a v-encoded, additive group of order n, and fix integers $k, n', h, b, u \geq 0$ such that $v \notin \{u+8, h+u+8\}$. Let $\mathcal{AE}$ be an AEAD scheme with key-length k and nonce-length n'. Let $cl : \{0,1\}^b \to \mathbb{Z}_n \setminus \{0\}$, $vr : \{0,1\}^* \to \{0,1\}^u$, and $\mathcal{H} : \{0,1\}^* \to \{0,1\}^h$ be functions. Function $\mathcal{H}$ is a hash function that will serve multiple purposes, one of which is to derive symmetric keys using HKDF [20]. We will ignore the details of HKDF in this section and simply denote key derivation by a function $\mathcal{F} : (\{0,1\}^*)^3 \to (\{0,1\}^h)^3$ that maps an "information" string id, a "salt" X, and input key material Y to a triple of h-bit strings $\mathcal{F}(id, X, Y)$. We will model $\mathcal{F}$ as a random oracle in our analysis; in the full version [29] we address the implications of this modeling choice.

```
Gen()                              Op(sk, ctx, op, in)
 1  K ⟵ {0,1}^b                    10  dec st hs; msg req; bool f, r; str u, pat, err
 2  s ← cl(K)                      11  s ← Scal(sk); o, f, r, pat ← op; hs, in ← in
 3  ret (sG, s)                    12  if o ≠ noise ∨ hs.id ≠ vr(ctx) ∨ |hs.L| ≠ h∨
                                   13    |hs.psk| ∈ {u + 8, h + u + 8} then ret ⊥
                                   14  if f then // outbound payload
 4  dec struct {                   15    (resp, err) ⟵ Write(&hs, s, r, pat, in)
 5    str P, E, S } msg            16    if ¬err then ret hs, resp, ◇
 6  dec struct { str id, psk;      17  else req ← in // inbound message
 7    int seq; str K, N;           18    (out, err) ⟵ Read(&hs, s, r, pat, req)
 8    str L, A;                    19    if ¬err then ret hs, out, ◇
 9    Q, R ∈ G; e ∈ ℤ_n } st       20  if err ret ◇, ◇, err
```

Fig. 7. Simple DL interface $\mathcal{N}$ for noise. Let $\mathbb{G} = \langle G \rangle$ be a v-encoded, additive group of order n and let $h, b, u \geq 0$ be integers such that $v \notin \{u + 8, h + u + 8\}$. Let $cl : \{0,1\}^b \to \mathbb{Z}_n \setminus \{0\}$ and $vr : \{0,1\}^* \to \{0,1\}^u$ be functions. Procedures Write and Read are defined in the full version [29].

Figure 7 specifies our Noise interface $\mathcal{N}$ at a high level and defines structures **st** and **msg** for the handshake state and messages respectively. The key generator $\mathcal{N}$.Gen chooses a random, b-bit string K, sets $s \leftarrow cl(K)$, and returns (sG, s). (Thus, $\mathcal{N}$ is simple in the sense of Definition 8.) Function cl serves the same purpose as cl in our specification of EdDSA; it maps a bit string of a particular length to a suitable scalar s for use with the given group. The key operator $\mathcal{N}$.Op is defined in terms of two procedures:

- Read($\&$**st** hs, **int** s, **bool** r, **str** pat, **msg** req) $\mapsto$ **str** out, err. Called when consuming an inbound message. It takes as input the static key s and processes the action $(0, r, pat)$ on the message req and current handshake state hs. It outputs a payload out.
- Write($\&$**st** hs, **int** s, **bool** r, **str** pat, in) $\mapsto$ **msg** $resp$, **str** err. Called when producing an outbound message. It takes as input the static key s and processes the action $(1, r, pat)$ on the payload in and current handshake state hs. It outputs a message $resp$.

Read and Write are defined in terms of $\mathcal{T}$, $\mathcal{AE}$, $\mathcal{F}$, and $\mathcal{H}$. The operand encodes the current handshake state hs and the input in, and the operator op encodes an action (f, r, pat). If $f = 1$, then the host interprets in as a payload to send to its peer in its next handshake message; it calls Write and returns the updated state and outbound message. If $f = 0$, then the host interprets in as a message sent by the peer; it calls Read and returns the updated state and inbound payload.

Context-to-Action Binding. The context ctx is bound to the handshake state via a field $hs.id$, which should be equal to $vr(ctx)$ (7:12). Each call to $\mathcal{F}$ made by either Read or Write uses $hs.id$ as the label. In this way, interface $\mathcal{N}$ binds the string $hs.id = vr(ctx)$ to each key derivation, thereby binding the context to the *action* being performed. We call this *context-to-action* binding. This differs from Noise as it is, which uses an empty string as the information string for key derivation via HKDF (see [30, Sect. 4.3]). (Formally, the processing rules as they are specified are recovered by defining $vr(ctx) = \varepsilon$ for all ctx.) Noise binds the context to *initialization* of the handshake state (see [30, Sect. 5.3]), but action binding is required in our attack model in order to provide context separation when the game leaks its internal handshake state to the adversary. We will discuss the issue that arises in the next section.

In order to save space, we defer detailed explanation of the Noise parameters, as well as the complete specifications of Read and Write, to the full version of this paper [29]. These details are essential to understanding the proof of our main result (Theorem 7), but since the low-level details are cumbersome, we will focus the remainder on stating and interpreting our results.

6.3   Security

Interface $\mathcal{N}$ is GAP1 secure for any game $\mathcal{G}$ subject to the following restrictions. First, the tokenizer must exclude any write action involving DH on the static secret. (It may, however, read messages that depend on the static secret.) And second, each time $\mathcal{G}$ invokes $\mathcal{F}$ on an input (id, u, v) it must hold that $id = vr(\alpha)$, where α is the game context.

Fix Noise parameters $(\mathbb{G}, \mathcal{AE}, \mathcal{T}, \mathcal{H}, \mathcal{F}, cl, vr, k, n', h, b, u)$ and let $\mathcal{N}$ be the DL interface instantiated with these parameters as specified in Fig. 7. Let $n = |\mathbb{G}|$ and let $\mathcal{X} = (1, 0, \mathsf{es}), (1, 0, \mathsf{ss}), (1, 1, \mathsf{se}), (1, 1, \mathsf{ss})$. Define $\psi : \{0,1\}^* \times (\{0,1\}^*)^3 \rightarrow \{0,1\}$ as the map $(ctx, (id, u, v)) \mapsto (vr(ctx) = id)$.

Theorem 7. *Suppose that n is prime. Let $\mathcal{G}$ be a regular game and suppose that $\mathcal{T}$ is $\mathcal{X}$-excluding and has action count ℓ. Let **DDH** be as defined in Fig. 4. When $\mathcal{F}$ is modeled as a random oracle, there exists a regular, **DDH**- and **Q**-relative simulator $\mathcal{S}$ such that for all $t, q_G, q_I, q_R, c \geq 0$ there exists a $\hat{t}$-time CR-adversary $\mathcal{C}$ such that*

$$\mathbf{Adv}_{\mathcal{N}, \mathcal{G}}^{\mathrm{gap1}}(\mathcal{S}, \boldsymbol{r}) \leq 2cq_I \mathbf{Adv}_{vr}^{\mathrm{cr}}(\mathcal{C}) + 2\ell q_I \mathbf{Adv}_{\mathcal{AE}}^{\mathrm{int\text{-}ctxt}}(\hat{t}, 0, q_I),$$

*where $\mathcal{G}$ is c-ro-bound and ψ-ro-regular; $\mathcal{AE}$, $\mathcal{T}$, $\mathcal{H}$, cl, and vr are 0-ro-bound; simulator $\mathcal{S}$ is $(O(t/(q_I + 1)), q_I, \ell)$-resource, $\ell q_R q_I$-**DDH**-bound, and 2-**Q**-bound; $\boldsymbol{r} = (t, q_G, q_I, q_R)$; and $\hat{t} = O(t + q_R q_I)$.*

We will sketch the main ideas of the proof; refer to the full version for the details [29]. To simulate static DH computations on an input Y (either the peer's static or ephemeral key), the simulator $\mathcal{S}$ computes the set $\mathcal{V}$ of points incident to the adversary's RO queries. For each $Z \in \mathcal{V}$ it uses its DDH oracle to check if $(\log_G P)(\log_G Y) = \log_G Z$, where P is the host's static key. If so, then it uses Z to simulate the output of the interface. This is only possible in general for read actions, since these require the adversary to compute a ciphertext under the correct symmetric key, which can be obtained by querying the RO first.

In fact, what we show is that, short of breaking the CR security of vr or INT-CTXT security of $\mathcal{AE}$, the only way to get a valid response from **Op** is to compute the inbound message as specified by the processing rules.

The need for context-to-action binding and the restriction of the game's RO queries arise in order to ensure there is no "subliminal channel" between the game and the adversary conveying information about the RO to the adversary beyond what it learns by making RO queries on its own. If the game provides the outputs of its RO queries to the adversary (e.g., by compromising the hand-shake state), then without action binding, these can be used by the adversary to compute ciphertexts without interacting with the RO. Hence, there is no way for the simulator to correctly respond given only knowledge of the adversary's RO queries. (Allowing the simulator to observe more RO queries than this—in particular, the game's—would make composition impossible.)

Finally, as we did in Sect. 5.2, we apply the GAP1 security of $\mathcal{N}$ and the composition theorem to the IDH problem for $\mathcal{N}$. We cannot reduce the CDH problem to it as we did in Corollary 1, since the simulator requires a **DDH** oracle. Of course, this is precisely what the GDH experiment provides. The following is obtained by applying Theorems 1 and 7. (We will not prove it, but the details are closely related to Corollary 1.)

Corollary 2. *Suppose that n is prime and that $\mathcal{T}$ is $\mathcal{X}$-excluding and has maximum action count ℓ. Let $r = |Rng\,cl|$ and suppose that $r \,|\, 2^b$. Then for all $t, q_I, q_R \geq 0$ it holds that*

$$\mathbf{Adv}^{\mathrm{idh}}_{\mathbb{G},\mathcal{N}}(t, q_I, q_R) \leq n/r\,\mathbf{Adv}^{\mathrm{gdh}}_{\mathbb{G}}(O(t+\hat{q}), \ell q_R q_I) + 2\ell q_I\,\mathbf{Adv}^{\mathrm{int\text{-}ctxt}}_{\mathcal{AE}}(\hat{t}, 0, q_I),$$

where $\mathcal{F}$ is modeled as a random oracle; $\mathcal{AE}$, $\mathcal{T}$, $\mathcal{H}$, cl, and vr are 0-ro-bound; $\hat{q} = q_R + \ell(q_I + 1)$; and $\hat{t} = O(t + q_R q_I)$.

Remark 1. The use of the DDH oracle by the simulator in Theorem 7 is standard; it is used, for instance, to prove joint security of encryption and signing in the ROM [13]. In fact, the Noise spec calls for a group for which the GDH problem is hard; see [30, Sect. 4.1].

Acknowledgements. This work was made possible by NSF grant CNS-1816375. We thank the anonymous reviewers for their useful comments. We thank Trevor Perrin for his valuable feedback on our analysis of Noise.

References

1. Acar, T., Belenkiy, M., Bellare, M., Cash, D.: Cryptographic agility and its relation to circular encryption. In: Gilbert, H. (ed.) EUROCRYPT 2010. LNCS, vol. 6110, pp. 403–422. Springer, Heidelberg (2010). https://doi.org/10.1007/978-3-642-13190-5_21
2. Acar, T., Nguyen, L., Zaverucha, G.: A TPM Diffie-Hellman oracle. Cryptology ePrint Archive, Report 2013/667 (2013). https://eprint.iacr.org/2013/667

3. Acar, Y., et al.: Comparing the usability of cryptographic APIs. In: 2017 IEEE Symposium on Security and Privacy (SP), pp. 154–171, May 2017
4. Barnes, R., Iyengar, S., Sullivan, N., Rescorla, E.: Delegated credentials for TLS. Internet-Draft draft-ietf-tls-subcerts-03, IETF Secretariat, February 2019. http://www.ietf.org/internet-drafts/draft-ietf-tls-subcerts-03.txt
5. Bellare, M., Rogaway, P.: Random oracles are practical: a paradigm for designing efficient protocols. In: Proceedings of the 1st ACM Conference on Computer and Communications Security, CCS 1993, pp. 62–73. ACM, New York (1993)
6. Bellare, M., Rogaway, P.: The security of triple encryption and a framework for code-based game-playing proofs. In: Vaudenay, S. (ed.) EUROCRYPT 2006. LNCS, vol. 4004, pp. 409–426. Springer, Heidelberg (2006). https://doi.org/10.1007/11761679_25
7. Bellare, M., Tackmann, B.: The multi-user security of authenticated encryption: AES-GCM in TLS 1.3. In: Robshaw, M., Katz, J. (eds.) CRYPTO 2016. LNCS, vol. 9814, pp. 247–276. Springer, Heidelberg (2016). https://doi.org/10.1007/978-3-662-53018-4_10
8. Bernstein, D.J., Duif, N., Lange, T., Schwabe, P., Yang, B.Y.: High-speedhigh-security signatures. J. Crypt. Eng. 2(2), 77–89 (2012)
9. Bhargavan, K., Boureanu, I., Fouque, P., Onete, C., Richard, B.: Content delivery over TLS: a cryptographic analysis of Keyless SSL. In: 2017 IEEE European Symposium on Security and Privacy (EuroS&P), pp. 1–16, April 2017. https://doi.org/10.1109/EuroSP.2017.52
10. Bleichenbacher, D.: Chosen ciphertext attacks against protocols based on the RSA encryption standard PKCS #1. In: Krawczyk, H. (ed.) CRYPTO 1998. LNCS, vol. 1462, pp. 1–12. Springer, Heidelberg (1998). https://doi.org/10.1007/BFb0055716
11. Brown, D.R.L., Gallant, R.P.: The static Diffie-Hellman problem. Cryptology ePrint Archive, Report 2004/306 (2004). https://eprint.iacr.org/2004/306
12. Camenisch, J., Chen, L., Drijvers, M., Lehmann, A., Novick, D., Urian, R.: One TPM to bind them all: fixing TPM 2.0 for provably secure anonymous attestation. In: 2017 IEEE Symposium on Security and Privacy (SP), pp. 901–920, May 2017
13. Degabriele, J.P., Lehmann, A., Paterson, K.G., Smart, N.P., Strefler, M.: On the joint security of encryption and signature in EMV. In: Dunkelman, O. (ed.) CT-RSA 2012. LNCS, vol. 7178, pp. 116–135. Springer, Heidelberg (2012). https://doi.org/10.1007/978-3-642-27954-6_8
14. Dowling, B., Paterson, K.G.: A cryptographic analysis of the wireguard protocol. In: Preneel, B., Vercauteren, F. (eds.) ACNS 2018. LNCS, vol. 10892, pp. 3–21. Springer, Cham (2018). https://doi.org/10.1007/978-3-319-93387-0_1
15. Gleeson, S., Zimman, C.: PKCS #11 cryptographic token interface base specification version 2.40. Online white paper, July 2015. http://docs.oasis-open.org/pkcs11/pkcs11-base/v2.40/pkcs11-base-v2.40.html
16. Haber, S., Pinkas, B.: Securely combining public-key cryptosystems. In: Proceedings of the 8th ACM Conference on Computer and Communications Security, CCS 2001, pp. 215–224. ACM, New York (2001)
17. Josefsson, S., Liusvaara, I.: Edwards-curve digital signature algorithm (EdDSA). RFC 8032, RFC Editor, January 2017
18. Kelsey, J., Schneier, B., Wagner, D.: Protocol interactions and the chosen protocol attack. In: Christianson, B., Crispo, B., Lomas, M., Roe, M. (eds.) Security Protocols 1997. LNCS, vol. 1361, pp. 91–104. Springer, Heidelberg (1998). https://doi.org/10.1007/BFb0028162

19. Kobeissi, N., Bhargavan, K.: Noise explorer: fully automated modeling and verification for arbitrary noise protocols. Cryptology ePrint Archive, Report 2018/766 (2018). https://eprint.iacr.org/2018/766
20. Krawczyk, H., Eronen, P.: HMAC-based extract-and-expand key derivation function (HKDF). RFC 5869, RFC Editor, May 2010. http://www.rfc-editor.org/rfc/rfc5869.txt
21. Künnemann, R., Steel, G.: YubiSecure? Formal security analysis results for the Yubikey and YubiHSM. In: Jøsang, A., Samarati, P., Petrocchi, M. (eds.) STM 2012. LNCS, vol. 7783, pp. 257–272. Springer, Heidelberg (2013). https://doi.org/10.1007/978-3-642-38004-4_17
22. Lim, C.H., Lee, P.J.: A key recovery attack on discrete log-based schemes using a prime order subgroup. In: Kaliski, B.S. (ed.) CRYPTO 1997. LNCS, vol. 1294, pp. 249–263. Springer, Heidelberg (1997). https://doi.org/10.1007/BFb0052240
23. Lipp, B., Blanchet, B., Bhargavan, K.: A mechanised cryptographic proof of the wireguard virtual private network protocol. Research Report RR-9269, Inria, Paris, April 2019. https://hal.inria.fr/hal-02100345
24. Maurer, U., Renner, R., Holenstein, C.: Indifferentiability, impossibility results on reductions, and applications to the random oracle methodology. In: Naor, M. (ed.) TCC 2004. LNCS, vol. 2951, pp. 21–39. Springer, Heidelberg (2004). https://doi.org/10.1007/978-3-540-24638-1_2
25. Namprempre, C., Rogaway, P., Shrimpton, T.: Reconsidering generic composition. In: Nguyen, P.Q., Oswald, E. (eds.) EUROCRYPT 2014. LNCS, vol. 8441, pp. 257–274. Springer, Heidelberg (2014). https://doi.org/10.1007/978-3-642-55220-5_15
26. Okamoto, T., Pointcheval, D.: The gap-problems: a new class of problems for the security of cryptographic schemes. In: Kim, K. (ed.) PKC 2001. LNCS, vol. 1992, pp. 104–118. Springer, Heidelberg (2001). https://doi.org/10.1007/3-540-44586-2_8
27. Oliveira, D., Rosenthal, M., Morin, N., Yeh, K.C., Cappos, J., Zhuang, Y.: It's the psychology stupid: how heuristics explain software vulnerabilities and how priming can illuminate developer's blind spots. In: Proceedings of the 30th Annual Computer Security Applications Conference, ACSAC 2014, pp. 296–305. ACM, New York (2014)
28. Oliveira, D.S., et al.: API blindspots: why experienced developers write vulnerable code. In: Fourteenth Symposium on Usable Privacy and Security (SOUPS 2018), pp. 315–328. USENIX Association, Baltimore (2018)
29. Patton, C., Shrimpton, T.: Security in the presence of key reuse: context-separable interfaces and their applications. Cryptology ePrint Archive, Report 2019/519 (2019). https://eprint.iacr.org/2019/519
30. Perrin, T.: The noise protocol framework. Online white paper, July 2018. https://noiseprotocol.org/noise.html
31. Pollard, J.M.: Kangaroos, monopoly and discrete logarithms. J. Cryptol. 13(4), 437–447 (2000)
32. Rescorla, E.: The transport layer security (TLS) protocol version 1.3. RFC 8446, RFC Editor, August 2018
33. Ristenpart, T., Shacham, H., Shrimpton, T.: Careful with composition: limitations of the indifferentiability framework. In: Paterson, K.G. (ed.) EUROCRYPT 2011. LNCS, vol. 6632, pp. 487–506. Springer, Heidelberg (2011). https://doi.org/10.1007/978-3-642-20465-4_27

34. Rogaway, P., Stegers, T.: Authentication without elision: partially specified protocols, associated data, and cryptographic models described by code. In: 2009 22nd IEEE Computer Security Foundations Symposium, pp. 26–39, July 2009
35. Shrimpton, T., Stam, M., Warinschi, B.: A modular treatment of cryptographic APIs: the symmetric-key case. In: Robshaw, M., Katz, J. (eds.) CRYPTO 2016. LNCS, vol. 9814, pp. 277–307. Springer, Heidelberg (2016). https://doi.org/10.1007/978-3-662 53018-4_11
36. Trusted Computing Group: TPM 2.0 library specification, September 2016. https://trustedcomputinggroup.org/resource/tpm-library-specification/

Author Index

Printed in the United States
By Bookmasters